HARRAP'S
MINI
Italian

HARRAP'S

MINI

Italian

DICTIONARY

PARRAGON

Hanno Collaborato alla redazione del presente dizionario
Annamaria Fattore Maioechi e Ada Bichiacchi

First published as
Harrap's Compact Italian and English Dictionary
in 1968

First published in this edition in Great Britain 1988
by HARRAP BOOKS Ltd
Chelsea House, 26 Market Square, Bromely, Kent BR1 1NA
© Copyright 1967 U. Mursia & Co., Milano, Via Tadimo 29

This edition published in 1993
by Parragon Book Service, Bristol

Printed and bound in Great Britain by BPCC Paperbacks Ltd

NORME, REGOLE E INFORMAZIONI

NORME PER L'USO DEL DIZIONARIO

1. La parte iniziale del presente **Piccolo dizionario** comprende una serie di informazioni che valgono a completare l'opera, a facilitarne la consultazione o ad arricchire le conoscenze del lettore; tali si debbono considerare le **regole di pronuncia**, l'elenco dei **verbi irregolari inglesi**, la tabella di raffronto fra le **unità inglesi o americane** e il sistema metrico, le indicazioni relative al **sistema monetario inglese e americano**, l'elenco dei **numeri ordinali e cardinali** e, infine, l'**elenco delle abbreviazioni** usate nel dizionario stesso.

Inoltre comprende una serie di informazioni in inglese a facilitarne la consultazione per il lettore inglese.

2. La seconda parte comprende il **Compact English-Italian Dictionary** e reca in appendice un ampio elenco di **nomi propri, storici e geografici** (con la relativa traduzione in italiano), nonché l'elenco delle **sigle e abbreviazioni** usate nei **Paesi di lingua inglese** con l'indicazione dell'equivalente italiano.

3. La terza parte comprende il **Piccolo dizionario italiano-inglese** e reca in appendice un ampio elenco di **nomi propri, storici e geografici** (con la relativa traduzione in inglese), nonché l'elenco delle **sigle e abbreviazioni** usate in **Italia** con l'indicazione dell'equivalente inglese.

4. Nella parte **italiano-inglese**, i lemmi italiani non recano accento se si tratta di parole piane (es.: *violino, rosa, determinazione*); recano l'accento se si tratta di parole tronche (es.: *così, però, lassù*) o sdrucciole (es.: *richiùdere, rimpròvero, nàutico*) o bisdrucciole o terminanti in *ia, io* con l'accento sulla *i* (es.: *filosofìa, mormorìo*). Tali accenti sono tutti gravi, salvo nelle parole con accento su una *e*, nel qual caso ci si è attenuti a un criterio strettamente ortoepico (es.: *règola, desèrtico, maneggévole, pregévole*): si è, cioè, distinto fra accento grave (pronuncia aperta) e accento acuto (pronuncia chiusa).

5. Nel corpo delle singole voci sono stati ampiamente adottati, secondo la consuetudine generale dei grandi dizionari, i seguenti **segni grafici**:

a) la **doppia barra** (‖) che sta a segnalare la peculiarità della fraseologia o una certa differenza di significato nell'ambito del lemma o il passaggio da un senso proprio a uno figurato o il passaggio dal significato corrente a uno più specialistico o, infine, l'inizio dell'elencazione di parole composte e di analoghe associazioni semantiche;

b) i **numeri arabi in neretto** (1., 2., 3. ecc.) che valgono ad attirare l'attenzione sui diversi significati in cui è stato possibile articolare una determinata voce del dizionario;

c) la **losanga nera** (♦) che sta a indicare il cambiamento di natura grammaticale che sopravviene internamente a due omonimi appartenenti a un medesimo gruppo etimologico (es.: passaggio da sostantivo maschile a sostantivo femminile; da sostantivo ad aggettivo; da aggettivo ad avverbio; da verbo transitivo a verbo riflessivo ecc.);

d) gli **esponenti in numeri arabi** (¹, ², ³ ecc.) che servono a distinguere parole omonime appartenenti però a gruppi etimologici diversi.

6. In entrambe le parti, nel caso di sostantivi che abbiano **numero diverso** nelle due lingue, si è data l'indicazione del numero stesso sùbito dopo il lemma. Es.: **fare** *sm.* manners (*pl.*) - **postage** *s.* spese postali (*pl.*) - **embers** *s. pl.* brace (*sing.*).

7. Per i **plurali irregolari inglesi** si sono usati i seguenti criteri:

a) nella parte **inglese-italiano** si è fatta seguire al lemma, fra parentesi, la forma plurale irregolare, per esteso - es.: **child** *s.* (*pl.* children) - nei casi generali o abbreviata - es.: **diagnosis** *s.* (*pl.* -ses) - nei casi di parole derivanti da altre lingue antiche o moderne. Nel primo caso i plurali sono stati elencati anche come voce a sé e con rimando: es.: **children** V. *child*;

b) nella parte **italiano-inglese** si è fatta seguire alla traduzione, fra parentesi, la forma plurale irregolare, per esteso - es.: **bambino** *sm.* child (*pl.* children) - nei casi generali o abbreviata - es.: **diàgnosi** *sf.* diagnosis (*pl.* -ses) - nei casi di parole derivanti da altre lingue antiche o moderne.

8. Per i **verbi irregolari inglesi** si sono usati i seguenti criteri:

a) nella parte **inglese-italiano** si è fatto seguire al lemma, fra parentesi, il paradigma: es.: to **bring** (brought, brought). Le due forme del passato remoto e del participio passato sono state elencate anche come voce a sé e con rimando: es.: **brought** V. *to bring*;

b) nella parte **italiano-inglese** si è fatta seguire alla traduzione, fra parentesi, l'indicazione dell'irregolarità - es.: **costare** *vi.* to cost (*v. irr.*) - a meno che lo stesso verbo inglese ricorra più volte nell'ambito della stessa voce e escludendo inoltre i due verbi ausiliari *to be* e *to have* (per i quali ultimi si suppone una costante attenzione del lettore circa l'irregolarità).

9. Per i **comparativi** e i **superlativi irregolari inglesi** sono stati seguiti analoghi criteri.

REGOLE DI PRONUNCIA

Alfabeto

L'alfabeto inglese è composto di 26 lettere, 5 in più dell'alfabeto italiano e precisamente: *j, k, w, x, y*. L'elenco completo delle lettere è il seguente:

a	(pron. *ei*)	n	(pron. *en*)
b	(pron. *bi*, con la *i* allungata)	o	(pron. *ou*)
c	(pron. *si*, con la *i* allungata e la *s* aspra, come in *sordo*)	p	(pron. *pi*, con la *i* allungata)
d	(pron. *di*, con la *i* allungata)	q	(pron. *chiù*)
e	(pron. *i*, con la *i* allungata)	r	(pron. *ar*, con la *a* allungata)
f	(pron. *ef*)	s	(pron. *es*, con la *s* aspra)
g	(pron. *gi*, con la *i* allungata)	t	(pron. *ti*, con la *i* allungata)
h	(pron. *eic*, con la *c* dolce)	u	(pron. *iù*)
i	(pron. *ai*)	v	(pron. *vi*, con la *i* allungata)
j	(pron. *gei*)	w	(pron. *dabliu*)
k	(pron. *kei*)	x	(pron. *ecs*)
l	(pron. *el*)	y	(pron. *uai*)
m	(pron. *em*)	z	(pron. *sed*, con la *s* dolce, come in *rosa*).

La pronuncia inglese è particolarmente difficile da apprendere ed è altresì difficile dare norme precise per l'apprendimento della stessa. Diamo comunque, qui di seguito, un elenco delle vocali, dei gruppi vocalici, delle consonanti e di alcuni gruppi consonantici con indicazioni approssimative sulla pronuncia.

Vocali

La vocale A ha vari suoni:

1. *ei* in sillaba tonica aperta come nella parola *tale* (racconto); nei gruppi *ange* e *aste* come nelle parole *danger* (pericolo) e *haste* (fretta);

2. *e* aperta in sillaba tonica chiusa come nella parola *cat* (gatto);

3. ha un suono incerto tra *e* aperta e *a* in sillabe atone iniziali o mediane come nelle parole *about* (circa) e *final* (finale);

4. *a* allungata quando è seguita da *r* finale (*r* muta) come nelle parole *car* (automobile) e *far* (lontano);

5. *ea* se *a* è seguita da *re* finale (*e* aperta e *a* appena accennata) come nelle parole *care* (cura) e *dare* (sfida);

6. *o* breve in molti vocaboli che cominciano con il gruppo *qua* come in *quality* (qualità) e in *quantity* (quantità);

7. *o* aperta e prolungata se seguita da *l* o *ll* come in *all* (tutto), *tall* (alto);

nel gruppo **alk** (1 muta) come in *talk* (chiacchiera); preceduta da **w** (ma non seguita da **k** o **g**) come in *war* (guerra);

8. **a** allungata nei gruppi **ance, and, ant, ask, alf** (1 muta), **ast, alm** (1 muta), **aff, aft, asp** e **ath** quando la **a** è tonica;

9. **i** breve e velata nelle desinenze **age** e **ate** non accentate.

La vocale E ha vari suoni:

1. **i** allungata in sillaba tonica aperta come in *these* (questi) e nei monosillabi, come in *me* (me);

2. **e** aperta come nella parola italiana *bello*, in sillaba tonica chiusa, come in *let* (lasciare);

3. **i** come nella parola italiana *vita*, in sillaba atona, come in *repeat* (ripetere);

4. **i** brevissima quando è preceduta da **s, z, x, ch, sh, g** e seguita da **s** come in *roses* (rose) e quando è tra due dentali come in *rested* (riposato);

5. **è** muta in fine di parola come in *love* (amore) e nelle desinenze **es, ed,** come in *loves* (amori) e *loved* (amato);

6. **eu** francese quando è seguita da **r** in sillaba tonica, come in *term* (termine);

7. **a** gutturale quando è nel gruppo **er** in fine di parola, come in *letter* (lettera);

8. **ia** con la **a** appena accennata quando è seguita da **re** in fine di parola come in *severe* (severo) e in *mere* (semplice).

La vocale I ha vari suoni:

1. **ai** in sillaba tonica aperta, come in *fine* (bello) e in sillaba chiusa quando è seguita dai gruppi **gh** (muto), come in *high* (alto); **ght** (gh muto) come in *night* (notte); **gn** (g muta) come in *sign* (segno); **ld**, come in *child* (bambino) e **nd**, come in *mind* (mente);

2. **i** breve in sillaba tonica chiusa, come in *tin* (stagno);

3. **eu** francese, se seguita da **r** come in *fir* (abete);

4. **aia**, se seguita da **re** come in *fire* (fuoco).

La vocale O ha vari suoni:

1. **ou** (con la **o** chiusa) in sillaba tonica aperta, come in *home* (casa) e se seguita da **ld** come in *cold* (freddo);

2. **o** aperta e breve in sillaba tonica chiusa come in *not* (non);

3. **ò** aperta e lunga se seguita da **r** come in *morning* (mattino);

4. **oa** se seguita da **re** in fine di parola come in *more* (più);

5. **eu** francese se preceduta da **w** e seguita da **r** come in *work* (lavoro);

6. **u** allungata nei seguenti vocaboli: *to do* (fare); *to move* (muovere); *to prove* (provare); *to lose* (perdere); *who* (chi); *two* (due); *tomb* (tomba); *womb* (grembo); *shoe* (scarpa); *wolf* (lupo); *woman* (donna);

7. a se preceduta da w e seguita da n come in *won* (vinto);
8. ua in *one* (uno).

La vocale U ha vari suoni:

1. iù in sillaba tonica aperta, come in *tune* (tono);
2. a in sillaba tonica chiusa, come in *but* (ma);
3. u allungata se preceduta da l o r, come in *Lucy* (Lucia) e *rule* (regola);
4. u breve, se preceduta da b, f, p e seguita da l, ll, sh, come in *bush* (cespuglio); *to push* (spingere); *bull* (toro); *full* (pieno); *to pull* (tirare);
5. eu francese se seguita da r in sillaba aperta, come in *fur* (pelliccia);
6. iua se seguita da re in fine di parola, come in *pure* (puro).

Gruppi vocalici

AI si pronuncia ea se seguito da r, come in *air* (aria).

AU, AW si pronunciano o allungata, come in *fraud* (frode) e *law* (legge).

EA si pronuncia in circa 40 parole e loro composti: *bread* (pane); *dead* (morto); *death* (morte); *head* (testa); *heavy* (pesante) ecc.;
   i lunga in moltissime sillabe toniche: *beat* (calore); *meat* (carne);
   ei nelle seguenti parole: *great* (grande); *break* (rompere); *steak* (bistecca);
   eu francese se all'inizio di parola e seguito da r come in *earth* (terra);
   i se in fine di parola seguito da r, come in *bear* (sopportare); in molte parole suona però ia, come in *tear* (lacrima), o a allungata, come in *heart* (cuore).

EE si pronuncia i allungata, come in *feeling* (sentimento).

EI si pronuncia ei in genere, come in *rein* (briglia);
   i se preceduto da sibilante, come in *ceiling* (soffitto).

EY si pronuncia ei in sillaba tonica, come in *prey* (preda);
   i in sillaba atona, come in *money* (denaro). L'eccezione più comune è *key* (chiave) che si pronuncia ki.

EU, EW si pronunciano iù come in *Europe* (Europa) e in *new* (nuovo).

IE si pronuncia i allungata come in *piece* (pezzo).

OI, OY si pronunciano oi come in *soil* (suolo) e *royal* (reale).

OA si pronuncia ou come in *boat* (barca).

OO si pronuncia u allungata come in *moon* (luna);
   u breve se seguita da k come in *book* (libro).
   Vi sono alcune eccezioni come *door* (porta) e *floor* (pavimento) dove il gruppo oo viene pronunciato oa e *blood* (sangue) e *flood* (alluvione) dove il gruppo oo viene pronunciato a.

OU, OW si pronunciano au come in *mouth* (bocca) e *now* (ora).

Consonanti

B è in generale pronunciata come in italiano; è però muta nei gruppi **bt** e **mb** in fine di parola, come in *debt* (debito) e *comb* (pettine).

C suona **s** aspra come nell'italiano *sordo* davanti a **e, i, y**, come in *cellar* (cantina), *city* (città) e *cyder* (sidro); suona **k** in fine di parola, come in *logic* (logico);

cce, cci, suonano **kse** e **ksi**;

ch suona **c** palatale come nell'italiano *città*, se seguito da vocale o in fine di parola; suona **k** in parole di origine greca o orientale. Suona **sc** come in italiano *sciare*, in parole di origine francese, come *machine* (macchina);

ck suona **k**;

tch suona **c** dolce.

G in fine di parola suona **g** gutturale come nell'italiano *gomma*;

ge, gi hanno suono palatale come nell'italiano *gesto*, *gita* in parole di origine latina; hanno suono gutturale in parole di origine germanica;

gh seguito da **t** o in fine di parola è muto;

gn ha la **g** muta quando le due lettere fanno parte della stessa sillaba, come in *sign* (segno); si pronunciano separate e la **g** ha suono gutturale quando le due lettere appartengono a due sillabe diverse, come in *signal* (segnale);

dge suona **g** palatale.

H è sempre aspirata tranne in *heir* (erede); *honest* (onesto); *honour* (onore) e *hour* (ora) e loro derivati.

J suona **g** palatale.

K è muta davanti a **n** come in *knee* (ginocchio).

L come in italiano.

M come in italiano.

N è nasale nei gruppi **ng** come in *ring* (anello) (la **g** è muta).

P suona **f** nei gruppi **ph**; è muta nel gruppo iniziale **psy**.

Q come in italiano.

R in genere, se mediana, non si pronuncia, ma allunga il suono della vocale che precede, come in *farm* (fattoria). Se è finale non si pronuncia.

S è in genere aspra all'inizio di parola o sillaba; è dolce se è posta tra due vocali;

sc suona **s** aspra se è seguita da **e, i, y**;

sh suona **sc** come nell'italiano *sciare*.

La **s** è muta in *aisle* (navata); *isle* e *island* (isola); *viscount* (visconte).

T ha due pronunce caratteristiche nel gruppo **th**:

a) un suono duro pronunciato con la lingua tra i denti, come in *thin* (sottile);

b) un suono dolce pronunciato con la lingua tra i denti, come in *this* (questo).

V come in italiano.

W in principio di parola suona **u** come in *west*; seguita da **r** è muta, come in *wrong* (sbagliato).

X finale ha il suono sordo **ks**; mediana può avere il suono sordo **ks** o il suono dolce **gs**; in principio di parola suona come la **s** dolce di *rosa*.

Y è semivocale; all'inizio di parola ha il suono consonantico **i**, come in *yes* (sì); ha tale suono anche in fine di polisillabi, come in *dignity* (dignità), e nel corpo della parola, come in *graveyard* (cimitero); in fine di monosillabi, invece, si pronuncia **ai**, come in *fly* (mosca) e in *cry* (grido).

Z è **s** dolce di *rosa*.

Osservazioni

1. I gruppi finali **ble, cle, kle, gle** hanno la **l** appena accennata e le due consonanti vengono pronunciate staccate.

2. Nei gruppi **gua, gue, gui, build** e **cuit** finale la **u** è muta, come in *building* (fabbricato).

3. **ough** seguito da **t** si pronuncia **o** allungato, come in *thought* (pensiero); **ough** suona **of** in: *cough* (tosse) e *trough* (trogolo); suona **af** in: *enough* (abbastanza), *rough* (ruvido) e *tough* (duro); suona **au** in: *plough* (arare) e *bough* (ramo); suona **ou** in *though* (sebbene) e *dough* (pasta); suona **u** allungato in *through* (attraverso).

4. I gruppi **ci, sci, si, ti, xi** seguiti da vocale suonano **sc** come in *scelto.*

5. I gruppi finali **sten** e **stle** suonano rispettivamente **sn** e **sl.**

6. Il gruppo finale **sure** suona **ja** (**j** francese).

7. Il gruppo finale **ture** suona **cia** con la **a** allungata.

I SEGNI D'INTERPUNZIONE (PUNCTUATION MARKS)

,	*comma*	virgola
;	*semicolon*	punto e virgola
:	*colon*	due punti
.	*full stop*	punto
?	*question mark*	punto di domanda
!	*exclamation mark*	punto esclamativo
'	*apostrophe*	apostrofo
—	*dash*	lineetta
-	*hyphen*	trattino d'unione
« »	*quotation marks*	virgolette basse o quadre
' '	*inverted commas*	virgolette alte o inglesi
( )	*brackets*	parentesi rotonde
[ ]	*square brackets*	parentesi quadre
*	*asterisk*	asterisco
...	*dots*	puntini
	new paragraph	a capo
	full stop and new paragraph	punto e a capo
	capital letter	lettera maiuscola
	small letter	lettera minuscola

VERBI IRREGOLARI INGLESI [1]

Infinito	Passato	Participio passato	
to abide	abode	abode	dimorare
to arise	arose	arisen	sorgere
to awake*	awoke	awoke, awaked	svegliare, svegliarsi
to be	was	been	essere
to bear	bore	born, borne	sopportare, generare
to beat	beat	beaten, beat	battere
to become	became	become	diventare
to befall	befell	befallen	accadere
to beget	begot	begot, begotten	generare
to begin	began	begun	cominciare
to behold	beheld	beheld	mirare
to bend	bent	bent	piegare
to bereave*	bereft	bereft	orbare
to bet	bet	bet	scommettere
to bid	bade, bid	bidden, bid	ordinare
to bind	bound	bound	(ri)legare
to bite	bit	bitten, bit	mordere
to bleed	bled	bled	sanguinare
to blow	blew	blown	soffiare
to break	broke	broken	rompere
to breed	bred	bred	allevare
to bring	brought	brought	portare
to build	built	built	costruire
to burn*	burnt	burnt	bruciare
to burst	burst	burst	scoppiare
to buy	bought	bought	comperare
to cast	cast	cast	gettare, fondere
to catch	caught	caught	prendere, acchiappare
to chide*	chid	chid	sgridare
to choose	chose	chosen	scegliere
to cleave	cleft	cleft	fendere
to cling	clung	clung	attaccarsi
to come	came	come	venire
to cost	cost	cost	costare
to creep	crept	crept	strisciare
to cut	cut	cut	tagliare
to deal	dealt	dealt	trattare, commerciare
to dig*	dug	dug	scavare
to do	did	done	fare
to draw	drew	drawn	tirare, disegnare
to dream*	dreamt	dreamt	sognare
to drink	drank	drunk	bere
to drive	drove	driven	guidare
to dwell*	dwelt	dwelt	dimorare

[1] L'elenco, compilato per comodità del lettore, comprende i verbi di uso più comune
L'asterisco apposto accanto a un verbo indica l'esistenza, per il verbo stesso, di
forme anche regolari.

to eat	ate, eat	eaten	mangiare
to fall	fell	fallen	cadere
to feed	fed	fed	nutrire
to feel	felt	felt	sentire, tastare
to fight	fought	fought	combattere
to find	found	found	trovare
to flee	fled	fled	fuggire
to fling	flung	flung	scagliare
to fly	flew	flown	volare
to forbid	forbade	forbidden	proibire
to forecast	forecast	forecast	predire
to forget	forgot	forgotten	dimenticare
to forgive	forgave	forgiven	perdonare
to forsake	forsook	forsaken	abbandonare
to freeze	froze	frozen	gelare
to get	got	got, gotten	ottenere, diventare
to gird	girt	girt	cingere
to give	gave	given	dare
to go	went	gone	andare
to grind	ground	ground	macinare
to grow	grew	grown	crescere, coltivare
to hang	hung	hung, hanged	appendere
to have	had	had	avere
to hear	heard	heard	udire
to hew*	hewed	hewn	recidere
to hide	hid	hidden, hid	nascondere
to hit	hit	hit	colpire
to hold	held	held	tenere, trattenere
to hurt	hurt	hurt	far male, ferire
to keep	kept	kept	tenere, conservare
to kneel*	knelt	knelt	inginocchiarsi
to knit*	knit	knit	lavorare a maglia
to know	knew	known	conoscere, sapere
to lay	laid	laid	deporre, posare
to lead	led	led	condurre, guidare
to lean	leant	leant	appoggiarsi, inclinarsi
to leap	leapt	leapt	saltare
to learn*	learnt	learnt	imparare
to leave	left	left	lasciare, partire
to lend	lent	lent	prestare
to let	let	let	lasciare
to lie	lay	lain	giacere, trovarsi
to light*	lit	lit	accendere
to lose	lost	lost	perdere
to make	made	made	fare
to mean	meant	meant	intendere, significare
to meet	met	met	incontrare
to mislay	mislaid	mislaid	smarrire
to mislead	misled	misled	sviare
to mistake	mistook	mistaken	sbagliare
to mow*	mowed	mown	falciare
to pay	paid	paid	pagare
to put	put	put	mettere

to read	read	read	leggere
to rend	rent	rent	strappare
to ride	rode	ridden	cavalcare
to ring	rang	rung	suonare
to rise	rose	risen	alzarsi, sorgere
to run	ran	run	correre
to saw	sawed	sawn	segare
to say	said	said	dire
to see	saw	seen	vedere
to seek	sought	sought	cercare
to sell	sold	sold	vendere
to send	sent	sent	mandare
to set	set	set	porre
to sew	sewed	sewn	cucire
to shake	shook	shaken	scuotere, tremare
to shear*	sheared	shorn	tosare
to shed	shed	shed	spargere
to shine	shone	shone	brillare, splendere
to shoe	shod	shod	calzare
to shoot	shot	shot	sparare
to show	showed	shown	mostrare
to shred	shred	shred	tagliuzzare
to shrink	shrank, shrunk	shrunk, shrunken	restringersi
to shut	shut	shut	chiudere
to sing	sang	sung	cantare
to sink	sank, sunk	sunk	affondare
to sit	sat	sat	sedere
to slay	slew	slain	trucidare
to sleep	slept	slept	dormire
to slink	slunk	slunk	svignarsela
to smell*	smelt	smelt	fiutare, odorare
to sow*	sowed	sown	seminare
to speak	spoke	spoken	parlare
to spell	spelt	spelt	compitare
to spend	spent	spent	spendere
to spill*	spilt	spilt	spandere, versare
to spin	spun, span	spun	filare
to spit	spat, spit	spat, spit	sputare
to split	split	split	spaccare
to spoil	spoilt	spoilt	guastare, viziare
to spread	spread	spread	diffondere, stendere
to spring	sprang	sprung	saltare
to stand	stood	stood	stare (in piedi)
to steal	stole	stolen	rubare
to stick	stuck	stuck	appiccicare
to sting	stung	stung	pungere
to stink	stank, stunk	stunk	puzzare
to strike	struck	struck	battere, colpire
to strive	strove	striven	sforzarsi
to swear*	swore	sworn	giurare
to sweat*	sweat	sweat	sudare
to sweep	swept	swept	spazzare
to swell*	swelled	swollen	gonfiare
to swim	swam	swum	nuotare
to swing	swung	swung	dondolare
to take	took	taken	prendere

to teach	taught	taught	insegnare
to tear	tore	torn	lacerare
to tell	told	told	dire, raccontare
to think	thought	thought	pensare
to thrive	throve	thriven	prosperare
to throw	threw	thrown	gettare
to thrust	thrust	thrust	spingere, gettare
to tread	trode	trod, trodden	calpestare
to understand	understood	understood	capire
to upset	upset	upset	capovolgere
to wake	woke	woke, woken	svegliare, svegliarsi
to wear	wore	worn	indossare, logorare
to weave	wove	woven	intrecciare, tessere
to weep	wept	wept	piangere
to win	won	won	vincere
to wind	wound	wound	serpeggiare
to withdraw	withdrew	withdrawn	ritirare, ritirarsi
to wring	wrung	wrung	torcere
to write	wrote	written	scrivere

TABELLA DI RAFFRONTO FRA LE UNITÀ INGLESI O AMERICANE E IL SISTEMA METRICO

	denominazione delle unità inglesi o americane	valore	equivalenza col sistema metrico *	equivalenza del sistema metrico con le unità inglesi **
misure lineari	pollice (inch - in)	—	2,54 cm	0,3937 (cm)
	piede (foot - ft)	12 in	0,304 m	3,28 (m)
	yarda (yard - yd)	3 ft	0,914 m	1,09 (m)
	fathom	6 ft	1,828 m	0,546 (m)
	miglio terrestre (statute mile)	5280 ft	1,609 km	0,621 (km)
	miglio inglese	5000 ft	1,523 km	0,656 (km)
	nodo (nautical mile)	6080 ft	1,853 km	0,539 (km)
superfici	pollice quadr. (square inch - sq.in)	144 sq.in	6,45 cm²	0,155 (cm²)
	piede quadr. (square foot - sq.ft)		829 cm²	10,76 (m²)
	yarda quadr. (square yard - sq.yd)	1296 sq.in	0,836 m²	1,196 (m²)
	miglio quadr. (square mile)		2,59 km²	0,386 (km²)
volumi e capacità	pollice cubo (cubic inch - cu.in)		16,38 cm³	0,061 (cm³)
	piede cubo (cubic foot - cu.ft)	1728 cu.in	28,32 dm³	0,0353 (dm³)
	yarda cubica (cubic yard - cu.yd)	27 cu.ft	0,764 m³	1,308 (m³)
	register ton	100 cu.ft	2,832 m³	0,353 (m³)
	oncia fluida americana (U.S. fl.oz)	1,8 cu.in	29,57 cm³	0,0338 (cm³)
	oncia fluida inglese (imp. fl.oz)	1,73 cu.in	28,4 cm³	0,0353 (cm³)
	bushel	8 gals	28,3 l	0,035 (l)
	gallone americano (U.S. gal)	231 cu.in	3,78 l	0,26 (l)
	gallone inglese (imp. gal)	277 cu.in	4,54 l	0,22 (l)
	pinta (pint)	1/8 gal	0,47 l	2,11 (l)
pesi	oncia avoirdupois (ounce - oz)	—	28,35 g	0,0352 (g)
	oncia troy (ounce troy - oz)		31,1 g	0,0321 (g)
	libbra avoirdupois (pound - lb)	16 oz.a.d.p.	453 g	2,204 (kg)
	libbra troy (pound - lb)	12 oz.t.	373 g	2,679 (kg)
	tonnellata americana (short ton - ton)	2000 lbs	907 kg	0,102 (t)
	tonnellata ingl. (long ton - ton)	2240 lbs	1016 kg	0,984 (t)

Con la graduale introduzione del sistema metrico, le unità di misura inglesi e americane diventeranno progressivamente meno diffuse

* Coefficiente per il quale si deve moltiplicare il valore della grandezza per ottenere la misura nel sistema metrico.

** Coefficiente per il quale si deve moltiplicare il valore espresso nell'unità metrica segnato tra parentesi per ottenere la misura nel sistema inglese.

SISTEMA MONETARIO INGLESE
(Denaro circolante)
Unità base = **pound**, sterlina.

Monete *(coins)*

½p piece (half-penny), duecentesima parte della sterlina;
1p piece (one penny), centesima parte della sterlina;
2p piece (two pence), cinquantesima parte della sterlina;
5p piece (five pence), ventesima parte della sterlina;
10p piece (ten pence), decima parte della sterlina;
50p piece (fifty pence), metà della sterlina.

Banconote *(banknotes)*

pound note (£1), sterlina carta;
five-pound note (£5), cinque sterline;
ten-pound note (£10), dieci sterline;
twenty-pound note (£20), venti sterline

Monete nominali *(nominal coins* – usate nelle parcelle dei professionisti, prezzi par articoli di lusso, per libri, ecc.)

guinea (£1.05, 105p), ghinea, centocinque pence;
half (a) guinea (52 ½p), mezza ghinea, cinquantadue pence e mezzo

SISTEMA MONETARIO AMERICANO
(Denaro circolante)
Unità base = **dollar**, dollaro.

Rame *(copper)*:
    cent o penny (1 c.), un centesimo di dollaro.

Lega di rame e nichel *(copper and nickel alloy)*:
    nickel o five cents (5 c.), cinque centesimi di dollaro.

Argento *(silver)*:
    dime (10 c.), dieci centesimi di dollaro;
    quarter (25 c.), un quarto di dollaro;
    half-dollar (50 c.), mezzo dollaro, cinquanta centesimi;
    dollar ($ 1), dollaro (generalmente in banconota).

Banconote *(bills)*:
    si hanno tagli da $ 1, 2, 5, 10, 20, 50, 100, 500.
    Esistono inoltre, sebbene non in circolazione normale, banconote da
    $ 1,000, 5,000 e 10,000.

I NUMERI

CARDINALI	ORDINALI		
1 one	1° -	1st -	the first
2 two	2° -	2nd -	the second
3 three	3° -	3rd -	the third
4 four	4° -	4th -	the fourth
5 five	5° -	5th -	the fifth
6 six	6° -	6th -	the sixth
7 seven	7° -	7th -	the seventh
8 eight	8° -	8th -	the eighth
9 nine	9° -	9th -	the ninth
10 ten	10° -	10th -	the tenth
11 eleven	11° -	11th -	the eleventh
12 twelve	12° -	12th -	the twelfth
13 thirteen	13° -	13th -	the thirteenth
14 fourteen	14° -	14th -	the fourteenth
15 fifteen	15° -	15th -	the fifteenth
16 sixteen	16° -	16th -	the sixteenth
17 seventeen	17° -	17th -	the seventeenth
18 eighteen	18° -	18th -	the eighteenth
19 nineteen	19° -	19th -	the nineteenth
20 twenty	20° -	20th -	the twentieth
21 twenty-one	21° -	21st -	the twenty-first
22 twenty-two	22° -	22nd -	the twenty-second
30 thirty	30° -	30th -	the thirtieth
40 forty	40° -	40th -	the fortieth
50 fifty	50° -	50th -	the fiftieth
60 sixty	60° -	60th -	the sixtieth
70 seventy	70° -	70th -	the seventieth
80 eighty	80° -	80th -	the eightieth
90 ninety	90° -	90th -	the ninetieth
100 one hundred	100° -	100th -	the (one) hundredth
101 one hundred and one	101° -	101st -	the one hundred and first
200 two hundred	200° -	200th -	the two hundredth
1.000 one thousand	1.000° -	1,000th -	the (one) thousandth
1.001 one thousand and one	1.001° -	1,001st -	the one thousand and first
1.010 one thousand and ten	1.010° -	1,010th -	the one thousand and tenth
10.000 ten thousand	10.000° -	10,000	the ten thousandth
100.000 one hundred thousand	100.000° -	100,000	the one hundred thousandth
200.000 two hundred thousand	200.000° -	200,000	the two hundred thousandth
1.000.000 one million	1.000.000° -	1,000,000	the one millionth

ELENCO DELLE ABBREVIAZIONI

abbr.	abbreviazione	gen.	genitivo
(aer.)	aeronautica	general.	generalmente
agg.	aggettivo	(geogr.)	geografia
(agr.)	agricoltura	(geol.)	geologia
(amer.)	americano, americanismo	(geom.)	geometria
		ger.	gerundio
amm.	amministrativo, amministrazione	(gergo)	gergo, gergale
		(giorn.)	giornalismo, giornalistico
(anat.)	anatomia		
(ant.)	anticamente, antiquato	(giur.)	giuridico
(arch.)	architettura	(gramm.)	grammatica
art.	articolo	i.	intransitivo
(arte)	arte, artistico	id.	idem
assol.	assoluto	imp.	impersonale
(astr.)	astronomia	imperat.	imperativo
attr.	attributo, attributivo	ind.	indicativo
aus.	ausiliare	indef.	indefinito
(auto)	automobilismo	inf.	infinito
avv.	avverbio	int.	interrogativo
(bot.)	botanica	inter.	interiezione, interiettivo
(biol.)	biologia	(iron.)	ironico
(chim.)	chimica	irr.	irregolare
(chir.)	chirurgia	(itt.)	ittiologia
(cine)	cinematografia	(lat.)	latino, latinismo
coll.	collettivo	loc. avv.	locuzione avverbiale
(comm.)	commercio, commerciale	loc. cong.	locuzione congiuntiva
comp.	comparativo	loc. prep.	locuzione prepositiva
compl.	complemento	(lett.)	letteratura, letterario
condiz.	condizionale	m.	maschile
cong.	congiunzione	(mar.)	marina, marittimo, marinaresco
(costr.)	costruzioni		
(cuc.)	cucina	(mat.)	matematica
(dial.)	dialettale	(mecc.)	meccanica
dif.	difettivo	(med.)	medicina
dim.	diminutivo	(metal.)	metallurgia
dimostr.	dimostrativo	(mil.)	militare
ecc., etc.	eccetera	(min.)	mineralogia, minerario
(eccl.)	ecclesiastico	(mit.)	mitologia
(econ.)	economia	(mus.)	musica
(edil.)	edilizia	neg.	negazione, negativo
(elettr.)	elettricità, elettrotecnica	(neol.)	neologismo
escl.	esclamativo, in esclamazione	ogg.	oggetto
		(ott.)	ottica
f.	femminile	p.	participio
(fam.)	familiare	pass.	passato
(farm.)	farmacia, farmaceutico	pers.	persona, personale
(ferr.)	ferrovia	(pitt.)	pittura
(fig.)	figurato	pl.	plurale
(fil)	filosofia	(poet.)	poetico
(fis)	fisica	(pol.)	politica
(foto)	fotografia	(pop.)	popolare
fut.	futuro	poss.	possessivo

pp.	participio passato	*sost.*	sostantivato
prep.	preposizione	*spec.*	specialmente
pred.	predicato, predicativo	*(sport)*	sport, sportivo
pres.	presente	*(spreg.)*	spregiativo
pron.	pronome, pronominale	*sthg.*	something
prov.	proverbio, proverbiale	*(stor.)*	storia
(psicol.)	psicologia	*superl.*	superlativo
qc.	qualcosa	*t.*	transitivo
qu.	qualcuno	*(teat.)*	teatro
r.	riflessivo	*(tec.)*	tecnica
(radio)	radiofonia	*(tel.)*	telefonia, telefono
rec.	reciproco	*(teol.)*	teologia
reg.	regolare	*(tip.)*	tipografia
rel.	relativo	*(tv.)*	televisione
(relig.)	religione	*(us.)*	uso, usato
s.	(dall'inglese) sostantivo	*v.*	verbo
s.	(dall'italiano) sostantivo	*V.*	vedi
	maschile e femminile	*(vezz.)*	vezzeggiativo
semidif.	semidifettivo	*v. dif.*	verbo difettivo
sf.	sostantivo femminile	*vi.*	verbo intransitivo
sm.	sostantivo maschile	*(v. irr.)*	verbo irregolare
(scherz.)	scherzoso	*(volg.)*	volgare
(scol.)	scolastico	*vr.*	verbo riflessivo
(scult.)	scultura	*v. semidif.*	verbo semidifettivo
sing.	singolare	*vt.*	verbo transitivo
so.	someone	*(zool.)*	zoologia
sogg.	soggetto		

INGLESE-ITALIANO

A

a *art.* 1. un, uno, una 2. un certo ‖ *once a week*, una volta alla settimana.

A *s.* (*mus.*) la.

aback *avv.* alla sprovvista.

abacus *s.* 1. abaco 2. pallottoliere.

abandon *s.* abbandono.

to abandon *vt.* abbandonare.

abase *vt.* abbassare, umiliare.

abasement *s.* umiliazione.

to abash *vt.* confondere.

abashment *s.* confusione.

to abate *vt.* diminuire. ♦ to abate *vi.* placarsi (*di tempo atmosferico*).

abatement *s.* diminuzione.

abbess *s.* badessa.

abbey *s.* abbazia.

abbot *s.* abate.

abbreviation *s.* abbreviazione.

to abdicate *vt.* e *vi.* 1. abdicare a 2. dimettersi.

abdication *s.* abdicazione.

abdomen *s.* addome.

abdominal *agg.* addominale.

to abduct *vt.* rapire.

abduction *s.* rapimento.

abductor *s.* 1. rapitore 2. (*anat.*) abduttore.

aberration *s.* aberrazione.

abetter *s.* fautore.

abeyance *s.* sospensione.

to abhor *vt.* aborrire.

abhorrence *s.* aborrimento.

to abide (abode, abode) *vi.* abitare ‖ *to — by*, conformarsi a.

ability *s.* abilità, capacità.

abject *agg.* abietto.

abjection *s.* abiezione.

abjuration *s.* abiura.

to abjure *vt.* abiurare.

ablation *s.* ablazione.

ablative *agg.* e *s.* ablativo.

able *agg.* capace ‖ *to be — to*, essere in grado di, potere.

ablution *s.* abluzione.

abnegation *s.* 1. abnegazione 2. rinuncia.

abnormal *agg.* anormale.

aboard *avv.* e *prep.* a bordo.

abode V. *to abide.* ♦ abode *s.* dimora.

to abolish *vt.* abolire.

abolishment, abolition *s.* abolizione.

abolitionism *s.* abolizionismo.

abolitionist *agg.* e *s.* abolizionista.

abominable *agg.* abominevole.

to abominate *vt.* detestare.

abomination *s.* abominazione.

aboriginal *agg.* e *s.* aborigeno.

to abort *vi.* abortire.

abortion *s.* aborto.

abortive *agg.* abortivo.

to abound *vi.* abbondare.

about *avv.* 1. circa 2. intorno ‖ *to be —*, stare per. ♦ about *prep.* 1. intorno a 2. presso di 3. riguardo a.

above *prep.* 1. al di sopra di 2. più di ‖ *— mentioned*, suddetto. ♦ above *avv.* in alto, sopra.

abrasion *s.* abrasione.

to abridge *vt.* 1. abbreviare 2. privare di.

abridg(e)ment *s.* 1. abbreviazione, sommario 2. privazione.

abroad *avv.* 1. all'estero 2. fuori.

to abrogate *vt.* abrogare.

abrogation *s.* abrogazione.

abrupt *agg.* 1. scosceso 2. brusco 3. inaspettato.

abruptness *s.* 1. ripidezza 2. rudezza 3. precipitazione.

abscess *s.* ascesso.

abscissa *s.* ascissa.

absence *s.* assenza.

absent *agg.* assente ‖ *— -minded*, distratto; *— -mindedness*, distrazione.

to absent *vt.* *to — oneself*, assentarsi.

absenteeism *s.* assenteismo.

absinth(e) *s.* assenzio.

absolute *agg.* e *s.* assoluto.

absolution *s.* assoluzione.

absolutism *s.* assolutismo.

absolutist *agg.* e *s.* assolutista.

to absolve *vt.* assolvere.

to absorb *vt.* assorbire.

absorbent *agg.* e *s.* assorbente.

absorption *s.* assorbimento.

to abstain *vi.* astenersi.

abstemious *agg.* sobrio.

abstention *s.* astensione.

abstentionist *s.* astensionista.

abstinence *s.* astinenza.

abstract *agg.* astratto. ♦ abstract *s.* 1. astrazione 2. estratto.

to abstract *vt.* 1. astrarre 2. estrarre 3. sottrarre 4. riassumere.

abstraction *s.* 1. astrazione 2. distrazione 3. furto.

abstractly *avv.* astrattamente.

abstruse *agg.* astruso.

abstruseness *s.* astrusità.

absurd *agg.* assurdo.

absurdity *s.* assurdità.

absurdly *avv.* assurdamente.

abundance *s.* abbondanza.

abundant *agg.* abbondante.

abuse *s.* 1. abuso 2. ingiuria.

to abuse *vt.* 1. abusare 2. ingiuriare.

abusive *agg.* 1. abusivo 2. ingiurioso.

abysm, abyss *s.* abisso.

abysmal, abyssal *agg.* abissale.

academic *agg.* e *s.* accademico.

academician *s.* accademico.

academy *s.* accademia: — *of music,* conservatorio.

acanthus *s.* acanto.

acarus *s.* (*pl.* -ri) acaro.

to accelerate *vt.* accelerare.

acceleration *s.* accelerazione.

accelerative *agg.* accelerativo.

accelerator *s.* acceleratore.

accent *s.* accento.

to accent *vt.* 1. accentare 2. accentuare.

to accentuate V. *to accent.*

accentuation *s.* accentuazione.

to accept *vt.* accettare, approvare.

acceptable *agg.* accettabile.

acceptance *s.* 1. accettazione 2. consenso.

acceptation *s.* accezione, significato.

access *s.* accesso.

accessible *agg.* accessibile.

accession *s.* 1. assunzione (*al trono*) 2. adesione 3. aggiunta.

accessory *agg.* e *s.* 1. accessorio 2. complice.

accident *s.* 1. caso: by —, per caso 2. incidente 3. irregolarità.

accidental *agg.* accidentale.

to acclaim *vt.* acclamare.

acclamation *s.* acclamazione.

acclimation, acclimatization *s.* acclimazione, acclimatazione.

to acclimate, to acclimatize *vt.* acclimatare. ♦ to acclimate, to acclimatize *vi.* acclimatarsi.

to accommodate *vt.* 1. adattare 2. ospitare 3. fornire.

accommodating *agg.* accomodante.

accommodation *s.* 1. accomodamento 2. comodità 3. alloggio 4. (*comm.*) facilitazione.

accompaniment *s.* accompagnamento.

accompanist *s.* (*mus.*) accompagnatore.

to accompany *vt.* accompagnare

(*anche mus.*).

accomplice *s.* complice.

to accomplish *vt.* compiere, realizzare.

accomplishment *s.* 1. compimento 2. compitezza 3. dote.

accord *s.* accordo.

to accord *vt.* accordare. ♦ to accord *vi.* accordarsi.

accordance *s.* accordo.

accordant *agg.* concorde, conforme.

according *agg.* 1. concordante, conforme 2. armonioso. ♦ according *avv.* — as, secondo che; — to, secondo.

accordingly *avv.* 1. in conseguenza 2. conformemente.

accordion *s.* fisarmonica.

accordionist *s.* fisarmonicista.

account *s.* 1. (*comm.*) conto 2. (*comm.*) acconto 3. valore 4. resoconto || *to take into* —, prendere in considerazione; *on* — *of,* a causa di.

to account *vt.* considerare || *to* — *for,* essere responsabile di.

accountable *agg.* responsabile.

accountancy *s.* ragioneria.

accountant *s.* contabile || *chartered* —, ragioniere.

to accredit *vt.* accreditare.

to accrue *vi.* 1. derivare 2. accumularsi.

to accumulate *vt.* accumulare. ♦ to accumulate *vi.* accumularsi.

accumulation *s.* accumulazione.

accumulative *agg.* accumulativo.

accumulator *s.* accumulatore.

accuracy *s.* esattezza.

accurate *agg.* esatto.

accusation *s.* accusa.

accusative *agg.* e *s.* accusativo.

to accuse *vt.* accusare.

accused *s.* accusato.

accuser *s.* accusatore.

to accustom *vt.* abituare.

accustomed *agg.* 1. abituale 2. abituato.

ace *s.* asso.

acetone *s.* acetone.

acetylene *s.* acetilene.

ache *s.* dolore.

to ache *vi.* far male: *my head aches,* mi fa male la testa.

to achieve *vt.* 1. compiere 2. ottenere.

achievement *s.* 1. compimento 2. conseguimento 3. gesta.

aching *agg.* 1. doloroso 2. afflitto.

♦ **aching** s. dolore.

acid agg. e s. acido.

acidity s. acidità.

acidulous agg. acidulo.

to **acknowledge** vt. riconoscere || to — receipt of, accusare ricevuta di.

acknowledg(e)ment s. riconoscimento.

acolyte s. accolito.

acorn s. ghianda.

acoustic(al) agg. acustico.

acoustics s. acustica.

to **acquaint** vt. informare || to become acquainted with, fare la conoscenza di.

acquaintance s. conoscenza.

acquiescence s. acquiescenza.

to **acquire** vt. acquisire, acquistare.

acquisition s. acquisto.

to **acquit** vt. 1. pagare 2. liberare 3. assolvere.

acquittal s. (giur.) assoluzione.

acquittance s. 1. saldo 2. quietanza.

acrid agg. acre.

acridity s. asprezza.

acrimony s. acrimonia.

acrobat s. acrobata.

acrobatic(al) agg. acrobatico.

acrobatics s. pl. acrobazia (sing.).

acropolis s. acropoli.

across avv. per traverso. ♦ **across** prep. attraverso || to come —. incontrare.

act s. atto, legge.

to **act** vt. e vi. 1. agire, fare 2. (teat.) recitare.

acting agg. facente funzione di. ♦ **acting** s. 1. azione 2. (teat.) rappresentazione.

action s. 1. azione 2. (giur.) processo 3. (mecc.) funzionamento.

active agg. attivo.

activism s. attivismo.

activist s. attivista.

activity s. attività.

actor s. attore.

actress s. attrice.

actual agg. reale.

actuality s. realtà.

actually avv. realmente.

to **actuate** vt. mettere in moto.

acuminate agg. acuminato.

acute agg. acuto.

ad s. V. advertisement.

adamantine agg. adamantino.

to **adapt** vt. adattare.

adaptable agg. adattabile.

adaptation s. adattamento.

to **add** vt. aggiungere || to — up, fare una somma.

addendum s. (pl. -da) aggiunta.

adder s. vipera.

addict s. tossicomane.

addition s. 1. (mat.) addizione 2. aggiunta.

additional agg. supplementare.

address s. 1. indirizzo 2. abilità. ♦ **addresses** s. pl. omaggi.

to **address** vt. e vi. indirizzare, arringare. ♦ to **address** vi. rivolgersi.

addressee s. destinatario.

addresser s. mittente.

to **adduce** vt. addurre.

adenoids s. pl. adenoidi.

adept agg. e s. perito, esperto.

adequate agg. adeguato.

to **adhere** vi. aderire.

adherence s. aderenza, adesione.

adherent agg. e s. aderente.

adhesion s. V. adherence.

adhesive agg. e s. adesivo.

adipose agg. adiposo.

adjacent agg. adiacente.

adjective agg. 1. aggettivale 2. addizionale. ♦ **adjective** s. aggettivo.

to **adjoin** vt. 1. aggiungere 2. essere contiguo.

adjoining agg. adiacente.

to **adjourn** vt. aggiornare.

adjournment s. aggiornamento.

adjunct s. 1. aggiunta 2. aggiunto 3. (gramm.) complemento.

adjuration s. implorazione.

to **adjust** vt. 1. aggiustare 2. adattare 3. regolare.

adjustment s. 1. adattamento, compromesso 2. (comm.) liquidazione.

adjutant s. aiutante.

to **administer** vt. 1. amministrare 2. fornire. ♦ to **administer** vi. contribuire.

administration s. 1. amministrazione 2. somministrazione.

administrative agg. amministrativo.

administrator s. amministratore.

admirable agg. ammirabile.

admiral s. ammiraglio.

admiralty s. ammiragliato.

admiration s. ammirazione.

to **admire** vt. ammirare.

admirer s. ammiratore.

admiringly avv. con ammirazione.

admissible agg. ammissibile.

admission s. 1. ammissione 2. confessione.

to **admit** *vt.* **1.** ammettere **2.** contenere.

admittance *s.* ammissione, ingresso.

to **admonish** *vt.* ammonire.

admonition *s.* ammonimento.

ado *s.* **1.** fatica **2.** confusione.

adolescence *s.* adolescenza.

adolescent *agg.* e *s.* adolescente.

to **adopt** *vt.* adottare.

adoption *s.* adozione.

adoptive *agg.* adottivo.

adorable *agg.* adorabile.

adoration *s.* adorazione.

to **adore** *vt.* adorare.

to **adorn** *vt.* adornare.

adornment *s.* ornamento.

adrenalin *s.* adrenalina.

adrift *avv.* alla deriva.

to **adulate** *vt.* adulare.

adulation *s.* adulazione.

adulator *s.* adulatore.

adult *agg.* e *s.* adulto.

to **adulterate** *vt.* adulterare.

adulteration *s.* adulterazione.

adulterer *s.* adultero.

adulteress *s.* adultera.

adulterine *agg.* adulterino.

adultery *s.* adulterio.

advance *s.* **1.** avanzamento **2.** anticipo **3.** approccio.

to **advance** *vt.* **1.** portar avanti **2.** anticipare (*denaro*) **3.** (*comm.*) aumentare. ♦ to **advance** *vi.* avanzare.

advancement *s.* **1.** avanzamento **2.** (*comm.*) rialzo.

advantage *s.* vantaggio || to take — of, approfittare di.

to **advantage** *vt.* avvantaggiare.

advantageous *agg.* vantaggioso.

advent *s.* avvento.

adventure *s.* avventura.

to **adventure** *vt.* rischiare. ♦ to **adventure** *vi.* avventurarsi.

adventurer *s.* avventuriero.

adventurous *agg.* avventuroso.

adverb *s.* avverbio.

adverbial *agg.* avverbiale.

adversary *s.* avversario.

adverse *agg.* avverso.

adversity *s.* avversità.

to **advert** *vi.* alludere, riferirsi.

to **advertise** *vt.* e *vi.* fare pubblicità a, divulgare.

advertisement *s.* **1.** avviso **2.** cartellone pubblicitario **3.** inserzione.

advertiser *s.* inserzionista.

advertising *agg.* pubblicitario. ♦ **advertising** *s.* pubblicità.

advice *s.* **1.** consiglio **2.** notizia.

advisability *s.* opportunità.

advisable *agg.* consigliabile.

to **advise** *vt.* **1.** consigliare **2.** avvisare || to — with so., consultarsi con qu.

advised *agg.* giudizioso.

adviser *s.* consigliere.

advocacy *s.* avvocatura.

advocate *s.* difensore.

aegis *s.* egida.

Aeolian *agg.* eolio.

to **aerate** *vt.* **1.** aerare **2.** gassare.

aeration *s.* **1.** aerazione **2.** (*chim.*) aggiunta di acido carbonico.

aerial *agg.* aereo. ♦ **aerial** *s.* (*radio*) antenna.

aerodrome *s.* aerodromo.

aerodynamics *s.* aerodinamica.

aeronaut *s.* aeronauta.

aeronautics *s.* aeronautica.

aeroplane *s.* aeroplano.

aerostat *s.* aerostato.

aerostatics *s.* aerostatica.

aesthete *s.* esteta.

aesthetic(al) *agg.* estetico.

aestheticism *s.* estetismo.

aesthetics *s.* estetica.

aestivation *s.* letargo estivo.

aether *s.* etere.

afar *avv.* lontano.

affability *s.* affabilità.

affable *agg.* affabile.

affair *s.* **1.** affare **2.** tresca.

to **affect**[1] *vt.* **1.** ostentare **2.** simulare.

to **affect**[2] *vt.* **1.** concernere **2.** commuovere **3.** (*med.*) intaccare.

affectation *s.* affettazione.

affected *agg.* **1.** affettato **2.** affetto **3.** commosso **4.** disposto.

affection *s.* **1.** affetto **2.** (*med.*) affezione.

affectionate *agg.* affezionato, affettuoso.

affective *agg.* affettivo.

to **affiliate** *vt.* affiliare. ♦ to **affiliate** *vi.* affiliarsi.

affiliation *s.* affiliazione.

affinity *s.* affinità, parentela.

to **affirm** *vt.* **1.** affermare **2.** ratificare.

affirmation *s.* **1.** affermazione **2.** ratificazione.

affirmative *agg.* affermativo || in the —, affermativamente.

to **affix** *vt.* aggiungere, apporre.

to **afflict** *vt.* affliggere.

affliction *s.* afflizione.

affluence *s.* 1. affluenza 2. abbondanza.

affluent *agg.* ricco. ♦ **affluent** *s.* (*geogr.*) affluente.

afflux *s.* afflusso.

to **afford** *vt.* offrire || *can* —, potersi permettere.

to **afforest** *vt.* imboschire.

afforestation *s.* imboschimento.

affront *s.* affronto || *to take* — *at*, offendersi per.

to **affront** *vt.* 1. affrontare 2. insultare.

afloat *avv.* a galla. ♦ **afloat** *agg.* 1. galleggiante 2. in circolazione.

afore *avv.* precedentemente. ♦ **afore** *prep.* prima di.

aforementioned, aforesaid *agg.* predetto.

afraid *agg.* spaventato || *to be* —, temere.

African *agg.* e *s.* africano.

after *agg.* seguente. ♦ **after** *prep.* 1. dopo, dietro 2. secondo 3. alla maniera di. ♦ **after** *avv.* dopo. ♦ **after** *cong.* dopo che.

afternoon *s.* pomeriggio.

afterthought *s.* riflessione.

afterward(s) *avv.* poi.

again *avv.* ancora, di nuovo.

against *prep.* 1. contro 2. in previsione di.

agape *agg.* e *avv.* a bocca aperta.

age *s.* 1. età 2. secolo || *old* —, vecchiaia; *to be of* —, essere maggiorenne; *to be under* —, essere minorenne; *Middle Ages*, Medioevo.

to **age** *vt.* e *vi.* invecchiare.

aged *agg.* 1. vecchio 2. dell'età di.

agency *s.* 1. causa, azione 2. (*comm.*) agenzia, rappresentanza.

agent *s.* agente.

agglomerate *agg.* e *s.* agglomerato.

to **agglomerate** *vt.* agglomerare. ♦ to **agglomerate** *vi.* agglomerarsi.

agglomeration *s.* agglomerazione.

to **agglutinate** *vt.* agglutinare. ♦ to **agglutinate** *vi.* agglutinarsi.

to **aggravate** *vt.* 1. aggravare 2. irritare.

aggravation *s.* 1. aggravamento 2. esasperazione.

aggregate *agg.* e *s.* aggregato.

to **aggregate** *vt.* 1. aggregare 2. ammontare a. ♦ to **aggregate** *vi.* aggregarsi.

aggregation *s.* aggregazione.

aggression *s.* aggressione.

aggressive *agg.* aggressivo.

aggressiveness *s.* aggressività.

aggressor *s.* aggressore.

aghast *agg.* 1. atterrito 2. stupefatto.

agile *agg.* agile.

agility *s.* agilità.

to **agitate** *vt.* agitare.

agitation *s.* agitazione.

agitator *s.* agitatore.

agnostic *agg.* e *s.* agnostico.

ago *agg.* e *avv.* fa.

agonistic(al) *agg.* agonistico.

to **agonize** *vt.* tormentare. ♦ to **agonize** *vi.* 1. tormentarsi 2. agonizzare.

agony *s.* 1. agonia 2. dolore.

agrarian *agg.* e *s.* agrario.

to **agree** *vt.* e *vi.* 1. accordarsi 2. accettare 3. essere adatto.

agreeable *agg.* 1. gradevole 2. conforme.

agreement *s.* 1. accordo 2. conformità 3. consenso.

agricultural *agg.* agricolo.

agriculture *s.* agricoltura.

agronomist *s.* agronomo.

agronomy *s.* agronomia.

ague *s.* febbre malarica.

ahead *avv.* avanti.

aid *s.* aiuto.

to **aid** *vt.* aiutare, soccorrere.

to **ail** *vt.* affliggere. ♦ to **ail** *vi.* sentirsi male.

aileron *s.* alettone.

aim *s.* 1. mira 2. scopo.

to **aim** *vt.* e *vi.* 1. mirare 2. aspirare a.

aimless *agg.* senza scopo.

air *s.* aria || — *conditioning*, condizionamento d'aria; — *lift*, ponte aereo; —*line*, aviolinea; —*raid*, incursione aerea; — *mail*, posta aerea.

to **air** *vt.* aerare.

aircraft *s.* aereo, aerei || -*carrier*, portaerei.

airfield *s.* campo d'aviazione.

airiness *s.* leggerezza, disinvoltura.

airing *s.* 1. ventilazione 2. passeggiata.

to **air-mail** *vt.* trasportare per via aerea.

airman *s.* aviatore.

airport *s.* aeroporto.

airship *s.* aeronave.

airsickness *s.* mal d'aria.

airstrip *s.* pista (*d'areoporto*).

airtight *agg.* a tenuta d'aria.

airway *s.* via aerea.

airy *agg.* **1.** arioso **2.** aereo **3.** gaio.

aisle *s.* navata (*laterale*).

ajar *avv.* socchiuso.

akin *agg.* **1.** consanguineo **2.** simile.

alacrity *s.* alacrità.

alarm *s.* allarme || — *-clock*, sveglia; *to take —*, allarmarsi.

to alarm *vt.* allarmare.

alas *inter.* ahimè.

Albanian *agg.* e *s.* albanese.

albatross *s.* albatro.

albumen *s.* albume.

albumin *s.* albumina.

alchemist *s.* alchimista.

alchemy *s.* alchimia.

alcohol *s.* alcool: *wood —*, alcool metilico.

alcoholic *agg.* alcolico. ◆ **alcoholic** *sm.* alcolizzato.

alcoholism *s.* alcoolismo.

alcove *s.* alcova.

alder *s.* ontano.

alderman *s.* assessore.

ale *s.* birra || *—house*, birreria.

aleatory *agg.* aleatorio.

alembic *s.* alambicco.

alert *agg.* **1.** all'erta **2.** svelto. ◆ **alert** *s.* allarme.

algebraic(al) *agg.* algebrico.

alien *agg.* e *s.* **1.** estraneo **2.** straniero.

to alienate *vt.* alienare.

alienation *s.* alienazione.

alienist *s.* alienista.

alight *agg.* illuminato.

to alight *vi.* **1.** scendere **2.** posarsi, atterrare.

to align *vt.* allineare. ◆ **to align** *vi.* allinearsi.

alignment *s.* allineamento.

alike *agg.* simile. ◆ **alike** *avv.* similmente.

aliment *s.* alimento.

alimentary *agg.* alimentare.

alimentation *s.* alimentazione.

aliquot *agg.* e *s.* aliquota.

alive *agg.* **1.** vivo **2.** vivace **3.** sensibile.

alkaline *agg.* alcalino.

all *agg.* tutto, tutti, ogni || — *the way*, lungo tutto il cammino. ◆ **all** *pron.* tutto, tutti || *not at —*, niente affatto; — *the better*, tanto meglio || — *of us*, noi tutti; *it is — up*, tutto è finito. ◆ **all** *avv.* completamente, interamente || —

right, va bene; — *but*, quasi. ◆ **all** *s.* tutto, totalità.

to allege *vt.* addurre.

allegiance *s.* fedeltà.

allegoric(al) *agg.* allegorico.

allegory *s.* allegoria.

allergic *agg.* allergico.

allergy *s.* allergia.

to alleviate *vt.* alleviare.

alleviation *s.* alleviamento.

alley *s.* vialetto, vicolo.

alliance *s.* **1.** alleanza **2.** unione.

allied *agg.* alleato.

alligator *s.* alligatore.

alliteration *s.* allitterazione.

alliterative *agg.* allitterativo.

to allocate *vt.* assegnare, distribuire.

allocution *s.* allocuzione.

to allot *vt.* assegnare.

allotment *s.* **1.** distribuzione **2.** lotto (*di terreno*).

to allow *vt.* **1.** permettere **2.** riconoscere **3.** concedere.

allowance *s.* **1.** permesso **2.** assegno, indennità **3.** razione **4.** riconoscimento **5.** sconto.

alloy *s.* (*metal.*) lega.

to allude *vi.* alludere.

to allure *vt.* attrarre.

allurement *s.* allettamento.

allusion *s.* allusione.

allusive *agg.* allusivo.

alluvion *s.* alluvione.

ally *s.* alleato.

to ally *vt.* **1.** unire **2.** alleare. ◆ **to ally** *vi.* allearsi.

almanac *s.* almanacco.

almighty *agg.* onnipotente: *the Almighty*, l'Onnipotente.

almond *s.* mandorla || — *-tree*, mandorlo.

almost *avv.* quasi.

alms *s.* elemosina || *-house*, ospizio per i poveri; — *-man*, accattone.

alone *agg.* e *avv.* solo.

along *avv.* e *prep.* **1.** lungo **2.** avanti.

alongside *avv.* (*mar.*) accanto, accosto. ◆ **alongside** *prep.* a fianco di, lungo.

aloof *avv.* a distanza. ◆ **aloof** *agg.* riservato, scontroso.

aloofness *s.* freddezza.

aloud *avv.* ad alta voce.

alp *s.* alpe.

alpha *s.* alfa.

alphabet *s.* alfabeto.

alphabetic(al) *agg.* alfabetico.

alpine *agg.* alpino.

already *avv.* già.

also *avv.* anche, inoltre.

altar *s.* altare ‖ — *-boy,* chierichetto; — *-piece,* pala d'altare.

to alter *vt.* alterare. ♦ to alter *vi.* alterarsi, trasformarsi.

alteration *s.* alterazione.

altercation *s.* alterco.

alternacy *s.* alternanza.

alternate *agg.* alterno, alternato.

to alternate *vt.* alternare. ♦ to alternate *vi.* alternarsi.

alternation *s.* alternazione.

alternative *agg.* alternativo. ♦ alternative *s.* alternativa.

alternator *s.* (*elettr.*) alternatore.

although *cong.* benché.

altimeter *s.* altimetro.

altitude *s.* 1. altitudine 2. (*aer.*) quota.

altogether *avv.* interamente.

altruism *s.* altruismo.

altruist *s.* altruista.

altruistic *agg.* altruistico.

aluminium *s.* alluminio.

always *avv.* sempre.

amalgam *s.* amalgama.

to amalgamate *vt.* amalgamare. ♦ to amalgamate *vi.* amalgamarsi.

amalgamation *s.* amalgamazione.

amaranth *s.* amaranto.

to amass *vt.* ammucchiare.

amateur *agg. e s.* amatore, dilettante.

amateurism *s.* dilettantismo.

to amaze *vt.* stupire.

amazement *s.* sorpresa.

amazing *agg.* sorprendente.

Amazon *s.* amazzone.

ambages *s. pl.* ambagi.

ambassador *s.* ambasciatore.

amber *s.* ambra.

ambient *agg.* circostante. ♦ ambient *s.* ambiente.

ambiguity *s.* ambiguità.

ambiguous *agg.* ambiguo.

ambit *s.* ambito.

ambition *s.* ambizione.

ambitious *agg.* ambizioso.

ambivalence *s.* ambivalenza.

ambivalent *agg.* ambivalente.

amble *s.* ambio.

ambo *s.* ambone.

ambulance *s.* ambulanza.

ambush *s.* imboscata.

to ambush *vt. e vi.* tendere una imboscata (a).

to ameliorate *vt. e vi.* migliorare.

to amend *vt.* emendare. ♦ to amend *vi.* emendarsi.

amendment *s.* emendamento.

amends *s.* ammenda.

amenity *s.* amenità.

American *agg. e s.* americano.

Americanism *s.* americanismo.

amethyst *s.* ametista.

amiability *s.* amabilità.

amiable *agg.* amabile.

amiably *avv.* amabilmente.

amianthus *s.* amianto.

amicable *agg.* amichevole.

amid *prep.* in mezzo a, tra, fra.

amiss *avv.* a male; *to take sthg.* —, aversene a male. ♦ amiss *agg.* inopportuno, errato.

amity *s.* amicizia.

ammonia *s.* ammoniaca.

ammunition *s.* munizioni.

amnesty *s.* amnistia.

to amnesty *vt.* amnistiare.

amoeba *s.* ameba.

among(st) *prep.* tra, fra (*più di due*); in mezzo a.

amoral *agg.* amorale.

amorality *s.* amoralità.

amorous *agg.* amoroso.

amorphous *agg.* amorfo.

to amortize *vt.* (*comm.*) ammortizzare.

amount *s.* 1. somma 2. totale 3. valore 4. quantità.

to amount *vi.* 1. ammontare 2. equivalere.

amperometer *s.* amperometro.

amphibian *agg. e s.* anfibio.

amphibious *agg.* anfibio.

amphitheatre *s.* anfiteatro.

amphitryon *s.* anfitrione.

amphora *s.* anfora.

ample *agg.* ampio.

amplification *s.* amplificazione.

amplifier *s.* amplificatore.

to amplify *vt.* amplificare. ♦ to amplify *vi.* dilungarsi.

to amputate *vt.* amputare.

amputation *s.* amputazione.

amulet *s.* amuleto.

to amuse *vt.* divertire.

amusement *s.* divertimento.

an *art.* V. a.

anachronic *agg.* anacronistico.

anachronism *s.* anacronismo.

anachronistic(al) *agg.* anacronistico.

anaemia *s.* anemia.

anaemic *agg.* anemico.

anaesthesia *s.* anestesia.

anaesthetic *agg.* e *s.* anestetico.
anaesthetist *s.* anestesista.
to anaesthetize *vt.* anestetizzare.
anagram *s.* anagramma.
anal *agg.* anale.
analgesic *agg.* e *s.* analgesico.
analogic(al) *agg.* analogico.
analogous *agg.* analogo.
analogy *s.* analogia.
to analyse *vt.* analizzare.
analysis *s.* (*pl.* -ses) analisi.
analyst *s.* analista.
analytic(al) *agg.* analitico.
anarchic(al) *agg.* anarchico.
anarchism *s.* anarchia.
anarchist *s.* anarchico.
anarchy *s.* anarchia.
anathema *s.* anatema.
anatomic(al) *agg.* anatomico.
anatomist *s.* anatomista.
to anatomize *vt.* anatomizzare.
anatomy *s.* anatomia.
ancestor *s.* antenato.
ancestral *agg.* ancestrale.
ancestry *s.* stirpe.
anchor *s.* (*mar.*) ancora.
to anchor *vt.* ancorare. ♦ to anchor *vi.* ancorarsi.
anchorage *s.* ancoraggio.
anchoret *s.* anacoreta.
anchovy *s.* acciuga.
ancient *agg.* e *s.* antico.
and *cong.* e.
androgynous *agg.* androgino.
anecdote *s.* aneddoto.
anecdotic(al) *agg.* aneddotico.
anew *avv.* di nuovo.
anfractuosity *s.* anfrattuosità.
anfractuous *agg.* anfrattuoso.
angel *s.* angelo: *guardian —*, angelo custode.
angelic(al) *agg.* angelico.
anger *s.* collera.
to anger *vt.* irritare.
angle *s.* (*geom.*) angolo || *at right
   angles*, perpendicolarmente.
to angle *vi.* 1. pescare (*con l'amo*)
   2. *to — for*, andare in cerca di.
angler *s.* pescatore (*con l'amo*).
Anglican *agg.* e *s.* anglicano.
Anglo-Saxon *agg.* e *s.* anglosassone.
angrily *avv.* irosamente.
angry *agg.* irato, arrabbiato || *to
   get —*, adirarsi.
anguish *s.* angoscia.
to anguish *vt.* angosciare. ♦ to
   anguish *vi.* angosciarsi.
angular *agg.* angolare.
anhydride *s.* anidride.

aniline *s.* anilina.
animadversion *s.* biasimo.
to animadvert *vi.* criticare: *to —
   on so., stbg.*, criticare qu., qc.
animal *agg.* e *s.* animale.
to animate *vt.* animare.
animatedly *avv.* animatamente.
animation *s.* animazione.
animator *s.* animatore.
animism *s.* animismo.
animosity *s.* animosità.
anise *s.* anice.
ankle *s.* caviglia.
ankylosis *s.* anchilosi.
annals *s. pl.* annali.
Annelida *s. pl.* anellidi.
to annex *vt.* annettere.
annexation *s.* annessione.
to annihilate *vt.* annichilire.
annihilation *s.* annichilimento.
anniversary *s.* anniversario.
to annotate *vt.* e *vi.* annotare.
annotation *s.* annotazione.
to announce *vt.* annunciare.
announcement *s.* annuncio.
announcer *s.* annunciatore.
to annoy *vt.* infastidire.
annoyance *s.* fastidio.
annoying *agg.* fastidioso.
annual *agg.* annuale. ♦ annual *s.*
   annuario.
annuity *s.* rendita annuale.
to annul *vt.* annullare.
annulment *s.* annullamento.
to annunciate *vt.* annunciare.
annunciation *s.* annuncio, annun-
   ciazione.
anode *s.* anodo.
anodyne *agg.* e *s.* anodino.
to anoint *vt.* ungere, consacrare.
anomalous *agg.* anomalo.
anomaly *s.* anomalia.
anonym *s.* anonimo.
anonymous *agg.* anonimo.
another *agg.* e *pron.* un altro ||
   one —, l'un l'altro.
answer *s.* risposta.
to answer *vt.* e *vi.* rispondere.
ant *s.* formica || *— -bear*, formi-
   chiere.
antagonism *s.* antagonismo.
antagonist *s.* antagonista.
Antarctic *agg.* antartico.
antecedent *agg.* e *s.* antecedente.
   ♦ antecedents *s. pl.* antenati.
to antedate *vt.* 1. antidatare 2. anticipare.
antediluvian *agg.* e *s.* antidiluviano.

antelope *s.* antilope.
anteroom *s.* anticamera.
anthem *s.* inno.
anthological *agg.* antologico.
anthology *s.* antologia.
anthracite *s.* antracite.
anthropocentric *agg.* antropocentrico.
anthropologist *s.* antropologo.
anthropology *s.* antropologia.
anthropomorphic *agg.* antropomorfo.
anthropomorphism *s.* antropomorfismo.
anthropomorphous *agg.* antropomorfo.
anthropophagous *agg.* e *s.* (*pl.* -gi) antropofago.
anthropophagy *s.* antropofagia.
antiaesthetic *agg.* antiestetico.
anti-aircraft *agg.* antiaereo.
antibiotic *agg.* e *s.* antibiotico.
antibody *s.* anticorpo.
to anticipate *vt.* 1. anticipare 2. prevedere 3. pregustare.
anticipation *s.* 1. anticipo 2. previsione 3. pregustazione.
anticlerical *agg.* anticlericale.
anticlericalism *s.* anticlericalismo.
anticonceptive *s.* antifecondativo.
anticonstitutional *agg.* anticostituzionale.
anticyclone *s.* anticiclone.
anti-dazzle *agg.* antiabbagliante.
antidote *s.* antidoto.
anti-freeze *s.* anticongelante.
anti-gas *agg.* antigas.
antimilitarism *s.* antimilitarismo.
antimilitarist *s.* antimilitarista.
antimony *s.* antimonio.
antinomy *s.* antinomia.
antiparticle *s.* antiparticella.
antipathetic(al) *agg.* avverso.
antipathy *s.* antipatia.
antiphon(y) *s.* antifona.
antipodal *agg.* degli, agli antipodi.
antipode *s.* antipodo.
antiquarian *agg.* e *s.* antiquario.
antiquary *s.* antiquario.
antiquated *agg.* antiquato.
antique *agg.* antico. ♦ antique *s.* antichità || — dealer, antiquario.
antiquity *s.* antichità.
antirheumatic *agg.* antireumatico.
anti-rust *agg.* e *s.* antiruggine.
anti-Semite *s.* antisemita.
anti-Semitism *s.* antisemitismo.
antiseptic *agg.* e *s.* antisettico.
antisocial *agg.* antisociale.

antispasmodic *agg.* e *s.* antispasmodico.
anti-tank *agg.* anticarro.
antitetanic *agg.* antitetanico.
anti-theft *agg.* e *s.* antifurto.
antithesis *s.* (*pl.* -ses) antitesi.
antithetic(al) *agg.* antitetico.
antitoxic *agg.* antitossico.
anus *s.* ano.
anvil *s.* incudine.
anxiety *s.* ansietà.
anxious *agg.* ansioso.
any *agg.* 1. qualunque 2. (*in frasi neg.; int.; dubitative*) qualche, nessuno, del || at — rate, in ogni modo. ♦ any *pron.* 1. alcuno, nessuno 2. ne || have you — bread?, hai del pane?; I haven't —, non ne ho.
anybody *pron.* 1. chiunque 2. (*in frasi neg.; int.; dubitative*) qualcuno, nessuno.
anyhow *avv.* e *cong.* comunque.
anyone *pron.* V. *anybody*.
anything *pron.* 1. qualunque cosa 2. (*in frasi neg.; int.; dubitative*) qualche cosa, niente.
anyway *avv.* in ogni modo, comunque.
anywhere *avv.* dovunque.
apace *avv.* presto.
apanage *s.* appannaggio.
apart *avv.* 1. a parte 2. lontano.
apartheid *s.* discriminazione razziale.
apartment *s.* alloggio (*in affitto*).
apathy *s.* apatia.
ape *s.* scimmia.
to ape *vt.* scimmiottare.
aperitif *s.* aperitivo.
apex *s.* apice.
aphaeresis *s.* aferesi.
aphonia *s.* afonia.
aphorism *s.* aforisma.
aphrodisiac *agg.* e *s.* afrodisiaco.
aphtha *s.* afta.
apiece *avv.* a testa.
apish *agg.* scimmiesco.
apocalypse *s.* apocalisse.
apocalyptic(al) *agg.* apocalittico.
apocrypha *s. pl.* libri apocrifi.
apocryphal *agg.* apocrifo.
apogee *s.* apogeo.
apologetic(al) *agg.* apologetico.
apologist *s.* apologista.
to apologize *vi.* scusarsi.
apologue *s.* apologo.
apology *s.* scusa.
apoplexy *s.* apoplessia.

apostasy s. apostasia.
apostate agg. e s. apostata.
apostle s. apostolo.
apostolate s. apostolato.
apostolic(al) agg. apostolico.
apostrophe s. apostrofo.
to **apostrophize** vt. apostrofare.
apothecary s. farmacista.
apotheosis s. (pl. -ses) apotcosi.
to **appal** vt. spaventare.
appalling agg. spaventoso.
apparatus s. apparato.
apparent agg. 1. visibile, evidente 2. (giur.) legittimo.
apparition s. apparizione.
appeal s. 1. appello 2. attrattiva.
to **appeal** vi. 1. appellarsi 2. attrarre.
appealing agg. 1. supplichevole 2. attraente.
to **appear** vi. 1. apparire 2. sembrare.
appearance s. 1. apparenza, aspetto 2. apparizione.
to **appease** vt. placare.
appeasement s. pacificazione, tregua.
appellative agg. e s. appellativo.
appendicitis s. appendicite.
appendix s. appendice.
appetite s. appetito.
appetizer s. aperitivo.
appetizing agg. appetitoso.
to **applaud** vt. e vi. applaudire.
applauding agg. plaudente.
applause s. applauso.
apple s. mela || — -tree, melo.
appliance s. 1. applicazione 2. apparecchio.
applicant s. richiedente.
application s. 1. applicazione 2. domanda.
to **apply** vt. applicare. ♦ to **apply** vi. 1. applicarsi 2. rivolgersi.
to **appoint** vt. 1. fissare 2. nominare, assegnare.
appointee s. persona designata.
appointment s. 1. appuntamento 2. nomina 3. impiego.
apposition s. apposizione.
appraisal s. stima.
to **appraise** vt. stimare.
appreciable agg. apprezzabile.
to **appreciate** vt. 1. apprezzare 2. rendersi conto di. ♦ to **appreciate** vi. aumentare di valore.
appreciation s. 1. apprezzamento 2. aumento di valore.
to **apprehend** vt. assodare.

apprehension s. 1. apprensione 2. percezione 3. arresto.
apprehensive agg. 1. apprensivo 2. perspicace.
apprentice s. apprendista.
apprenticeship s. apprendistato.
approach s. 1. avvicinamento 2. approccio 3. impostazione (di una pratica ecc.).
to **approach** vt. avvicinare. ♦ to **approach** vi. avvicinarsi.
approachable agg. accessibile.
appropriate agg. appropriato.
to **appropriate** vt. 1. appropriarsi di 2. stanziare.
appropriation s. 1. appropriazione 2. stanziamento.
approval s. 1. approvazione 2. (comm.) prova: on —, in prova.
to **approve** vt. 1. approvare 2. mostrare.
approximate agg. approssimativo.
to **approximate** vt. approssimare. ♦ to **approximate** vi. approssimarsi.
approximation s. approssimazione.
approximative agg. approssimativo
apricot s. albicocca || — -tree, albicocco.
April s. aprile.
apron s. 1. grembiale 2. riparo 3. (teat.) proscenio.
apse s. abside.
apt agg. 1. atto 2. intelligente 3. proclive.
aptitude, aptness s. 1. idoneità 2. intelligenza 3. proprietà (di vocabolo).
aqualung s. autorespiratore.
aquamarine s. acquamarina.
aquarium s. acquario.
aquatic(al) agg. acquatico.
aqueduct s. acquedotto.
aqueous agg. acqueo, acquoso.
Arab agg. e s. arabo.
arabesque s. arabesco.
Arabian agg. e s. arabo.
Arabic agg. arabico.
arable agg. arabile.
arbiter s. arbitro.
arbitrage s. arbitraggio.
arbitrary agg. arbitrario.
to **arbitrate** vt. e vi. arbitrare.
arbitrator s. (giur.) arbitro.
arboreal, arboreous agg. arboreo
arboriculture s. arboricoltura.
arbour s. pergolato.
arc s. arco.
arcade s. galleria.

Arcadian agg. e s. arcadico.

arch s. arco.

to arch vt. **1.** fabbricare ad arco **2.** inarcare. ◆ **to arch** vi. inarcarsi.

archaeologic(al) agg. archeologico.

archaeologist s. archeologo.

archaeology s. archeologia

archaic(al) agg. arcaico.

archaism s. arcaismo.

archangel s. arcangelo.

archbishop s. arcivescovo

archduke s. arciduca.

archer s. arciere.

archetype s. archetipo.

archipelago s. arcipelago.

architect s. architetto.

architectonic, architectural agg. architettonico.

architecture s. architettura.

archive s. archivio.

archivist s. archivista.

Arctic agg. e s. artico.

ardent agg. ardente.

ardour s. ardore.

arduous agg. arduo.

area s. area.

arena s. (arch.) arena.

Areopagus s. areopago.

argent s. argenteo.

Argentine agg. e s. argentino.

argil s. argilla.

to argue vi. **1.** discutere **2.** ragionare. ◆ **to argue** vt. dimostrare.

argument s. **1.** discussione **2.** argomentazione.

arid agg. arido.

aridity s. aridità.

to arise (arose, arisen) vi. **1.** alzarsi **2.** (fig.) nascere.

aristocracy s. aristocrazia.

aristocrat s. aristocratico.

aristocratic(al) agg. aristocratico.

Aristotelian agg. e s. aristotelico.

arithmetic s. aritmetica.

arithmetic(al) agg. aritmetico.

arm[1] s. braccio || — -in- —, a braccetto.

arm[2] s. arma || coat of arms, stemma.

to arm vt. armare. ◆ **to arm** vi. armarsi.

armament s. armamento.

armchair s. poltrona.

armful s. bracciata.

armistice s. armistizio.

armless agg. inerme.

armlet s. braccialetto.

armour s. corazza.

to armour vt. corazzare || armour-ed-car, autoblinda.

armoury s. **1.** arsenale **2.** armeria.

armpit s. ascella.

army s. esercito.

aromatic(al) agg. aromatico.

arose V. to arise.

around avv. intorno. ◆ **around** prep. **1.** intorno a **2.** circa.

to arouse vt. **1.** destare **2.** eccitare.

to arrange vt. **1.** accomodare **2.** predisporre **3.** (mus.) arrangiare.

arrangement s. **1.** accomodamento **2.** (mus.) arrangiamento **3.** dispositivo. ◆ **arrangements** s. pl. preparativi.

arras s. arazzo.

array s. **1.** apparato **2.** (mil.) spiegamento.

to array vt. **1.** ornare **2.** (mil.) schierare.

arrest s. arresto.

to arrest vt. arrestare.

arrival s. arrivo.

to arrive vi. arrivare.

arrogance s. arroganza.

arrogant agg. arrogante.

to arrogate vt. arrogarsi.

arrow s. freccia.

arsenal s. arsenale.

arsenic s. arsenico.

art s. arte.

arteriosclerosis s. arteriosclerosi.

artery s. arteria.

artesian agg. artesiano.

artful agg. **1.** abile **2.** artificioso **3.** astuto.

arthritic(al) agg. artritico.

arthritis s. artrite.

artichoke s. carciofo.

article s. articolo.

articulate agg. **1.** articolato **2.** chiaro.

to articulate vt. articolare. ◆ **to articulate** vi. articolarsi.

articulation s. articolazione.

artifice s. **1.** artificio **2.** abilità.

artificial agg. artificiale.

artificiality s. artificiosità.

artillery s. artiglieria.

artilleryman s. artigliere.

artist s. artista.

artistic(al) agg. artistico.

artistry s. abilità artistica.

artless agg. ingenuo.

Aryan agg. e s. ariano.

as avv. come || — ... —, tanto ... quanto; so — (con infinito), in modo da; — for, quanto a; — far —, sin dove, fino a; — much, al-

trettanto; — *well*, come pure. ♦
as *cong.* 1. poiché 2. mentre.

asbestos *s.* asbesto.

to **ascend** *vi.* ascendere. ♦ ∞
ascend *vt.* risalire, scalare.

ascendancy *s.* ascendente.

ascendant *agg. e s.* ascendente.

ascension *s.* ascensione.

ascent *s.* ascesa.

to **ascertain** *vt.* accertarsi di.

ascertainment *s.* accertamento.

ascetic *s.* asceta.

ascetic(al) *agg.* ascetico.

asceticism *s.* ascetismo.

to **ascribe** *vt.* ascrivere.

asepsis *s.* asepsi.

aseptic *agg. e s.* asettico.

asexual *agg.* asessuale.

ash *s.* cenere || — -*tray*, portacenere.

ash(-tree) *s.* frassino.

ashamed *agg.* vergognoso || *to be*
—, aver vergogna. ♦

ashore *avv.* a terra.

ashy *agg.* cinereo.

Asiatic *agg. e s.* asiatico.

aside *avv.* a parte, da parte.

asininity *s.* asinità.

to **ask** *vt. e vi.* 1. chiedere 2. invi-
tare || *to — so. for sthg.*, chiedere
a qu. qc.; *to — for trouble*, cer-
car fastidi.

askance *avv.* di traverso.

asker *s.* interrogante.

asleep *agg.* addormentato.

asocial *agg.* asociale.

asp *s.* aspide.

asparagus *s. coll.* asparago, aspa-
ragi.

aspect *s.* aspetto.

aspen *s.* pioppo tremulo.

aspergillum *s.* aspersorio.

asperity *s.* 1. asperità 2. (*fig.*)
asprezza.

aspersion *s.* 1. aspersione 2. calunnia.

asphalt *s.* asfalto.

asphyxia *s.* asfissia.

to **asphyxiate** *vt.* asfissiare.

aspirant *agg. e s.* aspirante.

to **aspirate** *vt.* aspirare.

aspiration *s.* aspirazione.

aspirator *s.* aspiratore.

to **aspire** *vi.* aspirare.

aspirin *s.* aspirina.

aspiring *agg.* ambizioso.

asquint *avv.* di traverso.

ass *s.* asino || *to make an — of one-
self*, rendersi ridicolo.

to **assail** *vt.* assalire.

assailant, assailer *s.* assalitore.

assassin *s.* assassino.

to **assassinate** *vt.* assassinare.

assassination *s.* assassinio.

assault *s.* assalto, aggressione.

to **assault** *vt.* assalire.

assaulter *s.* assalitore.

to **assay** *vt.* saggiare.

assayer *s.* (as)saggiatore.

to **assemble** *vt.* riunire. ♦ to **assemble** *vi.* riunirsi.

assembly *s.* 1. assemblea 2. (*mil.*)
adunata 3. (*mecc.*) montaggio: —
line, catena di montaggio.

assent *s.* consenso.

to **assent** *vt.* approvare.

to **assert** *vt.* asserire || *to — one-
self*, farsi valere.

assertion *s.* asserzione.

assertor *s.* assertore.

to **assess** *vt.* 1. tassare 2. (*comm.*)
ripartire.

assessment *s.* 1. valutazione 2. tassazione.

assessor *s.* agente delle tasse.

asset *s.* 1. bene, vantaggio. ♦ as-
sets *s. pl.* patrimonio, attività
(*sing.*).

assiduity *s.* assiduità.

assiduous *agg.* assiduo.

to **assign** *vt.* 1. assegnare 2. trasferire 3. designare.

assignation *s.* 1. assegnazione 2.
(*giur.*) cessione 3. appuntamento.

assignment *s.* 1. assegnazione 2.
(*giur.*) cessione.

assimilable *agg.* assimilabile.

to **assimilate** *vt.* 1. assimilare 2.
confrontare. ♦ to **assimilate** *vi.*
assimilarsi.

assimilation *s.* 1. assimilazione 2.
confronto.

to **assist** *vt. e vi.* assistere.

assistance *s.* assistenza.

assistant *agg. e s.* assistente || *shop*
—, commesso.

assize *s.* 1. (*giur.*) seduta. ♦ **Assizes** *s. pl.* Assise.

associate *agg. e s.* associato.

to **associate** *vt.* associare. ♦ to
associate *vi.* associarsi.

association *s.* associazione.

assonance *s.* assonanza.

to **assort** *vt.* 1. assortire 2. classificare. ♦ to **assort** *vi.* 1. armonizzarsi 2. frequentare: *to — with
so.*, frequentare qu.

to **assume** *vt.* 1. assumere 2. fingere 3. presumere.

assuming *agg.* presuntuoso.
assumption *s.* 1. assunzione 2. finzione 3. supposizione 4. presunzione.
assurance *s.* 1. assicurazione 2. sicurezza 3. fiducia.
to **assure** *vt.* 1. assicurare 2. rassicurare.
assurer *s.* assicuratore.
asterisk *s.* asterisco.
astern *avv.* a poppa.
asteroid *s.* asteroide.
asthenia *s.* astenia.
asthma *s.* asma.
asthmatic *agg.* e *s.* asmatico.
astigmatic *agg.* astigmatico.
astigmatism *s.* astigmatismo.
astir *agg.* e *avv.* in moto.
to **astonish** *vt.* stupire.
astonishing *agg.* sorprendente
astonishment *s.* sorpresa.
to **astound** *vt.* sbalordire.
astragal(us) *s.* astragalo.
astrakhan *s.* astracan.
astral *agg.* astrale.
astray *agg.* e *avv.* fuori strada.
astride *agg.* e *avv.* a cavalcioni. ◆
　astride *prep.* a cavalcioni di.
astringent *agg.* e *s.* astringente.
astrolabe *s.* astrolabio.
astrologer *s.* astrologo.
astrology *s.* astrologia.
astronaut *s.* astronauta.
astronautics *s.* astronautica.
astronomer *s.* astronomo.
astronomic(al) *agg.* astronomico.
astronomy *s.* astronomia.
astute *agg.* astuto.
asunder *avv.* 1. separatamente 2. in pezzi.
asylum *s.* 1. asilo, ricovero 2. manicomio.
asymmetric(al) *agg.* asimmetrico.
asymmetry *s.* asimmetria.
at *prep.* (*stato, tempo, modo*) a, da, in: *to arrive — a place*, arrivare in un luogo; *— that time*, in quel momento; *— will*, a volontà.
atavistic *agg.* atavico.
atavism *s.* atavismo.
ataxy *s.* atassia.
ate V. *to eat.*
atheism *s.* ateismo.
atheist *s.* ateo.
atheistic(al) *agg.* ateistico.
athlete *s.* atleta.
athletic *agg.* atletico.
athletics *s.* atletica.
atlas *s.* atlante.

atmosphere *s.* atmosfera.
atmospheric(al) *agg.* atmosferico.
atoll *s.* atollo.
atom *s.* atomo.
atomic(al) *agg.* atomico.
atomism *s.* atomismo.
to **atomize** *vt.* nebulizzare.
atomizer *s.* atomizzatore, nebulizzatore.
atomy *s.* atomo.
to **atone** *vt.* espiare.
atonement *s.* espiazione.
atonic *agg.* 1. atono 2. atonico.
atrocious *agg.* atroce.
atrocity *s.* atrocità.
atrophic *agg.* atrofico.
atrophy *s.* atrofia.
to **atrophy** *vt.* atrofizzare. ◆ to.
　atrophy *vi.* atrofizzarsi.
atropin(e) *s.* atropina.
to **attach** *vt.* 1. attaccare, unire 2. attribuire 3. attrarre. ◆ to **attach** *vi.* attaccarsi.
attaché *s.* addetto.
attachment *s.* 1. attaccamento 2. (*mecc.*) accessorio.
attack *s.* attacco.
to **attack** *vt.* attaccare.
attacker *s.* assalitore.
to **attain** *vt.* raggiungere. ◆ to **attain** *vi.* giungere.
attainable *agg.* raggiungibile.
attainment *s.* 1. raggiungimento 2. cultura.
attempt *s.* 1. tentativo 2. attentato.
to **attempt** *vt.* 1. tentare 2. attentare a.
to **attend** *vi.* 1. badare a 2. obbedire ‖ *to — on*, essere al servizio di. ◆ to **attend** *vt.* 1. assistere 2. accompagnare 3. frequentare.
attendance *s.* 1. servizio 2. assistenza 3. frequenza.
attendant *s.* 1. servitore 2. assistente 3. assiduo frequentatore.
attention *s.* attenzione: *to pay —*, fare attenzione.
attentive *agg.* 1. attento 2. sollecito.
to **attenuate** *vt.* 1. assottigliare 2. attenuare. ◆ to **attenuate** *vi.* 1. assottigliarsi 2. attenuarsi.
attenuation *s.* 1. assottigliamento 2. attenuazione.
to **attest** *vt.* attestare.
attic *agg.* e *s.* attico.
to **attire** *vt.* vestire, agghindare. ◆ to **attire** *vi.* vestirsi.
attitude *s.* atteggiamento.

attorney s. 1. procura 2. procuratore || — (-at-law), procuratore legale.

to attract vt. attrarre.

attraction s. 1. attrazione 2. attrattiva.

attractive agg. attraente.

attribute s. attributo.

to attribute vt. attribuire.

attribution s. attribuzione.

attributive agg. attributivo. ♦ **attributive** s. attributo.

aubergine s. melanzana.

auction s. asta: — sale, vendita all'asta.

to auction vt. vendere all'asta.

auctioneer s. banditore.

audible agg. udibile.

audience s. 1. udienza 2. uditorio.

audiovisual agg. audiovisivo.

audit s. verifica, revisione.

audition s. audizione.

auditory agg. e s. uditorio.

auger s. trivella, succhiello.

to augment vt. aumentare. ♦ **to augment** vi. crescere.

augmentative agg. e s. accrescitivo.

to augur vt. e vi. predire.

august agg. augusto.

August s. agosto.

aunt s. zia || great- —, prozia.

auricle s. 1. padiglione auricolare 2. (med.) orecchietta.

auricular agg. auricolare.

auriferous agg. aurifero.

to auscultate vt. auscultare.

auscultation s. auscultazione.

auscultator s. stetoscopio.

auspice s. auspicio.

auspicious agg. propizio.

austere agg. austero.

austerity s. austerità.

austral agg. australe.

Australian agg. e s. australiano.

Austrian agg. e s. austriaco.

autarky s. autarchia.

authentic(al) agg. autentico.

to authenticate vt. autenticare.

authentication s. autenticazione.

authenticity s. autenticità.

author s. autore.

authoress s. autrice.

authoritative agg. 1. autoritario 2. autorevole.

authoritativeness s. autorevolezza.

authority s. autorità.

authorization s. autorizzazione.

to authorize vt. autorizzare.

authorless agg. anonimo.

authorship s. paternità (di un libro).

autobiographic(al) agg. autobiografico.

autobiography s. autobiografia.

autochthon s. autoctono.

autochthonous agg. autoctono.

autocracy s. autocrazia.

autocrat s. autocrate.

autocriticism s. autocritica.

autoeducation s. autoeducazione.

autofinancing s. autofinanziamento.

autograph s. autografo.

autography s. autografia.

autolesion s. autolesione.

automatic agg. automatico. ♦ **automatic** s. arma automatica.

automation s. automazione.

automatism s. automatismo.

automaton s. automa.

autonomist s. autonomista.

autonomous agg. autonomo.

autonomy s. autonomia.

autopsy s. autopsia.

auto-suggestion s. autosuggestione.

autumn s. autunno.

autumnal agg. autunnale.

auxiliary agg. e s. ausiliare.

avail s. utilità.

to avail vt. e vi. servire a || to — oneself of, approfittare di.

availability s. 1. disponibilità 2. validità.

available agg. 1. disponibile 2. valevole.

avalanche s. valanga.

avarice s. 1. avarizia 2. cupidigia.

avaricious agg. 1. avaro 2. cupido.

to avenge vt. vendicare.

avenger s. vendicatore.

avenue s. viale.

to aver vt. asserire, dichiarare.

average agg. medio. ♦ **average** s. 1. media 2. (comm.) avaria.

averse agg. avverso.

aversion s. avversione.

to avert vt. sviare.

aviary s. uccelliera.

aviation s. aviazione.

aviator s. aviatore.

avid agg. avido.

avidity s. avidità.

to avoid vt. 1. evitare 2. (giur.) annullare.

avoidable agg. 1. evitabile 2. (giur.) annullabile.

to avow vt. dichiarare, ammettere.

avowal s. dichiarazione, ammissione.

to **await** *vt.* attendere.

awake *agg.* 1. sveglio 2. conscio.

to **awake (awoke, awoke)** *vt.* svegliare. ♦ to **awake (awoke, awoke)** *vi.* svegliarsi.

to **awaken** *vt.* risvegliare, far aprire gli occhi. ♦ to **awaken** *vi.* risvegliarsi, aprire gli occhi.

awakening *s.* risveglio.

award *s.* 1. sentenza 2. ricompensa.

to **award** *vt.* aggiudicare.

aware *agg.* conscio.

away *avv.* via, lontano || *right* —, subito, seduta stante.

awe *s.* timore reverenziale.

awful *agg.* 1. terribile 2. imponente.

awkward *agg.* 1. goffo, imbarazzato 2. scomodo 3. inopportuno 4. delicato.

awkwardness *s.* 1. goffaggine 2. imbarazzo.

awl *s.* lesina.

awning *s.* tenda.

awoke V. *to awake.*

awry *agg.* 1. storto 2. bieco. ♦ **awry** *avv.* 1. per traverso 2. perversamente.

ax(e) *s.* scure.

axiom *s.* assioma.

axiomatic(al) *agg.* assiomatico.

axis *s.* (*pl.* axes) asse.

axle *s.* (*mecc.*) asse.

azimuth *s.* azimut.

azote *s.* azoto.

to **azotize** *vt.* azotare.

Aztec *agg.* e *s.* azteco.

azure *agg.* e *s.* azzurro.

B

b *s.* (*mus.*) si.

babble *s.* balbettio.

to **babble** *vi.* e *vt.* 1. balbettare 2. mormorare (*di acque*).

babe *s.* bambino.

babel *s.* babele.

baboon *s.* babbuino.

baby *s.* bimbo, neonato || — -*sitter*, chi accudisce i bambini.

babyhood *s.* infanzia.

babyish *agg.* infantile.

baccarat *s.* baccarà.

Bacchanal *s.* 1. baccante 2. baccanale (*anche fig.*).

Bacchante *s.* baccante.

bacchic(al) *agg.* bacchico.

bachelor *s.* scapolo || *Bachelor of Arts*, titolo universitario in lettere.

bachelorhood *s.* celibato.

bacillus *s.* (*pl.* -li) bacillo.

back[1] *agg.* posteriore. ♦ **back** *avv.* dietro, indietro || *to be* —, essere di ritorno; *to go, to come* —, ritornare.

back[2] *s.* 1. dorso, schiena 2. spalle 3. rovescio 4. schienale 5. fondo.

to **back** *vt.* 1. sostenere 2. fare indietreggiare || *to — a bill*, avallare una cambiale. ♦ to **back** *vi.* indietreggiare || — *down*, abbandonare la contesa.

to **backbite** *vt.* denigrare.

backbiter *s.* calunniatore.

backbiting *agg.* maldicente. ♦ **backbiting** *s.* maldicenza.

backbone *s.* 1. spina dorsale 2. (*fig.*) fermezza.

backer *s.* 1. scommettitore 2. sostenitore.

backfire *s.* ritorno di fiamma.

background *s.* 1. sfondo 2. curriculum 3. ambiente.

backing *s.* 1. sostegno 2. marcia indietro.

backlash *s.* rimbalzo.

backslider *s.* apostata.

backward *agg.* 1. lento 2. tardo.

backward(s) *avv.* indietro.

backwash *s.* risacca.

bacon *s.* lardo affumicato, pancetta.

bacterial *agg.* batterico.

bacteriology *s.* batteriologia.

bacterium *s.* (*pl.* -ia) batterio.

bad (worse, worst) *agg.* 1. cattivo 2. brutto. ♦ **bad** *s.* 1. male 2. rovina.

bade V. *to bid.*

badge *s.* insegna.

badger *s.* tasso.

badly *avv.* male, malamente.

badness *s.* 1. cattiveria 2. cattiva qualità.

baffle *s.* (-*plate*) deflettore, diaframma.

to **baffle** *vt.* 1. eludere 2. confondere.

bag *s.* 1. sacco 2. borsa || *sleeping-* —, sacco a pelo.

to **bag** *vt.* 1. gonfiare 2. rubare 3. insaccare.

baggage *s.* bagaglio.

bagpipe *s.* cornamusa.

bail[1] *s.* 1. cauzione 2. garante.

to **bail**[1] *vt.* 1. dar garanzia per 2.

affidare (*dietro cauzione*).

to **bail**[2] *vt.* e *vi.* (*mar.*) aggottare || *to — out*, lanciarsi col paracadute.

bailiff *s.* 1. magistrato inquirente 2. ufficiale fiscale.

bain-marie *s.* bagnomaria.

bait *s.* 1. esca 2. sosta (*per ristoro*).

to **bait** *vt.* 1. adescare 2. tormentare. ♦ to **bait** *vi.* fermarsi (*per prendere ristoro*).

to **bake** *vt.* e *vi.* cuocere al forno.

baker *s.* fornaio.

bakery *s.* forno.

baking *s.* cottura al forno.

balance *s.* 1. bilancia 2. bilanciere 3. equilibrio 4. bilancio.

to **balance** *vt.* 1. pesare 2. pareggiare. ♦ to **balance** *vi.* 1. bilanciarsi 2. oscillare.

balanced *agg.* equilibrato.

balancer *s.* acrobata.

balcony *s.* 1. balcone 2. (*teat.*).balconata.

bald *agg.* 1. calvo, pelato 2. povero, nudo.

baldness *s.* 1. calvizie 2. (*fig.*) nudità.

baldric *s.* bandoliera.

bale *s.* (*comm.*) balla.

Balkan *agg.* balcanico.

ball *s.* 1. palla 2. ballo || *—-bearing*, cuscinetto a sfere.

to **ball** *vt.* appallottolare. ♦ tn **ball** *vi.* appallottolarsi.

ballad *s.* ballata.

ballast *s.* zavorra.

to **ballast** *vt.* zavorrare.

ballet *s.* balletto || *—-dancer*, ballerino classico.

ballistics *s.* balistica.

balloon *s.* 1. pallone 2. lambicco 3. fumetto.

ballot *s.* 1. pallina, scheda (*per votazione*) 2. voto 3. scrutinio || *—-box*, urna.

to **ballot** *vt.* mettere in ballottaggio.

balm *s.* balsamo.

balm-cricket *s.* (*zool.*) cicala.

balmy *agg.* balsamico.

Baltic *agg.* baltico.

balustrade *s.* balaustrata.

bamboo *s.* bambù.

ban *s.* bando.

to **ban** *vt.* proibire.

banal *agg.* banale.

banality *s.* banalità.

banana *s.* 1. banana 2. banano.

band *s.* 1. legame 2. benda 3. nastro 4. banda.

to **band** *vt.* 1. legare 2. bendare.

bandage *s.* bendaggio.

to **bandage** *vt.* bendare.

banderole *s.* banderuola.

bandit *s.* bandito.

bandmaster *s.* capobanda.

bandog *s.* cane da guardia.

bandsman *s.* bandista.

bane *s.* 1. calamità 2. veleno.

baneful *agg.* velenoso.

bang *s.* 1. botta 2. detonazione.

to **bang** *vt.* e *vi.* sbattere violentemente.

banging *s.* 1. colpi violenti 2. detonazioni.

to **banish** *vt.* bandire, esiliare.

banishment *s.* bando, esilio.

banister *s.* ringhiera (*di scala*).

bank *s.* 1. banca 2. banco 3. argine 4. terrapieno.

to **bank** *vt.* 1. arginare 2. depositare in banca || *to — upon*, contare su. ♦ to **bank** *vi.* gestire una banca.

bankbook *s.* libretto bancario.

banker *s.* banchiere.

banking *agg.* bancario. ♦ **banking** *s.* tecnica, professione bancaria.

bank note *s.* banconota.

bankrupt *agg.* e *s.* fallito || *to go —*, fallire.

bankruptcy *s.* fallimento.

banner *s.* vessillo.

banns *s. pl.* pubblicazioni matrimoniali.

banquet *s.* banchetto.

to **banquet** *vi.* banchettare.

banter *s.* scherzo, beffa.

to **banter** *vt.* canzonare.

baptism *s.* battesimo.

baptist(e)ry *s.* battistero.

to **baptize** *vt.* battezzare.

bar *s.* 1. sbarra 2. diga 3. striscia 4. ostacolo 5. (*fig.*) tribunale 6. bar 7. (*mus.*) battuta.

to **bar** *vt.* 1. sbarrare 2. ostacolare 3. proibire.

barbarian *agg.* e *s.* barbaro.

barbaric *agg.* barbarico.

barbarism *s.* 1. barbarie 2. (*gramm.*) barbarismo.

barbarous *agg.* barbaro.

barbarousness *s.* barbarie.

barbecue *s.* 1. animale arrostito intero 2. festa campestre.

to **barbecue** *vt.* arrostire un animale intero.

barbed *agg.* dentato.

barber *s.* barbiere.

barbiturate s. barbiturico.

bard s. bardo, trovatore.

bare agg. 1. nudo 2. logoro.

to **bare** vt. 1. denudare 2. snudare 3. smascherare.

barefoot agg. scalzo.

barehanded agg. e avv. 1. a mano nuda 2. senz'armi.

bareheaded agg. a capo scoperto.

barely avv. 1. apertamente 2. appena.

bargain s. affare.

to **bargain** vt. e vi. contrattare.

bargaining s. contrattazione.

barge s. chiatta.

baritone s. baritono.

bark[1] s. corteccia.

bark[2] s. latrato.

to **bark**[1] vt. scortecciare.

to **bark**[2] vi. latrare, abbaiare.

barking[1] s. scortecciamento.

barking[2] s. abbaiamento.

barley s. orzo.

barmaid s. barista (donna).

barman s. barista.

barn s. granaio.

barometer s. barometro.

barometric(al) agg. barometrico

baron s. barone.

baroness s. baronessa.

baroque agg. e s. barocco.

barracks s. pl. caserma (sing.).

barrage s. sbarramento.

barrel s. 1. barile 2. cilindro 3. canna (di arma da fuoco) || —organ, organetto.

to **barrel** vt. mettere in barili.

barrelled agg. double- — gun, fucile a due canne.

barren agg. sterile.

barrenness s. sterilità.

barricade s. barricata.

to **barricade** vt. barricare.

barrier s. barriera || transonic —, muro del suono.

barrister s. avvocato (che può discutere cause nelle corti superiori).

barrow s. 1. barella 2. carriola.

bartender s. barista.

barter s. baratto.

to **barter** vt. e vi. barattare.

basal agg. basilare.

basalt s. basalto.

base[1] agg. basso, vile.

base[2] s. base.

to **base** vt. basare.

baseless agg. senza base.

basement s. 1. fondamento 2. seminterrato.

baseness s. bassezza.

to **bash** vt. colpire.

bashful agg. timido.

bashfulness s. timidezza.

basic agg. 1. fondamentale 2. (chim.) basico.

basil s. basilico.

basilar agg. basilare.

basilisk s. basilisco.

basin s. 1. bacino 2. catino, lavabo || sugar —, zuccheriera.

basis s. (pl. -ses) base.

to **bask** vi. crogiolarsi (al sole, al fuoco).

basket s. cesto || —ball, pallacanestro; - -chair, poltroncina di vimini.

Basque agg. e s. basco.

bas-relief s. bassorilievo.

bass agg. e s. (mus.) basso.

bass s. pesce persico.

bassoon s. (mus.) fagotto.

bastard agg. e s. bastardo.

to **baste** vt. imbastire.

basting s. imbastitura.

bastion s. bastione.

bat[1] s. pipistrello.

bat[2] s. (sport) mazza.

batch s. 1. infornata 2. gruppo.

to **bate** vt. ridurre.

bath s. bagno || - —robe, accappatoio; - -tub, vasca da bagno.

to **bath** vt. bagnare. ♦ to **bath** vi. bagnarsi, fare il bagno.

bathe s. bagno (in mare, lago ecc.)

to **bathe** vt. bagnare. ♦ to **bathe** vi. bagnarsi, fare il bagno (in mare, lago ecc.).

bather s. bagnante.

bathing s. il bagnarsi || - -suit, costume da bagno.

bathroom s. stanza da bagno.

bathysphere s. batisfera.

batiste s. batista.

batman s. attendente.

baton s. 1. bastone 2. bacchetta (di direttore d'orchestra).

batrachian s. batrace.

batsman s. (sport) battitore.

battalion s. battaglione.

to **batten** vt. (mar.) chiudere (i boccaporti).

batter s. (cuc.) pastella.

to **batter** vt. battere || to — down, abbattere; to — in, sfondare.

battering s. cannoneggiamento.

battery s. batteria || storage —, accumulatore.

battle s. battaglia.

to **battle** vt. e vi. combattere.

battledore s. racchetta di legno ||
— and shuttlecock, volano.

battlement s. (arch.) merlo.

battleship s. nave da guerra.

bauxite s. bauxite.

bawdiness s. oscenità.

bawdy agg. osceno || — house, bordello.

bawl s. grido.

to **bawl** vt. e vi. gridare, vociare.

bay[1] s. 1. baia 2. insenatura, recesso (nelle montagne).

bay[2] s. alloro || — tree, lauro.

bay[3] s. 1. rientranza 2. campata ||
-window, bovindo.

bay[4] s. latrato || at —, senza scampo.

bay[5] agg. e s. baio.

to **bay**[1] vt. arginare.

to **bay**[2] vi. latrare.

bayonet s. baionetta.

baza(a)r s. 1. bazar 2. vendita di beneficenza.

to **be** (was, been) vi. 1. essere 2. stare 3. andare 4. costare: how much is it?, quanto costa? 5. dovere || to — in, essere in casa; to — about, stare per; so be it, così sia.

beach s. spiaggia.

beacon s. faro.

to **beacon** vt. guidare con segnalazioni luminose.

bead s. 1. goccia 2. perlina. ♦ **beads** s. pl. rosario (sing.).

to **bead** vt. imperlare. ♦ to **bead** vi. imperlarsi.

beak[1] s. becco, rostro 2. beccuccio.

to **beak** vt. beccare.

beaker s. boccale.

beam s. 1. trave 2. raggio 3. asta (di bilancia) 4. fiancata (di nave).

to **beam** vi. brillare. ♦ to **beam** vt. irradiare.

beaming agg. raggiante.

bean s. fagiolo || French —, fagiolino; coffee —, grano di caffè.

bear s. orso.

to **bear**[1] vt. e vi. speculare al ribasso (in Borsa).

to **bear**[2] (bore, born(e)) vt. 1. portare 2. sopportare 3. generare. ♦ to **bear** (bore, borne) vi. 1. resistere 2. appoggiarsi 3. pazientare || to — with, aver pazienza con.

bearable agg. sopportabile.

beard s. 1. barba 2. chioma (di cometa).

to **beard** vt. affrontare, sfidare.

bearded agg. barbuto.

beardless agg. senza barba.

bearer s. portatore.

bearing s. 1. sopportazione 2. portamento 3. condotta 4. relazione 5. sostegno 6. raccolto || to lose one's bearings, perdere l'orientamento; to take the bearings of a coast (mar.), rilevare una costa.

beast s. bestia.

beastliness s. bestialità.

beastly agg. bestiale. ♦ **beastly** avv. bestialmente.

beat s. 1. battito 2. (mus.) battuta.

to **beat** (beat, beat(en)) vt. e vi. battere || to — down, abbattere; to — back, respingere.

beaten agg. abbattuto, vinto.

beater s. battitore.

beatification s. beatificazione.

beating s. 1. battito 2. bastonatura 3. sconfitta.

beatitude s. beatitudine.

beautiful agg. bello.

beautifully avv. magnificamente.

to **beautify** vt. abbellire. ♦ to **beautify** vi. abbellirsi.

beauty s. bellezza.

beaver s. castoro.

became V. to become.

because cong. perché || — of, a causa di.

beck[1] s. ruscello.

beck[2] s. cenno, gesto.

to **become** (became, become) vi. 1. divenire 2. avvenire. ♦ to **become** (became, become) vt. addirsi a.

becoming agg. adatto.

bed s. 1. letto 2. fondo 3. (geol.) strato || double —, letto matrimoniale || flower- —, aiuola; — -cover, copriletto.

bedclothes s. pl. lenzuola.

bedlam s. manicomio.

bedouin agg. e s. beduino.

bedroom s. camera da letto.

bedside s. capezzale.

bedstead s. telaio del letto.

bedtime s. ora di andare a letto.

bee s. ape.

beech s. faggio || — -marten, faina.

beef s. manzo.

beefsteak s. bistecca.

beehive s. alveare.

beeline s. linea diretta, linea d'aria.

been V. to be.

beer s. birra.

beet s. barbabietola.

beetle s. coleottero, scarafaggio.

beetroot s. V. beet.

to befall (befell, befallen) vt. e vi. accadere.

before avv. prima, già || —mentioned, già citato. ♦ before prep. 1. prima (di) 2. davanti a. ♦ before cong. 1. prima che 2. piuttosto che.

beforehand avv. anticipatamente.

to beg vt. e vi. 1. chiedere, pregare 2. elemosinare.

began V. to begin.

to beget (begot, begot(ten)) vt. generare.

beggar s. mendicante.

beggarly agg. misero. ♦ beggarly avv. miseramente.

beggary s. mendicità.

begging agg. mendicante. ♦ begging s. accattonaggio.

to begin (began, begun) vt. e vi. cominciare || to — with, in primo luogo, per cominciare.

beginner s. 1. iniziatore 2. principiante.

beginning s. inizio.

begot V. to beget.

begotten V. to beget.

to begrime vt. insudiciare.

begun V. to begin.

behalf s. profitto, favore: on — of, da parte di, a nome di.

to behave vi. comportarsi: to — oneself, comportarsi bene || ill -behaved, maleducato.

behaviour s. comportamento, condotta.

to behead vt. decapitare.

beheld V. to behold.

behind avv. dietro, indietro. ♦ behind prep. dietro (a). ♦ behind s. parte posteriore.

to behold (beheld, beheld) vt. guardare.

beholder s. spettatore.

to behove vt. imp. convenire, essere doveroso.

being agg. presente. ♦ being s. 1. esistenza 2. essere vivente.

belch s. 1. rutto 2. eruzione.

to belch vi. ruttare. ♦ to belch vt. eruttare.

belfry s. campanile.

Belgian agg. e s. belga.

to belie vt. 1. smentire 2. deludere.

belief s. credenza, fede.

to believe vt. e vi. credere, aver

fede.

believer s. credente.

to belittle vt. sminuire.

bell s. 1. campana 2. campanello || — -boy, fattorino d'albergo; — -ringer, campanaro; — -tower, campanile.

belligerency s. belligeranza.

belligerent agg. e s. belligerante.

bellow s. muggito.

to bellow vi. muggire.

bellows s. pl. mantice, soffietto (sing.).

belly s. ventre.

to belong vi. 1. appartenere 2. concernere.

belongings s. pl. proprietà (sing.).

beloved agg. e s. amato.

below avv. giù, al di sotto. ♦ below prep. sotto: — zero, sotto zero.

belt s. 1. cintura 2. zona.

to belt vt. 1. cingere 2. staffilare.

to bemire vt. infangare. ♦ to bemire vi. impantanarsi.

bench s. 1. panca 2. banco 3. seggio 4. corte giudiziaria.

bend s. 1. curva 2. curvatura 3. (mar.) nodo.

to bend (bent, bent) vt. 1. piegare 2. tendere. ♦ to bend (bent, bent) vi. piegarsi.

bending s. V. bend.

beneath avv. e prep. V. below.

benediction s. benedizione.

benefactor s. benefattore.

benefactress s. benefattrice.

benefice s. beneficio.

beneficence s. beneficenza.

beneficent agg. benefico.

beneficiary agg. e s. beneficiario.

benefit s. 1. vantaggio 2. indennità 3. (giur.) beneficio.

to benefit vt. giovare, beneficare. ♦ to benefit vi. approfittare.

benevolence s. benevolenza.

benevolent agg. benevolo.

Bengal-light s. bengala.

benign agg. benigno.

benignity s. benignità.

bent V. to bend. ♦ bent agg. risoluto. ♦ bent s. inclinazione.

to benumb vt. intorpidire.

benumbing s. intorpidimento.

benzol s. benzolo.

to bequeath vt. lasciare per testamento.

bequest s. lascito.

Berber agg. e s. berbero.

to bereave (bereaved, bereft) *vt.* privare.

bergamot *s.* bergamotto.

berlin(e) *s.* berlina.

berry *s.* bacca.

berth *s.* 1. cuccetta 2. (*mar.*) ancoraggio 3. (*fig.*) posto.

to berth *vt.* ancorare.

beryllium *s.* berillio.

to beseech (besought, besought) *vt.* supplicare.

beseeching *s.* supplica.

to beseem *vt.* addirsi a.

beseeming *agg.* adatto.

beside *prep.* 1. vicino a 2. fuori di.

besides *avv.* inoltre. ♦ **besides** *prep.* oltre a.

to besiege *vt.* assediare.

besieger *s.* assediante.

besought V. *to* **beseech.**

to besprinkle *vt.* spruzzare.

best *agg.* (*superl. di good*) il migliore || — -*seller*, libro molto venduto. ♦ **best** *s.* il meglio. ♦ **best** *avv.* 1. nel modo migliore 2. maggiormente.

bestial *agg.* bestiale.

bestiality *s.* bestialità.

to bestialize *vt.* abbrutire.

to bestir *vt.* agitare.

to bestow *vt.* concedere.

bestowal *s.* conferimento.

to bestrew (bestrewed, bestrewn) *vt.* cospargere, disseminare.

bet *s.* scommessa.

to bet (bet, bet) *vt. e vi.* scommettere.

to betake (betook, betaken) *vr.* — *oneself*: dirigersi, recarsi.

to betray *vt.* tradire.

betrayal *s.* tradimento.

betrayer *s.* traditore.

betrothal *s.* fidanzamento.

betrothed *agg. e s.* fidanzato.

better[1] *s.* scommettitore.

better[2] *agg.* (*comp. di good*) migliore. ♦ **better** *avv.* meglio || *bad* —, sarebbe meglio che; *all the* —, so much the —, tanto meglio. ♦ **better** *s.* 1. il meglio 2. superiore.

to better *vt. e vi.* migliorare.

between *avv.* in mezzo. ♦ **between** *prep.* tra, fra (*due cose, due persone*).

beverage *s.* bevanda.

bevy *s.* stormo, frotta.

to beware *vi.* guardarsi, diffidare.

to bewilder *vt.* sconcertare.

bewildering *agg.* sbalorditivo.

bewilderment *s.* confusione.

to bewitch *vt.* incantare.

bewitcher *s.* incantatore.

bewitching *agg.* affascinante.

beyond *avv.* più in là. ♦ **beyond** *prep.* al di là di. ♦ **beyond** *s.* l'al di là.

bias *s.* 1. pregiudizio 2. predisposizione.

to bias *vt.* influenzare.

bib *s.* bavaglino.

Bible *s.* Bibbia.

biblical *agg.* biblico.

bibliographic(al) *agg.* bibliografico.

bibliography *s.* bibliografia.

bicameral *agg.* bicamerale.

bicarbonate *s.* bicarbonato.

bicentennial *agg. e s.* bicentenario.

bicephalous *agg.* bicipite.

biceps *s.* bicipite.

to bicker *vi.* litigare.

bicoloured *agg.* bicolore.

biconcave *agg.* biconcavo.

bicycle *s.* bicicletta.

bid[1] *s.* 1. offerta (*a un'asta*) 2. appalto.

to bid[1] **(bid, bid)** *vt.* offrire (*a un'asta*). ♦ **to bid (bid, bid)** *vi.* fare offerta di appalto.

to bid[2] **(bade, bidden)** *vt. e vi.* 1. comandare 2. dire || *to* — *goodbye,* accomiatarsi.

biennial *agg.* biennale.

biennium *s.* (*pl.* -biennia) biennio.

bier *s.* bara.

big *agg.* 1. grosso 2. gravido 3. importante.

bigamous *agg.* bigamo.

bigamy *s.* bigamia.

bigness *s.* grossezza.

bigot *s.* bigotto.

bigoted *agg.* bigotto, fanatico.

bilateral *agg.* bilaterale.

bilberry *s.* mirtillo.

bile *s.* bile.

bilingual *agg.* bilingue.

bilious *agg.* 1. biliare 2. collerico.

bill[1] *s.* becco.

bill[2] *s.* 1. progetto di legge 2. certi- 5. lista 6. affisso || — *of lading,* polizza di carico; — *of rights,* dichiarazione dei diritti.

to bill *vt.* 1. fatturare 2. affiggere 3. (*teat.*) mettere in programma.

billhook *s.* falcetto.

billiard *s.* di, da bigliardo: —

-*cue*, stecca da bigliardo.
billiards *s. pl.* bigliardo (*sing.*).
billion *s.* 1. bilione 2. (*amer.*) miliardo.
billow *s.* onda.
bimestrial *agg.* bimestrale.
bimonthly *agg. e s.* bimestrale. ♦ **bimonthly** *avv.* bimestralmente.
bin *s.* recipiente || *dust—*, bidone della spazzatura.
bind *s.* 1. legame 2. fascia.
to bind (bound, bound) *vt.* 1. legare 2. fasciare 3. rilegare 4. obbligare.
binder *s.* 1. rilegatore 2. (*mecc.*) legatrice.
binding *agg.* impegnativo. ♦ **binding** *s.* 1. legame 2. fasciatura 3. rilegatura.
binocular *s.* binocolo.
binomial *s.* binomio.
biochemistry *s.* biochimica.
biographer *s.* biografo.
biographic(al) *agg.* biografico.
biography *s.* biografia.
biological *agg.* biologico.
biologist *s.* biologo.
biology *s.* biologia.
biophysics *s.* biofisica.
biosphere *s.* biosfera.
bipartite *agg.* bipartito.
bipartition *s.* bipartizione.
biped *agg. e s.* bipede.
biplane *s.* biplano.
bipolar *agg.* bipolare.
birch *s.* 1. betulla 2. verga.
bird *s.* uccello.
birdcage *s.* gabbia (*per uccelli*).
birdseed *s.* miglio.
birth *s.* 1. nascita 2. stirpe.
birthday *s.* compleanno.
birthmark *s.* voglia, segno caratteristico (*di persona*).
birthplace *s.* luogo di nascita.
biscuit *s.* biscotto.
bisection *s.* bisezione.
bisector *s.* bisettrice.
bisexual *agg.* ermafrodito.
bishop *s.* vescovo.
bishopric *s.* vescovato.
bismuth *s.* bismuto.
bison *s.* bisonte.
bistoury *s.* bisturi.
bistre *s.* bistro.
bit *s.* 1. pezzettino 2. un poco 3. (*mecc.*) parte tagliente di un utensile 4. morso (*del cavallo*).
bit V. *to bite.*
bitch *s.* cagna.

bite *s.* 1. morso 2. presa.
to bite (bit, bit(ten)) *vt.* mordere. ♦ **to bite (bit, bit(ten))** *vi.* abboccare || *to — in*, corrodere.
biting *agg.* 1. mordente 2. mordace.
bitten V. *to bite.*
bitter *agg.* 1. amaro 2. aspro 3. (*di clima*) rigido || *-sweet*, agrodolce. ♦ **bitter** *s.* amaro.
bitterish *agg.* amarognolo.
bitterness *s.* 1. amarezza 2. rancore 3. rigidità (*di clima*).
bitumen *s.* bitume.
bivalent *agg.* bivalente.
bivouac *s.* bivacco.
bi-weekly *agg. e s.* bisettimanale. ♦ **bi-weekly** *avv.* due volte alla settimana.
to blab *vt. e vi.* 1. chiacchierare 2. spifferare.
black *agg.* 1. nero 2. negro 3. (*fig.*) malvagio, minaccioso. ♦ **black** *s.* 1. colore nero 2. negro.
to black *vt.* annerire. ♦ **to black** *vi.* annerirsi.
to blackball *vt.* votare contro, bocciare.
blackberry *s.* mora selvatica.
blackbird *s.* merlo.
blackboard *s.* lavagna.
to blacken *vt.* 1. annerire 2. (*fig.*) diffamare. ♦ **to blacken** *vi.* diventare nero.
blackguard *s.* mascalzone.
blackish *agg.* nerastro.
blackleg *s.* 1. truffatore 2. crumiro.
blackmail *s.* ricatto.
to blackmail *vt.* ricattare.
blackmailer *s.* ricattatore.
blackness *s.* 1. nerezza 2. oscurità.
blackout *s.* oscuramento.
blacksmith *s.* fabbro ferraio.
bladder *s.* vescica.
blade *s.* 1. stelo 2. lama.
blamable *agg.* biasimevole.
blame *s.* 1. biasimo 2. colpa.
to blame *vt.* 1. biasimare 2. incolpare.
blameful *agg.* biasimevole.
blameless *agg.* irreprensibile.
bland *agg.* blando.
blandishment *s.* blandizie (*pl.*).
blandly *avv.* blandamente.
blank *agg.* 1. vuoto 2. in bianco || *— verse*, verso sciolto. ♦ **blank** *s.* 1. vuoto 2. spazio in bianco 3. mira || *point—*, di punto in bianco.
blanket *s.* coperta.

blankly *avv.* **1.** senza espressione **2.** decisamente.

blare *s.* squillo (*di tromba*).

to blaspheme *vt.* e *vi.* bestemmiare.

blasphemous *agg.* blasfemo.

blasphemously *avv.* empiamente.

blasphemy *s.* bestemmia, empietà.

blast *s.* **1.** raffica **2.** squillo **3.** scoppio **4.** flagello || — -*furnace*, altoforno.

to blast *vt.* **1.** far esplodere **2.** rovinare.

blaze *s.* **1.** fiamma **2.** scoppio.

to blaze *vi.* ardere. ♦ **to blaze** *vt.* **1.** bruciare **2.** divulgare.

blazer *s.* giacca sportiva.

blazing *s.* **1.** fiamma **2.** splendore **3.** vanteria.

blazon *s.* **1.** blasone **2.** ostentazione.

bleach *s.* imbianchimento, candeggio.

to bleach *vt.* imbiancare, candeggiare. ♦ **to bleach** *vi.* imbiancarsi.

bleacher *s.* recipiente per candeggio.

bleaching *s.* V. *bleach*.

bleak *agg.* **1.** brullo **2.** desolato **3.** incolore.

bleakness *s.* **1.** freddezza **2.** squallore.

blear *agg.* **1.** cisposo **2.** ottuso.

bleat *s.* belato.

to bleat *vi.* belare.

to bleed (**bled, bled**) *vi.* sanguinare. ♦ **to bleed** (**bled, bled**) *vt.* salassare.

bleeding *s.* **1.** emorragia **2.** salasso **3.** fuga.

blemish *s.* difetto.

blend *s.* miscela.

to blend *vt.* mescolare. ♦ **to blend** *vi.* mescolarsi.

to bless *vt.* benedire.

blessed *agg.* beato, santo.

blessing *s.* benedizione.

blew V. *to blow*.

blind *agg.* cieco. ♦ **blind** *s.* **1.** tenda **2.** persiana **3.** paraocchi **4.** finzione.

to blind *vt.* **1.** accecare **2.** oscurare **3.** nascondere.

blindness *s.* cecità.

to blink *vi.* **1.** battere le palpebre **2.** lampeggiare **3.** (*fig.*) chiudere gli occhi.

blinker *s.* **1.** lampeggiatore **2.** paraocchi.

blinking *agg.* **1.** ammiccante **2.** scintillante. ♦ **blinking** *s.* ammicco.

bliss *s.* beatitudine.

blissful *agg.* **1.** beato **2.** delizioso.

blister *s.* bolla.

blithe *agg.* gaio.

blizzard *s.* tormenta (*di neve*).

block *s.* **1.** ceppo **2.** masso **3.** isolato (*di case*) **4.** ostacolo **5.** persona stupida || — *letters*, stampatello.

to block *vt.* bloccare.

blockade *s.* blocco.

blockhead *s.* stupido.

blonde *s.* donna bionda.

blood *s.* sangue.

bloodhound *s.* segugio.

bloodless *agg.* **1.** esangue **2.** incruento **3.** (*fig.*) insensibile.

bloodshed *s.* spargimento di sangue.

bloodshot *agg.* iniettato di sangue.

bloody *agg.* **1.** sanguinante **2.** sanguinoso **3.** sanguinario **4.** maledetto.

bloom *s.* **1.** fiore **2.** rossore.

to bloom *vi.* **1.** fiorire **2.** arrossire.

blossom *s.* fiore.

to blossom *vi.* **1.** fiorire **2.** diventare.

blot *s.* macchia.

to blot *vt.* **1.** macchiare **2.** assorbire.

blotch *s.* **1.** macchia **2.** pustola.

blotting *s.* **1.** il macchiare **2.** l'asciugare || — -*paper*, carta assorbente; — -*pad*, tampone di carta assorbente.

blouse *s.* camicetta.

blow *s.* **1.** soffio **2.** colpo **3.** fioritura || *to come to blows*, venire alle mani.

to blow (**blew, blown**) *vt.* **1.** soffiare **2.** suonare (*strumenti a fiato*) || *to* — *up*, (far) saltare in aria. ♦ **to blow** (**blew, blown**) *vi.* sboccare.

blower *s.* **1.** soffiatore **2.** sfiatatoio.

blown V. *to blow*.

blowpipe *s.* **1.** cannello per soffiare **2.** cerbottana.

blue *agg.* **1.** azzurro, blu **2.** livido **3.** triste.

bluebell *s.* campanula.

bluebottle[1] *s.* fiordaliso.

bluebottle[2] *s.* tafano.

blueprint *s.* cianografia.

bluff *s.* ripida scogliera.

bluish *agg.* bluastro.

blunder *s.* errore.

blunt *agg.* **1.** smussato **2.** ottuso **3.** schietto.

blush *s.* rossore.

to **blush** *vi.* arrossire.

board *s.* **1.** asse, tavola **2.** vitto **3.** pensione **4.** consiglio, ministero **5.** (*mar.*) bordo || *on —*, a bordo; *full —*, pensione completa. ◆ **boards** *s. pl.* palcoscenico (*sing.*).

to **board** *vt.* **1.** fornire di assi **2.** prendere a pensione **3.** (*mar.*) abbordare. ◆ to **board** *vi.* **1.** essere a pensione **2.** imbarcarsi.

boarder *s.* pensionante.

boarding *s.* assito || *— -house*, pensione; *— -school*, collegio.

boast *s.* vanto.

to **boast** *vt.* vantare. ◆ to **boast** *vi.* vantarsi.

boaster *s.* spaccone.

boastful *agg.* vanaglorioso.

boastfulness *s.* millanteria.

boasting *s.* vanteria.

boat *s.* barca, battello || *flying—*, idrovolante; *sauce—*, salsiera; *ferry—*, traghetto.

boating *s.* canottaggio.

boatman *s.* barcaiolo.

boatswain *s.* nostromo.

to **bob** *vi.* dondolarsi, oscillare || *to — up*, venire a galla.

bobbin *s.* bobina.

bobsled *s.* guidoslitta.

bodice *s.* busto.

bodkin *s.* punteruolo, stiletto.

body *s.* **1.** corpo **2.** corporazione, ente **3.** massa || *— belt*, panciera.

bodymaker *s.* carrozziere.

Boeotian *agg. e s.* beota.

bog *s.*

boggy *agg.* paludoso.

bogy *s.* spauracchio.

boil *s.* bollitura.

to **boil** *vt. e vi.* bollire, ribollire || *to — away*, consumarsi; *to — over*, traboccare bollendo.

boiler *s.* bollitore, caldaia.

boiling *agg.* bollente. ◆ **boiling** *s.* ebollizione.

boisterous *agg.* **1.** rumoroso **2.** violento.

boisterousness *s.* fracasso.

bold *agg.* **1.** audace **2.** sfacciato **3.** vigoroso || *— -face*, neretto.

boldness *s.* **1.** audacia **2.** sfacciataggine.

bolide *s.* bolide.

Bolshevism *s.* bolscevismo.

Bolshevist *agg. e s.* bolscevico.

holster *s.* **1.** cuscino **2.** support'.

bolt *s.* **1.** catenaccio **2.** bullone **3.** otturatore **4.** freccia **5.** fulmine.

to **bolt**[1] *vt.* **1.** sprangare **2.** imbullonare.

to **bolt**[2] *vt.* setacciare, vagliare.

bolter *s.* setaccio.

bomb *s.* bomba.

to **bomb** *vt.* bombardare.

to **bombard** *vt.* bombardare.

bombardier *s.* bombardiere.

bombardment *s.* bombardamento.

bombastic *agg.* ampolloso.

bomber *s.* bombardiere.

bond *s.* **1.** vincolo **2.** patto **3.** (*comm.*) titolo **4.** cauzione || *— -holder*, portatore di obbligazioni; *goods in —*, merci in attesa di sdoganamento.

bondage *s.* schiavitù.

bone *s.* **1.** osso **2.** lisca.

to **bone** *vt.* **1.** disossare **2.** spinare.

bonfire *s.* falò.

bonnet *s.* **1.** cuffia **2.** (*auto*) cofano.

bonus *s.* gratifica || *cost of living —*, carovita.

bony *agg.* **1.** osseo **2.** ossuto.

bonze *s.* bonzo.

booby *s.* sciocco.

book *s.* **1.** libro **2.** registro || *note—*, taccuino; *copy—*, quaderno.

to **book** *vt.* **1.** registrare **2.** prenotare.

bookbinding *s.* rilegatura.

bookcase *s.* libreria.

booking *s.* **1.** registrazione **2.** prenotazione || *— -office*, biglietteria.

bookish *agg.* **1.** studioso **2.** libresco.

bookkeeper *s.* contabile.

bookkeeping *s.* contabilità.

booklet *s.* libretto.

bookmaker *s.* allibratore.

bookseller *s.* libraio.

bookshelf *s.* (*pl. -lves*) scaffale.

bookshop *s.* libreria.

bookstall *s.* edicola, bancarella (*di libri*).

boom *s.* **1.** rombo **2.** periodo di prosperità.

to **boom** *vi.* **1.** rimbombare **2.** essere in periodo di prosperità.

boor *s.* persona zotica.

boorish *agg.* rustico.

boorishness *s.* rozzezza.

boot *s.* **1.** stivale, scarpa **2.** (*auto*) portabagagli.

bootblack *s.* lustrascarpe.

booth *s.* baracca || *telephone —*, cabina telefonica.

booty *s.* bottino.

border s. **1.** orlo **2.** frontiera.
to border vt. orlare || to — on, confinare con.
borderer s. abitante di confine.
bordering s. **1.** il bordare **2.** il confinare.
bore V. to bear.
bore[1] s. **1.** buco **2.** calibro (di arma).
bore[2] s. **1.** seccatura **2.** seccatore.
to bore[1] vt. forare.
to bore[2] vt. annoiare.
boreal agg. boreale.
boredom s. noia.
boric agg. borico.
boring[1] agg. noioso.
boring[2] s. perforazione || — test, sondaggio.
born V. to bear. ♦ **born** agg. nato, generato || to be —, nascere.
borne V. to bear.
borough s. **1.** municipio **2.** circoscrizione elettorale.
to borrow vt. prendere a prestito.
borrower s. chi prende a prestito.
bosom s. seno || — friend, amico intimo.
boss[1] s. **1.** protuberanza **2.** (arch.) bugna.
boss[2] s. capo, padrone.
bossy[1] agg. a bugnato.
bossy[2] agg. (gergo) prepotente.
botanist s. botanico.
botany s. botanica.
botch s. pasticcio.
to botch vt. **1.** rattoppare **2.** arruffare.
botcher s. pasticcione.
both agg. e pron. entrambi, tutti e due. ♦ **both** avv. nel medesimo tempo || — ... and, sia... sia, tanto... quanto.
bother s. seccatura.
to bother vt. infastidire. ♦ **to bother** vi. preoccuparsi.
bothersome agg. fastidioso.
bottle s. bottiglia || feeding—, poppatoio; — -feeding, allattamento artificiale.
to bottle vt. imbottigliare.
bottling s. imbottigliamento.
bottom agg. inferiore 2. basilare.
♦ **bottom** s. **1.** fondo **2.** fondamento **3.** deretano **4.** (mar.) chiglia.
to bottom vt. **1.** mettere il fondo (a) **2.** impagliare **3.** capire. ♦ **bottom** vi. posare, essere posato.
bottomless agg. **1.** senza fondo **2.**

senza fine.
bough s. ramo (d'albero).
bought V. to buy.
boulder s. macigno.
boulevard s. viale.
bounce s. **1.** balzo **2.** vanteria.
to bounce vt. far rimbalzare. ♦ **to bounce** vi. **1.** rimbalzare **2.** gloriarsi.
bouncer s. fanfarone.
bound[1] s. limite, confine.
bound[2] s. salto.
bound[3] V. to bind.
bound[4] agg. **1.** destinato **2.** diretto a **3.** certo.
to bound[1] vt. confinare, limitare.
to bound[2] vi. balzare.
boundary s. limite, frontiera.
boundless agg. illimitato.
bounteous agg. generoso.
bounty s. generosità.
bourgeois agg. e s. borghese.
bourgeoisie s. borghesia.
bow[1] s. **1.** arco **2.** archetto **3.** fiocco || — -window, bovindo.
bow[2] s. inchino.
bow[3] s. prua.
to bow vt. piegare. ♦ **to bow** vi. **1.** piegarsi **2.** inclinarsi.
bowels s. pl. viscere.
bower s. **1.** pergolato **2.** dimora.
bowl[1] s. ciotola.
bowl[2] s. boccia.
to bowl vt. far rotolare. ♦ **to bowl** vi. **1.** rotolare **2.** giocare a bocce.
bowler s. giocatore di bocce || — hat, bombetta.
bowling s. gioco delle bocce.
bowman s. arciere.
bowshot s. tiro d'arco.
box[1] s. **1.** scatola **2.** stanzetta **3.** stalla **4.** (teat.) palco **5.** (giur.) banco || letter— , buca per le lettere; money— , salvadanaio; strong— , cassaforte.
box[2] s. pugno, ceffone.
to box[1] vt. mettere in scatola.
to box[2] vt. schiaffeggiare. ♦ **to box** vi. fare del pugilato.
boxer s. pugile.
boxing s. pugilato.
boy s. ragazzo.
to boycott vt. boicottare.
boyhood s. fanciullezza.
boyish agg. fanciullesco.
bra s. reggipetto.
brace s. **1.** sostegno **2.** coppia, paio **3.** (mar.) braccio. ♦ **braces** s. pl. bretelle.

to **brace** *vt.* 1. legare 2. fortificare.

bracelet *s.* braccialetto.

brachycardia *s.* brachicardia.

bracket *s.* 1. mensola, sostegno 2. parentesi.

brackish *agg.* salato, salso.

brag *s.* 1. millanteria 2. millantatore.

to **brag** *vt.* vantare. ♦ to **brag** *vi.* vantarsi.

braggart *agg. e s.* spaccone.

bragging *s.* millanteria.

braid *s.* 1. treccia 2. gallone.

to **braid** *vt.* 1. intrecciare 2. guarnire.

brain *s.* cervello.

brainless *agg.* scervellato.

brake[1] *s.* 1. felce 2. boschetto.

brake[2] *s.* freno.

to **brake** *vt.* frenare.

brakesman *s.* frenatore.

bramble *s.* rovo.

bran *s.* crusca.

branch *s.* 1. ramo 2. filiale. ♦ to **branch** *vt.* ramificare. ♦ to **branch** *vi.* ramificarsi || to — out, estendersi (*di attività commerciale, affari*).

branching *s.* ramificazione.

brand *s.* 1. tizzone 2. marchio (*a fuoco*) 3. marca || — -new, nuovo fiammante.

to **brand** *vt.* 1. marchiare 2. stigmatizzare.

to **brandish** *vt.* brandire.

brass *agg.* 1. di ottone 2. (*fig.*) sfacciato. ♦ **brass** *s.* 1. ottone 2. (*mecc.*) bronzina 3. (*fig.*) sfacciataggine || — band, fanfara.

brassy *agg.* V. *brass*.

bravado *s.* bravata.

brave *agg. e s.* prode, coraggioso.

bravely *avv.* coraggiosamente.

bravery *s.* 1. coraggio 2. splendore.

brawl *s.* rissa.

to **brawl** *vi.* rissare.

brawn *s.* muscolo, forza muscolare.

brawny *agg.* muscoloso.

bray *s.* raglio.

to **bray**[1] *vi.* 1. ragliare 2. (*fig.*) stonare.

to **bray**[2] *vt.* frantumare, sminuzzare.

brazen *agg.* V. *brass*.

brazier[1] *s.* calderaio.

brazier[2] *s.* braciere.

Brazilian *agg. e s.* brasiliano.

breach *s.* 1. rottura 2. breccia 3. infrazione || — of promise, rottura di fidanzamento.

bread *s.* pane.

to **bread** *vt.* rimpanare.

breadth *s.* 1. larghezza 2. altezza (*di stoffe*).

breadthwise *avv.* in larghezza (*di stoffe*).

break *s.* 1. rottura 2. interruzione, intervallo 3. infrazione || — -up, collasso, smembramento, fine.

to **break** (broke, broken) *vt.* 1. rompere 2. interrompere 3. domare 4. rovinare. ♦ to **break** (broke, broken) *vi.* 1. rompersi 2. irrompere || to — down, demolire, (*auto*) restare in panne, esaurirsi; to — off, mandare a monte; to — up, fare a pezzi.

breakdown *s.* 1. collasso 2. rottura 3. dissesto || nervous —, esaurimento nervoso.

breaker *s.* 1. rompitore 2. violatore 3. domatore 4. (*mecc.*) macchina rompitrice 5. (*mar.*) frangente 6. (*elett.*) interruttore.

breakfast *s.* prima colazione.

to **breakfast** *vi.* fare la prima colazione.

breaking *s.* 1. rottura 2. (*comm.*) fallimento.

breakneck *agg.* a rotta di collo.

breakwater *s.* frangiflutti.

breast *s.* petto || — -bone, sterno.

breasted *agg.* dal petto || double-—, a doppio petto.

breath *s.* 1. soffio 2. respiro.

breathable *agg.* respirabile.

to **breathe** *vi.* 1. respirare 2. spirare. ♦ to **breathe** *vt.* 1. infondere 2. sussurrare.

breathing *s.* V. *breath*.

breathless *agg.* 1. ansante 2. esanime.

breathlessness *s.* affanno.

bred V. to *breed*. ♦ **bred** *agg.* ill-—, maleducato.

breech *s.* 1. parte posteriore 2. culatta (*di arma*).

breeches *s. pl.* calzoni.

breed *s.* razza.

to **breed** (bred, bred) *vt.* 1. generare 2. allevare. ♦ to **breed** (bred, bred) *vi.* nascere.

breeder *s.* 1. chi genera 2. allevatore.

breeding *s.* 1. generazione 2. allevamento 3. educazione.

breeze *s.* brezza.

breezy *agg.* 1. ventilato 2. cordiale.

brethren *s. pl.* confratelli.

breviary *s.* breviario.

brevity *s.* brevità.

brew *s.* 1. mistura 2. fermentazione (*di birra*).

to brew *vt.* 1. mescolare 2. (*fig.*) macchinare. ♦ **to brew** *vi.* fare la birra.

brewer *s.* birraio.

brewery *s.* fabbrica di birra.

bribe *s.* dono (*a scopo di corruzione*), allettamento.

to bribe *vt.* corrompere.

briber *s.* corruttore.

bribery *s.* corruzione.

brick *s.* mattone.

bricklayer *s.* muratore.

brickwork *s.* muratura in mattoni.

brickyard *s.* mattonaia.

bride *s.* sposa.

bridegroom *s.* sposo.

bridge *s.* ponte || **swing— **, ponte girevole; **toll— **, ponte a pedaggio; **— -head**, testa di ponte.

bridle *s.* briglia, freno.

to bridle *vt.* imbrigliare.

bridling *s.* imbrigliamento.

brief *agg.* breve. ♦ **brief** *s.* riassunto.

to brief *vt.* 1. riassumere 2. (*giur.*) nominare (il proprio avvocato) 3. dare istruzioni.

briefness *s.* brevità, concisione.

brier *s.* 1. rovo 2. rosa selvatica.

brig *s.* brigantino.

brigade *s.* brigata.

bright *agg.* 1. chiaro, splendente 2. vivace.

to brighten *vt.* 1. far brillare 2. animare. ♦ **to brighten** *vi.* 1. brillare 2. animarsi.

brightness *s.* 1. splendore 2. gaiezza.

brill *s.* (*itt.*) rombo.

brilliance, brilliancy *s.* brillantezza.

brilliant *agg.* e *s.* brillante.

brilliantine *s.* brillantina.

brim *s.* 1. orlo 2. ala (*di cappello*).

brimful *agg.* colmo.

brindled *agg.* pezzato.

brine *s.* acqua salata.

to bring (brought, brought) *vt.* 1. portare 2. indurre || **to — about**, causare; **to — back**, richiamare alla memoria; **to — forth**, dare alla luce; **to — up**, educare, allevare.

brink *s.* orlo.

brisk *agg.* 1. vivace 2. frizzante.

briskness *s.* vivacità.

bristle *s.* setola.

to bristle *vi.* essere irto di.

bristly *agg.* 1. setoloso 2. ruvido.

British *agg.* britannico.

Briton *agg.* e *s.* britanno.

broad *agg.* 1. ampio 2. chiaro 3. marcato 4. volgare || **— daylight**, pieno giorno. ♦ **broad** *s.* larghezza. ♦ **broad** *avv.* ampiamente.

broadcast *s.* 1. radiodiffusione 2. radiocomunicazione.

to broadcast (broadcast, broadcast) (*anche reg.*) *vt.* e *vi.* radiotrasmettere.

broadcaster *s.* trasmettitore.

broadcasting *s.* radiodiffusione.

to broaden *vt.* allargare. ♦ **to broaden** *vi.* allargarsi, estendersi.

broadness *s.* 1. larghezza 2. grossolanità.

broadside *s.* (*mar.*) 1. bordo, fiancata 2. bordata.

brocade *s.* broccato.

bro(c)coli *s.* broccolo.

broil *s.* rissa.

to broil *vt.* cuocere alla griglia. ♦ **to broil** *vi.* abbrustolirsi (*al sole*).

broke V. **to break**.

broken V. **to break**. ♦ **broken** *agg.* 1. variabile (*di tempo*) 2. accidentato (*di terreno*) 3. indebolito 4. avvilito 5. scorretto.

broker *s.* 1. (*comm.*) agente 2. mediatore.

bromide *s.* bromuro.

bromine *s.* bromo.

bronchial *agg.* bronchiale.

bronchia *s. pl.* bronchi.

bronchitis *s.* bronchite.

broncho-pneumonia *s.* broncopolmonite.

bronze *s.* bronzo.

to bronze *vt.* abbronzare. ♦ **to bronze** *vi.* abbronzarsi.

brooch *s.* spilla.

brood *s.* covata.

to brood *vt.* 1. covare 2. (*fig.*) rimuginare, meditare.

brooding *s.* 1. cova 2. meditazione.

brook *s.* ruscello.

to brook *vt.* sopportare, tollerare.

brooklet *s.* ruscelletto.

broom *s.* 1. ginestra 2. scopa.

broth *s.* brodo.

brothel *s.* bordello.

brother *s.* 1. fratello 2. collega || **— -in-law**, cognato; **half— **, fratellastro.

brotherhood s. 1. fratellanza 2. confraternita.

brotherlike agg. fraterno.

brotherly agg. fraterno. ♦ **brotherly** avv. fraternamente.

brought V. to bring.

brow s. fronte. ♦ **brows** s. pl. sopracciglia.

brown agg. 1. bruno 2. marrone. ♦ **brown** s. marrone.

to **brown** vt. 1. rendere bruno 2. rosolare. ♦ to **brown** vi. 1. diventare bruno 2. abbronzarsi

to **browse** vt. e vi. brucare.

bruise s. contusione.

to **bruise** vt. ammaccare. ♦ to **bruise** vi. ammaccarsi.

bruiser s. 1. pugilatore 2. (fig.) gradasso.

brush s. 1. spazzola, spazzolino 2. spazzolata 3. pennello 4. rissa || — -up, ripasso.

to **brush** vt. 1. spazzolare 2. sfiorare || to — aside (fig.), ignorare; to — up, ripassare.

brushwood s. sottobosco.

brushy agg. 1. ispido 2. folto (di bosco).

brusque agg. brusco.

brutal agg. brutale.

brutality s. brutalità.

to **brutalize** vt. 1. abbrutire 2. maltrattare. ♦ to **brutalize** vi. abbrutirsi.

brute agg. brutale. ♦ **brute** s. bruto.

brutish agg. brutale, rozzo.

bubble s. 1. bolla 2. gorgoglio.

to **bubble** vi. gorgogliare || to — over, traboccare.

bubo s. bubbone.

bubonic agg. bubbonico.

buccaneer s. bucaniere.

buck s. 1. daino 2. maschio (di molti animali).

to **buck** vi. sgroppare.

bucket s. secchio.

buckle s. fibbia.

to **buckle** vt. 1. affibbiare 2. piegare. ♦ to **buckle** vi. piegarsi.

bucolic agg. bucolico.

bud s. 1. gemma 2. germe.

to **bud** vi. germogliare.

Buddhism s. buddismo.

Buddhist agg. e s. buddista.

budget s. 1. raccolta (di documenti) 2. bilancio.

buffalo s. bufalo.

buffer s. respingente.

buffet[1] s. schiaffo.

buffet[2] s. credenza.

to **buffet** vt. schiaffeggiare.

buffoon s. buffone.

bug s. 1. coleottero 2. cimice || big —, (gergo) pezzo grosso.

bugbear s. spauracchio.

bugger s. sodomita.

build s. costruzione, struttura.

to **build** (**built**, **built**) vt. costruire || to — up, murare.

builder s. costruttore.

building agg. edilizio. ♦ **building** s. edificio.

built V. to build.

bulb s. 1. bulbo 2. lampadina || — socket, portalampada.

Bulgarian agg. e s. bulgaro.

bulge s. gonfiore.

to **bulge** vi. gonfiarsi. ♦ to **bulge** vt. 1. sporgere 2. gonfiare.

bulgy agg. rigonfio.

bulk s. 1. massa 2. carico.

bulkhead s. paratia.

bulky agg. massiccio.

bull s. 1. toro 2. maschio (di alcuni mammiferi) || —'s eye, oblò.

bulldog s. mastino.

bullet s. pallottola.

bulletin s. bollettino || news —, giornale radio.

bullfight s. corrida.

bullfighter s. torero.

bullock s. torello.

bully agg. borioso.

to **bully** vt. e vi. fare il prepotente (verso).

bulwark s. 1. bastione 2. (mar.) parapetto.

bumble-bee s. calabrone.

bump s. 1. urto 2. bernoccolo.

to **bump** vt. e vi. urtare, andare a sbattere contro.

bumper s. 1. paraurti 2. respingente.

bun s. 1. focaccia 2. crocchia.

bunch s. 1. mazzo 2. grappolo.

bundle s. 1. fagotto 2. fascio.

to **bundle** vt. riunire in fascio, fare un involto.

bung s. tappo.

bungler agg. e s. confusionario.

bunny s. coniglietto.

buoy s. boa.

buoyancy s. 1. galleggiabilità 2. ottimismo.

buoyant agg. 1. galleggiante 2. ottimista.

burden s. 1. peso 2. tonnellaggio.

to **burden** vt. caricare.
burdensome agg. gravoso.
bureau s. (pl. bureaux) ufficio.
bureaucracy s. burocrazia.
bureaucrat s. burocrate.
bureaucratic agg. burocratico.
burglar s. scassinatore (notturno).
burglary s. furto (notturno) con scasso.
to **burgle** vt. e vi. svaligiare con scasso.
burgomaster s. borgomastro.
burial s. sepoltura || — -ground, cimitero; — -service, ufficio funebre.
burin s. bulino.
burly agg. corpulento.
burn s. ustione.
to **burn** (**burnt, burnt**) (anche reg.) vt. e vi. bruciare, ardere.
burner s. bruciatore.
burning s. 1. incendio 2. (metal.) fusione.
to **burnish** vt. lustrare.
burnt V. to burn.
burrow s. tana, buca.
bursar s. economo.
bursary s. 1. ufficio dell'economato 2. borsa di studio.
burst s. 1. scoppio 2. squarcio.
to **burst** (**burst, burst**) vt. 1. far esplodere 2. sfondare. ◆ to **burst** (**burst, burst**) vi. 1. scoppiare 2. irrompere.
bursting s. scoppio.
to **bury** vt. seppellire.
bus s. autobus.
busby s. colbac.
bush s. cespuglio.
bushel s. staio.
bushy agg. folto.
busily avv. attivamente.
business s. 1. affare 2. mestiere 3. ditta 4. scopo || —-man, uomo d'affari; — -like, metodico, sistematico.
bust s. busto.
bustle s. trambusto.
to **bustle** vi. agitarsi.
busy agg. occupato.
to **busy** vt. occupare.
busybody s. ficcanaso.
but cong. ma. ◆ but avv. solo. ◆ but prep. tranne || — for, se non fosse per; — that, se non; cannot —, non poter far a meno di; all —, pressoché.
butane s. butano.
butcher s. macellaio.
butchery s. macello.

butler s. maggiordomo.
butt[1] s. 1. calcio (di arma) 2. impugnatura (di utensile) 3. mozzicone.
butt[2] s. urto.
to **butt** vt. e vi. cozzare.
butter s. burro.
to **butter** vt. imburrare.
buttercup s. ranuncolo.
butterfly s. farfalla.
buttery agg. burroso.
buttock s. natica.
button s. bottone.
to **button** vt. abbottonare.
button-hole s. occhiello.
to **button-hole** vt. 1. fare asole a 2. (fig.) attaccar bottone.
button-holer s. attaccabottoni.
buttress s. contrafforte.
buxom agg. formoso, avvenente (di donna).
to **buy** (**bought, bought**) vt. comprare || to — off, riscattare; to — up, accaparrare.
buyable agg. acquistabile.
buyer s. acquirente.
buzz s. ronzio.
buzzard s. poiana.
to **buzz** vi. e vt. ronzare, bisbigliare.
buzzer s. 1. insetto che ronza 2. cicala, segnale acustico.
by avv. 1. vicino 2. da parte, in disparte || — and —, fra poco; — and large, complessivamente. ◆ by prep. 1. (agente, causa, mezzo) per, da, con, di || a book (written) — Shakespeare, un libro di Shakespeare; to travel — train, viaggiare col treno 2. (tempo) entro, per, durante || day — day, di giorno in giorno; — night, di notte 3. (luogo) vicino a, a fianco di, attraverso || a house — the sea, una casa sul mare. ◆ by agg. secondario.
bye-bye inter. arrivederci.
bygone agg. e s. passato.
by-line s. (giorn.) firma.
byname s. soprannome.
by-pass s. 1. circonvallazione 2. deviazione.
by-product s. sottoprodotto.
byroad s. strada secondaria.
byssus s. bisso.
bystander s. spettatore.
bystreet s. viuzza.
byway s. via traversa.
byword s. proverbio, epiteto.
bywork s. lavoro supplementare (a tempo perso).
Byzantine agg. e s. bizantino.

C

C (*mus.*) do.
cab *s.* vettura di piazza.
cabal *s.* intrigo, cospirazione.
cabbage *s.* cavolo.
cab(b)ala *s.* cabala.
cab(b)alistic *agg.* cabalistico.
cabin *s.* 1. capanna 2. (*aer.; fer.; mar.*) cabina.
cabinet *s.* 1. stanzino 2. stipo, armadietto 3. (*pol.*) gabinetto, consiglio dei ministri || *—-maker*, ebanista; *— -minister*, membro del gabinetto.
cable *s.* 1. cavo 2. cablogramma || *— -way*, teleferica.
to cable *vt. e vi.* 1. fornire di cavo 2. trasmettere un cablogramma.
cablegram *s.* cablogramma.
cabman *s.* tassista.
caboose (*mar.*) cambusa.
cabotage *s.* cabotaggio.
cacao *s.* cacao.
cacophony *s.* cacofonia.
cactus *s.* cactus.
cadaverous *agg.* 1. cadaverico 2. esangue.
cadence *s.* cadenza, ritmo.
cadet *s.* cadetto.
caducity *s.* caducità.
Caesarean *agg.* cesareo, imperiale || *— operation*, parto cesareo.
caesura *s.* cesura.
café *s.* caffè (*locale pubblico*).
caffeine *s.* caffeina.
cage *s.* 1. gabbia 2. impalcatura.
to cage *vt.* mettere in gabbia.
cake *s.* torta, focaccia.
calamary *s.* calamaro.
calamitous *agg.* calamitoso.
calamity *s.* calamità.
calcareous *agg.* calcareo.
calcification *s.* calcificazione.
to calcify *vt.* calcificare. ♦ to calcify *vi.* calcificarsi.
calcination *s.* calcinazione.
to calcine V. *to calcify.*
calcite *s.* calcite.
calcium *s.* calcio.
to calculate *vt.* 1. calcolare 2. contare. ♦ to calculate *vi.* fare affidamento.
calculated *agg.* 1. calcolato 2. premeditato 3. (*fig.*) idoneo.
calculating *agg.* calcolatore || *— machine*, macchina calcolatrice.
calculation *s.* calcolo.

calculator *s.* calcolatore, calcolatrice.
calendar *s.* calendario, almanacco.
calf[1] *s.* (*pl.* calves) vitello.
calf[2] *s.* polpaccio.
to calibrate *vt.* 1. calibrare 2. (*mecc.*) tarare.
calibration *s.* calibratura, taratura.
calibre *s.* calibro.
calico *s.* calicò.
call *s.* 1. richiamo, chiamata 2. breve visita: *to pay* (*v. irr.*) *so. a —*, fare una breve visita a qu. 3. (*giur.*) appello 4. (*mil.*) adunata 5. (*mar.*) scalo || *— -bird*, uccello da richiamo; *— box*, cabina telefonica; *— up*, chiamata alle armi; *— trunk —*, chiamata intercontinentale.
to call *vt. e vi.* 1. chiamare, richiamare: *to — aside*, chiamare in disparte; *to — to arms*, chiamare alle armi; *to — to mind*, richiamare alla mente 2. esortare, ordinare || *to — into being*, creare; *to — out*, chiamare ad alta voce, esclamare; *to — up*, telefonare; *to — at*, fare scalo a; *to — for*, passare a prendere; *to — on*, fare una breve visita a; *to — upon*, implorare, invocare.
caller *s.* visitatore, visitatrice.
calligrapher *s.* calligrafo.
calligraphic *agg.* calligrafico.
calling *s.* 1. appello 2. mestiere, professione 3. vocazione.
callosity *s.* 1. callosità 2. (*fig.*) insensibilità.
callous *agg.* 1. calloso 2. (*fig.*) insensibile.
calm *agg.* calmo. ♦ calm *s.* calma.
to calm *vt.* calmare. ♦ to calm *vi.* to — down, calmarsi (*di tempesta ecc.*).
calming *agg.* calmante.
calmly *avv.* con calma.
calmness *s.* calma, tranquillità.
calorific *agg.* calorifico.
calorimeter *s.* calorimetro.
calory *s.* caloria.
to calumniate *vt.* calunniare.
Calvary *s.* Calvario.
calves V. *calf.*
Calvinism *s.* calvinismo.
Calvinist *agg. e s.* calvinista.
came V. *to come.*
camel *s.* cammello.
camellia *s.* camelia.
cameo *s.* cammeo.
camera *s.* 1. (*foto*) macchina foto-

grafica **2.** (*giur.*) Camera di Consiglio.

camisole *s.* corpetto, farsetto.

camouflage *s.* **1.** mascheramento **2.** (*mil.*) mimetizzazione.

to **camouflage** *vt.* **1.** mascerare **2.** (*mil.*) mimetizzare.

camp *s.* **1.** (*mil.*) campo **2.** campeggio || — *-bed*, brandina.

to **camp** *vt.* (*mil.*) accampare. ◆ to **camp** *vi.* **1.** accamparsi **2.** attendarsi.

campaign *s.* (*mil.*) campagna.

camper *s.* campeggiatore.

camphor *s.* canfora.

camping *s.* **1.** (*mil.*) accampamento **2.** campeggio.

can[1] *s.* recipiente di latta, bidone.

can[2] *v. dif.* (*ind. cong. pres.*) **could** (*ind. cong. pass. e condiz.*) potere, essere in grado di.

Canadian *agg.* e *s.* canadese.

canal *s.* canale.

canalization *s.* canalizzazione.

to **canalize** *vt.* canalizzare.

canary *agg.* giallo canarino. ◆ **canary** *s.* canarino.

to **cancel** *vt.* annullare, cancellare.

cancellation *s.* annullamento, cancellatura.

cancer *s.* cancro.

candid *agg.* sincero, candido.

candidate *s.* candidato.

candidature *s.* candidatura.

candidly *avv.* sinceramente, candidamente.

candied *agg.* candito.

candle *s.* candela || — *-end*, moccolo; — *-holder*, candelabro; *by* — *-light*, a lume di candela.

candlestick *s.* candeliere.

candour *s.* candore, ingenuità.

candy *s.* candito.

to **candy** *vt.* candire. ◆ to **candy** *vi.* cristallizzarsi (*di zucchero*).

cane *s.* **1.** giunco, canna **2.** bastone da passeggio.

to **cane** *vt.* bastonare (*con una canna*).

canine *s.* dente canino.

caning *s.* bastonatura.

canned *agg.* conservato in scatola.

cannibal *s.* cannibale.

cannibalism *s.* cannibalismo.

cannon *s.* **1.** cannone **2.** carambola (*al biliardo*).

to **cannon** *vi.* **1.** cannoneggiare **2.** far carambola.

canoe *s.* canoa.

canon *s.* **1.** canone **2.** (*eccl.*) canonico: — *law*, diritto canonico.

canonical *agg.* canonico.

to **canonize** *vt.* canonizzare.

canopy *s.* **1.** baldacchino **2.** volta (*del cielo*).

cant *s.* **1.** (*arch.*) angolo esterno **2.** inclinazione **3.** gergo.

canteen *s.* **1.** (*mil.*) dispensa **2.** mensa aziendale.

canvas *s.* **1.** canovaccio **2.** (*mar*) velatura **3.** tela **4.** tendone.

canyon *s.* burrone.

cap *s.* **1.** berretto **2.** (*arch.*) capitello **3.** (*mecc.*; *elettr.*) cappuccio, capsula.

capability *s.* capacità, abilità.

capable *agg.* abile, capace.

capacitor *s.* condensatore.

capacity *s.* **1.** capacità **2.** (*elettr*) potenza (*di motore*).

cape[1] *s.* capo, promontorio.

cape[2] *s.* cappa.

caper[1] *s.* cappero.

caper[2] *s.* piroetta, capriola.

to **caper** *vi.* far capriole.

capercaillie *s.* gallo cedrone.

capillarity *s.* capillarità.

capillary *agg.* capillare. ◆ **capillary** *s.* (*anat.*) vaso capillare.

capital[1] *agg.* e *s.* capitale.

capital[2] *s.* (*arch.*) capitello.

capitalism *s.* capitalismo.

capitalist *s.* capitalista.

capitalistic *agg.* capitalistico.

to **capitalize** *vt.* capitalizzare.

capitular *agg.* capitolare.

capitulary *s.* capitolare.

to **capitulate** *vi.* capitolare.

capitulation *s.* capitolazione.

capon *s.* cappone.

caprice *s.* capriccio.

capsize *vt.* capovolgere. ◆ to **capsize** *vi.* capovolgersi.

capstan *s.* argano.

capsule *s.* capsula.

to **capsule** *vt.* incapsulare.

captain *s.* **1.** capitano **2.** (*comm*) magnate.

captious *agg.* capzioso.

to **captivate** *vt.* cattivare, ammaliare.

captivating *agg.* cattivante, ammaliante.

captive *s.* prigioniero: *to take* —, far prigioniero.

captivity *s.* prigionia, cattività.

capture *s.* cattura.

to **capture** *vt.* far prigioniero, prendere (di città ecc.).

Capuchin s. 1. (eccl.) Cappuccino 2. scimmia cappuccina.

car s. 1. carro 2. automobile 3. (ferr.) vagone || — -licence, permesso di circolazione; dining—, vagone ristorante; sleeping—, vagone letto.

carabin s. carabina.

carabineer s. carabiniere.

to caracole vi. caracollare.

carafe s. caraffa.

caramel s. caramello.

carat s. carato.

caravan s. 1. carovana 2. carro (di zingari ecc.).

caravel s. caravella.

carbon s. carbonio || — paper, carta carbone.

carbonate s. carbonato.

carboniferous agg. carbonifero.

to carbonize vt. carbonizzare.

carbuncle s. carbonchio.

carburation s. carburazione.

carburetter, carburettor s. carburatore.

carcase s. carcassa.

carcinogen s. sostanza cancerogena.

card s. 1. cartoncino, biglietto 2. carta da giuoco.

to card vt. schedare.

cardan s. cardano || — joint, giunto cardanico.

cardboard s. cartone.

cardiac agg. cardiaco.

cardigan s. giacca di lana.

cardinal agg. e s. cardinale.

cardiogram s. cardiogramma

cardiologist s. cardiologo.

cardiopathy s. cardiopatia.

care s. 1. cura, attenzione, protezione: take —!, attenzione!; to take — of, aver cura 2. preoccupazione || — -free, senza pensieri; — -worn, pieno di pensieri.

to care vi. curarsi, interessarsi.

career s. 1. carriera 2. andatura veloce.

careful agg. 1. accurato 2. prudente.

carefully avv. 1. accuratamente 2. attentamente.

careless agg. noncurante.

carelessly avv. negligentemente.

carelessness s. trascuratezza.

caress s. carezza.

to caress vt. accarezzare.

caressing agg. carezzevole.

caretaker s. guardiano, custode.

caricature s. caricatura.

Carmelite s. carmelitano.

carmine agg. e s. carminio.

carnage s. carneficina, strage.

carnal agg. carnale, sensuale.

carnation agg. carnicino. ♦ **carnation** s. garofano.

carnival s. carnevale.

carnivore s. carnivoro.

carnivorous agg. carnivoro.

carol s. canto, inno.

carotid s. carotide.

carousel s. carosello.

carp s. carpa.

carpenter s. carpentiere, falegname.

carpet s. tappeto || bedside —, scendiletto.

carriage s. 1. carrozza, vettura 2. (comm.) trasporto.

carrier s. 1. portatore, spedizioniere 2. (mecc.) trasportatore 3. supporto.

carrion s. carogna.

carrot s. carota.

carry s. portata (di arma da fuoco ecc.).

to carry vt. e vi. 1. portare (un peso), trasportare 2. trasmettere (suoni) || to — about, portare addosso; to — on, continuare; to — out, eseguire, realizzare, compiere; to — through, portare a buon fine.

carrying s. trasporto.

cart s. carro.

cartel s. (econ.; pol.) cartello.

cartilage s. cartilagine.

cartography s. cartografia.

cartomancy s. cartomanzia.

carton s. scatola di cartone.

cartoon s. 1. vignetta 2. (cine) disegno animato.

cartridge s. 1. cartuccia 2. (foto) rotolo.

to carve vt. e vi. scolpire, incidere, cesellare.

carver s. intagliatore, scultore (in legno e avorio).

carving s. scultura, intaglio (in legno e avorio).

caryatid s. cariatide.

cascade s. piccola cascata (d'acqua).

case¹ s. 1. caso, avvenimento 2. (giur.) causa.

case² s. 1. astuccio 2. cassa, cassetta.

to case vt. imballare.

casement s. telaio di finestra (a due battenti), finestra.

cash *s.* cassa, contanti ‖ — *on delivery*, pagamento alla consegna; *by ready —*, in contanti.

to cash *vt.* incassare, riscuotere.

cashier *s.* cassiere.

to cashier *vt.* destituire.

casing *s.* involucro, copertura.

cask *s.* barile, botte.

casket *s.* scrigno.

cassation *s.* cassazione.

cassock *s.* tunica (*del clero anglicano*).

cast *s.* 1. getto, lancio 2. (*metal.*) gettata, stampo 3. complesso (*di attori*) ‖ — *-iron*, ghisa.

to cast (cast, cast) *vt.* e *vi.* 1. gettare, lanciare 2. (*metal.*) fondere (*in stampo*) ‖ *to — aside*, gettare da parte; *to — down*, abbassare (*gli occhi*).

castanets *s. pl.* nacchere.

castaway *agg.* arenato, respinto. ♦

castaway *s.* naufrago, reprobo.

caste *s.* casta.

caster *s.* V. *castor*.

to castigate *vt.* castigare, punire.

casting *s.* 1. il gettare 2. (*metal.*) getto, colata 3. distribuzione (*delle parti agli attori*).

castle *s.* castello.

castor *s.* 1. pepaiuola, saliera 2. rotella da mobili.

castor-oil *s.* olio di ricino.

to castrate *vt.* castrare.

casual *agg.* casuale, fortuito.

casually *avv.* per caso.

casualness *s.* irregolarità, noncuranza.

casualty *s.* 1. infortunio 2. infortunato.

casuistry *s.* casistica.

cat *s.* gatto.

cataclysm *s.* cataclisma.

catacomb *s.* catacomba.

catalepsy *s.* catalessi.

cataleptic *agg.* e *s.* catalettico.

catalogue *s.* catalogo.

to catalogue *vt.* e *vi.* catalogare.

catalyst *s.* catalizzatore.

cataplasm *s.* cataplasma.

catapult *s.* catapulta.

cataract *s.* cateratta.

catarrh *s.* catarro.

catastrophe *s.* catastrofe, calamità.

catastrophic(al) *agg.* catastrofico.

catch *s.* 1. presa, cattura 2. trappola ‖ *-as- -can*, lotta libera.

to catch (caught, caught) *vt.* 1. afferrare, acchiappare, prendere: *to*

— *the train*, prendere il treno 2. pescare, sorprendere.

catching *agg.* 1. attraente 2. orecchiabile (*di melodia*) 3. (*med.*) contagioso.

catchy *agg.* 1. attraente 2. orecchiabile (*di melodia*) 3. insidioso.

catechism *s.* catechismo.

to catechize *vt.* catechizzare.

catechumen *s.* catecumeno.

categoric(al) *agg.* categorico.

category *s.* categoria.

to cater *vi.* 1. provvedere cibo 2. procurare svaghi.

caterpillar *s.* 1. bruco 2. (*mecc.*) cingolo 3. trattore a cingoli.

catharsis *s.* catarsi.

cathartic *agg.* catartico.

cathedral *s.* cattedrale.

Catherine-wheel *s.* girandola.

cathode *s.* catodo.

cathodic *agg.* catodico.

catholic *agg.* e *s.* cattolico.

Catholicism *s.* cattolicesimo.

cation *s.* catione.

cattish *agg.* felino.

cattle *s.* bestiame, armenti ‖ — *-dealer*, negoziante di bestiame; — *-lifter*, ladro di bestiame.

caught V. *to catch.*

cauldron *s.* caldaia.

cauliflower *s.* cavolfiore.

causal *agg.* causale.

causality *s.* causalità.

causative *agg.* causativo.

cause *s.* 1. causa, ragione, motivo 2. (*giur.*) processo, causa.

to cause *vt.* causare, cagionare.

causeway *s.* strada rialzata.

caustic *agg.* caustico (*anche fig.*).

caustically *avv.* causticamente (*anche fig.*).

causticity *s.* causticità (*anche fig.*).

cauterization *s.* cauterizzazione.

to cauterize *vt.* cauterizzare.

caution *s.* 1. prudenza, cautela 2. cauzione, garanzia ‖ — *-money*, cauzione, pegno.

to caution *vt.* mettere in guardia.

cautious *agg.* cauto, prudente.

cautiously *avv.* cautamente.

cavalier *s.* cavaliere.

cavalry *s.* cavalleria.

cave *s.* caverna, spelonca.

to cave *vt.* e *vi.* scavare ‖ *to — in*, sprofondare.

cavernous *agg.* cavernoso (*anche fig.*).

caviar(e) *s.* caviale.

cavil s. cavillo.

to cavil vi. cavillare.

cavity s. cavità.

cavy s. cavia.

cayman s. caimano.

to cease vt. e vi. cessare, finire.

cedar s. cedro.

cedilla s. cediglia.

ceiling s. soffitto.

to celebrate vt. e vi. celebrare, solennizzare.

celebrated agg. famoso.

celebration s. celebrazione.

celebrity s. celebrità, persona famosa.

celerity s. celerità.

celery s. sedano.

celestial agg. celestiale, paradisiaco.

celibacy s. celibato.

cell s. 1. cella 2. cellula.

cellar s. cantina.

cellarman s. cantiniere.

cellular agg. cellulare, alveolare.

cellulitis s. cellulite.

celluloid agg. e s. celluloide.

cellulose s. cellulosa.

Celt s. celta.

Celtic agg. celtico.

cement s. 1. cemento 2. stucco, mastice.

to cement vt. cementare (anche fig.).

cemetery s. cimitero.

to cense vt. incensare.

censer s. turibolo.

censor s. censore.

to censor vt. censurare.

censorial agg. censorio.

censorship s. censura, censorato.

censure s. censura.

to censure vt. censurare.

census s. censo.

cent s. centesimo (di dollaro).

centaur s. centauro.

centenarian agg. e s. centenario.

centenary agg. e s. centenario.

centennial agg. centennale.

centesimal agg. centesimale.

centigrade agg. centigrado.

centigramme s. centigrammo.

centilitre s. centilitro.

centimetre s. centimetro.

central agg. 1. centrale 2. fondamentale.

centralism s. accentramento.

centralization s. concentrazione (di poteri).

to centralize vt. e vi. accentrare.

centre s. centro, parte centrale, interno.

centrifugal agg. centrifugo.

centripetal agg. centripeto.

centrism s. centrismo.

to centuplicate vt. centuplicare.

centurion s. centurione.

century s. 1. secolo 2. (stor.) centuria.

cephalalgia s. cefalea.

ceramics s. (arte della) ceramica.

cereal agg. e s. cereale.

cerebral agg. cerebrale.

cerebro-spinal agg. cerebro-spinale.

cerebrum s. cervello.

ceremonial agg. da cerimonia. ♦ ceremonial s. cerimoniale.

ceremonious agg. cerimonioso.

ceremony s. cerimonia || to stand on —, far complimenti.

certain agg. 1. certo, sicuro 2. indeterminato, certo.

certainly avv. certamente.

certainty s. certezza.

certificate s. certificato.

to certify vt. certificare, attestare.

certitude s. certezza.

cervical agg. cervicale. ♦ cervical s. vertebra cervicale. ♦ cervicals s. pl. nervi cervicali.

cessation s. cessazione.

cession s. cessione.

cess-pit, cess-pool s. pozzo nero.

cetacean agg. di cetaceo. ♦ cetacean s. cetaceo.

to chafe vt. 1. riscaldare 2. irritare. to chafe vi. 1. strofinarsi 2. irritarsi.

chaff s. 1. pula, paglia trinciata 2. (fig.) oggetto di nessun valore.

chaffer s. contrattazione, baratto.

chain s. 1. catena 2. serie, concatenamento.

to chain vt. 1. incatenare 2. (fig.) mettere in ceppi.

chain-stores s. pl. catene (di negozi o grandi magazzini).

chair s. 1. sedia: deck- —, sedia a sdraio; easy- —, poltrona 2. cattedra (universitaria).

chairman s. presidente (di consiglio, assemblea ecc.).

chalice s. calice.

chalk s. 1. gesso 2. (min.) calcare || —-drawing, disegno a pastello; —-stone (pat.), calcolo.

chalky agg. gessoso.

challenge s. 1. sfida 2. (mil.) intimazione.

to challenge vt. 1. sfidare 2. (mil.) intimare.

challenger s. sfidatore, sfidante.

chamber s. 1. sala, aula 2. (pol ; comm.) camera || — -music, musica da camera; —maid, cameriera (specialmente d'albergo).

chamberlain s. 1. ciambellano 2. tesoriere.

chameleon s. camaleonte.

chamois s. camoscio.

champion s. 1. campione 2. difensore.

championship s. campionato.

chance s. 1. avvenimento fortuito, caso 2. occasione.

to chance vi. accadere.

chancellery s. cancelleria.

chancellor s. cancelliere.

chancery s. cancelleria.

chandelier s. candeliere, lampadario.

change s. 1. cambio, mutamento || — for a —, tanto per cambiare 2. moneta spicciola.

to change vt. e vi. cambiare.

changeability s. mutabilità.

changeable agg. 1. mutabile 2. incostante (di tempo).

changing agg. cangiante, mutevole. ♦ **changing** s. cambio.

channel s. 1. canale, stretto. ♦ **channels** s. pl. vie di comunicazione.

chant s. canto, cantilena.

to chant vt. 1. fare canali 2. incanalare.

chaos s. caos.

chap[1] s. (fam.) individuo, ragazzo.

chap[2] s. screpolatura.

chapel s. cappella.

chaplain s. cappellano.

chaplet s. ghirlanda, corona (di fiori).

chapter s. capitolo.

to char vt. carbonizzare. ♦ **to char** vi. carbonizzarsi.

character s. 1. carattere, indole 2. scrittura 3. (lett.) personaggio.

characteristic agg. caratteristico. ♦ **characteristic** s. caratteristica.

characterization s. caratterizzazione.

to characterize vt. caratterizzare.

charade s. sciarada.

charcoal s. carbone di legna.

charge s. 1. prezzo richiesto, spesa 2. incarico, sorveglianza 3. (giur.) accusa.

to charge vt. 1. far pagare, addebitare 2. incaricare 3. accusare: to

— so. with a crime, accusare qu. di un delitto.

chargeable agg. 1. a carico di, da addebitarsi a 2. accusabile.

chariot s. cocchio.

charitable agg. caritatevole.

charitably avv. caritatevolmente.

charity s. 1. carità, benevolenza 2. istituzione benefica.

charlatan s. ciarlatano.

charm s. 1. fascino 2. incantesimo, malia.

to charm vt. 1. affascinare 2. sottoporre a magia.

charming agg. affascinante.

charmingly avv. in modo affascinante.

charnel(-house) s. ossario.

chart s. 1. grafico 2. carta marina

charter s. 1. licenza, brevetto 2. carta costituzionale.

chartography s. cartografia.

charwoman s. domestica ad ore.

charwork s. lavoro di domestica ad ore.

chase s. 1. inseguimento, caccia 2. riserva di caccia, cacciagione.

to chase[1] vt. inseguire, cacciare.

to chase[2] vt. cesellare.

chaser[1] s. cacciatore, inseguitore.

chaser[2] s. cesellatore.

chasing s. 1. cesellatura 2. filettatura (di una vite).

chasm s. baratro, abisso.

chaste agg. casto, puro.

chastely avv. castamente, virtuosamente.

chastity s. castità.

chat s. chiacchiera.

to chat vi. chiacchierare.

chatter s. 1. chiacchiera, chiacchierio 2. il battere dei denti.

to chatter vi. 1. chiacchierare 2. battere i denti.

chatterbox s. chiacchierone, chiacchierona.

chattering s. 1. chiacchierio 2. il battere dei denti.

chauvinism s. sciovinismo.

chauvinist s. sciovinista.

cheap agg. e avv. a buon mercato

cheaply avv. economicamente, in modo poco costoso.

cheat s. 1. frode 2. imbroglione.

to cheat vt. e vi. imbrogliare.

cheater s. truffatore, baro.

cheating s. inganno.

check[1] s. 1. scacco 2. controllo, verifica 3. scontrino, contromarca

check² s. disegno a scacchi.
to check vi. dare scacco. ♦ to check vt. controllare, verificare.
checked agg. quadrettato.
checkmate s. scacco matto.
to checkmate vt. dare scacco matto.
cheek s. guancia.
cheekily avv. sfacciatamente.
cheeky agg. sfacciato.
to cheer vt. rallegrare, incoraggiare. ♦ to cheer vi. essere di buon umore, rallegrarsi.
cheerful agg. di buon umore.
cheerfully avv. allegramente.
cheerfulness s. buon umore.
cheering agg. incoraggiante. ♦ cheering s. acclamazioni (pl.).
cheese s. formaggio.
cheetah s. ghepardo.
chemical agg. chimico.
chemically avv. chimicamente.
chemicals s. pl. prodotti chimici.
chemisette s. camicetta.
chemist s. 1. chimico 2. farmacista.
chemistry s. chimica.
cheque s. assegno: to cash a —, cambiare un assegno; — -book, libretto d'assegni; blank —, assegno in bianco; crossed —, assegno sbarrato.
to cherish vt. 1. (fig.) nutrire 2. curare teneramente, coccolare.
cherry s. ciliegia.
cherub s. cherubino.
chess s. giuoco degli scacchi || -board, scacchiera; — -men, pezzi degli scacchi.
chest s. 1. cassetta, cassone 2. torace.
chestnut agg. castano. ♦ chestnut s. 1. castagno 2. castagna.
to chew vt. e vi. masticare.
chicanery s. cavillo (legale).
chick s. 1. pulcino 2. (fig.) bambino.
chicken s. gallinella, pollo.
chicory s. cicoria.
to chide (chid, chid) (anche reg.) vt. e vi. redarguire, sgridare.
chief agg. principale. ♦ chief s. capo, comandante.
chiefly avv. principalmente.
chieftain s. capo (di tribù, clan ecc.).
chilblain s. gelone.
child s. (pl. children) 1. bambino, bambina 2. figlio, figlia.
childhood s. infanzia.
childish agg. infantile.

childishness s. fanciullaggine, puerilità.
childless agg. senza figli.
childlike agg. infantile.
children V. child.
Chilean agg. e s. cileno.
chill s. 1. colpo di freddo 2. (metal.) conchiglia.
to chill vt. 1. raffreddare, agghiacciare (anche fig.) 2. (metal.) fondere in conchiglia. ♦ to chill vi. raffreddarsi.
chilled agg. 1. congelato 2. (metal.) fuso in conchiglia.
chilliness s. 1. freddo 2. (fig.) freddezza.
chilly agg. 1. freddoloso (di persona) 2. fresco (di tempo).
chime s. scampanio.
to chime vt. e vi. scampanare, suonare a festa.
chiming s. lo scampanare.
chimney s. camino, comignolo || -sweeper, spazzacamino.
chimpanzee s. scimpanzè.
chin s. mento || -strap, sottogola.
china s. 1. porcellana fine 2. (fam.) stoviglie di porcellana.
chinchilla s. cincillà.
chine s. spina dorsale.
Chinese agg. e s. cinese.
chink s. fessura, crepa.
chip s. 1. scheggia 2. (cuc.) patatina fritta.
to chip vt. 1. scheggiare 2. rompere. ♦ to chip vi. scheggiarsi, frantumarsi.
chiromancer s. chiromante.
chiromancy s. chiromanzia.
chiropodist s. pedicure.
chirp s. 1. cinguettio, pigolio 2. stridio, il frinire (di cicale ecc.).
to chirp vi. 1. cinguettare, pigolare 2. frinire, stridere (di cicale ecc.).
chisel s. cesello.
to chisel vt. cesellare.
chiseller s. cesellatore.
chitterlings s. pl. trippa.
chivalrous agg. cavalleresco.
chivalry s. 1. cavalleria 2. condotta cavalleresca.
chloride s. cloruro.
chlorine s. cloro.
chlorite s. clorito.
chloroform s. cloroformio.
chlorophyll(l) s. clorofilla.
chock s. 1. cuneo, bietta 2. (mar.) passacavi.
chocolate agg. 1. di cioccolato 2.

color cioccolata. ♦ **chocolate** *s.* cioccolato: *cake of* —, tavoletta di cioccolato.

choice *agg.* di prima qualità, scelto. ♦ **choice** *s.* **1.** scelta **2.** la cosa scelta **3.** assortimento.

choir *s.* coro.

choke *s.* **1.** soffocamento **2.** strozzatura (*di tubo*).

to **choke** *vt.* **1.** soffocare (*anche fig.*) **2.** ingorgare. ♦ to **choke** *vi.* ostruirsi.

choker *s.* soffocatore.

cholera *s.* colera.

cholesterol *s.* colesterolo.

to **choose** (**chose, chosen**) *vt.* scegliere.

chooser *s.* chi sceglie.

chop *s.* **1.** (*cuc.*) braciola **2.** colpo (*di scure ecc.*).

to **chop** *vt. e vi.* **1.** fendere, tagliare **2.** (*cuc.*) tritare || to — *down*, abbattere (*alberi*); to — *off*, tagliar via.

chopper *s.* **1.** ascia **2.** chi taglia con l'ascia **3.** tagliatrice.

choppy *agg.* **1.** screpolato **2.** increspato (*del mare*).

choral *agg.* corale.

chord *s.* **1.** (*mus.; anat.; geom.*) corda **2.** (*mus.*) accordo.

choreographer *s.* coreografo.

choreographic *agg.* coreografico.

choreography *s.* coreografia.

chorus *s.* coro || — *singer*, corista.

chose V. *to choose*.

chosen V. *to choose*.

chrism *s.* crisma.

to **christen** *vt.* battezzare.

Christendom *s.* cristianità.

christening *s.* battesimo.

Christian *agg. e s.* cristiano || — *name*, nome di battesimo.

Christianity *s.* cristianesimo.

to **christianize** *vt.* convertire al cristianesimo.

Christmas *s.* Natale.

chromatic *agg.* cromatico.

chromatically *avv.* cromaticamente.

chromatism *s.* cromatismo.

chromatography *s.* cromatografia.

chrome *s.* cromo.

to **chrome** *vt.* cromare.

chromium *s.* cromo || — *-plated*, cromato; — *-plating*, cromatura.

chromolithograph *s.* cromolitografia.

chromosome *s.* cromosoma.

chromosphere *s.* cromosfera.

chronic *agg.* cronico (*anche fig.*).

chronicle *s.* cronaca.

chronicler *s.* cronista.

chronologic(al) *agg.* cronologico.

chronologically *avv.* cronologicamente.

chronology *s.* cronologia.

chronometer *s.* cronometro.

chrysalid *s.* crisalide.

chrysanthemum *s.* crisantemo.

chubby *agg.* paffuto.

church *s.* **1.** chiesa **2.** comunità religiosa || — *-going*, assiduità ai servizi religiosi; — *-living*, beneficio ecclesiastico; — *-service*, funzione religiosa.

churchman *s.* **1.** ecclesiastico **2.** membro della chiesa anglicana.

churchy *agg.* bigotto.

churchyard *s.* cimitero.

chyle *s.* (*fisiol.*) chilo.

ciborium *s.* ciborio.

cicada *s.* cicala.

to **cicatrize** *vt.* cicatrizzare. ♦ to **cicatrize** *vi.* cicatrizzarsi.

cider *s.* sidro.

cigar *s.* sigaro || — *-case*, portasigari, — *-end*, mozzicone; — *-holder*, bocchino per sigari.

cigarette *s.* sigaretta || — *-case*, portasigarette, — *-end*, mozzicone, — *-holder*, bocchino; — *paper*, cartina per sigaretta.

cilice *s.* cilicio.

cinder *s.* **1.** brace **2.** scoria.

cine-camera *s.* macchina da presa.

cinema *s.* cinematografo.

cinematograph *s.* **1.** proiettore cinematografico **2.** macchina da presa.

cinematographer *s.* **1.** operatore cinematografico **2.** cineasta.

cinematographic *agg.* cinematografico.

cinematography *s.* cinematografia.

cine-projector *s.* proiettore cinematografico.

cinerary *agg.* cinerario.

cinnabar *s.* cinabro.

cinnamon *s.* cannella.

cipher *s.* **1.** cifrario **2.** monogramma **3.** (*mat.; anche fig.*) zero, nullità.

to **cipher** *vt. e vi.* cifrare.

circle *s.* **1.** cerchio, circolo (*anche fig.*) **2.** orbita (*dei pianeti*) **3.** galleria (*di teatro*).

circlet *s.* cerchietto.

circuit s. **1.** cinta, circonvallazione **2.** rivoluzione, rotazione (di astri) **3.** (elettr.; sport) circuito.

circular agg. circolare. ♦ **circular** s. lettera circolare.

to **circulate** vt. mettere in circolazione, diffondere. ♦ to **circulate** vi. circolare.

circulating agg. circolante.

circulation s. **1.** circolazione **2.** diffusione **3.** (giorn.) tiratura.

circulatory agg. circolatorio.

to **circumcise** vt. circoncidere.

circumcision s. circoncisione.

circumference s. circonferenza.

circumflex agg. circonflesso.

circumlocution s. circonlocuzione.

to **circumnavigate** vt. circumnavigare.

circumnavigation s. circumnavigazione.

circumnavigator s. circumnavigatore.

to **circumscribe** vt. circoscrivere.

circumscription s. circoscrizione.

circumspect agg. circospetto.

circumspection s. circospezione.

circumstance s. circostanza.

circumstantial agg. **1.** circostanziale **2.** circostanziato.

circumstantiality s. abbondanza di particolari.

circumstantially avv. circostanziatamente.

to **circumvent** vt. circuire.

circumvention s. raggiro.

circumvolution s. circonvoluzione.

circus s. **1.** circo, arena **2.** piazza rotonda.

cirrhosis s. cirrosi.

cisalpine agg. cisalpino.

cistern s. cisterna.

citadel s. cittadella.

to **cite** vt. citare.

citizen s. cittadino.

citizenhood s. cittadinanza.

citizenship s. diritto di cittadinanza.

citrate s. citrato.

citric agg. citrico.

citron s. cedro.

city s. **1.** città (grande) **2.** centro di grande traffico di una città.

civic agg. civico.

civil agg. civile, cortese.

civilian agg. e s. civile, borghese.

civility s. civiltà, cortesia.

civilization s. civilizzazione, civiltà.

to **civilize** vt. civilizzare.

civilly avv. civilmente.

civism s. civismo.

claim s. **1.** richiesta **2.** (giur.) rivendicazione **3.** (comm.) reclamo.

to **claim** vt. **1.** esigere, chiedere **2.** (giur.) rivendicare **3.** (comns.) reclamare.

claimant s. **1.** rivendicatore **2.** richiedente.

clairvoyance s. chiaroveggenza.

clairvoyant agg. e s. chiaroveggente.

to **clamber** vi. arrampicarsi.

clammy agg. vischioso.

clamour s. clamore, vocio.

to **clamour** vt. e vi. vociferare.

clan s. gruppo familiare, tribù.

clandestine agg. clandestino.

to **clang** vi. emettere un suono, un grido. ♦ to **clang** vt. far risonare.

clangour s. fragore.

to **clank** vi. tintinnare. ♦ to **clank** vt. far tintinnare.

clap s. **1.** applauso **2.** rumore improvviso **3.** piccolo colpo (con la mano).

to **clap** vt. e vi. **1.** applaudire **2.** dare un colpo (con la mano) **3.** battere (le ali).

clapper s. **1.** battente (di porta) **2.** (teat.) membro della « claque ».

claret s. **1.** color rosso-violetto **2.** vino chiaretto.

clarification s. chiarificazione.

to **clarify** vt. chiarificare. ♦ to **clarify** vi. chiarificarsi.

clarinet s. clarinetto.

clarity s. chiarità.

clash s. **1.** cozzo, urto **2.** scontro (d'opinioni).

to **clash** vt. e vi. **1.** cozzare, far strepito **2.** scontrarsi (d'opinioni).

clasp s. fermaglio, fibbia.

to **clasp** vt. afferrare.

class s. **1.** classe, categoria **2.** (scol.) classe **3.** (fig.) distinzione.

classic agg. e s. classico.

classical agg. classico.

classically avv. classicamente.

classicism s. classicismo.

classification s. classificazione.

to **classify** vt. classificare.

classmate s. compagno di classe.

classroom s. aula.

classy agg. (fam.) di classe.

clatter s. fracasso.

to **clatter** vi. far fracasso.

clause s. clausola.

claustrophobia s. claustrofobia.

claw *s.* 1. artiglio, zampa con artigli 2. uncino 3. chela.

to claw *vt.* artigliare.

clawed *agg.* munito di artigli.

clay *s.* argilla: *fire* —, argilla refrattaria || — *pigeon*, piattello.

clayey *agg.* argilloso.

clean *agg.* 1. pulito 2. netto, nitido 3. (*fig.*) puro, schietto.

to clean *vt.* pulire.

cleaner *s.* pulitore, pulitrice || *dry* —, smacchiatore a secco.

cleaning *s.* pulitura.

cleanliness *s.* pulizia.

cleanly *agg.* pulito. ◆ **cleanly** *avv.* in modo pulito.

cleanness *s.* 1. pulizia (*anche fig.*) 2. nitidezza.

to cleanse *vt.* 1. pulire 2. purificare.

cleanser *s.* 1. pulitore 2. detersivo.

cleansing *agg.* purificante. ◆ **cleansing** *s.* 1. purificazione 2. depurazione.

clear *agg.* 1. chiaro, limpido 2. distinto, evidente || — *cut*, nettamente stagliato; — *sighted*, dalla vista buona.

to clear *vt.* 1. chiarire, schiarire 2. discolpare 3. (*comm.*) svincolare || *to* — *away*, sparecchiare, dissiparsi (*di nebbia*); *to* — *up*, rassettare (*una stanza*), chiarire (*un malinteso*). ◆ **to clear** *vi.* schiarirsi.

clearance *s.* 1. chiarificazione 2. sgombero 3. (*comm.*) sdoganamento.

clearing *s.* 1. chiarimento 2. rimozione.

clearly *avv.* chiaramente.

clearness *s.* 1. chiarezza 2. (*fig.*) limpidezza.

cleavage *s.* 1. spaccatura 2. (*min.*) clivaggio.

to cleave (**cleft, cleft**) *vt.* e *vi.* fendere, spaccare.

cleft *s.* fenditura.

clemency *s.* clemenza.

clement *agg.* 1. clemente 2. dolce, gentile (*di carattere*) 3. mite (*di tempo*).

to clench *vt.* 1. stringere (*mani, denti ecc.*) 2. ribadire.

clergy *s.* clero.

clergyman *s.* ecclesiastico.

clerical *agg.* 1. clericale 2. impiegatizio.

clericalism *s.* clericalismo.

clerk *s.* impiegato || *chief* —, ca-

poufficio.

to clerk *vi.* lavorare come impiegato.

clever *agg.* intelligente, abile, ingegnoso.

cleverly *avv.* intelligentemente.

cleverness *s.* intelligenza, abilità, ingegnosità.

clew *s.* gomitolo (*di filo*).

click *s.* scatto, rumore secco.

client *s.* cliente.

cliff *s.* scogliera.

climate *s.* clima.

climatic *agg.* climatico.

climax *s.* apice, culmine.

climb *s.* 1. rampa 2. ascesa.

to climb *vt.* e *vi.* 1. arrampicarsi 2. scalare (*anche fig.*).

climber *s.* 1. scalatore 2. (*fig.*) arrivista 3. pianta rampicante.

climbing *s.* 1. scalata 2. (*fig.*) arrivismo. ◆ **climbing** *agg.* rampicante.

to cling (**clung, clung**) *vi.* attaccarsi, aggrapparsi (*anche fig.*): *to* — *to a hope*, aggrapparsi ad una speranza.

clinical *agg.* clinico.

clinician *s.* clinico.

clinking *s.* tintinnio.

clip *s.* 1. fermaglio, molletta || *hair* —, forcina per capelli 2. graffa (*per ferite*) 3. tosatura (*di pecore*).

to clip *vt.* 1. tenere insieme (*con un fermaglio*) 2. tosare (*pecore ecc.*).

clipper *s.* 1. tosatore 2. (*mar.*) "clipper". ◆ **clippers** *s. pl.* 1. forbici 2. macchinetta per tosare (*sing.*).

cloak *s.* 1. mantello 2. (*fig.*) manto, velo.

clock *s.* orologio (*da muro, da tavolo*) || *alarm* —, sveglia.

clockwise *agg.* in senso orario || *counter* —, in senso antiorario.

clockwork *s.* meccanismo a orologeria.

clod *s.* zolla.

clog *s.* 1. impedimento, intoppo 2. zoccolo.

to clog *vt.* ostruire, impedire (*anche fig.*). ◆ **to clog** *vi.* incepparsi.

cloister *s.* chiostro.

close *agg.* 1. chiuso 2. serrato: — *combat*, combattimento corpo a corpo 3. afoso, viziato (*di aria*) 4. intimo: — *friend*, amico intimo 5. accurato, attento || — *fitting*, aderente (*di vestiti*); —

-mouthed, riservato; — -shaven, rasato con cura.

close s. 1. spazio cintato 2. fine, termine 3. corpo a corpo.

close avv. vicino, presso.

to close vt. chiudere || to — up, turare, sbarrare (di strada). ◆ to close vi. chiudersi || to — in, avvicinarsi, accorciarsi (di giorni); to — with, venire a un accordo.

closed agg. chiuso.

closely avv. 1. da vicino 2. attentamente.

closeness s. 1. afa, mancanza d'aria 2. compattezza 3. intimità 4. vicinanza 5. accuratezza.

closet s. 1. studio, salotto privato 2. armadio a muro 3. gabinetto.

close-up s. (cine) primo piano.

closing s. chiusura (di negozi, teatri ecc.).

clot s. grumo.

to clot vt. raggrumare, coagulare. ◆ to clot vi. raggrumarsi, coagularsi.

cloth s. tessuto, stoffa, tela || (table-) —, tovaglia.

to clothe vt. vestire.

clothes s. pl. abiti, indumenti || -hook, attaccapanni; — -line, corda (per stendere il bucato); — -peg, molletta (fermabucato).

clothing s. 1. vestiario 2. copertura.

cloud s. 1. nuvola, nube 2. nugolo (di insetti).

to cloud vt. e vi. annuvolare, oscurare || to — (up, over), annuvolarsi.

clouded agg. 1. coperto (di nubi) 2. torbido (di liquidi).

cloudily avv. nebulosamente.

cloudy agg. 1. nuvoloso 2. torbido.

clover s. trifoglio.

clown s. pagliaccio.

clownish agg. pagliaccesco.

club s. 1. mazza, randello 2. circolo, associazione 3. (carte) fiori.

clue s. 1. indizio, traccia 2. filo di un racconto.

clumsily avv. goffamente.

clumsiness s. goffaggine.

clumsy agg. goffo, senza grazia.

clung V. to cling.

cluster s. 1. grappolo (d'uva), mazzo (di fiori), gruppo 2. folla, capannello (di gente) 3. sciame.

clutch s. 1. stretta, grinfia 2. (auto) frizione.

to clutch vt. e vi. afferrare, afferrarsi, agguantare.

coach s. 1. carrozza, cocchio 2. pullman 3. carrozza ferroviaria 4. (sport) allenatore, istruttore || -house, rimessa; mourning- —, carro funebre; stage- —, diligenza.

coachman s. cocchiere.

coachwork s. carrozzeria.

coadjutor s. coadiutore.

coagulant s. sostanza coagulante.

to coagulate vt. coagulare. ◆ to coagulate vi. coagularsi.

coagulation s. coagulazione.

coagulator s. coagulante.

coal s. carbone; — -bed, bacino carbonifero; — -black, nero come il carbone; — -fed, alimentato a carbone; — -mine, miniera di carbone.

to coalesce vi. 1. coalizzarsi, unirsi 2. fondersi.

coalition s. coalizione.

coarse agg. 1. grossolano, rozzo 2. ruvido, grosso (di materiale).

coarsely avv. grossolanamente.

coarseness s. 1. grossolanità 2. ruvidezza (di stoffe ecc.).

coast s. costa || — -guard, polizia costiera.

coastal agg. costiero.

coaster s. 1. nave cabotiera 2. sottobicchiere.

coat s. 1. giacca, soprabito 2. manto (anche fig.), pelliccia (di animale) 3. rivestimento, intonaco || — of arms, stemma.

to coat vt. rivestire, coprire.

coating s. rivestimento, mano di vernice.

to coax vt. blandire, circuire. ◆ to coax vi. far moine.

coaxial agg. coassiale.

cobalt s. cobalto.

cobble s. ciottolo.

to cobble vt. 1. pavimentare (con ciottoli) 2. rappezzare (scarpe).

cobbler s. ciabattino.

cobra s. cobra.

cobweb s. ragnatela.

cocaine s. cocaina.

coccyx s. (pl. -cyges) coccige.

cock s. 1. gallo 2. cane di fucile.

cockade s. coccarda.

cockatoo s. cacatoa.

cockboat s. (mar.) lancia.

cockerel s. galletto.

cock-eyed agg. strabico.

cockish agg. sfrontato.

cockney *agg. e s.* dialetto londinese.

cockpit *s.* 1. arena (*per combattimento di galli*) 2. (*mar.*) castello di poppa.

cockroach *s.* scarafaggio.

cockscomb *s.* 1. cresta (*di gallo*) 2. (*fig.*) zerbinotto.

cocktail *s.* 1. cavallo con coda mozzata 2. cocktail.

cocoa *s.* cacao.

coconut *s.* noce di cocco.

cocoon *s.* bozzolo.

cod *s.* merluzzo.

code *s.* codice.

to code *vt.* 1. codificare 2. cifrare (*un dispaccio*).

codeine *s.* codeina.

codex *s.* codice, manoscritto antico.

codfish *s.* merluzzo.

codicil *s.* codicillo.

codification *s.* codificazione.

to codify *vt.* codificare.

co-director *s.* condirettore.

co-education *s.* istruzione nella scuola mista.

co-educational *agg.* (*scol.*) misto.

coefficient *agg. e s.* coefficiente.

coenobium *s.* cenobio.

coercible *agg.* coercibile.

coercion *s.* coercizione.

coercive *agg.* coercitivo.

coeval *agg. e s.* coevo.

to coexist *vi.* coesistere.

coexistence *s.* coesistenza.

coffee *s.* caffè: — -*bean*, chicco di caffè; — -*grounds*, fondi di caffè || — -*house*, caffè, bar; — -*mill*, macinino; — -*pot*, caffettiera.

coffer *s.* cassa, cofano.

coffin *s.* bara.

cog *s.* dente (*di ruota*).

cognate *agg. e s.* consanguineo, congiunto.

cognition *s.* cognizione.

cognitive *agg.* avente conoscenza.

cognizable *agg.* 1. conoscibile 2. (*giur.*) entro la giurisdizione di una corte.

to cohabit *vi.* coabitare.

cohabitation *s.* coabitazione.

coheir *s.* coerede.

coheiress *s.* (*donna*) coerede.

coherence *s.* 1. coerenza 2. aderenza.

coherent *agg.* 1. coerente 2. aderente.

coherently *avv.* coerentemente.

cohesion *s.* coesione.

cohesive *agg.* coesivo.

cohort *s.* coorte.

coil *s.* 1. rotolo, spira 2. (*elettr.; mecc.*) bobina.

coin *s.* moneta (*di metallo*).

to coin *vt.* coniare (*anche fig.*).

coinage *s.* conio.

to coincide *vi.* coincidere.

coincidence *s.* coincidenza.

coiner *s.* falsario.

colander *s.* colino.

cold *agg.* 1. freddo: *to be* —, aver freddo 2. freddo (*di carattere*), apatico: *in* — *blood*, a sangue freddo. ◆ **cold** *s.* 1. freddo 2. raffreddore: *to catch a* —, prendere il raffreddore.

coldness *s.* freddezza (*anche fig.*).

Coleoptera *s. pl.* coleotteri.

colic *s.* colica.

colitis *s.* colite.

to collaborate *vi.* collaborare.

collaboration *s.* collaborazione.

collaborationist *s.* collaborazionista.

collaborator *s.* collaboratore.

collapse *s.* 1. crollo (*anche fig.*) 2. collasso.

to collapse *vi.* crollare (*anche fig.*).

collar *s.* 1. colletto 2. collare.

to collate *vt.* 1. collezionare, confrontare 2. riordinare (*pagine di un'opera*).

collateral *agg.* collaterale.

colleague *s.* collega.

to collect *vt.* 1. riunire 2. incassare, riscuotere 3. fare una raccolta. ◆ **to collect** *vi.* 1. riunirsi 2. riscuotere.

collecting *s.* il raccogliere: *stamp* —, il raccogliere francobolli.

collection *s.* 1. raccolta, collezione 2. riunione di persone 3. questua, colletta.

collective *agg.* collettivo || — *title* (*tip.*), titolo generale.

collectivism *s.* collettivismo.

collectivity *s.* collettività.

collectivization *s.* collettivizzazione.

to collectivize *vt.* collettivizzare.

collector *s.* 1. collezionista 2. esattore.

college *s.* 1. collegio 2. scuola secondaria (*con internato*).

collegial *agg.* collegiale.

collier *s.* minatore.

colliery *s.* miniera di carbone.

collimator *s.* collimatore.

collision *s.* 1. collisione 2. urto, conflitto (*d'interessi*).

collocation *s.* collocazione.

colloidal *agg.* colloidale.

colloquial *agg.* d'uso corrente, familiare.

colloquialism *s.* espressione familiare.

colloquially *avv.* nella lingua parlata.

colloquy *s.* colloquio.

collusion *s.* collusione.

colon *s.* (*gramm.*) due punti.

colonel *s.* colonnello.

colonial *agg.* coloniale.

colonialism *s.* sistema coloniale.

colonialist *s.* colonialista.

colonist *s.* 1. colono 2. colonizzatore.

colonization *s.* colonizzazione.

to **colonize** *vt.* colonizzare. ♦ to **colonize** *vi.* stabilirsi in colonia.

colonizer *s.* colonizzatore.

colonnade *s.* colonnato.

colony *s.* colonia.

colossal *agg.* colossale.

colossus *s.* colosso.

colour *s.* 1. colore 2. colorito ‖ — -*bearer*, portabandiera; — -*blind*, daltonico; — -*print*, stampa a colori. ♦ **colours** *s. pl.* bandiera (*sing.*) ‖ *with the* —, sotto le armi.

to **colour** *vt.* colorare, tingere. ♦ to **colour** *vi.* colorirsi, prender colore.

colourable *agg.* verosimile.

colouration *s.* colorazione.

coloured *agg.* colorato, colorito (*anche fig.*).

colourful *agg.* colorito, pittoresco.

colouring *s.* 1. colorante 2. coloramento.

colourless *agg.* incolore.

colt *s.* 1. puledro 2. (*fig.*) novellino.

columbarium *s.* (*pl.* -ria) colombario.

column *s.* colonna (*anche fig.*).

columnist *s.* giornalista (*che cura una rubrica*).

coma *s.* coma.

comatose *agg.* comatoso.

comb *s.* 1. pettine 2. cresta (*gallo, onde ecc.*).

to **comb** *vt.* pettinare. ♦ to **comb** *vi.* frangersi (*di onde*) ‖ to — *one's hair*, pettinarsi.

combat *s.* combattimento, lotta.

combination *s.* 1. combinazione 2. associazione.

to **combine** *vt.* 1. unire 2. (*chim.*) combinare 3. contribuire. ♦ to **combine** *vi.* 1. unirsi 2. combinarsi.

combing *s.* pettinata.

comb-out *s.* rastrellamento.

combustible *agg.* e *s.* combustibile.

combustion *s.* combustione.

to **come** (**came**, **come**) *vi.* venire, arrivare, giungere, provenire ‖ to — *about*, accadere; to — *across*, incontrare per caso; to — *along* (*fam.*), capitare; to — *back*, ritornare; to — *down*, scendere; to — *in*, entrare, salire (*di marea*); to — *on*, avanzare, sopraggiungere (*di malattie, stagioni ecc.*), entrare in scena (*di attori*); to — *through*, superare; to — *under*, essere soggetti, essere catalogati; to — *upon*, trovare per caso.

comedian *s.* autore, attore di commedie.

comedy *s.* commedia.

comeliness *s.* avvenenza.

comely *agg.* avvenente.

comer *s.* chi viene.

comet *s.* cometa.

comfit *s.* confetto.

comfort *s.* 1. conforto 2. comodità.

to **comfort** *vt.* 1. confortare 2. ristorare.

comfortable *agg.* comodo, confortevole ‖ to *be* —, sentirsi a proprio agio.

comfortably *avv.* comodamente.

comforting *agg.* confortante.

comic *agg.* comico, buffo. ♦ **comic** *s.* 1. attore comico 2. il ridicolo, il comico. ♦ **comics** *s. pl.* (*fam.*) fumetti.

comical *agg.* comico, buffo.

comicality *s.* comicità.

coming *agg.* prossimo, futuro. ♦ **coming** *s.* 1. venuta, arrivo ‖ — *away*, partenza; — *back*, ritorno; — *down*, discesa, calo (*dei prezzi*).

comity *s.* cortesia, gentilezza.

comma *s.* virgola ‖ *inverted commas*, virgolette.

command *s.* 1. comando, ordine 2. padronanza.

to **command** *vt.* e *vi.* 1. comandare 2. dominare (*anche fig.*).

commandant *s.* comandante.

commander *s.* comandante.

commandership *s.* funzioni di comandante.

commandment *s.* comandamento.

to commemorate *vt.* commemorare.

commemoration *s.* commemorazione.

commemorative *agg.* commemorativo.

to commend *vt.* lodare, encomiare.

commendable *agg.* lodevole.

commendably *avv.* lodevolmente.

commendation *s.* elogio, lode.

commendatory *agg.* laudativo.

commensal *s.* commensale.

commensurability *s.* commensurabilità.

commensurable *agg.* commensurabile.

commensurate *agg.* proporzionato.

comment *s.* 1. commento 2. critica.

to comment *vt.* e *vi.* commentare: *to — up (on) a test*, commentare un testo.

commentary *s.* commentario.

commentation *s.* annotazione, commento.

commentator *s.* 1. commentatore 2. radiocronista.

commerce *s.* commercio.

commercial *agg.* commerciale.

commercialism *s.* mercantilismo.

commercialist *s.* commercialista.

to commercialize *vt.* rendere commerciabile.

commercially *avv.* commercialmente.

commination *s.* comminazione.

to commiserate *vt.* e *vi.* commiserare.

commissary *s.* commissario, delegato.

commissaryship *s.* commissariato.

commission *s.* 1. commissione, comitato 2. commissione, incarico || *— agent (o merchant)*, commissionario.

to commission *vt.* 1. commissionare 2. delegare.

commissioned *agg.* munito di autorità || *non — officer*, sottufficiale.

commissioner *s.* (*pol.*) delegato.

to commit *vt.* 1. affidare, rimettere: *to — one's soul to God*, rimettere la propria anima a Dio 2. commettere.

commitment, committal *s.* 1. consegna 2. incarico.

committed *agg.* (*neol.*) impegnato.

committee *s.* comitato.

commodity *s.* merce, oggetto di prima necessità || *free commodities*, merci esenti da dogana.

common *agg.* 1. comune 2. solito, abituale || *— law*, legge consacrata dalla consuetudine.

commoner *s.* 1. cittadino (*non nobile*) 2. membro della Camera dei Comuni.

commonness *s.* 1. banalità 2. frequenza (*di un avvenimento*).

commonplace *s.* luogo comune.

commons *s. pl.* il popolo (*sing.*) || *the House of —*, la Camera dei Comuni.

commonwealth *s.* 1. confederazione 2. repubblica (*anche fig.*).

commotion *s.* 1. agitazione, confusione 2. insurrezione, tumulto.

communal *agg.* della comunità.

commune *s.* comune.

communicability *s.* comunicabilità.

communicable *agg.* comunicabile.

to communicate *vt.* comunicare, trasmettere (*malattie, calore ecc.*).
♦ to **communicate** *vi.* mettersi in comunicazione.

communication *s.* 1. comunicazione, informazione 2. relazione, rapporto.

communicative *agg.* comunicativo.

communicativeness *s.* comunicativa.

communion *s.* comunione, comunanza || *Holy Communion*, Eucarestia.

communism *s.* comunismo.

communist *s.* comunista.

communistic *agg.* comunista.

community *s.* 1. comunanza (*di beni ecc.*) 2. collettività, società 3. (*eccl.*) comunità.

commutability *s.* permutabilità, commutabilità.

commutable *agg.* permutabile, commutabile.

commutative *agg.* commutativo.

commutator *s.* commutatore.

to commute *vt.* commutare.

compact¹ *s.* patto, contratto.

compact² *agg.* 1. compatto 2. ridotto.

compactness *s.* 1. compattezza 2. concisione (*di stile*).

companion¹ *s.* compagno.

companion² *s.* (*mar.*) boccaporto: *— -way*, scaletta (*di boccaporto*), scalandrone.

companionable *agg.* socievole.

companionship *s.* amicizia, cameratismo.

company *s.* **1.** compagnia **2.** comitiva **3.** (*comm.*) società.

comparable *agg.* paragonabile.

comparative *agg.* **1.** comparativo **2.** comparato. ◆ **comparative** *s.* (*gramm.*) comparativo.

comparatively *avv.* **1.** comparativamente **2.** relativamente.

to **compare** *vt.* paragonare, verificare. ◆ to **compare** *vi.* competere, rivaleggiare, reggere al confronto.

comparison *s.* **1.** paragone, confronto **2.** (*gramm.*) comparazione.

compartment *s.* compartimento, scompartimento.

compass *s.* **1.** circonferenza, spazio, estensione **2.** bussola. ◆ **compasses** *s. pl.* (*a pair of* —) compasso (*sing.*).

to **compass** *vt.* circondare.

compassion *s.* compassione: *out of* —, per compassione.

compassionate *agg.* compassionevole.

to **compassionate** *vt.* compassionare.

compassionately *avv.* con compassione.

compatibility *s.* compatibilità.

compatible *agg.* compatibile.

compatibly *avv.* compatibilmente.

to **compel** *vt.* costringere, obbligare.

compelling *agg.* irresistibile.

compendious *agg.* compendioso.

to **compensate** *vt.* ricompensare, risarcire. ◆ to **compensate** *vi.* supplire.

compensation *s.* **1.** compenso **2.** (*mecc.*) compensazione **3.** indennità, risarcimento.

compensator *s.* compensatore.

compensatory *agg.* compensativo.

to **compete** *vi.* competere, gareggiare.

competence *s.* **1.** competenza **2.** mezzi sufficienti per vivere (*pl.*).

competent *agg.* competente, abile.

competently *avv.* con competenza.

competition *s.* **1.** competizione, gara **2.** rivalità.

competitive *agg.* **1.** di competizione **2.** (*comm.*) di concorrenza.

competitively *avv.* per mezzo di concorso.

competitor *s.* concorrente, rivale.

compilation *s.* compilazione.

to **compile** *vt.* compilare.

compiler *s.* compilatore.

complacency *s.* **1.** soddisfazione **2.** compiacenza di sé.

complacent *agg.* **1.** compiacente **2.** soddisfatto di sé.

to **complain** *vi.* lagnarsi, dolersi.

complaint *s.* **1.** lamento **2.** reclamo.

complaisant *agg.* compiacente.

complement *s.* complemento.

complemental *agg.* complementare.

complementary *agg.* complementare.

complete *agg.* completo.

to **complete** *vt.* **1.** completare **2.** riempire (*moduli ecc.*).

completely *avv.* completamente.

completeness *s.* completezza.

completion *s.* compimento.

complex *agg.* **1.** complicato **2.** (*gramm.*) composto. ◆ **complex** *s.* complesso.

complexion *s.* carnagione, colorito.

complexity *s.* complessità.

compliance *s.* **1.** condiscendenza **2.** servilismo.

compliant *agg.* **1.** compiacente **2.** servile.

to **complicate** *vt.* complicare.

complicated *agg.* complicato.

complication *s.* complicazione.

complicity *s.* complicità.

compliment *s.* complimento: *to pay so. a* —, far un complimento a qu.

to **compliment** *vt.* complimentare, congratularsi con.

complimentary *agg.* **1.** complimentoso **2.** di favore: — *tickets*, biglietti di favore.

to **comply** *vi.* accondiscendere, conformarsi.

component *agg.* e *s.* componente.

to **comport** *vi.* comportarsi.

to **compose** *vt.* **1.** comporre, costituire **2.** (*mus.*) comporre || *to — a quarrel*, comporre una vertenza.

composed *agg.* **1.** composto **2.** calmo.

composer *s.* compositore.

composing *agg.* calmante. ◆ **composing** *s.* **1.** il comporre **2.** (*tip.*) composizione.

composite *agg.* composto.

composition *s.* **1.** composizione **2.** compromesso **3.** concordato, intesa.

compositor *s.* (*tip.*) compositore.

composure *s.* posatezza, sangue freddo.

compote s. conserva di frutta.

compound 1. miscela **2.** (*chim.*) composto **3.** (*gramm.*) parola composta.

to compound vt. e vi. **1.** comporre, mescolare **2.** combinare (*ingredienti, elementi ecc.*).

to comprehend vt. **1.** contenere **2.** capire.

comprehensibility s. comprensibilità.

comprehensible agg. **1.** comprensibile **2.** delimitato.

comprehension s. **1.** comprensione **2.** portata.

comprehensive agg. **1.** di vasta portata **2.** comprensivo.

comprehensively avv. comprensivamente.

compress s. compressa (*di garza*).

to compress vt. **1.** comprimere **2.** (*fig.*) condensare (*idee ecc.*).

compressibility s. compressibilità.

compression s. **1.** compressione **2.** (*fig.*) concentrazione.

to comprise vt. contenere, includere.

compromise s. compromesso.

to compromise vt. compromettere. ♦ **to compromise** vi. venire a un compromesso.

compromising agg. compromettente.

compulsion s. costrizione: *under* —, per costrizione.

compulsive agg. coercitivo.

compulsory agg. obbligatorio.

compunction s. compunzione.

computable agg. calcolabile.

computation s. calcolo.

to compute vt. computare, calcolare.

computer s. calcolatore.

comrade s. camerata, compagno.

comradeship s. cameratismo.

to concatenate vt. concatenare.

concatenation s. concatenazione.

concave agg. concavo.

to conceal vt. nascondere.

concealment s. **1.** occultamento **2.** nascondiglio.

conceit s. vanità, presunzione.

conceited agg. presuntuoso, vanitoso.

conceivability s. concepibilità.

conceivable agg. concepibile.

to conceive vt. **1.** concepire, generare **2.** immaginare, ide re.

to concentrate vt. **1.** concentrare

2. convergere. ♦ **to concentrate** vi. concentrarsi.

concentration s. **1.** concentrazione **2.** concentramento.

concentric agg. concentrico.

concept s. concetto.

conception s. **1.** concezione, concepimento **2.** concetto.

conceptional agg. concezionale.

conceptual agg. concettuale.

conceptualism s. concettualismo.

concern s. **1.** interesse, rapporto **2.** affare **3.** sollecitudine **4.** (*comm*) ditta, azienda.

to concern vt. concernere, riguardare.

concerned agg. **1.** interessato **2.** ansioso, preoccupato || *as far as I am* —, per quanto mi riguarda.

concerning prep. riguardo a, circa.

concert s. **1.** concerto **2.** accordo.

concerted agg. **1.** (*mus.*) concertato **2.** convenuto.

concession s. concessione.

concessionary agg. e s. concessionario.

concettism s. concettismo.

conch s. conchiglia, mollusco.

conchoid s. concoide.

conchoidal agg. concoidale.

to conciliate vt. conciliare.

conciliation s. conciliazione.

conciliator s. conciliatore, conciliatrice.

conciliatory agg. conciliante.

concise agg. conciso, succinto.

concision s. concisione.

conclave s. conclave.

to conclude vt. terminare, concludere. ♦ **to conclude** vi. terminare, concludersi.

conclusion s. conclusione.

conclusive agg. conclusivo.

to concoct vt. **1.** mescolare (*di ingredienti*) **2.** preparare, tramare.

concomitance s. concomitanza.

concomitant agg. concomitante.

concomitantly avv. simultaneamente.

concord s. **1.** concordia **2.** (*mus.*) accordo **3.** (*gramm.*) concordanza.

concordant agg. **1.** concorde **2.** (*mus.*) armonioso.

concordat s. concordato.

concourse s. concorso, affluenza (*di persone ecc.*).

concrete agg. concreto. ♦ **concrete** s. calcestruzzo.

concreteness *s.* concretezza.

concretion *s.* concrezione.

concubinage *s.* concubinato.

concubine *s.* concubina.

concupiscence *s.* concupiscenza.

to **concur** *vi.* concorrere, contribuire (*di cause, avvenimenti*).

concurrence *s.* 1. concorso (*di circostanze*) 2. cooperazione (*di persone*) 3. (*geom.*) convergenza.

concurrent *agg.* concorrente, simultaneo.

to **concuss** *vt.* 1. urtare 2. (*med.*) provocare un trauma 3. intimidire.

concussion *s.* 1. urto 2. (*med.*) commozione cerebrale, trauma.

to **condemn** *vt.* 1. condannare 2. biasimare, censurare.

condemnable *agg.* 1. condannabile 2. censurabile.

condemnation *s.* 1. condanna 2. biasimo, censura.

condensability *s.* condensabilità.

condensable *agg.* condensabile.

condensate *s.* (*fis.; chim.*) condensamento.

condensation *s.* condensazione.

to **condense** *vt.* condensare, abbreviare. ♦ to **condense** *vi.* condensarsi, concentrarsi.

condenser *s.* condensatore.

to **condescend** *vi.* accondiscendere.

condescending *agg.* condiscendente.

condescendingly *avv.* con condiscendenza.

condescension *s.* 1. condiscendenza 2. affabilità.

condition *s.* condizione, clausola: *on — that,* a condizione che.

to **condition** *vt.* condizionare.

conditional *agg.* e *s.* condizionale.

conditionally *avv.* condizionatamente.

conditioned *agg.* condizionato: — *air,* aria condizionata.

conditioning *s.* 1. condizionatura (*di tessili*) 2. condizionamento.

condolence *s.* condoglianza.

conduct *s.* 1. condotta, comportamento 2. metodo.

to **conduct** *vi.* 1. condurre, guidare, dirigere 2. (*fis.*) condurre, trasmettere. ♦ to **conduct** *vi.* 1. comportarsi 2. indicare la via.

conductibility *s.* conducibilità.

conductivity *s.* conducibilità.

conductor *s.* 1. guida (*di persone*) 2. (*mus.*) direttore 3. bigliettario.

conduit *s.* 1. conduttura 2. passaggio segreto.

cone *s.* 1. cono 2. pigna.

to **confabulate** *vi.* confabulare.

confectionary *agg.* di pasticceria.

confectioner *s.* pasticciere.

confectionery *s.* pasticceria.

confederate *agg.* confederato. ♦ **confederate** *s.* 1. confederato 2. complice.

to **confederate** *vt.* confederare. ♦ to **confederate** *vi.* confederarsi.

confederation *s.* confederazione.

to **confer** *vt.* conferire, dare. ♦ to **confer** *vi.* conferire, consultarsi.

conference *s.* 1. conferenza 2. congresso.

to **confess** *vt.* e *vi.* confessare, professare.

confessedly *avv.* apertamente, dichiaratamente.

confession *s.* confessione, professione: — *of faith,* professione di fede.

confessional *agg.* e *s.* confessionale.

confessionary *agg.* confessionale.

confessor *s.* 1. confessore 2. chi si confessa.

confetti *s. pl.* coriandoli.

confidant *s.* confidente.

to **confide** *vt.* confidare. ♦ to **confide** *vi.* confidarsi: *to — in so.,* confidarsi con qu.

confidence *s.* 1. fiducia 2. confidenza 3. sicurezza in se stessi.

confident *agg.* fiducioso.

confidential *agg.* confidenziale, riservato.

confidently *avv.* con sicurezza, con fiducia.

confiding *agg.* senza sospetti.

configuration *s.* configurazione.

to **configure** *vt.* configurare.

to **confine** *vt.* relegare, limitare. ♦ to **confine** *vi.* confinare, essere contiguo.

confinement *s.* 1. reclusione 2. limitazione 3. puerperio.

to **confirm** *vt.* 1. confermare 2. cresimare.

confirmation *s.* 1. conferma 2. cresima 3. (*pol.; giur.*) ratifica.

confirmatory *agg.* confermativo.

confiscable *agg.* confiscabile.

to **confiscate** *vt.* confiscare.

confiscation *s.* confisca.

conflagration *s.* conflagrazione.

conflict *s.* conflitto, contrasto.

confluence s. 1. confluenza 2. incrocio (di strade ecc.).

confluent agg. confluente.

to **conform** vt. conformare. ◆ to **conform** vi. conformarsi, ottemperare.

conformation s. 1. conformazione 2. adattamento.

conformist s. conformista.

conformity s. 1. conformità 2. conformismo.

to **confound** vt. 1. confondere, disorientare 2. sconvolgere.

confounded agg. attonito, confuso.

confraternity s. confraternita.

to **confront** vt. 1. affrontare 2. trovarsi di fronte a.

confrontation s. confronto.

Confucianism s. confucianesimo.

to **confuse** vt. 1. disorientare, sconcertare 2. confondere.

confusedly avv. confusamente.

confusion s. 1. disordine, confusione 2. turbamento.

confutation s. confutazione.

to **confute** vt. confutare.

to **congeal** vt. ghiacciare. ◆ to **congeal** vi. gelarsi.

congenial agg. 1. congeniale, affine 2. amabile, simpatico.

congeniality s. 1. affinità 2. carattere simpatico.

congenially avv. amabilmente.

congenital agg. congenito.

conger s. anguilla marina.

congeries s. congerie.

to **congest** vt. congestionare. ◆ to **congest** vi. congestionarsi.

congested agg. congestionato.

congestion s. congestione.

to **conglobate** vt. conglobare. ◆ to **conglobate** vi. conglobarsi.

conglobation s. conglobazione.

conglomerate agg. e s. conglomerato.

to **conglomerate** vt. conglomerare. ◆ to **conglomerate** vi. conglomerarsi.

conglomeration s. conglomerazione.

to **congratulate** vt. congratulare, congratularsi con.

congratulation s. congratulazione.

congratulatory agg. congratulatorio.

to **congregate** vt. adunare. ◆ to **congregate** vi. adunarsi.

congregation s. 1. unione, adunata, assemblea 2. (relig.) congregazione.

congregational agg. della congregazione.

congress s. congresso, riunione.

congressional agg. di congresso.

congruence s. congruenza.

congruent agg. congruente, conforme.

congruity s. conformità.

congruous agg. congruente, conforme.

conic(al) agg. conico.

conifer s. conifera.

coniferous agg. conifero.

conjecture s. congettura.

to **conjecture** vt. o vi. congetturare, ipotizzare.

conjointly avv. congiuntamente.

conjugal agg. coniugale. ◆ **conjugate** agg. congiunto. ◆ **conjugate** s. 1. (mat.) coniugato 2. (biol.) fusione.

to **conjugate** vt. coniugare. ◆ to **conjugate** vi. coniugarsi.

conjugation s. coniugazione.

conjunction s. congiunzione.

conjunctiva s. (anat.) congiuntiva.

conjunctive agg. 1. (biol.) connettivo 2. (gramm.) congiuntivo. ◆ **conjunctive** s. congiuntivo.

conjunctivitis s. congiuntivite.

conjuncture s. congiuntura, circostanza.

conjuration s. 1. incantesimo 2. evocazione solenne.

to **conjure** vt. 1. scongiurare 2. evocare. ◆ to **conjure** vi. fare giochi di prestigio.

conjurer s. prestigiatore.

conjuring s. prestidigitazione.

connatural agg. connaturale.

to **connect** vt. 1. connettere, collegare, unire 2. associare (mentalmente). ◆ to **connect** vi. 1. avere relazioni, collegarsi 2. (ferr.) far coincidenza.

connecting agg. che connette. ◆ **connecting** s. (elettr.) collegamento.

connection s. 1. collegamento, connessione 2. relazione, parentela 3. coincidenza 4. (comm.) clientela.

connective agg. connettivo.

conning-tower s. (mar.) torretta di comando.

connivance s. connivenza.

to **connive** vi. essere connivente.

connotation s. significato implicito.

to **connote** vt. implicare, significare.

to **conquer** *vt.* conquistare.
conqueror *s.* conquistatore.
conquest *s.* conquista.
consanguine *agg.* consanguineo.
consanguinity *s.* consanguineità.
conscience *s.* coscienza: *for — '
sake*, per scrupolo di coscienza; *to
be — -stricken*, sentirsi rimordere
la coscienza.
conscienceless *agg.* senza scrupoli.
conscientious *agg.* scrupoloso ||
— objector, obiettore di coscienza.
conscientiously *avv.* coscienziosamente.
conscious *agg.* consapevole, conscio.
consciousness *s.* coscienza, consapevolezza.
conscript *agg.* e *s.* coscritto.
conscription *s.* coscrizione.
to **consecrate** *vt.* consacrare, dedicare.
consecration *s.* consacrazione, dedizione.
consecutive *agg.* consecutivo.
consecutively *avv.* consecutiva-
mente.
consensual *agg.* consensuale.
consensus *s.* consenso, accordo ||
— of opinion, unanimità.
consent *s.* consenso, accordo || *by
mutual —*, amichevolmente.
to **consent** *vi.* acconsentire.
consequence *s.* 1. conseguenza, effetto 2. importanza.
consequent *agg.* conseguente, risultante.
consequential *agg.* consequenziale.
consequently *avv.* di conseguenza.
conservatism *s.* conservatorismo.
conservative *agg.* conservativo. ♦
Conservative *s.* conservatore.
conservator *s.* 1. conservatore 2.
sovrintendente (*di museo ecc.*).
conserve *s.* conserva di frutta.
to **consider** *vt.* considerare, riflettere, stimare.
considerable *agg.* considerevole,
importante.
considerate *agg.* rispettoso, pieno
di riguardi.
consideration *s.* 1. considerazione
2. rimunerazione 3. (*comm.*) provvigione.
considering *prep.* tenuto conto di,
considerando.
to **consign** *vt.* 1. (*comm.*) inviare,
consegnare 2. depositare (*soldi in
banca*).

consignation *s.* 1. (*comm.*) pagamento 2. consegna (*di merce*).
consignee *s.* consegnatario.
consigner *s.* mittente.
consignment *s.* 1. invio, spedizione
2. consegna, deposito.
to **consist** *vi.* consistere, essere composto.
consistence, consistency *s.* 1.
consistenza, compattezza 2. costanza.
consistent *agg.* coerente, logico.
consistently *avv.* coerentemente.
consistory *s.* concistoro.
consolation *s.* consolazione.
consolatory *agg.* consolante.
to **console** *vt.* consolare.
to **consolidate** *vt.* consolidare. ♦
to **consolidate** *vi.* consolidarsi.
consolidation *s.* consolidazione.
consoling *agg.* consolante.
consonance *s.* consonanza, accordo.
consonant *agg.* consono. ♦ **consonant** *s.* consonante.
consort *s.* 1. consorte 2. compagno,
collega.
to **consort** *vi.* associarsi, unirsi. ♦
to **consort** *vt.* associare, unire.
conspicuous *agg.* cospicuo, notevole.
conspicuousness *s.* cospicuità.
conspiracy *s.* congiura.
conspirator *s.* cospiratore.
to **conspire** *vt.* e *vi.* cospirare.
constable *s.* 1. agente di polizia 2.
conestabile.
constabulary *s.* corpo della polizia.
constancy *s.* costanza.
constant *agg.* costante, fedele. ♦
constant *s.* (*mat.*) costante.
constantly *agg.* costantemente.
constellation *s.* costellazione.
consternation *s.* costernazione.
constipation *s.* stitichezza.
constituency *s.* 1. gli elettori (*pl.*)
2. circoscrizione elettorale.
constituent *agg.* costituente. ♦
constituent *s.* 1. elemento costitutivo 2. (*pol.*) elettore.
to **constitute** *vt.* 1. costituire 2.
eleggere.
constitution *s.* 1. costituzione, statuto 2. costituzione, composizione
(*del corpo, dell'aria ecc.*).
constitutional *agg.* costituzionale.
constitutionalism *s.* costituzionalismo.
constitutionality *s.* costituzionalità.

constitutive *agg.* costitutivo.
to constrain *vt.* costringere.
constrained *agg.* costretto, forzato.
constraint *s.* 1. costrizione 2. imbarazzo.
to constrict *vt.* costringere.
constriction *s.* costrizione.
to construct *vt.* costruire (*anche fig.*).
construction *s.* 1. costruzione 2. (*giur.*) interpretazione.
constructive *agg.* costruttivo.
to construe *vt.* 1. costruire grammaticalmente 2. interpretare. ♦ to **construe** *vi.* fare l'analisi grammaticale.
consuetudinary *agg.* consuetudinario: — *law*, diritto consuetudinario.
consul *s.* console.
consular *agg.* consolare.
consulate *s.* consolato.
to consult *vt.* consultare. ♦ to **consult** *vi.* consultarsi.
consultation *s.* 1. consultazione 2. consulto.
consultative *agg.* consultativo.
consulting *agg.* consulente || — -room, ambulatorio.
to consume *vt.* consumare. ♦ to **consume** *vi.* consumarsi.
consumer *s.* consumatore, utente.
consummate *agg.* consumato, perfetto.
consumption *s.* 1. consumo 2. sciupio 3. distruzione 4. tubercolosi.
consumptive *s.* tisico, tubercolotico.
contact *s.* contatto, relazione.
to contact *vt.* e *vi.* mettere, mettersi in contatto con, prender contatto.
contagion *s.* contagio.
contagious *agg.* contagioso.
to contain *vt.* 1. contenere, comprendere 2. reprimere, frenare (*i sentimenti*).
contained *agg.* frenato, contenuto (*di comportamento*).
container *s.* recipiente.
contamination *s.* contaminazione.
to contemplate *vt.* e *vi.* contemplare, meditare.
contemplation *s.* contemplazione.
contemplative *agg.* contemplativo.
contemplator *s.* contemplatore.
contemporaneousness *s.* contemporaneità.
contemporary *agg.* e *s.* contemporaneo.

contempt *s.* disprezzo || — *of Court* (*giur.*), vilipendio della Corte.
contemptibility *s.* spregevolezza.
contemptible *agg.* spregevole.
contemptuous *agg.* sprezzante.
contemptuously *avv.* sprezzantemente.
to contend *vi.* 1. contendere. ♦ to **contend** *vt.* sostenere, affermare.
contending *agg.* contendente, rivale.
content *s.* 1. volume, capacità 2. contenuto. ♦ **contents** *s. pl.* indice (*di libro*) (*sing.*). ♦ **content** *agg.* contento, soddisfatto.
to content *vt.* contentare, soddisfare.
contented *agg.* contento, pago.
contention *s.* 1. contesa 2. emulazione 3. controversia.
contentious *agg.* litigioso.
contest *s.* contestazione, contesa.
to contest *vt.* contestare, contendere. ♦ to **contest** *vi.* competere, rivaleggiare.
context *s.* contesto.
contiguity *s.* contiguità.
continence *s.* continenza.
continent *agg.* continente. ♦ **continent** *s.* (*geogr.*) continente.
continental *agg.* e *s.* continentale.
contingency *s.* contingenza, caso.
contingent *agg.* eventuale, imprevisto.
continual *agg.* continuo.
continuation *s.* continuazione, seguito.
to continue *vt.* e *vi.* continuare, far continuare.
continuity *s.* 1. continuità 2. (*ctne*) sceneggiatura.
continuous *agg.* continuo.
to contort *vt.* contorcere.
contortion *s.* contorsione.
contortionist *s.* contorsionista.
contour *s.* contorno, profilo.
contraband *s.* contrabbando.
contraceptive *s.* anticoncezionale.
contract *s.* contratto, patto.
to contract *vt.* 1. contrarre (*matrimonio, amicizia ecc.*) 2. (*comm*) contrattare 3. contrarre, restringere. ♦ to **contract** *vi.* contrarsi, restringersi.
contractile *agg.* contrattile.
contraction *s.* accorciamento.
contractor *s.* 1. contraente 2. appaltatore 3. imprenditore.

contractual *agg.* contrattuale.

to **contradict** *vt.* contraddire.

contradiction *s.* contraddizione.

contradictory *agg.* contraddittorio.

to **contraindicate** *vt.* controindicare.

contraindication *s.* controindicazione.

contraposition *s.* opposizione, antitesi.

contrarily *avv.* contrariamente.

contrary *agg.* contrario, opposto. ♦ **contrary** *s.* il contrario: on the —, al contrario. ♦ **contrary** *avv.* contrariamente, all'opposto.

contrast *s.* contrasto, opposizione.

to **contrast** *vt.* e *vi.* far contrasto, mettere in contrasto.

to **contravene** *vt.* contravvenire.

to **contribute** *vt.* contribuire. ♦ to **contribute** *vi.* collaborare (a un giornale).

contribution *s.* 1. contributo 2. (*comm.*) apporto di capitale 3. collaborazione (a un giornale).

contributor *s.* 1. contributore 2. collaboratore (di giornale ecc.).

contrite *agg.* contrito.

contrition *s.* contrizione.

contrivance *s.* 1. espediente 2. apparato, congegno 3. invenzione.

to **contrive** *vt.* escogitare. ♦ to **contrive** *vi.* adoperarsi, riuscire.

control *s.* autorità, influenza, dominio, controllo || — device (*mecc.*), dispositivo di controllo; — room, camera di manovra; birth- —, limitazione delle nascite; self- —, autocontrollo. ♦ **controls** *s. pl.* (*mecc.*) comandi.

to **control** *vt.* controllare, dirigere.

controller *s.* controllore, sovrintendente.

controversial *agg.* controverso.

controversy *s.* controversia, polemica.

controvertible *agg.* controvertibile.

contumacious *agg.* 1. insubordinato 2. contumace.

contumacy *s.* 1. ribellione 2. contumacia.

contumely *s.* onta, contumelia.

contusion *s.* contusione.

contusive *agg.* contundente.

convalescence *s.* convalescenza.

convalescent *agg.* e *s.* convalescente.

to **convene** *vt.* 1. convocare, riunire 2. (*giur.*) citare. ♦ to **convene** *vi.* riunirsi, incontrarsi.

convenience *s.* 1. comodo, vantaggio. ♦ **conveniences** *s. pl.* comodità.

convenient *agg.* conveniente, comodo, adatto.

convent *s.* convento.

conventicle *s.* conventicola.

convention *s.* 1. patto, convenzione 2. assemblea 3. regola (di gioco). ♦ **conventions** *s. pl.* convenzioni (sociali).

conventional *agg.* convenzionale, comune.

conventionality *s.* convenzionalità.

conventual *agg.* e *s.* conventuale.

to **converge** *vi.* convergere. ♦ to **converge** *vt.* far convergere.

convergence *s.* convergenza.

convergent *agg.* convergente.

conversation *s.* conversazione.

converse *agg.* e *s.* inverso, contrario.

conversely *avv.* viceversa.

conversion *s.* conversione, trasformazione.

convert *s.* convertito.

to **convert** *vt.* 1. convertire 2. trasformare.

converter *s.* 1. convertitore 2. (*elettr.; mecc.*) convertitore, trasformatore.

convertible *agg.* convertibile || — car, automobile decappottabile.

convex *agg.* convesso.

convexity *s.* convessità.

to **convey** *vt.* 1. trasportare, convogliare 2. trasmettere (suoni, odori ecc.) 3. dare l'idea, suggerire.

conveyable *agg.* trasportabile, trasmissibile.

conveyance *s.* 1. trasporto 2. trasmissione 3. convogliamento.

conveyancer *s.* notaio.

conveyer *s.* 1. trasportatore 2. trasmettitore 3. convogliatore.

convict *s.* condannato, forzato.

to **convict** *vt.* condannare, dichiarare colpevole.

conviction *s.* 1. (giur.) verdetto di colpevolezza, condanna 2. convinzione.

to **convince** *vt.* convincere.

convincing *agg.* convincente.

convincingly *avv.* in modo convincente.

convivial *agg.* allegro, conviviale, gioviale.

conviviality *s.* giovialità.

convivially avv. convivialmente.

to convocate vt. convocare.

convocation s. convocazione.

convolution s. circonvoluzione.

convoy s. 1. (mar.; mil.) convoglio 2. scorta.

to convoy vt. 1. (mar.; mil.) convogliare 2. scortare.

convulsion s. 1. convulsione 2. rivolgimento.

convulsive agg. convulso.

to coo vi. tubare.

cook s. cuoco, cuoca: *head —*, capocuoco.

to cook vt. e vi. cucinare, cuocere.

cookery s. arte culinaria, cucina.

cooking s. 1. cottura 2. arte culinaria, cucina.

cool agg. 1. fresco 2. leggero (di abito) 3. calmo 4. freddo, senza entusiasmo 5. sfacciato.

to cool vt. 1. rinfrescare 2. calmare. ♦ **to cool** vi. 1. rinfrescarsi 2. calmarsi.

cooling agg. rinfrescante. ♦ **cooling** s. abbassamento di temperatura.

coolness s. 1. frescura 2. freddezza, calma, sangue freddo.

coop s. stia.

to coop vt. mettere nella stia.

cooper s. bottaio.

to co-operate vi. cooperare.

co-operation s. cooperazione.

co-operative agg. cooperativo.

co-operator s. cooperatore.

to co-opt vt. eleggere membro (di comitato).

co-ordinate agg. 1. dello stesso rango 2. coordinato. ♦ **co-ordinate** s. (mat.) coordinata.

to co-ordinate vt. coordinare.

co-ordination s. coordinazione.

co-ordinative agg. coordinativo.

co-owner s. comproprietario.

co-ownership s. comproprietà.

cop[1] s. cima (di collina ecc.).

cop[2] s. (gergo) poliziotto.

copartnership s. società, associazione.

to cope vi. fronteggiare, tener testa.

co-pilot s. (aer.) secondo pilota.

copper s. 1. rame 2. moneta di rame.

to copper vt. rivestire di rame.

copperplate s. 1. lastra di rame (per incisione) 2. incisione in rame.

Coptic agg. copto.

copulation s. copulazione.

copulative agg. copulativo.

copy s. 1. copia, trascrizione 2. riproduzione 3. esemplare || *—book*, quaderno; *— -reader*, revisore di stampa; *fair —*, bella copia; *rough —*, brutta copia.

to copy vt. 1. copiare 2. imitare.

copyist s. copista.

copyright s. diritto d'autore, proprietà letteraria.

coquetry s. civetteria.

coral s. corallo.

cord s. corda, spago || *spinal —*, midollo spinale.

cordage s. cordame.

cordial agg. cordiale. ♦ **cordial** s. (bevanda) cordiale.

cordiality s. cordialità.

cordially avv. cordialmente.

cordon s. cordone.

core s. 1. torsolo 2. centro, cuore.

co-respondent s. (giur.) correo (in adulterio).

coriaceous agg. coriaceo.

cork s. 1. sughero 2. tappo, turacciolo || *— jacket*, cintura di salvataggio.

corkscrew s. cavaturaccioli.

cormorant s. cormorano.

corn[1] s. 1. grano 2. cereale || *ear of —*, spiga di grano; *— -cob*, pannocchia.

corn[2] s. callo, durone.

cornea s. cornea.

corner s. 1. angolo 2. (comm.) accaparramento (di merci).

to corner vt. 1. mettere, spingere in un angolo 2. (fig.) mettere con le spalle al muro. ♦ **to corner** vi. formare un angolo.

cornet s. cornetta.

cornice s. cornicione.

corolla s. corolla.

corollary s. corollario.

coronary agg. coronario.

coronation s. incoronazione.

coroner s. magistrato inquirente.

corporal[1] agg. corporale.

corporal[2] s. caporale.

corporation s. 1. corporazione 2. azienda municipale.

corporative agg. corporativo: *— system*, sistema corporativo.

corporeal agg. corporeo.

corpse s. cadavere.

corpulent agg. corpulento.

corpuscle s. corpuscolo.

corral s. recinto (per bestiame).

correct *agg.* corretto.

to correct *vt.* correggere.

correction *s.* correzione, rettifica.

corrective *agg.* e *s.* correttivo.

correctness *s.* correttezza.

corrector *s.* correttore: — *of the press* (*tip.*), correttore di bozze.

to correlate *vt.* essere, mettere in correlazione. ♦ **to correlate** *vi.* essere in correlazione.

correlation *s.* correlazione.

correlative *agg.* correlativo.

to correspond *vi.* 1. corrispondere, essere in rapporti epistolari 2. rispondere a (*esigenze ecc.*) 3. equivalere.

correspondence 1. corrispondenza 2. accordo, rispondenza.

correspondent *s.* corrispondente.

corridor *s.* corridoio.

corroborant *agg.* corroborante.

corroboration *s.* conferma, convalida.

to corrode *vt.* corrodere. ♦ **to corrode** *vi.* corrodersi.

corrosion *s.* corrosione.

corrosive *agg.* e *s.* corrosivo.

to corrugate *vt.* corrugare.

corrugation *s.* corrugamento.

corrupt *agg.* corrotto, guasto, depravato.

to corrupt *vt.* corrompere, alterare. ♦ **to corrupt** *vi.* corrompersi, alterarsi.

corruption *s.* corruzione.

corsair *s.* corsaro.

corset *s.* corsetto.

cortisone *s.* cortisone.

corvette *s.* corvetta.

corvine *agg.* corvino.

coryphaeus *s.* (*pl.* -aei) corifeo.

cosecant *s.* cosecante.

cosily *avv.* comodamente.

cosine *s.* coseno.

cosmetic *agg.* e *s.* cosmetico.

cosmic(al) *agg.* cosmico.

cosmogony *s.* cosmogonia.

cosmographer *s.* cosmografo.

cosmography *s.* cosmografia.

cosmology *s.* cosmologia.

cosmopolitan *agg.* e *s.* cosmopolita.

cosmopolitanism *s.* cosmopolitismo.

cosmopolite *agg.* e *s.* cosmopolita.

cosmopolitism *s.* cosmopolitismo.

cosmos *s.* cosmo.

Cossack *s.* cosacco.

cost *s.* costo, prezzo ‖ — *of living*, carovia; *at all costs*, ad ogni costo;

extra —, spesa supplementare.

to cost (cost, cost) *vt.* e *vi.* costare.

costal *agg.* costale.

coster, costermonger *s.* venditore ambulante (*di frutta, verdura ecc.*).

costly *agg.* costoso.

costume *s.* 1. costume 2. abito.

cosy *agg.* comodo, intimo.

cot¹ *s.* capanna.

cot² *s.* (*mar.*) cuccetta 2. culla.

cotangent *s.* cotangente.

cotenant *s.* coaffittuario.

cothurnus *s.* (*pl.*-ni) coturno.

cottage *s.* villino.

cotton *s.* cotone ‖ — *mill*, cotonificio; — *-spinner*, operaio di filatura; — *-wool*, ovatta; — *-waste*, cascame.

couch *s.* divano.

cough *s.* tosse.

to cough *vt.* e *vi.* tossire.

could *v.* **can.**

council *s.* 1. consiglio (*adunanza di persone*) 2. (*eccl.*) concilio.

councillor *s.* consigliere.

counsel *s.* 1. consultazione 2. consiglio 3. legale.

to counsel *vt.* e *vi.* consigliare.

counsellor *s.* 1. consigliere 2. legale.

count¹ *s.* 1. conto, calcolo 2. (*pol.*) scrutinio 3. (*giur.*) capo d'accusa.

count² *s.* conte.

to count *vt.* e *vi.* 1. contare, calcolare 2. considerare, avere importanza.

countable *agg.* numerabile.

countenance *s.* espressione del volto, aria.

counter¹ *s.* calcolatore, contatore ‖ *revolution* —, contagiri.

counter² *s.* volta di poppa.

counter³ *s.* 1. banco, cassa (*di negozio*) 2. sportello 3. gettone (*da gioco*).

counter⁴ *agg.* contrario, opposto ‖ — *clockwise*, in senso antiorario; — *poison*, antidoto. ♦ **counter** *avv.* in senso ontario.

to counteract *vt.* agir contro, contrapporsi a.

counter-attack *s.* contrattacco.

to counter-attack *vt.* e *vi.* contrattaccare.

counterbalance *s.* contrappeso.

to counterbalance *vt.* controbilanciare.

counterblow *s.* contraccolpo.

countercharge s. controaccusa.

counterfeit agg. contraffatto, simulato. ◆ **counterfeit** s. contraffazione, simulazione.

counterfeiter s. **1.** falsario **2.** simulatore.

counterfoil s. matrice.

countermand s. revoca, contrordine.

counterpane s. copriletto.

counterpart s. **1.** sostituto **2.** duplicato, sosia **3.** complemento.

counterpoint s. contrappunto.

countershaft s. contralbero.

countersign s. contrassegno.

counterweight s. contrappeso.

countess s. contessa.

countless agg. innumerevole.

countrified agg. campagnolo, rurale.

country s. **1.** paese, regione **2.** campagna **3.** patria **4.** nazione.

countryman s. **1.** compaesano, compatriota **2.** contadino.

countryside s. campagna.

countrywoman s. **1.** compaesana, compatriota **2.** contadina.

county s. contea, provincia.

coup s. **1.** colpo **2.** (fig.) impressione.

couple s. coppia, paio.

to couple vt. accoppiare. ◆ **to couple** vi. accoppiarsi.

coupling s. accoppiamento.

coupon s. cedola, tagliando.

courage s. coraggio, ardire.

courageous agg. coraggioso.

course s. **1.** corso (del tempo), corso (di lezioni, conferenze) **2.** serie **3.** portata (dei pasti) **4.** (sport) circuito || of —, naturalmente; in due — a tempo debito.

court s. **1.** corte, cortile **2.** (giur.) corte || — of justice, tribunale.

to court vt. corteggiare.

courtier s. cortigiano.

courting s. corteggiamento.

courtyard s. cortile.

courtship s. corteggiamento.

cousin s. cugino, cugina.

cove s. **1.** insenatura **2.** grotta.

covenant s. convenzione, patto.

cover s. **1.** coperta, copertura **2.** calotta **3.** copertina (di libro) **4.** riparo, ricovero **5.** coperto (a tavola).

to cover vt. **1.** coprire, ricoprire **2.** proteggere **3.** percorrere **4.** nascondere **5.** comprendere, includere.

covering s. copertura, rivestimento.

coverlet s. copriletto.

covert s. ricovero, rifugio.

covertly avv. nascostamente.

to covet vt. agognare.

covetousness s. cupidigia.

cow s. mucca, vacca || — bell, campanaccio; — -grass, trifoglio di campo; — -shed, stalla.

coward s. codardo, vile.

cowardice s. codardia, viltà.

cowardly agg. codardo. ◆ **cowardly** avv. vilmente.

cowboy s. bovaro.

cowherd s. vaccaro.

cowl s. **1.** cappuccio, tonaca (di frate) **2.** (auto; aer.) cofano del motore.

coxswain s. timoniere.

coy agg. timido, riservato.

crab s. granchio.

crabbed agg. sgarbato, bisbetico.

crack s. **1.** schianto, detonazione, schiocco **2.** incrinatura, rottura.

to crack **1.** vt. schiantare, rompere, incrinare **2.** schioccare. ◆ **to crack** vi. **1.** screpolarsi, spezzarsi **2.** scricchiolare.

cracked agg. **1.** incrinato **2.** fesso (di voce).

cracker s. petardo || nut-crackers, schiaccianoci; — of jokes, burlone.

crackle s. **1.** crepitio **2.** screpolatura, incrinatura.

to crackle vi. scoppiettare, scricchiolare. ◆ **to crackle** vt. screpolare.

crackling s. scoppiettio.

cradle s. culla (anche fig.).

craft s. **1.** abilità, mestiere, professione **2.** astuzia, inganno.

craftsman s. artigiano.

craftsmanship s. artigianato.

crafty agg. astuto, abile.

crag s. rupe, cresta.

to cram vt. riempire, stipare, rimpinzare. ◆ **to cram** vi. rimpinzarsi.

cramp s. crampo.

to cramp vt. (fig.) bloccare, paralizzare.

crane s. gru (anche mecc.).

to crane vt. e vi. **1.** sollevare o abbassare (mediante una gru) **2.** allungare (il collo).

cranium s. cranio.

crank[1] s. manovella, manubrio.

crank[2] agg. **1.** piegato **2.** disinnestato.

to **crank** vt. e vi. **1.** piegare a gomito **2.** mettere in moto (con *manovella*).

cranking s. avviamento (di motore).

crash s. **1.** strepito, fracasso **2.** caduta **3.** scontro, collisione **4.** rovina (anche morale).

to **crash** vt. e vi. **1.** abbattere, precipitare, crollare con grande rumore **2.** scontrare, scontrarsi.

crate s. cassa da imballaggio.

crater s. cratere.

to **crawl** vi. **1.** strisciare, andar carponi **2.** brulicare **3.** avere la pelle d'oca.

crawl s. **1.** strisciamento **2.** (nuoto) « crawl ».

crayfish s. gambero (d'acqua dolce).

craze s. mania, smania.

craziness s. pazzia, follia.

crazy agg. **1.** folle **2.** maniaco, entusiasta.

to **creak** vi. cigolare, stridere.

cream s. **1.** panna, crema **2.** ogni sostanza densa e untuosa.

creamery s. caseificio.

creamy agg. cremoso.

crease s. piega, grinza.

to **crease** vt. fare pieghe, sgualcire.
♦ to **crease** vi. sgualcirsi.

to **create** vt. **1.** creare, produrre, suscitare **2.** nominare.

creation s. **1.** creazione **2.** universo, natura, il creato.

creative agg. creativo.

creator s. creatore.

creature s. **1.** essere vivente **2.** creatura (anche fig.), favorito.

credence s. credenza, fede.

credentials s. pl. credenziali.

credibility s. credibilità.

credible agg. credibile.

credit s. **1.** fiducia **2.** credito, reputazione, autorità **3.** (comm.) fido, credito.

to **credit** vt. **1.** prestar fede **2.** attribuire **3.** (comm.) accreditare

creditor s. creditore.

credulity s. credulità.

credulous agg. credulo.

creed s. credo, credenza religiosa.

creek s. **1.** insenatura **2.** (amer.) torrente.

to **creep** (**crept**, **crept**) vi. **1.** strisciare, avanzare lentamente **2.** arrampicarsi (di piante) || to — along, avanzare strisciando; to — away, allontanarsi strisciando.

creeper s. **1.** rettile, verme **2.** persona strisciante **3.** pianta rampicante.

creepy agg. **1.** strisciante **2.** che dà i brividi.

to **cremate** vt. cremare.

cremation s. cremazione.

crematory s. crematoio.

creole agg. e s. creolo.

crept V. to **creep**.

crepuscular agg. crepuscolare.

crescent agg. **1.** crescente **2.** a mezzaluna. ♦ **crescent** s. **1.** luna crescente **2.** mezzaluna (emblema turco) **3.** strada a semicerchio.

cress s. crescione.

crest s. **1.** cresta **2.** ciuffo, pennacchio **3.** criniera.

to **crest** vt. ornare di pennacchio.
♦ to **crest** vi. incresparsi (di onde).

crevasse s. crepaccio.

crevice s. fessura.

crew[1] s. equipaggio, ciurma.

crew[2] V. to **crow**.

crib s. **1.** greppia **2.** presepio **3.** stalla, capanna.

crick s. crampo || a — in the neck, torcicollo.

cricket s. grillo.

crime s. delitto, crimine.

criminal agg. e s. criminale.

criminalist s. penalista.

criminality s. criminalità.

criminology s. criminologia.

crimson s. cremisi.

to **cringe** vi. (fig.) farsi piccolo, umiliarsi.

cripple agg. e s. storpio, zoppo.

to **cripple** vt. storpiare. ♦ to **cripple** vi. essere zoppo.

crisis s. crisi.

crisp agg. **1.** croccante **2.** crespo **3.** tonificante. ♦ **crisp** s. patatina fritta, croccante.

criss-cross agg. incrociato.

critic s. critico.

critical agg. critico.

criticism s. critica.

to **criticize** vt. criticare.

critique s. critica, recensione.

croak s. gracidamento.

to **croak** vt. e vi. **1.** gracidare **2.** (fig.) brontolare.

Croatian agg. e s. croato.

crochet s. lavoro all'uncinetto || -book (o — -pin), uncinetto.

crock[1] s. coccio, vaso di terracotta.

crock[2] s. **1.** ronzino **2.** persona vecchia e malandata.

crock[3] s. fuliggine, sudiciume.

crockery s. terraglia.

crocodile s. coccodrillo.

croft s. piccolo podere, campicello.

crook s. 1. gancio, uncino 2. curva, flessione 3. (gergo) truffatore.

crookback s. gobba.

crooked agg. 1. curvo, storto, deforme 2. (fig.) perverso.

crookedly avv. 1. tortuosamente 2. indirettamente 3. perversamente.

crop s. 1. raccolto, messe 2. gozzo (di uccello) 3. (fig.) gruppo 4. rapata (di capelli).

to crop vt. 1. mietere 2. tosare.

cropper[1] s. mietitore.

cropper[2] s. (fam.) capitombolo.

cross agg. 1. obliquo, trasversale 2. adirato || — -bar, traversa; — -road, incrocio. ♦ cross s. 1. croce 2. tribolazione, pena.

to cross vt. e vi. 1. fare il segno della croce 2. attraversare 3. incrociare 4. cancellare || to — one's legs, accavallare le gambe.

crossbeam s. trave maestra.

crossbelt s. cartucciera a tracolla.

crossbow s. balestra.

crossbreed s. ibrido, incrocio.

cross-country agg. campestre.

cross-examination s. controinterrogatorio.

to cross-examine vt. controinterrogare.

cross-hatch s. tratteggio.

crossing s. 1. passaggio, traversata 2. incrocio || level —, passaggio a livello.

crossly avv. di malumore.

crosswise avv. 1. di traverso 2. a forma di croce.

crossword s. parole incrociate (pl.) || — puzzle, cruciverba.

crouch s. l'accovacciarsi.

to crouch vi. accovacciarsi, rannicchiarsi.

crow[1] s. corvo, cornacchia || a white —, una mosca bianca; to eat (v. irr.) a —, inghiottire un rospo.

crow[2] s. canto del gallo.

to crow (crew, crowed) vi. cantare (del gallo).

crowd s. folla, massa, moltitudine.

to crowd vt. affollare. ♦ to crowd vi. affollarsi, accalcarsi || to — together, stringere insieme.

crown s. 1. corona 2. cocuzzolo 3. coronamento, successo 4. (moneta) corona: half a —, mezza corona.

to crown vt. 1. incoronare 2. coronare, ricompensare.

crowning s. 1. incoronazione 2. coronamento.

crucial agg. cruciale.

crucible s. 1. crogiuolo 2. (fig.) dura prova.

crucifix s. crocifisso.

crucifixion s. crocifissione.

to crucify vt. crocifiggere.

crude agg. grezzo, rozzo, primitivo.

crudity s. asprezza.

cruel agg. crudele.

cruelty s. crudeltà.

cruet s. ampolla.

cruise s. crociera: to go on a —, fare una crociera.

cruiser s. incrociatore.

cruising s. crociera.

crumb s. 1. briciola 2. mollica.

to crumb vt. 1. sbriciolare 2. impanare.

crumble vt. sbriciolare. ♦ to crumble vi. sbriciolarsi.

crumbly agg. friabile.

to crumple vt. spiegazzare. ♦ to crumple vi. spiegazzarsi.

to crunch vt. e vi. sgranocchiare rumorosamente.

crusade s. crociata.

crusader s. crociato.

crush s. 1. folla, calca 2. frantumazione 3. (gergo) infatuazione.

to crush vt. 1. frantumare, torchiare 2. (fig.) annientare, sconfiggere. ♦ to crush vi. accalcarsi, affollarsi.

crushing agg. schiacciante (anche fig.).

crust s. 1. crosta 2. incrostazione.

Crustacea s. pl. crostacei.

crutch s. 1. gruccia, stampella 2. forcella (di ramo).

cry s. grido, lamento, pianto || within —, a portata di voce.

to cry vt. e vi. 1. gridare 2. piangere || to — out, alzare la voce, protestare.

crypt s. cripta.

cryptogam s. crittogama.

cryptogram s. crittogramma.

cryptography s. crittografia.

crystal agg. cristallino. ♦ crystal s. cristallo || — work, cristalleria.

crystalline agg. cristallino (anche fig.).

crystallization s. cristallizzazione.

to crystallize vt. cristallizzare. ♦ to crystallize vi. cristallizzarsi.

crystallography s. cristallografia.
cub s. 1. volpacchiotto 2. (fam.) ragazzaccio.
cubage s. cubatura.
Cuban agg. e s. cubano.
cubature s. cubatura.
cube s. cubo || — root, radice cubica.
cubic agg. cubico.
cubism s. cubismo.
cubit s. cubito.
cuckold s. becco, cornuto.
to **cuckold** vt. tradire (il marito).
cuckoo s. cuculo.
cucumber s. cetriolo.
cudgel s. randello.
to **cudgel** vt. randellare.
cuff s. polsino (di camicia).
cuirass s. corazza.
cuirassier s. corazziere.
culinary agg. culinario.
to **cull** vt. scegliere.
culminant agg. culminante.
to **culminate** vi. culminare, giungere al culmine.
culottes s. pl. gonna pantaloni.
culprit s. 1. colpevole 2. imputato.
cult s. culto.
cultivable agg. coltivabile.
to **cultivate** vt. coltivare (anche fig.).
cultivation s. coltivazione.
cultural agg. culturale.
culture s. 1. coltura, coltivazione 2. cultura.
cultured agg. colto, educato.
cumbersome agg. ingombrante.
cumulative agg. cumulativo.
cumulus s. (pl. -li) cumulo.
cuneiform agg. cuneiforme.
cunette s. cunetta (di trincea).
cunning agg. astuto, furbo. ♦ **cunning** s. astuzia.
cup s. 1. tazza 2. (sport) coppa, trofeo || — -bearer, coppiere; tea- —, tazza da tè.
cupboard s. credenza, armadio.
cupel s. coppella.
cupidity s. cupidigia.
cupreous agg. cupreo.
cupric agg. ramico.
cur s. 1. cane bastardo 2. mascalzone.
curable agg. curabile.
curacy s. vicariato, cura.
curare s. curaro.
curate s. curato, vicario.
curative agg. curativo.
curator s. direttore (di museo, istituto ecc.).

curb s. 1. cordone del marciapiede 2. freno (fig.) || — -bit, morso della briglia.
curd s. giuncata.
to **curdle** vt. cagliare, coagulare. ♦ to **curdle** vi. cagliarsi, coagularsi.
curdy agg. cagliato, coagulato.
cure s. 1. cura, rimedio: to take a —, fare una cura 2. (eccl.) cura 3. vulcanizzazione (di gomma).
to **cure** vt. 1. curare, rimediare 2. salare, affumicare (di cibi) 3. vulcanizzare (una gomma). ♦ to **cure** vi. curarsi.
cureless agg. incurabile.
curette s. (chir.) raschiatoio.
curfew s. coprifuoco.
curio s. oggetto raro.
curiosity s. curiosità: out of —, per curiosità.
curious agg. 1. curioso 2. strano, singolare.
curl s. 1. ricciolo 2. curva, spirale.
to **curl** vt. 1. arricciare 2. torcere. ♦ to **curl** vi. 1. arricciarsi 2. torcersi 3. sollevarsi in spire.
curler s. ferro per arricciare i capelli, bigodino.
curly agg. 1. ricciuto 2. a spirale.
currency s. 1. (comm.) circolazione monetaria 2. corso, credito, voga.
current agg. corrente. ♦ **current** s. corrente (anche fig.) || alternating —, corrente alternata; direct —, corrente continua.
currently avv. comunemente.
curriculum s. curriculum.
to **curry** vt. 1. strigliare 2. conciare (di cuoio).
curry-comb s. striglia.
curse s. maledizione, anatema: a — upon him!, sia maledetto!
to **curse** vt. 1. maledire 2. scomunicare. ♦ to **curse** vi. imprecare, pronunciare bestemmie.
cursed agg. maledetto.
cursive agg. e s. corsivo.
to **curtail** vt. accorciare, abbreviare.
curtain s. 1. tenda, tendina 2. cortina 3. sipario || — -call, chiamata alla ribalta.
curtain-raiser s. avanspettacolo.
curtly avv. brevemente, bruscamente.
curtsey s. riverenza, inchino (di donna).
curve s. curva, svolta.
to **curve** vt. curvare. ♦ to **curve** vi.

curvarsi.
curvet *s.* falcata.
curvilinear *agg.* curvilineo.
cushion *s.* cuscino.
cusp *s.* **1.** cuspide **2.** (*geom.*) vertice.
custard *s.* crema (*di uova e latte*).
custody *s.* **1.** custodia, vigilanza **2.** arresto, detenzione.
custom *s.* costume, consuetudine. ◆ **customs** *s. pl.* dogana (*sing.*) ‖ - -*house officer*, doganiere.
customary *agg.* **1.** abituale, d'uso comune **2.** (*giur.*) consuetudinario.
customer *s.* cliente, avventore.
cut *s.* **1.** taglio **2.** decurtazione **3.** (*sport*) colpo secco.
to cut (**cut, cut**) *vt. e vi.* **1.** tagliare, tagliarsi ‖ *to — a poor figure*, fare una brutta figura **2.** (*comm.*) ridurre **3.** praticare un'apertura ‖ *to — down*, abbattere; *to — out*, ritagliare; *to — up*, trinciare (*il pollo*), sradicare (*alberi*).
cutlet *s.* costoletta.
cut-off *s.* **1.** scorciatoia **2.** ritaglio di giornale.
cutter[1] *s.* **1.** tagliatore **2.** (*mecc.*) fresa.
cutter[2] *s.* (*mar.*) "cutter".
cut-throat *agg.* spietato. ◆ **cut-throat** *s.* tagliagole.
cutting *agg.* tagliente, sferzante. ◆ **cutting** *s.* **1.** taglio, incisione **2.** ritaglio, truciolo **3.** (*comm.*) riduzione.
cuttlefish *s.* seppia.
cyanide *s.* cianuro.
cybernetics *s.* cibernetica.
cycle *s.* ciclo.
cycling *s.* ciclismo.
cyclostyle *s.* ciclostile.
cyclotron *s.* ciclotrone.
cyclist *s.* ciclista.
cyclometer *s.* contachilometri.
cylinder *s.* **1.** cilindro **2.** rullo.
cylindrical *agg.* cilindrico.
cynic *agg. e s.* cinico.
cynicism *s.* cinismo.
cypress *s.* cipresso.
Cyprian *agg. e s.* cipriota.
Cyrillic *agg.* cirillico.
cyst *s.* cisti.
cystitis *s.* cistite.
cytology *s.* citologia.
Czar *s.* zar.
Czech *agg. e s.* ceco.
Czecho-Slovak *agg. e s.* cecoslovacco.

D

D *s.* (*mus.*) re.
dab *s.* **1.** colpo **2.** macchia.
to dab *vt.* **1.** sfiorare **2.** applicare.
to dabble *vt.* inumidire. ◆ **to dabble** *vi.* **1.** inumidirsi **2.** sguazzare ‖ *to — in* (*at*), dilettarsi di.
dachshund *s.* cane bassotto.
dad(dy) *s.* (*fam.*) papà, babbo.
daffodil *s.* narciso selvatico.
daft *agg.* sciocco, pazzoide.
dagger *s.* **1.** pugnale **2.** (*tip.*) croce ‖ *at daggers drawn*, ai ferri corti.
daguerreotype *s.* dagherrotipo.
daguerreotypy *s.* dagherrotipia.
dahlia *s.* dalia.
daily *agg.* quotidiano, giornaliero. ◆ **daily** *s.* (*giornale*) quotidiano. ◆ **daily** *avv.* ogni giorno.
daintily *avv.* delicatamente.
daintiness *s.* squisitezza.
dainty *agg.* **1.** squisito **2.** esigente **3.** raffinato (*di gusti*). ◆ **dainty** *s.* leccornia.
dairy *s.* latteria.
dairymaid *s.* lattaia.
dairyman *s.* lattaio.
dais *s.* piattaforma.
daisy *s.* margherita.
dalliance *s.* amoreggiamento.
to dally *vi.* gingillarsi, oziare.
Dalmatian *agg. e s.* dalmata.
daltonism *s.* daltonismo.
dam[1] *s.* diga, sbarramento.
dam[2] *s.* madre (*di animali*).
to dam *vt.* arginare.
damage *s.* danno. ◆ **damages** *s. pl.* (*giur.*) indennizzo, risarcimento (*sing.*).
to damage *vt.* danneggiare.
damaging *agg.* dannoso.
damask *s.* damasco.
to damask *vt.* damascare.
dame *s.* dama, gentildonna.
damn *s.* maledizione.
to damn *vt.* **1.** dannare **2.** (*spesso scritto* d-) maledire, mandare all'inferno.
damnation *s.* dannazione.
damnatory *agg.* compromettente (*di prove*).
damp *agg.* umido. ◆ **damp** *s.* **1.** umidità **2.** (*fig.*) depressione ‖ *fire-*, grisù.
to damp *vt.* **1.** inumidire **2.** (*fig.*) deprimere, smorzare.

damper s. **1.** regolatore (*di stufa, fornace ecc.*) **2.** (*mus.*) sordina.

dampness s. umidità.

dance s. danza.

to **dance** vt. e vi. danzare || *to — attendance on*, essere a disposizione di.

dancer s. ballerino.

dancing s. danza.

dandelion s. (*bot.*) soffione.

dandruff s. forfora.

dandy *arg.* elegante, raffinato. ◆ **dandy** s. zerbinotto.

Dane s. danese.

danger s. pericolo.

dangerous agg. pericoloso.

to **dangle** vi. ciondolare, penzolare ◆ to **dangle** vt. far penzolare.

dangling agg. penzolante.

Danish agg. danese.

dank agg. umido.

Dantean, Dantesque agg. dantesco.

dapple s. macchia || *—-grey*, leardo pomellato.

to **dapple** vt. chiazzare.

dare (**dared, durst**) v. *dif.* osare.

to **dare** vt. **1.** affrontare **2.** sfidare.

daredevil s. scavezzacollo.

daring agg. audace. ◆ **daring** s. audacia.

dark agg. **1.** scuro **2.** triste **3.** segreto. ◆ **dark** s. **1.** oscurità **2.** (*fig.*) ignoranza.

to **darken** vt. oscurare. ◆ to **darken** vi. oscurarsi.

darkling agg. oscuro. ◆ **darkling** avv. nell'oscurità.

darkness s. oscurità.

darling agg. e s. caro.

darn s. rammendo.

to **darn** vt. rammendare.

darnel s. loglio.

darner s. rammendatrice.

darning s. rammendo.

dart s. **1.** dardo **2.** slancio.

to **dart** vt. lanciare. ◆ to **dart** vi. lanciarsi (*in avanti*).

darting agg. dardeggiante.

Darwinism s. darwinismo.

dash s. **1.** slancio **2.** attacco **3.** tonfo **4.** spruzzo **5.** lineetta || *—-board*, cruscotto (*di automobili*).

to **dash** vt. **1.** frantumare **2.** macchiare. ◆ to **dash** vi. **1.** precipitarsi **2.** infrangersi.

dashing agg. impetuoso.

dastard s. vigliacco, furfante.

date[1] s. **1.** data **2.** appuntamento || *up to —*, aggiornato; *out of —*, antiquato.

date[2] s. dattero.

to **date** vt. e vi. datare || *to — a girl*, dare un appuntamento a una ragazza.

dating s. datazione.

dative agg. e s. dativo.

datum s. (*pl.* data) dato, elemento.

to **daub** vt. **1.** intonacare **2.** impiastrare.

dauber s. imbrattatore.

daughter s. figlia || *— -in-law*, nuora; *grand- — (di nonni)*, nipotina.

to **daunt** vt. spaventare, intimidire.

dauntless agg. intrepido.

to **dawdle** vi. oziare, bighellonare.

dawn s. alba.

to **dawn** vi. **1.** albeggiare **2.** apparire, balenare (*nella mente*).

day s. giorno || *— labourer*, lavoratore a giornata; *the — after tomorrow*, dopodomani; *the — before yesterday*, l'altro ieri; *this — week*, oggi a otto; *— off*, giorno di riposo; *— out*, giorno di libera uscita.

daybook s. (*comm.*) brogliaccio.

daybreak s. alba.

daydream s. fantasticheria.

to **daydream** vi. fantasticare.

daydreamer s. sognatore.

daylight s. luce del giorno.

daylong agg. che dura tutto il giorno. ◆ **daylong** avv. per tutto il giorno.

daytime s. giornata.

daze s. sbalordimento.

to **daze** vt. sbalordire.

dazzle s. abbagliamento || *— lamps (auto)*, fari abbaglianti.

to **dazzle** vt. abbagliare.

deacon s. diacono.

dead agg. **1.** morto **2.** assoluto || *— drunk*, ubriaco fradicio. ◆ **dead** avv. assolutamente || *— sure*, arcisicuro.

to **deaden** vt. **1.** attutire **2.** isolare (*acusticamente*). ◆ to **deaden** vi. attutirsi.

deadening s. isolamento acustico.

deadline s. **1.** linea non superabile **2.** scadenza, termine massimo.

deadly agg. mortale. ◆ **deadly** avv. mortalmente.

deadness s. torpore.

deaf agg. sordo.

to **deafen** vt. assordare.

deaf-mute s. sordomuto.

deafness s. sordità.

deal s. 1. quantità 2. accordo 3. affare 4. mano (del gioco delle carte) || a great —, moltissimo.

to deal (dealt, dealt) vt. distribuire, dare. ♦ **to deal (dealt, dealt)** vi. trattare, comportarsi || to — in, commerciare in.

dealer s. 1. commerciante 2. mazziere (delle carte).

dealing s. 1. commercio 2. distribuzione 3. relazione || double- —, slealtà.

dealt V. to deal.

deambulatory agg. deambulatorio.

dean s. 1. decano 2. preside (di facoltà universitaria).

dear agg. caro || — me!, povero me!

dearly avv. 1. caramente 2. a caro prezzo.

dearness s. amorevolezza.

dearth s. penuria.

death s. morte || — -rattles, rantoli dell'agonia; — -warrant, ordine di esecuzione capitale.

deathly agg. e avv. V. deadly.

to debase vt. 1. avvilire 2. svalutare.

to debar vt. escludere, privare.

to debark vt. e vi. sbarcare.

debate s. dibattito.

to debate vt. e vi. 1. discutere 2. ponderare.

debauch s. intemperanza, corruzione.

debauched agg. corrotto.

debauchery s. 1. corruzione 2. dissolutezza.

debenture s. (comm.) obbligazione.

debit s. debito.

to debit vt. addebitare.

to debouch vi. sfociare.

debris s. detriti (pl.).

debt s. debito.

debtor s. debitore.

début s. debutto.

decadence s. decadenza.

decadent agg. e s. decadente.

decagram(m)e s. decagrammo.

decahedron s. decaedro.

to decalcify vt. decalcificare.

decalitre s. decalitro.

decalogue s. decalogo.

decametre s. decametro.

to decamp vi. levare le tende.

to decant vt. travasare.

decantation s. decantazione.

decanter s. caraffa.

to decapitate vt. decapitare.

decasyllabic agg. decasillabico.

decay s. 1. decadimento 2. rovina 3. carie (dei denti).

to decay vt. 1. far decadere 2. mandare in rovina. ♦ **to decay** vi. 1. decadere 2. andare in rovina 3. cariarsi.

decayable agg. deperibile.

decease s. decesso.

to decease vi. morire.

deceit s. 1. inganno 2. falsità.

deceitful agg. 1. ingannevole 2. falso.

to deceive vt. ingannare.

deceiving agg. ingannatore.

to decelerate vt. e vi. rallentare.

deceleration s. rallentamento.

decelerator s. rallentatore.

December s. dicembre.

decency s. decenza. 2. ♦ **decencies** s. pl. convenienze.

decennary agg. decennale. ♦ **decennary** s. decennio.

decennial agg. e s. decennale.

decent agg. decente || a — fellow, un buon diavolo.

decentralization s. decentramento.

to decentralize vt. decentrare.

deception s. inganno.

deceptive agg. ingannevole.

to decide vt. decidere. ♦ **to decide** vi. decidersi, pronunciarsi.

decigram(me) s. decigrammo.

decimal agg. e s. decimale.

to decimate vt. decimare.

decimation s. decimazione.

decimetre s. decimetro.

to decipher vt. decifrare.

deciphering s. decifrazione.

decision s. decisione.

decisive agg. 1. decisivo 2. deciso.

deck s. (mar.) ponte, coperta || — -chair, sedia a sdraio; quarter-—, cassero.

to deck vt. ornare.

decker s. double- —, autobus a due piani.

to declaim vt. e vi. declamare.

declaimer s. declamatore.

declamation s. declamazione.

declamatory agg. declamatorio.

declaration s. dichiarazione.

to declare vt. e vi. dichiarare.

declension s. 1. declino 2. (gramm.) declinazione.

declinable agg. declinabile.

declination s. 1. inclinazione 2. declino.

decline s. declino, deperimento.

to **decline** *vt.* e *vi.* declinare.
declining *s.* **1.** declinazione **2.** deperimento **3.** rifiuto.
declivity *s.* declivio.
to **decode** *vt.* decifrare, tradurre (*testi in codice*).
decolorization *s.* decolorazione.
decoloration *s.* decolorazione.
to **decolour(ize)** *vt.* decolorare.
decomposable *agg.* scomponibile.
to **decompose** *vt.* **1.** decomporre **2.** scomporre. ♦ to **decompose** *vi.* **1.** decomporsi **2.** scomporsi.
decomposition *s.* decomposizione.
to **deconsecrate** *vt.* sconsacrare.
to **decorate** *vt.* decorare.
decoration *s.* decorazione.
decorative *agg.* decorativo.
decorator *s.* decoratore.
decorous *agg.* decoroso.
decoy *s.* esca, richiamo.
decrease *s.* diminuzione.
to **decrease** *vt.* e *vi.* diminuire.
decree *s.* decreto.
to **decree** *vt.* decretare.
decrepit *agg.* decrepito.
decrepitude *s.* decrepitezza.
to **decry** *vt.* stigmatizzare, denigrare.
to **decuple** *vt.* decuplicare.
to **dedicate** *vt.* dedicare.
dedicatee *s.* persona a cui è dedicato qc.
dedication *s.* **1.** dedica **2.** consacrazione.
dedicative, dedicatory *agg.* dedicatorio.
to **deduce** *vt.* **1.** dedurre **2.** derivare.
to **deduct** *vt.* detrarre.
deduction *s.* **1.** deduzione **2.** detrazione.
deductive *agg.* deduttivo.
deed *s.* atto, azione.
to **deem** *vt.* giudicare.
deep *agg.* **1.** profondo **2.** cupo || --freeze, surgelamento; -- mourning, lutto stretto. ♦ **deep** *s.* abisso, profondità. ♦ **deep** *avv.* profondamente || -- into the night, fino a notte tarda.
to **deepen** *vt.* **1.** approfondire **2.** incupire. ♦ to **deepen** *vi.* **1.** approfondirsi **2.** incupirsi.
deeply *avv.* profondamente.
deepness *s.* profondità.
deep-rooted *agg.* radicato.
deer *s.* cervo || (fallow) --, daino.
to **deface** *vt.* sfregiare.

defacement *s.* sfregio.
defamation *s.* diffamazione.
defamatory *agg.* diffamatorio.
to **defame** *vt.* diffamare.
defamer *s.* diffamatore.
default *s.* **1.** mancanza **2.** inadempienza **3.** (giur.) contumacia: judgement by --, giudizio in contumacia.
defaulting *agg.* (comm.) insolvente.
defeat *s.* **1.** sconfitta **2.** fallimento.
to **defeat** *vt.* **1.** sconfiggere **2.** frustrare.
defeatism *s.* disfattismo.
defeatist *agg.* e *s.* disfattista.
to **defecate** *vt.* purificare. ♦ to **defecate** *vi.* defecare.
defect *s.* difetto.
defection *s.* defezione.
defective *agg.* **1.** difettoso **2.** (gramm.) difettivo. ♦ **defective** *s.* anormale.
defence *s.* difesa.
defenceless *agg.* indifeso.
to **defend** *vt.* difendere.
defendant *s.* imputato.
defender *s.* difensore.
defenestration *s.* defenestrazione.
defensible *agg.* difensibile.
defensive *agg.* difensivo. ♦ **defensive** *s.* difensiva.
to **defer**[1] *vt.* e *vi.* differire || deferred payment, pagamento a rate.
to **defer**[2] *vt.* rimettere. ♦ to **defer** *vi.* rimettersi.
deference *s.* deferenza.
deferential *agg.* deferente.
deferment *s.* differimento.
defiance *s.* sfida.
defiant *agg.* ardito.
deficiency *s.* **1.** deficienza **2.** disavanzo.
deficient *agg.* e *s.* deficiente.
deficit *s.* (comm.) disavanzo.
to **defile** *vi.* marciare in fila. ♦ to **defile** *vt.* **1.** insozzare **2.** profanare.
defilement *s.* **1.** contaminazione **2.** profanazione.
definable *agg.* definibile.
to **define** *vt.* definire.
definite *agg.* definito.
definitely *avv.* in modo preciso.
definiteness *s.* precisione.
definition *s.* **1.** definizione **2.** nitidezza.
definitive *agg.* definitivo.
to **deflagrate** *vt.* far deflagrare. ♦ to **deflagrate** *vi.* deflagrare.

deflagration s. deflagrazione.
to deflate vt. sgonfiare. ♦ **to deflate** vi. sgonfiarsi.
deflation s. 1. sgonfiamento 2. deflazione.
to deflect vt. e vi. deviare.
deflection s. deviazione.
defloration s. deflorazione.
to deflower vt. 1. deflorare 2. devastare 3. spogliare (dei fiori).
to deforest vt. disboscare.
deforestation s. disboscamento.
to deform vt. deformare. ♦ **to deform** vi. deformarsi.
deformation s. deformazione.
deformed agg. deforme.
deformity s. deformità.
to defraud vt. defraudare.
defrauder s. frodatore.
to defray vt. pagare, risarcire.
to defrost vt. sgelare.
defroster s. riscaldatore.
deft agg. abile, destro.
to defy vt. sfidare.
degenerate agg. e s. degenerato.
to degenerate vt. e vi. degenerare.
degeneration s. degenerazione.
degradation s. degradazione.
to degrade vt. degradare.
degree s. 1. grado 2. rango 3. laurea, diploma || by degrees, gradatamente.
to dehydrate vt. disidratare.
dehydration s. disidratazione.
to deify vt. deificare.
deism s. deismo.
deity s. divinità.
to deject vt. abbattere, scoraggiare.
dejected agg. triste, abbattuto.
dejectedly avv. con aria abbattuta.
dejection s. abbattimento.
delation s. delazione.
delator s. delatore.
delay s. 1. ritardo 2. proroga.
to delay vt. e vi. ritardare.
delegacy s. delegazione.
delegate s. delegato.
to delegate vt. delegare.
delegation s. delegazione.
to delete vt. cancellare (anche fig.).
deliberate agg. 1. deliberato 2. cauto.
to deliberate vt. e vi. deliberare.
deliberately avv. deliberatamente.
deliberation s. 1. deliberazione 2. ponderatezza.
delicacy s. 1. delicatezza 2. ghiottoneria.

delicate agg. 1. delicato 2. esigente.
delicatessen s. pl. 1. ghiottonerie 2. salumeria (sing.).
delicious agg. delizioso.
delict s. (giur.) delitto.
delight s. delizia, gioia.
to delight vt. deliziare. ♦ **to delight** vi. dilettarsi.
delighted agg. lietissimo, entusiasta.
delightful agg. delizioso.
to delimit(ate) vt. delimitare.
delimitation s. delimitazione.
to delineate vt. delineare.
delineation s. delineazione.
delinquency s. 1. delinquenza 2. colpevolezza.
delinquent agg. colpevole. ♦ **delinquent** s. delinquente.
delirious agg. delirante.
deliriously avv. in modo delirante.
delirium s. delirio, frenesia.
to deliver vt. 1. liberare 2. consegnare 3. partorire 4. pronunciare (un discorso).
deliverance s. liberazione.
delivery s. 1. liberazione 2. consegna 3. parto 4. resa 5. dizione, pronuncia || — -man, fattorino.
deltoid agg. triangolare.
to delude vt. ingannare.
deluge s. diluvio.
delusion s. illusione.
delusive agg. illusorio.
to delve vt. scavare, esumare. ♦ **to delve** vi. compiere ricerche, frugare.
demagnetization s. demagnetizzazione.
to demagnetize vt. demagnetizzare.
demagogic(al) agg. demagogico.
demagogue s. demagogo.
demagogy s. demagogia.
demand s. 1. domanda 2. esigenza || on —, a richiesta.
to demand vt. 1. domandare 2. esigere.
demarcation s. demarcazione.
demeanour s. contegno.
demerit s. demerito.
demesne s. dominio, proprietà terriera.
demigod s. semidio.
demijohn s. damigiana.
demilitarization s. smilitarizzazione.
to demilitarize vt. smilitarizzare.
demise s. 1. trapasso (di proprietà)

2. decesso.
demiurge s. demiurgo.
demobilization s. smobilitazione.
to **demobilize** vt. smobilitare.
democracy s. democrazia.
democrat s. democratico.
democratic(al) agg. democratico.
democratization s. democratizzazione.
to **democratize** vt. democratizzare.
demographic(al) agg. demografico.
demography s. demografia.
to **demolish** vt. demolire.
demolisher s. demolitore.
demolition s. demolizione.
demon s. demonio.
demoniac(al) agg. demoniaco.
demonology s. demonologia.
demonstrability s. dimostrabilità.
demonstrable agg. dimostrabile.
demonstrant s. dimostrante.
to **demonstrate** vt. e vi. dimostrare.
demonstration s. dimostrazione.
demonstrative agg. 1. dimostrativo 2. espansivo.
demonstrativeness s. 1. dimostrazione 2. espansività.
demonstrator s. 1. dimostratore 2. dimostrante.
demoralization s. 1. depravazione 2. demoralizzazione.
to **demoralize** vt. 1. depravare 2. demoralizzare.
to **demur** vi. titubare, esitare.
demure agg. riservato, pudico.
demureness s. riservatezza, pudore.
den s. tana.
to **denationalize** vt. snazionalizzare.
to **denature** vt. denaturare.
deniable agg. negabile.
denial s. rifiuto || self- —, abnegazione.
to **denigrate** vt. denigrare.
denigration s. denigrazione.
denigrator s. denigratore.
to **denominate** vt. denominare.
denomination s. 1. denominazione 2. setta 3. valore (di monete).
denominational agg. confessionale.
denominative agg. denominativo.
denominator s. denominatore.
denotation s. 1. indicazione 2. significato.
to **denote** vt. denotare, indicare.
to **denounce** vt. denunciare.
dense agg. 1. denso 2. opaco 3. stupido.
density s. 1. densità 2. opacità 3.

stupidità.
dent s. incavo, tacca.
dental agg. e s. dentale.
dentary agg. dentario.
dentine s. dentina.
dentist s. dentista.
dentistry s. odontoiatria.
dentition s. dentizione.
denture s. dentiera.
denudation s. denudazione.
to **denude** vt. denudare.
denunciation s. denunzia.
to **deny** vt. negare, rifiutare.
deodorant agg. e s. deodorante.
to **deodorize** vt. deodorare.
deontology s. deontologia.
deoxidization s. disossidazione.
to **deoxidize** vt. disossidare.
to **depart** vi. partire, allontanarsi.
department s. 1. reparto 2. (amer.) ministero || — store, grande magazzino.
departure s. 1. partenza 2. allontanamento.
to **depend** vi. 1. dipendere: it all depends on circumstances, tutto dipende dalle circostanze 2. contare: — on so., contare su qu.
dependable agg. fidato.
dependant agg. e s. dipendente.
dependence s. 1. dipendenza 2. fiducia.
dependency s. territorio dipendente.
dependent agg. dipendente.
to **depict** vt. dipingere.
to **depilate** vt. depilare.
depilatory agg. e s. depilatorio.
to **deplete** vt. 1. vuotare 2. esaurire.
depletion s. esaurimento.
deplorable agg. deplorevole.
to **deplore** vt. deplorare.
to **deploy** vt. schierare, spiegare. ♦
to **deploy** vi. schierarsi (di truppe ecc.).
to **depone** vt. deporre (in un processo).
deponent s. testimone.
to **depopulate** vt. spopolare.
to **deport** vt. deportare || to — oneself, comportarsi.
deportation s. deportazione.
deportment s. atteggiamento.
deposal s. deposizione.
to **depose** vt. e vi. deporre.
deposit s. deposito.
to **deposit** vt. depositare.
deposition s. 1. deposizione 2. de-

posito.
depositor s. depositante.
depot s. deposito.
to deprave vt. depravare.
depravity s. depravazione.
deprecable agg. deprecabile.
to deprecate vt. disapprovare.
deprecation s. disapprovazione.
deprecative, deprecatory agg. disapprovante.
to depreciate vt. svalutare. ♦ **to depreciate** vi. svalutarsi.
depreciation s. 1. svalutazione 2. ammortamento: — charge, quota d'ammortamento.
depreciative, depreciatory agg. spregiativo.
depredation s. saccheggio.
depredatory agg. predatorio.
to depress vt. 1. deprimere 2. abbassare.
depression s. 1. depressione 2. (econ.) crisi.
depressor s. depressore.
deprivation s. privazione.
to deprive vt. privare.
depth s. 1. profondità 2. (mar.) fondale.
to depurate vt. depurare. ♦ **to depurate** vi. depurarsi.
depuration s. depurazione.
depurative agg. e s. depurativo.
depurator s. depuratore.
deputation s. delega.
to depute vt. deputare.
deputy s. 1. deputato 2. sostituto.
derailment s. deragliamento.
to derange vt. sconvolgere.
derangement s. sconvolgimento.
deratization s. derattizzazione.
to deride vt. deridere.
derision s. 1. derisione 2. zimbello.
derisive, derisory agg. derisorio.
derivable agg. derivabile.
derivation s. derivazione.
derivative agg. e s. derivato.
derivatively avv. per derivazione.
to derive vt. e vi. derivare.
derm s. derma.
dermatologist s. dermatologo.
dermatology s. dermatologia.
to derogate vi. derogare.
derogation s. deroga.
derogatory agg. derogatorio.
derrick s. 1. argano 2. torre di trivellazione.
descant s. 1. melodia 2. dissertazione.
to descend vt. e vi. (di)scendere ‖

to — upon so., aggredire qu.
descendance s. discendenza.
descendant s. discendente.
descent s. 1. discesa 2. incursione 3. lignaggio 4. caduta.
describable agg. descrivibile.
to describe vt. descrivere.
description s. descrizione.
descriptive agg. descrittivo.
to descry vt. scoprire.
to desecrate vt. profanare.
desert[1] agg. deserto. ♦ **desert** s. deserto.
desert[2] s. 1. merito 2. compenso.
to desert vt. abbandonare. ♦ **to desert** vi. disertare.
deserted agg. deserto.
deserter s. disertore.
desertion s. 1. abbandono 2. diserzione.
to deserve vt. meritare.
deservedly avv. meritatamente.
deserving agg. meritevole.
design s. disegno.
to design vt. 1. destinare 2. progettare 3. disegnare.
designate agg. designato.
to designate vt. 1. designare 2. indicare.
designation s. designazione.
designer s. disegnatore.
designing agg. astuto. ♦ **designing** s. 1. disegno 2. complotto.
desirable agg. desiderabile.
desire s. desiderio.
to desire vt. 1. desiderare 2. domandare.
desirous agg. desideroso.
to desist vi. desistere.
desk s. 1. scrivania 2. cassa ‖ school-master's —, cattedra (di insegnante).
desolate agg. desolato.
to desolate vt. 1. affliggere 2. devastare.
desolation s. desolazione.
despair s. disperazione.
to despair vi. disperare.
despairing agg. disperato.
desperate agg. disperato.
despicable agg. spregevole.
despicableness s. spregevolezza.
despisable agg. spregevole.
to despise vt. disprezzare.
despite prep. malgrado.
despiteful agg. maligno, dispettoso.
despondency s. scoraggiamento.
despondent agg. scoraggiato.
despot s. despota.

despotic(al) agg. dispotico.
despotism s. dispotismo.
destination s. destinazione.
to **destine** vt. destinare.
destiny s. destino.
destitute agg. 1. povero 2. privo.
destitution s. 1. povertà 2. privazione.
to **destroy** vt. distruggere.
destroyable agg. distruggibile.
destroyer s. 1. distruttore 2. cacciatorpediniere.
destroying agg. distruttore.
destruction s. distruzione, rovina.
destructive agg. distruttivo.
destructor s. distruttore.
desuetude s. disuso.
desultory agg. saltuario.
to **detach** vt. distaccare.
detachable agg. staccabile.
detached agg. 1. distaccato 2. isolato.
detachment s. 1. distacco 2. (mil.) distaccamento.
detail s. 1. dettaglio, particolare 2. pattuglia.
to **detail** vt. 1. dettagliare 2. (mil.) distaccare (una pattuglia).
to **detain** vt. 1. detenere 2. trattenere.
to **detect** vt. scoprire.
detectable agg. scopribile.
detection s. scoperta.
detective s. investigatore || — novel, romanzo poliziesco.
detector s. (radio) rivelatore.
detent s. (mecc.) arpione.
detention s. 1. detenzione 2. ritardo forzato.
to **deter** vt. trattenere.
to **deterge** vt. detergere.
detergent agg. e s. detergente, detersivo.
to **deteriorate** vt. deteriorare. ♦ to **deteriorate** vi. deteriorarsi.
deterioration s. deterioramento.
determinable agg. determinabile.
determinant s. causa determinante.
determinate agg. determinato.
determination s. determinazione.
determinative agg. determinativo.
to **determine** vt. determinare, decidere. ♦ to **determine** vi. risolversi || to — on, fissarsi su.
determined agg. deciso.
determinism s. determinismo.
determinist agg. e s. determinista.
deterrent agg. e s. (neol.) deterrente.

detersive agg. e s. detersivo.
to **detest** vt. detestare.
detestable agg. detestabile.
detestation s. 1. odio 2. esecrazione.
to **dethrone** vt. deposizione (dal trono).
to **detonate** vt. e vi. esplodere.
detonator s. detonatore.
detour s. deviazione, giravolta.
to **detract** vt. e vi. diminuire.
detraction s. detrazione.
detractor s. detrattore.
detriment s. detrimento.
detrimental agg. dannoso.
to **devaluate** vt. svalutare.
devaluation s. svalutazione.
to **devastate** vt. devastare.
devastation s. devastazione.
to **develop** vt. sviluppare. ♦ to **develop** vi. svilupparsi.
developer s. sviluppatore.
development s. sviluppo.
to **deviate** vt. e vi. deviare.
deviation s. deviazione.
deviationism s. deviazionismo.
device s. 1. trovata 2. dispositivo. ♦ **devices** s. pl. capriccio, inclinazione (sing.).
devil s. diavolo.
devilish agg. diabolico.
devious agg. 1. remoto 2. errante.
to **devise** vt. 1. escogitare 2. lasciare in eredità.
deviser s. inventore.
devising s. invenzione.
devoid agg. privo.
devolution s. 1. trasmissione (di beni) 2. degenerazione.
to **devolve** vt. trasmettere. ♦ to **devolve** vi. trasferirsi.
to **devote** vt. dedicare.
devoted agg. 1. devoto 2. votato.
devotion s. devozione.
devotional agg. devoto.
to **devour** vt. divorare.
devourer s. divoratore.
devout agg devoto, pio, religioso.
dew s. rugiada.
dewy agg. rugiadoso.
dexterity s. destrezza.
dexterous agg. destro.
dextrin(e) s. destrina.
diabetes s. diabete.
diabetic agg. e s. diabetico.
diabolic(al) agg. diabolico.
diadem s. diadema.
to **diagnose** vt. diagnosticare.
diagnosis s. (pl. -ses) diagnosi.

diagnostic *agg.* diagnostico.

diagonal *agg.* e *s.* diagonale.

diagram *s.* diagramma.

dial *s.* quadrante.

to dial *vt.* comporre (*un numero telefonico*) || *to — so.,* telefonare a qu.

dialect *s.* dialetto.

dialectal *agg.* dialettale.

dialectic(al) *agg.* dialettico.

dialectics *s.* dialettica.

dialogue *s.* dialogo.

to dialogue *vt.* e *vi.* dialogare.

diameter *s.* diametro.

diametrically *avv.* diametralmente.

diamond *s.* 1. diamante 2. losanga.

diaper *s.* 1. arabesco 2. pannolino.

diaphanous *agg.* diafano.

diaphragm *s.* diaframma.

diapositive *s.* diapositiva.

diarchy *s.* diarchia.

diarist *s.* diarista.

diarrhoea *s.* diarrea.

diary *s.* diario.

diatribe *s.* diatriba.

dice V. *die.*

to dice *vt.* 1. giocare ai dadi 2. tagliare a dadi 3. quadrettare.

dictaphone *s.* dittafono.

dictate *s.* dettame.

to dictate *vt.* e *vi.* dettare.

dictation *s.* 1. dettato 2. dettame.

dictator *s.* dittatore.

dictatorial *agg.* dittatoriale.

dictatorship *s.* dittatura.

diction *s.* 1. stile 2. dizione.

dictionary *s.* dizionario.

dictograph *s.* dittografo.

did V. *to do.*

didactic *agg.* didattico.

didactics *s.* didattica.

die *s.* (*pl.* dice) dado.

to die *vi.* morire || *to — away,* svanire; *to — out,* estinguersi.

dielectric *agg.* e *s.* dielettrico.

diet *s.* dieta.

to diet *vt.* mettere a dieta. ♦ **to diet** *vi.* essere a dieta.

dietarian *s.* chi sta a dieta.

dietary *agg.* dietetico. ♦ **dietary** *s.* dieta.

dietetic(al) *agg.* dietetico.

to differ *vi.* differire.

difference *s.* 1. differenza 2. divergenza.

different *agg.* differente.

differential *agg.* e *s.* differenziale.

to differentiate *vt.* differenziare. ♦ **to differentiate** *vi.* differenziarsi.

differentiation *s.* differenziazione.

differently *avv.* differentemente.

differing *agg.* 1. differente, discordante.

difficult *agg.* difficile.

difficulty *s.* difficoltà.

diffidence *s.* timidezza.

diffident *agg.* esitante.

diffraction *s.* difrazione.

diffuse *agg.* diffuso.

to diffuse *vt.* diffondere. ♦ **to diffuse** *vi.* diffondersi.

diffusedly, diffusely *avv.* 1. diffusamente 2. ovunque.

diffuser *s.* (*foto*) diffusore.

diffusion *s.* 1. diffusione 2. prolissità.

diffusive *agg.* 1. diffusivo 2. prolisso.

diffusor *s.* diffusore.

to dig (**dug, dug**) *vt.* vangare, scavare || *to — in,* affondare; *to — out,* estrarre.

digest *s.* 1. sommario 2. condensato.

to digest *vt.* classificare, condensare, redigere. ♦ **to digest** *vt.* e *vi.* digerire.

digestibility *s.* digeribilità.

digestible *agg.* digeribile.

digestion *s.* digestione.

digestive *agg.* e *s.* digestivo.

digger *s.* 1. zappatore 2. scavatrice.

digging *s.* 1. scavo 2. miniera. ♦ **diggings** *s. pl.* (*gergo*) alloggio (*sing.*).

digital *agg.* digitale.

dignified *agg.* dignitoso.

to dignify *vt.* elevare, nobilitare.

dignitary *s.* dignitario.

dignity *s.* 1. dignità 2. dignitario.

digression *s.* digressione.

digressive *agg.* digressivo.

dike *s.* diga.

to dike *vt.* arginare.

to dilapidate *vt.* dilapidare. ♦ **to dilapidate** *vi.* andare in rovina.

dilatability *s.* dilatabilità.

dilatable *agg.* dilatabile.

dilatation *s.* dilatazione.

to dilate *vt.* dilatare. ♦ **to dilate** *vi.* dilatarsi.

dilatory *agg.* 1. dilatorio 2. lento.

diligence *s.* diligenza.

diligent *agg.* diligente.

diluent *agg.* e *s.* diluente.

to dilute *vt.* diluire.

dilution *s.* 1. diluzione 2. sostanza

diluita.
diluvial *agg.* diluviale.
dim *agg.* **1.** debole **2.** appannato **3.** oscuro.
to **dim** *vt.* **1.** indebolire **2.** oscurare. ◆ to **dim** *vi.* **1.** indebolirsi **2.** oscurarsi.
dime *s.* quarto di dollaro.
dimension *s.* dimensione.
dimeter *s.* dimetro.
to **diminish** *vt. e vi.* diminuire.
diminishable *agg.* diminuibile.
diminution *s.* diminuzione.
diminutive *agg.* minuscolo. ◆ **diminutive** *s.* diminutivo.
dimissory *agg.* dimissorio.
dimly *avv.* **1.** debolmente **2.** oscuramente.
dimness *s.* **1.** debolezza **2.** offuscamento (*di vista*).
dimple *s.* fossetta.
din *s.* baccano.
to **din** *vt. e vi.* rintronare.
to **dine** *vi.* pranzare.
diner *s.* commensale.
to **ding** *vt. e vi.* suonare, scampanellare.
dingy *agg.* scuro, sporco.
dining *s.* il pranzare || — *room*, sala da pranzo.
dinner *s.* pranzo || — *wagon*, carrello (*per i pasti*); — *car*, vagone ristorante.
dinosaur *s.* dinosauro.
dint *s.* tacca || *by* — *of*, a forza di.
diocesan *agg. e s.* diocesano.
diocese *s.* diocesi.
diode *s.* diodo.
Dionysiac, Dionysian *agg.* dionisiaco.
diopter *s.* diottria.
dioptric *agg.* diottrico.
dioxid(e) *s.* biossido.
dip *s.* **1.** bagno **2.** inclinazione **3.** (*aer.*) picchiata **4.** tuffo.
to **dip** *vt.* **1.** immergere **2.** abbassare. ◆ to **dip** *vi.* **1.** immergersi **2.** abbassarsi **3.** tuffarsi.
diphtheria *s.* difterite.
diphtheric *agg.* difterico.
diphthong *s.* dittongo.
diplomacy *s.* diplomazia.
diplomat *s.* diplomatico.
diplomatic *agg.* diplomatico.
diplomatically *avv.* diplomaticamente.
diplomatics *s.* diplomazia.
diplomatist *s.* diplomatico.
dipody *s.* dipodia.

dipper *s.* **1.** tuffatore **2.** mestolo || *the Big* —, l'Orsa Maggiore.
dipsomaniac *s.* dipsomane.
dipteral *agg.* dittero.
diptych *s.* dittico.
dire *agg.* terribile, orrendo.
direct *agg.* diretto.
to **direct** *vt.* **1.** dirigere **2.** ordinare.
direction *s.* **1.** direzione **2.** indicazione.
directional *agg.* direzionale.
directive *agg.* direttivo. ◆ **directive** *s.* direttiva.
directly *avv.* **1.** direttamente **2.** subito.
director *s.* **1.** direttore **2.** regista.
directorial *agg.* direttivo.
directory *agg.* direttivo. ◆ **directory** *s.* **1.** (*tel.*) guida **2.** (*amer.*) consiglio di amministrazione.
direful *agg.* orrendo.
dirge *s.* canto funebre.
diriment *agg.* dirimento.
dirt *s.* sporcizia.
dirtiness *s.* sozzura.
dirty *agg.* **1.** sporco **2.** brutto **3.** sboccato.
to **dirty** *vt.* sporcare. ◆ to **dirty** *vi.* sporcarsi.
disability *s.* **1.** incapacità **2.** invalidità.
to **disable** *vt.* rendere incapace, inabile.
to **disabuse** *vt.* disingannare.
to **disaccustom** *vt.* disabituare.
disadvantage *s.* svantaggio.
disadvantageous *agg.* svantaggioso.
to **disagree** *vi.* dissentire.
disagreeable *agg.* sgradevole.
disagreeableness *s.* sgradevolezza.
disagreement *s.* dissenso.
to **disappear** *vi.* scomparire.
disappearance *s.* sparizione.
to **disappoint** *vt.* deludere.
disappointingly *avv.* in modo deludente.
disappointment *s.* delusione.
disapprobation, disapproval *s.* disapprovazione.
to **disapprove** *vt. e vi.* disapprovare.
disapprovingly *avv.* con disapprovazione.
to **disarm** *vt. e vi.* disarmare.
disarmament *s.* disarmo.
to **disarrange** *vt.* scompigliare.
disarrangement *s.* scompiglio.
disarray *s.* scompiglio, confusione.

to **disassemble** *vt.* smontare.
disassembling *s.* smontaggio.
disaster *s.* disastro.
disastrous *agg.* disastroso.
to **disavow** *vt.* ripudiare.
to **disband** *vt.* sciogliere. ◆ to **disband** *vi.* sbandarsi.
disbelief *s.* incredulità.
to **disbelieve** *vt.* e *vi.* non credere.
disbeliever *s.* incredulo.
disbursement *s.* pagamento.
to **discard** *vt.* scartare.
to **discern** *vt.* discernere.
discernible *agg.* visibile.
discernment *s.* discernimento.
discharge *s.* 1. scarico 2. scarica 3. congedo 4. assoluzione 5. liberazione 6. pagamento.
to **discharge** *vt.* 1. scaricare 2. congedare 3. assolvere 4. liberare. ◆ to **discharge** *vi.* scaricarsi.
disciple *s.* discepolo.
disciplinable *agg.* disciplinabile.
disciplinary *agg.* disciplinare.
discipline *s.* disciplina.
to **disclaim** *vt.* rifiutare, declinare (*responsabilità*).
disclaimer *s.* rinuncia, rifiuto.
to **disclose** *vt.* svelare.
disclosure *s.* rivelazione.
discoid *agg.* e *s.* discoide.
to **discolour** *vt.* scolorire. ◆ to **discolour** *vi.* scolorirsi.
discolouration *s.* scoloramento.
to **discomfit** *vt.* 1. sconfiggere 2. disorientare.
discomfort *vt.* mettere a disagio.
to **discompose** *vt.* agitare.
to **disconcert** *vt.* turbare.
to **disconnect** *vt.* separare, disunire.
disconnected *agg.* 1. sconnesso 2. disinnestato.
disconnectedness *s.* sconnessione.
disconsolate *agg.* sconsolato.
discontent *s.* scontento.
to **discontinue** *vt.* e *vi.* cessare.
discontinuity *s.* discontinuità.
discontinuous *agg.* discontinuo.
discord *s.* 1. discordia, dissenso 2. (*mus.*) dissonanza.
discordance *s.* 1. disaccordo 2. discordanza (*di suoni*).
discordant *agg.* discorde.
discordantly *avv.* in disaccordo.
discount *s.* sconto || *at a* —, sottocosto.
to **discount** *vt.* 1. scontare 2. tenere in poco conto.

discountable *agg.* 1. scontabile 2. poco attendibile.
to **discourage** *vt.* scoraggiare.
discouragement *s.* scoraggiamento.
to **discover** *vt.* scoprire.
discoverer *s.* scopritore.
discovery *s.* scoperta.
discredit *s.* 1. discredito 2. dubbio.
to **discredit** *vt.* 1. screditare 2. mettere in dubbio.
discreditable *agg.* vergognoso, infamante.
discreet *agg.* prudente, discreto.
discrepancy *s.* disaccordo.
discrete *agg.* separato, distinto.
discretion *s.* 1. discrezione 2. saggezza.
discretionary *agg.* discrezionale.
discriminate *agg.* discriminato.
to **discriminate** *vt.* e *vi.* discriminare.
discriminating *agg.* 1. sagace 2. discriminante.
discrimination *s.* 1. discriminazione 2. discernimento.
discursive *agg.* divagante.
discus *s.* disco || — *-thrower*, discobolo.
to **discuss** *vt.* discutere.
discussion *s.* discussione.
disdain *s.* sdegno.
to **disdain** *vt.* disdegnare.
disdainful *agg.* sdegnoso.
disease *s.* malattia.
to **disembark** *vt.* e *vi.* sbarcare.
to **disembarrass** *vt.* sbarazzare.
to **disembody** *vt.* 1. disincarnare 2. congedare.
to **disembowel** *vt.* sventrare.
disembowelment *s.* sventramento.
to **disenchant** *vt.* disincantare.
disenchantment *s.* disincanto.
to **disengage** *vt.* 1. disimpegnare 2. disinnestare. ◆ to **disengage** *vi.* liberarsi.
disengagement *s.* 1. liberazione 2. disinnesto.
to **disentangle** *vt.* districare. ◆ to **disentangle** *vi.* districarsi.
disentanglement *s.* districamento.
disesteem *s.* disistima.
to **disesteem** *vt.* disprezzare.
disfavour *s.* 1. disgrazia 2. disapprovazione.
to **disfigure** *vt.* sfigurare.
disfigurement *s.* deturpamento.
to **disfranchise** *vt.* privare dei diritti (*civili o di voto*).
to **disgorge** *vt.* 1. emettere 2. vomi-

tare (*anche fig.*).

disgrace *s*. **1.** vergogna **2.** disgrazia.

to **disgrace** *vt*. disonorare.

disgraceful *agg*. vergognoso.

disgregation *s*. disgregazione.

disguise *s*. travestimento || *in* —, travestito, camuffato.

to **disguise** *vt*. mascherare.

disgust *s*. disgusto.

to **disgust** *vt*. disgustare.

disgustedly *avv*. con disgusto.

disgustful, disgusting *agg*. disgustoso.

dish *s*. **1.** piatto **2.** vivanda || --washer, lavapiatti.

to **dish** *vt*. servire || *to* — *up*, servire in tavola.

to **disharmonize** *vt*. disarmonizzare.

to **dishearten** *vt*. scoraggiare.

disheartenment *s*. scoraggiamento.

to **dishevel** *vt*. arruffare.

dishonest *agg*. disonesto.

dishonesty *s*. disonestà.

dishonour *s*. **1.** disonore **2.** mancato pagamento.

to **dishonour** *vt*. **1.** disonorare **2.** rifiutare di pagare.

dishonourable *agg*. disonorevole.

dishonourableness *s*. disonorabilità.

disillusion(ment) *s*. disillusione.

to **disinfect** *vt*. disinfettare.

disinfectant *s*. disinfettante.

disinfection *s*. disinfezione.

to **disinfest** *vt*. disinfestare.

disinfestation *s*. disinfestazione.

to **disinherit** *vt*. diseredare.

to **disintegrate** *vt*. disintegrare. ♦ to **disintegrate** *vi*. disintegrarsi.

disintegration *s*. disintegrazione.

disintegrator *s*. disintegratore.

to **disinter** *vt*. dissotterrare.

disinterested *agg*. disinteressato.

disinterment *s*. dissotterramento.

to **disjoin** *vt*. disgiungere. ♦ to **disjoin** *vi*. disgiungersi.

to **disjoint** *vt*. **1.** disgregare **2.** disarticolare. ♦ to **disjoint** *vi*. disgregarsi.

disjunction *s*. separazione.

disjunctive *agg*. disgiuntivo.

disjunctively *avv*. disgiuntamente.

disk *s*. disco.

dislike *s*. avversione.

to **dislike** *vt*. detestare, provar avversione per.

to **dislocate** *vt*. **1.** spostare **2.** slogare **3.** disorganizzare.

dislocation *s*. **1.** dislocazione **2.** slogatura **3.** disorganizzazione.

to **dislodge** *vt*. sloggiare.

disloyal *agg*. sleale.

disloyalty *s*. slealtà.

dismal *agg*. tetro.

to **dismantle** *vt*. smantellare.

dismantlement *s*. smantellamento.

to **dismast** *vt*. (*mar*.) disalberare.

dismay *s*. costernazione.

to **dismay** *vt*. costernare.

to **dismember** *vt*. smembrare.

dismemberment *s*. smembramento.

to **dismiss** *vt*. **1.** congedare **2.** licenziare **3.** bandire.

dismissal *s*. **1.** congedo **2.** licenziamento **3.** destituzione **4.** rigetto.

to **dismount** *vt. e vi*. smontare.

disobedience *s*. disubbidienza.

disobedient *agg*. disubbidiente.

to **disobey** *vt*. disubbidire.

to **disoblige** *vt*. essere scortese con.

disobliging *agg*. scortese.

disorder *s*. **1.** disordine **2.** disturbo.

to **disorder** *vt*. **1.** scompigliare **2.** disturbare.

disorderly *agg*. **1.** disordinato **2.** turbolento.

disorganization *s*. disorganizzazione.

to **disorganize** *vt*. disorganizzare.

to **disorient(ate)** *vt*. disorientare.

disorientation *s*. disorientamento.

to **disown** *vt*. rinnegare.

disowning *s*. rinnegamento.

to **disparage** *vt*. **1.** deprezzare **2.** screditare.

disparagement *s*. **1.** deprezzamento **2.** denigrazione.

disparaging *agg*. **1.** sprezzante **2.** denigratorio.

disparate *agg*. disparato.

disparity *s*. disparità.

dispassionate *agg*. spassionato.

dispatch *s*. **1.** spedizione **2.** dispaccio **3.** disbrigo **4.** celerità.

to **dispatch** *vt*. **1.** spedire **2.** sbrigare.

to **dispel** *vt*. dissipare.

dispensary *s*. dispensario.

dispensation *s*. **1.** (*eccl*.) dispensa **2.** distribuzione **3.** beneficio.

to **dispense** *vt*. dispensare. ♦ to **dispense** *vi*. fare a meno di: *to* — *with so.*, fare a meno di qu.

dispersal *s*. dispersione.

to **disperse** *vt*. disperdere. ♦ to **disperse** *vi*. disperdersi.

dispersion *s*. dispersione.

dispersive *agg.* dispersivo.

dispirited *agg.* depresso.

to displace *vt.* 1. spostare 2. destituire.

displacement *s.* 1. spostamento 2. sostituzione 3. (*mar.*) dislocamento.

display *s.* mostra, esibizione.

to display *vt.* mostrare, esporre.

to displease *vt.* dispiacere.

displeasing *agg.* spiacevole.

displeasure *s.* dispiacere.

disposal *s.* 1. disposizione 2. cessione.

to dispose *vt. e vi.* disporre || *to — of,* disfarsi di, smerciare.

disposition *s.* 1. disposizione 2. indole.

to dispossess *vt.* spogliare.

dispossession *s.* 1. spoliazione 2. (*giur.*) esproprio.

disproportion *s.* sproporzione.

disproportionate, disproportioned *agg.* sproporzionato.

to disprove *vt.* 1. confutare 2. dimostrare la falsità di.

disputable *agg.* discutibile.

dispute *s.* controversia, disputa.

to dispute *vt.* 1. disputare 2. contestare.

disqualification *s.* 1. incapacità 2. (*giur.*) interdizione 3. squalifica.

to disqualify *vt.* 1. rendere incapace 2. (*giur.*) interdire 3. squalificare.

disquieting *agg.* inquietante.

disquisition *s.* 1. disquisizione 2. inchiesta.

disregard *s.* noncuranza.

to disregard *vt.* ignorare.

disreputable *agg.* 1. sconveniente 2. screditato.

disreputably *avv.* disonorevolmente.

disrepute *s.* discredito.

disrespectful *agg.* irrispettoso.

to disrobe *vt.* svestire. ♦ **to disrobe** *vi.* svestirsi.

disruption *s.* rottura.

disruptive *agg.* 1. che sembra 2. dirompente.

dissatisfaction *s.* insoddisfazione.

dissatisfactory *agg.* insoddisfacente.

dissatisfied *agg.* scontento.

to dissatisfy *vt.* scontentare.

to dissect *vt.* sezionare.

dissection *s.* 1. sezionamento 2. parte sezionata.

to dissemble *vt. e vi.* dissimulare,

ignorare.

dissembling *s.* dissimulazione. ♦ **dissembling** *agg.* ipocrita.

dissemblingly *avv.* ingannevolmente.

to disseminate *vt.* (dis)seminare.

dissemination *s.* disseminazione.

disseminator *s.* propagatore.

dissension *s.* divergenza.

dissent *s.* 1. dissenso 2. (*relig.*) separazione, scisma.

to dissent *vi.* dissentire.

dissenter *s.* dissidente.

dissenting *agg.* dissenziente.

to dissertate *vi.* dissertare.

dissertation *s.* dissertazione.

dissertator *s.* dissertatore.

disservice *s.* cattivo servizio.

to dissever *vt.* scindere. ♦ **to dissever** *vi.* scindersi.

dissidence *s.* dissidio.

dissident *agg. e s.* dissidente.

dissimilar *agg.* dissimile.

dissimilarity *s.* dissomiglianza.

dissimilation *s.* dissimilazione.

to dissimulate *vt. e vi.* dissimulare.

dissimulation *s.* dissimulazione.

dissimulator *s.* dissimulatore.

to dissipate *vt.* dissipare. ♦ **to dissipate** *vi.* dissiparsi.

dissipation *s.* dissipazione.

dissociable *agg.* 1. dissociabile 2. riservato.

to dissociate *vt.* dissociare. ♦ **to dissociate** *vi.* dissociarsi.

dissociation *s.* 1. dissociazione 2. sdoppiamento (*della personalità*).

dissolubility *s.* dissolubilità.

dissoluble *agg.* dissolubile.

dissolute *agg.* dissoluto.

dissoluteness *s.* dissolutezza.

dissolution *s.* dissoluzione.

to dissolve *vt.* dissolvere. ♦ **to dissolve** *vi.* dissolversi.

dissolvent *agg. e s.* dissolvente.

dissonance *s.* dissonanza.

dissonant *agg.* dissonante.

to dissuade *vt.* dissuadere.

dissuasion *s.* dissuasione.

dissyllabic *agg.* bisillabico.

dissyllable *s.* bisillabo.

dissymmetry *s.* asimmetria.

distaff *s.* conocchia.

distance *s.* distanza || *long — call,* telefonata interurbana; *at a —,* da lontano.

distant *agg.* 1. lontano 2. riservato.

distantly *avv.* (da) lontano.

distaste *s.* ripugnanza.

distasteful *agg.* repellente.

distemper[1] *s.* **1.** turbamento fisico **2.** cimurro **3.** tumulto.

distemper[2] *s.* tempera.

to distend *vt.* distendere. ♦ **to distend** *vi.* distendersi.

to distil(l) *vt.* e *vi.* (di)stillare.

distillate *s.* distillato.

distillation *s.* distillazione.

distiller *s.* distillatore.

distillery *s.* distilleria.

distinct *agg.* distinto.

distinction *s.* distinzione.

distinctive *agg.* distintivo.

to distinguish *vt.* e *vi.* distinguere.

distinguished *agg.* **1.** distinto **2.** illustre.

to distort *vt.* distorcere.

distortion *s.* distorsione.

to distract *vt.* **1.** distrarre **2.** turbare, far impazzire.

distraction *s.* **1.** distrazione **2.** follia: *to love to —*, amare alla follia.

to distrain *vi.* sequestrare.

distrait *agg.* distratto, smarrito.

distraught *agg.* **1.** folle **2.** sconvolto.

distress *s.* **1.** angoscia **2.** pericolo **3.** sequestro.

to distress *vt.* **1.** affliggere **2.** sequestrare.

distressful *agg.* penoso.

distributable *agg.* distribuibile.

to distribute *vt.* distribuire.

distribution *s.* distribuzione.

distributive *agg.* distributivo.

distributor *s.* distributore.

district *s.* distretto.

distrust *s.* diffidenza.

to distrust *vt.* diffidare di.

distrustful *agg.* diffidente.

to disturb *vt.* **1.** disturbare **2.** turbare.

disturbance *s.* agitazione.

disturber *s.* disturbatore.

disunion *s.* separazione.

to disunite *vt.* disunire. ♦ **to disunite** *vi.* separarsi.

disunited *agg.* disunito.

disuse *s.* disuso.

disused *agg.* disusato.

ditch *s.* fosso || *to die in the last —*, resistere ad oltranza.

to ditch *vi.* scavare fossi.

dithyramb *s.* ditirambo.

dithyrambic *agg.* ditirambico.

ditty *s.* **1.** canzone **2.** poemetto.

diuretic *agg.* e *s.* diuretico.

diurnal *agg.* **1.** diurno **2.** quotidiano.

diuturnal *agg.* diuturno.

diuturnity *s.* diuturnità.

divan *s.* divano.

dive *s.* **1.** tuffo **2.** (*aer.*) picchiata.

to dive *vi.* **1.** tuffarsi **2.** (*aer.*) lanciarsi in picchiata.

diver *s.* **1.** tuffatore **2.** palombaro.

to diverge *vi.* divergere.

divergence *s.* divergenza.

divergent *agg.* divergente.

diverse *agg.* **1.** diverso **2.** mutevole.

to diversify *vt.* rendere diverso.

diversion *s.* **1.** diversione **2.** passatempo.

diversity *s.* diversità.

to divert *vt.* **1.** deviare **2.** divertire.

to divest *vt.* spogliare.

to divide *vt.* dividere. ♦ **to divide** *vi.* dividersi.

dividend *s.* dividendo.

dividing *s.* divisione.

divination *s.* divinazione.

divinatory *agg.* divinatorio.

divine *agg.* divino. ♦ **divine** *s.* (*eccl.*) teologo.

to divine *vt.* e *vi.* predire.

diviner *s.* indovino || *water —*, rabdomante.

diving *s.* tuffo || *— -bell*, campana subacquea; *— -board*, trampolino.

divining *s.* divinazione.

divinity *s.* **1.** divinità **2.** teologia.

divisibility *s.* divisibilità.

divisible *agg.* divisibile.

division *s.* divisione.

divisional *agg.* di divisione.

divisor *s.* divisore.

divorce *s.* divorzio.

to divorce *vt.* divorziare.

divulgation *s.* divulgazione.

to divulge *vt.* divulgare.

divulger *s.* divulgatore.

dizzily *avv.* vertiginosamente.

dizziness *s.* vertigine.

dizzy *agg.* **1.** vertiginoso **2.** preso da vertigine **3.** stordito.

to do (did, done) *vt.* e *vi.* **1.** (*v. aus.* in frasi *int.*, *neg.*, *int.-neg.*) *— you understand English?*, capisci l'inglese?; *I do not (I don't*), non capisco; *he does not (he doesn't) speak English*, non parla l'inglese **2.** (*uso enfatico*) *I do study!*, studio veramente! **3.** (*sostitutivo*) *he said he would come and he did*, disse che sarebbe venuto e venne **4.** fare (*in senso generale, astratto*) *what are you doing?*, che cosa stai facendo?; *to*

— *one's duty*, fare il proprio dovere **3**. bastare: *that will do*, ciò basta **6**. addirsi, convenire: *this house will do me*, questa casa mi va bene ‖ *to* — *without*, fare a meno.

docile *agg.* docile.

docility *s.* docilità.

dock[1] *s.* bacino: *dry*— —, bacino di carenaggio ‖ — *-master*, capitano di porto; *wet*— —, darsena.

dock[2] *s.* banco degli imputati (*in tribunale*).

docker *s.* scaricatore.

docket *s.* **1**. (*giur.*) estratto verbale **2**. etichetta.

dockyard *s.* cantiere.

doctor *s.* dottore.

doctoral *agg.* dottorale.

doctorate *s.* dottorato.

doctrinaire *agg.* e *s.* dottrinario.

doctrinal *agg.* dottrinale.

doctrine *s.* dottrina.

document *s.* documento.

to document *vt.* documentare.

documentary *agg.* e *s.* documentario.

documentation *s.* documentazione.

to dodder *vi.* tremare, vacillare.

dodecagon *s.* dodecagono.

dodecahedron *s.* dodecaedro.

dodge *s.* **1**. schivata **2**. balzo.

to dodge *vt.* schivare. ♦ **to dodge** *vi.* scansarsi.

doe *s.* femmina (*di daino, cervo ecc.*).

doer *s.* chi agisce, chi fa.

dog *s.* **1**. cane **2**. (*mecc.*) gancio ‖ — *-cart*, calesse; — *catcher*, accalappiacani; — *-days*, giorni di canicola; — *-ear*, orecchia (*a una pagina*); — *-tired*, stanco morto.

to dog *vt.* inseguire.

dogged *agg.* ostinato.

doggerel *s.* filastrocca.

dogmatic(al) *agg.* dogmatico.

dogmatism *s.* dogmatismo.

doily *s.* tovagliolino.

doings *s. pl.* azioni, imprese.

dole *s.* **1**. ripartizione **2**. sussidio.

doleful *agg.* triste.

dolichocephalic *agg.* dolicocefalo.

doll *s.* bambola.

dollar *s.* dollaro.

dolly *s.* **1**. bambola **2**. (*cine*) carrello.

dolomitic *agg.* dolomitico.

dolphin *s.* **1**. delfino **2**. boa.

dolt *s.* stupido.

domain *s.* dominio.

dome *s.* cupola.

domestic *agg.* **1**. domestico **2**. nazionale. ♦ **domestic** *s.* domestico.

domicile *s.* domicilio.

domiciliary *agg.* domiciliare.

dominant *agg.* dominante.

to dominate *vt.* e *vi.* dominare.

domination *s.* dominazione.

domineering *agg.* dispotico.

Dominican *agg.* e *s.* domenicano.

dominion *s.* dominio, possedimento (*di territori*).

donation *s.* donazione.

donative *s.* dono.

done V. *to do* ‖ *over*— —, troppo cotto; *under*— —, poco cotto.

donjon *s.* torrione.

donkey *s.* asino.

donor *s.* donatore.

doodle *s.* ghirigoro.

doom *s.* **1**. destino **2**. giudizio.

to doom *vt.* condannare.

doomsday *s.* giudizio universale.

door *s.* porta, portiera ‖ — *-keeper*, portinaio; — *-post*, stipite; — *-way*, soglia.

dope *s.* **1**. vernice **2**. stupefacente.

to dope *vt.* **1**. verniciare **2**. drogare.

doping *s.* drogaggio.

Doric *agg.* dorico.

dormer (window) *s.* abbaino.

dormitory *s.* dormitorio.

dormouse *s.* (*pl.* dormice) ghiro.

dorsal *agg.* dorsale.

dosage *s.* dosaggio.

to dose *vt.* **1**. dosare **2**. adulterare.

dosimeter *s.* dosatore.

dossal *s.* dossale.

dossier *s.* incartamento.

dot *s.* punto, puntino.

to dot *vt.* punteggiare.

dotage *s.* **1**. rimbambimento **2**. infatuazione.

dotal *agg.* dotale.

doting *agg.* **1**. senile **2**. infatuato. ♦ **doting** *s.* senilità.

double *agg.* doppio. ♦ **double** *s.* **1**. doppio **2**. (*cine*) controfigura. ♦ **double** *avv.* **1**. doppiamente **2**. in due.

to double *vt.* **1**. raddoppiare **2**. doppiare **3**. piegare. ♦ **to double** *vi.* **1**. raddoppiarsi **2**. piegarsi.

double-dealing *s.* imbroglio.

doubleness *s.* doppiezza.

doubling *s.* raddoppiamento.

doubly *avv.* doppiamente.

doubt *s.* dubbio ‖ *no* —, indubbiamente.

to doubt *vt.* e *vi.* dubitare.

doubtful *agg.* incerto, dubbio.
doubtfulness *s.* dubbiosità.
doubtless *agg.* indubbio. ◆ **doubtless** *avv.* indubbiamente.
dough *s.* pasta.
dove *s.* colomba || — *-cot(e)*, colombaia.
dowdy *agg.* sciatto.
dower *s.* dote.
down[1] *s.* 1. duna 2. collina.
down[2] *s.* 1. piumino 2. lanugine.
down[3] *agg.* 1. diretto verso il basso 2. depresso.
down[4] *avv.* (in) giù || — *with!*, abbasso: — *with the tyrant!*, abbasso il tiranno! ◆ **down** *prep.* giù per.
to down *vt.* abbattere, rovesciare.
downcast *agg.* abbattuto.
downfall *s.* rovescio.
downhearted *agg.* scoraggiato.
downhill *agg.* discendente, inclinato. ◆ **downhill** *avv.* in discesa.
downpour *s.* acquazzone.
downright *agg.* vero, sincero. ◆ **downright** *avv.* completamente.
downstairs *avv.* giù. ◆ **downstairs** *agg.* dabbasso. ◆ **downstairs** *s.* pianterreno.
downtrodden *agg.* calpestato, oppresso.
downward *agg.* in giù, discendente.
downward(s) *avv.* in giù.
downy[1] *agg.* ondulato.
downy[2] *agg.* 1. lanuginoso 2. morbido.
dowry *s.* dote.
dowser *s.* rabdomante.
doze *s.* sonnellino.
to doze *vi.* sonnecchiare.
dozen *s.* dozzina.
drab *s.* 1. sciattona 2. sgualdrina.
draff *s.* feccia.
draft *s.* 1. tiro 2. sorso 3. abbozzo 4. corrente d'aria 5. (*comm.*) tratta 6. (*mar.*) pescaggio.
to draft *vt.* 1. tirare 2. abbozzare.
drag *s.* 1. erpice 2. (*mar.*) draga 3. ostacolo.
to drag *vt.* 1. trascinare 2. dragare. ◆ **to drag** *vi.* trascinarsi || — *on*, tirare in lungo.
to draggle *vt.* inzaccherare. ◆ **to draggle** *vi.* inzaccherarsi.
dragon *s.* drago || *-fly*, libellula.
drain *s.* 1. canale, fogna 2. fuga.
to drain *vt.* prosciugare. ◆ **to drain** *vi.* 1. prosciugarsi 2. defluire.
drainage *s.* 1. fognatura 2. drenaggio.

draining *s.* 1. scolatura 2. drenaggio.
dram *s.* dramma (*unità di peso*).
drama *s.* dramma.
dramatic(al) *agg.* drammatico.
dramatics *s. pl.* produzioni drammatiche (*di dilettanti*).
dramatist *s.* drammaturgo.
to dramatize *vt. e vi.* drammatizzare.
dramaturgy *s.* drammaturgia.
drank V. *to drink.*
to drape *vt.* drappeggiare.
draper *s.* negoziante di tessuti.
drapery *s.* 1. tessuti 2. drappeggi.
drastic *agg.* drastico.
draught *s.* V. *draft.* ◆ **draughts** *s. pl.* gioco della dama (*sing.*).
draught-board *s.* scacchiera.
draw *s.* 1. tiro 2. estrazione 3. attrazione.
to draw (**drew, drawn**) *vt.* 1. tirare 2. attirare 3. disegnare 4. estrarre 5. (*comm.*) emettere || *to — up*, compilare. ◆ **to draw** (**drew, drawn**) *vi.* tirarsi || *to — on*, avvicinarsi; *to — in*, ritirarsi; *to — up*, fermarsi.
drawback *s.* ostacolo.
drawbridge *s.* ponte levatoio.
drawer *s.* 1. estrattore 2. disegnatore 3. cassetto.
drawers *s. pl.* mutande.
drawing *s.* 1. disegno 2. estrazione 3. attrazione || *— -pen*, tiralinee; *— -pin*, puntina da disegno.
drawing-room *s.* salotto.
to drawl *vt.* strascicare la voce.
drawn V. *to draw.*
dread *s.* spavento.
dreadful *agg.* terribile.
dreadnought *s.* 1. impavido 2. (*mar.*) corazzata.
dream *s.* sogno.
to dream (**dreamt, dreamt**) (*anche reg.*) *vt. e vi.* sognare.
dreamer *s.* sognatore.
dreamt V. *to dream.*
dreamless *agg.* senza sogni.
dreamy *agg.* 1. sognante 2. vago.
dreariness *s.* tristezza.
dreary *agg.* tetro, squallido.
dredge *s.* draga.
to dredge[1] *vt. e vi.* dragare.
to dredge[2] *vt.* cospargere, spolverizzare.
dredger[1] *s.* draga.
dredger[2] *s.* spolverizzatore.
dredging *s.* dragaggio.

dregs s. pl. 1. feccia (sing.) 2. sedimento (sing.).

to **drench** vt. inzuppare || to get drenched, inzupparsi.

dress s. abito, abbigliamento.

to **dress** vt. 1. vestire 2. bendare 3. condire, rifinire. ♦ to **dress** vi. vestirsi.

dressing s. 1. abbigliamento 2. medicazione 3. condimento || —-gown, vestaglia; —-table, toletta.

dressmaker s. sarta.

dressmaking s. sartoria.

drew V. to draw.

dribble s. 1. gocciolamento 2. (sport) palleggio.

to **dribble** vt. e vi. 1. stillare 2. (sport) palleggiare.

dribbling s. V. dribble.

drier s. essiccatore.

drift s. 1. spinta 2. deriva 3. raffica 4. (fig.) significato.

to **drift** vt. sospingere. ♦ to **drift** vi. andare alla deriva, essere trascinato.

drill s. 1. trapano, trivella 2. esercitazione.

to **drill** vt. 1. trapanare, trivellare 2. esercitare.

drilling s. 1. trapanazione, trivellazione 2. esercitazione || —-machine, trapano.

drink s. 1. il bere 2. bevanda.

to **drink (drank, drunk)** vt. e vi. bere.

drinkable agg. bevibile.

drinker s. bevitore.

drinking s. il bere.

drip s. gocciolamento.

to **drip** vt. e vi. gocciolare.

dripping s. gocciolìo.

drive s. 1. gita (in auto) 2. viale (carrozzabile) 3. spinta.

to **drive (drove, driven)** vt. 1. condurre 2. guidare 3. azionare || to — away, scacciare; to — in, conficcare. ♦ to **drive (drove, driven)** vi. andare (in veicolo) || to — off, partire (in veicolo); to — up, arrivare (in veicolo).

drive-in s. cinema, banca ecc. in cui si entra in auto.

driver s. conducente.

driving s. 1. guida 2. comando.

drizzle s. pioggerella.

to **drizzle** vi. piovigginare.

drizzly agg. piovigginoso.

droll agg. buffo.

drollery s. 1. buffoneria 2. scherzo.

dromedary s. dromedario.

drone s. 1. fuco 2. ronzio.

to **drone** vt. e vi. ronzare.

to **droop** vt. abbassare. ♦ to **droop** vi. affosciarsi, languire.

drooping agg. 1. pendente, abbassato 2. abbattuto.

drop s. 1. goccia 2. caduta 3. ribasso.

to **drop** vt. lasciar cadere. ♦ to **drop** vi. cadere || to — in, fare una visitina; to — away, scomparire.

dropper s. contagocce.

dropsical agg. idropico.

dropsy s. idropisia.

dross s. scoria.

drought s. siccità.

drove V. to drive.

to **drown** vt. 1. annegare 2. smorzare. ♦ to **drown** vi. annegare.

drowning s. annegamento.

to **drowse** vi. sonnecchiare, assopirsi.

drowsily avv. in modo sonnolento.

drowsiness s. sonnolenza.

drowsy agg. sonnolento.

to **drub** vt. percuotere, bastonare.

drudge s. sgobbone.

to **drudge** vi. sfacchinare.

drudgery s. lavoro faticoso.

drug s. 1. medicina 2. droga || —-store, farmacia (in cui si vendono articoli vari).

to **drug** vt. drogare.

druggist s. farmacista.

Druid s. druido.

drum s. 1. tamburo 2. timpano.

to **drum** vi. suonare il tamburo. ♦ to **drum** vt. (fig.) inculcare.

drummer s. tamburino.

drumming s. tamburreggiamento.

drunk V. to drink. ♦ **drunk** agg. ubriaco.

drunkard s. ubriacone.

drunken agg. ubriaco.

drunkenness s. ubriachezza.

dry agg. asciutto, arido, secco || — cleaning, lavaggio a secco.

to **dry** vt. 1. seccare 2. asciugare. ♦ to **dry** vi. 1. seccarsi 2. asciugarsi || to — up, ammutolire.

dryad s. driade.

drying agg. essiccante. ♦ **drying** s. essiccamento.

dual agg. duplice.

dualism s. dualismo.

dualist s. dualista.

dualistic agg. dualistico.

duality s. dualità.

to dub[1] vt. creare cavaliere.

to dub[2] vt. (cine) doppiare.

dubbing s. doppiaggio.

dubious agg. 1. dubbio 2. dubbioso.

dubiousness s. dubbiosità.

dubitative agg. dubitativo.

ducal agg. ducale.

duchess s. duchessa.

duchy s. ducato.

duck[1] s. anitra.

duck[2] s. tela.

duck[3] s. tuffo.

to duck vt. 1. tuffare 2. piegare. ♦ to duck vi. 1. tuffarsi 2. piegarsi.

duckling s. anatroccolo.

duct s. condotto.

ductile agg. duttile.

ductility s. duttilità.

due agg. e s. dovuto || to be —, dover arrivare; to fall —, scadere.

duel s. duello.

to duel vi. duella.e.

duet s. duetto.

dug V. to dig.

duke s. duca.

dukedom s. ducato.

dull agg. 1. tardo, sciocco 2. sordo 3. triste 4. noioso 5. opaco.

to dull vt. 1. istupidire 2. intorpidire 3. smorzare. ♦ to dull vi. 1. istupidirsi 2. intorpidirsi 3. smorzarsi.

dullard s. imbecille.

dul(l)ness s. 1. lentezza 2. noia 3. opacità 4. ottusità.

dully avv. 1. ottusamente 2. lentamente 3. in modo noioso 4. debolmente.

duly avv. debitamente.

dumb agg. muto || — -show, pantomima.

to dumbfound vt. confondere.

dumbness s. mutismo.

dumb-waiter s. montavivande.

dummy agg. 1. muto 2. falso. ♦ dummy s. fantoccio.

dump s. 1. colpo sordo 2. ammasso.

dumping s. « dumping » (tipo di vendita concorrenziale sui mercati esteri).

dunce s. ignorante.

dune s. duna.

dung s. 1. sterco 2. letame.

dungarees s. pl. tuta (da lavoro) (sing.).

dungeon s. 1. torrione 2. prigione sotterranea.

dunghill s. letamaio.

to dunk vt. e vi. inzuppare.

duodenal agg. duodenale.

duodenum s. (pl. -na) duodeno.

dupe s. gonzo.

duplex agg. duplice.

duplicate agg. doppio. ♦ duplicate s. duplicato.

to duplicate vt. duplicare.

duplication s. 1. raddoppiamento 2. riproduzione.

duplicator s. copialettere.

duplicity s. doppiezza.

durability s. durata.

durable agg. durevole.

duralumin s. duralluminio.

duration s. durata.

duress s. 1. prigionia 2. coercizione.

during prep. durante.

durst V. dare.

dusk s. 1. oscurità 2. crepuscolo.

dusky agg. oscuro.

dust s. polvere || — -bin, pattumiera.

to dust vt. 1. impolverare 2. spolverare. ♦ to dust vi. impolverarsi.

duster s. 1. strofinaccio (per la polvere) 2. polverizzatore.

dustman s. spazzino.

dusty agg. polveroso.

Dutch agg. olandese.

Dutchman s. olandese.

dutiful agg. rispettoso.

duty s. 1. ubbidienza 2. dovere 3. tassa.

duumvirate s. duumvirato.

dwarf s. nano.

dwarfish agg. nano.

to dwell (dwelt, dwelt) vi. 1. abitare 2. fermarsi.

dweller s. abitatore.

dwelling s. abitazione.

dwelt V. to dwell.

dye s. tintura.

to dye vt. tingere. ♦ to dye vi. tingersi.

dyer s. tintore.

dyerworks s. pl. tintoria (sing.).

dying agg. morente.

dynamic(al) agg. dinamico.

dynamics s. dinamica.

dynamism s. dinamismo.

dynamite s. dinamite.

dynamiter s. dinamitardo.

dynamo s. dinamo.

dynamometer s. dinamometro.

dynast s. dinasta.

dynastic(al) agg. dinastico.

dynasty s. dinastia.

dyne s. dina.

dysenteric *agg.* dissenterico.
dysentery *s.* dissenteria.
dyspepsia *s.* dispepsia.
dyspeptic(al) *agg.* dispeptico.

E

E (*mus.*) mi.
each *agg.* ogni, ciascuno. ♦ **each** *pron.* ognuno, ciascuno || — *other*, l'un l'altro.
eager *agg.* 1. ardente, appassionato 2. avido, desideroso.
eagerly *avv.* 1. ardentemente 2. avidamente.
eagerness *s.* 1. ardore 2. impazienza, premura.
eagle *s.* aquila.
ear[1] orecchio || — *-ache* mal d'orecchi — *-drum;* timpano; — *-ring,* orecchino; — *-vax,* cerume; *within* — *-shot,* a portata di voce.
ear[2] *s.* spiga (*di grano*).
earl *s.* conte.
earldom *s.* 1. titolo di conte 2. contea.
early *agg.* 1. primo, il principio, la prima parte (*di qualsiasi tempo*) 2. mattiniero 3. prematuro 4. remoto || — *train,* treno del primo mattino.
early *avv.* 1. presto, di buon'ora, per tempo 2. al principio.
earmark *s.* 1. marchio, caratteristica 2. (*comm.*) contrassegno.
to earn *vt.* guadagnare, meritare.
earnest *agg.* 1. serio, zelante 2. ardente. ♦ **earnest** *s.* caparra, pegno.
earnestly *avv.* 1. seriamente 2. con ardore.
earnestness *s.* 1. serietà 2. ardore.
earnings *s. pl.* 1. guadagni 2. (*comm.*) utili.
earth *s.* 1. terra, mondo 2. terreno.
earth-bound *agg.* radicato, attaccato ai beni terreni.
earthen *agg.* di terra, di terracotta.
earthenware *s.* terraglia.
earthly *agg.* terrestre.
earthquake *s.* terremoto.
earthworm *s.* lombrico.
earthy *agg.* terroso, di terra.
ease *s.* 1. tranquillità (*di spirito*),

benessere 2. facilità, agevolezza 3. sollievo.
to ease *vt. e vi.* 1. alleviare, calmare 2. liberare, alleggerire.
easeful *agg.* tranquillo.
easel *s.* cavalletto, telaio.
easily *avv.* 1. facilmente 2. comodamente.
easiness *s.* 1. comodità, benessere 2. facilità.
east *s.* est, oriente: *the Far East,* l'Estremo Oriente. ♦ **east** *avv.* ad est, verso est.
Easter *s.* Pasqua.
easterly *agg.* dell'est, dall'est, orientale.
eastern *agg.* dell'est, orientale.
eastward *agg.* verso est.
easy *agg.* 1. facile 2. agiato, modo 3. piacevole.
easy *avv.* facilmente, comodamente.
easygoing *agg.* facilone, indolente.
to eat (ate, eaten) *vt. e vi.* 1. mangiare 2. rodere, corrodere.
eatable *agg.* mangiabile, commestibile.
eatables *s. pl.* vivande, viveri.
eaten V. *to eat.*
eater *s.* mangiatore.
eating *s.* il mangiare.
eaves *s. pl.* gronda, cornicione (*sing.*).
to eavesdrop *vi.* origliare.
ebb *s.* 1. riflusso, l'abbassarsi della marea 2. (*fig.*) decadenza || —*-tide,* bassa marea.
ebbing *agg.* 1. defluente 2. in declino.
ebonist *s.* ebanista.
ebonite *s.* ebanite.
ebony *s.* ebano.
ebullition *s.* ebollizione.
eccentric *agg. e s.* eccentrico (*anche fig.*).
eccentricity *s.* eccentricità.
ecclesiastic *agg. e s.* ecclesiastico.
ecclesiastical *agg.* ecclesiastico.
echelon *s.* scaglione.
echinoderm *s.* echinoderma.
echo *s.* eco.
to echo *vt. e vi.* 1. far eco (a) 2. echeggiare.
eclectic *agg. e s.* eclettico.
eclecticism *s.* eclettismo.
eclipse *s.* eclissi.
to eclipse *vt.* eclissare.
ecliptic *agg.* eclittico.
eclogue *s.* egloga.
ecology *s.* ecologia.

economic *agg.* economico.

economical *agg.* economico.

economics *s.* scienze economiche.

economist *s.* economista.

to **economize** *vt.* e *vi.* economizzare.

economy *s.* economia.

ecstasy *s.* estasi.

ecstatic *agg.* estatico.

ecstatically *avv.* estaticamente.

ecumenic(al) *agg.* ecumenico.

eczema *s.* eczema.

eddy *s.* 1. turbine d'aria, vortice 2. gorgo, risucchio.

edge *s.* 1. orlo, margine 2. ciglio, sponda 3. taglio (*di lama*) 4. spigolo.

to **edge** *vt.* e *vi.* 1. bordare, fare un bordo 2. affilare, arrotare, aguzzare (*anche fig.*).

edged *agg.* affilato, tagliente ‖ *double-* —, a doppio taglio (*anche fig.*).

edgeless *agg.* 1. senza bordo 2. smussato, che non taglia.

edging *s.* orlatura, fettuccia.

edible *agg.* mangereccio.

edibles *s. pl.* commestibili.

edict *s.* editto.

edifice *s.* edificio (*anche fig.*).

edifying *agg.* edificante.

to **edit** *vt.* 1. pubblicare, curare (*un libro*) 2. redigere 3. (*cine*) montare.

editing *s.* 1. redazione, commento (*di un testo*) 2. direzione (*di un giornale, ecc.*).

edition *s.* edizione.

editor *s.* 1. commentatore, curatore (*di un testo*) 2. direttore, redattore (*di un giornale*).

editorial *s.* editoriale, articolo di fondo. ♦ **editorial** *agg.* editoriale.

editorship *s.* direzione, redazione (*di giornali*).

to **educate** *vt.* 1. istruire, educare 2. affinare, esercitare.

educated *agg.* 1. istruito, colto 2. addestrato (*di animali*).

education *s.* 1. cultura, educazione 2. istruzione, insegnamento.

educational *agg.* educativo.

educative *agg.* istruttivo.

educator *s.* educatore.

to **educe** *vt.* estrarre, sviluppare.

educible *agg.* che si può estrarre.

to **edulcorate** *vt.* dolcificare.

eel *s.* anguilla.

eerie, eery *agg.* irreale, sovrannaturale.

to **efface** *vt.* cancellare, distruggere.

effect *s.* 1. effetto, risultato 2. impressione. ♦ **effects** *s. pl.* effetti personali.

to **effect** *vt.* effettuare, eseguire.

effective *agg.* 1. efficace 2. effettivo.

effectiveness *s.* efficacia.

effectual *agg.* efficace.

effectuality *s.* efficacia, validità.

effectuation *s.* effettuazione.

effeminacy *s.* effeminatezza.

effeminate *agg.* effeminato.

effervescence *s.* 1. effervescenza 2. (*fig.*) eccitamento.

effete *agg.* logoro, esaurito.

efficacious *agg.* efficace.

efficaciousness *s.* 1. efficacia 2. rendimento (*di una macchina*).

efficiency *s.* efficienza, rendimento.

efficient *agg.* 1. efficiente, di alto rendimento 2. abile, capace.

effigy *s.* effigie.

to **effloresce** *vi.* fiorire, germogliare.

effluent *s.* defluente.

effort *s.* sforzo, fatica.

effortless *agg.* senza sforzo, facile.

effrontery *s.* sfrontatezza.

effulgence *s.* splendore.

effusion *s.* effusione, esuberanza.

effusive *agg.* espansivo, esuberante.

egg *s.* uovo ‖ *boiled* —, uovo alla coque; *hard-boiled* —, uovo sodo.

to **egg** *vt.* to — *on so.*, istigare, incitare qu.

egocentric *agg.* egocentrico.

egocentrism *s.* egocentrismo.

egoism *s.* egoismo.

egoist *s.* egoista.

egoistic(al) *agg.* egoistico.

egotism *s.* egotismo.

egotist *s.* egotista.

egregious *agg.* insigne, eminente.

egress *s.* uscita.

Egyptian *agg.* e *s.* egiziano.

eider-down *s.* piumino (*da letto*)

eight *agg.* otto.

eighteen *agg.* diciotto.

eighteenth *agg.* diciottesimo.

eighth *agg.* ottavo.

eightieth *agg.* ottantesimo.

eighty *agg.* ottanta.

either *agg.* 1. l'uno o l'altro 2. ciascuno dei due, tutti e due. ♦ **either** *avv.* anche, pure. ♦ **either** *avv.* (*in frasi neg.*) neanche, neppure. ♦ **either** *cong.* (*seguito da or*) o, oppure.

to **ejaculate** *vt.* 1. eiaculare 2. e-

sclamare.
ejaculation s. 1. eiaculazione 2. esclamazione.
to eject vt. gettar fuori.
ejection s. 1. espulsione 2. (fig.) destituzione.
ejector s. espulsore.
elaborate agg. elaborato, accurato.
to elaborate vt. e vi. elaborare.
elaboration s. elaborazione.
to elapse vi. trascorrere, passare (del tempo).
elastic agg. elastico (anche fig.).
elasticity s. elasticità.
to elate vt. inebriare, esaltare.
elbow s. gomito.
to elbow vt. e vi. spingere con il gomito, andare avanti a gomitate.
elder agg. (comp. di old) maggiore, più vecchio (tra due persone). ◆
elder s. maggiore, più vecchio (fra due).
elderly agg. attempato.
eldest agg. (superl. di old) maggiore (tra fratelli), primogenito.
elect agg. eletto, scelto.
to elect vt. eleggere.
election s. 1. elezione 2. scelta.
elective agg. 1. elettivo 2. elettorale.
elector s. elettore.
electoral agg. elettorale.
electorate s. elettorato.
electric(al) agg. elettrico.
electrician s. elettricista.
electricity s. elettricità.
to electrify vt. 1. elettrificare 2. elettrizzare.
electrization s. elettrizzazione.
electrocardiogram s. elettrocardiogramma.
to electrocute vt. fulminare mediante elettricità.
electrocution s. elettroesecuzione.
electrode s. elettrodo.
electrodynamics s. elettrodinamica.
electrolysis s. elettrolisi.
electro-magnet s. elettromagnete.
electromagnetic agg. elettromagnetico.
electron s. elettrone.
electronic agg. elettronico.
electronics s. elettronica.
electrostatics s. elettrostatica.
elegance s. eleganza.
elegant agg. elegante, raffinato.
elegiac agg. elegiaco.
elegy s. elegia.

element s. 1. elemento 2. principio costitutivo.
elemental agg. 1. dei quattro elementi 2. elementare 3. fondamentale.
elementary agg. elementare.
elephant s. elefante.
elephantiasis s. elefantiasi.
elephantine agg. elefantesco.
to elevate vt. innalzare, elevare (anche fig.).
elevated agg. 1. elevato 2. sopraelevato.
elevation s. 1. elevazione 2. collina, luogo alto.
elevator s. ascensore, montacarichi.
eleven agg. undici.
elevenses s. (fam.) spuntino a metà mattina.
eleventh agg. undicesimo.
elf s. (pl. elves) elfo, folletto.
elfish agg. 1. incantato 2. vivace.
to elicit vt. estrarre, strappare.
eligibility s. eleggibilità.
eligible agg. eleggibile.
to eliminate vt. eliminare.
elimination s. eliminazione.
elision s. elisione.
elixir s. elisir.
elk s. alce.
ellipse s. ellisse.
ellipsis s. ellissi.
elliptic(al) agg. ellittico.
elm s. olmo.
elocution s. 1. elocuzione 2. dizione.
to elope vi. fuggire (con un amante).
elopement s. fuga (con un amante).
eloquence s. eloquenza.
eloquent agg. eloquente (anche fig.).
else avv. (dopo avv. e pron. int., indef.) altro.
elsewhere avv. altrove.
to elude vt. eludere, schivare.
elusive agg. 1. elusivo, ambiguo 2. sfuggevole.
elytron s. (pl. elytra) elitra.
Elzevir agg. e s. elzeviro.
to emaciate vt. far deperire, far dimagrire.
emaciated agg. emaciato.
to emanate vi. emanare.
emanation s. emanazione.
to emancipate vt. emancipare.
emancipation s. emancipazione.
to embalm vt. 1. imbalsamare 2. profumare.
embalmer s. imbalsamatore.

embankment *s.* 1. argine, diga 2. alzaia.

embarcation *s.* imbarco.

embargo *s.* embargo, fermo.

to embark *vt.* imbarcare (*truppe, merci*). ♦ to embark *vi.* imbarcarsi.

embarkation *s.* imbarco.

to embarrass *vt.* mettere in imbarazzo.

embarrassing *agg.* imbarazzante.

embarrassment *s.* 1. imbarazzo 2. difficoltà.

embassy *s.* ambasciata.

to embattle *vt.* disporre in ordine di battaglia, fortificare.

to embed *vt.* incassare, conficcare.

to embellish *vt.* abbellire, ornare.

embellishment *s.* abbellimento, ornamento.

ember *s.* tizzone. ♦ embers *s. pl.* brace (*sing.*).

embezzler *s.* malversatore.

to embitter *vt.* 1. rendere amaro 2. (*fig.*) amareggiare.

embitterment *s.* amarezza, inasprimento.

to emblazon *vt.* 1. decorare 2. celebrare.

emblem *s.* emblema, simbolo (*fig.*).

emblematic(al) *agg.* emblematico.

embodiment *s.* 1. incarnazione 2. incorporazione.

to embody *vt.* 1. incarnare 2. personificare 3. incorporare.

to embolden *vt.* incoraggiare.

embolism *s.* embolia.

embolus *s.* (*pl.* -li) embolo.

to emboss *vt.* 1. scolpire 2. stampare in rilievo.

embossed *agg.* 1. sbalzato 2. fatto in rilievo.

embrace *s.* abbraccio, amplesso.

to embrace *vt.* abbracciare (*anche fig.*). ♦ to embrace *vi.* abbracciarsi.

embrasure *s.* 1. vano (*di porta, finestra*) 2. feritoia.

to embroider *vt.* ricamare.

embroiderer *s.* ricamatore.

embroidery *s.* ricamo.

to embroil *vt.* coinvolgere in una disputa.

embryo *s.* embrione.

embryonic *agg.* embrionale (*anche fig.*).

to emend *vt.* emendare.

emendation *s.* emendamento.

emerald *s.* smeraldo.

to emerge *vi.* 1. emergere, affiorare 2. (*fig.*) risultare.

emergency *s.* emergenza, caso imprevisto || - -door, uscita di sicurezza; — means, mezzi di fortuna.

emersion *s.* emersione.

emery *s.* smeriglio || - -paper, carta smerigliata.

emetic *agg. e s.* emetico.

emigrant *agg. e s.* emigrante.

to emigrate *vi.* emigrare.

emigration *s.* enigrazione.

eminence *s.* 1. luogo, parte eminente 2. (*anat.*) protuberanza 3. (*fig.*) eminenza, eccellenza.

eminent *agg.* eminente (*anche fig.*).

eminently *avv.* eminentemente.

emir *s.* emiro.

emissary *s.* emissario, agente segreto.

emission *s.* emissione.

to emit *vt.* 1. emettere 2. esalare.

emollient *agg. e s.* emolliente.

emolument *s.* remunerazione, salario.

emotion *s.* emozione, turbamento.

emotional *agg.* 1. emotivo, impressionabile 2. commovente.

emotionalism *s.* emotività.

emotionally *avv.* con emozione.

emotive *agg.* 1. commovente 2. emotivo.

emperor *s.* imperatore.

emphasis *s.* 1. accentuazione, rilievo 2. enfasi.

to emphasize *vt.* accentuare.

emphatic *agg.* 1. accentuato 2. enfatico.

emphysema *s.* enfisema.

emphyteusis *s.* enfiteusi.

empire *s.* impero.

empiric *s.* empirico.

empirical *agg.* empirico.

empiricism *s.* empirismo.

emplacement *s.* 1. collocazione 2. (*mil.*) piazzuola.

to employ *s.* impiego: out of —, senza impiego.

to employ *vt.* 1. impiegare, adoperare 2. assumere.

employee *s.* impiegato.

employer *s.* datore di lavoro.

employment *s.* impiego, occupazione.

to empoison *vt.* avvelenare.

emporium *s.* 1. centro commerciale 2. emporio.

to empower *vt.* dare pieni poteri a.

emptiness s. 1. vuoto 2. vanità.

empty agg. 1. vuoto 2. vano 3. vacante || — *-handed*, a mani vuote.

to empty vt. vuotare. ♦ **to empty** vi. vuotarsi.

to emulate vt. emulare.

emulation s. emulazione.

emulator s. emulatore.

emulous agg. emulo.

to emulsify vt. emulsionare.

emulsion s. emulsione.

emulsive agg. emulsivo.

to enable vt. mettere in grado.

to enact vt. decretare, emanare (*una legge*).

enactment s. 1. promulgazione 2. legge.

enamel s. smalto.

to enamel vt. smaltare.

to encamp vi. accamparsi.

encaustic agg. encaustico.

encephalic agg. encefalico.

encephalitis s. encefalite.

to enchant vt. incantare, affascinare.

enchanter s. incantatore, mago.

enchanting agg. incantevole.

enchantment s. incanto, incantesimo.

enchantress s. incantatrice.

to encircle vt. circondare, cingere.

enclitic agg. enclitico.

to enclose vt. 1. racchiudere, cingere 2. accludere.

enclosed agg. 1. racchiuso, circondato 2. accluso.

enclosure s. 1. recinto, staccionata 2. allegato.

encomiast s. encomiasta.

to encompass vt. circondare (*anche fig.*).

encore avv. (*teat.*) bis.

to encore vt. chiedere il bis.

encounter s. scontro.

to encourage vt. incoraggiare, animare.

encouragement s. incoraggiamento.

encouraging agg. incoraggiante.

to encroach vt. 1. usurpare, invadere 2. (*giur.*) ledere.

to encrust vt. incrostare.

to encumber vt. 1. ingombrare, imbarazzare 2. ostruire.

encumbrance s. ingombro, impedimento.

encyclic(al) agg. enciclico. ♦ **encyclic(al)** s. enciclica.

encyclop(a)edia s. enciclopedia.

encyclop(a)edic(al) agg. enciclo-

pedico.

end s. 1. estremità, fine, termine 2. scopo, mira 3. morte.

to end vt. e vi. finire, concludere.

to endanger vt. mettere in pericolo, compromettere.

to endear vt. affezionare, rendere caro.

endearing agg. affettuoso, tenero.

endearment s. tenerezza. ♦ **endearments** s. pl. blandizie.

to endeavo(u)r vi. sforzarsi. ♦ **to endeavo(u)r** vt. tentare.

endemic agg. endemico.

ending agg. finale, ultimo. ♦ **ending** s. fine, conclusione.

endless agg. senza fine, eterno, continuo.

endocarditis s. endocardite.

endocardium s. endocardio.

endocarp s. endocarpo.

endocrine agg. endocrino.

endocrinology s. endocrinologia.

endogeny s. endogenesi.

to endorse vt. (*comm.*) girare, vistare.

endorsee s. (*comm.*) giratario.

endorsement s. (*comm.*) girata.

endorser s. (*comm.*) girante.

to endow vt. 1. dotare 2. fare una donazione.

endowment s. 1. costituzione di dote, donazione 2. (*fig.*) talento.

endurance s. 1. resistenza, sopportazione 2. durata.

to endure vt. tollerare, sopportare. ♦ **to endure** vi. resistere, durare.

enduring agg. 1. tollerante, paziente 2. durevole.

enema s. clistere.

enemy agg. e s. nemico.

energetic(al) agg. 1. energico 2. energetico.

to energize vt. infondere energia.

energumen s. energumeno.

energy s. energia, forza.

to enervate vt. snervare, indebolire.

enervation s. indebolimento.

to enfeeble vt. indebolire.

to enfold vt. 1. avvolgere 2. cingere.

to enforce vt. 1. imporre, far rispettare 2. mettere in vigore (*una legge*).

to enframe vt. incorniciare.

to enfranchise vt. affrancare, liberare.

enfranchisement s. affrancamento,

liberazione.

to engage *vt.* 1. impegnare 2. ingaggiare 3. attrarre (*l'attenzione*). ♦ **to engage** *vi.* impegnarsi || *to — in conversation*, prendere parte alla conversazione.

engaged *agg.* 1. impegnato 2. fidanzato 3. occupato, riservato.

engagement *s.* 1. impegno 2. fidanzamento 3. assunzione, impiego.

engaging *agg.* attraente, avvincente.

engagingly *avv.* in modo attraente.

to engender *vt.* produrre, causare.

engine *s.* 1. macchina, motore 2. (*ferr.*) locomotrice || *fire-* —, autopompa.

engineer *s.* 1. ingegnere 2. tecnico.

engineering *s.* 1. ingegneria 2. costruzione meccanica.

English *agg.* inglese. ♦ **English** *s.* lingua inglese.

Englishman *s.* (*uomo*) inglese.

Englishwoman *s.* (*donna*) inglese.

to engrave *vt.* 1. intagliare, incidere 2. (*fig.*) imprimere.

engraver *s.* incisore.

engraving *s.* arte dell'incisione || *wood-* —, xilografia.

to engross *vt.* 1. copiare (*un atto legale*), redigere (*un documento*) 2. assorbire (*l'attenzione*).

engrossment *s.* copiatura (*di documento*).

to enhance *vt.* accrescere.

enigma *s.* enigma.

enigmatic(al) *agg.* enigmatico.

to enjoy *vt.* 1. godere, gioire 2. gustare, provar piacere di || *to — oneself*, divertirsi.

enjoyable *agg.* piacevole, gradevole.

enjoyably *avv.* piacevolmente.

enjoyment *s.* godimento, piacere.

to enkindle *vt.* infiammare, eccitare. ♦ **to enkindle** *vi.* infiammarsi, eccitarsi.

to enlarge *vt.* 1. allargare, ampliare 2. (*foto*) ingrandire. ♦ **to enlarge** *vi.* allargarsi, ampliarsi.

enlargement *s.* 1. allargamento 2. (*foto*) ingrandimento.

enlarger *s.* (*foto*) ingranditore.

to enlighten *vt.* rischiarare, illuminare (*anche fig.*).

enlightenment *s.* 1. spiegazione, schiarimento 2. (*lett.*) l'illuminismo.

to enlist *vt.* arruolare. ♦ **to enlist** *vt.* arruolarsi.

enlistment *s.* arruolamento, ingaggio.

to enliven *vt.* rianimare, ravvivare.

to enmesh *vt.* impegolare, irretire.

enmity *s.* ostilità, inimicizia.

to ennoble *vt.* nobilitare.

enormity *s.* mostruosità.

enormous *agg.* enorme, immenso.

enough *avv.* abbastanza, sufficientemente. ♦ **enough** *agg.* sufficiente. ♦ **enough** *s.* il necessario, quanto basta.

to enrage *vt.* far arrabbiare, esasperare.

to enrapture *vt.* rapire, estasiare.

to enrich *vt.* 1. arricchire (*anche fig.*) 2. abbellire.

enrichment *s.* 1. arricchimento 2. abbellimento.

to enrol *vt.* 1. arruolare, ingaggiare 2. iscrivere.

enrolment *s.* 1. arruolamento, iscrizione 2. (*giur.*) registrazione.

ensign *s.* 1. bandiera, stendardo 2. portabandiera.

to enslave *vt.* assoggettare, far schiavo (*anche fig.*).

enslavement *s.* asservimento, schiavitù (*anche fig.*).

to ensnare *vt.* adescare, intrappolare (*anche fig.*).

to ensue *vt.* e *vi.* seguire.

to ensure *vt.* assicurare, garantire.

to entail *s.* eredità, ordine di successione (*vincolato*).

to entangle *vt.* impigliare, intralciare (*anche fig.*).

entanglement *s.* groviglio, impiccio.

to enter *vt.* e *vi.* 1. entrare, penetrare 2. iscrivere 3. (*comm.*) registrare || *to — upon*, intraprendere (*una carriera*).

enteric *agg.* enterico.

enteritis *s.* enterite.

enterocolitis *s.* enterocolite.

enterogastritis *s.* gastroenterite.

enterprise *s.* 1. impresa 2. iniziativa, intraprendenza.

enterprising *agg.* intraprendente.

to entertain *vt.* 1. ricevere, ospitare 2. intrattenere, divertire 3. carezzare (*un'idea*), nutrire (*dubbi, speranze*).

entertainer *s.* 1. anfitrione, ospite 2. comico.

entertaining *agg.* divertente.

entertainment *s.* 1. trattenimento, spettacolo 2. ricevimento, festa 3. divertimento.

to **enthral** *vt.* (*fig.*) affascinare, incantare.

enthralment *s.* incanto, malia.

to **enthrone** *vt.* mettere sul trono.

enthronement *s.* investitura, intronizzazione.

enthusiasm *s.* entusiasmo.

enthusiast *s.* entusiasta.

enthusiastic(al) *agg.* entusiastico.

enthusiastically *avv.* entusiasticamente.

to **entice** *vt.* sedurre, allettare.

enticement *s.* **1.** attrattiva **2.** adescamento, istigazione.

enticing *agg.* seducente, attraente.

entire *agg.* intero, completo.

entirely *avv.* interamente, completamente.

to **entitle** *vt.* **1.** intitolare (*un libro*) **2.** dare un titolo.

entity *s.* entità, esistenza.

entomological *agg.* entomologico.

entomologist *s.* entomologo.

entomology *s.* entomologia.

entrails *s. pl.* intestino (*sing.*), visceri.

entrance *s.* **1.** ingresso, entrata **2.** ammissione || — *hall*, vestibolo.

to **entrap** *vt.* prendere in trappola, truffare.

to **entreat** *vt.* pregare, supplicare.

entreaty *s.* supplica, istanza.

to **entrench** *vt. e vi.* trincerare, fortificare (*anche fig.*) || *to* — *upon*, usurpare.

entrepreneur *s.* **1.** (*teat.*) impresario **2.** imprenditore.

to **entrust** *vt.* affidare, commettere.

entry *s.* **1.** entrata **2.** ingresso, passaggio **3.** (*comm.*) registrazione.

to **entwine** *vt.* attorcigliare, intrecciare. ♦ to **entwine** *vi.* arrotolarsi.

to **enucleate** *vt.* spiegare, chiarire.

enucleation *s.* spiegazione, chiarimento.

to **enumerate** *vt.* enumerare.

enumeration *s.* enumerazione.

enumerator *s.* numeratore.

to **enunciate** *vt.* enunciare, proclamare.

enunciation *s.* enunciazione.

to **envelop** *vt.* avvolgere, avviluppare.

envelope *s.* busta, involucro.

envelopment *s.* avvolgimento.

enviable *agg.* invidiabile.

envious *agg.* invidioso.

to **environ** *vt.* circondare, accer-

chiare.

environment *s.* ambiente.

environs *s. pl.* dintorni.

envy *s.* invidia.

to **envy** *vt.* invidiare.

enzyme *s.* enzima.

epaulet(te) *s.* (*mil.*) spallina.

ephebe *s.* efebo.

ephemeral *agg.* effimero.

ephemeris *s.* (*pl.* -ides) effemeride.

epic *agg.* epico. ♦ **epic** *s.* poema epico.

epically *avv.* epicamente.

epicentre *s.* epicentro.

epicurean *agg. e s.* epicureo.

epidemic(al) *agg.* epidemico.

epidemically *avv.* epidemicamente.

epidermal *agg.* epidermico.

epidermis *s.* epidermide.

epigastric *agg.* epigastrico.

epigram *s.* epigramma.

epigrammatic *agg.* epigrammatico.

epigrammatist *s.* epigrammista.

epigraph *s.* epigrafe.

epigraphy *s.* epigrafia.

epilepsy *s.* epilessia.

epileptic *agg.* epilettico.

epilogue *s.* epilogo.

Epiphany *s.* Epifania.

episcopacy *s.* episcopato.

episcopal *agg.* episcopale.

episcopate *s.* episcopato.

episode *s.* episodio.

episodic(al) *agg.* episodico.

epistle *s.* epistola.

epistolary *agg.* epistolare.

epitaph *s.* epitaffio.

epithalamium *s.* epitalamio.

epithet *s.* epiteto.

epitome *s.* epitome, riassunto.

epoch *s.* epoca, età.

epopee *s.* epopea.

equability *s.* uguaglianza, uniformità.

equal *agg.* uguale, simile, stesso. ♦ **equal** *s.* pari (*di rango*).

equality *s.* uguaglianza, parità.

equalization *s.* eguagliamento.

to **equalize** *vt. e vi.* uguagliare.

equally *avv.* ugualmente, imparzialmente.

equanimity *s.* equanimità.

equanimous *agg.* equanime.

equation *s.* **1.** equazione **2.** pareggio.

equator *s.* equatore.

equatorial *agg.* equatoriale.

equestrian *agg.* equestre.

equidistant *agg.* equidistante.

equilateral *agg.* equilatero.

equine *agg.* equino.

equinoctial *agg.* equinoziale.

equinox *s.* equinozio.

to equip *vt.* 1. equipaggiare 2. fornire, arredare.

equipment *s.* 1. equipaggiamento 2. attrezzatura.

equipoise *s.* equilibrio.

equipollent *agg.* equipollente.

equitation *s.* equitazione.

equity *s.* giustizia, equità.

equivalence *s.* equivalenza.

equivalent *agg.* e *s.* equivalente.

equivocal *agg.* 1. ambiguo, equivoco 2. sospetto, losco.

equivocally *avv.* 1. ambiguamente 2. in modo losco.

to equivocate *vi.* equivocare, giocare sull'equivoco.

equivocation *s.* 1. l'equivocare 2. equivoco.

equivoke *s.* 1. gioco di parole 2. ambiguità (*d'espressione*).

era *s.* era, epoca.

eradicable *agg.* estirpabile.

to eradicate *vt.* sradicare, estirpare.

to erase *vt.* raschiare, cancellare.

eraser *s.* 1. raschietto 2. gomma per cancellare.

erasure *s.* raschiatura, cancellatura.

erect *agg.* diritto, ritto.

to erect *vt.* 1. raddrizzare 2. costruire.

erection *s.* 1. raddrizzamento 2. erezione.

eremite *s.* eremita.

ermine *s.* ermellino.

to erode *vt.* corrodere, logorare.

erosion *s.* erosione.

erosive *agg.* corrosivo.

erotic *agg.* erotico.

eroticism *s.* erotismo.

to err *vi.* 1. sbagliare 2. errare, vagabondare.

errand *s.* commissione || — *boy*, fattorino.

errant *agg.* 1. errante 2. che sbaglia.

erratic *agg.* 1. erratico 2. irregolare.

erratically *avv.* 1. irregolarmente 2. eccentricamente.

erring *agg.* 1. errante 2. che sbaglia.

erroneous *agg.* erroneo.

error *s.* 1. errore 2. torto.

erudite *agg.* erudito.

erudition *s.* erudizione.

to erupt *vi.* eruttare.

eruption *s.* eruzione.

eruptive *agg.* eruttivo.

escalade *s.* scalata.

escalator *s.* scala mobile.

escape *s.* 1. fuga, evasione 2. scampo, salvezza.

to escape *vt.* e *vi.* 1. fuggire, evadere 2. scampare.

escapism *s.* evasione dalla realtà.

escapist *s.* chi cerca di evadere dalla realtà.

eschatology *s.* escatologia.

to eschew *vt.* evitare, astenersi da.

escort *s.* scorta.

to escort *vt.* scortare, accompagnare.

Eskimo *s.* esquimese.

esoteric *agg.* esoterico.

especial *agg.* speciale.

especially *avv.* specialmente.

espionage *s.* spionaggio.

esplanade *s.* spianata.

to espy *vt.* scorgere, avvistare.

esquire *s.* (*titolo di cortesia*) John Smith Esq., egregio sig. John Smith.

essay *s.* 1. esperimento, prova 2. (*lett.*) saggio.

to essay *vt.* provare, mettere alla prova.

essayist *s.* saggista.

essence *s.* essenza.

essential *agg.* essenziale.

to establish *vt.* 1. affermare (*un diritto ecc.*) 2. instaurare 3. (*comm.*) fondare, costituire.

established *agg.* 1. stabilito, affermato 2. fondato.

establishment *s.* 1. affermazione, conferma 2. instaurazione 3. stabilimento, azienda.

estate *s.* 1. terra, proprietà (*terriera*) 2. stato, gruppo politico 3. condizione, classe sociale || — *agent*, mediatore.

esteem *s.* stima, considerazione.

to esteem *vt.* 1. stimare, tenere in gran conto 2. considerare.

estimable *agg.* degno di stima.

estimate *s.* 1. stima, giudizio 2. (*comm.*) preventivo.

to estimate *vt.* 1. stimare, valutare 2. preventivare.

estimator *s.* perito, stimatore.

to estrange *vt.* alienare, alienarsi, allontanare.

estrangement *s.* alienazione, allontanamento.

estuary *s.* estuario.

etching *s.* acquaforte.

eternal *agg.* eterno.

eternity *s.* eternità.

ether s. etere.
ethereal agg. etereo.
ethic(al) agg. etico.
ethics s. etica.
Ethiopian agg. etiopico. ♦ Ethiopian s. etiope.
Ethiopic agg. etiopico.
ethnic(al) agg. etnico.
ethnography s. etnografia.
ethnologist s. etnologo.
ethnology s. etnologia.
ethylene s. etilene.
ethylic agg. etilico.
etiquette s. 1. etichetta 2. cerimoniale.
Etrurian, Etruscan agg. e s. etrusco.
etymologic(al) agg. etimologico.
etymology s. etimologia.
eucalyptus s. eucalipto.
Eucharist s. Eucaristia.
eucharistic(al) agg. eucaristico.
eugenics s. eugenetica.
eulogist s. elogiatore.
to eulogize vt. elogiare.
eulogy s. elogio, panegirico.
eunuch s. eunuco.
euphemism s. eufemismo.
euphonic agg. eufonico.
euphony s. eufonia.
euphoria s. euforia.
euphuism s. eufuismo.
euphuist s. affettato.
euphuistic agg. affettato, ricercato (di stile).
European agg. e s. europeo.
Eurovision s. eurovisione.
euthanasia s. eutanasia.
to evacuate vt. e vi. evacuare, sfollare.
evacuation s. evacuazione, sfollamento.
to evade vt. evitare, schivare, eludere.
to evaluate vt. valutare.
evaluation s. valutazione.
evanescent agg. evanescente.
evangelic(al) agg. evangelico.
evangelist s. evangelista.
evangelistic agg. di un evangelista, missionario.
evangelization s. evangelizzazione.
to evangelize vt. evangelizzare.
to evaporate vi. evaporare. ♦ to evaporate vt. far evaporare.
evaporation s. evaporazione.
evasion s. 1. evasione, scappatoia 2. scusa, pretesto.
evasive agg. evasivo.

evasively avv. evasivamente.
evasiveness s. ambiguità.
eve s. vigilia.
even agg. 1. uguale, uniforme, costante, regolare 2. pari, equo. ♦ even avv. 1. ancora (con comp.) 2. persino, anche || — as, nel momento in cui.
evening s. 1. sera, serata 2. (fig.) declino, fine.
evenly avv. in modo uguale, uniformemente.
evensong s. vespro.
event s. 1. caso, eventualità 2. avvenimento 3. (sport) prova.
eventful agg. ricco di avvenimenti, movimentato.
eventual agg. finale, definitivo.
eventuality s. eventualità.
eventually avv. alla fine.
ever avv. 1. mai 2. sempre.
evergreen s. sempreverde.
everlasting agg. eterno.
everliving agg. immortale.
evermore avv. perpetuamente.
every agg. ogni, ciascuno, tutti.
everybody pron. indef. ognuno, tutti.
everyday agg. di tutti i giorni, quotidiano.
everyone pron. indef. V. everybody.
everything pron. indef. ogni cosa, tutto.
everywhere avv. ovunque.
to evict vt. sfrattare, espellere.
eviction s. sfratto.
evidence s. 1. evidenza 2. prova.
to evidence vt. provare, dimostrare.
evident agg. evidente, chiaro.
evil agg. cattivo, malvagio || —-eye, malocchio. ♦ evil s. male, peccato.
to evirate vt. evirare.
to evocate vt. evocare.
evocation s. evocazione.
evocative agg. evocatore.
to evoke vt. evocare.
evolution s. evoluzione.
evolutional agg. evolutivo.
evolutionism s. evoluzionismo.
to evolve vt. evolvere. ♦ to evolve vi. evolversi.
evolvement s. evoluzione, sviluppo.
ewe s. pecora (femmina).
to exacerbate vt. esacerbare, inasprire.
exacerbation s. esacerbazione, inasprimento.
exact agg. 1. esatto, giusto 2. puntuale, rigoroso.

to **exact** *vt.* **1.** esigere **2.** rendere necessario.

exacting *agg.* **1.** esigente **2.** impegnativo.

exaction *s.* esazione, estorsione.

exactitude *s.* esattezza, precisione.

exactly *avv.* esattamente.

exactness *s.* esattezza, precisione.

to **exaggerate** *vt.* esagerare, ingrandire.

exaggeration *s.* esagerazione.

to **exalt** *vt.* **1.** innalzare, elevare **2.** esaltare, lodare.

exaltation *s.* **1.** innalzamento **2.** esaltazione.

exalted *agg.* **1.** elevato (*di grado ecc.*) **2.** esaltato, eccitato.

examination *s.* **1.** esame, ispezione **2.** esame scolastico **3.** (*giur.*) interrogatorio.

to **examine** *vt.* **1.** verificare, ispezionare **2.** esaminare **3.** (*giur.*) istruire un processo.

examiner *s.* esaminatore.

example *s.* esempio.

to **exasperate** *vt.* **1.** peggiorare, aggravare **2.** esasperare.

exasperatingly *avv.* in modo esasperante.

exasperation *s.* esasperazione.

to **excavate** *vt.* scavare, fare scavi (*archeologici*).

excavation *s.* **1.** scavo **2.** fossa, buca.

excavator *s.* **1.** operaio scavatore **2.** (*mecc.*) escavatore.

to **exceed** *vt. e vi.* **1.** eccedere, superare (*i limiti*) **2.** essere superiore.

exceeding *agg.* esagerato.

exceedingly *avv.* eccessivamente, troppo.

to **excel** *vt.* superare. ♦ to **excel** *vi.* primeggiare.

excellence *s.* **1.** eccellenza **2.** pregio, superiorità.

Excellency *s.* (*titolo*) Eccellenza.

excellent *agg.* eccellente.

except *prep.* eccetto, tranne.

to **except** *vt.* eccettuare, escludere. ♦ to **except** *vi.* obiettare, sollevare eccezioni.

excepting *prep.* eccetto, tranne.

exception *s.* eccezione.

exceptional *agg.* eccezionale, straordinario.

excerpt *s.* brano scelto.

excess *s.* **1.** eccesso, intemperanza **2.** supplemento.

exchange *s.* **1.** scambio **2.** (*finanza*)

excessive *agg.* eccessivo, smoderato, cambio **3.** borsa, mercato || *bill of —*, cambiale; — *-broker*, agente di cambio.

to **exchange** *vt.* cambiare, scambiare. ♦ to **exchange** *vi.* fare un cambio.

exchangeable *agg.* scambiabile.

exchanger *s.* cambiavalute.

exchequer *s.* Tesoro, Scacchiere, fisco.

excise *s.* imposta indiretta || *— duty*, dazio.

to **excise**[1] *vt.* tassare.

to **excise**[2] *vt.* estirpare, mutilare (*un testo*).

exciseman *s.* daziere, funzionario degli uffici delle imposte.

excision *s.* taglio, recisione.

excitability *s.* eccitabilità.

excitable *agg.* eccitabile.

excitant *agg. e s.* eccitante.

excitation *s.* eccitazione.

to **excite** *vt.* **1.** provocare, far nascere (*una rivolta, un sentimento ecc.*) **2.** eccitare, animare.

excited *agg.* eccitato.

excitement *s.* eccitazione.

to **exclaim** *vt. e vi.* esclamare.

exclamation *s.* esclamazione.

exclamatory *agg.* esclamativo.

to **exclude** *vt.* escludere.

exclusion *s.* esclusione.

exclusive *agg.* **1.** altezzoso **2.** chiuso, scelto (*di ambiente*) **3.** esclusivo.

exclusiveness *s.* esclusività.

to **excogitate** *vt.* escogitare.

excommunicable *agg.* scomunicabile.

excommunicate *agg. e s.* scomunicato.

to **excommunicate** *vt.* scomunicare.

excommunication *s.* scomunica.

excrement *s.* escremento.

excrescence *s.* escrescenza, protuberanza.

excruciating *agg.* tormentoso, straziante.

to **exculpate** *vt.* giustificare, scolpare.

excursion *s.* **1.** escursione, gita **2.** (*mil.*) sortita.

excursionist *s.* escursionista, gitante.

excusable *agg.* scusabile.

excuse *s.* **1.** scusa, giustificazione **2.**

pretesto.

to **excuse** *vt.* scusare, giustificare.

execrable *agg.* esecrabile.

to **execrate** *vt.* e *vi.* 1. esecrare, detestare 2. maledire.

execration *s.* 1. esecrazione 2. maledizione.

executant *s.* esecutore.

to **execute** *vt.* 1. eseguire, mettere in esecuzione 2. (*giur.*) convalidare 3. giustiziare.

execution *s.* 1. compimento, attuazione 2. esecuzione.

executioner *s.* esecutore, boia.

executive *agg.* esecutivo.

executor *s.* esecutore.

exedra *s.* esedra.

exegesis *s.* (*pl.* -ses) esegesi.

exegete *s.* esegeta.

exemplary *agg.* esemplare.

exemplification *s.* esemplificazione.

to **exemplify** *vt.* esemplificare.

exempt *agg.* esente, esonerato.

to **exempt** *vt.* esentare, esonerare.

exemption *s.* esenzione, esonero.

exequies *s. pl.* esequie.

exercise *s.* esercizio, esercitazione ‖ — -book, quaderno.

to **exercise** *vt.* esercitare, usare. ♦ to **exercise** *vi.* esercitarsi, allenarsi.

exercitation *s.* esercizio, uso (*di una facoltà*).

to **exert** *vt.* esercitare.

exertion *s.* 1. esercizio (*di autorità*) 2. sforzo.

exhalation *s.* esalazione.

to **exhale** *vt.* e *vi.* esalare, emettere.

exhaust *s.* 1. (*mecc.*) scarico, scappamento 2. apparato aspiratore.

to **exhaust** *vt.* e *vi.* 1. aspirare (*aria, gas ecc.*) 2. esaurire (*anche fig.*).

exhausted *agg.* 1. aspirato 2. esausto, spossato.

exhausting *agg.* che esaurisce.

exhaustion *s.* 1. aspirazione 2. esaurimento.

exhaustive *agg.* 1. esauriente 2. spossante.

exhibit *s.* 1. insieme di oggetti in mostra 2. (*giur.*) documento.

to **exhibit** *vt.* 1. esibire, mostrare 2. (*giur.*) produrre (*documenti ecc.*).

exhibition *s.* 1. presentazione (*di documenti*) 2. esposizione, mostra.

exhibitionism *s.* esibizionismo.

exhibitionist *s.* esibizionista.

exhibitor *s.* espositore.

to **exhilarate** *vt.* rallegrare, esilarare.

exhilarating *agg.* esilarante.

to **exhort** *vt.* esortare, ammonire.

exhortation *s.* esortazione.

exhortative *agg.* esortativo.

exhumation *s.* esumazione.

to **exhume** *vt.* esumare.

exigence *s.* 1. esigenza, necessità 2. situazione critica.

exigent *agg.* 1. pressante, urgente 2. esigente.

exigible *agg.* esigibile.

exiguity *s.* esiguità.

exiguous *agg.* esiguo.

exile *s.* 1. esilio, bando 2. esule.

to **exile** *vt.* esiliare.

to **exist** *vi.* esistere.

existence *s.* esistenza.

existent *agg.* esistente.

existential *agg.* esistenziale.

existentialism *s.* esistenzialismo.

existentialist *agg.* e *s.* esistenzialista.

existing *agg.* esistente, attuale.

exit *s.* uscita.

exode, exodus *s.* esodo.

exogenous *agg.* esogeno.

to **exonerate** *vt.* 1. esonerare, dispensare 2. giustificare.

exoneration *s.* 1. dispensa, esonero 2. giustificazione.

exorbitant *agg.* esorbitante.

to **exorcise** *vt.* esorcizzare.

exorciser *s.* esorcista.

exorcism *s.* esorcismo.

exorcist *s.* esorcista.

exothermic *agg.* esotermico.

exotic *agg.* esotico.

exoticism *s.* esotismo.

to **expand** *vt.* espandere, dilatare, allargare. ♦ to **expand** *vi.* espandersi, dilagare, dilatarsi, allargarsi, svilupparsi.

expanse *s.* distesa, estensione, spazio.

expansion *s.* espansione, dilatazione, allargamento.

expansionism *s.* espansionismo.

expansive *agg.* 1. espansivo 2. dilatabile.

to **expatiate** *vi.* 1. errare, vagabondare 2. parlare e scrivere diffusamente.

expatiation *s.* 1. dissertazione 2. prolissità.

expatriate *agg.* e *s.* espatriato.

to **expatriate** *vt.* esiliare. ♦ to

expatriate *vi.* espatriare.
expatriation *s.* espatrio.
to expect *vt.* **1.** aspettare, aspettarsi **2.** esigere, insistere **3.** pensare, credere || *to — somebody to come*, prevedere la venuta di qu.
expectance *s.* aspettativa, attesa.
expectant *s.* **1.** chi attende **2.** candidato.
expectation *s.* attesa, aspettativa. ♦ **expectations** *s. pl.* speranze.
expectorant *agg. e s.* espettorante.
expectoration *s.* espettorazione.
expediency *s.* **1.** convenienza **2.** opportunism.o.
expedient *s.* espediente, ripiego.
to expedite *vt.* affrettare.
expedition *s.* **1.** spedizione **2.** prontezza, celerità.
expeditious *s.* svelto, sbrigativo.
to expel *vt.* espellere, cacciare.
expense *s.* **1.** spesa, sborso **2.** (*fig.*) sacrificio, prezzo.
expensive *agg.* costoso, caro.
experience *s.* esperienza.
to experience *vt.* sperimentare, provare.
experienced *agg.* pratico, esperto.
experiment *s.* esperimento, prova.
experimental *agg.* sperimentale.
experimentation *s.* sperimentasmo.
experimentalist *s.* sperimentalista.
experimentation *s.* sperimentazione.
expert *agg.* esperto. ♦ **expert** *s.* esperto, perito, competente.
expertly *avv.* abilmente.
to expiate *vt.* espiare.
expiation *s.* espiazione.
expiatory *agg.* espiatorio.
expiration *s.* **1.** fine, scadenza **2.** espirazione.
expiratory *agg.* espiratorio.
to expire *vt. e vi.* **1.** finire, scadere **2.** spirare, morire.
expiring *agg.* **1.** che scade **2.** spirante, morente.
expiry *s.* fine, cessazione.
to explain *vt. e vi.* spiegare, chiarire.
explanation *s.* spiegazione, delucidazione.
expletive *agg.* espletivo, pleonastico. ♦ **expletive** *s.* **1.** imprecazione **2.** pleonasmo.
explicable *agg.* spiegabile.
to explicate *vt.* sviluppare (*un prin-*

cipio, un'idea ecc.).
explication *s.* spiegazione, sviluppo.
explicit *agg.* esplicito, chiaro.
to explode *vt.* esplodere, far esplodere. ♦ **to explode** *vi.* scoppiare, esplodere.
to exploit *vt.* **1.** utilizzare, sfruttare **2.** approfittare di.
exploitation *s.* sfruttamento, utilizzazione.
exploiter *s.* **1.** chi valorizza (*idea, invenzione ecc.*) **2.** sfruttatore.
exploration *s.* esplorazione.
to explore *vt.* esplorare.
explorer *s.* esploratore, esploratrice.
explosion *s.* esplosione, scoppio.
explosive *agg. e s.* esplosivo.
exponent *s.* **1.** divulgatore **2.** esponente.
exponential *agg.* esponenziale.
export *s.* esportazione.
to export *vt.* esportare.
exportation *s.* esportazione.
exporter *s.* esportatore.
to expose *vt.* **1.** esporre **2.** (*foto*) impressionare.
exposé *s.* esposto, resoconto.
exposition *s.* **1.** spiegazione, commento **2.** mostra, esposizione.
expositive *agg.* espositivo.
expositor *s.* commentatore.
expository *agg.* esplicativo.
exposure *s.* **1.** esposizione (*al freddo, al caldo ecc.*) **2.** mostra **3.** (*foto*) (tempo di) esposizione.
to expound *vt.* spiegare (*una teoria*).
express *agg.* **1.** chiaro, preciso **2.** espresso, diretto. ♦ **express** *s.* espresso, corriere || *— train*, direttissimo.
to express *vt.* esprimere, manifestare.
expression *s.* espressione.
expressionism *s.* espressionismo.
expressionist *s.* espressionista.
expressive *agg.* espressivo, significativo.
expressly *avv.* espressamente.
to expropriate *vt.* espropriare.
expropriation *s.* espropriazione.
expulsion *s.* espulsione.
expulsive *agg.* espulsivo.
expunction *s.* cancellatura.
to expurgate *vt.* espurgare (*uno scritto*).
expurgation *s.* espurgazione (*di uno scritto*).

exquisite *agg.* 1. squisito 2. fine, sensibile. ♦ exquisite *s.* raffinato.

exquisiteness *s.* squisitezza, finezza.

extant *agg.* ancora esistente.

extemporaneous, extemporary *agg.* estemporaneo.

extempore *agg.* improvvisato.

extemporization *s.* improvvisazione.

to extemporize *vt.* e *vi.* improvvisare.

to extend *vt.* 1. estendere, allungare, prolungare. ♦ to extend *vi.* estendersi, allungarsi, prolungarsi.

extendible *agg.* estendibile.

extensible *agg.* estensibile.

extension *s.* 1. estensione, allungamento 2. (*comm.*) proroga.

extensive *agg.* 1. esteso, ampio 2. estensivo.

extent *s.* 1. estensione 2. volume 3. limite, grado.

to extenuate *vt.* attenuare.

extenuation *s.* attenuazione.

exterior *agg.* esterno, esteriore. ♦ exterior *s.* 1. l'esterno 2. esteriorità.

exteriority *s.* esteriorità.

exteriorization *s.* esteriorizzazione.

to exteriorize *vt.* esternare.

to exterminate *vt.* sterminare.

extermination *s.* sterminio.

external *agg.* esteriore, esterno.

externality *s.* superficialità.

to externalize *vt.* esternare.

externally *avv.* esternamente, esteriormente.

exterritorial *agg.* estraterritoriale.

extinct *agg.* 1. estinto 2. spento.

extinction *s.* estinzione.

to extinguish *vt.* 1. estinguere, spegnere 2. pagare, ammortizzare.

extinguisher *s.* spegnitore, estintore.

to extirpate *vt.* estirpare, sradicare.

extirpation *s.* estirpazione, sradicamento.

to extol *vt.* lodare, magnificare

to extort *vt.* estorcere, strappare.

extorter *s.* chi estorce.

extortion *s.* estorsione.

extortioner *s.* ricattatore.

extra *agg.* 1. straordinario 2. in più, extra. ♦ extra *s.* 1. supplemento 2. (*giorn.*) edizione straordinaria 3. (*cine*) comparsa. ♦ extra *avv.* extra, di più, in più, insolitamente.

extract *s.* 1. estratto 2. citazione.

to extract *vt.* estrarre, togliere.

extractable *agg.* estraibile.

extraction *s.* 1. estrazione 2. origine, stirpe.

extractive *agg.* estrattivo.

extractor *s.* estrattore.

to extradite *vt.* estradare.

extradition *s.* estradizione.

extraneous *agg.* estraneo.

extraordinary *agg.* straordinario, eccezionale.

extraterritorial *agg.* estraterritoriale.

extraterritoriality *s.* estraterritorialità.

extravagance *s.* 1. prodigalità, sperpero 2. stravaganza.

extravagant *agg.* 1. prodigo 2. stravagante.

extreme *agg.* 1. estremo, ultimo 2. grave. ♦ extreme *s.* estremo, estremità.

extremely *avv.* estremamente.

extremism *s.* estremismo.

extremist *s.* estremista.

extremity *s.* estremità.

extrinsic(al) *agg.* estrinseco.

extrovert *s.* estroverso.

to extrude *vt.* estromettere.

exuberance *s.* esuberanza.

exuberant *agg.* 1. copioso, abbondante 2. esuberante, pieno di vita.

exudation *s.* essudazione.

to exude *vt.* e *vi.* trasudare.

to exult *vi.* gioire, esultare.

exultant *agg.* esultante.

exultation *s.* esultanza.

eye *s.* occhio.

eyeball *s.* bulbo oculare.

eyebrow *s.* sopracciglio.

eyeglass *s.* lente, monocolo.

eyehole *s.* orbita, occhiaia.

eyelash *s.* ciglio.

eyelet *s.* occhiello, asola.

eyelid *s.* palpebra.

eyesight *s.* vista.

eyesore *s.* cosa brutta e spiacevole.

eyewitness *s.* testimone oculare.

F

F *s.* (*mus.*) fa.

fable *s.* favola.

fabled *agg.* 1. mitico 2. inventato.

fabric *s.* 1. tessuto 2. manufatto 3.

struttura 4. fabbricazione.

to **fabricate** *vt.* 1. fabbricare 2. inventare.

fabrication *s.* 1. fabbricazione 2. invenzione.

fabulist *s.* 1. favolista 2. bugiardo.

fabulosity *s.* favolosità.

fabulous *agg.* favoloso.

façade *s.* facciata.

face *s.* 1. faccia 2. aspetto 3. sfrontatezza 4. facciata 5. quadrante (*di orologio*) ‖ to pull faces, fare boccacce ‖ *-powder*, cipria; — *value*, (*comm.*) valore nominale.

to **face** *vt.* 1. fronteggiare 2. affrontare 3. ricoprire ‖ to — about, fare dietro-front.

facet *s.* sfaccettatura.

facetious *agg.* faceto.

facetiousness *s.* lepidezza.

facial *agg.* facciale.

facile *agg.* 1. facile 2. pronto 3. accomodante.

to **facilitate** *vt.* facilitare.

facilitation *s.* facilitazione.

facility *s.* facilità. ♦ **facilities** *s. pl.* facilitazioni.

facing *agg.* che sta di fronte. ♦ **facing** *s.* rivestimento. ♦ **facings** *s. pl.* mostrine.

fact *s.* 1. fatto 2. realtà ‖ in —, infatti, di fatto; *as a matter of* —, effettivamente.

faction *s.* 1. fazione 2. faziosità.

factious *agg.* fazioso.

factiousness *s.* faziosità.

factitious *agg.* fittizio.

factitiousness *s.* artificiosità.

factor *s.* 1. fattore 2. agente.

factory *s.* fabbrica.

factual *agg.* effettivo.

facultative *agg.* 1. facoltativo 2. casuale.

faculty *s.* facoltà.

fad *s.* 1. mania 2. capriccio.

faddist *s.* maniaco.

faddy *agg.* capriccioso.

fade *s.* (*radio*) variazione graduale.

to **fade** *vi.* 1. appassire 2. sbiadire 3. svanire ‖ to — in (*cine*) aprire in dissolvenza; to — out, (*cine*) chiudere in dissolvenza. ♦ to **fade** *vt.* 1. far sbiadire 2. far svanire.

fading *s.* 1. appassimento 2. scolorimento 3. affievolimento 4. dissolvenza.

to **fag** *vt.* affaticare. ♦ to **fag** *vi.* 1. affaticarsi 2. sfacchinare.

fag(g)ot *s.* fascina.

faience *s.* terracotta.

fall *s.* fallo.

to **fail** *vi.* 1. fallire 2. mancare, venir meno 3. indebolirsi 4. esser bocciato. ♦ to **fail** *vt.* 1. mancare di 2. bocciare 3. abbandonare.

failing[1] *agg.* debole. ♦ **failing** *s.* 1. debolezza 2. mancanza 3. fallimento.

failing[2] *prep.* in mancanza di.

failure *s.* 1. fallimento 2. incapacità 3. mancanza 4. indebolimento 5. guasto ‖ to be a —, essere un fallito.

fain *agg.* contento, disposto. ♦ **fain** *avv.* volentieri ‖ I would — stay, preferirei restare.

faint *agg.* 1. debole 2. timido 3. vago.

faint *s.* svenimento ‖ -hearted, codardo.

to **faint** *vi.* svenire.

faintness *s.* 1. debolezza 2. timidezza.

fair[1] *agg.* 1. onesto 2. biondo 3. gentile 4. bello 5. sereno (*di tempo*) 6. (*comm.*) libero ‖ — *-play*, comportamento leale. ♦ **fair** *avv.* 1. con onestà 2. con precisione.

fair[2] *s.* fiera ‖ fun —, Luna Park.

fairly *avv.* 1. onestamente 2. abbastanza.

fairness *s.* 1. bellezza 2. onestà 3. color biondo 4. bianchezza (*di carnagione*).

fairway *s.* canale navigabile.

fairy *s.* 1. fatato 2. immaginario. ♦ **fairy** *s.* fata ‖ -tale, fiaba.

fairyland *s.* paese delle fate.

fairylike *agg.* simile a fata.

faith *s.* 1. fede 2. promessa ‖ —-healer, guaritore.

faithful *agg.* 1. fedele 2. degno di fiducia.

faithfulness *s.* fedeltà.

faithless *agg.* 1. senza fede 2. sleale.

to **fake** *vt.* (*gergo*) falsificare.

fakir *s.* fachiro.

falcon *s.* falcone.

falconry *s.* falconeria.

fall *s.* 1. caduta, cascata 2. (*amer.*) autunno.

to **fall** (fell, fallen) *vi.* 1. cadere 2. abbassarsi 3. capitare in sorte 4. dividersi ‖ to — back, ritirarsi; to — behind, restare indietro; to — in with, imbattersi; to — short, essere insufficiente; to — away, deperire; to — down, far fiasco; to — due, scadere.

fallacious agg. fallace.

fallaciousness s. fallacia.

fallacy s. 1. fallacia 2. errore 3. sofisma.

fallen V. to fall.

fallibility s. fallibilità.

fallible agg. fallibile.

falling agg. cadente. ◆ **falling** s. caduta || — back, ripiegamento; — off, diminuzione; — short, insufficienza.

fall-out s. pioggia radioattiva.

fallow agg. incolto.

false agg. 1. falso 2. stonato 3. ingannevole || — bottom, doppio fondo.

falsehood s. falsità.

falsely avv. falsamente.

falseness s. falsità.

falsifiable agg. falsificabile.

falsification s. falsificazione.

falsifier s. falsificatore.

to **falsify** vt. 1. falsificare 2. smentire.

falsity s. falsità.

to **falter** vi. vacillare. ◆ to **falter** vt. balbettare.

fame s. fama.

famed agg. celebre.

familiar agg. familiare. ◆ **familiar** s. amico intimo || to be — with, esser pratico di.

familiarity s. familiarità.

familiarization s. familiarità.

to **familiarize** vt. familiarizzare.

family s. famiglia.

famine s. carestia.

to **famish** vt. far morire di fame. ◆ to **famish** vi. morire di fame.

famous agg. famoso.

fan[1] s. 1. ventaglio 2. ventilatore 3. pala (d'elica).

fan[2] s. (gergo) tifoso, ammiratore.

to **fan** vt. 1. sventolare 2. (agr.) vagliare.

fanatic agg. e s. fanatico.

fanatical agg. fanatico.

fanaticism s. fanatismo.

to **fanaticize** vt. rendere fanatico. ◆ to **fanaticize** vi. agire da fanatico.

fanciful agg. 1. fantasioso 2. fantastico.

fancifulness s. 1. fantasia 2. capriccio.

fancy agg. 1. immaginario 2. stra-

vagante 3. decorato. ◆ **fancy** s. 1. fantasia 2. capriccio 3. inclinazione || — ball, ballo in costume; — -dress, costume.

to **fancy** vt. 1. immaginare 2. ritenere.

fang s. 1. zanna 2. dente (velenoso).

fanning s. ventilazione.

fantastic(al) agg. 1. immaginario 2. bizzarro.

to **fantasticate** vt. e vi. fantasticare.

fantasy s. 1. fantasia 2. capriccio.

far agg. (farther, farthest) (further, furthest) lontano. ◆ **far** avv. 1. lontano 2. di gran lunga || — away, — off, lontano; as — as, fino a, per quanto; so —, finora; — -gone, a uno stadio avanzato (di malattie).

farce s. farsa.

farcical agg. farsesco.

farcicality s. qualità farsesca.

fare s. 1. tariffa 2. vitto 3. passeggero || bill of —, lista delle vivande.

to **fare** vi. 1. andare 2. riuscire 3. nutrirsi || to — badly, andar male.

farewell s. congedo. ◆ **farewell** inter. addio.

farfetched agg. remoto.

farinaceous agg. farinaceo.

farinose agg. farinoso.

farm s. fattoria || — -yard, aia.

to **farm** vt. coltivare. ◆ to **farm** vi. fare l'agricoltore.

farmer s. agricoltore.

farmhouse s. casa colonica.

farming s. agricoltura.

farmstead s. cascina.

farraginous agg. farraginoso.

farrier s. maniscalco.

farsighted agg. e s. presbite.

farther agg. (comp. di far) più lontano, ulteriore. ◆ **farther** avv. 1. (di) più 2. più lontano 3. inoltre.

farthermost agg. il più lontano.

farthest agg. (superl. di far) il più lontano, estremo. ◆ **farthest** avv. (il) più lontano.

farthing s. "farthing" (moneta inglese: un quarto di penny).

fascicle s. fascicolo.

to **fascinate** vt. affascinare.

fascinating agg. affascinante.

fascination s. fascino.

fascinator s. affascinatore.

fascism s. fascismo.

fascist agg. e s. fascista.

fashion s. 1. modo 2. abitudine 3. moda ‖ - -*plate*, figurino; *a man of —*, un uomo di mondo.

to **fashion** vt. foggiare.

fashionabie agg. 1. alla moda 2. elegante.

fast agg. 1. fermo 2. fedele 3. inalterabile 4. rapido 5. (*fig.*) dissoluto 6. in anticipo (*di orologio*). ♦ **fast** avv. 1. fermamente 2. fortemente 3. velocemente 4. in modo dissoluto.

fast s. digiuno.

to **fast** vi. digiunare.

to **fasten** vt. 1. attaccare 2. allacciare 3. chiudere 4. fissare. ♦ **fasten** vi. 1. allacciarsi 2. chiudersi 3. fissarsi.

fastener s. 1. fermaglio 2. legaccio, chiusura ‖ *snap —*, automatico.

fastening s. 1. legatura 2. gancio, chiavistello.

faster s. digiunatore.

fastidious agg. schizzinoso.

fastidiousness s. schizzinosità.

fastness s. 1. velocità 2. fermezza 3. solidità 4. dissolutezza.

fat agg. 1. grasso 2. (*fig.*) proficuo. ♦ **fat** s. grasso ‖ - -*head*, zuccone.

to **fat** V. *to fatten*.

fatal agg. fatale.

fatalism s. fatalismo.

fatalist s. fatalista.

fatalistic agg. fatalistico.

fatality s. 1. fatalità 2. fatalismo.

fatally avv. 1. in modo fatale 2. fatalmente.

fate s. fato.

father s. padre ‖ - -*in-law*, suocero.

fatherhood s. paternità.

fatherland s. madrepatria.

fatherless agg. senza padre.

fatherlike agg. paterno. ♦ **fatherlike** avv. paternamente.

fatherly agg. e avv. V. *fatherlike*.

fathom s. (*mar.*) braccio (*misura di profondità*).

to **fathom** vt. scandagliare.

fathomless agg. 1. incommensurabile 2. incomprensibile.

fatidic(al) agg. fatidico.

fatigue s. fatica.

to **fatigue** vt. affaticare. ♦ to **fatigue** vi. affaticarsi.

fatness s. grassezza.

to **fatten** vt. ingrassare. ♦ to **fatten** vi. ingrassarsi.

fattener s. ingrassatore.

fattening s. ingrassamento.

fattiness s. grassezza.

fatty agg. grasso.

fatuity s. fatuità.

fatuous agg. fatuo.

fault s. 1. fallo 2. colpa 3. difetto ‖ - -*finder*, criticone.

faultiness s. imperfezione.

faultless agg. 1. perfetto 2. irreprensibile.

faulty agg. difettoso.

faun s. fauno.

favour s. favore.

to **favour** vt. 1. favorire 2. sostenere 3. (*fam.*) assomigliare a.

favourable agg. favorevole.

favourite agg. e s. favorito.

favouritism s. favoritismo.

fawn s. cerbiatto.

to **fawn** vt. fare le feste ‖ *to — on*, adulare.

fawner s. adulatore.

fawning s. servilismo.

fear s. paura, timore.

to **fear** vt. e vi. temere, aver paura.

fearful agg. 1. terribile 2. timoroso.

fearfulness s. 1. aspetto terribile 2. timore.

fearless agg. intrepido.

feasibility s. fattibilità.

feasible agg. fattibile.

feast s. 1. festa 2. banchetto.

to **feast** vt. 1. rallegrare 2. festeggiare. ♦ to **feast** vi. banchettare.

feaster s. convitato.

feat s. impresa, prodezza.

feather s. penna, piuma.

to **feather** vt. 1. coprire di penne, piume 2. (*mar.*) spalare.

feathered agg. 1. pennuto 2. (*fig.*) alato.

feathering s. piumaggio.

featherless agg. implume.

feature s. 1. lineamento 2. (*cine*) attrazione 3. caratteristica ‖ -*film*, parte principale di un film.

to **feature** vt. 1. caratterizzare 2. (*teat.*) dare una parte importante a.

featureless agg. senza caratteristiche.

febrifuge s. febbrifugo.

febrile agg. febbrile.

February s. febbraio.

fecal agg. fecale.

fecund agg. fecondo.

to **fecundate** vt. fecondare.

fecundation s. fecondazione.

fecundity s. fecondità.
fed V. to feed.
federacy s. federazione.
federal agg. federale.
federalism s. federalismo.
federate agg. confederato.
to federate vt. confederare. ♦ to federate vi. confederarsi.
federation s. (con)federazione.
federative agg. federativo.
fee s. 1. onorario 2. tassa 3. (giur) proprietà ereditaria.
feeble agg. debole.
feebleness s. debolezza.
feed s. 1. alimentazione 2. pascolo.
to feed (fed, fed) vt. 1. nutrire 2. pascere 3. rifornire || to be fed up, essere stufo. ♦ to feed (fed, fed) vi. nutrirsi || to — up, ingrassare.
feeder s. 1. ciò che, chi nutre 2. cavo di alimentazione 3. affluente 4. serbatoio.
feeding s. alimentazione.
feel s. tatto.
to feel (felt, felt) vt. 1. sentire (col tatto o col sentimento) 2. tastare, sondare. ♦ to feel (felt, felt) vi. 1. sentirsi 2. andare a tastoni.
feeling agg. sensibile. ♦ feeling s. 1. sentimento 2. sensibilità 3. sensazione.
feet V. foot.
to feign vt. 1. inventare 2. falsificare. ♦ to feign vi. fingersi.
feignedly avv. simulatamente.
feigner s. simulatore.
feint s. 1. finta 2. simulazione.
to feint vi. fare una finta.
feldspar s. feldspato.
to felicitate vt. felicitarsi con || to — so. on sthg., felicitarsi con qu. di qc.
felicitation s. felicitazione.
felicitous agg. appropriato.
feline agg. e s. felino.
fell¹ V. to fall.
fell² agg. 1. crudele 2. funesto.
to fell vt. abbattere.
felling s. taglio (di un bosco).
fellow s. 1. individuo 2. compagno, collega || — -citizen, concittadino; — -creature, simile; a good —, un buon diavolo.
fellowship s. 1. amicizia 2. associazione.
felon agg. e s. criminale.
felony s. crimine, delitto.

felt¹ V. to feel.
felt² s. feltro.
to felt vt. feltrare.
felucca s. feluca.
female agg. 1. femminile 2. (mecc) femmina. ♦ female s. femmina.
feminine agg. e s. femminile.
femininity s. femminilità.
feminism s. femminismo.
femur s. femore.
fen s. palude || — -berry, mirtillo; — -fire, fuoco fatuo.
fence s. 1. recinto 2. scherma 3. (fam.) ricettatore.
to fence vt. cintare. ♦ to fence vi. tirar di scherma.
fencer s. schermidore.
fencing s. 1. cinta 2. scherma.
fender s. 1. riparo 2. paraurti 3. (mar.) parabordo.
fennel s. finocchio.
feracity s. feracità.
feral¹ agg. ferale, funesto.
feral² agg. ferino.
ferial agg. feriale.
ferine agg. ferino.
ferment s. fermento.
to ferment vi. 1. fermentare 2. agitarsi. ♦ to ferment vt. 1. far fermentare 2. eccitare.
fermentation s. 1. fermentazione 2. fermento.
fermentative agg. fermentativo.
fern s. felce.
ferocious agg. feroce.
ferocity s. ferocia.
ferreous agg. 1. ferroso 2. ferreo.
ferret¹ s. furetto.
ferret² s. nastro, fettuccia.
ferro-concrete s. cemento armato.
ferrous agg. ferroso.
ferruginous agg. ferruginoso.
ferry s. traghetto.
to ferry vt. e vi. traghettare.
ferryman s. traghettatore.
fertile agg. fertile.
fertility s. fertilità.
fertilization s. fertilizzazione.
to fertilize vt. 1. fertilizzare 2. fecondare.
fertilizer s. fertilizzante.
fervency s. fervore.
fervent, fervid agg. ardente.
fervour s. ardore.
festal agg. festivo.
fester s. suppurazione, piaga.
to fester vi. suppurare (di ferita)
festival s. 1. festa 2. festival.
festive agg. 1. festivo 2. festoso.

festivity s. festività. ✦ **festivities** s. pl. festeggiamenti.

festoon s. festone.

to fetch vt. 1. andare a prendere 2. tirare 3. fruttare, rendere ‖ to — back, riportare.

fetid agg. fetido.

fetish s. feticcio.

fetishism s. feticismo.

fetishist s. feticista.

fetter s. ceppo, catena.

to fetter vt. incatenare.

fettle s. condizione ‖ in fine —, in forma.

feud[1] s. ostilità.

feud[2] s. feudo.

feudal agg. feudale.

feudalism s. feudalesimo.

feudality s. 1. feudalesimo 2. feudo.

feudatory agg. e s. feudatario.

fever s. febbre ‖ to be in a —, avere la febbre.

feverish agg. 1. febbricitante 2. febbrile.

few agg. e pron. pochi ‖ a —, alcuni; quite a —, un numero considerevole; a good —, parecchi.

fewness s. scarsità, esiguità.

fiancé s. fidanzato.

fib s. fandonia.

to fib vi. dire fandonie.

fibre s. fibra.

fibroid, fibrous agg. fibroso.

fickle agg. incostante.

fickleness s. incostanza.

fictile agg. fittile.

fiction s. 1. narrativa 2. finzione.

fictional agg. immaginario.

fictitious agg. fittizio.

fiddle s. violino ‖ fit as a —, in ottima salute.

to fiddle vi. 1. suonare il violino 2. gingillarsi.

fiddler s. violinista.

fiddlestick s. archetto. ✦ **fiddlesticks** s. pl. sciocchezze.

fidelity s. fedeltà.

to fidget vt. agitare. ✦ **to fidget** vi. agitarsi.

fidgety agg. irrequieto.

fiduciary agg. e s. fiduciario.

field s. campo ‖ — -glass, binocolo; — -day, giorno di esercitazioni; — -officer, ufficiale superiore.

fiend s. demonio.

fiendish agg. diabolico.

fierce agg. 1. fiero 2. selvaggio 3. ardente.

fierceness s. 1. ferocia 2. ardore.

fiery agg. 1. di fuoco 2. focoso 3. infiammabile.

fife s. piffero.

fifteen agg. e s. quindici.

fifteenth agg. e s. quindicesimo.

fifth agg. e s. quinto.

fiftieth agg. e s. cinquantesimo.

fifty agg. e s. cinquanta ‖ — - —, a metà.

fig[1] s. fico.

fig[2] s. tenuta, vestiario.

fight s. 1. lotta 2. spirito combattivo.

to fight (fought, fought) vt. e vi. combattere ‖ to — down, vincere; to — off, respingere; to — shy of, tenersi alla larga da.

fighter s. 1. combattente 2. (aer.) caccia.

fighting s. combattimento, rissa.

figuration s. figurazione.

figurative agg. 1. figurativo 2. figurato.

figure s. 1. figura, forma 2. cifra 3. diagramma.

to figure vt. raffigurare. ✦ **to figure** vi. 1. immaginarsi 2. passare per.

figurehead s. 1. prestanome 2. (mar.) polena.

filament s. filamento.

filamentary, filamentous agg. filamentoso.

filcher s. ladruncolo.

file[1] s. lima.

file[2] s. 1. schedario, archivio 2. fila 3. raccolta.

to file[1] vt. limare.

to file[2] vt. 1. archiviare 2. ordinare. ✦ **to file** vi. marciare in fila.

filial agg. filiale.

filiation s. filiazione.

filibuster s. filibustiere.

filigree s. filigrana.

filing[1] s. limatura.

filing[2] s. 1. archiviazione 2. sfilata.

fill s. sazietà.

to fill vt. 1. riempire 2. occupare 3. otturare (di denti) ‖ to — in, to — up, riempire, compilare. ✦ **to fill** vi. riempirsi.

fillet s. 1. nastro 2. (cuc.) filetto.

filling s. 1. riempitura 2. otturazione 3. (cuc.) ripieno ‖ — station, stazione di rifornimento.

fillip s. 1. schiocco (delle dita) 2. stimolo.

film s. 1. pellicola 2. velo 3. membrana.

to film vt. 1. coprire con una pellicola 2. filmare. ◆ to **film** *vi.* 1. coprirsi con una pellicola 2. girare un film.

filmy *agg.* velato.

filter *s.* filtro.

to **filter** *vt.* e *vi.* filtrare.

filth *s.* sozzura.

filthily *avv.* in modo sudicio.

filthiness *s.* 1. sozzura 2. corruzione morale.

filthy *agg.* 1. sozzo 2. corrotto.

filtration *s.* filtrazione.

fin *s.* 1. pinna 2. *(mecc.)* aletta.

final *agg.* e *s.* finale.

finalist *s.* finalista.

finality *s.* 1. finalità 2. carattere definitivo.

finally *avv.* alla fine.

finance *s.* finanza.

to **finance** *vt.* finanziare.

financial *agg.* finanziario.

financier *s.* 1. finanziere 2. finanziatore.

financing *s.* finanziamento.

finch *s.* fringuello.

find *s.* scoperta, ritrovamento.

to **find (found, found)** *vt.* 1. trovare 2. provvedere 3. ritenere || *to — out*, scoprire.

finding *s.* 1. scoperta 2. sentenza.

fine[1] *agg.* 1. bello 2. fine. ◆ **fine** *avv.* bene.

fine[2] *s.* multa.

to **fine**[1] *vt.* raffinare. ◆ to **fine** *vi.* raffinarsi.

to **fine**[2] *vt.* multare.

finely *avv.* 1. bene 2. finemente.

finger *s.* dito || *—print*, impronta digitale; *— -tip*, punta delle dita; *— -post*, cartello segnavia.

to **finger** *vt.* 1. toccare con le dita 2. rubare || *to be light-fingered (fig.)*, avere le mani lunghe.

finish *s.* 1. fine 2. finezza 3. finitura.

to **finish** *vt.* e *vi.* finire.

finished *agg. (fig.)* perfetto.

finishing *agg.* ultimo, conclusivo. ◆ **finishing** *s.* (ri)finitura.

finite *agg.* limitato.

Finn *s.* finlandese.

Finnic, Finnish *agg.* finlandese.

fir (-tree) *s.* abete || *— -wood*, abetaia.

fire *s.* 1. fuoco 2. incendio || *on —*, in fiamme; *— -guard*, parafuoco; *— -plug*, bocca da incendio; *— station*, caserma dei pompieri; *— -works*, fuochi d'artificio.

to **fire** *vt.* 1. dar fuoco 2. far fuoco

3. *(fig.)* infiammare. ◆ to **fire** *vi.* 1. prender fuoco 2. *(fig.)* infiammarsi.

firedamp *s.* grisù.

fire escape *s.* 1. scala di sicurezza 2. scala dei pompieri.

firefly *s.* lucciola.

fireman *s.* pompiere.

fireplace *s.* caminetto.

fireproof *agg.* incombustibile.

fireside *s.* angolo del focolare.

firewood *s.* legna da ardere.

firing *s.* 1. accensione 2. sparo 3. alimentazione *(di un fuoco)* || *— squad*, plotone d'esecuzione.

firm[1] *agg.* 1. fisso 2. solido 3. deciso.

firm[2] *s.* azienda, ditta.

firmament *s.* firmamento.

firmly *avv.* 1. fermamente 2. solidamente.

firmness *s.* 1. fermezza 2. stabilità.

first *agg.* primo || *— -aid*, pronto soccorso; *— -born*, primogenito; *— -class*, di prima qualità; *— -name*, nome di battesimo. ◆ **first** *avv.* 1. prima di tutto 2. per la prima volta || *at —*, sulle prime. ◆ **first** *s.* 1. primo 2. principio.

firth *s.* fiordo.

fiscal *agg.* fiscale.

fish *s.* pesce || *— -hook*, amo.

to **fish** *vi.* 1. pescare 2. cercare. ◆ to **fish** *vt.* pescare.

fisher *s.* pescatore.

fisherman *s.* pescatore.

fishery *s.* pesca.

fishing *s.* pesca || *— -boat*, pescherccio; *— -line*, lenza.

fishmonger *s.* pescivendolo.

fishy *agg.* 1. di pesce 2. pescoso 3. *(fig.)* equivoco.

fission *s.* fissione.

fist *s.* pugno.

fit[1] *agg.* 1. adatto 2. pronto.

fit[2] *s.* 1. giusta misura 2. attacco, accesso *(di febbre, ira ecc.)*.

to **fit** *vt.* 1. adattare 2. andar bene a 3. provare || *to — out*, equipaggiare.

fitful *agg.* 1. irregolare 2. spasmodico.

fitfulness *s.* irregolarità.

fitness *s.* convenienza.

fitter *s.* 1. aggiustatore 2. montatore.

fitting *agg.* adatto, conveniente. ◆ **fitting** *s.* 1. adattamento, prova 2. equipaggiamento. ◆ **fittings**

s. pl. **1.** accessori **2.** arredamento (*sing.*).

five *agg.* e *s.* cinque.

fix *s.* **1.** difficoltà **2.** (*mar.*) punto.

to fix *vt.* fissare || — *to — up*, sistemare, riparare. ♦ **to fix** *vi.* stabilirsi.

fixation *s.* fissazione.

fixed *agg.* **1.** fisso **2.** stabilito.

fixer *s.* **1.** montatore **2.** fissatore.

fixing *s.* **1.** collocamento **2.** messa in opera **3.** fissaggio.

fixity *s.* **1.** stabilità **2.** fissità.

fizz *s.* **1.** effervescenza **2.** bevanda effervescente.

to fizz *vi.* frizzare.

fjord *s.* fiordo.

flabbiness *s.* **1.** mollezza **2.** fiacchezza (*di carattere ecc.*).

flabby *agg.* **1.** floscio **2.** fiacco.

flaccid *agg.* flaccido.

flaccidness *s.* flaccidezza.

flag[1] *s.* bandiera || — *-ship*, nave ammiraglia.

flag[2] *s.* lastra di pietra (*per pavimentazione*).

to flag[1] *vt.* **1.** imbandierare **2.** pavesare. ♦ **to flag** *vi.* **1.** pendere **2.** avvizzire.

to flag[2] *vt.* lastricare.

to flagellate *vt.* flagellare.

flagellation *s.* flagellazione.

flagellator *s.* flagellatore.

flagrancy *s.* flagranza.

flagrant *agg.* flagrante.

flagstaff *s.* asta di bandiera.

flair *s.* fiuto, intuizione.

flake *s.* **1.** fiocco (*di neve, lana ecc.*) **2.** favilla **3.** lamina **4.** scaglia.

to flake *vt.* **1.** sfaldare **2.** squamare **3.** coprire di fiocchi. ♦ **to flake** *vi.* **1.** sfaldarsi **2.** squamarsi **3.** cadere in fiocchi.

flaky *agg.* **1.** a falde **2.** a lamine, a scaglie.

flame *s.* fiamma || — *-thrower*, lanciafiamme.

to flame *vi.* fiammeggiare.

flaming *agg.* ardente.

flange *s.* orlo, frangia.

flank *s.* fianco.

to flank *vt.* **1.** fiancheggiare **2.** (*mil.*) attaccare il fianco di.

flannel *s.* flanella. ♦ **flannels** *s. pl.* calzoni di flanella.

flap *s.* **1.** lembo, falda **2.** colpo, agitazione **3.** linguetta **4.** (*aer.*) alettone.

flare *s.* **1.** fiammata improvvisa **2.**

chiarore.

to flare *vi.* **1.** brillare (*di luce incerta*) **2.** agitarsi **3.** divampare.

flash *s.* **1.** lampo **2.** chiusa || — *-back*, scena retrospettiva; — *-light*, lampo al magnesio.

to flash *vt.* **1.** proiettare **2.** diffondere. ♦ **to flash** *vi.* **1.** lampeggiare **2.** muoversi rapidamente.

flashing *agg.* risplendente. ♦ **flashing** *s.* splendore, scintillio.

flask *s.* fiasca.

flat[1] *agg.* **1.** piatto, piano **2.** disteso **3.** deciso **4.** sgonfio (*di pneumatico*).

flat[2] *s.* **1.** superficie piana **2.** pianura **3.** bassofondo **4.** chiatta **5.** appartamento **6.** (*mus.*) bemolle || — *-iron*, ferro da stiro.

flatly *avv.* **1.** pianamente **2.** scialbamente **3.** recisamente.

flatness *s.* **1.** piattezza **2.** decisione.

to flatten *vt.* **1.** appiattire **2.** smorzare. ♦ **to flatten** *vi.* **1.** appiattirsi **2.** indebolirsi.

to flatter *vt.* **1.** adulare **2.** illudere.

flatterer *s.* adulatore.

flattery *s.* adulazione.

flatulence, flatulency *s.* **1.** flatulenza **2.** vanità.

flatus *s.* flatulenza.

to flaunt *vt.* **1.** sventolare **2.** ostentare.

flavour *s.* gusto, aroma.

to flavour *vt.* aromatizzare, dare gusto a.

flavoured *agg.* **1.** profumato **2.** saporito.

flavouring *s.* **1.** aroma **2.** condimento.

flavourless *agg.* insipido.

flaw *s.* **1.** screpolatura **2.** falla, pecca.

flawless *agg.* perfetto.

flax *s.* lino.

flaxen *agg.* **1.** di lino **2.** biondo.

to flay *vt.* **1.** scorticare **2.** criticare aspramente.

flea *s.* pulce || — *-bite* (*fig.*), inezia.

fleck *s.* **1.** macchia **2.** scaglia.

to flee (**fled, fled**) *vt.* **1.** abbandonare **2.** evitare, schivare. ♦ **to flee** (**fled, fled**) *vi.* **1.** fuggire **2.** svanire.

fleece *s.* vello.

fleecy *agg.* lanoso.

to fleer *vt.* e *vi.* far beffe (a).

fleet *s.* flotta.

fleeting *agg.* fugace.

Flemish *agg.* fiammingo.

flesh *s.* carne || *to lose —*, dimagrire; *to put on —*, ingrassare.

fleshiness *s.* 1. carnosità 2. corpulenza.

fleshless *agg.* scarno.

fleshly *agg.* carnale, sensuale.

flew V. *to fly.*

to flex *vt.* flettere, piegare. ◆ **to flex** *vi.* flettersi.

flexibility *s.* 1. flessibilità 2. docilità.

flexible *agg.* 1. flessibile 2. docile.

flexion *s.* 1. flessione 2. curva.

flexuosity *s.* flessuosità.

flexuous *agg.* flessuoso.

flicker *s.* tremolio, bagliore.

to flicker *vi.* 1. tremolare 2. guizzare. ◆ **to flicker** *vt.* far tremolare.

flight[1] *s.* 1. volo 2. stormo 3. rampa (*di scale*).

flight[2] *s.* fuga.

flimsiness *s.* leggerezza, frivolezza.

flimsy *agg.* leggero, sottile.

to flinch *vi.* indietreggiare, ritirarsi.

fling *s.* 1. getto 2. beffa 3. tentativo.

to fling (**flung, flung**) *vt.* gettare. || *to — open*, spalancare. ◆ **to fling** (**flung, flung**) *vi.* gettarsi.

flint *s.* selce, pietra focaia.

to flip *vt.* 1. far schioccare 2. sbattere.

flippancy *s.* leggerezza.

flippant *agg.* leggero.

flipper *s.* pinna.

flirt *s.* 1. movimento rapido 2. amoreggiamento.

to flirt *vt.* muovere rapidamente. ◆ **to flirt** *vi.* amoreggiare.

flirtation *s.* amoreggiamento.

to flit *vi.* 1. volare 2. scorrere.

float *s.* galleggiante.

to float *vt.* 1. trasportare 2. inondare 3. (*comm.*) varare (*un progetto ecc.*). ◆ **to float** *vi.* 1. galleggiare 2. spandersi.

floatage *s.* 1. galleggiamento 2. relitto.

floatation *s.* (*comm.*) varo.

floater *s.* galleggiante.

floating *agg.* 1. galleggiante 2. oscillante, fluttuante.

flock[1] *s.* 1. bioccolo 2. gregge 3. cascame.

to flock *vi.* affollarsi.

floe *s.* banchisa.

to flog *vt.* fustigare || *to — a dead horse*, fare una fatica inutile.

flogger *s.* fustigatore.

flood *s.* inondazione, diluvio.

to flood *vt.* inondare. ◆ **to flood** *vi.* straripare.

flooding *s.* 1. inondazione 2. emorragia.

floodlight *s.* illuminazione con riflettore.

flood tide *s.* flusso della marea.

floor *s.* 1. pavimento 2. piano || *-lamp*, lampada a stelo.

to floor *vt.* pavimentare.

flooring *s.* impiantito.

flop *s.* 1. tonfo 2. insuccesso.

floral *agg.* floreale.

floriculture *s.* floricultura.

floriculturist *s.* floricultore.

florid *agg.* 1. florido 2. fiorito (*di stile*).

floridity *s.* floridezza.

florin *s.* fiorino.

florist *s.* fiorista.

flotilla *s.* flottiglia.

to flounce *vi.* agitarsi || *to — out*, andarsene furibondo.

flour *s.* farina || *potato- —*, fecola.

to flour *vt.* 1. infarinare 2. macinare.

flourish *s.* 1. ornamento 2. squillo di tromba.

to flourish *vi.* 1. prosperare 2. essere attivo.

flourishing *agg.* 1. fiorente 2. pomposo.

floury *agg.* 1. farinoso 2. infarinato.

flow *s.* corrente, flusso.

to flow *vi.* 1. scorrere 2. derivare da. ◆ **to flow** *vt.* inondare.

flower *s.* fiore || *— -bed*, aiuola; *— -bud*, bocciuolo.

to flower *vi.* fiorire. ◆ **to flower** *vt.* infiorare.

flowering *agg.* in fiore. ◆ **flowering** *s.* fioritura.

flowerless *agg.* senza fiori.

flowery *agg.* fiorito.

flowing *agg.* 1. fluente 2. fluido.

flown V. *to fly.*

flu *s.* influenza.

to fluctuate *vi.* 1. fluttuare 2. ondeggiare.

fluctuation *s.* oscillazione.

flue *s.* condotto per l'aria.

fluency *s.* 1. fluidità 2. scioltezza.

fluent *agg.* 1. fluente 2. dalla parola facile.

fluently *avv.* 1. fluentemente 2. speditamente.

fluff *s.* peluria.

fluffy agg. 1. soffice, vaporoso 2. coperto di peluria.

fluid agg. e s. fluido.

fluidity s. fluidità.

flung V. to fling.

fluorescence s. fluorescenza.

fluorescent agg. fluorescente.

fluoride s. fluoruro.

fluorine s. fluoro.

flurry s. 1. ventata 2. agitazione.

to flurry vt. agitare.

flush agg. 1. abbondante 2. pieno di vita 3. a pari livello 4. ben fornito. ◆ **flush** s. 1. flusso 2. vampata 3. vigore.

to flush vt. 1. lavare 2. far scorrere 3. rianimare. ◆ **to flush** vi. 1. scorrere 2. arrossire.

flute s. 1. flauto 2. increspatura.

fluted agg. 1. flautato 2. increspato.

flutter s. 1. battito, movimento rapido 2. eccitazione.

to flutter vt. agitare. ◆ **to flutter** vi. 1. agitarsi 2. battere le ali.

fluttering agg. 1. svolazzante 2. palpitante. ◆ **fluttering** s. 1. svolazzamento 2. palpitazione.

fluxion s. flusso.

fly[1] s. 1. volo 2. calesse 3. (mecc.) volano.

fly[2] s. mosca.

to fly (flew, flown) vi. volare. ◆ **to fly** (flew, flown) vt. 1. far volare 2. sventolare || to — about, svolazzare; to — away, fuggire; to off (aer.), decollare.

flying agg. 1. rapido 2. sventolante || —boat, idrovolante.

flypaper s. carta moschicida.

foam s. schiuma || — rubber gommapiuma.

to foam vi. spumeggiare.

foamy agg. spumeggiante.

focal agg. focale.

focus s. 1. fuoco 2. focolaio.

to focus vt. mettere a fuoco.

fodder s. foraggio.

to fodder vt. foraggiare.

foe s. nemico.

foetus s. feto.

fog s. nebbia.

foggy agg. nebbioso (anche fig.).

foible s. debolezza.

foil[1] s. 1. fioretto 2. traccia.

foil[2] s. lamina.

fold[1] s. ovile.

fold[2] s. 1. piega 2. spira.

to fold[1] vt. 1. piegare 2. avvolgere 3. abbracciare. ◆ **to fold** vi. pie-

garsi.

to fold[2] vt. chiudere nell'ovile.

folder s. 1. volantino 2. cartelletta.

folding agg. pieghevole. ◆ **folding** s. 1. piega, piegatura 2. avvolgimento 3. abbraccio.

foliage s. fogliame.

folio s. (tip.) fo(g)lio.

folk s. gente, popolo.

folklore s. folclore.

folkloristic agg. folcloristico.

to follow vt. e vi. seguire.

follower s. seguace.

following agg. seguente. ◆ **following** s. seguito.

folly s. follia.

to foment vt. fomentare.

fomentation s. fomentazione.

fomenter s. fomentatore.

fond agg. 1. amante 2. affettuoso.

to fondle vt. vezzeggiare.

fondly avv. 1. amorevolmente 2. ingenuamente.

fondness s. tenerezza, amore.

font s. 1. fonte battesimale 2. acquasantiera.

food s. cibo.

foodstuff s. alimenti (pl.).

fool s. 1. sciocco 2. buffone || to make a — of, beffarsi di.

to fool vt. ingannare. ◆ **to fool** vi. fare lo sciocco || to — away, sperperare.

foolery s. follia.

foolhardiness s. folle temerarietà.

foolhardy agg. temerario.

foolish agg. sciocco.

foolishness s. sciocchezza.

foot s. (pl. feet) 1. piede 2. zampa || on —, a piedi.

football s. pallone.

footballer s. calciatore.

foot-bath s. pediluvio.

footboard s. predellino.

footbridge s. cavalcavia.

footfall s. passo.

footing s. punto d'appoggio.

footlights s. pl. luci della ribalta.

footman s. domestico.

footmark s. orma.

footnote s. poscritto.

footpath s. sentiero.

footprint, footstep s. orma.

footstool s. sgabello.

footway s. passaggio pedonale.

fop s. damerino.

foppery s. fatuità.

foppish agg. fatuo.

for[1] prep. per || — all that, ciò nonostante; *as* —, in quanto a.

for¹ *cong.* poiché.

forage *s.* foraggio.

foray *s.* incursione, saccheggio.

forbade V. *to forbid.*

to **forbear** (**forbore, forborne**) *vi.* 1. astenersi 2. essere paziente.

forbearance *s.* 1. astensione 2. pazienza.

forbearing *agg.* paziente.

to **forbid** (**forbade, forbidden**) *vt.* proibire, impedire.

forbidding *agg.* 1. severo 2. ripugnante.

forbore V. *to forbear.*

forborne V. *to forbear.*

force *s.* forza. ♦ **forces** *s. pl.* truppe ‖ *the Armed Forces*, le Forze Armate.

to **force** *vt.* 1. forzare 2. costringere ‖ *to — back*, respingere; *to — in*, sfondare; *to — on*, far avanzare.

forceful *agg.* forte.

forceps *s.* 1. forcipe 2. pinza.

forcible *agg.* 1. violento 2. potente.

ford *s.* guado.

to **ford** *vt.* guadare.

fordable *agg.* guadabile.

fore *agg.* anteriore. ♦ **fore** *s.* prua.

forearm *s.* avambraccio.

to **forearm** *vt.* premunire.

to **forebode** *vt.* presagire (*un male*).

foreboding *s.* presagio.

forecast *s.* previsione.

to **forecast** (**forecast, forecast**) *vt.* prevedere.

forecastle *s.* castello di prua.

forefather *s.* antenato.

forefinger *s.* indice.

foreground *s.* primo piano.

forehead *s.* fronte.

foreign *agg.* 1. straniero 2. estraneo ‖ *— Office*, Ministero degli Esteri.

foreigner *s.* straniero.

forelock *s.* ciuffo.

foreman *s.* caposquadra, caporeparto.

foremast *s.* albero di trinchetto.

forename *s.* nome di battesimo.

forensic(al) *agg.* forense.

to **forerun** (**foreran, forerun**) *vt.* precorrere.

forerunner *s.* 1. precursore 2. messaggero.

foresail *s.* vela di trinchetto.

to **foresee** (**foresaw, foreseen**) *vt.* prevedere.

foreseeable *agg.* prevedibile.

foreseeing *s.* previsione.

foreseen V. *to foresee.*

to **foreshadow** *vt.* adombrare.

foreshortening *s.* scorcio.

foresight *s.* 1. previsione 2. previdenza.

forest *s.* foresta.

forestal *agg.* forestale.

to **forestall** *vt.* 1. prevenire 2. accaparrare.

forestalling *s.* 1. anticipazione 2. accaparramento.

forester *s.* 1. guardia forestale 2. abitante di foreste.

forestry *s.* 1. foresta 2. silvicultura.

foretaste *s.* pregustazione.

to **foretaste** *vt.* pregustare.

to **foretell** (**foretold, foretold**) *vt.* predire.

forethought *agg.* premeditato. ♦ **forethought** *s.* 1. premeditazione 2. previdenza.

foretold V. *to foretell.*

forever *avv.* per sempre.

to **forewarn** *vt.* avvertire.

foreword *s.* prefazione.

forfeit *s.* 1. perdita 2. ammenda 3. penitenza.

forfeiture *s.* 1. multa 2. confisca.

to **forgather** *vi.* riunirsi, associarsi.

forgave V. *to forgive.*

forge *s.* fucina.

to **forge** *vt.* 1. foggiare, fabbricare 2. contraffare.

forger *s.* 1. fabbro 2. falsario.

forgery *s.* contraffazione.

to **forget** (**forgot, forgotten**) *vt.* e *vi.* dimenticare, dimenticarsi.

forgetful *agg.* immemore 2. negligente.

forgetfulness *s.* 1. oblio 2. negligenza.

forget-me-not *s.* non-ti-scordar-di-me.

to **forgive** (**forgave, forgiven**) *vt.* perdonare.

forgiveness *s.* perdono.

forgot V. *to forget.*

forgotten V. *to forget.*

fork *s.* 1. forchetta 2. forca 3. forcella 4. biforcazione.

to **fork** *vi.* biforcarsi ‖ *to — out*, (*gergo*) pagare. ♦ to **fork** *vt.* biforcare.

forked *agg.* biforcuto.

forlorn *agg.* abbandonato.

form *s.* 1. forma 2. modulo 3. banco.

to **form** vt. formare. ♦ to **form** vi. formarsi.

formal agg. formale || — dress, abito da cerimonia.

formalism s. formalismo.

formalist s. formalista.

formality s. formalità.

to **formalize** vt. 1. formare 2. formalizzare.

format s. formato.

formation s. formazione.

formative agg. formativo.

forme s. (tip.) forma di stampa.

former[1] agg. e pron. precedente, il primo (fra due).

former[2] s. 1. artefice 2. stampo.

formerly avv. precedentemente.

formic agg. formico.

formidable agg. 1. formidabile 2. spaventoso.

formless agg. informe.

formulary s. formulario.

to **formulate** vt. formulare.

formulation s. formulazione.

to **forsake** (**forsook, forsaken**) vt. abbandonare.

forsaking s. abbandono.

forsook V. to forsake.

to **forswear** (**forswore, forsworn**) vt. 1. abiurare 2. spergiurare.

fort s. (mil.) fortezza.

forth avv. 1. avanti 2. fuori || and so —, e così via.

forthcoming agg. prossimo.

fortieth agg. e s. quarantesimo.

fortification s. fortificazione.

to **fortify** vt. fortificare.

fortitude s. forza d'animo.

fortnight s. due settimane.

fortnightly agg. quindicinale. ♦ **fortnightly** avv. ogni due settimane.

fortress s. (mil.) fortezza.

fortuitous agg. fortuito.

fortunate agg. 1. fortunato 2. propizio.

fortune s. 1. sorte: to tell fortunes, predire la sorte 2. fortuna.

fortune-teller s. indovino.

forty agg. e s. quaranta.

forward[1] agg. 1. avanzato 2. precoce 3. pronto.

to **forward**[2] vt. 1. promuovere 2. spedire.

forwarder s. spedizioniere.

forwarding s. spedizione.

forward(s) avv. avanti, in avanti.

fossil agg. e s. fossile.

fossilization s. fossilizzazione.

to **fossilize** vt. fossilizzare. ♦ to **fossilize** vi. fossilizzarsi.

to **foster** vt. 1. favorire 2. allevare, nutrire.

fought V. to fight.

foul agg. 1. sporco 2. tempestoso.

foulmouthed agg. sboccato.

to **foul** vt. 1. sporcare 2. urtare. ♦ to **foul** vi. 1. sporcarsi 2. urtarsi.

found V. to find.

to **found**[1] vt. fondare.

to **found**[2] vt. fondere.

foundation s. 1. fondazione 2. fondamenta 3. fondamento.

founder[1] s. fondatore.

founder[2] s. fonditore.

to **founder** vi. crollare. ♦ to **founder** vt. affondare.

foundling s. trovatello || — hospital, brefotrofio.

foundry s. fonderia.

fountain s. 1. fontana 2. sorgente || —pen, penna stilografica.

four agg. e s. quattro || — handed, quadrumane; — footed, quadrupede.

fourscore agg. ottanta.

fourteen agg. e s. quattordici.

fourteenth agg. e s. quattordicesimo.

fourth agg. e s. quarto.

fowl s. pollo, pollame.

fox s. volpe: — hunt, caccia alla volpe.

foxglove s. digitale.

foxy agg. 1. volpino 2. rossiccio 3. scolorito 4. aspro.

foyer s. ridotto.

fraction s. frazione.

fractional agg. frazionario.

to **fractionize** vt. frazionare.

fracture s. frattura.

to **fracture** vt. fratturare. ♦ to **fracture** vi. fratturarsi.

fragile agg. fragile.

fragility s. fragilità.

fragment s. frammento.

fragmentary agg. frammentario.

fragrance s. fragranza.

fragrant agg. fragrante.

frail agg. 1. debole 2. caduco.

frailness, frailty s. debolezza.

frame s. 1. cornice 2. struttura, intelaiatura.

to **frame** vt. 1. incorniciare 2. formare.

framework s. struttura.

framing s. incorniciatura.

franc s. franco.
franchise s. franchigia.
Franciscan agg. e s. francescano.
frank agg. franco.
frankness s. franchezza.
frantic agg. frenetico.
fraternal agg. fraterno.
fraternity s. 1. fraternità 2. confraternita.
fraternization s. affratellamento.
to fraternize vi. fraternizzare.
fratricidal agg. fratricida.
fratricide s. 1. fratricida 2. fratricidio.
fraud s. 1. frode 2. impostura 3.
(fam.) impostore.
fraudulence s. frode.
fraudulent agg. fraudolento.
fray s. zuffa.
to fray vt. consumare. ♦ to fray
vi. consumarsi.
freak s. 1. capriccio 2. macchiolina.
freakish, freaky agg. capriccioso.
freckle s. lentiggine.
freckled, freckly agg. lentigginoso.
free agg. 1. libero 2. (comm.) franco
3. abbondante 4. gratuito || — on
board, franco porto. ♦ free avv.
gratuitamente.
to free vt. liberare.
freedom s. libertà.
freely avv. 1. liberamente 2. gratul-
tamente.
freemason s. massone.
freemasonry s. massoneria.
freethinker s. libero pensatore.
freethinking s. libertà di pensiero.
freetrade s. libero scambio.
freetrader s. libero scambista.
freeze s. gelo, congelamento.
to freeze (froze, frozen) vt. e vi.
1. gelare 2. (imp.) far freddo.
freezer s. cella frigorifera.
freezing agg. glaciale, congelante.
♦ freezing s. congelamento.
freight s. 1. trasporto 2. nolo.
to freight vt. 1. trasportare 2. noleggiare 3. caricare.
French agg. francese. ♦ French s.
lingua francese.
to frenchify vt. francesizzare. ♦
to frenchify vi. francesizzarsi.
Frenchman s. francese (uomo).
Frenchwoman s. francese (donna).
frenzied agg. frenetico.
frenzy s. frenesia, delirio.
frequency s. frequenza.
frequent agg. frequente.
to frequent vt. frequentare.

fresco s. affresco.
fresh agg. fresco, nuovo, puro ||
— water, acqua dolce. ♦ fresh
s. sorgente.
fresh-water agg. d'acqua dolce.
to freshen vt. 1. rinfrescare 2. de-
salinizzare. ♦ to freshen vi. rinfrescarsi.
freshly avv. 1. in modo fresco 2.
recentemente.
freshman s. matricola.
freshness s. 1. freschezza 2. inesperienza.
fret³ s. agitazione.
fret² s. 1. fregio 2. traforo.
to fret¹ vt. rodere. ♦ to fret vi.
1. affliggersi 2. agitarsi.
to fret² vt. 1. ornare 2. traforare.
fretful agg. irritabile.
fretfully avv. con irritazione.
fretfulness s. irritabilità.
fretwork s. intaglio ornamentale.
friability s. friabilità.
friable agg. friabile.
friar s. frate || Black-—, domeni-
cano; Grey-—, francescano;
White-—, carmelitano.
friction s. frizione, attrito.
Friday s. venerdì; Good -—, Venerdì Santo.
fried agg. fritto.
friend s. amico || to make friends,
fare amicizia; the Society of
Friends, i quaccheri.
friendless agg. senza amici.
friendliness s. cordialità.
friendly agg. amichevole. ♦ friendly avv. amichevolmente.
friendship s. amicizia.
frigate s. fregata.
fright s. spavento.
to frighten vt. spaventare.
frightful agg. spaventevole.
frightfulness s. spavento.
frigid agg. 1. glaciale 2. frigido.
frigidity s. 1. freddezza 2. frigidità.
frill s. 1. fronzolo 2. gala increspata.
to frill vt. ornare di gale.
fringe s. 1. frangia 2. bordo.
to fringe vt. orlare.
frippery s. cianfrusaglie (pl.).
to frisk vi. fare capriole.
frisky agg. gaio.
frivolity s. frivolezza.
frivolous agg. frivolo.
frizzly, frizzy agg. crespo.
frock s. 1. abito 2. tonaca.
frog¹ s. rana.

frog[2] s. alamaro.

frogman s. sommozzatore.

frolic s. scherzo.

frolicsome agg. scherzoso.

from prep. da, di.

front agg. anteriore. ♦ **front** s. 1. fronte 2. sfrontatezza.

to **front** vt. fronteggiare.

frontal agg. frontale.

frontier s. frontiera.

frontispiece s. frontespizio.

frost s. 1. gelo 2. brina || —*bite*, congelamento; *hoar*—, brinata.

to **frost** vt. 1. gelare 2. (*cuc.*) glassare 3. smerigliare.

frosty agg. 1. gelato 2. gelido 3. canuto.

froth s. 1. schiuma 2. frivolezza.

to **froth** vi. far schiuma.

frothy agg. 1. schiumoso 2. leggero.

frown s. 1. l'aggrottare le ciglia 2. cipiglio.

to **frown** vi. 1. aggrottare le ciglia 2. acciugliarsi.

frowning agg. accigliato.

froze V. *to freeze.*

frozen V. *to freeze.*

fructiferous agg. fruttifero.

to **fructify** vi. fruttificare. ♦ to **fructify** vt. fertilizzare.

frugal agg. frugale.

frugalist s. persona frugale.

frugality s. frugalità.

fruit s. 1. frutta 2. frutto.

fruiterer s. fruttivendolo.

fruitful agg. 1. fruttifero 2. fertile 3. redditizio.

fruitfulness s. 1. fertilità 2. vantaggio.

fruition s. 1. godimento 2. realizzazione.

fruitless agg. infruttuoso.

to **frustrate** vt. frustrare.

frustration s. frustrazione.

frustum s. (*pl.* -ta) (*geom.*) tronco.

fry s. fritto, frittura.

to **fry** vt. e vi. friggere.

fudge s. fandonia, sciocchezza.

to **fudge** vt. rattoppare.

fuel s. combustibile || — *oil*, nafta.

to **fuel** vt. alimentare di combustibile.

fugacity s. fugacità.

fugitive agg. 1. fuggitivo 2. effimero. ♦ **fugitive** s. 1. fuggitivo 2. rifugiato.

fugitiveness s. fuggevolezza.

fugue s. (*mus.*) fuga.

fulcrum s. (*pl.* fulcra) fulcro.

to **fulfil** vt. 1. compiere 2. adempiere, esaurire.

fulfilment s. 1. compimento 2. adempimento, esaudimento.

fulgency s. fulgidezza.

fulgent agg. fulgente.

fulgid agg. fulgido.

fulguration s. folgorazione.

full agg. pieno || — *up*, completo; — -*stop*, punto. ♦ **full** avv. interamente. ♦ **full** s. 1. intero 2. massimo.

fullness s. pienezza.

fully avv. completamente.

fulminant agg. fulminante.

fulmination s. 1. fulminazione 2. imprecazione.

fumarole s. fumarola.

to **fumble** vi. annaspare. ♦ to **fumble** vt. maneggiare goffamente.

fume s. 1. fumo 2. eccitazione.

to **fume** vi. 1. fumare 2. irritarsi.

fun s. 1. divertimento 2. facezia || *to make* — *of so.*, canzonare qu.; *to have good* —, divertirsi molto.

funambulism s. funambolismo.

funambulist s. funambolo.

function s. funzione.

to **function** vi. 1. funzionare 2. fungere da.

functional agg. funzionale.

functionary s. funzionario.

fund s. fondo, riserva.

to **fund** vt. 1. accumulare 2. investire in obbligazioni.

fundament s. base.

fundamental agg. fondamentale. ♦ **fundamental** s. fondamento.

funeral agg. funebre. ♦ **funeral** s. funerale.

funerary, funereal agg. funereo.

funicular agg. e s. funicolare.

funnel s. 1. imbuto 2. camino, ciminiera.

funny agg. 1. comico 2. strano.

fur s. 1. pelliccia 2. patina, rivestimento.

to **fur** vt. coprire con pelliccia.

furbelow s. falpalà.

furious agg. furioso.

to **furl** vt. 1. piegare, chiudere 2. ammainare (*vele ecc.*). ♦ to **furl** vi. piegarsi, chiudersi.

furnace s. fornace.

to **furnish** vt. 1. fornire 2. ammobiliare.

furnisher s. fornitore.

furnishings s. pl. arredamento (*sing.*).

furniture s. 1. mobilio 2. contenuto.
furrier s. pellicciaio.
furriery s. pellicceria.
furrow s. 1. solco 2. scia.
to furrow vt. 1. solcare 2. arare.
further agg. (comp. di far) 1. più lontano 2. ulteriore. ◆ **further** avv. 1. più in là 2. ancora.
to further vt. favorire.
furthermore avv. inoltre.
furthermost agg. il più lontano.
furthest agg. (superl. di far) estremo. ◆ **furthest** avv. all'estremo limite.
furtive agg. furtivo.
furunculosis s. furuncolosi.
fury s. furia.
fuse s. 1. valvola, fusibile 2. spoletta 3. miccia.
to fuse vt. 1. fondere 2. liquefare. ◆ **to fuse** vi. 1. fondersi 2. saltare (di valvola).
fuselage s. fusoliera.
fusible agg. fusibile.
fusion s. fusione.
fuss s. 1. trambusto 2. smancerie.
to fuss vi. far confusione. ◆ **to fuss** vt. irritare.
fussily avv. 1. con inutile scalpore 2. con esagerata importanza.
fussy agg. 1. che fa confusione 2. meticoloso.
fusty agg. stantio.
futility s. futilità.
future agg. e s. futuro.
futurism s. futurismo.
fuzz s. lanuggine.
fuzzily avv. confusamente.
fuzziness s. 1. increspatura (di capelli) 2. (foto) sfocatura.
fuzzy agg. 1. lanuginoso 2. confuso 3. (foto) sfocato.

G

G s. (mus.) sol.
to gabble vt. e vi. parlare in modo confuso.
gabbler s. chiacchierone.
gable s. frontone.
gadfly s. 1. tafano 2. (fig.) persona irritante.
gadget s. aggeggio.
Gael s. gaelico.
Gaelic agg. e s. gaelico.

gaff s. uncino, rampone.
gag s. 1. bavaglio 2. improvvisazione 3. trovata geniale.
xo gag vt. imbavagliare. ◆ **to gag** vi. improvvisare (motti di spirito).
gage s. garanzia.
to gage vt. dare in pegno.
gaiety s. gaiezza. ◆ **gaieties** s. pl. divertimenti.
gaily avv. gaiamente.
gain s. 1. guadagno 2. aumento, miglioramento.
to gain vt. e vi. 1. guadagnare 2. aumentare || to — on, guadagnar terreno su.
gainer s. chi guadagna.
gainful agg. lucroso.
gainings s. pl. guadagni.
to gainsay vt. contraddire.
gainsaying s. contraddizione.
gait s. andatura.
gaiter s. ghetta.
galalith s. galalite.
galantine s. galantina.
galaxy s. galassia.
gale s. tempesta.
galenic agg. galenico.
Galilean agg. e s. galileo.
gall¹ s. bile, fiele || — -bladder, cistifellea.
gall² s. 1. scorticatura 2. irritazione.
to gall vt. irritare. ◆ **to gall** vi. irritarsi.
gallant agg. 1. prode 2. galante. ◆ **gallant** s. uomo di mondo.
gallantry s. 1. galanteria 2. coraggio 3. atto, discorso amoroso.
galleon s. galeone.
gallery s. galleria || picture- —, pinacoteca.
galley s. 1. (mar.) galea 2. (mar.) cambusa 3. (tip.) vantaggio || — proof (tip.), bozza in colonna; — slave, galeotto.
Gallic agg. e s. gallico.
gallicism s. francesismo.
gallinacean agg. e s. gallinaceo.
gallium s. gallio.
gallon s. gallone (misura).
galloon s. gallone (ornamento).
gallooned agg. gallonato.
gallop s. 1. galoppo: at a —, al galoppo 2. galoppata.
to gallop vt. far galoppare. ◆ **to gallop** vi. galoppare.
gallows s. pl. patibolo (sing.).
galore s. abbondanza. ◆ **galore** avv. in abbondanza.
galosh(e) s. galoscia.

galvanic(al) *agg.* **1.** galvanico **2.** (*fig.*) galvanizzante.

galvanization *s.* galvanizzazione.

to galvanize *vt.* galvanizzare.

galvanometer *s.* galvanometro.

galvanoplastic *agg.* galvanoplastico.

gamble *s.* gioco d'azzardo.

to gamble *vt. e vi.* giocare (*d'azzardo*).

gambler *s.* giocatore d'azzardo.

gambling *s.* V. *gamble* || — *-house*, casa da gioco.

gambol *s.* piroetta.

game *agg.* risoluto. ♦ **game** *s.* **1.** gioco (*con regole*), mano (*in una partita*) **2.** (*fig.*) progetto **3.** selvaggina (*coll.*).

to game V. *to gamble.*

gamekeeper *s.* guardacaccia.

gamely *avv.* coraggiosamente.

gamesome *agg.* scherzoso.

gamester *s.* giocatore.

gammon *s.* (*mar.*) trinca di bompresso.

gang *s.* **1.** squadra **2.** banda.

to gang *vt. e vi.* formare una banda.

ganglion *s.* (*pl.* ganglia) ganglio.

gangrene *s.* cancrena.

to gangrene *vi.* andare in cancrena.

gangster *s.* bandito.

gangsterism *s.* banditismo.

gangway *s.* **1.** passaggio (*tra file di sedie ecc.*) **2.** (*mar.*) passerella.

gaol *s.* prigione.

to gaol *vt.* imprigionare.

gaoler *s.* carceriere.

gap *s.* **1.** apertura, breccia **2.** intervallo **3.** divergenza **4.** lacuna.

gape *s.* **1.** sbadiglio **2.** apertura **3.** stupore.

to gape *vi.* **1.** spalancare la bocca **2.** sbadigliare **3.** restare a bocca aperta.

gaping *agg.* **1.** aperto **2.** stupito.

garage *s.* autorimessa || — *keeper*, garagista.

garb *s.* costume.

garbage *s.* rifiuto.

garden *s.* giardino.

to garden *vi.* fare del giardinaggio.

gardener *s.* giardiniere.

gardening *s.* giardinaggio.

gargarism *s.* gargarismo.

gargle *s.* liquido per gargarismi.

to gargle *vt. e vi.* gargarizzare.

gargoyle *s.* doccione.

garish *agg.* **1.** abbagliante **2.** appariscente.

garland *s.* ghirlanda.

garlic *s.* aglio.

garment *s.* abito, indumento.

garnet¹ *agg.* granato.

garnet² *s.* (*mar.*) paranco.

to garnish *vt.* guarnire.

garnish(ment) *s.* ornamento.

garret *s.* soffitta.

garrison *s.* guarnigione.

to garrison *vt.* presidiare.

garrulity *s.* garrulità.

garrulous *agg.* garrulo.

garter *s.* giarrettiera || *knight o, the Garter,* Cavaliere dell'Ordine della Giarrettiera.

gas *s.* gas || — *-fitter*, gassista; — *-mask*, maschera antigas; — *-meter*, contatore del gas.

to gas *vt.* **1.** fornire di gas **2.** asfissiare col gas.

Gascon *agg. e s.* guascone.

gasconade *s.* guasconata.

gaseous *agg.* gassoso.

gash *s.* sfregio.

to gash *vt.* sfregiare.

gas oil *s.* gasolio.

gasoline *s.* (*amer.*) benzina.

gasp *s.* respiro affannoso.

to gasp *vi.* **1.** ansare **2.** restare senza fiato **3.** parlare affannosamente.

gassy *agg.* gassoso.

gastric *agg.* gastrico.

gastritis *s.* gastrite.

gastroenteritis *s.* gastroenterite.

gastronome *s.* gastronomo.

gastronomic(al) *agg.* gastronomico.

gastronomy *s.* gastronomia.

gate *s.* **1.** cancello **2.** porta.

gatekeeper *s.* portiere, custode.

gateway *s.* portone, ingresso.

to gather *vt.* **1.** raccogliere **2.** acquistare **3.** dedurre. ♦ **to gather** *vi.* raccogliersi.

gathering *s.* **1.** raccolta **2.** (*med.*) ascesso.

gaud *s.* fronzolo.

gaudiness *s.* sfarzo.

gaudy *agg.* sfarzoso. ♦ **gaudy** *s.* festa (*universitaria*).

gauge *s.* **1.** misura **2.** calibro **3.** (*ferr.*) scartamento **4.** pescaggio || *narrow* —, scartamento ridotto.

to gauge *vt.* misurare.

gaunt *agg.* scarno.

gauze *s.* garza, velo, mussolina.

gauzy *agg.* trasparente.

gave V. *to give.*

gay *agg.* **1.** gaio **2.** licenzioso.

gayety *s.* gaiezza.

gaze *s.* sguardo fisso.

to gaze *vi.* fissare.

gazelle *s.* gazzella.

gazette *s.* gazzetta.

gazetteer *s.* 1. giornalista 2. dizionario geografico.

gear *s.* 1. meccanismo 2. (*auto*) marcia, cambio 3. (*mecc.*) ingranaggio.

to gear *vt.* ingranare || *to — up, down*, aumentare, diminuire la velocità.

gearing *s.* ingranaggio, innesto.

geese V. goose.

gelatin(e) *s.* gelatina.

gelatinous *agg.* gelatinoso.

to geld *vt.* castrare.

gelid *agg.* gelido.

gem *s.* gemma.

gemmy *agg.* pieno di gemme.

gender *s.* genere.

genderless *agg.* di genere comune.

genealogical *agg.* genealogico.

genealogy *s.* genealogia.

generable *agg.* generabile.

general *agg.* e *s.* generale.

generality *s.* 1. generalità 2. maggioranza.

generalization *s.* generalizzazione.

to generalize *vt.* e *vi.* generalizzare.

generally *avv.* generalmente.

to generate *vt.* generare.

generation *s.* generazione.

generative *agg.* generativo.

generator *s.* generatore.

generic(al) *agg.* generico.

generosity *s.* generosità.

generous *agg.* 1. generoso 2. abbondante.

genesis *s.* (*pl.* -ses) genesi.

genetic(al) *agg.* genetico.

genetics *s.* genetica.

genial *agg.* 1. gioviale 2. geniale 3. mite (*di clima*).

geniality *s.* 1. giovialità 2. mitezza (*di clima*).

genital *agg.* e *s.* genitale.

genitive *agg.* e *s.* genitivo.

genius *s.* genio.

genocide *s.* genocidio.

genre *s.* genere.

genteel *agg.* raffinato.

gentian *s.* genziana.

gentile *agg.* e *s.* pagano.

gentility *s.* signorilità.

gentle *agg.* 1. nobile 2. garbato 3. moderato 4. facile.

gentleman *s.* 1. signore 2. gentiluomo.

gentlemanlike, gentlemanly *agg.*

da gentiluomo.

gentleness *s.* gentilezza.

gentlewoman *s.* gentildonna.

gently *avv.* 1. gentilmente, con delicatezza 2. gradualmente.

gentry *s.* classe gentilizia.

to genuflect *vi.* genuflettersi.

genuflection *s.* genuflessione.

genuine *agg.* 1. autentico 2. sincero 3. puro.

genuineness *s.* 1. autenticità 2. sincerità.

genus *s.* (*pl.* -nera) genere.

geodesy *s.* geodesia.

geographer *s.* geografo.

geographic(al) *agg.* geografico.

geography *s.* geografia.

geologic(al) *agg.* geologico.

geologist *s.* geologo.

geology *s.* geologia.

geometer *s.* geometra.

geometric(al) *agg.* geometrico.

geometrician *s.* geometra.

geometry *s.* geometria.

geophysics *s.* geofisica.

geopolitics *s.* geopolitica.

georgic *agg.* georgico.

geranium *s.* geranio.

gerent *s.* gerente.

germ *s.* germe.

german *agg.* germano.

German *agg.* e *s.* tedesco.

Germanic *agg.* germanico.

Germanism *s.* germanesimo.

Germanist *s.* germanista.

germanium *s.* germanio.

germinal *agg.* germinale.

to germinate *vt.* far germinare. ♦ to germinate *vi.* germinare.

germination *s.* germinazione.

gerontology *s.* gerontologia.

gerund *s.* gerundio.

gerundial *agg.* gerundivo.

gerundive *agg.* e *s.* gerundivo.

gestation *s.* gestazione.

to gesticulate *vi.* gesticolare.

gesticulation *s.* gesticolazione.

gesture *s.* 1. gesto 2. il gestire.

to gesture *vi.* far gesti.

to get (got, got) *vt.* 1. ottenere, procurare 2. prendere 3. portare 4. fare. ♦ to get (got, got) *vi.* 1. andare 2. divenire || *to — off*, scendere; *to — over*, scavalcare; *to — out*, (far) uscire; *to — up*, alzarsi; *to — married*, sposarsi; *to — hold of*, impossessarsi di.

getaway *s.* 1. fuga 2. (*sport*) partenza.

gettable *agg.* ottenibile.

get-up *s.* 1. equipaggiamento 2. presentazione (*di libro, giornale ecc.*).

geyser *s.* 1. geyser 2. scaldabagno.

ghastliness *s.* 1. aspetto spaventoso 2. pallore spettrale.

ghastly *agg.* 1. spaventoso 2. spettrale.

gherkin *s.* cetriolo.

Ghibelline *agg.* e *s.* ghibellino.

ghost *s.* 1. spirito 2. spettro || *to give up the* —, spirare.

ghostliness *s.* 1. l'essere spettrale 2. spiritualità.

ghostly *agg.* 1. spettrale 2. spirituale.

giant *s.* gigante.

giantism *s.* gigantismo.

gibbet *s.* patibolo.

to gibbet *vt.* 1. impiccare 2. (*fig.*) mettere alla berlina.

gibbosity *s.* gibbosità.

gibbous *agg.* gibboso.

gibe *s.* scherno.

to gibe *vt.* e *vi.* schernire.

giblets *s. pl.* regaglie.

giddily *avv.* vertiginosamente.

giddiness *s.* 1. capogiro 2. (*fig.*) frivolezza.

giddy *agg.* 1. stordito 2. vertiginoso 3. frivolo.

to giddy *vt.* stordire. ♦ **to giddy** *vi.* aver le vertigini.

gift *s.* 1. dono 2. dote.

to gift *vt.* dotare.

gig *s.* 1. calessino 2. (*mar.*) iole.

gig 2 *s.* rampone, fiocina.

gigantean, gigantic *agg.* gigantesco.

giggle *s.* risatina.

to giggle *vi.* fare risatine.

to gild (gilt, gilt) (*anche reg.*) *vt.* (in)dorare.

gilder *s.* doratore.

gilding *s.* doratura.

gill *s.* 1. branchia 2. pappagorgia.

gilt V. *to gild.*

gilt *s.* doratura.

gimlet *s.* succhiello.

gin 1 *s.* "gin" (*liquore*).

gin 2 *s.* 1. elevatore 2. trappola (*per animali*).

ginger *s.* zenzero.

gingerly *agg.* cauto. ♦ **gingerly** *avv.* cautamente.

gipsy *s.* zingaro.

gipsydom *s.* gli zingari (*pl.*).

gipsyish *agg.* zingaresco.

giraffe *s.* giraffa.

to gird (girt, girt) (*anche reg.*) *vt.* cingere.

girder *s.* 1. trave maestra 2. sbarra

girdle *s.* 1. cintura 2. reggicalze.

to girdle *vt.* cingere.

girl *s.* ragazza || *flower* —, fioraia.

girlhood *s.* adolescenza (*di ragazza*).

Girondist *agg.* e *s.* girondino.

girt V. *to gird.*

girth *s.* 1. circonferenza 2. cinghia.

to give (gave, given) *vt.* dare || *to* — *in*, cedere; *to* — *out*, annunciare, venir meno; *to* — *up*, smettere, abbandonare; *to* — *birth to*, generare; *to* — *oneself up*, costituirsi (*alla polizia*); *to* — *oneself up to*, dedicarsi (a); *to* — *off*, emettere (*luce ecc.*).

giver *s.* datore.

glacial *agg.* glaciale.

glaciation *s.* glaciazione.

glacier *s.* ghiacciaio.

glacis *s.* spalto.

glad *agg.* lieto.

to gladden *vt.* rallegrare. ♦ **to gladden** *vi.* rallegrarsi.

glade *s.* radura.

gladiator *s.* gladiatore.

gladiolus *s.* (*pl.* -li) gladiolo.

gladly *avv.* con piacere.

gladness *s.* contentezza.

glair *s.* albume.

gladsome *agg.* gioioso.

glair *s.* albume.

glamorous *agg.* affascinante.

glamour *s.* 1. fascino 2. incantesimo

glance *s.* 1. occhiata 2. colpo obliquo.

to glance *vt.* e *vi.* 1. gettare uno sguardo 2. sfiorare 3. balenare || *to* — *off*, sorvolare su.

gland *s.* 1. ghiandola 2. ghianda.

glandiferous *agg.* ghiandifero.

glandular *agg.* glandolare.

glare *s.* 1. luce abbagliante 2. sguardo truce 3. abbagliamento.

to glare *vi.* 1. splendere 2. guardare torvamente.

glaring *agg.* 1. abbagliante 2. evidente.

glass *s.* 1. vetro 2. bicchiere 3. specchio || —*ware*, articoli in vetro; —*work*, fabbrica di vetro; —-*paper*, carta vetrata. ♦ **glasses** *s. pl.* occhiali, cannocchiale (*sing.*).

to glass *vt.* 1. specchiare 2. imbottigliare.

glassy *agg.* 1. vitreo 2. cristallino.

glaucous agg. glauco.

glaze s. superficie vetrosa.

to glaze vt. 1. smaltare 2. mettere vetri a. ♦ **to glaze** vi. diventare vitreo.

glazier s. vetraio.

glazy agg. vitreo.

gleam s. barlume.

to gleam vi. scintillare.

gleamy agg. scintillante.

to glean vt. e vi. spigolare.

gleaner s. spigolatore.

gleaning s. spigolatura.

glee s. allegria.

gleeful agg. allegro.

glib agg. 1. liscio 2. facondo 3. sciolto.

glibness s. 1. disinvoltura 2. facondia.

glide s. scivolata.

to glide vt. 1. far scorrere 2. trascorrere. ♦ **to glide** vi. 1. scivolare 2. passare.

glider s. aliante.

gliding agg. scorrevole. ♦ **gliding** s. volo a vela.

glimmer s. barlume.

to glimmer vi. brillare.

glimpse s. 1. visione 2. occhiata 3. vaga idea.

to glimpse vt. e vi. intravedere.

glitter s. scintillio.

to glitter vi. scintillare.

gloaming s. crepuscolo.

to gloat vi. fissare avidamente.

global agg. globale.

globe s. 1. globo 2. pianeta.

globous, globular agg. sferico.

globule s. globulo.

gloom s. 1. oscurità 2. tristezza.

to gloom vt. 1. oscurare 2. rattristare. ♦ **to gloom** vi. 1. oscurarsi 2. rattristarsi.

gloomy agg. cupo.

glorification s. glorificazione.

to glorify vt. glorificare.

glorious agg. 1. glorioso 2. splendido.

gloriousness s. V. glory.

glory s. 1. gloria 2. splendore.

to glory vi. vantarsi.

gloss s. 1. glossa 2. lucentezza 3. apparenza.

glossarist s. glossatore.

glossary s. glossario.

glossy agg. lucido.

glottis s. glottide.

glottologist s. glottologo.

glottology s. glottologia.

glove s. guanto || **to be hand in —** with, essere molto intimo con.

gloved agg. inguantato.

glover s. guantaio.

glow s. 1. calore 2. splendore 3. colorito || **—worm,** lucciola.

to glow vi. ardere.

glucose s. glucosio.

glue s. colla.

to glue vt. incollare.

glut s. 1. scorpacciata 2. saturazione.

to glut vt. 1. saziare 2. saturare. ♦ **to glut** vi. fare una scorpacciata.

gluten s. glutine.

gluteus s. (pl. glutei) gluteo.

glutton s. ghiottone.

gluttonous agg. ghiottone.

gluttony s. ghiottoneria.

glycerin(e) s. glicerina.

glycogen s. glicogeno.

gnarled agg. nodoso.

to gnash vt. e vi. digrignare.

gnat s. zanzara.

to gnaw vt. rodere.

gnawing agg. 1. rosicante 2. corrodente.

gnome[1] s. gnomo.

gnome[2] s. massima.

gnomic agg. gnomico.

gnosis s. gnosi.

gnostic agg. e s. gnostico.

gnosticism s. gnosticismo.

go s. 1. movimento 2. energia 3. colpo || **—between,** intermediario; **— by,** evasione; **—cart,** girello.

to go (**went, gone**) vi. 1. andare 2. divenire || **to — by,** passare; **to — for,** andare a cercare; **to — on,** continuare.

goad s. pungolo.

to goad vt. stimolare.

goal s. 1. traguardo 2. (sport) rete || **— keeper,** portiere.

goat s. capra.

goatish agg. 1. caprino 2. lascivo.

to gobble vt. tranguiare, inghiottire.

goblin s. folletto.

god s. 1. dio, divinità 2. Dio.

godchild s. (pl. -children) figlioccio.

goddaughter s. figlioccia.

goddess s. dea.

godfather s. padrino.

godless agg. 1. ateo 2. empio.

godlike agg. divino.

godliness s. devozione.

godly agg. religioso.

godmother s. madrina.

godown s. deposito.

godsend s. dono del cielo.

godship s. divinità.

godson s. figlioccio.

goggle agg. 1. stralunato 2. sporgente (di occhi).

to goggle vt. stralunare. ♦ to goggle vi. essere sporgenti (di occhi).

goggles s. pl. occhiali di protezione.

going s. 1. l'andare 2. partenza.

goitre s. gozzo.

goitrous agg. gozzuto.

gold s. agg. d'oro. ♦ gold s. oro || — -field, zona aurifera; — -dig'', cercatore d'oro.

golden agg. dorato, d'oro.

goldfinch s. cardellino.

goldsmith s. orefice.

gone s. to go.

gonfalon s. gonfalone.

goniometer s. goniometro.

goniometry s. goniometria.

good (better, best) agg. 1. buono 2. bravo 3. bello. ♦ good inter. bene!

good s. 1. bene 2. utilità || for —, per sempre.

good-bye inter. e s. addio, arrivederci.

good-for-nothing s. buono a nulla.

goodly agg. bello.

goodness s. 1. bontà 2. il meglio || my —!, Dio mio!

goods s. pl. merce (sing.).

goodwill s. 1. buona volontà 2. benevolenza.

goody agg. troppo buono. ♦ goody inter. bene!

goose s. (pl. geese) oca.

gooseberry s. uva spina.

goose-step s. passo dell'oca.

gore s. sangue rappreso.

gorge s. gola.

to gorge V. to glut.

gorgeous agg. magnifico.

gorgeousness s. magnificenza.

gospel s. vangelo.

gossamer s. ragnatela.

gossip s. 1. pettegolezzo 2. pettegolo.

to gossip vi. far pettegolezzi.

gossiper s. pettegolo.

gossipy agg. pettegolo.

got V. to get.

Gothic agg. e s. gotico.

gothicism s. 1. stile gotico 2. rozzezza.

gouache s. guazzo.

gouge s. sgorbia.

gourd s. zucca.

gourmand s. goloso.

gourmet s. buongustaio.

gout s. 1. gotta 2. goccia.

gouty agg. gottoso.

to govern vt. 1. governare 2. controllare 3. (gramm.) reggere.

governable agg. docile.

governess s. istitutrice.

government s. governo.

governmental agg. governativo.

governor s. 1. governatore 2. regolatore.

gown s. 1. veste 2. toga || dressing- —, veste da camera; night- —, camicia da notte.

grab s. presa.

to grab vt. 1. afferrare 2. (mecc.) bloccare.

grace s. grazia.

to grace vt. adornare.

graceful agg. grazioso.

gracefulness s. grazia.

graceless agg. 1. sgraziato 2. depravato.

gracile agg. gracile.

gracility s. gracilità.

gracious agg. benigno || good —!, mio Dio!

gradation s. gradazione.

grade s. 1. grado 2. pendio.

to grade vt. 1. graduare 2. livellare.

gradient agg. che sale, scende gradatamente. ♦ gradient s. pendenza.

gradual agg. graduale.

graduality s. gradualità.

graduate s. laureato.

to graduate vt. 1. graduare 2. laureare. ♦ to graduate vi. laurearsi.

graduation s. 1. graduazione 2. laurea.

graft s. innesto.

to graft vt. innestare.

grain s. 1. granaglie (pl.) 2. chicco 3. grano.

grainy agg. 1. granuloso 2. granoso.

gram s. grammo.

Gramineae s. pl. graminacee.

grammar s. grammatica.

grammarian s. grammatico.

grammatic(al) agg. grammaticale.

gramophone s. grammofono.

granary s. granaio.

grand agg. 1. grande 2. nobile || -aunt, prozia; — -uncle, prozio; — -nephew, pronipote (maschio); — -niece, pronipote (femmina).

grandchild *s.* (*pl.* -children) nipote (*di nonni*).

granddaughter *s.* nipote (*femmina*) (*di nonni*).

grandeur *s.* grandiosità.

grandfather *s.* nonno.

grandiloquence *s.* magniloquenza.

grandiloquent *agg.* magniloquente.

grandiose *agg.* grandioso.

grandiosity *s.* grandiosità.

grandmother *s.* nonna.

grandmotherly *agg.* protettivo.

grandparents *s. pl.* nonni.

grandson *s.* nipote (*maschio*) (*di nonni*).

grange *s.* fattoria, casa colonica.

granite *s.* granito.

granitic *agg.* granitico.

granivorous *agg.* granivoro.

grant *s.* concessione.

to grant *vt.* concedere || *to take for granted*, dare per scontato.

granular *agg.* granulare.

granularity *s.* granulosità.

to granulate *vt.* granulare. ♦ **to granulate** *vi.* granularsi.

granulation *s.* granulazione.

granulous *agg.* granuloso.

grape *s.* 1. acino || *-shot*, mitraglia. ♦ **grapes** *s. pl.* uva.

grapefruit *s.* pompelmo.

grapevine *s.* 1. vigna 2. (*fam.*) notizia ufficiosa.

graph *s.* grafico.

graphic(al) *agg.* 1. grafico 2. pittoresco.

graphite *s.* grafite.

graphologist *s.* grafologo.

graphology *s.* grafologia.

graphomania *s.* grafomania.

graphomaniac *s.* grafomane.

grapnel *s.* (*mar.*) grappino.

to grapple *vt.* afferrare. ♦ **to grapple** *vi.* lottare.

grappling *s.* (*mar.*) aggancio || *-irons*, grappini d'abbordaggio.

grasp *s.* 1. stretta 2. manico 3. potere.

to grasp *vt. e vi.* afferrare.

grasping *agg.* avido.

grass *s.* erba.

grasshopper *s.* cavalletta.

grass-widow *s.* donna separata dal marito.

grassy *agg.* erboso.

grate *s.* 1. grata 2. graticola.

to grate *vt.* 1. fornire di grata 2. grattugiare. ♦ **to grate** *vi.* stridere.

grateful *agg.* grato.

gratefulness *s.* gratitudine.

grater *s.* grattugia.

to gratify *vt.* 1. ricompensare 2. appagare.

gratifying *agg.* soddisfacente.

grating[1] *agg.* 1. irritante 2. stridente. ♦ **grating** *s.* stridore.

grating[2] *s.* 1. grata 2. (*ott.*) reticolo.

gratitude *s.* gratitudine.

gratuitous *agg.* gratuito.

gratuity *s.* mancia.

grave[1] *agg.* grave.

grave[2] *s.* tomba.

gravel *s.* ghiaia.

to gravel *vt.* inghiaiare.

gravelly *agg.* ghiaioso.

graven *agg.* intagliato.

graver *s.* 1. incisore 2. bulino.

gravestone *s.* pietra tombale.

graveyard *s.* cimitero.

gravid *agg.* gravido.

to gravitate *vi.* gravitare.

gravitation *s.* gravitazione.

gravitational *agg.* gravitazionale.

gravity *s.* gravità.

gravy *s.* sugo.

gray *agg. e s.* grigio.

to graze[1] *s.* 1. colpo di striscio 2. escoriazione.

to graze[1] *vt. e vi.* 1. graffiare 2. sfiorare.

to graze[2] *vt. e vi.* pascolare, condurre al pascolo.

grazier *s.* allevatore (*di bestiame*).

grazing[1] *s.* abrasione.

grazing[2] *s.* pascolo.

grease *s.* grasso.

to grease *vt.* ungere, lubrificare.

greaser *s.* ingrassatore.

greasiness *s.* untuosità.

greasy *agg.* 1. grasso 2. unto, untuoso 3. scivoloso.

great *agg.* grande || *-grandchild*, pronipote (*di nonni*); — *-grandfather*, bisnonno; — *-grandmother*, bisnonna.

greatness *s.* grandezza.

Grecian *agg. e s.* greco.

greed(iness) *s.* avidità.

greedy *agg.* avido.

Greek *agg. e s.* greco.

green *agg.* 1. verde 2. inesperto 3. vigoroso 4. recente. ♦ **green** *s.* prato. ♦ **greens** *s. pl.* frasche, verdura (*sing.*).

greenery *s.* 1. vegetazione 2. serra.

greengrocer *s.* erbivendolo.

greenhouse *s.* serra.

greenish *agg.* verdastro.

greenness *s.* **1.** color verde **2.** acerbezza **3.** ingenuità **4.** vigore.

greenroom *s.* (*teat.*) camerino.

to **greet** *vt.* e *vi.* salutare.

greeting *s.* saluto.

Gregorian *agg.* gregoriano.

grenadier *s.* granatiere.

grenadine *s.* granatina.

grew V. *to grow*.

grey *agg.* e *s.* grigio.

greyhound *s.* levriere.

greyness *s.* grigiore.

grid *s.* griglia.

gridiron *s.* graticola.

grief *s.* **1.** dolore **2.** fallimento || *to come to* —, fare fiasco.

grievance *s.* **1.** lagnanza **2.** torto.

to **grieve** *vt.* affliggere. ◆ to **grieve** *vi.* affliggersi.

grievous *agg.* **1.** doloroso **2.** grave.

griffon *s.* grifone.

grill *s.* **1.** graticola **2.** cibo ai ferri || — *room*, rosticceria.

to **grill** *vt.* e *vi.* arrostire (*alla graticola*).

grille *s.* inferriata.

grim *agg.* cupo.

grimace *s.* smorfia.

grime *s.* sudiciume.

to **grime** *vt.* insudiciare.

grimly *avv.* cupamente.

grimy *agg.* sudicio.

grin *s.* **1.** largo sorriso **2.** sogghigno.

to **grin** *vi.* **1.** fare un largo sorriso **2.** sogghignare.

to **grind** (**ground, ground**) *vt.* **1.** macinare **2.** molare **3.** digrignare **4.** (*fig.*) opprimere.

grinder *s.* **1.** mola **2.** molare **3.** arrotino || *organ*— —, suonatore di organetto.

grinding *agg.* irritante. ◆ **grinding** *s.* **1.** macinatura **2.** stridore **3.** affilatura **4.** (*fig.*) oppressione.

grindstone *s.* mola.

grip *s.* **1.** stretta **2.** manico **3.** (*fig.*) padronanza || *to lose one's grips*, perdere le staffe.

to **grip** *vt.* e *vi.* afferrare.

gripe *s.* **1.** presa **2.** freno. ◆ **gripes** *s. pl.* colica (*sing.*).

gripper *s.* pinza.

grist *s.* grano da macinare || *to bring* — *to one's mill*, tirar l'acqua al proprio mulino.

grit *s.* sabbia, arenaria.

grizzly *agg.* grigio. ◆ **grizzly** *s.* orso grigio.

groan *s.* gemito.

to **groan** *vi.* gemere.

groaning *s.* gemito.

grocer *s.* droghiere.

grocery *s.* drogheria. ◆ **groceries** *s. pl.* droghe e coloniali.

groggy *agg.* vacillante.

groin *s.* inguine.

groom *s.* stalliere.

to **groom** *vt.* strigliare.

groove *s.* solco.

to **grope** *vi.* brancolare.

gropingly *avv.* a tastoni.

gross *agg.* **1.** grossolano **2.** pesante **3.** lussureggiante **4.** (*comm.*) lordo.

grotesque *agg.* grottesco.

grotto *s.* grotta.

ground[1] V. *to grind*.

ground[2] *s.* **1.** suolo, terreno **2.** distanza, territorio **3.** motivi, ragioni (*general. pl.*) || — *-floor*, pianterreno.

to **ground** *vt.* fondare. ◆ to **ground** *vi.* **1.** fondarsi **2.** arenarsi.

grounded *agg.* interrato.

groundless *agg.* infondato.

groundlessness *s.* infondatezza.

grounds *s. pl.* **1.** fondi, sedimenti **2.** parco (*sing.*).

group *s.* gruppo.

to **group** *vt.* raggruppare. ◆ to **group** *vi.* raggrupparsi.

grouping *s.* raggruppamento.

grove *s.* boschetto || *olive* —, oliveto.

to **grovel** *vi.* **1.** strisciare a terra **2.** (*fig.*) umiliarsi.

grovelling *s.* strisciamento. ◆ **grovelling** *agg.* **1.** strisciante **2.** (*fig.*) abbietto.

to **grow** (**grew, grown**) *vi.* **1.** crescere **2.** diventare || *to* — *better*, migliorare; *to* — *old*, invecchiare; *to* — *up*, crescere, diventare maturo (*di persone*). ◆ to **grow** (**grew, grown**) *vt.* coltivare.

grower *s.* coltivatore.

growing *s.* coltivazione.

growl *s.* brontolio.

to **growl** *vt.* e *vi.* brontolare.

growler *s.* brontolone.

grown V. *to grow*.

grown-up *agg.* e *s.* adulto.

growth *s.* **1.** crescita **2.** produzione.

grub *s.* **1.** verme **2.** larva.

to **grub** *vt.* e *vi.* scavare.

grubby *agg.* **1.** bacato **2.** sporco.

grudge *s.* malanimo || *to bear a* — *against so.*, nutrire rancore verso qu.

to **grudge** *vt.* **1.** dare a malincuore **2.** invidiare.

grudging *agg.* **1.** riluttante **2.** invidioso.

gruesome *agg.* raccapricciante.

gruff *agg.* burbero.

grumble *s.* brontolio.

to **grumble** *vt.* e *vi.* brontolare.

grumbler *s.* brontolone.

grumbling *s.* brontolio.

grumpy *agg.* burbero, tetro.

grunt *s.* grugnito.

to **grunt** *vt.* e *vi.* grugnire.

gruyère *s.* gruviera.

guarantee *s.* **1.** garanzia **2.** garante.

to **guarantee** *vt.* garantire.

guard *s.* **1.** guardia **2.** capotreno **3.** parapetto.

to **guard** *vt.* custodire.

guardian *s.* **1.** guardiano **2.** tutore.

guardianship *s.* **1.** protezione **2.** tutela.

guardless *agg.* indifeso.

guardrail *s.* **1.** spartitraffico **2.** corrimano (*di scala*).

Guelph *s.* guelfo.

guerrilla *s.* **1.** guerriglia **2.** guerrigliere.

guess *s.* supposizione.

to **guess** *vt.* e *vi.* **1.** supporre **2.** indovinare.

guess-work *s.* congettura.

guest *s.* ospite || — -*house*, pensione.

guffaw *s.* riso sguaiato.

guide *s.* guida.

to **guide** *vt.* guidare.

guild *s.* corporazione.

guile *s.* insidia.

guileful *agg.* insidioso.

guileless *agg.* sincero.

guillotine *s.* ghigliottina.

guilt *s.* colpa.

guiltiness *s.* colpevolezza.

guiltless *agg.* innocente.

guilty *agg.* colpevole.

guinea *s.* ghinea.

Guinea-pig *s.* cavia.

guise *s.* **1.** aspetto, apparenza **2.** falso aspetto.

guitar *s.* chitarra.

guitarist *s.* chitarrista.

gulf *s.* golfo.

gull[1] *s.* gabbiano.

gull[2] *s.* sciocco.

to **gull** *vt.* truffare.

gully *s.* condotto (*di scolo*) || —

-*hole*, tombino.

gulp *s.* **1.** boccone **2.** sorso.

to **gulp** *vt.* inghiottire.

gum[1] *s.* gengiva.

gum[2] *s.* gomma.

to **gum** *vt.* ingommare.

gummy *agg.* gommoso.

gun *s.* **1.** cannone **2.** fucile **3.** rivoltella, pistola || — -*barrel*, canna da fucile; — -*carriage*, affusto di cannone.

gunfire *s.* sparatoria.

gunner *s.* artigliere.

gunpowder *s.* polvere da sparo.

gun-room *s.* armeria.

gunshot *s.* colpo di arma da fuoco.

gunsmith *s.* armaiolo.

gurgle *s.* gorgoglio.

to **gurgle** *vi.* gorgogliare.

gush *s.* **1.** getto **2.** effusione.

to **gush** *vi.* **1.** sgorgare **2.** essere espansivo.

gusher *s.* pozzo petrolifero.

gushing *agg.* **1.** sgorgante **2.** esuberante.

gust *s.* **1.** raffica **2.** (*fig.*) impeto.

gustative, gustatory *agg.* gustativo.

gusty *agg.* ventoso.

gut *s.* budello.

to **gut** *vt.* sventrare.

gutter *s.* **1.** grondaia **2.** rigagnolo.

to **gutter** *vt.* scanalare. ♦ to **gutter** *vi.* colare.

guttural *agg.* e *s.* gutturale.

to **guzzle** *vt.* tracannare.

gymkhana *s.* gincana.

gymnasium *s.* palestra.

gymnast *s.* ginnasta.

gymnastic(al) *agg.* ginnastico.

gymnastics *s.* ginnastica.

gynaeceum *s.* (*pl.* -cea) gineceo.

gynaecologic *agg.* ginecologico.

gynaecologist *s.* ginecologo.

gynaecology *s.* ginecologia.

gypsy *s.* V. gipsy.

to **gyrate** *vi.* girare.

gyroscope *s.* giroscopio.

gyves *s. pl.* ceppi, catene.

H

haberdasher *s.* merciaio.

haberdashery *s.* merceria.

habit *s.* **1.** abitudine **2.** temperamento **3.** costume.

habitable *agg.* abitabile.

habitation *s.* abitazione.

habitual *agg.* abituale, consueto.

habitude *s.* abitudine.

hack¹ *s.* **1.** tacca, incisione **2.** piccone, mazza **3.** tosse secca.

hack² *s.* **1.** ronzino **2.** (*fig.*) scribacchino.

to **hack¹** *vt.* sminuzzare. ♦ to **hack** *vi.* tossire a colpi secchi.

to **hack²** *vt. e vi.* **1.** adoperare cavalli da nolo **2.** adibire a un lavoro da scribacchino.

hackney *s.* **1.** cavallo da nolo **2.** vettura da nolo.

hacksaw *s.* seghetto.

had V. *to have.*

haematoma *s.* ematoma.

haemoglobin *s.* emoglobina.

haemophilia *s.* emofilia.

haemoptysis *s.* emottisi.

haemorrhage *s.* emorragia.

haemorrhoids *s. pl.* emorroidi.

haemostasia *s.* emostasi.

haemostatic *agg. e s.* emostatico.

haft *s.* manico, impugnatura.

hag *s.* **1.** strega, megera **2.** (*zool.*) lampreda.

haggard *agg.* sparuto, emaciato.

to **haggle** *vi.* mercanteggiare.

hagiographer *s.* agiografo.

hagiography *s.* agiografia.

hail¹ *s.* grandine || — *-stone*, chicco di grandine; — *-storm*, grandinata.

hail² *inter.* salve!, salute!

to **hail¹** *vi.* grandinare.

to **hail²** *vt. e vi.* salutare, chiamare.

hair *s.* **1.** capelli, capigliatura **2.** pelo, crine, setola || — *-breadth*, spessore di un capello; — *-cut*, taglio dei capelli; — *-do*, acconciatura.

hairdresser *s.* parrucchiere.

hairiness *s.* pelosità.

hairless *agg.* senza capelli.

hairpin *s.* forcella (*per capelli*).

hairy *agg.* **1.** capelluto **2.** peloso.

halation *s.* alone.

halberd *s.* alabarda.

hale *agg.* robusto, gagliardo.

half *agg.* mezzo.

half *s.* (*pl.* halves) metà, mezzo. ♦ **half** *avv.* a mezzo, a metà || — *-brother*, fratellastro; — *-length*, di media lunghezza; — *-mast*, a mezz'asta; — *-pay*, stipendio ridotto; — *-processed*, semilavorato; — *-sister*, sorellastra; — *-year*, se-

mestre.

halfpenny *s.* mezzo penny.

halfway *agg. e avv.* a mezza strada.

hall *s.* **1.** sala, salone **2.** refettorio, sala di ritrovo.

hallo! *int.* pronto (*al telefono*).

to **hallow** *vt.* santificare.

to **hallucinate** *vt.* allucinare.

hallucination *s.* allucinazione.

halo *s.* alone, aureola.

to **halt¹** *vt.* fermare. ♦ to **halt** *vi.* fermarsi.

to **halt²** *vi.* zoppicare.

halter *s.* **1.** capestro **2.** cavezza.

to **halve** *vt.* dividere a metà.

halyard *s.* (*mar.*) drizza.

ham *s.* **1.** prosciutto. ♦ **hams** *s. pl.* natiche.

hamlet *s.* piccolo villaggio.

hammer *s.* martello, martelletto: — *-blow*, colpo di martello, di maglio || to bring under the —, mettere all'asta.

to **hammer** *vt. e vi.* martellare.

hammering *s.* martellamento.

hammock *s.* amaca.

hamper¹ *s.* cesta.

hamper² *s.* impedimento.

to **hamper** *vt.* imbarazzare, ostacolare.

to **hamstring** *vt.* azzoppare.

hand *s.* **1.** mano: *hands off!*, via le mani!; *hands up!*, mani in alto! **2.** operaio, lavoratore **3.** calligrafia || *at* —, a portata di mano; *first* —, di prima mano.

to **hand** *vt.* porgere, dare || *to* — *in*, consegnare; *to* — *out*, distribuire; *to* — *over*, rimettere.

handbag *s.* borsetta.

handbill *s.* volantino.

handbook *s.* manuale.

handcuffs *s. pl.* manette.

to **handcuff** *vt.* mettere le manette.

handful *s.* **1.** manciata **2.** piccolo numero (*di persone*).

handgrip *s.* stretta di mano, morsa della mano.

handicap *s.* svantaggio.

to **handicap** *vt.* svantaggiare, ostacolare.

handicraft *s.* **1.** lavoro manuale **2.** abilità manuale.

handicraftsman *s.* artigiano.

handily *avv.* **1.** abilmente **2.** a portata di mano.

handiwork *s.* lavoro fatto a mano.

handkerchief *s.* fazzoletto.

handle *s.* **1.** manico, impugnatura

2. *(fig.)* pretesto || — *-bar*, manubrio *(di bicicletta)*.

to **handle** *vt.* 1. maneggiare 2. comportarsi verso.

handler *s.* manipolatore.

handling *s.* 1. maneggiamento 2. maniera di trattare.

handmade *agg.* fatto a mano.

handrail *s.* corrimano.

handshake *s.* stretta di mano.

handsome *agg.* bello, di bell'aspetto.

handwriting *s.* calligrafia.

handy *agg.* 1. abile, destro 2. a portata di mano || — *-man*, factotum.

hang *s.* inclinazione, pendio.

to **hang (hung, hung)** *vt.* appendere, attaccare.

to **hang (hung, hung)** *vi.* 1. pendere 2. appoggiarsi. ♦ to **hang** *(reg.)* *vt.* impiccare.

hanger *s.* gancio, uncino || — *on*, seguace, parassita; *dress* —, attaccapanni; *paper* —, tappezziere.

hanging *agg.* pendente, sospeso. ♦ **hanging** *s.* impiccagione.

hangman *s.* boia, carnefice.

hank *s.* matassa.

hapless *agg.* sfortunato.

to **happen** *vi.* avvenire, accadere.

happening *s.* avvenimento.

happily *avv.* felicemente.

happiness *s.* felicità.

happy *agg.* felice, contento.

harangue *s.* arringa.

to **harangue** *vt.* e *vi.* arringare, pronunciare un discorso solenne.

to **harass** *vt.* tormentare, molestare.

harbinger *s.* precursore.

harbour *s.* 1. porto 2. *(fig.)* rifugio.

to **harbour** *vt.* 1. accogliere, dare asilo a 2. nutrire *(pensieri ecc.)*. ♦ to **harbour** *vi.* entrare in porto.

hard *agg.* 1. duro 2. severo, spietato 3. difficile 4. rigido *(di tempo)*. ♦ **hard** *avv.* 1. energicamente 2. con difficoltà, duramente 3. vicino, accanto || — *-boiled*, bollito fino a diventar duro; — *-headed*, ostinato; — *-set*, in bisogno.

to **harden** *vt.* indurire. ♦ to **harden** *vi.* indurirsi.

hardening *agg.* temprante. ♦ **hardening** *s.* tempra.

hardihood *s.* ardire, coraggio.

hardily *avv.* arditamente.

hardiness *s.* 1. ardire 2. robustezza.

hardly *avv.* 1. a stento, a malapena 2. quasi 3. duramente, severamente.

hardness *s.* durezza *(anche fig.)*.

hardship *s.* 1. avversità 2. stento.

hardware *s.* ferramenta.

hardy *agg.* ardito.

hare *s.* lepre || — *-brained*, scervellato; — *-lip*, labbro leporino.

to **hark** *vt.* e *vi.* ascoltare || to — *back*, risalire a *(col pensiero)*.

harlequin *s.* arlecchino.

harlequinade *s.* arlecchinata.

harlot *s.* prostituta.

harm *s.* danno *(morale e fisico)* || *out of* — *'s way*, in salvo.

to **harm** *vt.* far male, far torto.

harmful *agg.* nocivo, dannoso.

harmfulness *s.* l'essere nocivo.

harmless *agg.* innocuo.

harmonic *agg.* 1. armonico, armonioso 2. *(mat.)* in progressione.

harmonious *agg.* armonioso.

harmonium *s.* armonium.

to **harmonize** *vt.* armonizzare. ♦ to **harmonize** *vi.* armonizzarsi.

harmony *s.* armonia, accordo.

harness *s.* finimenti *(pl.)*.

to **harness** *vt.* bardare, mettere i finimenti a.

harp *s.* arpa.

harpist *s.* arpista.

harpoon *s.* rampone, fiocina.

harpsichord *s.* clavicembalo.

harrow *s.* erpice.

harsh *agg.* 1. duro, ruvido 2. aspro 3. discordante *(di suono)*.

harshness *s.* asprezza, durezza.

harvest *s.* raccolto, messe.

harvester *s.* 1. mietitore 2. mietitrice meccanica.

haste *s.* fretta, rapidità || *to make* —, far presto.

to **haste**, to **hasten** *vt.* affrettare. ♦ to **haste**, to **hasten** *vi.* affrettarsi.

hastily *avv.* 1. frettolosamente 2. precipitosamente.

hasty *agg.* 1. frettoloso, affrettato 2. avventato, impetuoso.

hat *s.* cappello.

hatch *s.* 1. portello, mezza porta 2. *(mar.)* boccaporto.

hatchet *s.* accetta.

hate *s.* odio.

to **hate** *vt.* odiare, avere in odio.

hateful *agg.* 1. odioso 2. pieno di odio.

hatred *s.* odio.

hatstand *s.* attaccapanni.

hatter *s.* cappellaio.

haughtily *avv.* altezzosamente.

haughtiness s. alterigia, boria.

haughty agg. altezzoso, arrogante.

haul s. 1. trazione, tiro 2. raccolta, retata.

to **haul** vt. tirare, trainare. ♦ to **haul** vi. cambiare (di vento).

haulage s. 1. trasporto 2. costo del trasporto.

haunt s. 1. ricovero, ritiro 2. covo, tana.

to **haunt** vt. 1. frequentare assiduamente 2. perseguitare (di ricordi, pensieri ecc.).

haunted agg. 1. frequentato 2. perseguitato.

haunting agg. che perseguita.

to **have (had, had)** vt. 1. (ausiliare) avere: I — gone, sono andato; I — not (I haven't) read the book, non ho letto il libro 2. avere, possedere || — breakfast, far colazione 3. dovere: I — to go there, devo andarci 4. ricevere, ottenere || had better, sarebbe meglio che; I had rather, preferirei.

ɫ-**aven** s. (fig.) porto, rifugio.

havoc s. strage, rovina.

hawk s. 1. falco, sparviero 2. (fig.) avvoltoio.

hawker[1] s. falconiere.

hawker[2] venditore ambulante.

hawser s. gomena.

hawthorn s. biancospino.

hay s. fieno, paglia || — -loft, fienile; — -making, falciatura.

haycock s. mucchio di fieno.

hayseed s. seme di erba.

haystack s. mucchio di fieno.

hazard s. 1. azzardo, rischio 2. giuoco di dadi.

to **hazard** vt. azzardare, arrischiare.

haze s. foschia, nebbia.

hazel s. nocciuolo || — -nut, nocciuola.

hazily avv. indistintamente.

haziness s. 1. foschia 2. (fig.) confusione.

hazy agg. 1. nebbioso 2. indistinto (anche fig.).

he pron. sogg. m. egli, lui, colui.

head s. 1. testa 2. capo, direttore 3. individuo 4. parte alta di una cosa 5. capo, unità di bestiame || — -first, a capofitto; — -master, direttore di una scuola; — -money, taglia; — -work, lavoro mentale.

to **head** vt. 1. colpire con la testa 2. dirigere, comandare 3. intestare. ♦ to **head** vi. dirigersi.

headache s. mal di testa.

headed agg. munito di testa || hot-—, esaltato; pig-—, ostinato; swollen-—, tronfio; wrong-—, caparbio.

heading s. 1. intestazione, titolo (di un capitolo) 2. (aer.) rotta.

headland s. promontorio.

headless agg. senza testa (anche fig.).

headlight s. faro anteriore.

headline s. intestazione di capitolo, articolo.

headlong avv. a capofitto, precipitosamente.

headquarters s. pl. quartier generale (sing.).

headstone s. pietra tombale.

to **heal** vt. 1. guarire, curare 2. (fig.) sanare. ♦ to **heal** vi. 1. guarire 2. sanarsi.

healer s. guaritore.

healing agg. salutare.

health s. 1. salute 2. salvezza divina.

healthful agg. salubre.

healthily avv. salubremente.

healthiness s. 1. salute 2. salubrità.

healthy agg. 1. sano, robusto 2. salutare.

heap s. mucchio, cumulo.

to **heap** vt. ammucchiare, accumulare.

to **hear (heard, heard)** vt. e vi. 1. sentire, udire 2. sentir dire, venire a sapere.

hearing s. 1. udito 2. udienza.

hearsay s. diceria, voce.

hearse s. carro funebre.

heart s. 1. cuore (anche fig.) 2. affetto, coraggio 3. centro, parte principale || — -beat, pulsazione; — -break, crepacuore; — -breaking, straziante; — -failure, collasso cardiaco; — -felt, sincero, di cuore.

heartache s. angoscia, angustia.

heartburn s. bruciore di stomaco.

hearted agg. dal cuore, di cuore || broken-—, desolato; chicken-—, pauroso; down-—, depresso; lion-—, dal cuore di leone; whole-—, generoso.

to **hearten** vt. incoraggiare. ♦ to **hearten** vi. prendere coraggio.

hearth s. 1. focolare (anche fig.) 2. (metal.) crogiuolo, letto di fusione.

heartily avv. cordialmente.

heartiness s. 1. cordialità.

heartless *agg.* senza cuore.

hearty *agg.* **1.** sincero, cordiale **2.** sano, robusto.

heat *s.* **1.** calore, caldo **2.** animosità || — -*stroke*, colpo di calore; — -*wave*, ondata di calore.

to heat *vt.* **1.** scaldare **2.** animare. ◆ **to heat** *vi.* **1.** scaldarsi **2.** animarsi.

heater *s.* bollitore, riscaldatore.

heath *s.* brughiera.

heathen *agg.* e *s.* pagano.

heather *s.* erica.

heating *s.* riscaldamento.

heave *s.* **1.** sforzo **2.** rigonfiamento (*di onde*) **3.** sollevamento.

heaven *s.* **1.** cielo, paradiso (*anche fig.*) **2.** stato di gioia.

heavenly *agg.* divino, celeste.

heavenward *agg.* rivolto al cielo.

heavily *avv.* pesantemente, gravemente.

heaviness *s.* pesantezza.

heavy *agg.* **1.** pesante **2.** violento, forte **3.** fangoso, pesante (*di terreno*).

Hebrew *agg.* e *s.* ebreo.

hecatomb *s.* ecatombe.

hectare *s.* ettaro.

hectic *agg.* **1.** tisico, etico **2.** febbricitante.

hectogram(me) *s.* ettogrammo.

hectolitre *s.* ettolitro.

hectometre *s.* ettometro.

hedge *s.* **1.** siepe **2.** barriera.

to hedge *vt.* circondare con una siepe. ◆ **to hedge** *vi.* essere evasivo.

hedgehog *s.* riccio, porcospino.

hedonism *s.* edonismo.

hedonist *s.* edonista.

heed *s.* attenzione, cura.

heedful *agg.* attento, vigile.

heedless *agg.* sventato.

heedlessness *s.* sventatezza, trascuratezza.

heel *s.* **1.** calcagno, tallone **2.** sperone (*di uccelli*).

Hegelian *agg.* hegeliano.

hegemony *s.* egemonia.

heifer *s.* giovenca.

heigh *inter.* ehi!

height *s.* **1.** altezza **2.** altitudine **3.** altura, collina **4.** sommità, il più alto grado.

to heighten *vt.* **1.** innalzare **2.** accrescere, intensificare. ◆ **to heighten** *vi.* innalzarsi.

heinous *agg.* atroce.

heir *s.* erede.

heiress *s.* ereditiera.

held V. **to hold**.

helicoid *agg.* elicoidale.

helicopter *s.* elicottero.

heliocentric(al) *agg.* eliocentrico.

heliotherapy *s.* elioterapia.

heliport *s.* eliporto.

helium *s.* elio.

hell *s.* inferno (*anche fig.*).

Hellenic *agg.* ellenico.

Hellenism *s.* ellenismo.

Hellenist *s.* ellenista.

hellish *agg.* infernale.

hello *inter.* salve!

helm[1] *s.* elmo, casco.

helm[2] *s.* timone (*anche fig.*).

helmet *s.* elmetto, casco.

helmsman *s.* timoniere.

help *s.* aiuto, soccorso.

to help *vt.* **1.** aiutare, soccorrere **2.** servire (*cibo*) || *cannot* —, non poter fare a meno di; *to* — *oneself to*, servirsi di (*cibo*).

helper *s.* aiutante.

helpful *agg.* utile, servizievole.

helpless *agg.* senza aiuto, indifeso.

helpmate *s.* collaboratore.

Helvetic *agg.* elvetico.

hem[1] *s.* orlo, bordo.

hem[2] *inter.* ehm!.

to hem[1] *vt.* orlare || *to* — *in*, circondare, accerchiare.

to hem[2] *vi.* schiarirsi la gola.

hemicycle *s.* emiciclo.

hemiplegia *s.* emiplegia.

hemisphere *s.* emisfero.

hemispheric(al) *agg.* emisferico.

hemlock *s.* cicuta.

hemp *s.* canapa.

hen *s.* **1.** gallina **2.** femmina (*di uccelli*) || — -*house*, pollaio.

hence *avv.* **1.** di qui, da questo momento **2.** donde.

henceforth *avv.* d'ora innanzi.

hendecasyllabic *agg.* endecasillabico.

hendecasyllable *s.* endecasillabo.

henna *s.* alcanna.

hepatic *agg.* epatico.

hepatitis *s.* epatite.

heptagon *s.* ettagono.

heptagonal *agg.* ettagonale.

her *agg. poss. f.* suo, sua, suoi, sue. ◆ **her** *pron. compl. f.* la, lei, le, colei.

herald *s.* **1.** araldo **2.** nunzio **3.** (*fig.*) precursore.

heraldic *agg.* araldico.
herb s. 1. erba 2. pianta medicinale.
herbaceous *agg.* erbaceo.
herbal *agg.* di erba.
herbarium s. erbario.
herbivorous *agg.* erbivoro.
herborist s. erborista.
Herculean *agg.* erculeo.
herd s. gregge, mandria.
herdsman s. mandriano.
here *avv.* qui, qua || — *I am*, eccomi.
hereabouts *avv.* qui intorno.
hereafter *avv.* d'ora innanzi.
hereby *avv.* 1. con questo mezzo 2. qui vicino.
hereditary *agg.* ereditario.
heredity s. (*biol.*) ereditarietà.
herein *avv.* 1. in questo 2. (*comm.*) nella presente.
heresiarch s. eresiarca.
heresy s. eresia.
heretic(al) *agg.* e s. eretico.
herewith *avv.* qui accluso.
heritable *agg.* ereditabile.
heritage s. eredità.
hermaphrodite *agg.* e s. ermafrodito.
hermeneutics s. ermeneutica.
hermetic(al) *agg.* ermetico.
hermetically *avv.* ermeticamente.
hermit s. eremita.
hermitage s. eremo, eremitaggio.
hernia s. ernia.
hernial *agg.* erniario.
hero s. eroe.
heroic(al) *agg.* eroico.
heroin s. (*chim.*) eroina.
heroine s. eroina.
heroism s. eroismo.
heron s. airone.
herpes s. erpete.
herring s. aringa || — *-bone*, spina di pesce (*nei tessuti ecc.*).
hers *pron. poss. f.* il suo, la sua, i suoi, le sue.
herself *pron. r. f.* 1. se stessa, sé, si 2. ella stessa.
hesitant *agg.* esitante.
to hesitate *vi.* esitare.
hesitatingly *avv.* con esitazione.
hesitation s. esitazione.
heteroclite *agg.* eteroclito.
heterodox *agg.* eterodosso.
heterodoxy s. eterodossia.
heterogeneity s. eterogeneità.
heterogeneous *agg.* eterogeneo.
to hew (hewed, hewn) *vt.* fendere, recidere || *to — down*, abbat-

tere.
hexagon s. esagono.
hexagonal *agg.* esagonale.
hexahedron s. esaedro.
hexameter s., esametro.
hiatus s. iato.
to hibernate *vi.* (*zool.*) cadere in letargo invernale.
hibernation s. 1. svernamento 2. ibernazione.
hiccough, hiccup s. singhiozzo, singulto.
hid V. *to hide.*
hidden V. *to hide.*
hide[1] s. pelle, cuoio.
hide[2] s. nascondiglio || — *-and-seek*, rimpiattino.
to hide[1] **(hid, hidden)** *vt.* nascondere, celare. ♦ **to hide (hid, hidden)** *vi.* nascondersi, celarsi.
to hide[2] *vt.* 1. spellare, scorticare 2. frustare.
hideous *agg.* orrendo, odioso.
hideousness s. odiosità, aspetto orribile.
hiding s. il nascondere.
hierarchy s. gerarchia.
hieratic *agg.* ieratico.
hieroglyph s. geroglifico.
hieroglyphic(al) *agg.* geroglifico.
high *agg.* 1. alto, elevato (*anche fig.*) 2. altezzoso 3. forte, intenso (*di luce, colori*) || — *-born*, di alto lignaggio; — *-class*, di prim'ordine; — *-coloured*, dal colore acceso; — *-hearted*, pieno di coraggio; — *-life*, vita di alta società; — *-school*, scuola media; — *-sea*, mare aperto; — *-speed*, ad alta velocità. ♦ **high** *avv.* 1. alto, in alto 2. fortemente.
highbrow *agg.* e s. intellettuale.
highland s. regione montuosa.
highlander s. montanaro.
highly *avv.* 1. molto, assai 2. altamente, nobilmente.
highness s. 1. altezza, elevatezza 2. eccellenza, valore.
highway s. strada maestra.
highwayman s. bandito, rapinatore.
hilarious *agg.* ilare.
hill s. collina, altura.
hillock s. collinetta.
hillside s. pendio.
hilltop s. sommità della collina.
hilly *agg.* collinoso.
hilt s. elsa.
him *pron. pers. m.* lo, lui, gli, colui, sé.
himself *pron. r. m.* 1. si, sé, se

stesso 2. egli stesso.

hind² s. cerva, daina.

hind² s. colono, fattore.

hind(er) agg. posteriore.

to **hinder** vt. e vi. 1. impedire, ostruire 2. imbarazzare.

hindrance s. ostacolo, impaccio.

Hindu agg. e s. indù.

hinge s. 1. cardine 2. (fig.) perno.

to **hinge** vt. munire di cardini. ◆ to **hinge** vi. 1. girare sui cardini 2. essere imperniato.

hint s. 1. cenno, allusione 2. consiglio.

to **hint** vt. e vi. alludere, accennare, suggerire.

hinterland s. retroterra.

hip s. anca, fianco.

hippocampus s. (pl. -pi.) ippocampo.

hippopotamus s. ippopotamo.

hire s. affitto, nolo.

to **hire** vt. prendere a servizio, noleggiare.

hireling s. mercenario.

his agg. poss. m. suo, sua, suoi, sue. ◆ **his** pron. poss. m. il suo, la sua, i suoi, le sue.

Hispanic agg. ispanico.

Hispanicism s. ispanismo.

Hispanist s. ispanista.

hispid agg. ispido.

hiss s. sibilo, fischio.

to **hiss** vt. e vi. 1. sibilare 2. fischiare.

histology s. istologia.

historian s. storico.

historic(al) agg. storico.

historicity s. storicità.

historiographer s. storiografo.

historiography s. storiografia.

history s. storia.

histrion s. istrione.

histrionic(al) agg. istrionico.

histrionism s. istrionismo.

hit s. 1. colpo, botta 2. osservazione sarcastica 3. caso fortunato 4. (teat.) successo.

to **hit** (hit, hit) vt. e vi. 1. battere, picchiare 2. urtare, venire a contatto 3. (fig.) toccare, colpire || to — the mark, colpire nel segno.

hitch s. 1. colpo, strattone, balzo repentino 2. nodo.

to **hitch** vt. 1. muovere a sbalzi 2. legare, attaccare. ◆ to **hitch** vi. muoversi a sbalzi.

to **hitchhike** vi. fare l'autostop.

hitchhiker s. autostoppista.

hitchhiking s. autostop.

hive s. 1. alveare, arnia 2. sciame (anche fig.).

hives s. pl. orticaria, eruzione cutanea.

hoar s. candore, vecchiaia || — -frost, brina.

hoard s. gruzzolo.

to **hoard** vt. ammassare, ammucchiare. ◆ to **hoard** vi. ammucchiarsi.

hoarder s. incettatore.

hoarding s. recinto provvisorio.

hoarse agg. rauco, fioco.

hoarseness s. raucedine.

hoary agg. 1. bianco, canuto 2. venerando.

hobble s. 1. zoppicamento 2. imbarazzo.

to **hobble** vi. zoppicare. ◆ to **hobble** vt. azzoppare.

hobby s. svago preferito, passatempo.

hobnail s. chiodo (per scarponi).

hobnailed agg. chiodato.

hodman s. manovale.

hoe s. zappa.

to **hoe** vt. zappare, estirpare le erbacce.

hog s. maiale.

hogshead s. barilotto (per tabacco, zucchero).

hoist s. montacarichi.

to **hoist** vt. alzare, sollevare.

hold¹ s. 1. presa 2. (fig.) ascendente.

hold² s. (mar.) stiva.

to **hold** (held, held) vt. e vi. 1. tenere, sostenere 2. contenere 3. ritenere, credere, pensare 4. occupare una carica, possedere 5. resistere, aggrapparsi || to — up, sollevare; to — back, esitare.

holder s. 1. possessore, detentore, proprietario 2. sostegno, supporto 3. dente canino.

holdings s. pl. beni, titoli.

hold-up s. intoppo nel traffico, panna di automobile.

hole s. 1. foro, apertura, buco 2. antro, tana.

holiday s. 1. festa, giorno festivo 2. vacanza.

holiness s. santità.

hollow agg. 1. concavo, infossato 2. cupo, cavernoso 3. (fig.) falso, irreale, vuoto.

to **hollow** vt. scavare, incavare.

hollow avv. (fam.) completamente.

hollowness s. 1. cavità 2. timbro

holly s. agrifoglio.

holocaust s. olocausto.

holograph agg. e s. documento olografo.

holy agg. santo, sacro.

homage s. omaggio.

home¹ s. 1. casa, focolare domestico 2. patria 3. rifugio, asilo, ospizio.

home² agg. domestico, casalingo.

home³ avv. 1. a casa, in patria 2. direttamente, al segno || — -born, indigeno, locale; — -bred, allevato in casa; — -made, fatto in casa; — -market, mercato nazionale; — -town, città natia; — -trade, commercio interno

homeland s. patria.

homeless agg. senza casa.

homelike agg. domestico, familiare.

homely agg. 1. semplice, modesto 2. domestico.

homeopathic agg. omeopatico

homeopathy s. omeopatia.

Homeric agg. omerico.

homesick agg. nostalgico.

homesickness s. nostalgia.

homeward agg. e avv. verso casa, verso la patria

homework s. coll. compiti per casa.

homicidal agg. omicida.

homicide s. omicidio.

homily s. omelia.

homogeneity s. omogeneità.

homogeneous agg. omogeneo.

to homogenize vt. omogeneizzare.

to homologate vt. omologare.

homologation s. omologazione.

homologous agg. omologo.

homology s. omologia.

homonymous agg. omonimo.

homonymy s. omonimia.

homosexual agg. e s. omosessuale.

homosexuality s. omosessualità.

homy agg. casalingo.

honest agg. 1. onesto, integro 2. leale.

honesty s. 1. onestà, probità 2. lealtà.

honey s. miele.

honeycomb s. favo.

honeyed agg. 1. coperto di miele 2. (fig.) sdolcinato, adulatorio.

honeymoon s. luna di miele.

honeysuckle s. caprifoglio.

honorary agg. onorario, onorifico.

honorific agg. onorifico.

honour s. 1. onore, reputazione 2. stima, reverenza 3. Eccellenza.

to honour vt. onorare, fare onore a.

honourable agg. stimato, onorevole.

honourableness s. onorabilità.

hood s. cappuccio.

to hood vt. incappucciare, fornire di cappuccio.

hoof s. zoccolo (di animale).

hook s. 1. uncino, gancio 2. amo 3. tagliola 4. falce per grano || by — or by crook, di riffa o di raffa.

to hook vt. agganciare. ♦ to hook vi. agganciarsi.

hooked agg. 1. fornito di uncini 2. adunco, uncinato.

hoop s. collare, cerchio (di botte, ruota ecc.).

to hoop vt. cerchiare (una botte).

to hoot vt. e vi. 1. urlare, gridare 2. suonare il clacson.

hop¹ s. salto (su una gamba sola).

hop² s. luppolo.

to hop vt. e vi. saltare su una gamba sola.

hope s. speranza.

to hope vt. e vi. sperare, essere fiducioso.

hopeful agg. pieno di speranza, fiducioso.

hopefulness s. fiducia, buona speranza.

hopeless agg. senza speranza, irrimediabile.

hopelessness s. disperazione.

hopper s. persona od insetto che saltella.

horde s. orda.

horizon s. orizzonte.

horizontal agg. orizzontale.

horizontally avv. orizzontalmente.

hormone s. ormone.

horn s. 1. corno, tentacolo, antenna 2. (mus.) corno, tromba.

to horn vt. 1. fornire di corna 2. ferire con le corna.

hornet s. vespa, calabrone.

hornpipe s. cornamusa.

horology s. orologeria.

horoscope s. oroscopo: to cast a —, fare un oroscopo.

horrible agg. 1. orribile, orrendo 2. (fam.) eccessivo.

horribly avv. orribilmente.

horrid agg. orrido, orrendo.

horrific agg. orribile, orripilante.

to horrify vt. 1. atterrire, incutere timore 2. scandalizzare.

horror s. 1. orrore, spavento 2. cosa orribile || — -stricken, atterrito.

hors-d'oeuvre *s.* antipasto.

horse *s.* cavallo || — *-bean*, fava; — *-boy*, mozzo di stalla; — *-chestnut*, ippocastano; — *-doctor*, veterinario; — *-race*, corsa ippica; — *-shoe*, ferro di cavallo.

horseback *s.* dorso di cavallo || *on* —, a cavallo.

horseman *s.* cavaliere.

horticultural *agg.* attinente all'orticultura.

horticulture *s.* orticultura.

hosanna *inter.* osanna.

hose *s.* 1. idrante 2. calze (*pl.*).

hosier *s.* commerciante in calze.

hosiery *s.* maglieria.

hospice *s.* alloggio, ospizio.

hospitable *agg.* ospitale.

hospital *s.* ospedale.

hospitality *s.* ospitalità.

host[1] *s.* folla, moltitudine.

host[2] *s.* ospite, anfitrione.

hostage *s.* ostaggio.

hostel *s.* pensionato (*per giovani, studenti, militari ecc.*).

hostess *s.* 1. ospite, padrona di casa 2. assistente di volo.

hostile *agg.* ostile, nemico.

hostility *s.* inimicizia, ostilità.

hot *agg.* 1. caldo, ardente 2. forte, piccante 3. violento, impetuoso || — *-headed*, scalmanato.

hotel *s.* albergo || — *-keeper*, albergatore.

hothead *s.* testa calda.

hothouse *s.* serra.

hotly *avv.* caldamente.

hotspur *s.* persona impulsiva.

hound *s.* bracco, segugio.

to **hound** *vt.* cacciare (*con bracchi*).

hour *s.* 1. ora 2. periodo. ♦ **hours** *s. pl.* orario (*sing.*).

hourly *agg.* 1. continuo 2. all'ora 3. ad ogni ora. ♦ **hourly** *avv.* 1. continuamente 2. ad ogni ora 3. d'ora in ora.

house *s.* 1. casa, abitazione 2. albergo, pensione 3. clinica 4. convento 5. casato, dinastia 6. teatro 7. (*comm.*) ditta 8. (*mar.*) tuga.

to **house** *vt.* 1. alloggiare, ricevere in casa 2. (*fig.*) offrire un rifugio. ♦ to **house** *vi.* 1. prendere alloggio 2. rifugiarsi.

housebreaker *s.* scassinatore.

housebreaking *s.* demolizione edilizia.

household *s.* famiglia: *Royal Household*, la famiglia reale.

householder *s.* capofamiglia.

housekeeper *s.* governante, domestica.

housekeeping *s.* il governo della casa.

houseless *agg.* senza casa.

housemaid *s.* domestica, cameriera.

housewife *s.* (*pl.* -wives) massaia, casalinga.

housework *s.* lavoro domestico.

housing *s.* 1. il ricevere, l'accogliere 2. alloggio, rifugio, riparo.

hovel *s.* 1. tana 2. baracca.

to **hover** *vi.* 1. librarsi, svolazzare 2. gironzolare.

how *avv.* come, in che modo.

however *avv.* 1. comunque 2. però, tuttavia.

howitzer *s.* obice.

howl *s.* urlo, grido.

to **howl** *vt.* e *vi.* urlare, ululare.

howling *agg.* urlante, ululante.

hub *s.* mozzo di ruota.

hubbub *s.* tumulto, fracasso.

huddle *s.* calca, folla.

to **huddle** *vt.* ammucchiare. ♦ to **huddle** *vi.* affollarsi, accalcarsi.

hue *s.* tinta, colore.

hug *s.* abbraccio.

to **hug** *vt.* abbracciare (*anche fig.*) || to — *oneself*, compiacersi.

huge *agg.* enorme, vasto.

hugeness *s.* grandezza, enormità.

hull *s.* scafo.

hullabaloo *s.* tumulto, fracasso.

hullo *inter.* 1. (*fam.*) salve 2. (*tel.*) pronto.

hum *s.* ronzio, mormorio.

to **hum** *vt.* e *vi.* 1. ronzare, mormorare 2. cantare a bocca chiusa.

human *agg.* 1. umano 2. sensibile.

humane *agg.* umano, compassionevole.

humaneness *s.* benevolenza, umanità.

humanism *s.* umanesimo.

humanist *s.* umanista.

humanistic *agg.* umanistico.

humanitarian *agg.* filantropico, umanitario.

humanity *s.* 1. umanità, il genere umano 2. bontà, benevolenza.

to **humanize** *vt.* 1. rendere umano 2. adattare alla natura umana. ♦ to **humanize** *vi.* acquisire sentimenti migliori.

humankind *s.* il genere umano.

humble *agg.* umile, modesto.

to **humble** *vt.* umiliare.

humbleness *s.* umiltà.

humbly *avv.* umilmente.

humbug *s.* frode, impostura.

humdrum *s.* monotonia, tedio. ◆ **humdrum** *agg.* monotono.

humeral *agg.* omerale.

humerus *s.* (*pl.* -ri) omero.

humid *agg.* umido.

humidity *s.* umidità.

to **humiliate** *vt.* umiliare, mortificare.

humiliation *s.* umiliazione.

humility *s.* umiltà.

humming *agg.* ronzante. ◆ **humming** *s.* ronzio.

humorist *s.* umorista.

humorous *agg.* arguto, dotato di senso dell'umorismo.

humour *s.* 1. umorismo 2. umore.

hump *s.* 1. gobba, gibbosità 2. collinetta, cresta.

humpback *s.* 1. gobba 2. gobbo.

hunch *s.* gobba, gibbosità.

hunchback *s.* persona gobba.

hundred *agg.* cento. ◆ **hundred** *s.* centinaio.

hundredth *agg.* centesimo.

hung V. to *hang*.

Hungarian *agg.* e *s.* ungherese.

hunger *s.* 1. fame, appetito 2. (*fig.*) ingordigia.

hungrily *avv.* 1. con grande appetito 2. avidamente.

hungry *agg.* 1. affamato || to be —, aver fame 2. (*fig.*) avido, bramoso.

hunt *s.* 1. caccia 2. ricerca, inseguimento.

to **hunt** *vt.* e *vi.* 1. cacciare, andare a caccia 2. cercare affannosamente.

hunter *s.* cacciatore (*anche fig.*).

hunting *s.* 1. caccia 2. ricerca.

huntsman *s.* cacciatore.

hurdle *s.* ostacolo (*anche fig.*).

hurl *s.* lancio violento.

to **hurl** *vt.* lanciare, scagliare (*anche fig.*).

hurrah *inter.* urrah!

hurricane *s.* uragano, ciclone (*anche fig.*).

hurried *agg.* affrettato, precipitoso.

hurry *s.* fretta, precipitazione: to be in a —, aver fretta.

to **hurry** *vt.* affrettare. ◆ to **hurry** *vi.* affrettarsi || — up!, fa presto!

hurt *s.* lesione, ferita (*anche fig.*).

to **hurt** (hurt, hurt) *vt.* e *vi.* 1. dolere 2. recar dolore, offendere.

hurtful *agg.* 1. dannoso 2. offensivo.

husband *s.* marito.

husbandry *s.* 1. agricoltura 2. amministrazione domestica.

hush *inter.* silenzio.

to **hush** *vt.* 1. zittire, tacere 2. (*fig.*) calmare.

husk *s.* 1. guscio, baccello 2. involucro 3. (*pl.*) rifiuti.

to **husk** *vt.* sgusciare, sbucciare.

husky *agg.* rugoso, secco.

hussar *s.* ussaro.

hut *s.* 1. capanna, casupola 2. rifugio alpino.

hyacinth *s.* giacinto.

hybrid *agg.* e *s.* ibrido.

hybridism *s.* ibridismo.

hybridization *s.* ibridazione.

hydra *s.* idra.

hydrangea *s.* ortensia.

hydrant *s.* idrante.

hydrate *s.* idrato.

to **hydrate** *vt.* idratare.

hydraulic *agg.* idraulico.

hydraulics *s.* idraulica.

hydric *agg.* contenente idrogeno.

hydrocarbon *s.* idrocarburo.

hydrocephalus *s.* idrocefalo.

hydroelectric *agg.* idroelettrico.

hydrofluoric *agg.* fluoridrico.

hydrofoil boat *s.* aliscafo.

hydrogen *s.* idrogeno.

hydrology *s.* idrologia.

hydrolysis *s.* (*pl.* -ses) idrolisi.

hydrostatic(al) *agg.* idrostatico.

hyena *s.* iena.

hygiene *s.* igiene.

hygienics *s.* la scienza dell'igiene.

hygienist *s.* igienista.

hygrometry *s.* igrometria.

hymn *s.* inno.

hyperbole *s.* iperbole.

hyperbolic(al) *agg.* iperbolico.

hyperborean *agg.* e *s.* iperboreo.

hypercritical *agg.* ipercritico.

hypermetropy *s.* ipermetropia.

hypernutrition *s.* supernutrizione.

hypersensitive *agg.* ipersensibile.

hypersensitivity *s.* ipersensibilità.

hypertension *s.* ipertensione.

hypertrophy *s.* ipertrofia.

hyphen *s.* lineetta d'unione.

hypnosis *s.* (*pl.* -ses) ipnosi.

hypnotic *agg.* e *s.* ipnotico.

hypnotism *s.* ipnotismo.

to **hypnotize** *vt.* ipnotizzare.

hypochondria *s.* ipocondria.

hypochondriac *agg.* e *s.* ipocondriaco.

hypocrisy *s.* ipocrisia.

hypocrite s. ipocrita.
hypocritic(al) agg. ipocrita.
hypodermic agg. ipodermico.
hypodermoclysis s. ipodermoclisi.
hyposulphite s. iposolfito.
hypotenuse s. ipotenusa.
hypothecary agg. ipotecario.
to **hypothecate** vt. ipotecare.
hypothesis s. (pl. -ses) ipotesi.
to **hypothesize** vi. fare ipotesi.
hypothetic(al) agg. ipotetico.
hypothetically avv. ipoteticamente.
hysteria s. isterismo.
hysteric(al) agg. isterico.
hysterics agg. attacco isterico.

I

I pron. pers. io.
iamb s. giambo.
iambic agg. giambico.
Iberian agg. e s. iberico.
ice s. ghiaccio || — -box, ghiacciaia;
  — -breaker, rompighiaccio; —
  -cream, gelato.
to **ice** vt. 1. ghiacciare 2. (cuc.) glassare.
iceboat s. nave rompighiaccio.
Icelander s. islandese.
Icelandic agg. islandese.
ichtyologist s. ittiologo.
ichthyology s. ittiologia.
icicle s. ghiacciuolo.
iciness s. gelo.
icing s. glassatura.
icon s. icona.
iconoclast s. iconoclasta.
iconoclastic agg. iconoclastico.
iconography s. iconografia.
icy agg. gelido, gelato.
idea s. idea.
ideal agg. e s. ideale.
idealism s. idealismo.
idealist s. idealista.
idealistic(al) agg. idealistico.
idealization s. idealizzazione.
to **idealize** vt. idealizzare.
ideally avv. idealmente.
to **ideate** vt. ideare.
ideation s. ideazione.
identic(al) agg. identico.
identifiable agg. identificabile.
identification s. identificazione.
to **identify** vt. identificare || to —
  oneself with, immedesimarsi con.

identity s. identità.
ideogram s. ideogramma.
ideography s. ideografia.
ideologic(al) agg. ideologico.
ideologist s. ideologo.
ideology s. ideologia.
idiocy s. idiozia.
idiom s. 1. idioma 2. idiotismo.
idiomatic(al) agg. idiomatico.
idiosyncrasy s. idiosincrasia.
idiot s. idiota.
idiotic(al) agg. idiota.
idle agg. 1. ozioso 2. vano.
to **idle** vi. oziare.
idleness s. 1. ozio 2. futilità.
idler s. ozioso.
idly avv. oziosamente.
idol s. idolo.
idolater s. idolatra.
to **idolatrize** vt. idolatrare.
idolatrous agg. idolatrico.
idolatry, idolism s. idolatria.
idyl(l) s. idillio.
idyllic agg. idillico.
if cong. se || as —, come se.
igneous agg. igneo.
to **ignite** vt. accendere. ♦ to **ignite**
  vi. accendersi.
ignition s. accensione || battery
  coil —, spinterogeno.
ignobility s. ignobilità.
ignoble agg. ignobile.
ignominious agg. ignominioso.
ignominy, ignomy s. ignominia.
ignorance s. ignoranza.
ignorant agg. ignorante.
to **ignore** vt. ignorare.
ilex s. leccio.
iliac agg. iliaco.
ill (worse, worst) agg. 1. ammala-
  to 2. cattivo. ♦ ill avv. male ||
  — -advised, sconsiderato; — -dis-
  posed, malevolo; — -fated, sfortunato; — -mannered, maleducato.
  ♦ ill s. male.
illation s. illazione.
illegal agg. 1. illegale 2. illecito.
illegality s. illegalità.
illegible agg. illeggibile.
illegitimacy s. illegittimità.
illegitimate agg. illegittimo.
illiberal agg. 1. illiberale 2. meschino.
illiberality s. 1. illiberalità 2. meschinità.
illicit agg. illecito.
illimitable agg. illimitato.
illiteracy s. 1. analfabetismo 2. i-
  gnoranza.

illiterate agg. e s. **1.** analfabeta **2.** ignorante.

illness s. malattia.

illogical agg. illogico.

illogicality s. illogicità.

to **ill-treat** vt. maltrattare.

to **illuminate** vt. illuminare.

illumination s. illuminazione.

to **illumine** vt. illuminare.

illuminism s. illuminismo.

ill-usage s. maltrattamento.

to **ill-use** vt. maltrattare.

illusion s. illusione.

illusionism s. illusionismo.

illusionist s. illusionista.

illusive agg. illusorio.

illusiveness s. illusorietà.

illusory agg. illusorio.

to **illustrate** vt. illustrare.

illustration s. illustrazione.

illustrative agg. illustrativo.

illustrator s. illustratore.

illustrious agg. illustre.

ill-will s. malevolenza.

ill-wisher s. malevolo.

image s. immagine.

to **image** vt. **1.** immaginare **2.** descrivere **3.** riflettere.

imagery s. raffigurazione.

imaginable agg. immaginabile.

imaginary agg. immaginario.

imagination s. immaginazione.

imaginative agg. immaginativo.

to **imagine** vt. e vi. immaginare.

imagining s. immaginazione.

imbecile agg. e s. **1.** debole **2.** imbecille.

imbecility s. **1.** debolezza **2.** imbecillità.

to **imbibe** vt. assorbire. ◆ to **imbibe** vi. imbeversi.

to **imbue** vt. impregnare.

imitable agg. imitabile.

to **imitate** vt. imitare.

imitation s. imitazione.

imitative agg. imitativo.

imitator s. imitatore.

immaculate agg. immacolato.

immanence s. immanenza.

immanent agg. immanente.

immanentism s. immanentismo.

immaterial agg. **1.** immateriale **2.** irrilevante.

immaterialism s. immaterialismo.

immaterialist s. immaterialista.

immateriality s. immaterialità.

immature agg. immaturo.

immaturity s. immaturità.

immeasurability s. incommensura-

bilità.

immeasurable agg. incommensurabile.

immediacy s. **1.** immediatezza **2.** rapporto diretto.

immediate agg. **1.** immediato **2.** diretto.

immediateness s. V. immediacy.

immemorial agg. immemorabile.

immense agg. immenso.

immenseness, immensity s. immensità.

immensurability s. immensurabilità.

immensurable agg. immensurabile.

to **immerge**, to **immerse** vt. immergere. ◆ to **immerge** vi. immergersi.

immersion s. **1.** immersione **2.** eclisse.

immigrant agg. e s. immigrante.

to **immigrate** vi. immigrare.

immigration s. immigrazione.

imminence s. **1.** imminenza **2.** pericolo.

imminent agg. **1.** imminente **2.** sovrastante.

immobile agg. immobile.

immobility s. immobilità.

immobilization s. immobilizzazione.

to **immobilize** vt. immobilizzare.

immoderate agg. smodato.

immoderateness s. smoderatezza.

immodest agg. **1.** immodesto **2.** indecente.

immodesty s. **1.** immodestia **2.** indecenza.

to **immolate** vt. immolare.

immolation s. immolazione.

immolator s. immolatore.

immoral agg. immorale.

immorality s. immoralità.

immortal agg. e s. immortale.

immortality s. immortalità.

immortalization s. l'immortalare.

to **immortalize** vt. immortalare.

immovability s. **1.** immobilità **2.** inamovibilità.

immovable agg. **1.** immobile **2.** inamovibile.

immovables s. pl. beni immobili.

immune agg. **1.** immune **2.** esente.

immunity s. **1.** immunità **2.** esenzione.

immunization s. immunizzazione.

to **immunize** vt. immunizzare.

to **immure** vt. **1.** murare **2.** impri-

gionare 3. chiudere fra mura.
immutability s. immutabilità.
immutable agg. immutabile.
imp s. diavoletto.
impact s. urto, collisione.
to **impact** vt. conficcare.
to **impair** vt. menomare.
impairment s. menomazione.
to **impale** vt. impalare.
impalpability s. impalpabilità.
impalpable agg. impalpabile.
imparity s. imparità.
to **impart** vt. 1. impartire 2. rivelare.
impartial agg. imparziale.
impartiality s. imparzialità.
impassable agg. invalicabile, impraticabile.
impassibility s. impassibilità.
impassible agg. impassibile.
to **impassion** vt. appassionare.
impassionate, impassioned agg. eccitato, ardente.
impassive agg. impassibile.
impatience s. 1. impazienza 2. avversione.
impatient agg. 1. impaziente 2. intollerante.
impavid agg. impavido.
to **impeach** vt. 1. imputare 2. biasimare || to — so. for high treason, accusare qu. di alto tradimento.
impeachable agg. accusabile.
impeacher s. accusatore.
impeachment s. accusa.
impeccability s. impeccabilità.
impeccable agg. impeccabile.
impecunious agg. povero.
to **impede** vt. 1. impedire 2. ostacolare.
impediment s. impedimento.
to **impel** vt. spingere, incitare.
impellent agg. impellente. ♦ **impellent** s. incentivo.
to **impend** vi. incombere.
impendence s. imminenza.
impendent agg. incombente.
impenetrability s. impenetrabilità.
impenetrable agg. impenetrabile.
impenitence s. impenitenza.
impenitent agg. impenitente.
imperative agg. e s. imperativo.
imperator s. imperatore.
imperceptibility s. impercettibilità.
imperceptible agg. impercettibile.
imperfect agg. 1. imperfetto 2. incompiuto.
imperfection s. 1. imperfezione 2.

incompiutezza.
imperial agg. imperiale.
imperialism s. imperialismo.
imperialist s. imperialista.
imperialistic agg. imperialistico.
to **imperil** vt. mettere in pericolo.
imperious agg. 1. imperioso 2. impellente.
imperiousness s. 1. imperiosità 2. urgenza.
imperishability s. indistruttibilità.
imperishable agg. indistruttibile, imperituro.
impermeability s. impermeabilità.
impermeable agg. impermeabile.
impersonal agg. impersonale.
impersonality s. l'essere impersonale.
to **impersonate** vt. impersonare.
impersonation s. personificazione.
impertinence s. 1. impertinenza 2. non pertinenza.
impertinent agg. 1. impertinente 2. non pertinente.
imperturbability s. imperturbabilità.
imperturbable agg. imperturbabile.
impervious agg. 1. impervio 2. impermeabile.
to **impetrate** vt. impetrare.
impetration s. impetrazione.
impetuosity s. impetuosità.
impetuous agg. impetuoso.
impetus s. impeto.
impiety s. empietà.
impious agg. empio.
impish agg. birichino.
implacability s. implacabilità.
implacable agg. implacabile.
to **implant** vt. 1. impiantare 2. inculcare.
implement s. utensile.
to **implement** vt. 1. compiere 2. attrezzare.
to **implicate** vt. implicare.
implication s. implicazione.
implicit, implied agg. implicito.
to **implore** vt. implorare.
imploring agg. supplichevole.
to **imply** vt. implicare.
impolite agg. scortese.
impoliteness s. scortesia.
impolitic agg. impolitico.
imponderability s. imponderabilità.
imponderable agg. imponderabile.
import s. 1. importanza 2. significato 3. (comm.) importazione.
to **import** vt. 1. importare 2. si-

gnificare 3. (*comm.*) importare.

importance *s.* importanza.

important *agg.* importante.

importer *s.* importatore.

importunate, importune *agg.* urgente.

to **importune** *vt.* importunare.

importunity *s.* 1. insistenza 2. urgenza.

to **impose** *vt.* 1. imporre 2. (*tip.*) impaginare. ♦ to **impose** *vi.* imporsi || to — on, ingannare.

imposing *agg.* imponente.

imposition *s.* 1. imposizione 2. imposta 3. inganno 4. (*tip.*) messa in macchina.

impossibility *s.* impossibilità.

impossible *agg.* impossibile.

impostor *s.* impostore.

imposture *s.* impostura.

impotence *s.* impotenza.

impotent *agg.* impotente.

to **impoverish** *vt.* impoverire.

impoverishment *s.* impoverimento.

impracticability *s.* 1. inattuabilità 2. impraticabilità 3. intrattabilità.

impracticable *agg.* 1. inattuabile 2. impraticabile 3. intrattabile.

imprecation *s.* imprecazione.

imprecatory *agg.* imprecatorio.

impregnable *agg.* inespugnabile.

to **impregnate** *vt.* 1. impregnare 2. fecondare.

impregnation *s.* fecondazione.

to **impress** *vt.* 1. imprimere, stampare 2. impressionare.

impression *s.* 1. impressione 2. ristampa.

impressionability *s.* impressionabilità.

impressionable *agg.* impressionabile.

impressionism *s.* impressionismo.

impressionist *agg.* e *s.* impressionista.

impressive *agg.* impressionante.

imprint *s.* 1. impronta 2. stampa.

to **imprint** *vt.* 1. imprimere 2. stampare.

to **imprison** *vt.* imprigionare.

imprisonment *s.* prigionia.

improbability *s.* improbabilità.

improbable *agg.* improbabile.

improbably *avv.* improbabilmente.

impromptu *agg.* improvvisato. ♦ **impromptu** *s.* improvvisazione.

improper *agg.* 1. erroneo 2. inadatto 3. sconveniente, irregolare.

impropriety *s.* 1. scorrettezza 2. sconvenienza.

to **improve** *vt.* 1. migliorare 2. valorizzare. ♦ to **improve** *vi.* migliorare, perfezionarsi.

improvement *s.* miglioramento.

improvidence *s.* imprevidenza.

improvident *agg.* imprevidente.

improvisation *s.* improvvisazione.

improvisator *s.* improvvisatore.

to **improvise** *vt.* e *vi.* improvvisare.

imprudence *s.* imprudenza.

imprudent *agg.* imprudente.

impudence *s.* impudenza.

impudent *agg.* impudente.

to **impugn** *vt.* (*giur.*) impugnare.

impugnable *agg.* (*giur.*) impugnabile.

impugner *s.* oppositore.

impulse, impulsion *s.* impulso.

impulsive *agg.* impulsivo.

impulsiveness, impulsivity *s.* impulsività.

impunity *s.* impunità.

impure *agg.* impuro.

impurity *s.* impurità.

imputable *agg.* imputabile.

imputation *s.* imputazione.

to **impute** *vt.* imputare.

in *avv.* e *prep.* a, in, dentro, entro, durante || to be — Paris, essere a Parigi; the best — the world, il migliore del mondo; — my opinion, secondo me; — all, in tutto; — that, in quanto che.

inability *s.* incapacità.

inaccessibility *s.* inaccessibilità.

inaccessible *agg.* inaccessibile.

inaccuracy *s.* inesattezza.

inaccurate *agg.* inesatto.

inaction *s.* inattività.

inactive *agg.* inattivo.

inactivity *s.* inattività.

inadaptability *s.* inadattabilità.

inadequacy *s.* inadeguatezza.

inadequate *agg.* inadeguato.

inadmissibility *s.* inammissibilità.

inadmissible *agg.* inammissibile.

inadvertence *s.* inavvertenza.

inadvertent *agg.* 1. disattento 2. involontario.

inalienability *s.* inalienabilità.

inalienable *agg.* inalienabile.

inalterability *s.* inalterabilità.

inalterable *agg.* inalterabile.

inane *agg.* e *s.* vuoto.

inanimate *agg.* 1. inanimato 2. fiacco.

inanity *s.* inanità.

inappeasable *agg.* implacabile.
inappellable *agg.* inappellabile.
inappetence *s.* inappetenza.
inapplicable *agg.* inapplicabile.
inappropriate *agg.* inadeguato.
inapt *agg.* 1. inadatto 2. inetto.
inarticulate *agg.* inarticolato.
inattention *s.* 1. disattenzione 2. negligenza.
inattentive *agg.* 1. disattento 2. negligente.
inaudible *agg.* impercettibile.
inaugural *agg.* inaugurale.
to inaugurate *vt.* inaugurare.
inauguration *s.* inaugurazione.
inboard *agg.* interno. ♦ **inboard** *avv.* internamente.
inborn, inbred *agg.* innato.
incalculable *agg.* 1. incalcolabile 2. incerto.
incandescence *s.* incandescenza.
incandescent *agg.* incandescente.
incantation *s.* incantesimo.
incapability *s.* incapacità.
incapable *agg.* incapace.
incapacity *s.* incapacità.
to incarnate *vt.* 1. incarnar 2. realizzare.
incarnation *s.* incarnazione.
incatenation *s.* incatenamento.
incautious *agg.* incauto.
incendiary *agg.* e *s.* 1. incendiario 2. sovversivo.
incensation *s.* incensamento.
incense *s.* incenso.
to incense[1] *vt.* incensare.
to incense[2] *vt.* provocare.
incensurable *agg.* incensurabile.
incentive *agg.* stimolante. ♦ **incentive** *s.* incentivo.
incertitude *s.* incertezza.
incessant *agg.* incessante.
incest *s.* incesto.
incestuous *agg.* incestuoso.
inch *s.* pollice (*misura*).
incidence *s.* incidenza.
incident *agg.* probabile. ♦ **incident** *s.* avvenimento.
incidental *agg.* fortuito. ♦ **incidental** *s.* caso.
incipient *agg.* incipiente.
to incise *vt.* incidere.
incisive *agg.* incisivo.
incisiveness *s.* incisività.
incisor *s.* incisivo.
incitation *s.* incitamento.
to incite *vt.* incitare.
incivility *s.* villania.
inclemency *s.* inclemenza.

inclement *agg.* inclemente.
inclinable *agg.* incline.
inclination *s.* inclinazione.
to incline *vt.* inclinare. ♦ **to incline** *vi.* propendere.
inclined *agg.* 1. inclinato 2. incline.
to include *vt.* includere.
included *agg.* incluso, compreso.
inclusion *s.* inclusione.
inclusive *agg.* compreso.
incoherence *s.* incoerenza.
incoherent *agg.* incoerente.
incombustible *agg.* incombustibile.
income *s.* rendita, reddito || — -tax, imposta sul reddito.
incoming *s.* entrata. ♦ **incoming** *agg.* entrante.
incommensurability *s.* incommensurabilità.
incommensurable *agg.* incommensurabile.
incommensurate *agg.* 1. inadeguato 2. smisurato.
incommunicability *s.* incomunicabilità.
incommunicable *agg.* incomunicabile.
incommutable *agg.* incommutabile.
incomparable *agg.* incomparabile.
incompatibility *s.* incompatibilità.
incompatible *agg.* incompatibile.
incompetence *s.* incompetenza.
incompetent *agg.* e *s.* incompetente.
incomplete *agg.* incompleto.
incompleteness, incompletion *s.* incompletezza.
incomprehensibility *s.* incomprensibilità.
incomprehensible *agg.* incomprensibile.
incomprehension *s.* incomprensione.
inconceivability *s.* inconcepibilità.
inconceivable *agg.* inconcepibile.
inconclusive *agg.* inconcludente.
inconclusiveness *s.* inconcludenza.
incongruity *s.* incongruenza.
incongruous *agg.* incongruo.
inconsequence *s.* incongruenza.
inconsequent *agg.* incongruente.
inconsequential *agg.* 1. incoerente 2. irrilevante.
inconsiderate *agg.* sconsiderato.
inconsistence *s.* incoerenza.
inconsistent *agg.* incoerente.
inconsolable *agg.* inconsolabile.
inconstancy *s.* incostanza.
inconstant *agg.* incostante.

incontestability s. incontestabilità.

incontestable agg. incontestabile.

incontinence s. incontinenza.

incontinent agg. incontinente.

incontinently avv. smoderatamente.

incontrollable agg. incontrollabile.

incontrovertible agg. incontrovertibile.

inconvenience s. 1. disturbo 2. scomodità.

to **inconvenience** vt. scomodare.

inconvenient agg. incomodo.

inconvertible agg. inconvertibile.

to **incorporate** vt. 1. incorporare 2. (comm.) costituire. ◆ to **incorporate** vi. incorporarsi.

incorporated agg. 1. (comm.) anonimo 2. incorporato.

incorporation s. 1. incorporazione 2. (comm.) costituzione.

incorporeal agg. incorporeo.

incorrect agg. scorretto.

incorrectness s. scorrettezza.

incorrigible agg. incorreggibile.

incorrupt agg. incorrotto.

incorruptibility s. incorruttibilità.

incorruptible agg. incorruttibile.

increase s. aumento.

to **increase** vt. e vi. aumentare.

increasing agg. crescente.

increasingly avv. sempre più.

incredibility s. incredibilità.

incredible agg. incredibile.

incredulity s. incredulità.

incredulous agg. incredulo.

increment s. incremento.

to **incriminate** vt. incriminare.

incrimination s. incriminazione.

incriminatory agg. incriminante.

incrustation s. incrostazione.

incubation s. incubazione.

incubator s. incubatrice.

to **inculcate** vt. inculcare.

inculcation s. inculcazione.

inculpable agg. innocente.

inculpation s. accusa.

incumbent agg. incombente.

to **incur** vt. incorrere in.

incurability s. incurabilità.

incurable agg. incurabile.

incursion s. incursione.

indebted agg. 1. indebitato 2. obbligato.

indecency s. indecenza.

indecent agg. indecente.

indecipherable agg. indecifrabile.

indecision s. indecisione.

indecisive agg 1. indeciso 2. non decisivo.

indeclinable agg. indeclinabile.

indecomposable agg. indecomponibile.

indecorous agg. indecoroso.

indeed avv. in verità, davvero.

indefatigable agg. infaticabile.

indefeasible agg. irrevocabile.

indefinable agg. indefinibile.

indefinite agg. indefinito.

indefiniteness s. indeterminatezza.

indelible agg. indelebile.

indelicacy s. 1. rozzezza 2. sconvenienza.

indelicate agg. 1. sgarbato 2. sconveniente.

to **indemnify** vt. 1. indennizzare 2. assicurare.

indemnity s. 1. indennità 2. assicurazione.

indemonstrable agg. indimostrabile.

indent s. 1. dentellatura 2. incavo 3. (comm.) ordinazione 4. (tip.) capoverso.

to **indent** vt. 1. dentellare, frastagliare 2. intagliare 3. (comm.) ordinare (merci).

indentation, indention s. 1. dentellatura 2. incisione.

indenture s. 1. dentellatura 2. contratto.

independence s. indipendenza.

independent agg. e s. indipendente.

indescribable agg. indescrivibile.

indestructibility s. indistruttibilità.

indestructible agg. indistruttibile.

indeterminable agg. indeterminabile.

indeterminate agg. indeterminato.

indetermination s. indeterminazione.

index s. indice.

Indian agg. e s. indiano.

to **indicate** vt. indicare.

indicating agg. indicatore.

indication s. 1. indicazione 2. segno.

indicative agg. e s. indicativo.

indicator s. indicatore.

to **indict** vt. accusare.

indictment s. (giur.) accusa.

indifference s. 1. indifferenza 2. imparzialità 3. mancanza di valore.

indifferent agg. 1. indifferente 2.

imparziale 3. mediocre.

indifferentism s. indifferentismo.

indifferentist s. indifferentista.

indigence s. indigenza.

indigenous agg. indigeno.

indigent agg. indigente.

indigestible agg. indigesto.

indigestion s. dispepsia.

indignant agg. indignato.

indignation s. indignazione.

indignity s. 1. indegnità 2. offesa.

indigo s. indaco.

indirect agg. 1. indiretto 2. tortuoso.

indiscernible agg. indistinguibile.

indiscipline s. indisciplina.

indiscreet agg. 1. sconsiderato 2. indiscreto.

indiscrete agg. compatto.

indiscretion s. 1. sconsideratezza 2. indiscrezione.

indiscriminate agg. indiscriminato.

indispensable agg. indispensabile.

indisposed agg. indisposto.

indisposition s. 1. avversione 2. indisposizione.

indisputability s. indiscutibilità.

indisputable agg. indiscutibile.

indisputed agg. indiscusso.

indissolubility s. indissolubilità.

indissoluble agg. indissolubile.

indistinct agg. indistinto.

indistinguishable agg. indistinguibile.

individual agg. individuale. ♦ **individual** s. individuo.

individualism s. individualismo.

individualist agg. e s. individualista.

individualistic agg. individualistico.

individuality s. individualità.

individualization s. individualizzazione.

to **individualize** vt. individualizzare.

indivisibility s. indivisibilità.

indivisible agg. indivisibile.

indocility s. indocilità.

Indo-European agg. e s. indo-europeo.

indolence s. indolenza.

indolent agg. indolente.

indomitable agg. indomabile.

indoor agg. in casa.

indoors avv. in casa.

indraft, indraught s. risucchio, vortice.

indubitable agg. indubitabile.

to **induce** vt. indurre.

inducement s. 1. allettamento 2. movente.

induction s. 1. induzione 2. insediamento.

inductive agg. induttivo.

inductor s. induttore.

to **indulge** vt. essere indulgente verso. ♦ to **indulge** vi. indulgere.

indulgence s. 1. indulgenza 2. proroga.

indulgent agg. indulgente.

indult s. indulto.

industrial agg. industriale. ♦ **industrial** s. lavoratore dell'industria.

industrialism s. industrialismo.

industrialist s. industriale.

industrialization s. industrializzazione.

to **industrialize** vt. industrializzare.

industrious agg. industrioso.

industry s. 1. industria 2. operosità, diligenza.

inebriate agg. e s. ubriaco.

to **inebriate** vt. inebriare.

inedited agg. inedito.

ineffable agg. ineffabile.

ineffective agg. 1. inefficace 2. inefficiente.

ineffectiveness s. 1. inefficacia 2. inefficienza.

ineffectual agg. inutile.

inefficacy s. inefficacia.

inefficient agg. V. ineffective.

inelegance s. ineleganza.

inelegant agg. inelegante.

ineligibility s. ineleggibilità.

ineligible agg. ineleggibile.

ineluctable agg. ineluttabile.

inept agg. inadatto.

ineptitude, ineptness s. inettitudine.

inequality s. diseguaglianza.

inequity s. ingiustizia.

ineradicable agg. inestirpabile.

inerrability s. infallibilità.

inerrable agg. infallibile.

inert agg. inerte.

inertness s. inerzia.

inescapable agg. inevitabile.

inestimable agg. inestimabile.

inevitability s. inevitabilità.

inevitable agg. inevitabile.

inevitableness s. inevitabilità.

inexact agg. inesatto.

inexactitude s. inesattezza.

inexcusability s. inescusabilità.

inexcusable agg. imperdonabile.

inexecutable *agg.* ineseguibile.
inexhaustibility *s.* inesauribilità.
inexhaustible *agg.* inesauribile.
inexistence *s.* inesistenza.
inexistent *agg.* inesistente.
inexorability *s.* inesorabilità.
inexorable *agg.* inesorabile.
inexpedient *agg.* inopportuno.
inexpensive *agg.* poco costoso.
inexperience *s.* inesperienza.
inexperienced, inexpert *agg.* inesperto.
inexpiable *agg.* inespiabile.
inexplicable *agg.* inesplicabile.
inexplorable *agg.* inesplorabile.
inexpressible *agg.* inesprimibile.
inexpressive *agg.* inespressivo.
inexpressiveness *s.* inespressività.
inexpugnability *s.* inespugnabilità.
inexpugnable *agg.* inespugnabile.
inextinguishable *agg.* inestinguibile.
inextricable *agg.* inestricabile.
infallibility *s.* infallibilità.
infallible *agg.* infallibile.
infamous *agg.* infame.
infamy *s.* infamia.
infancy *s.* infanzia.
infant *agg.* infantile. ♦ **infant** *s.* 1. neonato 2. (*giur.*) minore.
infanticide *s.* 1. infanticida 2. infanticidio.
infantile *agg.* infantile.
infantilism *s.* infantilismo.
infantry *s.* fanteria || — -man, fante.
infarct *s.* infarto.
to infatuate *vt.* infatuare.
infatuation *s.* infatuazione.
to infect *vt.* contagiare.
infection *s.* contagio.
infectious *agg.* contagioso.
infective *agg.* infettivo.
infecund *agg.* infecondo.
infelicitous *agg.* infelice.
infelicity *s.* infelicità.
to infer *vt.* dedurre.
inferable *agg.* deducibile.
inference *s.* deduzione.
inferior *agg.* e *s.* inferiore.
inferiority *s.* inferiorità.
infernal *agg.* infernale.
to infest *vt.* infestare.
infestation *s.* infestamento.
infidel *agg.* e *s.* infedele.
infidelity *s.* 1. miscredenza 2. infedeltà.
to infiltrate *vt.* infiltrare. ♦ **to infiltrate** *vi.* infiltrarsi.
infiltration *s.* infiltrazione.

infinite *agg.* e *s.* infinito.
infinitesimal *agg.* infinitesimale.
infinitive *agg.* e *s.* infinito.
infinitude *s.* infinità.
infinity *s.* infinità, infinito.
infirm *agg.* 1. infermo 2. irresoluto.
infirmary *s.* infermeria.
infirmity *s.* 1. infermità 2. irresolutezza.
to inflame *vt.* infiammare. ♦ **to inflame** *vi.* infiammarsi.
inflammability *s.* infiammabilità.
inflammable *agg.* infiammabile.
inflammation *s.* 1. l'infiammare, l'infiammarsi 2. infiammazione.
inflammatory *agg.* infiammatorio.
to inflate *vt.* gonfiare.
inflation *s.* 1. gonfiore, gonfiatura 2. (*comm.*) inflazione.
inflationary *agg.* inflazionistico.
to inflect *vt.* 1. flettere 2. modulare.
inflection *s.* 1. flessione 2. inflessione.
inflexibility *s.* inflessibilità.
inflexible *agg.* inflessibile.
to inflict *vt.* infliggere.
infliction *s.* 1. inflizione 2. pena.
inflorescence *s.* inflorescenza.
influence *s.* 1. influenza 2. (*elettr.*) induzione.
to influence *vt.* influenzare.
influential *agg.* influente.
influenza *s.* (*med.*) influenza.
influx *s.* 1. affluenza 2. sbocco (*di fiume*).
inform *agg.* informe.
to inform *vt.* 1. informare 2. dar forma a.
informal *agg.* non ufficiale.
informality *s.* assenza di formalità.
information *s.* (*solo sing.*) 1. informazione 2. sapere 3. accusa.
informative, informatory *agg.* informativo.
informed *agg.* istruito.
informer *s.* 1. informatore 2. accusatore.
infraction *s.* 1. infrazione 2. violazione.
infrangibility *s.* infrangibilità.
infrangible *agg.* 1. infrangibile 2. inviolabile.
infrared *agg.* infrarosso.
infrequent *agg.* raro.
to infringe *vt.* violare.
infringement *s.* violazione.
infringer *s.* trasgressore.
infructuous *agg.* infruttuoso.

to **infuse** *vt.* **1.** versare **2.** infondere **3.** mettere in infusione.

infusible *agg.* infusibile.

infusion *s.* **1.** infusione **2.** infuso.

ingenious *agg.* ingegnoso.

ingenuity *s.* ingegnosità.

ingenuous *agg.* **1.** ingenuo **2.** franco.

ingenuousness *s.* ingenuità.

to **ingest** *vt.* ingerire.

ingestion *s.* ingestione.

inglorious *agg.* inglorioso.

ingot *s.* lingotto.

ingratitude *s.* ingratitudine.

ingredient *s.* ingrediente.

inguen *s.* inguine.

inguinal *agg.* inguinale.

to **inhabit** *vt.* abitare.

inhabitable *agg.* abitabile.

inhabitancy *s.* domicilio.

inhabitant *s.* abitante.

inhalant *s.* **1.** inalatore **2.** sostanza da inalare.

inhalation *s.* inalazione.

to **inhale** *vt. e vi.* **1.** aspirare **2.** inalare.

inhaler *s.* inalatore.

inherent *agg.* inerente.

to **inherit** *vt. e vi.* ereditare.

inheritance *s.* eredità.

to **inhibit** *vt.* **1.** inibire **2.** interdire.

inhibition *s.* **1.** inibizione **2.** interdizione.

inhibitory *agg.* inibitorio.

inhospitable *agg.* inospitale.

inhospitality *s.* inospitalità.

inhuman *agg.* inumano.

inhumanity *s.* inumanità.

inhumation *s.* inumazione.

inimical *agg.* nemico.

inimitable *agg.* inimitabile.

iniquitous *agg.* iniquo.

iniquity *s.* iniquità.

initial *agg. e s.* iniziale.

to **initial** *vt.* siglare.

initiate *agg. e s.* iniziato.

to **initiate** *vt.* iniziare.

initiation *s.* **1.** inizio **2.** iniziazione.

initiative *agg.* introduttivo. ♦ **initiative** *s.* iniziativa.

initiator *s.* iniziatore.

to **inject** *vt.* iniettare.

injection *s.* iniezione.

injector *s.* iniettore.

injunction *s.* ingiunzione.

to **injure** *vt.* ledere, ferire.

injurer *s.* **1.** danneggiatore **2.** feritore.

injury *s.* **1.** torto, danno **2.** ferita.

injustice *s.* ingiustizia.

ink *s.* inchiostro || — *-pot,* calamaio.

inkholder *s.* calamaio.

inkling *s.* indizio.

inky *agg.* **1.** di, simile a inchiostro **2.** macchiato d'inchiostro.

inlaid V. *to inlay.*

inland *agg. e s.* interno. ♦ **inland** *avv.* all'interno.

inlay *s.* intarsio.

to **inlay (inlaid, inlaid)** *vt.* intarsiare.

inlet *s.* **1.** piccola insenatura **2.** apertura.

inmate *s.* **1.** inquilino **2.** ricoverato.

inmost *agg.* più interno.

inn *s.* locanda || — *-keeper,* locandiere; — *of court,* scuola di legge.

innate *agg.* innato.

innavigable *agg.* non navigabile.

inner *agg.* interno, intimo.

innermost *agg.* V. *inmost.*

innervation *s.* innervazione.

innocence *s.* innocenza.

innocent *agg. e s.* innocente.

innoculty *s.* innocuità.

innocuous *agg.* innocuo.

innominate *agg.* innominato.

to **innovate** *vt. e vi.* innovare.

innovation *s.* innovazione.

innovator *s.* innovatore.

innumerability *s.* innumerabilità.

innumerable *agg.* innumerevole.

inobservance *s.* **1.** inosservanza **2.** disattenzione.

inobservant *agg.* **1.** inosservante **2.** disattento.

to **inoculate** *vt.* **1.** inoculare **2.** inculcare.

inoculation *s.* inoculazione.

inodorous *agg.* inodoro.

inoffensive *agg.* inoffensivo.

inopportune *agg.* inopportuno.

inopportuneness *s.* inopportunità.

inordinate *agg.* smoderato.

inorganic *agg.* inorganico.

inoxidizable *agg.* inossidabile.

inpouring *agg.* affluente. ♦ **inpouring** *s.* afflusso.

input *s.* (*mecc.; elettr.*) alimentazione, entrata.

inquest *s.* **1.** inchiesta **2.** giuria.

inquietude *s.* inquietudine.

to **inquire** *vt. e vi.* chiedere || — *after,* chiedere informazioni su; *to — into,* indagare su.

inquirer *s.* investigatore.

inquiring *agg.* **1.** indagatore **2.** curioso.

inquiry s. 1. ricerca 2. domanda 3. inchiesta.

inquisition s. 1. ricerca 2. inchiesta.

inquisitive agg. V. *inquiring*.

inquisitiveness s. curiosità

inrush s. irruzione.

insalubrity s. insalubrità.

insane agg. insano.

insanitary agg. malsano.

insanity s. insania.

insatiability s. insaziabilità.

insatiable, insatiate agg. insaziabile.

to **inscribe** vt. 1. iscrivere 2. scolpire 3. dedicare.

inscription s. 1. iscrizione 2. dedica.

inscrutability s. inscrutabilità.

inscrutable agg. inscrutabile.

inscrutableness s. inscrutabilità.

insect s. insetto.

insecticide s. insetticida.

insectivorous agg. insettivoro.

insecure agg. insicuro.

insecurity s. insicurezza.

insensate agg. 1. insensibile 2. insensato.

insensibility s. insensibilità.

insensible agg. 1. insensibile 2. inconscio.

insensitive agg. insensibile.

inseparable agg. inseparabile.

insert s. inserzione.

to **insert** vt. inserire.

insertion s. inserzione.

to **inset (inset, inset)** vt inserire.

inside agg. e s. interno. ♦ **inside** avv. e prep. dentro.

insidious agg. insidioso.

insight s. 1. intuito 2. penetrazione.

insignificant agg. insignificante.

insincere agg. insincero.

insincerity s. falsità.

to **insinuate** vt. insinuare.

insinuation s. insinuazione.

insinuative agg. insinuante.

insipid agg. insipido.

insipidity, insipidness s. insipidezza.

insipience s. insipienza.

insipient agg. insipiente.

to **insist** vi. insistere.

insistence s. insistenza.

insistent agg. insistente.

insolation s. insolazione.

insolence s. insolenza.

insolent agg. e s. insolente.

insolubility s. insolubilità.

insoluble agg. insolubile.

insolvable agg. insolubile.

insolvency s. insolvenza.

insolvent agg. insolvente. ♦ **insolvent** s. debitore insolvente.

insomnia s. insonnia.

to **inspect** vt. ispezionare.

inspection s. ispezione.

inspector s. ispettore.

inspectoral agg. di ispettore, di ispezione.

inspectorate s. ispettorato.

inspiration s. 1. inspirazione 2. ispirazione.

to **inspire** vt. 1. inspirare 2. ispirare.

inspirer s. ispiratore.

inspiring agg. ispiratore.

instability s. instabilità.

to **install** vt. installare.

installation s. installazione.

instalment s. 1. rata 2. puntata.

instance s. 1. esempio 2. caso 3. istanza.

instancy s. 1. urgenza 2. insistenza.

instant agg. 1. urgente 2. corrente. ♦ **instant** s. istante.

instantaneous agg. istantaneo.

instantly avv. all'istante. ♦ **instantly** cong. non appena che.

instead avv. invece.

instep s. 1. collo del piede 2. collo di scarpa.

to **instigate** vt. istigare.

instigation s. istigazione.

instigator s. istigatore.

to **instil(l)** vt. instillare.

instinct agg. imbevuto. ♦ **instinct** s. istinto.

instinctive agg. istintivo.

institute s. istituto. ♦ **institutes** s. pl. istituzioni.

to **institute** vt. istituire.

institution s. istituto.

institutional agg. istituzionale.

institutor s. istitutore.

to **instruct** vt. 1. istruire 2. informare 3. ordinare.

instruction s. istruzione.

instructive agg. istruttivo.

instructor s. istruttore.

instrument s. 1. strumento 2. atto giuridico.

to **instrument** vt. 1. strumentare 2. redigere.

instrumental agg. 1. strumentale 2. utile.

instrumentation s. 1. orchestrazio-

ne 2. uso di strumenti.
insubordinate *agg.* insubordinato.
insubordination *s.* insubordinazione.
insubstantial *agg.* incorporeo.
insufferable *agg.* insopportabile.
insufficiency *s.* insufficienza.
insufficient *agg.* insufficiente.
insular *agg.* **1.** insulare **2.** (*fig.*) di mentalità ristretta.
to insulate *vt.* isolare.
insulation *s.* isolamento.
insulator *s.* isolatore.
insulin *s.* insulina.
insult *s.* insulto.
to insult *vt.* insultare.
insuperable *agg.* insuperabile.
insuppressible *agg.* insopprimibile.
insurance *s.* assicurazione.
insurant *s.* assicurato.
to insure *vt.* assicurare.
insurer *s.* assicuratore.
insurgency *s.* insurrezione.
insurgent *agg.* e *s.* insorto.
insurmountable *agg.* insormontabile.
insurrection *s.* insurrezione.
insurrectional, insurrectionary *agg.* insurrezionale.
insurrectionist *s.* insorto.
intact *agg.* intatto.
intake *s.* **1.** presa **2.** energia assorbita.
intangible *agg.* intangibile.
integrable *agg.* integrabile.
integral *agg.* integrale.
integrant *agg.* integrante.
to integrate *vt.* integrare.
integration *s.* integrazione.
integrity *s.* integrità.
intellect *s.* intelletto.
intellective *agg.* intellettivo.
intellectual *agg.* e *s.* intellettuale.
intellectualism *s.* intellettualismo.
intelligence *s.* **1.** intelligenza **2.** informazioni (*pl.*).
intelligent *agg.* intelligente.
intelligibility *s.* intelligibilità.
intelligible *agg.* intelligibile.
intemperance *s.* intemperanza.
intemperate *agg.* **1.** smoderato **2.** rigido (*di clima*).
to intend *vt.* **1.** intendere **2.** destinare.
intendant *s.* intendente.
intended *agg.* progettato.
intense *agg.* intenso.
intensification *s.* intensificazione.
to intensify *vt.* intensificare. ♦ **to**

intensify *vi.* intensificarsi.
intensity *s.* **1.** intensità **2.** vigore.
intensive *agg.* intensivo, intenso.
intent *agg.* intento, dedito. ♦ **intent** *s.* intenzione, scopo.
intention *s.* intenzione.
intentional *agg.* intenzionale.
intently *avv.* intensamente.
to inter *vt.* seppellire.
to intercalate *vt.* intercalare.
to intercede *vi.* intercedere.
to intercept *vt.* intercettare.
interception *s.* intercettamento.
interceptor *s.* intercettatore.
intercession *s.* intercessione.
intercessor *s.* intercessore.
interchange *s.* scambio.
to interchange *vt.* scambiare. ♦ **to interchange** *vi.* scambiarsi.
interchangeable *agg.* scambievole.
intercom *s.* citofono.
intercommunication *s.* intercomunicazione.
intercontinental *agg.* intercontinentale.
intercostal *agg.* intercostale.
intercourse *s.* rapporto, relazione || **trade** —, scambi commerciali.
interdependence *s.* interdipendenza.
interdependent *agg.* interdipendente.
interdict *s.* **1.** interdizione **2.** interdetto **3.** proibizione.
to interdict *vt.* **1.** interdire **2.** proibire.
interdiction *s.* V. *interdict*.
interest *s.* interesse.
to interest *vt.* interessare.
interested *agg.* interessato || *those* —, gli interessati.
interesting *agg.* interessante.
to interfere *vi.* **1.** interferire **2.** scontrarsi.
interference *s.* **1.** interferenza **2.** collisione.
interior *agg.* e *s.* interno.
to interject *vt.* intromettere.
interjection *s.* intromissione.
to interlace *vt.* intrecciare. ♦ **to interlace** *vi.* intrecciarsi.
interlacing *s.* intreccio.
to interline *vt.* interlineare.
interlinear *agg.* interlineare.
interlineation *s.* interlineazione.
to interlink *vt.* concatenare.
to interlock *vt.* sincronizzare.
interlocution *s.* interlocuzione.
interlocutor *s.* interlocutore.

to **interlope** vi. immischiarsi.
interlude s. 1. intervallo 2. intermezzo.
intermarriage s. matrimonio tra membri di famiglie, razze diverse.
to **intermarry** vt. e vi. imparentarsi per mezzo di matrimonio.
to **intermeddle** vi. intromettersi.
intermeddler s. intrigante.
intermediary agg. intermedio, frapposto. ♦ **intermediary** s. 1. intermediario, mediatore 2. cosa intermedia.
intermediate agg. V. *intermediary*.
intermediation s. mediazione.
interment s. sepoltura.
interminable agg. interminabile.
to **intermingle** vt. mescolare. ♦ to **intermingle** vi. mescolarsi.
intermission s. sosta, pausa.
to **intermit** vt. interrompere. ♦ to **intermit** vi. interrompersi, essere intermittente.
intermittence s. intermittenza.
intermittent agg. intermittente.
to **intern** vt. internare.
internal agg. interno.
international agg. internazionale.
internationalism s. internazionalismo.
internationalist s. internazionalista.
to **internationalize** vt. internazionalizzare.
internment s. internamento.
to **interpellate** vt. interpellare.
interpellation s. interpellanza.
interphone s. citofono.
interplanetary agg. interplanetario.
interplay s. azione reciproca.
to **interpolate** vt. interpolare.
interpolation s. interpolazione.
to **interpose** vt. interporre. ♦ to **interpose** vi. interporsi.
interposition s. interposizione.
to **interpret** vt. interpretare. ♦ to **interpret** vi. fare l'interprete.
interpretation s. interpretazione.
interpretative agg. interpretativo.
interpreter s. interprete.
interpunction s. interpunzione.
interregnum s. 1. interregno 2. intervallo.
interrelation s. relazione.
interrelationship s. interdipendenza.
to **interrogate** vt. interrogare.
interrogation s. interrogazione || — -mark, punto interrogativo.

interrogative agg. e s. interrogativo.
interrogatory agg. interrogativo. ♦ **interrogatory** s. 1. interrogazione 2. interrogatorio.
to **interrupt** vt. e vi. interrompere.
interrupter s. interruttore.
interruption s. interruzione.
to **intersect** vt. intersecare. ♦ to **intersect** vi. intersecarsi.
intersection s. intersezione.
interspace s. intervallo, spazio.
to **intersperse** vt. cospargere.
interstice s. interstizio.
to **intertwine** vt. attorcigliare. ♦ to **intertwine** vi. attorcigliarsi.
interurban agg. interurbano.
interval s. intervallo.
to **intervene** vi. intervenire.
intervener s. chi interviene.
intervention s. intervento.
interventionist s. interventista.
interview s. intervista.
to **interview** vt. intervistare.
interviewer s. intervistatore.
to **interweave (interwove, interwoven)** vt. intessere, intrecciare.
intestinal agg. intestinale.
intestine agg. e s. intestino.
intimacy s. intimità.
intimate agg. intimo. ♦ **intimate** s. amico intimo.
to **intimate** vt. 1. intimare 2. accennare.
intimation s. 1. intimazione 2. preannunzio.
intimidation s. intimidazione.
intimidatory agg. intimidatorio.
into prep. in, dentro || to go — the, park, entrare nel parco; far — the night, fino a tarda notte.
intolerable agg. intollerabile.
intolerance s. intolleranza.
intolerant agg. e s. intollerante.
to **intonate** vt intonare.
intonation s. intonazione.
to **intone** vt. intonare.
to **intoxicate** vt. inebriare.
intoxication s. ebbrezza.
intractable agg. intrattabile.
intramuscular agg. intramuscolare.
intransgressible agg. che non può essere trasgredito.
intransigence s. intransigenza.
intransigent agg. e s. intransigente.
intransitive agg. intransitivo.
intravenous agg. endovenoso.
intrepid agg. intrepido.

intrepidity s. intrepidezza.
intricacy s. complicazione.
intricate agg. intricato.
intrigant s. intrigante.
intrigue s. intrigo.
to **intrigue** vt. 1. ingannare 2. rendere perplesso 3. affascinare. ♦ to **intrigue** vi. avere una tresca.
intriguer s. intrigante.
intrinsic agg. intrinseco.
to **introduce** vt. 1. introdurre 2. presentare.
introduction s. 1. introduzione 2. presentazione.
introductive, introductory agg. introduttivo.
intromission s. interferenza.
to **intromit** vt. introdurre.
to **introspect** vi. autoesaminarsi.
introspection s. introspezione.
introspective agg. introspettivo.
introversion s. introversione.
introvert agg. e s. introverso.
to **intrude** vt. imporre. ♦ to **intrude** vi. intromettersi.
intruder s. 1. intruso 2. importuno.
intrusion s. intrusione.
intrusive agg. 1. intruso 2. importuno.
intrusiveness s. indiscrezione.
intuition s. intuizione.
intuitional agg. intuitivo.
intuitionism s. intuizionismo.
intuitive agg. intuitivo.
to **inundate** vt. inondare.
inundation s. inondazione.
inurbane agg. inurbano.
inurbanity s. inurbanità.
to **inure** vt. abituare. ♦ to **inure** vi. venire in uso.
inurement s. abitudine.
inutility s. inutilità.
to **invade** vt. 1. invadere 2. violare.
invader s. invasore.
invalid agg. 1. invalido 2. nullo. ♦ **invalid** s. invalido.
to **invalid** vt. 1. rendere invalido 2. riformare.
to **invalidate** vt. invalidare.
invalidation s. invalidazione.
invalidity s. invalidità.
invaluable agg. inestimabile.
invariability s. invariabilità.
invariable agg. invariabile.
invasion s. invasione.
invective s. invettiva.
to **inveigh** vi. inveire.

to **invent** vt. inventare.
invention s. 1. invenzione 2. inventiva.
inventive agg. inventivo.
inventor s. inventore.
inventory s. inventario.
to **inventory** vt. fare l'inventario di.
inverse agg. e s. inverso.
inversion s. inversione.
invert agg. e s. invertito.
to **invert** vt. invertire.
invertebrate agg. e s. invertebrato.
invertible agg. invertibile.
to **invest** vt. 1. investire 2. rivestire.
to **investigate** vt. e vi. investigare.
investigation s. investigazione.
investigative agg. investigativo.
investigator s. investigatore.
investiture s. investitura.
investment s. investimento.
investor s. investitore.
inveterate agg. inveterato.
invidious agg. odioso.
invidiousness s. odiosità.
to **invigorate** vt. rinvigorire.
invigorative agg. rinforzante.
invincibility s. invincibilità.
invincible agg. invincibile.
inviolability s. inviolabilità.
inviolable agg. inviolabile.
inviolate agg. inviolato.
invisibility s. invisibilità.
invisible agg. invisibile.
invitation s. invito.
to **invite** vt. 1. invitare 2. provocare.
invocation s. invocazione.
invoice s. fattura.
to **invoice** vt. fatturare.
to **invoke** vt. 1. invocare 2. evocare.
involuntary agg. involontario.
involute agg. 1. involuto 2. a spirale.
involution s. 1. involuzione 2. intrico 3. (mat.) elevazione a potenza.
to **involve** vt. 1. avvolgere 2. implicare 3. complicare.
invulnerability s. invulnerabilità.
invulnerable agg. invulnerabile.
inward agg. interiore.
inwardness s. interiorità.
inwards avv. internamente.
iodine s. iodio.
to **iodize** vt. iodare.
ion s. ione.
Ionic agg. ionico.

ionization s. ionizzazione.
ionosphere s. ionosfera.
Iranian agg. e s. iraniano.
Iraqi agg. e s. iracheno.
irascibility s. irascibilità.
irascible agg. irascibile.
irate agg. adirato.
ireful agg. irato.
iridescence s. iridescenza.
iridescent agg. iridescente.
iris s. iride.
Irish agg. irlandese.
Irishman s. irlandese.
irksome agg. noioso.
iron agg. di ferro. ♦ **iron** s. ferro
|| -foundry, ferriera. ♦ **irons**
s. pl. catene.
to **iron** vt. 1. rivestire di ferro 2.
stirare.
ironclad agg. corazzato. ♦ **iron-**
clad s. corazzata.
ironic(al) agg. ironico.
ironing s. stiratura.
ironmonger s. negoziante in ferramenta.
ironsmith s. fabbro ferraio.
ironware s. ferramenta.
ironwork s. lavoro in ferro. ♦
ironworks s. pl. ferriera (sing.).
irony s. ironia.
to **irradiate** vt. irradiare. ♦ to **ir-**
radiate vi. risplendere.
irradiation s. 1. illuminazione 2.
irradiazione.
irrational agg. irrazionale.
irrationalism, irrationality s. irrazionalità.
irrealizable agg. irrealizzabile.
irreconcilability s. inconciliabilità.
irreconcilable agg. irreconciliabile.
irrecoverable agg. 1. irrecuperabile 2. irrimediabile.
irredentism s. irredentismo.
irredentist s. irredentista.
irreducible agg. irriducibile.
irreflection s. irriflessione.
irreflective agg. irriflessivo.
irrefutable agg. irrefutabile.
irregular agg. e s. irregolare.
irregularity s. irregolarità.
irrelevant agg. 1. non pertinente
2. insignificante.
irreligious agg. irreligioso.
irremediable agg. irrimediabile.
irremissible agg. irremissibile.
irremovability s. irremovibilità.
irremovable agg. irremovibile.
irreparable agg. irreparabile.
irreplaceable agg. insostituibile.

irreprehensible agg. irreprensibile.
irrepressible agg. irrefrenabile.
irrepressibleness s. irrefrenabilità.
irreproachable agg. irreprensibile.
irreprovable agg. irreprensibile.
irresistible agg. irresistibile.
irresolute agg. irresoluto.
irresoluteness, irresolution s.
irresolutezza.
irresolvable agg. insolubile.
irrespective agg. noncurante.
irresponsibility s. irresponsabilità.
irresponsible agg. 1. irresponsabile 2. insolvibile.
irresponsive agg. che non risponde.
irretrievable agg. irrecuperabile.
irreverence s. irriverenza.
irreverent agg. irriverente.
irreversibility s. irreversibilità.
irreversible agg. irreversibile.
irrevocable agg. irrevocabile.
irrigable agg. irrigabile.
to **irrigate** vt. irrigare.
irrigation s. irrigazione.
irritability s. irritabilità.
irritable agg. irritabile.
irritant agg. e s. irritante.
to **irritate** vt. irritare.
irritation s. irritazione.
irritative agg. irritante.
irruption s. irruzione.
Islamic agg. islamico.
Islamism s. islamismo.
island s. 1. isola 2. salvagente stradale.
islander s. isolano.
isle s. piccola isola || the British
Isles, le isole britanniche.
islet s. isolotto.
isochronism s. isocronismo.
to **isolate** vt. isolare.
isolation s. isolamento.
isolationism s. isolazionismo.
isolationist s. isolazionista.
isolator s. isolatore.
isomorphism s. isomorfismo.
isomorphous agg. isomorfo.
isosceles agg. isoscele.
isotherm s. isoterma.
isothermal agg. isotermico.
isotope s. isotopo.
isotrope s. isotropo.
Israeli agg. e s. israeliano.
Israelite s. israelita.
issue s. 1. uscita, sbocco, foce 2.
conclusione 3. prole, stirpe 4. problema 5. emissione, pubblicazione.
to **issue** vt. 1. emettere, pubblicare
2. rilasciare. ♦ to **issue** vi. 1.

uscire 2. risultare 3. discendere.

Issueless *agg.* 1. senza sbocco 2. senza prole.

isthmus *s.* istmo.

it *pron. neutro* esso, essa, ciò, lo, gli, le, ne, sé || *I don't believe —,* non ci credo; *— is raining,* piove; *— is Sunday,* è domenica.

Italian *agg.* e *s.* italiano.

to italicize *vt.* e *vi.* 1. stampare in corsivo 2. sottolineare.

itch *s.* 1. prurito 2. scabbia.

to itch *vi.* 1. prudere 2. aver voglia di.

itching *s.* prurito.

item *s.* (*comm.*) voce.

to itemize *vt.* specificare, elencare.

to iterate *vt.* ripetere.

itinerant *agg.* ambulante.

itinerary *s.* itinerario.

its *agg.* e *pron. poss. neutro* suo, sua, suoi, sue.

itself *pron. r. neutro* esso stesso, essa stessa, sé, si || *by —,* da solo.

ivory *s.* avorio.

ivy *s.* edera.

J

jab *s.* 1. stoccata 2. colpo improvviso.

jack *s.* 1. (*fam.*) marinaio 2. fante (*gioco delle carte*) 3. bandiera (*di nave*) 4. maschio (*di certi animali*) 5. uomo di fatica 6. (*mecc.*) cricco.

jackal *s.* sciacallo.

jackass *s.* somaro.

jackdaw *s.* cornacchia.

jacket *s.* 1. giacchetta 2. rivestimento protettivo, isolante.

Jacobin *s.* giacobino.

jade¹ *s.* giada.

jade² *s.* 1. cavallo, ronzino 2. megera.

to jag *vt.* frastagliare, dentellare.

jaguar *s.* giaguaro.

jail *s.* carcere.

to jail *vt.* incarcerare.

jailer *s.* carceriere.

to jam *vt.* premere, serrare, pigiare. ♦ **to jam** *vi.* bloccarsi, incepparsi.

jam¹ *s.* marmellata.

jam² *s.* 1. ammasso 2. compressione 3. ingorgo.

jamb *s.* stipite.

Jansenism *s.* giansenismo.

Jansenist *s.* giansenista.

January *s.* gennaio.

Japanese *agg.* e *s.* giapponese.

jar *s.* rumore aspro, stridio.

to jar *vi.* 1. discordare 2. stridere. ♦ **to jar** *vt.* 1. far discordare 2. far stridere.

jargon *s.* 1. gergo 2. linguaggio professionale.

jarring *agg.* discorde, stridente.

jasmin(e) *s.* gelsomino.

jasper *s.* diaspro.

jaundice *s.* itterizia.

javelin *s.* giavellotto.

jaw *s.* 1. mascella, mandibola 2. morsa, ganascia. ♦ **jaws** *s. pl.* stretta, gola.

jealous *agg.* geloso.

jealously *avv.* gelosamente.

jealousness, jealousy *s.* gelosia.

jeer *s.* beffa, scherno.

jelly *s.* gelatina (*anche di frutta*).

to jeopardize *vt.* mettere a repentaglio.

jeopardy *s.* rischio, pericolo.

jerk *s.* 1. scatto, strattone 2. spinta 3. sussulto, tic nervoso.

to jerk *vt.* dare uno strattone. ♦ **to jerk** *vi.* sobbalzare || *to — along,* avanzare a scatti.

jerky *agg.* 1. sussultante 2. convulso.

jersey *s.* camicetta a maglia con maniche.

jest *s.* facezia, scherzo.

to jest *vi.* scherzare, dire delle facezie.

jester *s.* burlone.

jestful *agg.* incline allo scherzo.

Jesuit *s.* gesuita.

Jesuitical *agg.* gesuitico.

jet¹ *agg.* nero lucido.

jet² *s.* 1. getto, spruzzo 2. spruzzatore || *— engine,* motore a reazione; *— plane,* aeroplano a reazione.

to jet *vt.* schizzare, sprizzare. ♦ **to jet** *vi.* slanciarsi.

jetty *s.* molo || *landing —,* imbarcadero.

Jew *s.* ebreo.

jewel *s.* gioiello.

jewelcase *s.* scrigno.

jeweller *s.* gioielliere.

jewellery *s.* 1. gioielli 2. commercio delle gemme.

Jewish *agg.* ebraico, ebreo.

to jib *vi.* recalcitrare, impuntarsi.

jig *s.* 1. giga 2. (*mecc.*) maschera.

jigsaw s. sega da traforo.

to jingle vt. far tintinnare. ♦ **to jingle** vi. tintinnare.

job s. 1. lavoro, impiego 2. (fam.) faccenda, situazione.

jobber s. 1. noleggiatore 2. lavoratore a cottimo 3. trafficante disonesto.

jockey s. fantino.

jocose agg. giocoso, allegro.

jocosity s. giocondità.

jocund agg. giocondo, gaio.

jocundity s. allegria, giocondità.

join s. giuntura.

to join vt. 1. unire 2. raggiungere. ♦ **to join** vi. 1. unirsi 2. essere contiguo.

joiner s. falegname.

joinery s. falegnameria.

joining s. congiunzione.

joint agg. unito, associato || — account, conto di partecipazione; — -heir, coerede; — -stock, capitale sociale; — -tenant, comproprietario.

joint s. 1. giuntura, congiunzione 2. trancio di carne 3. articolazione.

jointer s. pialla.

jointly avv. unitamente.

joke s. scherzo, burla, facezia.

to joke vt. burlarsi di, canzonare. ♦ **to joke** vi. celiare.

joker s. tipo ameno, burlone.

jolly agg. gaio, vivace.

to jolt vt. far sobbalzare, scuotere. ♦ **to jolt** vi. traballare.

to jostle vt. spingere. ♦ **to jostle** vi. spingersi.

journal s. 1. giornale 2. diario.

journalism s. giornalismo.

journalist s. giornalista.

journalistic agg. giornalistico.

journey s. viaggio (general. per terra).

to journey vi. fare un viaggio.

journey-man s. operaio specializzato.

jovial agg. gioviale, allegro.

joviality s. giovialità.

jowl¹ s. 1. mascella 2. guancia.

jowl² s. gozzo.

joy s. gioia, contentezza.

joyful agg. giulivo, allegro.

joyfully avv. gaiamente, allegramente.

joyless agg. mesto, senza gioia.

joyous agg. gioioso, gaio.

joyously avv. gioiosamente.

jubilant agg. giubilante, trionfante.

to jubilate vi. esultare.

jubilation s. giubilo.

jubilee s. giubileo.

Judaic agg. giudaico.

Judaism s. giudaismo.

judge s. 1. giudice 2. intenditore.

to judge vt. e vi. 1. fare da giudice, giudicare 2. supporre, stimare.

judgement s. 1. giudizio 2. verdetto, sentenza 3. parere.

judicial agg. giudiziale, giudiziario.

judiciary agg. giudiziario. ♦ **Judiciary** s. magistratura.

judicious agg. giudizioso.

jug s. 1. boccale 2. caraffa, bricco.

juggler s. 1. giocoliere 2. impostore.

jugular agg. e s. giugulare.

juice s. succo (di frutta ecc.).

juiciness s. succosità.

juicy agg. succoso.

jujube s. giuggiola.

Julian agg. giuliano.

July s. luglio.

jumble s. guazzabuglio.

jump s. salto, balzo: high — (sport), salto in alto.

to jump vt. 1. saltare, superare con un salto 2. mangiare (giuoco della dama). ♦ **to jump** vi. 1. saltare 2. trasalire.

jumper¹ s. saltatore.

jumper² s. maglione.

jumping agg. saltatore.

junction s. 1. congiunzione 2. nodo ferroviario.

juncture s. 1. articolazione 2. (fig.) congiuntura, momento critico.

June s. giugno.

jungle s. giungla.

junior agg. 1. minore, di secondaria importanza 2. il più giovane. ♦ **junior** s. 1. cadetto 2. minore.

juniper s. ginepro.

junk¹ s. 1. avanzo, rifiuto 2. gomena vecchia 3. carne salata.

junk² s. (mar.) giunca.

juridic(al) agg. giuridico.

jurisdiction s. giurisdizione.

jurisdictional agg. giurisdizionale.

jurisprudence s. giurisprudenza.

jurisprudent s. giurisprudente.

jurisprudential agg. legale.

jurist s. giurista.

jury s. giuria, giurì.

juryman s. giurato.

just agg. giusto, retto. ♦ **just** avv. appena, appunto, esattamente || — now, proprio ora; — so., proprio così; — then, proprio allora.

justice s. giustizia, imparzialità.
justiciable agg. processabile.
justiciary agg. giudiziario.
justifiability s. legittimità di difesa.
justifiable agg. giustificabile, legittimo || — homicide, omicidio per legittima difesa.
justification s. giustificazione.
justificative agg. giustificativo.
to justify vt. 1. giustificare 2. difendere 3. perdonare.
justly avv. giustamente, esattamente.
jut s. sporgenza.
to jut vt. e vi. sporgere.
jute s. iuta.
juvenile agg. giovanile.
juxtaposition s. accostamento.

K

kaleidoscope s. caleidoscopio.
kalends s. pl. calende.
kangaroo s. canguro.
kaolin(e) s. caolino.
karting s. andare in « go-kart ».
kathode s. catodo.
keel s. 1. chiglia 2. chiatta (da carbone).
to keel vt. 1. rovesciare 2. (mar.) carenare.
keen agg. 1. aguzzo, affilato 2. pungente 3. forte 4. appassionato 5. acuto.
keenly avv. 1. in modo penetrante 2. dolorosamente 3. avidamente 4. (comm.) al minimo.
keenness s. 1. sottigliezza 2. intensità 3. ardore 4. acume.
keep s. 1. sostentamento 2. torrione.
to keep (kept, kept) vi. 1. restare 2. conservarsi || to — on, continuare; to — off, tenersi in disparte. ◆ to keep (kept, kept) vt. 1. tenere 2. mantenere 3. custodire 4. rispettare || to — back, dissimulare; to — up, tener alto, sostenere.
keeper s. guardiano.
keeping s. 1. sorveglianza 2. mantenimento 3. armonia.
keepsake s. oggetto ricordo.
keg s. barilotto.
kennel s. 1. canile 2. muta di cani 3. rigagnolo.

to kennel vt. tenere in un canile.
◆ to kennel vi. rintanarsi.
kepi s. chepì.
kept V. to keep.
kerbstone s. cordonatura (del marciapiede).
kerchief s. fazzoletto.
kernel s. 1. gheriglio 2. seme 3. (fig.) essenza.
kettle s. bollitore, bricco.
key s. 1. chiave 2. tasto || — money, buonuscita.
to key vt. 1. (mecc.) inchiavettare 2. (mus.) accordare 3. chiudere a chiave || to — up (fig.), eccitare.
keyboard s. tastiera.
keyed agg. 1. munito di chiavi 2. (mus.) a tasti.
keyhole s. buco della serratura.
keyless agg. senza chiave.
keystone s. chiave di volta.
kick s. 1. calcio 2. rinculo || — -off (sport), calcio d'inizio.
to kick vt. prendere a calci. ◆ to kick vi. 1. tirar calci 2. rinculare (di armi) 3. recalcitrare.
kicker s. chi scalcia.
kid¹ s. 1. capretto 2. bimbo.
kid² s. tinozza.
to kidnap vt. rapire.
kidnapper s. rapitore.
kidnapping s. ratto.
kidney s. 1. rene 2. temperamento || stones in the kidneys, calcoli renali.
kier s. caldaia.
to kill vt. 1. uccidere 2. respingere 3. smorzare 4. fermare.
killer s. uccisore || lady- —, dongiovanni.
killing agg. mortale. ◆ killing s. uccisione.
killjoy s. guastafeste.
kiln s. fornace.
kilo, kilogram(me) s. chilo(grammo).
kilometer s. chilometro.
kilt s. gonnellino degli scozzesi.
kin s. consanguineo, affine. ◆ kin s. parentela.
kind¹ agg. gentile || very — of you, molto gentile da parte tua.
kind² s. specie, tipo.
to kindle vt. accendere. ◆ to kindle vi. accendersi.
kindliness s. gentilezza.
kindling s. 1. accensione 2. legna facilmente infiammabile.
kindly agg. gentile. ◆ kindly avv.

gentilmente.
kindness *s.* gentilezza.
kindred *agg.* 1. imparentato 2. affine. ♦ **kindred** *s.* parentela.
kinematics *s.* cinematica.
kinetic *agg.* cinetico.
kinetics *s.* cinetica.
king *s.* re || *king's English*, la lingua inglese ufficiale.
kingdom *s.* regno.
kinghood *s.* regalità.
kingly *agg.* regale, regio.
kingship *s.* regalità.
kinless *agg.* senza parenti.
kinsfolk *s. pl.* parenti.
kinship *s.* parentela.
kinsman *s.* parente.
kinswoman *s.* parente (*donna*).
kiosk *s.* chiosco || *newspaper* —, edicola.
kipper *s.* aringa, salmone affumicato.
to kipper *vt.* affumicare (*pesce*).
kiss *s.* bacio.
to kiss *vt.* baciare || *to* — *the dust*, mordere la polvere.
kit *s.* 1. cassetta 2. equipaggiamento.
kitchen *s.* cucina || — *garden*, orto.
kitchener *s.* cuciniere.
kitchenette *s.* cucinino.
kitchenware *s.* batteria da cucina.
kite *s.* 1. nibbio 2. aquilone 3. aliante.
kitten *s.* gattino.
kleptomania *s.* cleptomania.
kleptomaniac *agg. e s.* cleptomane.
knack *s.* 1. abilità 2. dispositivo ingegnoso.
knapsack *s.* zaino (*per soldati*).
knave *s.* furfante.
knavery *s.* disonestà.
knavish *agg.* disonesto.
to knead *vt.* impastare.
kneader *s.* 1. chi impasta 2. impastatrice.
kneading *s.* impasto || — *trough*, madia.
knee *s.* 1. ginocchio 2. tubo a gomito || — *cap*, rotula, ginocchiera.
to kneel (knelt, knelt) *vi.* inginocchiarsi.
kneeler *s.* 1. chi s'inginocchia 2. inginocchiatoio.
knell *s.* rintocco funebre.
to knell *vt.* chiamare a raccolta. ♦ **to knell** *vi.* sonare a morto.
knelt V. *to kneel.*

knew V. *to know.*
knickerbockers *s. pl.* calzoni alla zuava.
knick-knack *s.* ninnolo.
knick-knackery *s.* cianfrusaglie.
knife *s.* (*pl.* knives) 1. coltello 2. bisturi || *pen*— , temperino; *pruning*— , falcetto || — *grinder*, arrotino.
to knife *vt.* 1. tagliare 2. accoltellare.
knight *s.* cavaliere.
knighthood *s.* 1. rango di cavaliere 2. cavalleria.
knightliness *s.* cavalleria.
knightly *agg.* cavalleresco. ♦ **knightly** *avv.* cavallerescamente.
to knit (knit, knit) (*anche reg.*) *vt.* 1. lavorare a maglia 2. corrugare 3. unire. ♦ **to knit** (knit, knit) (*anche reg.*) *vi.* unirsi, saldarsi.
knitter *s.* 1. magliaia 2. telaio per maglieria.
knitting *s.* lavoro a maglia.
knitwear *s.* maglieria.
knob *s.* 1. protuberanza 2. pomo, manopola.
knobby *agg.* nodoso.
knock *s.* 1. colpo 2. (*mecc.*) battito in testa.
to knock *vt.* urtare. ♦ **to knock** *vi.* 1. bussare 2. detonare || *to* — *down*, abbattere; *to* — *out*, sopraffare.
knocker *s.* battente.
knot *s.* 1. nodo 2. coccarda 3. gruppo 4. difficoltà.
to knot *vt.* annodare. ♦ **to knot** *vi.* annodarsi.
knottiness *s.* 1. nodosità 2. (*fig.*) difficoltà.
knotty *agg.* 1. nodoso 2. (*fig.*) difficile.
to know (knew, known) *vt.* 1. conoscere 2. sapere 3. riconoscere || *to* — *of*, aver sentito parlare di; *to* — *about*, essere al corrente di.
knowable *agg.* 1. comprensibile 2. riconoscibile.
knowing *agg.* 1. intelligente 2. istruito.
knowledge *s.* conoscenza.
known V. *to know.*
knuckle *s.* articolazione, nocca || — *-duster*, pugno di ferro.
to knuckle *vi.* 1. (*fig.*) cedere 2. applicarsi || *to* — *under*, sottomettersi.

knurl s. zigrinatura.
to **knurl** vt. zigrinare.
Korean agg. e s. coreano.

L

la s. (mus.) la.
label s. etichetta.
to **label** vt. 1. mettere l'etichetta a
2. classificare.
labial agg. e s. labiale.
laboratory s. laboratorio.
laborious agg. laborioso.
laboriousness s. laboriosità.
labour s. 1. lavoro, fatica 2. mano
d'opera 3. doglie (pl.) || *hard* —,
lavori forzati; — *party*, partito la-
borista.
to **labour** vi. 1. lavorare, faticare
2. avere le doglie. ♦ to **labour**
vt. elaborare, sviluppare.
laboured agg. 1. elaborato 2. penoso.
labourer s. lavoratore.
labouring agg. laborioso.
labourism s. laburismo.
labourist s. laburista.
labyrinth s. labirinto.
lace s. 1. laccio 2. pizzo 3. passamaneria.
to **lace** vt. 1. allacciare 2. guarnire
con merletti, galloni.
to **lacerate** vt. lacerare.
lachrymal agg. lacrimale.
lachrymator s. gas lacrimogeno.
lack s. mancanza.
to **lack** vt. mancare di. ♦ to **lack**
vi. mancare, scarseggiare.
lacker s. 1. lacca 2. oggetto lac-
cato.
to **lacker** vt. laccare.
laconic(al) agg. laconico.
to **lacquer** V. to *lacker.*
lactation s. 1. lattazione 2. allattamento.
lacteal, lacteous agg. latteo.
lactose s. lattosio.
lacunar agg. lacunoso. ♦ **lacunar**
s. soffitto a cassettoni.
lacustrine agg. lacustre.
lacy agg. simile a pizzo.
lad s. ragazzo.
ladder s. 1. scala a pioli 2. smagliatura.
to **ladder** vt. munire di scala. ♦ to

ladder vi. smagliarsi.
to **lade (laded, laden)** vt. caricare.
laden agg. (fig.) oppresso.
lading s. carico: *bill of* —, polizza di carico.
ladle s. mestolo.
to **ladle** vt. versare con un mestolo.
lady s. signora || *Our Lady*, la Ma-
donna; — *doctor*, dottoressa.
ladybird s. coccinella.
ladykiller s. (fam.) dongiovanni.
ladylike agg. signorile, raffinato.
ladyship s. 1. rango di nobildonna
2. Signoria.
lag s. ritardo, rallentamento.
to **lag** vi. ritardare, restare indietro.
laggard agg. e s. pigro.
lagoon s. laguna.
to **laicize** vt. laicizzare.
laid V. to *lay.*
lain V. to *lie.*
lair s. tana.
laity s. 1. i laici 2. i profani.
lake s. lago.
laky agg. lacustre.
lamb s. agnello.
lambent agg. 1. lambente 2. scintillante.
lame agg. 1. zoppo 2. (fig.) debole
(di argomenti).
to **lame** vt. storpiare.
lamellar agg. lamellare.
lameness s. 1. zoppaggine 2. imperfezione.
lament s. lamento.
to **lament** vt. lamentare. ♦ to **lament** vi. lamentarsi.
lamentable agg. lamentevole.
lamentation s. lamento.
lamented agg. 1. deplorato 2. compianto.
to **laminate** vt. laminare.
lamination s. 1. laminazione 2. lamina.
lamp s. lampada || — *-black*, nero-
fumo; — *-shade*, paralume.
lamplight s. luce artificiale.
lampoon s. libello.
lamprey s. lampreda.
lance s. 1. lancia 2. fiocina.
to **lance** vt. (med.) incidere.
lancer s. lanciere.
lancet s. bisturi.
land s. 1. terra 2. paese, contrada
3. campagna, terreno || — *-sur-
veying*, agrimensura; — *surveyor*,
agrimensore.
to **land** vi. 1. sbarcare 2. atterrare.
♦ to **land** vt. 1. sbarcare 2. de-

porre **3.** prendere possesso di.
landed *agg.* fondiario.
landing *s.* **1.** sbarco **2.** atterraggio
3. pianerottolo || — *-stage*, pontile di sbarco; — *-strip*, pista d'atterraggio.
landlady *s.* **1.** padrona di casa **2.** albergatrice.
landless *agg.* senza terreni.
landlord *s.* **1.** padrone di casa, di terra **2.** albergatore.
landmark *s.* **1.** punto di riferimento **2.** pietra miliare.
landowner *s.* proprietario terriero.
landscape *s.* paesaggio || — *-painter*, paesaggista.
landslide, landslip *s.* frana.
lane *s.* **1.** viottolo, vicolo **2.** (*mar.*) rotta **3.** corsia (*di strada*).
language *s.* linguaggio.
languid *agg.* languido.
languish *s.* languore.
to **languish** *vi.* languire.
languor *s.* languore.
languorous *agg.* languido.
lank *agg.* **1.** allampanato **2.** liscio (*di capelli*).
lanolin(e) *s.* lanolina.
lantern *s.* lanterna.
lap[1] *s.* **1.** grembo **2.** valletta **3.** lembo.
lap[2] *s.* **1.** sovrapposizione **2.** (*sport*) giro di pista.
to **lap** *vt.* **1.** piegare **2.** avvolgere **3.** lambire **4.** bere avidamente. ♦ to **lap** *vi.* ripiegarsi.
laparotomy *s.* laparotomia.
lapel *s.* risvolto (*di giacca, soprabito*).
lapidary *agg.* lapidario. ♦ **lapidary** *s.* tagliatore di pietre.
lapidation *s.* lapidazione.
Lapp *agg.* e *s.* lappone.
lappet *s.* **1.** falda **2.** lobo dell'orecchio.
lapse *s.* **1.** errore **2.** intervallo.
to **lapse** *vi.* **1.** errare **2.** scivolare.
larboard *s.* fiancata sinistra (*di nave*).
larceny *s.* furto.
larch *s.* larice.
lard *s.* lardo.
to **lard** *vt.* **1.** ungere con lardo **2.** lardellare.
larder *s.* dispensa.
large *agg.* **1.** largo **2.** grande, ampio **3.** generoso || *at* —, in genere; *to be at* —, essere in libertà.
largeness *s.* **1.** ampiezza, grandezza **2.** generosità.

lark *s.* allodola.
laryngitis *s.* laringite.
larynx *s.* laringe.
lascivious *agg.* lascivo.
lasciviousness *s.* lascivia.
lash *s.* **1.** frusta **2.** frustata **3.** (*eye*)—, ciglio.
to **lash** *vt.* frustare || *to* — *at*, sferzare.
lashing *s.* **1.** frustata **2.** legatura.
lass, lassie *s.* ragazzina.
last *agg.* (*superl. di* late) **1.** ultimo **2.** scorso **3.** massimo || *the* — *but one*, il penultimo. ♦ **last** *s.* **1.** fine **2.** ultimo. ♦ **last** *avv.* **1.** ultimo **2.** l'ultima volta || *at* —, alla fine.
to **last** *vi.* durare.
lasting *agg.* durevole. ♦ **lasting** *s.* durata.
latch *s.* chiavistello.
late (later, latter; latest, last) *agg.* **1.** tardi **2.** in ritardo **3.** tardo **4.** precedente **5.** defunto. ♦ **late** *avv.* **1.** tardi **2.** in ritardo.
lately *avv.* recentemente.
latent *agg.* latente.
later *agg.* (*comp. di* late) posteriore. ♦ **later** *avv.* più tardi.
lateral *agg.* laterale.
latest *agg.* (*superl. di* late) ultimo, recentissimo || *at the* —, al più tardi.
latex *s.* lattice.
lathe *s.* tornio.
lather *s.* schiuma.
to **lather** *vt.* insaponare. ♦ to **lather** *vi.* schiumare.
Latin *agg.* e *s.* latino.
Latinism *s.* latinismo.
Latinist *s.* latinista.
Latinity *s.* latinità.
latitude *s.* **1.** latitudine **2.** ampiezza.
latter *agg.* (*comp. di* late) **1.** posteriore **2.** ultimo **3.** secondo.
latterly *avv.* recentemente.
lattice *s.* grata, traliccio.
latticed *agg.* munito di grata.
laudable *agg.* lodevole.
laudanum *s.* laudano.
laudatory *agg.* laudatorio.
laugh *s.* risata.
to **laugh** *vi.* ridere || *to* — *at*, deridere.
laughable *agg.* comico.
laughing *s.* risata || — *-stock*, zimbello.
laughter *s.* riso || *to burst into* —, scoppiare a ridere.

launch¹ s. varo.

launch² s. (mar.) lancia.

to launch vt. 1. lanciare 2. varare.

to launder vt. e vi. 1. fare il bucato 2. lavare e stirare.

launderette s. lavanderia con macchine automatiche.

laundress s. lavandaia.

laundry s. 1. lavanderia 2. bucato.

laureate agg. coronato d'alloro.

laurel s. lauro, alloro.

to laurel vt. coronare d'alloro.

lavatory s. gabinetto.

lavender s. lavanda.

lavish agg. prodigo.

to lavish vt. prodigare.

lavishness s. prodigalità.

law s. 1. legge 2. professione legale 3. processo, causa || — -court, tribunale; to go to —, ricorrere in giudizio.

lawful agg. 1. legale 2. legittimo.

lawfulness s. 1. legalità 2. legittimità.

lawgiver s. legislatore.

lawless agg. 1. illegale 2. sregolato.

lawn s. prato (rasato).

lawsuit s. (giur.) processo.

lawyer s. avvocato.

lax agg. allentato.

laxative agg. e s. lassativo.

laxity s. 1. negligenza 2. rilassatezza.

lay V. to lie.

lay agg. 1. laico 2. profano || — -brother, converso; — -sister, conversa. ♦ lay s. configurazione.

to lay (laid, laid) vt. 1. porre 2. deporre 3. preparare 4. calmare || to — aside, mettere da parte; to — out, stendere, spendere.

lay-by s. piazzola di sosta.

layer s. 1. strato 2. gallina che fa uova 3. (mil.) puntatore.

laying s. 1. posa 2. covata.

layoff s. stagione morta (di lavoro).

layout s. 1. esposizione 2. schema.

lazaret s. lazzaretto.

laziness s. pigrizia.

lazy agg. pigro.

lead¹ s. 1. piombo 2. grafite || red- —, minio; white- —, biacca.

lead² s. 1. comando 2. guinzaglio 3. mano (di carte).

to lead¹ vt. impiombare.

to lead² (led, led) vt. 1. condurre, capeggiare 2. indurre.

leaden agg. di piombo, plumbeo.

leader s. 1. capo 2. articolo di fondo.

leadership s. direzione.

leading¹ agg. 1. dominante 2. primo. ♦ leading s. guida.

leading² s. impiombatura.

leaf s. (pl. leaves) 1. foglia 2. foglio.

to leaf vt. sfogliare. ♦ to leaf vi. mettere le foglie.

leafless agg. senza foglie.

leaflet s. 1. fogliolina 2. volantino.

league s. lega.

to league vi. allearsi.

leak s. 1. fessura 2. (mar.) falla 3. perdita.

to leak vi. perdere || to — out, trapelare.

leakage s. 1. colatura 2. dispersione.

leaky agg. che cola, perde.

lean¹ agg. magro, esile.

lean² s. inclinazione.

to lean (leant, leant) (anche reg.) vt. e vi. 1. pendere 2. appoggiarsi 3. sporgersi 4. inclinare.

leaning s. 1. inclinazione 2. l'appoggiarsi.

leanness s. magrezza.

leant V. to lean.

leap s. salto || — -year, anno bisestile.

to leap (leapt, leapt) (anche reg.) vt. e vi. saltare.

to learn (learnt, learnt) (anche reg.) vt. e vi. imparare, apprendere.

learned agg. colto.

learner s. allievo.

learning s. cultura.

learnt V. to learn.

lease s. 1. contratto d'affitto 2. durata (di contratto) || on —, in affitto.

to lease vt. affittare.

leash s. guinzaglio.

to leash vt. tenere al guinzaglio.

least agg. (superl. di little) il minimo. ♦ least s. (il) meno. ♦ least avv. (il) meno.

leather s. 1. cuoio 2. oggetto in cuoio || patent —, vernice.

leathern agg. di cuoio.

leave s. 1. permesso 2. congedo.

to leave (left, left) vt. lasciare. ♦ to leave (left, left) vi. partire || to — off, smettere.

leaven s. 1. lievito 2. (fig.) fermento.

to leaven vt. far lievitare.

leaves V. *leaf.*

leaving *s.* partenza.

lecherous *agg.* lascivo.

lechery *s.* lascivia.

lecture *s.* **1.** conferenza **2.** lezione **3.** rimprovero.

to lecture *vt.* rimproverare. ♦ **to lecture** *vi.* fare una conferenza.

lecturer *s.* **1.** conferenziere **2.** lettore universitario.

led V. *to lead.*

ledger *s.* (*comm.*) libro mastro.

lee *s.* feccia.

leech *s.* sanguisuga (*anche fig.*).

to leer *vt.* e *vi.* guardare di sbieco.

leeward *agg.* e *avv.* sottovento.

leeway *s.* deriva.

left *agg.* sinistro. ♦ **left** *s.* sinistra || — *-handed*, mancino.

left V. *to leave.*

leftist *s.* (*pol.*) uomo di sinistra.

leg *s.* **1.** gamba **2.** (*cuc.*) cosciotto || *to pull so.'s* —, canzonare qu.

legacy *s.* legato.

legal *agg.* legale.

legality *s.* legalità.

legalization *s.* legalizzazione.

to legalize *vt.* legalizzare.

legatee *s.* legatario.

legation *s.* legazione.

legend *s.* leggenda.

legendary *agg.* leggendario.

leggins *s. pl.* gambali.

legible *agg.* leggibile.

legion *s.* legione.

legionary *agg.* e *s.* legionario.

to legislate *vi.* fare leggi. ♦ **to legislate** *vt.* trasformare per mezzo di leggi.

legislation *s.* legislazione.

legislative *agg.* legislativo.

legislator *s.* legislatore.

legislature *s.* **1.** legislatura **2.** corpo legislativo.

legitimacy *s.* legittimità.

legitimate *agg.* legittimo.

to legitimate *vt.* legittimare.

legitimation *s.* legittimazione.

legume *s.* legume.

leguminous *agg.* leguminoso.

leisure *s.* **1.** agio **2.** tempo libero.

leisurely *agg.* e *avv.* con comodo.

lemon *s.* limone.

lemonade *s.* limonata.

to lend (lent, lent) *vt.* prestare.

lender *s.* prestatore.

length *s.* **1.** lunghezza **2.** durata, spazio di tempo || *at —*, alla f.ne.

to lengthen *vt.* allungare. ♦ **to**

lengthen *vi.* allungarsi.

lengthy *agg.* lungo, prolisso.

lenient *agg.* **1.** emolliente **2.** mite.

lenitive *agg.* e *s.* calmante.

lens *s.* **1.** (*ott.*) lente **2.** (*foto*) obiettivo.

lent V. *to lend.*

Lent *s.* quaresima.

lentil *s.* lenticchia.

leonine *agg.* leonino.

leopard *s.* **1.** leopardo **2.** gatto-pardo.

leper *s.* lebbroso || — *hospital*, lebbrosario.

leporine *agg.* leporino.

leprosy *s.* lebbra.

leprous *agg.* lebbroso.

lesbian *agg.* e *s.* lesbica.

lesion *s.* lesione.

less *agg.* (*comp. di little*) minore, meno. ♦ **less** *s.* meno. ♦ **less** *avv.* meno. ♦ **less** *prep.* meno.

lessee *s.* affittuario.

to lessen *vt.* e *vi.* diminuire.

lesser *agg.* minore.

lesson *s.* lezione.

lest *cong.* per paura che.

to let (let, let) *vt.* **1.** lasciare, permettere **2.** affittare || *to — in*, far entrare; *to — off*, lasciar andare; *to — out*, lasciar uscire.

lethal *agg.* letale.

lethargy *s.* letargo.

letter *s.* lettera.

lettered *agg.* **1.** letterato **2.** intestato.

lettuce *s.* lattuga.

leucocyte *s.* leucocito.

leucocythaemia, leukemia *s.* leucemia.

levant *s.* levante.

level *agg.* **1.** livellato **2.** a livello **3.** regolato. ♦ **level** *s.* **1.** livello **2.** superficie piana **3.** livella || *on a — with*, sullo stesso piano di.

to level *vt.* **1.** livellare **2.** puntare (*un'arma*).

levelling *s.* **1.** livellamento **2.** puntamento (*di arma*).

lever *s.* **1.** manubrio **2.** leva.

to lever *vi.* far leva.

to levigate *vt.* **1.** levigare **2.** polverizzare.

levigation *s.* **1.** levigazione **2.** polverizzazione.

levity *s.* leggerezza.

levy *s.* **1.** leva **2.** imposta.

to levy *vt.* **1.** arruolare **2.** imporre (*di tasse*).

lewd *agg.* impudico.

lewdness *s.* impudicizia.

lexical *agg.* lessicale.

lexicographer *s.* lessicografo.

lexicography *s.* lessicografia.

lexicology *s.* lessicologia.

lexicon *s.* lessico.

liability *s.* 1. obbligo 2. tendenza 3. (*giur.*) responsabilità. ♦ **liabilities** *s. pl.* passività (*sing.*).

liable *agg.* 1. soggetto a 2. (*giur.*) responsabile.

liar *s.* bugiardo.

libation *s.* libagione.

libel *s.* 1. libello 2. (*giur.*) diffamazione.

to libel *vt.* 1. scrivere un libello contro 2. (*giur.*) sporgere querela.

liberal *agg.* 1. liberale 2. umanistico. ♦ **liberal** *s.* liberale.

liberalism *s.* liberalismo.

liberalist *s.* liberalista.

liberality *s.* liberalità.

to liberalize *vt.* rendere liberale.

to liberate *vt.* liberare.

liberation *s.* liberazione.

liberator *s.* liberatore.

liberticide *s.* 1. liberticida 2. liberticidio.

libertinage *s.* libertinaggio.

libertine *agg. e s.* libertino.

libertinism *s.* libertinaggio.

liberty *s.* libertà.

libidinous *agg.* libidinoso.

libido *s.* libidine.

librarian *s.* bibliotecario.

library *s.* biblioteca || *film* —, cineteca; *record* —, discoteca.

lice V. *louse.*

licence *s.* licenza || *driving* —, patente automobilistica.

to license *vt.* dare una licenza a.

licensed *agg.* autorizzato.

licentious *agg.* licenzioso.

licentiousness *s.* dissolutezza.

lichen *s.* lichene.

lick *s.* leccata.

to lick *vt.* 1. leccare 2. lambire.

lid *s.* coperchio.

lie¹ *s.* menzogna || *the* —, smentita.

lie² *s.* posizione.

to lie¹ *vi.* mentire.

to lie² (lay, lain) *vi.* giacere, trovarsi || *to* — *down,* coricarsi; *to* — *in,* partorire.

lieutenant *s.* tenente.

life *s.* (*pl.* lives) vita || —*-belt,* cintura di salvataggio; — *preserver,* salvagente.

lifeboat *s.* lancia di salvataggio.

lifeless *agg.* senza vita.

lifelike *agg.* vivido.

lift *s.* 1. ascensore 2. passaggio (*su un veicolo*) 3. sollevamento.

to lift *vt.* 1. alzare 2. rubare. ♦ **lift** *vi.* alzarsi.

light¹ *agg.* 1. chiaro 2. biondo 3. leggero 4. agile 5. insignificante.

light² *s.* 1. luce 2. fuoco 3. lampada || *traffic lights,* semaforo.

to light (lit, lit) *vt.* (*anche reg.*) *vt.* 1. accendere 2. illuminare. ♦ **to light (lit, lit)** (*anche reg.*) *vi.* 1. accendersi 2. illuminarsi 3. posarsi.

to lighten *vt.* 1. alleggerire, alleviare 2. illuminare. ♦ **to lighten** *vi.* 1. alleggerirsi 2. illuminarsi 3. (*imp.*) lampeggiare.

lighter *s.* 1. accenditore 2. (*mar.*) chiatta.

lighthouse *s.* faro.

lighting *s.* 1. accensione 2. luce (*di quadro*)

lightless *agg.* oscuro.

lightness *s.* 1. leggerezza 2. gaiezza 3. illuminazione.

lightning *s.* fulmine || —*rod,* parafulmine.

Ligurian *agg. e s.* ligure.

like *agg.* 1. simile 2. caratteristico di. ♦ **like** *prep.* come || — *this,* — *that,* così; *to feel* —, aver voglia di; *to look* —, avere l'aria di.

like *s.* simile. ♦ **likes** *s. pl.* gusti.

to like *vt.* piacere. ♦ **to like** *vi.* volere.

likelihood *s.* probabilità.

likely *agg.* 1. probabile 2. adatto. ♦ **likely** *avv.* probabilmente.

likeness *s.* 1. somiglianza 2. immagine.

likewise *avv.* 1. allo stesso modo 2. anche.

liking *s.* 1. gusto 2. preferenza.

lilac *agg. e s.* lilla.

lily *agg.* bianco. ♦ **lily** *s.* giglio || *water* —, ninfea.

limb *s.* 1. membro 2. ramo.

lime¹ *s.* 1. calce 2. pania.

lime² *s.* cedro.

lime³ *s.* tiglio.

to lime *vt.* 1. cementare 2. invischiare.

limelight *s.* luce della ribalta.

limestone *s.* calcare.

limit *s.* limite.

to limit *vt.* limitare.

limitary *agg.* **1.** limitato **2.** limitativo **3.** situato alla frontiera.

limitation *s.* limitazione.

limitative *agg.* limitativo.

limited *agg.* limitato || — *company*, società a responsabilità limitata; — *monarchy*, monarchia costituzionale.

limp *agg.* molle.

to **limp** *vi.* zoppicare.

limpid *agg.* limpido.

limpidity *s.* limpidezza.

limping *s.* zoppicamento.

line *s.* **1.** linea, riga **2.** ruga **3.** discendenza **4.** attività **5.** verso **6.** (*comm.*) articolo.

to **line** *vt.* **1.** rigare **2.** fiancheggiare **3.** foderare || *to — up*, allineare, allinearsi.

lineage *s.* lignaggio.

lineal *agg.* in linea diretta.

lineament *s.* lineamento.

linear *agg.* lineare.

linen *agg.* di lino. ♦ **linen** *s.* **1.** tela di lino **2.** biancheria.

liner *s.* **1.** transatlantico **2.** aereo di linea.

to **linger** *vt.* e *vi.* indugiare.

linguist *s.* linguista.

linguistic(al) *agg.* linguistico.

linguistics *s.* linguistica.

liniment *s.* linimento.

lining *s.* **1.** rigatura **2.** allineamento **3.** fodera **4.** rivestimento.

link *s.* **1.** anello **2.** (*fig.*) legame || *cuff-links*, gemelli da polso.

to **link** *vt.* collegare. ♦ to **link** *vi.* collegarsi.

linotyping *s.* linotipia.

linotypist *s.* linotipista.

lint *s.* garza.

lintel *s.* architrave.

lion *s.* leone.

lioness *s.* leonessa.

lip *s.* **1.** labbro **2.** margine || — *-stick*, rossetto per labbra.

to **lip** *vt.* **1.** toccare (con le labbra) **2.** sussurrare.

liquefaction *s.* liquefazione.

to **liquefy** *vt.* liquefare. ♦ to **liquefy** *vi.* liquefarsi.

liqueur *s.* rosolio.

liquid *agg.* **1.** liquido **2.** chiaro **3.** armonioso **4.** instabile. ♦ **liquid** *s.* liquido.

to **liquidate** *vt.* liquidare.

liquidation *s.* liquidazione.

liquidator *s.* liquidatore.

liquor *s.* **1.** liquido **2.** bevanda alcolica.

liquorice *s.* liquirizia.

to **lisp** *vi.* parlare bleso.

lisping *agg.* bleso. ♦ **lisping** *s.* pronuncia blesa.

list[1] *s.* **1.** lista **2.** striscia **3.** cimosa. ♦ **lists** *s. pl.* lizza (*sing.*).

list[2] *s.* (*mar.*) sbandamento.

to **list**[1] *vt.* elencare, catalogare.

to **list**[2] *vi.* (*mar.*) sbandare.

to **listen** *vi.* ascoltare: *to — so.*, ascoltare qu.; *to — in*, ascoltare la radio.

listener *s.* ascoltatore.

listening *s.* ascolto.

listless *agg.* disattento.

lit V. *to light*.

litany *s.* litania.

literal *agg.* **1.** letterale **2.** prosaico **3.** di lettera alfabetica.

literalism *s.* interpretazione letterale.

literary *agg.* letterario.

literate *agg.* e *s.* letterato.

literature *s.* letteratura.

lithe *agg.* agile.

lithograph *s.* litografia.

to **lithograph** *vt.* litografare.

lithographic(al) *agg.* litografico.

lithography *s.* (*arte della*) litografia.

litigant *s.* (*giur.*) contendente.

litmus *s.* tornasole.

litre *s.* litro.

litter *s.* **1.** lettiga, barella **2.** strame **3.** rifiuti **4.** figliata.

little (*less, least*) *agg.* **1.** piccolo **2.** breve **3.** poco || *a —*, un po' di. ♦ **little** *s.* poco. ♦ **little** *avv.* poco || *a —*, piuttosto.

liturgic(al) *agg.* liturgico.

liturgy *s.* liturgia.

live *agg.* **1.** vivo **2.** ardente **3.** carico (*di armi*).

to **live** *vi.* e *vt.* vivere, abitare.

livelihood *s.* mezzi di sussistenza.

liveliness *s.* vivacità.

lively *agg.* vivace.

liver *s.* fegato.

livery[1] *agg.* bilioso.

livery[2] *s.* **1.** livrea **2.** (*giur.*) passaggio di proprietà.

lives V. *life*.

livestock *s.* bestiame.

livid *agg.* livido.

living *agg.* **1.** vivo **2.** perfetto (*di somiglianza*). ♦ **living** *s.* **1.** mezzo di mantenimento **2.** vita || — *-room*, soggiorno.

lizard s. lucertola.

llama s. (zool.) lama.

load s. 1. carico, peso 2. (elettr.) carica, tensione.

to load vt. 1. caricare 2. adulterare.

loader s. caricatore.

loading s. caricamento.

loadstar s. stella polare.

loaf s. (pl. loaves) pagnotta || sugar— —, pan di zucchero.

to loaf vi. oziare.

loafer s. fannullone.

loan s. prestito: on —, a prestito.

to loan vt. prestare.

loath agg. riluttante.

to loathe vt. detestare.

loathing s. disgusto.

loathsome agg. 1. odioso 2. disgustoso.

loaves V. loaf.

lobby s. anticamera.

lobe s. lobo.

lobster s. aragosta.

local agg. e s. locale.

locality s. località.

to localize vt. localizzare.

to locate vt. 1. situare 2. individuare 3. indicare.

location s. 1. posizione 2. locazione.

lock¹ s. 1. ricciolo 2. fiocco.

lock² s. 1. serratura 2. diga 3. otturatore (di arma).

to lock vt. serrare. ♦ to lock vi. (mecc.) incepparsi.

locker s. armadio, bauletto a chiave.

locket s. medaglione.

lockout s. (econ.) serrata.

locomotion s. locomozione.

locomotive agg. locomotorio. ♦ locomotive s. locomotiva.

locust s. locusta || —-tree, carrubo, robinia.

locution s. locuzione.

lodge s. 1. loggia 2. padiglione.

to lodge vt. 1. alloggiare 2. collocare. ♦ to lodge vi. 1. alloggiare 2. entrare.

lodging s. alloggio, dimora.

loftiness s. 1. altezza 2. nobiltà.

lofty agg. 1. alto, elevato 2. orgoglioso, altero.

log s. ceppo || —-book, giornale di bordo.

logarithm s. logaritmo.

logic s. logica.

logical agg. logico.

logistic(al) agg. logistico.

logistics s. pl. (mil.) logistica (sing.).

logomachy s. logomachia.

loin s. lombo. ♦ loins s. pl. reni.

to loiter vt. sprecare (tempo ecc.). ♦ to loiter vi. bighellonare, oziare.

loitering s. il bighellonare, l'andare a zonzo.

Lombard agg. e s. lombardo.

Londoner s. londinese.

Londonese agg. londinese.

loneliness s. solitudine.

lonely, lonesome agg. solo, solitario.

long agg. lungo || —-distance call, telefonata interurbana. ♦ long s. molto tempo. ♦ long avv. a lungo || how —?, quanto tempo?; all day —, tutto il giorno; as — as, fino a, purché; so —!, arrivederci!; before —, tra poco.

to long vi. desiderare ardentemente: to — for sthg., desiderare ardentemente qc.

longanimity s. longanimità.

longboat s. lancia.

longevity s. longevità.

longevous agg. longevo.

longing agg. bramoso. ♦ longing s. brama.

longitude s. longitudine.

longitudinal agg. longitudinale.

long-sighted agg. 1. presbite 2. preveggente.

look s. sguardo. ♦ looks s. pl. aspetto (sing.).

to look vi. 1. sembrare 2. guardare || to — after, badare a; to — at, guardare; to — for, cercare; to — forward to, non veder l'ora di; to — like, somigliare; to — up, consultare (orario, dizionario ecc.); to — through, esaminare attentamente; to — up to, rispettare; to — down on, disprezzare.

looker-on s. spettatore.

looking-glass s. specchio.

lookout s. 1. guardia 2. vista panoramica 3. prospettiva.

loom s. telaio.

to loom vt. tessere. ♦ to loom vi. apparire indistintamente.

loop s. 1. cappio 2. gancio.

loophole s. feritoia.

loose agg. 1. sciolto 2. ampio 3. vago 4. licenzioso 5. allentato.

to loose vt. 1. sciogliere 2. liberare 3. lanciare.

to **loosen** *vt.* **1.** sciogliere **2.** allentare.

looseness *s.* **1.** scioltezza **2.** ampiezza **3.** libertinaggio **4.** imprecisione.

to **lop** *vt.* potare, mozzare.

loquacious *agg.* loquace.

loquacity *s.* loquacità.

lord *s.* **1.** signore **2.** Pari || — Mayor, sindaco.

to **lord** *vt.* dominare.

lordly *agg.* **1.** fastoso, imponente **2.** altero.

lordship *s.* signoria, autorità.

lorry *s.* autocarro.

to **lose** (lost, lost) *vt.* e *vi.* perdere.

loser *s.* perdente.

losing, loss *s.* perdita.

lost V. *to lose.*

lot *s.* **1.** sorte **2.** parte **3.** lotto (*di terreno ecc.*) || a — of, una quantità di.

to **lot** *vt.* lottizzare.

lotion *s.* lozione.

lottery *s.* lotteria.

loud *agg.* forte, fragoroso, rumoroso || -speaker, altoparlante. ◆ **loud(ly)** *avv.* ad alta voce.

lounge *s.* **1.** atrio (*di albergo, teat. ecc.*) **2.** lo stare in ozio.

to **lounge** *vi.* bighellonare.

lounger *s.* fannullone.

louse *s.* (*pl.* lice) pidocchio.

lousy *agg.* pidocchioso.

lovable *agg.* amabile.

love *s.* amore.

to **love** *vt.* amare.

loveless *agg.* senza amore.

loveliness *s.* bellezza.

lovely *agg.* bello.

lover *s.* amante, innamorato.

loving *agg.* amoroso.

lovingness *s.* affettuosità.

low[1] *agg.* **1.** basso **2.** debole || -spirited, depresso. ◆ **low** *avv.* **1.** in basso **2.** a voce bassa **3.** a basso prezzo.

low[2] *s.* muggito.

to **low** *vi.* muggire.

to **lower** *vt.* **1.** abbassare **2.** abbattere. ◆ **to lower** *vi.* abbattersi.

lowering *s.* abbassamento.

lowland *s.* pianura.

lowly *agg.* **1.** basso **2.** umile. ◆ **lowly** *avv.* umilmente.

loyal *agg.* leale.

loyalty *s.* lealtà.

lozenge *s.* **1.** (*geom.*) rombo **2.** pastiglia.

lubber *s.* zoticone.

lubricant *agg.* e *s.* lubrificante.

to **lubricate** *vt.* lubrificare.

lubricating, lubrication *s.* lubrificazione.

lubricator *s.* lubrificatore.

lubricity *s.* **1.** viscosità **2.** (*fig.*) lascivia.

lubricous *agg.* lubrico.

lucent *agg.* lucente.

lucid *agg.* lucido, chiaro.

lucidity *s.* lucidità, chiarezza.

luck *s.* **1.** sorte **2.** fortuna || to be in —, out of —, essere fortunato, sfortunato.

luckily *avv.* fortunatamente.

luckless *agg.* sfortunato.

lucky *agg.* fortunato.

lucrative *agg.* lucrativo.

to **lucubrate** *vi.* fare delle elucubrazioni.

lucubration *s.* elucubrazione.

ludicrous *agg.* ridicolo.

ludicrousness *s.* comicità.

luggage *s.* bagaglio.

lugubrious *agg.* lugubre.

lukewarm *agg.* tiepido, apatico.

to **lull** *vt.* **1.** cullare **2.** calmare.

lullaby *s.* ninna-nanna.

lumbago *s.* lombaggine.

lumbar *agg.* lombare.

lumber *s.* **1.** cianfrusaglie (*pl.*) **2.** legname || -room, ripostiglio.

to **lumber** *vt.* **1.** ammucchiare **2.** ingombrare. ◆ **to lumber** *vi.* **1.** tagliare legname **2.** muoversi pesantemente e rumorosamente.

lumbering *s.* commercio di legname.

luminary *s.* **1.** corpo luminoso **2.** luminare.

luminous *agg.* luminoso.

luminousness *s.* luminosità.

lump *s.* **1.** mucchio **2.** gonfiore **3.** zolletta **4.** (*comm.*) blocco **5.** persona goffa.

to **lump** *vt.* ammassare. ◆ **to lump** *vi.* raggrumarsi.

lumpy *agg.* **1.** granuloso **2.** increspato (*di mare*) **3.** pesante.

lunacy *s.* pazzia.

lunar *agg.* lunare.

lunatic *agg.* e *s.* pazzo.

lunation *s.* lunazione.

lunch *s.* seconda colazione, pasto del mezzogiorno.

to **lunch** *vi.* fare la seconda colazione. ◆ **to lunch** *vt.* offrire la colazione a.

luncheon *s.* spuntino.

lunette *s.* (*arch.*) lunetta.

lung *s.* polmone: iron —, polmone d'acciaio.

lupine *s.* lupino.

lure *s.* esca.

to lure *vt.* adescare.

lurid *agg.* 1. spettrale 2. orribile.

lurk *s.* nascondiglio.

to lurk *vi.* nascondersi.

luscious *agg.* 1. dolce 2. sensuale.

lust *s.* 1. lussuria 2. brama.

to lust *vi.* bramare: to — for so., sthg., bramare qu., qc.

lustful *agg.* 1. sensuale 2. bramoso.

lustfulness *s.* 1. sensualità 2. brama.

lustral *agg.* lustrale.

lustre[1] *s.* lustro, splendore.

lustre[2] *s.* lustro, quinquennio.

lusty *agg.* vigoroso, gagliardo.

lute *s.* liuto.

Lutheran *agg. e s.* luterano.

Lutheranism *s.* luteranesimo.

to luxate *vt.* (*med.*) lussare.

luxation *s.* lussazione.

luxuriant *agg.* lussureggiante.

to luxuriate *vi.* lussureggiare || to — in, deliziarsi di.

luxurious *agg.* lussuoso, sontuoso.

luxury *s.* 1. lusso 2. oggetto di lusso.

lye *s.* lisciva.

lying[1] *agg.* bugiardo.

lying[2] *agg.* giacente, situato.

lymph *s.* linfa.

lymphatic *agg.* linfatico. ♦ lymphatic *s.* vaso linfatico.

to lynch *vt.* linciare.

lynch law *s.* linciaggio.

lynx *s.* lince.

lyre *s.* lira.

lyric(al) *agg.* lirico. ♦ lyric *s.* lirica.

lyricism, lyrism *s.* lirismo.

lyrist *s.* poeta lirico.

M

macabre *agg.* macabro.

macaroni *s.* maccheroni.

macaroon *s.* amaretto.

mace *s.* mazza || — -bearer, mazziere.

to macerate *vt.* macerare. ♦ to

macerate *vi.* macerarsi.

maceration *s.* macerazione.

Machiavellian *agg.* machiavellico.

Machiavellism *s.* machiavellismo.

to machinate *vt.* macchinare.

machination *s.* macchinazione.

machine *s.* macchina || sewing- —, macchina da cucire.

to machine *vt. e vi.* lavorare a macchina.

machine-gun *s.* mitragliatrice.

to machine-gun *vt.* mitragliare.

machine-gunner *s.* mitragliere.

machinery *s.* 1. macchinario 2. meccanismo.

machining *s.* lavorazione (*a macchina*).

machinist *s.* macchinista.

mackerel *s.* sgombro || — sky, cielo a pecorelle.

mackintosh *s.* impermeabile.

macrocephalic *agg.* macrocefalo.

macrocosm *s.* macrocosmo.

macrocosmic *agg.* macrocosmico.

macromolecule *s.* macromolecola.

macroscopic *agg.* macroscopico.

to maculate *vt.* maculare.

maculation *s.* maculamento.

mad *agg.* 1. pazzo 2. idrofobo || to go —, impazzire.

madam *s.* signora.

madcap *s.* scervellato.

to madden *vt.* far impazzire. ♦ to madden *vi.* diventare matto.

madding *agg.* folle.

made V. to make.

madhouse *s.* manicomio.

madly *avv.* pazzamente.

madman *s.* pazzo.

madness *s.* 1. pazzia 2. idrofobia.

madrepore *s.* madrepora.

madrigal *s.* madrigale.

Maecenas *s.* mecenate.

magazine *s.* 1. magazzino 2. rivista 3. arsenale.

maggot *s.* 1. bruco 2. (*fig.*) capriccio.

maggoty *agg.* 1. bacato 2. (*fig.*) capriccioso.

magic *s.* magia.

magic(al) *agg.* magico.

magician *s.* mago.

magisterial *agg.* 1. di magistrato 2. autoritario.

magistracy *s.* magistratura.

magistrate *s.* magistrato.

magistrature *s.* magistratura.

magnanimity *s.* magnanimità.

magnanimous *agg.* magnanimo.

magnesium *s.* magnesio.
magnet *s.* magnete, calamita.
magnetic(al) *agg.* magnetico.
magnetism *s.* magnetismo.
magnetization *s.* **1.** magnetizzazione **2.** forza d'attrazione.
to **magnetize** *vt.* magnetizzare.
magnetizer *s.* magnetizzatore.
magneto *s.* magnete.
magnetometer *s.* magnetometro.
magnification *s.* **1.** esaltazione **2.** ingrandimento.
magnificence *s.* magnificenza.
magnificent *agg.* magnifico.
magnifier *s.* **1.** esaltatore **2.** lente d'ingrandimento.
to **magnify** *vt.* **1.** esaltare **2.** ingrandire.
magniloquence *s.* magniloquenza.
magniloquent *agg.* magniloquente.
magnitude *s.* grandezza.
magpie *s.* gazza.
Magyar *agg.* e *s.* magiaro.
mahogany *s.* mogano.
maid *s.* **1.** fanciulla **2.** cameriera || *old* —, zitella.
maiden[1] *agg.* **1.** vergine, puro **2.** esordiente.
maiden[2] *s.* fanciulla || — *name*, nome da ragazza.
maidenhead, maidenhood *s.* verginità.
maidenliness *s.* modestia, verecondia.
maidenly *agg.* verginale.
maidservant *s.* cameriera.
maieutics *s.* maieutica.
maigre *agg.* magro.
mail *s.* posta || — *-train*, treno postale.
to **mail** *vt.* mandare per posta.
to **maim** *vt.* storpiare.
main[1] *agg.* **1.** principale **2.** vigoroso || — *road*, strada maestra.
main[2] *s.* **1.** alto mare **2.** l'essenziale **3.** condotto principale.
mainland *s.* terraferma.
mainly *avv.* principalmente.
mainmast *s.* (*mar.*) albero maestro.
mainsail *s.* vela maestra.
mainspring *s.* molla principale.
to **maintain** *vt.* **1.** mantenere **2.** asserire.
maintenance *s.* **1.** mantenimento **2.** manutenzione **3.** difesa.
maize *s.* granturco.
majestic(al) *agg.* maestoso.
majesty *s.* maestà.
major *agg.* maggiore, principale. ♦

major *s.* **1.** maggiorenne **2.** (*mil.*) maggiore.
majority *s.* **1.** maggioranza **2.** maggiore età.
make *s.* **1.** fattura **2.** costituzione **3.** marca.
to **make (made, made)** *vt.* e *vi.* **1.** fare **2.** rendere **3.** fabbricare || *to* — *for*, dirigersi; *to* — *up*, preparare, truccare; *to* — *up for*, compensare per || *to* — *oneself understood*, farsi capire; *to* — *so. confess*, obbligare qu. a confessare; *to* — *so. do what one likes*, far fare a qu. ciò che si vuole.
make-believe *s.* finzione.
maker *s.* **1.** creatore **2.** costruttore || — *-up*, truccatore.
makeshift *s.* espediente.
make-up *s.* **1.** composizione **2.** trucco **3.** (*tip.*) impaginazione.
making *s.* **1.** fattura **2.** formazione. ♦ **makings** *s. pl.* il necessario (*sing.*).
maladjusted *agg.* **1.** disadatto **2.** disadattato.
maladjustment *s.* inadattabilità.
maladministration *s.* cattiva amministrazione.
maladroit *agg.* maldestro.
malady *s.* malattia.
malaise *s.* malessere.
Malayan *agg.* e *s.* malese.
malcontent *agg.* e *s.* malcontento.
male *agg.* maschio, maschile. ♦ **male** *s.* maschio.
malediction *s.* maledizione.
malefactor *s.* malfattore.
malefic *agg.* malefico.
maleficence *s.* malvagità.
maleficent *agg.* malefico.
malevolence *s.* malevolenza.
malevolent *agg.* malevolo.
malformation *s.* malformazione.
malformed *agg.* malformato.
malice *s.* **1.** malignità **2.** astio: *to bear* — *to so.*, nutrire rancore verso qu.
malicious *agg.* **1.** maligno **2.** premeditato.
malign *agg.* maligno.
malignancy *s.* malignità.
malignant *agg.* maligno.
malignity *s.* V. *malignancy*.
malleability *s.* malleabilità.
malleable *agg.* malleabile.
mallet *s.* mazzuolo.
mallow *s.* malva.
malnutrition *s.* malnutrizione.

malpractice s. pratica illecita.

malt s. malto.

Malthusian agg. e s. maltusiano.

Malthusianism s. maltusianesimo.

maltose s. maltosio.

to **maltreat** vt. maltrattare.

maltreatment s. maltrattamento.

malversation s. malversazione.

mama s. mamma.

mamma[1] s. mamma.

mamma[2] s. mammella.

mammal s. mammifero.

mammalian agg. e s. mammifero.

mammiferous agg. mammifero.

mammoth agg. enorme. ♦ **mam-moth** s. mammut.

mammy s. mammina.

man s. (pl. men) 1. uomo 2. marito || — -bour, ora lavorativa; — -of--war, nave da guerra.

to **man** vt. munire, equipaggiare (di uomini).

manacle s. manetta.

to **manacle** vt. ammanettare.

to **manage** vt. 1. dirigere 2. ma-neggiare 3. riuscire. ♦ to **manage** vi. destreggiarsi, cavarsela.

manageable agg. 1. maneggevole 2. fattibile.

management s. 1. direzione, am-ministrazione 2. abilità.

manager s. 1. direttore 2. ammini-stratore 3. impresario 4. organiz-zatore.

manageress s. 1. direttrice 2. am-ministratrice.

managerial agg. direttivo.

managership s. 1. direzione 2. am-ministrazione.

managing agg. dirigente || — di-rector, consigliere delegato.

mandarin s. mandarino.

mandatary s. mandatario.

mandate s. mandato.

mandator s. mandante.

mandatory agg. e s. mandatario.

mandible s. mandibola.

mandolin s. mandolino.

mandrake s. mandragora.

mandrel s. anima metallica.

mandrill s. mandrillo.

mane s. criniera.

manful agg. valoroso.

manganate s. manganato.

mange s. rogna.

manger s. mangiatoia.

to **mangle** vt. 1. lacerare 2. stor-piare.

mangy agg. 1. lacero 2. rognoso 3. spregevole.

to **manhandle** vt. manovrare (a mano).

manhole s. botola.

manhood s. 1. virilità 2. vigore 3. genere umano.

maniac agg. e s. maniaco, pazzo.

Manich(a)eism s. manicheismo.

manicurist s. manicure.

manifest agg. manifesto.

to **manifest** vt. manifestare.

manifestant s. manifestante.

manifestation s. manifestazione.

manifold agg. molteplice.

manifoldness s. molteplicità.

manikin s. 1. omiciattolo 2. mani-chino.

maniple s. manipolo.

to **manipulate** vt. manipolare.

manipulation s. manipolazione.

manipulator s. manipolatore.

mankind s. umanità.

manlike agg. 1. civile 2. antropo-morfo.

manliness s. virilità.

manly agg. maschio, virile.

manner s. 1. maniera 2. contegno ♦ **manners** s. pl. 1. modi 2. usanze.

mannered agg. manierato || ill- —, maleducato.

mannerism s. manierismo.

mannerly agg. cortese.

manoeuvrable agg. manovrabile.

manoeuvre s. manovra.

to **manoeuvre** vt. manovrare. ♦ to **manoeuvre** vi. fare le manovre.

manoeuvrer s. stratega.

manometer s. manometro.

manor s. feudo || — -house, ca-stello.

manorial agg. feudale.

mansard s. mansarda.

manservant s. domestico.

mansion s. palazzo.

manslaughter s. omicidio preter-intenzionale.

mantelpiece, mantelshelf s. men-sola di caminetto.

mantle s. manto, mantello.

to **mantle** vt. ammantare. ♦ to **mantle** vi. coprirsi.

manual agg. e s. manuale.

manufactory s. fabbrica.

manufacturable agg. fabbricabile.

manufacture s. 1. manifattura 2. manufatto.

to **manufacture** vt. fabbricare.

manufacturer s. fabbricante.

manufacturing *agg.* manifatturiero. ♦ **manufacturing** *s.* fabbricazione.

manure *s.* concime.

manuscript *agg. e s.* manoscritto.

many (more, most) *agg. e pron.* molti ‖ — *a*, più di uno; —*-sided*, molteplice; *so* —, tanti; *too* —, troppi; *as* — *as*, tanti... quanti; *how* —?, quanti?

map *s.* carta geografica.

maple *s.* acero.

to mar *vt.* guastare.

marathon *s.* maratona.

to maraud *vt. e vi.* saccheggiare.

marauder *s.* predatore.

marble *s.* **1.** marmo **2.** biglia.

to marble *vt.* marmorizzare.

marble-cutter *s.* marmista.

March *s.* marzo.

march¹ *s.* confine.

march² *s.* marcia.

to march *vi.* **1.** camminare **2.** marciare ‖ *to* — *in*, entrare marciando.

marching *agg.* in, di marcia.

marchioness *s.* marchesa.

mare *s.* cavalla.

margarine *s.* margarina.

margin *s.* margine.

marginal *agg.* marginale.

marine *agg.* marino, marittimo. ♦ **marine** *s.* **1.** marina **2.** fante di marina.

marital *agg.* maritale.

maritime *agg.* marittimo.

mark *s.* **1.** segno **2.** bersaglio **3.** voto **4.** marchio **5.** importanza **6.** marco ‖ *question* —, punto interrogativo.

to mark *vt.* **1.** segnare **2.** dare i voti a **3.** scegliere **4.** osservare.

marked *agg.* notevole.

marker *s.* **1.** chi segna **2.** segnalibro.

market *s.* mercato.

to market *vt.* **1.** vendere al mercato **2.** introdurre sul mercato. ♦ **market** *vi.* comprare, vendere sul mercato.

marketing *s.* **1.** compra-vendita **2.** « marketing » (*ricerche di mercato*).

marking *s.* segno.

marksman *s.* tiratore scelto.

marl *s.* marna.

marmalade *s.* marmellata (*d'arance*).

marmoreal *agg.* marmoreo.

marmot *s.* marmotta.

to maroon *vt.* abbandonare un luogo deserto.

marquee *s.* tendone.

marquess, marquis *s.* marchese.

marquise *s.* marchesa.

marriage *s.* matrimonio, unione.

married *agg.* **1.** sposato **2.** coniugale.

marrow *s.* midollo ‖ (*vegetable*) —, zucca.

to marry *vt.* sposare. ♦ **to marry** *vi.* sposarsi.

marsh *s.* palude ‖ — *-fever*, malaria; — *gas*, metano.

marshal *s.* maresciallo.

to marshal *vt.* **1.** schierare **2.** introdurre.

marshy *agg.* paludoso.

marsupial *agg. e s.* marsupiale.

marten *s.* martora.

martial *agg.* **1.** marziale **2.** di Marte.

Martian *agg. e s.* marziano.

martyr *s.* martire.

martyrdom *s.* martirio.

to martyrize *vt.* martirizzare.

martyrology *s.* martirologio.

marvel *s.* meraviglia.

to marvel *vi.* meravigliarsi.

marvellous *agg.* meraviglioso.

Marxism *s.* marxismo.

Marxist *agg. e s.* marxista.

marzipan *s.* marzapane.

mascot(te) *s.* mascotte.

masculine *agg. e s.* maschile.

masculinity *s.* mascolinità.

mash *s.* **1.** mistura **2.** purè.

to mash *vt.* **1.** mescolare **2.** schiacciare.

mask *s.* maschera.

to mask *vt.* mascherare.

masking *s.* il mascherarsi.

masochism *s.* masochismo.

mason *s.* muratore ‖ *Free Mason*, massone.

masonry *s.* **1.** arte del muratore **2.** costruzione in muratura **3.** massoneria.

masquerade *s.* mascherata.

to masquerade *vi.* **1.** mascherarsi **2.** fingersi.

mass¹ *s.* messa.

mass² *s.* massa, ammasso.

to mass *vt.* ammassare. ♦ **to mass** *vi.* ammassarsi.

massacre *s.* massacro.

to massacre *vt.* massacrare.

massage *s.* massaggio.

to massage *vt.* massaggiare.

masseur s. massaggiatore.

masseuse s. massaggiatrice.

massif s. massiccio.

massive agg. 1. massiccio 2. potente.

massiveness s. compattezza.

to **mass-produce** vt. produrre in serie.

mass-producer s. produttore in serie.

mass-production s. produzione in serie.

massy agg. massiccio.

mast s. (mar.) albero.

to **mast** vt. (mar.) alberare.

master s. 1. padrone 2. maestro || — builder, capomastro; Master of Arts, laureato in lettere.

to **master** vt. 1. conoscere a fondo 2. dominare.

masterful agg. 1. autoritario 2. abile.

masterhood s. padronanza.

masterly agg. magistrale.

masterpiece s. capolavoro.

mastership s. 1. autorità 2. abilità.

masterstroke s. colpo magistrale.

mastery s. 1. maestria 2. signoria.

mastication s. masticazione.

mastiff s. mastino.

mastitis s. mastite.

mastodon s. mastodonte.

mastoid s. mastoide.

mastoiditis s. mastoidite.

masturbation s. masturbazione.

mat s. stuoia || door- —, zerbino.

to **mat** vt. 1. intrecciare 2. coprire con stuoie 3. smerigliare.

match[1] s. 1. gara, incontro 2. avversario 3. l'uguale 4. matrimonio.

match[2] s. fiammifero.

to **match** vt. 1. accoppiare, maritare 2. uguagliare. ♦ to **match** vi. 1. accoppiarsi 2. accordarsi 3. rivaleggiare.

matchless agg. impareggiabile.

mate s. 1. compagno 2. aiuto 3. (mar.) ufficiale in seconda.

to **mate** vt. accoppiare. ♦ to **mate** vi. accoppiarsi.

material agg. 1. materiale 2. essenziale. ♦ **material** s. 1. materia, materiale 2. stoffa. ♦ **materials** s. pl. articoli || raw —, materie prime.

materialism s. materialismo.

materialist agg. e s. materialista.

materialistic agg. materialistico.

materialization s. materializzazione.

to **materialize** vt. materializzare. ♦ to **materialize** vi. 1. materializzarsi 2. avverarsi.

maternal agg. materno.

maternity s. maternità.

mathematic(al) agg. matematico.

mathematician s. matematico.

mathematics s. matematica.

matriarchy s. matriarcato.

matricidal agg. matricida.

matricide s. 1. matricida 2. matricidio.

to **matriculate** vt. immatricolare. ♦ to **matriculate** vi. immatricolarsi.

matriculation s. immatricolazione.

matrimonial agg. matrimoniale.

matrimony s. matrimonio.

matrix s. 1. matrice 2. (anat.) utero.

matron s. 1. matrona 2. direttrice 3. governante.

matronal, matronly agg. matronale.

matter s. 1. materia 2. faccenda || what is the — with you?, che cosa vi succede?; what is the —?, che succede?

to **matter** vi. 1. importare: it matters little, poco importa 2. (med.) suppurare.

matter-of-fact agg. pratico.

matting s. stuoia.

mattock s. piccone.

mattress s. materasso.

to **maturate** vi. 1. maturare 2. suppurare.

maturation s. 1. maturazione 2. suppurazione.

mature agg. maturo.

to **mature** vt. e vi. maturare.

maturity s. 1. maturità 2. (comm.) scadenza.

matutine agg. mattutino.

maudlin agg. 1. sdolcinato 2. querulo.

to **maunder** vi. 1. parlare a vanvera 2. girovagare.

mausoleum s. mausoleo.

mawkish agg. 1. nauseante 2. sdolcinato.

mawkishness s. 1. sapore nauseante 2. sdolcinatezza.

maxim s. massima.

maximalist s. massimalista.

maximum s. e agg. massimo.

May s. maggio || — Day, primo maggio.

may (might) v. dif. potere (*pres. ind. e congiuntivo*) || — I go out?, posso uscire?; he — arrive to day, può darsi che arrivi oggi; — be live to repent it, possa egli vivere tanto da pentirsene

maybe avv. forse.

maybug s. maggiolino.

mayflower s. biancospino.

mayonnaise s. maionese.

mayor s. sindaco.

maze s. labirinto.

to **maze** vt. disorientare, confondere.

mazily avv. confusamente.

mazy agg. intricato.

me pron. pers. me, mi.

meadow s. prato.

meagre agg. **1.** magro **2.** scarso.

meal[1] s. farina.

meal[2] s. pasto.

mealy agg. **1.** farinoso **2.** infarinato **3.** pallido **4.** chiazzato.

mean[1] agg. **1.** meschino **2.** mediocre.

mean[2] s. punto medio, mezzo. ♦ **means** s. pl. mezzi || by no means, ben lungi da.

to **mean (meant, meant)** vt. e vi. **1.** intendere, significare **2.** destinare.

meander s. meandro.

to **meander** vi. serpeggiare.

meaning agg. **1.** disposto **2.** significativo. ♦ **meaning** s. **1.** significato **2.** idea.

meaningful agg. significativo.

meaningless agg. senza senso.

meanly avv. **1.** meschinamente **2.** umilmente.

meanness s. meschinità.

meant V. to mean.

meantime s. frattempo. ♦ **meantime** avv. frattanto.

meanwhile avv. frattanto.

measles s. morbillo || German —, rosolia.

measurable agg. misurabile.

measure s. **1.** misura **2.** ritmo.

to **measure** vt. e vi. misurare.

measureless agg. smisurato.

measurement s. misurazione.

measurer s. misuratore.

meat s. carne.

meaty agg. **1.** polposo **2.** sostanzioso.

mechanic s. meccanico.

mechanical agg. meccanico.

mechanics s. meccanica.

mechanism s. **1.** meccanismo **2.**

tecnica.

mechanization s. meccanizzazione.

to **mechanize** vt. meccanizzare.

medal s. medaglia.

to **meddle** vi. immischiarsi.

meddler s. intrigante.

meddlesome agg. importuno.

medi(a)eval agg. medievale.

medi(a)evalism s. medievalismo.

medi(a)evalist s. medievalista.

medial agg. medio.

median agg. mediano.

mediate agg. mediato.

to **mediate** vt. conseguire con mediazione. ♦ to **mediate** vi. fare da intermediario.

mediation s. mediazione.

mediator s. mediatore.

medical agg. medico.

medicament s. medicamento.

medication s. medicazione.

medicative agg. curativo.

medicinal agg. medicinale.

medicine s. medicina || — -man, stregone.

mediocrity s. mediocrità.

to **meditate** vt. e vi. meditare.

meditation s. meditazione.

meditative agg. meditativo.

Mediterranean agg. mediterraneo.

medium agg. medio. ♦ **medium** s. mezzo.

mediumistic agg. medianico.

medlar s. nespola || — -tree, nespolo.

medley agg. misto. ♦ **medley** s. miscuglio.

medulla s. midollo.

medullar(y) agg. midollare.

meek agg. mite.

meekness s. mansuetudine.

to **meet (met, met)** vt. **1.** incontrare **2.** far fronte a. ♦ to **meet (met, met)** vi. incontrarsi || to — with, imbattersi in.

meeting s. **1.** incontro **2.** riunione || political —, comizio.

megalomaniac s. megalomane.

megaphone s. megafono.

melancholic agg. malinconico.

melancholy agg. malinconico. ♦ **melancholy** s. malinconia.

mellifluous agg. mellifluo.

mellow agg. **1.** maturo **2.** pastoso **3.** ubertoso.

to **mellow** vt. e vi. maturare.

mellowness s. **1.** maturità **2.** pastosità **3.** ubertosità.

melodic agg. melodico.

melodious *agg.* melodioso.
melodiousness *s.* melodiosità.
melodrama *s.* melodramma.
melodramatic *agg.* melodrammatico.
melody *s.* melodia.
melomaniac *s.* melomane.
melon *s.* melone || *water— —*, anguria.
melt *s.* fusione.
to melt *vt.* 1. sciogliere 2. intenerire. ♦ **to melt** *vi.* 1. sciogliersi 2. intenerirsi || *to — away*, svanire.
melter *s.* fonditore.
melting *s.* fusione || *— -pot*, crogiuolo.
meltingly *avv.* teneramente.
member *s.* membro.
membership *s.* 1. qualifica di membro 2. i membri.
membrane *s.* membrana.
memoirs *s. pl.* memorie.
memorable *agg.* memorabile.
memorandum *s.* (*pl.* -da) promemoria.
memorial *agg.* commemorativo. ♦ **memorial** *s.* 1. monumento 2. memoriale.
memorialist *s.* memorialista.
to memorize *vt.* imparare a memoria.
memory *s.* memoria.
men V. *man*.
menace *s.* minaccia.
to menace *vt.* e *vi.* minacciare.
menacing *agg.* minaccioso.
menagerie *s.* serraglio.
mend *s.* rattoppo.
to mend *vt.* 1. riparare 2. correggere. ♦ **to mend** *vi.* 1. correggersi 2. migliorare.
mendacious *agg.* mendace.
mendacity *s.* 1. abitudine di mentire 2. bugia.
mender *s.* 1. riparatore 2. rammendatrice.
mendicant *agg.* e *s.* mendicante.
mendicity *s.* mendicità.
mending *s.* 1. riparazione 2. rammendo.
menial *agg.* servile. ♦ **menial** *s.* servo.
meninx *s.* (*pl.* meninges) meninge.
meniscus *s.* menisco.
menopause *s.* menopausa.
menses *s. pl.* mestruazioni.
menstruation *s.* mestruazione.
mental *agg.* mentale || *— -hospi-*

tal, manicomio.
mentality *s.* 1. mentalità 2. intelligenza.
menthol *s.* mentolo.
mention *s.* menzione || *don't — it*, non c'è di che (risposta a « grazie »).
to mention *vt.* nominare.
mentionable *agg.* menzionabile.
mentor *s.* mentore.
mephitic *agg.* mefitico.
mercantile *agg.* mercantile.
mercantilism *s.* mercantilismo.
mercenary *agg.* e *s.* mercenario.
merchandise *s.* merce.
to merchandise *vt.* e *vi.* commerciare.
merchant *s.* mercante || *— -ship*, nave mercantile.
merciful *agg.* pietoso.
merciless *agg.* spietato.
mercury *s.* mercurio.
mercy *s.* pietà, misericordia.
mere[1] *agg.* 1. mero 2. solo.
mere[2] *s.* confine.
mere[3] *s.* laghetto, stagno.
to merge *vt.* assorbire. ♦ **to merge** *vi.* 1. essere assortito 2. immergersi.
merger *s.* (*comm.*) fusione (*di società*).
meridian *agg.* 1. meridiano 2. culminante. ♦ **meridian** *s.* 1. meridiano 2. culmine.
meridional *agg.* e *s.* meridionale.
merit *s.* merito.
to merit *vt.* meritare.
meritorious *agg.* meritorio.
mermaid *s.* sirena.
merman *s.* tritone.
merrily *avv.* allegramente.
merry *agg.* gaio.
merry-go-round *s.* giostra.
merrymaking *s.* festa.
mesh *s.* maglia. ♦ **meshes** *s. pl.* reti.
mesocarp *s.* mesocarpo.
mesozoic *agg.* e *s.* mesozoico.
mess *s.* 1. mensa 2. confusione 3. pasticcio.
to mess *vt.* mettere in disordine || *to — up*, mettere a soqquadro.
message *s.* 1. messaggio 2. commissione.
messenger *s.* messaggero || *— -boy*, fattorino.
Messiah *s.* Messia.
Messianic *agg.* messianico.
mestizo *s.* meticcio.

met V. *to meet.*
metabolism *s.* metabolismo.
metal *s.* 1. metallo 2. pietrisco.
metallic *agg.* metallico.
metallization *s.* metallizzazione.
to **metallize** *vt.* metallizzare.
metalloid *s.* metalloide.
metallurgic(al) *agg.* metallurgico.
metallurgist *s.* metallurgico.
metallurgy *s.* metallurgia.
metamorphic *agg.* metamorfico.
metamorphism *s.* metamorfismo.
metamorphosis *s.* (*pl.* -ses) metamorfosi.
metaphor *s.* metafora.
metaphoric(al) *agg.* metaforico.
metaphysic(al) *agg.* metafisico.
metaphysics *s.* metafisica.
metapsychic(al) *agg.* metapsichico.
metapsychics *s.* metapsichica.
metastasis *s.* (*pl.* -ses) metastasi.
metayage *s.* mezzadria.
metayer *s.* mezzadro.
mete *s.* segno di confine ‖ *metes and bounds* (*giur.*), limiti e confini.
metempsychosis *s.* metempsicosi.
meteor *s.* meteora.
meteoric *agg.* 1. meteorico 2. transitorio.
meteoroid *s.* meteorite.
meteorologic(al) *agg.* meteorologico.
meteorologist *s.* meteorologo.
meteorology *s.* meteorologia.
meter *s.* 1. contatore 2. tassametro.
methane *s.* metano.
method *s.* metodo.
methodic(al) *agg.* metodico.
methodist *s.* metodista.
methodological *agg.* metodologico.
methodology *s.* metodologia.
meticulosity *s.* meticolosità.
meticulous *agg.* meticoloso.
metre *s.* 1. metro 2. (*mus.*) tempo.
metrical *agg.* metrico.
metrics *s.* metrica.
metronome *s.* metronomo.
metropolis *s.* metropoli.
metropolitan *agg.* metropolitano.
♦ **metropolitan** *s.* abitante di una metropoli.
mettle *s.* tempra.
mettled, mettlesome *agg.* focoso.
mew[1] *s.* gabbiano.
mew[2] *s.* miagolio.
to **mew**[1] *vt.* rinchiudere in gabbia.
to **mew**[2] *vi.* miagolare.
to **mewl** *vi.* vagire.

Mexican *agg.* e *s.* messicano.
mezzanine *s.* mezzanino.
miaul *s.* miagolio.
mice V. *mouse.*
microbe *s.* microbo.
microbial *agg.* microbico.
microbiology *s.* microbiologia.
microcosm *s.* microcosmo.
micrometer *s.* micrometro.
micrometry *s.* micrometria.
micro-organism *s.* microorganismo.
microphone *s.* microfono.
microphotography *s.* microfotografia.
microscope *s.* microscopio.
microscopic(al) *agg.* microscopico.
microscopy *s.* microscopia.
mid *agg.* medio, mezzo.
midday *s.* mezzogiorno.
middle *agg.* medio ‖ *Middle Ages*, medioevo; — -*aged*, di mezza età.
♦ **middle** *s.* 1. mezzo 2. cintola.
middle class *s.* borghesia.
middleman *s.* intermediario.
middling *agg.* medio.
midge *s.* moscerino.
midget *s.* nano.
midland *agg.* centrale. ♦ **midlands** *s. pl.* regione centrale (*sing.*).
midnight *s.* mezzanotte.
midriff *s.* 1. diaframma 2. costume da bagno a due pezzi.
midshipman *s.* guardiamarina.
midst *s.* mezzo.
midsummer *s.* solstizio d'estate.
midway *agg.* e *avv.* a mezza strada.
mid-week *agg.* di metà settimana.
midwife *s.* (*pl.* -wives) levatrice.
midwinter *s.* solstizio d'inverno.
mien *s.* portamento.
might *s.* potenza.
might V. *may.*
mighty *agg.* potente.
migrant *agg.* e *s.* migratore.
to **migrate** *vi.* (e)migrare.
migration *s.* (e)migrazione.
migratory *agg.* migratore.
milady *s.* nobildonna.
mild *agg.* dolce.
mildew *s.* muffa.
mildness *s.* dolcezza.
mile *s.* miglio.
milestone *s.* pietra miliare.
milfoil *s.* millefoglie.
miliary *agg.* migliare.
militant *agg.* militante. ♦ **militant** *s.* attivista.

militarily *avv.* militarmente.

militarism *s.* militarismo.

militarist *s.* militarista.

militarization *s.* militarizzazione.

to **militarize** *vt.* militarizzare.

military *agg.* e *s.* militare.

militiaman *s.* milite.

milk *s.* latte || — -*jug*, lattiera.

to **milk** *vt.* mungere. ♦ to **milk** *vi.* 1. produrre latte 2. mungere.

milker *s.* 1. mungitore 2. mucca da latte.

milking *s.* mungitura.

milkmaid *s.* mungitrice.

milkman *s.* lattaio.

milky *agg.* 1. latteo 2. (*fig.*) gentile || *the Milky Way*, la Via Lattea.

mill *s.* 1. mulino 2. macinino 3. fabbrica || *saw-* —, segheria.

to **mill** *vt.* 1. macinare 2. segare 3. frullare.

millenary *agg.* millenario. ♦ **millenary** *s.* 1. millennio 2. millenario.

millennium *s.* millennio.

millepede *s.* millepiedi.

miller *s.* 1. mugnaio 2. fresatore 3. fresa.

millet *s.* (*bot.*) miglio.

milliard *s.* 1. miliardo 2. (*amer.*) bilione.

milligram(me) *s.* milligrammo.

millimetre *s.* millimetro.

milliner *s.* modista.

millinery *s.* modisteria.

milling *s.* 1. macinatura 2. fresatura.

million *s.* milione.

millionaire *s.* milionario.

millstone *s.* macina.

mime *s.* mimo.

to **mime** *vi.* e *vt.* mimare.

to **mimeograph** *vt.* ciclostilare.

mimetic *agg.* mimetico.

mimic *agg.* imitativo || — *art*, mimica. ♦ **mimic** *s.* imitatore.

to **mimic (mimicked, mimicked)** *vt.* imitare.

mimicry *s.* 1. imitazione 2. mimetismo.

minaret *s.* minareto.

minatory *agg.* minatorio.

mince *s.* carne tritata.

to **mince** *vt.* 1. tritare 2. tagliuzzare 3. mitigare. ♦ to **mince** *vi.* camminare, parlare in modo affettato.

mincer *s.* tritacarne.

mincing *agg.* affettato.

mind *s.* 1. mente 2. opinione.

to **mind** *vt.* 1. badare a 2. spiacere || *never* —!, non importa!; *I do not* —, non mi preoccupo di.

minded *agg.* incline || *broad-* —, di larghe vedute; *narrow-* —, di idee ristrette || *if you are so* —, se la pensate così.

mindful *agg.* memore.

mindless *agg.* 1. disattento 2. stupido.

mine[1] *pron. poss.* il mio, la mia, i miei, le mie || *a friend of* —, un mio amico.

mine[2] *s.* 1. miniera 2. mina || — -*sweeper*, dragamine.

to **mine** *vt.* 1. scavare 2. estrarre 3. minare.

miner *s.* minatore.

mineral *agg.* e *s.* minerale.

to **mineralize** *vt.* mineralizzare.

mineralogy *s.* mineralogia.

to **mingle** *vt.* mescolare. ♦ to **mingle** *vi.* mescolarsi.

miniature *agg.* in miniatura. ♦ **miniature** *s.* miniatura.

to **miniature** *vt.* e *vi.* fare miniature.

miniaturist *s.* miniaturista.

minim *s.* 1. (*mus.*) minima 2. quantità minima 3. inezia.

minimal *agg.* minimo.

to **minimize** *vt.* minimizzare.

minimum *s.* (*pl.* -ma) minimo.

mining *agg.* minerario. ♦ **mining** *s.* 1. scavo 2. estrazione 3. posa di mine.

minion *s.* favorito.

miniskirt *s.* minigonna.

minister *s.* ministro.

to **minister** *vi.* assistere.

ministerial *agg.* ministeriale.

ministry *s.* ministero.

mink *s.* visone.

minor *agg.* minore. ♦ **minor** *s.* minorenne.

minority *s.* 1. minoranza 2. età minore.

minstrel *s.* menestrello.

mint[1] *s.* zecca.

mint[2] *s.* menta.

to **mint** *vt.* coniare.

mintage *s.* conio.

minuend *s.* minuendo.

minuet *s.* minuetto.

minus *s.* e *prep.* meno.

minute *agg.* minuto, minuscolo.

minute[1] *s.* 1. minuto 2. nota || — -*band*, lancetta dei minuti.

minutely¹ *avv.* minutamente.

minutely² *avv.* di minuto in minuto.

minuteness *s.* 1. minutezza 2. minuziosità.

miracle *s.* miracolo.

miraculous *agg.* miracoloso.

mirage *s.* miraggio.

mire *s.* fango.

to mire *vt.* infangare. ◆ to mire *vi.* infangarsi.

mirror *s.* specchio || driving- —, specchietto retrovisore.

to mirror *vt.* rispecchiare.

mirth *s.* allegria.

mirthful *agg.* allegro.

mirthless *agg.* triste.

miry *agg.* fangoso.

misadventure *s.* disavventura.

misanthrope *s.* misantropo.

misanthropy *s.* misantropia.

misapplication *s.* applicazione erronea.

to misapply *vt.* applicare erroneamente.

misapprehension *s.* malinteso.

misbehaviour *s.* cattivo contegno.

misbelief *s.* falsa credenza.

to misbelieve *vi.* avere una falsa credenza.

misbeliever *s.* miscredente.

misbelieving *agg.* eretico.

to miscalculate *vt.* e *vi.* calcolare male.

miscarriage *s.* 1. disguido 2. fallimento 3. aborto.

to miscarry *vi.* 1. smarrirsi 2. fallire 3. abortire.

miscellaneous *agg.* miscellaneo.

miscellany *s.* miscellanea.

mischance *s.* sfortuna.

mischief *s.* 1. danno, male 2. malizia 3. birichinata.

mischievous *agg.* 1. nocivo 2. malizioso.

misconduct *s.* cattiva condotta.

miscount *s.* conteggio errato.

misdeed *s.* misfatto.

misdemeanour *s.* misfatto.

to misdirect *vt.* mandare in direzione sbagliata.

misdirection *s.* indicazione sbagliata.

misdoing *s.* misfatto.

miser *s.* avaro.

miserable *agg.* 1. triste 2. miserabile.

miserliness *s.* avarizia.

miserly *agg.* avaro.

misery *s.* 1. miseria 2. sofferenza.

misfire *s.* cilecca.

misfit *s.* 1. cosa che si adatta male 2. (*fig.*) pesce fuor d'acqua.

misfortune *s.* sventura.

to misgive (misgave, misgiven) *vt.* preoccupare. ◆ to misgive (misgave, misgiven) *vi.* preoccuparsi.

misgiving *s.* 1. presentimento 2. timore.

to misgovern *vt.* governare male.

misgovernment *s.* malgoverno.

to misguide *vt.* 1. guidare male 2. traviare.

to mishandle *vt.* maltrattare.

mishap *s.* infortunio.

to misinform *vt.* informare male.

misinformation *s.* informazione sbagliata.

to misinterpret *vt.* interpretare male.

misinterpretation *s.* interpretazione errata.

to misjudge *vt.* giudicare male.

misjudgement *s.* giudizio erroneo.

to mislay (mislaid, mislaid) *vt.* smarrire.

to mislead (misled, misled) *vt.* 1. traviare 2. ingannare.

misogamy *s.* misogamia.

misogynist *s.* misogino.

misogyny *s.* misoginia.

misoneism *s.* misoneismo.

to misplace *vt.* collocare male, fuori posto.

misplacement *s.* spostamento.

misprint *s.* errore di stampa, refuso.

to misprint *vt.* stampare con errori.

to mispronounce *vt.* pronunciare male.

mispronunciation *s.* pronuncia scorretta.

misquotation *s.* citazione erronea.

to misquote *vt.* citare erroneamente.

to misread (misread, misread) *vt.* leggere erroneamente.

mesreading *s.* falsa interpretazione.

to misrepresent *vt.* travisare.

misrepresentation *s.* travisamento.

miss¹ *s.* 1. colpo mancato 2. difetto.

miss² *s.* signorina: *Miss Jane Smith*, la signorina Jane Smith.

to miss *vt.* 1. mancare (*il colpo*) 2. perdere 3. notare, sentire la mancanza di **4.** evitare.

missal s. messale.

missile s. missile.

missing agg. mancante || the —, i dispersi.

mission s. missione.

missionary agg. e s. missionario.

missioner s. missionario.

to **misspell** vt. sbagliare l'ortografia.

mist s. **1.** bruma **2.** pioggerella **3.** appannamento.

to **mist** vt. appannare. ◆ to **mist** vi. appannarsi.

mistakable agg. suscettibile d'errore.

mistake s. errore.

to **mistake** (**mistook, mistaken**) vt. **1.** sbagliare **2.** scambiare **3.** non capire.

mistaken agg. **1.** in errore **2.** erroneo.

mister s. signore: Mr. Brown, il signor Brown.

mistletoe s. vischio.

mistook V. to mistake.

mistral s. maestrale.

mistranslation s. traduzione errata.

mistress s. **1.** signora: Mrs. Brown, la signora Brown **2.** insegnante **3.** amante.

mistrust s. diffidenza.

to **mistrust** vt. e vi. diffidare di, sospettare.

mistrustful agg. diffidente.

misty agg. **1.** nebbioso **2.** confuso.

to **misunderstand** (**misunderstood, misunderstood**) vt. e vi. fraintendere.

misunderstanding s. **1.** malinteso **2.** disaccordo.

misunderstood V. to misunderstand.

misusage, misuse s. **1.** cattivo uso **2.** maltrattamento.

to **misuse** vt. **1.** usar male **2.** maltrattare.

to **miswrite** (**miswrote, miswritten**) vt. scrivere scorrettamente.

mithridatic agg. immunizzante (contro veleni).

mithridatism s. immunizzazione (contro un veleno).

to **mitigate** vt. mitigare.

mitigation s. mitigazione.

mitral agg. mitrale.

mitre s. **1.** (eccl.) mitra **2.** giunto ad angolo.

mitt(en) s. manopola, guantone.

to **mix** vt. mescolare || to — up, confondere. ◆ to **mix** vi. mescolarsi.

mixed agg. misto, eterogeneo.

mixer s. (mecc.) mescolatore.

mixing s. mescolanza.

mixture s. **1.** mescolanza **2.** miscela.

mizzen s. (mar.) mezzana.

mnemonic agg. mnemonico.

mnemonics s. mnemonica.

moan s. gemito.

to **moan** vt. e vi. gemere.

moanful agg. lamentoso.

moaning s. lamento.

moat s. fossato.

mob s. **1.** folla **2.** plebaglia.

to **mob** vt. **1.** assalire **2.** affollare.

mobile agg. **1.** mobile **2.** mutevole.

mobility s. **1.** mobilità **2.** mutevolezza.

mobilization s. mobilitazione.

to **mobilize** vt. mobilitare.

moccasin s. mocassino.

mock agg. **1.** ironico **2.** finto || —-heroic, eroicomico. ◆ **mock** s. **1.** derisione **2.** imitazione.

to **mock** vt. e vi. beffare, prendersi gioco di.

mocker s. burlone.

mockery s. **1.** derisione **2.** contraffazione.

mocking agg. beffardo.

modal agg. modale.

modality s. modalità.

model agg. modello. ◆ **model** s. **1.** modello **2.** copia.

to **model** vt. modellare.

modeller s. **1.** modellatore **2.** modellista.

modelling s. **1.** modellatura **2.** creazione di modelli.

moderate agg. e s. moderato.

to **moderate** vt. moderare. ◆ to **moderate** vi. moderarsi.

moderateness s. moderatezza.

moderation s. moderazione.

moderator s. moderatore.

modern agg. e s. moderno.

modernism s. modernismo.

modernist s. modernista.

modernity s. modernità.

modernization s. **1.** rimodernamento **2.** aggiornamento.

to **modernize** vt. modernizzare. ◆ to **modernize** vi. modernizzarsi.

modest agg. **1.** modesto **2.** pudico.

modesty s. **1.** modestia **2.** pudore.

modifiable agg. modificabile.

modification s. modificazione.

modifier s. modificatore.

to **modify** vt. modificare.

to **modulate** vt. e vi. modulare.

modulation s. modulazione.

modulator s. modulatore.

mofette s. mofeta.

Mohammedan agg. e s. maomettano.

moist agg. umido.

to **moisten** vt. inumidire. ◆ to **moisten** vi. inumidirsi.

moistness s. umidità.

moisture s. vapore umido.

molar agg. e s. molare.

molasses s. melassa.

mole[1] s. neo.

mole[2] s. talpa.

mole[3] s. molo.

molecular agg. molecolare.

molecule s. molecola.

moleskin s. **1.** pelle di talpa **2.** fustagno. ◆ **moleskins** s. pl. calzoni di fustagno.

to **molest** vt. molestare.

molestation s. molestia.

molester s. molestatore.

to **mollify** vt. addolcire.

mollusc s. mollusco.

molybdenum s. molibdeno.

moment s. **1.** momento **2.** importanza.

momentary agg. momentaneo.

momentous agg. importante.

monachal agg. monacale.

monad s. monade.

monarch s. monarca.

monarchic(al) agg. monarchico.

monarchist s. monarchico.

monarchy s. monarchia.

monastery s. monastero.

monastic(al) agg. monastico.

Monday s. lunedì.

monetary agg. monetario.

monetization s. monetazione.

to **monetize** vt. monetizzare.

money s. denaro ‖ — *-bag*, portamonete; — *-order*, vaglia; *earnest* —, caparra; *paper* —, valuta cartacea; *ready* —, contanti.

moneyed agg. **1.** di, in denaro **2.** ricco.

moneyless agg. squattrinato.

monger s. mercante ‖ *fish* —, pescivendolo.

Mongolian agg. e s. mongolo.

mongolism s. mongolismo.

mongoloid agg. e s. mongoloide.

mongrel agg. misto. ◆ **mongrel** s. **1.** bastardo **2.** incrocio.

monism s. monismo.

monition s. **1.** ammonizione **2.** (giur.) citazione.

monitor s. **1.** consigliere **2.** capoclasse **3.** dispositivo di controllo.

monitory agg. ammonitore.

monk s. monaco.

monkey s. scimmia.

monkeyish agg. scimmiesco.

monkhood s. monacato.

monkish agg. monastico, manacale.

monochromatic agg. monocromatico.

monochrome s. monocromia.

monocle s. monocolo.

monody s. monodia.

monogamist s. monogamo.

monogamy s. monogamia.

monogram s. monogramma.

monograph s. monografia.

monographic(al) agg. monografico.

monolith s. monolito.

monolithic agg. monolitico.

monologue s. monologo.

monometallic agg. monometallico.

monomial s. monomio.

monomolecular agg. monomolecolare.

monoplane s. monoplano.

monopolist s. monopolista.

to **monopolize** vt. monopolizzare.

monopoly s. monopolio.

monorail s. monorotaia.

monosyllabic agg. monosillabico.

monosyllable s. monosillabo.

monotheism s. monoteismo.

monotheist s. monoteista.

monotheistic(al) agg. monoteistico.

monotone s. tono uniforme.

monotonous agg. monotono.

monotony s. **1.** tono uniforme **2.** monotonia.

monotype s. monotipo.

monsoon s. monsone.

monster agg. colossale. ◆ **monster** s. mostro.

monstrance s. ostensorio.

monstrosity s. mostruosità.

monstrous agg. mostruoso.

montage s. montaggio.

month s. mese.

monthly agg. e s. mensile. ◆ **monthly** avv. mensilmente.

monument s. monumento.

monumental agg. monumentale.

mood *s.* 1. umore 2. (*gramm.*) modo.
♦ **moods** *s. pl.* capricci.

moodily *avv.* di malumore.

moodiness *s.* malumore.

moody *agg.* di malumore.

moon *s.* luna.

to **moon** *vi.* 1. gingillarsi 2. allunare || *to — about*, bighellonare.

mooncalf *s.* (*pl.* -lves) idiota.

mooning *s.* vagabondaggio.

moonlight *s.* chiaro di luna.

moonlit *agg.* illuminato dalla luna.

moonshine *s.* V. *moonlight*.

moonshiny *agg.* V. *moonlit*.

moony *agg.* 1. lunare 2. distratto.

Moor *s.* moro.

moor¹ *s.* brughiera.

to **moor** *vt. e vi.* ormeggiare.

moorage *s.* ormeggio. ♦ **moorings** *s. pl.* 1. gomena (*sing.*) 2. ormeggi.

mop¹ *s.* 1. scopa 2. zazzera.

mop² *s.* smorfia.

to **mop¹** *vt.* 1. pulire 2. asciugare || *to — up* (*mil.*), rastrellare.

to **mop²** *vi.* fare smorfie.

mope *s.* 1. persona avvilita 2. tristezza.

to **mope** *vt.* avvilire. ♦ to **mope** *vi.* avvilirsi.

mopish *agg.* avvilito.

moraine *s.* morena.

moral *agg.* morale. ♦ **moral** *s.* 1. morale 2. principio morale. ♦ **morals** *s. pl.* costumi.

morale *s.* il morale.

moralism *s.* moralismo.

moralist *s.* moralista.

moralistic *agg.* moralistico.

morality *s.* moralità.

moralization *s.* moralizzazione.

to **moralize** *vt.* moralizzare. ♦ to **moralize** *vi.* trarre la morale.

morass *s.* palude.

moratory *agg.* moratorio.

moratorium *s.* (*pl.* -ria) moratoria.

moray *s.* murena.

morbid *agg.* 1. morboso 2. patologico.

morbidity *s.* 1. morbosità 2. stato patologico.

mordacity, mordancy *s.* mordacità.

mordant *agg. e s.* mordente.

more (*comp.* di *much*, *many*) *agg.*, *pron. e avv.* più, di più, maggiormente || *— and —*, sempre più; *once —*, ancora una volta.

moreover *avv.* inoltre.

morganatic *agg.* morganatico.

morgue *s.* obitorio.

Mormon *agg. e s.* mormone.

morning *s.* mattino.

Moroccan *agg. e s.* marocchino.

moron *s.* deficiente.

morose *agg.* tetro.

morphia, morphine *s.* morfina.

morphinomaniac *agg. e s.* morfinomane.

morphologic(al) *agg.* morfologico.

morphology *s.* morfologia.

morsel *s.* boccone.

mortal *agg. e s.* mortale.

mortality *s.* mortalità.

mortally *avv.* mortalmente.

mortar¹ *s.* mortaio.

mortar² *s.* calcina.

mortgage *s.* ipoteca.

to **mortgage** *vt.* ipotecare.

mortgagee *s.* creditore ipotecario.

mortgager *s.* debitore ipotecario.

mortification *s.* mortificazione.

to **mortify** *vt.* 1. mortificare 2. incancrenire. ♦ to **mortify** *vi.* 1. mortificarsi 2. incancrenirsi.

mortuary *agg.* mortuario. ♦ **mortuary** *s.* camera mortuaria.

mosaic *agg.* musivo. ♦ **mosaic** *s.* mosaico.

Moslem *agg. e s.* mussulmano.

mosque *s.* moschea.

mosquito *s.* zanzara || *—-net*, zanzariera.

moss *s.* 1. acquitrino 2. muschio.

mossy *agg.* muscoso.

most *agg. e pron.* (*superl.* di *much*, *many*) il più, la maggior parte di, il massimo. ♦ **most** *avv.* 1. il più 2. molto 3. maggiormente.

mostly *avv.* per lo più.

mote *s.* particella.

moth *s.* 1. falena 2. tignola.

mother *s.* madre || *-country*, madrepatria; *— in-law*, suocera.

motherhood *s.* maternità.

motherless *agg.* senza madre.

motherly *agg.* materno.

mothproof *agg.* inattaccabile dalle tarme.

motif *s.* motivo.

motion *s.* 1. moto, movimento 2. mozione || *— -picture*, film.

motionless *agg.* immobile.

to **motivate** *vt.* 1. motivare 2. stimolare.

motivation *s.* 1. motivazione 2. stimolo.

motive *agg.* motore. ♦ **motive** *s.*

motivo, movente.

motley agg. 1. screziato 2. eterogeneo. ◆ **motley** s. miscuglio.

motor agg. e s. motore || — *-cycle*, motocicletta; — *-car*, automobile. — *-boat*, motobarca; — *ship*, motonave.

to **motor** vi. andare in automobile.

motoring s. automobilismo.

motorist s. automobilista.

motorization s. motorizzazione.

to **motorize** vt. motorizzare.

mottle s. chiazza.

to **mottle** vt. chiazzare.

moufflon s. muflone.

mould[1] s. stampo.

mould[2] s. muffa.

mould[3] s. terriccio.

to **mould**[1] vt. modellare.

to **mould**[2] vi. ammuffire.

moulding s. 1. il modellare 2. cornice 3. fusione.

mouldy agg. ammuffito.

mound s. monticello.

mount[1] s. monte, montagna.

mount[2] 1. cavalcatura 2. intelaiatura 3. affusto di cannone 4. montatura.

to **mount** vt. salire. ◆ to **mount** vi. 1. montare 2. ammontare.

mountain s. montagna.

mountaineer s. 1. montanaro 2. alpinista.

mountaineering s. alpinismo.

mountainous agg. montuoso.

mountebank s. ciarlatano.

mounter s. montatore.

to **mourn** vt. e vi. piangere.

mourner s. chi è in lutto.

mournful agg. lugubre.

mourning s. 1. dolore 2. lutto: *to go into —*, mettere il lutto.

mouse s. (pl. mice) topo.

moustache s. baffi (pl.).

mouth s. bocca.

to **mouth** vt. declamare. ◆ to **mouth** vi. fare smorfie.

mouthful s. boccone.

mouthpiece s. 1. bocchino 2. portavoce.

movable agg. mobile.

movables s. pl. beni mobili.

move s. 1. movimento 2. mossa 3. trasloco.

to **move** vt. 1. muovere 2. commuovere. ◆ to **move** vi. 1. muoversi.

movement s. 1. movimento, moto. 2. traslocare 3. commuoversi.

mover s. promotore.

movie s. film. ◆ **movies** s. pl. cinema (sing.).

moving s. 1. spostamento 2. trasloco.

mow s. covone.

to **mow** (**mowed**, **mown**) vt. falciare.

mower s. falciatore.

mowing s. falciatura.

mown V. to **mow**.

much (**more**, **most**) agg., s. e avv. molto || *so —*, tanto; *too —*, troppo; *as — as*, tanto quanto; *how —?*, quanto?

muck s. letame.

mucous agg. mucoso.

mucus s. muco.

mud s. fango || — *-guard*, parafango.

to **mud** vt. infangare.

muddle s. confusione, pasticcio.

to **muddle** vt. confondere.

muddleheaded agg. confusionario.

muddler s. confusionario.

muddy agg. 1. fangoso 2. torbido 3. infangato.

to **muddy** vt. infangare.

muff[1] s. manicotto.

muff[2] s. 1. colpo mancato 2. babbeo.

to **muffle** vt. 1. avvolgere 2. smorzare.

muffler s. 1. sciarpa 2. guantone 3. silenziatore.

mug s. (fam.) faccia || — *shot* (tv), primo piano.

mulberry s. mora || — *(-tree)* gelso.

mule s. mulo.

mulish agg. (fig.) testardo.

muller s. pestello.

multiform agg. multiforme.

multimillionaire s. multimilionario.

multiple agg. e s. multiplo.

multiplicable agg. moltiplicabile.

multiplicand s. moltiplicando.

multiplication s. moltiplicazione.

multiplicity s. molteplicità.

multiplier s. moltiplicatore.

to **multiply** vt. moltiplicare. ◆ to **multiply** vi. moltiplicarsi.

multitude s. moltitudine.

multitudinous agg. 1. innumerevole 2. vasto.

mumble s. borbottio.

to **mumble** vt. e vi. borbottare.

mumbling s. V. *mumble*.

mummer s. guitto.

mummification s. mummificazione.
to **mummify** vt. mummificare.
mummy[1] s. mummia.
mummy[2] s. mammina.
mumps s. pl. orecchioni.
to **munch** vt. e vi. biascicare.
municipal agg. municipale.
municipality s. municipalità.
municipalization s. municipalizzazione.
to **municipalize** vt. municipalizzare.
munificence s. munificenza.
munificent agg. munifico.
munitions s. pl. munizioni.
mural agg. murale. ♦ **mural** s. affresco.
murder s. assassinio.
to **murder** vt. assassinare.
murderer s. assassino.
murderous agg. omicida.
muriatic agg. muriatico.
murky agg. tenebroso.
murmur s. 1. mormorio 2. brontolio.
to **murmur** vt. mormorare. ♦ to **murmur** vi. brontolare.
murmuring s. V. murmur.
muscat(el) s. moscato.
muscle s. muscolo.
muscled agg. muscoloso.
muscular agg. 1. muscolare 2. muscoloso.
musculature s. muscolatura.
Muse s. musa.
to **muse** vi. meditare.
museum s. museo.
mushroom s. fungo.
mushy agg. infrollito.
music s. musica.
musical agg. 1. musicale 2. appassionato di musica.
musicality s. musicalità.
musician s. musicista || street —, suonatore ambulante.
musicologist s. musicologo.
musicology s. musicologia.
musing agg. meditabondo. ♦ **musing** s. meditazione.
musk s. muschio.
musket s. moschetto.
musketeer s. moschettiere.
musky agg. muschiato.
Muslim agg. e s. mussulmano.
muslin s. mussola.
muss s. stato di confusione.
mussel s. mitilo.
must[1] s. mosto.
must[2] s. muffa.

must v. dif. (pres. ind.) dovere || be — return here, deve ritornare qui, it — be true, deve essere vero; you — know him!, non puoi non conoscerlo!
mustard s. senape.
muster s. adunata.
to **muster** vt. adunare. ♦ to **muster** vi. adunarsi.
mutability s. mutabilità.
mutable agg. mutevole.
mutation s. cambiamento.
mute agg. muto. ♦ **mute** s. 1. muto 2. sordina.
to **mutilate** vt. mutilare.
mutilation s. mutilazione.
mutineer s. ammutinato.
mutinous agg. ammutinato, ribelle.
mutiny s. ammutinamento.
to **mutiny** vi. ammutinarsi.
mutism s. mutismo.
to **mutter** V. to murmur.
mutton s. montone.
mutual agg. 1. reciproco 2. comune.
muzzle s. 1. muso 2. museruola 3. bocca (di arma).
to **muzzle** vt. mettere la museruola a.
my agg. poss. mio, mia, miei, mie.
mycosis s. (pl. -ses) micosi.
myocardial agg. miocardico.
myocarditis s. miocardite.
myocardium s. miocardio.
myopia s. miopia.
myopic agg. miope.
myosote s. miosotide.
myriad s. miriade.
myriagram s. miriagrammo.
myriametre s. miriametro.
Myriapoda s. pl. miriapodi.
myrrh s. mirra.
myrtle s. mirto.
myself pron. r. io stesso, me stesso, mi.
mysterious agg. misterioso.
mystery s. mistero.
mystic agg. e s. mistico.
mystical agg. mistico.
mysticism s. misticismo.
mystification s. mistificazione.
mystifier s. mistificatore.
to **mystify** vt. 1. disorientare 2. avvolgere nel mistero.
myth s. mito.
mythic(al) agg. mitico.
to **mythicize** vt. volgere in mito.
mythologic(al) agg. mitologico.
to **mythologize** vi. studiare i miti.
mythology s. mitologia.

mythomania s. mitomania.
mythomaniac agg. e s. mitomane.

N

nabob s. nababbo.
nacre s. madreperla.
to nag vt. e vi. brontolare.
naiad s. naiade.
nail s. 1. unghia, artiglio 2. chiodo.
to nail vt. 1. inchiodare 2. munire di chiodi.
nailer s. fabbricante di chiodi.
naïve agg. ingenuo, semplice.
naïveté s. ingenuità.
naked agg. 1. nudo, spogliato 2. spoglio, indifeso.
nakedness s. nudità.
name s. 1. nome 2. fama, reputazione || -- -day, onomastico; full --, generalità.
to name vt. 1. nominare, dare un nome 2. designare.
nameless agg. 1. senza nome 2. innominabile.
namely avv. cioè.
nanny s. bambinaia, balia.
nap¹ s. siesta, sonnellino.
nap² s. pelo (di stoffe).
to nap vi. schiacciare un sonnellino, sonnecchiare.
nape s. nuca.
naphtha s. nafta.
napkin s. 1. tovagliolo: -- -ring, anello per tovagliolo 2. pannolino.
narcissism s. narcisismo.
narcosis, narcotism s. narcosi.
narcotic agg. s. narcotico.
narcotization s. narcotizzazione.
to narcotize vt. narcotizzare.
to narrate vt. narrare.
narration s. narrazione, racconto.
narrative agg. narrativo. ♦ narrative s. resoconto, narrazione.
narrator s. narratore.
narrow agg. 1. stretto, angusto, ristretto (anche fig.) 2. esatto, minuzioso || -- -minded, di idee ristrette. ♦ narrow s. stretto, strettoia.
to narrow vt. stringere, ridurre. ♦ to narrow vi. stringersi, contrarsi.
narrowness s. strettezza, limitatezza.
narwhal s. narvalo.
nasal agg. nasale. ♦ nasal s. 1.

suono nasale 2. osso nasale.
nascent agg. nascente.
nastily avv. 1. sgradevolmente 2. con cattiveria.
nastiness s. 1. cattivo gusto 2. cattiveria.
nasty agg. 1. sporco, sgradevole 2. cattivo, tempestoso (di tempo).
natal agg. natale.
natality s. natalità.
natant agg. natante.
natation s. nuoto.
natatorial agg. natatorio.
nation s. nazione.
national agg. nazionale.
nationalism s. nazionalismo.
nationalist s. nazionalista.
nationality s. 1. nazionalità 2. patriottismo.
nationalization s. 1. nazionalizzazione 2. naturalizzazione.
to nationalize vt. 1. nazionalizzare 2. naturalizzare.
native agg. 1. innato 2. natio, indigeno. ♦ native s. indigeno, nativo.
nativity s. nascita, natività.
natural agg. 1. naturale, fisico 2. spontaneo 3. istintivo, innato.
naturalism s. naturalismo.
naturalist s. naturalista.
naturalistic agg. naturalistico.
naturalization s. 1. naturalizzazione 2. acclimatamento.
to naturalize vi. 1. naturalizzare 2. acclimatare.
nature s. 1. natura 2. carattere, temperamento || good --, bontà.
natured agg. di natura, per natura || good --, buono, di buon carattere.
naturism s. naturismo, nudismo.
naturist s. naturista.
naughtily avv. con cattiveria.
naughtiness s. cattiveria.
naughty agg. cattivo, impertinente.
to nauseate vt. nauseare, disgustare. ♦ to nauseate vi. avere la nausea, disgustarsi.
nauseating agg. nauseabondo.
nautical agg. nautico.
naval agg. navale.
nave¹ s. mozzo di ruota.
nave² s. navata centrale (di chiesa).
navel s. 1. ombelico 2. (fig.) centro.
navigability s. navigabilità.
navigable agg. navigabile.
to navigate vt. e vi. 1. navigare 2. regolare la rotta.

navigation *s.* 1. navigazione 2. rotta.

navigator *s.* navigatore, ufficiale di rotta.

navvy *s.* sterratore.

navy *s.* marina da guerra, flotta.

nay *avv.* anzi, non solo.

Nazi *agg.* e *s.* nazista.

Neapolitan *agg.* e *s.* napoletano.

near *agg.* 1. vicino, prossimo 2. affine, intimo 3. fedele, esatto. ◆ **near** *prep.* vicino a, presso a. ◆ **near** *avv.* vicino, presso, accanto.

to near *vt.* e *vi.* avvicinarsi (a).

nearby *agg. avv. prep.* assai vicino.

nearly *avv.* quasi.

neat *agg.* 1. pulito, lindo 2. grazioso, di buon gusto 3. chiaro, conciso.

neatly *avv.* 1. lindamente, ordinatamente 2. con semplicità, con buon gusto 3. concisamente.

neatness *s.* 1. pulizia, ordine 2. grazia, armonia 3. semplicità 4. concisione.

nebula *s.* nebulosa.

nebular *agg.* nebulare.

nebulosity *s.* nebulosità.

nebulous *agg.* nebuloso, vago.

necessary *agg.* necessario.

to necessitate *vt.* 1. rendere necessario 2. obbligare.

necessity *s.* necessità.

neck *s.* collo ‖ *stiff* —, torcicollo.

neckerchief *s.* fazzoletto da collo.

necklace *s.* collana, vezzo.

neckline *s.* scollatura.

necktie *s.* cravatta.

necrology *s.* necrologia.

necromancer *s.* negromante.

necromancy *s.* negromanzia.

necropolis *s.* necropoli.

necrosis *s.* (*pl.* -ses) necrosi.

nectar *s.* nettare.

need *s.* necessità, bisogno.

to need *vt.* e *vi.* essere necessario, occorrere, abbisognare, mancare di.

needful *agg.* necessario, indispensabile.

neediness *s.* bisogno, povertà.

needle *s.* 1. ago 2. puntina di grammofono.

to needle *vt.* 1. cucire, pungere (*con un ago*) 2. irritare.

needleful *s.* gugliata.

needless *agg.* inutile, superfluo.

needlewoman *s.* cucitrice.

needlework *s.* lavoro ad ago.

needs *avv.* necessariamente.

needy *agg.* povero, indigente.

ne'er *avv.* (*contrazione di* never) mai.

negation *s.* diniego.

negative *agg.* negativo. ◆ **negative** *s.* 1. negazione 2. qualità negativa.

neglect *s.* negligenza, trascuratezza.

to neglect *vt.* trascurare.

neglectful *agg.* negligente, noncurante.

negligence *s.* negligenza, trascuratezza.

negligent *agg.* negligente, trascurato.

negligible *agg.* trascurabile.

negotiable *agg.* negoziabile.

to negotiate *vt.* e *vi.* negoziare, trattare.

negotiation *s.* trattativa.

negress *s.* negra.

negro *agg.* e *s.* negro.

negroid *agg.* negroide.

neigh *s.* nitrito.

to neigh *vi.* nitrire.

neighbour *s.* vicino.

to neighbour *vi.* essere vicini di casa.

neighbourhood *s.* 1. i vicini, vicinato 2. paraggi, dintorni (*pl.*).

neighbouring *agg.* vicino, contiguo.

neither¹ *agg.* né l'uno né l'altro.

neither² *avv.* né, neppure, nemmeno: — ... *nor*, né ... né.

nemesis *s.* (*pl.* -ses) nemesi.

neo-classic(al) *agg.* neoclassico.

neo-classicism *s.* neoclassicismo.

neo-criticism *s.* neocriticismo.

neolithic *agg.* neolitico.

neologism *s.* neologismo.

neology *s.* neologia.

neon *s.* neon.

neophyte *s.* neofito.

neoplatonic *agg.* neoplatonico.

Neoplatonism *s.* neoplatonismo.

neopositivism *s.* neopositivismo.

neorealism *s.* neorealismo.

neorealist *s.* neorealista.

nephew *s.* nipote (*di zio*).

nephritic *agg.* nefritico.

nephritis *s.* nefrite.

nepotism *s.* nepotismo.

nerve *s.* 1. nervo 2. nervatura 3. forza, energia, sangue freddo.

to nerve *vt.* tonificare, rinvigorire.

nerveless *agg.* snervato, inerte.

nervous *agg.* 1. nervoso 2. forte, vigoroso 3. timido, apprensivo.

nervously *avv.* 1. nervosamente 2.

timidamente.

nervousness *s.* **1.** nervosismo, irritazione **2.** timidezza.

nervy *agg.* **1.** muscoloso, forte **2.** nervoso.

nescient *agg.* ignorante.

nest *s.* **1.** nido **2.** (*fig.*) covo, tana **3.** colonia (*di uccelli, insetti ecc.*).

to **nest** *vi.* fare il nido, nidificare.

to **nestle** *vt.* ospitare. ♦ to **nestle** *vi.* annidarsi, rifugiarsi.

nestling *s.* uccellino di nido.

net[1] *agg.* e *s.* netto.

net[2] *s.* **1.** rete **2.** (*fig.*) trappola.

to **net** *vt.* **1.** coprire con reti **2.** pescare con reti.

netful *s.* retata.

netting *s.* rete, reticolato.

nettle *s.* ortica || — *rash*, orticaria.

to **nettle** *vt.* pungere (*di ortica*).

network *s.* rete, reticolato.

neuralgia *s.* nevralgia.

neuralgic *agg.* nevralgico.

neurasthenia *s.* nevrastenia.

neurasthenic *agg.* nevrastenico.

neuritis *s.* nevrite.

neurologist *s.* neurologo.

neurology *s.* neurologia.

neuropathic *agg.* neuropatico.

neuropathology *s.* neuropatologia.

neurosis *s.* (*pl.* -ses) nevrosi.

neurotic *agg.* neuropatico.

neuter *s.* parola neutra, neutro.

neutral *agg.* neutrale.

neutralism *s.* neutralismo.

neutralist *s.* neutralista.

neutrality *s.* neutralità.

neutralization *s.* neutralizzazione.

to **neutralize** *vt.* neutralizzare.

neutron *s.* neutrone.

never *avv.* mai, giammai || — *again*, mai più; — *mind*, non importa; *now or* —, ora o mai più; — *-ending*, eterno.

nevermore *avv.* mai più.

nevertheless *avv.* nonostante, ciò nondimeno.

new *agg.* nuovo, recente || — *-born*, neonato; — *-comer*, nuovo venuto; — *-made*, appena fatto.

newish *agg.* piuttosto nuovo.

newly *avv.* recentemente.

news *s.* notizia, notizie || — *-man*, strillone (*di giornali*); — *-reel*, cinegiornale.

newsmonger *s.* persona pettegola e curiosa.

newspaper *s.* giornale, quotidiano.

New Zealander *s.* neozelandese.

next *agg.* **1.** prossimo, vicino, il più vicino **2.** futuro, venturo **3.** primo, contiguo. ♦ **next** *avv.* dopo, in seguito, poi. ♦ **next** *prep.* presso, accanto.

nib *s.* pennino.

nibble *s.* morso.

to **nibble** *vt.* **1.** mordicchiare, sgranocchiare **2.** abboccare.

nibbler *s.* roditore.

nice *agg.* **1.** piacevole, bello, simpatico **2.** buono, gustoso **3.** accurato, minuzioso.

nicely *avv.* **1.** amabilmente, piacevolmente **2.** esattamente.

nicety *s.* **1.** finezza, precisione. ♦ **niceties** *s. pl.* minuzie.

niche *s.* nicchia.

nick *s.* tacca, intaccatura || *in the* — *of time*, al momento giusto.

to **nick** *vt.* **1.** intaccare **2.** colpire, afferrare al momento opportuno.

nickel *s.* nichel.

to **nickel** *vt.* nichelare.

nickname *s.* soprannome, nomignolo.

to **nickname** *vt.* soprannominare.

nicotine *s.* nicotina.

niece *s.* nipote (*femmina*) (*di zio*).

niggard *agg.* spilorcio.

niggardliness *s.* spilorceria.

niggardly *agg.* avaro, spilorcio.

nigger *s.* (*spreg.*) negro.

night *s.* **1.** notte, sera **2.** buio, oscurità || *by* —, di notte, *good* —, buona notte; — *-bird*, uccello notturno, nottambulo; — *-dress*, camicia da notte; — *-shift*, turno di notte.

nightcap *s.* berretto da notte.

nightfall *s.* tramonto.

nightingale *s.* usignolo.

nightly *agg.* notturno. ♦ **nightly** *avv.* di notte.

nightmare *s.* incubo.

nightpiece *s.* « notturno » (*dipinto che rappresenta una scena notturna*).

nihilism *s.* nichilismo.

nihilist *s.* nichilista.

nimble *agg.* **1.** agile, leggero **2.** acuto, sveglio.

nimbleness *s.* **1.** agilità **2.** prontezza, acutezza.

nimbly *avv.* **1.** agilmente, leggermente **2.** prontamente.

nine *agg.* nove.

ninepins *s. pl.* birilli.

nineteen *agg.* diciannove.

nineteenth *agg.* e *s.* diciannovesimo.

ninetieth *agg.* novantesimo.

ninety *agg.* novanta.

ninth *agg.* nono.

nip *s.* **1.** pizzicotto, morso **2.** stretta, presa **3.** morso (*di freddo, gelo ecc.*).

to nip *vt.* **1.** pizzicare, mordere (*anche di freddo ecc.*) **2.** stroncare.

nipple *s.* capezzolo.

nitrate *s.* nitrato.

nitric *agg.* nitrico.

nitrite *s.* (*chim.*) nitrito.

nitroglycerin(e) *s.* nitroglicerina.

no *agg.* nessuno. ✦ **no** *avv.* **1.** no **2.** in nessun modo.

nobiliary *agg.* nobiliare.

nobility *s.* nobiltà (*anche fig.*).

noble *agg.* **1.** nobile (*anche fig.*) **2.** superbo, grandioso. ✦ **noble** *s.* nobile.

nobleman *s.* nobiluomo.

nobleness *s.* nobiltà (*anche fig.*).

noblewoman *s.* nobildonna.

nobly *avv.* nobilmente.

nobody *pron. indef.* nessuno.

nocturnal *agg.* notturno.

nocturne *s.* (*pitt.; mus.*) notturno.

nod *s.* **1.** cenno del capo **2.** ordine, comando.

to nod *vt.* e *vi.* **1.** annuire col capo **2.** assopirsi, chinare il capo dal sonno **3.** inclinarsi (*di edifici ecc.*).

nodding *agg.* chinato, inclinato. ✦ **nodding** *s.* cenno del capo.

nodose *agg.* nodoso.

nodosity *s.* nodosità.

nodular *agg.* a forma di nodo.

nodule *s.* nodulo.

noise *s.* rumore, fragore, chiasso.

noiseless *agg.* senza rumore, silenzioso.

noisily *avv.* rumorosamente.

noisy *agg.* **1.** rumoroso, turbolento **2.** (*fig.*) vistoso, chiassoso.

nomad *agg.* e *s.* nomade.

nomadism *s.* nomadismo.

nomenclature *s.* nomenclatura.

nominal *agg.* nominale.

nominalism *s.* nominalismo.

nominalist *s.* nominalista.

nominalistic *agg.* nominalistico.

nominative *agg.* e *s.* nominativo.

nominator *s.* nominatore.

nonagenarian *agg.* e *s.* nonagenario.

non-aligned *agg.* non allineato.

non-alignment *s.* non allineamento.

non-appearance *s.* contumacia.

non-attendance *s.* assenza.

non-commital *agg.* evasivo.

non-conducting *agg.* isolante, non conduttore.

non-conductor *s.* isolante.

nonconformist *agg.* e *s.* anticonformista.

nonconformity *s.* anticonformismo.

non-delivery *s.* mancata consegna.

none *pron. sing.* e *pl.* nessuno, non uno. ✦ **none** *avv.* affatto, niente affatto.

nonentity *s.* **1.** cosa o persona insignificante **2.** inesistenza.

non-existence *s.* inesistenza.

non-resistance *s.* resistenza passiva.

nonsense *s.* assurdità, sciocchezza.

nonsensical *agg.* assurdo, sciocco.

non-stop *agg.* continuo, senza fermate. ✦ **non-stop** *avv.* di continuo, senza fermate.

non-transferable *agg.* non trasferibile.

noodle *agg.* sciocco, gonzo.

nook *s.* **1.** cantuccio, angolo **2.** ripostiglio.

noon *s.* mezzogiorno.

noose *s.* **1.** nodo scorsoio **2.** tranello.

nor *cong.* né, neppure || *neither I — be*, né io né lui.

normal *agg.* **1.** normale, regolare **2.** perpendicolare.

normality *s.* normalità.

normalization *s.* normalizzazione.

to normalize *vt.* normalizzare.

Norman *agg.* e *s.* normanno.

normative *agg.* normativo.

north *s.* nord, settentrione || *— wind*, vento di tramontana.

north-east *s.* nord-est.

northerly *agg.* del nord, settentrionale. ✦ **northerly** *avv.* verso il nord.

northern *agg.* nordico, settentrionale.

northerner *s.* abitante del nord.

northward(s) *agg.* e *avv.* verso nord.

Norwegian *agg.* e *s.* norvegese.

nose *s.* **1.** naso **2.** muso (*di animali*) **3.** prua (*mar.*).

to nose *vt.* e *vi.* **1.** fiutare **2.** indagare **3.** ficcare il naso.

nostril *s.* narice.

not *avv.* non || *— at all*, niente affatto.

notability *s.* notabilità.
notable *agg.* degno di nota, notevole.
notarial *agg.* notarile.
notary *s.* notaio.
notation *s.* 1. (*mus.*) notazione 2. (*mat.*) numerazione.
notch *s.* tacca, dentellatura.
to notch *vt.* 1. intaccare 2. intagliare.
note *s.* 1. (*mus.*) nota, tono 2. marchio, segno 3. nota, appunto, commento 4. (*comm.*) cedola, acconto 5. banconota.
to note *vt.* notare.
notebook *s.* taccuino.
notehead *s.* intestazione.
noteless *agg.* privo di interesse.
noteworthiness *s.* importanza.
noteworthy *agg.* notevole.
nothing *pron. indef.* nulla, niente, nessuna cosa.
nothingness *s.* 1. il nulla 2. nullità.
notice *s.* 1. avviso, avvertimento 2. (*giur.*) intimazione 3. licenziamento 4. attenzione, cura 5. recensione || — *-board*, cartello pubblicitario, tabella.
to notice *vt.* 1. osservare, fare attenzione a 2. recensire.
noticeable *agg.* notevole.
notifiable *agg.* da denunciarsi.
notification *s.* notifica.
to notify *vt.* notificare; far sapere.
notion *s.* 1. nozione 2. idea, teoria.
notional *agg.* 1. immaginario 2. speculativo.
notoriety *s.* notorietà.
notorious *agg.* 1. noto, conosciuto 2. famigerato.
notoriously *avv.* notoriamente.
notwithstanding *prep.* nonostante, malgrado.
nougat *s.* torrone.
nought *s.* 1. nulla 2. (*mat.*) zero.
noumenon *s.* (*pl.* -ena) noumeno.
noun *s.* (*gramm.*) nome, sostantivo.
to nourish *vt.* nutrire (*anche fig.*).
nourishing *agg.* nutriente.
nourishment *s.* nutrimento.
novel *s.* romanzo.
novelist *s.* romanziere.
to novelize *vt.* romanzare.
novelty *s.* novità.
November *s.* novembre.
novice *s.* 1. (*eccl.*) novizio 2. apprendista.
novitiate *s.* noviziato.

now *avv.* 1. ora, adesso, subito, al presente 2. allora 3. a dire il vero. ♦ **now** *cong.* ora che. ♦ **now** *s.* ora, il presente.
nowadays *avv.* al giorno d'oggi.
nowhere *avv.* in nessun luogo.
noxious *agg.* nocivo, dannoso.
nozzle *s.* becco, beccuccio (*di teiera, pompa ecc.*).
nuclear *agg.* nucleare.
nuclein *s.* nucleina.
nucleonics *s. pl.* fisica nucleare.
nucleus *s.* (*pl.* -ei) 1. nucleo 2. nocciolo, centro.
nude *agg.* 1. nudo 2. (*fig.*) semplice. ♦ **nude** *s.* (*pitt.; scult.*) nudo.
nudism *s.* nudismo.
nudist *agg.* e *s.* nudista.
nugget *s.* pepita.
nuisance *s.* 1. noia, seccatura 2. danno.
null *agg.* nullo.
nullification *s.* annullamento.
to nullify *vt.* annullare.
nullity *s.* 1. nullità 2. il non essere valido.
numb *agg.* 1. intorpidito, intirizzito 2. tramortito, intontito.
to numb *vt.* 1. intorpidire, intirizzire 2. (*fig.*) istupidire.
number *s.* 1. numero, cifra 2. numero, quantità 3. numero di giornale.
to number *vt.* 1. contare, numerare 2. annoverare 3. ammontare.
numberless *agg.* innumerevole.
numbness *s.* torpore (*anche fig.*).
numerable *agg.* numerabile, calcolabile.
numeral *agg.* e *s.* numerale.
numerator *s.* numeratore.
numerical *agg.* numerico.
numerically *avv.* numericamente.
numerous *agg.* numeroso.
numismatic *agg.* numismatico.
numismatics *s.* numismatica.
numismatist *s.* numismatico.
numismatology *s.* numismatica.
nun *s.* 1. monaca, suora 2. piccione dal cappuccio.
nuncio *s.* (*eccl.*) nunzio.
nunnery *s.* convento (*di suore*).
nuptial *agg.* nuziale.
nuptials *s. pl.* nozze, sponsali.
nurse *s.* 1. nutrice, balia 2. infermiera.
to nurse *vt.* 1. allattare, nutrire 2. allevare 3. curare (*ammalati*).
nursling *s.* lattante.

nursery s. **1.** camera dei bambini **2.** scuola materna **3.** vivaio || — *rhyme*, filastrocca per bambini.

nursing agg. **1.** che allatta, nutre **2.** che cura || — *home*, casa di cura. ♦ **nursing** s. **1.** allattamento **2.** il curare **3.** professione di infermiera.

nurture s. vitto, nutrimento.

to **nurture** vt. nutrire, allevare.

nut s. **1.** noce **2.** (mecc.) dado.

nutcracker s. schiaccianoci.

nutmeg s. noce moscata.

nutrition s. nutrizione.

nutritive agg. nutritivo.

nutshell s. guscio di noce.

nylon s. nailon.

nymph s. ninfa.

O

oak s. quercia.

oakum s. stoppa.

oar s. remo || — *-blade*, pala di remo.

to **oar** vi. remare.

oarsman s. rematore.

oasis s. (pl. -ses) oasi.

oats s. pl. avena (sing.).

oath s. **1.** giuramento **2.** bestemmia.

obduracy s. **1.** inesorabilità **2.** ostinazione.

obdurate agg. **1.** inesorabile **2.** ostinato.

obedience s. ubbidienza.

obedient agg. ubbidiente.

obeisance s. riverenza.

obelisk s. obelisco.

obese agg. obeso.

obesity s. obesità.

to **obey** vt. e vi. ubbidire.

to **obfuscate** vt. **1.** offuscare **2.** confondere.

obituary s. necrologio.

object s. oggetto.

to **object** vt. e vi. obiettare.

objectification s. oggettivazione.

to **objectify** vt. oggettivare.

objection s. **1.** obiezione **2.** avversione.

objectionable agg. **1.** biasimevole **2.** sgradevole.

objective agg. oggettivo. ♦ **objective** s. obiettivo.

objectiveness s. oggettività.

objectivism s. oggettivismo.

objectivity s. oggettività.

objector s. oppositore || *conscientious* —, obiettore di coscienza.

obligation s. obbligo.

obligatoriness s. obbligatorietà.

obligatory agg. obbligatorio.

to **oblige** vt. **1.** obbligare **2.** fare un favore a.

obliging agg. cortese.

oblique agg. obliquo.

obliqueness, obliquity s. obliquità.

to **obliterate** vt. cancellare.

obliteration s. cancellatura.

oblivion s. oblio || *Act of* —, amnistia.

oblivious agg. dimentico.

oblong agg. **1.** oblungo **2.** rettangolare. ♦ **oblong** s. (geom.) rettangolo.

obnoxious agg. odioso.

obscene agg. osceno.

obscenity s. oscenità.

obscurantism s. oscurantismo.

obscurantist agg. e s. oscurantista.

obscuration s. oscuramento.

obscure agg. oscuro. ♦ **obscure** s. oscurità.

to **obscure** vt. oscurare.

obscurity s. oscurità.

obsecration s. supplica.

obsequies s. pl. esequie.

obsequious agg. ossequioso.

observable agg. **1.** visibile **2.** notevole.

observance s. **1.** osservanza **2.** (relig.) regola.

observant agg. osservante.

observation s. osservazione.

observatory s. osservatorio.

to **observe** vt. e vi. osservare.

observer s. osservatore.

observing agg. attento.

to **obsess** vt. ossessionare.

obsession s. ossessione.

obsessive agg. ossessivo.

obsolescence s. disuso.

obsolescent agg. che sta cadendo in disuso.

obsolete agg. **1.** antiquato **2.** scaduto (di prezzi).

obstacle s. ostacolo.

obstetric(al) agg. ostetrico.

obstetrician s. ostetrico.

obstetrics s. ostetricia.

obstinacy s. ostinazione.

obstinate agg. ostinato.

to **obstruct** vt. **1.** ostruire **2.** ritardare 3. intasare.

obstruction *s.* ostruzione, ostacolo.

obstructionism *s.* ostruzionismo.

obstructionist *s.* ostruzionista.

to **obtain** *vt.* ottenere. ♦ to **obtain** *vi.* prevalere.

obtainable *agg.* ottenibile.

to **obtrude** *vt.* imporre. ♦ to **obtrude** *vi.* **1.** imporsi **2.** intromettersi.

obtruder *s.* **1.** intruso **2.** importuno.

obtrusion *s.* intrusione.

obtrusive *agg.* **1.** intruso **2.** importuno.

obtrusiveness *s.* **1.** intrusione **2.** invadenza.

to **obtund** *vt.* ottundere.

obtundent *agg.* ottundente.

to **obturate** *vt.* otturare.

obturation *s.* otturazione.

obturator *s.* otturatore.

obtuse *agg.* **1.** ottuso **2.** sordo.

obtuseness *s.* ottusità.

to **obviate** *vt.* ovviare.

obvious *agg.* ovvio.

obviousness *s.* chiarezza.

occasion *s.* **1.** occasione **2.** motivo.

occasional *agg.* occasionale.

occident *s.* occidente.

occidental *agg.* occidentale.

occidentalism *s.* occidentalismo.

to **occidentalize** *vt.* occidentalizzare.

occidentally *avv.* all'occidentale.

occipital *agg.* occipitale.

occiput *s.* (*pl.* -pita) occipite.

to **occlude** *vt.* occludere.

occlusion *s.* occlusione.

occlusive *agg.* occlusivo.

occult *agg.* occulto.

to **occult** *vt.* occultare. ♦ to **occult** *vi.* occultarsi.

occultation *s.* occultamento.

occultism *s.* occultismo.

occultist *s.* occultista.

occupant *s.* occupante.

occupation *s.* occupazione.

occupational *agg.* professionale.

occupier *s.* occupante.

to **occupy** *vt.* occupare: *to — oneself with,* occuparsi di.

to **occur** *vi.* **1.** accadere **2.** venire in mente **3.** ricorrere.

occurrence *s.* avvenimento.

ocean *s.* oceano.

oceanic *agg.* oceanico.

oceanography *s.* oceanografia.

ocellus *s.* (*pl.* -li) ocello.

ochre *s.* ocra.

octagon *s.* ottagono.

octagonal *agg.* ottagonale.

octahedron *s.* ottaedro.

octane *s.* ottano.

octave *s.* ottava.

October *s.* ottobre.

octogenarian *agg.* e *s.* ottuagenario.

octonarian *agg.* e *s.* ottonario.

octonary *agg.* di otto in otto. ♦ **octonary** *s.* strofa di otto versi.

octopus *s.* (*pl.* -pi) polipo, piovra.

octosyllabic *agg.* ottosillabico.

octosyllable *s.* verso, parola di otto sillabe.

ocular *agg.* e *s.* oculare.

oculate(d) *agg.* maculato.

oculist *s.* oculista.

oculistic *agg.* oculistico.

odalisque *s.* odalisca.

odd *agg.* **1.** dispari **2.** scompagnato **3.** in più **4.** occasionale **5.** bizzarro. ♦ **odd** *s.* cosa extra.

oddity, oddness *s.* stranezza.

odds *s. pl.* **1.** differenza **2.** disaccordo **3.** pronostico || — *and ends,* rimanenze.

ode *s.* ode.

odious *agg.* odioso.

odontological *agg.* odontoiatrico.

odontologist *s.* odontoiatra.

odontology *s.* odontoiatria.

odoriferous *agg.* odorifero.

odorous *agg.* odoroso.

odour *s.* odore.

odourless *agg.* inodoro.

oedema *s.* edema.

oenologist *s.* enologo.

oenology *s.* enologia.

oesophagus *s.* (*pl.* -gi) esofago.

of *prep.* **1.** di **2.** (*tempo*) a, in **3.** da parte di: *very kind — you,* molto gentile da parte vostra || — *late,* ultimamente.

off *avv.* **1.** lontano, via **2.** completamente || *to be* —, essere finito, fermo, in libertà. ♦ **off** *prep.* **1.** lontano, via da **2.** giù da. ♦ **off** *agg.* **1.** destro **2.** esterno **3.** lontano **4.** secondario **5.** libero || — *day,* giorno di libertà.

offence *s.* **1.** offesa **2.** colpa, delitto **3.** scandalo.

offenceless *agg.* **1.** inoffensivo **2.** innocente.

to **offend** *vt.* offendere. ♦ to **offend** *vi.* **1.** peccare **2.** violare la legge.

offender *s.* **1.** peccatore **2.** colpevole.

offensive agg. 1. offensivo 2. sgradevole. ♦ **offensive** s. offensiva.

offensiveness s. aggressività.

offer s. offerta.

to offer vt. offrire. ♦ **to offer** vi. offrirsi.

offerer s. offerente.

offering s. offerta.

offertory s. offertorio.

offhand agg. 1. improvvisato 2. spontaneo. ♦ **offhand** avv. lì per lì.

office s. ufficio, carica || box-, botteghino.

officer s. ufficiale, funzionario || non-commissioned —, sottufficiale.

official agg. ufficiale. ♦ **official** s. funzionario.

officiant s. ufficiante.

to officiate vi. 1. esercitare le funzioni di 2. (relig.) ufficiare.

officious agg. 1. ufficioso 2. intrigante.

offing s. (mar.) largo.

offscourings s. pl. rifiuti, scarti.

offset s. 1. compenso 2. sperone (di monte) 3. germoglio, progenie 4. (tip.) fotolito.

offshoot s. 1. germoglio 2. ramo.

offshore agg. 1. di terra 2. lontano dalla costa. ♦ **offshore** avv. al largo.

offside s. (sport) fuori gioco.

offspring s. 1. prole 2. frutto.

often avv. spesso || how —?, quante volte?

ogive s. ogiva.

oil s. 1. olio 2. petrolio || — cloth, tela cerata; — field, giacimento petrolifero; — mill, frantoio; — paper, carta oleata; — pipeline, oleodotto.

to oil vt. ungere, oliare.

oiler s. oliatore.

oily agg. oleoso, untuoso.

ointment s. unguento.

O.K. avv. bene: to be —, andar bene.

old (elder, older; eldest, oldest) agg. vecchio || how — are you?, quanti anni hai?; — -fashioned, antiquato. ♦ **old** s. passato.

oldish agg. attempato.

oleander s. oleandro.

oleograph s. oleografia.

oleographic agg. oleografico.

olfactory agg. olfattivo.

oligarch s. oligarchia.

oligarchic(al) agg. oligarchico.

oligarchy s. oligarchia.

olive agg. 1. d'oliva 2. olivastro. ♦ **olive** s. 1. oliva 2. (-tree) olivo.

Olympiad s. olimpiade.

Olympian agg. olimpico, olimpionico. ♦ **Olympian** s. olimpionico.

Olympic agg. V. Olympian.

omelet(te) s. frittata.

omen s. auspicio.

ominous agg. di cattivo augurio.

omission s. omissione.

to omit vt. omettere.

omnipotence s. onnipotenza.

omnipotent agg. e s. onnipotente.

omnipresent agg. onnipresente.

omniscience s. onniscienza.

omniscient agg. e s. onnisciente.

omnivorous agg. onnivoro.

on prep. 1. su 2. a, in, di, per || on purpose, apposta. ♦ **on** avv. 1. su, indosso 2. (in) avanti || to be —, essere in funzione, essere rappresentato; and so —, eccetera.

once avv. una volta || at —, subito; all at —, improvvisamente. ♦ **once** cong. una volta che.

on-coming agg. prossimo.

one agg. 1. uno 2. uno solo. ♦ **one** pron. 1. (dimostr.) questo, quello 2. (indef.) (l') uno || — by —, uno a uno. ♦ **one's** uno || — John Brown, un certo John Brown.

one-eyed agg. guercio.

oneness s. unità, unicità.

onerous agg. oneroso.

oneself pron. r. se stesso.

one-sided agg. unilaterale.

one-sidedly avv. unilateralmente.

oneway agg. a senso unico.

ongoings s. pl. avvenimenti.

onion s. cipolla || spring-, cipollina.

onlooker s. spettatore.

only agg. e avv. solo.

onomastic agg. onomastico.

onomatopoeia s. onomatopea.

onomatopoeic agg. onomatopeico.

onset s. 1. attacco 2. inizio.

onto prep. su, in cima a.

ontological agg. ontologico.

ontology s. ontologia.

onus s. onere.

onward agg. avanzato.

onward(s) avv. avanti.

onyx s. onice.

to ooze vt. e vi. stillare || to — out, trapelare.

oozy agg. melmoso.

opacity s. opacità.

opal *s.* opale.

opalescent *agg.* opalescente.

opaque *agg.* opaco.

open *agg.* aperto || — *wide* —, spalancato; *in the* — *air*, all'aperto.

to open *vt.* aprire. ♦ to open *vi.* aprirsi.

open-handed *agg.* generoso.

opening *s.* 1. apertura 2. radura.

openly *avv.* apertamente.

open-minded *agg.* di larghe vedute.

open-mindedness *s.* larghezza di vedute.

openness *s.* 1. apertura 2. franchezza.

opera *s.* opera lirica || — *-house*, teatro dell'opera; — *glass*, binocolo.

to operate *vt.* 1. operare 2. far funzionare 3. gestire. ♦ to operate *vi.* 1. operare 2. funzionare.

operatic *agg.* di opera.

operation *s.* 1. operazione 2. funzionamento 3. azione.

operative *agg.* 1. attivo 2. operatorno, operaio (*meccanico*). sentenza. ♦ operative *s.* artigianista, telegrafista.

operator *s.* 1. operatore 2. telefonrio || — *part*, dispositivo di una

ophthalmia *s.* oftalmia.

ophthalmic *agg.* oftalmico.

ophthalmology *s.* oftalmologia, oculistica.

ophthalmoscopy *s.* oftalmoscopia.

opiate *agg.* 1. oppiato 2. soporifero. ♦ opiate *s.* narcotico.

opinion *s.* opinione.

opinionated, opinionative *agg.* ostinato.

opium *s.* oppio.

opponent *s.* avversario.

opportune *agg.* opportuno.

opportunism *s.* opportunismo.

opportunist *s.* opportunista.

opportunist(ic) *agg.* opportunistico.

opportunity *s.* occasione.

opposable *agg.* opponibile.

to oppose *vt.* opporre. ♦ to oppose *vi.* opporsi.

opposed *agg.* 1. opposto 2. ostile.

opposer *s.* oppositore.

opposite *agg.* e *s.* opposto. ♦ opposite *avv.* di fronte. ♦ opposite *prep.* di fronte a, dirimpetto a.

opposition *s.* opposizione.

to oppress *vt.* opprimere.

oppression *s.* oppressione.

oppressive *agg.* opprimente.

oppressor *s.* oppressore.

opprobrious *agg.* obbrobrioso.

to opt *vi.* optare.

optic(al) *agg.* ottico.

optician *s.* ottico.

optics *s.* ottica.

optimism *s.* ottimismo.

optimist *s.* e *s.* ottimista.

optimistic(al) *agg.* ottimistico.

option *s.* opzione.

optional *agg.* facoltativo.

opulence *s.* opulenza.

opulent *agg.* opulento.

or *cong.* o, oppure || *either...* —, sia... sia.

oracle *s.* oracolo.

oracular *agg.* profetico.

oral *agg.* e *s.* orale.

orange *s.* 1. arancia 2. arancio.

orangeade *s.* aranciata.

orangery *s.* aranceto.

oration *s.* discorso.

orator *s.* oratore.

oratorical *agg.* oratorio.

oratory[1] *s.* oratorio.

oratory[2] *s.* oratoria.

orb *s.* 1. cerchio 2. sfera.

orbit *s.* orbita.

orbital *agg.* orbitale.

orchard *s.* frutteto.

orchestra *s.* orchestra.

orchestral *agg.* orchestrale.

to orchestrate *vt.* orchestrare.

orchestration *s.* orchestrazione.

orchid, orchis *s.* orchidea.

to ordain *vt.* ordinare (*anche eccl.*).

ordeal *s.* 1. ordalia 2. dura prova.

order *s.* 1. ordine 2. classe || *in* — *that*, affinché; *in* — *to*, allo scopo di; *postal* —, vaglia postale; *made to* —, eseguito su ordinazione. ♦ orders *s. pl.* (*relig.*) ordini: *to take* —, farsi prete.

to order *vt.* 1. ordinare 2. riordinare.

ordering *s.* ordinamento. ♦ orderly *s.* 1. (*mil.*) ordinanza 2. (*mil.*) attendente.

ordinal *agg.* e *s.* ordinale.

ordinance *s.* 1. ordinanza 2. (*relig.*) rito.

ordinary *agg.* ordinario. ♦ ordinary *s.* 1. condizione ordinaria 2. pranzo a prezzo fisso.

ordinate *s.* ordinata.

ordination *s.* 1. ordine 2. (*relig.*) ordinazione.

ore *s.* minerale.

organ *s.* organo ‖ *barrel— —,* organetto; *mouth— —,* armonica.

organic *agg.* organico.

organism *s.* organismo.

organist *s.* organista.

organizable *agg.* organizzabile.

organization *s.* organizzazione. ♦ to **organize** *vt.* organizzare. ♦ to **organize** *vi.* organizzarsi.

organizer *s.* organizzatore.

organzine *s.* organzino.

orgasm *s.* orgasmo.

orgeat *s.* orzata.

orgiastic *agg.* orgiastico.

orgy *s.* orgia.

orient *s.* oriente.

to orient *vt.* 1. orientare 2. volgere verso oriente.

oriental *agg.* e *s.* orientale.

orientalist *s.* orientalista.

orientation *s.* orientamento.

orifice *s.* orifizio.

origan *s.* origano.

origin *s.* origine.

original *agg.* e *s.* originale.

originality *s.* originalità.

originally *avv.* 1. originalmente 2. originariamente.

to originate *vt.* dare origine. ♦ to **originate** *vi.* aver origine.

originator *s.* iniziatore.

ornament *s.* ornamento.

ornamental *agg.* ornamentale.

ornamentation *s.* decorazione.

ornate *agg.* ornato.

ornithological *agg.* ornitologico.

ornithologist *s.* ornitologo.

ornithology *s.* ornitologia.

orographic(al) *agg.* orografico.

orography *s.* orografia.

orphan *agg.* e *s.* orfano.

orphanage *s.* 1. la condizione di orfano 2. orfanotrofio.

orthodox *agg.* ortodosso.

orthodoxy *s.* ortodossia.

orthogonal *agg.* ortogonale.

orthographic(al) *agg.* 1. ortografico 2. ortogonale.

orthography *s.* 1. ortografia 2. (*geom.*) proiezione ortogonale.

orthop(a)edic(al) *agg.* ortopedico.

orthop(a)edics *s.* ortopedia.

orthop(a)edist *s.* ortopedico.

to oscillate *vi.* oscillare.

oscillation *s.* oscillazione.

oscillator *s.* oscillatore.

oscillatory *agg.* oscillatorio.

oscillograph *s.* oscillografo.

osier *s.* vimine.

osmose, osmosis *s.* osmosi.

osseous *agg.* osseo.

ossification *s.* ossificazione.

to ossify *vt.* ossificare. ♦ to **ossify** *vi.* ossificarsi.

ostensible *agg.* apparente.

ostensory *s.* ostensorio.

ostentation *s.* ostentazione.

ostentatious *agg.* ostentato.

osteological *agg.* osteologico.

osteology *s.* osteologia.

ostracism *s.* ostracismo.

to ostracize *vt.* dare l'ostracismo a.

ostrich *s.* struzzo.

other *agg.* e *pron.* altro ‖ *each —,* l'un l'altro; *every — day,* un giorno sì e un giorno no. ♦ **others** *pron. pl.* altri ‖ *some... —...,* gli uni... gli altri.

otherwise *agg.* diverso. ♦ **otherwise** *avv.* altrimenti.

otherworld *s.* mondo ultraterreno.

otitis *s.* otite.

otorhinolaryngologist *s.* otorinolaringoiatra.

otter *s.* lontra.

Ottoman *agg.* e *s.* ottomano.

ought *s.* zero.

ought *v. dif.* (*condiz.*) dovere: *you — to wait,* dovresti aspettare.

ounce *s.* oncia.

our *agg. poss.* nostro, nostra, nostri, nostre.

ours *pron. poss.* il nostro, la nostra, i nostri, le nostre.

ourselves *pron. r. pl.* noi stessi.

out *agg.* esterno. ♦ **out** *avv.* fuori. ♦ **out** (*of*) *prep.* 1. fuori (*di*) 2. senza 3. per ‖ *— -of-date,* fuori moda; *— -of-work,* disoccupato; *— -of-the-way,* remoto.

to outbid (**outbade, outbidden**) *vt.* offrire di più.

outboard *agg.* e *avv.* fuoribordo.

outbreak *s.* 1. scoppio 2. sommossa.

outburst *s.* scoppio.

outcast *s.* proscritto.

to outclass *vt.* surclassare.

outcome *s.* risultato.

outcry *s.* grido, scalpore.

outdid V. *to outdo.*

to outdistance *vt.* distanziare.

to outdo (**outdid, outdone**) *vt.* superare.

outdoor *agg.* all'aperto.

outdoors *avv.* all'aperto.

outer *agg.* esteriore.

outfit(ting) *s.* equipaggiamento.

to outfit *vt.* rifornire di equipaggiamento. ♦ **to outfit** *vi.* rifornirsi di equipaggiamento.

outfitter *s.* fornitore.

to outfly (outflew, outflown) *vt.* sorpassare nel volo.

outgone V. *to outgo.*

outgo *s.* uscita.

to outgo (outwent, outgone) *vt.* sorpassare.

outgoing *agg.* uscente, in partenza.

to outgrow (outgrew, outgrown) *vt.* 1. diventare troppo grande per 2. sorpassare (*in statura*).

outgrowth *s.* 1. escrescenza 2. risultato.

outhouse *s.* 1. tettoia 2. dipendenza.

outing *s.* escursione ‖ — *clothes*, abiti sportivi.

outlandish *agg.* 1. strano 2. remoto.

outlaw *s.* fuorilegge.

outlawry *s.* (*giur.*) proscrizione.

outlay *s.* spesa.

outlet *s.* 1. sbocco 2. cortile.

outline *s.* 1. contorno 2. schema 3. lineamento.

to outline *vt.* 1. delineare 2. abbozzare.

outliner *s.* bozzettista.

to outlive *vt.* sopravvivere a.

outlook *s.* 1. veduta 2. prospettiva 3. vigilanza.

to outnumber *vt.* superare numericamente.

outpost *s.* avamposto.

outpour *s.* 1. scroscio di pioggia 2. (*fig.*) sfogo.

output *s.* produzione, rendimento.

outrage *s.* oltraggio.

to outrage *vt.* oltraggiare.

outrageous *agg.* 1. oltraggioso 2. violento.

outrageousness *s.* 1. oltraggio 2. violenza.

outran V. *to outrun.*

to outrange *vt.* avere una portata maggiore di.

to outreach *vt.* sorpassare.

outrider *s.* battistrada.

outright *agg.* 1. franco 2. completo. ♦ **outright** *avv.* 1. francamente 2. completamente.

outrightness *s.* 1. immediatezza 2. franchezza.

outroar *s.* fracasso.

to outrun (outran, outrun) *vt.* oltrepassare.

outrush *s.* fuga.

to outsell (outsold, outsold) *vt.* 1. vendere in quantità superiore 2. vendere a prezzo superiore.

outset *s.* esordio.

to outshine (outshone, outshone) *vt.* eclissare (*anche fig.*).

outside *agg.* e *s.* 1. esterno 2. massimo. ♦ **outside** *avv.* 1. all'esterno 2. all'aperto. ♦ **outside** *prep.* fuori di.

outsider *s.* 1. profano 2. estraneo 3. (*sport*) non favorito.

outsize *agg.* fuori misura. ♦ **outsize** *s.* taglia fuori misura.

outskirt *s.* orlo. ♦ **outskirts** *s. pl.* periferia (*sing.*).

outsold V. *to outsell.*

outspoken *agg.* franco.

to outspread (outspread, outspread) *vt.* spiegare. ♦ **to outspread (outspread, outspread)** *vi.* spiegarsi.

outstanding *agg.* 1. prominente 2. resistente 3. in sospeso.

to outstretch *vt.* distendere.

to outstrip *vt.* superare (*in velocità*).

outward *agg.* e *s.* esterno. ♦ **outward(s)** *avv.* esternamente.

outwent V. *to outgo.*

oval *agg.* e *s.* ovale.

ovary *s.* ovaia.

ovation *s.* ovazione.

oven *s.* forno.

over *avv.* 1. di sopra 2. eccessivamente ‖ *to be* —, essere finito; — *and* — *again*, più e più volte. ♦ **over** *prep.* 1. su 2. più di 3. durante ‖ — *there*, dall'altra parte; — *and above*, oltre a.

overalls *s. pl.* tuta da lavoro (*sing.*).

overate V. *to overeat.*

to overbear (overbore, overborne) *vt.* dominare, sopraffare.

overbearing *agg.* imperioso.

overbearingness *s.* imperiosità.

overboard *avv.* in mare.

overbore V. *to overbear.*

overborne V. *to overbear.*

to overburden *vt.* sovraccaricare.

overcame V. *to overcome.*

overcast *agg.* scuro, nuvoloso.

to overcast (overcast, overcast) *vt.* oscurare. ♦ **to overcast (overcast, overcast)** *vi.* oscurarsi.

overcharge s. 1. sovraccarico 2. sovrapprezzo.

to **overcharge** vt. 1. sovraccaricare 2. far pagare troppo caro.

to **overcloud** vi. rannuvolarsi.

overcoat s. soprabito.

to **overcome** (overcame, overcome) vt. superare, vincere.

overcoming s. superamento, vittoria.

overconfident agg. troppo sicuro di sé.

overcredulity s. credulità eccessiva.

overcrowded agg. sovraffollato.

overcrowding s. sovraffollamento.

to **overdo** (overdid, overdone) vt. 1. esagerare 2. stancare.

overdone agg. troppo cotto.

overdose s. dose eccessiva.

overdrank V. to overdrink.

to **overdraw** (overdrew, overdrawn) vt. 1. esagerare 2. scoprire il conto in banca.

to **overdrink** (overdrank, overdrunk) vi. bere troppo.

overdue agg. scaduto.

to **overeat** (overate, overeaten) vi. mangiare troppo.

to **overestimate** vt. sopravvalutare.

overexcitability s. sovreccitabilità.

overexcitable agg. sovreccitabile.

to **overexcite** vt. sovreccitare.

overexcitement s. sovreccitazione.

to **overexert** vt. stancare.

to **overexpose** vt. sovresporre.

overfeeding s. superalimentazione.

overflew V. to overfly.

to **overflow** vt. inondare. ♦ to **overflow** vi. trabocare.

overflowing s. inondazione.

to **overfly** (overflew, overflown) vt. 1. sorvolare 2. superare in volo.

overfond agg. troppo appassionato.

to **overgrow** (overgrew, overgrown) vt. 1. coprire 2. superare. ♦ to **overgrow** (overgrew, overgrown) vi. 1. coprirsi 2. crescere troppo.

overgrowth s. 1. crescita eccessiva 2. vegetazione sovrabbondante.

overhang s. sporgenza, aggetto.

to **overhang** (overhung, overhung) vt. 1. sovrastare 2. ornare con tendaggi ecc.

to **overhaul** vt. 1. revisionare 2. sorpassare.

overhaul(ing) s. revisione.

overhead agg. 1. alto 2. (comm.) generale. ♦ **overhead** avv. in alto.

to **overhear** (overheard, overheard) vt. 1. udire per caso 2. origliare.

to **overheat** vt. surriscaldare. ♦ to **overheat** vi. surriscaldarsi.

overheating s. surriscaldamento.

overhung V. to overhang.

overindulgence s. eccessiva indulgenza.

overladen agg. sovraccarico.

overland avv. via terra.

overlap s. sovrapposizione.

overlay s. copertura.

to **overleap** vt. saltare di là da.

overload s. sovraccarico.

to **overload** vt. sovraccaricare.

to **overlook** vt. 1. guardare dall'alto 2. trascurare 3. ispezionare.

overlooker s. ispettore.

overnight agg. 1. compiuto durante la notte 2. per una notte. ♦ **overnight** avv. durante la notte.

overpaid V. to overpay.

to **overpass** vt. 1. attraversare 2. sorpassare 3. trasgredire.

overpast agg. passato.

to **overpay** (overpaid, overpaid) vt. pagare più del dovuto.

overpayment s. pagamento eccessivo.

to **overpeopled** agg. sovrappopolato.

overplus s. soprappiù.

overpopulated agg. sovrappopolato.

overpopulation s. sovrappopolazione.

to **overpower** V. to overbear.

overpowering agg. 1. schiacciante 2. prepotente.

overpressure s. sovrapressione.

to **overprint** vt. sovrastampare.

to **overprize** vt. sopravvalutare.

to **overproduce** vt. produrre in eccesso.

overproduction s. sovraproduzione.

overproud agg. troppo orgoglioso.

overran V. to overrun.

to **overrate** vt. sopravvalutare.

to **overreach** vt. 1. oltrepassare 2. imbrogliare.

to **overrule** vt. 1. dirigere 2. annullare 3. dominare.

to **overrun** (overran, overrun) vt. 1. invadere 2. devastare 3. oltrepassare.

oversaw V. *to oversee.*

oversea(s) *agg. e avv.* d'oltremare.

to oversee (**oversaw, overseen**) *vt.* ispezionare.

overseer *s.* **1.** ispettore **2.** capo squadra.

to overset (**overset, overset**) *vt.* rovesciare. ♦ **to overset** (**overset, overset**) *vi.* rovesciarsi.

to overshadow *vt.* **1.** ombreggiare **2.** adombrare **3.** proteggere.

overshoe *s.* soprascarpa.

to overshoot (**overshot, overshot**) *vt.* lanciare di là da || *to — the mark,* passare i limiti.

overside *avv.* lungo il fianco.

oversight *s.* **1.** svista **2.** sorveglianza.

to oversleep (**overslept, overslept**) *vi.* dormire oltre l'ora fissata.

to overspread (**overspread, overre.** ♦ **to overspread** (**overspread, overspread**) *vi.* spargersi.

to overstate *vt.* esagerare.

to overtake (**overtook, overtaken**) *vt.* **1.** cogliere **2.** superare.

overtaking *s.* sorpasso: *no —,* divieto di sorpasso.

overthrew V. *to overthrow.*

overthrow *s.* **1.** rovesciamento **2.** disfatta.

to overthrow (**overthrew, overthrown**) *vt.* **1.** rovesciare **2.** sconfiggere.

overtime *s.* straordinario (*orario di lavoro*).

overtook V. *to overtake.*

to overturn V. *to overthrow.*

overturnable *agg.* rovesciabile.

overturn(ing) *s.* rovesciamento.

overweary *agg.* stremato.

overweight *agg.* che supera il peso. ♦ **overweight** *s.* sovraccarico.

to overwhelm *vt.* **1.** sommergere **2.** sopraffare.

overwhelming *agg.* schiacciante.

overwork *s.* **1.** lavoro eccessivo **2.** straordinario.

to overwork *vt.* **1.** far lavorare troppo **2.** far eccessivo uso di. ♦ **to overwork** *vi.* lavorare troppo.

to overwrite (**overwrote, overwritten**) *vi.* scrivere troppo.

overwrought *agg.* **1.** esausto **2.** ricercato (*di stile*).

ovine *agg.* ovino.

oviparous *agg.* oviparo.

ovulation *s.* ovulazione.

ovule *s.* ovulo.

to owe *vt.* dovere, essere debitore di || *you must pay what is owing,* dovete pagare il vostro debito.

owing *agg.* dovuto.

owing *to prep.* a causa di.

owl *s.* gufo.

own *agg. e pron.* proprio.

to own *vt.* **1.** possedere **2.** ammettere || *to — to,* confessare.

owner *s.* proprietario || *shipowner,* armatore.

ownership *s.* proprietà.

ox (*pl.* oxen) *s.* bue.

oxidation *s.* ossidazione.

oxide *s.* ossido.

oxidizable *agg.* ossidabile.

to oxidize *vt.* ossidare. ♦ **to oxidize** *vi.* ossidarsi.

oxygen *s.* ossigeno || *— tent,* tenda ad ossigeno.

to oxygenate *vt.* ossigenare.

oxygenation *s.* ossigenazione.

to oxygenize *vt.* ossigenare.

oxyhydrogen *agg.* ossidrico: *— blowpipe,* cannello ossidrico.

oyster *s.* **1.** ostrica **2.** persona silenziosa, riservata.

ozone *s.* ozono.

to ozonize *vt.* ozonizzare.

P

pace *s.* passo.

to pace *vi.* andare al passo. ♦ **to pace** *vt.* percorrere. ♦ **to pace** *vi.* andare al passo, marciare.

paced *agg.* misurato (*a passi*) || *slow —,* a passi lenti.

pachyderm *s.* pachiderma.

pacific *agg.* pacifico.

to pacificate *vt.* pacificare.

pacification *s.* pacificazione.

pacificator, pacifier *s.* pacificatore.

pacificatory *agg.* conciliante.

pacifism *s.* pacifismo.

pacifist *agg. e s.* pacifista.

to pacify *vt.* pacificare.

pack *s.* **1.** pacco, balla, fagotto **2.** carico **3.** imballaggio **4.** muta (*di cani*) **5.** (*med.*) impacco || *— ice,* banchisa; *— saddle,* basto.

to pack *vt.* **1.** impacchettare **2.** imballare 3. raggruppare. ♦ to **pack** *vi.* raggrupparsi || *to* — *up*, fare i bagagli.

package *s.* 1. imballaggio 2. pacco.

to **package** *vt.* 1. imballare 2. impacchettare.

packer *s.* 1. imballatore 2. impacchettatrice (*macchina*).

packet *s.* 1. pacchetto 2. (*mar.*) — (-*boat*), postale.

packing *s.* 1. imballaggio 2. (*mecc.*) guarnizione 3. (*mar.*) baderna || — -*free*, franco d'imballaggio.

pact *s.* patto.

pad[1] *s.* 1. imbottitura 2. zampa (*di cane, lupo, volpe*) 3. (*med.*) tampone.

pad[2] *s.* rumore sordo.

to **pad** *vt.* imbottire.

paddle *s.* 1. pala 2. pagaia.

to **paddle** *vi.* remare con pagaie.

paddy *s.* risaia.

padlock *s.* lucchetto.

to **padlock** *vt.* chiudere con lucchetto.

paediatric *agg.* pediatrico.

paediatrician *s.* pediatra.

paediatrics *s.* pediatria.

paediatrist *s.* pediatra.

pagan *agg.* e *s.* pagano.

paganism *s.* paganesimo.

page[1] *s.* paggio.

page[2] *s.* pagina.

to **page** *vt.* 1. (*tip.*) impaginare 2. numerare le pagine.

pageant *s.* 1. (*teat.*) scena (*di sacra rappresentazione*) 2. parata, corteo.

pageantry *s.* 1. pompa, fasto 2. ostentazione.

to **paginate** *vt.* V. *to page.*

pagination *s.* 1. paginatura 2. impaginazione.

paid V. *to pay.*

pail *s.* secchio.

paillasse *s.* pagliericcio.

pain *s.* 1. pena 2. dolore, sofferenza. ♦ **pains** *s. pl.* doglie.

to **pain** *vt.* far male, far soffrire.

painful *agg.* penoso.

painless *agg.* indolore.

painstaking *agg.* diligente. ♦ **painstaking** *s.* cura.

paint *s.* 1. pittura 2. belletto.

to **paint** *vt.* dipingere. ♦ to **paint** *vi.* imbellettarsi.

painter *s.* 1. pittore 2. imbianchino.

painting *s.* 1. pittura 2. dipinto, quadro.

paintress *s.* pittrice.

pair *s.* paio, coppia.

to **pair** *vt.* accoppiare. ♦ to **pair** *vi.* accoppiarsi.

palace *s.* palazzo.

paladin *s.* paladino.

palatable *agg.* 1. gustoso 2. (*fig.*) gradevole.

palatal *agg.* e *s.* palatale.

palatalization *s.* palatalizzazione.

palate *s.* palato.

pale[1] *agg.* pallido.

pale[2] *s.* 1. paio 2. palizzata.

to **pale** *vt.* far impallidire. ♦ to **pale** *vi.* impallidire.

paleness *s.* pallore.

paleochristian *agg.* paleocristiano.

paleographer *s.* paleografo.

paleography *s.* paleografia.

paleolithic *agg.* paleolitico.

paleologist *s.* paleologo.

paleology *s.* paleologia.

paleontologic(al) *agg.* paleontologico.

paleontologist *s.* paleontologo.

paleontology *s.* paleontologia.

paleozoic *agg.* paleozoico.

palette *s.* tavolozza.

palfrey *s.* palafreno.

palinode *s.* palinodia.

palisade *s.* palizzata.

pall *s.* 1. drappo funebre 2. (*eccl.*) pallio.

to **pall**[1] *vt.* coprire con un drappo.

to **pall**[2] *vt.* saziare. ♦ to **pall** *vi.* saziarsi.

pallet[1] *s.* pagliericcio.

pallet[2] *s.* 1. paletta 2. tavolozza.

to **palliate** *vt.* 1. attenuare 2. scusare.

palliation *s.* 1. attenuazione 2. scusante.

palliative *agg.* e *s.* palliativo.

pallid *agg.* pallido.

pallor *s.* pallore.

palm[1] *s.* palma (*anche fig.*).

palm[2] *s.* (*anat.*) palmo.

to **palm** *vt.* toccare con la mano.

palmaceous *agg.* (*bot.*) di palma.

palmar *agg.* palmare.

palmate, palmated, *agg.* palmato.

palmiped *agg.* e *s.* palmipede.

palmistry *s.* chiromanzia.

palmy *agg.* 1. coperto di palme 2. prosperoso, vittorioso.

palpability *s.* palpabilità.

palpable *agg.* palpabile.

to **palpate** *vt.* palpare.

to **palpitate** *vi.* palpitare.

palpitation s. palpitazione.

palsy s. paralisi.

to **palsy** vt. paralizzare.

to **palter** vi. tergiversare.

paltriness s. meschinità.

paltry agg. meschino.

to **pamper** vt. viziare.

pamphlet s. opuscolo.

pamphleteer s. autore di opuscoli.

pan s. **1.** padella **2.** vaschetta **3.** bacino **4.** piatto di bilancia || *baking* —, teglia.

pancake s. frittella.

panchromatic agg. pancromatico.

pancreatic agg. pancreatico.

pandemonium s. pandemonio.

pander s. mezzano, ruffiano.

to **pander** vi. fare il mezzano.

pane s. **1.** lastra di vetro **2.** (edil.) pannello **3.** faccia (di brillante).

panegyric s. panegirico.

panegyric(al) agg. laudativo.

panel s. **1.** pannello **2.** (neol.) commissione, comitato **3.** (giur.) lista di giurati.

pang s. **1.** fitta **2.** (fig.) stretta al cuore.

panic agg. e s. panico.

panicky agg. allarmato.

panicle s. pannocchia.

panification s. panificazione.

pannier s. paniere.

panoramic agg. panoramico.

pansy s. viola del pensiero.

pant s. **1.** palpito **2.** ansito.

to **pant** vi. **1.** palpitare **2.** ansimare.

pantagruelian agg. pantagruelico.

pantheism s. panteismo.

pantheist s. panteista.

pantheistic(al) agg. panteistico.

panther s. pantera.

panties s. pl. (fam.) mutandine.

panting s. **1.** palpitazione **2.** ansito **3.** ansia.

pantograph s. pantografo.

pantomime s. pantomima.

pantry s. dispensa.

pants s. pl. (fam.) mutande.

pap s. pappa.

papacy s. papato.

papal agg. papale.

paper s. **1.** carta **2.** prova d'esame

paper s. **1.** carta **2.** certificato, documento **3.** prova d'esame **4.** giornale || — *back*, libro in brossura; — *board*, cartone; — *hanger*, tappezziere; — *hanging*, tappezzeria.

to **paper** vt. **1.** incartare **2.** tappezzare.

papery agg. cartaceo.

papillary agg. papillare.

papism s. papismo.

papist s. papista.

papyrology s. papirologia.

papyrus s. (pl. -ri) papiro.

parable s. parabola.

parabolic(al) agg. **1.** parabolico **2.** di parabola.

paraboloid s. paraboloide.

parachute s. paracadute.

to **parachute** vt. paracadutare. ♦ to **parachute** vi. paracadutarsi.

parachutism s. paracadutismo.

parachutist s. paracadutista.

parade s. **1.** (mil.) parata **2.** mostra, sfoggio **3.** viale, passeggiata.

to **parade** vt. disporre in parata. ♦ to **parade** vi. marciare in parata.

paradigm s. paradigma.

paradisaic(al) agg. paradisiaco.

paradise s. paradiso.

paradisiac(al) agg. paradisiaco.

paradox s. paradosso.

paradoxical agg. paradossale.

paraffin s. paraffina.

paragon s. modello (di perfezione ecc.).

paragraph s. paragrafo.

to **paragraph** vt. dividere in paragrafi.

parallel agg. parallelo. ♦ **parallel** s. **1.** parallelo **2.** parallela.

to **parallel** vt. **1.** mettere in posizione parallela **2.** paragonare.

parallelepiped s. parallelepipedo.

parallelism s. parallelismo.

parallelogram s. parallelogramma.

paralogism s. paralogismo.

to **paralyse** vt. paralizzare.

paralysis s. (pl. -ses) paralisi.

paralytic agg. e s. paralitico.

parameter s. parametro.

paramount agg. supremo. ♦ **paramount** s. capo supremo.

paramour s. amante.

paranoia s. paranoia.

paranoiac agg. e s. paranoico.

paranymph s. paraninfo.

parapet s. parapetto.

paraphrase s. parafrasi.

to **paraphrase** vt. e vi. parafrasare.

parasite s. parassita.

parasitic(al) agg. parassitico.

parasitism s. parassitismo.

parasol s. parasole.

paratrooper s. paracadutista.

paratyphoid s. paratifo.

parcel s. 1. pacco 2. lotto, appezzamento di terreno 3. gruppo.

to parcel vt. spartire.

parcelling s. spartizione.

parcener s. coerede.

to parch vt. 1. arrostire 2. disseccare. ♦ to parch vi. 1. bruciarsi 2. disseccarsi.

parchment s. pergamena.

pardon s. perdono.

to pardon vt. perdonare.

pardonable agg. perdonabile.

to pare vt. 1. tagliare 2. sbucciare.

parenchyma s. parenchima.

parent s. 1. genitore 2. causa, origine.

parentage s. 1. discendenza 2. nascita.

parental agg. paterno, materno.

parenthesis s. (pl. -ses) parentesi.

parenthetic(al) agg. parentetico.

parenthood s. paternità, maternità.

parentless agg. orfano.

paresis s. paresi.

pariah s. paria.

parietal agg. parietale.

parish s. parrocchia || — priest, parroco.

parishioner s. parrocchiano.

Parisian agg. e s. parigino.

parisyllabic agg. e s. parisillabo.

parity s. parità.

park s. 1. parco 2. posteggio.

to park vt. 1. adibire a parco 2. parcheggiare.

parking s. parcheggio || no —, divieto di sosta.

parkway s. (amer.) viale.

parley s. colloquio.

to parley vi. parlamentare.

parliament s. parlamento.

parliamentarian s. parlamentare.

parliamentarianism s. parlamentarismo.

parliamentary agg. parlamentare.

parlour s. 1. salotto 2. parlatorio || beauty —, istituto di bellezza.

Parmesan agg. parmigiano.

parochial agg. 1. parrocchiale 2. (fig.) ristretto.

parochialism s. ristrettezza di vedute.

parodist s. parodista.

parody s. parodia.

to parody vt. parodiare.

parole s. 1. parola d'onore 2. parola d'ordine.

paroxysm s. parossismo.

parricidal agg. parricida.

parricide s. 1. parricidio 2. parricida.

parrot s. pappagallo.

to parrot vt. ripetere pappagallescamente.

parry v. parare, schivare.

parsley s. prezzemolo.

parson s. parroco (anglicano).

parsonage s. (eccl.) canonica, parrocchia.

part s. parte.

to part vt. dividere. ♦ to part vi. dividersi.

to partake (partook, partaken) vi. partecipare, prendere parte.

parthenogenesis s. partenogenesi.

partial agg. parziale.

partiality s. parzialità.

partially avv. parzialmente.

participant agg. e s. partecipante.

to participate vi. 1. partecipare 2. condividere.

participation s. partecipazione.

participial agg. participiale.

participle s. participio.

particle s. particella (anche gramm.).

particular agg. 1. particolare 2. particolareggiato 3. esigente. ♦ particular s. particolare.

particularism s. particolarismo.

particularist s. particolarista.

particularity s. 1. particolarità 2. meticolosità.

to particularize vt. e vi. dettagliare.

parting s. separazione.

partisan agg. e s. partigiano.

partition s. 1. divisione 2. tramezzo.

to partition vt. dividere.

partitive agg. e s. partitivo.

partly avv. in parte.

partner s. 1. socio 2. coniuge.

partnership s. 1. associazione 2. (comm.) società.

partook V. to partake.

partridge s. pernice.

parturient agg. partoriente.

parturition s. parto.

party s. 1. parte 2. partito 3. brigata 4. trattenimento 5. pattuglia.

pasha s. pascià.

pass¹ s. passo, gola.

pass² s. 1. passaggio 2. trapasso 3. promozione 4. lasciapassare.

to pass vt. e vi. passare || to — away, sparire; to — by, passar oltre.

passable *agg.* passabile.

passage *s.* **1.** passaggio **2.** corridoio **3.** brano.

passementerie *s.* passamaneria.

passenger *s.* passeggero.

passer *s.* — *-by*, passante.

passible *agg.* passibile.

passing *agg.* **1.** passeggero **2.** casuale. ♦ **passing** *s.* passaggio.

passion *s.* passione ‖ — *-flower*, passiflora.

passional *agg.* passionale.

passionate *agg.* appassionato, passionale.

passionless *agg.* impassibile.

passive *agg.* e *s.* passivo.

passivism, passivity *s.* passività.

passport *s.* passaporto.

password *s.* parola d'ordine.

past *agg.* passato. ♦ **past** *s.* passato. ♦ **past** *avv.* vicino. ♦ **past** *prep.* al di là di.

paste *s.* pasta ‖ *tooth* —, dentifricio.

to paste *vt.* **1.** incollare, appiccicare **2.** (*gergo*) attaccare.

pasteboard *agg.* di cartone. ♦ **pasteboard** *s.* cartone.

pastel *s.* pastello.

pasteurization *s.* pastorizzazione.

to pasteurize *vt.* pastorizzare.

pastime *s.* passatempo.

pastoral *agg.* e *s.* pastorale.

pastry *s.* dolci (*pl.*).

pasture *s.* pascolo.

to pasture *vt.* e *vi.* pascolare.

pasty *agg.* pastoso. ♦ **pasty** *s.* (*cuc.*) pasticcio.

pat *agg.* adatto. ♦ **pat** *avv.* esattamente. ♦ **pat** *s.* **1.** colpetto **2.** panetto di burro.

to pat *vt.* battere leggermente.

patch *s.* **1.** pezza, toppa **2.** macchia.

to patch *vt.* aggiustare, rattoppare, raffazzonare.

patching *s.* rattoppo.

patchy *agg.* **1.** rappezzato **2.** a macchie.

patent *s.* **1.** chiaro, manifesto, evidente **2.** brevettato. ♦ **patent** *s.* brevetto.

to patent *vt.* brevettare.

patentee *s.* detentore di brevetto.

paternal *agg.* paterno.

paternalism *s.* paternalismo.

paternalistic *agg.* paternalistico.

paternity *s.* paternità.

path *s.* **1.** sentiero **2.** pista **3.** percorso, traiettoria.

pathetic *agg.* patetico.

pathfinder *s.* esploratore.

pathless *agg.* **1.** senza sentieri **2.** inesplorato.

pathogenic *agg.* patogeno.

pathologic(al) *agg.* patologico.

pathologist *s.* patologo.

pathology *s.* patologia.

pathway *s.* sentiero.

patience *s.* pazienza.

patient *agg.* **1.** paziente **2.** suscettibile. ♦ **patient** *s.* paziente.

patriarch *s.* patriarca.

patriarchal *agg.* patriarcale.

patriarchate *s.* patriarcato.

patrician *agg.* e *s.* patrizio.

patricide *s.* V. *parricide*.

patrimonial *agg.* patrimoniale.

patrimony *s.* patrimonio.

patriot *s.* patriota.

patriotic *agg.* patriottico.

patriotism *s.* patriottismo.

patrol *s.* pattuglia, ronda.

to patrol *vt.* e *vi.* pattugliare, fare la ronda.

patron *s.* patrono.

patronage *s.* patronato.

patronal *agg.* patronale.

patroness *s.* patronessa.

to patronize *vt.* **1.** patrocinare **2.** trattare con condiscendenza.

patronizing *agg.* **1.** protettivo **2.** condiscendente.

patter[1] *s.* gergo.

patter[2] *s.* picchiettìo.

to patter *vi.* picchiettare.

pattern *s.* **1.** modello, campione **2.** disegno (*di stoffa ecc.*).

to pattern *vt.* modellare (su).

paunch *s.* pancia.

pauper *s.* povero.

pauperism *s.* povertà.

pause *s.* pausa.

to pause *vi.* **1.** fare una pausa **2.** esitare, indugiare.

pauseless *agg.* incessante.

to pave *vt.* **1.** pavimentare **2.** (*fig.*) appianare.

pavement *s.* **1.** pavimentazione **2.** marciapiede.

paver *s.* lastricatore.

pavilion *s.* padiglione.

paving *s.* pavimentazione.

paw *s.* zampa.

to paw *vt.* dare zampate. ♦ **to paw** *vi.* scalpitare (*di cavalli*).

pawn *s.* **1.** pegno **2.** pedina (*di scacchi*).

to **pawn** *vt.* impegnare (*dare in pegno*).
pawnbroker *s.* prestatore su pegno.
pawnbroking *s.* il prestare su pegno.
pawner *s.* chi dà qualcosa in pegno.
pawnshop *s.* agenzia di prestiti su pegno.
pay *s.* paga.
to **pay (paid, paid)** *vt.* e *vi.* 1. pagare 2. rendere, fruttare || *to — off*, liquidare.
payable *agg.* 1. pagabile 2. redditizio.
payee *s.* creditore.
payer *s.* pagatore.
paying out *s.* esborso.
payment *s.* pagamento.
payoff *s.* 1. giorno di paga 2. liquidazione.
payroll *s.* libro paga.
pea *s.* pisello || *chick —*, cece.
peace *s.* pace.
peaceable *agg.* pacifico.
peaceful *s.* pacifico, tranquillo.
peacefulness *s.* pace, calma.
peaceless *agg.* agitato.
peacemaker *s.* pacificatore.
peach *s.* (*bot.*) pesca.
peach-tree *s.* pesco.
peachy *agg.* simile a pesca.
peacock *s.* pavone.
to **peacock** *vi.* pavoneggiarsi.
peak *s.* 1. picco 2. punta 3. visiera.
peaky *agg.* appuntito.
peal *s.* 1. scampanio 2. scoppio, fragore, scroscio (*di risa, applausi*).
to **peal** *vi.* scampanare. ♦ to **peal** *vt.* far rimbombare.
peanut *s.* arachide.
pear *s.* pera.
pear-tree *s.* pero.
pearl *s.* perla.
to **pearl** *vt.* imperlare, ornare di perle. ♦ to **pearl** *vi.* imperlarsi.
pearly *agg.* 1. perlaceo 2. ricco di perle.
peasant *s.* contadino.
peasantry *s.* 1. condizione di contadino 2. i contadini (*pl.*).
peat *s.* torba || *-bog*, torbiera.
pebble *s.* 1. ciottolo 2. cristallo di rocca.
to **pebble** *vt.* coprire con ciottoli.
peccary *s.* pecari.
peck *s.* beccata.
to **peck** *vt.* e *vi.* beccare.
pectoral *agg.* e *s.* pettorale.

peculation *s.* peculato.
peculiar *agg.* 1. particolare 2. strano.
peculiarity *s.* 1. particolarità 2. bizzarria, eccentricità.
pecuniary *agg.* pecuniario.
pedagogic(al) *agg.* pedagogico.
pedagogics *s.* pedagogia.
pedagogist *s.* pedagogista.
pedagogue *s.* pedagogo.
pedagogy *s.* pedagogia.
pedal *s.* pedale.
to **pedal** *vt.* e *vi.* pedalare.
pedant *s.* pedante.
pedantic *agg.* pedante.
pedantry *s.* pedanteria.
pedestal *s.* piedistallo.
pedestrian *agg.* pedestre. ♦ **pedestrian** *s.* pedone.
pediatrics *ecc.* V. *paediatrics ecc.*
pediment *s.* (*arch.*) frontone.
pedlar *s.* venditore ambulante.
peel *s.* buccia.
to **peel** *vt.* sbucciare. ♦ to **peel** *vi.* sbucciarsi.
peeling *s.* buccia.
peep[1] *s.* 1. sguardo furtivo 2. fessura.
peep[2] *s.* pigolio.
to **peep**[1] *vi.* 1. guardare furtivamente 2. far capolino.
to **peep**[2] *vi.* pigolare.
peeper[1] *s.* ficcanaso, persona curiosa.
peeper[2] *s.* piccincino.
peer *s.* 1. pari 2. Pari, membro della Camera dei Lord.
to **peer** *vt.* uguagliare. ♦ to **peer** *vi.* 1. scrutare 2. far capolino.
peerage *s.* 1. i Pari 2. nobiltà.
peerless *agg.* senza pari.
peevish *agg.* irritabile.
peg *s.* piuolo.
to **peg** *vt.* fissare.
pejorative *agg.* e *s.* peggiorativo.
pelagic *agg.* oceanico.
pelican *s.* pellicano.
pellet *s.* 1. pallottolina (*di carta ecc.*) 2. pallottola 3. pillola.
pellucid *agg.* trasparente.
pelt[1] *s.* colpo (*di proiettile ecc.*).
pelt[2] *s.* pelle (*di animale*).
to **pelt** *vt.* colpire.
pelvic *agg.* pelvico.
pelvis *s.* bacino.
pen[1] *s.* penna || *-nib*, pennino; *fountain— —*, penna stilografica.
pen[2] *s.* recinto (*per animali*).
to **pen**[1] *vt.* scrivere.
to **pen**[2] *vt.* rinchiudere animali in un recinto.

penal *agg.* penale.

to penalize *vt.* (*sport.*) penalizzare.

penalty *s.* penalità, punizione.

penance *s.* penitenza.

pence *s.* V. *penny.*

pencil *s.* matita.

pendant, pendent *agg.* e *s.* pendente.

pending *prep.* 1. durante 2. fino a.

pendular *agg.* pendolare.

pendulous *agg.* pendulo.

pendulum *s.* pendolo || — -*clock*, pendola.

penetrable *agg.* penetrabile.

to penetrate *vt.* e *vi.* penetrare.

penetration *s.* penetrazione.

penetrative *agg.* penetrante.

penguin *s.* pinguino.

penicillin *s.* penicillina.

peninsula *s.* penisola.

peninsular *agg.* peninsulare.

penis *s.* pene.

penitence *s.* penitenza.

penitent *agg.* e *s.* penitente.

penitential *agg.* penitenziale.

penitentiary *agg.* penitenziale. ♦ **penitentiary** *s.* (*eccl.*) penitenziere 2. riformatorio 3. (*amer.*) penitenziario.

penknife *s.* (*pl.* -*knives*) temperino.

pennant *s.* (*mar.*) pennone.

penniless *agg.* senza un soldo.

pennon *s.* pennone.

penny *s.* (*numero delle monete*), **pence** (*loro valore*) *s.* "*penny*".

pension *s.* pensione.

to pension *vt.* pensionare.

pensionable *agg.* pensionabile.

pensioner *s.* pensionato.

pensive *agg.* pensoso.

pent *agg.* chiuso.

pentagon *s.* pentagono.

pentagonal *agg.* pentagonale.

pentagram *s.* pentagono.

pentahedron *s.* pentaedro.

pentameter *s.* pentametro.

pentane *s.* pentano.

pentathlon *s.* pentatlon.

Pentecost *s.* Pentecoste.

Pentecostal *agg.* pentecostale.

penthouse *s.* tettoia.

pentode *s.* (*elettr.*) pentodo.

pentose *s.* pentosio.

penult(imate) *agg.* e *s.* penultimo.

penury *s.* povertà.

peony *s.* peonia.

people *s.* (*costruzione al pl.*) 1. popolo 2. gente 3. folla.

to people *vt.* popolare.

pepper *s.* pepe || — -*mill*, macinapepe.

to pepper *vt.* condire con pepe.

peppercorn *s.* grano di pepe.

peppermint *s.* menta peperita.

peppery *agg.* 1. pepato 2. collerico.

pepsin(e) *s.* pepsina.

per *prep.* per: — *cent*, per cento.

peracid *s.* peracido.

to perambulate *vt.* 1. attraversare 2. ispezionare. ♦ **to perambulate** *vi.* passeggiare.

perambulation *s.* 1. ispezione 2. passeggiata.

perambulator *s.* carrozzella per bambini.

percale *s.* percalle.

percelvable *agg.* percettibile.

to perceive *vt.* percepire, scorgere. ♦ **to perceive** *vi.* accorgersi.

percentage *s.* percentuale.

perceptible *agg.* percettibile.

perception *s.* percezione.

perceptive *agg.* percettivo.

perch[1] *s.* gruccia.

perch[2] *s.* pesce persico.

to perch *vi.* appollaiarsi.

perchlorate *s.* perclorato.

percipience *s.* percezione.

to percolate *vt.* e *vi.* filtrare, colare.

percolator *s.* filtro.

percussion *s.* percussione || — -*pin*, percussore.

perdition *s.* perdizione.

perdurable *agg.* durevole.

to peregrinate *vi.* peregrinare.

peregrination *s.* peregrinazione.

peremptory *agg.* perentorio.

perennial *agg.* perenne.

perfect *agg.* perfetto.

to perfect *vt.* perfezionare.

perfectibility *s.* perfettibilità.

perfectible *agg.* perfettibile.

perfecting *s.* 1. perfezionamento 2. completamento.

perfection *s.* 1. perfezione 2. perfezionamento.

perfectionism *s.* perfezionismo.

perfectionist *s.* perfezionista.

perfectly *avv.* perfettamente.

perfidious *agg.* perfido, sleale.

perfidy *s.* perfidia, slealtà.

to perforate *vt.* perforare.

perforation *s.* perforazione.

to perform *vt.* 1. eseguire 2. (*teat.*) rappresentare.

performable *agg.* 1. eseguibile 2. rappresentabile.

performance *s.* **1.** esecuzione **2.** atto **3.** (*teat.*) rappresentazione.
performer *s.* **1** esecutore **2.** attore.
performing *agg.* ammaestrato.
perfume *s.* profumo.
to perfume *vt.* profumare.
perfumer *s.* profumiere.
perfumery *s.* **1.** profumeria **2.** profumi.
perfunctory *agg.* superficiale.
to perfuse *vt.* aspergere.
perfusion *s.* aspersione.
perhaps *avv.* forse.
pericardium *s.* pericardio.
perigee *s.* perigeo.
peril *s.* pericolo.
perilous *agg.* pericoloso.
perimeter *s.* perimetro.
period *s.* **1.** periodo **2.** ora di lezione **3.** stadio, fase (*di una malattia*) **4.** (*gramm.*) punto.
periodic *agg.* periodico.
periodical *agg.* e *s.* periodico.
periodicity *s.* periodicità.
peripheral *agg.* periferico.
periphery *s.* **1.** perimetro **2.** superficie.
periphrase, periphrasis *s.* (*pl.* -ses) perifrasi.
periphrastic *agg.* perifrastico.
periscope *s.* periscopio.
to perish *vi.* perire.
perishable *agg.* **1.** deperibile **2.** mortale.
perishables *s. pl.* merci deteriorabili.
peristyle *s.* peristilio.
peritonitis *s.* peritonite.
periwig *s.* parrucca.
periwigged *agg.* imparruccato.
periwinkle *s.* pervinca.
to perjure *vt.* giurare falsamente.
perjurer, perjury *s.* spergiuro.
permanence *s.* permanenza.
permanent *agg.* permanente.
permanganate *s.* permanganato.
permeability *s.* permeabilità.
permeable *agg.* permeabile.
to permeate *vt.* permeare. ◆ **to permeate** *vi.* permearsi.
permission, permit *s.* permesso.
to permit *vt.* e *vi.* permettere.
to permute *vt.* permutare.
pernicious *agg.* pernicioso.
to perorate *vi.* perorare.
peroration *s.* perorazione.
peroxid(e) *s.* perossido || *hydrogen* —, acqua ossigenata.
to peroxide *vt.* ossigenare.

perpendicular *agg.* perpendicolare. ◆ **perpendicular** *s.* **1.** perpendicolare **2.** filo a piombo.
perpendicularity *s.* perpendicolarità.
to perpetrate *vt.* perpetrare.
perpetration *s.* perpetrazione.
perpetual *agg.* perpetuo.
to perpetuate *vt.* perpetuare.
perpetuity *s.* **1.** perpetuità **2.** rendita vitalizia.
to perplex *vt.* **1.** rendere perplesso **2.** complicare.
perplexed *agg.* perplesso.
perplexity *s.* **1.** perplessità **2.** complicazione.
to persecute *vt.* perseguitare.
persecution *s.* persecuzione.
persecutor *s.* persecutore.
perseverance *s.* perseveranza.
to persevere *vi.* perseverare.
Persian *agg.* e *s.* persiano.
persimmon *s.* (*bot.*) cachi.
to persist *vi.* persistere.
persistence *s.* persistenza.
persistent *agg.* persistente.
person *s.* persona.
personable *agg.* ben fatto.
personage *s.* personaggio.
personal *agg.* personale.
personality *s.* personalità.
personalization *s.* personificazione.
to personalize *vt.* personificare.
personally *avv.* personalmente.
personification *s.* personificazione.
to personify *vt.* personificare.
personnel *s.* personale.
perspective *agg.* prospettico. ◆ **perspective** *s.* prospettiva.
perspicacious *agg.* perspicace.
perspicacity *s.* perspicacia.
perspicuity *s.* perspicuità.
perspicuous *agg.* perspicuo.
perspiration *s.* traspirazione.
to perspire *vt.* e *vi.* sudare, trasudare.
to persuade *vt.* persuadere.
persuasion *s.* **1.** persuasione **2.** credenza.
persuasive *agg.* persuasivo.
pert *agg.* impertinente.
to pertain *vi.* appartenere.
pertinacious *agg.* pertinace.
pertinacy, pertinacity *s.* pertinacia.
pertinence *s.* pertinenza.
pertinent *agg.* pertinente.
pertly *avv.* insolentemente.
pertness *s.* insolenza.

to **perturb** *vt.* perturbare.
perturbation *s.* perturbazione.
perusal *s.* lettura attenta.
to **peruse** *vt.* leggere attentamente.
to **pervade** *vt.* pervadere.
pervasion *s.* penetrazione.
pervasive *agg.* penetrante.
perverse *agg.* **1.** perverso **2.** errato **3.** ostinato.
perversion *s.* perversione.
perversity *s.* perversità.
pervert *s.* **1.** pervertito **2.** apostata.
to **pervert** *vt.* pervertire.
pessimism *s.* pessimismo.
pessimist *s.* pessimista.
pessimistic *agg.* pessimistico.
pessimistically *avv.* in modo pessimistico.
pest *s.* peste (*anche fig.*).
to **pester** *vt.* importunare.
pestiferous *agg.* pestifero.
pestilence *s.* pestilenza.
pestilent *agg.* **1.** nocivo **2.** molesto.
pestilential *agg.* pestilenziale.
pestle *s.* pestello.
pet *agg.* e *s.* favorito || — *name*, vezzeggiativo.
to **pet** *vt.* vezzeggiare.
petal *s.* petalo.
petard *s.* petardo.
petition *s.* petizione, istanza.
to **petition** *vt.* e *vi.* fare una petizione (a).
petitioner *s.* postulante.
to **petrify** *vt.* pietrificare. ♦ to **petrify** *vi.* pietrificarsi.
petrography *s.* petrografia.
petrol *s.* benzina.
petticoat *s.* sottoveste.
pettifogger *s.* azzeccagarbugli.
petty *agg.* **1.** meschino **2.** subalterno.
petulant *agg.* petulante.
pew *s.* banco (*di chiesa*).
pewter *s.* peltro.
phagocyte *s.* fagocita.
phalanstery *s.* falansterio.
phalanx *s.* (*pl.* -ges) falange.
phallic *agg.* fallico.
phantasm *s.* fantasma.
phantasmagoria *s.* fantasmagoria.
phantasmagorial, phantasmagoric(al) *agg.* fantasmagorico.
phantom *s.* **1.** fantasma **2.** apparizione.
Pharaoh *s.* faraone.
Pharisee *s.* fariseo.
pharmaceutic(al) *agg.* farmaceutico.

pharmaceutics *s.* farmaceutica.
pharmacology *s.* farmacologia.
pharmacopoeia *s.* farmacopea.
pharmacy *s.* farmacia.
pharyngitis *s.* faringite.
pharynx *s.* (*pl.* -ges) faringe.
phase *s.* fase.
pheasant *s.* fagiano.
phenic *agg.* fenico.
phenol *s.* fenolo.
phenomenal *agg.* **1.** fenomenico **2.** fenomenale.
phenomenalism *s.* fenomenismo.
phenomenology *s.* fenomenologia.
phenomenon *s.* (*pl.* -na) fenomeno.
phial *s.* fiala.
to **philander** *vi.* fare il cascamorto.
philanderer *s.* cascamorto.
philanthrope *s.* filantropo.
philanthropic(al) *agg.* filantropico.
philanthropism *s.* filantropia.
philanthropist *s.* filantropo.
philanthropy *s.* filantropia.
philatelic(al) *agg.* filatelico.
philatelist *s.* filatelico.
philately *s.* filatelia.
philharmonic *agg.* filarmonico.
philippic *s.* filippica.
Philippine *agg.* filippino.
philologian, philologist *s.* filologo.
philology *s.* filologia.
philosopher *s.* filosofo.
philosophic(al) *agg.* filosofico.
philosophist *s.* pseudofilosofo.
to **philosophize** *vi.* filosofare.
philosophy *s.* filosofia.
phlebitis *s.* flebite.
phleboclysis *s.* fleboclisi.
phlegm *s.* flemma.
phlegmatic(al) *agg.* flemmatico.
phlegmon *s.* flemmone.
phlogistic *agg.* flogistico.
phobia *s.* fobia.
phoenix *s.* fenice.
phone *s.* V. *telephone.*
phones *s.* *pl.* cuffie.
phoneme *s.* fonema.
phonetics *s.* fonetica.
phonogram *s.* fonogramma.
phonograph *s.* fonografo.
phonology *s.* fonologia.
phosphate *s.* fosfato.
phosphor *s.* fosforo.
phosphorescence *s.* fosforescenza.
phosphorescent *agg.* fosforescente.
phosphoric *agg.* fosforico.
phosphorous *agg.* fosforoso.

PHOTO 204 **PILING**

photo s. foto.

photocell s. cellula fotoelettrica.

photocopy s. fotocopia.

photoelectric(al) agg. fotoelettrico.

photogenic agg. fotogenico.

photograph s. fotografia.

to **photograph** vt. fotografare.

photographer s. fotografo.

photography s. fotografia (come arte).

photometry s. fotometria.

photomontage s. fotomontaggio.

phrase s. 1. locuzione, frase 2. stile.

to **phrase** vt. esprimere.

phraseology s. fraseologia.

phrenetic(al) agg. frenetico.

phrenologist s. frenologo.

phrenology s. frenologia.

phthisiology s. tisiologia.

phthisis s. tisi.

phylloxera s. fillossera.

physic s. medicina.

physical agg. fisico.

physician s. medico.

physicist s. fisico.

physics s. fisica.

physiognomist s. fisionomista.

physiognomy s. fisionomia.

physiologic(al) agg. fisiologico.

physiologist s. fisiologo.

physiology s. fisiologia.

physiotherapy s. fisioterapia.

physique s. fisico.

pianist s. pianista.

picaresque agg. picaresco.

pick[1] s. 1. piccone 2. colpo di piccone || — tooth —, stuzzicadenti.

pick[2] s. scelta, il meglio (di qc.).

to **pick** vt. 1. scavare 2. pulire 3. raccogliere 4. rubare.

pickax(e) s. piccone.

picker s. 1. piccone 2. zappatore 3. raccoglitore.

picket s. 1. piolo, palo 2. (mil.) picchetto.

pickle s. 1. salamoia 2. sottaceti (pl.).

to **pickle** vt. mettere in salamoia, sotto aceto.

picklock s. 1. scassinatore 2. grimaldello.

pickpocket s. borsaiolo.

pickup s. 1. raccolta 2. (mecc.) accelerazione 3. fonorivelatore.

pictorial agg. 1. illustrato 2. pittorico. ◆ **pictorial** s. giornale illustrato.

picture s. 1. quadro, dipinto, ritrat-

to 2. illustrazione. ◆ **pictures** s. pl. cinema (sing.) || — fook, libro illustrato.

to **picture** vt. dipingere || to — to oneself, immaginarsi, figurarsi.

picturesque agg. pittoresco.

pidgin agg. — English, inglese scorretto (usato tra cinesi ed europei).

pie[1] s. pica, gazza.

pie[2] s. torta, pasticcio.

pie[3] s. (tip.) refuso.

piece s. 1. pezzo 2. pezza (di tessuto) || by the —, a cottimo.

to **piece** vt. rappezzare, raggiustare.

piecemeal avv. pezzo per pezzo. ◆ **piecemeal** agg. frammentario.

piecework s. (lavoro a) cottimo.

pieceworker s. cottimista.

pied agg. screziato.

pier s. 1. molo 2. pilone || — -glass, specchiera.

to **pierce** vt. 1. forare 2. trafiggere.

piercer s. 1. punzone 2. punzonatore.

piercing agg. penetrante. ◆ **piercing** s. perforamento.

pietism s. pietismo.

piety s. pietà, reverenza.

pig s. 1. maiale 2. (metal.) lingotto.

pigeon s. piccione || — -house, piccionaia; carrier —, piccione viaggiatore.

pigeonhole s. 1. colombaia 2. casella 3. (giur.) casellario.

to **pigeonhole** vt. incasellare.

piggish agg. porcino.

pigheaded agg. testardo.

pigment s. pigmento.

pigmentation s. pigmentazione.

pigmy agg. e s. pigmeo.

pigsty s. porcile.

pike[1] s. picca.

pike[2] s. (amer.) pedaggio.

pilaster s. pilastro.

pile s. 1. mucchio 2. fabbricato 3. rogo 4. (elettr.) pila 5. (fig.) gruzzolo.

to **pile**[1] vt. ammucchiare. ◆ to **pile** vi. ammucchiarsi.

to **pile**[2] vt. conficcare pali in, fare palizzate.

piles s. pl. emorroidi.

to **pilfer** vt. e vi. rubacchiare.

pilferer s. ladruncolo.

pilgrim s. pellegrino.

pilgrimage s. pellegrinaggio.

piling[1] s. ammucchiamento.

piling[2] s. palificazione di sostegno.

pill s. pillola: *contraceptive (pill)*, pillola anticoncezionale.
pillage s. 1. saccheggio 2. bottino.
to pillage vt. saccheggiare.
pillar s. colonna, guanciale ‖ -*box*, cassetta delle lettere.
pillory s. berlina.
to pillory vt. mettere alla berlina.
pillow s. cuscino, guanciale ‖ -*case*, federa.
pilot s. pilota.
to pilot vt. pilotare.
pilotage s. pilotaggio.
pimple s. foruncolo.
pin s. 1. spillo 2. perno ‖ *pins* and *needles*, formicolio.
to pin vt. 1. puntare 2. (*fig.*) inchiodare.
pinafore s. grembiulino.
pinaster s. pinastro.
to pincer vt. attanagliare.
pincers s. pl. tenaglie.
pinch s. 1. pizzico, pizzicotto 2. (*fig.*) angustia.
to pinch vt. 1. pizzicare 2. stringere 3. causare dolore. ◆ **to pinch** vi. essere avaro.
pinchbeck s. principisbecco.
pincushion s. puntaspilli.
Pindaric agg. pindarico.
pine s. pino ‖ — -*apple*, ananasso; — -*cone*, pigna; — -*wood*, pineta.
to pine vi. struggersi.
pinion[1] s. penna remigante.
pinion[2] s. (*mecc.*) pignone.
to pinion vt. tarpare le ali a.
pink agg. rosa. ◆ **pink** s. 1. colore rosa 2. garofano 3. (*fig.*) quintessenza.
to pink vt. 1. traforare 2. trafiggere.
pinky agg. roseo.
pinnacle s. 1. pinnacolo 2. sommità.
pinpoint s. capocchia di spillo.
pint s. pinta.
pioneer s. pioniere.
pious agg. 1. pio 2. pietoso.
piousness s. pietà.
pip s. seme di frutto.
to pip vi. pigolare.
pipage s. 1. tubatura 2. trasporto per tubatura.
pipe s. 1. tubo 2. pipa 3. strumento a fiato 4. condotta.
to pipe vi. 1. suonare (*piffero ecc.*) 2. stridere. ◆ **to pipe** vt. 1. suonare 2. trasportare con tubature 3.

fornire di tubature.
pipeline s. oleodotto.
piper s. pifferaio.
pipet(te) s. (*chim.*) pipetta.
piping agg. 1. flautato 2. acuto. ◆ **piping** s. 1. suono (*di piffero ecc.*) 2. suono acuto 3. tubatura.
piquancy s. gusto piccante.
piquant agg. piccante.
pique s. ripicco, risentimento.
piracy s. 1. pirateria 2. plagio.
pirate s. 1. pirata 2. plagiario.
pirogue s. piroga.
pirouette s. piroetta.
to pirouette vi. piroettare.
pistil s. pistillo.
pistol s. pistola.
piston s. pistone.
pit[1] s. 1. fossa 2. cavità 3. platea.
to pit vt. 1. bucare 2. mettere in una fossa.
pitch[1] s. 1. lancio 2. beccheggio 3. (*mecc.*) passo 4. (*mus.*) intonazione 5. inclinazione.
pitch[2] s. pece, bitume ‖ -*dark*, nero come la pece.
to pitch[1] vt. 1. sistemare 2. gettare 3. intonare. ◆ **to pitch** vi. 1. beccheggiare 2. (*aer.*) picchiare.
to pitch[2] vt. impeciare.
pitcher s. brocca.
pitchfork s. forcone.
to pitchfork vt. 1. rimuovere 2. spingere (*col forcone*).
pitching s. beccheggio.
pitchy agg. 1. impeciato 2. simile a pece.
piteous agg. pietoso.
pitfall s. trappola.
pith s. 1. midollo 2. (*fig.*) essenza.
pithy agg. (*fig.*) vigoroso.
pitiable, pitiful agg. pietoso.
pitiless agg. spietato.
pittance s. poco denaro.
pitted agg. butterato.
pity s. pietà ‖ *what a* —!, che peccato!
to pity vt. aver pietà di, compatire.
pitying agg. pietoso.
pivot s. cardine.
to pivot vt. montare su cardini. ◆ **to pivot** vi. girare su cardini.
placable agg. placabile.
placard s. manifesto.
to placate vt. placare.
placatory agg. conciliante.
place s. 1. posto 2. brano ‖ *to take* —, aver luogo, accadere.

to **place** *vt.* mettere, porre, situare.
placement *s.* collocamento.
placid *agg.* placido.
placidity *s.* placidità.
placing *s.* sistemazione.
plagiarism *s.* plagio.
plagiarist *s.* plagiario.
to **plagiarize** *vt.* plagiare.
plagiary *s.* 1. plagio 2. plagiario.
plague *s.* peste.
to **plague** *vt.* affliggere.
plaguer *s.* tormentatore.
plaid *s.* 1. mantello scozzese 2. tessuto a quadri.
plain *agg.* 1. piano, chiaro, evidente 2. semplice 3. comune, scialbo. ♦ **plain** *s.* pianura. ♦ **plain** *avv.* 1. chiaramente 2. semplicemente.
plain-clothes *s. pl.* abiti borghesi.
plainness *s.* 1. chiarezza 2. semplicità 3. aspetto scialbo.
plaint *s.* 1. lamento, lagnanza 2. *(giur.)* querela.
plaintiff *s.* *(giur.)* attore *(nei processi civili)*.
plaintive *agg.* lamentoso.
plait *s.* 1. piega *(di abiti)* 2. treccia.
to **plait** *vt.* 1. pieghettare 2. intrecciare.
plan *s.* 1. piano, progetto 2. pianta *(di una città)*.
to **plan** *vt.* progettare.
plane[1] *agg.* piano. ♦ **plane** *s.* 1. piano 2. aereo.
plane[2] *s.* pialla.
plane[3] *s.* — *-tree*, platano.
to **plane**[1] *vi.* volare.
to **plane**[2] *vt.* piallare.
planer *s.* *(mecc.)* piallatrice.
planet *s.* *(astr.)* pianeta.
planetary *agg.* planetario.
planimetric(al) *agg.* planimetrico.
planimetry *s.* planimetria.
planisphere *s.* planisfero.
plank *s.* tavola, asse.
to **plank** *vt.* coprire di tavole.
planking *s.* tavolato.
plankton *s.* plancton.
planner *s.* progettista.
planning *s.* progettazione.
plant *s.* 1. pianta 2. impianto, apparato 3. fabbrica, stabilimento.
to **plant** *vt.* (im)piantare.
plantation *s.* piantagione.
planter *s.* 1. piantatore 2. colonizzatore.
plantigrade *agg. e s.* plantigrado.
plaque *s.* placca.
plash *s.* pozzanghera.

plaster *s.* 1. cerotto 2. gesso 3. intonaco.
to **plaster** *vt.* 1. incerottare 2. ingessare 3. intonacare 4. ricoprire.
plastering *s.* 1. intonacatura 2. ingessatura.
plastic *agg.* plastico, malleabile.
plasticine *s.* plastilina.
plasticity *s.* plasticità.
to **plasticize** *vt.* rendere plastico.
plastics *s. pl.* materie plastiche.
plate *s.* 1. lastra, lamina 2. piatto 3. tavola fuori testo 4. targa 5. squama 6. vasellame.
to **plate** *vt.* 1. placcare 2. rivestire di piastre.
plateau *s.* altipiano.
platen *s.* 1. piastra metallica 2. rullo di macchina da scrivere.
platform *s.* 1. piattaforma 2. *(ferr.)* marciapiede 3. impalcatura 4. *(amer.)* programma politico.
plating *s.* 1. placcatura 2. rivestimento metallico.
to **platinize** *vt.* platinare.
platinum *s.* platino.
platitude *s.* banalità.
Platonic *agg.* platonico.
Platonism *s.* platonismo.
platoon *s.* plotone.
plausibility *s.* plausibilità.
plausible *agg.* plausibile.
play *s.* 1. gioco 2. dramma 3. *(mus.)* esecuzione 4. azione || — *bill*, cartellone teatrale; — *time*, ricreazione.
to **play** *vt. e vi.* 1. giocare 2. recitare 3. agire 4. suonare || *to — down*, dare poca importanza a.
playboy *s.* *(fam.)* gaudente.
player *s.* 1. giocatore 2. attore 3. suonatore.
playful *agg.* giocoso.
playfulness *s.* allegria.
playground *s.* terreno di giochi.
playhouse *s.* teatro.
playing *s.* 1. gioco 2. rappresentazione 3. *(mus.)* esecuzione.
plaything *s.* giocattolo.
playwright, **playwriter** *s.* commediografo.
plea *s.* 1. giustificazione 2. *(giur.)* eccezione difensiva.
to **plead** *vt.* 1. patrocinare 2. addurre a pretesto 3. *(giur.)* perorare *(una causa)*. ♦ to **plead** *vi.* 1. difendersi 2. supplicare.
pleader *s.* patrocinatore.
pleading *agg.* supplichevole. ♦

pleading *s.* difesa. ♦ **pleadings** *s. pl.* comparse.

pleasant *agg.* piacevole.

pleasantry *s.* piacevolezza.

to **please** *vt. e vi.* piacere (a) || — God, a Dio piacendo.

pleased *agg.* lieto.

pleasing *agg.* piacevole.

pleasure *s.* piacere.

pleat *s.* piega (*di abiti ecc.*).

to **pleat** *vt.* pieghettare.

plebeian *agg. e s.* plebeo.

plebiscitary *agg.* plebiscitario.

plebiscite *s.* plebiscito.

plectrum *s.* plettro.

pledge *s.* **1.** pegno **2.** promessa **3.** brindisi.

to **pledge** *vt.* **1.** impegnare **2.** brindare a.

pledgee *s.* (*giur.*) creditore pignoratizio.

plenary *agg.* plenario || — session, seduta plenaria.

plenilune *s.* plenilunio.

plenipotentiary *agg. e s.* plenipotenziario.

plentiful *agg.* abbondante.

plenty *s.* abbondanza, quantità.

pleonasm *s.* pleonasma.

pleonastic *agg.* pleonastico.

plethora *s.* pletora.

plethoric *agg.* pletorico.

pleurisy *s.* pleurite.

plexus *s.* plesso.

pliability *s.* pieghevolezza.

pliable *agg.* pieghevole.

pliancy *s.* V. *pliability*.

pliant *s.* V. *pliable*.

pliers *s. pl.* pinze.

plight[1] *s.* situazione critica.

plight[2] *s.* impegno, promessa.

to **plight** *vt.* impegnare, promettere.

plod *s.* **1.** passo pesante **2.** lavoro faticoso.

to **plod** *vt. e vi.* **1.** camminare faticosamente **2.** sgobbare.

plodder *s.* **1.** chi cammina faticosamente **2.** sgobbone.

plot *s.* **1.** appezzamento **2.** trama **3.** congiura.

to **plot** *vt. e vi.* **1.** fare la pianta di **2.** tramare.

plotter *s.* cospiratore.

plough *s.* aratro.

to **plough** *vt. e vi.* **1.** arare **2.** solcare.

ploughing *s.* aratura.

ploughman *s.* aratore.

ploughshare *s.* vomere.

plover *s.* piviere.

pluck *s.* **1.** strappo **2.** coraggio.

to **pluck** *vt.* **1.** strappare **2.** spennare **3.** tirare || *to — up*, sradicare.

plucky *agg.* coraggioso.

plug *s.* **1.** tappo (*di lavandino ecc.*) **2.** (*elettr.; tel.*) spina || *spark(ing)- — (mecc.)*, candela.

to **plug** *vt.* **1.** tappare **2.** tamponare || *to — in*, inserire la corrente; *to — away*, sgobbare:

plugging *s.* chiusura.

plum *s.* **1.** prugna, susina **2.** uva passa **3.** (*fig.*) il meglio.

plumage *s.* piumaggio.

plumb *agg.* **1.** a piombo **2.** completo. ♦ **plumb** *s.* **1.** filo a piombo **2.** scandaglio. ♦ **plumb** *avv.* **1.** a piombo **2.** esattamente.

to **plumb** *vt.* **1.** rendere verticale **2.** scandagliare **3.** impiombare.

plumber *s.* idraulico.

plumbery *s.* negozio di idraulico.

plumbing *s.* **1.** piombatura **2.** lavori idraulici.

plumbum *s.* piombo.

plume *s.* piuma, penna.

plummet *s.* piombino.

plump[1] *agg.* grassottello.

plump[2] *agg.* brusco, netto. ♦ **plump** *avv.* **1.** improvvisamente **2.** direttamente.

to **plump** *vt.* **1.** ingrassare **2.** far cadere. ♦ to **plump** *vi.* **1.** ingrassare **2.** cadere.

to **plunder** *s.* depredare.

plunderer *s.* saccheggiatore.

plunge *s.* tuffo.

to **plunge** *vt.* tuffare. ♦ to **plunge** *vi.* tuffarsi.

plunger *s.* **1.** tuffatore **2.** stantuffo.

plunk *s.* colpo metallico.

to **plunk** *vt.* far cadere pesantemente. ♦ **plunk** *vi.* cadere pesantemente.

plural *agg. e s.* plurale.

pluralism *s.* pluralismo.

plurality *s.* pluralità.

plus *agg.* **1.** in più **2.** (*elettr.*) positivo || — *value*, plusvalore. ♦ **plus** *s.* **1.** più **2.** quantità positiva. ♦ **plus** *prep.* più.

plush *agg.* « peluche », felpa.

plutocracy *s.* plutocrazia.

plutocrat *s.* plutocrate.

ply *s.* piega || — *-wood*, compensato.

to **ply** *vt.* **1.** maneggiare **2.** importunare. ♦ to **ply** *vi.* **1.** lavorare assiduamente **2.** fare la spola.

pneumatic *agg.* e *s.* pneumatico.

pneumonia *s.* polmonite.

pneumothorax *s.* pneumotorace.

to poach *vt.* **1.** calpestare **2.** cacciare di frodo **3.** interferire.

poacher *s.* bracconiere.

poaching *s.* bracconaggio.

pocket *s.* **1.** tasca **2.** buca (*di biliardo*) || — *-book*, lib.o tascabile.

to pocket *vt.* **1.** intascare **2.** nascondere, soffocare (*sentimenti ecc.*).

pocketful *s.* tascata.

pod *s.* **1.** baccello **2.** gruppetto.

poem *s.* **1.** poesia **2.** poema.

poet *s.* poeta.

poetic(al) *agg.* poetico.

poetic(s) *s.* poetica.

poetry *s.* poesia.

pc:gnant *agg.* **1.** pungente **2.** commovente.

point *s.* **1.** punto **2.** punta, estremità **3.** caratteristica.

to point *vt.* **1.** indicare, segnare a dito **2.** appuntire **3.** dirigere || *to* — *out*, indicare, porre in rilievo.

point-blank *agg.* diretto. ◆ **point-blank** *avv.* direttamente.

pointed *agg.* **1.** appuntito **2.** mordace **3.** evidente.

pointer *s.* **1.** indicatore **2.** lancetta (*di orologio*).

pointless *agg.* **1.** spuntato **2.** inutile, senza scopo.

pointsman *s.* (*ferr.*) deviatore.

poise *s.* equilibrio.

to poise *vt.* bilanciare. ◆ **to poise** *vi.* bilanciarsi.

poison *s.* veleno.

to poison *vt.* avvelenare.

poisoning *agg.* velenoso. ◆ **poisoning** *s.* avvelenamento.

poisonous *agg.* velenoso (*anche fig.*).

poke *s.* spinta, urto.

to poke *vt.* e *vi.* **1.** spingere **2.** andare a tastoni.

poker *s.* attizzatoio.

poky *agg.* meschino.

polar *agg.* polare.

polarity *s.* polarità.

polarization *s.* polarizzazione.

to polarize *vt.* polarizzare.

pole[1] *s.* palo.

pole[2] *s.* polo.

Pole[3] *s.* polacco.

polecat *s.* puzzola.

polemic *s.* **1.** polemica **2.** polemista.

polemic(al) *agg.* polemico.

polemi(ci)st *s.* polemista.

to polemize *vi.* polemizzare.

police *s.* polizia || — *-force*, corpo di polizia.

police court *s.* pretura.

policeman *s.* poliziotto.

policy[1] *s.* **1.** linea di condotta **2.** sagacia.

policy[2] *s.* polizza.

polio(myelitis) *s.* poliomielite.

Polish[1] *agg.* polacco.

polish[2] *s.* **1.** lucidatura **2.** lucido **3.** raffinatezza || *shoe* —, lucido per le scarpe.

to polish *vt.* **1.** lucidare **2.** raffinare. ◆ **to polish** *vi.* **1.** divenire lucido **2.** raffinarsi.

polisher *s.* **1.** lucidatore **2.** lucido.

polishing *s.* lucidatura.

polite *agg.* cortese.

politeness *s.* cortesia.

politic *agg.* abile.

political *agg.* politico.

politician *s.* uomo politico.

politics *s.* politica.

poll *s.* **1.** votazione, scrutinio **2.** referendum.

to poll *vt.* radere. ◆ **to poll** *vi.* votare, raccogliere voti.

pollen *s.* polline.

to pollinate *vt.* impollinare.

pollination *s.* impollinazione.

to pollute *vt.* contaminare.

pollution *s.* contaminazione.

polyandry *s.* poliandria.

polychrome *agg.* policromo.

polychromy *s.* policromia.

polyclinic *s.* policlinico.

polygamist *s.* poligamo.

polygamous *agg.* poligamo.

polygamy *s.* poligamia.

polyglot *agg.* e *s.* poliglotta.

polygon *s.* poligono.

polyhedral *agg.* poliedrico.

polyhedron *s.* poliedro.

polymerization *s.* polimerizzazione.

polymorphic *agg.* polimorfo.

polymorphism *s.* polimorfismo.

polyp *s.* polipo.

polyphonic *agg.* polifonico.

polyphony *s.* polifonia.

polysyllabic(al) *agg.* polisillabico.

polysyllable *s.* polisillabo.

polytechnic *agg.* e *s.* politecnico.

polytheism *s.* politeismo.

polytheist *s.* politeista.

polytheistic(al) *agg.* politeistico.

polyvalent *agg.* polivalente.

pomade s. pomata.
to pomade vt. impomatare.
pomegranate s. 1. melagrana 2. melograno.
pomp s. pompa, fasto.
pomposity s. pomposità.
pompous agg. pomposo.
pond s. stagno.
to pond vt. e vi. stagnare.
to ponder vt. e vi. ponderare.
ponderable agg. ponderabile.
ponderous agg. ponderoso.
pontiff s. pontefice.
pontifical agg. pontificio. ♦ **pontifical** s. pontificato.
pontificate s. pontificato.
to pontificate vi. pontificare.
pontoon s. pontone.
pony s. « pony », piccolo cavallo.
poodle s. barboncino.
pool[1] s. 1. stagno 2. pozza || **swimming** —, piscina.
pool[2] s. (comm.) 1. fondo comune 2. (comm.) consorzio, sindacato.
poor agg. povero.
poorly avv. male.
poorness s. povertà.
pop s. scoppio.
to pop vi. scoppiare. ♦ **to pop** vt. 1. far scoppiare 2. ficcare.
popcorn s. fiocco di granoturco.
pope s. papa.
popery s. papismo.
poplar s. pioppo.
poppied agg. coperto di papaveri.
poppy s. papavero.
populace s. plebaglia.
popular agg. popolare.
popularity s. popolarità.
popularization s. popolarizzazione.
to popularize vt. popolarizzare.
to populate vt. popolare.
population s. popolazione.
Populism s. populismo.
Populist s. populista.
populous agg. popoloso.
porch s. portico.
porcupine s. porcospino.
pore s. poro.
to pore vi. esaminare.
pork s. carne di maiale.
pornographic agg. pornografico.
pornography s. pornografia.
porosity s. porosità.
porous agg. poroso.
porphyry s. porfido.
port[1] s. porto.
port[2] s. 1. (mecc.) apertura, foro 2. (mar.) portello.

port[3] s. fianco sinistro di nave.
portable agg. portatile.
portal s. portale.
portcullis s. saracinesca (di fortezza).
to portend vt. preannunciare.
portent s. 1. presagio 2. portento.
portentous agg. 1. sinistro 2. portentoso.
porter[1] s. facchino.
porter[2] s. custode, portiere.
porter[3] s. birra scura.
portfolio s. 1. cartella, busta 2. (pol.) portafoglio.
porthole s. 1. (mar.) portello 2. feritoia.
portion s. porzione, parte.
to portion vt. dividere, distribuire.
portrait s. ritratto.
portraitist s. ritrattista.
to portray vt. ritrarre.
portrayal s. ritratto.
portrayer s. ritrattista.
Portuguese agg. e s. portoghese.
pose s. posa.
to pose[1] vt. proporre.
to pose[2] vi. posare.
poser s. posatore.
position s. posizione.
positive agg. 1. positivo 2. sicuro. ♦ **positive** s. 1. realtà 2. (foto) positiva.
positivism s. positivismo.
positivist s. positivista.
positivistic agg. positivistico.
posology s. posologia.
to possess vt. possedere.
possessed agg. indemoniato.
possession s. possesso.
possessive agg. possessivo.
possessor s. possessore.
possibility s. possibilità.
possible agg. possibile.
possibly avv. possibilmente.
post[1] s. posta, corrispondenza || — card, cartolina; by return of —, a giro di posta.
post[2] s. 1. palo, sostegno, puntello 2. stipite || sign- —, indicatore stradale.
to post[1] vt. imbucare, inviare per posta.
to post[2] vt. affiggere.
postage s. spese postali (pl.).
postage stamp s. francobollo.
postal agg. postale.
to postdate vt. posdatare.
poster s. 1. affisso 2. attacchino.
poste-restante s. fermo posta.

posterior *agg.* posteriore.
posterity *s.* posterità.
postern *s.* postierla.
post-free *agg.* franco di porto.
posthumous *agg.* postumo.
postil(l)ion *s.* postiglione.
postman *s.* postino.
postmark *s.* timbro postale.
postmaster *s.* direttore di ufficio postale.
to **postpone** *vt.* rimandare.
postponement *s.* rinvio.
to **post-score** *vt.* (cine) sonorizzare.
postscript *s.* poscritto.
postulate *s.* postulato.
to **postulate** *vt.* 1. porre come postulato 2. chiedere.
postulator *s.* postulante.
posture *s.* posizione.
to **posture** *vi.* assumere una posizione.
post-war *agg.* postbellico.
posy *s.* mazzolino di fiori.
pot *s.* 1. recipiente 2. pentola || — -bellied, panciuto.
to **pot** *vt.* conservare (in vaso).
potable *agg.* potabile.
potash *s.* potassa.
potassic *agg.* potassico.
potassium *s.* potassio.
potato *s.* patata.
potent *agg.* potente.
potential *agg. e s.* potenziale.
potentiality *s.* potenzialità.
potion *s.* pozione.
potter *s.* vasaio.
pottery *s.* 1. terraglie 2. fabbrica di terraglie.
pouch *s.* borsa.
to **pouch** *vt.* intascare.
poulterer *s.* pollivendolo.
poultry *s.* pollame.
pounce *s.* balzo.
to **pounce** *vi.* avventarsi su, contro.
pound[1] *s.* 1. libbra 2. sterlina.
pound[2] *s.* recinto.
to **pound**[1] *vt. e vi.* pestare.
to **pound**[2] *vt.* rinchiudere.
pour *s.* acquazzone.
to **pour** *vt.* versare. ♦ to **pour** *vi.* 1. versarsi 2. diluviare.
pout *s.* broncio.
to **pout** *vi.* fare il broncio.
poverty *s.* povertà.
powder *s.* 1. polvere 2. cipria, talco.
to **powder** *vt.* 1. polverizzare 2. incipriare. ♦ to **powder** *vi.* 1. pol-

verizzarsi 2. incipriarsi.
powdery *agg.* 1. friabile 2. polveroso.
power *s.* potenza, potere || *horse* —, cavallo vapore; — *-station*, centrale elettrica.
to **power** *vt.* motorizzare.
powerful *agg.* potente.
powerless *agg.* debole.
pox *s.* sifilide || *chicken* —, varicella, *small* —, vaiolo.
practicability *s.* praticabilità.
practicable *agg.* 1. praticabile 2. fattibile.
practical *agg.* pratico.
practicality *s.* praticità.
practice *s.* 1. pratica 2. abitudine, regola 3. esercizio 4. professione 5. (coll.) clienti (di medico ecc.).
to **practise** *vt.* 1. praticare 2. esercitare. ♦ to **practise** *vi.* esercitarsi.
practitioner *s.* professionista.
praetorian *agg.* pretoriano.
pragmatic(al) *agg.* prammatico.
pragmatism *s.* pragmatismo.
pragmatist *agg. e s.* pragmatista.
prairie *s.* prateria.
praise *s.* lode.
to **praise** *vt.* lodare.
praiser *s.* lodatore.
praiseworthy *agg.* lodevole.
prance *s.* impennata.
prank *s.* monelleria.
to **prank** *vt.* ornare, agghindare vistosamente. ♦ to **prank** *vi.* mettersi in mostra.
prate *s.* chiacchiera, sproloquio.
to **prate** *vi.* chiacchierare, proferire parole senza senso.
prattle *s.* balbettio.
to **prattle** *vt. e vi.* balbettare.
praxis *s.* prassi.
to **pray** *vt. e vi.* pregare.
prayer *s.* preghiera.
to **preach** *vt. e vi.* predicare.
preacher *s.* predicatore.
to **preachify** *vi.* predicare in modo noioso.
preaching *s.* predicazione.
preachy *agg.* (fam.) incline a far prediche.
to **pre-announce** *vt.* preannunziare.
to **prearrange** *vt.* predisporre.
prearrangement *s.* predisposizione.
prebend *s.* prebenda.
prebendary *s.* prebendario.
precarious *agg.* precario.

precariousness s. precarietà.
precatory agg. supplichevole.
precaution s. precauzione.
precautional agg. precauzionale.
to precede vt. e vi. precedere.
precedence s. precedenza.
precedent agg. e s. precedente.
preceding agg. precedente.
precept s. precetto.
preceptive agg. istruttivo
preceptor s. precettore.
precession s. precessione.
precinct s. 1. recinto 2. limiti 3. vicinanze (pl.).
preciosity s. preziosità.
precious agg. prezioso.
preciousness s. preziosità.
precipice s. precipizio.
precipitate agg. e s. precipitato.
to precipitate vt. e vi. precipitare.
precipitation s. precipitazione.
precipitous agg. ripido.
précis s. riassunto.
precise agg. preciso.
precision s. precisione.
to preclude vt. precludere.
precocious agg. precoce.
precociousness, precocity s. precocità.
preconceived agg. preconcetto.
precursor s. precursore, predecessore.
precursory agg. 1. preliminare 2. premonitore.
predaceous agg. rapace.
to predate vt. predatare.
predatory agg. rapace.
to predecease vt. premorire a.
predecessor s. predecessore.
to predesignate vt. predesignare.
predestination s. predestinazione.
to predestine vt. predestinare.
predetermination s. predeterminazione.
to predetermine vt. predeterminare.
predicable agg. asseribile.
predicament s. situazione scabrosa.
predicate agg. e s. predicato.
to predicate vt. 1. asserire 2. implicare.
predication s. affermazione.
predicative agg. 1. predicativo 2. affermativo.
predicatory agg. predicatorio.
to predict vt. e vi. predire.
prediction s. predizione.
predilection s. predilezione.

to predispose vt. predisporre.
predisposition s. predisposizione.
predominance s. predominanza.
to predominate vi. predominare.
pre-eminence s. preminenza.
pre-eminent agg. preminente.
pre-emption s. prelazione, priorità.
to pre-engage vt. impegnare in anticipo.
to pre-establish vt. prestabilire.
to pre-exist vi. preesistere.
pre-existence s. preesistenza.
to prefabricate vt. prefabbricare.
prefabricated agg. — house, casa prefabbricata.
preface s. prefazione.
to preface vt. 1. fare una prefazione a 2. iniziare.
prefatory agg. introduttivo.
prefect s. prefetto.
prefecture s. prefettura.
to prefer vt. 1. preferire 2. promuovere, elevare.
preferable agg. preferibile.
preference s. preferenza.
preferential agg. preferenziale.
preferment s. avanzamento, promozione.
prefiguration s. prefigurazione.
to prefigure vt. prefigurare.
prefix s. prefisso.
pregnancy s. 1. gravidanza 2. (fig.) significato, importanza.
pregnant agg. 1. incinta 2. significativo, importante 3. fecondo.
prehension s. 1. prensione 2. apprendimento.
prehistoric(al) agg. preistorico.
prehistory s. preistoria.
prejudice s. pregiudizio.
to prejudice vt. 1. pregiudicare 2. influenzare.
prejudicial agg. pregiudizievole.
prelate s. prelato.
prelatic(al) agg. prelatizio.
preliminary agg. preliminare. ◆ preliminaries s. pl. preliminari.
prelude s. preludio.
to prelude vt. preludere. ◆ to prelude vi. eseguire un preludio.
premature agg. prematuro.
to premeditate vt. premeditare.
premeditation s. premeditazione.
premier s. primo ministro.
premise s. 1. premessa 2. stabile con terreni annessi.
to premise vt. premettere.
premolar agg. e s. premolare.
premonitory agg. premonitore.

preoccupation *s.* preoccupazione.
to preoccupy *vt.* **1.** preoccupare **2.** occupare in precedenza.
preparation *s.* preparazione, preparativo.
preparative, preparatory *agg.* preparatorio.
to prepare *vt.* preparare. ♦ **to prepare** *vi.* prepararsi.
preponderance *s.* preponderanza.
preponderant *agg.* preponderante.
preposition *s.* preposizione.
prepositional *agg.* di preposizione.
to prepossess *vt.* **1.** occupare in precedenza **2.** influenzare.
prepossessing *agg.* attraente.
prepossession *s.* prevenzione.
preposterous *agg.* assurdo.
prepotence *s.* predominio.
prepotent *agg.* predominante.
Pre-Raphaeli(ti)sm *s.* preraffaellismo.
prerogative *agg.* privilegiato. ♦ **prerogative** *s.* prerogativa.
presage *s.* presagio.
presbyope *s.* presbite.
presbyopic *agg.* presbite.
Presbyterian *agg.* e *s.* presbiteriano.
Presbyterianism *s.* presbiterianismo.
presbytery *s.* presbiterio.
prescience *s.* prescienza.
to prescribe *vt.* prescrivere.
prescript *s.* ordinanza.
prescription *s.* prescrizione.
presence *s.* presenza.
present[1] *agg.* presente || — -*day*, contemporaneo. ♦ **present** *s.* presente, tempo presente || *at* —, attualmente. ♦ **presents** *s. pl.* (*giur.*) documento (*sing.*).
present[2] *s.* dono, regalo.
to present *vt.* **1.** presentare **2.** regalare.
presentable *agg.* presentabile.
presentation *s.* **1.** presentazione **2.** dono.
presenter *s.* **1.** presentatore **2.** donatore.
presentiment *s.* presentimento.
presently *avv.* presto, quanto prima.
presentment *s.* presentazione.
preservable *agg.* conservabile.
preservation *s.* conservazione.
preservative *agg.* e *s.* preservativo.
preserve *s.* **1.** riserva **2.** conserva (*di pomodoro, frutta ecc.*).
to preserve *vt.* **1.** preservare **2.** conservare **3.** mettere in conserva.

to preside *vi.* presiedere.
presidency *s.* presidenza.
president *s.* presidente.
presidential *agg.* presidenziale.
press *s.* **1.** stretta, pressione **2.** pressa **3.** (*fig.*) stampa **4.** calca, ressa || — *conference*, conferenza stampa.
to press *vt.* **1.** premere, comprimere **2.** costringere. ♦ **to press** *vi.* affollarsi.
pressing *agg.* **1.** urgente **2.** insistente.
pressman *s.* **1.** cronista (*di giornale*) **2.** (*tip.*) stampatore.
pressure *s.* pressione || — -*cooker*, pentola a pressione.
to pressurize *vt.* pressurizzare.
prestige *s.* prestigio.
presumable *agg.* presumibile.
to presume *vt.* e *vi.* **1.** presumere **2.** avere la presunzione di.
presuming *agg.* presuntuoso.
presumption *s.* **1.** presunzione **2.** supposizione.
presumptive *agg.* presunto.
presumptuous *agg.* presuntuoso.
presumptuousness *s.* presunzione.
to presuppose *vt.* presupporre.
presupposition *s.* presupposizione.
pretence *s.* **1.** pretesa **2.** pretesto **3.** simulazione.
to pretend *vi.* **1.** pretendere **2.** fingere.
pretender *s.* **1.** pretendente **2.** simulatore.
pretension *s.* **1.** pretesa **2.** presunzione.
pretentious *agg.* pretenzioso.
preternatural *agg.* soprannaturale.
pretext *s.* pretesto.
prettiness *s.* grazia.
pretty *agg.* grazioso. ♦ **pretty** *avv.* abbastanza.
to prevail *vi.* prevalere.
prevailing *agg.* **1.** prevalente **2.** efficace.
prevalence *s.* prevalenza.
to prevaricate *vi.* **1.** tergiversare **2.** mentire.
prevarication *s.* **1.** tergiversazione **2.** menzogna.
prevaricator *s.* **1.** chi tergiversa **2.** mentitore.
to prevent *vt.* impedire.
prevention *s.* **1.** impedimento **2.** prevenzione.
preventive *agg.* preventivo.

preview s. anteprima.
previous agg. precedente.
prevision s. previsione.
pre-war agg. prebellico.
prey s. preda.
to **prey** vi. 1. (de)predare 2. (fig.) consumare.
price s. prezzo, costo.
to **price** vt. fissare il prezzo di.
priceless agg. inestimabile.
prick s. 1. punta 2. puntura 3. (fig.) pungolo, rimorso.
to **prick** vt. 1. pungere 2. segnare 3. rizzare le orecchie. ♦ to **prick** vi. 1. formicolare 2. pungersi.
prickle s. 1. spina 2. pungiglione.
prickly agg. pungente.
pride s. orgoglio.
to **pride** vt. to — oneself upon, essere orgoglioso di.
priest s. prete.
priesthood s. 1. clero 2. sacerdozio.
prig s. presuntuoso.
prim agg. affettato.
primary agg. primo, primario.
primate s. (eccl.) primate.
prime agg. 1. primo 2. di prima qualità. ♦ **prime** s. 1. principio 2. (fig.) fiore.
to **prime** vt. caricare, innescare.
primer[1] s. sillabario.
primer[2] s. innesco.
primeval agg. primordiale.
primigenial agg. primigenio.
priming s. 1. innesco 2. prima mano (di vernice ecc.).
primitive agg. e s. primitivo.
primitiveness s. primitività.
primogeniture s. primogenitura.
primordial agg. primordiale.
primrose s. primula.
prince s. principe.
princely agg. principesco.
princess s. principessa.
principal agg. principale. ♦ **principal** s. 1. principale, direttore 2. (edil.) trave maestra 3. (comm.) mandante.
principality s. principato.
principle s. principio.
print s. 1. impronta 2. stampa 3. stampatello 4. (foto) copia.
to **print** vt. 1. stampare 2. scrivere a stampatello 3. imprimere.
printer s. 1. tipografo 2. (mecc.) stampatrice.
printing s. 1. stampa 2. tiratura ‖ — -press, pressa tipografica.
prior agg. precedente. ♦ **prior** s.

priore. ♦ **prior** avv. prima.
priorate s. priorato.
prioress s. priora.
priority s. priorità.
prism s. prisma.
prismatic(al) agg. prismatico.
prison s. prigione.
prisoner s. prigioniero.
privacy s. 1. intimità 2. riserbo.
private agg. 1. privato 2. appartato 3. segreto, riservato, personale. ♦ **private** s. soldato semplice.
privation s. privazione.
privative agg. privativo.
privilege s. privilegio.
to **privilege** vt. privilegiare.
privy agg. 1. nascosto 2. al corrente di.*
prize s. premio.
to **prize** vt. stimare.
probabilism s. probabilismo.
probability s. probabilità.
probable agg. probabile.
probate s. omologazione.
probation s. prova.
probative agg. probativo.
probatory agg. probatorio.
probe s. sonda.
to **probe** vt. sondare.
probity s. probità.
problem s. problema.
problematic(al) agg. problematico.
procedural agg. procedurale.
procedure s. 1. procedimento 2. procedura.
to **proceed** vi. 1. procedere 2. provenire.
proceeding s. V. procedure.
proceeds s. pl. profitto (sing.).
process s. 1. procedimento 2. processo.
to **process** vt. 1. processare 2. (chim.) trattare.
procession s. processione.
processionary s. (zool.) processionaria.
proclaim s. proclama.
to **proclaim** vt. proclamare.
proclamation s. proclama(zione).
proconsul s. proconsole.
to **procrastinate** vt. e vi. procrastinare.
procrastination s. procrastinazione.
to **procreate** vt. procreare.
procreation s. procreazione.
procreator s. procreatore.
proctor s. 1. censore 2. (giur.) procuratore.

procurator *s.* procuratore.
to **procure** *vt.* 1. procurare, procurarsi 2. adescare.
procurer *s.* mezzano.
prod *s.* pungolo.
to **prod** *vt.* pungolare.
prodigal *agg. e s.* prodigo.
prodigality *s.* prodigalità.
prodigious *agg.* 1. prodigioso 2. enorme.
prodigiousness *s.* prodigiosità.
prodigy *s.* prodigio.
produce *s.* prodotto || *farm* —, prodotto agricolo; *raw* —, materia prima.
to **produce** *vt.* 1. produrre 2. presentare.
producer *s.* 1. produttore 2. (*teat.*) regista.
product *s.* prodotto.
production *s.* 1. esibizione 2. produzione.
productive *agg.* produttivo.
productivity *s.* produttività.
proem *s.* proemio.
profanation *s.* profanazione.
profane *agg.* 1. profano 2. empio.
to **profane** *vt.* profanare.
profaner *s.* profanatore.
profanity *s.* 1. profanità 2. empietà.
to **profess** *vt.* 1. professare 2. pretendere.
profession *s.* professione.
professional *agg.* professionale || — *man*, professionista. ◆ **professional** *s.* professionista.
professionalism *s.* professionismo.
professor *s.* professore (*d'università*).
professorial *agg.* professorale.
proficiency *s.* competenza || — *in English*, buona conoscenza dell'inglese.
proficient *agg. e s.* esperto, competente.
profile *s.* profilo.
to **profile** *vt.* 1. profilare 2. tracciare il profilo di.
profit *s.* profitto, guadagno.
to **profit** *vt.* giovare. ◆ to **profit** *vi.* approfittare.
profitable *agg.* vantaggioso.
profiteer *s.* profittatore.
profligacy *s.* 1. sregolatezza 2. spergero.
profligate *agg. e s.* 1. dissoluto 2. scialacquatore.
profound *agg.* profondo.

profuse *agg.* 1. abbondante 2. prodigo.
profusion *s.* 1. profusione 2. prodigalità.
progenitor *s.* progenitore.
progeny *s.* progenie.
prognathism *s.* prognatismo.
prognathous *agg.* prognato.
prognosis *s.* (*pl.* -ses) prognosi.
prognostic *agg.* rivelatore. ◆ **prognostic** *s.* 1. pronostico 2. sintomo.
prognostication *s.* 1. pronostico 2. prognosi.
program(me) *s.* programma.
to **program(me)** *vt.* programmare.
programming *s.* programmazione.
programmist *s.* programmista.
progress *s.* 1. progresso 2. avanzata 3. sviluppo 4. andamento, corso.
to **progress** *vi.* 1. progredire 2. avanzare 3. svilupparsi.
progression *s.* 1. progressione 2. avanzamento.
progressive *agg.* progressivo, progressista. ◆ **progressive** *s.* progressista.
to **prohibit** *vt.* proibire.
prohibition *s.* 1. proibizione 2. proibizionismo.
prohibitionist *s.* proibizionista.
prohibitive *agg.* proibitivo.
project *s.* progetto.
to **project** *vt.* 1. progettare 2. proiettare. ◆ to **project** *vi.* sporgere.
projectile *s.* proiettile.
projection *s.* 1. progetto 2. proiezione.
projector *s.* 1. progettista 2. proiettore.
proletarian *agg. e s.* proletario.
proletariat *s.* proletariato.
to **proliferate** *vt.* proliferare. ◆ to **proliferate** *vi.* moltiplicarsi.
proliferation *s.* proliferazione.
prolific *agg.* prolifico.
prolix *agg.* prolisso.
prolixity *s.* prolissità.
prologue *s.* prologo.
to **prolong** *vt.* 1. prolungare 2. (*comm.*) prorogare.
promenade *s.* passeggiata, passeggio pubblico, lungomare.
prominence *s.* prominenza.
prominent *agg.* prominente.
promiscuity *s.* promiscuità.
promiscuous *agg.* promiscuo.
promise *s.* promessa.
to **promise** *vt. e vi.* promettere.

promissory *agg.* contenente una promessa || — *note* (*comm.*), pagherò cambiario.

promontory *s.* promontorio.

to promote *vt.* 1. promuovere 2. dare impulso a, favorire.

promoter *s.* promotore.

promotion *s.* 1. promozione 2. incoraggiamento.

prompt *agg.* 1. sollecito 2. (*comm.*) in contanti. ♦ **prompt** *s.* 1. (*comm.*) termine di pagamento 2. suggerimento.

to prompt *vt.* 1. spingere 2. suggerire.

prompter *s.* suggeritore.

promptness *s.* prontezza.

to promulgate *vt.* promulgare.

promulgation *s.* promulgazione.

promulgator *s.* promulgatore.

prone *agg.* prono.

prong *s.* 1. dente (*di forca*) 2. forca.

pronominal *agg.* pronominale.

pronoun *s.* pronome.

to pronounce *vt.* 1. pronunciare 2. dichiarare. ♦ **to pronounce** *vi.* pronunciarsi.

pronouncement *s.* dichiarazione.

pronouncing, pronunciation *s.* pronuncia.

proof *agg.*-a prova di. ♦ **proof** *s.* 1. prova 2. bozza 3. gradazione alcoolica || — *reader,* correttore di bozze; *burden of* — (*giur.*), onere della prova.

prop *s.* puntello.

to prop *vt.* 1. sostenere 2. appoggiare.

propaedeutic(al) *agg.* propedeutico.

propaedeutics *s.* propedeutica.

propagandist *s.* propagandista.

to propagandize *vt.* propagandare.

to propagate *vt.* propagare. ♦ **to propagate** *vi.* propagarsi.

propagation *s.* 1. propagazione 2. (*bot.; zool.*) riproduzione.

propagator *s.* propagatore.

propane *s.* propano.

to propel *vt.* spingere avanti.

propellant *agg. e s.* propulsore, propellente.

propeller *s.* propulsore || (*screw-*) —, elica.

propensity *s.* propensione.

proper *agg.* 1. proprio 2. adatto 3. corretto 4. propriamente detto.

property *s.* 1. proprietà 2. (*teat.*) costumi, arredi per la scena (*pl.*) ||

real —, beni immobili (*pl.*).

prophecy *s.* profezia.

to prophesy *vt. e vi.* profetizzare.

prophet *s.* profeta.

prophetic(al) *agg.* profetico.

prophylactic *agg. e s.* profilattico.

prophylaxis *s.* profilassi.

to propitiate *vt.* propiziare.

propitiation *s.* propiziazione.

propitiator *s.* propiziatore.

propitiatory *agg.* propiziatorio.

propitious *agg.* propizio.

proportion *s.* 1. proporzione 2. parte. ♦ **proportions** *s. pl.* dimensioni.

to proportion *vt.* 1. proporzionare 2. dividere in parti proporzionate.

proportional *agg.* proporzionale.

proportionality *s.* proporzionalità.

proportionate *agg.* proporzionato.

to proportionate V. *to proportion.*

proportioning *s.* proporzionamento.

proposal *s.* proposta.

to propose *vt.* proporre. ♦ **to propose** *vi.* 1. prefiggersi, intendere 2. fare richiesta di matrimonio || *to* — *the health of so.,* bere alla salute di qu.

proposition *s.* 1. proposta 2. proposizione 3. asserzione 4. problema.

proprietary *agg.* di proprietà. ♦ **proprietary** *s.* proprietario || — *rights,* diritti di proprietà.

proprietor *s.* proprietario.

propriety *s.* 1. proprietà 2. opportunità 3. decoro, decenza. ♦ **proprieties** *s. pl.* convenienze.

propulsion *s.* propulsione.

propulsive *agg.* propulsivo.

propylaeum *s.* (*pl.* -laea) propileo.

propylene *s.* propilene.

prosaic *agg.* prosaico.

prosaism *s.* prosaicità.

proscenium *s.* (*pl.* -nia) proscenio.

to proscribe *vt.* 1. bandire 2. vietare.

proscription *s.* 1. proscrizione 2. proibizione.

prose *s.* 1. prosa 2. prosaicità || — *writer,* prosatore.

prosecutable *agg.* perseguibile.

to prosecute *vt.* 1. proseguire 2. perseguire.

prosecution *s.* 1. proseguimento 2. processo 3. (*giur.*) accusa.

prosecutor *s.* 1. prosecutore 2. accusatore || *Public* — (*giur.*), l'accusa pubblica.

proselyte s. proselito.
proselytism s. proselitismo.
prosiness s. 1. prosaicità 2. banalità.
prosody s. prosodia.
prospect s. 1. panorama 2. prospettiva 3. speranza, aspettativa.
to prospect vt. 1. esplorare 2. ricercare.
prospecting s. ricerca.
prospective agg. 1. futuro 2. eventuale.
to prosper vt. far prosperare. ♦ to **prosper** vi. prosperare.
prosperity s. prosperità.
prosperous agg. prospero.
prostate s. prostata.
prostatic agg. prostatico.
prosthesis s. (med.) protesi.
prostitute s. prostituta.
to prostitute vt. prostituire.
prostitution s. prostituzione.
prostrate agg. prostrato.
to prostrate vt. prostrare.
prostration s. 1. prostrazione 2. prosternazione.
prostyle agg. e s. prostilo.
prosy agg. 1. prosaico 2. noioso.
protagonist s. protagonista.
to protect vt. proteggere.
protection s. 1. protezione 2. salvacondotto.
protectionism s. protezionismo.
protectionist s. protezionista.
protective agg. protettivo.
protector s. protettore.
protectorate s. protettorato.
protectory s. patronato.
protein s. proteina.
protest s. 1. protesta 2. (comm.) protesto.
to protest vt. e vi. protestare.
protestant agg. e s. protestante.
Protestantism s. protestantesimo.
protestation s. dichiarazione.
protocol s. protocollo.
proton s. protone.
protoplasm s. protoplasma.
prototype s. prototipo.
Protozoa s. pl. protozoi.
to protract vt. 1. protrarre 2. rilevare.
protraction s. 1. protrazione 2. rilievo.
protractor s. 1. protrattore 2. goniometro.
to protrude vt. 1. sporgere 2. imporre. ♦ to **protrude** vi. 1. sporgersi 2. imporsi.

protrusion, protuberance s. protuberanza.
proud agg. orgoglioso, superbo.
to prove vt. 1. provare, verificare 2. omologare. ♦ to **prove** vi. risultare.
provender s. foraggio, biada.
proverb s. proverbio.
proverbial agg. proverbiale.
to provide vt. 1. provvedere 2. premunirsi 3. stabilire (di leggi). ♦ to **provide** vt. 1. procurare 2. rifornire.
provided cong. purché, a patto che.
providence s. 1. provvidenza 2. previdenza.
provident agg. 1. provvido 2. previdente.
providential agg. provvidenziale.
province s. 1. provincia 2. (fig.) sfera, campo d'attività.
provincial agg. e s. provinciale.
provincialism s. provincialismo.
provision s. 1. preparativo 2. provvedimento 3. clausola 4. (giur.) disposizione. ♦ **provisions** s. pl. provviste.
to provision vt. approvvigionare.
provisional agg. provvisorio.
provisioning s. approvvigionamento.
provocation s. provocazione.
provocative agg. 1. provocante 2. stimolante.
provocativeness s. provocazione.
to provoke vt. 1. provocare 2. irritare.
provoker s. provocatore.
provost s. prevosto.
prow s. prora.
prowess s. 1. prodezza, valore.
proximity s. prossimità.
proxy s. 1. procura 2. procuratore.
prude s. persona eccessivamente pudica.
prudence s. prudenza.
prudent agg. prudente.
prudential agg. prudenziale.
prudentials s. pl. provvedimenti precauzionali.
prudery s. ritrosia eccessiva.
prudish agg. pudibondo.
prune s. prugna secca.
to prune vt. potare.
pruner s. potatore.
pruning s. potatura ‖ — -hook, falcetto.
prussic agg. prussico.
pry[1] s. ficcanaso.

pry² s. leva.

to pry¹ vi. indagare.

to pry¹ vt. muovere con una leva.

psalm s. salmo.

psalmody s. salmodia.

pseudonym s. pseudonimo.

psyche s. psiche.

psychiatric(al) agg. psichiatrico.

psychiatrist s. psichiatra.

psychiatry s. psichiatria.

psychic s. 1. medium 2. psicologia.

psychic(al) agg. psichico.

psychoanalysis s. psicanalisi.

psychoanalyst s. psicanalista.

psychoanalytic(al) agg. psicanalitico.

to psychoanalyze vt. psicanalizzare.

psychologic(al) agg. psicologico.

psychologist s. psicologo.

psychology s. psicologia.

psychometry s. psicometria.

psychopathic agg. e s. psicopatico.

psychopathology s. psicopatologia.

psychopathy s. psicopatia.

psychosis s. psicosi.

psychotherapy s. psicoterapia.

ptisan s. tisana.

pub s. bar (in Gran Bretagna).

puberty s. pubertà.

pubis s. (pl. -bes) pube.

public agg. e s. pubblico || the reading —, i lettori (pl.).

publican s. 1. oste 2. (stor.) pubblicano.

publication s. pubblicazione.

publicity s. pubblicità.

to publish vt. 1. pubblicare 2. divulgare.

publishable agg. pubblicabile.

publisher s. editore.

pucker s. ruga, grinza.

to pucker vt. raggrinzare, corrugare. ♦ to pucker vi. raggrinzarsi, corrugarsi.

pudding s. 1. budino 2. pasticcio || black —, sanguinaccio.

puddle s. 1. pozzanghera 2. malta.

to puddle vt. 1. infangare 2. coprire di malta.

puerility s. puerilità.

Puerto Rican agg. e s. portoricano.

puff s. 1. soffio, sbuffo 2. piumino.
♦ to puff vt. 1. soffiare 2. gonfiare.

puffy agg. 1. gonfio 2. ansimante 3. paffuto, grasso.

pugilist s. pugile.

pugnacious agg. pugnace.

pugnacity s. combattività.

puke s. vomito.

to puke vt. e vi. vomitare.

pull s. 1. strappo 2. sforzo, tensione 3. maniglia (di cassetto).

to pull vt. 1. tirare 2. strappare || to — down, demolire. ♦ to pull vi. 1. trascinarsi 2. remare || to — back, ritirarsi; to — up, fermarsi.

puller s. (mecc.) estrattore.

pulley s. puleggia.

pulmonary agg. polmonare.

pulp s. polpa.

to pulp vt. ridurre in polpa. ♦ to pulp vi. diventare polposo.

pulpit s. pulpito.

pulpy agg. polposo.

pulsation s. pulsazione.

pulsatory agg. pulsante.

pulse s. 1. pulsazione, polso, battito 2. (radio) impulso.

to pulse vi. pulsare.

to pulverize vt. polverizzare. ♦ to pulverize vi. polverizzarsi.

pumice s. pomice.

pump s. pompa || petrol —, distributore di benzina.

to pump vt. e vi. pompare || to — up, gonfiare.

pumpkin s. zucca.

pun s. gioco di parole.

punch¹ s. punzone.

punch² s. pugno.

punch³ s. « punch » (bevanda alcoolica).

to punch¹ vt. (per)forare.

to punch² vt. prendere a pugni.

punching s. perforazione.

punctilio s. meticolosità.

punctilious agg. meticoloso.

punctual agg. puntuale.

punctuality s. puntualità.

punctually avv. puntualmente.

to punctuate vt. 1. punteggiare 2. (fig.) sottolineare.

punctuation s. punteggiatura.

puncture s. 1. puntura 2. foratura.

to puncture vt. 1. pungere 2. forare.

pungency s. 1. asprezza 2. acutezza (di dolore).

pungent agg. 1. pungente 2. acuto, cocente 3. piccante.

to punish vt. punire.

punishable agg. punibile.

punishment s. punizione.

punitive, punitory agg. punitivo.

punt s. chiatta.

punter s. puntatore (*di corse ecc.*).

puny agg. sparuto.

pup s. cucciolo.

pupil[1] s. 1. allievo 2. (*giur.*) pupillo.

pupil[2] s. pupilla.

pupil(l)age s. (*giur.*) minorità: *child in* —, bambino sotto tutela.

pupil(l)ary agg. (*giur.*) pupillare.

puppet s. burattino || — *show*, spettacolo di burattini; — *player*, burattinaio.

puppy s. cucciolo.

purchase s. acquisto.

to purchase vt. acquistare.

purchaser s. acquirente.

purchasing s. acquisto || — *power*, potere di acquisto.

pure agg. puro, schietto, casto.

purely avv. puramente, semplicemente.

purgative agg. purgativo. ♦ **purgative** s. purgante.

purgatory s. purgatorio.

purge s. 1. purga 2. epurazione.

to purge vt. 1. purgare 2. epurare. ♦ **to purge** vi. purgarsi.

purification s. purificazione.

purificatory agg. purificatore.

to purify vt. purificare.

purism s. purismo.

purist s. purista.

Puritan agg. e s. puritano.

Puritanism s. puritanismo.

purity s. purezza.

to purloin vt. rubare.

purloiner s. frodatore.

purple agg. 1. purpureo, paonazzo 2. ornato. ♦ **purple** s. porpora.

to purple vt. imporporare. ♦ **to purple** vi. imporpórarsi.

purport s. significato.

to purport vt. 1. significare 2. pretendere.

purpose s. 1. intenzione, scopo 2. fermezza || *on* —, di proposito.

to purpose vi. proporsi (*di*).

purposeful agg. 1. premeditato 2. avveduto.

purposefully avv. intenzionalmente, espressamente.

purposeless agg. 1. inutile 2. senza intenzione.

purpurin s. porporina.

to purr vi. fare le fusa.

purse s. borsellino.

to purse vt. contrarre. ♦ **to purse** vi. incresparsi, contrarsi.

purser s. commissario di bordo.

pursuant agg. conforme.

to pursue vt. 1. (in)seguire 2. continuare.

pursuer s. 1. inseguitore 2. continuatore.

pursuit s. 1. inseguimento 2. occupazione, impiego.

purulence s. suppurazione.

purulent agg. purulento.

push s. 1. spinta, influenza, pressione 2. bisogno 3. (*elettr.*) pulsante.

to push vt. 1. spingere, incalzare, fare pressione 2. lanciare (*una moda, un articolo ecc.*) ♦ **to push** vi. spingersi.

pusher s. chi, ciò che spinge.

pusillanimity s. pusillanimità.

pusillanimous agg. pusillanime.

puss(y) s. micino.

pustule s. pustola.

to put (put, put) vt. 1. mettere, porre 2. esporre, sottoporre || *to* — *off*, rimandare, togliere (*vestiti ecc.*); *to* — *on*, indossare, accendere; *to* — *through*, mettere in comunicazione telefonica; *to* — *up*, alzare. ♦ **to put** (put, put) vi. dirigersi.

putative agg. putativo.

putrefaction s. putrefazione.

to putrefy vt. putrefare. ♦ **to putrefy** vi. putrefarsi.

putrescence s. putrescenza.

putrescible agg. putrescibile.

putrid agg. putrido.

putridness s. putridità.

puttees s. pl. mollettiere.

putty s. mastice, stucco.

puzzle s. 1. enigma 2. imbarazzo 3. intrigo.

to puzzle vt. imbarazzare. ♦ **to puzzle** vi. essere imbarazzato.

pygmy agg. e s. pigmeo.

pyjamas s. pl. pigiama (*sing.*).

pylon s. pilone || *steel* —, traliccio.

pylorus s. piloro.

pyorrh(o)ea s. piorrea.

pyramid s. piramide.

pyramidal agg. piramidale.

pyre s. pira.

pyrites s. pirite.

pyrography s. pirografia.

pyromancy s. piromanzia.

pyromaniac s. piromane.

pyrope s. piropo.

pyrotechnic(al) agg. pirotecnico.

pyrotechnics s. pirotecnica.

Pythagorean agg. e s. pitagorico.

python s. pitone.

pyx s. pisside.

Q

quack¹ s. ciarlatano.

quack² s. schiamazzare (di anitra).

to **quack¹** vi. fare il ciarlatano.

to **quack²** vi. schiamazzare (di anitra).

quadrangle s. quadrangolo.

quadrangular agg. quadrangolare.

quadrant s. quadrante.

quadrennial agg. quadriennale.

quadrilateral agg. e s. quadrilatero.

quadrille s. quadriglia.

quadrumane s. quadrumane.

quadrumanous agg. quadrumane.

quadruped agg. e s. quadrupede.

quadruple agg. e s. quadruplo.

to **quadruple** vt. quadruplicare. ◆ to **quadruple** vi. quadruplicarsi.

quagmire s. pantano.

quail s. quaglia.

to **quail** vi. avvilirsi, sgomentarsi.

quaint agg. strano, bizzarro.

quake s. scossa, tremito.

to **quake** vi. 1. avere i brividi 2. tremare (anche di terra).

Quaker s. Quacchero.

quaky agg. tremante.

qualifiable agg. qualificabile.

qualification s. 1. qualificazione, capacità, requisito 2. condizione, riserva 3. qualifica.

qualified agg. 1. qualificato, competente 2. limitato || — acceptance (comm.), accettazione con riserva.

qualifier s. (gramm.) parola che modifica.

to **qualify** vt. 1. qualificare, definire 2. abilitare 3. (giur.) autorizzare. ◆ to **qualify** vi. 1. qualificarsi 2. abilitarsi.

qualitative agg. qualitativo.

quality s. qualità, caratteristica.

qualm s. 1. nausea 2. scrupolo.

qualmish agg. 1. soggetto a nausee 2. nauseante 3. scrupoloso.

quantitative agg. quantitativo.

quantity s. quantità.

quarantine s. quarantena.

quarrel s. lite, contesa.

to **quarrel** vi. litigare, venire a contesa.

quarreller s. attaccabrighe, contendente.

quarrelsome agg. attaccabrighe, rissoso.

quarry¹ s. 1. cava 2. (fig.) fonte d'informazione.

quarry² s. selvaggina, preda.

to **quarry** vt. 1. cavare (pietre, marmo ecc.) 2. ricavare informazioni da.

quarter s. 1. quarto: a — of an hour, un quarto d'ora 2. quartiere, rione. ◆ **quarters** s. pl. 1. alloggio 2. (mil.) acquartieramento.

to **quarter** vt. e vi. 1. dividere in quattro parti 2. alloggiare 3. (mil.) acquartierarsi.

quarterly agg. trimestrale. ◆ **quarterly** s. pubblicazione trimestrale. ◆ **quarterly** avv. trimestralmente.

quartermaster s. 1. commissario 2. quartiermastro.

quartet s. quartetto.

quartz s. quarzo.

to **quash** vt. (giur.) annullare.

quaternary agg. quaternario.

quatrain s. quartina.

quaver s. trillo, vibrazione.

to **quaver** vt. e vi. 1. vibrare, tremare (di voce) 2. gorgheggiare.

quay s. banchina, molo.

queasy agg. 1. nauseabondo 2. schizzinoso.

queen s. regina.

queenlike agg. regale.

queenly agg. regale, da regina.

queer agg. strano, eccentrico.

to **queer** vt. mettere in ridicolo.

queerly avv. stranamente.

to **quench** vt. 1. spegnere, estinguere 2. calmare.

quencher s. estintore.

quenchless agg. inestinguibile.

querulous agg. querulo, gemebondo.

query s. domanda, quesito.

to **query** vt. e vi. 1. chiedere, indagare 2. mettere in dubbio.

quest s. ricerca.

to **quest** vt. e vi. cercare, far ricerche.

question s. 1. domanda, interrogazione 2. dubbio, obiezione 3. questione, problema || — mark, punto interrogativo.

to **question** vt. 1. interrogare 2. mettere in dubbio.

questionable agg. incerto, discutibile.

questionably avv. discutibilmente.

questionary s. questionario.

queue s. 1. coda 2. fila di persone: to stand in a —, fare la coda.

to **queue** vt. e vi. fare la coda, mettere in coda.

quibble *s.* giuoco di parole, doppio senso.

to quibble *vi.* **1.** fare giuochi di parole **2.** cavillare.

quibbling *agg.* a doppio senso.

quick *agg.* **1.** rapido, veloce **2.** pronto, intelligente, acuto || — *-eyed*, dagli occhi penetranti; — *-eared*, dall'orecchio fino; — *-lime*, calce viva; — *-sighted*, dalla vista acuta; — *-tempered*, irascibile.

to quicken *vt.* **1.** affrettare **2.** animare. ♦ **to quicken** *vi.* **1.** affrettarsi **2.** animarsi.

quickly *avv.* rapidamente, prontamente.

quickness *s.* **1.** rapidità **2.** vivacità, acutezza.

quicksand *s.* sabbia mobile.

quickset *s.* siepe di sempreverdi.

quicksilver *s.* mercurio, argento vivo (*anche fig.*).

quickstep *s.* passo cadenzato.

quickthorn *s.* biancospino.

quiescence *s.* quiescenza.

quiescent *agg.* quiescente.

quiescently *avv.* tranquillamente.

quiet *agg.* **1.** quieto, tranquillo **2.** sobrio, tenue (*di colore*) **3.** docile, dolce.

to quiet *vt.* acquietare. ♦ **to quiet** *vi.* acquietarsi.

quietism *s.* quietismo.

quietist *s.* quietista.

quietly *avv.* tranquillamente, con calma.

quietness *s.* quiete, tranquillità.

quill *s.* **1.** penna, penna d'oca **2.** piccolo galleggiante (*per canna da pesca*).

to quill *vt.* pieghettare, increspare.

quilt *s.* trapunta.

to quilt *vt.* trapuntare.

quince *s.* cotogna || — *jam*, marmellata di cotogne.

quinine *s.* chinino.

quinquennial *agg.* quinquennale.

quintal *s.* quintale.

quintessence *s.* quintessenza.

quintet *s.* quintetto.

quintuple *agg.* e *s.* quintuplo.

to quintuple *vt.* quintuplicare. ♦ **to quintuple** *vi.* quintuplicarsi.

quisling *s.* collaborazionista.

to quit *vt.* **1.** abbandonare, lasciare **2.** quietanzare, saldare.

quite *avv.* **1.** completamente, interamente **2.** piuttosto, abbastanza || — *young*, giovanissimo; *to be*

— *well*, stare proprio bene.

quiver *s.* fremito, brivido.

to quiver *vt.* e *vi.* **1.** tremare, fremere **2.** palpitare.

quivering *agg.* fremente, tremolante. ♦ **quivering** *s.* tremolio.

quixotic *agg.* donchisciottesco.

quiz *s.* (*pl.* quizzes) burlone.

to quiz *vt.* burlare.

quotation *s.* **1.** citazione **2.** (*comm.*) quotazione.

quote *s.* (*fam.*) citazione. ♦ **quotes** *s. pl.* virgolette.

to quote *vt.* **1.** citare **2.** (*comm.*) quotare (*in borsa*).

quotidian *agg.* quotidiano.

quotient *s.* quoziente.

R

rabbi *s.* rabbino.

rabbit *s.* coniglio.

rabble *s.* plebaglia.

to rabble *vt.* assaltare, linciare.

rabid *agg.* **1.** rabbioso **2.** irragionevole **3.** idrofobo.

rabidity *s.* **1.** rabbia **2.** fanatismo.

rabies *s.* idrofobia.

race[1] *s.* **1.** corso **2.** corsa || — *meeting*, concorso ippico.

race[2] *s.* razza.

to race *vi.* **1.** correre **2.** imballarsi (*di motori*) **3.** prendere parte a una corsa **4.** allevare cavalli da corsa.

racecourse *s.* ippodromo.

racehorse *s.* cavallo da corsa.

racer *s.* **1.** corridore **2.** cavallo da corsa **3.** mezzo da corsa.

racial *agg.* razziale.

racialism *s.* razzismo.

racialist *s.* razzista.

racially *avv.* dal punto di vista razziale.

racily *avv.* vivacemente.

raciness *s.* vivacità.

racing *s.* corsa || — *car*, automobile da corsa.

racism *s.* razzismo.

racist *s.* razzista.

rack[1] *s.* **1.** rastrelliera **2.** reticella portabagagli **3.** (*mecc.*) cremagliera || *clothes* —, attaccapanni.

rack[2] *s.* ruota, strumento di tortura.

rack[3] *s.* nembo, nuvolaglia.

rack[4] *s.* rovina, distruzione.

to **rack¹** *vt.* **1.** torturare **2.** pretendere troppo.

to **rack²** *vi.* fuggire (*di nubi*).

racket¹ *s.* racchetta.

racket² *s.* **1.** fracasso **2.** baldoria **3.** (*gergo*) associazione a delinquere.

racy *agg.* **1.** genuino **2.** vivace, pungente.

radial *agg.* radiale.

radiance *s.* radiosità.

radiant *agg.* **1.** radiante **2.** raggiante.

to **radiate** *vt.* e *vi.* irradiare.

radiation *s.* (ir)radiazione.

radiator *s.* radiatore.

radical *agg.* e *s.* radicale.

radicalism *s.* radicalismo.

radio *s.* radio || — *-beacon*, radiofaro; — *-control*, radiocomando; — *-operator*, radiotelegrafista.

radioactive *agg.* radioattivo.

radioactivity *s.* radioattività.

radioengineering *s.* radiotecnica.

radiogoniometer *s.* radiogoniometro.

radiogram *s.* **1.** marconigramma **2.** radiogrammofono.

radiograph *s.* radiografia.

radiography *s.* radiografia.

radiologist *s.* radiologo.

radiology *s.* radiologia.

radioscopy *s.* radioscopia.

radiostatics *s. pl.* disturbi atmosferici.

radiotelegraphy *s.* radiotelegrafia.

radiotelephony *s.* radiotelefonia.

radiotherapeutics *s.* radioterapia.

radish *s.* ravanello.

radium *s.* radio.

radius *s.* raggio.

raffia *s.* rafia.

raft *s.* zattera || — *-bridge*, ponte di barche.

rag *s.* straccio.

ragamuffin *s.* pezzente.

rage *s.* **1.** furore **2.** passione.

to **rage** *vi.* infuriare || *the plague raged*, la peste infieriva.

ragged *agg.* **1.** lacero **2.** frastagliato **3.** spettinato **4.** rozzo.

raggedly *avv.* **1.** a brandelli **2.** in modo non uniforme.

raggedness *s.* **1.** cenciosità **2.** ineguaglianza.

raging *agg.* furioso.

raid *s.* incursione, scorreria.

to **raid** *vt.* e *vi.* fare un'incursione.

rail, railing *s.* **1.** sbarra **2.** ringhiera **3.** rotaia || *to go by* —, viaggiare per ferrovia.

raillery *s.* canzonatura.

railroad, railway *s.* ferrovia || — *companies*, società ferroviarie.

railwayman *s.* ferroviere.

rain *s.* pioggia || *it looks like* —, vuol piovere; *to be drenched with* —, essere inzuppato || — *-glass*, barometro.

to **rain** *v. imp.* piovere. ♦ to **rain** *vt.* far piovere.

rainbow *s.* arcobaleno.

raincoat *s.* impermeabile.

rainfall *s.* **1.** piovosità **2.** scroscio di pioggia.

rainproof *agg.* impermeabile.

rainy *agg.* piovoso.

raise *s.* aumento.

to **raise** *vt.* **1.** alzare **2.** innalzare **3.** allevare **4.** coltivare **5.** (*mil.*) arruolare.

raisin *s.* uva passa.

raising *s.* **1.** innalzamento **2.** aumento **3.** allevamento **4.** coltivazione **5.** educazione.

rake¹ *s.* rastrello.

rake² *s.* inclinazione.

rake³ *s.* libertino.

to **rake¹** *vt.* **1.** rastrellare **2.** raschiare || — *up*, ammucchiare.

to **rake²** *vi.* essere inclinato.

rally¹ *s.* riunione, raduno.

rally² *s.* canzonatura.

to **rally¹** *vt.* raccogliere. ♦ to **rally** *vi.* rianimarsi.

to **rally²** *vt.* canzonare.

ram *s.* **1.** ariete **2.** (*mar.*) sperone.

to **ram** *vt.* **1.** (*mar.*) speronare **2.** conficcare **3.** comprimere.

ramble *s.* vagabondaggio.

to **ramble** *vi.* **1.** vagare **2.** divagare.

rambler *s.* **1.** vagabondo **2.** rampicante.

rambling *agg.* **1.** errante **2.** sconnesso || — *thoughts*, divagazioni.

ramification *s.* ramificazione.

to **ramify** *vt.* ramificare. ♦ to **ramify** *vi.* ramificarsi.

rammer *s.* (*mil.*) pestello.

ramp¹ *s.* rampa.

ramp² *s.* (*gergo*) truffa.

rampage *s.* contegno iroso.

rampant *agg.* **1.** rampante **2.** violento **3.** predominante **4.** lussureggiante.

rampart *s.* bastione.

to **rampart** *vt.* fortificare.

ramshackle *agg.* sgangherato, che cade in rovina.

ran V. *to run.*

rancid agg. rancido.

rancour s. rancore.

rand s. soletta (*di scarpa*).

random agg. fatto a caso || at —, a casaccio.

rang V. *to ring.*

range s. 1. fila 2. catena (*di monti*) 3. spazio 4. sfera, raggio 5. gamma 6. fornello 7. (*aer.*) autonomia.

to range vt. 1. allineare 2. classificare 3. puntare. ♦ to range vi. 1. vagare 2. avere una portata di 3. oscillare (*di prezzi*).

ranger s. 1. guardia forestale 2. vagabondo.

rank agg. 1. rigoglioso 2. volgare 3. puzzolente. ♦ rank s. 1. fila 2. rango, grado 3. truppa.

to rank vi. 1. schierarsi 2. essere classificato.

to ransack vt. 1. frugare 2. saccheggiare.

ransom s. riscatto.

to ransom vt. riscattare.

to rant vt. e vi. declamare.

rap s. colpo.

to rap vt. e vi. 1. battere 2. bussare.

rapacious agg. rapace.

rapacity s. rapacità.

rape¹ s. violenza carnale.

rape² s. rapa.

to rape vt. violentare.

rapid agg. rapido. ♦ rapid s. rapida.

rapidity s. rapidità.

rapt agg. rapito.

raptorial agg. rapace.

rapture s. rapimento.

rare agg. 1. raro 2. rarefatto.

rarefaction s. rarefazione.

to rarefy vt. 1. rarefare 2. raffinare. ♦ to rarefy vi. rarefarsi.

rarely avv. 1. raramente 2. in modo eccellente.

rareness, rarity s. 1. rarità 2. rarefazione.

rascal s. furfante.

rascalism, rascality s. furfanteria.

rash agg. avventato. ♦ rash s. eruzione cutanea.

rashness s. avventatezza.

rasp s. 1. raspa 2. stridore.

to rasp vt. 1. raspare 2. irritare.

raspberry s. lampone.

rasping agg. stridente.

rat s. 1. topo 2. (*fig.*) traditore.

rate s. 1. tasso, quota 2. tassa 3. prezzo, tariffa 4. ritmo, andamento || first —, di prim'ordine; — of discount, tasso di sconto.

to rate¹ vt. 1. stimare 2. tassare 3. classificare.

to rate² vt. redarguire.

rateable agg. soggetto ad imposta.

ratepayer s. contribuente.

rather avv. piuttosto || I had —, preferirei; I would — not, non ci tengo.

ratification s. ratifica.

to ratify vt. ratificare.

rating¹ s. 1. stima 2. tassa 3. classificazione.

rating² s. sgridata.

ratio s. rapporto.

ration s. razione.

to ration vt. razionare.

rational agg. razionale.

rationalism s. razionalismo.

rationalist s. razionalista.

rationality s. razionalità.

to rationalize vt. 1. razionalizzare 2. spiegare razionalmente.

rationally avv. razionalmente.

rattle s. 1. sonaglio 2. rantolo 3. tintinnio.

to rattle vt. far risuonare. ♦ to rattle vi. 1. risuonare 2. cianciare.

rattling agg. 1. vivace 2. tintinnante.

ravage s. rovina.

to ravage vt. devastare.

rave s. delirio.

to rave vt. declamare. ♦ to rave vi. delirare || to — about sthg., andar pazzo per qc.

ravel s. 1. groviglio 2. lembo sfilacciato.

to ravel vt. ingarbugliare. ♦ to ravel vi. sfilacciarsi.

raven s. corvo.

to raven vt. e vi. saccheggiare.

ravenous agg. vorace.

ravine s. burrone.

raving agg. delirante. ♦ raving s. delirio.

to ravish vt. 1. rapire 2. violentare.

ravisher s. rapitore.

ravishing agg. (*fig.*) affascinante.

ravishment s. 1. rapimento 2. stupro.

raw agg. 1. crudo 2. greggio 3. inesperto 4. a nudo. ♦ raw s. punto vivo.

rawness s. 1. crudezza 2. rozzezza 3. inesperienza 4. escoriazione.

ray¹ s. 1. raggio 2. lampo.

ray² s. (zool.) razza.

to ray vt. irradiare. ♦ to ray vi. irradiarsi.

to raze vt. radere al suolo.

razor s. rasoio || — -blade, lametta.

to reabsorb vt. riassorbire.

reach s. 1. portata 2. penetrazione || beyond my —, irraggiungibile.

to reach vt. 1. raggiungere 2. porgere. ♦ to reach vi. estendersi.

to react vi. reagire.

reaction s. reazione.

reactionary agg. e s. reazionario.

reactive agg. reattivo.

read agg. colto. ♦ read s. lettura.

to read (read, read) vt. 1. leggere 2. interpretare 3. segnare || to — over, rileggere; to — through, esaminare.

readable agg. 1. leggibile 2. interessante.

reader s. 1. lettore 2. libro di lettura.

readily avv. prontamente.

readiness s. prontezza.

reading s. 1. lettura 2. interpretazione || — -desk, leggio.

to readjust vt. riaggiustare.

readjustment s. riordinamento.

to readmit vt. riammettere.

readmittance s. riammissione.

ready agg. pronto || — -made, confezionato; — money, contanti; — -made clothes, abito preconfezionato; — -built, prefabbricato.

to ready vt. preparare.

to reaffirm vt. riaffermare.

reafforestation s. rimboschimento.

reagent s. reagente.

real agg. e s. reale || — estate, beni immobili (pl.).

realism s. realismo.

realist s. realista.

realistic agg. realistico.

reality s. 1. realtà 2. realismo.

realizable agg. realizzabile.

realization s. 1. realizzazione 2. percezione.

to realize vt. 1. accorgersi di 2. realizzare 3. capire.

really avv. realmente.

realm s. reame.

realty s. beni immobili (pl.).

ream s. (tip.) risma.

to reap vt. 1. mietere 2. fare il raccolto (anche fig.).

reaper s. mietitore.

reaping s. mietitura.

to reappear vi. riapparire.

to reappoint vt. rinominare.

rear agg. posteriore. ♦ rear s. 1. retroguardia 2. retro.

to rear vt. 1. alzare, innalzare 2. allevare 3. coltivare.

to rearm vt. riarmare.

rearmament s. riarmo.

to rearrange vt. riordinare.

rearrangement s. riordinamento.

reason s. 1. ragione 2. causa, motivo 3. raziocinio.

to reason vt. e vi. 1. ragionare 2. persuadere || to — about a subject, discutere di un argomento.

reasonable agg. ragionevole.

reasonableness s. ragionevolezza.

reasonably avv. ragionevolmente.

reasoning s. ragionamento.

to reassert vt. riasserire.

reassurance s. rassicurazione.

to reassure vt. rassicurare.

to reawaken vt. risvegliare. ♦ to reawaken vi. risvegliarsi.

rebate s. riduzione, sconto.

rebel agg. e s. ribelle.

to rebel vi. ribellarsi.

rebellion s. ribellione.

rebellious agg. ribelle.

to rebind (rebound, rebound) vt. rilegare (un libro).

rebirth s. rinascita.

reborn agg. rinato.

rebound¹ V. to rebind.

rebound² s. rimbalzo.

to rebound vi. rimbalzare.

rebuff s. diniego, mortificazione.

to rebuild (rebuilt, rebuilt) vt. ricostruire.

rebuke s. rimprovero.

to rebuke vt. rimproverare.

to rebut vt. respingere, rifiutare.

recalcitrant agg. recalcitrante.

to recalcitrate vi. recalcitrare.

recall s. 1. richiamo 2. revoca.

to recall vt. 1. richiamare 2. rievocare, far tornare alla memoria.

to recant vt. e vi. ritrattare.

recantation s. ritrattazione.

to recapitulate vt. e vi. ricapitolare.

recapitulation s. ricapitolazione.

recapture s. riconquista.

to recapture vt. riconquistare.

recast s. nuova forma.

to recast (recast, recast) vt. 1. rifondere 2. rimaneggiare.

to recede vi. 1. indietreggiare 2. diminuire.

receding agg. **1.** rientrante **2.** sfuggente.

receipt s. **1.** ricevimento **2.** ricevuta **3.** ricetta.

to receipt vt. quietanzare.

to receive vt. **1.** ricevere **2.** accettare.

receiver s. **1.** ricevitore **2.** (giur.) ricettatore.

receiving s. ricezione.

recension s. revisione.

recent agg. recente.

receptacle s. ricettacolo.

reception s. **1.** ricevimento **2.** ricezione **3.** accoglienza.

receptive agg. ricettivo.

receptivity s. ricettività.

recess s. **1.** intervallo **2.** rientranza **3.** recesso.

recession s. **1.** ritiro **2.** recessione.

recessive agg. retrocedente.

recharge s. ricarica.

to recharge vt. ricaricare.

to rechristen vt. ribattezzare.

recidivism s. recidività.

recipe s. ricetta.

recipient agg. e s. ricevente.

reciprocal agg. reciproco. ♦ **reciprocal** s. (mat.) numero reciproco.

to reciprocate vt. **1.** contraccambiare **2.** muovere alternativamente. ♦ **to reciprocate** vi. muoversi alternativamente.

reciprocating agg. (mecc.) alternativo.

reciprocation s. **1.** moto alterno **2.** scambio.

reciprocity s. reciprocità.

recital s. **1.** relazione **2.** recitazione.

recitation s. **1.** recitazione **2.** recita **3.** narrazione.

recitative agg. e s. recitativo.

to recite vt. **1.** recitare **2.** riferire.

reckless agg. incurante.

recklessness s. noncuranza.

to reckon vt. **1.** contare, computare **2.** considerare.

reckoner s. calcolatore.

reckoning s. conto.

reclaim s. rivendicazione.

to reclaim vt. **1.** redimere **2.** bonificare **3.** rivendicare.

reclamation s. **1.** redenzione **2.** bonifica **3.** rivendicazione.

to recline vt. chinare. ♦ **to recline** vi. chinarsi.

reclining agg. chinato.

recluse agg. recluso. ♦ **recluse** s. eremita.

reclusion s. **1.** reclusione **2.** eremo.

recognition s. riconoscimento.

recognizable agg. riconoscibile.

to recognize vt. riconoscere.

recoil s. **1.** il ritrarsi **2.** rinculo.

to recoil vi. **1.** ritrarsi **2.** ricadere **3.** rinculare.

to recollect vt. **1.** raccogliere **2.** ricordare || to — oneself, riaversi.

recollection s. ricordo.

to recommence vt. e vi. ricominciare.

to recommend vt. raccomandare.

recommendation s. raccomandazione.

recommendatory agg. raccomandatorio.

recompense s. **1.** ricompensa **2.** risarcimento.

to recompense vt. **1.** ricompensare **2.** risarcire.

to recompose vt. ricomporre.

recomposition s. ricomposizione.

to reconcile vt. (ri)conciliare || to — oneself, rassegnarsi.

reconcilement s. **1.** riconciliazione **2.** rassegnazione.

reconnaissance s. ricognizione.

to reconnoitre vt. e vi. perlustrare.

to reconquer vt. riconquistare.

reconquest s. riconquista.

to reconsider vt. riconsiderare.

reconsideration s. revisione.

reconstitute vt. ricostituire.

to reconstruct vt. ricostruire.

reconstruction s. ricostruzione.

reconversion s. riconversione.

to reconvert vt. riconvertire.

record s. **1.** registrazione **2.** documento **3.** passato **4.** disco || — player, giradischi.

to record vt. registrare.

recorder s. **1.** cancelliere **2.** registratore **3.** archivista || tape —, magnetofono.

recording s. registrazione.

recordist s. (cine) tecnico del suono.

recourse s. ricorso.

to recover vt. ricuperare, riacquistare, riscoprire. ♦ **to recover** vi. ristabilirsi.

recoverable agg. **1.** ricuperabile **2.** guaribile.

recovery s. **1.** recupero **2.** guarigione **3.** (giur.) rivendicazione.

to recreate vt. divertire. ♦ **to recreate** vi. divertirsi.

to re-create vt. ricreare.

recreation s. ricreazione.

recreative *agg.* ricreativo.
to recriminate *vi.* recriminare.
recrimination *s.* recriminazione.
recrudescence *s.* recrudescenza.
recrudescent *agg.* che rincrudisce.
recruit *s.* recluta.
to recruit *vt.* 1. reclutare 2. rinforzare. ♦ **to recruit** *vi.* ristabilirsi.
recruitment *s.* reclutamento.
rectangle *s.* rettangolo.
rectangular *agg.* rettangolare.
rectification *s.* rettificazione.
rectifier *s.* (*mecc.*) rettificatrice.
to rectify *vt.* rettificare.
rectilineal *agg.* rettilineo.
rectitude *s.* rettitudine.
rector *s.* 1. rettore 2. parroco.
rectorate *s.* rettorato.
rectorship *s.* rettorato.
rectory *s.* 1. presbiterio 2. (*eccl.*) beneficio.
to recur *vi.* ritornare.
recurrence *s.* ricorso.
recurrent *agg.* ricorrente.
recusant *agg.* e *s.* dissidente.
red *agg.* e *s.* rosso || —*hot*, rovente; — *lead*, minio; — *letter day*, giorno festivo. ♦ **Reds** *s. pl.* comunisti.
to redact *vt.* 1. redigere 2. revisionare.
redactor *s.* redattore.
to redden *vt.* arrossare. ♦ **to redden** *vi.* arrossire.
reddish *agg.* rossiccio.
to redeem *vt.* 1. riscattare 2. ricuperare 3. estinguere: *to — a mortgage*, estinguere un'ipoteca.
redeemable *agg.* 1. riscattabile 2. ricuperabile.
redeemer *s.* redentore.
redemption *s.* 1. redenzione 2. (*comm.*) rimborso 3. (*giur.*) riscatto.
redness *s.* rossore.
to redouble *vt.* e *vi.* raddoppiare.
redress *s.* riparazione.
to redress *vt.* riparare, rimediare.
redskin *agg.* e *s.* pellerossa.
to reduce *vt.* 1. ridurre 2. degradare.
reduced *agg.* ridotto.
reducer *s.* riduttore.
reduction *s.* 1. riduzione 2. degradazione.
redundance *s.* sovrabbondanza.
redundant *agg.* ridondante.
redwood *s.* sequoia.
to re-echo *vt.* e *vi.* riecheggiare.
reed *s.* canna || *broken* —, perso-

na infida; — *pipe*, zampogna.
re-edification *s.* riedificazione.
to re-edify *vt.* riedificare.
to re-educate *vt.* rieducare.
reef *s.* secca || *coral*- —, banco di coralli.
to reek *vi.* puzzare. ♦ **to reek** *vt.* trasudare.
reel *s.* 1. bobina 2. giro vorticoso || *news*- —, cinegiornale.
to reel *vt.* avvolgere || *to — off*, snocciolare. ♦ **to reel** *vi.* girare.
to re-elect *vt.* rieleggere.
to re-emerge *vi.* riemergere.
to re-enact *vt.* richiamare in vigore (*una legge*).
to re-enter *vt.* rientrare.
re-entrance *s.* rientro.
re-entry *s.* 1. rientro 2. nuova registrazione.
to re-establish *vt.* ristabilire.
re-establishment *s.* ristabilimento.
re-examination *s.* riesame.
to re-examine *vt.* riesaminare.
refectory *s.* refettorio.
to refer *vt.* attribuire 2. rimandare. ♦ **to refer** *vi.* 1. riferirsi 2. rivolgersi.
referable *agg.* riferibile.
referee *s.* arbitro.
to referee *vt.* e *vi.* arbitrare.
reference *s.* 1. riferimento 2. consultazione 3. referenza 4. (*giur.*) rinvio.
referential *agg.* riferentesi a.
refill *s.* ricambio.
to refill *vt.* riempire di nuovo.
to refine *vt.* raffinare. ♦ **to refine** *vi.* raffinarsi.
refined *agg.* 1. raffinato 2. colto.
refinement *s.* 1. raffinamento 2. raffinatezza.
refiner *s.* raffinatore.
refinery *s.* raffineria.
refit *s.* riparazione.
to refit *vt.* riparare.
to reflect *vt.* e *vi* 1. riflettere 2. meditare.
reflection *s.* 1. riflessione, riflesso 2. biasimo || *to cast reflections on so.*, criticare qu.
reflective *agg.* riflessivo.
reflector *s.* riflettore.
reflex *agg.* e *s.* riflesso.
reflorescence *s.* rifioritura.
reflux *s.* riflusso.
reform *s.* riforma.
to reform *vt.* riformare.
reformation *s.* riforma.

reformational *agg.* di riforma.

reformatory *agg.* riformativo. ◆ **reformatory** *s.* riformatorio.

reformer *s.* riformatore.

to **refract** *vt.* rifrangere.

refraction *s.* rifrazione.

refractivity *s.* rifrangibilità.

refractor *s.* rifrattore.

refractory *agg.* **1.** refrattario **2.** ostinato.

refrain *s.* ritornello.

to **refrain** *vi.* trattenersi, astenersi.

to **refresh** *vt.* **1.** rinfrescare **2.** rinvigorire. ◆ to **refresh** *vi.* **1.** rinvigorirsi **2.** rifornirsi.

refreshment *s.* ristoro. ◆ **refreshments** *s. pl.* cibo, bevanda (*sing.*).

refrigerant *agg.* e *s.* refrigerante.

to **refrigerate** *vt.* refrigerare.

refrigeration *s.* refrigerazione.

refrigerator *s.* frigorifero.

refrigeratory *agg.* refrigerante.

to **refuel** *vt.* rifornire di carburante. ◆ to **refuel** *vi.* rifornirsi di carburante.

refuge *s.* rifugio.

refugee *s.* rifugiato, profugo.

refulgence *s.* fulgore.

refulgent *agg.* rifulgente.

refund *s.* rimborso.

to **refund** *vt.* rimborsare.

refusable *agg.* rifiutabile.

refusal *s.* **1.** rifiuto **2.** diritto di opzione.

refuse *s.* rifiuto.

to **refuse** *vt.* rifiutare. ◆ to **refuse** *vi.* rifiutarsi.

refuser *s.* ricusante.

refutal *s.* confutazione.

to **refute** *vt.* confutare.

to **regain** *vt.* riguadagnare.

regal *agg.* regale.

regality *s.* regalità.

regally *avv.* regalmente.

regard *s.* **1.** considerazione **2.** sguardo || *with — to*, riguardo a. ◆ **regards** *s. pl.* saluti.

to **regard** *vt.* **1.** considerare **2.** riguardare **3.** osservare.

regardful *agg.* **1.** attento **2.** rispettoso.

regardless *agg.* senza riguardo. ◆ **regardless** *avv.* senza riguardo a, senza badare a.

regatta *s.* regata.

regelation *s.* ricongelamento.

regency *s.* reggenza.

to **regenerate** *vt.* rigenerare. ◆ to **regenerate** *vi.* rigenerarsi.

regeneration *s.* rigenerazione.

regenerative *agg.* rigeneratore.

regenerator *s.* rigeneratore.

regent *agg.* e *s.* reggente.

regicide *s.* **1.** regicida **2.** regicidio.

regimen *s.* regime.

regiment *s.* reggimento.

to **regiment** *vt.* **1.** irreggimentare **2.** disciplinare.

regimental *agg.* reggimentale.

regimentals *s. pl.* (*mil.*) uniforme (*sing.*).

region *s.* regione.

regional *agg.* regionale.

register *s.* registro.

to **register** *vt.* registrare, iscrivere. ◆ to **register** *vi.* iscriversi.

registrar *s.* **1.** segretario **2.** ufficiale di stato civile.

registration *s.* registrazione, iscrizione.

registry *s.* **1.** registrazione **2.** ufficio del Registro.

regnant *agg.* regnante.

regress *s.* retrocessione.

to **regress** *vi.* retrocedere.

regression *s.* regresso.

regressive *agg.* regressivo.

regret *s.* rammarico.

to **regret** *vt.* **1.** rimpiangere **2.** rammaricarsi di.

regretful *agg.* pieno di rammarico.

regular *agg.* e *s.* regolare.

regularity *s.* regolarità.

regularization *s.* regolarizzazione.

to **regularize** *vt.* regolarizzare.

regularly *avv.* regolarmente.

to **regulate** *vt.* regolare.

regulation *s.* **1.** regolamento **2.** regolazione.

regulative *agg.* e *s.* regolatore.

regulator *s.* regolatore.

to **rehabilitate** *vt.* **1.** riabilitare **2.** ripristinare.

rehabilitation *s.* **1.** riabilitazione **2.** ripristino.

rehearsal *s.* **1.** ripetizione **2.** (*teat.*) prova.

to **rehearse** *vt.* **1.** ripetere **2.** provare.

reign *s.* regno.

to **reign** *vi.* regnare.

to **reimburse** *vt.* rimborsare.

reimbursement *s.* rimborso.

rein *s.* redine.

to **rein** *vt.* tenere a freno.

to **reincarnate** *vt.* reincarnare.

reincarnation *s.* reincarnazione.

reindeer *s.* renna.

to **reinforce** *vt.* rinforzare.
reinforce(ment) *s.* rinforzo.
to **reinstate** *vt.* ristabilire.
to **reintegrate** *vt.* reintegrare.
reinvestment *s.* nuovo investimento.
to **reinvigorate** *vt.* rinvigorire.
reinvigoration *s.* rinvigorimento.
to **reiterate** *vt.* reiterare.
reiteration *s.* reiterazione.
reject *s.* persona, cosa rifiutata.
to **reject** *vt.* rifiutare.
rejection *s.* rifiuto.
to **rejoice** *vt.* rallegrare. ♦ to rejoice *vi.* rallegrarsi.
rejoicing *s.* **1.** allegria **2.** festa.
rejuvenation *s.* ringiovanimento.
relapse *s.* ricaduta.
to **relapse** *vi.* **1.** ricadere **2.** avere una ricaduta.
to **relate** *vt.* **1.** narrare **2.** mettere in relazione. ♦ to relate *vi.* aver rapporto con.
relater *s.* narratore.
relation *s.* **1.** relazione **2.** parente.
relationship *s.* **1.** relazione **2.** parentela.
relative *agg.* relativo. ♦ relative *s.* parente.
relativism *s.* relativismo.
relativity *s.* relatività.
to **relax** *vt.* **1.** rilassare **2.** allentare. ♦ to relax *vi.* rilassarsi.
relaxation *s.* **1.** rilassamento **2.** svago **3.** mitigazione.
relay *s.* **1.** turno **2.** ricambio **3.** (*radio*) collegamento.
to **relay** *vt.* (*radio*) collegare.
release *s.* **1.** liberazione **2.** quietanza **3.** cessione **4.** scarico.
to **release** *vt.* **1.** liberare **2.** cedere.
releasee *s.* cessionario.
to **relegate** *vt.* **1.** relegare **2.** rimettere.
relegation *s.* relegazione.
relentless *agg.* inflessibile.
to **relent** *vi.* impietosirsi.
relevance *s.* **1.** relazione **2.** pertinenza.
relevant *agg.* **1.** relativo **2.** pertinente.
reliability *s.* attendibilità.
reliable *agg.* attendibile, fidato.
reliance *s.* **1.** fede **2.** persona, cosa di fiducia.
relic *s.* reliquia.
relief[1] *s.* **1.** sollievo **2.** aiuto **3.** esenzione **4.** cambio.
relief[2] *s.* **1.** rilievo **2.** (*pitt.*) prospettiva.

to **relieve** *vt.* **1.** alleviare, sollevare **2.** aiutare **3.** dare il cambio a **4.** dare rilievo a.
reliever *s.* soccorritore.
relieving *agg.* **1.** che allevia, soccorre **2.** (*mil.*) che dà il cambio.
religion *s.* religione.
religiosity *s.* religiosità.
religious *agg.* e *s.* religioso.
to **relinquish** *vt.* abbandonare.
relinquishment *s.* abbandono.
reliquary *s.* reliquario.
reliques *s. pl.* resti.
relish *s.* **1.** gusto **2.** sapore, profumo, aroma **3.** condimento.
to **relish** *vt.* **1.** gustare **2.** insaporire.
to **relive** *vt.* e *vi.* rivivere.
to **reload** *vt.* ricaricare.
to **reluct** *vi.* essere riluttante.
reluctance *s.* riluttanza.
reluctant *agg.* riluttante.
reluctantly *avv.* con riluttanza.
to **rely** *vi.* fidarsi.
remade V. *to remake*.
to **remain** *vi.* rimanere, restare.
remainder *s.* resto, avanzo, rimanenza.
remains *s. pl.* resti.
to **remake** (**remade, remade**) *vt.* rifare.
remark *s.* nota, osservazione, commento.
to **remark** *vt.* e *vi.* osservare.
remarkable *agg.* notevole.
remarkableness *s.* ragguardevolezza.
remarkably *avv.* notevolmente.
to **remarry** *vt.* risposare. ♦ to remarry *vi.* risposarsi.
remediable *agg.* rimediabile.
remedy *s.* rimedio, cura.
to **remedy** *vt.* rimediare.
to **remember** *vt.* ricordare. ♦ to remember *vi.* ricordarsi.
remembrance *s.* ricordo.
to **remind** *vt.* ricordare (*qc. a qu.*), far ricordare, rammentare.
reminder *s.* ricordo, promemoria.
remindful *agg.* **1.** memore **2.** che fa ricordare.
reminiscence *s.* ricordo.
reminiscent *agg.* che ricorda.
remise *s.* (*giur.*) cessione.
to **remise** *vt.* (*giur.*) rinunciare a, cedere (*diritti ecc.*).
remiss *agg.* negligente.
remissible *agg.* remissibile.

remission s. **1.** remissione **2.** esonero, annullamento **3.** (med.) remissione.

remissive agg. indulgente.

to **remit** vt. rimettere. ♦ to **remit** vi. diminuire, mitigarsi.

remittal s. (giur.) remissione (condono).

remittance s. rimessa (di denaro).

remittent agg. (med.) intermittente.

remnant agg. rimanente. ♦ **remnant** s. resto, rimanenza, avanzo.

to **remodel** vt. rimodellare.

remonstrance s. rimostranza.

to **remonstrate** vi. protestare.

remonstration s. rimostranza.

remorse s. rimorso.

remorseful agg. pieno di rimorso.

remorseless agg. senza rimorsi.

remote agg. remoto.

remoteness s. distanza, lontananza.

remotion s. rimozione, allontanamento.

remount s. rimonta (di cavalli).

to **remount** vt. e vi. **1.** rimontare (a cavallo, in bicicletta) **2.** risalire.

removable agg. rimovibile.

removal s. **1.** rimozione **2.** trasferimento, trasloco.

remove s. **1.** trasferimento **2.** grado (di parentela).

to **remove** vt. rimuovere. ♦ to **remove** vi. trasferirsi.

removed agg. lontano.

remover s. chi, ciò che toglie.

to **remunerate** vt. rimunerare.

remuneration s. rimunerazione.

remunerative agg. rimunerativo.

renaissance s. rinascimento.

renal agg. renale.

to **rename** vt. rinominare.

to **rend** (**rent, rent**) vt. lacerare. ♦ to **rend** (**rent, rent**) vi. lacerarsi.

to **render** vt. **1.** rendere **2.** consegnare.

rendering s. **1.** restituzione **2.** resa.

renegade s. rinnegato.

to **renew** vt. rinnovare. ♦ to **renew** vi. rinnovarsi.

renewable agg. rinnovabile.

renewal s. **1.** rinnovo **2.** ripresa.

renewer s. rinnovatore.

renitency s. riluttanza.

renitent agg. renitente, riluttante.

rennet s. ranetta.

to **renounce** vt. **1.** rinunciare a **2.** ripudiare.

renouncement s. rinuncia.

to **renovate** vt. rinnovare.

renown s. rinomanza, fama.

renowned agg. rinomato, famoso.

rent[1] s. affitto.

rent[2] s. **1.** strappo, squarcio **2.** spaccatura.

rent[3] V. to **rend**.

to **rent** vt. affittare. ♦ to **rent** vi. essere affittato.

rental s. affitto.

renunciation s. rinuncia.

to **reoccupy** vt. rioccupare.

to **reopen** vt. riaprire. ♦ to **reopen** vi. riaprirsi.

reopening s. riapertura.

reorganization s. riassetto, riorganizzazione.

repaid V. to **repay**.

repair s. **1.** riparazione, restaurazione **2.** stato, condizione.

to **repair** vt. riparare, restaurare.

repairer s. riparatore.

reparation s. riparazione.

repartee s. replica arguta.

repartition s. ripartizione.

to **repatriate** vt. e vi. rimpatriare.

repatriation s. rimpatrio.

to **repay** (**repaid, repaid**) vt. ripagare.

repayable agg. ripagabile.

repeal s. revoca.

to **repeal** vt. revocare.

repealer s. revocatore.

repeat s. ripetizione.

to **repeat** vt. ripetere. ♦ to **repeat** vi. ripetersi.

repeater s. **1.** ripetitore **2.** ripetente **3.** arma a ripetizione.

repeating agg. **1.** a ripetizione **2.** periodico (di numero).

to **repel** vt. respingere.

repellent agg. repellente.

to **repent** vt. e vi. pentirsi.

repentance s. pentimento.

repentant agg. pentito.

repenter s. penitente.

repercussion s. ripercussione.

repercussive agg. ripercussivo.

repertoire s. repertorio.

repertory s. **1.** repertorio **2.** raccolta.

repetition s. ripetizione.

to **repine** vi. lamentarsi.

to **replace** vt. **1.** ricollocare **2.** rimpiazzare, sostituire.

replaceable agg. sostituibile.

replacement s. **1.** ricollocamento **2.** sostituzione.

replete *agg.* pieno.
repletion *s.* pienezza.
replication *s.* replica.
reply *s.* risposta.
to reply *vi.* rispondere.
report *s.* 1. diceria 2. reputazione 3. rapporto 4. scoppio.
to report *vt.* riportare. ◆ to report *vi.* 1. stendere rapporto 2. fare il cronista 3. presentarsi.
reporter *s.* cronista (*di giornale*).
to repose *vt.* porre. ◆ to repose *vi.* riposare.
to reprehend *vt.* rimproverare.
reprehensible *agg.* biasimevole.
reprehension *s.* biasimo.
to represent *vt.* rappresentare, raffigurare.
representation *s.* 1. rappresentazione 2. rappresentanza.
representative *agg.* rappresentativo. ◆ representative *s.* rappresentante.
to repress *vt.* reprimere.
repressed *agg.* represso.
repressible *agg.* reprimibile.
repression *s.* repressione.
repressive *agg.* repressivo.
reprimand *s.* rimprovero.
to reprimand *vt.* rimproverare.
reprint *s.* ristampa.
to reprint *vt.* ristampare.
reprisal *s.* rappresaglia.
reproach *s.* 1. rimprovero 2. discredito.
to reproach *vt.* 1. rimproverare 2. discreditare.
reproachable *agg.* riprovevole.
reproachful *agg.* di rimprovero.
reprobate *agg.* corrotto. ◆ reprobate *s.* reprobo.
to reprobate *vt.* 1. riprovare 2. dannare.
reprobation *s.* 1. riprovazione 2. dannazione.
to reproduce *vt.* riprodurre. ◆ to reproduce *vi.* riprodursi.
reproducer *s.* riproduttore.
reproducible *agg.* riproducibile.
reproduction *s.* riproduzione.
reproductive *agg.* riproduttivo.
reproof *s.* rimprovero.
to reprove *vt.* rimproverare.
reptile *agg.* strisciante. ◆ reptile *s.* rettile.
republic *s.* repubblica.
republican *agg. e s.* repubblicano.
republication *s.* ripubblicazione.
to republish *vt.* ripubblicare.
to repudiate *vt.* ripudiare.

repudiation *s.* ripudio.
repugnance *s.* 1. ripugnanza 2. incompatibilità.
repugnant *agg.* 1. ripugnante 2. incompatibile.
repulse *s.* ripulsa, rifiuto.
to repulse *vt.* respingere.
repulsion *s.* repulsione.
repulsive *agg.* ripulsivo.
reputable *agg.* onorato.
reputation *s.* reputazione.
repute *s.* fama.
to repute *vt.* reputare.
reputed *agg.* 1. supposto 2. putativo.
request *s.* richiesta.
to request *vt.* (ri)chiedere.
to require *vt.* 1. richiedere 2. ordinare, obbligare.
requirement *s.* 1. richiesta 2. requisito.
requisite *agg.* richiesto. ◆ requisite *s.* requisito.
requisition *s.* 1. richiesta 2. requisito 3. requisizione.
to requisition *vt.* requisire.
requital *s.* 1. contraccambio 2. ricompensa.
to requite *vt.* 1. ricompensare 2. contraccambiare.
to reread (reread, reread) *vt.* rileggere.
to rescind *vt.* rescindere.
rescission *s.* rescissione.
rescue *s.* 1. liberazione 2. soccorso.
to rescue *vt.* 1. liberare 2. riacquistare 3. soccorrere.
research *s.* ricerca || — work, lavoro di ricerca.
to research *vi.* fare ricerche.
researcher *s.* ricercatore.
to resell (resold, resold) *vt.* rivendere.
resemblance *s.* rassomiglianza.
to resemble *vt.* assomigliare a.
to resent *vt.* risentirsi di.
resentful *agg.* 1. risentito 2. permaloso.
resentment *s.* risentimento.
reservation *s.* 1. riserva 2. prenotazione.
reserve *s.* 1. riserva 2. riserbo.
to reserve *vt.* riservare.
reservoir *s.* serbatoio.
to reset (reset, reset) *vt.* 1. rimettere a posto 2. (*tip.*) ricomporre.
to resettle *vt.* risistemare. ◆ to resettle *vi.* risistemarsi.
resettlement *s.* risistemazione.

to **reshape** *vt.* dare nuova forma a.
to **reside** *vi.* risiedere.
residence *s.* residenza.
resident *agg.* e *s.* residente.
residential *agg.* residenziale.
residual *agg.* residuo. ◆ **residual** *s.* 1. residuo 2. resto.
residue *s.* residuo, avanzo.
to **resign** *vt.* 1. consegnare 2. rinunciare || *to — oneself*, rassegnarsi. ◆ to **resign** *vi.* dimettersi.
resignation *s.* 1. dimissioni (*pl.*) 2. rinuncia 3. rassegnazione.
resigned *agg.* rassegnato.
resilience, resiliency *s.* elasticità.
resilient *agg.* elastico.
resin *s.* resina.
resinous *agg.* resinoso.
resipiscence *s.* resipiscenza.
resipiscent *agg.* resipiscente.
resist *s.* sostanza protettiva.
to **resist** *vt.* e *vi.* resistere.
resistance *s.* resistenza.
resistant, resistent *agg.* resistente.
resistive *agg.* resistente.
resold V. to *resell*.
to **resole** *vt.* risolare.
resolubile *agg.* (ri)solubile.
resolute *agg.* risoluto.
resoluteness *s.* risolutezza.
resolution *s.* 1. risolutezza 2. risoluzione 3. scissione.
resolutive *agg.* risolutivo.
resolvable *agg.* risolvibile.
resolve *s.* risoluzione.
to **resolve** *vt.* 1. risolvere 2. scindere. ◆ to **resolve** *vi.* risolversi.
resolvent *agg.* e *s.* solvente.
resonance *s.* risonanza.
resonant *agg.* risonante.
to **resorb** *vt.* riassorbire.
resorbent *agg.* riassorbente.
resort *s.* 1. ricorso 2. risorsa 3. ritrovo 4. luogo di soggiorno.
to **resort** *vi.* 1. ricorrere 2. recarsi.
to **resound** *vi.* risonare. ◆ to **resound** *vt.* proclamare.
resource *s.* risorsa.
resourceful *agg.* pieno di risorse.
resourceless *agg.* senza risorse.
respect *s.* 1. rispetto, stima 2. aspetto 3. punto di vista.
to **respect** *vt.* rispettare.
respectability *s.* 1. rispettabilità 2. convenzioni sociali (*pl.*).
respectable *agg.* rispettabile.
respectful *agg.* rispettoso.
respecting *prep.* rispetto a.
respective *agg.* rispettivo.

respiration *s.* respirazione.
respirator *s.* respiratore.
respiratory *agg.* respiratorio.
respite *s.* 1. dilazione 2. tregua.
to **respite** *vt.* concedere una dilazione, una tregua a.
resplendent *agg.* risplendente.
respond *s.* responsorio.
to **respond** *vi.* rispondere.
respondence *s.* rispondenza.
respondent *agg.* 1. rispondente 2. sensibile. ◆ **respondent** *s.* (*giur.*) convenuto.
response *s.* risposta.
responsibility *s.* responsabilità.
responsible *agg.* 1. responsabile 2. di responsabilità.
responsive *agg.* rispondente.
responsory *s.* responsorio.
rest[1] *s.* 1. riposo 2. appoggio.
rest[2] *s.* resto, residuo.
to **rest** *vt.* 1. riposare 2. appoggiare. ◆ to **rest** *vi.* 1. riposarsi 2. appoggiarsi.
to **restate** *vt.* riesporre.
restaurant *s.* ristorante || *— -car*, vagone ristorante.
restful *agg.* tranquillo.
restfulness *s.* tranquillità.
resting-place *s.* luogo di riposo.
restitution *s.* restituzione.
restive *agg.* 1. restio 2. irrequieto.
restless *agg.* 1. irrequieto 2. incessante.
restlessness *s.* irrequietezza.
restorable *agg.* 1. restituibile 2. restaurabile.
restoration *s.* 1. restituzione 2. restauro 3. restaurazione 4. ricostruzione.
to **restore** *vt.* 1. restituire 2. restaurare 3. ricostruire 4. ristabilire.
to **restrain** *vt.* 1. trattenere 2. confinare.
restrainable *agg.* reprimibile.
restraint *s.* 1. freno 2. detenzione.
to **restrict** *vt.* limitare.
restrictedly *avv.* limitatamente.
restriction *s.* restrizione.
restrictive *agg.* restrittivo.
result *s.* risultato.
to **result** *vi.* 1. risultare 2. risolversi.
resultant *agg.* e *s.* risultante.
resultful *agg.* utile, efficace.
resultless *agg.* inutile, inefficace.
to **resume** *vt.* riprendere.
resummons *s.* nuova convocazione.
resumption *s.* ripresa.

resurgent *agg.* risorgente.
to resurrect *vt.* (*fam.*) risuscitare.
resurrection *s.* risurrezione.
resurrectional *agg.* di risurrezione.
to resuscitate *vt.* e *vi.* risuscitare.
resuscitation *s.* risuscitamento.
to ret *vt.* macerare.
retail *s.* vendita al minuto || by —, al minuto.
to retail *vt.* e *vi.* vendere al minuto.
retailer *s.* dettagliante.
to retain *vt.* trattenere, conservare.
retainable *agg.* trattenibile, conservabile.
retainer *s.* caparra, anticipo.
retaining *agg.* — *wall*, muro di sostegno.
retake *s.* (*cine*) replica di una ripresa.
to retake (**retook, retaken**) *vt.* 1. riprendere 2. (*cine*) ripetere una ripresa.
to retaliate *vi.* far rappresaglia.
retaliation *s.* rappresaglia.
retaliative, retaliatory *agg.* vendicativo.
retard *s.* ritardo.
to retard *vt.* e *vi.* ritardare.
to retaste *vt.* riassaggiare.
to retch *vi.* avere conati di vomito.
to retell (**retold, retold**) *vt.* ripetere.
retention *s.* 1. ritenzione 2. memoria.
retentive *agg.* 1. che trattiene 2. tenace (*di memoria*).
reticence, reticency *s.* reticenza.
reticent *agg.* reticente.
reticle *s.* (*ott.*) reticolo.
reticular *agg.* reticolare.
reticulate *agg.* reticolato.
reticulum *s.* (*pl.* -la) reticolo.
retinue *s.* seguito.
to retire *vt.* ritirare. ◆ **to retire** *vi.* ritirarsi.
retired *agg.* 1. ritirato 2. a riposo, in ritiro.
retirement *s.* 1. ritiro 2. collocamento a riposo 3. (*mil.*) ritirata.
retiring *agg.* 1. riservato 2. che si ritira, uscente.
retold V. *to retell.*
retook V. *to retake.*
retorsion *s.* ritorsione.
retort *s.* storta.
to retort *vt.* ritorcere. ◆ **to retort** *vi.* ribattere.
retort(ion) *s.* ritorsione.
retouch *s.* ritocco.

to retouch *vt.* ritoccare.
to retrace *vt.* ripercorrere, risalire.
to retract *vt.* 1. ritrarre 2. ritrattare. ◆ **to retract** *vi.* ritrarsi.
retractable *agg.* ritraibile 2. ritrattabile.
retractation *s.* ritrattazione.
retractile *agg.* retrattile.
retractor *s.* (*med.*) divaricatore.
to retread (**retrod, retrodden**) *vt.* ripercorrere.
retreat *s.* eremo, luogo appartato.
to retreat *vi.* ritirarsi, retrocedere.
retreating *agg.* sfuggente. ◆ **retreating** *s.* (*mil.*) ritirata.
retribution *s.* punizione.
retrievable *agg.* 1. ricuperabile 2. riparabile.
retrieval *s.* 1. ricupero (*di beni*) 2. riparazione.
to retrieve *vt.* 1. ricuperare 2. riparare.
retroaction *s.* 1. reazione 2. azione retroattiva.
retroactive *agg.* retroattivo.
to retrocede[1] *vi.* retrocedere.
to retrocede[2] *vt.* restituire.
retrocession[1] *s.* retrocessione.
retrocession[2] *s.* restituzione.
retrod V. *to retread.*
retrodden V. *to retread.*
retrospect(ion) *s.* sguardo retrospettivo.
retrospective *agg.* retrospettivo.
retroversion *s.* retroversione.
return *s.* 1. ritorno 2. restituzione 3. guadagno, profitto 4. relazione || — *journey*, viaggio di ritorno; *election returns*, risultati elettorali.
to return *vi.* 1. ritornare 2. rispondere, ricambiare, replicare. ◆ **to return** *vt.* 1. restituire, rimandare 2. produrre, fruttare 3. (*pol.*) eleggere.
reunion *s.* riunione.
to reunite *vt.* riunire. ◆ **to reunite** *vi.* riunirsi.
revaluation *s.* rivalutazione.
to revalue *vt.* rivalutare.
to reveal *vt.* rivelare.
revel *s.* baldoria.
to revel *vi.* far baldoria.
revelation *s.* rivelazione.
reveller *s.* chi fa baldoria.
revelry *s.* baldoria.
revenge *s.* vendetta.
to revenge *vt.* vendicare. ◆ **to revenge** *vi.* vendicarsi.
revengeful *agg.* vendicativo.

revenger s. vendicatore.
revenue s. **1.** entrata **2.** fisco.
to **reverberate** vt. e vi. riverberare.
reverberation s. riverberazione, riverbero.
to **revere** vt. riverire.
reverence s. riverenza.
to **reverence** vt. riverire.
reverend agg. reverendo.
reverent(ial) agg. riverente.
reverie s. fantasticheria.
reversal s. **1.** rovesciamento **2.** (giur.) annullamento.
reverse agg. e s. rovescio || — gear, retromarcia.
to **reverse** vt. rovesciare. ◆ to **reverse** vi. innestare la retromarcia.
reversibility s. reversibilità.
reversible agg. reversibile, rovesciabile.
reversion s. reversione.
to **revert** vi. ritornare.
review s. **1.** revisione **2.** recensione **3.** rivista, periodico **4.** (mil.) rivista.
to **review** vt. **1.** rivedere **2.** recensire **3.** (mil.) passare in rivista.
reviewal s. revisione, recensione.
reviewer s. recensore, revisore.
to **revile** vt. e vi. ingiuriare.
to **revise** vt. rivedere, modificare.
reviser s. revisore.
revision s. revisione, correzione.
revival s. **1.** ripristino **2.** ripresa **3.** rinascita.
to **revive** vt. e vi. resuscitare.
reviver s. chi, ciò che rinvigorisce.
revivification s. rinascita.
to **revivify** vt. ravvivare.
revocable agg. revocabile.
revocation s. revoca.
revocatory agg. revocatorio.
to **revoke** vt. revocare.
revolt s. rivolta.
to **revolt** vt. disgustare. ◆ to **revolt** vi. rivoltarsi.
revolution s. rivoluzione.
revolutionary agg. e s. rivoluzionario.
to **revolutionize** vt. rivoluzionare.
to **revolve** vt. meditare. ◆ to **revolve** vi. girare, rotare.
revolver s. rivoltella.
revolving agg. **1.** rotante **2.** rotativo.
revulsion s. **1.** revulsione **2.** mutamento.
revulsive agg. revulsivo.

reward s. ricompensa.
to **reward** vt. ricompensare.
rewarding agg. rimunerativo. ◆ **rewarding** s. rimunerazione.
to **rewrite (rewrote, rewritten)** vt. riscrivere.
rhagades s. pl. ragadi.
rhapsody s. rapsodia.
rheostat s. reostato.
rhetoric s. retorica.
rhetorical agg. retorico.
rhetorician s. retore.
rheumatic agg. e s. reumatico.
rheumatism s. reumatismo.
rhinitis s. rinite.
rhinoceros s. rinoceronte.
rhizome s. rizoma.
rhododendron s. rododendro.
rhomb s. rombo.
rhombic(al) agg. rombico.
rhombohedron s. (pl. -dra) romboedro.
rhomboid agg. e s. romboide.
rhubarb s. rabarbaro.
rhyme s. rima.
to **rhyme** vt. far rimare. ◆ to **rhyme** vi. rimare.
rhymer s. rimatore.
Rhynchota s. pl. rincoti.
rhythm s. ritmo.
rhythmic(al) agg. ritmico.
rib s. **1.** costola **2.** costa, nervatura **3.** stecca.
to **rib** vt. **1.** munire (di coste ecc.) **2.** scanalare.
ribbing s. **1.** nervatura **2.** rigatura.
ribbon s. nastro.
rice s. riso || —field (o —swamp), risaia.
rich agg. ricco.
richly avv. riccamente.
richness s. ricchezza.
rick s. bica.
ricket(s) s. rachitismo.
rickety agg. **1.** rachitico **2.** malsicuro.
to **rid (rid, rid)** vt. liberare || to **get — of,** sbarazzarsi di.
ridden V. to **ride.**
riddle[1] s. indovinello.
riddle[2] s. vaglio, crivello.
to **riddle**[1] vt. risolvere.
to **riddle**[2] vt. **1.** vagliare **2.** setacciare.
ride s. passeggiata, percorso (a cavallo, su un veicolo).
to **ride (rode, ridden)** vt. **1.** montare (cavallo, bicicletta) **2.** percorrere (a cavallo, su un veicolo) **3.**

(fig.) opprimere. ♦ to **ride** (rode, **ridden**) *vi.* andare (*a cavallo, su un veicolo*).

rider *s.* cavaliere, fantino.

ridge *s.* cresta, catena di monti.

ridicule *s.* ridicolo.

to **ridicule** *vt.* schernire.

ridiculous *agg.* ridicolo.

riding *s.* corsa (*a cavallo, in veicolo*).

rifle *s.* fucile.

rifleman *s.* fuciliere.

rift *s.* crepa.

rigging *s.* attrezzatura.

right[1] *agg.* 1. giusto 2. (*geom.*) retto 3. destro.

right[2] *s.* 1. il giusto, il bene 2. diritto 3. destra, mano destra, lato destro.

right[3] *avv.* 1. giustamente, bene 2. direttamente 3. proprio 4. a destra.

righteous *agg.* giusto.

righteousness *s.* rettitudine.

rightful *agg.* 1. legittimo 2. giusto.

rightly *avv.* 1. rettamente 2. esattamente.

rigid *agg.* rigido.

rigidity, rigor *s.* rigidità.

rigorism *s.* rigorismo.

rigorist *s.* rigorista.

rigorous *agg.* rigido.

rigour *s.* rigore.

rim *s.* bordo, orlo.

to **rim** *vt.* bordare, cerchiare.

rind *s.* 1. buccia 2. corteccia 3. crosta 4. cotenna.

to **rind** *vt.* 1. sbucciare 2. scortecciare.

ring[1] *s.* 1. anello, cerchio 2. pista.

ring[2] *s.* 1. scampanellata 2. (*fig.*) accento, tono.

to **ring**[1] *vt.* circondare.

to **ring**[2] (rang, rung) *vt.* suonare || to — up, telefonare. ♦ to **ring** (rang, rung) *vi.* risuonare.

ringleader *s.* capobanda.

rink *s.* pista di pattinaggio.

to **rinse** *vt.* sciacquare.

rinsing *s.* risciacquatura.

riot *s.* 1. rivolta 2. gazzarra.

to **riot** *vi.* 1. tumultuare 2. gozzovigliare.

rioter *s.* rivoltoso.

riotous *agg.* 1. tumultuante 2. sregolato.

rip *s.* lacerazione, scucitura, strappo.

to **rip** *vt.* lacerare, strappare. ♦ to **rip** *vi.* lacerarsi.

ripe *agg.* maturo.

to **ripen** *vt.* e *vi.* maturare.

ripeness *s.* maturità.

ripple *s.* 1. increspatura, ondulatura 2. gorgoglio.

to **ripple** *vt.* increspare, ondulare. ♦ to **ripple** *vi.* incresparsi, ondularsi.

rise *s.* 1. il sorgere 2. salita, ascesa 3. aumento 4. sorgente.

to **rise** (rose, risen) *vi.* 1. sorgere 2. aumentare.

riser *s.* chi si alza.

risible *agg.* risibile.

rising *s.* 1. sorgere 2. salita, ascesa 3. aumento 4. rivolta.

risk *s.* rischio.

to **risk** *vt.* rischiare.

risky *agg.* rischioso.

rissole *s.* polpetta.

rite *s.* rito.

ritual *agg.* e *s.* rituale.

rival *agg.* e *s.* rivale.

to **rival** *vt.* rivaleggiare.

rivalry, rivalry *s.* rivalità.

river *s.* fiume.

riverside *s.* lungofiume.

to **rivet** *vt.* 1. ribadire 2. fissare.

rivulet *s.* fiumicello.

road *s.* strada || — -bed, fondo stradale; — sign, cartello stradale.

roadstead *s.* (*mar.*) rada.

roadway *s.* carreggiata.

to **roam** *vt.* e *vi.* vagare (*per*).

roar *s.* 1. ruggito 2. rombo.

to **roar** *vt.* e *vi.* 1. ruggire 2. tuonare || to — with laughter, ridere fragorosamente.

roaring *agg.* 1. rumoroso 2. ruggente, mugghiante. ♦ **roaring** *s.* V. roar.

roast *agg.* e *s.* arrosto.

to **roast** *vt.* 1. arrostire 2. tostare. ♦ to **roast** *vi.* arrostirsi.

roasting *agg.* rovente. ♦ **roasting** *s.* 1. arrostimento 2. torrefazione.

to **rob** *vt.* derubare. ♦ to **rob** *vi.* rubare.

robber *s.* ladro.

robbery *s.* furto.

robe *s.* 1. toga 2. vestiti (*pl.*).

to **robe** *vt.* vestire. ♦ to **robe** *vi.* vestirsi.

robin *s.* pettirosso.

robust *agg.* 1. robusto 2. faticoso.

robustness *s.* robustezza.

rock[1] *s.* 1. roccia 2. rocca.

rock[2] *s.* dondolio.

to **rock** *vt.* cullare, dondolare. ♦

to **rock** *vi.* dondolarsi, oscillare, barcollare.

rocker *s.* **1.** chi culla, dondola **2.** dondolo (*di sedia ecc.*) **3.** (*mecc.*) bilanciere.

rocket *s.* razzo.

rocking *agg.* **1.** a dondolo **2.** vacillante. ♦ **rocking** *s.* oscillazione, dondolio.

rocky *agg.* roccioso.

rod *s.* verga || *fishing* —, canna da pesca.

rode V. *to ride.*

rodent *agg.* e *s.* roditore.

roe[1] *s.* capriolo maschio.

roe[2] *s.* uova di pesce.

rogue *s.* briccone.

roguery *s.* bricconeria.

roguish *agg.* bricconesco.

role *s.* **1.** (*teat.*) ruolo, parte **2.** funzione.

roll[1] *s.* **1.** rotolo **2.** elenco, lista **3.** rullo, cilindro.

roll[2] *s.* **1.** (*mar.; aer.*) rollio **2.** rullo (*di tamburo*).

to **roll** *vt.* **1.** far rotolare **2.** arrotolare **3.** spianare. ♦ to **roll** *vi.* **1.** rotolare **2.** arrotolarsi **3.** ruotare **4.** rollare **5.** rullare.

roller *s.* **1.** rullo, cilindro **2.** cavallone || — *skates*, schettini.

rolling *s.* **1.** (ar)rotolamento || — *-mill*, laminatoio; — *pin*, matterello.

Roman *agg.* e *s.* romano.

Romance *agg.* romanzo, neolatino.

romance *s.* **1.** poema cavalleresco, racconto fantastico **2.** avventura romanzesca **3.** idillio **4.** poesia **5.** (*mus.*) romanza.

Romanesque *agg.* e *s.* romanico.

Romanian *agg.* e *s.* romeno.

Romanic *agg.* romanico.

Romanist *s.* romanista.

Romansh *agg.* e *s.* ladino.

romantic *agg.* romantico.

romanticism *s.* romanticismo.

to **romanticize** *vt.* romanzare.

to **romp** *vi.* giocare rumorosamente.

rompish *agg.* chiassoso.

rood *s.* croce.

roof *s.* tetto || — *-garden*, giardino pensile.

to **roof** *vt.* **1.** coprire con un tetto **2.** ospitare.

rook *s.* cornacchia.

room *s.* **1.** stanza **2.** spazio **3.** possibilità.

to **room** *vt.* e *vi.* (*amer.*) alloggiare.

roomy *agg.* spazioso.

root *s.* radice.

to **root**[1] *vt.* piantare || *to* — *away, out, up,* sradicare. ♦ to **root** *vi.* mettere radice.

to **root**[2] *vt.* e *vi.* grufolare.

rope *s.* fune, corda || — *-dancer*, funambolo.

to **rope** *vt.* legare.

rosary *s.* **1.** roseto **2.** (*eccl.*) rosario.

rose *agg.* e *s.* rosa || — *-bush*, rosaio; — *-diamond*, rosetta; — *-window*, rosone.

rose V. *to rise.*

rosemary *s.* rosmarino.

roseola *s.* rosolia.

rosery *s.* roseto.

rosette *s.* **1.** rosetta **2.** (*arch.*) rosone **3.** coccarda.

rosewood *s.* palissandro.

rosin *s.* pece greca.

rostrum *s.* (*pl.* rostra *o* rostrums) rostro.

rosy *agg.* roseo.

rot *s.* putrefazione.

to **rot** *vt.* e *vi.* imputridire.

rotary *agg.* rotante. ♦ **rotary** *s.* — (*press*), rotativa.

to **rotate** *vt.* e *vi.* rotare.

rotation *s.* rotazione.

rotative, rotatory *agg.* rotatorio.

rote *s.* abitudine, memoria meccanica.

rotogravure *s.* rotocalco.

rotor *s.* rotore.

rotten *agg.* marcio.

rottenness *s.* marciume.

rotund *agg.* **1.** rotondo **2.** enfatico.

rouble *s.* rublo.

rouge *agg.* rossetto.

rough *agg.* **1.** irregolare, ruvido, scabro **2.** tempestoso **3.** rozzo.

to **rough** *vt.* irruvidire || *to* — *il* (*fam.*), vivere primitivamente.

to **roughen** *vt.* irruvidire. ♦ to **roughen** *vi.* irruvidirsi.

to **rough-hew** *vt.* abbozzare.

roughly *avv.* ruvidamente.

roughness *s.* **1.** ruvidezza **2.** rudezza **3.** inclemenza (*di tempo*).

round *agg.* **1.** rotondo **2.** intero **3.** franco **4.** vigoroso **5.** considerevole. ♦ **round** *s.* **1.** cerchio **2.** sfera **3.** ciclo **4.** giro, ronda.

round *avv.* intorno. ♦ **round** *prep.* intorno a.

to **round** *vt.* arrotondare. ♦ to **round** *vi.* **1.** arrotondarsi **2.** girare

3. svilupparsi.

roundabout *agg.* indiretto. ♦
roundabout *s.* giostra.

roundly *avv.* 1. vigorosamente 2.
francamente.

roundness *s.* 1. rotondità 2. scorrevolezza 3. franchezza.

to **rouse** *vt.* (ri)svegliare (*anche fig.*).
♦ to **rouse** *vi.* (ri)svegliarsi.

rouser *s.* ridestatore.

rousing *agg.* stimolante.

rout *s.* 1. plebaglia 2. tumulto 3.
rotta.

to **rout** *vt.* sconfiggere.

route *s.* via, rotta.

routinist *s.* abitudinario.

rove *s.* vagabondaggio.

to **rove** *vi.* e *vi.* vagare.

rover *s.* 1. vagabondo 2. pirata.

roving *s.* vagabondaggio.

row[1] *s.* fila.

row[2] *s.* remata, gita in barca.

to **row** *vt.* trasportare (*remando*). ♦
to **row** *vi.* remare.

rowdy *agg.* e *s.* turbolento.

rower *s.* rematore.

rowlock *s.* scalmo.

royal *agg.* regale, reale.

royalist *s.* realista.

royalty *s.* 1. regalità 2. i reali 3. diritto d'autore.

rub *s.* 1. fregata, grattata 2. ineguaglianza 3. ostacolo, difficoltà.

to **rub** *vt.* fregare. ♦ to **rub** *vi.* fregarsi.

rubber *s.* 1. massaggiatore 2. strofinaccio 3. gomma || — *-solution*,
mastice.

rubbish *s.* rifiuti (*pl.*).

rubble *s.* pietrisco.

ruby *s.* rubino.

rucksack *s.* zaino.

rudder *s.* timone.

ruddy *agg.* rosso, rubicondo.

rude *agg.* 1. rude, violento 2. rudimentale 3. grezzo.

rudeness *s.* 1. rozzezza 2. violenza.

rudiment *s.* rudimento.

rudimentary *agg.* rudimentale.

ruffian *agg.* brutale. ♦ **ruffian** *s.*
ribaldo.

ruffle *s.* 1. increspatura 2. sconvolgimento 3. tumulto.

to **ruffle** *vt.* 1. increspare 2. arruffare
3. agitare.

rug *s.* 1. coperta 2. tappetino.

rugged *agg.* 1. ruvido 2. scompigliato 3. austero 4. rozzo.

ruggedness *s.* 1. ruvidezza 2. auste-

rità 3. rudezza.

ruin *s.* rovina.

to **ruin** *vt.* e *vi.* rovinare.

ruinous *agg.* 1. rovinoso 2. in rovina.

rule *s.* 1. regola 2. dominio 3. riga
da disegno.

to **rule** *vt.* 1. governare, dominare 2.
rigare.

ruler *s.* 1. dominatore 2. regolo.

ruling *s.* 1. governo 2. decisione.

Rumanian *agg.* e *s.* romeno.

rumble *s.* 1. rombo 2. brontolio.

to **rumble** *vt.* e *vi.* 1. rombare 2.
brontolare.

rumbling *s.* V. *rumble.*

rumen *s.* rumine.

ruminant *agg.* e *s.* ruminante.

to **ruminate** *vt* e *vi.* ruminare.

rummage *s.* ricerca, perquisizione.

to **rummage** *vt.* e *vi.* 1. rovistare
2. perquisire.

rumour *s.* diceria.

to **rumour** *vt.* far correre la voce.

rump *s.* 1. posteriore 2. resto.

to **rumple** *vt.* 1. spiegazzare 2. arruffare.

run *s.* 1. corsa 2. percorso, giro 3.
andamento 4. periodo 5. richiesta.

to **run** (ran, run) *vi.* 1. correre 2.
colare 3. diventare 4. estendersi 5.
essere in vigore, durare. ♦ to **run**
(ran, run) *vt.* 1. far funzionare
2. dirigere 3. seguire 4. passare ||
to — in, rodare; *to — over*, investire.

runaway *agg.* 1. fuggitivo 2. decisivo. ♦ **runaway** *s.* 1. fuggitivo
2. fuga.

rung[1] *s.* 1. piolo 2. raggio (*di ruota*).

rung[2] V. *to ring.*

runnel *s.* ruscello.

runner *s.* 1. corridore 2. messo 3.
passatoia 4. pattino 5. carrello.

running *s.* 1. corsa 2. esercizio 3.
flusso || *-in*, rodaggio.

runway *s.* pista.

rupture *s.* rottura.

rural *agg.* rurale.

rush[1] *s.* giunco.

rush[2] *s.* 1. attacco 2. impeto 3. afflusso || — *-hours*, ore di punta.

to **rush** *vt.* spingere. ♦ to **rush** *vi.*
precipitarsi.

rushy *agg.* 1. di giunchi 2. folto di
giunchi.

Russian *agg.* e *s.* russo.

rust *s.* ruggine.

to **rust** *vt.* arrugginire. ♦ to **rust** *vi.* arrugginirsi.

rustic(al) *agg.* rustico. ♦ **rustic(al)** *s.* campagnolo.

rustle *s.* fruscio, stormire (*di foglie*).

to **rustle** *vt.* far frusciare. ♦ to **rustle** *vi.* frusciare.

rusty *agg.* 1. rugginoso 2. (*fig.*) ombroso.

ruthless *agg.* spietato.

ruthlessness *s.* crudeltà.

rye *s.* segale.

S

Sabbath *s.* il giorno della settimana dedicato al riposo.

sable *s.* zibellino.

sabot *s.* zoccolo.

sabotage *s.* sabotaggio.

to **sabotage** *vt.* e *vi.* sabotare.

saboteur *s.* sabotatore.

sabre *s.* sciabola ‖ — *cut*, sciabolata.

to **sabre** *vt.* sciabolare.

saccharin(e) *s.* saccarina.

saccharose *s.* saccarosio.

sacerdotal *agg.* sacerdotale.

sack¹ *s.* 1. sacco 2. (*gergo*) licenziamento.

sack² *s.* (*mil.*) sacco, saccheggio.

sack³ *s.* vino bianco delle Canarie.

to **sack¹** *vt.* 1. insaccare 2. (*gergo*) licenziare.

to **sack²** *vt.* (*mil.*) saccheggiare.

sacking¹ *s.* tela da sacco.

sacking² *s.* saccheggio.

sacral¹ *agg.* (*anat.*) sacro.

sacral² *agg.* rituale.

sacrament *s.* sacramento.

sacramental *agg.* sacramentale.

sacred *agg.* 1. sacro, religioso 2. consacrato, dedicato.

sacrifice *s.* 1. sacrificio 2. abnegazione.

to **sacrifice** *vt.* e *vi.* 1. sacrificare, immolare 2. rinunziare.

sacrilege *s.* sacrilegio.

sacrist *s.* sagrestano.

sacristy *s.* sagrestia.

sacrosanct *agg.* sacrosanto.

sad *agg.* triste, mesto ‖ to *make so.* —, rattristare qu.

to **sadden** *vt.* rattristare. ♦ to **sadden** *vi.* rattristarsi.

saddle *s.* 1. sella, sellino 2. giogaia.

to **saddle** *vt.* sellare, mettere in sella.

saddler *s.* sellaio.

sadism *s.* sadismo.

sadist *s.* sadico.

sadistic *agg.* sadico.

sadly *avv.* tristemente, mestamente.

sadness *s.* tristezza, mestizia.

safe *agg.* 1. sicuro, al riparo 2. salvo, intatto 3. innocuo ‖ — *and sound*, sano e salvo; — *conduct*, salvacondotto; — *deposit*, cassetta di sicurezza. ♦ **safe** *s.* 1. cassaforte 2. sicura (*di armi*).

safeguard *s.* salvaguardia.

to **safeguard** *vt.* salvaguardare, difendere.

safekeeping *s.* custodia.

safety *s.* sicurezza, salvezza, scampo ‖ — *belt*, cintura di sicurezza; — *device*, dispositivo di sicurezza; — *pin*, spilla di sicurezza.

saffron *s.* zafferano.

sag *s.* 1. abbassamento, cedimento 2. (*mar.*) scarroccio.

sagacious *agg.* acuto, sagace.

sagaciousness, sagacity *s.* sagacia, perspicacia.

sage¹ *s.* salvia.

sage² *s.* saggio, dotto.

said V. *to say*.

sail¹ *s.* vela, velatura ‖ to *set* (v. *irr.*) —, spiegare le vele, salpare; to *strike* (v. *irr.*) —, ammainare le vele.

sail² *s.* gita su imbarcazione a vela.

to **sail** *vt.* e *vi.* 1. veleggiare, navigare, costeggiare 2. salpare 3. volare, veleggiare (*di uccelli, nuvole ecc.*).

sailer *s.* veliero.

sailing *s.* 1. navigazione, traversata 2. partenza (*di navi*).

sailor *s.* marinaio.

sailplane *s.* veleggiatore.

saint *agg.* e *s.* santo.

to **saint** *vt.* canonizzare, santificare.

sainthood, saintliness *s.* santità.

saintly *agg.* santo, di santo.

sake *s.* 1. amore, interesse 2. riguardo, rispetto ‖ *for God's* —, per l'amor di Dio.

salaam *s.* riverenza, salamelecco.

salacious *agg.* salace, lascivo.

salad *s.* insalata ‖ *fruit* —, macedonia di frutta.

salamander *s.* salamandra.

salariat s. categorie salariate.

salary s. stipendio.

sale s. 1. vendita || *bill of* —, fattura; *on* —, in vendita 2. asta: — *by auction*, vendita all'asta 3. liquidazione, svendita.

sal(e)able agg. vendibile, commerciabile.

salesman s. venditore, commesso.

saleswoman s. venditrice, commessa.

salicylate s. salicilato.

salient agg. 1. sporgente, prominente 2. saliente, notevole.

saline agg. salino, salso.

salinity s. salsedine, salinità.

saliva s. saliva.

salivary agg. salivare.

salivation s. salivazione.

sallow agg. giallastro.

sally s. 1. (*mil.*) sortita 2. escursione.

to sally vi. fare una sortita || *to — forth*, uscire (*per una passeggiata*).

salmon s. salmone.

saloon s. salone || *dancing* —, sala da ballo.

salt s. sale. ♦ **salt** agg. 1. salato 2. sotto sale 3. (*fig.*) amaro, piccante || —*cellar*, saliera; — -*mine*, salina.

to salt vt. 1. salare, cospargere di sale 2. rendere piccante (*anche fig.*).

salting s. palude costiera.

saltish agg. salmastro, salaticcio.

saltness s. salsedine.

saltpetre s. salnitro.

salty agg. 1. sala:o, salmastro 2. piccante (*anche fig.*).

salubrious agg. salubre.

salutary agg. salutare.

salutation s. saluto.

salute s. saluto, gesto di saluto || *to fire a* —, salutare a salve.

to salute vt. salutare, dare il benvenuto.

salvage s. salvataggio (*di navi, carico ecc.*).

salvation s. salvezza (*anche relig.*).

salve s. unguento, balsamo.

same agg. medesimo, stesso, uguale || *at the* — *time*, allo stesso tempo. ♦ **same** pron. lo stesso, il medesimo.

samely agg. monotono, uniforme.

sameness s. 1. somiglianza 2. monotonia.

sample s. campione, modello, esemplare || — *book*, campionario.

sanatorium s. sanatorio.

sanatory agg. curativo.

sanctification s. santificazione.

to sanctify vt. santificare.

sanction s. 1. autorizzazione, approvazione 2. (*giur.*) ratifica 3. sanzione.

to sanction vt. 1. autorizzare 2. (*giur.*) ratificare 3. aggiungere sanzioni penali (*ad una legge*).

sanctity s. santità.

sanctuary s. 1. santuario 2. asilo, rifugio.

sand s. sabbia, rena || — -*bath*, bagno di sabbia. ♦ **sands** s. pl. spiaggia (*sing.*).

to sand vt. 1. coprire di sabbia 2. arenare 3. smerigliare.

sandal s. sandalo.

sandpaper s. carta vetrata.

sandstone s. arenaria.

sandy agg. sabbioso.

sane agg. sano di mente, sensato.

sang V. *to sing*.

sanguinary agg. sanguinario, crudele.

sanguine agg. sanguigno.

sanguineous agg. del sangue, sanguigno.

sanitarian s. igienista. ♦ **sanitarian** agg. igienico.

sanitarist s. igienista.

sanitary agg. igienico, sanitario.

sanity s. V. *saneness*.

sank V. *to sink*.

Sanscrit, Sanskrit agg. e s. Sanscrito.

santon s. santone.

sap s. 1. linfa, succo 2. (*fig.*) vigore.

sapful agg. 1. succoso 2. vigoroso.

sapid agg. sapido, gustoso (*anche fig.*).

sapient agg. pedante.

sapless agg. 1. secco, avvizzito 2. fiacco.

saponification s. saponificazione.

to saponify vt. saponificare.

Sapphic agg. saffico.

sapphire s. zaffiro.

saraband s. sarabanda.

Saracen agg. e s. saraceno.

sarcasm s. sarcasmo.

sarcastic agg. sarcastico.

sarcophagus s. (*pl.* -gi) sarcofago.

sardine s. sardina.
sardonic agg. sardonico.
sash[1] s. fascia, cintura.
sash[2] s. telaio scorrevole (di finestra).
sat V. to sit.
satanic(al) agg. satanico.
satchel s. cartella (di scolaro).
to **sate** vt. saziare.
satellite s. satellite.
satiable agg. saziabile.
to **satiate** vt. saziare, satollare.
satiety s. sazietà.
satin s. raso.
satire s. satira.
satiric(al) agg. satirico.
satirist s. autore di satire.
to **satirize** vt. satireggiare.
satisfaction s. 1. soddisfazione 2. riparazione 3. (giur.) estinzione.
satisfactory agg. soddisfacente.
satisfiable agg. che può essere soddisfatto.
to **satisfy** vt. soddisfare, appagare || to — a claim, accogliere un reclamo. ♦ to **satisfy** vi. fare ammenda.
satrap s. satrapo.
saturate agg. saturo.
to **saturate** vt. saturare, impregnare.
saturation s. saturazione.
Saturday s. sabato.
satyr s. satiro.
satyric agg. satiresco.
sauce s. salsa, intingolo.
saucepan s. casseruola.
saucer s. piattino, sottocoppa.
saucily avv. sfacciatamente.
saucy agg. sfacciato, insolente.
sauerkraut s. crauti.
to **saunter** vi. bighellonare.
saunterer s. bighellone.
sausage s. salsiccia, salame.
savage agg. selvaggio, barbaro 2. feroce, crudele. ♦ **savage** s. selvaggio.
savagely avv. selvaggiamente, barbaramente.
savannah s. savana.
save prep. salvo, tranne, eccetto.
to **save** vt. e vi. 1. salvare, difendere 2. conservare, risparmiare.
saving s. liberazione, salvezza. ♦ **savings** s. pl. risparmi.
saviour s. salvatore, redentore.
to **savour** vi. aver sapore.
savoury agg. saporito, piccante.
saw s. sega || -mill, segheria.
to **saw** (**sawed, sawn**) vt. e vi.

segare.
saw V. to see.
sawdust s. segatura.
sawn V. to saw.
sawyer s. segatore.
Saxon agg. e s. sassone.
saxophone s. sassofono.
say s. il dire, detto, parola.
to **say** (**said, said**) vt. e vi. 1. dire, affermare 2. esprimere un'opinione || to — out, dire apertamente.
saying s. proverbio, massima: as the — goes, come dice il proverbio.
scabbard s. fodero.
scabby agg. coperto di croste.
scabies s. scabbia.
scaffold s. 1. impalcatura 2. patibolo, forca.
to **scaffold** vt. erigere impalcature.
scaffolding s. impalcatura.
scald s. scottatura.
to **scald** vt. 1. scottare 2. sterilizzare con acqua bollente. ♦ to **scald** vi. scottarsi.
scale[1] s. piatto (di bilancia). ♦ **scales** s. pl. bilancia (sing.).
scale[2] s. scaglia.
scale[3] s. scala, misura, gradazione.
to **scale**[1] vt. e vi. pesare.
to **scale**[2] vt. squamare, scrostare. ♦ to **scale** vi. squamarsi, scrostarsi.
to **scale**[3] vt. 1. scalare 2. graduare || to — down, diminuire; to — up, aumentare.
scalene agg. e s. scaleno.
scallop s. 1. conchiglia 2. dentellatura, festone, smerlo (di stoffa).
to **scallop** vt. 1. tagliare a festone 2. cuocere pesce in conchiglia.
scalp s. 1. cranio, cuoio capelluto 2. scalpo.
to **scalp** vt. 1. scalpare 2. criticare aspramente.
scalpel s. bisturi.
to **scan** vt. e vi. 1. scandire (versi) 2. esaminare, scrutare.
scandal s. 1. scandalo 2. maldicenza 3. (giur.) diffamazione.
to **scandalize** vt. scandalizzare.
scandalous agg. scandaloso.
Scandinavian agg. e s. scandinavo.
scanning s. 1. scansione (di versi) 2. osservazione || —-line, (tv), linea di scansione.
scansion s. scansione.
scantily avv. debolmente, scarsamente.
scantiness s. insufficienza, scarsezza.

scanty *agg.* **1.** scarso, insufficiente **2.** esiguo, angusto.

scapegoat *s.* capro espiatorio.

scapegrace *s.* **1.** scapestrato **2.** monello.

scapular *agg.* scapolare.

scar *s.* cicatrice, sfregio.

to scar *vt.* **1.** cicatrizzare **2.** sfregiare. ◆ **to scar** *vi.* cicatrizzarsi.

scarab *s.* scarabeo.

scarce *agg.* insufficiente, scarso.

scarcely *avv.* appena, a fatica, a malapena.

scare *s.* terrore, sgomento.

to scare *vt.* spaventare, sgomentare.

scarecrow *s.* **1.** spaventapasseri **2.** spauracchio.

scarf *s.* sciarpa, fascia.

to scarify *vt.* scarificare.

scarlet *agg.* scarlatto, porporino || — *fever*, scarlattina.

scarp(e) *s.* scarpata.

to scatter *vt.* **1.** spargere **2.** mettere in fuga, disperdere. ◆ **to scatter** *vi.* spargersi, diffondersi.

scattered *agg.* sparso, disseminato.

scattering *s.* sparpagliamento, dispersione.

scenario *s.* sceneggiatura || — *writer*, sceneggiatore.

scene *s.* **1.** scena **2.** episodio **3.** scenario, quinta **4.** vista, panorama || — *painter*, scenografo.

scenery *s.* **1.** scenario **2.** prospettiva, veduta.

scenographer *s.* scenografo.

scenographic *agg.* scenografico.

scenography *s.* scenografia.

scent *s.* **1.** odore, profumo **2.** traccia, pista (*anche fig.*).

to scent *vt.* **1.** fiutare, seguire la traccia **2.** profumare.

scented *agg.* profumato.

scentless *agg.* inodoro.

sceptical *agg.* scettico.

scepticism *s.* scetticismo.

sceptre *s.* scettro.

schedule *s.* **1.** catalogo, distinta, elenco **2.** (*amer.*) orario **3.** inventario.

to schedule *vt.* comporre una lista, un catalogo.

schematic(al) *agg.* schematico.

schematism *s.* schematismo.

scheme *s.* **1.** schema **2.** piano, progetto.

to scheme *vt. e vi.* **1.** progettare, fare un piano **2.** tramare.

schism *s.* scisma.

schismatic(al) *s.* scismatico.

schizophrenic *agg. e s.* schizofrenico.

scholar *s.* studioso, letterato.

scholarly *agg.* dotto, istruito.

scholarship *s.* **1.** dottrina, sapere **2.** borsa di studio.

scholastic *agg.* **1.** scolastico, pedante **2.** (*fil.*) scolastico.

scholastically *avv.* scolasticamente, secondo la scolastica.

scholasticism *s.* (*fil.*) scolastica.

school *s.* **1.** scuola, classe **2.** lezione, ora di lezione || — *book*, libro di testo; — *mate*, compagno di scuola; — *report*, pagella; — *term*, trimestre; — *time*, periodo scolastico; *boarding* —, collegio; *grammar* —, ginnasio; *night* —, serale.

to school *vt.* **1.** istruire **2.** controllare, disciplinare.

schoolboy *s.* scolaro.

schoolfellow *s.* compagno di scuola.

schoolmaster *s.* maestro, insegnante.

schoolmistress *s.* maestra, insegnante.

schoolroom *s.* aula scolastica.

schooner *s.* (*mar.*) goletta.

science *s.* scienza || — *fiction*, fantascienza; *man of* —, scienziato.

scientific *agg.* scientifico.

scientifically *avv.* scientificamente.

scientism *s.* scientismo.

scientist *s.* scienziato.

scimitar *s.* scimitarra.

scion *s.* **1.** germoglio **2.** rampollo, discendente.

scission *s.* scissione, divisione.

scissors *pl.* forbici, cesoie.

sclerosis *s.* (*pl.* -ses) sclerosi.

sclerotic *s.* sclerotico.

scoff *s.* derisione, scherno.

to scoff *vt. e vi.* deridere, schernire || *to* — *at so.*, farsi beffe di qu.

scold *s.* donna bisbetica.

to scold *vt.* sgridare, rimproverare. ◆ **to scold** *vi.* essere adirato.

scolding *s.* sgridata, rimprovero.

scoliosis *s.* scoliosi.

scooter *s.* **1.** monopattino **2.** motoretta.

scope *s.* **1.** portata, possibilità **2.** prospettiva, sfera, campo.

scorbutic *agg. e s.* scorbutico.

scorch *s.* bruciatura, scottatura.

to scorch *vt. e vi.* **1.** bruciacchiare **2.** inaridire (*di sole, gelo ecc.*).

scorching *agg.* **1.** bruciante, ardente **2.** (*fig.*) caustico, mordace.

score *s.* **1.** tacca, scanalatura **2.** linea, segno, linea di partenza, limite (*in corse, giuochi ecc.*) **3.** (*sport*) punteggio **4.** (*mus.*) spartito.

to score *vt. e vi.* **1.** intaccare, intagliare **2.** marcare, segnare **3.** (*sport*) segnare il punteggio **4.** (*mus.*) orchestrare || *to — up*, mettere in conto.

scorer *s.* (*sport*) marcatore.

scorn *s.* **1.** disprezzo, disdegno **2.** scherno.

to scorn *vt.* disprezzare, disdegnare.

scornful *agg.* sprezzante, sdegnoso.

scorpion *s.* scorpione || *— -fish*, scorfano.

Scot *s.* scozzese.

Scotch *agg.* scozzese.

Scotsman *s.* (*uomo*) scozzese.

Scottish *agg.* scozzese.

scoundrel *s.* furfante, farabutto.

scourge *s.* (*fig.*) flagello.

to scourge *vt.* sferzare, flagellare.

scout *s.* esploratore, ricognitore.

to scout *vi.* andare in esplorazione, in ricognizione. ♦ **to scout** *vt.* perlustrare.

scowl *s.* cipiglio, sguardo torvo.

to scowl *vt. e vi.* aggrottare le ciglia, guardare torvamente.

scramble *s.* **1.** arrampicata **2.** contesa, gara.

to scramble *vt.* **1.** arraffare **2.** mescolare alla rinfusa ♦ **to scramble** *vi.* **1.** inerpicarsi **2.** gareggiare **3.** (*cuc.*) strapazzare (*le uova*).

scrap *s.* pezzetto, frammento || *—-heap*, mucchio di rifiuti. ♦ **scraps** *s. pl.* rimasugli, scarti.

scrape *s.* **1.** graffio, scalfittura **2.** raschio.

to scrape *vt. e vi.* **1.** raschiare, grattare **2.** levigare, sfregare, strisciare || *to — a living*, sbarcare il lunario.

scraper *s.* **1.** raschietto **2.** strimpellatore.

scraping *s.* raschiatura.

scratch *s.* **1.** graffiatura, graffio **2.** grattata **3.** colpo fortunato (*al giuoco*).

to scratch *vt. e vi.* **1.** graffiare **2.** (*fig.*) scalfire **3.** grattare.

scrawl *s.* scarabocchio, sgorbio.

to scrawl *vt. e vi.* **1.** scarabocchiare **2.** scribacchiare.

scrawler *s.* chi scarabocchia.

scrawly *agg.* scarabocchiato || *— writing* (*fam.*), scritto a zampe di gallina.

scream *s.* grido acuto, strillo.

to scream *vt. e vi.* **1.** gridare, strillare **2.** fischiare (*di locomotiva*).

screamer *s.* strillone.

screaming *agg.* **1.** strillante, urlante **2.** sguaiato.

screech *s.* **1.** grido, strillo acuto **2.** stridore.

screen *s.* **1.** paravento **2.** (*cine; tv*) schermo **3.** (*mil.*) scorta.

to screen *vt. e vi.* **1.** riparare, schermare **2.** vagliare.

screenings *s. pl.* materiale vagliato (*sing.*).

screenplay *s.* (*cine*) sceneggiatura.

screenwriter *s.* sceneggiatore.

screw *s.* **1.** vite **2.** cavatappi, succhiello **3.** elica.

to screw *vt.* **1.** avvitare, stringere **2.** torcere. ♦ **to screw** *vi.* torcersi || *to — out*, svitare.

screwdriver *s.* cacciavite.

screwy *agg.* **1.** brillo **2.** tirchio, spilorcio.

scribble *s.* sgorbio, scarabocchio (*anche fig.*).

to scribble *vt. e vi.* scarabocchiare.

scribe *s.* copista.

scriber *s.* punta a tracciare.

scrip[1] *s.* **1.** pezzo di carta **2.** frammento di uno scritto.

scrip[2] *s.* certificato provvisorio, cedola.

scripture *s.* la sacra Scrittura.

to scrounge *vt. e vi.* rubacchiare.

scrounger *s.* ladruncolo, scroccone.

scrub *s.* **1.** boscaglia **2.** povero diavolo (*fam.*).

to scrub *vt. e vi.* sfregare.

scrubby *agg.* esile, debole.

scruff *s.* nuca, collottola.

scruple *s.* scrupolo.

scrupolosity *s.* scrupolosità.

scrupulous *agg.* scrupoloso.

to scrutinize *vt.* scrutinare, esaminare.

scrutiny *s.* **1.** esame minuzioso **2.** scrutinio **3.** esame (*di una legge*).

scuffle *s.* zuffa, tafferuglio.

to scuffle *vi.* azzuffarsi.

scullery *s.* retrocucina || *— -boy*, *-maid*, sguattero, sguattera.

sculptor *s.* scultore.

sculptress *s.* scultrice.

sculptural *agg.* scultorio, statuario.

sculpture s. scultura.
to **sculpture** vt. e vi. scolpire.
scum s. 1. schiuma, spuma 2. feccia (anche fig.).
to **scum** vt. e vi. 1. schiumare, far schiuma 2. produrre feccia.
scummer s. schiumarola.
scurf s. 1. squama, forfora 2. incrostazioni (pl.).
scurrility s. scurrilità, volgarità.
scurrilous agg. scurrile, triviale.
to **scurry** vi. precipitarsi.
scurvy agg. spregevole, meschino.
scuttle[1] s. recipiente per carbone.
scuttle[2] s. 1. (mar.) portellino 2. botola.
scuttle[3] s. fuga precipitosa.
to **scuttle**[1] vt. produrre falle (in una nave).
to **scuttle**[2] vi. correre via precipitosamente.
sea s. mare || — -bear, orso polare; — -biscuit, galletta; — calf, foca; — fight, battaglia navale; — food, frutti di mare; — front, lungomare; — quake, maremoto; — storm, mareggiata.
seacoast s. costa, spiaggia.
seafarer s. navigante, navigatore.
seafaring s. viaggi per mare.
seahorse s. ippocampo.
seal[1] s. foca.
seal[2] s. 1. sigillo, timbro 2. (fig.) suggello, vincolo.
to **seal**[1] vi. andare a caccia di foche.
to **seal**[2] vt. 1. sigillare 2. suggellare || — one's fate, decidere la propria sorte.
sealing s. suggellamento || — -wax, ceralacca.
seam s. 1. cucitura 2. sutura.
to **seam** vt. 1. unire con cucitura 2. rigare, segnare.
seamen s. pl. equipaggio (di una nave).
seamanship s. arte della navigazione.
seamless agg. senza cucitura.
seamstress s. cucitrice.
seaplane s. idrovolante.
seaport s. porto marittimo.
search s. 1. ricerca, indagine 2. perquisizione, visita doganale || — warrant, mandato di perquisizione.
to **search** vt. e vi. cercare, perlustrare, perquisire || to — out, rinvenire, scovare.
searcher s. ricercatore.
searching agg. indagatore, inquisi-

torio. ♦ **searching** s. 1. ricerca, esame 2. sondaggio.
searchlight s. riflettore.
seashore s. spiaggia, lido.
seasickness s. mal di mare.
seaside s. spiaggia, riva.
season s. stagione, epoca || — bill (teat.), cartellone; — ticket, abbonamento stagionale.
to **season** vt. 1. stagionare 2. acclimatare 3. condire. ♦ to **season** vi. 1. stagionarsi 2. invecchiarsi (di vino).
seasonable agg. 1. di stagione 2. opportuno.
seasonal agg. stagionale.
seasoned agg. 1. stagionato 2. condito.
seasoning s. 1. stagionatura 2. condimento.
seat s. 1. sedile, posto 2. seggio 3. sede.
to **seat** vt. 1. mettere a sedere 2. insediare, collocare.
seaward agg. che va verso il mare.
seaweed s. alga marina.
sebaceous agg. sebaceo.
secant agg. e s. secante.
to **secede** vi. separarsi, ritirarsi.
seceder s. secessionista, separatista.
secession s. secessione, scissione.
secessionism s. secessionismo.
to **seclude** vt. 1. appartare, isolare 2. rinchiudere.
secluded agg. appartato, isolato, solitario.
seclusion s. 1. isolamento 2. solitudine.
seclusive agg. che serve ad isolare.
second[1] s. minuto secondo.
second[2] agg. secondo.
secondary agg. secondario.
secrecy s. 1. segretezza 2. riserbo.
secret agg. 1. segreto 2. nascosto, intimo. ♦ **secret** s. segreto.
secretariat(e) s. 1. segretariato 2. segreteria.
secretary s. 1. segretario 2. ministro (preposto ad un dicastero).
to **secrete**[1] vt. secernere.
to **secrete**[2] vt. occultare, nascondere.
secretion s. secrezione.
secretly avv. 1. segretamente 2. in modo reticente.
sect s. setta.
sectarian s. settario.
sectarianism s. spirito di setta.
sectary s. settario.

section s. 1. sezione, parte 2. paragrafo 3. regione, quartiere.
to section vt. sezionare.
sectional agg. 1. parziale, di classe 2. a sezioni.
sector s. settore.
secular agg. 1. secolare 2. laico 3. mondano, profano. ♦ **secular** s. laico.
secularism s. secolarismo.
secularist agg. e s. laico.
to secularize vt. laicizzare.
secure agg. 1. sicuro, certo 2. salvo.
to secure vt. 1. assicurare, salvaguardare 2. (giur.; comm.) garantire 3. mettere al sicuro.
security s. 1. sicurezza, protezione 2. certezza 3. garanzia, cauzione. ♦ **securities** s. pl. titoli, valori.
sedan s. — (-chair), portantina.
sedate agg. 1. posato, composto 2. grave, serio.
sedative agg. e s. sedativo.
sedentary agg. e s. sedentario.
sediment s. sedimento.
sedimentary agg. sedimentario.
sedimentation s. sedimentazione.
sedition s. sedizione.
seditious agg. sedizioso.
to seduce vt. sedurre, corrompere.
seduction s. seduzione.
sedulous agg. assiduo.
to see (**saw**, **seen**) vt. e vi. 1. vedere, scorgere 2. capire, rendersi conto di 3. esaminare, giudicare 4. fare in modo che ‖ to — about, assumersi l'incarico di; to — off, accompagnare (alla partenza); to — over, ispezionare; to — through (fig.), indoviniare, penetrare.
see s. (eccl.) sede, diocesi.
seed s. 1. seme, semenza 2. (fig.) principio, germe 3. stirpe.
seedy agg. pieno di semi.
to seek (**sought**, **sought**) vt. e vi. 1. cercare, andare alla ricerca di 2. ottenere 3. chiedere, ricorrere a ‖ to — for sthg., ricercare qc.
seeker s. cercatore.
to seem vi. sembrare, apparire.
seeming agg. apparente, esteriore.
seemliness s. decenza, decoro.
seemly agg. decoroso, decente.
seen V. to see.
segment s. segmento, sezione.
segmentation s. segmentazione.
to segregate vt. segregare, separare. ♦ **to segregate** vi. separarsi, scindersi.

segregation s. segregazione.
seismograph s. sismografo.
seismologist s. sismologo.
seismology s. sismologia.
seizable agg. afferrabile.
to seize vt. e vi. 1. afferrare, prendere 2. capire, comprendere 3. (giur.) avere in possesso, sequestrare.
selzing s. 1. atto dell'afferrare 2. conquista, cattura.
seizure s. 1. (giur.) confisca, sequestro 2. conquista, cattura.
seldom avv. raramente.
select agg. 1. scelto, selezionato 2. schizzinoso.
to select vt. selezionare.
selection s. selezione, scelta.
selective agg. selettivo.
selectivity s. selettività.
selector s. selettore.
self s. (pl. selves) l'io, l'individuo. ♦ **self** agg. 1. della stessa materia 2. uniforme.
self-conceit s. presunzione.
self-control s. autocontrollo.
self-defence s. legittima difesa.
self-denial s. abnegazione.
self-determination s. autodeterminazione.
self-educated agg. autodidatta.
self-examination s. esame di coscienza.
self-government s. (pol.) autogoverno.
self-help s. (giur.) legittima difesa.
selfish agg. egoistico.
selfishness s. egoismo.
self-portrait s. autoritratto.
sell s. (fam.) delusione.
to sell (**sold**, **sold**) vt. e vi. 1. vendere 2. (fig.) vendere, tradire ‖ to — off (comm.), liquidare.
seller s. 1. venditore 2. articolo che si vende.
selling s. vendita, smercio ‖ — up, vendita fallimentare.
selves V. self.
semantic agg. semantico.
semantics s. semantica.
semester s. semestre.
semi prefisso semi, mezzo, metà.
semicircle s. semicerchio.
semicircular agg. semicircolare.
semicolon s. punto e virgola.
semifinal agg. e s. semifinale.
seminar s. seminario (d'università).
seminarist s. seminarista.
seminary s. seminario.
semination s. semina.

Semite *agg.* e *s.* semita.

Semitic *agg.* semitico.

Semitism *s.* semitismo.

semitone *s.* semitono.

semivowel *s.* semivocale.

senate *s.* senato.

senator *s.* senatore.

senatorial *agg.* senatoriale.

to send (sent, sent) *vt.* e *vi.* mandare, inviare, spedire || to — away, congedare; to — back, rinviare; to — for, mandare a chiamare; to — off, inviare (*per lettera*); to — out, emettere.

sender *s.* 1. mandante, mittente 2. (*comm.*) spedizioniere 3. (*radio, tv.*) emittente.

sending *s.* 1. invio 2. (*comm.*) spedizione 3. (*radio, tv.*) trasmissione.

senescence *s.* senescenza.

senile *agg.* senile.

senility *s.* senilità.

senior *agg.* 1. più vecchio, più anziano 2. più ragguardevole, che ha più anzianità. ♦ **senior** *s.* 1. decano, anziano 2. il superiore.

seniority *s.* anzianità (*d'anni, di grado*).

sensation *s.* 1. senso, sensazione 2. colpo, impressione.

sensational *agg.* 1. che dipende dai sensi 2. sensazionale.

sense *s.* 1. senso, sensazione, impressione 2. conoscenza 3. significato || common —, buon senso. ♦ **senses** *s. pl.* facoltà mentale (*sing.*).

senseful *agg.* significativo.

senseless *agg.* 1. inanimato 2. insensato.

sensibility *s.* 1. sensibilità, sensitività 2. emotività.

sensible *agg.* 1. sensato, giudizioso 2. percettibile 3. notevole, considerevole 4. consapevole.

sensibly *avv.* 1. assennatamente 2. percettibilmente.

sensism *s.* sensismo.

sensist *s.* sensista.

sensitive *agg.* 1. sensitivo, sensibile 2. suscettibile, impressionabile.

sensitively *avv.* sensibilmente.

sensitiveness *s.* 1. sensibilità 2. suscettibilità.

to sensitize *vt.* sensibilizzare.

sensitizer *s.* (*foto*) sensibilizzatore.

sensorial *agg.* sensorio.

sensory *agg.* sensoriale.

sensual *agg.* sensuale.

sensualism *s.* sensualismo.

sensuality *s.* sensualità.

sensually *avv.* sensualmente, voluttuosamente.

sensuous *agg.* sensoriale, voluttuoso.

sent V. *to send.*

sentence *s.* 1. giudizio, sentenza 2. (*gramm.*) frase || to pass a —, pronunciare una sentenza.

to sentence *vt.* giudicare, pronunciare una sentenza contro.

sententious *agg.* sentenzioso.

sententiously *avv.* sentenziosamente.

sentient *agg.* senziente, sensibile.

sentiment *s.* 1. sentimento 2. opinione, parere.

sentimental *agg.* sentimentale, romantico.

sentimentalism *s.* sentimentalismo.

sentimentalist *s.* persona sentimentale.

sentimentality *s.* sentimentalità.

sentinel *s.* sentinella, guardia.

sentry *s.* sentinella, guardia, scolta || — box, garitta.

separate *agg.* separato, staccato.

to separate *vt.* separare. ♦ **to separate** *vi.* separarsi.

separately *avv.* separatamente.

separation *s.* separazione, divisione.

separatism *s.* separatismo.

September *s.* settembre.

septicaemia *s.* setticemia.

septuagenarian *agg.* e *s.* settuagenario.

septuagenary *agg.* settuagenario.

septum *s.* (*pl.* -ta) diaframma.

sepulchral *agg.* sepolcrale.

sepulchre *s.* sepolcro.

sequacious *agg.* pedissequo, servile.

sequel *s.* 1. conseguenza 2. seguito.

sequence *s.* 1. successione, sequela 2. sequenza.

to sequestrate *vt.* sequestrare, confiscare.

sequestration *s.* sequestro, confisca.

sequin *s.* lustrino.

seraphic(al) *agg.* serafico.

serenade *s.* serenata.

serene *agg.* 1. sereno, senza nubi 2. calmo, tranquillo.

serenely *avv.* serenamente.

serenity *s.* 1. serenità, limpidezza 2. tranquillità.

sergeant *s.* 1. sergente 2. brigadiere.

serial *s.* romanzo a puntate, pubblicazione periodica.

serially *avv.* **1.** in serie **2.** periodicamente.

sericulture *s.* sericoltura.

sericulturist *s.* sericoltore.

series *s.* serie, successione.

serigraphy *s.* serigrafia.

serious *agg.* **1.** serio, pensieroso **2.** grave, importante.

seriousness *s.* **1.** serietà **2.** gravità.

sermon *s.* sermone, predica.

serotherapy *s.* sieroterapia.

serous *agg.* sieroso.

serpent *s.* serpente.

serum *s.* siero.

servant *s.* servo, servitore.

to serve *vt.* e *vi.* **1.** servire, essere al servizio di **2.** servire, essere utile **3.** essere sotto le armi **4.** (*giur.*) notificare (*di atti*) || *to — out*, distribuire.

server *s.* **1.** chi serve **2.** chierico **3.** vassoio.

service *s.* **1.** servizio (*anche militare*) **2.** servigio, favore **3.** funzione religiosa **4.** (*giur.*) notifica. ◆ **Services** *s. pl.* forze armate.

serviceable *agg.* utile, pratico.

serviette *s.* tovagliolo.

servile *agg.* servile.

servilism *s.* servilismo.

servility *s.* servilità.

serving *s.* **1.** il servire **2.** servizio (*di tavola*).

servitude *s.* servitù, schiavitù. ◆ **session** *s.* sessione, seduta. ◆ **sessions** *s. pl.* (*giur.*) udienze.

set¹ *agg.* **1.** fermo, fisso **2.** stabilito, prestabilito **3.** studiato, preparato. ◆ **set** *s.* **1.** il solidificarsi **2.** forma, serie **3.** gruppo **4.** direzione, corso **5.** (*poet.*) tramonto **6.** serie completa, insieme: *a — of teeth*, una dentiera; *the complete — of Shakespeare's works*, la raccolta completa delle opere di Shakespeare.

to set (set, set) *vt.* e *vi.* **1.** mettere, porre, collocare **2.** sistemare, mettere a punto (*anche fig.*) || *to — about*, accingersi; *to — back*, impedire; *to — in*, incominciare; *to — out*, esporre; *to — up*, fissare, installare; *to — aside* (*giur.*), annullare; *to — off*, compensare.

set-back *s.* contrattempo.

set-down *s.* rimprovero.

set-off *s.* **1.** contrasto **2.** compensazione.

setting *s.* **1.** messa in opera, mon-

taggio 2. ambiente **3.** scenario, messa in scena **4.** incastonatura.

to settle *vt.* e *vi.* **1.** fissare, decidere, determinare **2.** saldare, liquidare (*conti, questioni ecc.*) **3.** sistemare, sistemarsi **4.** stabilire **5.** calmare, calmarsi **6.** depositare, depositarsi (*di sedimenti ecc.*) || *to — down*, stabilirsi (*in un luogo*).

settled *agg.* fissato, stabilito.

settlement *s.* **1.** determinazione **2.** saldo, liquidazione **3.** sistemazione **4.** lo stabilirsi (*in un luogo*) **5.** colonia, distretto **6.** (*giur.*) transazione || *financial —*, regolamento di conti.

settler *s.* **1.** chi decide **2.** colonizzatore.

settling *s.* **1.** stabilizzazione **2.** saldo, pagamento.

set-to *s.* zuffa.

setup *s.* disposizione, organizzazione.

seven *agg.* sette.

sevenfold *agg.* settuplo. ◆ **sevenfold** *avv.* sette volte tanto.

seventeen *agg.* diciassette.

seventeenth *agg.* diciassettesimo.

seventh *agg.* settimo.

seventieth *agg.* settantesimo.

seventy *agg.* settanta.

to sever *vt.* staccare, dividere. ◆ **to sever** *vi.* staccarsi, dividersi.

several *agg.* **1.** parecchi, diversi (*pl.*) **2.** separato, distinto. ◆ **several** *pron.* alcuni, diversi (*pl.*) || *— of them*, alcuni di loro.

severally *avv.* separatamente, individualmente.

severe *agg.* **1.** severo, austero **2.** violento, forte **3.** rigido (*di clima*).

severely *avv.* **1.** severamente **2.** violentemente.

severity *s.* **1.** severità, durezza **2.** violenza.

to sew (sewed, sewn) *vt.* e *vi.* cucire.

sewage *s.* acque di scolatura.

to sew¹ *s.* chi cuce, cucitrice.

sewer² *s.* **1.** canale artificiale di drenaggio **2.** fogna.

sewing *s.* **1.** il cucire **2.** lavoro di cucito.

sewn V. *to sew*.

sex *s.* sesso.

sexagenarian *agg.* e *s.* sessagenario.

sextet(te) *s.* sestetto.

sexton *s.* sagrestano.

sextuple *agg.* e *s.* sestuplo.

sexual *agg.* sessuale.

shabbiness s. 1. l'essere male in arnese 2. meschinità.

shabby agg. 1. male in arnese, cencioso 2. meschino, gretto.

shackles s. pl. 1. manette, ceppi 2. (fig.) impedimenti.

shade s. 1. ombra (anche fig.) 2. sfumatura (di colore, significato ecc.) 3. spirito, ombra 4. schermo, riparo ‖ eye-—, visiera.

to shade vt. e vi. 1. ombreggiare, riparare (da luce, calore) 2. velare, oscurare (anche fig.).

shadiness s. ombrosità.

shading s. 1. ombreggiare 2. ombreggiatura, sfumatura.

shadow s. ombra (anche fig.). ◆ **shadows** s. pl. oscurità.

to shadow vt. pedinare, seguire come un'ombra.

shadowy agg. 1. ombroso, ombreggiato 2. indistinto, vago.

shady agg. ombreggiato, all'ombra.

shaft[1] s. 1. lancia, giavellotto 2. fulmine 3. gambo, stelo 4. asta, bastone 5. (mecc.) albero.

shaft[2] s. sfiatatoio, condotto.

shaggy agg. 1. ispido, irsuto 2. peloso (di tessuto) 3. incolto.

Shah s. scià.

shake s. 1. scossa, scuotimento 2. tremore, tremito 3. frullato.

to shake (shook, shaken) vt. e vi. 1. scuotere, agitare (liquidi) 2. tremare, far tremare 3. turbare 4. indebolire.

shakily avv. instabilmente.

shaking agg. tremante, vacillante. ◆ **shaking** s. scossa, scuotimento.

shaky agg. 1. instabile, tremolante 2. malsicuro.

shall v. dif. 1. (aus. per le prime pers. del fut. predicente) I — go to England next summer, andrò in Inghilterra l'estate prossima; we — work next week, lavoreremo la prossima settimana 2. (aus. per le seconde e terze pers. del fut. volitivo) you — go to bed!, andrai a letto! 3. dovere: you — wait for me, devi aspettarmi.

shallow agg. 1. poco profondo, basso 2. (fig.) superficiale.

sham s. 1. finta, inganno 2. ipocrita.

shaman s. sciamano.

shambles s. pl. 1. mattatoio (sing.) 2. carneficina (sing.).

shame s. 1. vergogna, pudore 2. disonore.

to shame vt. 1. svergognare, far arrossire 2. disonorare.

shamefaced agg. 1. vergognoso 2. timido.

shameful agg. vergognoso, disonorevole.

shameless agg. svergognato, sfacciato.

shamelessly avv. sfacciatamente.

shank s. 1. gamba, stinco 2. gambo, stelo 3. fusto (di colonna) ‖ -bone, tibia.

shape s. 1. forma, figura.

to shape vt. e vi. creare, dar forma a.

shapeless agg. informe.

shapely agg. ben fatto.

share s. 1. parte, porzione 2. (comm.) azione, titolo.

to share vt. dividere, spartire. ◆ **to share** vi. partecipare, condividere.

shareholder s. azionista.

share-out s. distribuzione.

shark s. 1. squalo, pescecane 2. (fig.) profittatore.

sharp agg. 1. tagliente, affilato 2. aguzzo 3. scosceso, ripido 4. netto, chiaro 5. intelligente, acuto.

sharp avv. puntualmente, in punto.

to sharpen vt. 1. affilare, aguzzare 2. (fig.) rendere più acuto.

sharper s. imbroglione.

sharply avv. acutamente.

sharpness s. 1. filo, affilatura 2. acutezza 3. vivacità, intelligenza.

sharp-sighted agg. dalla vista acuta.

to shatter vt. frantumare. ◆ **to shatter** vi. frantumarsi.

shattering s. disintegrazione.

shave[1] s. il radersi, rasatura.

shave[2] s. pialla.

to shave[1] vt. radere. ◆ **to shave** vi. radersi.

to shave[2] vt. piallare.

shaven agg. 1. rasato 2. (eccl.) tonsurato.

shaving s. 1. il radersi 2. truciolo.

shawl s. scialle.

she pron. pers. f. ella, lei, colei. ◆ **she** attr. indicante il sesso degli animali: a —-bear, un'orsa.

sheaf s. (pl. sheaves) 1. fascio, covone 2. (geom.) fascio (di rette ecc.).

to shear (sheared, shorn) vt. 1. cesoiare, tranciare 2. tosare.

shearing s. recisione, taglio.

shears s. pl. cesoie, forbici.

sheath s. guaina, fodero.

to **sheathe** vt. 1. mettere nel fodero 2. rivestire di.

sheaves V. sheaf.

to **shed (shed, shed)** vt. 1. versare, spandere 2. lasciar cadere.

shed s. tettoia, capannone.

shedding s. 1. spargimento 2. perdita, caduta (di foglie ecc.).

sheen s. splendore, lucentezza.

sheep s. (anche pl.) 1. pecora, ovino 2. (fig.) persona debole, timorosa.

sheepish agg. timido, impacciato.

sheepskin s. 1. pelle di pecora 2. cartapecora.

sheer[1] agg. 1. puro, semplice, mero 2. liscio, non diluito (di bevande).

sheer[2] s. virata, cambiamento di rotta.

sheet s. 1. lenzuolo 2. foglio 3. lamina, lamiera.

sheik(h) s. sceicco.

shelf s. (pl. shelves) mensola, scaffale.

shell s. 1. conchiglia, guscio 2. involucro, carcassa 3. bossolo (di cartuccia) 4. (fig.) apparenza.

to **shell** vt. e vi. sgusciare, sgranare.

shelter s. 1. riparo, rifugio 2. pensilina.

to **shelter** vt. riparare. ♦ to shelter vi. ripararsi.

to **shelve** vt. 1. provvedere di scaffali 2. mettere negli scaffali.

shelves V. shelf.

shelving s. scaffalatura.

shepherd s. pastore, pecoraio.

sherbet s. sorbetto.

shield s. 1. scudo 2. (fig.) protezione.

to **shield** vt. proteggere, difendere.

shift s. 1. cambiamento, sostituzione 2. risorsa, espediente 3. turno (di lavoro).

to **shift** vt. 1. spostare 2. cambiare. ♦ to shift vi. 1. spostarsi 2. arrangiarsi.

shilling s. scellino.

to **shilly-shally** vi. tentennare.

to **shimmer** vi. luccicare, mandare bagliori.

to **shine (shone, shone)** vt. e vi. 1. splendere, brillare (anche fig.) 2. essere brillante.

shine s. 1. splendore, luminosità 2. luce del sole.

Shintoist s. scintoista.

shiny agg. splendente, rilucente.

ship s. nave, bastimento || convoy- —, nave scorta; flag- —, nave ammiraglia; landing- —, nave da sbarco.

to **ship** vt. 1. imbarcare 2. (comm.) spedire. ♦ to ship vi. imbarcarsi.

shipboard s. bordo.

shipboy s. mozzo.

shipbuilder s. costruttore navale.

shipmate s. compagno di bordo.

shipment s. imbarco, spedizione di merci.

shipping s. 1. forze navali (pl.) 2. imbarco, spedizione.

shipwreck s. naufragio.

to **shipwreck** vi. naufragare.

shipyard s. cantiere navale.

shirker s. scansafatiche.

shirt s. camicia (da uomo).

shiver[1] s. scheggia.

shiver[2] s. brivido, fremito.

to **shiver**[1] vt. frantumare. ♦ to shiver vi. frantumarsi.

to **shiver**[2] vt. e vi. rabbrividire, tremare.

shivering s. V. shiver.

shivery agg. 1. fragile 2. tremante.

shoal[1] s. secca, bassofondo.

shoal[2] s. banco (di pesci).

shock s. 1. urto, collisione 2. forte impressione, violenta emozione.

to **shock** vt. 1. colpire, disgustare 2. provocare un collasso. ♦ to shock vi. 1. scandalizzarsi 2. scontrarsi.

shocking agg. 1. che colpisce 2. disgustoso.

shoe s. scarpa, calzatura || horse- —, ferro di cavallo.

shoeblack s. lustrascarpe.

shoemaker s. calzolaio.

shoe-string s. laccio (da scarpe)

shone V. to shine.

shook V. to shake.

shoot s. 1. spedizione di caccia 2. virgulto 3. puntura, fitta.

to **shoot (shot, shot)** vt. e vi. 1. lanciare 2. sparare, uccidere sparando 3. cacciare 4. fare un'istantanea.

shooter s. cacciatore.

shooting s. 1. tiro, sparo 2. caccia 3. il fotografare, il girare un film.

shop s. 1. bottega, negozio 2. officina, laboratorio || — -assistant, commesso; — -book, libro dei conti; — -lifter, taccheggiatore; — -window, vetrina.

shopkeeper s. negoziante.

shopman s. commesso di negozio.

shopping s. compere, acquisti (pl.).

shore s. spiaggia, lido.

shorn V. to shear.

short agg. **1.** corto, breve **2.** basso, piccolo (di statura) **3.** conciso **4.** brusco, rude. ♦ **short** s. **1.** compendio **2.** (cine) cortometraggio.

short avv. **1.** bruscamente, improvvisamente **2.** (comm.) allo scoperto.

shortage s. mancanza, carenza.

short-circuit s. corto circuito.

short-cut s. scorciatoia.

short-dated agg. (comm.) a breve scadenza.

to **shorten** vt. accorciare, abbreviare.

shortening s. accorciamento, abbreviazione.

shorthand s. stenografia.

shortly avv. **1.** fra breve **2.** brevemente.

shortness s. brevità.

short-sighted agg. miope.

shot[1] V. to shoot.

shot[2] s. **1.** sparo, colpo **2.** proiettile **3.** ripresa cinematografica.

shotgun s. fucile da caccia.

should s. dif. **1.** (aus. per le prime pers. del condiz.) I — be very happy, sarei felicissimo **2.** dovere: it — be so, dovrebbe essere così.

shoulder s. spalla.

to **shoulder** vt. e vi. **1.** spingere con le spalle **2.** portare sulle spalle.

shout s. grido, chiasso.

to **shout** vt. e vi. gridare, urlare.

shove s. spinta, urto.

to **shove** vt. spingere. ♦ **to shove** vi. spingersi.

shovel s. pala.

to **shovel** vt. spalare.

shoveller s. spalatore.

show s. **1.** mostra, esibizione **2.** apparenza **3.** pompa, ostentazione || — case, bacheca; — down, chiarificazione; — off, esibizionismo.

to **show (showed, shown)** vt. e vi. **1.** mostrare, far vedere **2.** rappresentare, indicare **3.** dimostrare, provare **4.** apparire, farsi vedere || to — down, mettere le carte in tavola; to — off, darsi delle arie.

shower s. acquazzone, rovescio.

showman s. presentatore.

shown V. to show.

showy agg. fastoso, appariscente.

shrank V. to shrink.

shred s. brandello, frammento.

shrew s. bisbetica.

shrewd agg. sagace, accorto.

shrewdly avv. sagacemente.

shrewdness s. sagacia, accortezza.

shrewish agg. brontolone.

shriek s. grido, strillo, suono lacerante.

to **shriek** vt. e vi. gridare, stridere.

shrill agg. stridulo, acuto.

to **shrill** vt. e vi. strillare, stridere.

shrimp s. gamberetto.

shrine s. reliquiario.

shrink s. restringimento.

to **shrink (shrank, shrunk)** vt. e vi. **1.** restringere, restringersi, contrarre **2.** indietreggiare.

shrinkable agg. restringibile.

shrinkage s. **1.** diminuzione, restringimento **2.** (comm.) deprezzamento.

shrinking s. contrazione, ritiro.

shroud s. sudario.

shrub s. arbusto, cespuglio.

shrubbery s. boscaglia d'arbusti.

shrug s. spallucciata.

to **shrug** vi. alzare le spalle.

shrunk V. to shrink.

shudder s. brivido.

to **shudder** vi. rabbrividire.

shuffle s. **1.** passo strascicato **2.** scompiglio **3.** il mescolare (le carte).

to **shuffle** vt. e vi. **1.** muoversi a fatica **2.** mescolare, scompigliare.

to **shun** vt. sfuggire, scansare.

shunt s. **1.** (elett.) derivazione **2.** (ferr.) scambio.

to **shunt** vt. e vi. **1.** (elett.) inserire in derivazione **2.** (ferr.) smistare, smistarsi.

shut agg. ben chiuso.

to **shut (shut, shut)** vt. e vi. chiudere, serrare || shut up!, taci.

shutter s. imposta, persiana.

shuttle s. spola, navetta.

shy agg. riservato, timido.

to **shy** vt. spaventare. ♦ **to shy** vi. scartare (di cavallo).

shyly avv. timidamente.

shyness s. timidezza, scontrosità.

Siberian agg. e s. siberiano.

sibilant agg. e s. sibilante.

Sibylline agg. sibillino.

Sicilian agg. e s. siciliano.

sick agg. **1.** ammalato **2.** nauseato || to fall —, ammalarsi.

to **sicken** vt. e vi. **1.** far ammalare, ammalarsi **2.** sfiorire **3.** sentir nausea.

sickening agg. nauseabondo, rivoltante.

sickle s. falce.

sickly agg. **1.** malaticcio **2.** pallido, debole **3.** nauseante.

sickness s. malattia.

side s. **1.** lato, fianco **2.** parte, partito, fazione **3.** discendenza || — -door, porta laterale; — -face, profilo; — -look, occhiata in tralice; — -note, nota marginale; — -post, stipite.

sideboard s. credenza.

sidecar s. motocarrozzetta.

sidelong agg. laterale, obliquo.

sidereal agg. sidereo.

sideways avv. lateralmente, obliquamente.

to **sidle** vi. camminare di fianco, andare a sghembo || to — up to so., avvicinarsi furtivamente a qu.

siege s. assedio.

sieve s. setaccio, crivello.

to **sieve** vt. setacciare, crivellare.

to **sift** vt. e vi. setacciare **2.** filtrare (di luce, polvere ecc.).

sigh s. sospiro.

to **sigh** vt. e vi. **1.** sospirare **2.** sibilare.

sight s. **1.** vista, visione **2.** veduta, panorama **3.** colpo d'occhio **4.** mirino.

to **sight** vt. e vi. **1.** avvistare **2.** prendere la mira.

sighted agg. **1.** fornito di vista || long—, presbite; short—, miope.

sightless agg. senza vista.

sign s. **1.** segno, cenno **2.** indicazione, traccia || traffic —, segnale stradale.

to **sign** vt. e vi. firmare, segnare, sottoscrivere.

signal s. segnale, segno.

to **signal** vt. segnalare. ♦ to **signal** vi. far segnali.

signalman s. segnalatore.

signatory s. firmatario.

signature s. **1.** firma, sigla **2.** (tip.) segnatura.

signboard s. insegna (di albergo, negozio ecc.).

significant agg. espressivo, significativo.

to **signify** vt. e vi. **1.** significare, voler dire **2.** denotare, indicare, presagire **3.** importare.

silence s. silenzio.

to **silence** vt. far tacere, imporre il silenzio.

silencer s. silenziatore.

silent agg. **1.** silenzioso, taciturno **2.** muto.

silently avv. silenziosamente.

silhouette s. profilo, contorno.

silica s. silice.

silicate s. silicato.

silicon s. silicio.

silicosis s. silicosi.

silk s. seta.

silken agg. serico, di seta.

silkworm s. baco da seta || — breeding, sericoltura.

silky agg. di seta, serico.

sill s. basamento, soglia.

silliness s. stupidità, sciocchezza.

silly agg. sciocco, stupido.

to **silo** vt. conservare, mettere in silo.

silt s. melma.

silver s. argento, argenteria || — -plate, argenteria; — -plating, argentatura || quick —, mercurio.

to **silver** vt. inargentare. ♦ to **silver** vi. inargentarsi.

silverware s. oggetti d'argento.

silvery agg. argenteo.

similar agg. simile, analogo.

similarity s. somiglianza, similitudine.

similitude s. **1.** similitudine **2.** somiglianza.

simoniac agg. e s. simoniaco.

simony s. simonia.

to **simper** vi. parlare in modo affettato.

simple agg. **1.** semplice, elementare **2.** sincero **3.** autentico.

simpleton s. sempliciotto.

simplicity s. semplicità, candore.

simplification s. semplificazione.

to **simplify** vt. semplificare.

simply avv. semplicemente.

simulation s. simulazione.

simulator s. simulatore.

simultaneity s. simultaneità.

simultaneous agg. simultaneo.

sin s. **1.** peccato, colpa **2.** offesa.

to **sin** vi. peccare.

since avv. da allora, da allora in poi || long —, molto tempo fa. ♦ **since** cong. **1.** da quando **2.** poiché. ♦ **since** prep. da, fin da.

sincere agg. sincero, schietto.

sincerely avv. sinceramente || yours —, cordialmente vostro (nelle lettere).

sincerity *s.* sincerità.

sinew *s.* **1.** tendine, nervo **2.** (*fig.*) vigore, nerbo.

sinful *agg.* peccaminoso, colpevole.

sinfully *avv.* peccaminosamente.

to sing (sang, sung) *vt. e vi.* cantare.

to singe *vt.* bruciacchiare, strinare (*anche fig.*). ♦ **to singe** *vi.* bruciarsi.

singer *s.* cantante.

singing *s.* **1.** canto **2.** fischio (*del vento ecc.*).

single *agg.* **1.** solo, unico **2.** individuale, particolare **3.** celibe || *every — day*, tutti i giorni.

to single *vt.* distinguere, scegliere: *to — out sthg.*, scegliere qc.

singleness *s.* **1.** unicità **2.** sincerità.

singly *avv.* **1.** separatamente, ad uno ad uno **2.** da solo, senza aiuto.

singsong *s.* cantilena, canto monotono.

singular *agg.* **1.** singolare, solo **2.** eccezionale **3.** bizzarro, strano.

singularity *s.* **1.** singolarità, rarità **2.** particolarità **3.** stranezza.

singularly *avv.* singolarmente.

sinister *agg.* sinistro, funesto, di cattivo augurio.

sink *s.* **1.** lavandino, acquaio **2.** scolo.

to sink (sank, sunk) *vi.* **1.** affondare, andare a fondo **2.** sprofondare **3.** abbassare, abbassarsi, calare **4.** cadere, cedere (*di terreno, muro ecc.*).

sinner *s.* peccatore.

sinuous *agg.* sinuoso.

sinus *s.* **1.** cavità **2.** seno.

sip *s.* sorso.

to sip *vt. e vi.* sorseggiare.

siphon *s.* sifone.

sir *s.* **1.** (*vocativo*) signore **2.** « sir » (*titolo*).

siren *s.* sirena.

siroc *s.* scirocco.

sirup *s.* sciroppo.

sister *s.* **1.** sorella **2.** suora || *— -in- law*, cognata.

sisterhood *s.* congregazione religiosa di suore.

sisterly *avv.* da sorella, amorevolmente.

to sit (sat, sat) *vt. e vi.* **1.** sedere, stare seduto, far sedere **2.** essere in seduta **3.** appollaiarsi, posare **4.** covare || *to — out*, rimanere fino alla fine; *to — up*, rimanere al-

zato.

site *s.* area fabbricabile.

sitting *s.* **1.** posa, seduta **2.** adunanza || *— -room*, stanza di soggiorno. ♦ **sittings** *s. pl.* sessioni (*di una Corte*).

situated *agg.* **1.** situato, collocato **2.** in una certa situazione (*di persona*).

situation *s.* **1.** situazione, posizione **2.** stato, circostanza **3.** posto, impiego: *to apply for a —*, fare una domanda di impiego.

six *agg.* sei.

sixfold *agg.* sestuplo. ♦ **sixfold** *avv.* sei volte tanto.

sixpence *s.* moneta da sei « pence », mezzo scellino.

sixpenny *agg.* del valore di sei « pence ».

sixteen *agg.* sedici.

sixteenth *agg.* sedicesimo.

sixth *agg.* sesto.

sixtieth *agg.* sessantesimo.

sixty *agg.* sessanta.

size *s.* **1.** grandezza, misura, dimensione **2.** formato, taglia **3.** colla.

to size *vt.* allineare || *to — up*, valutare.

sizzle *s.* sfrigolio.

skate *s.* pattino || *roller —*, pattino a rotelle.

to skate *vi.* pattinare.

skating *s.* pattinaggio.

skein *s.* matassa.

skeleton *s.* scheletro (*anche fig.*).

to skeletonize *vt.* scheletrire. ♦ **to skeletonize** *vi.* scheletrirsi (*anche fig.*).

skeptic *agg. e s.* scettico.

skeptical *agg.* scettico.

skepticism *s.* scetticismo.

sketch *s.* **1.** schizzo, abbozzo **2.** scenetta.

to sketch *vt.* abbozzare, schizzare.

skewness *s.* asimmetria.

ski *s.* sci || *-lift*, sciovia.

to ski *vi.* sciare.

skier *s.* sciatore.

skiff *s.* (*mar.*) schifo.

skilful *agg.* abile, esperto.

skilfully *avv.* abilmente.

skilfulness *s.* abilità.

skill *s.* abilità, destrezza.

skilled *agg.* esperto, abile, versato || *— worker*, operaio specializzato.

to skim *vt. e vi.* **1.** schiumare, scremare **2.** rasentare, sfiorare.

skimmer *s.* schiumarola.

skimming s. scrematura.

skin s. pelle, cute.

to **skin** vt. e vi. scuoiare || to — over, rimarginarsi (di ferite).

skinny agg. magro, scarno.

to **skip** vt. e vi. fare un balzo, saltare alla corda || to — a few pages, saltare qualche pagina.

skirmish s. scaramuccia.

skirt s. **1.** sottana, gonna **2.** orlo, lembo.

to **skirt** vt. e vi. orlare, costeggiare.

skittish agg. capriccioso, frivolo.

skittles s. pl. birilli.

skull s. cranio, teschio || — -cap, papalina.

sky s. cielo, firmamento.

skylark s. allodola.

skylight s. lucernario.

skyline s. linea, profilo (di montagne ecc.).

skyman s. paracadutista.

skyscraper s. grattacielo.

skyward agg. e avv. verso il cielo.

slab s. **1.** lastra, piastra **2.** pezzo, fetta.

slack agg. **1.** molle, allentato **2.** debole, fiacco **3.** (comm.) calmo, stagnante, debole. ♦ **slack** s. (comm.) stagione morta.

to **slacken** vt. **1.** allentare, mollare **2.** diminuire. ♦ to **slacken** vi. **1.** allentarsi **2.** smorzarsi.

slacker s. fannullone.

slain V. to slay.

siam s. sbatacchiamento.

to **slam** vt. sbattere, chiudere violentemente. ♦ to **slam** vi. chiudersi violentemente.

slander s. **1.** calunnia **2.** (giur.) diffamazione.

to **slander** vt. **1.** calunniare **2.** (giur.) diffamare.

slanderer s. **1.** calunniatore **2.** (giur.) diffamatore.

slanderous agg. calunnioso, maldicente.

slang s. gergo.

slant s. pendenza, inclinazione.

to **slant** vt. e vi. essere in pendenza, inclinare.

slanting agg. inclinato, obliquo, sghembo.

slap s. schiaffo, ceffone.

to **slap** vt. **1.** schiaffeggiare **2.** sbattere.

slash s. **1.** taglio, sfregio **2.** frustata.

to **slash** vt. tagliare, fendere.

slate s. ardesia, tegola d'ardesia.

slaughter s. **1.** macello **2.** carneficina, massacro.

to **slaughter** vt. **1.** macellare **2.** massacrare.

slaughterer s. **1.** macellatore **2.** massacratore.

slaughterhouse s. mattatoio.

Slav agg. e s. slavo.

slave s. schiavo.

slaver[1] s. schiavista.

slaver[2] s. saliva, bava.

slavery s. schiavitù.

to **slay** (**slew, slain**) vt. ammazzare.

sleek agg. lucido, levigato.

sleep s. sonno, dormita || — walker, sonnambulo.

to **sleep** (**slept, slept**) vt. e vi. **1.** dormire, riposare **2.** passare la notte.

sleeper s. **1.** dormiente, dormiglione **2.** (ferr.) traversina **3.** (ferr.) vettura letto.

sleepily avv. con aria assonnata.

sleeping agg. dormiente, addormentato || — bag, sacco a pelo; — -berth, cuccetta; — -car, vagone letto; — -draught, sonnifero.

sleepless agg. insonne.

sleeplessness s. insonnia.

sleepy agg. assonnato, sonnolento.

sleet s. nevischio.

sleeve s. manica.

sleeved agg. con maniche.

sleigh s. slitta.

slender agg. **1.** magro, snello **2.** debole, fiacco.

slenderness s. **1.** snellezza, magrezza **2.** debolezza.

slept V. to sleep.

slew V. to slay.

slice s. pezzo, fetta, porzione.

to **slice** vt. affettare.

slicer s. affettatrice.

slid V. to slide.

slide s. **1.** scivolata **2.** pendenza **3.** scivolo **4.** (mecc.) carrello, pattino.

to **slide** (**slid, slid**) vt. e vi. **1.** scivolare, far scivolare, scorrere, far scorrere **2.** sfuggire.

sliding agg. scorrevole.

slight agg. **1.** esile, minuto, magro **2.** leggero, scarso.

slim agg. **1.** magro, sottile **2.** debole.

slime s. melma, limo.

slimy agg. fangoso, viscoso.

sling[1] s. fionda.

sling[2] *s.* cinghia.

to sling[1] **(slung, slung)** *vt.* scagliare con la fionda.

to sling[2] *vt.* sospendere, appendere.

to slink (slunk, slunk) *vi.* sgattaiolare.

slip[1] *s.* 1. innesto 2. (*tip.*) bozza in colonna.

slip[2] *s.* 1. scalo, molo 2. guinzaglio 3. sottoveste 4. scivolone 5. papera, lapsus.

to slip *vt.* e *vi.* 1. scivolare, inciampare 2. entrare, uscire furtivamente 3. sguscire, liberarsi || *to — away*, scorrere (*di tempo*).

slipper *s.* pantofola.

slippery *agg.* sdrucciolevole, viscido (*anche fig.*).

slipshod *agg.* 1. scalcagnato 2. trasandato.

slit *s.* fessura, fenditura.

to slit (slit, slit) *vt.* fendere.

slope *s.* pendenza, pendio.

to slope *vi.* essere in pendenza, inclinarsi.

sloping *agg.* inclinato, obliquo.

slot *s.* fessura, scanalatura || *— machine*, distributore automatico a gettoni.

sloth *s.* pigrizia, indolenza.

slothful *agg.* pigro, indolente.

slouch *s.* andatura dinoccolata.

slouching *agg.* dinoccolato, goffo.

slovenliness *s.* sciatteria, sporcizia.

slovenly *agg.* sciatto, sudicio.

slow *agg.* 1. lento 2. tardo, ottuso || *—down*, rallentamento; *— -match*, miccia.

to slow *vt.* e *vi. to — up o down*, rallentare.

slowly *avv.* lentamente.

slowness *s.* lentezza, pigrizia.

sluggish *agg.* pigro, tardo, indolente.

sluggishness *s.* pigrizia, indolenza.

slum *s.* vicolo, tugurio. ◆ **slums** *s. pl.* quartieri poveri (*di una città*).

slumber *s.* dormiveglia, assopimento.

to slumber *vt.* e *vi.* dormire, dormicchiare.

slung V. *to sling*.

slunk V. *to slink*.

slush *s.* poltiglia, fango.

sly *agg.* 1. astuto, malizioso 2. infido.

smack *s.* 1. sapore, aroma 2. schiocco 3. schiaffo.

to smack *vt.* e *vi.* 1. schioccare 2. schioccare baci 3. schiaffeggiare.

small *agg.* 1. piccolo, minuto 2. leggero, debole 3. poco, scarso 4. di poca importanza.

small-arms *s. pl.* armi portatili.

smallness *s.* piccolezza.

smallpox *s.* vaiolo.

smart *agg.* 1. acuto, pungente 2. vivace, sveglio 3. elegante.

to smarten *vt.* e *vi.* abbellire || *to — up*, rianimarsi, farsi bello.

smartness *s.* 1. acutezza, vivacità, brio 2. eleganza.

smash *s.* 1. urto, scontro 2. rovina.

to smash *vt.* 1. frantumare, fracassare 2. sconfiggere, annientare. ◆ **to smash** *vi.* 1. frantumarsi 2. sfasciarsi 3. crollare.

smasher *s.* 1. chi frantuma 2. (*fam.*) caso eccezionale.

smear *s.* macchia, imbrattatura.

to smear *vt.* macchiare, imbrattare.

smell *s.* 1. odorato, olfatto 2. odore.

to smell (smelt, smelt) *vt.* e *vi.* 1. fiutare, sentire l'odore 2. avere odore || *to — of*, sapere di; *to — out*, scovare.

smile *s.* sorriso.

to smile *vt.* e *vi.* sorridere || *fortune smiled on you*, la fortuna ti fu favorevole.

smiling *agg.* sorridente, sereno.

smirch *s.* onta, macchia.

to smite (smote, smitten) *vt.* e *vi.* 1. colpire, percuotere 2. sconfiggere, sgominare || *to — down*, abbattere.

smith *s.* fabbro.

smitten V. *to smite*.

smoke *s.* 1. fumo 2. fumata || *—stack*, fumaiolo.

to smoke *vt.* e *vi.* 1. fumare 2. affumicare.

smoker *s.* fumatore, fumatrice.

smoking *s.* il fumare. ◆ **smoking** *agg.* fumante.

smoky *agg.* 1. fumoso 2. affumicato, annerito dal fumo 3. che sa di fumo.

smooth *agg.* 1. liscio, levigato 2. omogeneo 3. armonioso (*di suono*) 4. mellifluo 5. calmo, tranquillo (*di mare*).

to smooth *vt.* 1. lisciare, spianare 2. appianare.

smoothing *s.* lisciatura, spianatura.

smoothly *avv.* 1. pianamente 2. armonicamente 3. in modo mellifluo.

smoothness *s.* 1. levigatezza 2. armonia (*di verso, suono*) 3. affabilità.

smote V. *to smite.*

to **smother** *vt. e vi.* 1. soffocare, opprimere 2. ricoprire.

to **smoulder** *vi.* ardere sotto la cenere.

to **smuggle** *vt. e vi.* contrabbandare.

smuggler *s.* contrabbandiere.

smuggling *s.* contrabbando.

smut *s.* fuliggine.

snack *s.* 1. boccone, porzione 2. spuntino || — *-bar,* tavola calda.

snail *s.* chiocciola, lumaca.

snake *s.* serpente.

snakily *avv.* 1. tortuosamente 2. *(fig.)* slealmente.

snaky *agg.* serpentino.

snap *s.* 1. colpo secco, morso, schiocco 2. scatto 3. fermaglio, fibbia.

to **snap** *vt. e vi.* 1. schioccare, far schioccare 2. aprirsi di colpo, spezzare con un colpo secco 3. *(foto)* scattare un'istantanea.

snapshot *s.* *(foto)* istantanea.

snare *s.* 1. trappola, rete 2. insidia, tentazione.

to **snare** *vt.* prendere in trappola, al laccio *(anche fig.).*

snarl *s.* ringhio.

to **snarl** *vi.* ringhiare.

snatch *s.* 1. strappo, strattone 2. brano, frammento.

to **snatch** *vt. e vi.* afferrare, ghermire || — *off,* strappare.

sneak *s.* persona malfida.

sneer *s.* sogghigno beffardo.

to **sneer** *vt. e vi.* sorridere beffardamente, schernire.

sneeze *s.* starnuto.

to **sneeze** *vi.* starnutire.

to **sniff** *vt. e vi.* fiutare || *to — at sthg.* annusare qc.

snip *s.* 1. ritaglio, scampolo 2. forbiciata.

to **snip** *vt.* tagliuzzare.

snobbery *s.* snobismo.

to **snore** *vi.* russare.

snort *s.* sbuffo, rumore sbuffante.

to **snort** *vt. e vi.* sbuffare.

snout *s.* muso, grugno.

snow *s.* neve, nevicata || — *-plough,* spazzaneve; — *-slide,* valanga.

to **snow** *v. imp.* nevicare || *it is snowing,* nevica.

snowfall *s.* nevicata.

snowflake *s.* fiocco di neve.

snowy *agg.* 1. nevoso, coperto di neve 2. niveo.

snuff *s.* 1. l'aspirare col naso 2. tabacco da fiuto || — *-box,* tabacchiera.

to **snuff**[1] *vt. e vi.* 1. annusare aspirando 2. fiutare tabacco.

to **snuff**[2] *vt. e vi.* smoccolare *(una candela).*

to **snuffle** *vt. e vi.* pronunciare con tono nasale.

snug *agg.* 1. comodo 2. confortevole 3. nascosto.

to **snuggle** *vi.* 1. rannicchiarsi 2. accoccolarsi.

so *avv.* così, tanto, talmente || — *far,* fino ad ora; — *long as,* a patto che; *if* —, in tal caso; *that being* —, stando così le cose.

to **soak** *vt.* 1. immergere 2. bagnare. ♦ to **soak** *vi.* 1. inzupparsi, imbeversi 2. bagnarsi.

soaking *agg.* 1. che bagna, che inzuppa 2. bagnato. ♦ **soaking** *s.* immersione, bagnatura.

soap *s.* sapone || — *dish,* portasapone.

to **soap** *vt.* insaponare. ♦ to **soap** *vi.* insaponarsi.

soapbox *s.* 1. cassa per sapone 2. *(fam.)* palco improvvisato per oratori *(da strada).*

soapsuds *s. pl.* saponata *(sing.).*

soapwort *s.* saponaria.

sob *s.* singhiozzo.

to **sob** *vt. e vi.* singhiozzare.

sober *agg.* 1. sobrio *(nel bere)* 2. calmo, composto.

sobriety *s.* 1. sobrietà *(nel bere)* 2. moderazione, calma.

so-called *agg.* cosiddetto.

sociability *s.* socievolezza.

sociable *agg.* socievole.

social *agg.* 1. sociale 2. socievole.

socialism *s.* socialismo.

socialist *s.* socialista.

sociality *s.* socievolezza.

to **socialize** *vt.* socializzare.

society *s.* 1. società, compagnia 2. strato sociale 3. associazione.

sociological *agg.* sociologico.

sociologist *s.* sociologo.

sociology *s.* sociologia.

sock *s.* 1. calzino, calza corta 2. soletta.

socket *s.* 1. cavità 2. *(elett.)* presa di corrente, portalampada 3. *(anat.)* orbita.

Socratic *agg. e s.* socratico.

sod *s.* zolla erbosa.

soda *s.* carbonato di sodio.

sodium s. sodio.

soft agg. 1. molle, tenero 2. liscio, morbido, soffice 3. dolce, mite || — -boiled (egg), uovo alla coque.

to soften vt. 1. ammollire, ammorbidire 2. calmare, raddolcire. ♦ **to soften** vi. 1. ammorbidirsi 2. intenerirsi.

softening agg. che rende molle. ♦ **softening** s. 1. ammorbidimento 2. intenerimento.

softly avv. 1. teneramente 2. sommessamente 3. piano piano.

softness s. 1. morbidezza 2. dolcezza, mitezza.

soil s. 1. suolo, terreno 2. macchia (anche fig.).

to soil vt. macchiare. ♦ **to soil** vi. macchiarsi.

sojourn s. soggiorno.

to sojourn vi. soggiornare.

solace s. sollievo, conforto.

to solace vt. consolare.

solar agg. solare.

sold V. to sell.

solder s. lega per saldatura.

to solder vt. saldare.

soldering s. saldatura.

soldier s. 1. soldato 2. stratega || foot- —, soldato di fanteria; horse- —, soldato di cavalleria.

soldierlike agg. militaresco.

soldiery s. coll. soldatesca, truppe.

sole[1] agg. solo, unico.

sole[2] s. suola, pianta del piede.

sole[3] s. soglióla.

solecism s. solecismo.

solely avv. solamente.

solemn agg. solenne, serio, grave.

solemnity s. solennità.

to solemnize vt. solennizzare.

solemnly avv. solennemente.

sol-fa s. solfeggio.

to sol-fa vt. e vi. solfeggiare.

to solicit vt. 1. sollecitare 2. adescare. ♦ **to solicit** vi. fare sollecitazioni.

solicitation s. 1. sollecitazione 2. invito, adescamento.

solicitor s. 1. sollecitatore 2. procuratore legale.

solicitous agg. 1. sollecito 2. ansioso, desideroso.

solid agg. 1. solido, compatto 2. reale, fondato. ♦ **solid** s. solido.

solidarity s. solidarietà.

solidary agg. solidale.

solidification s. solidificazione.

to solidify vt. solidificare ♦ **to so**-

lidify vi. solidificarsi.

solidity s. 1. solidità 2. (comm.) solvenza.

solidly avv. 1. solidamente 2. all'unanimità.

soliloquy s. soliloquio.

solitaire s. solitario (pietra preziosa e giuoco delle carte).

solitary agg. 1. solo, unico 2. solitario 3. isolato, romito.

solitude s. solitudine, isolamento.

soloist s. solista.

solstice s. solstizio.

solubility s. solubilità.

soluble agg. 1. solubile 2. scomponibile 3. risolvibile.

solution s. 1. (chim.) soluzione 2. risoluzione.

solvability s. 1. (comm.) solvibilità 2. solubilità 3. risolvibilità.

solvable agg. 1. (comm.) solvibile 2. solubile 3. risolvibile.

to solve vt. risolvere, chiarire.

solvency s. (comm.) solvibilità.

solvent agg. 1. (comm.) solvibile 2. solvente. ♦ **solvent** s. solvente.

somatic(al) agg. somatico.

somatology s. somatologia.

sombre agg. 1. fosco, scuro 2. (fig.) tetro, triste.

some agg. 1. qualche, alcuni, certi 2. un certo, qualsiasi 3. (partitivo) un po' di, del, della, dei, degli, delle. ♦ **some** pron. 1. alcuni, alcune 2. un po'. ♦ **some** avv. circa.

somebody pron. indef. qualcuno.

somehow avv. in qualche modo, in un modo o nell'altro.

someone pron. indef. qualcuno: — else, qualcun altro.

somersault s. 1. salto mortale, capriola 2. (aer.) capottamento 3. (auto) ribaltamento.

to somersault, to somerset vi. 1. fare salti mortali 2. (aer.) capottare 3. (auto.) ribaltare.

something pron. indef. qualche cosa.

sometime avv. 1. un tempo 2. presto o tardi, un giorno o l'altro.

sometimes avv. qualche volta, alcune volte.

someway avv. in un modo o nell'altro.

somewhat pron. ind. un poco.

somewhere avv. in qualche luogo.

sonnambulism s. sonnambulismo.

somnambulist s. sonnambulo.

somnolent *agg.* **1.** sonnolento **2.** assopito.

son *s.* figlio, figliolo || — *-in-law,* genero.

song *s.* canto, canzone.

songbook *s.* canzoniere.

songful *agg.* **1.** melodioso **2.** che ama cantare.

songster *s.* cantante (*uomo*).

sonnet *s.* sonetto.

sonority *s.* sonorità.

sonorous *agg.* sonoro, risonante.

sonorously *avv.* sonoramente.

soon (*comp. di* sooner) *avv.* presto, tra poco || *the sooner the better,* prima è meglio è; *sooner or later,* presto o tardi; *I had sooner,* preferirei; *as — as,* non appena.

soot *s.* fuliggine.

to soot *vt.* macchiare, sporcare di fuliggine.

to soothe *vt.* calmare, placare.

soothsayer *s.* indovino.

sooty *agg.* fuligginoso.

sophism *s.* sofisma.

sophist *s.* sofista (*anche fig.*).

sophistic(al) *agg.* sofistico, pedante.

sophisticated *agg.* **1.** sofisticato, raffinato **2.** adulterato.

sophistry *s.* sofisma.

sorcerer *s.* stregone, mago.

sorceress *s.* strega, maga.

sorcery *s.* stregoneria, sortilegio.

sordid *agg.* **1.** sordido, avaro **2.** vile, meschino.

sore *agg.* **1.** doloroso, dolorante, infiammato **2.** triste, addolorato **3.** estremo, intenso.

sorrel *s.* sauro.

sorrow *s.* **1.** dispiacere, dolore **2.** rincrescimento **3.** sventura.

to sorrow *vi.* affliggersi, addolorarsi.

sorrowful *agg.* **1.** triste, infelice **2.** penoso, doloroso.

sorry *agg.* spiacente, dolente || *sorry!,* scusate!; *to be —,* dispiacersi.

sort *s.* sorta, specie.

to sort *vt.* raggruppare, selezionare.

♦ **to sort** *vi.* accordarsi, adattarsi.

sought V. *to seek.*

soul *s.* **1.** anima, animo, spirito **2.** essenza, personificazione.

sound¹ *avv.* profondamente.

sound² *agg.* **1.** sano, intero, in buono stato **2.** buono, solido **3.** profondo, completo || — *-headed* equilibra-

to, — *-minded,* di buon senso.

sound³ *s.* suono, rumore || — *wave,* onda sonora.

sound⁴ *s.* sondaggio.

sound⁵ *s.* braccio di mare, stretto.

to sound¹ *vt.* e *vi.* **1.** suonare, risuonare **2.** sembrare, aver l'aria di.

to sound² *vt.* e *vi.* sondare, scandagliare.

sounding *agg.* sonoro, sonante, risonante.

soundless *agg.* muto, senza suono.

soundly *avv.* **1.** sanamente **2.** profondamente.

soundness *s.* **1.** buona condizione (*di salute*) **2.** solidità (*di argomento*).

soup *s.* zuppa, minestra.

sour *agg.* **1.** acido, aspro, acerbo **2.** bisbetico.

to sour *vt.* e *vi.* **1.** inacidire **2.** inasprire, esacerbare.

source *s.* **1.** fonte, sorgente **2.** origine.

sourdine *s.* (*mus.*) sordina.

sourish *agg.* acidulo.

sourness *s.* acidità.

south *s.* sud, mezzogiorno.

southern *agg.* del sud, meridionale.

southerner *s.* abitante del sud, meridionale.

southward *avv.* verso sud.

sovereign *s.* sovrano.

sovereignty *s.* sovranità.

sow *s.* scrofa.

to sow (**sowed, sown**) *vt.* e *vi.* seminare, piantare.

sowing *s.* seminagione.

sown V. *to sow.*

spa *s.* sorgente minerale.

space *s.* spazio || — *-ship,* astronave.

to space *vt.* spaziare, disporre ad intervalli.

spaceman *s.* astronauta.

spacesuit *s.* tuta spaziale.

spacial *agg.* spaziale.

spacing *s.* spaziatura, interlineatura.

spacious *agg.* spazioso, ampio.

spade *s.* vanga, badile.

span V. *to spin.*

span *s.* **1.** spanna, palmo **2.** breve spazio di tempo.

to span *vt.* **1.** misurare a spanne **2.** attraversare.

spangle *s.* lustrino.

Spaniard *s.* spagnolo.

Spanish *agg.* spagnolo.

to spank *vt.* (*fam.*) sculacciare.

spar¹ *s.* (*mar.*) antenna.

spar² *s.* incontro di pugilato.

spare *agg.* 1. parco, frugale 2. d'avanzo, disponibile, in più || — *room*, camera in più (*per gli ospiti*); — *time*, tempo disponibile; — *wheel*, ruota di scorta.

to spare *vt.* 1. economizzare, risparmiare 2. privarsi, fare a meno di. ♦ **to spare** *vi.* essere frugale.

sparing *agg.* 1. parco, frugale 2. limitato, moderato.

spark *s.* 1. scintilla, favilla 2. (*fig.*) lampo, barlume.

to spark *vi.* scintillare, emettere scintille.

sparkle *s.* scintilla, favilla.

to sparkle *vi.* 1. emettere scintille (*di fuoco*) 2. sfavillare, brillare, risplendere (*anche fig.*).

sparkler *s.* stella filante.

sparkling *agg.* scintillante, vivace (*anche fig.*).

sparrow *s.* passero || — -*hawk*, sparviero.

Spartan *agg.* e *s.* spartano.

spasm *s.* 1. spasmo 2. attacco, spasimo (*anche fig.*).

spasmodic(al) *agg.* spasmodico.

spastic *agg.* spastico.

spat V. *to* spit.

spatial *agg.* spaziale.

spatiality *s.* spazialità.

spatter *s.* 1. schizzo 2. sgocciolio.

to spatter *vt.* e *vi.* 1. schizzare, inzaccherare 2. gocciolare.

to speak (spoke, spoken) *vt.* e *vi.* 1. parlare 2. esprimere, rivelare || *to — at*, alludere a; *to — out*, parlare francamente; *to — to*, garantire; *to — up*, alzare la voce.

speaker *s.* parlatore, oratore, annunciatore || *the — of the House of Commons*, il Presidente della Camera dei Comuni.

speaking *agg.* parlante, espressivo, eloquente. ♦ **speaking** *s.* 1. il parlare, discorso 2. eloquenza, declamazione.

spear *s.* 1. lancia, alabarda, asta 2. fiocina.

to spear *vt.* 1. trafiggere (*con lancia*) 2. fiocinare.

special *agg.* 1. speciale, particolare 2. eccezionale, straordinario.

specialist *s.* specialista.

speciality *s.* specialità, particolarità.

to specialize *vt.* specializzare. ♦

specialize *vi.* specializzarsi.

specially *avv.* specialmente, soprattutto.

specialty *s.* 1. (*comm.*) specialità 2. (*giur.*) contratto sigillato.

species *s.* 1. specie, classe 2. sorta, genere, tipo.

specific *agg.* specifico, particolare.

specification *s.* 1. specificazione 2. descrizione dettagliata.

to specify *vt.* specificare, precisare.

specimen *s.* modello, esemplare.

speck *s.* 1. macchiolina, punto 2. granello (*di polvere ecc.*).

speckled *agg.* macchiato, screziato.

speckless *agg.* senza macchia (*anche fig.*).

spectacle *s.* spettacolo, vista. ♦ **spectacles** *s. pl.* occhiali: *to put on one's* —, mettersi gli occhiali.

spectacled *agg.* che porta gli occhiali.

spectacular *agg.* spettacolare.

spectator *s.* spettatore.

spectral *agg.* spettrale.

spectre *s.* spettro, fantasma.

specular *agg.* speculare.

to speculate *vt.* e *vi.* 1. meditare, considerare 2. (*comm.*) speculare.

speculation *s.* 1. speculazione, meditazione 2. (*comm.*) speculazione.

speculative *agg.* contemplativo, speculativo (*anche comm.*).

speculator *s.* 1. spirito speculatore 2. (*comm.*) speculatore.

sped V. *to* speed.

speech *s.* 1. parola, favella 2. discorso, arringa 3. linguaggio.

speechless *agg.* senza parola, muto (*anche fig.*).

speed *s.* velocità, rapidità.

to speed *vi.* affrettarsi. ♦ **to speed** (**sped, sped**) *vt.* 1. aiutare 2. affrettare 3. regolare la velocità || *to — up the work*, affrettare i lavori.

speedometer *s.* tachimetro.

speedway *s.* 1. pista, circuito (*di autodromo*).

speedy *agg.* rapido, pronto.

spell¹ *s.* incantesimo.

spell² *s.* 1. turno di lavoro 2. intervallo.

to spell (spelt, spelt) (*anche reg.*) *vt.* e *vi.* compitare, sillabare.

to spellbind (spellbound, spellbound) *vt.* incantare, affascinare.

spelling *s.* 1. compitazione 2. ortografia.

spelt V. *to spell*.

to spend (spent, spent) *vt. e vi.* 1. spendere, sborsare 2. dedicare, impiegare 3. passare, trascorrere.

sperm *s.* sperma.

sphenoid *agg. e s.* sfenoide.

sphere *s.* sfera, globo.

spheric(al) *agg.* sferico.

sphericity *s.* sfericità.

sphincter *s.* sfintere.

Sphinx *s.* sfinge (*anche fig.*).

spice *s.* 1. aroma 2. (*fig.*) sapore, gusto 3. spezie (*pl.*).

to spice *vt.* 1. condire con spezie 2. (*fig.*) dar gusto a, rendere interessante.

spicery *s.* spezie, aromi (*pl.*).

spicily *avv.* 1. aromaticamente 2. (*fig.*) gustosamente.

spiciness *s.* 1. aroma, profumo 2. (*fam.*) arguzia.

spick-and-span *agg.* (*fam.*) lindo, lucente.

spicy *agg.* 1. aromatico, piccante 2. (*fig.*) arguto, mordace.

spider *s.* ragno.

spidery *agg.* 1. simile a ragno 2. infestato da ragni.

spike[1] *s.* punta, aculeo.

spike[2] *s.* spiga.

to spike *vt.* inchiodare || *to — so.'s guns*, guastare i piani di qu.

to spill (split, spilt) *vt.* 1. versare 2. disarcionare. ◆ to spill (spilt, spilt) *vi.* versarsi, traboccare.

spin *s.* (*aer.*) avvitamento.

to spin (span, spun) *vt. e vi.* 1. filare (*cotone ecc.*) 2. (*mecc.*) lavorare al tornio 3. girare, far girare.

spinach *s.* spinacio.

spinal *agg.* spinale.

spindle *s.* 1. fuso, fusello 2. (*mecc.*) asse, mandrino.

spine *s.* 1. spina, lisca 2. spina dorsale.

spineless *agg.* 1. senza spine 2. senza spina dorsale 3. (*fam.*) debole, molle.

spinner *s.* 1. ragno filatore 2. (*aer.*) ogiva 3. filatore.

spinning *s.* 1. filatura, filato 2. movimento rotatorio || *—-mill*, filanda.

spinster *s.* 1. filatrice 2. donna nubile, zitella.

spiral *agg.* spirale, a spirale. ◆ spiral *s.* spirale.

spire[1] *s.* guglia, cuspide.

spire[2] *s.* spira, spirale.

spirit *s.* 1. spirito, anima 2. folletto, fantasma 3. genio, intelletto 4. coraggio, vigore.

spirits[1] *s. pl.* umore, stato d'animo (*sing.*).

spirits[2] *s. pl.* bevande fortemente alcooliche.

spirited *agg.* brioso, vivace || *high- —*, fiero; *poor- —*, depresso.

spiritism *s.* 1. spiritismo.

spiritual *agg.* spirituale.

spiritualism *s.* 1. spiritualismo 2. spiritismo.

spiritualist *s.* 1. spiritualista 2. spiritista.

spirituality *s.* spiritualità.

spit *s.* sputo, saliva.

to spit (spat, spat) *vi.* sputare.

spite *s.* dispetto, ripicco: *out of —*, per dispetto; *in — of*, a dispetto di.

spiteful *agg.* dispettoso.

spittle V. *spit*.

spittoon *s.* sputacchiera.

splash *s.* 1. schizzo, spruzzo 2. tonfo.

to splash *vt. e vi.* ▲ schizzare, spruzzare 2. inzacchearre, infangare. ◆ to splash *vi.* 1. spruzzare 2. cadere con un tonfo.

splashy *agg.* bagnato, fangoso.

splay *agg.* largo e piatto. ◆ splay *s.* (*arch.*) strombatura.

to splay *vt.* (*arch.*) strombare. ◆ to splay *vi.* essere in posizione obliqua.

spleen *s.* 1. milza 2. (*fig.*) malumore, umore nero.

splendid *agg.* splendido, magnifico.

splendour *s.* splendore, lustro.

splenetic *agg. e s.* splenetico, bilioso.

splinter *s.* scheggia, frantume.

split *agg.* spaccato, diviso. ◆ split *s.* 1. fessura, crepaccio 2. scissione.

to split (split, split) *vt.* 1. fendere 2. spaccare, frazionare || *to — hairs*, spaccare un capello in quattro; *to — one's sides* (*with laughing*), ridere a crepapelle. ◆ to split (split, split) *vi.* fendersi.

splitting *agg.* che si fende, che fende. ◆ splitting *s.* fessura, spaccatura.

spoil(s) *s.* spoglia, preda.

to **spoil** (**spoilt, spoilt**) (*anche reg.*) *vt.* e *vi.* 1. rovinare, alterare, sciupare, viziare 2. saccheggiare, predare.

spoilt *agg.* 1. guasto, avariato 2. viziato.

spoke *s.* 1. raggio (*di ruota*) 2. piolo (*di scala*).

spoke V. *to speak.*

spoken V. *to speak.*

spokesman *s.* portavoce.

spoliation *s.* ruberia, saccheggio.

sponge *s.* spugna (*anche fig.*).

to **sponge** *vt.* 1. pulire, lavare con la spugna 2. fare spugnature 3. (*fig.; fam.*) scroccare.

sponger *s.* 1. pescatore di spugne 2. scroccone.

spongy *agg.* spugnoso, poroso.

sponsor *s.* 1. padrino, madrina 2. (*giur.*) garante, mallevadore.

to **sponsor** *vt.* 1. essere garante di 2. offrire (*programmi radio, tv*).

sponsorial *agg.* 1. di garanzia 2. di padrino, di madrina.

sponsorship *s.* 1. garanzia 2. qualità di padrino, di madrina.

spontaneity *s.* spontaneità.

spontaneous *agg.* spontaneo.

spontaneously *avv.* spontaneamente.

spool *s.* rocchetto, bobina.

spoon *s.* cucchiaio.

to **spoon** *vt.* prendere con un cucchiaio.

spoon-fed *agg.* coccolato, viziato.

spoonful *s.* cucchiaiata.

sporadic *agg.* sporadico, raro.

sport *s.* 1. giuoco, divertimento 2. scherzo 3. sport. ♦ **sports** *s. pl* gare, incontri.

to **sport** *vi.* 1. scherzare 2. giocare 3. fare dello sport.

sporting *agg.* sportivo.

sportive *agg.* 1. gioviale 2. sportivo.

sportsman *s.* 1. sportivo 2. uomo animato da spirito sportivo.

sportsmanlike *agg.* caratteristico di uno sportivo.

sportswoman *s.* donna sportiva.

spot *s.* 1. luogo, località 2. macchia (*anche fig.*) || *on the —*, sul colpo.

to **spot** *vt.* macchiare, punteggiare. ♦ to **spot** *vi.* macchiarsi.

spotless *agg.* senza macchia, immacolato (*anche fig.*).

spotlight *s.* riflettore, luce della ribalta.

spotty *agg.* macchiato, chiazzato.

spout *s.* 1. tubo di scarico, grondaia 2. getto, colonna (*d'acqua*).

to **spout** *vt.* scaricare, emettere. ♦ to **spout** *vi.* scaturire, zampillare.

sprain *s.* distorsione, strappo muscolare.

to **sprain** *vt.* storcere, slogare.

sprang V. *to spring.*

to **sprawl** *vi.* sdraiarsi in modo scomposto.

spray *s.* 1. spruzzo, schiuma 2. getto vaporizzato (*di acqua ecc.*) 3. spruzzatore.

to **spray** *vt.* 1. polverizzare, vaporizzare 2. aspergere, spruzzare.

sprayer *s.* spruzzatore.

spread *agg.* steso, aperto, spiegato.

to **spread** (**spread, spread**) *vt.* 1. stendere, spiegare, spalmare 2. (*fig.*) spargere, diffondere. ♦ to **spread** (**spread, spread**) *vi.* stendersi, spiegarsi.

spreader *s.* spruzzatore.

spreading *agg.* che si propaga. ♦ **spreading** *s.* (*fig.*) propagazione.

spree *s.* baldoria.

sprig *s.* 1. ramoscello 2. (*fig.*) rampollo.

spring *s.* 1. sorgente, fonte 2. primavera 3. salto, balzo 4. molla, elasticità || — *-board*, trampolino; — *-head*, fontana; — *-mattress*, materasso a molle.

to **spring** (**sprang, sprung**) *vi.* 1. nascere, discendere, scaturire (*di acqua*) 2. saltare 3. scattare || to — *up*, crescere (*di piante*). ♦ to **spring** (**sprang, sprung**) *vt.* 1. far scattare (*con una molla*) 2. far brillare (*una mina*) 3. saltare.

springiness *s.* elasticità.

springy *agg.* 1. pieno di sorgenti 2. elastico.

sprinkle *s.* aspersione, spruzzatina.

to **sprinkle** *vt.* e *vi.* spruzzare, aspergere.

sprinkler *s.* 1. spruzzatore, innaffiatoio 2. aspersorio.

sprint *s.* (*sport*) scatto finale.

to **sprout** *vi.* germogliare. ♦ to **sprout** *vt.* far germogliare.

to **spruce** *vt.* adornare, agghindare.

sprung V. *to spring.* ♦ **sprung** *agg.* 1. a molla 2. spaccato.

spun V. *to spin.*

spur *s.* 1. sperone 2. (*fig.*) sprone.

to **spur** *vt.* 1. spronare 2. (*fig.*) incitare.

to **spurn** vt. e vi. disdegnare, trattare con disprezzo.

s**purt** s. getto, vampata.

spy s. spia.

to **spy** vt. e vi. spiare, fare la spia.

squabble s. battibecco, lite.

to **squabble** vi. accapigliarsi, venire a parole.

squ**ad** s. squadra, plotone.

squalid agg. squallido, miserabile.

squall s. urlo, strepito.

squalor s. squallore.

to **squander** vt. sprecare, scialacquare.

squanderer s. sciupone, sperperatore.

square agg. 1. quadrato 2. robusto, massiccio 3. perpendicolare. ♦ **square** s. 1. quadrato 2. piazza 3. squadra || — -built, tarchiato; — -root, radice quadrata; — -shouldered, dalle spalle larghe e diritte. ♦ **square** avv. ad angolo retto, in squadra.

to **square** vt. e vi. 1. quadrare, squadrare 2. pareggiare un conto 3. elevare al quadrato.

squared agg. 1. squadrato, quadrato 2. elevato al quadrato.

squash s. 1. cosa schiacciata 2. spremuta (di frutta): orange— -, spremuta d'arancio.

to **squash** vt. 1. schiacciare, spiaccicare 2. spremere.

squat agg. rannicchiato, accoccolato.

to **squat** vi. accovacciarsi, accoccolarsi.

squatter s. pioniere.

squeak s. 1. grido acuto 2. pigolio, squittio, guaito 3. cigolio.

to **squeak** vt. e vi. 1. strillare in tono acuto 2. squittire, guaire 3. cigolare.

squeaky agg. 1. che strilla 2. che guaisce, squittisce 3. cigolante.

squeamish agg. 1. soggetto a nausee 2. schizzinoso.

squeeze s. 1. compressione 2. spremitura 3. stretta, abbraccio.

to **squeeze** vt. 1. spremere 2. stringere, abbracciare. ♦ to **squeeze** vi. accalcarsi.

squeezer s. 1. ciò che preme 2. (mecc.) torchio.

squid s. seppia.

squint agg. strabico. ♦ **squint** s. strabismo.

to **squint** vi. essere strabico. ♦ to **squint** vt. guardare di traverso.

squire s. gentiluomo, nobiluomo (di campagna).

squirrel s. scoiattolo.

stab s. coltellata, pugnalata.

to **stab** vt. pugnalare, accoltellare.

to **stabilize** vt. stabilizzare.

stabilizer s. stabilizzatore.

stable[1] agg. stabile, permanente.

stable[2] s. scuderia, stalla.

stack s. mucchio, cumulo || chimney— -, ciminiera.

to **stack** vt. ammucchiare, accumulare.

staff s. 1. bastone, sostegno (anche fig.) 2. stato maggiore 3. personale (di ufficio ecc.) || editorial —, corpo redazionale; flag —, asta della bandiera.

stag s. cervo.

stage s. 1. piattaforma 2. palcoscenico 3. (fig.) campo d'azione, scena 4. stadio, grado 5. tappa || — -direction, didascalia; — -director, regista (teat.); — -effect, effetto scenico; — -name, nome d'arte; landing— — (mar.), pontile.

to **stage** vt. 1. mettere in scena 2. inscenare (una dimostrazione ecc.).

stagger s. barcollamento, andatura a zig-zag.

to **stagger** vi. 1. vacillare 2. dubitare, esitare. ♦ to **stagger** vt. far vacillare.

staginess s. teatralità.

staging s. 1. (teat.) messa in scena 2. (edil.) impalcatura.

stagnancy s. ristagno.

stagnant agg. stagnante.

to **stagnate** vi. ristagnare.

stagnation s. ristagno, stasi.

staid agg. posato, serio.

stain s. 1. scolorimento, macchia 2. (fig.) taccia, onta.

to **stain** vt. 1. macchiare 2. tingere. ♦ to **stain** vi. macchiarsi, sporcarsi.

stained agg. macchiato, sporco.

stainless agg. senza macchia.

stair s. scalino, gradino. ♦ **stairs** s. pl. scale || winding— —, scala a chiocciola; flight of —, rampa di scale.

staircase s. 1. scala, scalone 2. tromba delle scale.

stairway s. scalinata.

stake[1] s. 1. palo, paletto 2. piccola incudine.

stake[2] s. posta, scommessa || at —, in giuoco. ♦ **stakes** s. pl. (ippica) premio, corsa.

to stake[1] vt. cintare, chiudere (con una palizzata).

to stake[1] vt. mettere in giuoco, scommettere.

stale agg. 1. vecchio, stantio 2. (fig.) trito, caduto in disuso.

stalk[1] s. stelo, gambo.

stalk[2] s. andatura rigida e maestosa.

stall s. 1. stalla 2. bancarella, chiosco.

stammer s. balbuzie, balbettamento.

to stammer vt. e vi. 1. balbettare 2. farfugliare.

stammering agg. balbuziente. ♦ **stammering** s. balbuzie.

stamp s. 1. impronta, segno 2. francobollo, bollo 3. stampo || -collector, filatelico; -paper, carta bollata.

to stamp vt. 1. imprimere, incidere 2. (fig.) dare l'impronta 3. timbrare || to — down, calpestare. ♦ **to stamp** vi. battere i piedi.

stamping s. 1. scalpitio 2. timbratura.

stand s. 1. pausa, fermata 2. punto di vista 3. posizione, luogo (d'appostamento) 4. palco, tribuna 5. bancarella, chiosco || test-—, banco di prova.

to stand (stood, stood) vi. 1. essere, stare in piedi 2. stare, trovarsi 3. fermarsi, indugiare 4. conservarsi, rimaner valido || to — by, stare accanto, restare fedele a; to — for, significare, implicare; to — out, resistere, tener duro, spiccare. ♦ **to stand (stood, stood)** vt. sopportare, resistere.

standard s. 1. stendardo, bandiera 2. modello, campione 3. livello, qualità 4. supporto, base 5. tipo.

standardization s. standardizzazione.

stand-by s. scorta, riserva.

standing agg. 1. eretto, che sta in piedi 2. fermo, inattivo 3. fisso, immutabile. ♦ **standing** s. 1. posizione eretta 2. posizione, rango 3. periodo di tempo.

standoffish agg. riservato, altezzoso.

standpoint s. 1. luogo di osservazione 2. punto di vista.

standstill agg. in riposo, fermo. ♦ **standstill** s. arresto, fermata.

stank V. to stink.

staple s. 1. prodotto principale (di

un paese ecc.) 2. (fig.) argomento principale (di una conversazione).

star s. 1. stella, astro 2. (fig.) fortuna, destino 3. (tip.) asterisco.

to star vt. 1. costellare 2. segnare con un asterisco. ♦ **to star** vi. (cine, teat.) avere il ruolo di protagonista.

starboard agg. di dritta. ♦ **starboard** s. (mar.) dritta.

starch s. 1. amido 2. (fig.) rigidezza, formalismo.

to starch vt. 1. inamidare 2. (fig.) rendere formale.

starchiness s. 1. inamidatura 2. (fig.) formalismo, rigidità.

stardom s. divismo.

stare s. sguardo fisso.

to stare vt. guardare intensamente, fissare. ♦ **to stare** vi. sgranare gli occhi.

starfish s. stella di mare.

staring agg. 1. fisso, stupefatto 2. sgargiante, vistoso.

staringly avv. fissamente, con occhi sbarrati.

stark agg. 1. rigido, duro 2. completo, vero e proprio.

starless agg. senza stelle.

starlet s. 1. piccola stella 2. (cine) stellina.

starlight agg. stellato, stellare. ♦ **starlight** s. luce stellare.

starlike agg. simile a stella.

starlit agg. illuminato dalle stelle.

starred agg. 1. stellato, adorno di stelle 2. a stella.

starry agg. stellato, trapunto di stelle, brillante come una stella.

start s. 1. inizio, partenza 2. soprassalto || by fits and starts, irregolarmente 3. vantaggio dato all'inizio di una corsa 4. (mecc.) avviamento.

to start vi. 1. partire, mettersi in viaggio 2. cominciare 3. trasalire || to — out, aver intenzione di; to — up, spuntare all'improvviso. ♦ **to start** vt. 1. cominciare 2. far trasalire.

starter s. 1. iniziatore, fondatore 2. (sport) "starter", mossiere.

starting s. 1. inizio, partenza 2. debutto 3. (mecc.) messa in moto, avviamento.

startle s. trasalimento.

to startle vt. spaventare, far trasalire. ♦ **to startle** vi. spaventarsi, trasalire.

startling *agg.* impressionante, sorprendente.

starvation *s.* inedia, fame.

to starve *vi.* 1. morire di fame 2. (*fig.*) bramare. ♦ **to starve** *vt.* far morire di fame.

state *s.* 1. stato, condizione 2. governo, nazione 3. rango, dignità || — *control*, statalizzazione; — -*documents*, documenti ufficiali; — -*prisoner*, prigioniero politico; — -*trial*, processo politico.

to state *vt.* 1. affermare, dichiarare 2. stabilire.

stateless *agg.* 1. senza patria 2. senza pompa 3. apolide.

stately *agg.* nobile, signorile.

statement *s.* 1. esposto, relazione 2. asserzione, affermazione 3. (*giur.*) deposizione, esposizione dei fatti.

statesman *s.* statista.

static(al) *agg.* statico.

statics *s.* statica.

station *s.* 1. posto, luogo, base 2. stazione 3. condizione sociale || *petrol* —, stazione di rifornimento; *through* —, stazione di transito.

stationary *agg.* stazionario.

stationer *s.* cartolaio || —'*s* (*shop*), cartoleria.

stationery *s.* articoli di cancelleria.

station house *s.* guardina.

stationmaster *s.* capostazione.

statist *s.* statista.

statistic(al) *agg.* statistico.

statistically *avv.* statisticamente.

statistics *s.* 1. scienza della statistica 2. statistiche (*pl.*).

statuary *agg.* statuario, scultorio.

statue *s.* statua.

statuesque *agg.* statuario.

stature *s.* statura.

status *s.* 1. stato, condizione sociale 2. situazione.

statute *s.* statuto, regolamento.

statutory *agg.* statutario.

to staunch *vt.* 1. arrestare 2. stagnare. ♦ **to staunch** *vi.* stagnarsi.

stave *s.* 1. doga (*di botte*) 2. piolo (*di scala*) 3. strofa.

stay[1] *s.* 1. soggiorno 2. pausa.

stay[2] *s.* 1. sostegno, supporto 2. (*mecc.*) puntello.

to stay[1] *vi.* 1. fermarsi, sostare, soggiornare 2. resistere || *to* — *away*, essere assente; *to* — *in*, stare in casa, (*mil.*) essere consegnato; *to*

— *up*, vegliare. ♦ **to stay** *vt.* 1. arrestare, fermare 2. resistere.

to stay[2] *vt.* (*mecc.*) puntellare.

steadfast *agg.* fermo, risoluto.

steadfastly *avv.* stabilmente, fermamente.

steadfastness *s.* fermezza, tenacia.

steadily *avv.* 1. saldamente, fermamente 2. costantemente.

steadiness *s.* 1. fermezza, sicurezza 2. assiduità, perseveranza.

steading *s.* tenuta agricola.

steady *agg.* 1. fermo, saldo 2. equilibrato 3. continuo, regolare 4. fedele, assiduo.

to steady *vt.* rafforzare, rendere fermo, equilibrato. ♦ **to steady** *vi.* rafforzarsi.

steak *s.* bistecca.

to steal (stole, stolen) *vt.* e *vi.* rubare || *to* — *along*, camminare furtivamente; *to* — *away*, svignarsela; *to* — *upon*, avvicinarsi pian piano.

stealing *s.* furto || *cattle* (*o horse*)- —, abigeato.

stealthily *avv.* furtivamente.

stealthy *agg.* furtivo.

steam *s.* vapore: — -*engine*, macchina a vapore.

to steam *vt.* 1. esporre al vapore 2. cucinare al vapore. ♦ **to steam** *vi.* emettere vapore.

steamboat *s.* imbarcazione a vapore.

steamer *s.* nave a vapore.

steamship *s.* piroscafo.

steamtight *agg.* a tenuta di vapore.

steamy *agg.* 1. che esala vapore 2. appannato, umido.

stearic *agg.* stearico.

steel *s.* 1. acciaio 2. arma, spada 3. acciarino || — *cap*, elmetto; — *company*, acciaieria || *stainless* —, acciaio inossidabile.

steelwork *s.* lavoro, struttura in acciaio.

steelwork *s. pl.* acciaieria (*sing.*).

steely *agg.* 1. di acciaio, simile ad acciaio 2. (*fig.*) severissimo.

steelyard *s.* stadera.

steep[1] *agg.* 1. ripido, scosceso 2. (*fig.*) ambizioso, arduo 3. esorbitante (*di prezzi*).

steep[2] *s.* macerazione, l'inzuppare.

to steep *vt.* immergere (*anche fig.*), inzuppare.

steeple *s.* guglia, campanile.

steeplechase *s.* (*ippica*) corsa ad

ostacoli.

steer *s.* bue giovane, manzo.

to **steer** *vt.* 1. governare, manovrare 2. dirigere. ♦ to **steer** *vi.* 1. dirigersi 2. (*auto*) sterzare.

steering *s.* guida, governo (*dello sterzo, del timone*).

stem *s.* 1. tronco, gambo, stelo 2. cannello (*di pipa*) 3. (*mar.*) prua.

to **stem** *vt.* arrestare, arginare.

stench *s.* puzzo, tanfo.

step *s.* 1. passo (*anche fig.*), andatura 2. orma, impronta 3. provvedimento 4. gradino || *to be in — with so.*, tenere il passo con qu.; *— by —*, gradualmente; *in —* (*elett.*), in fase.

to **step** *vi.* camminare || *to — aside*, farsi da parte; *to — forward*, avanzare; *to — in*, montare (*su un veicolo*). ♦ to **step** *vt.* misurare a passi.

stepbrother *s.* fratellastro.

stepchild *s.* (*pl.* **-children**) figliastro.

stepdaughter *s.* figliastra.

stepfather *s.* patrigno.

stepmother *s.* matrigna.

stepsister *s.* sorellastra.

stepson *s.* figliastro.

stereophonic *agg.* stereofonico.

stereophony *s.* stereofonia.

stereoscope *s.* stereoscopio.

stereotype *s.* stereotipo.

sterile *agg.* sterile.

sterility *s.* sterilità.

to **sterilize** *vt.* rendere sterile, sterilizzare.

stern¹ *agg.* severo, austero.

stern² *s.* (*mar.*) poppa.

sternly *avv.* severamente.

sternness *s.* severità, austerità.

stethoscope *s.* stetoscopio.

stevedore *s.* scaricatore (*di porto*).

stew *s.* (*cuc.*) umido, stufato.

to **stew** *vt.* e *vi.* cuocere in umido.

steward *s.* 1. amministratore, intendente 2. (*aer., mar.*) cameriere di bordo.

stewardess *s.* 1. dispensiere 2. (*aer., mar.*) cameriera di bordo.

stick *s.* 1. bastone 2. bastoncino 3. barra, stecca.

to **stick** (**stuck, stuck**) *vt.* 1. ficcare, conficcare 2. infilare 3. incollare, appiccicare. ♦ to **stick** (**stuck, stuck**) *vi.* 1. fissarsi, conficcarsi 2. incollarsi.

stickiness *s.* viscosità, adesività.

sticky *agg.* 1. appiccicaticcio, visco-

so 2. poco accomodante.

stiff *agg.* 1. rigido, duro 2. (*fig.*) inflessibile 3. indolenzito, intorpidito 4. freddo, riservato || *— collar*, colletto duro; *— -neck*, torcicollo.

to **stiffen** *vt.* 1. indurire 2. indolenzire, intorpidire 3. rassodare. ♦ to **stiffen** *vi.* 1. indurirsi, irrigidirsi (*anche fig.*) 2. rassodarsi.

stiffness *s.* 1. durezza, rigidezza 2. intorpidimento.

to **stifle** *vt.* 1. soffocare 2. (*fig.*) reprimere. ♦ to **stifle** *vi.* sentirsi soffocare.

stifling *agg.* soffocante.

to **stigmatize** *vt.* 1. marchiare 2. stigmatizzare.

stile *s.* scaletta.

still¹ *agg.* tranquillo, calmo, silenzioso || *— -life* (*pitt.*), natura morta.

still² *avv.* 1. ancora, tuttora 2. tuttavia, nondimeno.

still³ *s.* alambicco.

to **still** *vt.* acquietare, calmare. ♦ to **still** *vi.* acquietarsi, calmarsi.

stillness *s.* calma, quiete.

stilt *s.* trampolo.

stimulant *s.* 1. stimolante 2. bevanda alcolica.

to **stimulate** *vt.* stimolare, incitare.

stimulus *s.* (*pl.-* li) stimolo, incentivo.

sting *s.* 1. pungiglione, aculeo 2. puntura d'insetto 3. dolore acuto 4. pungolo, stimolo.

to **sting** (**stung, stung**) *vt.* e *vi.* 1. pungere 2. colpire, ferire (*anche fig.*).

stinginess *s.* avarizia, spilorceria.

stinging *agg.* pungente, mordace.

stingy *agg.* avaro, taccagno.

stink *s.* puzzo, fetore.

to **stink** (**stank, stunk**) *vt.* e *vi.* puzzare, riempire di puzzo.

stinking *agg.* puzzolente, fetido.

to **stipulate** *vt.* e *vi.* stipulare.

stipulation *s.* stipulazione, patto.

stir *s.* 1. il rimescolare, l'attizzare || *to give a —*, dare una rimescolata 2. animazione, tumulto.

to **stir** *vt.* 1. rimescolare 2. muovere, agitare. ♦ to **stir** *vi.* muoversi, agitarsi.

stirabout *s.* indaffarato.

stirrer *s.* incitatore, istigatore.

stirring *agg.* eccitante.

stirrup *s.* staffa.

stitch *s.* 1. punto 2. maglia.

stock s. 1. rifornimento, provvista || *to be out of* —, essere sprovvisto 2. titoli, azioni (*pl.*) 3. tronco, ceppo 4. (*fig.*) stirpe.

to stock vt. 1. approvvigionare 2. tenere in magazzino.

stockbroker s. agente di cambio.

stockbroking s. professione dell'agente di cambio.

stock company s. società per azioni.

Stock Exchange s. Borsa valori.

stockfish s. stoccafisso.

stockholder s. azionista.

stocking s. calza lunga.

stoic agg. e s. stoico.

stoicism s. stoicismo.

stoker s. fuochista.

stole V. *to steal*.

stolen V. *to steal*.

stolid agg. 1. imperturbabile 2. sciocco.

stolidity s. flemma.

stomach s. stomaco: — -*ache*, mal di stomaco.

stomatitis s. stomatite.

stomatology s. stomatologia.

stone s. 1. pietra, ciottolo, sasso 2. nocciolo 3. (*med.*) calcolo || — -*blind*, completamente cieco; — -*breaker*, spaccapietre; — *cutter*, tagliapietre.

to stone vt. 1. lapidare 2. rivestire di pietra 3. snocciolare.

stoneless agg. senza nocciolo.

stoneware s. ceramica.

stony agg. 1. pietroso, sassoso 2. (*fig.*) duro, insensibile.

stood V. *to stand*.

stool s. sgabello, seggiolino.

stoop s. curvatura, inchino.

to stoop vi. 1. curvare, inchinarsi 2. (*fig.*) accondiscendere, abbassarsi.

stop s. 1. sosta, arresto 2. segno di punteggiatura || — *watch*, cronometro.

to stop vt. 1. fermare 2. turare, otturare 3. impedire. ♦ **to stop** vi. fermarsi.

stopper s. 1. tappo, turacciolo 2. otturatore.

stopping s. 1. otturazione 2. (*comm.*) cessazione, sospensione (*di pagamenti ecc.*).

storage s. 1. immagazzinamento 2. deposito, magazzino.

store s. 1. provvista, riserva 2. magazzino || — -*keeper*, magazziniere; — -*ship*, nave da carico.

to store vt. 1. fornire, rifornire 2. immagazzinare, mettere da parte (*anche fig.*).

storehouse s. magazzino, deposito.

storey s. piano (*di edificio*).

stork s. cicogna.

storm s. 1. tempesta, temporale 2. tumulto, agitazione.

to storm vi. 1. infuriare, scatenarsi 2. (*fam.*) adirarsi. ♦ **to storm** vt. attaccare.

stormy agg. tempestoso, burrascoso.

story s. 1. storia, racconto, novella, favola || *to tell stories*, contar frottole.

stoup s. acquasantiera.

stout agg. 1. forte, robusto, resistente 2. fermo, risoluto 3. grosso, tozzo.

stove s. 1. stufa 2. cucina economica: *gas*- —, cucina a gas.

to stove vt. mettere in forno, stufa.

to stow vt. stivare, riempire.

stowage s. (*mar.*) stivaggio.

straddle s. posizione a gambe divaricate, il mettersi a cavalcioni.

to straddle vt. stare a cavalcioni di. ♦ **to straddle** vi. mettersi a gambe divaricate.

straight[1] agg. 1. diritto, rettilineo 2. onesto, retto 3. ordinato || *a* — *whisky*, un whisky liscio.

straight[2] s. 1. posizione diritta 2. (*fig.*) condotta onesta.

straight[3] avv. 1. diritto, in linea retta 2. direttamente.

to straighten vt. raddrizzare. ♦ **to straighten** vi. raddrizzarsi.

straightforward agg. 1. diritto, diretto 2. schietto, leale.

straightforwardly avv. 1. in linea retta 2. francamente, schiettamente.

strain s. 1. tensione (*anche fig.*) 2. sforzo, fatica 3. distorsione, strappo muscolare.

to strain vt. 1. sottoporre a tensione 2. sforzare. ♦ **to strain** vi. sforzarsi.

strained agg. 1. teso 2. indebolito 3. non spontaneo, forzato.

strainer s. colino, filtro.

strait s. (*geogr.*) stretto. ♦ **to strand** vi. incagliarsi.

stranding s. incagliamento (*di una nave*).

strange agg. 1. strano, bizzarro 2. estraneo, sconosciuto.

stranger s. estraneo, sconosciuto, forestiero.

to **strangle** vt. strangolare.

strangling s. strangolamento.

strap s. 1. cinghia, correggia 2. maniglia a pendaglio (su tram ecc.).

to **strap** vt. legare con cinghia.

stratagem s. stratagemma.

strategic(al) agg. strategico.

strategist s. stratega.

strategy s. strategia.

stratification s. stratificazione.

to **stratify** vt. stratificare.

stratosphere s. stratosfera.

stratospheric agg. stratosferico.

stratum s. (pl. -ta) 1. strato 2. strato sociale.

straw s. 1. paglia 2. fuscello, cannuccia || — (-hat), paglietta; — -colour, giallo paglierino.

strawberry s. fragola.

stray agg. 1. smarrito, randagio 2. casuale. ♦ **stray** s. animale domestico smarrito.

to **stray** vi. vagare, vagabondare (anche fig.).

streak s. 1. striscia, striatura 2. vena (anche fig.).

to **streak** vt. 1. striare 2. venare.

stream s. 1. corso d'acqua, ruscello 2. flusso, fiotto 3. corrente (anche fig.).

to **stream** vi. 1. scorrere, fluire 2. ondeggiare || to — out, effondersi. ♦ **stream** vt. far scorrere.

street s. via, strada || one-way —, strada a senso unico.

streetwalker s. passeggiatrice.

strength s. 1. forza, vigore 2. solidità, tenacia.

to **strengthen** vt. rafforzare, irrobustire. ♦ to **strengthen** vi. rafforzarsi, irrobustirsi.

strengthening s. fortificante.

strenuous agg. strenuo, energico.

strenuously avv. strenuamente.

strenuousness s. vigore.

streptococcus s. (pl. -cci) streptococco.

streptomycin s. streptomicina.

stress s. 1. sforzo, pressione 2. enfasi 3. accento tonico.

to **stress** vt. 1. forzare 2. accentuare 3. porre in rilievo.

stretch s. 1. stiramento, tensione 2. spazio di tempo 3. distesa, estensione.

to **stretch** vt. tirare, tendere, stendere. ♦ to **stretch** vi. estendersi.

stretcher s. 1. tenditore 2. lettiga.

to **strew** (**strewed**, **strewn**) vt. spargere, sparpagliare.

strict agg. 1. preciso, esatto 2. (fig.) severo, rigido.

strictly avv. 1. esattamente 2. severamente.

stridden V. to **stride**.

stride s. 1. passo lungo, andatura || to make great strides, avanzare a grandi passi.

to **stride** (**strode**, **stridden**) vi. camminare a grandi passi.

strident agg. stridente.

strife s. contesa, lotta.

strike s. 1. sciopero 2. scoperta (di giacimento) 3. attacco aereo.

to **strike** (**struck**, **struck**) vt. e vi. 1. battere, colpire 2. (fig.) impressionare, colpire 3. suonare le ore 4. accendere (un fiammifero) 5. scioperare || to — down, abbattere; to — in, frapporsi.

striker s. 1. scioperante 2. (mecc.) percussore.

striking agg. sorprendente.

string s. 1. spago, cordicella 2. laccio 3. (mus.) corda.

to **string** (**strung**, **strung**) vt. e vi. 1. legare con corde 2. accordare (uno strumento) || to — up, impiccare.

strip s. striscia, nastro.

to **strip** vt. svestire. ♦ to **strip** vi. svestirsi.

stripe s. striscia, lista.

to **stripe** vt. rigare, listare.

striped agg. a righe, a strisce.

to **strive** (**strove**, **striven**) vi. sforzarsi.

strode V. to **stride**.

stroke s. 1. colpo, percossa 2. movimento 3. bracciata (al nuoto), remata, battuta (al tennis) 4. tratto (di penna ecc.) 5. rintocco (d'orologio) 6. (med.) colpo 7. carezza.

to **stroke**[1] vi. vogare in cadenza.

to **stroke**[2] vt. accarezzare, lisciare.

stroll s. passeggiata, quattro passi.

to **stroll** vi. gironzolare.

strolling agg. errante, girovago.

strong agg. forte, robusto, energico.

stronghold s. roccaforte.

strontium s. stronzio.

strove V. to **strive**.

struck V. to **strike**.

structural agg. strutturale.

structure s. 1. struttura 2. costruzione.

struggle s. **1.** lotta, combattimento **2.** sforzo || *hand-to-hand* —, lotta corpo a corpo.

to struggle *vi.* **1.** lottare, divincolarsi **2.** (*fig.*) sforzarsi.

struggler s. contendente, chi lotta.

to strum *vt.* e *vi.* strimpellare.

strumpet s. prostituta.

strung V. *to string.*

strut s. andatura solenne.

to strut *vi.* incedere con sussiego.

stub s. **1.** ceppo **2.** mozzicone.

stubble s. stoppia.

stubborn *agg.* ostinato, cocciuto, tenace, ribelle.

stubbornness s. caparbietà, tenacia.

to stucco *vt.* stuccare.

stuck V. *to stick.*

stud s. **1.** chiodo a capocchia larga **2.** bottoncino (*da camicia*).

to stud *vt.* guarnire di borchie.

student s. studente.

studentship s. borsa di studio.

studied *agg.* **1.** studiato, ricercato **2.** colto.

studio s. **1.** studio (*d'artista*) **2.** teatro di posa.

studious *agg.* studioso, diligente.

study s. **1.** studio **2.** esame attento, investigazione.

to study *vt.* e *vi.* **1.** studiare **2.** esaminare attentamente.

stuff s. **1.** sostanza, materia prima **2.** cosa, roba **3.** stoffa, tessuto.

to stuff *vt.* **1.** imbottire **2.** (*cuc.*) farcire **3.** rimpinzare.

stuffing s. **1.** imbottitura **2.** (*cuc.*) ripieno.

stuffy *agg.* afoso || — *air*, aria viziata.

to stumble *vi.* **1.** inciampare **2.** (*fig.*) fare passi falsi.

stump s. **1.** ceppo, tronco **2.** radice (*di dente*) **3.** piattaforma, podio.

to stun *vt.* stordire, tramortire.

stung V. *to sting.*

stunk V. *to stink.*

stunt s. (*gergo*) **1.** bravata, esibizione **2.** trovata pubblicitaria, notizia sensazionale.

stupefaction s. **1.** stupore **2.** torpore provocato da stupefacenti.

to stupefy *vt.* **1.** istupidire **2.** abbrutire. ♦ **to stupefy** *vi.* **1.** istupidirsi **2.** abbrutirsi.

stupendous *agg.* splendido, stupendo.

stupid *agg.* stupido, ottuso.

stupidity s. stupidità.

stupidly *avv.* stupidamente.

sturdy *agg.* **1.** vigoroso, forte **2.** risoluto.

to stutter *vt.* e *vi.* balbettare.

stuttering s. balbuzie.

sty s. porcile.

style s. **1.** stile (*anche fig.*) **2.** modello, genere **3.** moda.

to style *vt.* chiamare, denominare.

stylist s. stilista.

stylistic *agg.* stilistico.

stylization s. stilizzazione.

to stylize *vt.* stilizzare.

stylographic *agg.* stilografico.

stylus s. stilo.

subalpine *agg.* subalpino.

subaltern s. subalterno.

subaquatic *agg.* subacqueo.

subclass s. sottoclasse.

subcommission s. sottocommissione.

subcommissioner s. vice-commissario.

subcommittee s. sottocomitato.

subconscious *agg.* e s. subcosciente.

subcutaneous *agg.* sottocutaneo.

subdeacon s. suddiacono.

to subdivide *vt.* suddividere. ♦ **to subdivide** *vi.* suddividersi.

subdivisible *agg.* suddivisibile.

subdivision s. suddivisione.

subdual s. **1.** soggiogamento **2.** attenuazione.

to subdue *vt.* **1.** conquistare, soggiogare **2.** ridurre, attenuare.

subgovernor s. vicegovernatore.

subject[1] *agg.* **1.** soggetto, assoggettato **2.** sottoposto, esposto a.

subject[2] s. **1.** argomento, materia di studio **2.** (*gramm.*) soggetto **3.** suddito.

to subject *vt.* **1.** assoggettare **2.** esporre.

subjection s. **1.** assoggettamento **2.** dipendenza.

subjective *agg.* soggettivo.

subjectivism s. soggettivismo.

subjunctive s. congiuntivo.

sublease s. subaffitto.

to sublease *vt.* subaffittare.

to sublet (sublet, sublet) *vt.* subaffittare.

sublieutenancy s. grado di sottotenente.

sublieutenant s. sottotenente.

sublimate *agg.* e s. sublimato.

to sublimate *vt.* sublimare.

sublime *agg.* e s. sublime.

sublimity s. sublimità.

submarine agg. subacqueo. ♦ **submarine** s. sommergibile.

submariner s. sommergibilista.

to **submerge** vt. immergere, sommergere. ♦ to **submerge** vi. immergersi.

submergence s. sommersione.

submersible agg. affondabile.

submersion s. immersione.

submission s. sottomissione, docilità.

submissive agg. remissivo, docile.

submissively avv. in modo remissivo.

submissiveness s. sottomissione.

to **submit** vt. sottomettere, sottoporre. ♦ to **submit** vi. sottomettersi, assoggettarsi.

submultiple agg. e s. sottomultiplo.

subnormal agg. al di sotto della norma.

subordinacy s. subordinazione.

subordinate agg. subordinato. ♦ **subordinate** s. subalterno, inferiore.

to **subordinate** vt. subordinare.

subordination s. subordinazione.

to **suborn** vt. subornare, corrompere.

subornation s. subornazione.

subplot s. trama secondaria.

to **subscribe** vt. e vi. **1.** sottoscrivere, firmare **2.** aderire, trovarsi d'accordo **3.** abbonarsi.

subscriber s. **1.** the —, il sottoscritto **2.** abbonato.

subscription s. **1.** sottoscrizione **2.** abbonamento **3.** consenso.

subsequence s. susseguenza.

subsequent agg. successivo, ulteriore.

subsequently avv. successivamente.

to **subside** vi. **1.** calare, decrescere **2.** quietarsi **3.** cadere (sul fondo), depositare (di liquidi).

subsidiary agg. sussidiario, supplementare, ausiliario.

to **subsidize** vt. sussidiare.

subsidy s. sussidio.

to **subsist** vt. e vi. sussistere.

subsistence s. esistenza, sussistenza.

subsistent agg. sussistente.

subsoil s. sottosuolo.

subspecies s. sottospecie.

substance s. **1.** sostanza, essenza **2.** contenuto, l'essenziale **3.** solidità, fondamento.

substantial agg. **1.** sostanzioso, solido **2.** importante, notevole.

substantialism s. sostanzialismo.

substantiality s. **1.** sostanzialità **2.** concretezza.

substantially avv. sostanzialmente.

substantive agg. considerevole, reale. ♦ **substantive** s. (gramm.) sostantivo.

substitute s. **1.** sostituto **2.** surrogato, imitazione.

to **substitute** vt. e vi. sostituire.

substitution s. sostituzione.

substratum s. (pl. -ta) **1.** sostrato (anche fig.).

subtenancy s. subaffitto.

subtenant s. subaffittuario.

subterfuge s. sotterfugio.

subterranean agg. sotterraneo.

sub-title s. sottotitolo, didascalia.

subtle agg. **1.** penetrante, acuto, sottile **2.** elusivo, indefinibile.

subtleness s. **1.** sottigliezza, acutezza **2.** carattere elusivo.

subtlety s. sottigliezza.

subtly avv. **1.** acutamente, sottilmente **2.** elusivamente.

to **subtract** vt. sottrarre, detrarre.

subtraction s. sottrazione.

subtractive agg. sottrattivo.

subtrahend s. sottraendo.

suburb s. sobborgo. ♦ **suburbs** s. pl. periferia (sing.).

suburban agg. suburbano, periferico.

subversion s. sovversione.

subversive agg. sovversivo.

to **subvert** vt. sovvertire.

subway s. **1.** sottopassaggio **2.** (amer.) metropolitana.

to **succeed** vt. succedere a, seguire, subentrare a. ♦ to **succeed** vi. **1.** succedere, seguire **2.** riuscire, aver successo.

success s. successo, riuscita.

successful agg. che ha successo.

successfully avv. con successo.

succession s. successione, serie.

successive agg. successivo, seguente.

successively avv. successivamente.

successor s. successore.

succinct agg. succinto, conciso.

succulent agg. succulento.

to **succumb** vi. soccombere, soggiacere.

succursal s. succursale.

such agg. tale, simile: — that, — as, tale che, tale da. ♦ **such** pron. tale, tali, questo, quello, questa, quella, questi, quelli, queste, quelle.

suchlike *agg.* simile, dello stesso genere.

suck *s.* succhiata, poppata.

to suck *vt.* e *vi.* 1. succhiare, poppare 2. assorbire.

sucker *s.* 1. (*mecc.*) pistone 2. ventosa.

to suckle *vt.* allattare.

suckling *s.* lattante.

sudden *agg.* improvviso, inaspettato.
♦ **sudden** *s.* evento improvviso.

suddenly *avv.* inaspettatamente.

suddenness *s.* subitaneità.

to sue *vt.* e *vi.* 1. ricorrere in giudizio 2. sollecitare.

to suffer *vt.* e *vi.* 1. subire, patire 2. tollerare 3. soffrire.

suffering *s.* 1. sofferenza, pena 2. tolleranza.

sufficiency *s.* sufficienza.

sufficient *agg.* sufficiente.

suffix *s.* (*gramm.*) suffisso.

to suffocate *vt.* e *vi.* soffocare.

suffocation *s.* soffocamento.

suffrage *s.* 1. suffragio, diritto di voto 2. preghiera.

to suffuse *vt.* coprire, cospargere.

sugar *s.* 1. zucchero 2. (*fig.*) atteggiamento mellifluo || —*beet*, barbabietola da zucchero; — *cane*, canna da zucchero; — *tongs*, mollette per lo zucchero; *lump* —, zucchero in zollette.

to sugar *vt.* 1. inzuccherare 2. (*fig.*) addolcire, adulare.

sugariness *s.* 1. dolcezza 2. mellifluità.

sugary *agg.* 1. zuccheroso, zuccherino 2. (*fig.*) mellifluo.

to suggest *vt.* 1. suggerire 2. far nascere un'idea 3. insinuare.

suggestible *agg.* suggeribile, suggestionabile.

suggestion *s.* 1. suggerimento 2. suggestione 3. associazione di idee.

suggestive *agg.* stimolante, che ispira.

suggestiveness *s.* carattere allusivo.

suicidal *agg.* suicida, che ha tendenze al suicidio.

suicide *s.* 1. suicidio 2. suicida.

suit *s.* 1. domanda, preghiera 2. (*giur.*) causa 3. abito completo (*da uomo*) || —*case*, valigia.

to suit *vt.* adattare, convenire a, far comodo a. ♦ **to suit** *vi.* essere conveniente, accordarsi, adattarsi.

suitability *s.* convenienza.

suitable *agg.* adatto, idoneo.

suitably *avv.* appropriatamente.

suite *s.* 1. seguito, corteo 2. serie.

suitor *s.* 1. postulante 2. corteggiatore.

sulkiness *s.* malumore.

sulks *s. pl.* malumore, broncio (*sing.*).

sulky[1] *agg.* 1. imbronciato, scontroso 2. tetro.

sulky[2] *s.* "sulky", sediolo.

sullen *agg.* 1. accigliato 2. tetro.

sullenly *avv.* accigliato; di malumore.

sulphate *s.* solfato.

sulphide *s.* solfuro.

sulphite *s.* solfito.

sulphonamide *s.* sulfamidico.

sulphur *s.* zolfo || — *mine* (o — *pit*), solfatara.

to sulphur, to sulphurate *vt.* solforare.

sulphuric *agg.* solforico.

sulphurous *agg.* solforoso.

sultan *s.* sultano.

sultanate *s.* sultanato.

sultriness *s.* afa, caldo soffocante.

sultry *agg.* afoso, soffocante.

sum *s.* 1. somma, quantità (*di denaro*) 2. addizione.

to sum *vt.* e *vi.* sommare, addizionare || — *up*, riassumere.

summarily *avv.* sommariamente.

to summarize *vt.* e *vi.* riassumere.

summary *s.* sommario, ricapitolazione.

summer *s.* estate.

to summer *vi.* trascorrere l'estate.

summertime *s.* stagione estiva.

summit *s.* 1. cima, vetta 2. (*fig.*) culmine || *at the* — (*pol.*), al vertice.

to summon *vt.* 1. chiamare, mandare a chiamare 2. convocare 3. (*giur.*) citare.

summons *s.* (*giur.*) citazione, ingiunzione 2. convocazione.

sumptuous *agg.* sontuoso.

sumptuously *avv.* sontuosamente.

sumptuousness *s.* sontuosità.

sun *s.* sole || —*bath*, bagno di sole; — *glasses*, occhiali da sole.

to sun *vt.* esporre al sole. ♦ **to sun** *vi.* esporsi al sole.

to sun-bathe *vi.* fare i bagni di sole.

sunbeam *s.* raggio di sole.

sunbow *s.* arcobaleno.

sunburn *s.* 1. abbronzatura 2. scottatura (solare).

sunburnt agg. **1.** abbronzato **2.** scottato dal sole.

sunburst s. sprazzo di sole.

Sunday s. domenica.

to **sunder** vt. separare, recidere. ◆ to **sunder** vi. separarsi, scindersi.

sundry agg. parecchi, vari.

sunflower s. girasole.

sung V. to sing.

sunk V. to sink.

sunlight s. luce del sole.

sunlit agg. soleggiato.

sunny agg. luminoso, soleggiato.

sunproof agg. inalterabile al sole.

sunrise s. il sorgere del sole.

sunset s. tramonto (anche fig.).

sunshade s. parasole.

sunshine s. luce del sole.

sunspot s. macchia solare.

sunstroke s. insolazione.

sun-worship s. culto del Sole.

sup s. sorso, goccia.

to **sup¹** vt. e vi. sorseggiare.

to **sup²** vi. cenare.

superable agg. superabile.

to **superabound** vi. sovrabbondare.

superabundance s. sovrabbondanza.

superabundant agg. sovrabbondante.

superb agg. superbo, magnifico.

superciliary agg. sopracciliare.

supercilious agg. altero.

superelevation s. sopraelevazione.

superficial agg. superficiale, poco profondo.

superficiality s. superficialità.

superfluous agg. superfluo.

superhuman agg. sovrumano.

to **superimpose** vt. sovrapporre.

superintendence s. sovrintendenza.

superintendent s. sovrintendente.

superior agg. superiore.

superiority s. superiorità.

superlative agg. superlativo.

superman s. superuomo.

supermarket s. supermercato.

supermundane agg. ultraterreno.

supernatural agg. soprannaturale.

supernutrition s. supernutrizione.

to **supersede** vt. rimpiazzare.

supersensitive agg. ipersensibile.

supersensitiveness s. ipersensibilità.

supersession s. sostituzione.

supersonic agg. ultrasonoro, supersonico.

superstition s. superstizione.

superstitious agg. superstizioso.

superstructure s. sovrastruttura.

supertax s. soprattassa.

superterrestrial agg. ultraterreno.

to **supervise** vt. e vi. sovrintendere.

supervision s. sorveglianza, sovrintendenza.

supervisor s. sovrintendente.

supervisory agg. di controllo.

supine agg. supino (anche fig.).

supinely avv. supinamente.

supper s. cena || to have —, cenare; — -time, ora di cena.

to **supplant** vt. soppiantare.

supple agg. **1.** pieghevole, flessibile **2.** elastico (anche fig.).

supplement s. supplemento.

supplementary agg. supplementare.

suppliant agg. supplichevole. ◆ **suppliant** s. supplicante.

supply s. **1.** rifornimento, approvvigionamento **2.** (comm.) fornitura **3.** sostituto, supplente.

to **supply** vt. fornire, rifornire. ◆ to **supply** vi. fare da sostituto.

support s. sostegno, appoggio || in — of, in favore di.

to **support** vt. **1.** sostenere, reggere **2.** dare appoggio a **3.** mantenere.

supportable agg. sostenibile, sopportabile.

supporter s. **1.** sostegno **2.** fautore, sostenitore.

to **suppose** vt. supporre, presupporre, presumere.

supposed agg. presunto, supposto.

supposition s. supposizione, ipotesi.

suppository s. (med.) supposta.

to **suppress** vt. **1.** sopprimere, reprimere **2.** (fig.) soffocare, trattenere.

suppression s. **1.** soppressione **2.** il mettere a tacere.

to **suppurate** vi. suppurare.

suppuration s. suppurazione.

suprarenal agg. surrenale.

supremacy s. supremazia.

supreme agg. sommo, supremo.

surcharge s. **1.** sovraccarico **2.** soprattassa **3.** sovrapprezzo.

sure agg. sicuro, certo, fidato.

surely avv. sicuramente, certamente.

surety s. garanzia, pegno.

suretyship s. garanzia.

surf s. **1.** risacca **2.** spuma dei marosi.

surface s. superficie (anche fig.).

surfeit s. **1.** eccesso **2.** sazietà. ◆ to **surfeit** vt. saziare. ◆ to **sur-**

feit *vi.* saziarsi.
surge *s.* **1.** maroso, cavallone **2.** *(fig.)* impeto.
to **surge** *vi.* gonfiarsi, sollevarsi, tumultuare.
surgeon *s.* chirurgo.
surgery *s.* chirurgia.
surgical *agg.* chirurgico.
surlily *avv.* sgarbatamente.
surly *agg.* sgarbato.
to **surmount** *vt.* sormontare, superare.
surname *s.* **1.** cognome **2.** soprannome.
to **surname** *vt.* soprannominare.
to **surpass** *vt.* sorpassare, superare.
surpassing *agg.* superiore, eccellente.
surpassingly *avv.* straordinariamente.
surplus *s.* **1.** sovrappiù, eccedenza **2.** residuati di guerra.
surprise *s.* **1.** sorpresa **2.** stupore, meraviglia.
to **surprise** *vt.* **1.** sorprendere, cogliere all'improvviso **2.** stupire.
surprisedly *avv.* con sorpresa.
surprising *agg.* sorprendente.
surrealism *s.* surrealismo.
surrealist *agg.* e *s.* surrealista.
surrender *s.* **1.** resa, capitolazione **2.** abbandono, cessione.
to **surrender** *vt.* cedere, consegnare. ♦ to **surrender** *vi.* arrendersi.
surreptitious *agg.* clandestino, furtivo.
surrogate *s.* sostituto, supplente.
surround *s.* bordura, bordo.
to **surround** *vt.* **1.** circondare **2.** accerchiare.
surrounding *agg.* circostante. ♦ **surroundings** *s. pl.* dintorni.
survey *s.* esame, sguardo generale.
to **survey** *vt.* e *vi.* esaminare, fare rivelazioni.
surveyor *s.* ispettore.
survival *s.* **1.** sopravvivenza **2.** avanzo, reliquia.
to **survive** *vi.* sopravvivere. ♦ to **survive** *vt.* vivere più a lungo di.
survivor *s.* superstite.
susceptibility *s.* suscettibilità.
susceptible *agg.* **1.** suscettibile **2.** impressionabile.
suspect *agg.* sospetto. ♦ **suspect** *s.* persona sospetta.
to **suspect** *vt.* sospettare. ♦ to **suspect** *vi.* essere sospettoso.
to **suspend** *vt.* **1.** appendere, tenere

sospeso **2.** sospendere.
suspender *s.* giarrettiera, bretella.
suspense *s.* incertezza, attesa ansiosa.
suspension *s.* sospensione.
suspensive *agg.* sospensivo.
suspicion *s.* sospetto, dubbio.
suspicious *agg.* sospettoso, diffidente.
suspiciously *avv.* sospettosamente.
to **sustain** *vt.* **1.** mantenere, sostenere **2.** prolungare **3.** reggere.
sustainable *agg.* sostenibile.
sustenance *s.* mezzi di sussistenza *(pl.).*
suture *s.* sutura.
to **suture** *vt.* suturare.
swab *s.* **1.** strofinaccio **2.** *(mar.)* radazza **3.** *(med.)* tampone.
to **swab** *vt.* pulire, strofinare.
swag *s.* movimento ondeggiante.
swagger *s.* sgargiante.
to **swagger** *vi.* **1.** pavoneggiarsi **2.** gloriarsi.
swallow[1] *s.* rondine.
swallow[2] *s.* **1.** baratro **2.** deglutizione.
to **swallow** *vt.* e *vi.* **1.** deglutire, inghiottire **2.** *(fig.)* ingoiare.
swam V. to *swim*.
swamp *s.* palude ‖ — *-fever*, febbre malarica.
to **swamp** *vt.* inondare, inzuppare. ♦ to **swamp** *vi.* affondare (*anche fig.*).
swan *s.* cigno ‖ — *song*, canto del cigno.
swarm *s.* sciame, folla.
to **swarm** *vi.* **1.** sciamare **2.** pullulare, brulicare, essere affollato.
swash *s.* **1.** sciacquio **2.** gradassata.
to **swash** *vi.* **1.** spruzzare, sguazzare **2.** turbinare, infrangersi. ♦ to **swash** *vt.* far sguazzare.
to **swat** *vt.* colpire, schiacciare (*mosche ecc.*).
swathe *s.* benda, fascia.
to **swathe** *vt.* bendare, fasciare.
sway *s.* **1.** oscillazione **2.** potere, potenza, preponderanza.
to **sway** *vt.* **1.** sballottolare **2.** dominare, influenzare **3.** maneggiare, impugnare **4.** *(mar.)* issare. ♦ to **sway** *vi.* **1.** ondeggiare **2.** propendere **3.** predominare.
swear *s.* bestemmia, imprecazione.
to **swear** (**swore**, **sworn**) *vt.* e *vi.* **1.** giurare, far giurare **2.** imprecare, bestemmiare.

sweat s. sudore, traspirazione.
to sweat vt. e vi. traspirare, sudare, sfacchinare.
sweater s. **1.** chi suda **2.** maglione di lana.
sweating s. sudore || – -bath, bagno turco.
sweaty agg. **1.** sudato **2.** che fa sudare.
Swede s. svedese.
Swedish agg. svedese.
sweep s. **1.** scopata **2.** movimento circolare **3.** curva, distesa.
to sweep (swept, swept) vi. **1.** spazzare, scopare **2.** muoversi rapidamente **3.** estendersi. ◆ **to sweep (swept, swept)** vt. **1.** spazzare **2.** sfiorare.
sweeping agg. **1.** vasto **2.** completo **3.** rapido, impetuoso (di corrente). ◆ **sweepings** s. pl. rifiuti.
sweet agg. **1.** dolce, amabile **2.** piacevole, gentile. ◆ **sweet** s. **1.** dolce, torta **2.** caramella.
to sweeten vt. **1.** zuccherare **2.** addolcire. ◆ **to sweeten** vi. addolcirsi.
sweetening s. **1.** addolcimento **2.** sostanza che addolcisce.
sweetheart s. innamorato.
sweetly avv. dolcemente.
sweetmeat s. dolciumi; frutta candita.
sweetness s. **1.** sapore dolce **2.** dolcezza, amabilità.
swell s. **1.** rigonfiamento **2.** il gonfiarsi (dell'acqua ecc.).
to swell (swelled, swollen) vi. **1.** gonfiarsi **2.** crescere, aumentare. ◆ **to swell (swelled, swollen)** vt. gonfiare.
swelling s. rigonfiamento, ingrossamento.
swept V. to sweep.
to swerve vt. deviare. ◆ **to swerve** vi. fare uno scarto.
swift agg. rapido, veloce.
swim s. nuotata.
to swim (swam, swum) vi. nuotare. ◆ **to swim (swam, swum)** vt. attraversare a nuoto.
swimmer s. nuotatore.
swimming s. nuoto || – -belt, salvagente; – -pool, piscina.
swindle s. truffa, frode.
to swindle vt. e vi. truffare.
swindler s. truffatore.
swine s. maiale, porco || – -herd, porcaro.

swing s. **1.** oscillazione **2.** libertà d'azione **3.** altalena.
to swing (swung, swung) vi. **1.** dondolare, oscillare **2.** ruotare **3.** camminare dondolandosi. ◆ **to swing (swung, swung)** vt. **1.** far dondolare **2.** far ruotare.
swinging s. dondolio.
swish s. **1.** sibilo **2.** sferzata.
Swiss agg. svizzero.
switch s. **1.** verga, frustino **2.** (elett.) interruttore.
to switch vt. e vi. **1.** colpire con un frustino **2.** muovere bruscamente **3.** (ferr.) smistare || to – off, spegnere (la luce); to – on, accendere (la luce).
swollen V. to swell.
swoon s. svenimento.
to swoon vi. svenire.
to swoop vi. calare improvvisamente, abbattersi.
sword s. spada.
swore V. to swear.
sworn V. to swear.
swum V. to swim.
swung V. to swing.
sycamore s. sicomoro.
syllable s. sillaba.
syllogism s. sillogismo.
syllogistic agg. sillogistico.
to syllogize vt. e vi. sillogizzare.
sylph s. silfo, silfide.
sylvan agg. silvano, silvestre.
symbiosis s. simbiosi.
symbol s. simbolo.
symbolic(al) agg. simbolico.
symbolism s. simbolismo.
to symbolize vt. simboleggiare.
symmetric(al) agg. simmetrico.
symmetry s. simmetria.
sympathetic agg. **1.** sensibile, comprensivo **2.** congeniale, adatto.
to sympathize vi. condividere i sentimenti altrui.
sympathizer s. **1.** chi è comprensivo **2.** simpatizzante (di un partito ecc.).
sympathy s. **1.** comprensione, partecipazione **2.** condoglianze (pl.).
symphonic agg. sinfonico.
symphony s. sinfonia.
symposium s. simposio, banchetto.
symptom s. sintomo.
symptomatic(al) agg. sintomatico.
synagogue s. sinagoga.
synchronism s. sincronismo.
synchronization s. sincronizza-

zione.

to **synchronize** vt. e vi. sincronizzare.

to **syncopate** vt. sincopare.

syncope s. sincope.

syndicalism s. sindacalismo.

syndicate s. sindacato.

synod s. sinodo.

synonym s. sinonimo.

synonymous agg. sinonimo.

synonymy s. sinonimia.

synovitis s. sinovite.

syntactic(al) agg. sintattico.

syntax s. sintassi.

synthesis s. (pl. -ses) sintesi.

to **synthesize** vt. sintetizzare.

synthetic(al) agg. sintetico.

syntony s. sintonia.

syphilis s. sifilide.

syphilitic agg. sifilitico.

Syrian agg. e s. siriano.

syringe s. siringa.

syrup s. sciroppo.

syrupy agg. sciropposo.

system s. 1. sistema 2. metodo || railway —, rete ferroviaria.

systematic(al) agg. sistematico, metodico.

systematically avv. sistematicamente, metodicamente.

systematization s. sistemazione.

to **systematize** vt. ridurre a sistema.

T

tab s. 1. linguetta (di scarpa) 2. (mil.) mostrina 3. talloncino.

tabernacle s. 1. tabernacolo 2. tempio.

table s. 1. tavola 2. tavolata 3. tabella || —cloth, tovaglia; time- —, orario.

tablet s. 1. tavoletta 2. pastiglia, compressa.

tabloid s. pasticca.

taboo agg. e s. tabù.

tabular agg. 1. a forma di tabella 2. catalogato 3. piano, piatto.

tabulate agg. piano.

to **tabulate** vt. disporre in tabelle.

tabulation s. classificazione.

tabulator s. tabulatore.

tachometer s. tachimetro.

tachycardia s. tachicardia.

tacit agg. tacito.

taciturn agg. taciturno.

tack s. 1. chiodo 2. imbastitura 3. bordata 4. (fig.) linea di condotta.

to **tack** vt. 1. inchiodare 2. imbastire. ♦ to **tack** vi. 1. bordeggiare 2. virare.

tacking s. 1. l'inchiodare 2. imbastitura 3. bordeggio.

tackle s. 1. arnesi (pl.) 2. (mar.) paranco.

to **tackle** vt. 1. afferrare 2. affrontare (difficoltà ecc.).

tacky agg. viscoso.

tact s. tatto.

tactful agg. pieno di tatto.

tactical agg. tattico.

tactician s. tattico.

tactics s. tattica.

tactile agg. 1. tattile 2. tangibile.

tactility s. 1. tattilità 2. tangibilità.

tactless agg. senza tatto.

tactlessness s. mancanza di tatto.

tactual agg. tattile.

tadpole s. (zool.) girino.

tag s. 1. lembo pendente 2. cartellino 3. aggiunta 4. luogo comune || licence —, bollo di circolazione.

to **tag** vt. mettere cartellini a.

tail s. coda || —coat, marsina.

to **tail** vt. munire di coda. ♦ to **tail** vi. 1. essere in coda 2. seguire da presso || to — away, affievolirsi.

tailor s. sarto || —made costume, tailleur.

to **tailor** vi. fare il sarto. ♦ to **tailor** vt. fare un abito.

taint s. 1. infezione 2. tara 3. marchio.

to **taint** vt. guastare. ♦ to **taint** vi. guastarsi.

taintless agg. incontaminato.

take s. 1. presa 2. incasso 3. (cine) ripresa.

to **take** (**took, taken**) vt. 1. prendere 2. portare 3. accompagnare 4. necessitare || to — after, assomigliare; to — in, ricevere, ridurre, capire; to — off, togliere, decollare; to — on, assumere; to — to, darsi a.

take-off s. (aer.) decollo.

taking agg. 1. attraente 2. contagioso. ♦ **taking** s. 1. presa 2. incasso.

talc(um) s. talco || talcum powder, talco in polvere.

tale *s.* racconto, storia, novella.

talent *s.* talento.

talented *agg.* che ha talento.

talentless *agg.* senza talento.

tales *s. pl.* (*giur.*) giudici supplenti.

talisman *s.* talismano.

talk *s.* 1. conversazione 2. chiacchiera.

to talk *vt. e vi.* parlare, conversare, discutere || *to — out,* discutere a fondo.

talkative *agg.* loquace.

talkativeness *s.* loquacità.

talker *s.* 1. parlatore 2. chiacchierone.

talkies *s. pl.* (*gergo*) film sonoro (*sing.*).

talking *s.* conversazione.

talky *agg.* loquace.

tall *agg.* 1. alto 2. incredibile.

tallness *s.* altezza, statura.

tallow *s.* sego.

tally *s.* 1. tacca 2. cartellino, talloncino, etichetta.

to tally *vt.* registrare. ♦ to tally *vi.* combaciare.

tallyshop *s.* negozio che vende a rate.

talon *s.* 1. artiglio 2. (*mecc.*) dente 3. (*comm.*) matrice.

tamarind *s.* tamarindo.

tambourine *s.* tamburello.

tame *agg.* 1. addomesticato 2. mansueto 3. insipido, banale.

to tame *vt.* domare, addomesticare. ♦ to tame *vi.* ammansirsi.

tameable *agg.* addomesticabile.

tameless *agg.* indomito.

tamely *avv.* docilmente.

tameness *s.* 1. docilità 2. banalità.

tamer *s.* domatore.

taming *s.* addomesticamento.

to tamp *vt.* pigiare.

tamper *s.* pestello.

to tamper *vi.* 1. manomettere 2. immischiarsi: *to — with,* immischiarsi in 3. corrompere.

tamperer *s.* 1. falsificatore 2. corruttore 3. ficcanaso.

tampering *s.* 1. manomissione 2. corruzione.

tampon *s.* tampone.

tan *agg.* marrone rossiccio. ♦ tan *s.* 1. tannino 2. concia 3. abbronzatura.

to tan *vt.* 1. conciare 2. abbronzare. ♦ to tan *vi.* abbronzarsi.

tanning *s.* abbronzatura.

tang[1] *s.* 1. punta 2. odore, sapore penetrante.

tang[2] *s.* suono acuto.

to tang *vt.* far risuonare. ♦ to tang *vi.* risuonare.

tangency *s.* tangenza.

tangent *agg. e s.* tangente.

tangential *agg.* tangenziale.

tangerine *s.* mandarino.

tangibility *s.* tangibilità.

tangible *agg.* tangibile.

tangle *s.* groviglio.

to tangle *vt.* 1. aggrovigliare 2. intrappolare. ♦ to tangle *vi.* aggrovigliarsi.

tanglesome, tangly *agg.* ingarbugliato.

tank *s.* 1. serbatoio, cisterna 2. carro armato || *—truck,* autobotte.

tankard *s.* boccale.

tanker *s.* nave cisterna || *air —,* aerocisterna; *oil —,* petroliera.

tanner *s.* conciatore.

tannery *s.* conceria.

tannin *s.* tannino.

tanning *s.* concia.

to tantalize *vt.* tormentare.

tantalizing *agg.* allettante.

tantamount *agg.* equivalente.

tap[1] *s.* rubinetto, spina.

tap[2] *s.* colpetto.

to tap[1] *vt.* 1. spillare 2. forare.

to tap[2] *vt.* battere leggermente.

tape *s.* nastro || *— -recorder,* magnetofono; *recording —,* nastro magnetico.

to tape *vt.* 1. legare con un nastro 2. misurare con un nastro 3. incidere su nastro magnetico.

taper *agg.* conico, rastremato ♦ taper *s.* 1. candela 2. conicità, rastremazione.

to taper *vt.* assottigliare. ♦ to taper *vi.* assottigliarsi, restringersi.

tapestry *s.* arazzo.

tapeworm *s.* tenia.

tapir *s.* tapiro.

tar *s.* catrame.

to tar *vt.* incatramare.

tardiness *s.* 1. lentezza 2. indolenza.

tardy *agg.* 1. lento 2. svogliato.

tare *s.* tara.

target *s.* bersaglio.

tariff *s.* tariffa.

tarnish *s.* 1. appannamento 2. macchia.

to tarnish *vi.* 1. appannarsi 2. macchiarsi. ♦ to tarnish *vt.* 1. macchiare 2. inquinare.

tarpaulin s. telone impermeabile.

tarry agg. 1. catramato 2. simile a catrame.

to **tarry** vi. indugiare.

tart agg. aspro.

tart s. torta di frutta, crostata.

tartan[1] s. tessuto scozzese.

tartan[2] s. (mar.) tartana.

tartar agg. e s. tartaro.

tartaric agg. tartarico.

tartlet s. pasticcino.

tartly avv. in modo acido.

task s. compito, dovere, impresa.

to **task** vt. 1. assegnare un compito a 2. affaticare.

task-work s. lavoro a cottimo.

tassel s. 1. nappa 2. segnalibro.

to **tassel** vt. adornare di nappe.

taste s. 1. gusto 2. assaggio.

to **taste** vt. 1. gustare 2. assaggiare. ♦ to **taste** vi. sapere di.

tasteful agg. raffinato.

tastefulness s. buon gusto.

tasteless agg. 1. insipido 2. di cattivo gusto.

tastelessness s. 1. scipitezza 2. mancanza di gusto.

taster s. assaggiatore.

tasty agg. 1. saporito 2. (gergo) di buon gusto.

tatter s. cencio.

to **tatter** vt. stracciare. ♦ to **tatter** vi. cadere a pezzi.

tattery agg. stracciato.

tattle s. chiacchiera.

to **tattle** vi. chiacchierare.

tattler s. chiacchierone.

tattoo[1] s. tatuaggio.

tattoo[2] s. (mil.) 1. ritirata 2. carosello militare.

to **tattoo**[1] vt. tatuare.

to **tattoo**[2] vi. tamburellare.

taught V. to teach.

taunt s. sarcasmo.

to **taunt** vt. 1. rimproverare 2. schernire.

taunting agg. beffardo. ♦ **taunting** s. rimprovero sarcastico.

taut agg. 1. teso 2. in ordine.

to **tauten** vt. tendere. ♦ to **tauten** vi. tendersi.

tautness s. tensione.

tautologic(al) agg. tautologico.

tautology s. tautologia.

tavern s. taverna || — -keeper, oste.

taw s. biglia.

tawdry agg. sgargiante.

tawny agg. bruno fulvo.

tax s. 1. tassa 2. peso || — -payer, contribuente.

to **tax** vt. 1. tassare 2. accusare.

taxability s. tassabilità.

taxable agg. tassabile.

taxation s. tassazione.

taxi s. tassì || — -driver, tassista; (aer.) — track, pista di rullaggio.

to **taxi** vi. (aer.) rullare.

taxicab s. autopubblica.

taximeter s. tassametro.

tea s. tè || — -pot, teiera; high —, cena fredda; — -set, servizio da tè.

to **teach** (taught, taught) vt. insegnare.

teachable agg. 1. che apprende facilmente 2. che si insegna facilmente.

teacher s. insegnante.

teachership s. insegnamento.

teaching agg. che insegna. ♦ **teaching** s. insegnamento.

teacup s. tazza da tè.

team s. 1. squadra 2. tiro (di cavalli).

to **team** vt. aggiogare, accoppiarsi, raggrupparsi. ♦ to **team** vi. accoppiarsi, associarsi.

tear[1] s. 1. lacrima 2. goccia || — -gas, gas lacrimogeno.

tear[2] s. strappo, lacerazione.

to **tear** (tore, torn) vt. strappare, lacerare. ♦ to **tear** (tore, torn) vi. strapparsi.

tearful agg. lacrimoso.

tearing agg. violento. ♦ **tearing** s. strappo, lacerazione.

tear-off s. parte da staccare.

tease s. chi stuzzica.

to **tease** vt. 1. stuzzicare 2. cardare (lana ecc.).

teaser s. 1. seccatore 2. cardatore 3. questione difficile.

teaspoon s. cucchiaino da tè.

technical agg. tecnico.

technicality s. tecnicismo.

technician s. tecnico.

technique s. tecnica.

technological agg. tecnologico.

technology s. tecnologia.

tectonics s. 1. edilizia 2. tettonica.

tedious agg. tedioso.

tediousness s. tedio.

to **teem** vi. brulicare.

teen-ager s. adolescente.

teens s. pl. età da tredici a diciannove anni.

teeth V. tooth.

teething s. dentizione.

teetotal(l)er *s.* astemio.

telecast *s.* teletrasmissione || — **news**, telegiornale.

to telecast (telecast, telecast) *vt.* teletrasmettere.

telecommunication *s.* telecomunicazione.

telecontrol *s.* telecomando.

telegram *s.* telegramma.

telegraph *s.* telegrafo.

to telegraph *vt. e vi.* telegrafare.

telegraphic *agg.* telegrafico.

telegraphist *s.* telegrafista.

telegraphy *s.* telegrafia.

telemeter *s.* telemetro.

telepathy *s.* telepatia.

telephone *s.* telefono || — **booth**, cabina telefonica; — **-book**, elenco telefonico.

to telephone *vt. e vi.* telefonare.

telephonist *s.* telefonista.

telephony *s.* telefonia.

telephoto *s.* telefoto.

telephotograph *s.* telefotografia.

telescope *s.* telescopio.

to telescope *vi.* incastrarsi.

teletype *s.* telescrivente.

teletyper *s.* telescrivintista.

teletypewriter *s.* telescrivente.

to teleview *vt. e vi.* guardare la televisione.

televiewer *s.* telespettatore.

to televise *vt.* riprendere con la televisione.

television *s.* televisione || — **set**, televisore.

televisional *agg.* televisivo.

to tell (told, told) *vt. e vi.* 1. dire 2. raccontare 3. distinguere.

teller *s.* 1. narratore 2. (*comm.*) cassiere.

telling *agg.* efficace. ♦ **telling** *s.* 1. il raccontare 2. rivelazione.

telltale *s.* 1. chiacchierone 2. (*tec.*) controllore.

telluric *agg.* tellurico.

telpher *s.* cabina di funivia.

telpherage *s.* trasporto per teleferica.

temper *s.* 1. indole 2. umore 3. collera 4. moderazione.

to temper *vt.* temperare.

temperament *s.* temperamento.

temperamental *agg.* capriccioso.

temperance *s.* temperanza.

temperate *agg.* 1. temperato (*di clima*) 2. moderato.

temperature *s.* temperatura || **to have a** —, avere la febbre.

tempered *agg.* 1. temprato 2. moderato 3. di indole, umore || **quick** —, irritabile.

tempest *s.* tempesta.

temple[1] *s.* tempio.

temple[2] *s.* (*anat.*) tempia.

temporal *agg.* temporale.

temporariness *s.* temporaneità.

temporary *agg.* temporaneo.

temporization *s.* temporeggiamento.

to temporize *vi.* temporeggiare.

to tempt *vt.* tentare.

temptation *s.* tentazione.

tempter *s.* tentatore.

tempting *agg.* seducente.

ten *agg. e s.* dieci.

tenacious *agg.* 1. tenace 2. viscoso.

tenacity *s.* tenacia.

tenancy *s.* locazione.

tenant *s.* 1. proprietario 2. locatario.

to tend[1] *vt.* curare, badare a, custodire.

to tend[2] *vi.* tendere.

tendency *s.* tendenza.

tendential, tendentious *agg.* tendenzioso.

tender[1] *agg.* tenero || — **of**, sollecito verso.

tender[2] *s.* 1. guardiano, custode 2. nave di appoggio.

tender[3] *s.* offerta, proposta.

to tender *vt.* offrire, presentare.

tenderness *s.* 1. tenerezza 2. delicatezza.

tendon *s.* (*anat.*) tendine.

tendril *s.* viticcio.

tenebrous *agg.* tenebroso.

tenement *s.* 1. podere 2. abitazione.

tenor *s.* 1. tenore (*di vita ecc.*) 2. (*giur.*) copia esatta 3. (*mus.*) tenore.

tense[1] *agg.* teso.

tense[2] *s.* (*gramm.*) tempo.

to tense *vt.* tendere. ♦ **to tense** *vi.* tendersi.

tension *s.* tensione.

tent *s.* tenda.

tentacle *s.* tentacolo.

tentative *agg.* sperimentale. ♦ **tentative** *s.* tentativo, prova.

tenth *agg. e s.* decimo.

tenuity *s.* 1. tenuità 2. rarefazione 3. fluidità.

tenuous *agg.* 1. tenue 2. rarefatto 3. fluido.

tenure *s.* 1. possesso 2. gestione.

tepid *agg.* tiepido.

tepidity *s.* tepidezza.

tercet *s.* terzina.

tergal *agg.* dorsale.

to tergiversate *vi.* tergiversare.

tergiversation *s.* tergiversazione.

term *s.* 1. termine 2. (*scol.*) trimestre 3. (*giur.*) sessione 4. condizione. ♦ **terms** *s. pl.* rapporti.

to term *vt.* definire.

terminable *agg.* terminabile.

terminal *agg.* estremo. ♦ **terminal** *s.* 1. estremità 2. stazione di testa, capolinea 3. (*elettr.*) morsetto.

to terminate *vt.* 1. limitare 2. terminare. ♦ **to terminate** *vi.* 1. essere limitato 2. terminare.

termination *s.* 1. termine 2. (*gramm.*) desinenza.

terminator *s.* 1. chi termina 2. limite.

terminology *s.* terminologia.

terminus *s.* (*pl.* -ni) 1. capolinea 2. meta.

termite *s.* (*zool.*) termite.

tern *s.* terno.

ternary *agg.* ternario.

terrace *s.* 1. terrapieno 2. terrazzo (*sul tetto*) 3. fila di case.

terraqueous *agg.* terracqueo.

terrestrial *agg.* e *s.* terrestre.

terrible *agg.* terribile.

terrific *agg.* 1. spaventoso 2. (*fam.*) straordinario.

to terrify *vt.* atterrire.

territorial *agg.* territoriale.

territory *s.* territorio.

terror *s.* terrore.

terrorism *s.* terrorismo.

terrorist *s.* terrorista.

terroristic *agg.* terroristico.

to terrorize *vt.* terrorizzare.

terse *agg.* conciso.

terseness *s.* concisione.

tertiary *agg.* e *s.* terziario.

test *s.* 1. prova, esperimento, saggio 2. "test", reattivo psicologico || — *driver*, collaudatore; — *film*, provino; — *-tube*, provetta.

to test *vt.* 1. controllare 2. mettere alla prova 3. analizzare.

testament *s.* testamento.

testamentary *agg.* testamentario.

tester *s.* 1. collaudatore 2. apparecchio di misura 3. baldacchino.

testicle *s.* testicolo.

to testify *vt.* e *vi.* testimoniare.

testimonial *s.* 1. benservito 2. dono.

testimony *s.* testimonianza.

testing *s.* collaudo, prova.

tetanic(al) *agg.* tetanico.

tetanus *s.* tetano.

tetchy *agg.* stizzoso.

tetrahedron *s.* tetraedro.

tetralogy *s.* tetralogia.

Teutonic *agg.* teutonico.

text *s.* 1. testo 2. argomento.

textile *agg.* e *s.* tessile.

textual *agg.* testuale.

texture *s.* trama, tessuto.

thallium *s.* tallio.

than *cong.* che, di, di quello che (non), di quanto (non): *he is older — you*, è più vecchio di te.

to thank *vt.* ringraziare || — *you!*, grazie!

thankful *agg.* riconoscente.

thankfulness *s.* riconoscenza.

thankless *agg.* ingrato.

thanks *s. pl.* grazie, ringraziamenti.

thanksgiving *s.* ringraziamento.

that *agg.* (*pl.* those) quello, quella. ♦ **that** *pron. dimostr.* quello, questo, ciò. ♦ **that** *pron. rel.* che, il quale, la quale, i quali, le quali.

that *cong.* 1. che 2. affinché 3. purché.

thatch *s.* copertura di paglia (*per tetti*).

to thatch *vt.* coprire con paglia.

thaumaturge *s.* taumaturgo.

thaumaturgic(al) *agg.* taumaturgico.

thaw *s.* sgelo, disgelo.

to thaw *vt.* sgelare. ♦ **to thaw** *vi.* sgelarsi.

the *art.* il, lo, la, i, gli, le.

theatre *s.* teatro.

theatrical *agg.* teatrale.

theft *s.* furto.

their *agg. poss.* loro.

theirs *pron. poss.* il, la loro; i, le loro.

theism *s.* teismo.

them *pron.* loro, li, le, sé.

thematic *agg.* tematico.

theme *s.* tema.

themselves *pron.* r. 1. se stessi, se stesse, sé, si 2. essi stessi, esse stesse.

then *avv.* 1. allora 2. poi.

theocracy *s.* teocrazia.

theocratic(al) *agg.* teocratico.

theologian *s.* teologo.

theologic(al) *agg.* teologico.

theology *s.* teologia.

theorem *s.* teorema.

theoretic(al) *agg.* teorico.

theoretics *s.* teoretica.

theorist *s.* teorico.

to theorize *vi.* teorizzare.

theory *s.* teoria.

therapeutic(al) *agg.* terapeutico.

therapeutics *s.* terapeutica.

therapy *s.* terapia.

there *avv.* 1. là, lì 2. ci, vi 3. in ciò. ◆ **there** *inter.* ecco! su!

thereabout(s) *avv.* 1. là vicino 2. all'incirca.

thereby *avv.* per mezzo di, perciò.

therefore *avv.* quindi, dunque.

thereupon *avv.* al che, tosto.

thermal *agg.* termico, termale.

thermic *agg.* termico.

thermionic *agg.* termoionico.

thermodynamics *s.* termodinamica.

thermoelectric *agg.* termoelettrico.

thermometer *s.* termometro.

thermonuclear *agg.* termonucleare.

thermostat *s.* termostato.

these (*pl. di* this), questi, queste.

thesis *s.* (*pl.* -ses) tesi, dissertazione.

thews *s. pl.* muscoli.

they *pron. pers.* 1. essi, esse, loro 2. (*in costruzioni impersonali*) si: — *say,* si dice.

thick *agg.* 1. spesso, grosso: *a — book,* un grosso libro 2. fitto, folto 3. denso, torbido.

to thicken *vt.* ispessire, addensare. ◆ **to thicken** *vi.* ispessirsi, addensarsi.

thickening *s.* ispessimento.

thicket *s.* boschetto.

thickly *avv.* fittamente, densamente.

thickness *s.* 1. spessore, grossezza 2. densità 3. strato.

thickset *agg.* 1. fitto, spesso 2. tarchiato.

thief *s.* (*pl.* thieves) ladro.

to thieve *vt. e vi.* rubare, essere ladro.

thievish *agg.* ladresco.

thigh *s.* coscia || — *bone,* femore.

thimble *s.* ditale.

thin *agg.* 1. sottile 2. magro, snello 3. rado, raro 4. fluido, rarefatto 5. debole, fiacco.

to thin *vt. e vi.* 1. assottigliare, assottigliarsi, dimagrire 2. diradare, sfoltire. ◆ **to thin** *vt.* 1. assottigliare 2. diradare, sfoltire. ◆ **to thin** *vi.* 1. assottigliarsi 2. diradarsi.

thing *s.* 1. cosa, oggetto 2. argomen-

to, soggetto.

to think (thought, thought) *vt. e vi.* 1. pensare, riflettere 2. ritenere, considerare 3. credere, aspettarsi || *to — of,* pensare, avere in animo di; *to — ill of so.,* avere una cattiva opinione di qu.; *to — out,* escogitare; *to — over,* riflettere.

thinkable *agg.* concepibile, immaginabile.

thinker *s.* pensatore.

thinking *agg.* pensante, ragionevole ◆ **thinking** *s.* pensiero, riflessione, opinione.

thinness *s.* sottigliezza, tenuità, magrezza, radezza.

third *agg. e s.* terzo.

thirdly *avv.* in terzo luogo.

third-rate *agg.* di terz'ordine.

thirst *s.* 1. sete, arsura 2. (*fig.*) avidità.

thirsty *agg.* assetato || *to be —,* aver sete; *to be — for* (*fig.*), bramare.

thirteen *agg.* tredici.

thirteenth *agg.* tredicesimo.

thirtieth *agg.* trentesimo.

thirty *agg.* trenta.

this *agg. e pron. dimostr.* (*pl.* these) questo, questa.

Thomism *s.* tomismo.

thomist *s.* tomista.

thorax *s.* torace.

thorn *s.* spina (*anche fig.*).

thorny *agg.* spinoso (*anche fig.*).

thorough *agg.* 1. completo, totale 2. perfetto, esperto 3. meticoloso.

thoroughbred *agg.* 1. purosangue (*di cavallo*) 2. di antico lignaggio. ◆ **thoroughbred** *s.* purosangue.

thoroughfare *s.* arteria di grande traffico || *no —,* passaggio vietato.

those (*pl. di* that) quelli, quelle.

though *avv.* comunque, tuttavia. ◆ **though** *cong.* benché, sebbene.

thought V. **to think**.

thought *s.* 1. pensiero, riflessione 2. idea, parere 3. concezione.

thoughtful *agg.* 1. pensoso, pensieroso 2. sollecito.

thoughtless *agg.* sconsiderato, sventato, negligente.

thoughtlessness *s.* sconsideratezza, negligenza.

thousand *agg.* mille. ◆ **thousand** *s.* migliaio.

thrall *s.* schiavo.

to thrash *vt. e vi.* 1. battere, sferzare 2. (*mar.*) navigare contro vento 3. trebbiare 4. bastonare || *to* — *out*, dibattere.

thrasher *s.* trebbiatore.

thrashing machine *s.* trebbiatrice.

thread *s.* 1. filo (*anche fig.*) 2. vena, filone.

to thread *vt.* 1. infilare 2. far passare attraverso.

threadbare *agg.* 1. consumato, consunto 2. (*fig.*) vieto, trito.

threading *s.* filettatura.

threadlike *agg.* filiforme.

threat *s.* minaccia.

to threaten *vt.* e *vi.* minacciare.

threatening *agg.* minaccioso.

three *agg.* e *s.* tre.

threescore *agg.* sessanta.

to thresh *vt.* e *vi.* trebbiare.

threshold *s.* 1. soglia, limitare 2. (*fig.*) esordio, inizio.

threw V. *to throw.*

thrice *avv.* tre volte.

thriftiness *s.* economia, parsimonia.

thrifty *agg.* frugale, economo.

thrill *s.* brivido, palpito.

to thrill *vt.* far fremere, elettrizzare. ♦ **to thrill** *vi.* fremere, vibrare, emozionarsi.

thriller *s.* (*gergo*) storia, film sensazionale, poliziesco.

thrilling *agg.* 1. sensazionale, emozionante 2. penetrante.

to thrive (throve, thriven) *vi.* 1. prosperare, fiorire 2. crescere vigorosamente.

thriving *agg.* 1. prospero, fiorente 2. rigoglioso.

throat *s.* gola || — *wash*, gargarismo; *sore* —, mal di gola.

throaty *agg.* gutturale.

throb *s.* battito, pulsazione, fremito.

to throb *vi.* battere, pulsare, fremere.

throbbing *agg.* palpitante, vibrante (*anche fig.*).

thrombosis *s.* trombosi.

throne *s.* trono.

throng *s.* folla, moltitudine.

to throng *vt.* affollare, stipare. ♦ **to throng** *vi.* affollarsi, affluire.

to throttle *vt.* strozzare, strangolare.

through *avv.* 1. attraverso, da una parte all'altra 2. (*ferr.*) direttamente || — *train*, treno diretto.

through *prep.* 1. attraverso, per 2. durante, per tutta la durata di

3. per mezzo.

throughout *avv.* da un capo all'altro, dal principio alla fine. ♦ **throughout** *prep.* in ogni parte di, durante tutto il, dal principio alla fine di.

throve V. *to thrive.*

throw *s.* lancio, gittata (*di missile ecc.*), tiro.

to throw (threw, thrown) *vt.* e *vi.* 1. gettare, scagliare, proiettare 2. atterrare, rovesciare || *to* — *away*, buttar via; *to* — *off*, buttar fuori; *to* — *out* espellere.

throwback *s.* 1. movimento brusco all'indietro 2. ostacolo.

thrown V. *to throw.*

thrush *s.* tordo.

thrust *s.* 1. colpo, botta 2. colpo con arma appuntita.

to thrust (thrust, thrust) *vt.* e *vi.* 1. spingere, ficcare 2. frapporre 3. forzare.

thud *s.* tonfo, rumore sordo.

to thud *vi.* fare un rumore sordo.

thumb *s.* pollice.

to thumb *vt.* 1. lasciare ditate su (*un foglio ecc.*) 2. strimpellare.

thump *s.* rumore sordo.

to thump *vt.* battere, percuotere, dar pugni.

thumping *agg.* pesante.

thunder *s.* 1. tuono: *a peal of* —, un colpo di tuono 2. scoppio, rombo 3. fulmine (*anche fig.*).

to thunder *vt.* e *vi.* 1. tuonare, rimbombare 2. minacciare.

thunderbolt *s.* fulmine, saetta (*anche fig.*).

thundering *agg.* 1. tonante, fulminante 2. (*fam.*) straordinario.

thundery *agg.* minaccioso.

Thursday *s.* giovedì.

thus *avv.* così, in questo modo.

to thwart *vt.* opporsi a, ostacolare.

thyme *s.* timo.

thyroid *s.* tiroide.

tibia *s.* tibia.

tick *s.* tic-tac, ticchettio (*di orologio*).

to tick *vt.* e *vi.* ticchettare.

ticket *s.* 1. biglietto, tessera, scontrino 2. (*mil.*) congedo || — *collector*, bigliettaio; — *inspector*, controllore; *single* —, biglietto di andata.

to ticket *vt.* 1. mettere il cartellino del prezzo a 2. fornire di biglietto.

ticking s. traliccio.

tickle s. solletico.

to **tickle** vt. fare il solletico, solleticare (anche fig.). ♦ to **tickle** vi. prudere.

tickler s. 1. chi solletica 2. questione delicata.

ticklish agg. 1. sensibile al solletico 2. scabroso.

tide s. 1. marea 2. (fig.) corrente, corso || − −gauge, mareografo.

to **tide** vi. salire, crescere come la marea.

tidily avv. lindamente.

tidings s. pl. novità.

tidy agg. ordinato, preciso, pulito.

to **tidy** vt. riordinare, mettere in ordine.

tie s. 1. laccio, legaccio 2. cravatta 3. (fig.) legame 4. (ferr.) traversina.

to **tie** vt. 1. legare, allacciare, congiungere (anche fig.) 2. annodare.

tied agg. vincolato, schiavo.

tier s. ordine, fila (di posti).

to **tier** vt. allineare.

tiff s. stizza, bisticcio || to be in a −, essere in collera.

to **tiff** vi. essere stizzito.

tiger s. tigre.

tight agg. 1. impermeabile, a perfetta tenuta 2. teso, tirato 3. stretto, aderente, attillato 4. scarso, a corto di denaro 5. (gergo) ubriaco. ♦ **tight** avv. 1. ermeticamente 2. in maniera tesa.

to **tighten** vt. 1. serrare 2. tirare, tendere. ♦ to **tighten** vi. 1. serrarsi 2. tendersi.

tightly avv. ermeticamente, strettamente.

tightness s. 1. impermeabilità, tenuta 2. tensione 3. (gergo) ubriachezza.

tights s. pl. calzamaglia.

tigress s. tigre (femmina).

tile s. 1. tegola, mattonella, piastrella 2. (fam.) cappello a cilindro.

to **tile** vt. coprire di tegole, piastrelle.

tilemaking s. fabbricazione di tegole.

tilery s. fabbrica di tegole.

tiling s. tegolato, piastrellatura.

till¹ prep. fino a: − now, fino ad ora. ♦ **till** cong. finché, fino al momento in cui.

till² s. cassetto in cui si custodisce il denaro.

to **till** vt. dissodare, arare.

tillage s. 1. dissodamento, aratura 2. terreno coltivato.

tiller s. 1. aratore 2. (mar.) barra del timone.

tilt¹ s. tenda, tendone.

tilt² s. 1. torneo, giostra 2. contesa, disputa 3. inclinazione, pendenza.

to **tilt** vt. 1. inclinare 2. rovesciare. ♦ to **tilt** vi. 1. oscillare 2. (mar.) beccheggiare.

timber s. 1. legname da costruzione 2. bosco con alberi d'alto fusto 3. trave 4. (fig.) tempra, carattere 5. (mar.) costola || − −work, costruzione in legno.

to **timber** vt. rivestire di legno.

timbre s. timbro (di suoni).

time s. 1. tempo, periodo di tempo, circostanza, epoca, età 2. volta, volte 3. orario, ora || with −, col passar del tempo; from − to −, di tanto in tanto; as times go, coi tempi che corrono; at times, a volte; in good −, per tempo; what − is it?, che ore sono?

to **time** vt. fissare l'orario di. ♦ to **time** vi. tenere il tempo.

timekeeper s. 1. cronometro 2. cronometrista.

timeliness s. tempestività.

timely agg. opportuno, tempestivo.

timepiece s. orologio (da tavolo).

timer s. cronometrista.

time-study agg. − engineer, analista tempi.

timid agg. timido.

timidity s. timidezza.

timing s. 1. calcolo del tempo (di pose fotografiche ecc.) 2. (mecc.) messa in fase.

timorous agg. timoroso.

tin s. 1. stagno, latta 2. recipiente. to **tin** vt. 1. stagnare 2. conservare in scatola.

tincture s. 1. (chim.) tintura, soluzione alcoolica 2. tinta 3. sfumatura, traccia 4. gusto, aroma.

to **tincture** vt. 1. tingere, colorare 2. aromatizzare.

tinder s. esca (per fuoco).

tinge s. 1. sfumatura, tocco 2. (fig.) pizzico.

to **tinge** vt. dare una sfumatura a (anche fig.).

to **tingle** vt. 1. pizzicare 2. far tintinnare. ♦ to **tingle** vi. arrossire (di guance).

tink s. tintinnio.

tinker *s.* calderaio (*ambulante*), stagnino.

to **tinker** *vt.* rabberciare, riparare.

tinkle *s.* tintinnio.

to **tinkle** *vt.* far tintinnare. ♦ to **tinkle** *vi.* tintinnare.

tinkling *s.* tintinnio.

tinsel *agg.* vistoso, sgargiante. ♦ **tinsel** *s.* orpello (*anche fig.*).

tint *s.* tinta, colore delicato, sfumatura.

to **tint** *vt.* colorire, tinteggiare.

tiny *agg.* minuscolo.

tip[1] *s.* **1.** punta, cima **2.** puntale.

tip[2] *s.* **1.** immondezzaio **2.** inclinazione.

tip[3] *s.* mancia.

to **tip**[1] *vt.* toccare, battere leggermente.

to **tip**[2] *vt.* **1.** rovesciare **2.** inclinare. ♦ to **tip** *vi.* **1.** rovesciarsi **2.** inclinarsi.

to **tip**[3] *vt.* e *vi.* **1.** dare la mancia **2.** (*gergo*) dare, passare.

tippet *s.* mantellina.

tipsy *agg.* ubriaco.

tiptoe *s.* punta dei piedi: *on* —, in punta di piedi.

to **tiptoe** *vi.* camminare in punta di piedi.

tire *s.* **1.** cerchione di ruota **2.** pneumatico || *flat* —, gomma a terra.

to **tire**[1] *vt.* stancare, annoiare. ♦ to **tire** *vi.* stancarsi, annoiarsi.

to **tire**[2] *vt.* fornire di cerchione, di pneumatico.

tired *agg.* stanco, affaticato, esausto || *to be* — *out*, essere stanco morto.

tireless *agg.* instancabile.

tiresome *agg.* faticoso, stancante, noioso.

tissue *s.* tessuto || —*paper*, carta velina.

Titan *s.* titano, gigante.

titanic *agg.* titanico (*anche fig.*).

title *s.* **1.** titolo **2.** titolo, grado, qualifica.

to **title** *vt.* **1.** intitolare, intestare **2.** conferire un titolo.

titular *s.* titolare.

to **toad** *s.* rospo.

toady *s.* adulatore.

to **toady** *vt.* adulare, comportarsi servilmente.

toast[1] *s.* pane abbrustolito, crostino.

toast[2] *s.* brindisi.

to **toast**[1] *vt.* abbrustolire, tostare.

to **toast**[2] *vt.* e *vi.* fare un brindisi.

toaster *s.* tostapane.

tobacco *s.* tabacco || —*box*, tabacchiera.

tobacconist *s.* tabaccaio || —'*s shop*, tabaccheria.

tocsin *s.* segnale d'allarme.

today *s.* oggi. ♦ **today** *avv.* oggigiorno.

toddle *s.* andatura incerta, vacillante.

to **toddle** *vi.* camminare a passi incerti, passeggiare.

toe *s.* dito del piede.

together *avv.* assieme, insieme, unitamente.

toil[1] *s.* fatica, duro lavoro || —*worn*, sfinito dalla fatica.

toil[2] *s.* laccio, trappola (*anche fig.*).

to **toil**[1] *vi.* faticare, lavorare duramente.

to **toil**[2] *vt.* prendere in trappola (*anche fig.*).

toilet *s.* **1.** toletta, pulizia **2.** abbigliamento **3.** bagno, gabinetto || —*paper*, carta igienica.

toilsome *agg.* faticoso, laborioso.

token *s.* **1.** segno, simbolo **2.** prova, pegno, ricordo.

tolerable *agg.* **1.** tollerabile **2.** discreto.

tolerance *s.* tolleranza.

tolerant *agg.* tollerante.

to **tolerate** *vt.* tollerare, sopportare.

toleration *s.* tolleranza.

toll[1] *s.* pedaggio, dazio, gabella.

toll[2] *s.* rintocco (*di campana*).

to **toll**[1] *vt.* suonare. ♦ to **toll** *vi.* rintoccare.

tomato *s.* pomodoro.

tomb *s.* tomba.

tomboy *s.* ragazza indiavolata.

tome *s.* tomo, volume.

tomfool *agg.* e *s.* sciocco, banale.

tommy *s.* **1.** pane, pagnotta **2.** provviste (*che l'operaio porta da casa*) (*pl.*).

tommy-gun *s.* fucile mitragliatore, mitra.

tomorrow *s.* e *avv.* domani.

ton *s.* tonnellata.

tonality *s.* tonalità.

tone *s.* tono, timbro, accento.

to **tone** *vt.* e *vi.* **1.** (*mus.*) dare il tono, intonare, accordare **2.** (*pitt.*) sfumare.

toneless *agg.* inespressivo, privo di colore, senza vigore.

tongs *s. pl.* pinze, molle, tenaglie.

tongue *s.* **1.** lingua **2.** lingua, linguaggio **3.** lingua (*di terra, fuoco*) || —*tied*, muto, taciturno; — —*twister*, scioglilingua.

to **tongue** *vt.* leccare, lambire.

tonic *agg.* tonico, corroborante. ♦ **tonic** *s.* (*med.*) tonico, energetico.

tonight *avv.* e *s.* stanotte, stasera.

tonnage *s.* tonnellaggio, stazza.

tonsil *s.* tonsilla.

tonsillitis *s.* tonsillite.

tonsure *s.* tonsura.

to **tonsure** *vt.* tonsurare.

too *avv.* **1.** troppo **2.** anche, pure **3.** inoltre.

took V. *to take.*

tool *s.* **1.** arnese, attrezzo, utensile **2.** (*fig.*) strumento.

tooth *s.* (*pl.* teeth) **1.** dente, zanna **2.** dente (*di pettine, forchetta ecc.*) || —*paste*, dentifricio; — *pick*, stuzzicadenti.

toothache *s.* mal di denti.

toothbrush *s.* spazzolino da denti.

toothing *s.* dentatura, dentellatura.

toothless *agg.* sdentato.

toothy *agg.* dai denti sporgenti.

top¹ *s.* **1.** cima, sommità **2.** (*fig.*) apice **3.** parte superiore, "capote" di automobile.

top² *s.* trottola.

topaz *s.* topazio.

topic *s.* argomento, soggetto.

topical *agg.* d'attualità.

topographer *s.* topografo.

topographic(al) *agg.* topografico.

topography *s.* topografia.

topology *s.* topologia.

toponymy *s.* toponomastica.

topsail *s.* vela di gabbia.

topsyturvy *agg.* sottosopra, capovolto. ♦ **topsyturvy** *s.* capovolgimento, disordine, scompiglio. ♦ **topsyturvy** *avv.* sottosopra.

to **topsyturvy** *vt.* mettere sossopra.

toque *s.* berretto, tocco.

torch *s.* torcia, fiaccola || *electric* —, lampadina tascabile.

torchlight *s.* luce di fiaccole, torce || —*procession*, fiaccolata.

tore V. *to tear.*

torment *s.* tormento, tortura.

to **torment** *vt.* tormentare.

torn V. *to tear.*

tornado *s.* ciclone.

torpedo *s.* **1.** (*zool.*) torpedine **2.** (*mar.*) siluro || — *boat*, torpediniera; — *boat destroyer*, cacciatorpediniere.

to **torpedo** *vt.* silurare.

torpid *agg.* torpido, apatico.

torpor *s.* torpore.

torrefaction *s.* torrefazione.

to **torrefy** *vt.* torrefare.

torrent *s.* torrente (*anche fig.*).

torrential *agg.* torrenziale.

torrid *agg.* torrido.

torsion *s.* torsione.

tortoise *s.* tartaruga.

torture *s.* tortura, tormento (*anche fig.*).

to **torture** *vt.* torturare, tormentare.

torturous *agg.* tormentoso.

toss *s.* **1.** lancio **2.** movimento del capo.

to **toss** *vt.* **1.** gettare, lanciare **2.** agitare, scuotere **3.** disarcionare. ♦ to **toss** *vi.* **1.** agitarsi, smaniare **2.** tirare a sorte **3.** (*mar.*) beccheggiare.

total *agg.* totale, completo. ♦ **total** *s.* totale.

totalitarian *agg.* totalitario.

totalitarianism *s.* totalitarismo.

totality *s.* totalità.

totalizator *s.* totalizzatore.

to **totalize** *vt.* e *vi.* totalizzare.

totalizer *s.* totalizzatore.

to **totter** *vi.* camminare barcollando.

tottering *agg.* vacillante, malsicuro.

touch *s.* **1.** tocco, colpetto **2.** tatto **3.** contatto, rapporto.

to **touch** *vt.* **1.** toccare **2.** sfiorare **3.** (*fig.*) colpire, commuovere. ♦ to **touch** *vi.* essere in contatto, confinare.

touchiness *s.* suscettibilità.

touching *agg.* toccante, commovente. ♦ **touching** *prep.* riguardo a.

touchstone *s.* pietra di paragone.

touchwood *s.* esca (*per accendere il fuoco*).

touchy *agg.* permaloso.

tough *agg.* **1.** duro **2.** forte, robusto **3.** (*fig.*) inflessibile **4.** difficile **5.** violento.

to **toughen** *vt.* indurire. ♦ to **toughen** *vi.* indurirsi.

toughness *s.* **1.** durezza **2.** inflessibilità.

tour *s.* giro, viaggio, escursione.

to **tour** *vt.* e *vi.* fare un viaggio.

tourism s. turismo.

tourist s. turista.

tourmalin(e) s. tormalina.

tournament s. torneo.

to **tousle** vt. scompigliare, arruffare.

tow s. rimorchio.

toward(s) prep. 1. verso, in direzione di 2. riguardo a 3. verso, circa (di tempo).

towel s. asciugamano || — -horse, porta-asciugamani.

tower s. torre.

to **tower** vi. torreggiare.

towing s. rimorchio.

town s. 1. città 2. cittadinanza || — -council, consiglio comunale; — -planning, piano regolatore; chief —, capoluogo.

townhall s. municipio.

townhouse s. residenza di città.

townscape s. veduta (di città).

townsfolk s. abitanti di una città.

township s. territorio, giurisdizione di una città.

townsman s. cittadino.

townspeople s. cittadinanza.

townward(s) avv. verso la città.

toxic(al) agg. tossico.

toxicity s. tossicità.

toxicologist s. tossicologo.

toxicology s. tossicologia.

toxin s. tossina.

toy s. 1. giocattolo 2. bazzecola, storiella.

to **toy** vi. giocherellare, trastullarsi.

toyish agg. 1. simile a giocattolo 2. insignificante.

toyshop s. negozio di giocattoli.

trabeation s. trabeazione.

trace s. traccia, orma.

to **trace** vt. 1. tracciare 2. seguire le tracce 3. rintracciare || to — back, risalire.

traceable agg. 1. rintracciabile 2. che si può tracciare.

trachea s. trachea.

tracheal agg. tracheale.

tracheitis s. tracheite.

trachyte s. trachite.

tracing s. 1. tracciato 2. calco, ricalco.

track s. 1. traccia, orma 2. sentiero, corso (anche fig.) 3. (sport) pista 4. (ferr.) binario || sound — (cine), colonna sonora.

to **track** vt. 1. inseguire, pedinare 2. tracciare un sentiero. ♦ to **track** vi. posare i binari.

tract[1] s. periodo, tratto, spazio.

tract[2] s. opuscolo.

tractability s. arrendevolezza.

tractable agg. arrendevole.

traction s. 1. trazione 2. contrazione.

tractor s. trattore.

trade s. 1. mestiere 2. commercio, traffico 3. commercianti (pl.) || — bank, banca commerciale; — dispute, vertenza sindacale; — -mark, marchio di fabbrica; — -show (cine), anteprima per la critica; free— —, libero scambio.

to **trade** vt. e vi. commerciare, negoziare.

trader s. 1. commerciante 2. nave mercantile.

trading s. commercio.

tradition s. tradizione.

traditional agg. tradizionale.

traditionalism s. tradizionalismo.

traditionalist s. tradizionalista.

to **traduce** vt. calunniare.

traffic s. 1. traffico, commercio 2. traffico, circolazione || — lights, semaforo; — jam, ingorgo stradale.

tragedian s. 1. tragediografo 2. attore tragico.

tragedy s. tragedia.

tragic(al) agg. tragico.

tragicomedy s. tragicommedia.

tragicomic(al) agg. tragicomico.

trail s. 1. traccia, striscia 2. pista, orma 3. cammino, sentiero.

to **trail** vt. 1. trascinare 2. seguire le tracce di. ♦ to **trail** vi. trascinarsi.

trailer s. 1. inseguitore, cacciatore 2. rimorchio 3. (cine) film di prossima programmazione.

train s. 1. treno: express — (o fast —), rapido; slow —, accelerato 2. seguito, corteo 3. serie, successione, fila.

to **train** vt. 1. allevare, educare 2. esercitare, allenare, addestrare. ♦ to **train** vi. 1. esercitarsi, allenarsi 2. viaggiare in ferrovia.

trainer s. istruttore, allenatore.

training s. educazione, ammaestramento, allenamento.

trait s. tratto, fattezza, caratteristica.

traitor s. traditore.

trajectory s. traiettoria.

tram s. 1. tram 2. carrello da miniera || — -conductor, tranviere.

trammel s. 1. tramaglio 2. intoppo.

tramp s. 1. calpestio 2. viaggio a piedi.

to **tramp** vt. 1. camminare pesantemente 2. viaggiare a piedi 3. vagabondare.

trample s. calpestio.

to **trample** vt. 1. calpestare 2. (fig.) offendere. ◆ to **trample** vi. camminare pesantemente.

tramway s. tranvia.

to **tranquillize** vt. tranquillizzare.

tranquillizer s. (med.) tranquillante.

to **transact** vt. e vi. negoziare, trattare affari.

transaction s. 1. affare, operazione 2. (giur.) transazione 3. atti (di congresso ecc.) (pl.).

transactor s. negoziatore.

transalpine agg. e s. transalpino.

transatlantic agg. transatlantico.

to **transcend** vt. trascendere, superare.

transcendence s. trascendenza.

transcendent agg. trascendente.

transcendental agg. trascendentale.

transcendentalism s. trascendentalismo.

transcontinental agg. transcontinentale.

to **transcribe** vt. trascrivere.

transcript s. riproduzione, copia.

transcription s. trascrizione.

transept s. transetto.

transfer s. 1. trasferimento, cessione 2. (giur.) trapasso 3. decalcomania.

to **transfer** vt. trasferire, cedere.

transferable agg. trasferibile.

transfiguration s. trasfigurazione.

to **transfigure** vt. trasfigurare.

to **transfix** vt. trafiggere.

transfocator s. (cine) teleobiettivo.

to **transform** vt. trasformare.

transformable agg. trasformabile.

transformation s. trasformazione.

transformer s. trasformatore.

transformism s. trasformismo.

to **transfuse** vt. 1. travasare 2. fare una trasfusione (di sangue).

transfusion s. trasfusione.

to **transgress** vt. trasgredire. ◆ to **transgress** vi. commettere una violenza, peccare.

transgression s. trasgressione.

transgressor s. trasgressore.

transient agg. passeggero, transitorio.

transistor s. (radio) transistor.

transit s. 1. transito, passaggio 2. trasporto.

transition s. transizione.

transitive agg. transitivo.

transitory agg. transitorio.

translatable agg. traducibile.

to **translate** vt. tradurre.

translation s. 1. traduzione 2. trasferimento, assunzione (al cielo).

translator s. traduttore.

translucent agg. traslucido, diafano, trasparente.

to **transmigrate** vi. trasmigrare.

transmigration s. trasmigrazione.

transmissible agg. trasmissibile.

transmission s. trasmissione.

to **transmit** vt. trasmettere.

transmitter s. trasmettitore.

transoceanic agg. transoceanico.

transparence s. trasparenza.

transparent agg. 1. trasparente, limpido 2. chiaro, evidente.

to **transpire** vt. e vi. traspirare.

to **transplant** vt. trapiantare.

transplantation s. trapianto.

transport s. 1. trasporto (anche fig.) 2. mezzo di trasporto.

transportable agg. trasportabile.

transposal s. trasposizione.

transposition s. trasposizione (di parole, cifre ecc.).

transubstantiation s. transustanziazione.

transversal agg. e s. trasversale.

trap s. trappola || - -door, botola.

to **trap** vt. prendere in trappola.

trapeziun s. trapezio.

trapper s. chi tende trappole.

trash[1] s. rifiuto.

trash[2] s. guinzaglio.

to **trash** vt. sfrondare.

trashy agg. senza valore.

traumatic agg. traumatico.

travel s. 1. viaggi (pl.): — agency, agenzia di viaggi 2. (mecc.) corsa.

to **travel** vi. viaggiare.

traveller s. viaggiatore.

travelling agg. 1. viaggiante 2. di, da viaggio 3. mobile. ◆ **travelling** s. il viaggiare.

traverse agg. trasversale. ◆ **traverse** s. 1. trasversale 2. traversata.

to **traverse** vt. 1. traversare 2. muovere lateralmente. ◆ to **traverse** vi. 1. fare una traversata 2. muoversi lateralmente 3. girare su un perno.

travertin(e) s. travertino.

travesty s. parodia.

trawl s. (mar.) strascico.

trawler s. peschereccio a strascico.

tray s. vassoio || *ash- —*, portacenere.

treacherous agg. traditore, sleale.

treacherousness, treachery s. tradimento, slealtà.

tread s. 1. passo 2. suola 3. battistrada.

to tread (trod, trodden) vt. e vi. camminare. ♦ **to tread (trod, trodden)** vt. 1. percorrere 2. calpestare.

treadle s. pedale.

treason s. tradimento.

treasure s. tesoro.

to treasure vt. 1. ammassare 2. custodire gelosamente.

treasurer s. tesoriere.

treasury s. 1. tesoreria 2. Ministero del Tesoro.

treat s. festa.

to treat vt. 1. trattare 2. offrire.

treatise s. trattato.

treatment s. 1. trattamento 2. (med.) cura.

treaty s. trattato.

treble agg. 1. triplo, triplice 2. (mus.) di soprano, parte di soprano.

to treble vt. triplicare. ♦ **to treble** vi. triplicarsi.

tree s. 1. albero 2. trave || *— -frog*, raganella.

trefoil s. trifoglio.

trellis s. graticcio.

tremble s. tremito.

to tremble vi. tremare.

trembling agg. tremante, tremolante. ♦ **trembling** s. tremito.

tremendous agg. tremendo.

tremor s. tremore.

tremulous agg. tremulo.

trench s. 1. fosso 2. trincea.

to trench vt. e vi. scavare, solcare, scavare trincee.

trenchant agg. tagliente, incisivo, efficace.

trencher s. tagliere.

trend s. direzione, orientamento, tendenza.

to trend vi. tendere.

trepan s. trapano.

to trepan vt. trapanare.

trepidation s. 1. tremito 2. trepidazione.

trespass s. 1. trasgressione 2. violazione.

to trespass vi. 1. commettere una violazione 2. peccare.

trespasser s. 1. trasgressore 2. peccatore.

trestle s. 1. cavalletto 2. intelaiatura.

trial s. 1. processo 2. prova, esperimento.

triangle s. triangolo.

triangular agg. triangolare.

triangulation s. triangolazione.

tribal agg. tribale.

tribe s. tribù.

tribune[1] s. tribuno.

tribune[2] s. tribuna.

tributary agg. e s. tributario.

tribute s. tributo.

trichromatic agg. tricromico.

trick s. 1. trucco 2. imbroglio 3. mania.

to trick vt. ingannare.

trickery s. inganno.

trickish agg. scaltro.

trickle s. gocciolio.

to trickle vi. gocciolare.

tricky agg. 1. scaltro 2. intricato.

tricolour agg. e s. tricolore.

tricycle s. triciclo.

trident s. tridente.

tridimensional agg. tridimensionale.

triennial agg. triennale.

trifle s. sciocchezza.

to trifle vi. scherzare.

trifler s. persona leggera.

trifling agg. 1. insignificante 2. frivolo.

trigeminal agg. e s. trigemino.

trigeminus s. trigemino.

trigger s. grilletto.

trigonometry s. trigonometria.

trihedron s. triedro.

trill s. trillo.

to trill vt. e vi. trillare.

trillion s. 1. trilione 2. (amer.) bilione.

trilogy s. trilogia.

trim agg. ordinato. ♦ **trim** s. 1. ordine 2. assetto 3. (cine) taglio.

to trim vt. 1. ordinare 2. tagliare.

trimester s. trimestre.

trimmer s. decoratore.

trimming s. 1. guarnizione 2. bastonatura.

trinity s. trinità.

trinket s. ninnolo.

trinomial s. trinomio.

trip s. 1. gita, viaggio 2. passo agile 3. passo falso.

to trip vi. 1. saltellare 2. inciampare. ♦ **to trip** vt. 1. far inciampare **2.** (*mecc.*) liberare.

tripartite *agg.* tripartito.

tripartition *s.* tripartizione.

tripe *s.* **1.** trippa **2.** (*gergo*) ciarpame, sciocchezze (*pl.*).

triple *agg.* triplo.

to triple *vt.* triplicare. ♦ **to triple** *vi.* triplicarsi.

triplicate *agg.* triplicato. ♦ **triplicate** *s.* triplice copia.

to triplicate *vt.* triplicare.

tripod *s.* **1.** treppiede **2.** tripode.

tripper *s.* gitante.

triptych *s.* trittico.

trisyllabic(al) *agg.* trisillabico.

trite *agg.* trito.

to triturate *vt.* triturare.

triumph *s.* trionfo.

to triumph *vi.* trionfare.

triumphant *agg.* trionfante.

triumvir *s.* triumviro.

triumvirate *s.* triumvirato.

trivalent *agg.* trivalente.

trivial *agg.* banale.

triviality *s.* banalità.

trod V. *to tread.*

trodden V. *to tread.*

troglodyte *s.* troglodita.

troglodytic(al) *agg.* trogloditico.

trolley *s.* carrello || — *bus*, filobus; — *line*, linea tranviaria.

troop *s.* **1.** gruppo **2.** truppe (*pl.*).

to troop *vi.* **1.** radunarsi **2.** sfilare.

trophy *s.* trofeo.

tropic *agg.* tropico.

tropical *agg.* tropicale.

tropism *s.* tropismo.

troposphere *s.* troposfera.

trot *s.* trotto.

to trot *vt.* far trottare. ♦ **to trot** *vi.* trottare.

trotter *s.* trottatore.

trouble *s.* guaio, disturbo.

to trouble *vt.* disturbare. ♦ **to trouble** *vi.* preoccuparsi.

troublesome *agg.* fastidioso.

trough *s.* **1.** truogolo **2.** condotto, solco **3.** depressione (*atmosferica*).

trousers *s. pl.* calzoni

trout *s.* trota.

trowel *s.* cazzuola.

truce *s.* tregua.

truck[1] *s.* **1.** baratto, scambio.

truck[1] *s.* **1.** carrello **2.** (*amer.*) autocarro.

to truck[1] *vt.* barattare.

to truck[2] *vt.* trasportare (*su carrello*).

trucker *s.* camionista.

truculent *agg.* truculento.

to trudge *vi.* camminare faticosamente.

true *agg.* vero, esatto || *out of* —, sfasato.

truffle *s.* tartufo.

truly *avv.* **1.** veramente **2.** esattamente.

to trump *vt.* ingannare || *to* — *up a charge*, inventare un'accusa.

trumpery *agg.* illusorio. ♦ **trumpery** *s.* orpello.

trumpet *s.* tromba.

to trumpet *vi.* **1.** suonare la tromba **2.** barrire. ♦ **to trumpet** *vt.* strombazzare.

trumpeter *s.* trombettiere.

truncate *agg.* tronco, troncato.

truncheon *s.* manganello.

trunk *s.* **1.** tronco **2.** baule **3.** proboscide || — -*call*, comunicazione interurbana. ♦ **trunks** *s. pl.* calzoni corti.

truss *s.* **1.** fascio **2.** (*arch.*) capriata.

trust *s.* **1.** fede, fiducia **2.** incarico di fiducia **3.** (*econ.*) "trust", consorzio monopolistico.

to trust *vt. e vi.* confidare, fidarsi di, dar credito || *to* — *so. with sthg.*, affidare qc. a qu.

trustee *s.* **1.** (*comm.*) fiduciario **2.** (*giur.*) curatore.

truster *s.* chi si fida.

trustful *agg.* fiducioso.

trustworthy *agg.* degno di fiducia.

truth *s.* verità.

truthful *agg.* **1.** vero **2.** fedele.

try *s.* tentativo || — -*on*, prova (*di abiti*); — -*out* (*mecc.*), prova.

to try *vt.* provare, tentare || *to* — *for sthg.*, cercare di ottenere qc.; *to* — *on*, provare (*di abiti*); *to* — *out*, sottoporre a dura prova.

trying *agg.* **1.** difficile **2.** difficilmente sopportabile.

tub *s.* tinozza, vasca.

tube *s.* **1.** tubo **2.** camera d'aria **3.** (*fam.*) ferrovia sotterranea.

tuber *s.* **1.** tubero **2.** tubercolo.

tubercular *agg.* **1.** tubercolare **2.** tubercoloso.

tuberculosis *s.* tubercolosi.

tuberculous *agg.* tubercoloso.

tubing *s.* tubatura.

tubular, tubulous *agg.* tubolare.

tuck *s.* piega (*di abito*).

to tuck *vt.* **1.** (ri)piegare **2.** pigiare || — *up*, rimboccare.

Tuesday *s.* martedì.

tuff *s.* tufo vulcanico.

tuft *s.* **1.** ciuffo **2.** fiocco **3.** cespuglio.

tug *s.* strappo || — *-of-war*, tiro alla fune.

to **tug** *vt.* e *vi.* **1.** tirare **2.** dare strattoni.

tugboat *s.* (*mar.*) rimorchiatore.

tuition *s.* istruzione.

tulip *s.* tulipano.

tumble *s.* **1.** caduta **2.** confusione.

to **tumble** *vi.* **1.** cadere **2.** agitarsi **3.** precipitarsi **4.** fare acrobazie. ♦ to **tumble** *vt.* **1.** far cadere **2.** scompigliare.

tumble-down *agg.* in rovina.

tumbler *s.* **1.** acrobata **2.** bicchiere (*senza piede*).

tumefaction *s.* tumefazione.

to **tumefy** *vt.* tumefare. ♦ to **tumefy** *vi.* tumefarsi.

tumescence *s.* tumescenza.

tumescent *agg.* gonfio.

tumid *agg.* tumido.

tumidity *s.* gonfiore.

tumour *s.* tumore.

tumult *s.* tumulto.

tumultuous *agg.* tumultuoso.

tumulus *s.* (*pl.* -li) tumulo.

tun *s.* botte.

tuna *s.* tonno.

tune *s.* **1.** tono **2.** accordo **3.** motivo || *in* —, intonato; *out of* —, stonato.

to **tune** *vt.* (*mus.*) accordare || *to* — *up*, mettere a punto. ♦ to **tune** *vi.* essere in armonia.

tuneful *agg.* armonioso.

tuner *s.* **1.** (*mus.*) accordatore **2.** (*radio*) sintonizzatore.

tungsten *s.* tungsteno.

tunic *s.* tunica.

Tunisian *agg.* e *s.* tunisino.

to **tunnel** *vi.* costruire un tunnel. ♦ to **tunnel** *vt.* perforare.

tunny *s.* tonno.

turban *s.* turbante.

turbid *agg.* torbido.

turbidity *s.* torbidezza.

turbine *s.* turbina.

turbojet *s.* turbogetto || — *engine*, turboreattore.

turbulence *s.* turbolenza.

turbulent *agg.* turbolento.

tureen *s.* zuppiera.

turf *s.* **1.** zolla erbosa **2.** torba **3.** campo da corse || — *-accountant*, allibratore.

turgid *agg.* turgido.

turgidity *s.* turgidezza.

Turk *agg.* e *s.* turco.

turkey *s.* tacchino.

Turkish *agg.* turco.

turmoil *s.* agitazione.

turn *s.* **1.** giro **2.** curva **3.** turno **4.** servizio **5.** attitudine || — *-out*, assemblea, sciopero, produzione; — *-table*, piattaforma girevole, giradischi.

to **turn** *vi.* **1.** girarsi, volgersi **2.** diventare. ♦ to **turn** *vt.* **1.** girare, volgere **2.** mutare **3.** tornire || *to* — *off*, chiudere, spegnere; *to* — *on*, aprire, accendere; *to* — *down*, abbassare; *to* — *out*, scacciare, produrre, spegnere, risultare; *to* — *over*, rovesciare.

turnabout *s.* **1.** giostra **2.** inversione (*di rotta*).

turncoat *s.* voltagabbana.

turner *s.* tornitore.

turning *s.* **1.** giro, svolta **2.** tornitura.

turning-point *s.* svolta decisiva, momento critico.

turnip *s.* rapa.

turnkey *s.* secondino.

turnout *s.* **1.** folla **2.** equipaggio.

turnover *s.* **1.** rovesciamento **2.** (*comm.*) giro **3.** torta.

turnpike *s.* strada a pedaggio.

turnspit *s.* girarrosto.

turpentine *s.* trementina.

turpitude *s.* turpitudine.

turquoise *s.* turchese.

turret *s.* torretta.

turtle *s.* **1.** tartaruga **2.** — (*-dove*), tortora.

Tuscan *agg.* e *s.* toscano.

tusk *s.* zanna.

tussle *s.* zuffa.

to **tussle** *vi.* azzuffarsi.

tutelar(y) *agg.* tutelare.

tutor *s.* istitutore.

to **tutor** *vt.* **1.** istruire **2.** controllare.

tutorial *agg.* di istitutore.

tutorship *s.* mansione di istitutore.

twang *s.* **1.** suono acuto **2.** suono nasale.

to **twang** *vi.* **1.** avere un suono acuto **2.** parlare con voce nasale.

tweet *s.* cinguettio.

to **tweet** *vi.* cinguettare.

tweezers *s. pl.* pinzette.

twelfth *agg.* e *s.* dodicesimo.

twelve *agg.* e *s.* dodici.

twentieth *agg.* e *s.* ventesimo.

twenty *agg.* e *s.* venti.

twice *avv.* due volte.

twig *s.* ramoscello.

twilight *s.* **1.** crepuscolo **2.** luce fioca.

twin *agg.* e *s.* gemello.

to **twin** *vt.* accoppiare. ♦ to **twin** *vi.* accoppiarsi.

twine *s.* **1.** spago, corda **2.** groviglio.

twinge *s.* fitta, dolore.

twinkle *s.* **1.** scintillio **2.** ammicco || *in a* —, in un batter d'occhio.

to **twinkle** *vi.* **1.** scintillare **2.** ammiccare.

twinkling *s.* balenio.

twirl *s.* piroetta, rotazione.

to **twirl** *vt.* e *vi.* girare, roteare.

twist *s.* **1.** filo ritorto **2.** torsione **3.** curva.

to **twist** *vt.* **1.** torcere **2.** travisare. ♦ to **twist** *vi.* **1.** torcersi **2.** serpeggiare.

twister *s.* **1.** torcitore **2.** truffatore.

twisty *agg.* **1.** tortuoso **2.** disonesto.

to **twit** *vt.* biasimare.

twitch *s.* **1.** strattone **2.** tic nervoso.

twitter *s.* **1.** pigolio **2.** agitazione.

to **twitter** *vi.* **1.** pigolare **2.** essere ansioso.

two *agg.* e *s.* due.

twofold *agg.* doppio. ♦ **twofold** *avv.* doppiamente.

twopence *s.* due penny (*valore*).

tycoon *s.* (*amer.*) magnate.

type *s.* **1.** tipo **2.** simbolo **3.** (*tip.*) carattere tipografico || — *setting* (*tip.*), composizione.

to **type** *vt.* **1.** rappresentare **2.** dattilografare.

written) *vt.* e *vi.* dattilografare.

to **typewrite** (**typewrote**, **typewriter** *s.* dattilografo.

typewriting *s.* dattilografia.

typewritten V. to *typewrite*.

typewrote V. to *typewrite*.

typhoon *s.* tifone.

typhus *s.* tifo.

typic(al) *agg.* tipico.

to **typify** *vt.* **1.** incarnare **2.** esemplificare.

typist *s.* dattilografo.

typographer *s.* tipografo.

typographic(al) *agg.* tipografico.

typography *s.* tipografia.

tyrannic(al) *agg.* tirannico.

tyrannicide *s.* **1.** tirannicida **2.** tirannicidio.

to **tyrannize** *vt.* e *vi.* tiranneggiare.

tyrannous *agg.* tirannico.

tyranny *s.* tirannia.

tyrant *s.* tiranno.

tyre *s.* V. *tire.*

Tyrrhene, Tyrrhenian *agg.* e *s.* tirreno.

Tzigane *agg.* e *s.* tzigano.

U

ubication *s.* ubicazione.

ugliness *s.* bruttezza.

ugly *agg.* **1.** brutto **2.** vile, turpe.

ulcer *s.* ulcera, piaga (*anche fig.*).

to **ulcerate** *vt.* ulcerare. ♦ to **ulcerate** *vi.* ulcerarsi.

ulceration *s.* ulcerazione.

ulcerous *agg.* ulceroso.

ulna *s.* (pl. -ae) (*anat.*) ulna.

ultimate *agg.* ultimo, finale, definitivo.

ultra *agg.* ultra, estremo, eccessivo. ♦ **ultra** *s.* estremista.

ultramarine *agg.* oltremarino.

ultramontane *agg.* e *s.* oltremontano.

ultramundane *agg.* oltremondano.

ultra-red *agg.* infrarosso.

ultrasonic *agg.* ultrasonico.

ultraviolet *agg.* ultravioletto.

umbilical *agg.* ombelicale.

umbrella *s.* ombrello || — *stand*, portaombrelli.

umpire *s.* (*giur.; sport*) arbitro.

unabashed *agg.* imperturbato.

unabated *agg.* non diminuito, non scemato.

unable *agg.* incapace, inabile.

unabridged *agg.* non abbreviato, completo || — *edition*, edizione integrale.

unacceptable *agg.* inaccettabile.

unaccomplished *agg.* incompleto, incompiuto.

unaccountability *s.* inesplicabilità.

unaccountable *agg.* inesplicabile.

unaccustomed *agg.* non abituale, insolito.

unachievable *agg.* inseguibile.

unacquainted *agg.* **1.** ignaro di, non al corrente di **2.** sconosciuto, poco familiare.

unacquired *agg.* non acquisito, innato.

unactive *agg.* inattivo.

unadapted *agg.* inadatto.

unadorned *agg.* disadorno.

unadvisable *agg.* non consigliabile, inopportuno.

unaffected *agg.* **1.** senza affettazione, semplice **2.** insensibile.

unafraid *agg.* impavido.

unalienable *agg.* inalienabile.

unallied *agg.* senza relazione, senza connessione.

unalterable *agg.* inalterabile.

unamendable *agg.* incorreggibile.

to **unanchor** *vi.* togliere l'ancora.
♦ to **unanchor** *vt.* disancorare.

unanimated *agg.* inanimato.

unanimity *s.* unanimità.

unanimous *agg.* unanime.

unannounced *agg.* non annunciato, imprevisto.

unanswerable *agg.* **1.** a cui non si può rispondere **2.** irrefutabile.

unanswered *agg.* senza risposta.

unappealable *agg.* inappellabile.

unappeasable *agg.* implacabile.

unappeased *agg.* insoddisfatto.

unapplied *agg.* non impiegato, inapplicato.

unappreciated *agg.* non apprezzato, incompreso.

unapprehensive *agg.* **1.** lento nell'apprendere **2.** non apprensivo.

unapproachable *agg.* inaccessibile.

unapt *agg.* **1.** inadatto **2.** inetto.

unargued *agg.* indiscusso.

to **unarm** *vt.* disarmare.

unarmed *agg.* disarmato, inerme.

unartful *agg.* privo di artifici, ingenuo.

unascertainable *agg.* non verificabile.

unascertained *agg.* sconosciuto, non accertato.

unasked *agg.* non richiesto.

unaspiring *agg.* senza ambizione.

unassailable *agg.* inattaccabile.

unassailed *agg.* inattaccato.

unasserted *agg.* non asserito.

unassuming *agg.* modesto, senza pretese.

unattackable *agg.* inattaccabile.

unattainable *agg.* inaccessibile.

unattempted *agg.* intentato.

unauthorized *agg.* **1.** non autorizzato **2.** illecito.

unavailable *agg.* **1.** inutile, vano **2.** non disponibile.

unavenged *agg.* impunito.

unavoidable *agg.* inevitabile.

unaware *agg.* inconsapevole, inconscio.

unawareness *s.* inconsapevolezza.

unawares *avv.* inconsapevolmente, inconsciamente.

unbalance *s.* squilibrio.

to **unbalance** *vt.* sbilanciare.

to **unbandage** *vt.* sbendare.

unbearable *agg.* insopportabile.

unbeaten *agg.* **1.** insuperato, non battuto **2.** non frequentato.

unbecoming *agg.* disdicevole.

unbelief *s.* incredulità, scetticismo.

unbelievable *agg.* incredibile.

unbelieving *agg.* incredulo; scettico.

to **unbend** (**unbent, unbent**) *vt.* **1.** raddrizzare **2.** allentare, slegare.
♦ to **unbend** (**unbent, unbent**) *vi.* raddrizzarsi.

unbias(s)ed *agg.* imparziale, senza preconcetti.

to **unbind** (**unbound, unbound**) *vt.* sciogliere, slegare.

to **unbolt** *vt.* disserrare, aprire.

unborn *agg.* non nato, nascituro, che deve venire.

to **unbosom** *vt.* rivelare, confidare.
♦ to **unbosom** *vi.* sfogarsi: — *oneself* to *so.*, aprirsi con qu.

unbound V. to *unbind.*

unbreakable *agg.* infrangibile.

unbreathable *agg.* irrespirabile.

to **unbreech** *vt.* togliere i calzoni.

to **unbridle** *vt.* sbrigliare, dare libero corso a (*anche fig.*).

unbridled *agg.* incontrollato, senza briglia.

unbroken *agg.* **1.** intatto, intero, inviolato **2.** incessante.

unbruised *agg.* non ammaccato, illeso.

to **unbuckle** *vt.* sfibbiare, slacciare.

to **unburden** *vt.* **1.** scaricare, alleggerire **2.** (*fig.*) alleviare.

unburied *agg.* insepolto.

to **unbury** *vt.* disseppellire.

to **unbutton** *vt.* sbottonare. ♦ to **unbutton** *vi.* sbottonarsi.

uncalled *agg.* non chiamato, non invitato: — *for*, superfluo, gratuito.

uncanny *agg.* misterioso, irreale.

uncared-for *agg.* negletto, abbandonato.

unceasing *agg.* incessante.

uncensurable *agg.* incensurabile.

uncertain *agg.* **1.** incerto, malsicuro **2.** irresoluto.

uncertainty *s.* **1.** incertezza **2.** irresolutezza.

to **unchain** *vt.* sciogliere da catene.

unchanged *agg.* immutato.

uncharged *agg.* **1.** non carico **2.** non incriminato.

uncharitable *agg.* poco caritatevole.

to **uncharm** *vt.* liberare da un incantesimo.

unchaste *agg.* impuro.

unchecked *agg.* sfrenato.

uncivil *agg.* **1.** scortese, maleducato **2.** indecoroso.

uncivilized *agg.* non civilizzato.

to **unclasp** *vt.* slacciare. ♦ to **unclasp** *vi.* allentare la stretta.

uncle *s.* zio.

uncombed *agg.* spettinato.

uncomely *agg.* **1.** sgraziato **2.** sconveniente.

uncomfortable *agg.* **1.** scomodo, a disagio **2.** spiacevole.

uncommon *agg.* insolito, raro.

uncompared *agg.* incomparato.

uncompelled *agg.* non costretto, spontaneo.

unconcerned *agg.* indifferente, noncurante.

unconcerning *agg.* irrilevante, che non interessa.

unconditional *agg.* incondizionato.

uncongenial *agg.* **1.** antipatico, spiacevole **2.** non congeniale.

unconquerable *agg.* invincibile, indomabile.

unconquered *agg.* invitto, indomito.

unconscionable *agg.* **1.** irragionevole **2.** senza scrupoli.

unconscious *agg.* **1.** inconscio, ignaro **2.** privo di sensi. ♦ **unconscious** *s.* inconscio.

unconsciousness *s.* **1.** inconsapevolezza **2.** stato di incoscienza.

unconsolable *agg.* inconsolabile.

unconstitutional *agg.* incostituzionale.

unconstrained *agg.* **1.** non costretto, libero **2.** disinvolto.

unconstraint *s.* **1.** assenza di costrizione, libertà **2.** spontaneità.

uncontrollable *agg.* incontrollabile.

uncontrolled *agg.* senza controllo, sfrenato.

unconventional *agg.* non convenzionale, disinvolto.

unconvertible *agg.* inconvertibile.

unconvincing *agg.* non convincente.

to **uncork** *vt.* sturare, stappare.

uncountable *agg.* innumerevole.

to **uncouple** *vt.* **1.** sguinzagliare **2.** staccare.

uncouth *agg.* **1.** ordinario, rozzo **2.** desolato.

to **uncover** *vt.* **1.** scoprire **2.** spogliare. ♦ to **uncover** *vi.* togliersi il cappello.

uncovered *agg.* **1.** scoperto, senza tetto **2.** spogliato **3.** senza cappello.

unction *s.* **1.** unzione **2.** unguento.

unctuous *agg.* grasso, untuoso (*anche fig.*).

uncultivable *agg.* non coltivabile.

uncultivated *agg.* incolto, non coltivato.

uncut *agg.* intonso, non tagliato.

undaunted *agg.* intrepido, impavido.

to **undeceive** *vt.* disingannare.

undecided *agg.* **1.** indeciso, non risolto **2.** indefinito **3.** irresoluto.

undeclinable *agg.* indeclinabile.

undecomposable *agg.* indecomponibile.

undefended *agg.* **1.** indifeso **2.** (*giur.*) non assistito da difesa legale.

undeniable *agg.* innegabile.

under *prep.* **1.** sotto, al di sotto di **2.** in corso di **3.** meno di. ♦ **under** *avv.* sotto, al di sotto ‖ — *-age*, minorenne.

underbrush *s.* sottobosco.

to **undercharge** *vt.* far pagare troppo poco.

underclothes *s. pl.* biancheria intima (*sing.*).

undercover *agg.* segreto.

undercurrent *s.* **1.** corrente sottomarina **2.** (*fig.*) attività, tendenza nascosta.

to **underdo** (**underdid, underdone**) *vt. e vi.* **1.** agire in modo insufficiente **2.** cuocere poco.

underdone V. to *underdo*. ♦ underdone *agg.* poco cotto.

to **underestimate** *vt.* sottovalutare.

underfed *agg.* denutrito.

to **underfeed** (**underfed, underfed**) *vt.* nutrire insufficientemente.

to **undergo** (**underwent, undergone**) *vt.* **1.** subire, essere sottoposto a **2.** sopportare.

undergraduate *s.* studente universitario.

underground *agg.* sotterraneo. ♦ **underground** *s.* **1.** sottosuolo **2.** metropolitana.

underground *avv.* 1. sottoterra 2. (*pol.*) clandestinamente.

underhand *agg.* 1. clandestino, segreto 2. furbo, astuto. ◆ **underhand** *avv.* segretamente, clandestinamente.

to underline *vt.* sottolineare.

underlining *s.* sottolineatura.

undermentioned *agg.* sottoindicato.

to undermine *vt.* 1. minare, scalzare 2. (*fig.*) indebolire, insidiare.

underneath *avv.* di sotto, al di sotto.

to underpay (underpaid, underpaid) *vt.* pagare inadeguatamente.

to underrate *vt.* sottovalutare.

underscriber *s.* sottoscrittore.

undersea *agg.* sottomarino.

to undersell (undersold, undersold) *vt.* svendere.

undershrub *s.* sottobosco.

undersignature *s.* firma in calce.

undersold V. *to undersell.*

to understand (understood, understood) *vt.* e *vi.* 1. capire, comprendere 2. dedurre, supporre 3. sentir dire.

understandable *agg.* comprensibile.

understanding *s.* 1. comprensione 2. patto, intesa ‖ *on this* —, a queste condizioni.

to understate *vt.* minimizzare.

understatement *s.* attenuazione del vero.

understood V. *to understand.*

to undertake (undertook, undertaken) *vt.* e *vi.* 1. intraprendere 2. incaricarsi di 3. prendere in appalto.

undertaker *s.* 1. impresario 2. imprenditore di pompe funebri.

undertaking *s.* 1. l'intraprendere 2. (*comm.*) impresa 3. (*giur.*) promessa, obbligazione.

undertook V. *to undertake.*

undervaluation *s.* 1. scarsa stima 2. svalutazione.

to undervalue *vt.* sottovalutare.

underwater *agg.* subacqueo ‖ *fishing* —, pesca subacquea.

underwent V. *to undergo.*

underworld *s.* 1. bassifondi (*pl.*) 2. oltretomba.

to underwrite (underwrote, underwritten) *vt.* e *vi.* 1. sottoscrivere, firmare 2. (*comm.*) assicurare.

undeserved *agg.* immeritato.

undeserving *agg.* immeritevole.

undesirable *agg.* indesiderabile.

undestroyable *agg.* indistruttibile.

undetected *agg.* non scoperto.

undetermined *agg.* 1. indeterminato 2. indeciso.

undid V. *to undo.*

undies *s.* *pl.* biancheria intima (*sing.*).

undine *s.* ondina.

undisciplined *agg.* indisciplinato.

undiscriminating *agg.* che non distingue, che non fa distinzioni.

undiscussed *agg.* indiscusso.

indisputed *agg.* incontestato.

undissembled *agg.* non dissimulato.

undistinguished *agg.* indistinto.

undisturbed *agg.* indisturbato.

undividable *agg.* indivisibile.

to undo (undid, undone) *vt.* 1. disfare, sciogliere 2. annullare, rovinare.

undoing *s.* 1. disfacimento 2. rovina.

undone[1] V. *to undo.* ◆ **undone** *agg.* disfatto, rovinato.

undone[2] *agg.* incompiuto.

undoubtable *agg.* indubitabile.

undoubted *agg.* indubbio.

undreamed *agg.* non sognato, impensato.

to undress *vt.* svestire. ◆ **to undress** *vi.* svestirsi.

undue *agg.* 1. non dovuto, indebito 2. inadatto.

to undulate *vi.* 1. ondeggiare 2. essere ondulato.

undulation *s.* ondulazione.

undulatory *agg.* ondulatorio.

unduly *avv.* indebitamente.

to unearth *vt.* 1. dissotterrare, portare alla luce 2. far uscire dalla tana (*un animale*).

unearthly *agg.* ultraterreno ‖ — *hour*, ora impossibile.

uneasily *avv.* 1. a disagio, con difficoltà 2. con ansia.

uneasiness *s.* 1. disagio, pena 2. ansia.

uneasy *agg.* 1. a disagio 2. ansioso, inquieto.

uneatable *agg.* immangiabile.

uneducated *agg.* rozzo, ignorante.

uneffected *agg.* non effettuato.

unembarrassed *agg.* a proprio agio, disinvolto.

unemployed *agg.* 1. disoccupato 2. non usato.

unemployment *s.* disoccupazione

|| — *benefit*, sussidio di disoccupazione.

unending *agg.* eterno, senza fine.

unequal *agg.* 1. ineguale 2. inadeguato, incapace.

unequalled *agg.* ineguagliato.

unerring *agg.* infallibile, sicuro.

uneven *agg.* 1. ineguale, irregolare 2. ruvido, non livellato.

unevenness *s.* 1. disuguaglianza, irregolarità 2. dislivello.

uneventful *agg.* pacifico, senza avvenimenti importanti.

unexceptionable *agg.* ineccepibile.

unexhausted *agg.* inesausto.

unexpected *agg.* inatteso.

unexpensive *agg.* poco costoso.

unexplored *agg.* inesplorato.

unextinguishable *agg.* inestinguibile.

unfadable *agg.* 1. che non può appassire 2. solido (*di colore*).

unfading *agg.* 1. che non appassisce 2. che non sbiadisce.

unfailing *agg.* 1. infallibile, sicuro 2. immancabile.

unfair *agg.* sleale: — *competition*, concorrenza sleale.

unfairness *s.* slealtà, ingiustizia.

unfaithful *agg.* 1. infedele, sleale 2. inesatto.

unfaithfulness *s.* 1. infedeltà 2. inesattezza.

unfaltering *agg.* fermo, non esitante.

unfamiliar *agg.* poco familiare.

unfashionable *agg.* fuori moda.

to **unfasten** *vt.* slacciare, slegare. ♦ to **unfasten** *vi.* slacciarsi, slegarsi.

unfathomable *agg.* insondabile.

unfavourable *agg.* sfavorevole.

unfeeling *agg.* insensibile, spietato.

unfinished *agg.* 1. incompleto 2. non rifinito.

unfit *agg.* 1. inadatto, disadatto 2. inabile.

unfitness *s.* 1. inidoneità 2. debole costituzione.

to **unfold** *vt.* 1. aprire, schiudere 2. svelare. ♦ to **unfold** *vi.* 1. aprirsi, schiudersi 2. svelarsi.

unforbearing *agg.* insofferente, impaziente.

unforeseeing *agg.* improvvidente.

unforeseen *agg.* imprevisto.

unforgettable *agg.* indimenticabile.

unforgiving *agg.* senza misericordia.

unforgotten *agg.* inobliato.

unfortunate *agg.* sfortunato.

unfortunately *avv.* sfortunatamente.

unfounded *agg.* infondato.

to **unfreeze** (**unfroze, unfrozen**) *vt.* disgelare, scongelare. ♦ to **unfreeze** (**unfroze, unfrozen**) *vi.* disgelarsi.

unfrequent *agg.* infrequente.

unfriendly *agg.* poco amichevole.

to **unfrock** *vt.* spretare.

unfroze V. to *unfreeze*.

unfrozen V. to *unfreeze*.

unfruitful *agg.* infruttuoso.

unfruitfulness *s.* infruttuosità.

to **unfurl** *vt.* e *vi.* spiegare, spiegarsi (*di bandiere ecc.*).

unfurnished *agg.* 1. non ammobiliato 2. sfornito.

ungainly *agg.* goffo, maldestro.

ungentlemanlike *agg.* indegno di un gentiluomo.

ungirt *agg.* senza cintura.

to **unglue** *vt.* scollare. ♦ to **unglue** *vi.* scollarsi.

ungodly *agg.* 1. empio 2. malvagio.

ungraceful *agg.* sgraziato.

ungrammatical *agg.* sgrammaticato.

ungrateful *agg.* ingrato.

ungrounded *agg.* 1. infondato 2. senza preparazione.

unguarded *agg.* sguarnito, senza difesa.

unguent *s.* unguento.

unhandy *agg.* 1. maldestro 2. poco maneggevole.

unhappiness *s.* infelicità.

unhappy *agg.* infelice, triste.

unharmed *agg.* intatto, illeso.

unharmful *agg.* innocuo.

unhealthily *avv.* in modo malsano, poco igienicamente.

unhealthy *agg.* 1. malsano, insalubre 2. (*fig.*) dannoso 3. malaticcio.

unheard *agg.* 1. non udito 2. non ascoltato 3. sconosciuto, strano || — *of*, inaudito.

to **unhinge** *vt.* scardinare.

unholy *agg.* profano, empio.

to **unhook** *vt.* sganciare. ♦ to **unhook** *vi.* sganciarsi.

unhoped *agg.* insperato, inatteso.

to **unhorse** *vt.* 1. disarcionare 2. staccare i cavalli da.

unhuman *agg.* sovrumano.

unhurt *agg.* illeso, incolume.

unhurtful *agg.* innocuo.

unicellular *agg.* unicellulare.
unification *s.* unificazione.
uniform *agg.* uniforme, costante. ♦
 uniform *s.* uniforme, divisa.
to uniform *vt.* uniformare.
uniformity *s.* uniformità.
to unify *vt.* unificare.
unilateral *agg.* unilaterale.
unilaterally *avv.* unilateralmente.
unimaginable *agg.* inimmaginabile.
unimpaired *agg.* inalterato, intatto.
unimpassioned *agg.* spassionato,
 calmo.
unimpeachable *agg.* incensurabile.
unimportance *s.* scarsa importanza.
unimportant *agg.* privo d'importanza.
unimposing *agg.* poco imponente,
 che non fa soggezione.
uninhabitable *agg.* inabitabile.
uninhabited *agg.* disabitato.
uninominal *agg.* uninominale.
unintelligent *agg.* stupido.
unintelligible *agg.* inintelligibile.
unintended *agg.* 1. involontario 2.
 (*giur.*) non intenzionale.
uninteresting *agg.* non interessante.
uninviting *agg.* poco attraente.
union *s.* unione, associazione, lega
 || (*trade*) —, sindacato; *the Union
 Jack*, la bandiera del Regno Unito.
unionism *s.* tendenza ad unirsi.
unionist *s.* unionista.
uniparous *agg.* uniparo.
unique *agg.* 1. unico, solo 2. eccezionale.
uniqueness *s.* unicità.
unisexual *agg.* unisessuale.
unison *s.* 1. (*mus.*) unisono 2. (*fig.*)
 concordia.
unit *s.* 1. unità, unità di misura 2.
 complesso, insieme.
unitary *agg.* unitario. ♦ **to unite** *vi.*
 1. unirsi 2. mettersi d'accordo.
united *agg.* unito, collegato.
unity *s.* 1. unità 2. armonia.
universal *agg.* universale.
universality *s.* universalità.
to universalize *vt.* universalizzare.
universe *s.* universo.
university *s.* università.
univocal *agg.* univoco, non ambiguo.
to unjoint *vt.* disgiungere.
unjust *agg.* ingiusto.
unjustifiable *agg.* ingiustificabile.
unjustified *agg.* ingiustificato.
unkempt *agg.* trascurato, sciatto.

unkind *agg.* 1. sgarbato, scortese 2.
 crudele.
unkindness *s.* scortesia.
unknown *agg.* sconosciuto, ignoto.
unlawful *agg.* illegale.
to unlearn (unlearnt, unlearnt)
 (*anche reg.*) *vt.* disimparare.
unleavened *agg.* non lievitato || —
 bread, pane azzimo.
unless *cong.* a meno che, salvo che.
unlike *agg.* dissimile, diverso. ♦
 unlike *avv.* diversamente. ♦ **unlike** *prep.* diversamente da.
unlikelihood *s.* inverosimiglianza,
 improbabilità.
unlikely *agg.* inverosimile, improbabile.
unlimited *agg.* illimitato, sconfinato.
to unline *vt.* sfoderare.
unlined[1] *agg.* senza fodera.
unlined[2] *agg.* senza rughe.
unliterary *agg.* non letterario.
to unload *vt.* 1. scaricare 2. (*fig.*)
 alleggerire.
to unlock *vt.* aprire (*con chiave*).
unlooked-for *agg.* imprevisto.
to unloose *vt.* slegare.
unlosable *agg.* che non può essere
 perso.
unlovable *agg.* poco amabile, antipatico.
unlucky *agg.* 1. sfortunato 2. di
 cattivo augurio.
to unman *vt.* 1. evirare 2. abbrutire 3. togliere forza.
unmarred *agg.* non sciupato.
unmarried *agg.* non coniugato.
to unmask *vt.* togliere la maschera
 (*anche fig.*). ♦ **to unmask** *vi.* togliersi la maschera.
unmatched *agg.* senza rivali.
unmentionable *agg.* innominabile,
 irripetibile.
unmerciful *agg.* spietato.
unmethodical *agg.* non metodico.
unminded *agg.* negletto.
unmindful *agg.* 1. immemore 2. incurante.
unmistakable *agg.* indubbio, ine-
 quivocabile.
to unmoor *vt.* e *vi.* togliere gli ormeggi a.
to unnail *vt.* schiodare.
unnatural *agg.* innaturale, contro
 natura.
unnavigable *agg.* non navigabile.
unnecessary *agg.* non necessario.
unneeded *agg.* inutile, non neces-

sario.

to **unnerve** vt. snervare.

unnoticed agg. inosservato.

unobjectionable agg. ineccepibile.

unobliging agg. poco compiacente.

unobservant agg. **1.** inosservante **2.** distratto.

unobserved agg. inosservato.

unobtrusive agg. discreto, modesto.

unoffending agg. inoffensivo.

unofficial agg. ufficioso.

to **unpack** vt. e vi. **1.** disfare (le valigie) **2.** disimballare.

unpalatable agg. di gusto sgradevole.

unpardonable agg. imperdonabile.

unpaved agg. non lastricato.

unperceivable agg. impercettibile.

unperceived agg. inavvertito.

unperishable agg. duraturo, imperituro.

unpleasant agg. spiacevole, sgradevole.

unpliable agg. poco piacevole.

unpoetic(al) agg. poco poetico.

to **unpoison** vt. svelenire.

unpolluted agg. incontaminato.

unpopular agg. impopolare.

unpopularity s. impopolarità.

unprecise agg. impreciso.

unpredictable agg. imprevedibile.

unpredicted agg. imprevisto.

unpremeditated agg. non premeditato.

unprepared agg. impreparato.

unpreparedness s. impreparazione.

unprepossessed agg. senza prevenzioni.

unprepossessing agg. senza attrattive, antipatico.

unpresentable agg. impresentabile.

unpriestly agg. che non si addice a un prete.

unprincely agg. che non si addice a un principe.

unprintable agg. non adatto ad essere pubblicato.

unproductive agg. improduttivo.

unprofitable agg. poco vantaggioso.

unprofitableness s. infruttuosità.

unpronounceable agg. impronunciabile.

unprovable agg. indimostrabile.

unpublished agg. inedito.

unqualified agg. **1.** incompetente **2.** non abilitato **3.** (giur.) senza restrizioni.

to **unqualify** vt. **1.** inabilitare **2.** squalificare.

unquenchable agg. inestinguibile, insaziabile (anche fig.).

unquestionable agg. incontestabile, indiscutibile.

unquestioned agg. indiscusso.

unquiet agg. inquieto.

unquoted agg. **1.** non citato **2.** (comm.) non quotato (di titoli).

to **unravel** vt. districare. ♦ to **unravel** vi. districarsi.

unreachable agg. irraggiungibile.

unready agg. **1.** impreparato **2.** tardo, lento.

unreal agg. irreale.

unreality s. irrealtà.

unrealizable agg. irrealizzabile.

unreasonable agg. irragionevole.

unrecognizable agg. irriconoscibile.

unredeemed agg. **1.** irredento **2.** non controbilanciato **3.** (comm.) non estinto.

unrelated agg. senza rapporti, senza legami.

unreliable agg. **1.** non fidato **2.** inattendibile.

unrepealed agg. (giur.) non abrogato.

unrequired agg. non richiesto.

unrest s. inquietudine.

unrestrained agg. non represso.

unrestricted agg. senza limitazioni.

unrevenged agg. invendicato.

unripe agg. immaturo, acerbo (anche fig.).

unrivalled agg. impareggiabile.

to **unroll** vt. svolgere. ♦ to **unroll** vi. svolgersi.

unruly agg. sregolato, indisciplinato.

to **unsaddle** vt. dissellare, disarcionare.

unsafe agg. malsicuro.

unsatisfied agg. **1.** insoddisfatto **2.** non convinto.

unsavoury agg. insipido, scipito.

unscholarly agg. **1.** indegno di un letterato **2.** non erudito.

to **unscrew** vt. svitare.

unscriptural agg. non conforme alle Sacre Scritture.

to **unseal** vt. dissigillare.

unseasonable agg. **1.** fuori stagione **2.** (fig.) intempestivo.

unseemliness s. indecenza

unseemly agg. sconveniente, indecente.

unseizable agg. inafferrabile.

unselfish agg. disinteressato.

unselfishness s. disinteresse.

unsettled *agg.* 1. disordinato 2. sconvolto, turbato 3. mutevole, indeciso.

to unsew (unsewed, unsewn) *vt.* scucire.

unshaken *agg.* non scosso, fermo.

to unsheathe *vt.* sguainare.

to unshoe (unshod, unshod) *vt.* 1. togliere le scarpe 2. togliere i ferri a (*un cavallo*).

unshrinkable *agg.* irrestringibile.

unskilfulness *s.* incapacità, imperizia.

unskilled *agg.* inesperto, inabile.

unsocial *agg.* asociale.

unsold *agg.* invenduto.

to unsolder *vt.* dissaldare.

unsolved *agg.* insoluto.

unsound *agg.* 1. malsano, malato 2. guasto, avariato.

unspeakable *agg.* 1. inesprimibile 2. inqualificabile.

unstable *agg.* 1. instabile 2. (*fig.*) mutevole.

unsteadiness *s.* incostanza, volubilità.

unsteady *agg.* instabile, incostante.

unsubstantial *agg.* 1. inconsistente 2. illusorio.

unsuccessful *agg.* mal riuscito, sfortunato.

unsuitable *agg.* inadatto, non appropriato.

unsure *agg.* 1. malsicuro, precario 2. incerto.

unsurpassed *agg.* insorpassato.

unsuspected *agg.* insospettato, non sospetto.

unsustainable *agg.* insostenibile.

untamable *agg.* indomabile.

untame *agg.* selvaggio, non addomesticato.

untaught *agg.* poco istruito, ignorante.

unteachable *agg.* 1. difficile da insegnare 2. non educabile.

unthinkable *agg.* inimmaginabile.

to unthread *vt.* sfilare, togliere il filo a.

untidily *avv.* disordinatamente.

untidy *agg.* disordinato, trasandato.

to untie *vt.* slegare. ♦ to untie *vi.* slegarsi.

until *prep.* fino a. ♦ until *cong.* finché.

untimeliness *s.* intempestività, inopportunità.

untimely *agg.* 1. prematuro 2. inopportuno. ♦ untimely *avv.* 1. pre-

maturamente 2. inopportunamente.

untiring *agg.* instancabile.

untitled *agg.* senza titolo.

to untomb *vt.* dissotterrare.

untouchable *agg.* 1. intoccabile 2. (*fig.*) irraggiungibile.

untouched *agg.* 1. non toccato, intatto 2. illeso, indenne.

untoward *agg.* 1. restio, caparbio 2. infausto.

untranslatable *agg.* intraducibile.

untravelled *agg.* che non ha viaggiato.

untrodden *agg.* non calpestato, non battuto.

untrue *agg.* 1. falso, menzognero 2. infedele.

untrustworthy *agg.* indegno di fiducia.

to untune *vt.* scordare (*uno strumento musicale*).

unusable *agg.* inutilizzabile.

unusual *agg.* insolito, inusitato.

unutterable *agg.* indescrivibile, impronunciabile.

unvarying *agg.* invariabile.

to unveil *vt.* 1. togliere il velo a 2. (*fig.*) rivelare.

unwary *agg.* incauto, sconsiderato.

unwatchful *agg.* non vigilante, disattento.

unweaned *agg.* non svezzato.

unweary *agg.* non stanco, indefesso.

unwell *agg.* indisposto, ammalato.

unwieldy *agg.* 1. ingombrante 2. impacciato.

unwilling *agg.* 1. riluttante 2. involontario.

unwillingly *avv.* malvolentieri.

unwillingness *s.* 1. riluttanza 2. malavoglia.

to unwind (unwound, unwound) *vt.* srotolare. ♦ to unwind (unwound, unwound) *vi.* srotolarsi.

unwise *agg.* malaccorto.

unwitting *agg.* inconsapevole.

unworldly *agg.* spirituale, non mondano.

unworthy *agg.* indegno, spregevole.

unwound *V.* to unwind.

to unwrap *vt.* disfare, svolgere.

unwritten *agg.* non scritto || — law, legge tramandata oralmente.

unwrought *agg.* 1. non lavorato 2. grezzo.

up¹ *avv.* 1. su, in su, in alto 2. in piedi || — to, fino a; hurry —, spicciati; *the game is* —, tutto è perduto. ♦ **up** *prep.* su, su per, in cima a || — *now*, fino ad ora.

up² *agg.* ascendente, che va verso l'alto || — *train*, treno per Londra.

up-and-down *agg.* 1. che va in su e in giù 2. oscillante.

to upbraid *vt.* rimproverare.

upheaval *s.* 1. sollevamento 2. agitazione.

uphill *agg.* 1. in salita 2. (*fig.*) difficile. ♦ **uphill** *avv.* in salita. ♦ **uphill** *s.* salita.

to uphold (upheld, upheld) *vt.* 1. sostenere, sorreggere 2. (*fig.*) appoggiare, patrocinare.

to upholster *vt.* tappezzare, imbottire.

upholsterer *s.* tappezziere.

upholstery *s.* tappezzeria, imbottitura.

upkeep *s.* mantenimento, manutenzione.

upland *agg.* montuoso. ♦ **upland** *s.* zona montuosa.

upon *prep.* V. on.

upper *agg.* 1. superiore, più alto 2. più lontano (*dall'ingresso ecc.*) || *the* Upper House, la Camera dei Lords.

uppercut *s.* (*sport*) "uppercut", colpo dal basso in alto.

upright *agg.* 1. ritto, diritto, eretto 2. retto, integro. ♦ **upright** *avv.* in piedi, perpendicolarmente.

uprightness *s.* 1. perpendicolarità 2. rettitudine.

uproar *s.* tumulto, chiasso.

uproarious *agg.* tumultuoso, chiassoso.

to uproot *vt.* sradicare, svellere.

ups and downs *s. pl.* 1. ondulazioni (*del terreno*) 2. (*fig.*) vicissitudini, alti e bassi.

to upset (upset, upset) *vt.* 1. rovesciare 2. disturbare, sconvolgere. ♦ **to upset (upset, upset)** *vi.* rovesciarsi, capovolgersi.

upset *agg.* 1. rovesciato, capovolto 2. (*fig.*) sconvolto, turbato. ♦ **upset** *s.* 1. rovesciamento 2. disordine.

upshot *s.* esito, risultato.

upside-down *avv.* capovolto, sottosopra.

upstairs *agg. e avv.* al piano superiore, di sopra.

upstanding *agg.* 1. eretto, diritto 2. (*fig.*) franco, leale.

up-to-date *agg.* aggiornato, all'ultima moda.

upward(s) *agg.* ascendente, rivolto verso l'alto. ♦ **upward** *avv.* 1. in su, in alto 2. al di sopra.

uranium *s.* uranio.

urban *agg.* urbano, di città.

urbane *agg.* urbano, cortese.

urbanity *s.* urbanità, cortesia.

urbanization *s.* urbanizzazione.

to urbanize *vt.* urbanizzare.

urchin *s.* monello.

uretic *agg. e s.* diuretico.

urge *s.* 1. impulso, stimolo 2. spinta, sprone.

to urge *vt. e vi.* 1. spingere, stimolare 2. consigliare, raccomandare.

urgency *s.* 1. urgenza, premura 2. bisogno urgente, necessità.

urgent *agg.* urgente, pressante.

uric *agg.* urico.

to urinate *vi.* orinare.

urine *s.* orina.

urn *s.* 1. urna 2. bricco.

us *pron. pers. compl. pl.* ci, noi: *three of* —, tre di noi.

usable *agg.* usabile, servibile.

usage *s.* 1. uso, trattamento, impiego 2. usanza.

use *s.* 1. uso, impiego 2. utilità, vantaggio 3. (*giur.*) usufrutto.

to use *vt.* 1. usare, adoperare 2. trattare || *to* — *up*, consumare.

used *agg.* 1. usato, adoperato 2. abituato || -*up*, esaurito.

useful *agg.* utile, pratico.

usefulness *s.* utilità, vantaggio.

useless *agg.* inutile, vano.

uselessness *s.* inutilità.

user *s.* 1. utente 2. (*giur.*) usufruttuario.

usher *s.* usciere.

to usher *vt.* precedere (*in qualità di usciere*).

usual *agg.* usuale, abituale || *as* —, come al solito.

usually *avv.* di solito, abitualmente.

usufruct *s.* (*giur.*) usufrutto.

usufructuary *agg. e s.* usufruttuario.

usurer *s.* usuraio.

to usurp *vt.* usurpare.

usurpation *s.* usurpazione.

usurper *s.* usurpatore.

usury *s.* usura (*anche fig.*).

utensil *s.* utensile, arnese.

uterine *agg.* uterino.

uterus *s.* (*pl.* -ri) utero.

utilitarian *s.* utilitarista.

utilitarianism *s.* utilitarismo.

utility *s.* utilità, vantaggio.

utilizable *agg.* utilizzabile.

utilization *s.* utilizzazione.

to **utilize** *vt.* utilizzare.

utmost *agg. e s.* 1. estremo, ultimo 2. massimo, sommo || *to do one's* —, fare del proprio meglio.

Utopian *s.* utopista.

utter *agg.* completo, totale.

to **utter** *vt.* 1. emettere 2. esprimere, pronunciare.

utterable *agg.* esprimibile.

utterance *s.* espressione, sfogo.

uttering *s.* 1. messa in circolazione 2. spaccio (*di assegni ecc.*).

utterly *avv.* completamente, totalmente.

uttermost *agg. e s.* V. *utmost.*

uxoricide *s.* 1. uxoricida 2. uxoricidio.

V

vacancy *s.* 1. vuoto, lacuna 2. posto vacante || *no* —, completo (*di alberghi ecc.*).

vacant *agg.* 1. vuoto, vacante 2. non occupato.

to **vacate** *vt.* lasciar vacante, sgomberare || *to* — *a seat,* dare le dimissioni.

vacation *s.* 1. il ritirarsi, il lasciar libero 2. vacanze: *long* —, vacanze estive (*pl.*).

to **vaccinate** *vt. e vi.* vaccinare.

vaccination *s.* vaccinazione.

vaccine *s.* vaccino.

to **vacillate** *vi.* 1. vacillare 2. (*fig.*) esitare.

vacillating *agg.* 1. vacillante 2. incostante, irresoluto.

vacillation *s.* 1. vacillamento 2. esitazione.

vacillatory *agg.* V. *vacillating.*

vacuity *s.* vacuità (*anche fig.*).

vacuous *agg.* 1. vacuo, vuoto 2. sciocco, ozioso.

vacuum *s.* vuoto pneumatico || — *cleaner,* aspirapolvere.

vagabond *s.* viandante, vagabondo.

vagary *s.* fantasticheria, capriccio.

vagrancy *s.* vagabondaggio, accattonaggio.

vagrant *agg. e s.* vagabondo.

vague *agg.* vago, impreciso.

vaguely *avv.* vagamente.

vagueness *s.* indeterminatezza.

vain *agg.* 1. vano, inutile 2. vanitoso.

vainglorious *agg.* vanaglorioso.

vainglory *s.* vanagloria.

vainly *avv.* 1. inutilmente 2. vanitosamente.

valance *s.* 1. drappeggio 2. cortina (*di un letto*).

valediction *s.* addio, commiato.

valedictory *agg.* d'addio, di saluto. ◆ **valedictory** *s.* discorso d'addio.

valence *s.* (*chim.*) valenza.

valerian *s.* valeriana.

valet *s.* valletto.

valiant *agg.* valoroso, prode.

valid *agg.* valido, legittimo.

to **validate** *vt.* render valido, convalidare.

validity *s.* validità.

validly *avv.* validamente.

valley *s.* valle, vallata.

valorization *s.* valorizzazione.

to **valorize** *vt.* valorizzare.

valour *s.* valore.

valuable *agg.* 1. di valore, prezioso 2. valutabile.

valuation *s.* 1. valutazione, stima 2. considerazione.

value *s.* 1. valore, prezzo 2. (*fig.*) pregio, importanza || — *in exchange,* valore effettivo.

to **value** *vt.* 1. valutare, stimare 2. considerare, dar valore.

valueless *agg.* di nessun valore.

valuer *s.* estimatore.

valve *s.* 1. valvola 2. valva.

vamp[1] *s.* 1. rappezzamento 2. (*mus*) accompagnamento.

vamp[2] *s.* (*gergo*) donna fatale.

vampire *s.* vampiro.

van *s.* 1. furgone 2. vagone ferroviario || *luggage* —, bagagliaio; *prison* —, cellulare.

Vandal *agg. e s.* vandalo.

Vandalic *agg.* vandalico.

vandalism *s.* vandalismo.

vane *s.* 1. banderuola 2. pala (*di mulino a vento ecc.*).

vanguard *s.* avanguardia (*anche fig.*).

vanilla *s.* vaniglia.

to **vanish** *vi.* svanire, sparire.

vanishing *s.* il dileguarsi, lo sparire.

vanity *s.* vanità || —*case,* borsetta col necessario per il trucco.

to **vanquish** *vt.* vincere, conquistare.

vanquisher *s.* conquistatore

vantage *s.* vantaggio.

vapid *agg.* insulso.

vaporization *s.* evaporazione.

to **vaporize** *vt.* far evaporare. ♦ to **vaporize** *vi.* 1. evaporare 2. (*fig.*) volatilizzarsi.

vaporizer *s.* vaporizzatore.

vaporous *agg.* vaporoso.

vapour *s.* vapore, esalazione.

to **vapour** *vi.* 1. evaporare 2. (*fig.*) vantarsi.

vapouring *agg.* che evapora. ♦ **vapouring** *s.* vanteria.

vapourish *agg.* 1. pieno di vapori 2. depresso.

vapours *s. pl.* depressione (*sing.*), allucinazioni.

variability *s.* variabilità, mutevolezza.

variable *agg.* variabile, incostante.

variance *s.* 1. variazione 2. disaccordo.

variant *agg.* differente, contrastante. ♦ **variant** *s.* variante.

variation *s.* variazione, modificazione. ♦ **variations** *s. pl.* (*mat.*) variazioni.

varicoloured *agg.* variopinto.

varicose *agg.* varicoso.

varied *agg.* 1. vario, variato 2. variopinto.

to **variegate** *vt.* variegare, screziare.

variegated *agg.* variegato, screziato.

variegation *s.* screziatura.

variety *s.* varietà, diversità || — **show** (*teat.*), spettacolo di varietà.

various *agg.* alcuni, molti (*pl.*).

variously *avv.* variamente.

varnish *s.* 1. vernice, lacca 2. (*fig.*) apparenza, aspetto esteriore || **nail** —, smalto per unghie.

to **varnish** *vt.* 1. verniciare, laccare 2. (*fig.*) mascherare.

varnishing *s.* verniciatura, laccatura.

to **vary** *vt.* variare, cambiare. ♦ to **vary** *vi.* essere differente.

vase *s.* vaso.

vaseline *s.* vaselina.

vassal *s.* vassallo.

vassallage *s.* vassallaggio.

vast *agg.* ampio, immenso, vasto.

vastness *s.* vastità.

vat *s.* tino, tinozza.

vault[1] *s.* 1. volta, soffitto a volta 2. cantina 3. sepolcro 4. (*fig.*) vol-ta celeste.

vault[2] *s.* volteggio.

to **vault** *vi.* volteggiare. ♦ to **vault** *vt.* saltare.

vaulting *s.* 1. il costruire volte 2. costruzione a volta.

to **vaunt** *vt.* vantare. ♦ to **vaunt** *vi.* vantarsi.

veal *s.* (*cuc.*) vitello.

vector *s.* vettore.

vectorial *agg.* vettoriale.

veer *s.* 1. cambiamento di direzione 2. (*mar.*) virata.

to **veer** *vi.* 1. cambiare direzione 2. (*mar.*) virare.

vegetable *agg.* vegetale. ♦ **vegetable** *s.* 1. vegetale 2. ortaggio. ♦ **vegetables** *s. pl.* verdura (*sing.*).

vegetal *agg.* vegetale.

vegetarian *agg.* e *s.* vegetariano.

to **vegetate** *vi.* vegetare (*anche fig.*).

vegetation *s.* 1. vegetazione 2. il vegetare.

vegetative *agg.* vegetativo.

vehemence *s.* veemenza.

vehement *agg.* veemente, impetuoso.

vehicle *s.* veicolo.

veil *s.* 1. velo, cortina 2. (*fig.*) apparenza, pretesto.

to **veil** *vt.* 1. velare, coprire 2. (*fig.*) dissimulare, nascondere.

veiling *s.* 1. il velare 2. velo, schermo.

vein *s.* 1. (*anat.; geol.; fig.*) vena 2. venatura, nervatura.

to **vein** *vt.* venare, coprire di venature.

veined *agg.* 1. venato 2. con venature, nervature.

velleity *s.* velleità.

velocipede *s.* velocipede.

velocity *s.* velocità.

velvet *agg.* di velluto, vellutato. ♦ **velvet** *s.* velluto.

velvety *agg.* vellutato, morbido.

venal *agg.* venale.

venality *s.* venalità.

to **vend** *vt.* vendere.

vendor *s.* venditore.

to **veneer** *vt.* 1. impiallacciare 2. (*fig.*) mascherare.

veneer, veneering *s.* 1. impiallacciatura 2. (*fig.*) maschera, vernice.

venerable *agg.* venerabile.

to **venerate** *vt.* venerare.

veneration *s.* venerazione.

venereal *agg.* venereo.

Venetian *agg.* e *s.* veneziano || —

blinds, shades, persiana alla veneziana.

vengeance *s.* vendetta ‖ *to take — on so.,* vendicarsi di qu.

vengeful *agg.* vendicativo, vendicatore.

venial *agg.* veniale.

venom *s.* veleno (*di animali*).

venomous *agg.* velenoso.

venous *agg.* **1.** venoso **2.** con nervature.

vent¹ *s.* spacco, apertura (*di abito*).

vent² *s.* **1.** sbocco, apertura, foro **2.** (*fig.*) sfogo ‖ *to give — to,* dar libero corso a.

to vent *vt.* **1.** svuotare, esalare **2.** (*fig.*) sfogare.

to ventilate *vt.* **1.** ventilare **2.** (*fig.*) discutere, rendere manifesto.

ventilation *s.* **1.** ventilazione **2.** discussione.

ventral *agg.* ventrale, addominale.

ventricle *s.* ventricolo.

ventriloquism *s.* ventriloquio.

ventriloquist *s.* ventriloquo.

venture *s.* **1.** avventura, azzardo **2.** (*comm.*) speculazione.

to venture *vt.* avventurare, arrischiare. ♦ **to venture** *vi.* avventurarsi, arrischiarsi.

venturer *s.* avventuriero.

venue *s.* sede giurisdizionale.

veracious *agg.* verace.

veracity *s.* veracità.

veranda(h) *s.* veranda.

verb *s.* verbo.

verbal *agg.* **1.** verbale **2.** orale, a parole.

verbally *avv.* verbalmente, oralmente.

verbiage *s.* verbosità.

verbose *agg.* verboso, prolisso.

verdant *agg.* verdeggiante.

verdict *s.* verdetto.

verdigris *s.* verderame.

verge *s.* **1.** orlo, limite ‖ *on the — of,* sul punto di **2.** bacchetta, verga.

to verge *vi.* **1.** confinare, essere contiguo, adiacente **2.** (*fig.*) rasentare: *to — on madness,* rasentare la pazzia.

verifiable *agg.* verificabile.

verification *s.* verifica.

verifier *s.* verificatore.

to verify *vt.* **1.** verificare, controllare **2.** (*giur.*) autenticare.

verily *avv.* in verità.

verisimilar *agg.* verosimile.

verisimilitude *s.* verosimiglianza.

verism *s.* verismo.

veritable *agg.* vero, genuino.

verity *s.* verità, realtà.

vermiform *agg.* vermiforme.

vermin *s. coll.* insetti parassiti.

verminous *agg.* infestato da parassiti.

vernacular *s.* vernacolo, dialetto nativo. ♦ **vernacular** *agg.* vernacolo, nativo.

versatile *agg.* versatile, multiforme.

versatility *s.* versatilità.

verse *s.* **1.** verso **2.** strofa **3.** componimento in versi.

versification *s.* versificazione.

to versify *vt. e vi.* **1.** comporre in versi **2.** narrare in versi.

version *s.* versione, traduzione.

vertebra *s.* (*pl.* -ae) vertebra.

vertebral *agg.* vertebrale.

vertebrate *agg. e s.* vertebrato.

vertex *s.* (*pl.* -tices) vertice, apice, sommità.

vertical *agg.* verticale. ♦ **vertical** *s.* piano verticale, verticale.

verticality *s.* posizione verticale, perpendicolarità.

very *agg.* **1.** vero e proprio, autentico **2.** (*uso enfatico*) esatto, stesso: *at that — moment,* in quello stesso istante. ♦ **very** *avv.* molto, assai.

vessel *s.* **1.** vaso, recipiente **2.** nave, vascello.

vest *s.* **1.** panciotto **2.** camiciola, davantino.

to vest *vt.* **1.** conferire, investire **2.** (*giur.*) assegnare **3.** parare (*di altari ecc.*). ♦ **to vest** *vi.* passare per eredità.

vestal *s.* vestale.

vestibule *s.* vestibolo, entrata, portico di chiesa.

vestige *s.* vestigio, traccia.

vestment *s.* veste (*spec. liturgica*).

vestry *s.* **1.** sagrestia **2.** assemblea parrocchiale.

vesture *s.* rivestimento, veste.

veteran *agg. e s.* veterano.

veterinary *agg. e s.* veterinario.

to vex *vt.* **1.** vessare, opprimere **2.** irritare.

vexation *s.* **1.** vessazione, oppressione **2.** irritazione.

vexatious *agg.* **1.** irritante, fastidioso **2.** (*giur.*) vessatorio.

vexed *agg.* **1.** vessato, oppresso **2.** irritato.

via *prep.* per, via, attraverso: — *air mail*, per via aerea.

viability *s.* vitalità.

viable *agg.* vitale.

viaduct *s.* viadotto.

vial *s.* fiala.

viand *s.* vivanda, cibo.

vibrant *agg.* vibrante, tremante.

to vibrate *vi.* vibrare, risuonare. ♦ to vibrate *vt.* far vibrare.

vibration *s.* vibrazione, tremolio.

vibrator *s.* vibratore.

vibratory *agg.* 1. vibratorio 2. vibrante.

vicar *s.* 1. curato (*nella Chiesa d'Inghilterra*) 2. vicario (*Chiesa Cattolica*).

vicariate *s.* vicariato.

vice[1] *s.* 1. immoralità, depravazione 2. vizio.

vice[2] *s.* (*mecc.*) morsa.

vice[3] *s.* sostituto, vice.

vice[4] *prep.* in luogo di.

viceroy *s.* vicerè.

vicinity *s.* 1. vicinanza, prossimità 2. affinità.

vicious *agg.* 1. vizioso, immorale 2. maligno 3. bizzarro (*di animali*) 4. difettoso, scorretto.

vicissitude *s.* vicissitudine.

victim *s.* vittima.

victor *s.* vincitore.

victorious *agg.* vittorioso.

victory *s.* vittoria.

to victual *vt.* vettovagliare, approvvigionare. ♦ to victual *vi.* approvvigionarsi.

victualling *s.* vettovagliamento, approvvigionamento.

victuals *s. pl.* vettovaglie, viveri.

to vie *vi.* gareggiare.

view *s.* 1. vista, sguardo 2. veduta, panorama 3. opinione 4. scopo, mira 5. (*giur.*) sopralluogo || *point of —*, punto di vista; — *-finder* (*foto*), mirino.

to view *vt.* 1. guardare attentamente 2. esaminare.

viewer *s.* 1. chi guarda 2. telespettatore 3. ispettore.

viewless *agg.* 1. senza vista (*di casa ecc.*) 2. invisibile.

viewpoint *s.* punto di vista.

vigil *s.* veglia.

vigilance *s.* vigilanza.

vigilant *agg.* vigilante, vigile.

vigorous *agg.* vigoroso, forte.

Viking *s.* vichingo.

vigour *s.* vigore, energia.

vigorously *avv.* vigorosamente.

vile *agg.* vile, spregevole.

vileness *s.* viltà, bassezza.

to vilify *vt.* diffamare.

villa *s.* villa.

village *s.* villaggio, paese.

villager *s.* abitante di villaggio.

villain *s.* furfante, scellerato.

villainous *agg.* scellerato, infame.

villainy *s.* scelleratezza.

to vindicate *vt.* 1. rivendicare 2. giustificare, difendere.

vindication *s.* 1. rivendicazione 2. giustificazione, difesa.

vindictive *agg.* vendicativo.

vine *s.* vite || — *-leaf*, pampino; — *-dresser*, vignaiuolo.

vinegar *s.* aceto.

vinery *s.* serra per viti.

vineyard *s.* vigneto, vigna.

vintage *s.* 1. vendemmia 2. annata.

vintager *s.* vendemmiatore.

vintner *s.* vinaio.

to violate *vt.* 1. violare, trasgredire 2. profanare.

violation *s.* 1. violazione, trasgressione 2. profanazione.

violator *s.* 1. violatore, trasgressore 2. profanatore.

violence *s.* violenza, veemenza.

violent *agg.* violento, impetuoso.

violet *agg.* violetto, viola. ♦ violet *s.* viola mammola.

violin *s.* violino.

violoncellist *s.* violoncellista.

viper *s.* vipera (*anche fig.*).

virgin *s.* agg. e *s.* vergine.

virginal *agg.* verginale.

virginity *s.* verginità.

virile *agg.* virile.

virility *s.* virilità.

virtual *agg.* virtuale, effettivo.

virtuality *s.* potenzialità, virtualità.

virtue *s.* 1. virtù, moralità, forza d'animo 2. qualità, merito.

virtuosity *s.* virtuosismo.

virtuous *agg.* virtuoso, morale.

virulence *s.* virulenza.

virulent *agg.* virulento.

virus *s.* virus.

visa *s.* visto consolare.

to visa *vt.* vistare (*un passaporto*).

visceral *agg.* viscerale.

viscid *agg.* viscido.

viscidity *s.* viscidità.

viscose *s.* viscosa.

viscosity *s.* viscosità.

viscount *s.* visconte.

viscous *agg.* viscoso.

visibility s. visibilità.

visible agg. visibile, evidente, manifesto.

vision s. 1. visione, immaginazione 2. vista, capacità visiva.

visional agg. irreale.

visionary s. visionario.

visit s. visita: to pay a —, fare una visita.

to visit vt. e vi. visitare, fare una visita.

visitation s. 1. visita ufficiale 2. castigo divino.

visitor s. visitatore, ospite.

visor s. visiera.

visual agg. visuale, visivo.

to visualize vt. 1. rendere visibile 2. prospettare. ♦ **to visualize** vi. diventare visibile.

vital agg. vitale, essenziale.

vifality s. vitalità.

to vitalize vt. vivificare.

vitals s. pl. organi vitali.

vitamin s. vitamina.

to vitiate vt. 1. viziare 2. (giur.) invalidare.

vitiation s. 1. corruzione 2. (giur.) l'invalidare.

viticulture s. viticoltura.

vitreous agg. vitreo.

vitrifiable agg. vetrificabile.

vitrification s. vetrificazione.

to vitrify vt. vetrificare. ♦ **to vitrify** vi. vetrificarsi.

vitriol s. vetriolo.

to vituperate vt. vituperare.

vituperation s. invettiva, biasimo.

vivacious agg. vivace, vispo.

vivacity s. vivacità, brio.

vivid agg. 1. vivace, vigoroso 2. vivido, colorito.

to vivify vt. vivificare, animare.

viviparous agg. viviparo.

vivisection s. vivisezione.

vixen s. 1. volpe femmina 2. megera.

vocabulary s. vocabolario.

vocal agg. vocale.

vocalization s. vocalizzazione.

to vocalize vt. e vi. vocalizzare.

vocation s. 1. vocazione 2. attitudine, inclinazione 3. professione.

vocational agg. professionale.

vocative agg. e s. vocativo.

vociferous agg. clamoroso, vociferante.

vogue s. voga, moda.

voice s. voce || with one —, all'unanimità.

to voice vt. esprimere, dire.

voiced agg. 1. dalla voce: deep- —, dalla voce profonda 2. sonoro.

voiceless agg. senza voce, muto.

void agg. 1. vuoto 2. privo 3. (giur.) nullo. ♦ **void** s. il vuoto.

to void vt. 1. vuotare, liberare 2. abrogare.

volatile agg. 1. volatile, alato 2. (fig.) incostante. ♦ **volatile** s. 1. volatile 2. (chim.) sostanza volatile.

to volatilize vt. volatilizzare. ♦ **to volatilize** vi. volatilizzarsi.

volcano s. vulcano.

volley s. 1. scarica, raffica, salva || — -ball, palla a volo.

voltage s. (elettr.) voltaggio, tensione.

voltameter s. voltametro.

volubility s. speditezza (di eloquio), loquacità.

voluble agg. spedito (di eloquio), loquace.

volume s. 1. volume 2. tomo, libro 3. massa.

volumetric(al) agg. volumetrico.

voluminous agg. 1. in molti volumi 2. (fig.) fecondo (di scrittore) 3. voluminoso.

voluntarily avv. volontariamente.

voluntary agg. 1. volontario, spontaneo 2. voluto, fatto di proposito 3. mantenuto da contributi non statali. ♦ **voluntary** s. azione volontaria.

volunteer s. volontario.

to volunteer vi. 1. offrirsi volontariamente 2. arruolarsi volontario.

voluptuary agg. 1. voluttuario 2. voluttuoso.

voluptuous agg. voluttuoso, sensuale.

voluptuousness s. voluttà, sensualità.

volute s. voluta, spirale.

vomit s. vomito.

to vomit vt. e vi. vomitare (anche fig.).

voracious agg. ingordo, vorace.

vortex s. vortice, gorgo.

vortical agg. vorticoso.

votary s. seguace, devoto.

vote s. voto, votazione.

to vote vt. e vi. votare.

voter s. elettore.

votive agg. votivo.

to vouch vt. e vi. 1. attestare, garantire 2. (giur.) citare come garante.

voucher *s.* 1. testimone 2. documento giustificativo.

to vouchsafe *vt.* concedere.

vow *s.* voto.

to vow *vi.* fare un voto.

vowel *s.* vocale.

voyage *s.* viaggio (*spec. per via d'acqua*) || outward —, viaggio di andata; *home* —, viaggio di ritorno.

to voyage *vi.* fare una traversata, navigare.

vulcanization *s.* vulcanizzazione.

vulgar *agg.* volgare, triviale.

vulgarism, vulgarity *s.* volgarità.

to vulgarize *vt.* 1. rendere volgare 2. divulgare.

vulnerability *s.* vulnerabilità.

vulnerable *agg.* vulnerabile.

vulture *s.* avvoltoio.

W

to wabble *vi.* vacillare, traballare.

wad *s.* 1. tampone 2. imbottitura 3. rotolo (*di banconote*).

to wad *vt.* 1. tamponare 2. imbottire.

wadable *agg.* guadabile.

wadding *s.* ovatta.

waddle *s.* andatura ondeggiante.

to waddle *vi.* camminare ondeggiando.

wade *s.* guado.

to wade *vt.* guadare. ♦ **to wade** *vi.* procedere faticosamente.

wader *s.* 1. chi passa a guado 2. (*zool.*) trampoliere. ♦ **waders** *s. pl.* stivaloni impermeabili.

wading *s.* il guadare.

wafer *s.* 1. cialda 2. disco adesivo.

waft *s.* soffio.

to waft *vt.* sospingere. ♦ **to waft** *vi.* fluttuare.

wag *s.* 1. cenno 2. scodinzolio.

to wag *vt.* scuotere. ♦ **to wag** *vi.* scuotersi || *to have a wagging tongue*, avere la lingua troppo lunga.

to wage *vt.* intraprendere (*guerra*).

to wager *vt.* e *vi.* scommettere.

wages *s. pl.* salario (*sing.*) || —-*earner*, salariato.

to waggle V. *to wag.*

wag(g)on *s.* carro || *tea*- —, car-

rello da tè.

waif *s.* relitto (*anche fig.*).

wail *s.* gemito.

to wail *vt.* e *vi.* gemere.

wainscot *s.* rivestimento in legno.

to wainscot *vt.* rivestire in legno.

waist *s.* cintola.

waistband *s.* cintura.

waistbelt *s.* cinturone.

waistcoat *s.* panciotto.

wait *s.* 1. attesa 2. agguato.

to wait *vt.* e *vi.* (*for so., sthg.*) aspettare (*qu., qc.*) || *to* — *on*, servire.

waiter *s.* 1. cameriere 2. vassoio.

waiting *s.* attesa || — *room*, sala d'aspetto; *to keep* —, fare aspettare.

waitress *s.* cameriera.

to waive *vt.* rinunciare a, mettere da parte.

wake[1] *s.* 1. scia 2. pista.

wake[2] *s.* 1. risveglio 2. veglia (*funebre*).

to wake (waked e woke, waked, woke(n)) *vt.* svegliare. ♦ **to wake** (waked e woke, waked, woke(n)) *vi.* svegliarsi.

wakeful *agg.* sveglio.

wakefulness *s.* veglia.

to waken V. *to wake.*

wakening *s.* risveglio.

waking *agg.* sveglio. ♦ **waking** *s.* 1. risveglio 2. veglia.

walk *s.* 1. passeggiata 2. andatura 3. (*fig.*) rango || *to take a* —, fare una passeggiata.

to walk *vi.* passeggiare, andare a piedi || *to* — *off*, andarsene.

walker *s.* camminatore.

walkie-talkie *s.* (*radio*) trasmettitore-ricevitore portatile.

walking *s.* il camminare || — *tour*, escursione a piedi.

walkover *s.* facile vittoria.

wall *s.* muro || — *paper*, carta da parato; *main* —, muro maestro.

to wall *vt.* circondare di mura || *to* — *up*, murare.

wallet *s.* portafoglio.

wall-eye *s.* glaucoma.

Walloon *agg.* e *s.* vallone.

to wallop *vt.* 1. bastonare 2. percuotere, sculacciare.

wallow *s.* pantano.

to wallow *vi.* sguazzare.

walnut *s.* noce.

walrus *s.* tricheco.

waltz *s.* valzer.

to **waltz** *vi.* ballare il valzer.
wan *agg.* pallido.
to **wan** *vi.* impallidire.
wand *s.* bacchetta magica.
wander *s.* vagabondaggio.
to **wander** *vi.* 1. vagare 2. vaneggiare.
wanderer *s.* vagabondo.
wandering *agg.* 1. errante 2. delirante. ♦ **wandering** *s.* 1. vagabondaggio 2. delirio.
wane *s.* declino.
to **wane** *vi.* 1. declinare 2. decrescere 3. essere in fase calante.
to **wangle** *vt.* ottenere con intrighi.
want *s.* 1. mancanza 2. bisogno: *to be in — of*, aver bisogno di.
to **want** *vt.* 1. volere 2. aver bisogno di 3. mancare.
wanted *agg.* ricercato: *to be — by the police*, essere ricercato dalla polizia.
wanting *prep.* senza, in mancanza di.
wanton *agg.* 1. licenzioso 2. capriccioso 3. arbitrario 4. lascivo.
to **wanton** *vi.* 1. scherzare 2. comportarsi dissolutamente.
wantonness *s.* 1. dissolutezza 2. capriccio.
war *s.* guerra: *— Office*, Ministero della Guerra.
to **war** *vi.* guerreggiare.
warble *s.* trillo.
to **warble** *vt.* e *vi.* trillare.
warbling *agg.* melodioso. ♦ **warbling** *s.* gorgheggio.
ward *s.* 1. guardia 2. reparto 3. rione 4. tutela 5. pupillo.
to **ward** *vt.* parare: *to — off a blow*, parare un colpo.
warden *s.* 1. guardiano 2. direttore 3. governatore.
wardenship *s.* carica di direttore, governatore.
warder *s.* 1. guardiano 2. carceriere.
wardrobe *s.* guardaroba.
wardroom *s.* (*mar.*) quadrato ufficiali.
wardship *s.* tutela.
ware *agg.* conscio, circospetto.
to **ware** *vt.* fare attenzione a.
wares *s. pl.* 1. articoli 2. vasellame (*sing.*).
warehouse *s.* magazzino.
to **warehouse** *vt.* depositare in magazzino.
warehouseman *s.* 1. magazziniere 2. commerciante all'ingrosso.

warfare *s.* operazione bellica.
warfaring *agg.* bellicoso.
warily *avv.* cautamente.
wariness *s.* cautela.
warlike *agg.* guerriero.
warlikeness *s.* bellicosità.
warlock *s.* stregone.
warm *agg.* 1. caldo 2. animato.
to **warm** *vt.* 1. scaldare 2. animare. ♦ to **warm** *vi.* 1. scaldarsi 2. animarsi.
warmer *s.* riscaldatore.
warm-hearted *agg.* bonario, cordiale.
warming *s.* riscaldamento.
warmonger *s.* guerrafondaio.
warmth *s.* calore.
to **warn** *vt.* avvertire || *to — off*, invitare ad allontanarsi.
warning *s.* 1. (pre)avviso || *— light*, spia luminosa.
warp *s.* 1. ordito 2. deformazione.
to **warp** *vt.* 1. curvare 2. (*fig.*) alterare. ♦ to **warp** *vi.* 1. curvarsi 2. (*fig.*) alterarsi.
warpath *s.* sentiero di guerra.
warping *s.* deformazione, pervertimento.
warrant *s.* 1. garanzia, garante 2. (*giur.; comm.*) ordine, autorizzazione.
to **warrant** *vt.* 1. garantire 2. giustificare.
warrantable *agg.* 1. giustificabile 2. legittimo.
warrantee *s.* chi riceve una garanzia.
warranter, -tor *s.* garante.
warranty *s.* 1. garanzia 2. autorizzazione.
warrior *s.* guerriero.
warship *s.* nave da guerra.
wart *s.* verruca.
wartime *s.* tempo di guerra.
wary *agg.* cauto.
was V. *tc be.*
wash *s.* 1. lavata 2. bucato 3. sciacquio 4. brodaglia 5. mano (*di colore*).
to **wash** *vt.* 1. lavare 2. bagnare 3. gettare. ♦ to **wash** *vi.* 1. lavarsi 2. essere lavabile || *to — up*, rigovernare (*le stoviglie*); *to — over*, sommergere.
washable *agg.* lavabile.
washbasin *s.* catino.
washboard *s.* asse per lavare.
washer *s.* 1. lavandaio 2. (*mecc.*) lavatrice 3. (*mecc.*) rondella.

washerwoman s. lavandaia.

washhouse s. lavanderia.

washing s. **1.** lavaggio **2.** bucato **3.** risciacquatura || — *-machine*, lavatrice.

whashout s. erosione, dilatamento.

washroom s. **1.** lavanderia **2.** gabinetto.

washstand s. lavabo.

washy agg. **1.** annacquato **2.** scialbo.

wasp s. vespa.

waspish agg. pungente.

waspishness s. irascibilità.

wastage s. logorio.

waste agg. **1.** deserto **2.** di scarto. ♦ **waste** s. **1.** spreco **2.** scarto **3.** deserto || — *-basket*, cestino per rifiuti; — *-paper*, carta straccia.

to waste vt. **1.** consumare **2.** sprecare **3.** rovinare. ♦ **to waste** vi. **1.** consumarsi **2.** rovinarsi.

wasteful agg. **1.** rovinoso **2.** prodigo.

waster s. dissipatore.

wasting agg. **1.** logorante **2.** devastante. ♦ **wasting** s. **1.** sciupio **2.** deperimento **3.** devastazione.

watch s. **1.** orologio (*da polso*) **2.** guardia || — *-fire*, fuoco di bivacco; *to be on the —*, stare in guardia.

to watch vt. **1.** osservare **2.** stare a guardia di. ♦ **to watch** vi. **1.** vegliare **2.** aspettare.

watcher s. **1.** spettatore **2.** sorvegliante.

watchful agg. attento.

watchfulness s. **1.** vigilanza **2.** cautela.

watchmaker s. orologiaio.

watchman s. guardia (*notturna*).

watchword s. parola d'ordine.

water s. acqua || *to hold —*, non fare acqua, (*fig.*) essere logico; — *-bottle*, borraccia; — *-colour*, acquarello; — *-colourist*, acquarellista; — *-closet*, gabinetto; — *-gate*, chiusa; — *-line*, linea di galleggiamento; — *-meadow*, marcita; — *-polo*, pallanuoto; *drinking —*, acqua potabile.

to water vt. **1.** bagnare **2.** diluire **3.** abbeverare **4.** secernere || *to make one's mouth —*, far venire l'acquolina in bocca. ♦ **to water** vi. **1.** abbeverarsi **2.** riempirsi d'acqua.

waterfall s. cascata.

watering s. **1.** annaffiamento **2.** diluizione **3.** abbeverarsi **4.** rifornimento d'acqua **5.** secrezione || — *-can*, — *-pot*, annaffiatoio.

waterman s. (pl. -men) barcaiolo.

watermark s. **1.** filigrana **2.** indicatore di livello **3.** livello d'acqua.

watermelon s. anguria.

waterproof agg. e s. impermeabile.

to waterproof vt. impermeabilizzare.

watershed s. **1.** spartiacque **2.** bacino idrico.

watertight agg. stagno.

waterway s. canale navigabile.

waterworks s. pl. impianto idrico (sing.).

watery agg. **1.** acquoso **2.** lacrimoso.

wattle s. **1.** fascina **2.** vimine.

wave s. **1.** onda, onda **2.** cenno (*della mano*).

to wave vi. **1.** ondeggiare **2.** far cenno (*con la mano*). ♦ **to wave** vt. **1.** far ondeggiare **2.** ondulare **3.** chiamare (*con un cenno di mano*).

waved agg. ondulato.

wave-length s. lunghezza d'onda.

waveless agg. liscio.

wavelet s. piccola onda.

wavelike agg. ondeggiante.

to waver vi. vacillare.

wavering s. **1.** oscillazione **2.** esitazione.

wavily avv. a onde.

waviness s. ondulazione.

waving s. **1.** ondeggiamento, ondulazione **2.** sventolio **3.** cenno.

wavy agg. **1.** ondulato **2.** ondeggiante.

wax s. **1.** cera **2.** paraffina.

to wax [1] vt. incerare.

to wax [1] vi. **1.** crescere **2.** aumentare.

waxen agg. di, come cera.

way s. **1.** via **2.** maniera **3.** punto di vista **4.** stato || *to make —*, far posto; *this —*, per di qua; *in a —*, in un certo senso; *by the —*, tra parentesi; *one- —*, senso unico; *out of the —*, fuori mano.

waybill s. lista dei passeggeri.

wayfarer s. viandante.

to waylay vt. tendere un agguato a.

wayside s. margine della strada.

wayward agg. **1.** indocile **2.** capriccioso.

waywardness s. ostinazione.

we pron. sogg. noi.

weak *agg.* 1. debole 2. diluito.

to weaken *vi.* indebolirsi. ♦ to weaken *vt.* indebolire.

weakling *s.* persona debole.

weakly *agg.* debole.

weakness *s.* debolezza.

weal¹ *s.* benessere, prosperità.

weal² *s.* livido.

wealth *s.* ricchezza.

wealthy *agg.* ricco.

to wean *vt.* 1. svezzare 2. togliere il vizio a.

weaning *s.* svezzamento.

weapon *s.* arma.

wear *s.* 1. uso, usura 2. durata 3. abbigliamento.

to wear (wore, worn) *vt.* 1. indossare 2. logorare 3. stancare ‖ to — out, logorare, stancare. ♦ to wear (wore, worn) *vi.* 1. logorarsi 2. stancarsi 3. durare ‖ to — out, logorarsi, stancarsi.

wearily *avv.* stancamente.

weariness *s.* 1. stanchezza 2. tedio.

wearing *agg.* 1. logorante 2. da indossare. ♦ wearing *s.* 1. logorio 2. l'indossare.

wearisome *agg.* 1. faticoso 2. tedioso.

weary *agg.* 1. stanco 2. annoiato.

to weary *vt.* 1. affaticare 2. annoiare. ♦ to weary *vi.* 1. affaticarsi 2. annoiarsi.

weasel *s.* donnola.

weather *s.* tempo (*atmosferico*) ‖ — -glass, barometro; — -report, bollettino metereologico.

to weather *vt.* 1. esporre all'aria 2. superare ‖ to — a storm, resistere a una burrasca. ♦ to weather *vi.* alterarsi.

weathercock *s.* banderuola.

weathering *s.* alterazione (*di tempo*).

weave *s.* tessuto.

to weave (wove, woven) *vt.* 1. tessere, intrecciare 2. (*fig.*) ideare.

weaver *s.* tessitore.

weaving *s.* 1. tessitura 2. orditura.

web *s.* 1. tela 2. (*fig.*) trama 3. membrana ‖ cob—, ragnatela.

to wed *vt.* sposare. ♦ to wed *vi.* sposarsi.

wedding *s.* nozze (*pl.*) ‖ — -breakfast, rinfresco di nozze; — -ring, fede nuziale.

wedge *s.* cuneo.

to wedge *vt.* 1. incuneare 2. fendere con cunei.

wedlock *s.* vincolo matrimoniale.

Wednesday *s.* mercoledì.

wee *agg.* minuscolo ‖ a — bit, un tantino.

weed *s.* erbaccia. ♦ weeds *s. pl.* gramaglie.

to weed *vt.* 1. sarchiare 2. estirpare.

weeding *s.* sarchiatura.

week *s.* settimana ‖ today —, oggi a otto; — in — out, una settimana dopo l'altra.

weekday *s.* giorno feriale.

week-end *s.* fine settimana.

weekly *agg.* e *s.* settimanale. ♦ weekly *avv.* settimanalmente.

weep *s.* pianto.

to weep (wept, wept) *vt.* e *vi.* 1. piangere 2. trasudare ‖ to — out, piangere disperatamente.

weeper *s.* 1. chi piange 2. velo, nastro di lutto.

weeping *s.* 1. pianto 2. trasudamento.

weft *s.* trama (*di tessuto*).

to weigh *vt.* e *vi.* 1. pesare 2. (*fig.*) ponderare ‖ to — down, piegare; to — anchor (*mar.*), levar l'ancora.

weigh-house *s.* pesa pubblica.

weighing *s.* pesatura ‖ — -machine, pesa.

weight *s.* 1. peso 2. importanza ‖ to put on —, ingrassare

to weight *vt.* appensantire, caricare.

weightiness *s.* 1. pesantezza 2. (*fig.*) importanza.

weightless *agg.* senza peso.

weighty *agg.* 1. pesante 2. (*fig.*) importante.

weir *s.* chiusa, diga.

weird *agg.* 1. fatale 2. misterioso.

welcome *agg.* gradito. ♦ welcome *s.* benvenuto.

to welcome *vt.* dare il benvenuto a, gradire.

to weld *vt.* saldare. ♦ to weld *vi.* saldarsi.

welding *s.* saldatura.

welfare *s.* benessere ‖ — contributions, oneri previdenziali; — state, stato assistenziale; — work, assistenza sociale.

well¹ *s.* 1. fonte, pozzo 2. tromba delle scale.

well² *avv.* e *s.* bene ‖ as —, pure; as — as, oltre a, oltre che; to be —, star bene; to get —, guarire.

to well *vi.* sgorgare.

well-advised *agg.* saggio.

well-being *s.* benessere.

well-bred *agg.* educato.
well-doing *s.* buona condotta.
well-done *agg.* (*cuc.*) ben cotto.
well-meaning *agg.* ben intenzionato.
well-off *agg.* agiato.
well-read *agg.* colto, ben educato.
well-timed *agg.* opportuno.
well-to-do *agg.* agiato.
Welsh *agg.* gallese.
Welshman *s.* gallese.
went V. *to go.*
wept V. *to weep.*
were V. *to be* ‖ *as it —,* per così dire.
west *agg.* occidentale. ♦ **west** *avv.* a, verso ovest. ♦ **west** *s.* ovest.
westerly *agg.* 1. dall'ovest 2. verso ovest. ♦ **westerly** *avv.* verso ovest.
western *agg.* occidentale.
westerner *s.* occidentale.
to westernize *vt.* occidentalizzare. ♦ **to westernize** *vi.* occidentalizzarsi.
westward *agg. e avv.* verso ovest.
westwards *avv.* verso ovest.
wet *agg.* 1. umido 2. piovoso ‖ *— blanket,* guastafeste. ♦ **wet** *s.* 1. umidità 2. tempo piovoso.
to wet *vt.* bagnare. ♦ **to wet** *vi.* bagnarsi.
wet-nurse *s.* nutrice.
wetting *s.* bagnatura.
whale *s.* balena ‖ *— -boat,* baleniera.
to whale *vi.* andare a caccia di balene.
whalebone *s.* stecca di balena.
whaler *s.* 1. baleniere 2. baleniera.
wharf *s.* banchina.
to wharf *vt.* attraccare.
what *agg.* 1. (*int.*) quale? quali? che? 2. (*rel.*) (quello) ... che 3. (*escl.*) che! ♦ **what** *pron.* 1. (*int.*) che?; che cosa? 2. (*rel.*) ciò che 3. (*escl.*) quanto! ‖ — *for?,* perché mai?; — *is he?,* che cosa fa? ♦ **what** *inter.* come!
whatever *agg.* qualunque. ♦ **whatever** *pron.* qualunque cosa. ♦ **whatever** *avv.* affatto.
whatsoever V. *whatever.*
wheat *s.* grano.
to wheedle *vt.* lusingare.
wheel *s.* 1. ruota 2. volante ‖ *wheels within wheels,* retroscena.
to wheel *vt.* 1. far ruotare 2. spingere (*su un veicolo a ruote*). ♦

to wheel *vi.* ruotare.
wheelbarrow *s.* carriola.
wheeze *s.* respiro affannoso.
to wheeze *vi.* ansimare.
whelp *s.* cucciolo.
when *avv. e cong.* quando.
whence *avv.* da dove.
whenever *avv.* tutte le volte che.
where *avv.* dove.
whereabout(s) *avv. e cong.* dove. ♦ **whereabout(s)** *s.* luogo.
whereas *cong.* mentre.
whereby *avv.* 1. (*int.*) come? 2. (*rel.*) per cui.
wherefore *avv.* 1. (*int.*) perché 2. (*rel.*) perciò.
wherein *avv.* 1. (*int.*) come? dove? 2. (*rel.*) in cui.
whereof *avv.* 1. (*int.*) di che? 2. (*rel.*) di cui.
whereon *avv.* 1. (*int.*) su che? 2. (*rel.*) su cui.
whereto *avv.* 1. (*int.*) verso dove? a che scopo? 2. (*rel.*) a cui.
whereupon *avv.* 1. (*int.*) su che? 2. (*rel.*) dopo di che.
wherever *avv.* dovunque.
whet *s.* 1. affilatura 2. (*fig.*) stimolante.
to whet *vt.* 1. affilare 2. stimolare.
whether *cong.* se ‖ ... *or,* o...o.
whey *s.* siero (*del latte*).
which *agg.* 1. (*int.*) quale?, quali? 2. (*rel.*) il, la quale, i, le quali. ♦ **which** *pron.* 1. (*int.*) quale?, quali?, chi? 2. (*rel.*) il, la quale, i, le quali; il che ‖ *I cannot tell — is —,* non so distinguerli l'uno dall'altro.
whichever *agg.* qualunque. ♦ **whichever** *pron.* qualunque cosa.
whiff *s.* 1. soffio 2. sbuffo.
to whiff *vt. e vi.* 1. soffiare 2. emettere sbuffi.
whig *agg. e s.* (*pol. inglese*) liberale.
while *cong.* 1. mentre 2. sebbene. ♦ **while** *s.* momento ‖ *once in a —,* una volta tanto; *the —,* frattanto.
to while *vt. to — away the time,* ammazzare il tempo.
whilst V. *while.*
whim *s.* capriccio.
whimper *s.* 1. piagnucolio 2. uggiolio.
to whimper *vi.* 1. piagnucolare 2. uggiolare.
whimsical *agg.* stravagante.

whimsicality *s.* stravaganza.

whimsy *agg.* capriccioso. ✦ **whimsy** *s.* capriccio.

whine *s.* piagnisteo.

to whine V. *to whimper.*

whinny *s.* nitrito.

to whinny *vi.* nitrire.

whip *s.* frusta.

to whip *vt.* 1. frustare 2. frullare. ✦ to whip *vi.* precipitarsi || to — away, partire improvvisamente; to — out, pronunciare con violenza, tirar fuori.

whipper-snapper *s.* gradasso.

whirl *s.* 1. vortice 2. *(fig.)* confusione.

to whirl *vt.* 1. far roteare 2. trascinare. ✦ to whirl *vi.* 1. roteare 2. correr via 3. *(fig.)* esser confuso.

whirligig *s.* giostra.

whirlpool *s.* gorgo.

whirlwind *s.* turbine.

whir(r) *s.* 1. ronzio 2. frullio *(d'ali)* 3. rombo *(di motore).*

to whir(r) *vi.* 1. ronzare 2. frullare *(d'ali)* 3. rombare *(di motore).*

whisk *s.* 1. scopino 2. frullino 3. movimento rapido.

to whisk *vt.* 1. spazzare 2. *(cuc.)* frullare 3. agitare. ✦ to whisk *vi.* guizzare via.

whisker *s.* 1. basetta 2. baffo.

whisper *s.* 1. mormorio 2. diceria.

to whisper *vt. e vi.* mormorare, bisbigliare.

whistle *s.* fischio.

to whistle *vt. e vi.* 1. fischiare 2. chiamare con un fischio.

whistler *s.* 1. chi fischia 2. marmotta canadese.

whit *s.* 1. inezia 2. atomo.

Whit *agg.* di Pentecoste.

white *agg. e s.* bianco || — feather, viltà; — -livered, codardo.

to whiten *vt. e vi.* imbiancare.

whitener *s.* 1. imbianchino 2. candeggiante.

whiteness *s.* bianchezza.

whitening *s.* 1. imbiancamento 2. candeggiamento.

whitesmith *s.* lattoniere.

whitethorn *s.* biancospino.

whitewash *s.* 1. calce 2. *(fig.)* riabilitazione.

to whitewash *vt.* 1. imbiancare 2. *(fig.)* riabilitare.

whitewasher *s.* imbianchino.

whitewashing *s.* 1. imbiancatura 2. riabilitazione.

whiting *s.* calce.

whitish *agg.* biancastro.

whitlow *s.* patereccio.

Whitsunday *s* Pentecoste.

whiz *s.* sibilo.

who *pron.* 1. *(int.)* chi? 2. *(rel.)* il, la quale, i, le quali.

whoever *pron.* chiunque.

whole *agg.* tutto, intero. ✦ **whole** *s.* il tutto, l'intero 2. il complesso || as a —, nell'insieme; on the —, nel complesso.

wholeness *s.* totalità.

wholesale *agg. e avv.* all'ingrosso. ✦ **wholesale** *s.* vendita all'ingrosso.

to wholesale *vt. e vi.* vendere all'ingrosso.

wholesaler *s.* venditore all'ingrosso.

wholesome *agg.* salutare.

wholly *avv.* totalmente.

whom *pron. compl.* di who.

whomever *pron. compl.* chiunque.

whomsoever V. *whomever.*

whoop *s.* ululato.

whooping-cough *s.* pertosse.

whorl *s.* spirale.

whose *pron.* 1. *(int.)* di chi? 2. *(rel.)* del, della quale, dei, delle quali.

whosever *pron.* di chiunque.

whosoever V. *whoever.*

why *avv.* 1. *(int.)* perché? 2. *(rel.)* per cui. ✦ why *cong.* perché. ✦ why *inter.* perbacco.

wick *s.* lucignolo.

wicked *agg.* malvagio.

wickedness *s.* malvagità.

wicker *s.* vimine.

wicket *s.* 1. sportello 2. cancelletto.

wide *agg.* 1. largo 2. alto *(di tessuto)* 3. spalancato: — open, spalancato. ✦ **wide** *avv.* largamente.

wide-awake *agg.* 1. completamente sveglio 2. *(fig.)* vigilante.

widely *avv.* largamente.

to widen *vt.* allargare. ✦ to widen *vi.* allargarsi.

widespread *agg.* esteso.

widow *s.* vedova.

widower *s.* vedovo.

widowhood *s.* vedovanza.

width *s.* 1. larghezza 2. altezza *(di stoffa).*

to wield *vt.* 1. brandire 2. esercitare *(autorità ecc.).*

wife *s.* *(pl.* wives) moglie.

wig *s.* *(fam.)* sgridata.

wild agg. **1.** selvaggio, selvatico **2.** agitato **3.** pazzo **4.** avventato **5.** disordinato. ♦ **wild** s. deserto.

wild avv. **1.** selvaggiamente **2.** impulsivamente **3.** sfrenatamente.

wilderness s. deserto.

wild-goose chase s. impresa vana, impossibile.

wildness s. **1.** selvatichezza **2.** furore.

wile s. astuzia.

wilful agg. **1.** ostinato **2.** premeditato.

wilfulness s. **1.** ostinazione **2.** premeditazione.

will s. **1.** volontà **2.** testamento ‖ free —, libero arbitrio.

will v. ausiliare (usato per il futuro) he — be, egli sarà **2.** v. dif. volere: I — go, io voglio andare, io andrò (futuro volitivo).

to will vt. e vi. **1.** disporre **2.** lasciare per testamento.

willed agg. strong —, di forte volontà.

willing agg. **1.** volonteroso **2.** disposto ‖ — or not, volente o nolente.

willingly avv. volentieri.

willow s. — -(tree), salice: weeping —, salice piangente.

willy-nilly agg. e avv. volente o nolente.

wily agg. astuto.

wimple s. **1.** soggolo **2.** arricciatura.

to win (won, won) vt. e vi. vincere ‖ to — back, riconquistare.

wince s. sussulto.

to wince vi. trasalire.

winch s. **1.** argano **2.** manovella.

wind¹ s. **1.** vento **2.** respiro ‖ to get — of, aver sentore di; — -breaker, giacca a vento; — -cone, manica a vento.

wind² s. **1.** svolta, curva **2.** giro di carica.

to wind¹ vt. **1.** fiutare **2.** sfiatare.

to wind² (wound, wound) vt. **1.** avvolgere **2.** (una molla) caricare **3.** girare ‖ to — off, svolgere. ♦

to wind (wound, wound) vi. **1.** serpeggiare **2.** avvolgersi ‖ to — off, svolgersi.

windbag s. **1.** otre (di cornamusa) **2.** (fig.) parolaio.

winder s. **1.** manovella **2.** avvolgitore.

winding agg. tortuoso. ♦ **winding** s. **1.** tortuosità **2.** tornante **3.** spira

4. caricamento **5.** ritorcitura.

windlass s. argano.

windmill s. mulino a vento.

window s. finestra, finestrino ‖ — -dresser, vetrinista; French- —, porta finestra.

windpipe s. trachea.

windscreen s. parabrezza ‖ — wiper, tergicristallo.

windshield s. (amer.) parabrezza.

windward agg. contro vento. ♦ **windward** s. sopravvento.

windy agg. **1.** ventoso **2.** verboso.

wine s. vino.

wing s. **1.** ala **2.** battente (di porta) **3.** (teat.) quinta ‖ on the —, in volo; to take —, spiccare il volo.

winged agg. alato.

wink s. **1.** battito di palpebre **2.** ammicco **3.** (fig.) istante.

to wink vi. **1.** battere le palpebre **2.** ammiccare **3.** scintillare.

winner s. vincitore.

winning agg. **1.** vincitore **2.** suadente. ♦ **winning** s. vittoria.

to winnow vt. e vi. vagliare.

winsome agg. incantevole.

winter s. inverno. ♦ **winter** agg. invernale.

to winter vi. svernare.

wintered agg. gelato.

winterly V. wintry.

wintriness s. rigore invernale.

wintry agg. invernale, fred.lo.

wipe s. **1.** asciugatura **2.** spolverata.

to wipe vt. **1.** asciugare **2.** strofinare ‖ to — off, cancellare.

wiper s. **1.** chi pulisce **2.** strofinaccio.

wire s. **1.** filo metallico **2.** telegramma ‖ — netting, rete metallica; barbed —, filo spinato.

to wire vt. e vi. **1.** legare con filo metallico **2.** prendere in trappola **3.** telegrafare.

wired agg. munito di filo metallico, di rete metallica.

wireless agg. senza fili. ♦ **wireless** s. radiotelegrafia.

to wireless vt. e vi. radiotelegrafare.

wire-puller s. intrigante, eminenza grigia.

wiry agg. **1.** di, simile a filo metallico **2.** (fig.) resistente.

wisdom s. saggezza.

wise agg. **1.** saggio **2.** edotto, informato.

wise s. modo, maniera.

wiseacre s. saccente.

wisely *avv.* saggiamente.

wish *s.* **1.** desiderio **2.** augurio: *best wishes*, i migliori auguri.

to wish *vt.* e *vi.* **1.** desiderare **2.** augurare || *I wish I were*, vorrei essere; *I wish I had*, vorrei avere; *I wish I could*, vorrei potere.

wisher *s.* **1.** chi desidera **2.** chi augura.

wishful *agg.* desideroso.

wishing *agg.* desideroso. ◆ **wishing** *s.* desiderio.

wistaria *s.* glicine.

wistful *agg.* **1.** desideroso **2.** pensoso.

wistfully *avv.* **1.** con desiderio **2.** pensosamente.

wistfulness *s.* **1.** bramosia **2.** raccoglimento.

wit *s.* **1.** ingegno **2.** spirito **3.** persona di spirito || *to live by one's wits*, vivere di espedienti; *to be at one's wits' end*, non saper più cosa fare.

witch *s.* strega.

to witch *vt.* stregare.

witchcraft *s.* **1.** stregoneria *2.* fascino.

witch-doctor *s.* stregone.

witchery *s.* V. *witchcraft*.

witching *agg.* magico.

with *prep.* **1.** con **2.** presso **3.** a causa di, per, da.

to withdraw (withdrew, withdrawn) *vt.* ritirare. ◆ **to withdraw (withdrew, withdrawn)** *vi.* ritirarsi.

withdrawal *s.* **1.** ritirata, ritiro **2.** ritrattazione.

withdrawn V. *to withdraw*.

withdrew V. *to withdraw*.

withe *s.* vimine.

to wither *vt.* e *vi.* avvizzire.

withering *s.* avvizzimento.

to withhold (withheld, withheld) *vt.* **1.** trattenere **2.** rifiutare **3.** nascondere.

within *prep.* entro. ◆ **within** *avv.* dentro.

without *prep.* senza, senza di. ◆ **without** *cong.* senza (che). ◆ **without** *avv.* fuori.

to withstand (withstood, withstood) *vt.* resistere a, fronteggiare.

withstander *s.* oppositore.

withstood V. *to withstand*.

witness *s.* **1.** testimone: *eye* —, testimone oculare **2.** testimonianza.

to witness *vt.* **1.** essere testimone a **2.** mostrare. ◆ **to witness** *vi.* testimoniare.

witticism *s.* arguzia.

wittily *avv.* spiritosamente.

wittiness *s.* spirito.

wittingly *avv.* consapevolmente.

witty *agg.* spiritoso.

wives V. *wife*.

wizard *s.* mago.

to wobble V. *to wabble*.

woe *s.* dolore.

woeful *agg.* doloroso.

woke V. *to wake*.

woken V. *to wake*.

wolf *s.* (*pl.* wolves) lupo || *she-* —, lupa.

to wolf *vt.* divorare.

wolfish *agg.* da lupo.

woman *s.* (*pl.* women) donna.

womanhood *s.* **1.** femminilità **2.** maturità (*della donna*) **3.** condizione di donna.

womanish *agg.* **1.** effeminato **2.** femminile.

womankind *s.* le donne (*in genere*).

womanlike *agg.* femminile. ◆ **womanlike** *avv.* femminilmente.

womanliness *s.* femminilità.

womanly *agg.* femminile.

womb *s.* **1.** ventre **2.** grembo **3.** utero.

women V. *woman*.

won V. *to win*.

wonder *s.* **1.** prodigio **2.** meraviglia.

to wonder *vi.* **1.** domandarsi **2.** stupirsi.

wonderful *agg.* meraviglioso.

wonderingly *avv.* con meraviglia.

wonderland *s.* paese delle meraviglie.

wondrous *agg.* mirabile.

wont *agg.* abituato. ◆ **wont** *s.* abitudine.

wonted *agg.* abituato, abituale.

to woo *vt.* corteggiare.

wood *s.* **1.** bosco **2.** legno || —*cutter*, boscaiolo.

woodcock *s.* beccaccia.

woodcut *s.* **1.** incisione su legno **2.** xilografia.

wooden *agg.* di legno.

woodiness *s.* **1.** boscosità **2.** legnosità.

woodland *s.* terreno boscoso.

woodman *s.* **1.** guardaboschi **2.** taglialegna.

woodpecker *s.* picchio.

woodwork *s.* lavoro in legno.

woody *agg.* 1. boscoso 2. legnoso.

wooer *s.* corteggiatore.

wool *s.* 1. lana 2. peluria di animale || *cotton —*, ovatta.

wool(l)en *agg.* di lana. ◆ **wool(l)en** *s.* stoffa di lana.

woolly *agg.* 1. di lana, lanoso 2. *(fig.)* confuso.

word *s.* parola || *by — of mouth*, oralmente.

to word *vt.* esprimere.

wordiness *s.* verbosità.

wording *s.* espressione.

wordy *agg.* verboso.

wore V. *to wear*.

work *s.* lavoro || *out of —*, disoccupato. ◆ **works** *s. pl.* 1. meccanismo *(sing.)* 2. fabbrica, officina *(sing.)*.

to work *vt.* 1. lavorare 2. far funzionare 3. dirigere || *to — in*, introdurre; *to — off*, liberarsi di; *to — out*, calcolare; *to — up*, elaborare. ◆ **to work** *vi.* 1. lavorare 2. funzionare 3. agitarsi.

workable *agg.* 1. eseguibile 2. lavorabile.

workaday *agg.* lavorativo.

workday *s.* giorno feriale.

worker *s.* lavoratore || *skilled —*, operaio qualificato.

workhouse *s.* ospizio di mendicità.

working *agg.* 1. laborioso 2. funzionante. ◆ **working** *s.* 1. lavorio 2. funzionamento 3. lavorazione || *-clothes*, abiti da lavoro; *— expenses*, spese d'esercizio.

workless *agg.* senza lavoro.

workman *s.* operaio.

workmanship *s.* 1. abilità 2. fattura.

workroom *s.* laboratorio.

workshop *s.* officina.

workwoman *s.* operaia.

world *s.* mondo: *all over the —*, in tutto il mondo.

worldliness *s.* 1. condizione terrena 2. mondanità.

worldly *agg.* 1. terreno 2. mondano.

world-wide *agg.* diffuso, noto in tutto il mondo.

worm *s.* verme || *— -screw*, vite senza fine.

to worm *vt.* carpire || *to — one's way*, insinuarsi.

wormwood *s.* assenzio.

worn V. *to wear*. ◆ **worn** *agg.* 1.

consumato 2. indebolito || *— -out*, logoro, *(fig.)* esausto.

worried *agg.* 1. preoccupato 2. tormentato.

worrier *s.* seccatore.

worrisome *agg.* 1. irritante 2. preoccupato.

worry *s.* 1. ansia 2. guaio.

to worry *vt.* tormentare. ◆ **to worry** *vi.* preoccuparsi.

worrying *agg.* 1. preoccupante 2. tormentoso.

worse *agg. (comp. di bad e ill)* peggiore, peggio. ◆ **worse** *avv.* e *s.* peggio || *all the —*, tanto peggio; *so much the — for*, tanto peggio per; *none the —*, ugualmente; *— and —*, di male in peggio.

worship *s.* adorazione.

to worship *vt.* e *vi.* adorare, venerare.

worshipper *s.* 1. adoratore 2. fedele.

worst *agg. (superl. di bad e ill)* peggiore, pessimo. ◆ **worst** *avv.* e *s.* peggio || *at (the) —*, nella peggiore delle ipotesi.

worsted *agg.* di lana pettinata.

worth *agg.* degno. ◆ **worth** *s.* valore.

worthily *avv.* degnamente.

worthiness *s.* 1. valore 2. dignità.

worthless *agg.* 1. senza valore 2. indegno.

worthlessness *s.* 1. mancanza di valore 2. indegnità.

worthy *agg.* degno, meritevole. ◆ **worthy** *s.* persona illustre.

would *v. dif.* 1. *(ausiliare del condiz.) he — go*, egli andrebbe 2. *(passato ind. imperfetto, congiuntivo, condiz.)* volere 3. *(imperfetto ind.)* solere: *he — come every day*, soleva venire ogni giorno.

would-be *agg.* sedicente.

wound *s.* ferita.

to wound *vt.* ferire.

wound V. *to wind*.

wove V. *to weave*.

woven V. *to weave*.

wrack *s.* distruzione, rovina.

to wrangle *vi.* discutere.

wrangler *s.* attaccabrighe.

wrap *s.* sciarpa, coperta, mantello.

to wrap *vt.* avvolgere || *to — up*, impacchettare. ◆ **to wrap** *vi.* avvolgersi.

wrapper *s.* 1. imballatore 2. carta da imballo 3. copertina.

wrapping s. involucro || — *paper*, carta da imballaggio.

wrath s. ira.

wrathful agg. irato.

wrathfulness s. ira

wreath s. ghirlanda.

to wreathe vt. 1. intrecciare 2. inghirlandare 3. attorcigliare. ♦ **to wreathe** vi. innalzarsi in spire.

wreathy agg. 1. inghirlandato 2. a forma di ghirlanda.

wreck s. 1. naufragio (*anche fig.*) 2. relitto.

to wreck vt. rovinare. ♦ **to wreck** vi. naufragare.

wreckage V. *wreck*.

wren s. scricciolo.

wrench s. 1. strappo 2. (*mecc.*) chiave inglese.

to wrench, **to wrest** vt. 1. strappare 2. torcere.

wrestle s. lotta.

to wrestle vi. lottare.

wrestler s. lottatore.

wrestling s. (*sport.*) lotta

wretch s. disgraziato.

wretched agg. 1. disgraziato 2. scadente.

wretchedness s. 1. disgrazia 2. squallore.

wriggle s. contorsione.

to wriggle vt. contorcere. ♦ **to wriggle** vi. 1. contorcersi 2. (*fig.*) dar risposte evasive.

wring s. 1. torsione 2. dolore acuto.

to wring (wrung, wrung) vt. 1. torcere 2. estorcere 3. stringere || *to — out*, spremere, (*fig.*) strappare.

wringer s. 1. torcitore 2. torchio.

wringing agg. lancinante (*di dolore*). ♦ **wringing** s. torcitura.

wrinkle[1] s. 1. ruga 2. grinza.

wrinkle[2] s. stratagemma.

to wrinkle vt. 1. corrugare 2. spiegazzare. ♦ **to wrinkle** vi. corrugarsi.

wrinkled, **wrinkly** agg. 1. corrugato 2. rugoso.

wrinkledness s. rugosità.

wrist s. polso.

wristband s. polsino.

to write (wrote, written) vt. scrivere || *to — back*, rispondere; *to — down*, annotare, descrivere; *to — off*, cancellare; *to — out*, copiare, emettere un assegno.

writer s. scrittore.

writhe s. contorcimento.

to writhe vt. contorcere. ♦ **to writhe** vi. 1. contorcersi 2. (*fig.*) fremere.

writing s. 1. lo scrivere 2. scrittura 3. scritto || — *desk*, scrivania; — *paper*, carta da lettere.

written V. *to write*.

wrong agg. 1. sbagliato 2. ingiusto 3. illegale. ♦ **wrong** avv. 1. erroneamente 2. ingiustamente.

wrong s. 1. torto 2. male || — *doer*, peccatore, offensore; — *doing*, peccato, offesa.

to wrong vt. 1. far torto a 2. imbrogliare.

wrongful agg. V. *wrong*.

wrongfulness s. ingiustizia.

wrongly avv. V. *wrong*.

wrote V. *to write*.

wrought agg. lavorato || — *iron*, ferro battuto.

wrung V. *to wring*.

wry agg. storto.

to wry vt. contorcere. ♦ **to wry** vi. contorcersi.

wryly avv. per traverso.

X

xenophobe s. xenofobo.

xenophobia s. xenofobia.

xerophilous agg. xerofilo.

Xmas s. Natale.

X-ray agg. attr. a, di raggi X.

to X-ray vt. sottoporre a raggi X.

X-rays s. pl. raggi X.

xylograph s. xilografia.

xylographer s. xilografo.

xylographic(al) agg. xilografico.

xylography s. xilografia.

xylophone s. xilofono.

xylophonist s. xilofonista.

Y

yacht s. panfilo.

to yacht vi. fare crociere su panfilo.

yachtsman s. (*pl.* -men) proprietario di panfilo.

to yank vt. e vi. strappare, dare uno

strattone.

yap s. guaito.

to **yap** vi. guaire.

yard s. 1. iarda 2. cortile 3. cantiere: ship— —, cantiere navale.

yarn s. 1. filo 2. (fig.) storia.

yawl s. (naut.) iole, piccola imbarcazione.

yawn s. 1. sbadiglio 2. apertura.

to **yawn** vi. 1. sbadigliare 2. aprirsi.

yawning agg. 1. sonnolento 2. spalancato.

yea avv. sì.

year s. anno: — by —, di anno in anno; all the — round, per tutto l'anno; New Year's Day, Capodanno.

yearbook s. annuario.

yearling agg. di un anno d'età.

yearling s. animale di un anno.

yearlong agg. che dura un anno.

yearly agg. annuale. ♦ **yearly** avv. annualmente.

to **yearn** vi. languire || to — for, after sthg., bramare qc.

yearning s. brama. ♦ **yearning** agg. bramoso.

yeast s. 1. lievito 2. fermento.

to **yeast** vi. 1. lievitare 2. fermentare.

yell s. urlo.

to **yell** vt. e vi. urlare.

yeller s. urlatore.

yellow agg. e s. giallo.

to **yellow** vt. e vi. ingiallire.

yellowish agg. giallastro.

yelp s. guaito.

to **yelp** vi. guaire.

yeoman s. piccolo proprietario terriero.

yes avv. sì.

yesterday avv. e s. ieri: the day before —, l'altro ieri; — week, ieri a otto.

yet avv. 1. ancora 2. già || as —, finora. ♦ **yet** cong. tuttavia.

yew s. — (-tree) tasso.

yield s. 1. produzione 2. (comm.) rendita.

to **yield** vt. e vi. 1. produrre, rendere 2. cedere || to — oneself up, arrendersi.

yielding agg. 1. pieghevole 2. docile.

yoke s. 1. giogo 2. barra (del timone) 3. coppia (di animali).

to **yoke** vt. aggiogare.

yolk s. tuorlo.

yonder agg. quello là, di laggiù. ♦ **yonder** avv. là.

you pron. pers. 1. tu, te, ti 2. voi, ve, vi 3. (forma di cortesia) Lei, Loro.

young agg. giovane || — people, i giovani (in genere).

youngster s. giovanetto.

your agg. poss. 1. tuo 2. vostro 3. (forma di cortesia) Suo.

yours pron. poss. 1. tuo 2. vostro 3. (forma di cortesia) Suo, Loro || — truly, — faithfully, distinti saluti.

yourself pron. r. 1. tu stesso, ti, te, te stesso 2. (forma di cortesia) Lei stesso.

yourselves pron. r. 1. voi stessi, vi 2. (forma di cortesia) Loro stessi.

youth s. 1. gioventù 2. ragazzo.

youthful agg. 1. giovane 2. giovanile.

youthfulness s. aspetto giovanile.

Yugoslav agg. e s. iugoslavo.

Z

zeal s. zelo.

zealot s. fanatico.

zealous agg. zelante.

zed s. zeta.

zenith s. zenit.

zephyr s. zeffiro.

zero s. 1. zero 2. (fig.) nullità.

zest s. 1. gusto 2. aroma.

zigzag agg. e avv. a zigzag.

to **zigzag** vi. andare a zigzag.

zinc s. zinco.

to **zinc** vt. zincare.

zincking s. zincatura.

zincograph s. zincografia.

to **zincograph** vt. imprimere su lastre di zinco.

zincographer s. zincografo.

zincography s. zincografia.

Zionism s. sionismo.

Zionist s. e agg. sionista.

zip s. fischio || — (-fastener), cerniera lampo.

to **zip** vi. sibilare.

zipper s. cerniera lampo.

zircon s. zircone.

zirconium s. zirconio.

zodiac s. zodiaco.

zodiacal agg. zodiacale.

zonal, zonary *agg.* zonale.
zonate(d) *agg.* a zone.
zonation *s.* zonatura.
zone *s.* zona.
zoo *s.* zoo.
zoological *agg.* zoologico.
zoologist *s.* zoologo.
zoology *s.* zoologia.
zoom *s.* **1.** rombo **2.** (*aer.*) salita a candela.
to zoom *vi.* **1.** rombare **2.** (*aer.*) salire a candela.

zoomorphic *agg.* zoomorfo.
zoomorphism *s.* zoomorfismo.
zoophilist *s.* zoofilo.
zoophilous *agg.* zoofilo.
zoophily *s.* zoofilia.
zoophobia *s.* zoofobia.
zootechnic *agg.* zootecnico.
zootechnics, zootechny *s.* zootecnica.
zootomic(al) *agg.* zootomico.
zouave *s.* zuavo.
zygoma *s.* (*pl.* zygomata) zigomo.

NOMI PROPRI, STORICI E GEOGRAFICI

Abel Abele.
Abraham Abramo.
Abyssinia Abissinia.
Achilles Achille.
Adam Adamo.
Adolph Adolfo.
Adonis Adone.
Adriatic Sea Mar Adriatico.
Aegean Sea Mar Egeo.
Aeneas Enea.
Aeschylus Eschilo.
Aesop Esopo.
Afghanistan Afganistan.
Agamemnon Agamennone.
Agatha Agata.
Agnes Agnese.
Ajax Aiace.
Albert Alberto
Aldous Aldo.
Alec, Alex dim. di Alexander.
Alexander Alessandro.
Alexandra Alessandra.
Alexis Alessio.
Alfred Alfredo.
Algiers Algeri.
Alps pl. Alpi.
Alsace Alsazia.
Amazon Rio delle Amazzoni.
Ambrose Ambrogio.
Andes pl. Ande.
Andrew Andrea.
Andy dim. di Andrew.
Angel Angelo.
Ann(e) Anna.
Annie dim. di Ann(e).
Antarctica Antartide.
Anthony Antonio.
Antoninus Antonino.
Antony Antonio.
Apennines pl. Appennini.
Aphrodite Afrodite.
Apulia Puglia.
Aragon Aragona.
Archimedes Archimede.
Ariadne Arianna.
Aristophanes Aristofane.
Aristotle Aristotele.
Armand Armando.
Arnold Arnaldo.
Arthur Arturo.
Athens Atene.
Atlantic Atlantico.

Augustin Agostino.
Augustus Augusto.
Azores pl. Azzorre.

Babel Babele.
Babylon Babilonia.
Bacchus Bacco.
Balearic Islands Baleari.
Balkans pl. Balcani.
Balthazar Baldassarre.
Baltic Sea Mar Baltico.
Baltimore Baltimora.
Baptist Battista.
Barcelona Barcellona.
Barnabas, Barnaby Barnaba.
Bartholomew Bartolomeo.
Basel Basilea.
Basil Basilio.
Beatrix Beatrice.
Belgium Belgio.
Belgrade Belgrado.
Benedict Benedetto.
Bengal Bengala.
Ben dim. di Benjamin.
Benjamin Beniamino.
Benny dim. di Benjamin.
Berlin Berlino.
Bermudas pl. Bermude.
Bern Berna.
Bernard Bernardo.
Bertha Berta.
Bess dim. di Elizabeth.
Bethlehem Betlemme.
Betty dim. di Elizabeth.
Bill(y) dim. di William.
Blanche Bianca.
Bob(by) dim. di Robert.
Bohemia Boemia.
Boniface Bonifacio.
Bosporus Bosforo.
Brandenburg Brandeburgo.
Brazil Brasile.
Brittany Bretagna.
Brutus Bruto.
Burma Birmania.

Cadiz Cadice.
Caesar Cesare.
Cain Caino.
Caius Caio.

Calvin Calvino.
Cambodia Cambogia.
Canada Canadà.
Capitol Campidoglio.
Caribbean Sea Mar dei Caraibi.
Caroline Carolina.
Carpathian Mountains pl. Carpazi.
Carthage Cartagine.
Cashmere Cascemir.
Caspian Sea Mar Caspio.
Cassiopeia Cassiopea.
Cassius Cassio.
Catherine Caterina.
Cato Catone.
Caucasus Caucaso.
Cecil Cecilio.
Channel (The) La Manica.
Charlemagne Carlomagno.
Charles Carlo.
Charlie dim. di Charles.
Charlotte Carlotta.
Chile Cile.
China Cina.
Christ Cristo.
Christine Cristina.
Christopher Cristoforo.
Cicero Cicerone.
Cinderella Cenerentola.
Clara Clara, Chiara.
Claude, Claudius Claudio.
Clement Clemente.
Clementine Clementina.
Clytemnestra Clitennestra.
Cologne Colonia.
Connie dim. di Constance.
Conrad Corrado.
Constance Costanza.
Constantine Costantino.
Constantinople Costantinopoli.
Corinth Corinto.
Cornelius Cornelio.
Cornwall Cornovaglia.
Crete Creta.
Cynthia Cinzia.
Cyprus Cipro.
Cyril Cirillo.
Cyrus Ciro.
Czechoslovakia Cecoslovacchia.

Daisy dim. di Margaret.
Damascus Damasco.
Damocles Damocle.
Dan dim. di Daniel.
Daniel Daniele.
Danny dim. di Daniel.
Danube Danubio.
Danzig Danzica.

Daphne Dafne.
Dardanelles pl. Dardanelli.
Darius Dario.
Dave dim. di David.
Deb(by) dim. di Deborah.
Deborah Debora.
Delphi Delfo.
Democritus Democrito.
Demosthenes Demostene.
Denmark Danimarca.
Dick dim. di Richard.
Dido Didone.
Diocletian Diocleziano.
Diogenes Diogene.
Dionysius Dionigi, Dionisio.
Dominic Domenico.
Domitian Domiziano.
Dorothy Dorotea.
Dublin Dublino.

Ed(dy) dim. di Edmund, Edward.
Edgar Edgardo.
Edinburgh Edimburgo.
Edmund Edmondo.
Edward Edoardo.
Egypt Egitto.
Eire (Stato Libero di) Irlanda.
Eleanor Eleonora.
Electra Elettra.
Elias, Elijah Elia.
Eliza Elisa.
Elizabeth Elisabetta.
Emanuel Emanuele.
Emily Emilia.
England Inghilterra.
Epaminondas Epaminonda.
Epicurus Epicuro.
Erasmus Erasmo.
Ernest Ernesto.
Esther Ester.
Ethiopia Etiopia.
Euclid Euclide.
Eugene Eugenio.
Euphrates Eufrate.
Euripides Euripide.
Europe Europa.
Eve Eva.
Evelyn Evelina.
Ezekiel Ezechiele.

Faust(us) Fausto.
Felix Felice.
Ferdinand Ferdinando.
Finland Finlandia.
Florence Firenze.
France Francia.
Frances Francesca.

Francis Francesco.
Frank Franco.
Frankfurt Francoforte.
Fred(dy) *dim. di* Frederic.
Frederic Federico.

Gabriel Gabriele.
Galilee Galilea.
Gascony Guascogna.
Gaule Gallia.
Geneva Ginevra.
Genoa Genova.
Geoffrey Goffredo.
George Giorgio.
Gerard Gerardo.
Germany Germania.
Gibraltar Gibilterra.
Gilbert Gilberto.
Golgotha Golgota.
Goliath Golia.
Grace Grazia.
Great Britain Gran Bretagna.
Greece Grecia.
Greenland Groenlandia.
Gregory Gregorio.
Guiana Guaiana.
Gustavus Gustavo.
Guy Guido.

Hadrian Adriano.
Hague (The) L'Aia.
Hamburg Amburgo.
Hamlet Amleto.
Hannibal Annibale.
Harold Aroldo.
Harriet Enrichetta.
Harry *dim. di* Harold, Henry.
Hebrides *pl.* Ebridi.
Hector Ettore.
Helen Elena.
Hellas Ellade.
Henrietta Enrichetta.
Henry Arrigo, Enrico.
Heraclitus Eraclito.
Herbert Erberto.
Hercules Ercole.
Hermes Ermete.
Herod Erode.
Herodotus Erodoto.
Hesiod Esiodo.
Hilary Ilario.
Himalaya Imalaia.
Hindustan Indostan.
Hippolytus Ippolito.
Holland Olanda.
Homer Omero.
Horace, Horatio Orazio.

Hubert Uberto.
Hugh Ugo.
Humbert Umberto.
Hungary Ungheria.

Icarus Icaro.
Iceland Islanda.
Ignatius Ignazio.
Innocent Innocente.
Ionian Sea Mar Ionio.
Ireland Irlanda.
Iris Iride.
Isaac Isacco.
Isabel Isabella.
Isaiah Isaia.
Ishmael Ismaele.
Isis Iside.
Israel Israele.
Italy Italia.

Jack(ie) *dim. di* John.
Jacob Giacobbe.
Jamaica Giamaica.
James Giacomo.
Jane Giovanna.
Janet *dim. di* Jane.
Japan Giappone.
Jason Giasone.
Java Giava.
Jean Giovanna.
Jeffrey Goffredo.
Jehovah Geova.
Jenny *dim. di* Jean.
Jeremiah Geremia.
Jericho Gerico.
Jerome Gerolamo.
Jerry *dim. di* Gerard, Jerome.
Jerusalem Gerusalemme.
Jesus Gesù.
Jim(my) *dim. di* James.
Jo *dim. di* Josephine.
Joan Giovanna.
Job Giobbe.
Joe *dim. di* Joseph.
John Giovanni.
Johnny *dim. di* John.
Jonah, Jonas Giona.
Jonathan Gionata.
Jordan Giordano.
Joseph Giuseppe.
Josephine Giuseppina.
Joshua Giosuè.
Jove Giove.
Judas, Jude Giuda.
Judea Giudea.
Judith Giuditta.
Judy *dim. di* Judith.

Julia Giulia.
Julian Giuliano.
Juliana Giuliana.
Julie Giulia.
Juliet Giulietta.
Julius Giulio.
Juno Giunone.
Jupiter Giove.
Juvenal Giovenale.

Kashmir Cascemir.
Kate, Kitty *dim. di* Catherine.
Korea Corea.

Lambert Lamberto.
Laocoon Laocoonte.
Lapland Lapponia.
Larry *dim. di* Lawrence.
Latium Lazio.
Launcelot Lancillotto.
Lausanne Losanna.
Lawrence Lorenzo.
Lazarus Lazzaro.
Leander Leandro.
Lebanon Libano.
Leghorn Livorno.
Leo(n) Leone.
Leonard Leonardo.
Leonidas Leonida.
Leopold Leopoldo.
Lethe Lete.
Letitia Letizia.
Lewis Luigi.
Libya Libia.
Liège Liegi.
Lisbon Lisbona
Livy Livio.
Liza, Lizzie, Liz(zy) *dim. di* Elizabeth.
Lombardy Lombardia.
London Londra.
Lou *dim. di* Louise.
Louis Luigi.
Louise Luigia, Luisa.
Louvain Lovanio.
Lucerne Lucerna.
Lucian Luciano.
Lucifer Lucifero.
Lucius Lucio.
Lucretius Lucrezio.
Lucy Lucia.
Luke Luca.
Luther Lutero.
Luxemburg Lussemburgo.
Lycurgus Licurgo.
Lydia Lidia.
Lyons Lione.

Magdalene Maddalena.
Mag(gie) *dim. di* Margaret.
Majorca Maiorca.
Malaya Malesia.
Manchuria Manciuria.
Manfred Manfredi.
Mantua Mantova.
Marathon Maratona.
Marcellus Marcello.
Margaret Margherita.
Margie *dim. di* Margaret.
Marianne Marianna.
Marius Mario.
Mark Marco.
Mars Marte.
Martha Marta.
Martial Marziale.
Martin Martino.
Mary Maria.
Matilda Matilde.
Matt *dim. di* Matthew.
Matthew Matteo.
Matty *dim. di* Martha, Matilda.
Maurice Maurizio.
Max *dim. di* Maximilian.
Maximilian Massimiliano.
May *dim. di* Mary.
Mediterranean Mediterraneo.
Meg *dim. di* Margaret.
Menelaus Menelao.
Mephistopheles Mefistofele.
Mercury Mercurio.
Merlin Merlino.
Methuselah Matusalemme.
Meuse Mosa.
Mexico Messico.
Michael Michele.
Mick(ey) *dim. di* Michael.
Midas Mida.
Mike *dim. di* Michael.
Milan Milano.
Minos Minosse.
Minotaur Minotauro.
Mithridates Mitridate.
Mohammed Maometto.
Moll(y) *dim. di* Mary.
Moluccas *pl.* Molucche.
Monaco (Principato di) Monaco.
Morocco Marocco.
Moscow Mosca.
Moses Mosè.
Mozambique Mozambico.
Munich Monaco di Baviera.
Mycenae Micene.

Naples Napoli.
Napoleon Napoleone.
Narcissus Narciso.

Nell(y) *dim. di* Helen.
Neptune Nettuno.
Nero Nerone.
Netherlands *pl.* Paesi Bassi.
Newfoundland Terranova.
New Zealand Nuova Zelanda.
Nice Nizza.
Nicholas Nicola.
Nick *dim. di* Nicholas.
Nile Nilo.
Noah Noè.
Normandy Normandia.
Norway Norvegia.

Oedipus Edipo.
Oliver Oliviero.
Olympus Olimpo.
Ophelia Ofelia.
Orestes Oreste.
Orion Orione.
Orkneys *pl.* Orcadi.
Orpheus Orfeo.
Osiris Osiride.
Oswald Osvaldo.
Othello Otello.
Ovid Ovidio.

Pacific Pacifico.
Paddy *dim. di* Patrick.
Padua Padova.
Palestine Palestina.
Pancras Pancrazio.
Papua Papuasia.
Paris¹ Paride.
Paris² Parigi.
Parnassus Parnaso.
Parthenon Partenone.
Pat *dim. di* Patricia, Patrick.
Patricia Patrizia.
Patrick Patrizio.
Paul Paolo.
Paula Paola.
Pauline Paolina.
Peg(gy) *dim. di* Margaret.
Peking Pechino.
Peloponnesus Peloponneso.
Pennsylvania Pensilvania.
Pericles Pericle.
Perseus Perseo.
Peru Perù.
Pete *dim. di* Peter.
Peter Pietro.
Phaedra Fedra.
Pharsalus Farsalo.
Philadelphia Filadelfia.
Philip Filippo.
Philippi Filippi.

Philippines *pl.* Filippine.
Piedmont Piemonte.
Pigmalion Pigmalione.
Pindar Pindaro.
Piraeus Pireo.
Plus Pio.
Plato Platone.
Pliny Plinio.
Plutarch Plutarco.
Poland Polonia.
Poll(y) *dim. di* Mary.
Polynesia Polinesia.
Pompey Pompeo.
Portugal Portogallo.
Prague Praga.
Prometheus Prometeo.
Ptolemy Tolomeo.
Pyrenees *pl.* Pirenei.
Pythagoras Pitagora.

Quentin Quintino.

Rachel Rachele.
Ramses Ramsete.
Raphael Raffaele, Raffaello.
Raymond Raimondo.
Remus Remo.
Rhine Reno.
Rhodes Rodi.
Rhone Rodano.
Richard Riccardo.
Rob *dim. di* Robert.
Robert Roberto.
Roderick Rodrigo.
Roger Ruggero.
Roland Orlando, Rolando.
Rome Roma.
Romulus Romolo.
Rosalie Rosalia.
Rosalind Rosalinda.
Rose Rosa.
Roumania Romania.
Roxana Rossana.
Rudolph Rodolfo.
Rudy *dim. di* Rudolph.

Sadie, Sally *dim. di* Sarah.
Sam *dim. di* Samuel.
Samson Sansone.
Samuel Samuele.
Sappho Saffo.
Sarah Sara.
Sardinia Sardegna.
Satan Satana.
Saturn Saturno.
Savoy Savoia.

Saxony Sassonia.
Scipion Scipione.
Scotland Scozia.
Sean Giovanni.
Sebastian Sebastiano.
Sibyl Sibilla.
Sicily Sicilia.
Silvester Silvestro.
Simeon Simeone.
Simon Simone.
Simplon Sempione.
Smyrna Smirne.
Socrates Socrate.
Sodom Sodoma.
Solomon Salomone.
Somaliland Somalia.
Sophia Sofia.
Sophocles Sofocle.
Soudan Sudan.
Spain Spagna.
Stephen Stefano.
Steve *dim. di* Stephen.
Stockholm Stoccolma.
Strasbourg Strasburgo.
Sue *dim. di* Susan(nah).
Sulla Silla.
Susy *dim. di* Susan(nah).
Susan(nah) Susanna.
Sweden Svezia.
Switzerland Svizzera.
Sylvia Silvia.
Syracuse Siracusa.
Syria Siria.

Tacitus Tacito.
Tangier(s) Tangeri.
Ted(dy) *dim. di* Edward.
Telemachus Telemaco.
Terence Terenzio.
Tess *dim. di* Theresa.
Thailand Tailandia.
Thames Tamigi.
Thebes Tebe.
Themistocles Temistocle.
Theodoric Teodorico.
Theresa Teresa.
Thermopylae *pl.* Termopili.
Theseus Teseo.
Thomas Tommaso.
Tiber Tevere.
Tiberius Tiberio.
Tirol Tirolo.
Titian Tiziano.
Titus Tito.
Tobias Tobia.
Toby *dim. di* Tobias.

Tom(my) *dim. di* Thomas.
Tonkin, Tonking Tonchino.
Tony *dim. di* Ant(h)ony.
Trajan Traiano.
Tristan, **Tristram** Tristano.
Troy Troia.
Tully Tullio.
Tunis Tunisi.
Turin Torino.
Turkey Turchia.
Tuscany Toscana.
Tyrol Tirolo.
Tyrrhenian Sea Mar Tirreno.

Ukraine Ucraina.
Ulysses Ulisse.
United States of America Stati
    Uniti d'America.
Urban Urbano.
Ursula Orsola.
USA Stati Uniti d'America.
USSR URSS (Unione Repubbliche
    Socialiste Sovietiche).

Valentine Valentino.
Valerius Valerio.
Vatican Vaticano.
Venetia Veneto.
Venice Venezia.
Venus Venere.
Vesuvius Vesuvio.
Victor Vittorio.
Victoria Vittoria.
Vincent Vincenzo.
Virgil Virgilio.
Vivian Viviana, Viviano.
Vulcan Vulcano.

Wales Galles.
Walter Gualtiero.
Warsaw Varsavia.
Will *dim. di* William.
William Guglielmo.
Willy *dim. di* William.

Xerxes Serse.

Yugoslavia Iugoslavia.

Zachary Zaccaria.
Zurich Zurigo.

SIGLE E ABBREVIAZIONI USATE
NEI PAESI DI LINGUA INGLESE

a., 1. *about:* c., circa **2.** *acre:* acro **3.** *approved:* approvato, riconosciuto dallo Stato.

A.A., *Automobile Association:* A.C., Automobile Club.

A.A.R., *against all risks:* contro ogni rischio.

Abp., *Archbishop:* arcivescovo.

abr., 1. *abridged:* ridotto (*di edizione*) **2.** *abridgment:* compendio.

A.C., *alternating current:* c.a., corrente alternata.

a/c, ac., *account:* c., conto.

A.D., *Anno Domini (= dopo Cristo):* d.C., dopo Cristo.

adj., *adjourned:* aggiornato.

Adm., *Admiral:* ammiraglio.

adv., *advertisement:* inserzione.

A.E.C., *Atomic Energy Commission:* C.E.A., Commissione per l'energia atomica.

A.F., *Air Force:* A.M., Aeronautica Militare.

Ala., *Alabama.*

Alas., *Alaska.*

alt., 1. *alternate:* alternata **2.** *alternating:* alternata.

a.m., *ante meridiem, before noon:* antimeridiano.

Am(er)., 1. *America:* Am., Amer., America **2.** *American:* am., amer., americano.

anon., *anonymous:* anonimo.

A.P., *Associated Press:* Stampa Associata.

app., *appendix:* app., appendice.

approx., *approximately:* appross., approssimativamente.

Apr., *April:* apr., aprile.

apt., *apartment:* appartamento.

Ariz., *Arizona.*

Ark., *Arkansas.*

arr., 1. *arrival:* arr., arrivo **2.** *arrived:* arr., arrivato.

ass., *association:* ass., associazione.

at. no., *atomic number:* n.a., numero atomico.

att(y)., *attorney:* proc., procuratore.

at. wt., *atomic weight:* p. at., peso atomico.

Aug., *August:* ago., agosto.

avdp., *avoirdupois:* avoirdupois.

ave., *avenue:* v.le, viale.

b., 1. *book:* l., libro **2.** *born:* n., nato.

B.A., *Bachelor of Arts:* diplomato in lettere.

Bap(t)., *Baptist:* Battista.

B.B.C., *British Broadcasting Corporation:* Ente Radiofonico Britannico.

B.C., *Before Christ:* a.C., avanti Cristo.

B/E, b.e., *bill of exchange:* cambiale.

B.E.A., *British European Airways:* Linee Aeree Europee Britanniche.

Beds., *Bedfordshire.*

Berks., *Berkshire.*

bet., *between:* fra.

B/L, *bill of lading:* polizza di carico.

blvd., *boulevard:* boulevard.

B.M., *British Museum:* Museo Britannico.

B.M.A., *British Medical Association:* Associazione Medica Britannica.

B.O.A.C., *British Overseas Airways Corporation:* Società aerea d'oltremare britannica.

B. of A., *Bank of America:* Banca d'America.

B. of E., *Bank of England:* Banca d'Inghilterra.

Bp., *Bishop:* vesc., vescovo.

bros., *brothers:* F.lli, Fratelli.

b.s., 1. *balance sheet:* bilancio di esercizio **2.** *bill of sale:* atto di vendita.

bsh., *bushel:* staio.

Bucks., *Buckinghamshire.*

bul(l)., *bulletin:* boll., bollettino.

c., 1. *centigrade:* c., centigrado **2.** *cent:* cent., centesimo **3.** *chapter:* cap., capitolo.

C/A, *current account:* c/c, conto corrente.

ca., 1. *cathode:* catodo 2. *about:* ca., circa.

Cal(if)., *California.*

Cam(b)., *Cambridge.*

Cambs., *Cambridgeshire.*

Can., 1. *Canada:* Canada 2. *Canadian:* canadese.

Cantab., *of Cambridge:* cantabrigense.

cap., 1. *chapter:* cap, capitolo 2. *capital:* capitale.

Capt., *Captain:* cap., capitano.

Card., *Cardinal:* card., cardinale.

cc., 1. *chapters:* capp., capitoli 2. *cubic centimetres:* cmc., centimetri cubi.

C.D., *Corps Diplomatique:* C.D., Corpo Diplomatico.

C.E.D., *Community for European Defence:* C.E.D., Comitato per la Difesa Europea.

Celt., *Celtic:* celtico.

cent., 1. *centigrade:* c., centigrado 2. *centimetre:* cm., centimetro 3. *central:* centrale 4. *century:* sec., secolo.

c.f., *cost and freight:* c.f., costo e nolo.

C.F.I., c.f.i., *cost, freight and insurance:* costo, nolo e assicurazione.

Ch., 1. *Church:* Chiesa 2. *China:* Cina 3. *Chinese:* cinese.

ch(ap)., *chapter:* cap., capitolo.

Ches(h)., *Cheshire.*

Chr., 1. *Christ:* Cristo 2. *Christian:* cristiano.

C.I.A., *Central Intelligence Agency:* Organizzazione centrale d'informazioni (Servizio segreto americano).

c.i.f., *cost, insurance, freight:* c.i.f., costo, assicurazione e nolo.

cm., *centimetre:* cm., centimetro.

Co., 1. *Company:* s., società 2. *County:* contea.

c/o, *care of:* c/o, presso.

C.O.D., c.o.d., *cash on delivery:* pagamento alla consegna.

Col., 1. *Colonel:* col., colonnello 2. *Colorado.*

coll., 1. *colleague:* collega 2. *college:* coll., collegio 3. *colloquial:* fam., familiare.

Colo., *Colorado.*

Conn., *Connecticut.*

Consol., *consolidated:* consolidato.

cont(d)., *continued:* continuo, ininterrotto.

coop., *co-operative:* coop., cooperativa.

corp., *corporation:* 1. corporazione 2. *(amer.)* s.r.l., società a responsabilità limitata.

Corn(w), *Cornwall.*

c.o.s., *cash on shipment:* pagamento alla spedizione.

C.P., *Communist Party:* P.C., Partito Comunista.

cp., *compare:* cfr., confrontare.

Ct., *Connecticut.*

cu., *cubic:* c., cubico.

Cumb., *Cumberland.*

C.U.P., *Cambridge University Press:* Edizioni dell'Università di Cambridge.

d., 1. *date:* data 2. *dead:* m., morto 3. *penny, pence:* penny, pence.

d.c., *direct current:* c.c., corrente continua.

D.A.B., *Dictionary of American Biography:* Dizionario della Biografia Americana.

Dak., *Dakota.*

D.C., *District of Columbia:* Distretto della Columbia.

D.D., *Doctor of Divinity:* dottore in teologia.

dd., *d/d, delivered:* consegnato.

Dec., *December:* dic., dicembre.

Del., *Delaware.*

dep., 1. *department:* reparto, ufficio; *(am.)* ministero 2. *deputy:* deputato.

Devon., *Devonshire.*

Dir., *director:* diret., direttore.

disc., *discount:* sconto.

D. Lit., *Doctor of Literature:* dottore in letteratura.

D.N.B., *Dictionary of National Biography:* Dizionario della Biografia Nazionale.

dol., *dollar:* dollaro.

Dorset., *Dorsetshire.*

doz., *dozen:* dozz., dozzina.

D.P., *Displaced Person:* profugo.

Dr., 1. *Doctor:* dott., dottore 2. *Debtor:* debitore.

dz., *dozen:* dozz., dozzina.

E., 1. *East:* E, Est 2. *English:* inglese.

ea., *each:* cad., cadauno.

E.B., *Encyclopaedia Britannica:* Enciclopedia Britannica.

E.C.A., *Economic Co-operation Administration:* Amministrazione della cooperazione economica.

E.C.M., *European Common Market:* M.E.C., Mercato Comune Europeo.

ed., 1. *edited:* ed., edito **2.** *edition:* ed., edizione.

E.D.C., *European Defence Community:* C.E.D., Comunità per la difesa europea.

edit., V. *ed.*

Edn., *Edinburgh.*

e.g., *for example:* p. es., per esempio.

Emp., *Emperor:* imperatore.

enc(l)., *enclosure:* all., allegato.

Eng., 1. *England:* Inghilterra **2.** *English:* inglese.

esp(ec)., *especially:* spec., specialmente.

Esq., *Esquire (titolo di cortesia usato negli indirizzi):* Egr., egregio.

etc., *and so on:* ecc., eccetera.

Eur., 1. *Europe:* Europa **2.** *European:* europeo.

ex., 1. *examined:* esaminato **2.** *example:* es., esempio **3.** *excepted:* eccetto **4.** *executive:* esecutivo.

exc., *except(ed):* eccettuato.

F., *Fahrenheit:* F., Fahrenheit.

f., *frequency:* f., frequenza.

F.A.O., *Food and Agricultural Organization:* Organizzazione per l'agricoltura e l'alimentazione.

F.B.I., *Federal Bureau of Investigation:* Ufficio federale d'investigazione.

Feb., *February:* feb., febbraio.

Fed., 1. *Federal:* fed., federale **2.** *Federation:* federazione.

Fla., Flor., *Florida.*

F.O., *Foreign Office:* M.A.E.E., Ministero degli affari esteri.

F.O.B., f.o.b., *free on board:* f.o.b., franco bordo.

fol., *folio:* folio.

fol(l)., *following:* seg., seguente.

Fr., 1. *Father:* P., padre **2.** *France:* Francia **3.** *French:* francese **4.** *Friday:* ven., venerdì.

Fri., *Friday:* ven., venerdì.

ft., *foot, feet:* piede, piedi.

g., 1. *conductance:* conduttanza **2.** *gender:* genere **3.** *gram:* g., grammo **4.** *guinea:* ghinea.

Ga., *Georgia.*

gal(l)., *gallon:* gallone.

G.B., *Great Britain:* Gran Bretagna.

Gen., *General:* gen., generale.

gen., 1. *gender:* genere **2.** *generally:* gen., generalmente.

gent., *gentleman:* gentiluomo, signore.

G.H.Q., *General Headquarters:* Q.G., quartier generale.

G.I., *Government Issue:* promulgazione ministeriale.

Gloster., *Gloucestershire.*

G-Man., *Government Man:* soldato governativo.

G.O.P., *Grand Old Party (U.S. Republican Party):* Partito Repubblicano Americano.

G.P.O., *General Post Office:* Posta centrale.

H, *hydrogen:* H., idrogeno.

h., 1. *hour:* h., ora **2.** *high:* A., alto.

H.B.M., *His (Her) Britannic Majesty:* S.M.B., Sua Maestà Britannica.

H.C., *House of Commons:* Camera dei Comuni.

H.E., *His Excellency:* S.E., Sua Eccellenza.

Hereford., *Herefordshire.*

Herts., *Hertfordshire.*

hf., *half:* metà.

H.H., 1. *His Holiness:* S.S., Sua Santità **2.** *His (Her) Highness:* S.A., Sua Altezza.

hhd., *hogshead:* hogshead *(misura di capacità l. 238,5).*

H.L., *House of Lords:* Camera Alta.

H.M., *His (Her) Majesty:* V.M., Vostra Maestà.

H.M.S., *His* . *(Her) Majesty's Service:* servizio di Sua Maestà.

Hon., *Honourable:* on., onorevole.

H.P., 1. *high pressure:* alta pressione **2.** *horse power:* H.P., cavalli vapore.

hr., *hour:* h., ora.

H.S., *High School:* scuola media superiore.

Hunts., *Huntingdonshire.*

I(a)., *Iowa.*

ib(id)., *in the same place:* ibid., nello stesso luogo.

I.D., *Intelligence Department:* reparto informazioni.

id., *the same:* id., come sopra.

Id(a)., *Idaho.*

i.e., *that is:* cioè.

Ill., *Illinois.*

in., *inch:* pollice *(misura).*

inc., 1. *incorporated*: incorporato 2. *including*: incluso.

inst., *instant (the present month)*: c.m., corrente mese.

I.O.U., *I owe you*: pagherò.

I.Q., *Intelligence Quotient*: Q.I., quoziente d'intelligenza.

Ire., *Ireland*.

Ja(n)., *January*: genn., gennaio.

J.P., *Justice of the Peace*: giudice di pace.

Jr., jun., *junior*: iun., junior.

Kan(s)., *Kansas*.

kg., *kilogram*: kg., chilogrammo.

kilo., 1. *kilogram*: chilogrammo 2. *kilometre*: km., chilometro.

K.K.K., *Ku Klux Klan*: K.K.K., Ku Klux Klan.

km., *kilometre*: km., chilometro.

K.O., *knock out*: fuori combattimento.

kw., *kilowatt*: kw., chilowatt.

Ky., *Kentucky*.

L., *pound*: L.st., lira sterlina.

l., 1. *litre*: l., litro 2. *long*: lungo.

La., *Louisiana*.

Lancs., *Lancashire*.

Lat., *Latin*: latino.

lat., *latitude*: latitudine.

lb., *pound*: libbra.

L.C.D., *lowest common denominator*: m.c.d., minimo comun denominatore.

L.C.M., *least common multiple*: m.c.m., minimo comune multiplo.

Leics., *Leicestershire*.

L.F., *low frequency*: b.f., bassa frequenza.

Lieut., *Lieutenant*: luogotenente.

Lincs., *Lincolnshire*.

LL.D., *Doctor of Laws*: dottore in legge.

Lon., *London*: Londra.

lon(g)., *longitude*: longitudine.

L.P., 1. *Labour Party*: Partito Laburista 2. *Long Play*: microsolco.

L.R., *Lloyd's Register*: Registro dei Lloyd.

Ltd., *limited*: s.r.l., società a responsabilità limitata.

m., 1. *male*: m., maschio 2. *metre*: m., metro 3. *mile*: miglio 4. *minute*: m., minuto 5. *month*: m., mese.

M.A., *Master of Arts*: laureato in lettere.

Mad., Madm., *Madam*: sig.ra, signora.

Maj., *Major*: magg., maggiore.

Mar., *March*: mar., marzo.

Mass., *Massachusetts*.

max., *maximum*: mass., massimo.

M.C., *Member of Congress*: membro del Congresso.

Md., *Maryland*.

M.D., *Doctor of Medicine*: dottore in medicina.

Mdx., *Middlesex*.

Me., *Maine*.

M.F., *medium frequency*: m.f., media frequenza.

mg(m)., *milligram*: mg., milligrammo.

Mich., *Michigan*.

Minn., *Minnesota*.

Miss., *Mississippi*.

mm., *millimetre*: mm., millimetro.

Mo., 1. *Missouri* 2. *Monday*: lun., lunedì.

M.O., *money order*: ordine di pagamento.

Mon., *Monday*: lun., lunedì.

Mont., *Montana*.

M.P., 1. *Military Police*: Polizia militare 2. *Member of Parliament*: membro del Parlamento.

mph., *miles per hour*: miglia orarie.

Mr., *Mister*: sig., signor.

Mrs., *Mistress*: sig.ra, signora.

M/S, *motorship*: M/n, motonave.

MS., *manuscript*: ms., manoscritto.

MSS., *manuscripts*: mss., manoscritti.

Mt., *mount*: M., monte.

mus., 1. *museum*: mus., museo 2. *music*: musica.

N., *North*: N, Nord.

n., 1. *born*: n., nato 2. *number*: n., numero.

N.A.T.O., *North Atlantic Treaty Organization*: P.A., Patto atlantico.

N.B.C., *National Broadcasting Company*: Compagnia radiofonica nazionale.

N.C., *North Carolina*.

N.C.O., *non-commissioned officer*: s. uff., sottufficiale.

N. D(ak)., *North Dakota*.

Neb(r)., *Nebraska*.

Nev., *Nevada*.

New M., *New Mexico*.

N.H., *New Hampshire.*

N.J., *New Jersey.*

N. M(ex)., *New Mexico.*

no., *number:* n., numero.

Norf., *Norfolk.*

Northum(b)., *Northumberland*

nos., *numbers:* numeri.

Notts., *Nottinghamshire.*

Nov., *November:* nov., novembre.

N.Y., *New York:* Nuova York.

O., *Ohio.*

Oct., *October:* ott., ottobre.

O.E.D., *Oxford English Dictionary:* Dizionario Inglese Oxford.

Okla., *Oklahoma.*

op. cit., *in the work cited:* op. cit., opera citata.

Ore(g)., *Oregon.*

O.U.P., *Oxford University Press:* Edizioni dell'Università di Oxford.

Ox(f)., *Oxford.*

Oxon., **1.** *Oxford* **2.** *of Oxford:* ossoniese **3.** *Oxfordshire ounce:* oncia.

P., *(car-)park:* P., parcheggio.

p., **1.** *page:* p., pagina **2.** *past:* pass., passato.

Pa., *Pennsylvania.*

P.A.A., *Pan American Airways:* Linee aeree panamericane.

par., *paragraph:* parag., paragrafo.

pat., **1.** *patent:* brev., brevetto **2.** *patented:* brevettato.

P.A.Y.E., *pay as you earn (trattenuta di ricchezza mobile):* R.M., ricchezza mobile.

pd., *paid:* pagato.

Penn(a). v. *Pa.*

Ph. D., *Doctor of Philosophy:* dottore in filosofia.

P.M., *Prime Minister:* Primo Ministro.

p.m., *post meridiem (after noon):* pomeridiano.

P.O., p.o., **1.** *Post Office:* U.P., fficio postale **2.** *postal order:* V., vaglia.

P.O.B., *post office box:* C.P., casella postale.

p.o.d., *pay on delivery:* pagamento alla consegna.

pp., *pages:* pagg., pagine.

prep., *preparation:* preparazione.

Pres., *President:* pres., presidente.

Prof., *Professor:* prof., professore.

prox., *next:* prossimo.

P.S., *postscript:* P.S., poscritto.

p.t.o., *please turn over:* voltare pagina.

Q.M.G., *Quartermaster General:* capo dipartimento amministrazione e alloggi.

qu., **1.** *quart:* misura di capacità (l. 1.136) **2.** *quarter:* quarto.

quot., *quotation:* citazione.

R., r., **1.** *river:* f., fiume **2.** *road:* strada.

R.A.C., *Royal Automobile Club:* Regio Automobile Club.

R.A.D.I.A.C., *Radioactivity Detection Identification and Computation:* Rivelazione, identificazione e calcolo della radioattività.

R.A.F., *Royal Air Force:* Regia Aviazione militare.

R.C., **1.** *Red Cross:* C.R., Croce Rossa **2.** *Roman Catholic:* Cattolico Romano.

R.C.A., *Radio Corporation of America:* Associazione Radiofonica Americana.

re., *reference* **1.** ref., referenza **2.** riferimento.

rec., **1.** *receipt:* ricevuta **2.** *record:* record.

reg., **1.** *region:* regione **2.** *register:* reg., registro **3.** *regular:* regolare.

Rev., *Reverend:* rev., reverendo.

R.H., *Royal Highness:* A.R., Altezza Reale.

R.N., *Royal Navy:* Regia Marina.

Rt. Hon., *Right Honourable:* molto onorevole.

Rt. Rev., *Right Reverend:* molto reverendo.

Ry., *Railway:* ferrovia.

S., *South:* S, Sud.

s., **1.** *second:* secondo **2.** *shilling:* scellino.

Sat., *Saturday:* sab., sabato.

S.C., *South Carolina.*

sch., *school:* sc., scuola.

Scot., **1.** *Scotland:* Scozia **2.** *Scottish:* scozzese.

S. D(ak)., *South Dakota.*

sec., **1.** *second:* secondo **2.** *section:* sezione **3.** *secretary:* segr., segretario

Sen., **1.** *Senate:* senato **2.** *senator:* senatore **3.** *senior:* senior.

Sept., *September:* sett., settembre.

Sergt., *sergeant:* serg., sergente.

sh., *shilling:* scellino.

S.H.A.P.E., *Supreme Headquarters Allied Powers Europe*: quartier generale delle Forze alleate in Europa.

Shrops., *Shropshire*.

So., 1. *South*: S, Sud 2. *Southern*: sudista.

Soc., *society*: s., società.

Somerset., *Somersetshire*.

spec., 1. *special*: spec., speciale 2. *specification*: specificazione.

sp. gr., *specific gravity*: gravità specifica.

sq., *square*: p.za, piazza.

Sr., 1. *senior*: senior 2. *Sir*: Sir 3. *sister*: sorella.

SS, S/S, *steamship*: piroscafo.

St., 1. *Saint*: s., santo 2. *street*: via.

st., *stone*: misura di peso (Kg. 6,350).

Staffs., *Staffordshire*.

ster., stg., *sterling*: L.st., lira sterlina.

St. Ex., *Stock Exchange*: Borsa valori.

Sun(d)., *Sunday*: dom., domenica.

Sup. Ct., *Supreme Court*: C.S., Corte suprema.

supp(l)., *supplement*: supplemento.

Sur., *Surrey*.

Sus., *Sussex*.

S.W., 1. *South Wales*: Galles del sud 2. *South West*: S.O., sud ovest.

Swit., Swtz., *Switzerland*: Svizzera.

syn., *synonym*: sinonimo

Sy., *Surrey*.

t., 1. *ton*: t., tonnellata 2. *volume*: v., volume.

T.B., *tuberculosis*: tbc, tuberculosi.

tel., 1. *telegram*: telegramma 2. *telegraph*: telegrafo 3. *telephone*: tel., telefono.

Tenn., *Tennessee*.

Tex., *Texas*.

Thur(s)., *Thursday*: giov., giovedì.

T.O., *turn over*: voltare.

T.U., *Trade-Union*: Sindacato.

Tu(es)., *Tuesday*: mar., martedì.

TV., *television*: TV, televisione.

T.W.A., *Trans World Airlines*: linee aeree intercontinentali.

U., 1. *Union*: U., unione 2. *University*: Università.

U.K., *United Kingdom*: R.U., Regno Unito.

U.N., *United Nations*: N.U., Nazioni Unite.

U.N.E.S.C.O., *United Nations Educational Scientific and Cultural Organization*: Organizzazione culturale, scientifica e per l'educazione delle Nazioni Unite.

U.N.I.C.E.F., *United Nations International Children's Emergency Fund*: Fondo d'emergenza internazionale per l'infanzia delle Nazioni Unite.

U.N.O., *United Nations Organization*: O.N.U., Organizzazione delle Nazioni Unite.

U.P., *United Press*: Stampa associata.

U.S., *United States*: S.U., Stati Uniti.

U.S.A., 1. *United States of America*: S.U.A., Stati Uniti d'America 2. *United States Army*: Esercito degli Stati Uniti.

U.S.A.E.C., *United States Atomic Energy Commission*: commissione per l'energia atomica degli Stati Uniti.

U.S.A.F., *United States Air Force*: Aviazione militare degli Stati Uniti.

U.S.I.S., *United States Information Service*: Servizio informazioni degli Stati Uniti.

U.S.N., *United States Navy*: Marina degli Stati Uniti.

U.S.S.R., *Union of Soviet Socialist Republics*: U.R.S.S., Unione delle repubbliche socialiste sovietiche.

U.S.S., *United States Ship*: nave degli Stati Uniti.

Ut., *Utah*.

v., *verse*: v., verso.

Va., *Virginia*.

Vat., *Vatican*: Vaticano.

Ven., *Venerable*: Ven., venerabile.

V.H.F., *very high frequency*: altissima frequenza.

Vic(t)., *Victoria*.

V.I.P., *Very Important Person*: Persona molto importante.

viz., *namely*: cioè.

vol., *volume*: vol., volume.

V.P., *Vice-President*: vicepresidente.

vs., *against*: contro.

Vt., *Vermont*.

Vul(g)., *Vulgate*: Vulgata.

vv., *verses*: vv., versi.

w., *watt*: W., watt.

W., 1. *West*: O, Ovest **2.** *Washington.*

w., 1. *week*: settimana **2.** *wife*: moglie **3.** *with*: con.

Warwick., *Warwickshire.*

Wash., *Washington.*

W.D., *War Department*: Ministero della Guerra.

Wed., *Wednesday*: mer., mercoledì.

Westm., *Westminster.*

Westmore., *Westmoreland.*

whf., *wharf*: pontile.

Wis(c)., *Wisconsin.*

wk., 1. *week*: settimana **2.** *work*: lavoro.

w.l., *wave length*: lunghezza d'onda.

Worcs., *Worcestershire.*

W.R.A.C., *Women's Royal Army Corps*: Regio corpo d'armata femminile.

wt., *weight*: peso.

W.Va., *West Virginia*: Virginia dell'ovest.

Wy(o)., *Wyoming.*

Xmas., *Christmas*: Natale.

y., 1. *yard*: iarda **2.** *year*: anno.

yd., *yard*: iarda.

Y.H.A., *Youth Hostels Association*: Associazione Ostelli per la gioventù.

Y.M.C.A., *Young men's Christian Association*: Associazione Cristiana per i giovani.

yr., 1. *year*: anno **2.** *your*: vostro.

Yorks., *Yorkshire.*

yrs., 1. *years*: anni **2.** *yours*: vostri.

Y.W.C.A., *Young Women's Christian Association*: Associazione Cristiana per le giovani.

Z., *atomic number*: n.a., numero atomico.

&, *and*: e.

&c., *and so forth*: etc., ecc., eccetera.

PREFACE TO THE ITALIAN-ENGLISH SECTION OF THE
PICCOLO DIZIONARIO ITALIANO-INGLESE

1. The first part of the English-Italian section of the Compact Dictionary contains information in Italian designed to help in its use. It gives rules of pronunciation, a list of irregular verbs, tables of comparison of the English and American units and metric system, information on the English and American currency, a list of cardinal and ordinal numbers, and an explanatory list of the abbreviations used.

A similar introduction is included here to help in the use of the Italian-English section.

2. Since Italian presents particular problems with its verbs we have provided a list of irregular verbs in general use. We have not included their compounds, as they are conjugated in the same way.

Those verbs which take *essere* as an auxiliary are indicated by means of a single star. Those which take *essere* when used intransitively and *avere* when used transitively have a double star.

With the past definite tense we have shown the 1st person singular only, since the 3rd person singular and the 3rd person plural follow the same pattern, while the 2nd person singular and plural are regular in form e.g.: *prendere – presi, prendesti, prese, prendemmo, prendeste*, presero.

3. There are two points concerning the current use of verbs which the student of Italian may well find helpful:

a) there is a tendency in modern Italian towards a more frequent use of the perfect tense to represent completed past action (though such irrefutable statements of the past as, for example, *Dante died in 1321* would still always be translated as *Dante morì . . .*);

b) though the polite form in the singular, with *Lei* and the 3rd person of the verb, is regularly used e.g.: *Lei scrive in inglese?* (Are you writing in English?), the plural form addressed to more than one person is now more frequently the 2nd person plural with *Voi*, instead of the 3rd person plural with *Loro* e.g.: *Voi scrivete in inglese?* rather than *Loro scrivono in inglese?*

4. As some Italian nouns have irregular plurals or do not change their form in the plural we have included a list of the more commonly used ones.

5. In illustrating the possible alternative translations for the Italian words listed, the following symbols have been adopted:

a) a double line (ll) after the initial translation or translations indicates a grammatical change from, for example, an adjective to a noun or a pronoun to an adverb;

b) a lozenge (◆) indicates something more than just an alternative translation, showing, for example, a figurative or idiomatic use;

c) the numbers printed in large type (**1.**, **2.**, **3.**, etc.) indicate the various alternative meanings;

d) the small numbers (¹, ², ³, etc.) indicate words of identical form but different meaning.

The Alphabet

The Italian alphabet consists of 21 letters only. j (*i lunga*), k (*cappa*), w (*doppio vu*), x (*ics*), y (*ipsilon*) do not occur in the alphabet, though they are used for the spelling of foreign words e.g.: *judo*, *kimono*, *watt*, *xenofobia*, *yacht*. In some cases y is replaced by i, e.g. *raion* for rayon. ch replaces k, e.g. *chilogramma* for kilogram. ph is represented by f, e.g. *fobia* for phobia. x occurs in certain expressions such as *ex-presidente*, *extraterritoriale*, etc.

Letter	Name	Letter	Name
a	*a*	m	*emme*
b	*bi*	n	*enne*
c	*ci*	o	*o*
d	*di*	p	*pi*
e	*e*	q	*cu*
f	*effe*	r	*erre*
g	*gi*	s	*esse*
h	*acca*	t	*ti*
i	*i*	u	*u*
l	*elle*	v	*vu*
		z	*zeta*

Pronunciation

Since Italian is a phonetic language, once the rules of pronunciation are learnt, it is possible to pronounce most words correctly, though it is not always easy to tell on which syllable the tonic stress falls.

The Vowels

Italian vowels are pure sounds and should be pronounced well forward in the mouth:

	A	like a in far	*gala*
close	E	like a in fate	*seta*
open	E	like e in ten	*pelle*
	I	like i in machine	*vino*
close	O	like o in store	*corte*
open	O	like o in spot	*motto*
	U	like oo in spoon	*uso*

The Consonants

In the case of double consonants each consonant is sounded, with the voice rising on them and falling on the following vowel.

The consonants B, D, F, L, M, N, P, Q, T and V are pronounced very much as in English. The rest are as follows:

C 1. before a, o, u, and consonants, including h: like c in cat, as in *casa*, *crema*, *chilo*;

2. before e or i: like ch in chip, as in *cena*, *cibo*.

G 1. before a, o, u and consonants, including h but not including l and n: like g in gap, as in *gala*, *grido*, *ghiro*;

2. before e or i: like g in gem, as in *gente*, *gita*.

gli like lli in billion, as in *figlia*; (a few exceptions have the gli pronounced as in English, e.g. *anglicano*, *negligente*).

gn like ni in onion, as in *signore*.

H is always silent and occurs in very few words, except as shown above to harden the c and g sounds before e and i.

Q is always followed by u, like qu in quick, as in *quinto*.

R is rolled, rather as in rr Scottish pronunciation, as in *pera*, *serra*.

S 1. is voiced, like s in rose, as in *rasa*, *esatto*, or when followed by b, d, g, l, m, n, r, v, the voiceless consonants, as in *sdegno*, *svelto*;

2. is unvoiced like s in sap, at the beginning of a word, or when it is doubled, as in *sega*, *rosso*.

sc 1. before e or i is like sh in shot, as in *scena*;

2. before a, o and u is like sk in skate, as in *scarpa*, *scopo*, *scudo*;

3. an h after it and before e or i makes it like sk, as in *schema*, *schiena*;

4. an i after it and before a, o or u makes it like sh, as in *scialle*, *sciocco*, *sciupare*.

Z 1. voiced like ds in treads, as in *zio*;

2. unvoiced like ts in wits, as in *forza*.

Accentuation

In printed and written Italian an accent is used to indicate when the tonic stress falls on a final vowel such as in *città* or *caffè*. It is also used to distinguish between two words which are spelt and pronounced alike but have different meanings:

è = is   *e* = and

dà = he gives   *da* = from, by, of, etc.

It also occurs on some monosyllabic words as in *già* and *più*.

In print the acute accent is used to indicate a stress on a final e as in *perché* or *né*, though in handwriting the grave accent is more usual. In modern Italian the grave accent is normally used elsewhere and we have followed this practice.

As a general rule the tonic stress is on the penultimate syllable, but this is not by any means always so. The grave and acute accents have been used to show where the stress falls when it does not fall on the penultimate syllable. The open and close e are distinguished in the accepted way by means of è and é, e.g. *créscere*, *crédere*, *festival*, *férvido*, and the grave accent is used everywhere else, e.g. *càndido*, *moltitùdine*.

IRREGULAR ITALIAN VERBS†

Accendere – *p. def.* accesi, *p.p.* acceso
Accludere – see alludere
Addurre – *pres.* adduco, *p. def.* addussi, *fut.* addurrò, *p.p.* addotto
Affliggere – *p. def.* afflissi, *p.p.* afflitto
Alludere – *p. def.* allusi, *p.p.* alluso
Andare* – *pres.* vado, vai, va, andiamo, andate, vanno *fut.* andrò
Annettere – *p. def.* annettei (annessi), *p.p.* annesso
Apparire* – *pres.* apparisco, *p. def.* apparii (apparvi, apparsi), *p.p* apparso
Appendere – *p. def.* appesi, *p.p.* appeso
Ardere – *p. def.* arsi, *p.p.* arso
Aspergere – *p. def.* aspersi, *p.p.* asperso
Assalire – *pres.* assalgo (assalisco), assalgono
Assolvere – *p. def.* assolsi (assolvei, assolvetti), *p.p.* assolto
Assumere – *p. def.* assunsi, *p.p.* assunto

Bere – *pres.* bevo, *p. def.* bevvi, *fut.* berrò

Cadere* – *p. def.* caddi, *fut.* cadrò
Cedere – *p. def.* cedei (cedetti)
Chiedere – *p. def.* chiesi, *p.p.* chiesto
Chiudere – *p. def.* chiusi, *p.p.* chiuso
Cingere – *p. def.* cinsi, *p.p.* cinto
Cogliere – *pres.* colgo, colgono, *p. def.* colsi, *p.p.* colto
Comprimere – *p. def.* compressi, *p.p.* compresso
Conoscere – *p. def.* conobbi, *p.p.* conosciuto
Consumare – *p. def.* consumai (consunsi), *p.p.* consumato (consunto)
Correre** – *p. def.* corsi, *p.p.* corso
Costruire – *p.p.* costruito (costrutto)
Crescere* – *p. def.* crebbi, *p.p.* cresciuto
Cucire – *pres.* cucio
Cuocere – *pres.* cuocio, cuoci, cuoce, cociamo, cocete, cuociono, *p. def.* cossi, *p.p.* cotto

Dare – *pres.* do, dai, dà, diamo, date, danno, *p. def.* diedi (detti), desti, *fut.* darò, *p.p.* dato

† Verbs which take *essere* are indicated by one star.
Those taking *avere* and *essere* have two stars.

Decidere – *p. def.* decisi, *p.p.* deciso

Difendere – *p. def.* difesi, *p.p.* difeso

Dipendere** – *p. def.* dipesi, *p.p.* dipeso

Dipingere – *p. def.* dipinsi, *p.p.* dipinto

Dire – *pres.* dico, dite, *p. def.* dissi, *fut.* dirò, *p.p.* detto

Dirigere – *p. def.* diressi, *p.p.* diretto

Discutere – *p. def.* discussi, *p.p.* discusso

Dissolvere – *p. def.* dissolsi (dissolvei), *p.p.* dissolto

Distinguere – *p. def.* distinsi, *p.p.* distinto

Dividere – *p. def.* divisi, *p.p.* diviso

Dolersi* – *pres.* mi dolgo, ti duoli, si duole, ci doliamo, vi dolete, si
  dolgono, *p. def.* mi dolsi, *fut.* mi dorrò

Dovere – *pres.* devo (debbo), devi, deve, dobbiamo, dovete, devono
  (debbono), *fut.* dovrò

Eccellere – *p. def.* eccelsi, *p.p.* eccelso

Emergere* – *p. def.* emersi, *p.p.* emerso

Ergere – *p. def.* ersi, *p.p.* erto

Erigere – *p. def.* eressi, *p.p.* eretto

Esigere – *p.p.* esatto

Espellere – *p. def.* espulsi, *p.p.* espulso

Esplodere** – *p. def.* esplosi, *p.p.* esploso

Evadere* – *p. def.* evasi, *p.p.* evaso

Fare – *pres.* faccio (fo), fai, fa, facciamo, fate, fanno, *imper.* facevo, *p. def.*
  feci, *fut.* farò, *p.p.* fatto

Fendere – *p. def.* fendei (fendetti), *p.p.* fesso (fenduto)

Figgere – *p. def.* fissi, *p.p.* fisso (fitto)

Fingere – *p. def.* finsi, *p.p.* finto

Fondere – *p. def.* fusi, *p.p.* fuso

Frangere – *p. def.* fransi, *p.p.* franto

Friggere – *p. def.* frissi, *p.p.* fritto

Giacere* – *pres.* giaccio, giacciono, *p. def.* giacqui, *p.p.* giaciuto

Giungere* – *p. def.* giunsi, *p.p.* giunto

Godere – *fut.* godrò

Incutere – *p. def.* incussi (incutei), *p.p.* incusso

Indulgere – *p. def.* indulsi, *p.p.* indulto

Intridere – *p. def.* intrisi, *p.p.* intriso

Invadere – *p. def.* invasi, *p.p.* invaso

Ledere – *p. def.* lesi, *p.p.* leso

Leggere – *p. def.* lessi, *p.p.* letto

Mettere – *p. def.* misi, *p.p.* messo

Mordere – *p. def.* morsi, *p.p.* morso

Morire* – *pres.* muoio, muori, muore, moriamo, morite, muoiono, *fut.* morrò, *p.p.* morto

Mungere – *p. def.* munsi, *p.p.* munto

Muovere – *pres.* moviamo, movete, *p. def.* mossi, *p.p.* mosso

Nascere* – *p. def.* nacqui, *p.p.* nato

Nascondere – *p. def.* nascosi, *p.p.* nascosto

Nuocere – *pres.* noccio, nociamo, nocete, nocciono, *p. def.* nocqui, *p.p.* nociuto

Offrire – *p. def.* offrii (offersi), *p.p.* offerto

Parere* – *pres.* paio, paiamo, paiono, *p. def.* parvi, *fut.* parrò, *p.p.* parso

Percuotere – *p.p.* percosso

Perdere – *p. def.* persi (perdei, perdetti), *p.p.* perduto (perso)

Persuadere – *p. def.* persuasi, *p.p.* persuaso

Piacere* – *pres.* piaccio, piaci, piace, piacciamo, piacete, piacciono, *p. def.* piacqui, *p.p.* piaciuto

Piangere – *p. def.* piansi, *p.p.* pianto

Piovere** – *p. def.* piovve, piovvero

Porgere – *p. def.* porsi, *p.p.* porto

Porre – *pres.* pongo, poni, pone, poniamo, ponete, pongono, *p. def.* posi, *fut.* porrò, *p.p.* posto

Potere – *pres.* posso, puoi, può, possiamo, potete, possono, *fut.* potrò

Prediligere – *p. def.* predilessi, *p.p.* prediletto

Prendere – *p. def.* presi, *p.p.* preso

Proteggere – *p. def.* protessi, *p.p.* protetto

Pungere – *p. def.* punsi, *p.p.* punto

Radere – *p. def.* rasi, *p.p.* raso

Redimere – *p. def.* redensi, *p.p.* redento

Reggere – *p. def.* ressi, *p.p.* retto

Rendere – *p. def.* resi, *p.p.* reso

Ridere – *p. def.* risi, *p.p.* riso

Rifulgere** – *p. def.* rifulsi, *p.p.* rifulso

Rispondere – *p. def.* risposi, *p.p.* risposto

Rodere – *p. def.* rosi, *p.p.* roso

Rompere – *p. def.* ruppi, *p.p.* rotto

Salire** – *pres.* salgo, salgono

Sapere – *pres.* so, sai, sa, sappiamo, sapete, sanno, *p. def.* seppi, *fut.* saprò

Scegliere – *pres.* scelgo, scelgono, *p. def.* scelsi, *p.p.* scelto

Scendere** – *p. def.* scesi, *p.p.* sceso

Scindere – *p. def.* scissi, *p.p.* scisso

Sciogliere – *pres.* sciolgo, sciolgono, *p. def.* sciolsi, *p.p.* sciolto

Scrivere – *p. def.* scrissi, *p.p.* scritto

Scuotere – *p. def.* scossi, *p.p.* scosso

Sedere* – *pres.* siedo (seggo), siedi, siede, sediamo, sedete, siedono (seggono)

Soddisfare – *pres.* soddisfo (soddisfaccio, soddisfò), soddisfi (soddisfai), soddisfa, soddisfiamo (soddisfacciamo), soddisfate, soddisfano (soddisfanno), *p. def.* soddisfeci, *p.p.* soddisfatto

Sorgere* – *p. def.* sorsi, *p.p.* sorto

Spargere – *p. def.* sparsi, *p.p.* sparso

Spegnere – *p. def.* spensi, *p.p.* spento

Spendere – *p. def.* spesi, *p.p.* speso

Spingere – *p. def.* spinsi, *p.p.* spinto

Stare* – *pres.* sto, stai, sta, stiamo, state, stanno, *imperf.* stavo, *p. def.* stetti, *p.p.* stato

Stringere – *p. def.* strinsi, *p.p.* stretto

Struggere – *p. def.* strussi, *p.p.* strutto

Svellere – *pres.* svello (svelgo), svellono (svelgono), *p. def.* svelsi, *p.p.* svelto

Svenire* – *p. def.* svenni

Tacere – *pres.* taccio, taci, tace, taciamo, tacete, tacciono, *p. def.* tacqui, *p.p.* taciuto

Tendere – *p. def.* tesi, *p.p.* teso

Tenere – *pres.* tengo, tieni, tiene, teniamo, tenete, tengono, *p. def.* tenni, *fut.* terrò

Tingere – *p. def.* tinsi, *p.p.* tinto

Togliere – *pres.* tolgo, tolgono, *p. def.* tolsi, *p.p.* tolto

Torcere – *p. def.* torsi, *p.p.* torto

Trarre – *pres.* traggo, trai, trae, traiamo, traete, traggono, *imperf.* traevo, *p. def.* trassi, *fut.* trarrò, *p.p.* tratto

Uccidere – *p. def.* uccisi, *p.p.* ucciso

Udire – *pres.* odo, odi, ode, udiamo, udite, odono, *fut.* udrò (udirò)

Ungere – *p. def.* unsi, *p.p.* unto

Uscire* – *pres.* esco, esci, esce, usciamo, uscite, escono

Valere** – *pres.* valgo, valgono, *p. def.* valsi, *fut.* varrò, *p.p.* valso

Vedere – *pres.* vedo (veggo), vedono (veggono), *p. def.* vidi, *fut.* vedrò, *p.p.* visto

Venire* – *pres.* vengo, vieni, viene, veniamo, venite, vengono, *p. def.* venni, *fut.* verrò

Vilipendere – *p. def.* vilipesi, *p.p.* vilipeso

Vincere – *p. def.* vinsi, *p.p.* vinto

Vivere** – *p. def.* vissi, *p.p.* vissuto

Volere – *pres.* voglio, vuoi, vuole, vogliamo, volete, vogliono, *p. def.*
    volli, *fut.* vorrò

Volgere – *p. def.* volsi, *p.p.* volto

IRREGULAR PLURALS OF NOUNS

l'autobus	gli autobus
il bar	i bar
il caffè	i caffè
la città	le città
la frutta	le frutta
il re	i re
il braccio	le braccia
il bue	i buoi
il centinaio	le centinaia
il dito	le dita
il ginocchio	le ginocchia
la guancia	le guance
il labbro	le labbra
il lenzuolo	le lenzuola
la mano	le mani
il migliaio	le migliaia
l'orecchio	le orecchie
il paio	le paia
l'uomo	gli uomini

ITALIAN MONEY

Italian bank notes are issued in the following denominations:

500 lire	10,000 lire
1000 lire	50,000 lire
2000 lire	100,000 lire.
5000 lire	

The one hundred thousand lire notes are not negotiable outside Italy.

Coins are issued in five, ten, twenty, fifty, one hundred and five hundred pieces.

NUMERALS

Cardinal		*Cardinal cont.*	
1	uno	3	tre
2	due	4	quattro

Cardinal		*Cardinal cont.*	
5	cinque	29	ventinove
6	sei	30	trenta
7	sette	31	trentuno
8	otto	32	trentadue
9	nove	38	trentotto
10	dieci	40	quaranta
11	undici	50	cinquanta
12	dodici	60	sessanta
13	tredici	70	settanta
14	quattordici	80	ottanta
15	quindici	90	novanta
16	sedici	100	cento
17	diciassette	101	centouno
18	diciotto	105	centocinque
19	diciannove	150	centocinquanta
20	venti	200	duecento
21	ventuno	300	trecento
22	ventidue	1000	mille
23	ventitré	1100	millecento
24	ventiquattro	1200	milleduecento
25	venticinque	2000	duemila
26	ventisei	100,000	centomila
27	ventisette	1,000,000	un milione
28	ventotto		

Ordinal	
1st	primo
2nd	secondo
3rd	terzo
4th	quarto
5th	quinto
6th	sesto
7th	settimo
8th	ottavo
9th	nono
10th	decimo
11th	undicesimo *or* decimo primo
12th	dodicesimo *or* decimo secondo
20th	ventesimo
21st	ventunesimo *or* ventesimo primo
22nd	ventiduesimo *or* ventesimo secondo

30th	trentesimo
40th	quarantesimo
50th	cinquantesimo
101st	centunesimo
200th	duecentesimo
1000th	millesimo
1205th	milleduecentocinquesimo
1,000,000th	milionesimo

ABBREVIATIONS USED IN THE DICTIONARY

abbr.	abbreviation	*(dial.)*	dialect
(aer.)	aviation	*dif.*	defective
agg.	adjective	*dim.*	diminutive
(agr.)	agriculture	*dimostr.*	demonstrative
(amer.)	American		
amm.	administrative	*ecc., etc.*	etcetera
(anat.)	anatomy	*(eccl.)*	ecclesiastical
(ant.)	archaic	*(econ.)*	economics
(arch.)	architecture	*(edil.)*	building industry
art.	article	*(elettr.)*	electricity
(arte)	art	*escl.*	exclamation
assol.	absolute		
(astr.)	astronomy	*f.*	feminine
attr.	attribute	*(fam.)*	familiar
aus.	auxiliary	*(farm.)*	pharmaceutical
(auto)	motoring	*(ferr.)*	railway
avv.	adverb	*(fig.)*	figurative
		(fil.)	philosophy
(bot.)	botany	*(fis.)*	physics
(biol.)	biology	*(foto)*	photography
		fut.	future
(chim.)	chemistry		
(chir.)	surgery	*gen.*	genitive
(cine)	cinematography	*general.*	generally
coll.	collective	*(geogr.)*	geography
(comm.)	commerce	*(geol.)*	geology
comp.	comparative	*(geom.)*	geometry
compl.	complement	*ger.*	gerund
condiz.	conditional	*(gergo)*	jargon, slang
cong.	conjunction	*(giorn.)*	journalism
(costr.)	building	*(giur.)*	legal
(cuc.)	cooking	*(gramm.)*	grammar

i.	intransitive	*pl.*	plural
id.	idem	*(poet.)*	poetical
imp.	impersonal	*(pol.)*	political
imperat.	imperative	*(pop.)*	popular
imperf.	imperfect	*poss.*	possessive
ind.	indicative	*p.p.*	past participle
indef.	indefinite	*prep.*	preposition
inf.	infinitive	*pred.*	predicate
int.	interrogative	*pres.*	present
inter.	interjection	*pron.*	pronoun
(iron.)	ironic	*prov.*	proverbial
irr.	irregular	*(psicol.)*	psychology
(itt.)	ichthyology		
		qc.	something
(lat.)	Latin, Latinism	*qu.*	someone
loc. avv.	adverbial phrase		
loc. cong.	conjunctive	*r.*	reflexive
	phrase	*(radio)*	radio
loc. prep.	prepositional	*rec.*	reciprocal
	phrase	*reg.*	regular
(lett.)	literature	*rel.*	relative
		(relig.)	religion
m.	masculine		
(mar.)	naval, maritime	*s.*	masculine and
(mat.)	mathematics		feminine noun
(mecc.)	mechanics	*semidif.*	partly defective
(med.)	medicine	*sf.*	feminine noun
(metal.)	metallurgy	*sm.*	masculine noun
(mil.)	military	*(scherz.)*	humourous
(min.)	mineralogy	*(scol.)*	scolastic
(mit.)	mythology	*(scult.)*	sculpture
(mus.)	music	*sing.*	singular
		so	someone
neg.	negative	*sogg.*	subject
(neol.)	neologism	*sost.*	noun
		spec.	especially
		(spreg.)	pejorative
ogg.	object	*sthg.*	something
(ott.)	optics	*(stor.)*	history
		superl.	superlative
p.	participle		
pass.	past		
p. def.	past definite	*t.*	transitive
pers.	personal	*(teat.)*	theatre
(pitt.)	painting	*(tec.)*	technical

(tel.)	telephony	*v. dif.*	defective verb
(teol.)	theology	*vi.*	instransitive verb
(tip.)	typography	*(v. irr.)*	irregular verb
(tv.)	television	*(volg.)*	vulgar
		vr.	reflexive verb
(us.)	usage	*v. semidif.*	partially defective verb
v.	verb	*vt.*	transitive verb
V.	cf.		
(vezz.)	diminutive	*(zool.)*	zoology

A

a, ad prep. **1.** (termine) to: l'ho dato a te, I gave it to you **2.** (moto a luogo) vado alla stazione, I am going to the station **3.** (stato in luogo) in, at: vivo a Milano, I live in Milan; sono a casa, I am at home **4.** (tempo determinato) at, on, in: al mio arrivo, on my arrival **5.** (iterativo): due, tre volte al giorno, twice, three times a day.

àbaco (arch.) sm. abacus.

abate sm. abbot.

abbacchiare vt. (di frutta) to beat (v. irr.) down. ♦ **abbacchiarsi** vr. to feel (v. irr.) down-hearted.

abbacchiato agg. down-hearted.

abbacinare vt. to dazzle.

àbbaco sm. elementary arithmetic book.

abbagliante agg. dazzling: fari abbaglianti, dazzling beams.

abbagliare vt. to dazzle, to blind (with).

abbaglio sm. **1.** dazzling **2.** (errore) blunder.

abbaiare vi. to bark.

abbaino sm. garret.

abbandonare vt. **1.** to leave (v. irr.), to forsake (v. irr.), to abandon **2.** (rinunciare) to give (v. irr.) up.

abbandonato agg. **1.** (trascurato) neglected **2.** (di casa) deserted **3.** (di persona) forsaken.

abbandono sm. **1.** (di persona che viene abbandonata) forsaking **2.** (rinuncia) giving up.

abbarbicare vi. to take (v. irr.) root. ♦ **abbarbicarsi** vr. to cling (v. irr.) (anche fig.).

abbaruffarsi vr. to quarrel.

abbassamento sm. lowering || — di temperatura, fall (in temperature).

abbassare vt. **1.** to lower, to pull down || — la testa, to bend (v. irr.) one's head **2.** (ridurre) to reduce. ♦ **abbassarsi** vr. to stoop (down).

abbasso avv. **1.** (al di sotto) below **2.** (giù) down **3.** (al piano terreno, dopo aver sceso le scale) downstairs. ♦ **abbasso!** inter. d∘wn with!

abbastanza avv. **1.** enough **2.** (discretamente) quite.

abbàttere vt. to pull down. ♦ **abbàttersi** vr. to be discouraged.

abbattimento sm. **1.** throwing down **2.** (morale) dejection.

abbattuto agg. disheartened.

abbazia sf. abbey.

abbecedario sm. primer.

abbellimento sm. embellishment.

abbellire vt. to embellish.

abbeverare vt. to water. ♦ **abbeverarsi** vr. to water.

abbeveratoio sm. trough.

abbicì sm. **1.** alphabet **2.** (principi elementari) primer.

abbiente agg. well-to-do, wealthy.

abbigliamento sm. clothes || industria dell'—, clothing industry.

abbigliare vt. to dress.

abbinare vt. to couple.

abbindolare vt. to cheat.

abbisognare vi. to need, to be necessary.

abboccamento sm. interview.

abboccare vt. e vi. **1.** to bite (v. irr.) **2.** (fig.) to be taken in. ♦ **abboccarsi** vr. to confer (with).

abbonacciarsi vi. **1.** (di vento) to drop **2.** (di mare) to smooth down.

abbonamento sm. **1.** subscription **2.** (ferr.) season-ticket.

abbonare vt. **1.** to make (v. irr.) (so.) a subscriber **2.** (defalcare) to make a discount. ♦ **abbonarsi** vr. to subscribe (to).

abbonato sm. **1.** subscriber **2.** (ferr.) season-ticket holder.

abbondante agg. plentiful.

abbondanza sf. plenty.

abbondare vi. to have plenty (of), to be plentiful.

abbonire vt. to calm.

abbordàbile agg. accessible.

abbordaggio sm. boarding.

abbordare vt. **1.** (mar.) to board **2.** (una persona) to open conversation (with).

abborracciare vi. to bungle.

abbottonare vt. to button (up). ♦ **abbottonarsi** vr. to button one's clothes (up).

abbottonatura sf. **1.** button-holes **2.** (l'abbottonarsi) buttoning.

abbozzare vt. to sketch || — un sorriso, to smile faintly.

abbozzo sm. sketch.

abbozzolarsi vr. to cocoon.

abbracciare vt. **1.** to embrace **2.** (comprendere) to include **3.** (afferrare) to grasp **4.** (con lo sguardo) to take (v. irr.) in. ♦ **abbracciarsi** vr. to embrace.

abbraccio sm. embrace.

abbrancare vt. to grasp. ♦ **abbrancarsi** vr. to cling (v. irr.) (to).

abbreviare vt. to shorten, to abridge.

abbreviazione sf. abbreviation.

abbrivare vt. to get (v. irr.) under way.

abbrivo sm. freshway.

abbronzare vt. 1. to bronze 2. (al sole) to tan. ♦ **abbronzarsi** vr. to get (v. irr.) tanned.

abbronzatura sf. tanning.

abbruciacchiare vt. to scorch.

abbrustolire vt. to toast, to roast.

abbrutimento sm. brutalization.

abbrutire vt. to brutalize.

abbuffarsi vr. to stuff oneself.

abbuiarsi vr. to get (v. irr.) dark.

abbuono sm. allowance.

abburattare vt. to sift.

abdicare vi. to abdicate.

abdicazione sf. abdication.

aberrare vi. to stray.

aberrazione sf. aberration.

abetaia sf. fir-wood.

abete sm. fir-tree.

abietto agg. abject, base.

abiezione sf. abjection.

abigeato sm. cattle-stealing.

àbile agg. 1. able, skilful 2. (a †are qc.) clever at.

abilità sf. ability, skill.

abilitare vt. to qualify.

abilitazione sf. qualification ‖ esame di —, qualifying examination.

abisso sm. abyss.

abitàbile agg. inhabitable.

abitàcolo sm. (aer.) cockpit.

abitante sm. inhabitant.

abitare vi. to inhabit, to live in.

abitato sm. inhabited place.

abitazione sf. habitation, house.

àbito sm. 1. (da uomo) suit 2. (da donna) dress.

abituale agg. usual, customary.

abituare vt. to accustom. ♦ **abituarsi** vr. to get (v. irr.) used (to).

abitudinario agg. methodical. ♦ **abitudinario** sm. routinist.

abitùdine sf. habit, custom.

abituro sm. slum dwelling.

abiura sf. abjuration.

abiurare vt. to abjure.

ablazione sf. ablation.

abluzione sf. ablution.

abnegazione sf. self-denial.

abnorme agg. abnormal.

abolire vt. to abolish.

abolizione sf. abolition, repeal.

abominare vt. to loathe.

abominévole agg. abominable.

aborigeni sm. pl. the natives.

aborrimento sm. abhorrence.

aborrire vt. to hate, to loathe.

abortire vi. to miscarry.

aborto sm. miscarriage.

abrasione sf. abrasion.

abrogare vt. 1. to abrogate 2. (giur.) to repeal.

abrogazione sf. 1. abrogation 2. (giur.) repeal.

àbside sf. apse.

abulia sf. (fig.) lack of will-power.

abùlico agg. (fig.) lacking in will-power.

abusare vi. to abuse.

abusivo agg. abusive.

abuso sm. abuse.

acacia sf. acacia.

acanto sm. acanthus.

acca sf. letter H.

accademia sf. academy.

accadèmico agg. academical. ♦ **accadèmico** sm. academician.

accademismo sm. academism.

accadere vi. to happen.

accaduto sm. event.

accagliarsi vr. 1. to curdle 2. (del sangue) to coagulate.

accalappiacani sm. dog-catcher.

accalappiare vt. 1. to catch (v. irr.) 2. (fig.) to ensnare.

accalcarsi vr. to crowd.

accaldarsi vi. 1. to get (v. irr.) heated 2. (fig.) to get excited.

accaldato agg. hot.

accalorarsi vr. to get (v. irr.) excited.

accampamento sm. camp.

accampare vt. to camp: — diritti, to lay (v. irr.) claims (to).

accanimento sm. 1. fury 2. (tenacia) tenacity.

accanirsi vr. 1. (infierire) to rage 2. (ostinarsi) to persist.

accanito agg. 1. (senza pietà) relentless 2. obstinate.

accanto avv. beside, near, by ‖ accanto a, by, near, at the side of.

accantonare vt. to set (v. irr.) aside.

accaparrare vt. to buy (v. irr.) up.

accapigliarsi vr. to come (v. irr.) to blows, to quarrel.

accappatoio sm. bath-gown.

accapponarsi vr. to get (v. irr.) goose-flesh.

accarezzare vt. 1. to caress, to stroke 2. (fig.) to entertain.

accartocciare vt. 1. to wrap up 2. (spiegazzare) to crumple.

accasare vt. to marry, to give (v. irr.) in marriage. ♦ **accasarsi** vr. to get (v. irr.) married.

accasciarsi vi. 1. to fall (v. irr.) to the ground 2. (fig.) to lose (v. irr.) heart.

accatastare vt. to heap up.

accattivarsi vi. to win (v. irr.).

accattonaggio sm. begging.

accattone sm. beggar.

accavallare vt. to overlap: — le gambe, to cross one's legs.

accecamento sm. 1. blinding 2. (fig.) lack of perception.

accecare vt. to blind. ♦ **accecarsi** vr. to blind oneself.

accèdere vi. 1. to approach 2. (entrare) to enter 3. (comm.) to comply (with).

accelerare vt. 1. to quicken 2. (di velocità) to accelerate.

accelerato sm. (ferr.) slow train.

acceleratore sm. accelerator.

accelerazione sf. acceleration.

accèndere vt. 1. to light 2. (di fiammiferi) to strike (v. irr.) 3. (di radio, luce ecc.) to switch on 4. (fig.) to inflame. ♦ **accèndersi** vr. 1. to light up 2. (prender fuoco) to catch (v. irr.) fire || — in volto, to blush.

accendino sm. **accendisigaro** sm. (cigarette)-lighter.

accennare vi. 1. to make (v. irr.) a sign 2. (menzionare) to mention 3. (alludere) to allude.

accenno sm. 1. sign 2. (fig.) hint.

accensione sf. 1. lighting 2. (mecc.) ignition || chiavetta d'—, ignition-key.

accentare vt. to accent, to stress.

accentazione sf. accentuation, stressing.

accento sm. 1. accent 2. (tonico) stress.

accentramento sm. centralization.

accentrare vt. to centralize.

accentuare vt. to accentuate, to stress. ♦ **accentuarsi** vr. to get (v. irr.) worse, to increase.

accerchiamento sm. surrounding.

accerchiare vt. to surround.

accertamento sm. 1. assurance 2. (controllo) verification.

accertare vt. 1. to assure 2. (verificare) to verify.

acceso agg. 1. lit up 2. (in volto) blushing 3. (d'ira) in a temper.

accessibile agg. 1. open to 2. (di persona) approachable.

accesso sm. 1. admission 2. (di malattia, passione) fit.

accessorio agg. accessory. ♦ **accessori** sm. pl. fittings.

accetta sf. hatchet.

accettare vt. 1. to accept 2. (consentire) to consent.

accetto agg. welcome.

accezione sf. meaning.

acchiappare vt. to catch (v. irr.).

acchito sm. di primo —, at first sight, at once.

acciacco sm. infirmity.

acciaieria sf. steel-mill.

acciaio sm. steel.

acciarino sm. 1. flint-lock 2. (di fucile) gun-lock.

accidentale agg. accidental.

accidentato agg. uneven.

accidente sm. chance, accident.

accidenti inter. damn.

accidia sf. sloth.

accigliarsi vr. to frown.

accingersi vr. to set (v. irr.) about (doing).

acciottolare vt. to cobble.

acciottolato sm. cobbled paving.

acciottolio sm. clatter.

acciuffare vt. to catch (v. irr.), to seize.

acciuga sf. anchovy.

acclamare vt. 1. to acclaim 2. (applaudire) to applaud.

acclamazione sf. acclamation, applause.

acclimatazione sf. acclimatization.

acclùdere vt. to enclose.

accluso agg. enclosed.

accoccolarsi vr. to squat down.

accodarsi vr. to follow.

accogliente agg. comfortable, hospitable.

accoglienza sf. reception, welcome.

accògliere vt. 1. to receive 2. (fare buona accoglienza) to welcome 3. (una richiesta) to grant.

accòlito sm. acolyte.

accollatura sf. neckline.

accoltellare vt. to stab.

accomiatare vt. 1. to give (v. irr.) leave 2. (licenziare) to dismiss. ♦ **accomiatarsi** vr. to take (v. irr.) leave (of).

accomodamento sm. 1. adjustment 2. (conciliazione) conciliation.

accomodante agg. yielding.

accomodare vt. 1. (riparare) to repair 2. (sistemare) to settle 3. (far comodo) to suit.

accompagnamento sm. 1. (l'accompagnare) accompanying 2. (seguito) retinue 3. (mus.) accompaniment.

accompagnare vt. 1. to accompany 2. (— qu. alla stazione) to see (v. irr.) so. off 3. (mus.) to accompany.

accompagnatore sm. 1. companion 2. (mus.) accompanist.

accomunare vt. 1. to join, to associate. ♦ **accomunarsi** vr. to join.

acconciare vt. 1. to adjust, to adorn 2. (capelli) to dress.

acconciatura sf. hair-style.

acconsentire vi. 1. to consent 2. (annuire) to assent.

accontentare vt. to satisfy. ♦ **accontentarsi** vr. to be content (with).

acconto sm. account.

accoppare vt. to kill.

accoppiamento sm. 1. coupling 2. (di buoi al giogo) yoking 3. (mecc.) connection.

accoppiare vt. 1. to couple 2. (fig.) to match. ♦ **accoppiarsi** vr. to couple, to mate.

accoppiata sf. (ippica) fourecast.

accorato agg. sorrowful.

accorciare vt. to shorten.

accordare vt. 1. to grant 2. (mus.) to tune 3. (armonizzare) to match. ♦ **accordarsi** vr. to agree (upon).

accordatore sm. tuner.

accordo sm. 1. agreement ‖ come d'—, as agreed 2. (mus.) chord 3. (fig.) harmony.

accorgersi vr. 1. (percepire) to perceive 2. (rendersi conto) to realize.

accorgimento sm. 1. sagacity 2. (stratagemma) clever device.

accorrere vi. to run (v. irr.), to hasten: — in aiuto, to rush to the help.

accortezza sf. sagacity.

accorto agg. shrewd.

accostare vt. 1. to draw (v. irr.) near 2. (porte, finestre ecc.) to set

(v. irr.) ajar. ♦ **accostarsi** vr. to come (v. irr.) near.

accotonare vt. to raise.

accotonatura sf. raising.

accozzaglia sf. huddle: un'— di gente, a motley crowd.

accozzare vt. to huddle. ♦ **accozzarsi** vr. to huddle.

accreditamento sm. (comm.) crediting.

accreditare vt. to credit. ♦ **accreditarsi** vr. to gain credit.

accréscere vt. to increase.

accrescimento sm. increase.

accrescitivo agg. e sm. augmentative.

accucciarsi vr. to crouch.

accudire vi. to look after: — alla casa, to do (v. irr.) the housework.

accumulare vt. to heap up.

accumulatore sm. accumulator.

accuratezza sf. accuracy, care.

accurato agg. careful, precise.

accusa sf. charge.

accusare vt. 1. to accuse, to charge (with) 2. (sentire) to feel (v. irr.) 3. (comm.) to acknowledge.

accusativo agg. e sm. accusative.

accusato sm. accused.

accusatore sm. prosecutor: pubblico —, public prosecutor.

acerbo agg. 1. unripe 2. (acido) sour.

àcero sm. maple.

acetilene sm. acetylene.

aceto sm. vinegar.

acetone sm. acetone.

acidità sf. 1. acidity 2. (di stomaco) hyperchlorhydria.

àcido agg. sour. ♦ **àcido** sm. acid.

acidulo agg. acidulous.

àcino sm. (di uva) grape.

acme sf. 1. acme 2. (di malattia) crisis (pl. -ses).

acne sf. acne.

aconfessionale agg. nondenominational.

acqua sf. 1. water: — marina, sea water; — piovana, rain water; — potabile, drinking water 2. (pioggia) rain: — a catinelle, heavy rain.

acquaforte sf. etching.

acquaio sm. sink.

acquamarina sf. aquamarine.

acquaragia sf. turpentine.

acquario sm. aquarium.

acquasanta sf. holy water.

acquasantiera *sf.* stoup.

acquàtico *agg.* aquatic.

acquattarsi *vr.* 1. to crouch 2. (*nascondersi*) to hide (*v. irr.*).

acquavite *sf.* brandy.

acquazzone *sm.* downpour.

acquedotto *sm.* aqueduct.

acquerellista *sm.* water-colourist.

acquerello *sm.* water-colour.

acquerùgiola *sf.* drizzle.

acquiescente *agg.* acquiescent.

acquiescenza *sf.* acquiescence.

acquirente *sm.* buyer.

acquisire *vt.* to acquire.

acquistare *vt.* 1. (*comperare*) to buy (*v. irr.*) 2. (*ottenere*) to get (*v. irr.*) 3. (*fig.*) to gain || — *terreno*, to make (*v. irr.*) progress.

acquisto *sm.* purchase || *fare acquisti*, to go (*v. irr.*) shopping.

acquitrino *sm.* marsh.

acquolina *sf.* drizzle: *far venire l'— in bocca*, to make (*v. irr.*) so.'s mouth water.

acre *agg.* 1. sour 2. (*fig.*) sarcastic 3. (*pungente*) pungent.

acrèdine *sf.* 1. acridity 2. (*fig.*) acrimony.

acrimonia *sf.* acrimony.

acròbata *s.* acrobat.

acrobàtico *agg.* acrobatic.

acrobazìa *sf.* acrobatics (*pl.*) || *fare delle acrobazie*, to perform stunts.

acròpoli *sf.* acropolis.

acuire *vt.* to sharpen: — *l'interesse*, to stimulate interest.

acùleo *sm.* 1. (*bot.*) prickle 2. (*zool.*) sting.

acume *sm.* insight.

acuminare *vt.* to sharpen.

acùstica *sf.* acoustics.

acutezza *sf.* 1. sharpness 2. (*di mente*) perspicacity.

acutizzare *vt.* to make (*v. irr.*) acute. ♦ **acutizzarsi** *vr.* to grow (*v. irr.*) acute.

acuto *agg.* 1. sharp 2. (*di angoli, accenti*) acute 3. (*intenso*) intense 4. (*di suono*) shrill. ♦ **acuto** *sm.* (*mus.*) high note.

adagiare *vt.* to lay (*v. irr.*) down with care. ♦ **adagiarsi** *vr.* to lie (*v. irr.*) down.

adagio[1] *avv.* 1. slowly 2. (*con cautela*) cautiously 3. (*con delicatezza*) gently.

adagio[2] *sm.* proverb, saying.

adamantino *agg.* adamantine.

adamìtico *agg.* adamic.

adattàbile *agg.* adaptable.

adattamento *sm.* 1. adaptation 2. (*assestamento*) adjustment.

adattare *vt.* to adapt, to fit. ♦ **adattarsi** *vr.* 1. to adapt oneself 2. (*attagliarsi*) to fit.

adatto *agg.* 1. fit, proper 2. (*che va bene*) suitable (for).

addebitare *vt.* to debit.

addèbito *sm.* charge: *fare un — a qu. per qc.*, to charge so. with sthg.

addendo *sm.* addendum (*pl.* -da).

addensamento *sm.* 1. thickening 2. (*di persone*) crowding.

addensare *vt.* 1. to thicken. ♦ **addensarsi** *vr.* 1. to thicken 2. (*di folla*) to crowd.

addentare *vt.* to bite (*v. irr.*).

addentellato *sm.* 1. (*arch.*) toothing 2. (*fig.*) stepping-stone.

addentrarsi *vr.* to penetrate: — *in una questione*, to probe a question.

addentro *avv.* inside.

addestramento *sm.* 1. training 2. (*mil.*) drilling.

addestrare *vt.* 1. to train 2. (*mil.*) to drill.

addetto *agg.* employed (in). ♦ **addetto** *sm.* attaché.

addietro *avv.* 1. (*di spazio*) behind 2. (*di tempo*) before, ago || *era venuto due giorni —*, he had come two days before.

addìo *inter.* good-bye.

addirittura *avv.* 1. quite 2. (*in esclamazioni*) really!

addirsi *vr.* to become (*v. irr.*).

additare *vt.* to point at.

addizionale *agg.* additional.

addizionare *vt.* to sum up.

addizionatrice *sf.* adding-machine, adder.

addizione *sf.* addition.

addobbare *vt.* to adorn.

addobbo *sm.* 1. decoration 2. (*eccl.*) sacred ornaments (*pl.*).

addolcire *vt.* 1. to sweeten 2. (*fig.*) to soften. ♦ **addolcirsi** *vr.* to soften(er).

addolorare *vt.* to grieve. ♦ **addolorarsi** *vr.* to be grieved.

addolorato *agg.* grieved, sorry.

addome *sm.* abdomen.

addomesticare *vt.* to tame.

addominale *agg.* abdominal.

addormentare *vt.* 1. to send (*v. irr.*) to sleep 2. (*med.*) to anaesthetize. ♦ **addormentarsi** vr. **1.** to fall (v. irr.) asleep **2.** (fig.) to go (v. irr.) to sleep.

addossare vt. **1.** to lean **2.** (attribuire) to lay (v. irr.). ♦ **addossarsi** vr. **1.** (affollarsi) to crowd **2.** (prendere su di sé) to take (v. irr.) upon oneself.

addosso avv. prep. **1.** on, upon: mettere qc. —, to put (v. irr.) sthg. on; togliere qc. d'—, to take (v. irr.) sthg. off **2.** (vicino a) close to: la casa è — alla montagna, the house is close to the mountain ‖ dare —, to assault, to contradict.

addottrinare vt. to instruct. ♦ **addottrinarsi** vr. to instruct oneself.

addurre vt. **1.** to put (v. irr.) forward: — una scusa, to plead **2.** (citare) to quote.

adeguamento sm. **1.** proportionment **2.** (adattamento) adaptation.

adeguare vt. **1.** to proportionate **2.** (adattare) to conform. ♦ **adeguarsi** vr. to conform oneself, to adapt oneself.

adeguato agg. **1.** proportionate **2.** (adatto) convenient, fit **3.** (giusto) fair.

adémpiere vt. **1.** (compiere) to fulfil **2.** (eseguire) to carry out. ♦ **adémpiersi** vr. (avverarsi) to come (v. irr.) true.

adempimento sm. **1.** fulfilment **2.** (esecuzione) carrying out.

adenòidi sf. pl. adenoids.

adepto sm. **1.** adept **2.** (seguace) follower.

aderente agg. **1.** adherent **2.** (di abito) close-fitting.

aderenza sf. **1.** adherence **2.** (med.) adhesion **3.** (pl.) connections.

aderire vi. **1.** (stare vicino e fig.) to adhere, to stick to **2.** (consentire) to comply with **3.** (parteggiare per) to take sides (with).

adescamento sm. **1.** enticement **2.** (seduzione) seduction.

adescare vt. **1.** to entice **2.** (sedurre) to seduce.

adesione sf. adhesion: dare la propria — ad un partito, to join a party.

adesivo agg. adhesive.

adesso avv. now, at present, at the moment.

adiacente agg. adjacent.

adibire vt. to use as.

àdipe sm. fat.

adiposo agg. adipose.

adirarsi vr. to get (v. irr.) angry.

adirato agg. angry.

adire vt. (giur.) to apply to: — le vie legali, to take (v. irr.) legal steps.

àdito sm. entry: dare —, to give (v. irr.) rise.

adocchiare vt. **1.** to glance **2.** (scorgere) to catch (v. irr.) sight of.

adolescente agg. teen-aged, adolescent. ♦ **adolescente** sm. teen-ager.

adolescenza sf. adolescence.

adombrare vt. **1.** to shade **2.** (nascondere) to conceal **3.** (simboleggiare) to symbolize. ♦ **adombrarsi** vr. **1.** to resent **2.** (di cavallo) to shy.

adoperare vt. to use. ♦ **adoperarsi** vr. to endeavour.

adoràbile agg. charming.

adorare vt. to adore, to worship.

adorazione sf. adoration, worship.

adornare vt. to adorn.

adorno agg. adorned.

adottare vt. to adopt.

adottivo agg. adoptive.

adozione sf. adoption: patria d'—, adopted country.

adrenalina sf. adrenalin.

adulare vt. to flatter.

adulatore agg. flattering. ♦ **adulatore** sm. flatterer.

adulazione sf. flattery.

adùltera sf. adulteress.

adulterare vt. **1.** to adulterate **2.** (fig.) to falsify.

adulterino agg. adulterine.

adultèrio sm. adultery.

adùltero agg. adulterous. ♦ **adùltero** sm. adulterer.

adulto agg. e sm. grown-up, adult.

adunanza sf. meeting.

adunco agg. hooked.

aerare vt. **1.** to air **2.** (chim.) to aerate.

aerazione sf. **1.** airing **2.** (chim.) aeration.

aèreo agg. aerial ‖ per via aerea, by air. ♦ **aèreo** sm. **1.** plane **2.** (radio) aerial.

aerodinàmica sf. aerodynamics.

aeròdromo sm. aerodrome.

aerolito sm. aerolite.

aeromodello sm. model aircraft.

aeronàuta sm. aeronaut.

aeronàutica sf. aeronautics.

aeronave *sf.* airship.

aeronavigazione *sf.* air navigation

aeroplano *sm.* (aero)plane, aircraft || — *a razzo*, rocket plane; — *passeggeri*, passenger plane; — *da bombardamento*, bomber.

aeroporto *sm.* airport.

aerosòl *sm.* aerosol.

aerostàtica *sf.* aerostatics.

aeròstato *sm.* aerostat.

aerostazione *sf.* air-terminal.

aerotassì *sm.* airtaxi.

aerotrasportare *vt.* to air-bear.

afa *sf.* sultriness.

afasìa *sf.* aphasia.

affàbile *agg.* affable.

affabilità *sf.* affability, kindness.

affaccendarsi *vr.* to busy oneself.

affaccendato *agg.* busy.

affacciare *vt.* **1.** to show (*v. irr.*) **2.** (*un dubbio*) to raise. ♦ **affacciarsi** *vr.* **1.** to show oneself **2.** (*su un luogo*) to face.

affamare *vt.* to starve (out).

affamato *agg.* **1.** hungry **2.** (*fig.*) eager. ♦ **affamato** *sm.* starveling.

affamatore *sm.* starver.

affannare *vt.* to trouble, to worry. ♦ **affannarsi** *vr.* **1.** to worry oneself **2.** (*affaccendarsi*) to busy oneself.

affanno *sm.* **1.** breathlessness **2.** (*pena*) worry.

affannoso *agg.* **1.** breathless || *respiro* —, difficult breathing **2.** (*ansioso*) anxious.

affare *sm.* **1.** affair, business: — *di cuore*, love affair; *questo è nostro*, this is our business **2.** (*comm.*) business: *fare affari*, to do (*v. irr.*) business || (*pol.*) *affari esteri*, foreign affairs; (*in Gran Bretagna*) *Ministero degli Affari Esteri*, Foreign Office.

affarista *sm.* speculator.

affascinante *agg.* charming.

affascinare *vt.* to charm.

affaticamento *sm.* weariness.

affaticare *vt.* to tire. ♦ **affaticarsi** *vr.* **1.** to get (*v. irr.*) tired **2.** (*lavorare molto*) to work hard.

affatto *avv.* **1.** completely, quite **2.** (*in frasi negative*) at all: *niente* —, not at all.

affatturare *vt.* to bewitch.

affermare *vt.* to affirm **2.** (*fig.*) to assert. ♦ **affermarsi** *vr.* to make (*v. irr.*) a name for oneself.

affermativo *agg.* affirmative.

affermazione *sf.* **1.** statement **2.** (*successo*) achievement.

afferrare *vt.* to grasp **2.** (*fig.*) to seize. ♦ **afferrarsi** *vr.* to grasp, to clutch at.

affettare[1] *vt.* (*tagliare a fette*) to slice.

affettare[2] *vt.* (*ostentare*) to affect.

affettato[1] *agg.* sliced.

affettato[2] *agg.* (*ostentato*) affected.

affettatrice *sf.* slicing machine.

affettazione *sf.* affectation, show.

affettivo *agg* emotional.

affetto[1] *sm.* affection: *portare — a qu.*, to set (*v. irr.*) one's affection on so.

affetto[2] *agg.* affected (with).

affettuosità *sf.* tenderness.

affettuoso *agg.* tender, affectionate.

affezionarsi *vr.* to grow (*v. irr.*) fond of.

affezione *sf.* **1.** affection **2.** (*med.*) affection, disease.

affiancare *vt.* to flank. ♦ **affiancarsi** *vr.* to line up (with).

affiatamento *sm.* concord.

affiatare *vt.* **1.** to bring (*v. irr.*) together **2.** (*mus.*) to tune. ♦ **affiatarsi** *vr.* to become (*v. irr.*) familiar (with).

affibbiare *vt.* **1.** to buckle **2.** (*fig.*) to shift (upon).

affidamento *sm.* trust, confidence: *dare* —, to inspire confidence.

affidare *vt.* **1.** to entrust **2.** (*consegnare*) to commit. ♦ **affidarsi** *vr.* to rely upon.

affievolire *vt.* to weaken. ♦ **affievolirsi** *vr.* to grow (*v. irr.*) weak.

affiggere *vt.* to post up: — *lo sguardo*, to fix one's eyes (on).

affilare *vt.* to sharpen. ♦ **affilarsi** *vr.* (*dimagrire*) to thin.

affilato *agg.* **1.** sharp **2.** (*di naso, viso*) thin.

affiliare *vt.* to affiliate.

affiliato *sm.* member, associate.

affiliazione *sf.* affiliation.

affinamento *sm.* **1.** refining **2.** (*fig.*) sharpening.

affinare *vt.* **1.** to refine **2.** (*assottigliare*) to make (*v. irr.*) thin. ♦ **affinarsi** *vr.* **1.** to refine, to improve **2.** (*assottigliarsi*) to become (*v. irr.*) thin.

affinché *cong.* so that, in order that.

affine *agg.* like, similar.

affinità *sf.* affinity.

affiorare vi. to appear on the surface.

affissare vt. to affix.

affissione sf. bill-posting.

affisso sm. 1. (avviso) bill 2. (cartello) placard 3. (manifesto) poster.

affittacàmere sm. e sf. landlord, landlady.

affittare vt. 1. (dare in affitto) to let (v. irr.) 2. (prendere in affitto) to rent 3. (noleggiare) to hire.

affitto sm. rent.

afflato sm. afflatus.

affliggere vt. 1. to distress 2. (di malattie) to afflict. ♦ **affliggersi** vr. to worry.

afflitto agg. sad, sorrowful.

afflizione sf. 1. affliction 2. (flagello) calamity.

afflosciarsi vr. 1. to become (v. irr.) flabby 2. (fig.) to weaken.

affluente sm. affluent.

affluenza sf. 1. (di acque) flow 2. (di persone) crowd 3. (abbondanza) plenty.

affluire vi. 1. (di acque) to flow 2. (di persone) to crowd 3. (di cose) to pour in.

afflusso sm. afflux.

affogamento sm. drowning.

affogare vt. 1. to drown 2. (fig.) to smother. ♦ **affogarsi** vr. to drown oneself.

affogato agg. 1. drowned 2. (fig.) oppressed || uova affogate, poached eggs.

affollamento sm. overcrowding, throng.

affollare vt. 1. to crowd 2. (fig.) to overwhelm. ♦ **affollarsi** vr. to press up.

affollato agg. crowded.

affondare vt. 1. (sommergere) to sink (v. irr.) 2. (immergere) to plunge.

affossamento sm. ditching.

affossare vt. to ditch. ♦ **affossarsi** vr. to become (v. irr.) hollow.

affrancamento sm. release.

affrancare vt. 1. to release 2. (con francobollo) to stamp. ♦ **affrancarsi** vr. to free oneself.

affrancato agg. 1. free 2. (con francobollo) stamped.

affrancatura sf. postage.

affranto agg. broken-hearted || (dalla fatica) worn out.

affratellarsi vr. to fraternize.

affresco sm. fresco.

affrettare vt. 1. to hasten 2. (anticipare) to anticipate. ♦ **affrettarsi** vr. to make (v. irr.) haste.

affrettatamente avv. hastily.

affrettato agg. 1. hasty 2. (trascurato) careless.

affrontare vt. 1. to face 2. (fig.) to deal (v. irr.) with. ♦ **affrontarsi** vr. (venire alle mani) to come (v. irr.) to blows.

affronto sm. insult.

affumicare vt. 1. to fill with smoke 2. (cuc.) to smoke.

affumicato agg. 1. blackened by smoke 2. (cuc.) smoked || lenti affumicate, sun-glasses.

affusolare vt. to taper.

afonia sf. aphonia.

àfono agg. voiceless.

aforisma sm. aphorism.

afoso agg. sultry.

africano agg. e sm. African.

afroasiàtico agg. Afro-Asiatic.

afta sf. aphtha.

àgata sf. agate.

àgave sf. agave.

agenda sf. note-book.

agente sm. agent.

agenzia sf. agency.

agevolare vt. to make (v. irr.) easy.

agevolazione sf. facilitation.

agévole agg. 1. easy 2. (di strada) smooth.

agevolmente avv. easily.

agganciare vt. 1. to hook 2. (ferr.) to couple up.

aggéggio sm. device.

aggettare vi. to jut out.

aggettivo sm. adjective.

agghiacciare vt. to freeze (v. irr.). ♦ **agghiacciarsi** vr. to freeze.

agghindare vt. to array. ♦ **agghindarsi** vr. to dress (oneself) up.

aggiogare vt. to yoke.

aggiornamento sm. 1. (rinvio) adjournment 2. (di un libro) revision.

aggiornare vt. 1. (rinviare) to adjourn 2. (mettere al corrente) to bring (v. irr.) up to date. ♦ **aggiornarsi** vr. to brush up one's knowledge.

aggiornato agg. up-to-date.

aggirare vt. to go (v. irr.) round || — l'ostacolo, to avoid an obstacle. ♦ **aggirarsi** vr. to wander about, to go about.

aggiudicare vt. to award. ♦ **ag-**

giudicarsi *vr.* to win (*v. irr.*).

aggiudicazione *sf.* award.

aggiungere *vt.* to add. ♦ aggiungersi *vr.* to join.

aggiunta *sf.* 1. addition 2. (*aumento*) increase.

aggiunto *agg.* added, joined. ♦ aggiunto *sm.* assistant.

aggiustare *vt.* 1. (*riparare*) to mend 2. (*sistemare*) to arrange. ♦ aggiustarsi *vr.* (*accomodarsi*) to make (*v. irr.*) oneself comfortable.

agglomerato *sm.* agglomerate.

agglutinare *vt.* to agglutinate.

aggraffare *vt.* to seize.

aggranchire *vt.* to benumb.

aggrapparsi *vr.* to cling (*v. irr.*) (to), to get (*v. irr.*) hold (of).

aggravante *agg.* aggravating. ♦ aggravante *sf.* (*giur.*) aggravating circumstance.

aggravare *vt.* to aggravate, to overburden. ♦ aggravarsi *vr.* to grow (*v. irr.*) worse.

aggravato *agg.* 1. overburdened 2. (*med.*) worse.

aggraziare *vt.* to make (*v. irr.*) graceful.

aggredire *vt.* to assault.

aggregare *vt.* to associate. ♦ aggregarsi *vr.* to join.

aggressione *sf.* aggression, assault.

aggressività *sf.* aggressiveness.

aggressivo *agg.* aggressive.

aggressore *sm.* aggressor.

aggrottare *vt.* to frown.

aggrovigliare *vt.* to entangle.

aggrovigliarsi *vr.* to get (*v. irr.*) entangled.

aggruppare *vt.* to group.

agguantare *vt.* to catch (*v. irr.*).

agguato *sm.* ambush.

agguerrire *vt.* to inure (for war). ♦ agguerrirsi *vr.* to get (*v. irr.*) inured.

agiatamente *avv.* in ease and comfort.

agiato *agg.* well-to-do.

àgile *agg.* nimble.

agilità *sf.* nimbleness.

agio *sm.* comfort, ease, leisure.

agiografia *sf.* hagiography.

agire *vi.* to act.

agitare *vt.* 1. to agitate 2. (*scuotere*) to shake (*v. irr.*) 3. to stir (*anche fig.*). ♦ agitarsi *vr.* to be agitated.

agitatore *sm.* 1. agitator 2. (*mecc.*) stirrer.

agitazione *sf.* 1. agitation 2. (*eccitazione*) excitement 3. (*di folla*) tumult.

aglio *sm.* garlic.

agnello *sm.* lamb.

agnosticismo *sm.* agnosticism.

ago *sm.* 1. needle 2. (*mecc.*) tongue.

agognare *vt.* to long (for sthg.).

agonìa *sf.* agony, pangs (*pl.*) of death.

agonismo *sm.* athletic spirit.

agonizzante *agg.* dying.

agonizzare *vi.* to be in one's death agony.

agorafobìa *sf.* agoraphobia.

agosto *sm.* August.

agraria *sf.* agriculture.

agrario *agg.* agrarian. ♦ agrario *sm.* 1. land-owner 2. (*esperto*) agriculturist.

agreste *agg.* agrestic, rustic.

agretto *agg.* sourish.

agricolo *agg.* agricultural.

agricoltore *sm.* farmer.

agricoltura *sf.* agriculture.

agrifoglio *sm.* holly.

agrimensore *sm.* land-surveyor.

agro *agg.* sour. ♦ agro *sm.* sourness.

agrodolce *agg.* bitter-sweet, sourish.

agronomìa *sf.* agronomy.

agronòmico *agg.* agronomical.

agrònomo *sm.* agronomist.

agrumi *sm. pl.* citrus fruit (*sing.*).

aguzzare *vt.* to sharpen.

aguzzino *sm.* 1. gaoler, jailer 2. (*fig.*) torturer.

aguzzo *agg.* sharp, pointed.

ahimè *inter.* alas.

aia *sf.* threshing-floor.

aio *sm.* tutor.

airone *sm.* heron.

aitante *agg.* vigorous, stout.

aiuola *sf.* flower-bed.

aiutante *sm.* 1. assistant 2. (*mil.*) adjutant: — di campo, aide-de-camp.

aiutare *vt.* to help. ♦ aiutarsi *vr.* (*ingegnarsi*) to make (*v. irr.*) shift. ♦ aiutarsi *vr. rec.* to help (one another).

aiuto *sm.* 1. help: chiedere —, to call for help 2. (*chi aiuta*) help, helper 3. (*pl.*) (*mil.*) reinforcements.

aizzare *vt.* to incite, to rouse.

ala *sf.* wing.

alabarda *sf.* halberd.

alabastro *sm.* alabaster.

àlacre *agg.* brisk, industrious.

alacrità *sf.* alacrity.

alamaro *sm.* frog.

alambicco *sm.* still.

alano *sm.* Great Dane.

alba *sf.* dawn.

albanese *agg. e sm.* Albanian.

àlbatro *sm.* albatross.

albeggiare *vi.* to dawn.

alberare *vt.* 1. to plant with trees 2. (*mar.*) to mast.

alberato *agg.* planted with trees.

alberatura *sf.* (*mar.*) masting.

albergatore *sm.* hotel-keeper.

alberghiero *agg.* hotel (*attributivo*): *industria alberghiera.* hotel trade.

albergo *sm.* hotel.

àlbero *sm.* 1. tree 2. (*mar.*) mast 3. (*mecc.*) shaft.

albicocca *sf.* apricot.

albino *agg. e sm.* albino.

albo *sm.* 1. list, roll: — *degli avvocati,* Law List; — *d'onore,* roll of honour 2. (*per fotografie ecc.*) album 3. (*tavola per affissione*) notice-board.

album *sm.* album.

albume *sm.* albumen.

albumina *sf.* albumin.

alca *sf.* auk.

alcalino *agg. e sm.* alkaline.

alce *sm.* elk.

alchimìa *sf.* alchemy.

alcòlico *agg.* alcoholic.

alcolismo *sm.* alcoholism.

alcolizzato *agg. e sm.* alcoholic.

alcool *sm.* alcohol.

alcova *sf.* alcove.

alcunché *pron.* anything, something.

alcuno *agg.* 1. (*frasi affermative*) some, a few 2. (*frasi negative*) any. ♦ **alcuno** *pron.* 1. (*frasi affermative*) somebody, someone 2. (*frasi negative*) anybody, anyone.

aldilà *sm.* hereafter.

aleatorio *agg.* aleatory.

aleggiare *vi.* 1. to flutter 2. (*fig.*) to hover (about).

alettone *sm.* aileron.

alfa *sf.* alpha.

alfabeto *sm.* alphabet.

aifiere *sm.* 1. ensign 2. (*scacchi*) bishop.

alga *sf.* seaweed.

àlgebra *sf.* algebra.

algèbrico *agg.* algebraic, algebraical.

aliante *sm.* glider.

àlibi *sm.* alibi.

alienare *vt.* to alienate, to estrange. ♦ **alienarsi** *vr.* to alienate oneself, to become (*v. irr.*) estranged.

alienato *agg.* lunatic, mad; estranged, alienated. ♦ **alienato** *sm.* 1. lunatic, madman (*pl. -men*) 2. alienated person, estranged person.

alienazione *sf.* alienation, estrangement.

alienista *sm.* alienist, psychiatrist.

alieno *agg.* averse, opposed.

alimentare[1] *vt.* to feed (*v. irr.*), to nourish.

alimentare[2] *agg.* alimentary ‖ *generi alimentari,* foodstuffs; *negozio di generi alimentari,* grocery store.

alimentazione *sf.* nourishment, feeding.

alimento *sm.* food.

alínea *sf.* paragraph.

alìquota *sf.* aliquot, rate.

aliscafo *sm.* hydrofoil boat.

aliseo *sm.* trade-wind.

àlito *sm.* breath.

allacciare *vt.* 1. to lace, to connect 2. (*fig.*) to establish. ♦ **allacciarsi** *vr.* 1. (*abbracciarsi*) to embrace 2. (*aggrovigliarsi*) to get (*v. irr.*) entangled, to be entangled.

allagare *vt.* to flood, to inundate.

allampanato *agg.* lean, lanky.

allargamento *sm.* widening, enlargement.

allargare *vt.* to widen, to enlarge, to extend. ♦ **allargarsi** *vr.* to widen, to extend, to spread (*v. irr.*).

allarmante *agg.* alarming.

allarmare *vt.* to alarm. ♦ **allarmarsi** *vr.* to get (*v. irr.*) frightened.

allarme *sm.* alarm, warning, alert.

allattamento *sm.* breast-feeding, nursing.

allattare *vt.* to suckle, to nurse.

alleanza *sf.* alliance.

allearsi *vr.* to ally, to become (*v. irr.*) allies.

alleato *agg.* allied. ♦ **alleato** *sm.* ally.

allegare *vt.* 1. to allege 2. (*accludere*) to enclose.

allegato *sm.* enclosure.

alleggerimento *sm.* lightening, relief.

alleggerìre *vt.* to lighten, to relieve, to unburden. ♦ **alleggerirsi** *vr.* to relieve oneself.

allegoria *sf.* allegory.

allegòrico *agg.* allegoric(al).

allegramente *agg.* cheerfully, merrily.

allegrìa *sf.* cheerfulness, mirth.

allegro *agg.* merry, cheerful, jolly.

allegrone *sm.* jolly fellow.

allenamento *sm.* training.

allenare *vt.* to train. ♦ **allenarsi** *vr.* to train (oneself).

allenatore *sm.* trainer; (*di squadre*) coach.

allentamento *sm.* **1.** loosening **2.** (*di velocità*) slackening.

allentare *vt.* to slacken, to loosen, to relax: — *il freno*, to release the brake. ♦ **allentarsi** *vr.* to slacken.

allergìa *sf.* allergy.

allèrgico *agg.* allergic.

allestimento *sm.* preparation, fitting out || — *scenico*, staging.

allestire *vt.* to prepare, to fit out.

allettamento *sm.* enticement, allurement.

allettante *agg.* alluring, enticing.

allettare *vt.* to allure, to entice.

allevamento *sm.* **1.** breeding, raising || (*di bambino*) bringing up **2.** (*luogo*) stock-farm || — *di cavalli*, stud-farm.

allevare *vt.* **1.** (*bambini*) to bring (*v. irr.*) up **2.** (*animali*) to breed (*v. irr.*), to rear.

allevatore *sm.* breeder.

alleviare *vt.* to relieve, to alleviate.

allibire *vi.* to be left speechless, to be struck dumb.

allibito *agg.* struck dumb, speechless.

allibratore *sm.* bookmaker.

allietare *vt.* to cheer. ♦ **allietarsi** *vr.* to cheer up.

allievo *sm.* **1.** pupil **2.** (*mil.*) cadet.

alligatore *sm.* alligator.

allineamento *sm.* **1.** alignment || (*tip.*) — *di caratteri*, ranging of characters **2.** (*mil.*) dressing.

allineare *vt.* **1.** to line up, to align: — *delle cifre*, to tabulate figures **2.** (*mil.*) to dress; (*in ordine di marcia*) to form up. ♦ **allinearsi** *vr.* **1.** to get (*v. irr.*) into line **2.** (*mil.*) to dress || *allinearsi*, draw up! **3.** (*pol.*) to be aligned with.

allocco *sm.* **1.** owl **2.** (*fig.*) fool.

allocuzione *sf.* allocution: *fare un'—*, to deliver a speech.

allòdola *sf.* skylark, lark.

allogare *vt.* to lodge.

allogazione *sf.* lease.

alloggiare *vt.* **1.** to lodge, to house, to put (*v. irr.*) up **2.** (*mil.*) to quarter; (*in casa privata*) to billet. ♦ **alloggiare** *vi.* **1.** to lodge, to live **2.** (*mil.*) to quarter; (*in casa privata*) to be billeted.

alloggio *sm.* **1.** lodging || *indennità di —*, living-out allowance **2.** (*mil.*) quarters (*pl.*).

allontanamento *sm.* **1.** removal **2.** (*licenziamento*) dismissal.

allontanare *vt.* **1.** to remove, to drive (*v. irr.*) away: — *un pericolo*, to evert a danger **2.** (*licenziare*) to dismiss, to turn out. ♦ **allontanarsi** *vr.* to go (*v. irr.*) away, to depart.

allora *avv.* **1.** then **2.** (*quindi*) so.

allorché *cong.* when.

alloro *sm.* laurel.

alluce *sm.* big toe.

allucinare *vt.* **1.** to dazzle **2.** (*dare allucinazioni*) to hallucinate.

allucinato *agg.* hallucinated.

allucinazione *sf.* hallucination.

allùdere *vi.* to allude (to), to hint (at).

alluminio *sm.* aluminium.

allunaggio *sm.* mooning.

allunare *vi.* to moon.

allungàbile *agg.* extensible.

allungamento *sm.* lengthening, stretching.

allungare *vt.* **1.** to lengthen, to extend, to stretch || — *il passo*, to quicken one's steps || — *il collo*, to stretch one's neck || — *gli orecchi*, to strain one's ears || (*fig.*) — *le mani su qc.*, to lay (*v. irr.*) hands on sthg. ♦ **allungarsi** *vr.* to lengthen, to grow (*v. irr.*) longer, to draw (*v. irr.*) out.

allusione *sf.* allusion, hint.

allusivo *agg.* allusive.

alluvionato *agg.* flooded || *zone alluvionate*, flood-areas. ♦ **alluvionato** *sm.* flood-victim.

alluvione *sf.* flood.

almanaccare *vi.* to fantasticate.

almanacco *sm.* almanac.

almeno *avv.* at least.

alno *sm.* alder-tree.

aloè *sm.* aloe.

alone sm. halo.

alpaca sm. alpaca.

alpe sf. alp.

alpestre agg. alpine.

alpinismo sm. (mountain-)climbing, mountaineering.

alpinista s. (mountain-)climber.

alpino agg. Alpine.

alquanto avv. somewhat, rather.

altalena sf. swing.

altana sf. roof-terrace.

altare sm. altar.

alterare vt. to alter; (salute) to impair; (cibo) to adulterate. ◆ **alterarsi** vr. 1. to alter, to change 2. (andare a male) to go (v. irr.) bad 3. (turbarsi) to be upset || la sua voce si alterò, his voice faltered.

alterazione sf. 1. alteration 2. (deterioramento) deterioration 3. (turbamento) emotion; (della voce) faltering.

alterco sm. altercation.

alterigia sf. haughtiness.

alternanza sf. alternation.

alternare vt. to alternate. ◆ **alternarsi** vr. to alternate.

alternativa sf. alternative.

alterno agg. alternate.

altero agg. lofty, proud.

altezza sf. 1. height 2. (di tessuto) width 3. (di suono) pitch 4. (fig.) essere all'— di qc., to be equal to sthg.; to be up to sthg. 5. (titolo) highness.

altezzoso agg. haughty.

alticcio agg. tight, tipsy.

altimetro sm. altimeter.

altitùdine sf. altitude.

alto agg. 1. high, tall: un uomo —, a tall man || alta direzione, top management 2. (di suono) loud || ad alta voce, aloud, loudly 3. (profondo) deep: acqua alta, deep water 4. (geogr.) northern, upper 5. (stor.) early. ◆ **alto** sm. height || alti e bassi, ups and downs. ◆ **alto** avv. high, up || mani in —, hands up.

altoforno sm. blast-furnace.

altolocato agg. high-ranking, high-class.

altoparlante sm. loud-speaker.

altopiano sm. plateau.

altresì avv. likewise, also.

altrettanto agg. correlativo as much (...as); (pl.) as many (...as) || (neg.) as (o so) much (...as); (pl.)

as (o so) many... (as): egli ha altrettante possibilità quanto me, he has as many chances as I. ◆ **altrettanto** pron. 1. as much; (pl.) as many 2. (lo stesso) the same: — a voi!, the same to you! ◆ **altrettanto** avv. 1. (con agg. e avv.) as (...as); (neg.) as (o so) ...as) 2. (coi verbi) as much (as).

altrimenti avv. otherwise. ◆ **altrimenti** cong. otherwise, else.

altro agg. indef. 1. other || un —, another 2. (differente) different 3. (con pronomi int.) else: chi altro?, who else? 4. (in più) more: leggerò altri due libri, I shall read two more books 5. (susseguente) next: verrò l'altra domenica, I shall come next Sunday 6. (antecedente) last: andai l'altro mese, I went last month.

altronde 1. (nella loc. avv.) d'—, on the other hand 2. (tuttavia) however.

altrove avv. elsewhere, somewhere else.

altrui agg. other people's, someone else's. ◆ **l'altrùi** sm. the property of others.

altruismo sm. unselfishness.

altruìstico agg. unselfish.

altura sf. height.

alunno sm. pupil.

alveare sm. beehive.

àlveo sm. river-bed.

alzàia sf. towing-line || strada d'—, towing-path.

alzare vt. 1. to lift, to raise 2. (erigere) to build (v. irr.) 3. (mar.) to hoist. ◆ **alzarsi** vr. (dal letto) to get (v. irr.) up 2. (in piedi) to stand (v. irr.) up 3. (in altezza) to grow (v. irr.) tall.

alzata sf. 1. raising 2. (l'alzarsi) rising.

amàbile agg. amiable.

amabilità sf. amiability.

amaca sf. hammock.

amàlgama sm. amalgam.

amalgamare vt. to amalgamate.

amante s. 1. lover 2. (fig.) fond.

amanuense sm. copyist.

amaranto sm. amaranth.

amare vt. 1. to love, to be fond of 2. (richiedere) to require.

amareggiare vt. 1. to make (v. irr.) bitter 2. (fig.) to sadden. ◆ **amareggiarsi** vr. to worry.

amarena sf. sour black cherry.

amaretto *sm.* macaroon.

amarezza *sf.* 1. bitterness 2. (*fig.*) sorrow.

amaro *agg.* bitter. ♦ amaro *sm.* (*liquore*) bitters (*pl.*).

amatore *sm.* 1. lover 2. (*chi si occupa d'arte per diletto*) amateur.

amàzzone *sf.* 1. Amazon 2. (*fig.*) masculine woman.

ambage *sf.* ambages (*pl.*) || *senza ambagi*, plainly.

ambasciata *sf.* 1. embassy 2. (*messaggio*) message.

ambasciatore *sm.* ambassador.

ambedue *agg. e pron.* both.

ambientare *vt.* 1. to acclimatize 2. (*fatti, personaggi ecc.*) to place. ♦ ambientarsi *vr.* to get (*v. irr.*) accustomed.

ambiente *sm.* 1. ambient 2. (*fig.*) milieu 3. (*stanza*) room.

ambiguità *sf.* ambiguity.

ambiguo *agg.* ambiguous.

ambio *sm.* amble.

ambire *vt.* to desire.

àmbito *sm.* ambit.

ambivalente *agg.* ambivalent.

ambivalenza *sf.* ambivalence.

ambizione *sf.* ambition.

ambizioso *agg.* ambitious.

ambo *sm.* ambo.

ambra *sf.* amber.

ambrosia *sf.* ambrosia.

ambulante *agg.* itinerant || *venditore* —, pedlar.

ambulanza *sf.* ambulance.

ambulatorio *sm.* surgery.

ameba *sf.* amoeba.

amebìasi *sf.* amoebiasis (*pl.* -es).

amenità *sf.* 1. amenity 2. (*facezia*) joke.

ameno *agg.* 1. pleasant 2. (*divertente*) funny: *un tipo* —, a funny chap.

americanismo *sm.* Americanism.

americano *agg. e sm.* American.

ametista *sf.* amethyst.

amianto *sm.* amianthus.

amichévole *agg.* friendly.

amicizia *sf.* friendship || *fare* —, to make (*v. irr.*) friends with.

amico *sm.* friend.

amidatura *sf.* starching.

àmido *sm.* starch.

ammaccare *vt.* to bruise.

ammaccatura *sf.* bruise.

ammaestramento *sm.* 1. (*addestramento*) training 2. (*insegnamento*) teaching 3. (*di animali*) taming.

ammaestrare *vt.* 1. (*addestrare*) to train 2. (*insegnare*) to teach (*v. irr.*) 3. (*di animali*) to tame.

ammainare *vt.* to furl.

ammalarsi *vr.* to fall (*v. irr.*) ill.

ammalato *agg.* 1. (*pred.*) ill 2. (*attr.*) sick. ♦ ammalato *sm.* sick person, patient.

ammaliare *vt.* to bewitch.

ammaliatrice *sf.* bewitcher.

ammanco *sm.* shortage || — *di cassa*, deficit.

ammanettare *vt.* to handcuff.

ammannire *vt.* to prepare.

ammansire *vt.* 1. to tame 2. (*fig.*) to calm. ♦ ammansirsi *vr.* 1. to become (*v. irr.*) tamed 2. to calm down.

ammarare *vi.* 1. to alight (on water) 2. (*di capsule spaziali*) to splash down.

ammassare *vt.* to heap. ♦ ammassarsi *vr.* to gather.

ammasso *sm.* heap.

ammattire *vi.* to get (*v. irr.*) mad.

ammazzare *vt.* to kill.

ammazzatoio *sm.* slaughter-house.

ammenda *sf.* amends (*pl.*).

ammèttere *vt.* 1. (*lasciar entrare*) to admit, to receive 2. (*concedere, supporre*) to acknowledge, to suppose.

ammezzato *sm.* mezzanine.

ammezzire *vi.* to become (*v. irr.*) over-ripe.

ammiccare *vi.* to wink (at).

ammina *sf.* amine.

amministrare *vt.* 1. to manage 2. (*giur.; eccl.*) to administer.

amministrativo *agg.* administrative.

amministratore *sm.* manager.

amministrazione *sf.* management.

ammiràbile *agg.* admirable.

ammiraglio *sm.* admiral.

ammirare *vt.* to admire.

ammiratore *sm.* 1. admirer 2. (*di attori ecc.*) fan.

ammirazione *sf.* admiration.

ammirévole *agg.* admirable.

ammissìbile *agg.* admissible.

ammobiliamento *sm.* furnishing.

ammobiliare *vt.* to furnish.

ammodernare *vt.* to modernize.

ammodo *agg.* nice, proper.

ammogliare *vt.* to marry. ♦ ammogliarsi *vr.* to get (*v. irr.*) married.

ammollare vt. **1.** to soak **2.** (ammorbidire) to soften.

ammollire vt. to soften.

ammoniaca sf. ammonia.

ammonire vt. **1.** to admonish **2.** (avvisare) to warn.

ammonizione sf. **1.** admonition **2.** (rimprovero) reproof **3.** (avvertimento) warning.

ammontare vi. to amount.

ammonticchiare vt. to heap (up).

ammorbare vt. to taint.

ammorbidire vt. to soften.

ammortamento sm. redemption || quota d'—, depreciation allowance.

ammortire vt. to numb.

ammortizzare vt. to redeem.

ammosciare vi. to become (v. irr.) flabby.

ammucchiare vt. to heap (up).

ammuffire vi. **1.** to grow (v. irr.) musty **2.** (fig.) to languish: — in casa, to languish at home.

ammutinamento sm. mutiny.

ammutinarsi vr. to mutiny.

ammutinato agg. mutinous. ♦ **ammutinato** sm. mutineer.

ammutolire vi. **1.** to become (v. irr.) dumb **2.** (essere ammutolito da altri) to be struck dumb.

amnesia sf. loss of memory.

amnistia sf. amnesty.

amnistiare vt. to amnesty.

amo sm. fish-hook.

amorale agg. amoral.

amoralità sf. amorality.

amore sm. **1.** love || — di sé, selfishness **2.** (persona o cosa amata) beloved || per amore di, for the sake of.

amoreggiare vi. to flirt.

amoretto sm. flirtation.

amorévole agg. loving.

amorevolezza sf. lovingness.

amorfo agg. amorphous.

amorino sm. Cupid.

amoroso agg. **1.** loving **2.** (fig.) amorous: poesia —, amorous verse.

amovibile agg. movable.

amperòmetro sm. amperometer.

ampiezza sf. width, (anche fig.) breadth.

ampio agg. **1.** wide **2.** (di abito) comfortable.

amplesso sm. embrace.

ampliamento sm. amplification.

ampliare vt. **1.** to amplify **2.** (aumentare) to increase. ♦ **ampliar-**

si vr. to widen.

amplificare vt. **1.** to enlarge **2.** (fig.; fis.) to amplify.

amplificatore sm. amplifier.

amplificazione sf. amplification.

ampolla sf. **1.** phial **2.** (per olio, aceto ecc.) cruet.

ampollosità sf. pomposity.

ampolloso agg. pompous: stile —, bombastic style.

amputare vt. to amputate.

amputazione sf. amputation.

amuleto sm. amulet.

anabbaglianti sm. pl. lower beams

anabolismo sm. anabolism.

anacoreta sm. anchorite.

anacronismo sm. anachronism.

anacronistico agg. anachronistic.

anàgrafe sf. registry office.

anagramma sm. anagram.

analcòlico agg. soft.

anale agg. anal.

analfabeta sm. illiterate.

analfabetismo sm. illiteracy.

analgesico agg. e sm. analgesic.

anàlisi sf. analysis (pl. -ses).

analitico agg. analytical.

analizzare vt. to analyse.

analogamente avv. likewise.

analogia sf. analogy.

anàlogo agg. similar.

ànanas sm. pine-apple.

anarchia sf. anarchy.

anàrchico agg. anarchic. ♦ **anàrchico** sm. anarchist.

anatema sm. anathema.

anatomìa sf. anatomy.

anatòmico agg. anatomic.

anatomista sm. anatomist.

ànatra sf. duck.

anatròccolo sm. duckling.

anca sf. hip.

ancestrale agg. ancestral.

anche avv. **1.** (pure) also, too **2.** (in frasi neg.) either: anch'io non verrò, I will not come either **3.** (con comp.) even, still: ciò è anche peggio, it is still worse **4.** (persino) even. ♦ **anche** cong. (anche se) even if, even though

ancheggiare vi. to waddle.

anchilosare agg. ankylosed.

anchilosi sf. ankylosis.

àncora sf. **1.** anchor: levar l'—, to weigh anchor **2.** (fig.) hope: — di salvezza, last hope.

ancora avv. **1.** (tuttora) still **2.** (in frasi neg.) yet **3.** (di nuovo) again **4.** (davanti a comp.) still, even

5. (*con pron. e agg. quantitativi*) more: — *molte persone*, many more people **6.** («*di più*» in *frasi affermative*) some more: *voglio ancora caffè*, I want some more coffee **7.** («*di più*» in *frasi neg. e dubitative*) any more: *hai ancora caffè?*, have you any more coffee? **8.** (*più a lungo*) longer: *leggi ancora un po'*, read a little longer.

ancoraggio *sm.* anchorage.

ancorare *vt.* to anchor.

ancorché *cong.* even if, even though.

andamento *sm.* **1.** (*tendenza*) trend **2.** (*procedimento*) proceeding.

andante *agg.* **1.** (*scadente*) plain **2.** (*comm.*) current **3.** (*mus.*) andante.

andare *vi.* **1.** (*anche fig.*) to go (*v. irr.*): — *a cavallo*, to go on horseback; — *a far compere*, to go shopping; — *a piedi*, to go on foot; — *a zonzo*, to lounge about; — *e venire*, to come (*v. irr.*) and go; — *in bicicletta*, to ride (*v. irr.*) a bicycle; — *in treno*, to go by train; — *a male*, to go bad **2.** (*essere molto venduto*) to be in demand **3.** (— *bene, di indumento*) to fit || — *avanti* (*di orologi*), to be fast; — *indietro* (*di orologi*), to be slow. ♦ **andàrsene** *vr.* to go away.

andata *sf.* going: — *e ritorno*, going there and back || *biglietto di sola* —, single ticket || *biglietto di* — *e ritorno*, return ticket.

andatura *sf.* **1.** gait **2.** (*velocità*) pace.

andazzo *sm.* habit, custom.

andicappare *vt.* to handicap.

andirivieni *sm.* coming and going.

àndito *sm.* passage.

andrògino *agg.* androgynous. ♦ **andrògino** *sm.* androgyne.

androne *sm.* lobby.

aneddòtico *agg.* anecdotic.

aneddòto *sm.* anecdote.

anelare *vi.* **1.** to gasp **2.** (*fig.*) to long for.

anèlito *sm.* **1.** gasp **2.** (*fig.*) longing for.

anello *sm.* ring: — *di fidanzamento*, engagement ring; — *di matrimonio*, wedding ring || — *di catena*, link of a chain.

anemìa *sf.* anaemia.

anèmico *agg.* anaemic.

anèmone *sm.* anemone.

anestesìa *sf.* anaesthesia.

anestesista *s.* anaesthetist.

anestètico *agg. e sm.* anaesthetic.

anestetizzare *vt.* to anaesthetize.

anfibio *agg.* amphibious. ♦ **anfibio** *sm.* (*zool.; mil.*) amphibian.

anfiteatro *sm.* amphitheatre.

anfitrione *sm.* amphitryon.

ànfora *sf.* amphora (*pl.* -ae).

anfrattuoso *agg.* anfractuous.

angèlico *agg.* angelic(al).

àngelo *sm.* angel.

angherìa *sf.* vexation.

angina *sf.* angina.

angioma *sm.* angioma.

anglicano *agg. e sm.* Anglican.

angolare *agg.* angular.

àngolo *sm.* **1.** corner **2.** (*fis.; geom.*) angle.

angoloso *agg.* angular.

angoscia *sf.* anguish.

angosciare *vt.* to anguish.

angoscioso *agg.* **1.** (*che dà angoscia*) distressing **2.** (*pieno di angoscia*) full of anguish.

anguilla *sf.* **1.** eel **2.** (*fig.*) elusive person.

anguria *sf.* water-melon.

angustia *sf.* **1.** narrowness **2.** (*tribolazione*) distress.

angustiare *vt.* to afflict. ♦ **angustiarsi** *vr.* to worry.

angusto *agg.* **1.** narrow **2.** (*fig.*) mean.

ànice *sm.* anise.

anidride *sf.* anhydride.

anilina *sf.* aniline.

ànima *sf.* **1.** soul || *esalare l'*—, to die || *vender l'*— *a caro prezzo*, to sell (*v. irr.*) one's life dearly. **2.** (*parte centrale, nerbo*) soul, heart **3.** (*cuore, sentimento*) feeling, heart **4.** (*persona*) person: *Torino ha oltre un milione di anime*, Turin has over one million persons.

animale *sm. e agg.* animal.

animalesco *agg.* beastly.

animare *vt.* to enliven, to give (*v. irr.*) life. ♦ **animarsi** *vr.* to become (*v. irr.*) lively.

animatamente *avv.* animatedly.

animato *agg.* **1.** living **2.** (*vivace*) lively.

animatore *sm.* animator.

animazione *sf.* briskness.

animismo *sm.* animism.

ànimo *sm.* **1.** mind: *ho in animo di fare ciò*, I have a mind to do that **2.** (*coraggio*) courage **3.** (*inclinazione*) disposition.

animosità *sf.* animosity.

animoso *agg.* **1.** brave **2.** (*ostile*) malevolent.

anisetta *sf.* anisette.

ànitra *sf.* duck.

annacquare *vt.* **1.** to water **2.** (*fig.*) to moderate.

annaffiare *vt.* to water.

annaffiatoio *sm.* watering-can.

annali *sm. pl.* annals.

annaspare *vi.* to grope.

annaspio *sm.* groping.

annata *sf.* **1.** year **2.** (*raccolto*) crop.

annebbiare *vt.* **1.** to dim **2.** (*fig.*) to dull. ♦ **annebbiarsi** *vr.* (*della vista*) to blur.

annegamento *sm.* drowning.

annegare *vt.* to drown. ♦ **annegarsi** *vr.* to drown oneself.

annegato *agg.* drowned.

annerimento *sm.* blackening.

annerire *vt.* to blacken.

annessione *sf.* annexation.

annesso *agg.* **1.** connected **2.** (*accluso*) enclosed.

annèttere *vt.* to annex.

annichilazione *sf.* annihilation.

annichilimento *sm.* annihilation.

annichilire *vt.* to annihilate.

annidarsi *vr.* **1.** to nestle **2.** (*nascondersi*) to hide (*v. irr.*).

annientamento *sm.* **1.** destruction **2.** (*di desideri*) frustration.

annientare *vt.* to destroy.

anniversario *agg. e sm.* anniversary.

anno *sm.* **1.** year: — *bisestile*, leap-year ‖ *Capo d'*—, New Year's Day ‖ *durante tutto l'*—, all the year round **2.** (*periodo lungo e indeterminato*) a long time **3.** (*nell'indicare l'età*) to be ... years old: *ho 10 anni*, I am 10 years old.

annodare *vt.* to knot: — *amicizie*, to make friends.

annoiare *vt.* to bore, to tire. ♦ **annoiarsi** *vr.* to be bored.

annoiato *agg.* bored.

annoiatore *sm.* tiresome person.

annoso *agg.* old.

annotare *vt.* **1.** (*corredare di note*) to annotate **2.** (*prendere nota*) to take (*v. irr.*) note (of).

annotazione *sf.* note.

annottare *vi.* to grow (*v. irr.*) dark.

annuale *agg.* yearly.

annuario *sm.* year-book.

annuire *vi.* to nod.

annullamento *sm.* cancellation.

annullare *vt.* **1.** to annul **2.** (*comm.*) to cancel.

annunciare *vt.* **1.** to announce **2.** (*predire*) to foretell (*v. irr.*).

annunciatore *sm.* announcer.

annuncio *sm.* **1.** notice **2.** (*presagio*) presage.

ànnuo *agg.* yearly.

annusare *vi.* **1.** to smell **2.** (*tabacco*) to take (*v. irr.*) snuff.

annuvolarsi *vr.* **1.** to get (*v. irr.*) cloudy **2.** (*fig.*) to become (*v. irr.*) gloomy.

ano *sm.* anus.

anòdino *agg.* anodyne.

ànodo *sm.* anode.

anomalìa *sf.* anomaly.

anòmalo *agg.* anomalous.

anònima *sf.* joint-stock company.

anònimo *agg.* anonymous. ♦ **anònimo** *sm.* anonym.

anormale *agg.* abnormal.

anormalità *sf.* abnormality.

ansa *sf.* **1.** (*insenatura*) creek **2.** (*di fiume*) bend **3.** (*manico*) handle.

ansante *agg.* panting.

ansare *vi.* to pant.

ansia *sf.* anxiety.

ansietà *sf.* anxiety.

ansimare *vi.* to pant.

ansioso *agg.* **1.** anxious **2.** (*desideroso*) eager.

ànsito *sm.* panting.

anta *sf.* **1.** shutter **2.** (*di armadio*) door.

antagonismo *sm.* antagonism.

antagonista *s.* antagonist.

antàrtico *agg.* Antarctic.

antecedente *agg.* previous. ♦ **antecedente** *sm.* antecedent.

antecessore *sm.* predecessor.

antefatto *sm.* antecedent fact.

anteguerra *sm.* pre-war time.

antenato *sm.* ancestor.

antenna *sf.* **1.** (*zool.*) antenna (*pl.* -nae) **2.** (*radio*) aerial.

anteporre *vt.* to place before, to put (*v. irr.*) before.

anteprima *sf.* preview.

anteriore *agg.* **1.** (*nello spazio*) fore **2.** (*nel tempo*) previous, former.

antiabbaglianti *sm. pl.* anti-dazzle.

antiaèreo *agg.* anti-aircraft.

antibattèrico *agg. e sm.* antibacterial.

antibiòtico *agg. e sm.* antibiotic.

anticaglia *sf.* worthless antique.

anticamente *avv.* in ancient times.

anticàmera *sf.* ante-room ‖ *fare* —,

to be kept waiting.
anticarro agg. anti-tank.
antichità sf. 1. antiquity 2. (oggetti antichi) antiques (pl.).
anticipare vt. 1. to anticipate 2. (di danaro) to pay in advance.
anticipatamente avv. in advance.
anticipato agg. 1. advanced 2. (comm.) in advance.
anticipazione sf. anticipation.
anticipo sm. advance: essere in —, to be before time 2. (caparra) earnest money.
anticlericale agg. e s. anticlerical.
anticlericalismo sm. anticlericali-sm.
antico agg. 1. ancient 2. (all'antica) old-fashioned.
anticonformista s. nonconformist.
anticongelante sm. anti-freeze.
anticorpo sm. antibody.
anticostituzionale agg. anticonstitutional.
antidatare vt. to antedate.
antidiluviano agg. e sm. antediluvian.
antidoto sm. antidote.
antiestetico agg. antiaesthetic.
antifascismo sm. antifascism.
antifascista s. e agg. antifascist.
antifebbrile sm. febrifuge.
antifecondativo sm. anti-conceptive.
antifona sf. antiphon: capire l'— to take (v. irr.) a hint.
antifurto sm. antitheft device.
antigas agg. anti-gas: maschera —, gas-mask.
antigienico agg. unhealthy.
antilope sf. antelope.
antimilitarismo sm. antimilitarism.
antincendio agg. antifire: pompa —, fire-pump.
antinebbia agg. faro —, fog-light.
antinevralgico agg. antineuralgic.
antinomìa sf. antinomy.
antiparticella sf. antiparticle.
antipasto sm. hors-d'oeuvre.
antipatìa sf. dislike.
antipàtico agg. disagreeable.
antipodi sm. pl. antipodes.
antiquariato sm. antique-dealing.
antiquario sm. antique-dealer.
antiquato agg. old-fashioned.
antireumàtico agg. antirheumatic.
antirùggine sf. anti-rust.
antisemitismo sm. anti-Semitism.
ғ **antisèttico** agg. e sm. antisepti..
antispàstico agg. antispasmodic.

antistante agg. before, in front of.
antìtesi sf. antithesis (pl. -ses).
antitetànico agg. antitetanic.
antitètico agg. antithetic(al).
antitòssico agg. antitoxic.
antivigilia sf. the day before the eve.
antologìa sf. anthology.
antològico agg. anthological.
antonomasia sf. antonomasia || per —, antonomastically.
antracite sf. anthracite.
antro sm. 1. cave 2. (tana) den.
antropocentrismo sm. anthropocentrism.
antropofagìa sf. anthropophagy.
antropòfago agg. anthropophagous.
♦ **antropòfago** sm. cannibal.
antropologìa sf. anthropology.
antropòlogo sm. anthropologist.
antropomorfo agg. anthropomorphous.
anulare agg. annular. ♦ **anulare** sm. ring-finger.
anzi cong. 1. (al contrario) on the contrary 2. (in più) moreover || — che, rather than; — che no, rather. ♦ **anzi** avv. before: — tempo, before time.
anzianità sf. seniority.
anziano agg. 1. elderly 2. (in cariche, uffici ecc.) senior.
anziché cong. 1. rather than 2. (invece di) instead of.
anzidetto agg. above-mentioned.
anzitempo avv. before time.
aorta sf. aorta.
apartìtico agg. non-sectarian.
apatìa sf. apathy, indifference.
apàtico agg. listless.
ape sf. bee.
aperitivo sm. aperitif.
apertamente avv. openly.
aperto agg. open.
apertura sf. 1. opening 2. (di mente) broad-mindedness 3. (ampiezza di un arco) span: — alare, wing-span.
àpice sm. apex.
apicoltura sf. bee-keeping.
apnea sf. apnoea.
apocalisse sf. apocalypse.
apocalìttico agg. apocalyptic(al).
apòcrifo agg. apocryphal || libri apocrifi, Apocrypha.
apòfisi sf. apophysis.
apogeo sm. apogee.
apòlide agg. stateless. ♦ **apòlide** sm. stateless person.

apolítico *agg.* non-political.
apologìa *sf.* apologia.
apologista *s.* apologist.
apòlogo *sm.* apologue.
apoplessìa *sf.* apoplexy.
apoplèttico *agg.* apoplectic: *colpo* —, apoplectic fit.
apostasìa *sf.* apostasy.
apòstata *sm.* apostate.
apòstolo *sm.* apostle.
apostrofare *vt.* to apostrophize.
apòstrofe *sf.* apostrophe.
apòstrofo *sm.* apostrophe.
apoteòsi *sf.* apotheosis.
appagare *vt.* 1. to satisfy, to gratify 2. (*la sete*) to quench one's thirst.
appalare *vt.* 1. to couple 2. (*armonizzare colori, vestiario ecc.*) to match.
appallottolare *vt.* to roll into a ball.
appaltare *vt.* to give (*v. irr.*) out by contract.
appaltatore *sm.* contractor.
appalto *sm.* contract, bid.
appannàggio *sm.* apanage.
appannamento *sm.* 1. (*di metalli*) tarnishing 2. (*di vetri ecc.*) clouding 3. (*di vista*) dimming.
appannare *vt.* 1. (*di metalli*) to tarnish 2. (*di vetri ecc.*) to cloud 3. (*di vista*) to dim.
apparato *sm.* 1. apparatus 2. (*mostra*) display.
apparecchiare *vt.* to prepare: — *la tavola*, to lay (*v. irr.*) the table.
apparecchio *sm.* 1. set 2. (*aereoplano*) aeroplane || — *fotografico*, camera; — *telefonico*, telephone; — *radio*, radio set.
apparentare *vt.* to relate.
apparente *agg.* 1. (*illusorio*) seeming 2. (*chiaro*) apparent, obvious.
apparentemente *avv.* seemingly.
apparenza *sf.* 1. appearance 2. (*aspetto*) look 3. (*pompa*) show.
apparire *vi.* 1. to appear 2. (*aver l'aspetto*) to look 3. (*risultare*) to result.
appariscente *agg.* 1. striking 2. (*vistoso*) showy.
apparizione *sf.* apparition.
appartamento *sm.* flat.
appartarsi *vr.* to retire.
appartenenza *sf.* belonging.
appartenere *vi.* 1. to belong (to) 2. (*essere membro*) to be a member (of).

appassionare *vt.* to impassion. ◆ **appassionarsi** *vr.* to become (*v. irr.*) fond of.
appassionato *agg.* 1. passionate 2. (*di musica, arte ecc.*) keen (on).
appassire *vi.* to wither.
appellare *vt.* to name, to call. ◆ **appellarsi** *vr.* to appeal.
appellativo *sm.* appellative.
appello *sm.* 1. (*giur.*) appeal 2. (*chiamata*) call 3. (*esortazione*) appeal.
appena *avv.* 1. (*a fatica*) hardly 2. (*molto poco*) very little 3. (*da poco*) just: *ero* — *arrivato*, I had just arrived || *non* —, as soon as.
appèndere *vt.* to hang (*v. irr.*).
appendice *sf.* appendix || *romanzo* d'—, serial.
appendicite *sf.* appendicitis.
appesantire *vt.* to make (*v. irr.*) heavy. ◆ **appesantirsi** *vr.* to grow (*v. irr.*) heavy.
appestare *vt.* 1. to infect 2. (*spargere odore*) to stink (*v. irr.*).
appestato *agg.* 1. plague-stricken 2. (*fig.*) tainted. ◆ **appestato** *sm.* plague-stricken person.
appetenza *sf.* 1. appetite 2. (*desiderio*) longing (for sthg.).
appetìbile *agg.* pleasing.
appetire *vt.* to desire.
appetito *sm.* appetite.
appezzamento *sm.* plot of land.
appianare *vt.* 1. to level 2. (*fig.*) to smooth.
appiattarsi *vr.* 1. to crouch 2. (*stare in agguato*) to lie (*v. irr.*) in wait 3. (*nascondersi*) to hide (*v. irr.*).
appiattire *vt.* to flatten.
appiccare *vt.* (*il fuoco*) to set (*v. irr.*) fire.
appiccicare *vt.* 1. to stick (*v. irr.*) 2. (*appioppare*) to palm off.
appiccicoso *agg.* sticky.
appiè *prep.* 1. (*al di sotto*) below 2. (*ai piedi*) at the foot: — *del letto*, at the foot of the bed.
appiedare *vt.* to dismount.
appiedato *agg.* dismounted.
appieno *avv.* fully.
appigliarsi *vr.* to get (*v. irr.*) hold of: — *ad un pretesto*, to take (*v. irr.*) a pretext.
appìglio *sm.* 1. support 2. (*fig.*) pretext.
appiombo *sm.* perpendicularity.
appioppare *vt.* 1. to give (*v. irr.*)

|| — *uno schiaffo*, to slap 2. (*af-fibbiare*) to palm off.

appisolarsi *vr.* to doze off.

applaudire *vt.* e *vi.* to applaud.

applauditore *sm.* applauder.

appláuso *sm.* 1. applause (*solo sing.*) 2. (*fig.*) praise.

applicare *vt.* 1. to apply 2. (*giur.*) to carry out 3. (*accostare*) to set (*v. irr.*). ◆ **applicarsi** *vr.* to apply oneself.

applicazione *sf.* 1. application 2. (*fig.*) care 3. (*guarnizione*) trimming.

appoggiare *vt.* 1. to lean (*v. irr.*) 2. (*posare*) to lay (*v. irr.*) 3. (*fig.*) to back. ◆ **appoggiarsi** *vr.* 1. to lean (*v. irr.*) 2. (*fig.*) to rely (on).

appoggio *sm.* 1. support 2. (*fig.*) assistance 3. (*colui che dà —*) supporter.

appollaiarsi *vr.* to perch.

apporre *vt.* to affix.

apportare *vt.* 1. to bring (*v. irr.*) 2. (*produrre*) to produce.

apporto *sm.* contribution.

appositamente *avv.* on purpose.

appósito *agg.* 1. special 2. (*adatto*) fit.

apposizione *sf.* 1. (*gramm.*) apposition 2. (*l'apporre*) affixing.

apposta *avv.* expressly.

appostare *vt.* (*mil.*) to place. ◆ **appostarsi** *vr.* to lie (*v. irr.*) in ambush.

apprèndere *vt.* to learn (*v. irr.*).

apprendista *sm.* apprentice.

apprendistato *sm.* apprenticeship.

apprensione *sf.* 1. concern 2. (*l'apprendere*) learning.

appresso *avv.* near, close by. ◆ **appresso** *prep.* near, close to.

apprestamento *sm.* preparation.

apprestare *vt.* to prepare.

apprettare *vt.* to dress.

apprezzàbile *agg.* appreciable.

apprezzamento *sm.* 1. appreciation 2. (*giudizio*) opinion.

apprezzare *vt.* 1. to appreciate 2. (*valutare*) to value.

approdare *vi.* 1. to land 2. (*fig.*) to be of use.

approfittare *vi.* to profit (by). ◆ **approfittarsi** *vr.* 1. to avail oneself 2. (*abusare*) to take (*v. irr.*) undue advantage.

approfondire *vt.* 1. to make (*v. irr.*) deeper 2. (*fig.*) to examine

closely.

approntare *vt.* to make (*v. irr.*) ready.

appropriarsi *vr.* to take (*v. irr.*) possession of.

appropriato *agg.* fit, suitable.

appropriazione *sf.* appropriation: — *indebita*, embezzlement.

approssimarsi *vr.* 1. to come (*v. irr.*) near 2. (*di tempo*) to draw (*v. irr.*) near.

approssimativamente *avv.* approximately.

approssimativo *agg.* approximative.

approssimazione *sf.* approximation.

approvare *vt.* 1. to approve (of) 2. (*promuovere*) to pass.

approvazione *sf.* approval.

approvvigionamento *sm.* 1. (*l'approvvigionare*) supplying 2. (*provviste*) supplies.

approvvigionare *vt.* to supply provisions (to).

appuntamento *sm.* appointment.

appuntare *vt.* 1. to sharpen 2. (*prender nota*) to note 3. (*biasimare*) to blame.

appuntellare *vt.* 1. to prop 2. (*fig.*) to support.

appuntino *avv.* nicely.

appuntito *agg.* pointed.

appunto[1] *sm.* 1. note 2. (*critica*) blame.

appunto[2] *avv.* exactly, just.

appurare *vt.* to verify.

apribottiglie *sm.* bottle-opener.

aprile *sm.* April: *pesce d'—*, April fool.

aprire *vt.* to open: — *le braccia a qc.*, to welcome so.

apriscàtole *sm.* tin-opener.

àquila *sf.* eagle.

aquilino *agg.* aquiline.

aquilone *sm.* 1. (*vento del nord*) north wind 2. (*giocattolo*) kite.

aquilotto *sm.* eaglet.

arabescare *vt.* to decorate with arabesques.

arabesco *sm.* arabesque.

aràbico *agg.* Arabic.

aràbile *agg.* arable.

àrabo *agg.* e *sm.* Arab.

aràchide *sf.* peanut.

aragosta *sf.* lobster.

aràldico *agg.* heraldic.

araldo *sm.* herald.

arancia *sf.* orange.

aranciata *sf.* orange squash.

aranciera *sf.* orangery.

arancio *agg.* (*colore*) orange. ♦ arancio *sm.* orange-tree.

arancione *agg.* orange-coloured.

arare *vt.* to plough.

aratore *sm.* ploughman (*pl.* -men).

aratro *sm.* plough.

aratura *sf.* ploughing.

arazzo *sm.* arras.

arbitraggio *sm.* 1. (*sport*) umpirage 2. (*comm.*) arbitrage.

arbitrare *vt.* 1. to arbitrate 2. (*calcio, boxe*) to referee.

arbitrario *agg.* arbitrary.

arbitrio *sm.* 1. will: *libero* —, free will 1. (*atto arbitrario*) arbitrary act.

àrbitro *sm.* 1. (*sport*) umpire 2. (*calcio, boxe*) referee 3. (*giur.*) arbitrator.

arboricoltore *sm.* arboriculturist.

arboricoltura *sf.* arboriculture.

arboscello *sm.* shrub.

arbusto *sm.* shrub || — *di scienza*, eminent scholar.

arca *sf.* ark.

arcàdico *agg. e sm.* Arcadian.

arcàico *agg.* 1. archaic 2. (*di parole, stile*) obsolete.

arcaismo *sm.* 1. archaism 2. (*parola arcaica*) obsolete word.

arcàngelo *sm.* archangel.

arcano *agg.* mysterious.

archeologìa *sf.* archaeology.

archeològico *agg.* archaeologic(al).

archeòlogo *sm.* archaeologist.

archètipo *sm.* archetype.

archetto *sm.* 1. small arch 2. (*mus.*) bow.

architettare *vt.* 1. to draw (*v. irr.*) the plans 2. (*fig.*) to devise.

architetto *sm.* architect.

architettònico *agg.* architectonic.

architettura *sf.* architecture.

architrave *sm.* architrave.

archiviare *vt.* 1. to place in the archives 2. (*comm.*) to file.

archivio *sm.* 1. archives (*pl.*) 2. (*comm.*) file.

archivista *sm.* archivist.

arciduca *sm.* archduke.

arciere *sm.* archer.

arcigno *agg.* gruff.

arcimiliardario *sm.* multimillionaire.

arcipèlago *sm.* archipelago (*pl.* -goes).

arcivescovado *sm.* archbishopric.

arcivéscovo *sm.* archbishop.

arco *sm.* 1. (*arma*) bow 2. (*geom.*) arc 3. (*arch*) arch 4. (*mus.*) bow.

arcobaleno *sm* rainbow.

arcolaio *sm.* wool-winder.

arcuare *vt.* 1. to arch 2. (*piegare*) to bend (*v. irr.*).

ardente *agg.* 1. burning 2. (*fig.*) passionate.

ardentemente *avv.* ardently.

àrdere *vt.* to burn (*v. irr.*).

ardesia *sf.* slate.

ardire *vi.* to dare 2. (*avere l'impudenza*) to have the impudence.

ardito *agg.* 1. bold 2. (*rischioso*) risky.

ardore *sm.* 1. fierce heat 2. (*fig.*) passion.

àrduo *agg.* 1. hard 2. (*erto*) steep.

àrea *sf.* 1. area 2. (*sfera d'azione*) sphere.

arena *sf.* 1. (*sabbia*) sand 2. (*arch*) arena.

arenarsi *vr.* to get (*v. irr.*) stranded (*anche fig.*).

arengario *sm.* tribune.

areòpago *sm.* Areopagus.

àrgano *sm.* 1. (*mar.*) capstan 2. (*mecc.*) windlass.

argentare *vt.* to silver.

argènteo *agg.* silvery.

argenterìa *sf.* silver ware.

argentino *agg.* silvery.

argento *sm.* silver.

argilla *sf.* clay.

argilloso *agg.* clayey.

arginare *vt.* 1. to dam 2. (*fig.*) to check.

àrgine *sm.* bank.

argomentare *vt.* to infer. ♦ argomentare *vi* to argue.

argomentazione *sf.* reasoning.

argomento *sm.* 1. subject 2. (*prova a sostegno*) argument.

arguire *vt.* to deduce.

argutezza *sf.* shrewdness.

arguto *agg.* 1. sharp 2. (*faceto*) witty.

arguzia *sf.* wit.

aria *sf.* 1. air: — *condizionata*, air conditioning || *corrente d'—*, draught || *camera d'—*, inner tube || *andare all'—*, to fall (*v. irr*) through 2. (*aspetto*) look 3. (*mus.*) tune.

ariano *agg. e sm* Aryan.

aridità *sf* 1. aridity 2. (*di cuore*) lack of feeling

àrido *agg.* 1. arid 2. (*di cuore*)

lacking feeling.

arieggiare vt. 1. to air 2. (rasso-migliare) to look like 3. (imitare) to imitate.

arieggiato agg. aired.

ariete sm. ram.

aringa sf. herring.

arioso agg. airy.

aristocràtico agg. aristocratic. ◆ **aristocràtico** sm. aristocrat.

aristocrazìa sf. aristocracy.

aristotèlico agg. e sm. Aristotelian.

aritmètica sf. arithmetic.

aritmètico agg. arithmetic(al).

arlecchinata sf. harlequinade.

arlecchino sm. harlequin.

arma sf. weapon, arm: armi bianche, side-arms; armi da fuoco, fire-arms || galleria d'armi, armoury.

armadietto sm. 1. (per medicinali, strumenti ecc.) cabinet 2. (per abiti) locker.

armadio sm. 1. (per stoviglie) cupboard 2. (per abiti) wardrobe.

armaiolo sm. armourer.

armamentario sm. 1. instruments (pl.) 2. (armeria) armoury.

armamento sm. arming.

armare vt. to arm.

armata sf. army.

armatore sm. 1. shipbuilder 2. (chi possiede una nave) shipowner.

armatura sf. 1. armour 2. (impalcatura) scaffolding.

armeggiare vi. 1. to handle arms 2. (darsi da fare) to busy oneself 3. (tramare) to manoeuvre.

armeggio sm. 1. handling of arms 2. (l'affaccendarsi) bustling 3. (intrigo) manoeuvre.

armento sm. herd.

armerìa sf. armoury.

armiere sm. gunsmith.

armistizio sm. armistice.

armonìa sf. harmony.

armònica sf. (a bocca) mouth-organ.

armònico agg. harmonic.

armonio sm. harmonium.

armonioso agg. harmonious.

armonista s. harmonist.

armonizzare vt. to harmonize. ◆ **armonizzare** vi. 1. to harmonize 2. (di colori) to match.

arnese sm. 1. (strumento) tool 2. (aggeggio) gadget.

arnia sf. beehive.

aroma sm. flavour.

aromàtico agg. aromatic.

aromatizzare vt. to flavour.

arpa sf. harp.

arpeggiare vi. to play the harp.

arpeggio sm. arpeggio.

arpista s. harpist.

arra sf. earnest.

arrabattarsi vr. to bestir oneself.

arrabbiare vi. 1. to become (v. irr.) angry 2. (di cane) to be affected with rabies. ◆ **arrabbiarsi** vr. to get (v. irr.) angry.

arrabbiato agg. 1. angry 2. (di cane) rabid.

arrabbiatura sf. rage.

arraffare vt. to grasp.

arrampicarsi vr. to climb.

arrampicata sf. climb.

arrampicatore sm. 1. mountain climber 2. (fig.) social climber.

arrancare vi. 1. to plod along 2. (zoppicare) to limp 3. (affaticarsi) to get (v. irr.) tired.

arrangiamento sm. arrangement.

arrangiare vt. to arrange. ◆ **arrangiarsi** vr. to manage.

arrecare vt. 1. to bring (v. irr.) 2. (causare) to cause.

arredamento sm. furnishing.

arredare vt. to furnish.

arredatore sm. internal decorator.

arredo sm. piece of furniture.

arrèndersi vr. 1. to surrender 2. (fig.) to give (v. irr.) it up.

arrendévole agg. 1. pliant 2. (fig.) docile.

arrestare vt. 1. to stop 2. (trarre in arresto) to arrest. ◆ **arrestarsi** vr. to stop.

arresto sm. arrest.

arretrare vt. 1. to pull back 2. (ritirare) to withdraw (v. irr.).

arretrato agg. backward.

arricchimento sm. enrichment.

arricchire vt. to enrich. ◆ **arricchirsi** vr. to grow (v. irr.) rich.

arricciare vt. to curl: — il naso, to turn up one's nose.

arridere vi. to be favourable.

arringare vt. to harangue.

arringatore sm. haranguer.

arrischiare vt. to risk. ◆ **arrischiarsi** vr. to venture.

arrivare vi. 1. to arrive (at), (in) 2. (fig.) to attain.

arrivato agg. (fig.) successful.

arrivederci inter. goodbye.

arrivismo sm. social climbing.

arrivista sm. social climber.

arrivo sm. arrival.

arrogante agg. arrogant.

arroganza sf. arrogance.

arrogarsi vr. to arrogate to oneself.

arrossire vi. to blush.

arrostire vt. 1. to roast 2. (di pane) to toast.

arrosto sm. roast.

arrotare vt. to grind (v. irr.): — i denti, to grind one's teeth.

arrotino sm. knife-grinder.

arrotolare vt. to roll up.

arrotondare vt. 1. to round 2. (di cifre) to make (v. irr.) a round figure.

arrovellarsi vr. to worry.

arroventare vt. to make (v. irr.) red-hot.

arruffare vt. to ruffle.

arruffone sm. muddler

arrugginire vi. to rust.

arruolare vt. to enrol.

arsenale sm. 1. (cantiere) ship-yard 2. (deposito di armi) arsenal.

arsènico sm. arsenic.

arsura sf. 1. (siccità) drought 2. (sete) parching thirst.

arte sf. art || belle arti, fine arts.

artefatto agg. adulterated.

artéfice sm. maker.

arteria sf. 1. artery 2. (di traffico) thoroughfare.

arteriosclerosi sf. arteriosclerosis.

artesiano agg. artesian.

àrtico agg. arctic.

articolare vt. to articulate.

articolazione sf. articulation.

articolo sm. 1. (gramm.; di giornale) article || — di fondo, editorial 2. (comm.) item.

artificiale agg. artificial.

artificio sm. 1. device 2. (astuzia) cunning.

artigianato sm. handicraft.

artigiano sm. craftsman (pl. -men).

artigliere sm. gunner.

artiglieria sf. artillery.

artiglio sm. claw.

artista sm. artist.

artistico agg. artistic(al).

arto sm. limb: — artificiale, artificial limb.

artrite sf. arthritis (pl. -ides).

artrosi sf. arthrosis.

arzigògolo sm. subtlety.

arzillo agg. lively, brisk.

ascella sf. armpit.

ascendente sm. 1. ascendancy 2. (antenato) ancestor.

ascendenza sf. ancestry.

ascéndere vi. (anche fig.) to rise (v. irr.).

ascensione sf. 1. ascension 2. (scalata) climb.

ascensore sm. lift.

ascesa sf. ascent.

ascesi sf. mystical practice.

ascesso sm. abscess.

asceta sm. ascetic.

ascètico agg. ascetical.

ascetismo sm. asceticism.

ascia sf. axe.

ascissa sf. abscissa (pl. -sae).

asciugacapelli sm. hair-drier.

asciugamano sm. towel.

asciugare vt. 1. to dry 2. (con un panno) to wipe. ♦ **asciugarsi** vr. to dry up.

asciugatoio sm. towel.

asciutto agg. 1. (anche fig.) dry 2. (magro) thin.

ascoltare vt. 1. to listen (to) 2. (assistere) to attend: — le lezioni, to attend classes.

ascolto sm. listening.

ascrìvere vt. 1. to count 2. (attribuire) to ascribe. ♦ **ascrìversi** vr. to claim.

asepsi sf. asepsis.

asessuale agg. asexual.

asèttico agg. aseptic.

asfaltare vt. to asphalt.

asfalto sm. asphalt.

asfissìa sf. 1. asphyxia 2. (da gas) gassing.

asfissiare vt. 1. to asphyxiate 2. (con gas) to gas.

asiàtico agg. e sm. Asiatic.

asilo sm. 1. shelter 2. (scuola materna) infant-school.

asimmetrìa sf. asymmetry.

asimmètrico agg. asymmetrical.

asinerìa sf. stupidity.

asinità sf. asininity.

àsino sm. 1. ass 2. (fig.) jackass.

asma sf. asthma.

asmàtico agg. asthmatical.

asociale agg. asocial.

àsola sf. buttonhole.

aspàrago sm. asparagus.

aspèrgere vt. to sprinkle.

asperità sf. 1. asperity 2. (di superfici) unevenness 3. (di carattere) harshness.

aspersorio sm. aspergillum.

aspettare vt. to wait (for). ♦ **aspettarsi** vr. to expect.

aspettativa sf. 1. expectation 2.

(esonero temporaneo) temporary retirement.

aspetto *sm.* look || *di bell'aspetto*, good-looking || *sala d'—*, waiting--room.

àspide *sm.* asp.

aspirante *agg.* aspirant. ♦ **aspirante** *sm.* candidate, applicant.

aspirapòlvere *sm.* vacuum cleaner, hoover.

aspirare *vt.* to inspire. ♦ **aspirare** *vi.* to aspire (to).

aspiratore *sm.* aspirator.

aspirazione *sf.* **1.** aspiration **2.** *(mecc.)* suction.

aspirina *sf.* aspirin.

asportare *vt.* **1.** to remove **2.** *(med.)* to extirpate.

asportazione *sf.* **1.** removal **2.** *(med.)* extirpation.

asprezza *sf.* **1.** sourness **2.** *(fig.)* harshness.

asprigno *agg.* sourish.

aspro *agg.* **1.** sour **2.** *(fig.)* harsh.

assaggiare *vt.* to taste.

assaggio *sm.* **1.** tasting **2.** *(campione)* sample.

assai *avv.* **1.** *(con agg. e avv.)* very **2.** *(con comp.)* much: *— meglio*, much better.

assalire *vt.* **1.** to assail **2.** *(di malattia)* to attack.

assalitore *sm.* assailer.

assaltare *vt.* to assault.

assalto *sm.* assault, attack.

assaporare *vt.* **1.** to savour **2.** *(fig.)* to enjoy.

assassinare *vt.* to murder.

assassìnio *sm.* murder.

assassino *sm.* murderer.

asse *sf.* **1.** *(tavola di legno)* board **2.** *(geom.)* axis *(pl.* axes) **3.** *(stor.)* Axis.

assecondare *vt.* to favour.

assediare *vt.* to besiege.

assèdio *sm.* siege.

assegnamento *sm.* assignment || *fare — su qualcuno*, to rely on so.

assegnare *vt.* **1.** to assign **2.** *(un premio)* to award.

assegno *sm.* cheque: *— al portatore*, cheque to bearer; *— circolare*, banker's draft; *— sbarrato*, crossed cheque.

assemblea *sf.* **1.** meeting **2.** *(corpo deliberante)* assembly.

assembramento *sm.* concourse of people.

assembrarsi *vr* to assemble.

assennatezza *sf.* common sense.

assennato *agg.* sensible.

assenso *sm.* assent.

assentarsi *vr.* to go *(v. irr.)* away.

assente *agg.* absent.

assenteismo *sm.* absenteeism.

assentire *vi.* **1.** to assent (to) **2.** *(col capo)* to nod (in assent).

assenza *sf.* absence.

assènzio *sm.* absinth.

asserire *vt.* to affirm.

asserragliarsi *vr.* to barricade oneself.

asserto *sm.* assertion.

assertore *sm.* **1.** assertor **2.** *(difensore)* defender, champion.

asservimento *sm.* enslavement.

asservire *vt.* to enslave, to subdue.

asserzione *sf.* statement.

assessorato *sm.* assessorship.

assessore *sm.* **1.** *(alle imposte)* assessor **2.** *(comunale)* councillor responsible for a municipal region.

assestamento *sm.* **1.** adjustment **2.** *(definitivo)* settlement **3.** *(del terreno)* settling.

assestare *vt.* to arrange: *— un colpo*, to deal *(v. irr.)* a blow. ♦ **assestarsi** *vr.* to settle (down).

assetato *agg.* **1.** thirsty **2.** *(fig.)* eager (for).

assetto *sm.* order.

assicurare *vt.* **1.** *(legare)* to fasten **2.** *(promettere)* to assure **3.** *(affermare)* to affirm **4.** *(comm.)* to insure.

assicurata *sf.* registered letter.

assicurato *agg.* insured, assured. ♦ **assicurato** *sm.* insurant.

assicuratore *sm.* insurer.

assicurazione *sf.* **1.** assurance **2.** *(comm.)* insurance.

assideramento *sm.* frost-bite.

assiduità *sf.* assiduity.

assìduo *agg.* assiduous.

assieme *avv.* V. *insieme.*

assieparsi *vr.* to crowd (round).

assillante *agg.* urging.

assillare *vt.* to urge.

assillo *sm.* **1.** urge **2.** *(fig.)* worry.

assimilàbile *agg.* assimilable.

assimilare *vt.* to assimilate, to absorb.

assimilazione *sf.* assimilation.

assioma *sm.* axiom.

assiomàtico *agg.* axiomatic.

assise *sf. pl.* assizes.

assistente *sm.* assistant.

assistenza *sf.* assistance.

assistenziale *agg.* charitable.

assistere *vt.* 1. to assist 2. (*curare*) to nurse. ♦ **assistere** *vi.* to attend (sthg.).

assito *sm.* 1. wooden partition 2. (*pavimento*) plank floor.

asso *sm.* 1. (*carte*) ace 2. (*sport*) champion || *piantare in* —, to leave (*v. irr.*) in the lurch.

associare *vt.* to join. ♦ **associarsi** *vr.* to associate.

associato *sm.* member.

associazione *sf.* association.

assodare *vt.* 1. to consolidate 2. (*accertare*) to ascertain.

assoggettare *vt.* to subject. ♦ **assoggettarsi** *vr.* to submit oneself.

assolato *agg.* sunny.

assoldare *vt.* to recruit.

assolo *sm.* (*mus.*) solo.

assolutamente *avv.* absolutely.

assolutismo *sm.* absolutism.

assolutista *agg.* e *sm.* absolutist.

assoluto *agg.* e *sm.* absolute.

assoluzione *sf.* 1. (*eccl.*) absolution 2. (*giur.*) discharge.

assòlvere *vt.* 1. (*teol.*) to absolve 2. (*giur.*) to discharge 3. (*eseguire*) to accomplish.

assomigliante *agg.* like.

assomigliare *vi.* to look like.

assommare *vt.* e *vi.* to add, to amount (to).

assonanza *sf.* assonance.

assonnarsi *vr.* to fall (*v. irr.*) asleep.

assonnato *agg.* sleepy.

assopimento *sm.* dozing.

assopire *vt.* to make (*v. irr.*) dozy. ♦ **assopirsi** *vr.* to doze off.

assorbente *agg.* absorbing || *carta* —, blotting-paper.

assorbimento *sm.* absorption.

assorbire *vt.* to absorb.

assordante *agg.* deafening.

assordare *vt.* to deafen.

assortimento *sm.* assortment.

assortire *vt.* 1. to stock 2. (*fig.*) to match.

assorto *agg.* absorbed.

assottigliamento *sm.* 1. thinning 2. (*riduzione*) reduction.

assottigliare *vt.* 1. to thin 2. (*diminuire*) to reduce. ♦ **assottigliarsi** *vr.* to grow (*v. irr.*) thin.

assuefare *vt.* to accustom. ♦ **assuefarsi** *vr.* to accustom oneself.

assuefazione *sf.* custom.

assùmere *vt.* 1. to assume 2. (*in*

servizio) to employ 3. (*informazioni*) to make (*v. irr.*) inquiries.

assunzione *sf.* 1. (*ascesa*) accession 2. (*impiego*) engagement 3. (*teol.*) Assumption.

assurdamente *avv.* absurdly.

assurdità *sf.* absurdity.

assurdo *agg.* absurd. ♦ **assurdo** *sm.* absurdity.

assùrgere *vi.* to rise (*v. irr.*).

asta *sf.* 1. pole 2. (*di bandiera*) flagstaff 3. (*di occhiali*) bar 4. (*di bilancia*) arm (of balance) 5. (*vendita all'asta*) auction(-sale).

astante *agg.* present. ♦ **astante** *sm.* on-looker.

astemio *agg.* abstemious. ♦ **astemio** *sm.* teetotaller.

astenersi *vr.* to abstain.

astenìa *sf.* asthenia.

astensione *sf.* abstention.

astensionista *sm.* abstentionist.

asterisco *sm.* asterisk.

asteròide *sm.* asteroid.

asticciola *sf.* pothook.

astigmàtico *agg.* astigmatic.

astigmatismo *sm.* astigmatism.

astinenza *sf.* abstinence.

astio *sm.* resentment.

astiosamente *avv.* resentfully.

astioso *agg.* resentful.

astracàn *sm.* astrakhan.

astràgalo *sm.* 1. (*bot.*) astragalus (*pl.* -li) 2. (*arch.*) astragal.

astrale *agg.* astral.

astrarre *vt.* to abstract. ♦ **astrarsi** *vr.* to think (*v. irr.*) about sthg. else.

astrattismo *sm.* (*arte*) abstractionism.

astratto *agg.* abstract.

astrazione *sf.* abstraction.

astringente *agg.* e *sm.* astringent.

astro *sm.* star.

astrolabio *sm.* astrolabe.

astrologìa *sf.* astrology.

astròlogo *sm.* astrologer.

astronàuta *sm.* astronaut.

astronave *sf.* space-ship.

astronomìa *sf.* astronomy.

astronòmico *agg.* astronomic(al).

astrònomo *sm.* astronomer.

astrusità *sf.* abstruseness.

astruso *agg.* abstruse.

astuccio *sm.* case, box: — *per occhiali*, spectacle-case.

astuto *agg.* cunning.

astuzia *sf.* 1. (*qualità*) cunning 2. (*atto*) trick.

ATASSIA 361 **ATTO**

atassìa sf. ataxy.

atàvico agg. atavic.

atavismo sm. atavism.

ateismo sm. atheism.

àteo agg. atheistic. ♦ **àteo** sm. atheist.

atleta sm. athlete.

atlètica sf. athletics.

atlètico agg. athletic.

atmosfera sf. atmosphere.

atollo sm. atoll.

atòmico agg. atomic.

atomismo sm. atomism.

atomìstica sf. atomic theory.

atomizzatore sm. atomizer.

àtomo sm. (anche fig.) atom.

atonìa sf. atony.

àtono agg. atonic.

atrio sm. (entrance-)hall.

atroce agg. dreadful.

atrocità sf. atrocity.

atrofìa sf. atrophy.

atrofizzare vt. to atrophy.

atrofizzato agg. atrophic.

atropìna sf. atropine.

attaccabottoni sm. buttonholer.

attaccabrighe sm. quarrelsome fellow.

attaccamento sm. attachment: avere dell'—, to entertain an attachment (for).

attaccante sm. attacker.

attaccapanni sm. cloak-stand.

attaccare vt. 1. (unire) to attack 2. (appiccicare) to stick (v. irr.) 3. (cucire) to sew (v. irr.) 4. (assalire) to attack 5. (mus.) to open. ♦ **attaccarsi** vr. 1. (appigliarsi) to cling (v. irr.) 2. (affezionarsi) to become (v. irr.) fond of.

attaccatura sf. junction: — della manica, arm-hole.

attacchino sm. bill-poster.

attacco sm. 1. (mil.) attack 2. (med.) fit 3. (mecc.) connection ∥ — elettrico, connecting plug.

attagliarsi vr. to suit.

attanagliare vt. to pinch.

attardarsi vr. to delay.

attecchire vi. 1. to take (v. irr.) root 2. (aver fortuna) to find (v. irr.) favour.

atteggiamento sm. attitude.

atteggiarsi vr. to assume an attitude: — a vittima, to pose as a victim.

attempato agg. elderly.

attendente sm. orderly.

attèndere vt. 1. (aspettare) to wait for 2. (aspettarsi) to expect 3. (accudire, frequentare) to attend.

attendìbile agg. reliable.

attenere vi. to concern. ♦ **attenersi** vr. 1. to cling (v. irr.) (on), (to) 2. (seguire) to conform.

attentamente avv. 1. attentively 2. (con cura) carefully.

attentare vi. to attempt. ♦ **attentarsi** vr. to dare.

attentato sm. attempt (upon).

attenti sm. attention: stare sull'—, to stand (v. irr.) at attention.

attento agg. attentive, careful.

attenuante agg. extenuating.

attenuare vt. 1. to attenuate 2. (giur.) to extenuate.

attenuazione sf. 1. attenuation 2. (di colpa) extenuation.

attenzione sf. 1. attention 2. care: fate —, take care 3. (riguardo) regard.

atterraggio sm. landing.

atterrare vt. to knock down. ♦ **atterrare** vi. (aer.) to land.

atterrire vt. to terrify. ♦ **atterrirsi** vr. to take (v. irr.) fright.

attesa sf. wait.

attestare vt. to attest.

attestato sm. 1. certificate 2. (prova) proof.

atticciato agg. sturdy.

àttico sm. attic.

attiguo agg. adjoining.

attillarsi vr. to spruce oneself up.

attillato agg. close-fitting.

àttimo sm. moment.

attinente agg. pertaining.

attinenza sf. relationship.

attingere vt. to draw (v. irr.): — acqua da un pozzo, to draw water from a well; — denaro da qu., to draw on so. for money.

attirare vt. to attract, to draw (v. irr.) (anche fig.).

attitùdine sf. turn, disposition.

attivare vt. to make (v. irr.) active.

attivista s. activist.

attività sf. 1. activity 2. (comm.) profit: — e passività, assets and liabilities.

attivizzare vt. to make (v. irr.) active.

attivo agg. active.

attizzare vt. to stir up.

attizzatoio sm. poker.

atto[1] sm. 1. act 2. (azione) action 3. (fatto) deed: un — buono, a good deed.

atto² *agg.* fit.

attònito *agg.* astonished.

attore *sm.* actor: — *cinematografico*, screen actor.

attorniare *vt.* to surround.

attorno *avv.* e *prep.* about, round, around: *non c'è nessuno* —, there is nobody about; — *alla tavola*, round the table; *le colline* — *al villaggio*, the hills around the village || *darsi d'* —, to busy oneself.

attraccaggio *sm.* mooring.

attraccare *vi.* to moor.

attraente *agg.* charming, attractive.

attrarre *vt.* to attract, to draw (*v. irr.*) (*anche fig.*).

attrattiva *sf.* attraction, appeal.

attraversamento *sm.* crossing.

attraversare *vt.* 1. to cross 2. (*ostacolare*) to thwart.

attraverso *avv.* 1. (*di luogo*) across, through: — *il fiume*, across the river 2. (*di tempo*) through.

attrazione *sf.* attraction, appeal.

attrezzare *vt.* to equip.

attrezzatura *sf.* equipment.

attrezzista *sm.* (*teat.*) property-man.

attrezzo *sm.* tool.

attribuire *vt.* 1. to attribute 2. (*assegnare*) to assign 3. (*addossare*) to put (on).

attributo *sm.* attribute.

attribuzione *sf.* attribution.

attrice *sf.* actress: — *cinematografica*, screen actress.

attrito *sm.* 1. friction 2. (*fig.*) dissension.

attruppamento *sm.* trooping.

attrupparsi *vr.* to troop.

attuàbile *agg.* feasible.

attuale *agg.* present.

attualità *sf.* the moment: *cosa d'*—, topical question.

attualmente *avv.* at present.

attuare *vt.* to carry out.

attutire *vt.* to mitigate: — *un rumore*, to deaden a noise.

audace *agg.* bold.

audacia *sf.* boldness.

audiovisivo *agg.* audiovisual.

auditore *sm.* listener.

auditorio *sm.* 1. auditorium 2. (*pubblico*) audience.

audizione *sf.* 1. (*fisiol.*) hearing 2. (*teat.*) performance.

àuge *sm.* summit: *essere in* —, to enjoy great favour.

augurale *agg.* augural.

augurare *vt.* to wish.

augurio *sm.* wish || *auguri di Natale e Capodanno*, season's greetings.

augusto *agg.* august.

àula *sf.* hall, room: — *di scuola*, school-room.

aumentare *vt.* to increase.

aumento *sm.* increase.

àureo *agg.* 1. gold 2. (*dorato*) golden.

aurèola *sf.* halo.

aurìcola *sf.* auricle.

auricolare *agg.* auricular.

aurìfero *agg.* auriferous.

aurora *sf.* dawn (*anche fig.*).

auscultare *vt.* to auscultate.

auscultazione *sf.* auscultation.

ausiliare *agg.* auxiliary.

ausilio *sm.* 1. help 2. (*difesa*) defence.

auspicare *vt.* to augur.

auspicio *sm.* 1. (*stor.*) auspice, omen: *di buon, cattivo* —, of good, ill omen 2. (*augurio*) wish.

austerità *sf.* austerity.

austero *agg.* austere.

australe *agg.* austral.

australiano *agg.* e *sm.* Australian.

austriaco *agg.* e *sm.* Austrian.

autarchìa *sf.* autarky.

autenticare *vt.* to certify.

autenticazione *sf.* authentication.

autenticità *sf.* authenticity.

autèntico *agg.* 1. authentic 2. (*genuino*) genuine.

autista *sm.* driver: — *di piazza*, taxi-driver.

àuto *sf.* car: — *da corsa*, racing car; — *aperta*, open car; — *di serie*, production-model car; — *fuori serie*, special-body car. -

autoambulanza *sf.* ambulance.

auto-attrezzi *sf.* breakdown-lorry.

autobiografìa *sf.* autobiography.

autobiògrafo *sm.* autobiographer.

autoblinda *sf.* armoured car.

autobotte *sf.* tank truck.

àutobus *sm.* (motor-) bus.

autoclave *sf.* autoclave.

autocontrollo *sm.* self-control.

autòcrate *sm.* autocrat.

autocrazìa *sf.* autocracy.

autocrìtica *sf.* self-criticism.

autòctono *agg.* autochthonous. ♦ autòctono *sm.* native.

autodafé *sm.* auto-da-fé (*pl.* autos--da-fé).

autodeterminazione sf. self-deter-mination.

autodidatta s. self-taught person.

autòdromo sm. motor-racing track.

autoeducazione sf. self-education.

autofinanziamento sm. self-financing.

autògeno agg. autogenous.

autogoverno sm. self-government.

autografare vt. to autograph.

autògrafo agg. autographic(al). ♦ **autògrafo** sm. autograph.

autolesione sf. self-injury.

autolesionismo sm. self-injuring.

autolettiga sf. ambulance.

autolinea sf. bus line.

automa sm. automaton, robot.

automàtico agg. automatic: pistola, fucile —, automatic pistol, gun || distributore —, slot machine.

automatismo sm. automatism.

automazione sf. automation.

automòbile sf. V. auto.

automobilismo sm. motoring.

automobilista sm. motorist.

automotrice sf. rail-car.

autonoleggio sm. car rental.

autonomia sf. autonomy: — di volo, flight range.

autonomismo sm. self-government.

autònomo agg. self-governing.

autoparco sm. car-park.

autopilota sm. automatic pilot.

autopompa sf. fire-engine.

autoposteggio sm. parking.

autopsìa sf. autopsy.

autoradio sf. car radio-set.

autore sm. author.

autorespiratore sm. aqualung.

autorévole agg. authoritative.

autorevolezza sf. authoritativeness.

autorimessa sf. garage.

autorità sf. authority.

autoritario agg. authoritative.

autoritratto sm. self-portrait.

autorizzare vt. 1. (dare autorità) to empower 2. (permettere) to permit.

autorizzazione sf. permission, consent.

autoscuola sf. driving school.

autostazione sf. filling station.

autostòp sm. hitch-hiking.

autostoppista sm. hitch-hiker.

autostrada sf. motor-way.

autosuggestione sf. auto-suggestion.

autotreno sm. motor-lorry.

autrice sf. authoress.

autunnale agg. autumnal.

autunno sm. autumn.

ava sf. 1. grandmother 2. (antenata) ancestress.

avallare vt. to guarantee.

avallo sm. guarantee.

avambraccio sm. forearm.

avamposto sm. outpost.

avanguardia sf. vanguard: essere all'—, to be in the van.

avannotto sm. fry.

avanscoperta sf. scouting party: andare all'—, to scout.

avanspettàcolo sm. introductory variety turn.

avanti avv. 1. (di luogo) forward: andare —, to move forward 2. (a chi bussa) « come in » 3. (di tempo) before || (di orologio) fast: il mio orologio è avanti di 20 minuti, my watch is twenty minutes fast: ♦ **avanti** prep. before. ♦ **avanti che** cong. before (con ger.).

avantieri avv. the day before yesterday.

avanzamento sm. 1. advancing 2. (progresso) advancement 3. (promozione) promotion.

avanzare vt. 1. to advance 2. (fig.) to put (v. irr.) forward 3. (promuovere) to promote. ♦ **avanzare** vi. to advance. ♦ **avanzarsi** vr. to advance.

avanzata sf. advance.

avanzato agg. 1. advanced 2. (promosso) promoted.

avanzo sm. remnant || — di galera, jail-bird || — di stoffa, scrap of cloth.

avarìa sf. damage.

avariato agg. damaged.

avarizia sf. avarice.

avaro agg. avaricious.

avena sf. oats (p).

avere vt. 1. (general. e come v. ausiliare) to have: ho molti libri, I have many books; ho letto questo giornae, I have read this newspaper 2. (possedere) to own, to have got: ha una grande casa, he owns, has got a big house 3. (ottenere) to get (v. irr.): ebbi quell'impiego, I got that job 4. (indossare) to wear (v. irr.): aveva (indosso) un abito rosso, she was wearing a red dress 5. (dovere) to have to: ho molte cose da fare,

I have many things to do **6.** (*di anni*) to be ... years old: *ho 10 anni*, I am ten years old.

aviatore *sm.* airman (*pl.* -men), pilot.

aviazione *sf.* **1.** aviation **2.** (*arma*) Air Force.

avicoltura *sf.* bird-rearing.

avidità *sf.* **1.** avidity **2.** (*ingordigia*) greed **3.** (*brama*) eagerness.

àvido *agg.* **1.** avid **2.** (*ingordo*) greedy **3.** (*desideroso*) eager.

aviere *sm.* airman (*pl.* -men).

aviogetto *sm.* jet(-plane).

aviolinea *sf.* airline.

aviotrasportare *vt.* to air-bear (*v. irr.*).

aviotrasporto *sm.* air-transport.

avitaminosi *sf.* avitaminosis.

avito *agg.* ancestral.

avo *sm.* **1.** grandfather **2.** (*antenato*) ancestor **3.** (*pl.*) forefathers.

avorio *sm.* ivory.

avulso *agg.* uprooted.

avvalersi *vr.* to avail oneself.

avvaloramento *sm.* strengthening.

avvalorare *vt.* **1.** to give (*v. irr.*) value to **2.** (*rafforzare*) to strengthen.

avvampare *vi.* to flare up (*anche fig.*).

avvantaggiare *vt.* to advantage, to better. ♦ **avvantaggiarsi** *vr.* to profit (by).

avvedersi *vr.* to perceive.

avvedutamente *avv.* shrewdly.

avvedutezza *sf.* shrewdness.

avveduto *agg.* shrewd.

avvelenamento *sm.* poisoning.

avvelenare *vt.* to poison.

avvelenatore *sm.* poisoner.

avvenente *agg.* charming, pretty.

avvenenza *sf.* charm, loveliness.

avvenimento *sm.* event.

avvenire¹ *vi. imp.* to happen.

avvenire² *sm.* future.

avventarsi *vr.* to throw (*v. irr.*) oneself.

avventatamente *avv.* rashly.

avventatezza *sf.* rashness.

avventato *agg.* rash.

avventizio *agg.* **1.** temporary **2.** (*giur.*) adventitious.

avvento *sm.* **1.** (*eccl.*) Advent **2.** arrival **3.** (*assunzione al trono*) accession.

avventore *sm.* customer.

avventura *sf.* adventure.

avventurarsi *vr.* to venture.

avventuriero *sm.* adventurer.

avventuroso *agg.* adventurous.

avverarsi *vr.* to come (*v. irr.*) true.

avverbiale *agg.* adverbial.

avverbio *sm.* adverb.

avversare *vt.* to oppose.

avversario *agg.* contrary. ♦ **avversario** *sm.* opponent.

avversione *sf.* aversion, dislike.

avversità *sf.* adversity, misfortune.

avverso *agg.* unfavourable.

avvertenza *sf.* **1.** (*avviso*) warning **2.** (*attenzione, cura*) attention, care.

avvertibile *agg.* perceptible.

avvertimento *sm.* warning.

avvertire *vt.* **1.** (*avvisare*) to inform **2.** (*mettere in guardia*) to warn **3.** (*osservare*) to notice.

avvezzare *vt.* to accustom.

avvezzo *agg.* accustomed, used.

avviamento *sm.* starting.

avviare *vt.* to start.

avvicinamento *sm.* approach.

avvicinare *vt.* to approach. ♦ **avvicinarsi** *vr.* **1.** to approach **2.** (*essere simile*) to be similar.

avvicendare *vt.* to alternate. ♦ **avvicendarsi** *vr.* to alternate.

avvicendamento *sm.* alternation.

avvilente *agg.* **1.** discouraging **2.** (*umiliante*) humiliating.

avvilimento *sm.* **1.** dejection **2.** (*umiliazione*) humiliation.

avvilire *vt.* **1.** (*scoraggiare*) to dishearten **2.** (*umiliare*) to humiliate. ♦ **avvilirsi** *vr.* **1.** to lose heart **2.** (*umiliarsi*) to abase oneself.

avvilito *agg.* **1.** downcast **2.** (*umiliato*) humbled.

avviluppare *vt.* **1.** to wrap up **2.** (*aggrovigliare*) to entangle. ♦ **avvilupparsi** *vr.* **1.** to wrap oneself up **2.** (*aggrovigliarsi*) to get (*v. irr.*) entangled.

avvinazzarsi *vr.* to get (*v. irr.*) drunk.

avvinazzato *agg.* tipsy.

avvincente *agg.* engaging.

avvincere *vt.* to enthral.

avvinghiarsi *vr.* to cling (*v. irr.*).

avvio *sm.* start: *prendere l'—*, to start off.

avvisaglia *sf.* (*primo segno*) foreshadowing.

avvisare *vt.* **1.** to inform, to let (*v. irr.*) know **2.** (*mettere in guardia*) to warn.

avviso *sm.* **1.** notice **2.** (*consiglio*) warning **3.** (*manifesto*) poster **4.**

(*opinione*) opinion.
avvistare *vt.* to sight.
avvitamento *sm.* spin.
avvitare *vt.* **1.** (*mecc.*) to screw **2.** (*aer.*) to spin.
avviticchiarsi *vr.* to twist round.
avvocato *sm.* **1.** lawyer **2.** (*civilista*) solicitor.
avvocatura *sf.* legal profession.
avvòlgere *vt.* **1.** to wrap (*anche fig.*) **2.** (*arrotolare*) to roll up.
avvolgimento *sm.* **1.** winding **2.** (*di pacchi*) wrapping up **3.** (*elettr.*) winding.
avvoltoio *sm.* vulture (*anche fig.*).
azalea *sf.* azalea.
azienda *sf.* firm, concern: — *industriale*, manufacturing concern; — *agricola*, farm.
aziendale *agg.* firm, concern.
àzimut *sm.* azimuth.
azimutale *agg.* azimuthal.
azionamento *sm.* working.
azionare *vt.* to set (*v. irr.*) in action, to work.
azionario *agg.* share: *capitale* —, share capital.
azione *sf.* **1.** action **2.** (*comm.*) share.
azionista *s.* shareholder.
azotare *vt.* to azotize.
azoto *sm.* azote.
aztecq *agg. e sm.* Aztec.
azzannare *vt.* to seize in the jaws.
azzardare *vt.* to risk, to venture.
azzardo *sm.* hazard || *gioco d'*—, game of chance.
azzeccare *vt.* to guess, to hit (*v. irr.*) the mark.
àzzimo *agg.* unleavened: *pane* —, unleavened bread.
azzoppare *vt.* to lame. ♦ **azzopparsi** *vr.* to become (*v. irr.*) lame.
azzuffarsi *vr.* to come (*v. irr.*) to blows.
azzurro *agg.* blue.
azzurrògnolo *agg.* bluish.

B

babbeo *sm.* blockhead.
babbo *sm.* father, daddy.
babbuccia *sf.* slipper.
babbuino *sm.* baboon.
babele *sf.* babel.
bacare *vi.* **bacarsi** *vr.* to rot.

bacato *agg.* rotten.
bacca *sf.* berry.
baccalà *sm.* stockfish.
baccanale *sm.* bacchanal.
baccano *sm.* uproar.
baccante *sf.* Bacchante.
baccarà *sm.* baccarat.
baccellierato *sm.* bachelorship.
baccelliere *sm.* bachelor.
baccello *sm.* pod.
bacchetta *sf.* **1.** rod **2.** (*di direttore d'orchestra*) baton **3.** (*di tamburo*) drumstick.
bacchettata *sf.* rod stroke.
bacchettone *sm.* bigot.
bacchiare *vt.* to beat (*v. irr.*) down.
bàcchico *agg.* Bacchic.
bacheca *sf.* show-case.
bachelite *sf.* bakelite.
bacherozzo *sm.* **1.** (*scarafaggio*) cockroach **2.** (*bruco*) maggot.
bachicoltura *sf.* silkworm breeding.
baciamano *sm.* hand-kissing.
baciapile *sm.* bigot.
baciare *vt.* to kiss. ♦ **baciarsi** *rec.* to kiss each other.
bacile *sm.* basin.
bacillo *sm.* bacillus (*pl.* -li).
bacinella *sf.* basin.
bacino *sm.* **1.** basin **2.** (*anat.*) pelvis **3.** (*mar.*) dock: — *di carenaggio*, dry dock.
bacio *sm.* kiss.
baciucchiare *vt.* to kiss repeatedly.
baco *sm.* worm: — *da seta*, silkworm.
bada *sf.* (*nella loc.*) *tenere a* — *qu.*, to hold (*v. irr.*) so. at bay.
badare *vi.* to mind (so., sthg.): *senza* — *a spese*, regardless of expense.
badessa *sf.* abbess.
badìa *sf.* abbey.
badilante *sm.* navvy.
badile *sm.* shovel.
baffo *sm.* **1.** moustache: *portare i baffi*, to wear (*v. irr.*) a moustache || *ridere sotto i baffi*, to laugh in one's sleeve **2.** (*sgorbio*) smear.
bagagliaio *sm.* luggage van.
bagaglio *sm.* luggage (*solo sing.*) || *fare i bagagli*, to pack || *disfare i bagagli*, to unpack.
bagarinaggio *sm.* cornering.
bagattella *sf.* trifle.
baggianata *sf.* **1.** (*azione*) foolish action **2.** (*discorso*) nonsense.
bagliore *sm.* flash.

bagnante sm. bather.

bagnare vt. **1.** to wet **2.** (immergere) to dip **3.** (di mare, fiume) to wash. ♦ **bagnarsi** vr. **1.** to get (v. irr.) wet **2.** (fare bagni in mare ecc.) to bathe.

bagnato agg. wet.

bagnino sm. bathing attendant.

bagno sm. **1.** bath: far un —, to take (v. irr.) a bath; — di sole, sun-bath **2.** (in mare ecc.) bathe || fare il —, to bathe || costume da —, bathing-costume.

bagnomaria sm. bain-marie.

bagordo sm. revelry.

baia¹ sf. (scherzo) joke || dare la — a qu., to make (v. irr.) fun of so.

baia² sf. (geogr.) bay.

baionetta sf. bayonet.

bàita sf. Alpine hut.

balaustrata sf. balustrade.

balbettare vt. e vi. to stammer.

balbettìo sm. stammer.

balbuzie sf. stammer.

balbuziente agg. stammering. ♦ **balbuziente** s. stammerer.

balconata sf. balcony.

balcone sm. balcony.

baldacchino sm. canopy.

baldanza sf. boldness.

baldanzoso agg. bold.

baldo agg. bold.

baldoria sf. revel: far —, to make (v. irr.) merry.

balena sf. whale: stecca di —, whalebone.

balenare vi. **1.** to lighten **2.** (di idea) to flash.

baleno sm. lightning || in un —, in the twinkling of an eye.

balestra sf. **1.** crossbow **2.** (mecc.) leaf spring.

balìa sf. wet nurse: — asciutta, dry-nurse.

balìa sf. mercy: in — di, at the mercy of.

balìstica sf. ballistics.

balla sf. **1.** (di cotone, di lana) bale **2.** (volg.; fandonia) tall story **3.** (fig.; mucchio) heap.

ballare vt. e vi. to dance.

ballata sf. ballad.

ballatoio sm. gallery.

ballerina sf. **1.** dancer **2.** (classica) ballerina.

ballerino sm. **1.** dancer **2.** (classico) ballet-dancer.

balletto sm. ballet.

ballo sm. **1.** dance **2.** (festa) ball || essere in —, to be on the go; tirare in —, to call in question.

ballottaggio sm. second ballot.

balneare agg. bathing || stazione —, seaside resort.

balocco sm. toy.

balordàggine sf. **1.** dullness **2.** (azione) foolish action **3.** (discorso) nonsense.

balordo agg. e sm. stupid.

bàlsamico agg. balmy.

bàlsamo sm. balm.

baluardo sm. bulwark.

balza sf. **1.** cliff **2.** (di vestito) flounce.

balzano agg. **1.** queer **2.** (di cavallo) white-footed.

balzare vi. to jump.

balzo sm. jump: cogliere la palla al —, to seize an opportunity.

bambagia sf. cotton-wool.

bambina sf. **1.** little girl, child (pl. children) **2.** (in fasce) baby.

bambinaia sf. nurse.

bambino sm. **1.** little boy, child (pl. children) **2.** (in fasce) baby || dare alla luce un —, to bring (v. irr.) forth a child.

bamboccio sm. **1.** (bambola) ragdoll **2.** (fig.) simpleton.

bàmbola sf. doll.

bambù sm. bamboo.

banale agg. banal.

banalità sf. banality.

banana sf. banana.

banano sm. banana-tree.

banca sf. bank.

bancarella sf. stall.

bancario agg. bank: libretto —, passbook. ♦ **bancario** sm. bank clerk.

bancarotta sf. bankruptcy: fare —, to go (v. irr.) bankrupt.

banchetto sm. banquet.

banchiere sm. banker.

banchina sf. **1.** (molo) wharf **2.** (terrapieno) bank.

banchisa sf. ice-pack.

banco sm. **1.** bench **2.** (di chiesa) pew **3.** (di negozio) counter **4.** (di nebbia, di sabbia, di gioco) bank.

banconota sf. banknote.

banda sf. **1.** (lato) side **2.** (mus.; striscia di stoffa) band **3.** (di delinquenti) gang.

banderuola sf. weathercock.

bandiera sf. flag, colours (pl.).

bandire vt. **1.** to proclaim **2.** (esi-

liare, eliminare) to banish.
bandito *sm.* outlaw.
bando *sm.* **1.** ban **2.** (*esilio*) banishment || *essere al* —, to be banished **3.** (*annunzio*) announcement.
bar *sm.* bar.
bara *sf.* coffin.
baracca *sf.* hut.
baraccone *sm.* booth.
baraonda *sf.* chaos.
barare *vi.* to cheat.
bàratro *sm.* abyss.
barattare *vt.* to exchange.
baratto *sm.* barter.
barattolo *sm.* **1.** jar **2.** (*di metallo*) tin.
barba *sf.* beard: *fare, farsi la* —, to shave || (*fig.*) *in* — *a*, in spite of.
barbabiètola *sf.* beet-root.
barbarie *sf.* **1.** barbarousness **2.** (*crudeltà*) barbarity.
bàrbaro *agg. e sm.* barbarian.
barbiere *sm.* barber.
barbone *sm.* **1.** (*straccione*) tramp **2.** (*cane*) poodle.
barbuto *agg.* bearded.
barca *sf.* boat: *andare in* —, to go (*v. irr.*) boating.
barcaiolo *sm.* boatman (*pl.* -men).
barcamenarsi *vr.* to wangle.
barcollare *vi.* to stagger.
barcone *sm.* long boat.
bardare *vt.* to harness. ♦ **bardarsi** *vr.* to dress up.
barella *sf.* stretcher.
barile *sm.* barrel.
barista *sm.* barman (*pl.* -men). ♦ **barista** *sf.* barmaid.
baritonale *agg.* baritone.
baritono *sm.* baritone.
barlume *sm.* glimmer.
baro *sm.* cheat.
barocco *agg. e sm.* baroque.
baromètrico *agg.* barometric(al).
baròmetro *sm.* barometer.
barone *sm.* baron.
baronessa *sf.* baroness.
barra *sf.* **1.** bar **2.** (*mar.*) helm.
barricare *vt.* to barricade.
barricata *sf.* barricade.
barriera *sf.* **1.** barrier **2.** (*fig.*) obstacle.
barrire *vi.* to trumpet.
barrito *sm.* trumpet.
barroccio *sm.* cart.
baruffa *sf.* quarrel.
barzelletta *sf.* joke.
basalto *sm.* basalt.

basamento *sm.* base.
basare *vt.* to base.
basco *agg. e sm.* Basque. ♦ **basco** *sm.* (*berretto*) beret.
base *sf.* base.
basette *sf.* *pl.* whiskers.
bàsico *agg.* basic.
basilare *agg.* basic.
basìlica *sf.* basilica.
basìlico *sm.* basil.
basilisco *sm.* basilisk.
bassezza *sf.* baseness.
basso *agg.* **1.** low **2.** (*di statura*) short **3.** (*abietto*) base. ♦ **basso** *avv.* low. ♦ **basso** *sm.* **1.** bottom **2.** (*mus.*) bass.
bassofondo *sm.* shallow || *i bassifondi della società*, the underworld.
bassopiano *sm.* lowland.
bassorilievo *sm.* bas-relief.
bassotto *agg.* thick-set. ♦ **bassotto** *sm.* (*cane*) dachshund.
bassoventre *sm.* belly.
basta *inter.* stop it!: — *con*, enough of.
bastardo *agg. e sm.* **1.** bastard **2.** (*di animali*) mongrel.
bastare *vi.* to be enough.
bastimento *sm.* ship.
bastione *sm.* **1.** rampart **2.** (*mil.*) bastion.
basto *sm.* pack-saddle.
bastonare *vt.* to cane.
bastonata *sf.* blow with a cane.
bastonatura *sf.* caning.
bastone *sm.* stick, staff.
batacchio *sm.* clapper.
batisfera *sf.* bathysphere.
batista *sf.* batiste.
batosta *sf.* blow.
batrace *sm.* batrachian.
battaglia *sf.* battle, fight || (*fig.*) *cavallo di* —, favourite subject, favourite piece.
battagliare *vi.* to battle, to fight (*v. irr.*), to struggle.
battagliero *agg.* **1.** warlike **2.** (*fig.*) fierce.
battaglione *sm.* battalion.
battelliere *sm.* boatman (*pl.* -men).
battello *sm.* boat.
battente *sm.* **1.** (*picchiotto*) knocker **2.** (*di porta*) wing.
bàttere *vt.* **1.** to beat (*v. irr.*), to strike (*v. irr.*) (*anche delle ore*) **2.** (*scrivere a macchina*) to type || — *le mani*, to clap hands; — *i piedi*, to stamp; *in un batter d'oc-*

chio, in the twinkling of an eye.
◆ **bàttere** *vi.* 1. to knock 2. (*pulsare*) to throb. ◆ **bàttersi** *vr.* to fight (*v. irr.*).

batterìa *sf.* 1. battery 2. (*da cucina*) kitchen utensils.

batter:o *sm.* bacterium (*pl.* -ia).

batteriologia *sf.* bacteriology.

battésimo *sm.* baptism: *nome di* —, Christian name.

battezzare *vt.* to baptize.

battibaleno *sm.* (*nella loc. avv.*) *in un* —, in a twinkling.

battibecco *sm.* squabble.

batticuore *sm.* 1. throb 2 (*fig.*) fear.

battimano *sm.* clap.

battipanni *sm.* carpet-beater.

battistero *sm.* baptistery.

battistrada *sm.* 1. outrider 2. (*di pneumatico*) tread ‖ *fare da* —, to lead (*v. irr.*) the way.

bàttito *sm.* 1. beat 2. (*mecc.*) knock.

battitore *sm.* 1. beater 2. (*cricket, baseball*) batsman (*pl.* -men).

battitura *sf.* thrashing.

battuta *sf.* 1. beating: — *di caccia*, beating 2. (*di spirito*) witty remark 3. (*mus.*) bar 4. (*teat.*) cue 5. (*tennis*) service.

batùffolo *sm.* flock.

baule *sm.* trunk.

bauxite *sf.* bauxite.

bava *sf.* 1. slaver 2. (*di lumaca*) slime.

bavaglino *sm.* bib.

bavaglio *sm.* gag: *mettere il* — *a qu.* (*fig.*), to gag so.

bàvero *sm.* collar.

bazàr *sm.* bazaar.

bazza *sf.* slipper-chin.

bazzècola *sf.* trifle.

bazzicare *vt.* e *vi.* to frequent.

bazzotto *agg.* soft-boiled.

be' *inter.* well.

beare *vt.* to make (*v. irr.*) so. happy.
◆ **bearsi** *vr.* to rejoice (at).

beatificazione *sf.* beatification.

beatitùdine *sf.* beatitude.

beato *agg.* 1. happy 2. (*relig.*) blessed.

beccaccia *sf.* woodcock.

beccaccino *sm.* snipe.

beccare *vt.* 1. to peck 2. (*fam. per acchiappare*) to catch (*v. irr.*). ◆ **beccarsi** *vr.* 1. (*procurarsi*) to get (*v. irr.*) 2. (*litigare*) to quarrel.

beccata *sf.* peck.

beccheggiare *vi.* to pitch.

beccheggio *sm.* pitching.

becchime *sm.* birdseed.

becchino *sm.* grave-digger.

becco *sm.* 1. beak 2. (*caprone*) billy-goat 3. (*fig.*) cuckold.

beccuccio *sm.* (*di teiera ecc.*) spout.

beduino *agg.* e *sm.* Bedouin.

befana *sf.* 1. "befana" 2. (*fig. fam.*) hag.

beffa *sf.* mockery: *farsi* — *di*, to laugh at; (*ingannare*) to make (*v. irr.*) a fool of.

beffardo *agg.* mocking. ◆ **beffardo** *sm.* mocker.

beffare *vt.* to mock. ◆ **beffarsi** *vr.* to laugh at.

beffeggiare *vt.* V. *beffare.*

bega *sf.* 1. quarrel 2. (*problema intricato*) entangled affair.

beghina *sf.* bigot.

begonia *sf.* (*bot.*) begonia.

belare *vi.* to bleat.

belato *sm.* bleat.

belga *agg.* e *sm.* Belgian.

bella *sf.* 1. beauty 2. (*innamorata*) sweetheart ‖ *copiare in* —, to make (*v. irr.*) a fair copy.

belladonna *sf.* (*bot.; farm.*) belladonna.

belletto *sm.* rouge.

bellezza *sf.* beauty: *istituto di* —, beauty parlour.

bellicismo *sm.* warlikeness.

bèllico *agg.* 1. war (*attributivo*) 2. (*del tempo di guerra*) wartime.

bellicoso *agg.* warlike.

belligerante *agg.* e *sm.* belligerent.

belligeranza *sf.* belligerence.

bellimbusto *sm.* dandy.

bello *agg.* 1. fine, beautiful 2. (*di uomo*) handsome ‖ *nel bel mezzo*, right in the middle. ◆ **bello** *sm.* 1. (*la bellezza*) beauty 2. (*innamorato*) sweetheart ‖ *sul più* —, at the right moment; *ora viene il* —, now you'll hear the best of it.

belva *sf.* wild beast.

belvedere *sm.* 1. observation post 2. (*arch.*) belvedere.

bemolle *sm.* (*mus.*) flat.

benché *cong.* though.

benda *sf.* bandage.

bendaggio *sm.* bandage.

bendare *vt.* to bandage.

bene *sm.* good: *per il tuo* —, for your sake; *voler* —, to love. ◆

beni sm. pl. property || — immobili, real estate; — di consumo, consumer goods. ◆ **bene** avv. 1. well 2. (molto) very 3. (nientemeno) no less than || star —, to be well; andar —, to suit.

benedetto agg. blessed.

benedire vt. to bless.

benedizione sf. blessing.

benefattore sm. benefactor.

beneficare vt. to help.

beneficenza sf. charity.

beneficiario agg. e sm. beneficiary.

beneficiata sf. benefit.

beneficio sm. 1. benefit 2. (eccl.; giur.) benefice.

benefico agg. 1. beneficent 2. (vantaggioso) beneficial.

benemerenza sf. merit.

benemerito agg. well-deserving.

beneplacito sm. consent: a tuo —, as you like.

benessere sm. welfare.

benestante agg. well-off. ◆ **benestante** s. well-to-do person.

benestare sm. assent.

benevolenza sf. benevolence.

benevolo agg. benevolent.

bengala sf. Bengal light.

beniamino sm. darling.

benignità sf. 1. benignity 2. (di clima) mildness.

benigno agg. 1. benign 2. (di clima) mild.

beninteso avv. of course.

benpensante agg. sensible || i benpensanti, the right thinking.

benservito sm. testimonial.

bensì cong. but.

benvenuto agg. sm. inter. welcome || dare il — a qu., to welcome so.

benvolere vt. to like: farsi —, to make (v. irr.) oneself liked.

benzina sf. petrol.

benzinaio sm. filling station attendant.

benzolo sm. benzol.

beone sm. drunkard.

beota agg. e sm. Bœotian.

berbero agg. e sm. Berber.

berciare vi. to bawl.

bere vt. to drink (v. irr.) || darla a — (fig.), to tell (v. irr.) tall stories.

bergamotto sm. (bot.; farm.) bergamot.

berillo sm. beryllium.

berlina sf. 1. (carrozza) berline 2. (automobile) limousine 3. (gogna)

pillory: mettere alla —, to pillory.

bernòccolo sm. bump.

berfetta sf. cap.

berretto sm. cap.: — con visiera, peaked cap.

bersagliare vt. 1. to shoot (v. irr.) (at) 2. (fig.) to torment.

bersaglio sm. target: tiro al —, target-shooting || colpire il —, to hit (v. irr.) the mark.

besciamella sf. cream-sauce.

bestemmia sf. swear.

bestemmiare vi. to swear (v. irr.).

bestia sf. beast || montare in —, to lose (v. irr.) one's temper.

bestiale agg. beastly.

bestialità sf. 1. beastliness 2. (fig.) foolishness || dire —, to talk nonsense; fare —, to make (v. irr.) blunders.

bestiame sm. cattle.

bèttola sf. tavern.

betulla sf. birch.

bevanda sf. drink.

beveraggio sm. beverage.

bevitore sm. drinker.

bevuta sf. 1. draught 2. (il bere) drinking.

biada sf. fodder.

biancastro agg. whitish.

biancheggiare vi. e vt. 1. (essere bianco) to be white 2. (diventare, far diventare bianco) to whiten.

biancheria sf. linen.

bianco agg. white || in —, blank; di punto in —, suddenly.

biancore sm. whiteness.

biancospino sm. hawthorn.

biascicare vt. to mumble.

biasimare vt. to blame.

biasimévole agg. blamable.

biàsimo sm. blame.

Bibbia sf. Bible.

bibita sf. drink.

biblico agg. biblical.

bibliografia sf. bibliography.

bibliogràfico agg. bibliographic(al).

biblioteca sf. 1. library 2. (scaffale) bookcase.

bibliotecario sm. librarian.

bica sf. stack.

bicamerale agg. (pol.) bicameral.

bicarbonato sm. bicarbonate.

bicchiere sm. glass.

bicèfalo agg. V. bicipite.

bicicletta sf. bicycle: andare in —, to cycle.

bicipite agg. two-headed. ◆ **bicipite** sm. biceps.

bicocca *sf.* hut.

bicolore *agg.* two-coloured.

bidè *sm.* bidet.

bidello *sm.* porter.

bidente *sm.* pitchfork.

bidone *sm.* 1. can 2. (*fam.*) swindle.

bieco *agg.* sinister.

biella *sf.* (*mecc.*) connecting rod.

biennale *agg.* biennial.

biètola *sf.* beet.

biennio *sm.* biennium (*pl.* -nia).

bifase *agg.* (*elettr.*) two-phase.

bifolco *sm.* boor.

biforcarsi *vr.* to fork.

biforcazione *sf.* fork.

biforcuto *agg.* forked.

bigamìa *sf.* bigamy.

bìgamo *agg.* bigamous. ♦ **bìgamo** *sm.* bigamist.

bighellonare *vi.* to lounge.

bighellone *sm.* lounger.

bigio *agg.* grey.

bigiotterìa *sf.* trinkets (*pl.*).

biglia *sf.* (billiard-)ball.

bigliettàio *sm.* 1. conductor 2. (*di stazione*) booking-clerk.

biglietterìa *sf.* 1. booking-office 2. (*di teatro*) box-office.

biglietto *sm.* 1. card: — *di visita*, visiting card 2. (*di tram ecc.*) ticket: — *di andata e ritorno*, return ticket; *mezzo* —, half-fare ticket 3. (*banconota*) bank-note.

bigodino *sm.* (hair-)curler.

bigotto *agg.* bigoted. ♦ **bigotto** *sm.* bigot.

bikini *sm.* bikini.

bilancia *sf.* balance, scales (*pl.*).

bilanciare *vt.* to balance.

bilanciere *sm.* 1. balance-wheel 2. (*mar.*) outrigger.

bilancio *sm.* budget: *fare il* —, to strike (*v. irr.*) the balance.

bilaterale *agg.* bilateral.

bile *sf.* 1. bile 2. (*ira*) anger.

biliardo *sm.* billiards (*pl.*).

bìlico *sm.* 1. balance 2. (*fig.*) uncertainty || *mettere in* —, to balance; *stare in* —, to be balanced.

bilingue *agg.* bilingual.

bilione *sm.* billion.

bilioso *agg.* bilious.

bimba *sf.* V. *bambina*.

bimbo *sm.* V. *bambino*.

bimensìle *agg.* fortnightly.

bimestrale *agg.* bimestrial.

bimestre *sm.* (period of) two months.

bimotore *agg.* two-engined: *aereo* —, two-engined plane.

binario *sm.* track: — *morto*, dead-end track.

binòcolo *sm.* binoculars (*pl.*).

binomio *sm.* binomial.

biòccolo *sm.* flock: — *di neve*, snow-flake.

biochìmica *sf.* biochemistry.

biofìsica *sf.* biophysics.

biografìa *sf.* biography.

biogràfico *agg.* biographic(al).

biògrafo *sm.* biographer.

biologìa *sf.* biology.

biològico *agg.* biologic(al).

biòlogo *sm.* biologist.

biondo *agg.* fair.

biosfera *sf.* biosphere.

biòssido *sm.* dioxide.

bipartizione *sf.* bipartitior

bìpede *agg. e sm.* biped.

biplano *sm.* biplane.

bipolare *agg.* bipolar.

birba *sf.* scapegrace.

birbante *s.* rogue.

birbonata *sf.* knavery.

birbone *sm.* rogue.

bireattore *sm.* two-engined jet.

birichino *sm.* urchin. ♦ **birichino** *agg.* naughty.

birillo *sm.* skittle.

biro *sf.* ball-point pen.

biròccio *sm.* cart.

birra *sf.* beer.

birrerìa *sf.* 1. beer-house 2. (*fabbrica*) brewery.

bisàccia *sf.* packsack.

bisbètico *agg.* cantankerous.

bisbigliare *vt.* to whisper.

bisbiglio *sm.* whisper.

bisbòccia *sf.* spree: *far* —, to revel.

bisca *sf.* gambling-house.

biscia *sf.* snake.

biscotto *sm.* biscuit.

bisessuale *agg.* bisexual.

bisestile *agg. anno* —, leap year.

bisettimanale *agg.* bi-weekly.

bisettrice *sf.* bisector.

bisìllabo *agg.* disyllabic. ♦ **bisìllabo** *sm.* disyllable.

bislacco *agg.* odd.

bislungo *agg.* oblong.

bismuto *sm.* bismuth.

bisnipote *s.* great-grandchild (*pl.* -children).

bisnonna *sf.* great-grandmother.

bisognare *vi. imp.* to be neces-

bisnonno *sm.* great-grandfather. sary, must.

bisogno *sm.* **1.** need **2.** (*povertà*) necessity ‖ *aver* —, to need.

bisognoso *agg.* needy.

bisonte *sm.* bison.

bissare *vt.* to give (*v. irr.*) an encore (of sthg.).

bistecca *sf.* beefsteak.

bisticciare *vi.* to squabble.

bisticcio *sm.* **1.** squabble **2.** (*gioco di parole*) pun.

bistrattare *vt.* to ill-treat.

bistro *sm.* bistre.

bisturì *sm.* lancet.

bitòrzolo *sm.* bump.

bitume *sm.* bitumen.

bivacco *sm.* bivouac.

bivalente *agg.* bivalent.

bivio *sm.* **1.** fork **2.** (*fig.*) alternative.

bizantino *agg. e sm.* Byzantine.

bizza *sf.* freak ‖ *fare le bizze*, to be peevish.

bizzarria *sf.* **1.** peculiarity **2.** (*cosa*) curiosity **3.** (*atto, detto*) extravagance.

bizzarro *agg.* strange.

bizzoso *agg.* **1.** freakish **2.** (*irascibile*) irascible.

blandire *vt.* to soothe.

blandizia *sf.* blandishment.

blando *agg.* bland.

blasone *sm.* **1.** blazon **2.** (*nobiltà*) nobility.

blaterare *vi. e vt.* to prate.

bleso *agg.* lisping ‖ *pronuncia blesa*, lisp. ♦ **bleso** *sm.* lisper.

blindare *vt.* (*mil.*) to armour.

bloccare *vt.* to block, to stop. ♦ **bloccarsi** *vr.* to jam.

blocco *sm.* **1.** block **2.** (*mil.*) blockade.

blu *agg. e sm.* blue.

bluff *sm.* bluff.

blusa *sf.* blouse.

boa[1] *sf.* (*mar.*) buoy.

boa[2] *sm.* (*zool.*) boa.

bobina *sf.* bobbin.

bocca *sf.* mouth: — *da incendio*, fire-plug; — *dello stomaco*, pit of the stomach; *chiudere la* — *a qu.*, to silence so.

boccaccia *sf.* grimace.

boccale *sm.* jug.

boccaporto *sm.* hatchway.

boccata *sf.* mouthful.

boccheggiare *vi.* to gasp.

bocchino *sm.* mouthpiece.

boccia *sf.* **1.** water-bottle **2.** (*sport*) bowl.

bocciare *vt.* **1.** (*respingere*) to reject **2.** (*agli esami*) to fail.

bocciatura *sf.* failure.

boccio *sm.* bud.

boccone *sm.* **1.** bit **2.** (*boccata*) mouthful **3.** (*esca*) bait.

bocconi *avv.* lying face downwards.

boia *sm.* executioner.

boicottare *vt.* to boycott.

bolgia *sf.* **1.** (*fig.*) bedlam **2.** (*di inferno*) pit.

bòlide *sm.* (*astr.*) bolide.

bolla *sf.* **1.** bubble **2.** (*vescica*) blister **3.** (*eccl.*) bull.

bollare *vt.* **1.** (*timbrare*) to stamp **2.** (*a fuoco e fig.*) to brand.

bollato *agg.* stamped: *carta bollata*, stamped paper **2.** (*a fuoco e fig.*) branded.

bollente *agg.* boiling.

bolletta *sf.* **1.** bill **2.** (*ricevuta*) receipt ‖ *essere in* — (*fig.*), to be (*v. irr.*) penniless.

bollettario *sm.* counterfoil-book.

bollettino *sm.* **1.** bulletin **2.** (*comm.*) list, note.

bollire *vi. e vt.* to boil.

bollito *sm.* boiled meat.

bollitore *sm.* **1.** boiler **2.** (*bricco*) kettle.

bollitura *sf.* boiling.

bollo *sm.* stamp.

bollore *sm.* **1.** boil **2.** (*fig.*) excitement.

bolscevico *agg. e sm.* Bolshevist.

bolscevismo *sm.* Bolshevism.

boma *sf.* (*mar.*) boom.

bomba *sf.* bomb.

bombardamento *sm.* bombardment.

bombardare *vt.* to bombard; (*generalmente da aereo*) to bomb.

bombardiere *sm.* **1.** (*soldato*) bombardier **2.** (*aereo*) bomber.

bombetta *sf.* bowler.

bòmbola *sf.* bottle.

bomboniera *sf.* candy-box.

bonaccia *sf.* dead calm.

bonaccione *agg.* good-natured. ♦ **bonaccione** *sm.* good-natured man (*pl.* men).

bonarietà *sf.* good nature.

bonario *agg.* good-natured, friendly.

bonifica *sf.* reclamation.

bonificare *vt.* **1.** to reclaim **2.** (*comm.*) to grant an allowance.

bonomìa *sf.* good nature.

bontà *sf.* goodness.

bonzo *sm.* bonze.

borbottare *vi. e vt.* **1.** to mumble

2. (*lamentarsi*) to grumble.
borbottio *sm.* 1. mumbling 2. (*protesta*) grumbling.
bordare *vt.* to border.
bordeggiare *vi.* to tack.
bordello *sm.* bawdyhouse.
bordo *sm.* 1. edge 2. (*mar.*) board: *a* —, on board.
bordura *sf.* border.
bòrea *sf.* Boreas.
boreale *agg.* boreal: *aurora* —, aurora borealis.
borgata *sf.* village.
borghese *agg.* 1. middle-class 2. (*comune*) plain 3. (*civile*) civilian: *in* —, in civilian dress. ♦ **borghese** *s.* middle-class person.
borghesìa *sf.* middle class(es): *l'alta* —, the upper middle class(es); *la piccola* —, the lower middle class(es).
borgo *sm.* village.
borgomastro *sm.* burgomaster.
boria *sf.* arrogance.
bòrico *agg.* boric.
borioso *agg.* arrogant.
borotalco *sm.* talcum powder.
borraccia *sf.* flask.
borsa[1] *sf.* bag || — *per documenti*, brief case; — *di studio*, scholarship.
borsa[2] *sf.* (*comm.*) Stock Exchange.
borsaiolo *sm.* pickpocket.
borseggiare *vt.* to pick pockets.
borsellino *sm.* purse.
borsetta *sf.* (hand-)bag.
boscaglia *sf.* brushwood.
boscaiolo *sm.* woodman (*pl.* -men).
boschetto *sm.* grove.
bosco *sm.* wood.
boscoso *agg.* woody.
bòssolo *sm.* cartridge-case.
botànica *sf.* botany.
bòtola *sf.* trap-door.
botta *sf.* 1. blow 2. (*battuta*) sarcastic remark || *dare un sacco di botte a qu.*, to whack so.
botte *sf.* barrel.
bottega *sf.* shop.
bottegaio *sm.* shop-keeper.
bottiglia *sf.* bottle.
bottiglieria *sf.* wine shop.
bottino *sm.* booty: *far* —, to plunder.
botto *sm.* blow || *di* —, suddenly.
bottone *sm.* button || *attaccare un* — (*fig.*), to buttonhole.
bovaro *sm.* cowherd.
bovini *sm. pl.* cattle (*sing.*).

bozza *sf.* 1. (*gonfiore*) swelling 2. (*tip.*) proof 3. (*abbozzo*) draft || *correggere le bozze*, to proofread.
bozzetto *sm.* sketch.
bòzzolo *sm.* cocoon.
braccare *vt.* to hunt.
braccetto (*nella loc. avv.*) *a* —, arm-in-arm.
bracciale *sm.* 1. (*fascia che si porta al braccio*) arm-band 2. (*braccialetto*) bracelet.
braccialetto *sm.* bracelet.
bracciante *sm.* labourer.
bracciata *sf.* 1. armful 2. (*di nuoto*) stroke.
braccio *sm.* arm: *essere in — a qu.*, to be in so.'s arms || — *di mare*, sound.
bracco *sm.* hound.
bracconaggio *sm.* poaching.
bracconiere *sm.* poacher.
brace *sf.* embers (*pl.*).
brache *sf. pl.* 1. trousers 2. (*mutande*) drawers.
brachicèfalo *agg.* brachycephalous.
braciere *sm.* brazier.
braciola *sf.* chop.
bradicardia *sf.* (*med.*) bradycardia.
brado *agg.* wild.
brama *sf.* longing.
bramare *vt.* to long for (sthg.).
bramosia *sf.* covetousness.
bramoso *agg.* eager for (sthg.).
branca *sf.* 1. claw 2. (*settore*) branch.
branchia *sf.* gill.
branco *sm.* 1. herd 2. (*di pecore*) flock 3. (*di pesci*) shoal 4. (*di lupi e fig.*) pack.
brancolare *vi.* to grope.
branda *sf.* 1. camp-bed 2. (*mar.*) bunk.
brandello *sm.* 1. rag 2. (*pezzetto*) bit || *coi vestiti a brandelli*, in rags; *fare a brandelli*, to tear (*v. irr.*) up.
brandire *vt.* to brandish.
brano *sm.* piece.
brasato *sm.* braised beef.
brasiliano *agg. e sm.* Brazilian.
bravata *sf.* bravado.
bravo *agg.* clever, good || —!, well done!; *su, da* —!, be a good boy!
bravura *sf.* 1. cleverness 2. (*coraggio*) bravery || (*mus.*) *pezzo di* —, bravura.
breccia *sf.* breach: *essere sulla* —, to stand (*v. irr.*) in the breach.
brefotrofio *sm.* foundling hospital.

bretella *sf.* brace.
breve *agg.* short.
brevettare *vt.* to patent.
brevetto *sm.* patent.
breviario *sm.* breviary.
brevità *sf.* brevity.
brezza *sf.* breeze.
bricco *sm.* kettle, pot.
bricconata *sf.* roguish trick.
briccone *sm.* rogue.
briciola *sf.* crumb.
briciolo *sm.* bit.
briga *sf.* 1. trouble 2. (*lite*) quarrel: *attaccar* —, to pick a quarrel.
brigadiere *sm.* 1. « brigadiere » 2. (*ufficiale nell'Esercito Britannico assegnato al comando di brigata*) brigadier.
brigante *sm.* robber.
brigantino *sm.* (*mar.*) brig.
brigare *vi.* to intrigue.
brigata *sf.* 1. party 2. (*mil.*) brigade.
briglia *sf.* bridle || *a* — *sciolta*, at full gallop.
brillante *agg. e sm.* brilliant.
brillantina *sf.* brilliantine.
brillare *vi.* to shine (*v. irr.*). ♦ **brillare** *vt.* 1. (*riso ecc.*) to hull 2. (*una mina*) to blast.
brillo *agg.* tipsy.
brina *sf.* hoarfrost.
brinare *vi. imp.*: *ha brinato*, there has been a frost.
brinata *sf.* hoarfrost.
brindare *vi.* to toast: — *a qu.*, to toast so.
brindello *sm.* rag.
brindisi *sm.* toast.
brio *sm.* liveliness.
brioso *agg.* lively.
britànnico *agg.* British.
brìvido *sm.* 1. shiver 2. (*di paura, orrore*) shudder.
brizzolato *agg.* grizzled.
brocca *sf.* jug.
broccato *sm.* brocade.
bròccolo *sm.* broccoli.
brodaglia *sf.* slops (*pl.*).
brodo *sm.* broth.
broglio *sm.* intrigue: — *elettorale*, gerry-mander.
bromo *sm.* bromine.
bromuro *sm.* bromide.
bronchiale *agg.* bronchial.
bronchite *sf.* bronchitis.
broncio *sm.* pout || *fare il* —, to pout.
bronco *sm.* bronchus (*pl.* -chi).

broncopolmonite *sf.* bronchopneumonia.
brontolare *vi. e vt.* to grumble.
brontolio *sm.* grumbling.
brontolone *sm.* grumbler.
brontosàuro *sm.* brontosaurus.
brònzeo *agg.* 1. bronze (*attributivo*) 2. (*simile a bronzo*) bronzy.
bronzo *sm.* bronze || *faccia di* —, brazen-faced person.
brossura *sf.* paper-back binding || *in* —, paper-bound.
brucare *vt.* to browse (on).
bruciacchiare *vt.* to scorch.
bruciacchiatura *sf.* scorching.
bruciapelo (*nella loc. avv.*) *a* —, point-blank.
bruciare *vt. e vi.* to burn (*v. irr.*).
bruciatore *sm.* burner.
bruciatura *sf.* burn.
bruciore *sm.* burning, smart (*anche fig.*).
bruco *sm.* caterpillar.
brùffolo *sm.* pimple.
brughiera *sf.* heath.
brulicare *vi.* to swarm (with).
brulichio *sm.* swarm.
brullo *agg.* bare.
bruma *sf.* mist.
brumoso *agg.* misty.
brunire *vt.* to burnish.
brunitura *sf.* burnishing.
bruno *agg.* brown.
bruscamente *avv.* roughly.
brusco *agg.* 1. rough 2. (*di sapore*) sour.
brusìo *sm.* buzz.
brutale *agg.* brutal.
brutalità *sf.* brutality.
bruto *agg. e sm.* brute.
bruttezza *sf.* ugliness.
brutto *agg.* 1. ugly 2. (*cattivo*) bad.
bruttura *sf.* 1. ugly thing 2. (*azione*) base action.
bùbbola *sf.* lie.
bubbone *sm.* bubo.
bubbònico *agg.* bubonic.
buca *sf.* hole: — *delle lettere*, letter-box.
bucaneve *sm.* snowdrop.
bucaniere *sm.* buccaneer.
bucare *vt.* 1. to pierce 2. (*una gomma*) to puncture 3. (*biglietti*) to punch.
bucato *sm.* 1. washing 2. (*i panni*) laundry.
buccia *sf.* peel.
bucherellare *vt.* to riddle.

buco *sm.* hole.

bucòlico *agg.* bucolic.

buddismo *sm.* Buddhism.

buddista *s.* Buddhist.

budello *sm.* **1.** bowel **2.** (*strada stretta*) alley **3.** (*tubo*) narrow tube.

budino *sm.* pudding.

bue *sm.* ox (*pl.* oxen): *carne di* —, beef.

bùfalo *sm.* buffalo.

bufera *sf.* **1.** storm **2.** (*di vento*) gale.

buffetto *sm.* fillip: *dare un* —, to fillip.

buffo *agg.* funny || *opera buffa*, comic opera.

buffonata *sf.* buffoonery.

buffone *sm.* **1.** clown, fool **2.** (*di corte*) court jester **3.** (*fig.*) unreliable person.

bugìa *sf.* **1.** lie **2.** (*portacandela*) flat candlestick.

bugiardo *agg.* false. ♦ **bugiardo** *sm.* liar.

bugigàttolo *sm.* lumber-room.

buio *agg.* e *sm.* dark: — *pesto*, pitch dark.

bulbo *sm.* **1.** bulb **2.** (*di occhio*) eyeball.

bùlgaro *agg.* e *sm.* Bulgarian.

bulinare *vt.* to engrave.

bulino *sm.* burin.

bullonare *vt.* (*mecc.*) to bolt.

bullone *sm.* bolt.

buonanotte *sf.* good night.

buonasera *sf.* good evening.

buoncostume *sm.*: *squadra del* —, vice squad.

buongiorno *sm.* **1.** (*di mattina*) good morning **2.** (*di pomeriggio*) good afternoon **3.** (*a ogni ora incontrandosi, fam.*) hullo **4.** (*a ogni ora lasciandosi*) goodbye.

buongustaio *sm.* gourmet.

buongusto *sm.* good taste.

buono *agg.* **1.** good **2.** (*di tempo*) fine || *alla buona*, informal; *a buon diritto*, by right; *di buon grado*, willingly. ♦ **buono** *sm.* **1.** good **2.** (*persona*) good person **3.** (*comm.*) bond **4.** (*tagliando*) coupon.

buonsenso *sm.* (common) sense.

buontempone *sm.* merry fellow.

buonumore *sm.* V. *umore.*

buonuomo *sm.* **1.** good-natured man (*pl.* men) **2.** simple man (*pl.* men).

burattinaio *sm.* puppet showman (*pl.* -men).

burattino *sm.* puppet.

burbanzoso *agg.* haughty.

bùrbero *agg.* gruff.

burla *sf.* trick || *per* —, in fun.

burlare *vt.* to play a trick on (so.). ♦ **burlarsi** *vr.* to make (*v. irr.*) fun of.

burlesco *agg.* farcical.

burlone *sm.* joker.

buròcrate *sm.* bureaucrat.

burocràtico *agg.* bureaucratic.

burocrazìa *sf.* bureaucracy; (*in Inghilterra*) Civil Service.

burrasca *sf.* storm.

burrascoso *agg.* stormy.

burrificio *sm.* dairy.

burro *sm.* butter.

burrone *sm.* ravine.

burroso *agg.* buttery.

buscarsi *vr.* to get (*v. irr.*) || *buscarle*, to get a thrashing.

bussare *vi.* to knock: — *alla porta*, to knock at the door.

busse *sf. pl.* blows: *prendere le* —, to get (*v. irr.*) a thrashing.

bùssola *sf.* compass: *perdere la* — (*fig.*), to lose (*v. irr.*) one's head.

bussolotto *sm.* dice-box || *fare il giuoco dei bussolotti* (*anche fig.*), to juggle.

busta *sf.* **1.** envelope **2.** (*astuccio*) case.

bustarella *sf.* bribe.

bustina *sf.* (*mil.*) service cap.

busto *sm.* **1.** bust **2.** (*indumento per donna*) corset.

butano *sm.* (*chim.*) butane.

buttare *vt.* **1.** to throw (*v. irr.*) **2.** (*sprecare*) to waste || — *all'aria*, to upset (*v. irr.*); — *a terra*, to knock down.

butterato *agg.* pitted.

buzzo *sm.* belly || *di* — *buono*, very eagerly.

C

càbala *sf.* cab(b)ala.

cabalistico *agg.* cab(b)alistic(al).

cabina *sf.* **1.** box, hut: — *balneare*, bathing hut; — *telefonica*, telephone box **2.** (*aer.; mar.*) cabin.

cablogramma *sm.* cable.

cabotaggio *sm.* cabotage: *nave di piccolo —*, coasting vessel.

cacao *sm.* 1. *(bot.)* cacao 2. *(polvere, bevanda)* cocoa.

cacare *vi.* to evacuate one's bowels.

cacarella *sf.* diarrhoea.

cacatoa, cacatùa *sm.* cockatoo.

cacca *sf.* excrement.

caccia *sf.* hunt, hunting || *— grossa*, big game || *cane da —*, sporting dog; *stagione di —*, shooting season; *andare a —*, to go *(v. irr.)* hunting; *andare a — di uccelli*, to go shooting. ♦ **caccia** *sm. (aer.)* fighter.

cacciagione *sf.* game.

cacciare *vt.* 1. to hunt 2. *(mil.; mar.)* to chase 3. *(scacciare)* to expel 4. *(mettere)* to put *(v. irr.)*.

cacciatore *sm.* hunter *(anche fig.)*.

cacciatorpediniere *sm.* (torpedo-boat) destroyer.

cacciavite *sm.* screwdriver.

cachi *sm.* persimmon.

cacio *sm.* cheese || *essere alto come un soldo di —*, to be very short.

cacofonia *sf.* cacophony.

cactus *sm.* cactus *(pl.* cacti*)*.

cadauno *agg.* e *pron. indef.* each.

cadàvere *sm.* corpse.

cadavèrico *agg.* 1. corpse-like 2. *(pallido)* deadly pale.

cadente *agg.* 1. falling 2. *(di astri)* setting || *stella —*, shooting star || *età —*, decrepit old age.

cadenza *sf.* 1. cadence 2. *(ritmo)* rhythm 3. *(accento)* accent.

cadere *vi.* 1. to fall *(v. irr.)* *(anche fig.)*: — *bocconi*, to fall flat on one's face; — *in mare*, to fall overboard; — *addormentato*, to fall asleep; — *a proposito*, to fall in the nick of time; — *dal sonno*, to be overcome by sleep; — *nell'errore*, to fall into error || *far —*, to knock down; *(fig.)* to bring *(v. irr.)* about the fall of 2. *(tramontare, di astri)* to set *(v. irr.)* 3. *(calare)* to drop 4. *(far fiasco)* to fail.

cadetto *agg.* e *sm.* cadet.

caducità *sf.* caducity.

caduco *agg.* perishable, decaying.

caduta *sf.* 1. fall, falling 2. *(fig.)* downfall, ruin 3. *(fis.)* drop.

caffè *sm.* 1. coffee: — *macinato*, ground coffee; — *nero*, black coffee 2. *(locale)* coffee-house.

caffeina *sf.* caffeine.

caffettiera *sf.* coffee-pot.

cafone *sm.* boor.

cagionévole *agg.* sickly, weak.

cagliarsi *vr.* to curdle.

cagna *sf.* bitch.

cagnara *sf.* 1. furious barking 2. *(fig.)* uproar.

cagnesco *agg. in —*, surlily || *guardare in —*, to scowl at.

cagnolino *s.: n.* 1. *(cucciolo)* puppy 2. *(cane piccolo)* small dog.

caimano *sm.* cayman.

cala *sf.* 1. creek 2. *(mar.)* hold.

calabrone *sm.* hornet.

calamaio *sm.* ink-stand.

calamaro *sm.* calamary.

calamita *sf.* magnet *(anche fig.)*.

calamità *sf.* calamity, misfortune.

calamitare *vt.* to magnetize *(anche fig.)*.

calamitoso *agg.* calamitous.

calandra *sf.* 1. *(zool.)* wood-lark 2. *(mecc.)* calender.

calare *vt.* to lower, to drop || *cala la tela*, the curtain drops. ♦ **calare** *vi.* 1. to descend 2. *(di astri)* to set *(v. irr.)* 3. *(di febbre)* to abate 4. *(comm.)* to fall *(v. irr.)*. ♦ **calarsi** *vr.* to let *(v. irr.)* oneself down.

calata *sf.* descent.

calca *sf.* crowd.

calcagno *sm.* heel || *stare alle calcagna di qu.*, to follow so. closely.

calcare[1] *vt.* 1. to tread *(v. irr.)* 2. *(premere)* to press down || — *la mano (fig.)*, to exaggerate.

calcare[2] *sm.* limestone.

calcàreo *agg.* calcareous.

calce *sf.* lime || *in —* *(loc. avv.)*, at the foot.

calcestruzzo *sm.* concrete.

calciare *vi.* to kick.

calciatore *sm.* footballer.

calcificare *vt.* to calcify.

calcificazione *sf.* calcification.

calcina *sf.* lime.

calcinaccio *sm.* debris *(solo sing.)*.

calcinare *vt.* to calcine.

calcio[1] *sm.* 1. kick 2. *(giuoco)* football || *d'inizio*, kick-off; — *di rigore*, penalty 3. *(di arma)* butt.

calcio[2] *sm. (chim.)* calcium.

calco *sm.* 1. *(scult.)* cast 2. *(di disegno)* drawing.

calcolàbile *agg.* computable.

calcolare *vt.* 1. to calculate, to compute 2. *(prevedere)* to estimate.

calcolatore *sm.* (electronic) computer || *regolo —*, slide-rule.

calcolatrice *sf.* calculating machine.
càlcolo *sm.* **1.** calculation **2.** (*med.*) stone.
calcomanìa *sf.* transfer.
caldaia *sf.* **1.** kier **2.** (*per produzione di vapore*) boiler.
caldamente *avv.* warmly.
caldeggiare *vt.* to favour.
caldeggiatore *sm.* supporter.
calderaio *sm.* tinker.
calderone *sm.* **1.** cauldron **2.** (*fig.*) medley.
caldo *agg.* **1.** warm; (*molto caldo*) hot **2.** (*fig.*) ardent. ♦ **caldo** *sm.* heat || *far —*, to be warm, to be hot.
caleidoscòpio *sm.* kaleidoscope.
calendàrio *sm.* calendar.
calende *sf. pl.* kalends || *rimandare alle — greche*, to put off till doomsday.
calesse *sm.* gig, calash.
calessino *sm.* gig.
calibrare *vt.* to calibrate.
calibratura *sf.* calibration.
càlibro *sm.* **1.** calibre **2.** (*di persona*) caliber, importance.
càlice *sm.* **1.** (*eccl.*) chalice **2.** (*bicchiere*) goblet, drinking-cup.
calìgine *sf.* thick fog, smog.
callifugo *sm.* corn-plaster.
calligrafìa *sf.* handwriting.
calligràfico *agg.* calligraphic.
calligrafo *sm.* calligrapher: *perito —*, handwriting expert.
callista *sm.* chiropodist.
callo *sm.* corn.
callosità *sf.* callosity.
calloso *agg.* callous.
calma *sf.* calm.
calmante *agg.* calming, soothing. ♦ **calmante** *sm.* (*farm.*) sedative.
calmare *vt.* **1.** to calm **2.** (*metter pace*) to appease.
calmo *agg.* calm, quiet.
calo *sm.* **1.** shrinkage **2.** (*comm.*) drop.
calore *sm.* **1.** (*forte*) heat; (*moderato*) warmth **2.** (*fig.*) warmth, eagerness.
calorìa *sf.* calory.
calorìfero *sm.* heating apparatus, radiator.
caloroso *agg.* **1.** warm, hearty **2.** (*che non sente freddo*) not feeling the cold.
calotta *sf.* **1.** cap: *— cranica*, skull-cap **2.** (*geom.*) bowl.
calpestare *vt.* to tread (*v. irr.*):

vietato — l'erba, keep off the grass.
calpestìo *sm.* trampling (of feet).
calunnia *sf.* slander.
calunniare *vt.* to slander.
calunniatore *sm.* slanderer.
caivizie *sf.* baldness.
calvo *agg.* bald.
calza *sf.* **1.** (*corta*) sock; (*da donna*) stocking **2.** (*lavoro a maglia*) knitting || *fare la —*, to knit.
calzamaglia *sf.* tights (*pl.*).
calzare *vt.* to put (*v. irr.*) on. ♦ **calzare** *vi.* to fit.
calzatura *sf.* shoe || *negozio di calzature*, shoe-shop.
calzaturificio *sm.* boot factory.
calzettone *sm.* heavy sock.
calzino *sm.* sock.
calzolàio *sm.* shoemaker.
calzolerìa *sf.* shoemaker's shop.
calzoni *sm. pl.* trousers.
camaleonte *sm.* chameleon (*anche fig.*).
cambiale *sf.* bill (of exchange): *— a vista*, bill at sight; *emettere una —*, to issue a bill; *girare una —*, to endorse a bill; *protestare una —*, to note a bill || *— pagherò*, promissory note.
cambiamento *sm.* change.
cambiare *vt.* to change (*anche fig.*). ♦ **cambiarsi** *vr.* to change.
cambio *sm.* **1.** change **2.** (*econ.*) exchange **3.** (*mecc.*) change-gear **4.** (*auto*) gear || *in —*, in exchange for, instead of.
camelia *sf.* (*bot.*) camellia.
càmera *sf.* **1.** room: *— da letto*, bedroom; *— dei bambini*, nursery; *— degli ospiti*, guest-room || *musica da —*, chamber music **2.** (*pol.*) Chamber House: *camera dei deputati*, Chamber of Deputies **3.** (*tec.*) chamber || *— oscura*, dark room; *— d'aria*, inner tube.
camerata[1] *sm.* comrade, mate.
camerata[2] *sf.* dormitory.
cameratismo *sm.* comradeship.
cameriera *sf.* **1.** maid **2.** (*di albergo*) chambermaid **3.** (*di ristorante*) waitress.
cameriere *sm.* **1.** man-servant (*pl.* men-) **2.** (*di ristorante*) waiter.
càmice *sm.* **1.** overall **2.** (*eccl.*) surplice.
camicetta *sf.* blouse.
camicia *sf.* **1.** (*da uomo*) shirt || *— da notte (da uomo)*, night-shirt

2. (*da donna*) chemise || — *da notte* (*da donna*), night-dress **3.** (*tec*) jacket || *è nato con la* —, he was born with a silver spoon in his mouth.

caminetto *sm.* fireplace.

camino *sm.* **1.** (*focolare*) fireplace **2.** (*comignolo*) chimney.

camion *sm.* lorry.

camioncino *sm.* van.

camionista *sm.* lorry-driver.

cammello *sm.* camel.

cammeo *sm.* cameo.

camminare *vi.* **1.** to walk || — *a grandi passi*, to stride (*v. irr.*) along; — *in punta di piedi*, to walk on tiptoe **2.** (*di meccanismi*) to go (*v. irr.*), to work **3.** (*discorsi, affari ecc.*) to proceed.

camminata *sf.* **1.** walk **2.** (*andatura*) gait.

camminatore *sm.* walker.

cammino *sm.* way.

camomilla *sf.* (*bot.*) camomile: *una tazza di* —, a cup of camomile-tea.

camoscio *sm.* chamois: *pelle di* —, chamois leather.

campagna *sf.* **1.** country: *casa di* —, country-house; *andare in* —, to go (*v. irr.*) into the country; *essere in* —, to be in the country **2.** (*tenuta*) estate **3.** (*mil.*) campaign **4.** (*villeggiatura*) holidays.

campana *sf.* bell.

campanaro *sm.* bell-ringer.

campanello *sm.* door-bell: — *d'allarme*, alarm-bell.

campanile *sm.* bell-tower.

campanilismo *sm.* parochialism.

campare *vi.* to live.

campeggiatore *sm.* camper.

campeggio *sm.* camping.

campestre *agg.* rural, rustic || *corsa* —, cross-country race.

campionario *sm.* set of samples, sample case || *fiera campionaria*, trade fair.

campionato *sm.* championship.

campione *sm.* **1.** champion **2.** (*comm.*) sample.

campo *sm.* **1.** (*mil.*) field **2.** (*sport*) sport ground || — *da tennis*, tennis court **3.** (*terreno*) field || — *di battaglia*, battle-field.

camuffare *vt.* to disguise.

canadese *agg. e sm.* Canadian.

canaglia *sf.* **1.** rabble **2.** (*di persona malvagia*) rascal.

canale *sm.* **1.** canal **2.** (*braccio di* mare) channel **3.** (*condotto*) pipe **4.** (*tv.*) channel.

cànapa *sf.* hemp.

canarino *sm.* canary.

cancellare *vt.* **1.** (*a penna*) to cross out; (*con una gomma*) to rub out; (*con un panno*) to wipe out **2.** (*fig.*) efface.

cancellatura *sf.* **1.** erasure **2.** (*fig.*) effacement.

cancelleria *sf.* **1.** (*pol.*) chancellery **2.** (*materiale di* —) stationery articles **3.** (*giur.*) record-office.

cancelliere *sm.* **1.** (*pol.*) chancellor **2.** (*giur.*) recorder.

cancello *sm.* gate.

cancrena *sf.* gangrene.

cancro *sm.* cancer.

candeggina *sf.* chloride.

candela *sf.* **1.** candle: — *di sego*, tallow candle; *al lume di* —, by candle-light **2.** (*auto*) sparking plug.

candelabro *sm.* branched candle-stick.

candeliere *sm.* candlestick.

candelotto *sm.* short thick candle: — *fumogeno*, smoke candle.

candidato *sm.* candidate.

candidatura *sf.* candidature.

càndido *agg.* **1.** snow-white **2.** (*innocente*) innocent.

candito *agg.* candied. ◆ **candito** *sm.* sugar candy.

candore *sm.* **1.** whiteness **2.** (*innocenza*) innocence.

cane *sm.* **1.** dog: — *da caccia*, sporting dog; — *pastore*, sheep dog; — *da guardia*, watch-dog **2.** (*persona spietata*) brute **3.** (*di fucile*) cock.

cànfora *sf.* camphor.

canguro *sm.* kangaroo.

canìcola *sf.* the height of summer.

canile *sm.* kennel.

canino *agg.* canine: *dente* —, canine tooth.

canna *sf.* **1.** reed **2.** (*coltivata*) cane || — *da zucchero*, sugar cane **3.** (*tubo*) pipe **4.** (*di arma*) barrel **5.** (*da pesca*) (fishing-)rod.

cannella *sf.* **1.** (*bot.*) cinnamon **2.** (*di botte*) spout.

cannello *sm.* **1.** torch **2.** (*chim.*) pipe.

canneto *sm.* canebrake.

cannibale *sm.* cannibal.

cannocchiale *sm.* binoculars (*pl.*) || — *da campagna*, field glasses; — *da teatro*, opera glasses.

cannone *sm.* 1. gun: — *antiaereo*, anti-aircraft gun; — *anticarro*, anti-tank gun 2. (*fig.*) ace.

cannuccia *sf.* 1. thin cane: — *per sorbire bibite*, straw.

cànone *sm.* canon: — *d'affitto*, rent; — *della radio*, radio-licence fee.

canònica *sf.* rectory.

canònico *agg.* canonical ‖ *diritti canonici*, canon law. ♦ **canònico** *sm.* canon.

canonizzare *vt.* to canonize.

canoro *agg.* singing.

canottaggio *sm.* 1. rowing, boating 2. (*come attività*) boating.

canottiera *sf.* vest.

canotto *sm.* small boat.

canovaccio *sm.* 1. (*per asciugare stoviglie*) dish-cloth; 2. (*per ricamo*) canvas 3. (*trama di un'opera*) plot.

cantante *sm.* singer.

cantare *vt.* 1. to sing (*v. irr.*) 2. (*del gallo*) to crow 3. (*fare la spia*) to squeal.

cantata *sf.* song.

canterellare *vt.* e *vi.* to sing (*v. irr.*) softly, to hum.

càntico *sm.* hymn.

cantiere *sm.* yard.

cantilena *sf.* sing-song.

cantina *sf.* cellar.

cantiniere *sm.* cellarman (*pl.* -men).

cantino *sm.* chanterelle.

canto[1] *sm.* singing.

canto[2] *sm.* (*angolo*) corner ‖ *canto — mio*, for my part; *da un —*, on one hand.

cantonata *sf.* corner: *prendere una —*, to make (*v. irr.*) a blunder.

cantone *sm.* 1. corner 2. (*geogr.*) canton.

cantoniera *sf.* 1. (*mobile*) corner cupboard 2. (*casa*) roadman's house 3. (*ferr.*) signalman's house.

cantoniere *sm.* signalman (*pl.* -men).

canuto *agg.* hoary.

canzonare *vt.* to make (*v. irr.*) fun of.

canzone *sf.* song.

canzonetta *sf.* 1. short song 2. (*poet.*) canzonet.

canzonettista *s.* 1. music-hall singer 2. (*autore di canzoni*) songwriter.

caolino *sm.* kaolin.

caos *sm.* chaos.

capace *agg.* 1. able 2. (*idoneo*) fit 3. (*abile*) clever.

capacità *sf.* 1. ability, cleverness 2. (*capienza*) capacity.

capanna *sf.* hut.

capanno *sm.* 1. (*da caccia*) shooting-box 2. (*per bagnanti*) bathing-box.

caparbieria *sf.* stubbornness.

caparbio *agg.* stubborn.

caparra *sf.* caution-money.

capeggiare *vt.* to lead (*v. irr.*).

capello *sm.* hair (*solo sing.*) ‖ *acconciatura dei capelli*, hairdress; *farsi tagliare i capelli*, to have one's hair cut; *avere un diavolo per —*, to be furious.

capezzale *sm.* bolster.

capèzzolo *sm.* nipple.

capienza *sf.* capacity.

capigliatura *sf.* hair.

capillare *agg.* capillary.

capillarità *sf.* capillarity.

capinera *sf.* blackcap.

capire *vt.* to understand (*v. irr.*).

capitale *sm.* capital. ♦ **capitale** *agg.* 1. (*che riguarda la vita*) capital 2. (*principale*) main.

capitalismo *sm.* capitalism.

capitalista *s.* capitalist.

capitalizzare *vt.* to capitalize. ♦ **capitalizzare** *vi.* (*accumulare denaro*) to save.

capitano *sm.* captain, leader.

capitare *vi.* 1. (*giungere*) to arrive 2. (*accadere*) to happen, to befall (*v. irr.*).

capitello *sm.* (*arch.*) capital.

capitolare *vi.* to capitulate.

capitolare *sm.* capitulary. ♦ **capitolare** *agg.* capitular.

capitolo *sm.* chapter.

capitòmbolo *sm.* tumble.

capo *sm.* 1. head ‖ *avere mal di —*, to have a headache; *senza — né coda*, without rhyme or reason 2. (*estremità*) end ‖ *da un — all'altro*, from end to end; *andare a —*, new line; *in — a un anno*, within a year; *Capo d'Anno*, New Year's day 3. (*geogr.*) cape 4. (*chi comanda*) leader.

capobanda *sm.* 1. (*mus.*) bandmaster 2. (*di una banda di criminali*) ringleader.

capocuoco *sm.* head cook.

capocordata *sm.* first man on the rope.

capodanno *sm.* New Year's day.

capofamiglia *s.* head of a family.

capofila *sm.* file-leader.

capofitto (*nella loc. avv.*) *a* —, headlong || *cadere, tuffarsi a* —, to fall (*v. irr.*), to dive head first.

capogiro *sm.* dizziness.

capolavoro *sm.* masterpiece.

capolinea *sm.* terminus (*pl.* -ni).

capolino *sm.* small head || *far* —, to peep in.

capoluogo *sm.* main town.

caporale *sm.* corporal.

caporedattore *sm.* editor in chief.

caposaldo *sm.* 1. datum point 2. (*mil.*) stronghold 3. (*fondamento*) main point.

caposcuola *sm.* leader of a movement.

capostazione *sm.* station-master.

capotare *vi.* 1. (*di aerei*) to somersault 2. (*di auto*) to turn over.

capoufficio *sm.* head-clerk.

capoverso *sm.* 1. (*in poesia*) beginning of a line 2. (*in prosa*) beginning of a paragraph.

capovòlgere *vt.* to turn upside down. ◆ **capovòlgersi** *vr.* to capsize.

cappa *sf.* 1. (*mantello*) cloak 2. (*di prete*) cape 3. (*fig.*) vault || — *del camino*, chimney.

cappella *sf.* chapel.

cappellano *sm.* chaplain.

cappello *sm.* 1. hat: — *a cilindro*, top-hat; — *di paglia*, straw hat; 2. (*introduzione*) preamble.

càppero *sm.* caper.

cappone *sm.* capon.

cappotto *sm.* 1. coat 2. (*di gioco*) capot.

cappuccino *sm.* 1. (*eccl.*) capuchin 2. (*bevanda*) white coffee.

cappuccio *sm.* hood.

capra *sf.* goat.

capretto *sm.* kid.

capriccio *sm.* whim: *fare i capricci*, to be naughty.

caprino *agg.* goatish.

capriola[1] *sf.* caper: *far capriole*, to cut (*v. irr.*) capers.

capriola[2] *sf.* (*femmina del capriolo*) doe.

capriolo *sm.* roe-deer.

càpsula *sf.* 1. capsule 2. (*di dente*) crown.

captare *vt.* (*radio*) to pick up.

capzioso *agg.* captious.

carabina *sf.* carabine.

carabiniere *sm.* carabineer.

caracollare *vi.* to caracole.

caraffa *sf.* 1. (*per acqua*) carafe 2. (*per vino*) decanter.

caràmbola *sf.* cannon: *far* —, to cannon.

carambolare *vi.* to cannon.

caramella *sf.* sugar-drop, toffee.

caramellare *vt.* to coat with burnt sugar.

caramello *sm.* caramel.

carato *sm.* carat.

caràttere *sm.* 1. character, temper 2. (*caratteristica*) character 3. (*tip.*) type.

caratterista *s.* character actor (actress).

caratterìstico *agg.* characteristic. ◆ **caratterìstica** *sf.* characteristic.

caravella *sf.* caravel.

carbonaio *sm.* coal merchant.

carbone *sm.* coal || — *di legna*, charcoal; — *fossile*, pit coal; *miniera di* —, coal-mine.

carbonerìa *sf.* Carbonarist movement.

carbonìfero *agg.* carboniferous.

carbonio *sm.* carbon.

carbonizzare *vt.* 1. to carbonize 2. (*di legno*) to char.

carburante *sm.* fuel.

carburatore *sm.* carburettor.

carburazione *sf.* carburation.

carcassa *sf.* carcass.

carcerazione *sf.* imprisonment.

càrcere *sm.* prison, jail.

carceriere *sm.* jailer.

carciofo *sm.* artichoke.

cardano *sm.* (*mecc.*) cardan joint.

cardare *vt.* to card.

cardìaco *agg.* cardiac || *disturbi cardiaci*, heart-disease.

cardinale *agg.* e *sm.* cardinal.

càrdine *sm.* 1. hinge, pivot 2. (*fig.*) foundation.

cardiòlogo *sm.* cardiologist.

cardiopatia *sf.* cardiopathy.

cardo *sm.* 1. (*bot.*) thistle 2. (*cuc.*) cardoon 3. (*mecc.*) carding machine.

carena *sf.* 1. (*mar.*) keel 2. (*aer.*) hull 3. (*zool.*) carina (*pl.* -nae).

carenza *sf.* want, lack.

carestìa *sf.* famine.

carezza *sf.* caress.

carezzare *vt.* to caress.

carezzévole *agg.* caressing.

cariàtide *sf.* caryatid.

cariato *agg.* decayed.

càrica *sf.* 1. (*pubblico ufficio*) office: *entrare in* —, to take (*v.*

irr.) office **2.** (*mil.*) charge **3.** (*di arma da fuoco; elettr.*) charge **4.** (*di orologio*) winding up.

caricare *vt.* **1.** to load **2.** (*mil.; elettr.*) to charge **3.** (*di orologio*) to wind (*v. irr.*) up.

caricatore *sm.* **1.** loader **2.** (*di arma*) magazine.

caricatura *sf.* caricature.

càrico[1] *agg.* **1.** loaded, laden (*anche fig.*) **2.** (*di caffè*) strong **3.** (*elettr.*) charged.

càrico[2] *sm.* **1.** (*di nave*) freight; (*di veicolo*) load; (*di animale da soma*) burden **2.** (*fig.*) load, weight **3.** (*accusa*) charge || (*comm.*) *essere a — di qu.*, to be charged to so.

carie *sf.* decay.

carino *agg.* pretty, nice.

carità *sf.* **1.** (*amore; teol.*) charity **2.** (*elemosina*) alms.

carlinga *sf.* cockpit.

carlona (*nella loc. avv.*) *alla —*, carelessly.

carminio *agg.* carmine.

carnagione *sf.* complexion.

carnale *agg.* carnal.

carne *sf.* **1.** flesh **2.** (*come alimento*) meat || *— di manzo*, beef; *— di vitello*, veal; *— in scatola*, tinned meat; *— congelata*, frozen meat.

carnéfice *sm.* executioner.

carneficina *sf.* slaughter.

carnevale *sm.* carnival.

carnivoro *agg.* carnivorous.

caro *agg.* **1.** dear **2.** (*costoso*) dear, expensive.

carogna *sf.* carrion.

carosello *sm.* carousel.

carota *sf.* carrot.

caròtide *sf.* carotid.

carovana *sf.* caravan.

carovita *sm.* high cost of living.

carpa *sf.* carp.

carpentiere *sm.* carpenter.

carpire *vt.* **1.** to snatch **2.** (*con astuzia*) to swindle.

carponi *avv.* on all fours.

carràbile *agg.* cart: *passo —*, driveway.

carreggiata **1.** (*solco*) track **2.** (*strada*) cartway.

carrellata *sf.* dolly shot.

carrello *sm.* **1.** (*ferr.*) wag(g)on **2.** (*aer.*) landing gear **3.** (*cine; tv.*) dolly **4.** (*di macchina per scrivere*)

carriage.

carriera *sf.* career || *di gran —*, at full speed.

carriola *sf.* wheelbarrow.

carrista *sm.* (*mil.*) tankman (*pl. -men*).

carro *sm.* **1.** (*a due ruote*) cart **2.** (*a quattro ruote*) wag(g)on || *— armato*, tank.

carrozza *sf.* carriage: *— diretta*, through coach; *— viaggiatori*, passenger car.

carrozzàbile *agg.* practicable.

carrozzella *sf.* **1.** cab **2.** (*per bambini*) perambulator; (*fam.*) pram.

carrozzeria *sf.* body.

carrozziere *sm.* body-maker.

carrozzone *sm.* **1.** lumbering coach **2.** (*di zingari*) caravan.

carruba *sf.*, **carrubo** *sm.* carob.

carrùcola *sf.* pulley.

carta *sf.* paper: *— da lettere*, writing-paper; *— carbone*, carbon paper; *— d'identità*, identity card; *— stradale*, road-map.

cartaio *sm.* paper-maker.

cartamodello *sm.* dressmaker's pattern.

cartamoneta *sf.* paper-money.

cartapesta *sf.* paper-pulp.

cartavetrata *sf.* sand-paper.

carteggio *sm.* correspondence **2.** (*collezione di lettere*) collection of letters.

cartella *sf.* **1.** (*da scuola*) satchel **2.** (*di cuoio*) brief-case.

cartello *sm.* **1.** bill **2.** (*pubblicitario*) poster **3.** (*stradale*) traffic sign **4.** (*econ.*) cartel.

cartellone *sm.* **1.** (*pubblicitario*) poster **2.** (*teat.*) bill.

cartellonista *sm.* commercial artist.

cartiera *sf.* paper-mill.

cartilàgine *sf.* cartilage.

cartoccio *sm.* paper-bag.

cartografia *sf.* cartography.

cartoleria *sf.* stationer's shop.

cartolina *sf.* postcard: *— illustrata*, picture postcard.

cartoncino *sm.* thin card.

cartone *sm.* cardboard || *cartoni animati*, cartoons.

cartuccia *sf.* cartridge || *mezza —* (*fig.*), shrimp.

casa *sf.* **1.** (*abitazione*) house **2.** (*ambiente familiare*) home || *amico di —*, family friend; *donna di —*, housewife; *nostalgia di —*, home-sickness; *andare a* —, to go (*v. irr.*) home; *restare a* —, to stay at home; *essere in* —, to be in 3. (*stirpe*) house, dynasty, family.

casacca *sf.* coat.

casaccio (*nella loc. avv.*) *a* —, at random.

casalinga *sf.* housewife.

casalingo *agg.* homely; *cucina casalinga*, plain cooking.

casato *sm.* 1. (*cognome*) surname 2. (*origine, nascita*) birth.

cascame *sm.* waste.

cascamorto *sm.* spoon: *fare il* —, to run (*v. irr.*) after.

cascante *agg.* 1. (*debole*) weak 2. (*floscio*) flabby (*anche fig.*).

cascare *vi.* 1. to fall (*v. irr.*) 2. (*con rumore*) to crash ‖ — *dalle nuvole*, to be struck with amazement; — *dal sonno*, to be overcome with sleep.

cascata *sf.* 1. (*caduta*) fall 2. (*d'acqua*) waterfall 3. (*fig.*) cascade.

cascina *sf.* 1. dairy farm 2. (*cascinale*) farmstead.

casco *sm.* 1. helmet 2. (*per asciugare i capelli*) dryer.

casella *sf.*: — *postale*, post-box.

casellante *sm.* 1. (*ferr.*) signalman (*pl.* -men) 2. (*di passaggio a livello*) crossing keeper.

casellario *sm.* 1. set of pigeon-holes 2. (*giur.*) — *penale*, records-office.

casereccio *agg.* homely: *pane* —, home-made bread.

caserma *sf.* barracks (*pl.*).

caso *sm.* 1. chance 2. (*fatto*) case 3. (*possibilità*) way, possibility ‖ *a* —, at random; *per* —, by chance.

càspita *inter.* good gracious!

cassa *sf.* 1. case, box 2. (*comm.*) cash ‖ *libro di* —, cash-book; *pagamento per* —, cash-payment; *sportello di* —, cashier's window 3. (*mus.*) case ‖ *gran* —, bass-drum.

cassaforte *sf.* safe.

cassapanca *sf.* chest.

cassazione *sf.* (*giur.*) cassation.

casseruola *sf.* saucepan.

cassetto *sm.* drawer.

cassettone *sm.* chest of drawers.

cassiere *sm.* cashier.

casta *sf.* caste.

castagna *sf.* chestnut.

castagnaccio *sm.* chestnut-tart.

castagno *sm.* chestnut-tree.

castano *agg.* nut-brown.

castellano *sm.* lord of a castle.

castello *sm.* castle.

castigare *vt.* to punish.

castigatezza *sf.* moderation.

castigato *agg.* 1. (*casto*) chaste 2. (*emendato*) castigated.

castigo *sm.* punishment.

castità *sf.* chastity.

casto *agg.* chaste.

castoro *sm.* beaver.

castrare *vt.* to castrate.

castrato *sm.* (*cuc.*) mutton.

castroneria *sf.* stupidity.

casuale *agg.* casual.

casualità *sf.* casualness.

cataclisma *sm.* cataclysm (*anche fig.*).

catacomba *sf.* catacomb.

catafalco *sm.* catafalque.

catafascio (*nella loc. avv.*) *andare a* —, to go (*v. irr.*) to rack and ruin; *a* —, topsyturvy.

catalessi *sf.* catalepsy.

catalizzatore *sm.* catalyst.

catalogare *vt.* to catalogue.

catàlogo *sm.* catalogue.

catapecchia *sf.* hovel.

catapulta *sf.* catapult.

catarifrangente *sm.* reflector.

catarro *sm.* catarrh.

catarsi *sf.* catharsis.

catasta *sf.* pile, heap.

catasto *sm.* cadastre.

catàstrofe *sf.* catastrophe.

catastròfico *agg.* catastrophic(al).

catechismo *sm.* catechism.

catechizzare *vt.* 1. to catechize 2. (*fig.*) to persuade.

catecùmeno *sm.* catechumen.

categorìa *sf.* category, class.

categòrico *agg.* categorical, absolute.

catena *sf.* 1. chain 2. (*fig.*) bond.

catenaccio *sm.* bolt.

cateratta *sf.* cataract.

caterva *sf.* 1. (*di persone*) crowd 2. (*di cose*) great quantity.

catino *sm.* basin.

catione *sm.* (*fis.*) cation.

càtodo *sm.* cathode.

catramare *vt.* to tar.

catrame *sm.* tar.

càttedra *sf.* 1. desk 2. (*l'ufficio dell'insegnare*) teaching post 3. (*di università*) chair.

cattedrale *sf.* cathedral.

cattiveria *sf.* wickedness.

cattività *sf.* captivity.

cattivo *agg.* e *sm.* bad || — *scritto-re*, poor writer.

cattolicésimo *sm.* catholicism.

cattòlico *agg.* catholic.

cattura *sf.* **1.** capture **2.** (*arresto*) arrest: *mandato di* —, warrant of arrest.

catturare *vt.* **1.** to capture **2.** (*arrestare*) to arrest.

caucciù *sm.* india-rubber.

càusa *sf.* **1.** cause **2.** (*giur.*) law suit || *far — a qu.*, to sue so. (for).

causare *vt.* to cause.

càustico *agg.* caustic (*anche fig.*)

cautèla *sf.* caution.

cautelare *vt.* to protect. ♦ **cautelarsi** *vr.* to take (*v. irr.*) precautions.

cauterizzare *vt.* to cauterize.

càuto *agg.* cautious, prudent.

cauzione *sf.* **1.** guarantee **2.** (*per essere rilasciato dalla polizia*) bail.

cava *sf.* quarry.

cavalcare *vt.* to ride (*v. irr.*). ♦ **cavalcare** *vi.* to ride on horseback.

cavalcavìa *sm.* fly-over bridge.

cavalcioni (a) *loc. avv.* astride.

cavaliere *sm.* **1.** rider **2.** (*di ordine cavalleresco*) knight.

cavalla *sf.* mare.

cavalleresco *agg.* knightly.

cavallerìa *sf.* **1.** (*mil.*) cavalry **2.** (*stor.*) chivalry.

cavalletta *sf.* grasshopper.

cavalletto *sm.* **1.** trestle **2.** (*foto*) tripod **3.** (*per pittori*) easel.

cavallo *sm.* **1.** horse: — *da corsa*, racehorse; — *a dondolo*, rocking-horse; — *da soma*, pack-horse; *ferro di* —, horse-shoe **2.** (*ginnastica*) vaulting-horse **3.** (*cavallo vapore*) horse-power (*abbr.* H.P.).

cavallone *sm.* (*maroso*) billow.

cavare *vt.* to take (*v. irr.*) off || — *un dente*, to pull out a tooth || *cavarsela*, to get (*v. irr.*) off.

cavatappi, **cavatùraccioli** *sm.* cork-screw.

caverna *sf.* cave.

cavernoso *agg.* cavernous || *voce cavernosa*, very deep voice.

cavezza *sf.* halter.

cavia *sf.* cavy.

caviale *sm.* caviar.

caviglia *sf.* ankle.

cavillare *vi.* to cavil (at).

cavillo *sm.* cavil.

cavità *sf.* cavity.

cavo *agg.* hollow, empty. ♦ **cavo** *sm.* cable, rope.

cavolfiore *sm.* cauliflower.

càvolo *sm.* cabbage.

cazzotto *sm.* punch || *fare a cazzotti*, to come (*v. irr.*) to blows.

cazzuola *sf.* trowel.

cece *sm.* chick-pea.

cecità *sf.* blindness (*anche fig.*).

cecoslovacco *agg.* e *sm.* Czechoslovak

cèdere *vt.* e *vi.* **1.** (*dare*) to give (*v. irr.*) **2.** (*trasferire*) to hand over **3.** (*vendere*) to dispose of. ♦ **cedere** *vi.* **1.** to surrender **2.** (*venir meno*) to subside **3.** (*essere inferiore*) to be second to.

cedimento *sm.* **1.** yielding **2.** (*fig.*) giving up.

cèdola *sf.* coupon.

cedrata *sf.* citron syrup.

cedrina *sf.* lemon-scented verbena.

cedro *sm.* **1.** citron-tree **2.** (*frutto*) citron.

cedrone *agg.* e *sm.* (*gallo*) capercaillie.

cefalea *sf.* cephalea.

cefalgìa *sf.* cephalalgy.

ceffone *sm.* slap in the face.

celare *vt.* to conceal, to hide (*v. irr.*).

celebrare *vt.* to celebrate || — *un anniversario*, to keep (*v. irr.*) an anniversary.

celebrazione *sf.* celebration.

cèlebre *agg.* celebrated.

celebrità *sf.* celebrity.

cèlere *agg.* quick, swift.

celerità *sf.* quickness.

celeste *agg.* **1.** light-blue **2.** (*del cielo*) heavenly.

celia *sf.* jest.

celiare *vi.* to jest.

celibato *sm.* bachelorhood.

cèlibe *agg.* e *sm.* single. ♦ **cèlibe** *sm.* bachelor.

cella *sf.* cell.

cèllula *sf.* cell.

cellulare *agg.* cellular || *segregazione* —, close confinement.

cellulite *sf.* cellulitis.

cellulòide *sf.* celluloid.

cellulosa *sf.* cellulose.

celta *sm.* Celt.

cèltico *agg.* Celtic.

cémbalo *sm.* **1.** (*tamburello*) tambourine **2.** (*spinetta*) spinet.

cementare *vt.* to cement (*anche fig.*).

cementazione *sf.* cementation.
cementificio *sm.* cement-factory.
cemento *sm.* cement: — *armato*, reinforced concrete.
cena *sf.* **1.** (*pasto serale leggero*) supper **2.** (*pranzo*) dinner ‖ *far* —, to have supper
cenàcolo *sm.* **1.** supper-room **2.** (*di artisti*) artistic coterie ‖ *il — di Leonardo da Vinci*, Leonardo's Last Supper.
cenare *vi.* to have (*v. irr.*) supper.
cenciaio *sm.* ragman (*pl.* -men).
cencio *sm.* **1.** rag **2.** (*vestito logoro*) tatters (*pl.*).
cencioso *agg.* ragged, tattered.
cénere *sf.* ash (*general. al pl.*).
cenno *sm.* **1.** (*segno*) sign **2.** (*allusione*) hint **3.** (*breve notizia*) notice ‖ *fare un — col capo*, to nod ‖ *a un vostro* — (*comm.*), on hearing from you.
cenobio *sm.* coenobium (*pl.* -ia).
cenone *sm.* **1.** (*di Natale*) Christmas eve dinner **2.** (*di Capodanno*) New Year's eve dinner.
censimento *sm.* census.
censire *vt.* **1.** to take (*v. irr.*) a census of **2.** (*di proprietà*) to assess.
censo *sm.* **1.** (*stor.*) census **2.** (*ricchezza*) wealth.
censore *sm.* **1.** censor **2.** (*fig.*) critic.
censorio *agg.* censorial.
censura *sf.* **1.** (*ufficio di censore*) censorship **2.** (*azione di censura*) censure.
censurare *vt.* **1.** to censor **2.** (*fig.*) to censure.
centàuro *sm.* **1.** centaur **2.** (*fig., motociclista*) motorcyclist.
centellinare *vt.* to sip.
centenario *agg. e sm.* **1.** centennial **2.** (*di persona*) centenarian. ◆ **centenario** *sm.* (*commemorazione*) centenary.
centesimale *agg.* centesimal.
centèsimo *agg.* (the) hundredth. ◆ **centèsimo** *sm.* **1.** (one) hundredth (of sthg.) **2.** (*di dollaro*) cent **3.** (*di franco*) centime ‖ *non avere un* —, to be penniless.
centigrado *agg.* centigrade.
centigrammo *sm.* centigramme.
centilitro *sm.* centilitre.
centimetro *sm.* centimetre.
centinaio *sm.* hundred.
cento *agg. e num. card.* hundred ‖ — *di questi giorni*, many happy

returns of the day.
centrale *agg.* central. ◆ **centrale** *sf.* **1.** — *elettrica*, power station **2.** — *telefonica*, exchange.
centralinista *s.* operator.
centralino *sm.* telephone exchange.
centralismo *sm.* centralism.
centrare *vt.* to hit (*v. irr.*) the centre.
centrìfuga *sf.* centrifuge.
centrìfugo *agg.* centrifugal.
centrino *sm.* doily.
centrìpeto *agg.* centripetal.
centrismo *sm.* centrism.
centro *sm.* **1.** centre **2.** (*istituto*) institute.
centuplicare *vt.* **1.** to centuplicate **2.** (*fig.*) to increase.
cèntuplo *agg. e sm.* centuple.
centuria *sf.* (*stor.*) century.
centurione *sm.* (*stor.*) centurion.
ceppo *sm.* **1.** stump **2.** (*fig.*) stock.
cera *sf.* **1.** wax **2.** (*aspetto*) look ‖ *avere bella* —, to look well.
ceralacca *sf.* sealing-wax.
ceràmica *sf.* **1.** (*arte*) ceramics **2.** (*pezzo*) piece of pottery.
ceramista *sm.* ceramist.
cerato *agg.* waxed ‖ *tela cerata*, wax-cloth.
cerbiatto *sm.* fawn.
cerbottana *sf.* **1.** blowgun **2.** (*giocattolo*) pea-shooter.
cercare *vt.* **1.** to look for **2.** (*per consultazione*) to look up **3.** (*a tentoni*) to fumble for **4.** (*chiedere*) to ask (for). ◆ **cercare** *vi.* to try.
cercatore *sm.* seeker: — *d'oro*, gold-digger; (*amer.*) prospector.
cerchia *sf.* circle.
cerchiare *vt.* to hoop.
cerchiatura *sf.* hooping.
cerchietto *sm.* **1.** small ring **2.** (*gioco*) quoit.
cerchio *sm.* **1.** circle **2.** (*gioco*) hoop.
cerchione *sm.* rim.
cereale *sm.* cereals (*pl.*).
cerebrale *agg.* cerebral.
cèreo *agg.* waxen.
ceretta *sf.* **1.** boot polish **2.** (*per depilare*) wax.
cerimonia *sf.* **1.** ceremony **2.** (*pompa*) pomp.
cerimoniale *sm.* ceremonial.
cerimoniere *sm.* Master of Ceremonies.
cerimonioso *agg.* ceremonious
cerino *sm.* match.

cerniera *sf.* **1.** (*di occhiali, porte, finestre*) hinge **2.** (*di borsetta*) clasp **3.** (*lampo*) zipper.

cèrnita *sf.* choice, selection.

cero *sm.* large candle.

cerone *sm.* make-up.

cerotto *sm.* plaster.

certamente *avv.* certainly, undoubtedly.

certezza *sf.* certainty.

certificare *vt.* to certify, to attest.

certificato *sm.* certificate.

certo[1] *agg. indef.* **1.** certain: *un — Mr. Smith,* a (certain) Mr. Smith **2.** (*qualche*) some: *certe persone lo riconobbero,* some people recognized him; *dopo un — tempo,* after some time **3.** (*tale, di tal genere*) such. ♦ **certi** *pron. indef. pl.* some people.

certo[2] *agg.* certain. ♦ **certo** *avv.* certainly.

certuni *pron. indef.* some.

cerùleo *agg.* sky-blue.

cerva *sf.* (*zool.*) hind.

cervella *sf.* brain.

cervelletto *sm.* cerebellum.

cervello *sm.* **1.** brain **2.** (*intelligenza, mente*) understanding, mind.

cervellòtico *agg.* far-fetched.

cervicale *agg.* cervical.

cervice *sf.* nape.

cèrvidi *sm. pl.* cervidae.

cervo *sm.* deer (*inv. al pl.*).

cesàreo *agg.* Caesarean ‖ *taglio* —, Caesarean operation.

cesarismo *sm.* Caesarism.

cesellare *vt.* to chisel (*anche fig.*).

cesellatura *sf.* chisel work.

cesello *sm.* chisel.

cesola *sf.* shears (*pl.*).

cespuglio *sm.* bush, thicket.

cespuglioso *agg.* bushy.

cessare *vt. e vi.* to cease, to stop.

cessazione *sf.* cessation.

cessione *sf.* transfer.

cesso *sm.* lavatory.

cesta *sf.* basket.

cestaio *sm.* **1.** basket-maker **2.** (*chi vende*) basket-vendor.

cestinare *vt.* (*fig.*) to refuse.

cestino *sm.* small basket: *— da lavoro,* work-basket; *— da viaggio,* luncheon-basket; *— per la carta straccia,* waste-paper basket.

cesto *sm.* (*sport*) basket.

cesura *sf.* caesura.

cetàceo *agg. e sm.* cetacean.

ceto *sm.* class, rank.

cetra *sf.* cithern, lyre.

cetriolino *sm.* gherkin.

cetriolo *sm.* cucumber.

che[1] *pron. rel.* **1.** (*sogg., riferito a persone*) who, that: *l'uomo — mi parlò,* the man who (that) spoke to me **2.** (*sogg., riferito a cose e animali*) which, that: *ecco il cane — mi ju regalato,* here is the dog which (that) was given to me **3.** (*ogg., riferito a persone*) whom: *è la ragazza più graziosa — abbia mai incontrato,* she is the prettiest girl whom I ever met **4.** (*ogg., riferito a cose e animali*) which: *questo è il libro — le darò,* this is the book which I shall give her **5.** *il —,* which **6.** (*riferito a tempo*) when.

che[2] *agg. int.* what: *— musica preferisci?,* what music do you prefer? **2.** which: *— libro scegli?,* which book do you choose? ♦ **che** *pron. int.* what: *— è questo?,* what is this? ♦ **che** *agg. escl.* what, what a. ♦ **che** *pron. ind.* something.

che[3] *cong.* **1.** that **2.** (*comparativo*) than: *è più bella che intelligente,* she is more beautiful than intelligent **3.** (*correlativo*) whether: *— tu venga o no,* whether you come or not. ♦ **che** *inter.* what!

checché *pron. indef.* whatever.

checchessia *pron. indef.* anything.

chepì *sm.* (*mil.*) shako.

cherosene *sm.* kerosene.

cherubino *sm.* cherub.

chetamente *avv.* quietly, secretly.

chetare *vt.* to quiet. ♦ **chetarsi** *vr.* to quiet down.

chetichella (*nella loc. avv.*) *alla* —, on the sly, secretly.

cheto *agg.* quiet.

chi *pron. rel.* **1.** (*colui che*) he (*ogg.* him) who (*ogg.* whom) **2.** (*colei che*) she (*ogg.* her) who (*ogg.* whom) **3.** (*coloro che*) they (*ogg.* them) who (*ogg.* whom) **4.** (*gen.*) those, the person who(m). ♦ **chi** *pron. indef.* **1.** whoever, anyone **2.** (*qualcuno che*) someone who. ♦ **chi** *pron. int.* **1.** (*sogg.*) who **2.** (*ogg.*) whom **3.** which: *— di voi?,* which of you? **4.** (*specificazione poss.*) whose: *di — è questa casa?,* whose house is this?

chiàcchiera *sf.* chatter.

chiacchierare *vi.* to chat.

chiacchierata *sf.* chat.

chiacchierone *sm.* chatterbox.

chiamare *vt.* to call || *mandare a —*, to send (*v. irr.*) for; *— al telefono*, to call up. ♦ **chiamarsi** *vr.* to be called || *come ti chiami?*, what's your name?

chiamata *sf.* call, appeal.

chiara *sf. — d'uovo*, white (of an egg).

chiaretto *sm.* (*vino*) claret.

chiarezza *sf.* 1. clearness 2. (*fig.*) evidence.

chiarificare *vt.* to clarify.

chiarificazione *sf.* 1. clarification 2. (*fig.*) frank explanation.

chiarimento *sm.* explanation.

chiarire *vt.* 1. to clarify, to clear up 2. (*spiegare*) to explain.

chiaro *agg.* 1. clear, evident 2. (*di luce*) light.

chiarore *sm.* 1. light 2. (*luce tenue*) faint light.

chiaroscuro *sm.* light and shade.

chiaroveggente *agg.* 1. clear--sighted 2. (*che ha facoltà divinatorie*) clairvoyant.

chiassata *sf.* row.

chiasso *sm.* noise, uproar.

chiassone *sm.* noisy person.

chiassoso *agg.* 1. noisy 2. (*fig.*) showy.

chiatta *sf.* barge.

chiavarda *sf.* bolt.

chiave *sf.* 1. key 2. (*mus.*) clef.

chiavistello *sm.* latch, bolt.

chiazza *sf.* spot, stain.

chicchessìa *pron. indef.* anyone.

chicco *sm.* 1. grain 2. (*di grandine*) hailstone 3. (*di caffè*) coffee-bean 4. (*di uva*) grape.

chièdere *vt.* 1. to ask: — *qc. a qu.*, (*per sapere*) to ask so. sthg., (*per avere*) to ask so. for sthg. 2. (*riferito a un prezzo*) to charge.

chierichetto *sm.* altar boy.

chiesa *sf.* church.

chiglia *sf.* (*mar.*) keel.

chilo[1] *sm.* (*med.*) chyle || *fare il —*, to take (*v. irr.*) a nap.

chilo[2] *sm.* kilo.

chilogrammo *sm.* kilogram.

chilometraggio *sm.* distance in kilometres.

chilòmetro *sm.* kilometre.

chilowatt *sm.* kilowatt.

chimera *sf.* chimera.

chimica *sf.* chemistry.

chìmico *agg.* chemical. ♦ **chìmico**

sm. chemist.

china *sf.* slope.

chinare *vt.* to bend (*v. irr.*), to bow. ♦ **chinarsi** *vr.* to bend (*v. irr.*) down.

chincaglierìa *sf.* 1. small fancy articles (*pl.*) 2. (*negozio*) fancy goods shop.

chinino *sm.* quinine.

chioccia *sf.* brooding-hen.

chiòcciola *sf.* snail || *scala a —*, spiral staircase.

chiodato *agg.* nailed.

chiodo *sm.* 1. nail 2. (*fig.*) fixed idea.

chioma *sf.* hair.

chiosco *sm.* 1. kiosk 2. (*per giornali, frutta e verdura*) stand.

chiostro *sm.* cloister.

chiromante *s.* chiromancer.

chiromanzìa *sf.* chiromancy.

chirurgìa *sf.* surgery.

chirurgo *sm.* surgeon.

chissà *inter.* goodness knows.

chitarra *sf.* guitar.

chiùdere *vt.* 1. to shut (*v. irr.*) || *— a chiave*, to lock 2. (*terminare*) to close 3. (*rinchiudere*) to shut (*v. irr.*) up.

chiunque *pron.* 1. (*sogg.*) anyone who, whoever 2. (*ogg.*) whomever, anyone 3. (*specificazione possessiva*) *di —*, whoever.

chiuso *agg.* closed, shut || *— a chiave*, locked.

chiusura *sf.* closing.

ci *pron.* 1. (*ogg.*) us: *essi — amano*, they love us 2. (*riflessivo*) ourselves: *noi — laviamo*, we wash ourselves 3. (*rec. fra due persone*) each other: *mia madre ed io — guardammo*, my mother and I looked at each other 4. (*rec. fra più persone*) one another 5. (*dimostrativo*) this, that, it: *non badarci*, pay no attention to it. ♦ **ci** *avv. di luogo* there (*là*), here (*qui*).

ciabatta *sf.* slipper.

ciambella *sf.* ring-shaped cake.

ciambellano *sm.* chamberlain.

ciancia *sf.* idle talk || *ciance!*, nonsense!

cianciare *vi.* to chatter.

cianografìa *sf.* blueprint.

cianuro *sm.* cyanide.

ciao *inter.* 1. (*incontrandosi*) hullo 2. (*congedandosi*) bye-bye.

ciarla *sf.* 1. loquacity 2. (*notizia*

falsa) false report.

ciarlare *vi.* to talk idly.

ciarlatano *sm.* charlatan.

ciascuno *agg.* every. ♦ **ciascuno** *pron.* 1. (*con valore distributivo*) each 2. (*tutti*) everybody, everyone.

cibernètica *sf.* cybernetics.

cibo *sm.* food.

ciborio *sm.* ciborium (*pl. -ia*).

cicala *sf.* cicada.

cicatrice *sf.* scar.

cicatrizzare *vt.* to cicatrize, to heal. ♦ **cicatrizzarsi** *vr.* to cicatrize, to heal.

cicerone *sm.* guide.

ciclamino *sm.* cyclamen.

cìclico *agg.* cyclic.

ciclismo *sm.* cycling.

ciclista *s.* cyclist.

ciclo *sm.* 1. cycle 2. (*di malattia*) course.

ciclone *sm.* hurricane.

ciclòpico *agg.* Cyclopean.

ciclostilare *vt.* to mimeograph.

ciclostile *sm.* cyclostyle.

ciclotrone *sm.* cyclotron.

cicogna *sf.* stork.

cicuta *sf.* hemlock.

cieco *agg.* blind (*anche fig.*). ♦ **cieco** *sm.* blind man.

cielo *sm.* 1. sky 2. (*aria*) air 3. (*paradiso*) Heaven.

cifra *sf.* 1. figure, number 2. (*segno di cifrario*) cipher.

cifrare *vt.* 1. to cipher 2. (*ricamare in cifra*) to mark.

ciglio *sm.* 1. eyelash 2. (*bordo*) edge.

cigno *sm.* swan.

cilecca *sf.* failure || *far —,* to miss fire, (*fig.*) to fail.

cileno *agg.* Chilean.

cilicio *sm.* 1. hairshirt 2. (*relig.*) cilice.

ciliegia *sf.* cherry.

ciliegio *sm.* cherry-tree.

cilindrata *sf.* (*auto*) displacement.

cilindro *sm.* 1. (*geom.; auto*) cylinder 2. (*cappello*) top-hat.

cima *sf.* 1. top, summit: *in —,* at the top 2. (*fig.*) genius.

cimbali *sm. pl.* *essere in —,* to be tipsy.

cimentare *vt.* to put (*v. irr.*) to the test. ♦ **cimentarsi** *vr.* to venture upon.

cimitero *sm.* cemetery, graveyard.

cinabro *sm.* cinnabar.

cincillà *sf.* chinchilla.

cineasta *sm.* cinematographer.

cinecàmera *sf.* cine-camera.

cinedilettante *sm.* film-amateur.

cinegiornale *sm.* news-reel.

cinema *sm.* 1. cinema, pictures (*pl.*) 2. (*locale*) cinema 3. (*amer.*) movies (*pl.*).

cinemàtica *sf.* kinematics.

cinematografìa *sf.* cinematography.

cinematògrafo *sm.* cinema.

cinèreo *agg.* cinereous, ashen-grey.

cinese *agg. e sm.* Chinese.

cineteca *sf.* film library.

cinètica *sf.* kinetics.

cingere *vt.* 1. to engird 2. (*circondare*) to surround.

cinghia *sf.* 1. strap 2. (*mecc.*) belt.

cinghiale *sm.* (*zool.*) wild boar.

cìnico *agg.* cynical. ♦ **cìnico** *sm.* cynic.

cinismo *sm.* cynicism.

cinocèfalo *sm.* cynocephalus (*pl. -ali*).

cinòdromo *sm.* greyhound racing--track.

cinofilìa *sf.* dog-love.

cinquanta *agg.* fifty.

cinquantenario *sm.* fiftieth anniversary.

cinque *agg.* five.

cinquecento *agg.* five hundred.

cinta *sf.* town-walls (*pl.*): *muro di —,* boundary walls.

cinto *sm.* belt. ♦ **cinto** *agg.* surrounded.

cìntola *sf.* waist: *dalla — in giù,* below the waist; *dalla — in su,* above the waist.

cintura *sf.* belt.

cinturone *sm.* belt.

ciò *pron.* that, this, it.

ciocca *sf.* (*di capelli*) lock.

cioccolata *sf.* chocolate.

cioccolatino *sm.* chocolate.

cioccolato *sm.* chocolate.

cioè *cong.* that is.

ciondolare *vi.* 1. to dangle 2. (*fig.*) to lounge.

ciòndolo *sm.* pendant.

ciondoloni *avv.* dangling.

ciòtola *sf.* cup, bowl.

ciòttolo *sm.* pebble.

cipolla *sf.* onion.

cipresso *sm.* cypress.

cipria *sf.* powder: *piumino per —,* powder puff.

circa *prep. e avv.* about, nearly || *— a,* as to.

circo *sm.* circus.

circolante *agg.* circulating: *moneta* —, currency.

circolare¹ *agg.* circular. ♦ **circolare** *sf.* circular letter.

circolare² *vi.* to circulate.

circolatorio *agg.* circulatory.

circolazione *sf.* **1.** circulation **2.** (*traffico*) traffic **3.** (*comm.*) currency.

circolo *sm.* **1.** circle **2.** (*associazione*) club.

circoncidere *vt.* to circumcise.

circoncisione *sf.* circumcision.

circondare *vt.* to surround (*anche fig.*).

circonferenza *sf.* circumference.

circonflesso *agg.* circumflex.

circonlocuzione *sf.* circumlocution.

circonvallazione *sf.* ring-road.

circonvenire *vt.* to circumvent.

circonvoluzione *sf.* circumvolution.

circoscrivere *vt.* to circumscribe.

circoscrizione *sf.* **1.** circumscription **2.** (*territorio*) area.

circospetto *agg.* circumspect.

circospezione *sf.* circumspection.

circostante *agg.* **1.** surrounding **2.** (*attr.*) neighbouring.

circostanza *sf.* circumstance, occasion: *in queste circostanze*, under these circumstances; *in quella* —, on that occasion.

circostanziale *agg.* circumstantial.

circostanziare *vt.* to detail.

circuire *vt.* **1.** to surround **2.** (*fig.*) to circumvent.

circuito *sm.* circuit.

cirillico *agg.* cyrillic.

cirrosi *sf.* cirrhosis.

cisalpino *agg.* cisalpine.

cisposo *agg.* blear.

ciste *sf.* cyst.

cisterna *sf.* **1.** cistern **2.** (*serbatoio*) tank.

cistifellea *sf.* gall-bladder.

cistite *sf.* cystitis.

citare *vt.* **1.** (*menzionare*) to mention **2.** (*da un libro o da un discorso ecc.*) to quote **3.** (*giur.*) to summon.

citazione *sf.* **1.** (*da un discorso, un libro ecc.*) quotation **2.** (*giur.*) summons (*pl.*).

citòfono *sm.* interphone.

citologìa *sf.* (*biol.*) cytology.

citrato *sm.* citrate.

cìtrico *agg.* citric.

città *sf.* **1.** town: — *di provincia*, country town; — *natale*, home town; *gente di* —, townspeople; *vita di* —, town life **2.** (*metropoli*) city.

cittadella *sf.* **1.** citadel **2.** (*baluardo*) stronghold.

cittadina *sf.* **1.** small town **2.** (*donna che abita in città*) woman citizen.

cittadinanza *sf.* **1.** (*abitanti*) people of the city **2.** (*nazionalità*) citizenship: *diritto di* —, right of citizenship.

cittadino *sm.* **1.** (*che abita in città*) town-dweller **2.** (*che appartiene a uno stato*) citizen. ♦ **cittadino** *agg.* town.

ciuffo *sm.* **1.** forelock **2.** (*di penne, peli, erba*) tuft.

ciurma *sf.* crew.

civetta *sf.* **1.** owl **2.** (*fig.*) coquette.

civetterìa *sf.* coquetry.

cìvico *agg.* civic.

civile *agg.* **1.** civil **2.** (*che riguarda la civiltà*) civilized **3.** (*gentile*) polite **4.** (*non ecclesiastico o non militare*) civilian.

civilizzare *vt.* to civilize.

civilizzazione *sf.* civilization.

civiltà *sf.* **1.** civilization **2.** (*cortesia*) politeness.

civismo *sm.* civic virtues (*pl.*).

clamore *sm.* uproar.

clamoroso *agg.* noisy.

clandestino *agg.* clandestine, secret.

clarinetto, clarino *sm.* clarinet.

classe *sf.* class || *di* — (*qualità*), first-rate.

classicismo *sm.* classicism.

clàssico *agg.* classical. ♦ **clàssico** *sm.* classic.

classìfica *sf.* **1.** classification **2.** (*sport*) position.

classificare *vt.* to classify.

classificazione *sf.* classification.

claudicare *vi.* to limp.

clàusola *sf.* **1.** clause **2.** (*riserva*) reserve.

claustrofobìa *sf.* claustrophobia.

clava *sf.* club.

clavicémbalo *sm.* harpsichord.

clavìcola *sf.* collar-bone.

clemente *agg.* clement, mild.

clemenza *sf.* clemency, mildness.

cleptòmane *agg. e sm.* kleptomaniac.

cleptomanìa *sf.* kleptomania.

clericale *agg.* clerical.

clero *sm.* clergy.

cliente *sm.* 1. customer 2. (*di medico, avvocato*) client.

clientela *sf.* 1. customers (*pl.*) 2. (*di medico, avvocato*) practice 3. (*comm.*) connection.

clima *sm.* climate.

clinica *sf.* nursing-home.

clinico *agg.* clinical. ♦ **clinico** *sm* clinician.

clistere *sm.* enema.

cloaca *sf.* cloaca.

cloro *sm.* chlorine.

clorofilla *sf.* chlorophyll.

cloroformio *sm.* chloroform.

cloruro *sm.* chloride.

coabitare *vi.* to cohabit.

coabitazione *sf.* cohabitation.

coadiuvante *agg.* coadjuvant.

coadiuvare *vt.* to help.

coagulare *vi.* 1. to coagulate 2. (*del latte*) to curdle.

coagulazione *sf.* coagulation.

coàgulo *sm.* 1. curd 2. (*di sangue*) blood-clot.

coalizione *sf.* alliance, coalition.

coalizzare *vt.* to unite. ♦ **coalizzarsi** *vr.* to form a coalition.

coartare *vt.* to force.

coatto *agg.* forced: *domicilio* —, forced residence.

cobalto *sm.* cobalt.

cobelligerante *agg.* e *sm.* co-belligerent.

cobra *sm.* cobra.

cocaina *sf.* cocaine.

cocainòmane *s.* cocainist.

coccarda *sf.* cockade.

cocchiere *sm.* coachman (*pl.* -men).

cocchio *sm.* coach.

còccige *sm.* cocyx (*pl.* -yges).

coccinella *sf.* ladybird.

cocciniglia *sf.* cochineal.

coccio *sm.* 1. (*terracotta*) crock, pot 2. (*pezzo rotto*) fragment of pottery.

cocciutàggine *sf.* stubbornness.

cocciuto *agg.* stubborn.

cocco *sm.* 1. (*frutto*) coconut 2. (*albero*) coconut-tree 3. (*fam. vezz.*) darling.

coccodrillo *sm.* crocodile.

coccolare *vt.* to pet, to fondle.

cocente *agg.* 1. hot, scalding 2. (*fig.*) deep, bitter.

cocòmero *sm.* water-melon.

cocùzzolo *sm.* 1. crown 2. (*vetta*) top.

coda *sf.* 1. tail 2. (*fila*) queue: *fare la* —, to queue up.

codardo *agg.* cowardly. ♦ **codardo** *sm.* coward.

codesto *agg.* 1. that (*pl.* those) 2. (*come « tale »*) such. ♦ **codesto** *pron.* that one (*pl.* those ones).

còdice *sm.* 1. code: — *civile*, Civil Law 2. (*manoscritto antico*) codex.

codificare *vt.* to codify.

coefficiente *sm.* coefficient.

coercitivo *agg.* coercive.

coercizione *sf.* compulsion.

coerente *agg.* coherent.

coerenza *sf.* coherence.

coesione *sf.* cohesion.

coesistenza *sf.* coexistence.

coesistere *vi.* to coexist.

coetàneo *agg.* e *sm.* contemporary || *Carlo ed io siamo coetanei*, Charles and I are the same age.

cofanetto *sm.* casket: — *di gioielli*, jewel box.

còfano *sm.* 1. coffer 2. (*auto*) bonnet.

cògliere *vt.* 1. to pick up, to pluck 2. (*sorprendere*) to catch (*v. irr.*) 3. (*colpire*) to hit (*v. irr.*) 4. (*afferrare*) to seize: — *la palla al balzo*, to seize the opportunity.

cognata *sf.* sister-in-law.

cognato *sm.* brother-in-law.

cognizione *sf.* 1. knowledge 2. (*giur.*) cognizance.

cognome *sm.* surname.

coincidenza *sf.* 1. coincidence 2. (*ferr.*) connection.

coincìdere *vi.* to coincide, to clash.

coinvòlgere *vt.* to involve.

còito *sm.* coition.

colabrodo *sm.* strainer.

colaggio *sm.* 1. (*di liquidi*) leakage 2. (*metal.*) casting.

colare *vt.* 1. to strain 2. (*fondere*) to cast (*v. irr.*) ♦ **colare** *vi.* to drip.

colata *sf.* 1. (*metal.*) casting 2. (*quantità di metallo fuso*) cast 3. (*di lava*) flow.

colato *agg.* strained, filtered.

colazione *sf.* 1. (*del mattino*) breakfast 2. (*di mezzogiorno*) lunch.

colbacco *sm.* busby.

colei *pron. dimostr.* 1. (*sogg.*) she; (*ogg.*) her 2. — *che*, she who, she whom (*sogg.*); her who, her whom (*ogg.*): — *che viene qui è mia sorella*, she who is coming here is my sister; — *che vedi è Maria*, she whom you see is Mary; *puoi — che viene?*, can you see her who is coming?; *sono stata aiutata da* —

che odiavo, I have been helped by her whom I hated.

coleòttero *sm.* coleopter.

colera *sm.* cholera.

colesterolo *sm.* cholesterol.

còlica *sf.* colic.

colino *sm.* strainer.

colite *sf.* colitis.

colla *sf.* glue || — *di farina*, paste.

collaborare *vi.* to collaborate.

collaboratore *sm.* collaborator.

collaborazione *sf.* collaboration.

collaborazionismo *sm.* collaborationism.

collaborazionista *sm.* collaborationist.

collana *sf.* **1.** necklace **2.** (*raccolta*) collection **3.** (*di libri*) series.

collare *sm.* collar.

collasso *sm.* breakdown: — *cardiaco*, heart failure.

collaterale *agg.* collateral.

collaudare *vt.* to test.

collaudatore *sm.* **1.** tester **2.** (*aer.*) test pilot **3.** (*auto*) test-driver.

collàudo *sm.* test: *fare un* — *di qc.*, to put (*v. irr.*) sthg. to the test.

collazionare *vt.* to collate.

colle *sm.* hill.

collega *sm.* colleague.

collegamento *sm.* **1.** connection **2.** (*mecc.*) linkwork || *essere in* —, to be in touch.

collegare *vt.* to connect, to link.

collegiale *agg.* collegial. ◆ **collegiale** *sm.* boarder.

collegio *sm.* **1.** college **2.** (*scuola con convitto*) boarding-school.

còllera *sf.* anger || *essere in* —, to be angry.

collèrico *agg.* hot-tempered.

colletta *sf.* collection.

collettivismo *sm.* collectivism.

collettività *sf.* collectivity.

collettivizzare *vt.* to collectivize.

collettivizzazione *sf.* collectivization.

collettivo *agg.* collective.

colletto *sm.* collar.

collettore *agg.* collecting. ◆ **collettore** *sm.* **1.** (*esattore; raccoglitore*) collector **2.** (*mecc.*) manifold **3.** (*elettr.*) commutator.

collezionare *vt.* to collect.

collezione *sf.* collection.

collezionista *sm.* collector.

collimare *vi.* **1.** (*essere d'accordo*) to agree (with) **2.** (*coincidere*) to

coincide.

collina *sf.* hill.

collinoso *agg.* hilly.

collirio *sm.* eye-wash.

collisione *sf.* collision (*anche fig.*), impact.

collo *sm.* **1.** neck: *allungare il* —, to crane one's neck || *a rotta di* —, at breakneck speed; *tra capo e* —, unexpectedly **2.** (*pacco*) parcel, package.

collocamento *sm.* **1.** placing **2.** (*impiego*) employment || *agenzia di* —, employment bureau **3.** (*comm.*) disposal.

collocare *vt.* **1.** to place **2.** (*impiegare*) to employ **3.** (*comm.*) to sell (*v. irr.*), to dispose (of sthg.). ◆ **collocarsi** *vr.* **1.** to place oneself **2.** (*impiegarsi*) to get a situation.

collocazione *sf.* **1.** placing **2.** (*comm.*) sale **3.** (*di libri in biblioteche*) press-mark.

colloidale *agg.* colloidal.

colloquio *sm.* **1.** conversation, talk **2.** (*intervista*) interview.

collusione *sf.* collusion.

colluttazione *sf.* scuffle: *venire a* —, to come (*v. irr.*) to grips.

colmare *vt.* **1.** to fill up **2.** (*fig.*) to fill, to overwhelm.

colmo *agg.* full, brimful. ◆ **colmo** *sm.* top, summit, climax || *per* — *di sfortuna*, as a crowning misfortune; *è il* —!, that beats everything.

colomba *sf.* dove.

colombaia *sf.* dove-cot.

colombo *sm.* pigeon: — *viaggiatore*, carrier-pigeon.

colonia *sf.* colony.

coloniale *agg.* colonial.

colonialismo *sm.* colonialism.

colonialista *sm.* colonialist.

colonizzare *vt.* to colonize.

colonizzatore *sm.* colonizer.

colonizzazione *sf.* colonization.

colonna *sf.* **1.** column (*anche fig.*), pillar || — *d'acqua*, fall of water.

colonnato *sm.* colonnade.

colonnello *sm.* colonel.

colono *sm.* **1.** farmer **2.** (*abitante di una colonia*) settler.

colorante *agg.* colouring. ◆ **colorante** *sm.* dye.

colorare *vt.* to colour. ◆ **colorarsi** *vr.* **1.** to colour **2.** (*di persona*) to blush, to flush.

colorazione *sf.* colouring.

colore *sm.* **1.** colour ‖ *biancheria di —*, coloured linen; *gente di —*, coloured people; *colori a olio*, oil-paints **2.** *(aspetto)* look.

colorire *vt.* to colour.

colorito *sm.* complexion.

coloritura *sf.* colouring.

coloro *pron. dimostr.* **1.** they *(sogg.)*; them *(compl.)* **2.** *— che*, they who, they whom *(sogg.)*; them who, them whom *(compl.)*: *— studiano saranno premiati*, they who study will be given a prize; *— tu vedi sono i miei amici*, they whom you see are my friends; *amerò sempre — mi amano*, I shall always love them who love me; *ti presenterò a — hai visto ieri*, I shall introduce you to them whom you saw yesterday.

colossale *agg.* colossal.

colosso *sm.* colossus *(pl. -si)*.

colpa *sf.* **1.** fault **2.** *(colpevolezza)* guilt.

colpévole *agg.* guilty.

colpevolezza *sf.* guilt, guiltiness.

colpire *vt.* **1.** to hit *(v. irr.)*, to strike *(v. irr.; anche fig.)* **2.** *(di arma da fuoco)* to shoot *(v. irr.)*.

colpo *sm.* **1.** blow, stroke *(anche fig.)*: *— di fortuna*, stroke of luck; *— apoplettico*, stroke of apoplexy ‖ *— d'aria*, draught; *a — d'occhio*, at a glance; *a — sicuro*, without any risk; *senza — ferire*, without resistance **2.** *(di arma da fuoco)* shot.

colposo *agg.* unpremeditated: *omicidio —*, manslaughter.

coltellata *sf.* stab.

coltello *sm.* knife: *a serramanico*, jack-knife; *affilare un —*, to sharpen a knife.

coltivàbile *agg.* cultivable.

coltivare *vt.* to cultivate *(anche fig.)*, to till, to farm.

coltivatore *sm.* **1.** tiller, farmer **2.** *(di patate, tabacco ecc.)* grower.

coltivazione *sf.* **1.** tilling, farming **2.** *(di patate, tabacco ecc.)* growing.

colto *agg.* *(istruito)* learned.

coltre *sf.* blanket, coverlet.

colui *pron. dimostr.* **1.** he *(sogg.)* him *(compl.)* **2.** *— che*, he who, he whom *(sogg.)*; him who, him whom *(compl.)*: *— che ti ha salutato è mio fratello*, he who has greeted you is my brother; *— che vedesti ieri è un mio vecchio ami-*

co, he whom you saw yesterday is an old friend of mine; *daranno il premio a — che studierà*, they will give the prize to him who studies; *fui aiutata da — che avevo aiutato*, I was helped by him whom I had helped.

coma *sm.* coma.

comandamento *sm.* **1.** command, precept **2.** *(relig.)* commandment.

comandante *sm.* commander.

comandare *vt.* **1.** to order, to command **2.** *(essere al comando)* to command, to be in command of.

comando *sm.* **1.** *(ordine)* order **2.** *(autorità)* command **3.** *(sede del comandante)* headquarters *(pl.)*.

comatoso *agg.* comatose.

combaciare *vi.* to fit together.

combattente *sm.* **1.** fighting man **2.** *(soldato)* soldier, service man.

combattístico *agg.* soldier (like) *(attr.)*.

combàttere *vt. e vi.* to fight *(v. irr.)* *(anche fig.)*.

combattimento *sm.* **1.** combat, fight, battle **2.** *(boxe)* match.

combattività *sf.* pugnacity.

combattivo *agg.* pugnacious.

combinare *vt.* **1.** to combine **2.** *(di colori)* to match **3.** *(concludere)* to conclude **4.** *(progettare)* to plan.

combinazione *sf.* **1.** combination **2.** *(sistemazione)* arrangement **3.** *(caso, coincidenza)* chance, coincidence.

combríccola *sf.* **1.** band **2.** *(comitiva)* party.

combustíbile *agg.* combustible. ♦ **combustíbile** *sm.* fuel.

combustione *sf.* combustion.

combutta *sf.* **1.** gang: *essere in —*, to be hand in glove **2.** *(congiura)* plot.

come *avv.* **1.** *(simile a)* like: *è proprio — suo padre*, he is just like his father **2.** *(in qualità di, modale)* as: *ti parlo — amico*, I am speaking to you as a friend **3.** *(in comp.)* as ... as; so ... as: *Carlo è studioso — me*, Charles is as studious as I; *Carlo non è studioso — me*, Charles is not so studious as I **4.** *(int.)* how: *— va?*, How are you? **5.** *(escl.)* how: *— è interessante questo libro!*, How interesting this book is! ♦ **come** *prep.* **1.** *(tempo-*

rale) as, as soon as: — *sentii la sua voce lo riconobbi*, as soon as I heard his voice I recognized him 2. (*come se*) as if: *mi guarda — se mi conoscesse*, he is looking at me as if he knew me || — *Dio volle*, in God's good time; — *segue*, as follows; — *d'accordo*, as agreed.

cometa *sf.* comet.

comicità *sf.* comicality.

còmico *agg.* comical, funny. ♦ **còmico** *sm.* comedian.

comìgnolo *sm.* chimney-pot.

cominciare *vt.* to begin (*v. irr.*), to start.

comitato *sm.* committee.

comitiva *sf.* party, company.

comizio *sm.* meeting.

comma *sm.* paragraph.

commedia *sf.* 1. comedy, play 2. (*fig.*) pretence || *recitare la* —, to play a part.

commediante *sm.* 1. player 2. (*fig.*) shammer.

commediògrafo *sm.* playwright.

commemorare *vt.* to commemorate.

commemorativo *agg.* memorial.

commemorazione *sf.* commemoration.

commendàbile *agg.* commendable.

commendatizia *sf.* letter of recommendation.

commensale *sm.* table-companion.

commentare *vt.* to comment (on).

commentario *sm.* (*lett.*) commentary.

commentatore *sm.* commentator.

commento *sm.* commentary.

commerciàbile *agg.* negotiable.

commerciale *agg.* commercial.

commercializzare *vt.* to commercialize.

commerciante *sm.* 1. trader 2. (*uomo d'affari*) business-man (*pl.* -men) || — *all'ingrosso*, wholesale dealer; — *al minuto*, retailer.

commerciare *vi.* to trade, to deal (*v. irr.*) (in).

commercio *sm.* 1. commerce, trade 2. (*affari*) business || — *all'ingrosso*, wholesale trade; — *al minuto*, retail trade; — *d'importazione*, *esportazione*, import, export trade; *essere in* —, to be on sale; *essere fuori* —, to be out of sale; *essere in* — (*di un commerciante*), to be in business.

commessa *sf.* shop assistant, shop-girl.

commesso *sm.* clerk, shopman (*pl.* -men), shop assistant || — *viaggiatore*, commercial traveller.

commestibili *agg.* eatable. ♦ **commestibili** *sm. pl.* foodstuffs.

commèttere *vt.* 1. to commit, to do (*v. irr.*), to make (*v. irr.*) 2. (*ordinare*) to order.

commiato *sm.* 1. (*preso*) leave 2. (*dato*) dismissal.

commilitone *sm.* fellow-soldier.

comminatoria *sf.* commination.

comminatorio *agg.* comminatory.

commiserare *vt.* to pity.

commiserazione *sf.* pity.

commissariato *sm.* 1. (*carica di commissario*) commissaryship 2. (*ufficio*) commissary's office.

commissario *sm.* commissary.

commissionare *vt.* (*comm.*) to order.

commissionario *sm.* (*comm.*) commission agent.

commissione *sf.* 1. errand: *fare una* —, to go (*v. irr.*) on an errand 2. (*comm.*) commission, order 3. (*comitato*) commission, committee.

commisurare *vt.* to compare.

committente *sm.* purchaser, buyer.

commosso *agg.* moved, affected.

commovente *agg.* moving, touching, affecting.

commozione *sf.* 1. emotion 2. (*med.*) concussion: — *cerebrale*, concussion of the brain.

commuòvere *vt.* to move, to touch. ♦ **commuòversi** *vr.* to be moved.

commutàbile *agg.* commutable.

commutare *vt.* to commute.

commutativo *agg.* commutative.

commutatore *sm.* commutator.

comò *sm.* chest of drawers.

comodino *sm.* night-table.

comodità *sf.* convenience, comfort.

còmodo *agg.* 1. useful 2. (*conveniente*) convenient 3. (*confortevole*) comfortable 4. (*maneggevole*) handy.

compagnìa *sf.* 1. company: *tener* —, to keep (*v. irr.*) company 2. (*gruppo di persone*) party 3. (*società*) company.

compagno *sm.* companion, mate, comrade || — *di giuochi*, playmate; — *di stanza*, room-mate; — *di studi*, fellow-student.

compagnone *sm.* jolly good fellow.

comparàbile *agg.* comparable.

comparare *vt.* to compare.

comparativo *agg.* (*gramm.*) comparative.

comparato *agg.* comparative.

compare *sm.* 1. (*compagno*) comrade, partner 2. (*padrino*) godfather 3. (*testimone di matrimonio*) witness 4. (*complice*) accomplice.

comparire *vi.* 1. to appear 2. (*sembrare*) to show (*v. irr.*) oneself 3. (*far bella mostra*) to show (*v. irr.*) off.

comparizione *sf.* appearance: (*giur.*) *mandato di —,* summons.

comparsa *sf.* 1. appearance 2. (*teat.; cine*) supernumerary 3. (*giur.*) appearance.

compartecipare *vi.* to share in.

compartimento *sm.* 1. compartment 2. (*circoscrizione*) department.

compartizione *sf.* distribution.

compassato *agg.* 1. stiff, formal 2. (*di discorso*) restrained.

compassione *sf.* pity, commiseration.

compasso *sm.* compasses (*pl.*).

compatibile *agg.* consistent.

compatibilità *sf.* consistency.

compatimento *sm.* pity, compassion.

compatire *vt.* to pity.

compatriota *sm.* fellow-countryman (*pl.* -men). ♦ **compatriota** *sf.* fellow-countrywoman (*pl.* -women).

compattezza *sf.* 1. compactness 2. (*di associazione, partito*) unity.

compatto *agg.* compact, solid.

compendiare *vt.* to abridge, to sum up.

compendio *sm.* 1. abridgement, summary.

compenetrare *vt.* to penetrate.

compensàbile *agg.* remunerable.

compensare *vt.* 1. to compensate 2. (*ricompensare*) to reward.

compensato *sm.* ply-wood.

compensazione *sf.* 1. compensation, indemnity 2. (*comm.*) clearing.

compenso *sm.* 1. compensation 2. (*rimunerazione*) reward, retribution.

còmpera *sf.* purchase.

competente *agg.* competent.

competenza *sf.* 1. competence 2. (*onorario*) fee.

compètere *vi.* 1. (*gareggiare*) to vie 2. (*spettare*) to be due, to belong.

competitivo *agg.* competitive.

competitore *sm.* competitor, rival.

competizione *sf.* competition.

compiacente *agg.* obliging.

compiacenza *sf.* 1. kindness 2. (*soddisfazione*) satisfaction.

compiacere *vt.* to please, to gratify. ♦ **compiacersi** *vr.* 1. to be pleased (with), to congratulate 2. (*degnarsi*) to condescend.

compiacimento *sm.* 1. satisfaction 2. (*congratulazione*) congratulation.

compiàngere *vt.* 1. to pity, to sympathise (with) 2. (*disprezzare*) to despise.

compianto *agg.* regretted. ♦ **compianto** *sm.* regret.

còmpiere *vt.* 1. (*finire*) to finish 2. (*eseguire*) to accomplish 3. (*adempiere*) to do (*v. irr.*): — *il proprio dovere,* to do one's duty 4. (*di età*) *ho compiuto 30 anni,* I am now 30 years old.

compilare *vt.* to compile: — *un documento,* to draw (*v. irr.*) up a document; — *una lista,* to make (*v. irr.*) a list.

compilazione *sf.* 1. compilation 2. (*comm.*) drawing up.

compimento *sm.* 1. (*il compire*) completion 2. (*conclusione*) achievement.

compitare *vt.* to spell (*v. irr.*).

compitezza *sf.* politeness, refinement.

compìto *agg.* polite.

còmpito *sm.* 1. task, duty 2. (*scolastico, a casa*) homework; (*a scuola*) class-work.

compiutamente *avv.* completely.

compiutezza *sf.* completeness.

compiuto *agg.* complete.

compleanno *sm.* birthday: *buon —!,* happy birthday!.

complementare *agg.* complementary.

complemento *sm.* 1. complement 2. (*gramm.*) — *indiretto,* indirect object 3. (*mil.*) *truppe di —,* reserve.

complessato *agg.* neurotic.

complessione *sf.* constitution.

complessità *sf.* complexity.

complessivamente *avv.* on the whole.

complessivo *agg.* total, inclusive.

complesso *agg.* complex, complicated. ♦ **complesso** sm. **1.** whole **2.** (*industriale*) plant, set **3.** (*mus.*) band.

completamente avv. completely.

completare vt. to complete, to finish.

completezza sf. completeness.

completo agg. **1.** complete, whole **2.** (*pieno*) full. ♦ **completo** sm. (*vestito*) suit.

complicare vt. to complicate.

complicato agg. complicated.

complicazione sf. complication: *salvo complicazioni*, if no complications set in.

còmplice s. accomplice.

complicità sf. accomplicity.

complimentare vt. to compliment. ♦ **complimentarsi** vr. to congratulate (so.).

complimento sm. **1.** compliment **2.** (*congratulazione*) congratulation.

complottare vi. to plot.

complotto sm. plot, conspiracy.

compluvio sm. (*arch.*) compluvium (*pl.* -ia).

componente agg. component. ♦ **componente** sm. **1.** member **2.** (*chim.*) component.

componimento sm. **1.** (*lett.; mus.; scol.*) composition **2.** (*giur.*) settlement.

comporre vt. **1.** to compose: — *una poesia*, to write (*v. irr.*) a poem; — *un numero telefonico*, to dial a number **2.** (*chim.*) to compound **3.** (*assestare*) to arrange.

comportamento sm. behaviour.

comportare vt. to involve, to require. ♦ **comportarsi** vr. to behave (oneself).

compòsito agg. composite.

compositore sm. **1.** (*mus.*) composer **2.** (*tip.*) compositor.

composizione sf. **1.** composition **2.** (*conciliazione*) composition, agreement **3.** (*tip.*) composing.

composta sf. compound.

compostezza sf. **1.** composure **2.** (*dignità*) self-respect.

composto agg. **1.** compound **2.** (*ordinato*) tidy **3.** (*calmo*) calm ‖ *stare* —, to sit (*v. irr.*) still. ♦ **composto** sm. compound.

comprare vt. **1.** to buy (*v. irr.*): — *a credito*, to buy on credit; — *per contanti*, to buy for cash; — *all'ingrosso*, to buy wholesale **2.** (*corrompere*) to bribe.

compratore sm. buyer, purchaser.

compravéndita sf. marketing.

comprèndere vt. **1.** (*includere*) to include, to take (*v. irr.*) in **2.** (*capire*) to understand (*v. irr.*) **3.** (*rendersi conto*) to realize.

comprensibile agg. intelligible.

comprensibilità sf. intelligibility.

comprensione sf. **1.** comprehension, understanding **2.** (*compassione*) sympathy.

comprensivo agg. **1.** comprehensive **2.** (*che capisce*) comprehending **3.** (*che prova simpatia*) sympathetic.

compressa sf. **1.** tablet **2.** (*di garza*) compress.

comprensibilità sf. compressibility.

compressione sf. compression.

comprimere vt. **1.** to compress **2.** (*fig.*) to restrain, to repress.

compromesso sm. compromise.

compromettente agg. compromising.

compromèttere vt. to compromise, to involve.

comproprietà sf. joint ownership.

comproprietario sm. joint owner.

comprovare vt. to prove.

compunto agg. filled with compunction, contrite.

computare vt. to compute.

computisteria sf. book-keeping.

còmputo sm. reckoning.

comunale agg. communal, municipal.

comunardo sm. (*stor.*) Communard.

comune¹ agg. **1.** common **2.** (*abituale*) frequent, usual.

comune² sm. **1.** commune **2.** (*edificio*) Town Hall.

comunella sf. cabal: *far* — *con qu.*, to consort.

comunemente avv. commonly, usually.

comunicàbile agg. communicable.

comunicabilità sf. communicability.

comunicante agg. communicating.

comunicare vt. **1.** to communicate, to transmit **2.** (*relig.*) to communicate. ♦ **comunicarsi** vr. to receive Holy Communion.

comunicativa sf. communicativeness.

comunicativo agg. communicative.

comunicato sm. bulletin.

comunicazione sf. communication.

comunione sf. **1.** communion: —

di idee, similarity of ideas **2.** (*relig.*) Holy Communion.

comunismo *sm.* communism.

comunista *s.* communist.

comunità *sf.* community.

comunque *avv.* however, anyhow.

con *prep.* **1.** (*compagnia, unione, strumento*) with: *venne — me,* he came with me; *scrivo — questa penna,* I write with this pen **2.** (*stato, condizione*) in: *— il freddo sto meglio,* in cold weather I feel better **3.** (*mezzo di trasporto*) by: *arriverò col treno delle 3,* I shall arrive by the three o'clock train **4.** (*per mezzo di*) by means of.

conato *sm.* effort || *avere conati di vomito,* to feel (*v. irr.*) sick.

conca *sf.* **1.** basin, pot **2.** (*valle*) valley.

concatenamento *sm.* concatenation.

concatenare *vt.* to concatenate.

concatenazione *sf.* concatenation.

còncavo *agg.* concave, hollow.

concèdere *vt.* **1.** to grant, to bestow **2.** (*permettere*) to allow.

concentramento *sm.* concentration: *campo di —,* concentration camp.

concentrare *vt.* to concentrate. ♦ **concentrarsi** *vr.* to concentrate.

concentrato *agg.* concentrated. ♦ **concentrato** *sm.* concentrated food.

concentrazione *sf.* concentration.

concèntrico *agg.* concentric.

concepìbile *agg.* conceivable.

concepimento *sm.* conception.

concepire *vt.* **1.** to conceive **2.** (*nutrire speranze, timori*) to entertain **3.** (*formulare*) to express.

conceria *sf.* tannery.

concèrnere *vt.* to concern, to relate to.

concertare *vt.* **1.** (*mus.*) to harmonize **2.** (*stabilire*) to plan, to arrange.

concertato *agg.* concerted (*anche mus.*), arranged.

concertista *s.* concert artist.

concertìstico *agg.* concert.

concerto *sm.* concert.

concessionario *sm.* concessionary agent.

concessione *sf.* **1.** concession **2.** (*permesso*) permission.

concetto *sm.* concept.

concettuale *agg.* conceptual.

concezionale *agg.* conceptional.

concezione *sf.* conception.

conchiglia *sf.* shell.

concia *sf.* **1.** (*di pelli*) tanning **2.** (*di tabacco*) curing.

conciare *vt.* **1.** (*pelli*) to tan **2.** (*tabacco*) to cure **3.** (*fig.*) to ill-treat **4.** (*insudiciare*) to soil. ♦ **conciarsi** *vr.* to get (*v. irr.*) dirty.

conciatore *sm.* tanner.

conciatura *sf.* tanning.

conciliàbile *agg.* compatible, consistent.

conciliabilità *sf.* compatibility.

conciliàbolo *sm.* conventicle, secret talk.

conciliante *agg.* conciliatory.

conciliare *vt.* **1.** to reconcile **2.** (*procacciare*) to win (*v. irr.*), to gain. ♦ **conciliarsi** *vr.* to win (*v. irr.*).

conciliare *agg.* conciliar.

conciliatore *agg.* conciliatory. ♦ **conciliatore** *sm.* peacemaker || *giudice —,* Justice of the Peace.

conciliazione *sf.* conciliation.

concilio *sm.* Council.

concimaia *sf.* dung-hill, dung-pit.

concimare *vt.* to dung.

concimazione *sf.* dunging.

concime *sm.* **1.** (*organico*) dung **2.** (*chimico*) fertilizer.

concio *sm.* dung.

concionare *vi.* to harangue.

concione *sf.* harangue.

concisione *sf.* concision.

conciso *agg.* concise, brief.

concistoro *sm.* (*eccl.*) concistory.

concitare *vt.* to excite, to stir (up).

concitazione *sf.* excitement, agitation.

concittadino *sm.* fellow-citizen.

conclamare *vt.* to acclaim.

conclave *sm.* (*eccl.*) conclave.

concludente *agg.* **1.** conclusive **2.** (*di persona*) energetic.

concludere *vt.* **1.** to conclude, to finish **2.** (*dedurre*) to infer **3.** (*fare*) to do (*v. irr.*).

conclusionale *sf.* (*giur.*) pleadings (*pl.*).

conclusione *sf.* **1.** conclusion **2.** (*risultato*) issue, result.

conclusivo *agg.* conclusive.

concomitante *agg.* concomitant.

concomitanza *sf.* concomitance.

concordanza *sf.* agreement.

concordare *vi.* to agree. ♦ **concordare** *vt.* **1.** to agree upon **2.**

(mettere d'accordo) to reconcile 3. *(gramm.)* to put *(v. irr.)* in concord.

concordatario *agg.* 1. *(eccl.)* of concordat 2. *(giur.; comm.)* composition.

concordato *sm.* 1. convention 2. *(eccl.)* concordat 3. *(giur.; comm.)* agreement, composition.

concorde *agg.* concordant, agreeing: *volontà —,* unanimous will.

concordemente *avv.* concordantly.

concordia *sf.* concord, agreement.

concorrente *agg.* 1. concurrent 2. *(rivale)* competing. ♦ **concorrente** *sm.* 1. candidate 2. *(rivale)* competitor.

concorrenza *sf.* 1. *(affluenza)* concourse 2. *(comm.)* competition ‖ *fare —,* to compete with; — *sleale,* unfair competition.

concorrenziale *agg.* competitive.

concòrrere *vi.* 1. to come *(v. irr.)* together 2. *(contribuire)* to concur, to contribute 3. *(partecipare)* to share in 4. *(mettersi in gara)* to compete.

concorso *sm.* 1. *(affluenza)* rush, crowd, concourse 2. *(gara)* competition 3. *(sport)* contest.

concretare *vt.* 1. to make *(v. irr.)* concrete 2. *(concludere)* to realize.

concretezza *sf.* concreteness.

concreto *agg.* 1. concrete, real 2. *(solido)* solid.

concrezione *sf.* concretion.

concubina *sf.* concubine.

concubinaggio, concubinato *sm.* concubinage.

conculcare *vt.* to trample on.

concupire *vt.* to covet, to lust after.

concupiscenza *sf.* concupiscence, lust.

concussione *sf.* *(giur.)* concussion.

condanna *sf.* 1. condemnation 2. *(sentenza)* sentence: — *a morte,* death sentence 3. *(pena)* penalty.

condannàbile *agg.* condemnable.

condannare *vt.* 1. to sentence 2. *(fig.)* to condemn 3. *(riprovare)* to blame.

condannato *agg.* sentenced. ♦ **condannato** *sm.* condemned man.

condensàbile *agg.* condensable.

condensabilità *sf.* condensability.

condensazione *sf.* condensation.

condensare *vt.* to condense.

condensatore *sm.* condenser.

condimento *sm.* seasoning, dressing.

condire *vt.* to season; *(anche fig.)* to flavour.

condirettore *sm.* joint manager.

condiscendente *agg.* complying.

condiscendenza *sf.* 1. compliance 2. *(degnazione)* condescension.

condiscèndere *vi.* 1. to comply with 2. *(degnarsi)* to condescend.

condiscépolo *sm.* schoolfellow.

condivìdere *vt.* to share *(anche fig.)*.

condizionale *agg. e sm.* conditional. ♦ **condizionale** *sf.* *(giur.)* conditional sentence.

condizionamento *sm.* conditioning.

condizionare *vt.* to condition.

condizione *sf.* 1. condition: *a — che:* on condition that 2. *(ceto)* rank, station.

condoglianza *sf.* condolence.

condominio *sm.* joint ownership.

condòmino *sm.* joint-owner.

condonare *vt.* to remit.

condono *sm.* remission.

condotta *sf.* 1. conduct, behaviour.

condotto *agg. medico —,* doctor employed by the local authority. ♦ **condotto** *sm.* 1. conduit, pipeline 2. *(anat.)* duct.

conducente *sm.* driver.

conducibilità *sf.* *(fis.)* conductibility.

condurre *vt.* 1. *(guidare)* to lead *(v. irr.)* 2. *(accompagnare)* to take *(v. irr.)* 3. *(governare, trattare)* to manage: — *i propri affari,* to manage one's business 4. *(vivere)* to lead *(v. irr.):* — *una vita triste,* to lead a sad life. ♦ **condurre** *vi.* to lead *(v. irr.):* questa strada conduce a Milano, this route leads to Milan. ♦ **condursi** *vr.* to behave.

conduttività *sf.* conductivity.

conduttivo *agg.* conducting. ♦ **conduttore** *agg.* conducting. ♦ **conduttore** *sm.* 1. leader, guide 2. *(di veicoli)* driver 3. *(fis.)* conductor.

conduttura *sf.* 1. duct, conduit 2. *(di tubazioni)* piping.

conduzione *sf.* 1. management 2. *(fis.)* conduction.

confabulare *vi.* to confabulate.

confacente *agg.* suitable, proper.

confarsi *vr.* to suit, to become *(v. irr.)*.

confederale *agg.* confederal.

confederare *vt.* to confederate.

confederazione *sf.* **1.** Confederation **2.** (*alleanza*) confederacy.

conferenza *sf.* **1.** lecture **2.** (*assemblea*) conference.

conferenziere *sm.* lecturer.

conferimento *sm.* bestowal.

conferire *vt.* to confer, to bestow. ◆ **conferire** *vi.* **1.** to have an interview **2.** (*giovare*) to be useful.

conferma *sf.* confirmation.

confermare *vt.* to confirm. ◆ **confermarsi** *vr.* to prove oneself.

confermazione *sf.* confirmation.

confessare *vt.* **1.** to confess **2.** (*riconoscere, ammettere*) to admit. ◆ **confessarsi** *vr.* (*eccl.*) to go (*v. irr.*) to confession.

confessionale *agg.* confessional. ◆ **confessionale** *sm.* confessional.

confessione *sf.* **1.** confession **2.** (*ammissione*) admission **3.** (*memorie*) memoirs (*pl.*).

confessore *sm.* confessor.

confetteria *sf.* confectionery.

confettiere *sm.* confectioner.

confetto *sm.* comfit.

confettura *sf.* **1.** (*confetti*) sweetmeats (*pl.*) **2.** (*marmellata*) jam || — *d'arance*, marmalade.

confezionare *vt.* **1.** to make (*v. irr.*) up **2.** (*di piatti*) to prepare **3.** (*di pacchi*) to pack up.

confezione *sf.* **1.** manufacture **2.** (*preparazione*) preparation **3.** (*pl.*) (*abiti*) ready-to-wear clothes **4.** (*imballaggio*) packing.

conficcare *vt.* to hammer, to drive (*v. irr.*). ◆ **conficcarsi** *vr.* to run (*v. irr.*) into.

confidare *vt.* to confide. ◆ **confidare** *vi.* **1.** to confide, to trust **2.** (*fare assegnamento*) to rely (on).

confidente *agg.* trustful. ◆ **confidente** *sm.* **1.** confidant **2.** (*di polizia*) police spy.

confidenza *sf.* **1.** (*fiducia*) confidence **2.** (*cosa confidata*) secret **3.** (*familiarità*) familiarity || *essere in — con qu.*, to be on familiar terms with so.

confidenziale *agg.* confidential: *strettamente —*, strictly confidential.

confidenzialmente *avv.* confidentially.

configgere *vt.* to drive (*v. irr.*) in.

configurare *vt.* to configure, to shape.

configurazione *sf.* configuration, shape.

confinante *agg.* **1.** neighbouring **2.** (*fig.*) bordering.

confinare *vi.* to border on. ◆ **confinare** *vt.* **1.** to banish **2.** (*fig.*) to confine.

confinario *agg.* border.

confinato *agg.* interned.

confine *sm.* **1.** border, frontier **2.** (*fig.*) limit, boundary.

confino *sm.* internment, political confinement.

confisca *sf.* confiscation.

confiscàbile *agg.* confiscable.

confiscare *vt.* to confiscate.

confitto *agg.* **1.** nailed, driven in **2.** (*fig.*) fixed.

conflagrare *vi.* to break (*v. irr.*) out.

conflagrazione *sf.* **1.** conflagration **2.** (*fig.*) sudden out-break (of war).

conflitto *sm.* **1.** conflict **2.** (*fig.*) clash.

confluente *agg.* confluent.

confluenza *sf.* confluence.

confluire *vi.* to flow together.

confóndere *vt.* **1.** to confuse **2.** (*scambiare una persona per un'altra*) to mistake (*v. irr.*) **3.** (*turbare*) to confound. ◆ **confóndersi** *vr.* **1.** to get (*v. irr.*) mixed up **2.** (*mescolarsi*) to mingle **3.** (*turbarsi*) to be disconcerted.

confondìbile *agg.* liable to be confused.

conformare *vt.* to conform. ◆ **conformarsi** *vr.* to conform.

conformato *agg.* shaped.

conformazione *sf.* conformation.

conforme *agg.* **1.** conforming **2.** (*simile*) similar **3.** (*fedele*) true || — *a*, in conformity with. ◆ **conforme** *a* *loc. avv.* in conformity with.

conformismo *sm.* time-serving.

conformista *s.* **1.** time-server **2.** (*relig.*) conformist.

conformìstico *agg.* conformist.

conformità *sf.* conformity.

confortàbile *agg.* consolable.

confortante *agg.* consoling.

confortare *vt.* **1.** to comfort **2.** (*incoraggiare*) to encourage.

confortatore *agg.* comforting. ◆ **confortatore** *sm.* comforter.

confortatorio *agg.* comforting.

confortévole *agg.* **1.** comforting **2.** (*comodo*) comfortable.

confortevolmente *avv.* comfortably.

conforto *sm.* 1. comfort, solace 2. (*incoraggiamento*) encouragement.

confratello *sm.* brother (*pl.* brethren).

confratèrnita *sf.* brotherhood.

confrontàbile *agg.* comparable.

confrontare *vt.* 1. to compare 2. (*giur.*) to confront.

confronto *sm.* 1. comparison 2. (*giur.*) confrontation ‖ *nei confronti di*, to, towards; *in* — *a*, in comparison with.

confucianésimo *sm.* confucianism.

confusamente *avv.* confusedly.

confusionario *agg.* blundering, unmethodical. ♦ **confusionario** *sm.* bungler, muddler.

confusione *sf.* confusion, medley.

confusionismo *sm.* general confusion.

confuso *agg.* 1. confused, mixed, vague 2. (*indistinto*) indistinct 3. (*imbarazzato*) embarrassed.

confutàbile *agg.* confutable.

confutare *vt.* to confute.

confutazione *sf.* confutation.

congedare *vt.* 1. to dismiss 2. (*mil.*) to discharge. ♦ **congedarsi** *vr.* to take (*v. irr.*) one's leave.

congedato *agg.* discharged.

congedo *sm.* 1. (*commiato*) leave 2. (*mil.*) leave, discharge ‖ *essere in* —, to be on leave.

congegnare *vt.* 1. (*mecc.*) to assemble 2. (*fig.*) to devise.

congegno *sm.* 1. device, gear 2. (*fig.*) device, scheme.

congelamento *sm.* 1. freezing 2. (*med.*) congelation.

congelare *vt.* to freeze (*v. irr.*), to congeal.

congelato *agg.* congealed, frozen (*anche comm.*).

congelatore *sm.* freezer.

congènere *agg.* 1. akin (*attr.*) 2. similar (*pred.*).

congeniale *agg.* congenial.

congènito *agg.* congenital, innate.

congestionare *vt.* to congest.

congestionato *agg.* congested: *viso* —, flushed face.

congestione *sf.* congestion.

congettura *sf.* conjecture, supposition.

congetturare *vt.* to conjecture.

congiùngere *vt.* 1. to join 2. (*collegare*) to connect.

congiuntiva *sf.* conjunctiva.

congiuntivite *sf.* conjunctivitis.

congiuntivo *agg.* conjunctive. ♦ **congiuntivo** *sm.* (*gramm.*) subjunctive.

congiunto *agg.* 1. joined, united 2. (*collegato*) connected. ♦ **congiunto** *sm.* relative.

congiuntura *sf.* 1. point of junction 2. (*circostanza, situazione*) circumstance, situation 3. (*econ.*) trend, trade cycle.

congiunzione *sf.* 1. connection 2. (*gramm.; astr.*) conjunction.

congiura *sf.* conspiracy, plot.

congiurare *vi.* to conspire, to plot.

congiurato *sm.* conspirator, plotter.

conglobamento *sm.* conglobation.

conglobare *vt.* 1. to conglobation 2. (*di tasse, debiti ecc.*) to combine.

conglobazione *sf.* conglobation.

conglomerato *sm.* 1. (*geol.*) conglomerate 2. (*etnico; pol.*) grouping.

congratularsi *vr.* to congratulate.

congratulazione *sf.* congratulation.

congregazione *sf.* assembly, congregation (*anche eccl.*).

congressista *s.* member of a congress.

congresso *sm.* congress.

congruo *agg.* 1. (*coerente*) congruous 2. (*adeguato*) adequate.

conguagliare *vt.* 1. to equalize 2. (*comm.*) to balance.

coniare *vt.* to coin (*anche fig.*).

cònico *agg.* conic(al).

conifera *sf.* conifer.

coniglio *sm.* 1. rabbit 2. (*fig.*) faint-hearted.

conio *sm.* 1. (*attrezzo per coniare*) minting die 2. (*impronta*) coin, brand 3. (*invenzione di nuove parole*) coinage.

coniugale *agg.* conjugal: *vita* —, married life.

coniugare *vt.* 1. to conjugate 2. (*unire in matrimonio*) to marry.

coniugato *agg.* married.

coniugazione *sf.* conjugation.

còniuge *sm.* husband. ♦ **còniuge** *sf.* wife.

connaturale *agg.* connatural, innate.

connaturato *agg.* deeply rooted.

connazionale *sm.* fellow-countryman (*pl.* -men). ♦ **connazionale** *sf.* fellow-countrywoman (*pl.* -women).

connessione sf. connection.

connesso agg. connected.

connèttere vt. 1. (unire) to connect, to join 2. (fig.) to associate, to link || non connettere, to talk at random.

connettivo agg. connective.

connivente agg. conniving (at).

connotato sm. description, feature || i connotati, description.

connubio sm. 1. marriage 2. (fig.) union.

cono sm. cone: — gelato, ice-cream cone.

conoscente sm. acquaintance.

conoscenza sf. 1. knowledge || venire a — di qc., to become (v. irr.) acquainted with sthg. 2. (persona) acquaintance 3. (sensi) consciousness.

conòscere vt. 1. to know (v. irr.): — di vista, to know by sight; — di fama, to know by reputation; — dalla voce, to recognize by one's voice 2. (fare la conoscenza) to meet (v. irr.).

conoscìbile agg. 1. knowable 2. (riconoscibile) recognizable.

conoscitivo agg. cognitive.

conoscitore sm. expert, good judge.

conosciuto agg. well-known, renowned.

conquista sf. conquest.

conquistare vt. 1. to conquer 2. (fig.) to win (v. irr.).

conquistatore sm. 1. conqueror 2. (rubacuori) lady-killer.

consacrare vt. 1. (eccl.) to consecrate 2. (dedicare) to devote.

consacrazione sf. consecration.

consanguineità sf. consanguinity.

consanguineo agg. consanguine, akin. ♦ **consanguineo** sm. kinsman (pl. -men).

consapévole agg. aware, conscious.

consapevolezza sf. 1. consciousness 2. (conoscenza) knowledge.

conscio agg. conscious.

consecutivo agg. 1. following 2. (di seguito) running: per due giorni consecutivi, for two days running 3. (gramm.) consecutive.

consegna sf. 1. (comm.) delivery: — contro assegno, cash on delivery; — mancata, nondelivery; ordine di —, delivery-note; effettuare la —, to effect delivery 2. (deposito) consignment 3. (mil.) orders (pl.) || — in caserma, confi-

nement to barracks.

consegnare vt. 1. to deliver 2. (mil.) to confine to barracks.

conseguente agg. consequent.

conseguenza sf. consequence.

conseguìbile agg. attainable.

conseguimento sm. attainment.

conseguire vt. to attain, to achieve, to get (v. irr.).

consenso sm. 1. consent 2. (matrimoniale) licence.

consensuale agg. by mutual consent.

consentire vi. to consent, to agree. ♦ **consentire** vt. to allow.

consenziente agg. consenting.

conserto agg. interwoven, folded: a braccia conserte, with folded arms.

conserva sf. preserve || — di frutta, jam; — di pomodoro, tomato sauce.

conservare vt. to preserve ♦ **conservarsi** vr. to keep (v. irr.).

conservativo agg. conservative.

conservatore agg. 1. preserving 2. (pol.) conservative. ♦ **conservatore** sm. 1. preserver 2. (pol.) conservative.

conservatorio sm. academy of music.

conservazione sf. preservation || istinto di —, instinct· of self-preservation.

considerare vt. 1. to consider, to think (v. irr.) of 2. (reputare) to deem, to judge. ♦ **considerarsi** vr. to consider oneself.

considerato agg. considerate || — che, considering that.

considerazione sf. 1. consideration 2. (stima) esteem, regard || avere — per qu., to have regard for so.

considerévole agg. considerable.

consigliare vt. to advise. ♦ **consigliarsi** vr. to ask so.'s advice, to consult (with).

consigliere sm. 1. counsellor 2. (membro di un consiglio) councillor.

consiglio sm. 1. advice (solo sing.) 2. (corpo di persone) council.

consiliare agg. of a council.

consìmile agg. similar.

consistente agg. firm, substantial.

consistenza sf. 1. consistence 2. (comm.) on hand: — di cassa, cash on hand.

consìstere vi. to consist.

consociare *vt.* to associate.

consociato *agg.* associated.

consociazione *sf.* association.

consocio *sm.* co-partner.

consolante *agg.* cheering.

consolare[1] *vt.* to console, to comfort. ♦ **consolarsi** *vr.* to be comforted.

consolare[2] *agg.* consular.

consolato *sm.* consulate.

consolatore *agg.* consoling. ♦ **consolatore** *sm.* consoler.

consolazione *sf.* consolation, solace.

cònsole *sm.* consul.

consolidamento *sm.* consolidation.

consolidare *vt.* to consolidate, to strengthen.

consolidato *agg.* consolidated.

consonante *sf.* consonant.

consonanza *sf.* consonance (*anche fig.*).

cònsono *agg.* in accordance (with).

consorella *sf.* (*eccl.*) sister.

consorte *sm.* consort, husband. ♦ **consorte** *sf.* consort, wife.

consorteria *sf.* faction.

consorzio *sm.* society: — *agrario*, agricultural union.

constare *vi.* 1. (*essere composto*) to consist 2. (*risultare*) to be within one's knowledge || *da quanto mi consta*, as far as I know.

constatare *vt.* V. *costatare*.

constatazione *sf.* V. *costatazione*.

consueto *agg.* usual, customary.

consuetudinario *agg.* customary, consuetudinary.

consuetùdine *sf.* 1. custom, habit 2. (*comm.*) rule.

consulente *sm.* adviser.

consulenza *sf.* advice.

consulta *sf.* 1. consultation 2. (*corpo consultivo*) council.

consultare *vt.* 1. to consult 2. (*esaminare*) to examine.

consultazione *sf.* consultation: *libro di —*, reference book.

consultivo *agg.* consultative.

consulto *sm.* consultation.

consumare *vt.* 1. to consume 2. (*di abiti*) to wear (*v. irr.*) 3. (*dissipare*) to waste 4. (*compiere*) to commit.

consumato *agg.* 1. (*perfetto*) accomplished 2. (*logoro*) worn out 3. (*divorato*) consumed.

consumatore *sm.* consumer.

consumazione *sf.* 1. consumption 2. (*giur.*) consummation 3. (*bibita*) drink.

consumo *sm.* consumption || *per proprio uso e —*, for one's private use.

consunzione *sf.* consumption.

contàbile *agg.* bookkeeping. ♦ **contàbile** *sm.* bookkeeper.

contabilità *sf.* bookkeeping.

contachilòmetri *sm.* speedometer.

contadino *sm.* countryman (*pl.* -men), peasant. ♦ **contadino** *agg.* rustic.

contado *sm.* countryside.

contagiare *vt.* to infect.

contagio *sm.* contagion (*anche fig.*), infection.

contagioso *agg.* contagious, infectious (*anche fig.*).

contagiri *sm.* revolution counter.

contagocce *sm.* dropper.

contaminare *vt.* 1. to pollute, to infect 2. (*un testo letterario*) to corrupt.

contaminazione *sf.* contamination (*anche fig.*), pollution.

contante *agg.* ready. ♦ **contante** *sm.* ready money || *pagare in contanti*, to pay cash.

contare *vt.* 1. to count, to number 2. (*considerare*) to consider 3. (*proporsi*) to think (*v. irr.*) of || *conto di andare a Milano domani*, I think of going to Milan tomorrow 4. (*aspettarsi*) to expect. ♦ **contare** *vi.* 1. (*avere importanza*) to count, to be important 2. (*fare assegnamento*) to rely on.

contatore *sm.* meter: — *del gas*, gas-meter; — *dell'acqua*, water-meter; — *della luce*, electric power-meter.

contatto *sm.* 1. contact, touch: *essere in —*, to be in touch 2. (*elettr.*) contact.

conte *sm.* 1. Count 2. (*in Gran Bretagna*) Earl.

contea *sf.* 1. earldom 2. (*divisione territoriale*) county.

conteggiare *vt.* to count.

conteggio *sm.* computation.

contegno *sm.* 1. behaviour 2. (*atteggiamento*) attitude.

contegnoso *agg.* 1. dignified 2. (*altero*) stiff.

contemperamento *sm.* adaptation.

contemperare *vt.* to adapt.

contemplare *vt.* 1. to behold (*v.*

irr.), to admire 2. (*giur.*) to consider.

contemplativo *agg.* contemplative.

contemplatore *sm.* contemplator.

contemplazione *sf.* contemplation.

contempo (*nella loc. avv.*) **nel —**, in the meantime.

contemporaneamente *avv.* at the same time.

contemporaneità *sf.* contemporaneousness.

contemporàneo *agg. e sm.* contemporary.

contendente *agg.* contending, opposing. ♦ **contendente** *sm.* opponent, rival.

contèndere *vt.* to contend, to refuse. ♦ **contèndersi** *vr. rec.* to contend.

contenere *vt.* 1. to contain, to hold (*v. irr.*) 2. (*trattenere*) to repress. ♦ **contenersi** *vr.* 1. (*comportarsi*) to behave 2. (*dominarsi*) to contain oneself.

contenitore *sm.* container.

contentare *vt.* to content. ♦ **contentarsi** *vr.* to be content (with).

contentezza *sf.* pleasure, joy.

contento *agg.* content, pleased.

contenuto *sm.* contents (*pl.*).

contenzioso *agg.* contentious.

conterìe *sf. pl.* glass beads.

conterràneo *sm.* fellow-countryman (*pl.* -men) || (*femm.*) fellow-countrywoman (*pl.* -women).

contesa *sf.* 1. contest 2. (*litigio*) quarrel.

contessa *sf.* countess.

contestàbile *agg.* questionable.

contestare *vt.* 1. to contest, to challenge, to deny 2. (*notificare*) to declare.

contestazione *sf.* dispute, objection: **sollevare contestazioni**, to raise objections.

contesto *sm.* context.

contiguità *sf.* contiguity.

contiguo *agg.* neighbouring.

continentale *agg.* continental.

continente *agg.* moderate. ♦ **continente** *sm.* continent.

continenza *sf.* continence.

contingentamento *sm.* allotment.

contingentare *vt.* to allot.

contingenza *sf.* 1. emergency 2. (*circostanza*) circumstance 3. (*fil.*) contingency.

continuamente *avv.* continuously.

continuare *vt. e vi.* 1. to go (*v.*

irr.) on (with) 2. (*riprendere*) to resume.

continuativo *agg.* continuative.

continuato *agg.* 1. (*ininterrotto*) continuous 2. (*che si ripete*) continua!.

continuatore *sm.* continuator.

continuazione *sf.* continuation.

continuità *sf.* continuity.

continuo *agg.* 1. (*ininterrotto*) continuous 2. (*che si ripete*) continual.

conto *sm.* 1. (*anche comm.*) account: **fare i conti**, to make (*v. irr.*) up accounts 2. (*di albergo ecc.*) bill 3. (*assegnamento*) reliance: **far — su**, to rely on 4. (*stima*) regard || **persona di poco —**, person of little account; **rendersi —**, to realize; **mettersi per proprio —**, to set (*v. irr.*) for oneself.

contòrcere *vt.* to twist. ♦ **contòrcersi** *vr.* to twist.

contorcimento *sm.* twisting.

contornare *vt.* 1. to surround 2. (*con guarnizioni*) to trim.

contorno *sm.* 1. outline 2. (*orlo*) border 3. (*cuc.*) vegetables (*pl.*).

contorsione *sf.* contortion.

contorsionismo *sm.* writhing.

contorsionista *s.* contorsionist.

contorto *agg.* twisted.

contrabbandare *vt.* to smuggle.

contrabbandiere *sm.* smuggler.

contrabbando *sm.* smuggling.

contrabbassista *sm.* double-bass player.

contrabbasso *sm.* double-bass.

contraccambiare *vt.* to return.

contraccambio *sm.* return || **rendere il —**, to retaliate (upon).

contraccolpo *sm.* 1. counterblow 2. (*fig.*) reaction.

contraccusa *sf.* countercharge.

contrada *sf.* 1. quarter 2. (*paese*) country.

contraddanza *sf.* country-dance.

contraddire *vt.* to contradict. ♦ **contraddirsi** *vr.* to contradict oneself. ♦ **contraddirsi** *v. rec.* to contradict one another, each other.

contraddistinguere *vt.* to mark.

contraddittore *sm.* opposer.

contraddittorio *agg.* contradictory. ♦ **contraddittorio** *sm.* debate.

contraddizione *sf.* contradiction, discrepancy.

contraente *agg.* contracting. ♦

contraènte sm. contractor.
contraèrea sf. anti-aircraft artillery.
contraèreo agg. anti-aircraft.
contraffare vt. to counterfeit.
contraffatto agg. counterfeit.
contraffattore sm. 1. (falsificatore) counterfeiter 2. (imitatore) imitator.
contrafforte sm. buttress.
contraggenio sm. dislike || a (di) —, unwillingly.
contràlbero sm. (mecc.) countershaft.
contralto sm. contralto.
contrammiraglio sm. rear-admiral.
contrappasso sm. retaliation.
contrappello sm. second roll-call.
contrappesare vt. to counterbalance.
contrappeso sm. counterbalance.
contrapporre vt. to oppose, to contrast || — qc. a qu., to set (v. irr.) sthg. against so.
contrapposizione sf. contraposition.
contrapposto agg. opposite || per —, on the contrary. ◆ **contrapposto** sm. opposite.
contrappunto sm. counterpoint.
contrariamente avv. on the contrary || — ad ogni aspettativa, contrary to all expectation.
contrariare vt. 1. to oppose 2. (irritare) to annoy.
contrarietà sf. 1. opposition 2. (avversità) misfortune.
contrario agg. 1. contrary, opposed 2. (nocivo) harmful 3. (riluttante) unwilling || al —, on the contrary. ◆ **contrario** sm. contrary.
contrarre vt. to contract.
contrassegnare vt. to mark.
contrassegno sm. 1. countersign 2. (segno) mark 3. (distintivo) badge.
contrastare vi. to be in contrast. ◆ **contrastare** vt. to oppose.
contrastato agg. opposed.
contrasto sm. 1. contrast 2. (dissidio) conflict.
contrattaccare vt. to counterattack.
contrattacco sm. counterattack.
contrattare vt. to negotiate: — il prezzo, to haggle about the price.
contrattazione sf. dealing, negotiation.
contrattempo sm. 1. (incidente) mishap 2. (inconveniente) inconvenience.

contràttile agg. contractile.
contratto sm. contract.
contratto agg. contracted.
contrattuale agg. contractual.
contravveleno sm. antidote.
contravvenire vi. to infringe.
contravventore sm. transgressor.
contravvenzione sf. 1. violation 2. (multa) fine.
contrazione sf. contraction.
contribuente sm. taxpayer.
contribuire vi. to contribute.
contributo sm. contribution.
contribuzione sf. contribution.
contristarsi vr. to grieve.
contrito agg. contrite.
contrizione sf. contrition.
contro prep. 1. against 2. (in opposizione a) contrary to || — assegno, cash on delivery.
controbàttere vt. (confutare) to disprove, to confute.
controbilanciare vt. to counterbalance.
controcampo sm. (cine) reverse shot.
controcorrente sf. counter-current. ◆ **controcorrente** loc. avv. against the stream.
controffensiva sf. counter-offensive.
controfigura sf. double.
controfirmare vt. to countersign.
controindicare vt. (med.) to contra-indicate.
controindicazione sf. (med.) contra-indication.
controllare vt. 1. to control 2. (verificare) to verify, to check 3. (ispezionare) to inspect 4. (comm.) to audit.
controllo sm. 1. control 2. (verifica) check, verification 3. (ispezione) inspection 4. (comm.) audit.
controllore sm. 1. controller 2. (ferr.) ticket-inspector.
controluce avv. against the light. ◆ **controluce** sf. counterlight.
contromarca sf. pass-out check (ticket).
controparte sf. counter-party.
contropartita sf. 1. (comm.) counter-item 2. (compenso) compensation.
contropelo sm. wrong way of the hair || fare il —, to shave against the lie of the hair.
controproducente agg. having opposite effect.

controproposta sf. counter-proposal.

controprova sf. 1. countercheck 2. (giur.) counter-evidence.

contròrdine sm. counter-order: dare un —, to countermand an order.

controriforma sf. counter-reformation.

controrivoluzione sf. counter-revolution.

controsenso sm. self-contradiction, absurdity.

controspionaggio sm. counter-espionage.

controstòmaco avv. reluctantly.

controvelaccio sm. (mar.) main royal.

controvento avv. against the wind.

controversia sf. controversy.

controverso agg. controversial.

controvertìbile agg. controvertible.

controvoglia avv. unwillingly.

contumace agg. guilty of default.

contumacia sf. default.

contumaciale agg. (giur.) judgement by default.

contumelia sf. insult, abuse.

contundente agg. blunt: corpo —, blunt instrument.

conturbare vt. 1. to perturb 2. (eccitare) to thrill.

contusione sf. bruise.

contuso agg. bruised.

convalescente agg. e sm. convalescent.

convalescenza sf. convalescence.

convalidare vt. to ratify, to confirm.

convegno sm. meeting.

convenévole agg. convenient, proper. ♦ **convenévoli** sm. pl. compliments.

conveniente agg. 1. convenient (for) 2. (economicamente vantaggioso) profitable.

convenienza sf. 1. convenience 2. (vantaggio economico) profit 3. (buona creanza) propriety.

convenire vi. 1. to convene 2. (essere d'accordo) to agree 3. (essere utile) to be convenient.

convento sm. 1. convent 2. (di suore) nunnery.

conventuale agg. conventual.

convenuto agg. agreed upon. ♦ **convenuto** sm. 1. agreement 2. i convenuti, the persons present.

convenzionale agg. conventional.

convenzionare vt. to make (v. irr.) an agreement.

convenzione sf. convention.

convergente agg. convergent.

convergenza sf. convergence.

convèrgere vi. to converge.

conversare vi. to talk.

conversatore sm. talker.

conversazione sf. conversation, talk.

conversione sf. 1. (anche fig.) conversion 2. (mil.) wheel.

convertìbile agg. convertible.

convertire vt. 1. (pol.; relig.) to convert 2. (mutare) to turn, to change. ♦ **convertirsi** vr. to be converted.

convessità sf. convexity.

convesso agg. convex.

convincere vt. to convince, to persuade.

convinto agg. convinced, persuaded.

convinzione sf. persuasion, firm belief.

convitato sm. guest.

convito sm. banquet.

convitto sm. boarding-school.

convivente agg. cohabiting.

convivenza sf. cohabitation, life in common.

convivere vi. to live together.

convocare vt. to convene, to summon.

convocazione sf. convocation, summoning.

convogliare vt. 1. (scortare) to escort 2. (trasportare) to carry away 3. (indirizzare) to address.

convoglio sm. 1. (treno) train 2. (mil.; mar.) convoy.

convolare vi. to fly (v. irr.) together: — a giuste nozze, to get (v. irr.) married.

convulsione sf. convulsion.

convulso agg. convulsive.

cooperare vi. to co-operate, to collaborate.

cooperativa sf. 1. co-operative society 2. (di consumo) co-operative store.

cooperativo agg. co-operative.

cooperatore sm. co-operator.

cooperazione sf. co-operation, collaboration.

coordinamento sm. co-ordination.

coordinare vt. to co-ordinate.

coordinata sf. co-ordinate.

coordinativo agg. co-ordinative.

coordinato agg. co-ordinate.

coordinatore *agg.* co-ordinative. ◆
 coordinatore *sm.* co-ordinator.

coordinazione *sf.* co-ordination.

coorte *sf.* 1. (*mil.*) cohort 2. (*folla*)
 crowd.

copale *sf.* 1. copal 2. (*pelle*) patent
 leather.

copeco *sm.* copeck.

coperchio *sm.* lid, cover (*anche
 mecc.*).

coperta *sf.* 1. blanket: — *da viaggio*, rug; — *scozzese*, plaid 2.
 (*mar.*) deck.

copertina *sf.* cover: — *di libro*,
 book-cover.

coperto *agg.* 1. (*riparato*) covered,
 sheltered || — *di ferro*, iron-clad;
 mettere al —, to shelter from 2.
 (*di cielo*) overcast 3. (*nascosto*)
 hidden. ◆ **coperto** *sm.* cover.

copertone *sm.* tyre.

copertura *sf.* 1. covering 2. (*di mobili*) cover.

copia *sf.* 1. copy 2. (*foto*) print.

copiare *vt.* to copy.

copiativo *agg.* *matita copiativa*,
 copying pencil.

copiatura *sf.* copying.

copione *sm.* script.

copiosamente *avv.* plentifully.

copioso *agg.* plentiful.

copista *sm.* copyist.

coppa *sf.* 1. cup 2. (*auto*) pan.

coppella *sf.* (*metal.*) cupel.

coppellare *vt.* (*metal.*) to cupel.

coppia *sf.* 1. (*di persone e cose*)
 couple 2. (*di animali*) pair || *una
 — di buoi*, a yoke.

copricapo *sm.* hat.

coprifuoco *sm.* curfew.

copriletto *sm.* coverlet.

coprire *vt.* 1. to cover 2. (*nascondere*) to conceal 3. (*coprire un suono*) to drown.

copto *agg.* coptic. ◆ **copto** *sm.*
 copt.

copulativo *agg.* (*gramm.*) copulative.

copulazione *sf.* copulation.

coraggio *sm.* 1. courage, bravery,
 heart 2. (*sfrontatezza*) impudence.

coraggiosamente *avv.* bravely.

coraggioso *agg.* brave, bold.

corale *agg.* choral.

corallifero *agg.* coralliferous.

corallo *sm.* coral.

corazza *sf.* 1. cuirass 2. (*bot.; zool.*)
 armour, carapace.

corazzare *vt.* 1. to armour 2. (*fig.*)

to strengthen. ◆ **corazzarsi** *vr.*
 to harden oneself.

corazzata *sf.* (*mar.*) battleship.

corazziere *sm.* cuirassier.

corbelleria *sf.* 1. foolish action 2.
 (*sciocchezza*) nonsense.

corda *sf.* 1. rope 2. (*mus.*) string.

cordaio *sm.* 1. (*chi fabbrica corde*)
 rope-maker 2. (*chi vende corde*)
 rope-seller.

cordame *sm.* cordage.

cordata *sf.* rope: *in* —, on the rope.

cordiale *agg.* cordial, hearty. ◆
 cordiale *sm.* (*liquore*) cordial.

cordialità *sf.* cordiality.

cordialmente *avv.* cordially.

cordicella *sf.* string.

cordigliera *sf.* cordillera.

cordite *sf.* cordite.

cordoglio *sm.* deep sorrow.

cordone *sm.* 1. cord 2. (*mil.*) cordon.

coreano *agg. e sm.* Korean.

coreografia *sf.* choreography.

coreografico *agg.* 1. choreographic
 2. (*fig.*) spectacular.

coreografo *sm.* choreographer.

coriaceo *agg.* coriaceous, tough.

coriandolo *sm.* confetti (*pl.*).

coricare *vt.* to lay (*v. irr.*) down.
 ◆ **coricarsi** *vr.* to lie (*v. irr.*)
 down.

corifeo *sm.* coryphaeus (*pl.* -aei).

corinzio *agg. e sm.* Corinthian.

corista *sm.* chorus-singer.

cormorano *sm.* (*zool.*) cormorant.

cornacchia *sf.* rook, crow.

cornamusa *sf.* bagpipe.

cornata *sf.* butt.

cornea *sf.* cornea.

cornetta *sf.* cornet.

cornice *sf.* frame.

cornicione *sm.* 1. (*arch.*) cornice
 2. (*di finestre, porte*) label 3. (*di
 gronda*) eaves (*pl.*).

cornificare *vt.* 1. (*di moglie*) to
 cuckold 2. (*di marito*) to be unfaithful to.

corno *sm.* horn || (*inter.*) *un* —, not
 at all.

cornuto *agg.* horned. ◆ **cornuto**
 sm. (*fig.*) cuckold.

coro *sm.* 1. chorus 2. (*eccl.*) choir.

corolla *sf.* corolla.

corollario *sm.* corollary.

corona *sf.* 1. crown: — *del rosario*,
 rosary crown; — *del dente*, crown
 2. (*mecc.*) rim 3. (*relig.*) (*tonsura*)
 tonsure.

coronamento *sm.* **1.** crowning **2.** (*completamento*) fulfilment.

coronare *vt.* to crown (*anche fig.*).

coronario *agg.* coronary.

corpo *sm.* **1.** body || *a — morto*, desperately; *combattere a — a —*, to fight (*v. irr.*) hand to hand; *passare sul — di qu.*, to pass over so. **2.** (*cadavere*) corpse **3.** (*collettività*) corps || *— insegnante*, teaching staff.

corporale *agg.* corporal.

corporativismo *sm.* (*econ.*) corporative system.

corporativo *agg.* (*econ.*) corporative.

corporatura *sf.* build, size.

corporazione *sf.* corporation.

corpòreo *agg.* corporeal.

corpulento *agg.* corpulent, stout.

corpulenza *sf.* stoutness.

corpuscolare *agg.* corpuscular.

corpùscolo *sm.* corpuscle.

corredare *vt.* **1.** to equip **2.** (*accompagnare*) to accompany.

corredino *sm.* baby's outfit.

corredo *sm.* **1.** outfit **2.** (*di sposa*) trousseau **3.** (*bagaglio*) wealth, store: *— di cultura*, store of knowledge.

corrèggere *vt.* **1.** to correct **2.** (*di bevande*) to lace. ♦ **corrèggersi** *vr.* to amend, to correct oneself.

correggia *sf.* leather strap.

correlativo *agg.* correlative.

correlazione *sf.* correlation.

corrente[1] *agg.* **1.** (*che scorre*) running **2.** (*circolante*) current **3.** (*comm.*) inst. (*abbrev. di instant*) || *conto —*, current account **4.** (*andante*) common.

corrente[2] *sf.* **1.** current (*anche fig.*), stream **2.** (*di aria*) draught.

correntemente *avv.* fluently.

còrrere *vi.* **1.** to run (*v. irr.*): *— dietro a qu.*, to run after; *— a gambe levate*, to run as hard as one can || *lasciar —*, to take (*v. irr.*) no notice of sthg. **2.** (*di tempo*) to pass **3.** (*di voci*) to be abroad.

corresponsàbile *agg.* jointly responsible.

corresponsione *sf.* payment.

correttezza *sf.* **1.** correctness **2.** (*onestà*) honesty **3.** (*decoro, educazione*) propriety, politeness.

correttivo *agg.* e *sm.* corrective.

corretto *agg.* **1.** correct, exact **2.** (*irreprensibile*) faultless **3.** (*di bevanda*) laced.

correttore *sm.* corrector || *— di bozze*, proof-reader.

correzionale *agg.* correctional.

correzione *sf.* correction || *— di bozze*, proof-reading; *casa di —*, house of correction.

corridoio *sm.* **1.** passage **2.** (*di treno*) corridor.

corridore *sm.* **1.** runner **2.** (*sport*) racer.

corriera *sf.* coach.

corriere *sm.* **1.** messenger **2.** (*chi trasporta merci*) carrier **3.** (*posta*) mail.

corrimano *sm.* handrail.

corrispettivo *agg.* correlative. ♦ **corrispettivo** *sm.* **1.** equivalent **2.** (*compenso*) compensation.

corrispondente *agg.* e *sm.* correspondent.

corrispondenza *sf.* correspondence.

corrispòndere *vi.* **1.** to correspond (with) **2.** (*ricambiare sentimenti ecc.*) to return. ♦ **corrispòndere** *vt.* to pay.

corrisposto *agg.* **1.** (*contraccambiato*) returned **2.** (*pagato*) paid.

corroborante *agg.* e *sm.* corroborant.

corroborare *vt.* to strengthen.

corròdere *vt.* to corrode.

corrómpere *vt.* **1.** to corrupt (*anche fig.*), to pollute **2.** (*con denaro*) to bribe.

corrosione *sf.* corrosion.

corrosivo *agg.* e *sm.* corrosive.

corrucciarsi *vr.* to get (*v. irr.*) angry.

corrucciato *agg.* angry, worried.

corruccio *sm.* anger, worry.

corrugamento *sm.* corrugation: *— della fronte*, wrinkling of the forehead.

corrugare *vt.* to wrinkle.

corruttibile *agg.* corruptible.

corruttore *agg.* corrupting. ♦ **corruttore** *sm.* **1.** corrupter **2.** (*con denaro*) briber.

corruzione *sf.* **1.** corruption **2.** (*con denaro*) bribery.

corsa *sf.* **1.** run **2.** (*sport*) race **3.** (*su veicolo pubblico*) trip || *prezzo della —*, fare; (*ferr.*) *perdere la —*, to miss the train.

corsaro *sm.* corsair.

corsetto *sm.* corset.

corsìa *sf.* **1.** passage **2.** (*di ospedale*) ward **3.** (*di strada*) lane.

corsiero *sm.* steed.

corsivo *agg.* cursive. ♦ **corsivo** *sm.* (*tip.*) italics (*pl.*).

corso *sm.* 1. course (*anche fig.*) 2. (*di acque*) water-course.

corte *sf.* 1. court 2. (*cortile*) courtyard 3. (*corteggiamento*) courtship.

corteccia *sf.* 1. bark 2. (*anat.*) cortex.

corteggiare *vt.* 1. to woo 2. (*adulare*) to flatter.

corteggiatore *sm.* suitor, lover.

corteo *sm.* train, procession: — *funebre*, funeral train.

cortese *agg.* kind.

cortesia *sf.* 1. kindness, politeness 2. (*favore*) favour || *per* —, please.

cortigiano *sm.* 1. courtier 2. (*adulatore*) flatterer.

cortile *sm.* courtyard || *animali da* —, poultry.

cortina *sf.* curtain: — *di ferro* (*pol.*), iron curtain.

cortisone *sm.* cortisone.

corto *agg.* short: *a* — *di*, short of.

cortocircuito *sm.* short circuit.

cortometraggio *sm.* short (film).

corvetta *sf.* (*mar.*) corvette.

corvino *agg.* 1. corvine 2. (*nero*) raven(-black).

corvo *sm.* raven.

cosa *sf.* 1. thing 2. (*faccenda*) matter || *nessuna* —, nothing; *ogni* —, everything; *che* —?, what?.

cosacco *agg. e sm.* Cossack.

coscia *sf.* 1. thigh 2. (*cuc.*) leg.

cosciente *agg.* 1. conscious 2. (*conscio*) aware.

coscienza *sf.* 1. conscience 2. (*consapevolezza*) consciousness.

coscienziosamente *avv.* conscientiously.

coscienzioso *agg.* conscientious.

cosciotto *sm.* leg: — *di manzo*, leg of beef.

coscritto *sm.* recruit.

coscrizione *sf.* conscription.

cosecante *sf.* cosecant.

coseno *sm.* (*mat.*) cosine.

così *avv.* so: *e* — *via*, and so on; — *come*, — *pure*, as well as; — *come*, — ... *quanto*, as ... as; — *da*, so ... as: *non è* — *sciocco da farlo*, he is not so foolish as to do that.

cosicché *cong.* so that.

cosiddetto *agg.* so-called.

cosiffatto *agg.* such, similar.

cosmesi *sf.* beauty culture.

cosmètico *agg. e sm.* cosmetic.

còsmico *agg.* cosmic.

cosmo *sm.* cosmos.

cosmogonìa *sf.* cosmogony.

cosmografia *sf.* cosmography.

cosmògrafo *sm.* cosmographer.

cosmologia *sf.* cosmology.

cosmonàuta *s.* astronaut.

cosmonàutica *sf.* astronautics.

cosmopolita *agg. e sm.* cosmopolitan.

cosmopolitismo *sm.* cosmopolitanism.

coso *sm.* (*fam.*) 1. (*cosa*) thing 2. (*individuo*) fellow.

cospàrgere *vt.* 1. to strew (*v. irr.*) 2. (*sale, zucchero ecc.*) to sprinkle.

cospetto *sm.* presence: *al* — *di*, in the presence of.

cospicuità *sf.* conspicuousness.

cospìcuo *agg.* 1. (*visibile*) conspicuous 2. (*notevole*) remarkable.

cospirare *vi.* to plot.

cospiratore *sm.* plotter.

cospirazione *sf.* plot.

costa *sf.* 1. coast, shore 2. (*venatura*) rib 3. (*di monte*) side 4. (*di libro*) back.

costà *avv.* there.

costaggiù *avv.* down there.

costale *agg.* costal.

costante *agg.* steady. ♦ **costante** *sf.* constant.

costanza *sf.* 1. firmness 2. (*perseveranza*) perseverance || *con* —, steadily.

costare *vi.* to cost (*v. irr.*).

costassù *avv.* up there.

costata *sf.* chop.

costatare *vt.* 1. (*accertare*) to ascertain 2. (*notare*) to notice.

costatazione *sf.* 1. ascertainment 2. (*osservazione*) remark.

costato *sm.* chest.

costeggiare *vt.* 1. to follow the coast of 2. (*per terra*) to skirt. ♦ **costeggiare** *vi.* to coast along.

costei *pron.* 1. (*sogg.*) she 2. (*compl.*) her 3. this woman, that woman.

costellare *vt.* to scatter.

costellazione *sf.* constellation.

costernare *vt.* to dismay. ♦ **costernarsi** *vr.* to be dismayed (at).

costernazione *sf.* dismay.

costì *avv.* there.

costiera *sf.* stretch of coast.

costiero *agg.* coastal || *nave costiera*, coaster.

costipare *vt.* 1. (*un terreno*) to tamp 2. (*ammassare*) to amass. ♦ **costiparsi** *vr.* 1. (*raffreddarsi*) to catch (*v. irr.*) a cold 2. (*di intestino*) to become (*v. irr.*) constipated.

costipato *agg.* essere —, to have a cold.

costipazione *sf.* 1. (*raffreddore*) cold 2. (*intestinale*) constipation 3. (*di terreno*) tamping.

costituente *agg.* constituent.

costituire *vt.* 1. to constitute, to form 2. (*nominare*) to appoint. ♦ **costituirsi** *vr.* (*consegnarsi*) to give (*v. irr.*) oneself up.

costituito *agg.* constituted.

costitutivo *agg.* constitutive.

costituto *sm.* (*giur.*) interrogation of the accused.

costituzionale *agg.* constitutional.

costituzionalismo *sm.* constitutionalism.

costituzionalità *sf.* constitutionality.

costituzione *sf.* 1. establishment 2. (*pol.; med.*) constitution.

costo *sm.* cost: ad ogni —, at all cost; a nessun —, in no case.

còstola *sf.* rib ‖ stare alle costole, to watch over.

costoletta *sf.* cutlet.

costone *sm.* side.

costoro *pron.* 1. (*sogg.*) they 2. (*compl.*) them 3. these people, those people.

costoso *agg.* expensive, dear.

costringere *vt.* 1. (*stringere*) to press 2. (*obbligare*) to compel.

costrizione *sf.* 1. (*restringimento*) constriction 2. (*obbligo*) compulsion.

costruire *vt.* to build (*v. irr.*).

costruttivo *agg.* constructive.

costruttore *agg.* building. ♦ **costruttore** *sm.* builder.

costruzione *sf.* construction, building.

costui *pron.* 1. (*sogg.*) he 2. (*compl.*) him 3. this man, that man.

costumato *agg.* 1. (*virtuoso*) virtuous 2. (*educato*) polite.

costume *sm.* 1. (*usanza*) custom 2. (*personale*) habit 3. (*condotta*) morals (*pl.*) 4. (*vestito*) costume.

costumista *sm.* costume-designer.

cotangente *sf.* (*mat.*) cotangent.

cotenna *sf.* 1. pigskin 2. (*del cranio*) scalp 3. (*del lardo*) rind.

còtica *sf.* V. cotenna.

cotogna *sf.* quince.

cotognata *sf.* quince jam.

cotoletta *sf.* cutlet.

cotone *sm.* cotton.

cotoniere *sm.* cotton-spinner.

cotoniero *agg.* cotton.

cotonificio *sm.* cotton-mill.

cotonina *sf.* calico.

cotta¹ *sf.* (*eccl.*) surplice.

cotta² *sf.* 1. (*cottura*) cooking 2. (*infornata*) batch 3. (*fam.*) prendere una — per, to have a crush on.

cottimista *sm.* pieceworker.

còttimo *sm.* piecework: lavorare a —, to work by the job; lavoro a —, job-work; contratto a —, job contract.

cotto *sm.* brickwork.

cottura *sf.* 1. cooking 2. (*in forno*) baking.

coturno *sm.* cothurnus (*pl.* -ni).

cova *sf.* 1. (*il covare*) brooding 2. (*nido*) nest.

covare *vt.* 1. to brood 2. (*fig.*) to brood over 3. (*di fuoco; passioni*) to smoulder 4. (*di malattia*) to be latent.

covata *sf.* brood.

covo *sm.* den.

covone *sm.* sheaf (*pl.* sheaves).

cozza *sf.* mussel.

cozzare *vi.* 1. to strike (*v. irr.*) 2. (*venire in collisione*) to collide.

cozzo *sm.* 1. clash, collision 2. (*conflitto*) conflict.

crampo *sm.* cramp.

cranio *sm.* skull.

crasso *agg.* crass, gross: ignoranza crassa, gross ignorance.

cratere *sm.* crater.

cràuti *sm. pl.* sauerkraut (*sing.*)

cravatta *sf.* neck-tie.

creanza *sf.* politeness.

creare *vt.* 1. to create 2. (*causare*) to cause 3. (*nominare*) to appoint 4. (*costituire*) to form.

creativo *agg.* creative.

creato *sm.* creation.

creatore *agg.* creating. ♦ **creatore** *sm.* creator.

creatura *sf.* creature.

creazione *sf.* creation.

credente *sm.* believer.

credenza¹ *sf.* belief.

credenza² *sf.* (*buffet*) sideboard.

credenziale *agg.* credential: lettera —, credential.

crédere vt. e vi. 1. (pensare) to think (v irr.) 2. (prestar fede) to believe. ♦ **crédersi** vr. to think (v. irr.) oneself.

credìbile agg. 1. credible 2. (di persona) trustworthy.

credibilità sf. credibility.

creditizio agg. credit.

crédito sm. 1. (comm.) credit: a —, on credit 2. (stima) esteem.

creditore sm. creditor.

credo sm. creed.

credulità sf. credulity.

credulone agg. credulous.

crema sf. cream.

cremagliera sf. rack: ferrovia a —, rack-railway.

cremare vt. to cremate.

crematorio agg. crematory: forno —, crematory.

cremazione sf. cremation.

cremeria sf. creamery.

crèmisi agg. e sm. crimson.

crèolo agg. e sm. creole.

crepa sf. crack.

crepaccio sm. crevasse.

crepacuore sm. heart-break: morire di —, to die of a broken heart.

crepapelle (nella loc. avv.) ridere a —, to roar with laughter; mangiare a —, to eat to excess.

crepare vi. to crack.

crepella sf. crepoline.

crepitare vi. to crackle.

crepitìo sm. crackle.

crepuscolare agg. crepuscular.

crepùscolo sm. twilight.

crescente agg. growing.

crescenza sf. growth.

créscere vi. 1. to grow (v. irr.) 2. (aumentare) to increase.

crescione sm. (bot.) water-cress.

créscita sf. 1. growth 2. (aumento) increase.

crèsima sf. confirmation.

cresimare vt. to confirm.

creso sm. Croesus.

crespo agg. crisp.

cresta sf. 1. crest 2. (di gallo) comb.

crestina sf. maid-servant's cap.

creta sf. clay.

cretineria sf. 1. idiocy 2. (azione) foolish action 3. (detto) nonsense.

cretinismo sm. idiocy.

cretino agg. e sm. idiot.

cricca sf. gang.

cricco sm. jack.

criminale agg. e sm. criminal.

criminalista s. 1. (avvocato) criminal lawyer 2. (studioso) criminologist.

criminalità sf. criminality.

crimine sm. crime.

criminologìa sf. criminology.

criminosità sf. criminality.

criminoso agg. criminal.

crine sm. horse-hair.

criniera sf. mane.

crinolina sf. crinoline.

criolite sf. cryolite.

cripta sf. crypt.

crisàlide sf. chrysalid.

crisantemo sm. chrysanthemum.

crisi sf. 1. crisis (pl. -ses) 2. (med.) fit.

crisma sm. 1. (eccl.) chrism 2. (fig.) approval || con tutti i crismi, approved, praised.

cristalleria sf. 1. crystal-ware 2. (fabbrica) crystal manufactory.

cristalliera sf. glass case.

cristallino agg. e sm. crystalline.

cristallizzare vt. e vi., **cristallizzarsi** vr. to crystallize.

cristallizzazione sf. crystallization.

cristallo sm. 1. crystal 2. (lastra di vetro) plate glass.

cristallografìa sf. crystallography.

cristianésimo sm. Christianity.

cristiania sm. (sport) Christiania.

cristianità sf. 1. (i cristiani) Christendom 2. (cristianesimo) Christianity.

cristiano agg. e sm. Christian.

criterio sm. 1. principle 2. opinion 3. (buon senso) sense.

critica sf. 1. criticism 2. (saggio) critical essay 3. (i critici) the critics (pl.).

criticamente avv. critically.

criticare vt. 1. to criticize 2. (biasimare) to blame.

criticismo sm. 1. criticism 2. (stor.) critical philosophy.

crìtico agg. critical. ♦ **crìtico** sm critic.

criticone sm. fault-finder.

crittògama sf. (bot.) cryptogam.

crittografìa sf. cryptography.

crittogramma sm. cryptogram.

crivellare vt. to riddle.

crivellatura sf. riddling.

crivello sm. riddle.

croato agg. e sm. Croatian.

croccante agg. crisp. ♦ **croccante** sm. almond sweetmeat.

crocchetta sf. croquette.
crocchia sf. bun.
crocchio sm. group.
croce sf. cross.
crocerossina sf. Red Cross nurse.
crociata sf. crusade.
crociato sm. crusader.
crocicchio sm. cross-road.
crociera sf. 1. cruise 2. (arch.) cross-vault.
crocifiggere vt. to crucify.
crocifissione sf. crucifixion.
crocifisso sm. crucifix.
croco sm. (bot.) crocus.
crogiuolo sm. crucible.
crollare vi. to fall (v. irr.) down.
crollo sm. 1. breakdown 2. (caduta) falling down.
croma sf. (mus.) quaver.
cromare vt. to chromium-plate.
cromàtico agg. chromatic.
cromatismo sm. chromatism.
cromatografia sf. chromatography.
cromatura sf. chromium plating.
cromo sm. chromium.
cromolitografia sf. chromolithography.
cromosomo sm. chromosome.
crònaca sf. 1. chronicle 2. (di giornale) news.
crònico agg. chronic. ♦ **crònico** sm. chronic invalid.
cronista sm. reporter.
cronistoria sf. chronicle.
cronologìa sf. chronology.
cronològico agg. chronological.
cronometraggio sm. time-study.
cronometrare vt. to time.
cronometrìa sf. timing.
cronòmetro sm. stop watch.
crosta sf. 1. crust 2. (tec.) coating.
crostàcei sm. pl. Crustacea.
crostata sf. (cuc.) tart.
cròtalo sm. rattlesnake.
crucciare vt., **crucciarsi** vr. to worry.
cruciale agg. crucial.
cruciverba sm. cross-word puzzle.
crudele agg. cruel.
crudeltà sf. cruelty.
crudezza sf. 1. (di stagione) harshness 2. (di parole) coarseness 3. (di cibo) rawness.
crudo agg. 1. raw 2. (poco cotto) underdone 3. (aspro, rigido) harsh 4. (rozzo) coarse.
cruento agg. bloody.
crumiro sm. blackleg.
cruna sf. needle's eye.

crusca sf. bran.
cruscotto sm. dashboard.
cubaggio sm. cubage.
cubano agg. e sm. Cuban.
cubatura sf. cubature.
cubetto sm. — di ghiaccio, ice cube.
cùbico agg. cubic.
cubismo sm. cubism.
cubitale agg. a caratteri cubitali, in very large letters.
cùbito sm. 1. (misura) cubit 2. (avambraccio) forearm.
cubo sm. cube.
cuccagna sf. abundance || albero della —, greasy pole.
cuccetta sf. berth.
cucchiaiata sf. spoonful.
cucchiaino sm. 1. tea-spoon, coffee-spoon 2. (il contenuto) tea-spoonful.
cucchiaio sm. spoon.
cuccia sf. dog-house.
cucciolo sm. puppy.
cùccuma sf. kettle.
cucina sf. 1. kitchen 2. (modo di cucinare) cooking 3. (culinaria) cookery 4. (stufa) stove.
cucinare vt. to cook.
cuciniere sm. man-cook.
cucire vt. 1. to sew (v. irr.) 2. (med.) to stitch.
cucito sm. needlework.
cucitrice sf. 1. seamstress 2. (macchinetta) stapler.
cucitura sf. 1. seam 2. (di fogli) stapling.
cucù sm. (zool.) cuckoo.
cucùrbita sf. gourd.
cuffia sf. 1. cap. 2. (radio) headphone.
cugina sf. cousin.
cugino sm. cousin.
cui pron. rel. 1. (di possesso) whose; (di possesso, solo per animali e cose) of which: l'uomo la — casa, the man whose house; il libro le — pagine, the book the pages of which 2. (altri casi, per persone) whom; (altri casi, per animali e cose) which: l'uomo con — parlai, the man to whom I spoke; il libro di — parlai, the book about which I spoke || in — (dove), where; in — (quando) when.
culaccio sm. rump.
culatta sf. breech.
culinaria sf. cookery.
culinario agg. culinary.

culla sf. cradle.

cullare vt. to rock, to lull (anche fig.).

culminante agg. culminant: momento —, climax.

culminare vi. to culminate.

cùlmine sm. 1. summit 2. (fig.) apex.

culo sm. bottom; (volg.) ass.

culto sm. 1. cult 2. (religione) religion 3. (adorazione) worship.

cultore sm. lover.

cultura sf. culture.

culturale agg. cultural.

cumulare vt. to heap up.

cumulativo agg. cumulative.

cumulatore sm. hoarder.

cumulazione sf. hoarding.

cùmulo sm. 1. heap 2. (nube) cumulus (pl. -li).

cuna sf. cradle.

cuneiforme agg. cuneiform, wedge-shaped.

cùneo sm. wedge.

cunetta sf. 1. (stradale) road bump 2. (scolo) gutter.

cunìcolo sm. underground passage, shaft.

cuòcere vt. 1. to cook 2. (in forno, fornace) to bake.

cuoco sm. cook.

cuolame sm. leather and hides.

cuoio sm. leather || — capelluto, scalp.

cuore sm. heart.

cupezza sf. 1. darkness 2. (tristezza) gloom.

cupidigia sf. cupidity, greed.

cùpido agg. greedy.

cupo agg. 1. dark 2. (triste) gloomy 3. (profondo) deep.

cùpola sf. dome.

cùpreo agg. cupreous.

cùprico agg. cupric.

cura sf. 1. care 2. (med.) treatment || casa di —, nursing-home.

curàbile agg. curable.

curante agg. medico —, attending physician.

curare vt. 1. (aver cura di) to take (v. irr.) care of 2. (med.) to treat 3. (una pubblicazione) to edit. ♦ **curarsi** vr. (seguire una cura) to follow a treatment.

curaro sm. curare.

curato sm. vicar.

curatore sm. trustee.

curdo agg. Kurdish. ♦ **curdo** sm. Kurd.

curia sf. 1. (eccl.) see 2. (giur.) court of justice.

curie sm. curie.

curiosare vi. to pry.

curiosità sf. 1. curiosity 2. (stranezza) oddity.

curioso agg. curious.

currìculum sm. curriculum (pl. -la).

cursore sm. 1. messenger 2. (mecc.) slider.

curva sf. bend.

curvare vt. to bend (v. irr.). ♦ **curvarsi** vr. 1. to bend (v. irr.) 2. (inclinarsi) to bow.

curvatura sf. 1. bending 2. (arch.) sweep.

curvilìneo agg. curvilinear.

curvo agg. bent.

cuscinetto sm. small cushion || — a sfera, ball bearing.

cuscino sm. 1. cushion 2. (guanciale) pillow 3. (mecc.) pillow.

custode sm. keeper.

custodia sf. 1. care 2. (tutela) guardianship 3. (astuccio) case.

custodire vt. 1. to keep (v. irr.) 2. (aver cura di) to look after.

cutàneo agg. skin: malattia cutanea, skin disease.

cute sf. skin.

D

da prep. 1. (provenienza) from: vengo — Milano, I come from Milan 2. (moto a luogo) to: andremo — loro, we shall go to their house 3. (stato in luogo) at: vivo — mia zia, I live at my aunt's 4. (moto per luogo) through: passai — Roma, I passed through Rome 5. (tempo, durata) for: siamo qui — due mesi, we have been here for two months; (a partire da) since: lo conosco dal 1955, I have known him since 1955 6. (agente) by: fu aiutato — sua sorella, he was helped by his sister 7. (come) like: si comportano — bambini, they are behaving like children || fare —, to act as.

dabbasso avv. 1. below, down below 2. (al piano inferiore) downstairs.

dabbenàggine *sf.* ingenuousness.
dabbene *agg.* honest.
daccapo *avv.* over again, from the beginning.
dacché *cong.* since.
dadaismo *sm.* dadaism.
dado *sm.* **1.** die (*pl.* dice) **2.** (*cuc.*) cube **3.** (*mecc.*) nut.
daffare *sm.* work || *darsi* —, to be on the go.
dagherrotipìa *sf.* daguerreotypy.
dagherròtipo *sm.* daguerreotype.
dàgli, dài *inter.* go on.
dàino *sm.* fallow-deer (*invariato al pl.*).
dàlia *sf.* dahlia.
daltònico *agg.* colour-blind.
daltonismo *sm.* colour-blindness.
d'altronde *avv.* on the other hand.
dama *sf.* **1.** lady of rank **2.** (*al ballo*) partner **3.** (*giuoco*) draughts (*pl.*).
damasco *sm.* damask.
damerino *sm.* dandy.
damiere *sm.* draughtboard.
damigella *sf.* maid of honour.
damigiana *sf.* demijohn.
danaroso *agg.* wealthy.
danese *agg.* Danish. ♦ **danese** *sm.* Dane.
dannare *vt.* to damn || *far* —, to drive (*v. irr.*) so. mad. ♦ **dannarsi 1.** to be damned **2.** (*fig.*) to strive (*v. irr.*) hard.
dannato *agg.* damned. ♦ **dannato** *sm.* damned soul.
dannazione *sf.* damnation: —!, damn!
danneggiamento *sm.* damage.
danneggiare *vt.* **1.** to damage **2.** (*di persone*) to injure.
danno *sm.* **1.** damage **2.** (*a persona*) injury || *recare* — *a qu.*, to do (*v. irr.*) so. harm.
dànnoso *agg.* harmful.
dantesco *agg.* Dantesque.
danza *sf.* dance.
danzante *agg.* dancing: *trattenimento* —, dance.
danzare *vt. e vi.* to dance.
danzatore *sm.* dancer.
dappertutto *avv.* everywhere.
dappocàggine *sf.* ineptitude.
dappoco *agg.* inept.
dappresso *avv.* near-by.
dapprima *avv.* at first.
dardeggiare *vt. e vi.* to dart.
dardo *sm.* dart.
dare *sm.* debit. ♦ **dare** *vt.* to give

(*v. irr.*): — *origine, luogo a qc.*, to give rise; — *a bere a qu. che*, to give so. to believe that; — *ad intendere*, to give to understand; — *a, pensare*, to give food for thought || — *atto di qc.*, to acknowledge; *può darsi, maybe*; — *ala testa*, to go (*v. irr.*) to one's head; — *nell'occhio*, to stand (*v. irr.*) out. ♦ **darsi** *vr.* to devote oneself || — *al bere*, to take (*v. irr.*) to drink; — *ammalato*, to pretend to be ill; — *da fare*, to busy oneself; *darsela a gambe*, to take (*v. irr.*) to one's heels.
dàrsena *sf.* wet dock.
darvinismo *sm.* Darwinism.
data *sf.* date: *in* — *d'oggi*, under to-day's date.
datare *vt.* to date.
dativo *sm.* dative.
dato *agg.* **1.** given **2.** (*stabilito*) stated **3.** (*dedito*) addicted || — *e non concesso*, supposing that. ♦ **dato** *sm.* datum (*pl.* -ta). ♦ **dato che** *cong.* since, as.
datore *sm.* giver || — *di lavoro*, employer.
dàttero *sm.* **1.** date **2.** (*albero*) date-palm.
dattilografare *vt.* to typewrite.
dattilografìa *sf.* typewriting.
dattilògrafo *sm.* typist.
dattiloscritto *agg.* typewritten. ♦ **dattiloscritto** *sm.* typescript.
dattorno *avv.* round, about.
davanti *avv.* before, in front. ♦ **davanti** *sm.* front. ♦ **davanti** *agg.* front. ♦ **davanti a** (*loc. prep.*) before.
davantino *sm.* ruffle.
davanzale *sm.* window-sill.
davvero *avv.* really, indeed.
daziario *agg.* toll.
daziere *sm.* exciseman (*pl.* -men).
dazio *sm.* **1.** toll, duty **2.** (*ufficio daziario*) toll-house **3.** (*di consumo*) excise.
dea *sf.* goddess.
deambulare *vi.* to walk about.
deambulatorio *agg. e sm.* deambulatory.
deambulazione *sf.* deambulation.
debellare *vt.* **1.** to defeat **2.** (*fig.*) to overcome (*v. irr.*).
debilitante *agg.* weakening.
debilitare *vt.* to weaken.
debilitazione debilitation.

debitamente *avv.* duly.

débito *agg.* due, proper. ♦ **débito** *sm.* debt: *fare un —*, to run (*v. irr.*) into debt.

debitore *sm.* debtor.

débole *agg.* weak.

debolezza *sf.* weakness.

debosciato *agg.* debauched.

debuttante *sm.* **1.** novice **2.** (*di ragazza in società*) debutante.

debuttare *vi.* **1.** to make (*v. irr.*) one's debut **2.** (*di ragazza in società*) to come (*v. irr.*) out.

debutto *sm.* **1.** debut **2.** (*di ragazza in società*) coming out.

dècade *sf.* **1.** (*di giorni*) ten days **2.** (*di anni*) ten years.

decadente *agg.* **1.** decaying **2.** (*lett.*) decadent.

decadenza *sf.* decay, decline.

decadere *vi.* to decline || — *da un diritto*, to lose (*v. irr.*) a right.

decaduto *agg.* impoverished.

decaedro *sm.* decahedron.

decagrammo *sm.* decagram.

decalcare *vt.* to transfer.

decalcificare *vt.* to decalcify.

decàlitro *sm.* decalitre.

decàlogo *sm.* decalogue.

decàmetro *sm.* decametre.

decampare *vi.* **1.** to decamp **2.** (*fig.*) to recede.

decano *sm.* **1.** senior **2.** (*eccl.*) dean.

decantare *vt.* **1.** to extol **2.** (*chim.*) to decant.

decantazione *sf.* (*chim.*) decantation.

decapitare *vt.* to behead.

decappottàbile *agg.* (*auto*) convertible.

decasìllabo *agg.* decasyllabic. ♦ **decasìllabo** *sm.* decasyllable.

decatissaggio *sm.* decatizing.

decèdere *vi.* to die.

decelerare *vt.* to decelerate.

decennale *agg.* decennial.

decenne *agg.* **1.** ten years old (*predicativo*) **2.** ten-year-old (*attributivo*).

decennio *sm.* ten-year period.

decente *agg.* decent, proper.

decentramento *sm.* decentralization.

decentrare *vt.* to decentralize.

decenza *sf.* decency.

decesso *sm.* death.

decìdere *vt.* to decide. ♦ **decìdersi** *vr.* to make (*v. irr.*) up one's

mind.

decifrare *vt.* **1.** to decipher **2.** (*fam.*) to make (*v. irr.*) out.

decifrazione *sf.* deciphering.

decigrammo *sm.* decigram.

decìlitro *sm.* decilitre.

decimale *agg. e sm.* decimal.

decimare *vt.* to decimate.

decimazione *sf.* decimation.

decimetro *sm.* decimetre.

dècimo *agg.* tenth.

decina *sf.* ten, half-a-score.

decisione *sf.* decision.

decisivo *agg.* decisive.

deciso *agg.* **1.** resolute, firm **2.** (*definito*) decided.

declamare *vt. e vi.* to declaim.

declamatòrio *agg.* declamatory.

declamazione *sf.* declamation.

declassare *vt.* to degrade.

declinàbile *agg.* declinable.

declinante *agg.* declining.

declinare *vt.* **1.** to decline || — *le proprie generalità*, to say (*v. irr.*) one's name and surname. ♦ **declinare** *vi.* **1.** (*del sole*) to set (*v. irr.*) **2.** (*degradare*) to slope **3.** (*venir meno*) to decline.

declinazione *sf.* (*gramm.*) declension.

declino *sm.* decline.

declivio *sm.* declivity.

decollaggio *sm.* (*aer.*) take-off.

decollare *vi.* to take (*v. irr.*) off.

decollo *sm.* take-off.

decolorante *agg.* decolorating. ♦ **decolorante** *sm.* decolorant.

decolorare *vt.* to decolorate.

decolorazione *sf.* decoloration || — *dei capelli*, hair bleaching.

decomponìbile *agg.* decomposable.

decomporre *vt.* to decompose.

decomposizione *sf.* **1.** decomposition **2.** (*putrefazione*) putrefaction.

decongelare *vt.* to defrost.

decongestionare *vt.* to decongest.

decorare *vt.* to decorate: — *al valore*, to decorate for bravery.

decorativo *agg.* decorative.

decoratore *sm.* decorator.

decorazione *sf.* decoration.

decoro *sm.* dignity.

decoroso *agg.* decorous, proper.

decorrenza *sf.* expiration: *con — da*, beginning from.

decòrrere *vi.* **1.** to pass || *a — da*, to begin (*v. irr.*) from **2.** (*comm.*) to run (*v. irr.*), to have effect.

decorso *sm.* **1.** period **2.** (*il passa-*

re) passing.

decrepitezza *sf.* decrepitude.

decrèpito *agg.* decrepit.

decréscere *vi.* to decrease.

decretare *vt.* **1.** to decree **2.** (*concedere*) to confer.

decreto *sm.* decree: — *legge*, Order in Council.

decuplicare *vt.* to decuple.

dècuplo *sm.* decuple, ten times as much.

decurtare *vt.* to reduce.

dèdalo *sm.* maze.

dèdica *sf.* dedication.

dedicare *vt.* to dedicate. ♦ **dedicarsi** *vr.* to devote oneself.

dedicatorio *agg.* dedicatory.

dèdito *agg.* **1.** given up **2.** (*a vizio*) addicted.

dedizione *sf.* devotion.

dedurre *vt.* **1.** to infer, to deduce **2.** (*defalcare*) to deduct.

deduttivo *agg.* deductive.

deduzione *sf.* deduction.

defalcare *vt.* to deduct.

defalco *sm.* deduction.

defecare *vi.* to defecate.

defenestrare *vt.* **1.** to throw (*v. irr.*) out of the window **2.** (*fig.*) to dismiss.

defenestrazione *sf.* defenestration.

deferente *agg.* deferential.

deferenza *sf.* compliance, deference.

deferire *vt.* **1.** to submit **2.** (*giur.*) to remit.

defezionare *vi.* to desert.

defezione *sf.* **1.** defection **2.** (*mil.*) desertion.

deficiente *agg.* **1.** insufficient **2.** (*idiota*) mentally deficient. ♦ **deficiente** *sm.* idiot.

deficienza *sf.* **1.** deficiency, lack **2.** (*idiozia*) mental deficiency.

dèficit *sm.* deficit.

definìbile *agg.* definable.

definire *vt.* **1.** to define **2.** (*determinare, risolvere*) to determine.

definitivo *agg.* final.

definito *agg.* definite.

definizione *sf.* **1.** definition **2.** (*risoluzione*) settlement.

deflagrante *agg.* deflagrating.

deflagrare *vi.* to deflagrate.

deflagrazione *sf.* deflagration.

deflazione *sf.* deflation.

deflèttere *vi.* to deflect.

deflettore *sm.* baffle.

deflorare *vt.* to deflower.

deflorazione *sf.* defloration.

defluire *vi.* to flow down.

deflusso *sm.* **1.** downflow **2.** (*di marea*) ebb-tide.

deformante *agg.* deforming.

deformare *vt.* **1.** to deform, to disfigure **2.** (*alterare*) to alter. ♦ **deformarsi** *vr.* **1.** (*mecc.*) to warp **2.** to get (*v. irr.*) deformed.

deformazione *sf.* **1.** deformation **2.** (*mecc.*) buckling.

deforme *agg.* deformed.

deformità *sf.* deformity.

defraudare *vt.* to defraud.

defunto *agg.* e *sm.* dead.

degenerare *vi.* to degenerate.

degenerazione *sf.* degeneration.

degènere *agg.* degenerate.

degente *sm.* patient.

degenza *sf.* stay in hospital.

deglutizione *sf.* swallowing.

degnarsi *vr.* to condescend.

degnazione *sf.* condescension.

degno *agg.* worthy, deserving.

degradante *agg.* degrading.

degradare *vt.* to degrade.

degradazione *sf.* degradation.

degustare *vt.* to taste.

deiezione *sf.* dejection.

deificare *vt.* to deify.

deismo *sm.* deism.

deità *sf.* deity.

delatore *sm.* delator.

delazione *sf.* delation, informing.

delèbile *agg.* erasable.

dèlega *sf.* **1.** delegation **2.** (*procura*) proxy.

delegare *vt.* to delegate.

delegato *sm.* delegate.

delegazione *sf.* **1.** delegation **2.** (*commissione*) committee.

deleterio *agg.* harmful.

delfino *sm.* **1.** (*zool.*) dolphin **2.** (*fig.*) probable successor **3.** (*stor.*) dauphin.

deliberare *vt.* to decide.

deliberazione *sf.* deliberation.

delicatezza *sf.* delicacy.

delicato *agg.* **1.** delicate **2.** (*scrupoloso*) scrupulous **3.** (*discreto*) discreet, tactful.

delimitare *vt.* to delimit.

delimitazione *sf.* delimitation.

delineare *vt.* to outline.

delineazione *sf.* delineation.

delinquente *sm.* delinquent.

delinquenza *sf.* criminality.

delinquere *vi.* to commit an offence.

deliquio *sm.* swoon.

delirare vi. to rave.
delirio sm. delirium, frenzy (anche fig.).
delitto sm. crime.
delittuoso agg. criminal.
delizia sf. delight.
deliziare vt. to delight.
delizioso agg. 1. delightful 2. (di sapore, profumo) delicious.
delta sm. delta.
deltòide agg. e sm. deltoid.
delucidare vt. to explain.
delucidazione sf. explanation.
delùdere vt. to disappoint.
delusione sf. disappointment.
demagogìa sf. demagogy.
demagògico agg. demagogic.
demagogo sm. demagogue.
demandare vt. to commit.
demaniale agg. (owned by the) State.
demanio sm. State property.
demarcare vt. to mark the boundaries of.
demarcazione sf. demarcation.
demente agg. insane. ♦ **demente** sm. madman (pl. -men).
demenza sf. insanity.
demeritare vt. to forfeit. ♦ **demeritare** vi. to deserve censure.
demèrito sm. demerit.
demiurgo sm. demiurge.
democràtico agg. democratic. ♦ **democràtico** sm. democrat.
democratizzare vt. to democratize.
democrazìa sf. democracy.
democristiano sm. christian-democrat.
demografìa sf. demography.
demogràfico agg. demographic(al).
demolire vt. to demolish.
demolitore sm. 1. demolisher 2. (fig.) iconoclast.
demolizione sf. 1. demolition 2. (fig.) destruction.
dèmone sm. 1. demon 2. (diavolo) devil.
demonìaco agg. demoniac(al).
demonio sm. 1. devil 2. (fig.) demon.
demonologìa sf. demonology.
demoralizzare vt. to demoralize. ♦ **demoralizzarsi** vr. to lose (v. irr.) heart.
demoralizzazione sf. demoralization.
denaro sm. 1. money 2. (moneta antica) denarius (pl. -rii).
denaturare vt. to denature.

dendrologìa sf. dendrology.
denegare vt. to deny.
denicotinizzare vt. to denicotinize.
denigrare vt. to denigrate.
denigratore sm. denigrator.
denigrazione sf. denigration.
denominare vt. to name.
denominativo agg. denominative.
denominatore sm. denominator.
denominazione sf. denomination.
denotare vt. to signify.
densità sf. density.
denso agg. thick.
dentale agg. dental.
dentario agg. dental, tooth (attr.).
dentato agg. toothed.
dentatura sf. 1. set of teeth 2. (di ingranaggio) toothing.
dente sm. tooth (pl. teeth).
dentellare vt. to indent.
dentellatura sf. indentation.
dentello sm. 1. (mecc.) tooth 2. (arch.) dentil 3. (tacca) notch.
dentiera sf. dental plate.
dentifricio agg. tooth (attr.). ♦ **dentifricio** sm. tooth-paste.
dentina sf. dentine.
dentista sm. dentist.
dentìstico agg. dental: gabinetto —, dentist's surgery.
dentizione sf. teething.
dentro avv. in, inside. ♦ **dentro** prep. 1. in, inside 2. (di tempo) (with)in.
denudare vt. 1. to strip 2. (scoprire) to lay (v. irr.) bare. ♦ **denudarsi** vr. to strip.
denudazione sf. denudation.
denuncia sf. 1. denunciation 2. (dichiarazione) statement: — dei redditi, statement of one's income.
denunciare vt. 1. to denounce 2. (dichiarare) to report 3. (giur.) — qu., to inform against so.
denutrito agg. underfed.
denutrizione sf. underfeeding.
deodorante agg. deodorizing. ♦ **deodorante** sm. deodorant.
deodorare vt. to deodorize.
deontologìa sf. deontology.
depauperamento sm. impoverishment.
depauperare vt. to impoverish.
depennare vt. to cross out.
deperìbile agg. perishable.
deperimento sm. 1. (di salute) wasting away 2. (per un dolore) pining away 3. (di cose) deterioration.

deperire vi. 1. (di salute) to waste away 2. (per un dolore) to pine. away 3. (di cose) to deteriorate.
depilare vt. to remove hair (from).
depilatore sm. hair-remover.
depilatorio agg. hair-removing.
depilazione sf. hair-removal.
deploràbile agg. deplorable.
deplorare vt. 1. (essere spiacenti) to deplore 2. (lagnarsi di) to complain of.
deplorazione sf. 1. (biasimo) blame 2. (rimpianto) regret.
deplorévole agg. 1. deplorable 2. (biasimevole) blamable.
deporre vt. 1. to lay (v. irr.) 2. (da una carica) to remove from (an) office 3. (depositare) to deposit 4. (giur.) to witness. ♦ **deporre** vi. (giur.) to give (v. irr.) evidence.
deportare vt. to deport.
deportato agg. deported. ♦ **deportato** sm. convict.
deportazione sf. deportation.
depositante sm. depositor.
depositare vt. to deposit: — merci, to store goods.
depositario sm. trustee.
depòsito sm. 1. deposit 2. (luogo in cui depositare) warehouse 3. (per bagagli) left-luggage room.
deposizione sf. deposition.
depravare vt. to corrupt.
depravazione sf. corruption.
deprecàbile agg. deprecable.
deprecare vt. to deprecate.
deprecativo agg. deprecatory.
deprecazione sf. deprecation.
depredamento sm. plunder.
depredare vt. to plunder, to ravage.
depressione sf. depression.
depressivo agg. depressing.
depresso agg. depressed.
depressore sm. depressor.
deprezzamento sm. depreciation.
deprezzare vt. to depreciate.
deprimente agg. depressing.
deprimere vt. to depress.
depurare vt. to depurate.
depurativo agg. depurative.
depuratore sm. 1. depurator 2. (mecc.) cleaner.
depurazione sf. purification, depuration.
deputare vt. to depute.
deputato sm. deputy.
deputazione sf. deputation.

deragliamento sm. derailment.
deragliare vi. to go (v. irr.) off the rails.
derattizzare vt. to clear by deratization.
derattizzazione sf. deratization.
derelitto agg. forlorn.
deretano sm. posterior.
deridere vt. to laugh at, to make (v. irr.) fun of.
derisibile agg. laughable.
derisione sf. mockery.
derisorio agg. derisory.
deriva sf. drift.
derivare vi. 1. to derive 2. (originarsi) to rise (v. irr.). ♦ **derivare** vt. to derive.
derivativo agg. derivative.
derivato agg. derived. ♦ **derivato** sm. 1. derivative 2. (sottoprodotto) by-product.
derivazione sf. 1. derivation 2. (elettr.) shunt.
derma sm. derm.
dermatologia sf. dermatology.
dermatològico agg. dermatological.
dermatòlogo sm. dermatologist.
dèroga sf. derogation.
derogare vi. to derogate.
derrata sf. 1. victual 2. (alimentare) food-stuff.
derubare vt. to rob (so. of).
desco sm. dinner table.
descrittivo agg. descriptive.
descrivere vt. to describe.
descrivibile agg. describable.
descrizione sf. description.
desèrtico agg. desert.
deserto agg. e sm. desert.
desideràbile agg. desirable.
desiderare vt. 1. to wish 2. (desiderare di avere) to wish for.
desiderio sm. wish.
desideroso agg. desirous, eager (for).
designare vt. to appoint.
designazione sf. designation.
desinare vi. to dine, to have dinner. ♦ **desinare** sm. dinner.
desinenza sf. ending.
desistere vi. to cease, to leave (v. irr.) off.
desolare vt. 1. to desolate 2. (addolorare) to distress.
desolato agg. (spiacente) sorry.
desolazione sf. 1. desolation 2. (dolore) grief, sorrow.
dèspota sm. despot.
destare vt. 1. to wake (v. irr.) 2.

(suscitare) to rouse. ♦ **destarsi** *vr.* to wake *(v. irr.)* up.

destinare *vt.* **1.** to destine **2.** *(devolvere)* to assign.

destinatario *sm.* addressee.

destinazione *sf.* destination.

destino *sm.* **1.** destiny **2.** *(sorte)* lot.

destituire *vt.* to dismiss.

destituzione *sf.* dismissal.

desto *agg.* awake.

destra *sf.* **1.** right hand **2.** *(parte destra)* right, right side: *alla tua* —, on your right; *tenere la* —, to keep *(v. irr.)* right.

destramente *avv.* skilfully.

destreggiarsi *vr.* to manage.

destrezza *sf.* dexterity.

destriero *sm.* steed.

destrina *sf.* dextrine.

destro *agg.* **1.** right **2.** *(abile)* clever. ♦ **destro** *sm.* opportunity.

desueto *agg.* unusual, obsolete.

desuetùdine *sf.* disuse.

desùmere *vt.* **1.** to infer **2.** *(trarre)* to draw *(v. irr.)*.

detenere *vt.* **1.** to hold *(v. irr.)* **2.** *(tener prigioniero)* to keep *(v. irr.)* in prison.

detentore *sm.* holder.

detenuto *agg.* imprisoned. ♦ **detenuto** *sm.* prisoner.

detenzione *sf.* **1.** possession **2.** *(il detenere)* holding **3.** *(galera)* detention.

detergente *agg.* e *sm.* detergent.

detèrgere *vt.* to cleanse.

deterioramento *sm.* deterioration.

deteriorare *vt.* **1.** to deteriorate **2.** *(danneggiare)* to damage.

deteriore *agg.* worse.

determinàbile *agg.* determinable.

determinante *agg.* determinant.

determinare *vt.* **1.** to determine **2.** *(causare)* to cause.

determinativo *agg.* determinative || *articolo* —, definite article.

determinato *agg.* **1.** determinate **2.** *(particolare)* special **3.** *(deciso)* resolute.

determinazione *sf.* determination.

determinismo *sm.* determinism.

deterrente *agg.* deterrent.

detersivo *agg.* e *sm.* detersive.

detestàbile *agg.* detestable.

detestare *vt.* to loathe.

detettore *sm.* detector.

detonante *agg.* explosive.

detonare *vi.* to detonate.

detonatore *sm.* detonator.

detonazione *sf.* explosion.

detrarre *vt.* to deduct.

detrattore *sm.* detractor.

detrazione *sf.* **1.** deduction **2.** *(fig.)* detraction.

detrimento *sm.* detriment.

detrìtico *agg.* detrital.

detrito *sm.* rubble, debris.

detronizzare *vt.* to depose.

detronizzazione *sf.* dethronement.

detta *(nella loc. avv.)* *a* — *di qu.,* according to what so. says.

dettagliante *sm.* retailer.

dettagliare *vt.* to detail.

dettagliatamente *avv.* in detail.

dettaglio *sm.* **1.** detail **2.** *(comm.)* retail.

dettame *sm.* dictate.

dettare *vt.* **1.** to dictate **2.** *(suggerire)* to suggest || — *la legge,* to lay *(v. irr.)* down the law.

dettato *sm.* dictation.

detto *agg.* **1.** called **2.** *(sopraddetto)* said, above-mentioned. ♦ **detto** *sm.* saying.

deturpare *vt.* to disfigure.

deturpazione *sf.* disfigurement.

devalutazione *sf.* depreciation.

devastare *vt.* to ravage, to ruin.

devastatore *agg.* ravaging. ♦ **devastatore** *sm.* ravager.

devastazione *sf.* devastation.

deviare *vi.* to deviate || *non* —! *(non cambiare discorso),* stick to the point! ♦ **deviare** *vt.* to divert.

deviazione *sf.* **1.** deviation **2.** *(stradale)* detour || — *ferroviaria,* shunting.

deviazionismo *sm.* deviationism.

devoluzione *sf.* devolution.

devòlvere *vt.* **1.** *(giur.)* to devolve, to assign **2.** *(adoperare)* to employ.

devoto *agg.* **1.** devout, affectionate **2.** *(relig.)* pious, religious.

devozione *sf.* devotion, piety.

di *prep.* **1.** of **2.** *(partitivo)* some, any: *dammi del pane,* give me some bread; *hai dello zucchero?,* have you any sugar? **3.** *(tempo)* in, during: — *mattina,* in the morning **4.** *(argomento)* of, about **5.** *(paragone coi comparativi)* than: *è più graziosa* — *sua sorella,* she is prettier than her sister **6.** *(nei superl.)* of, in **7.** *(modo)* with, in.

dì *sm.* day.

diabete *sm.* diabetes.

diabètico *agg.* e *sm.* diabetic.

diabòlico *agg.* diabolic(al).

diàcono *sm.* deacon.

diadema *sm.* diadem.

diàfano *agg.* diaphanous.

diaframma *sm.* diaphragm.

diàgnosi *sf.* diagnosis (*pl.* -ses).

diagnosticare *vt.* to diagnose.

diagnòstico *agg.* diagnostic.

diagonale *agg.* diagonal. ♦ diagonale *sf.* diagonal.

diagonalmente *avv.* diagonally.

diagramma *sm.* diagram.

dialettale *agg.* dialectal.

dialèttica *sf.* dialectics.

dialèttico *agg.* dialectic. ♦ dialèttico *sm.* dialectic.

dialetto *sm.* dialect.

diàlisi *sf.* dialysis (*pl.* -ses).

dialogare *vi.* to hold (*v. irr.*) a dialogue.

diàlogo *sm.* dialogue.

diamante *sm.* diamond.

diametralmente *avv.* diametrically.

diàmetro *sm.* diameter.

diàmine *inter.* good heavens!

dianzi *avv.* just, just now.

diapositiva *sf.* slide.

diarchia *sf.* diarchy.

diario *sm.* diary.

diarrea *sf.* diarrhoea.

diaspro *sm.* jasper.

diatonìa *sf.* diatony.

diatriba *sf.* diatribe.

diavoleria *sf.* 1. devilry 2. (*fam.*) trick.

diavoletto *sm.* imp.

diàvolo *sm.* devil.

dibàttere *vt.* to debate. ♦ dibàttersi *vr.* to struggle.

dibàttito *sm.* debate, discussion.

dibattuto *agg.* controversial.

diboscamento *sm.* deforestation.

diboscare *vt.* to deforest.

dicastero *sm.* office.

dicembre *sm.* December.

dicerìa *sf.* gossip, rumour.

dichiarare *vt.* to declare.

dichiarato *agg.* declared.

dichiarazione *sf.* declaration.

diciannove *agg.* nineteen.

diciannovenne *agg.* 1. nineteen years old (*pred.*) 2. nineteen-year-old (*attr.*).

diciannovèsimo *agg.* nineteenth.

diciassette *agg.* seventeen.

diciassettenne *agg.* 1. seventeen years old (*pred.*) 2. seventeen-year-old (*attr.*).

diciassettèsimo *agg.* seventeenth.

diciottenne *agg.* 1. eighteen years old (*pred.*) 2. eighteen-year-old (*attr.*).

diciottèsimo *agg.* eighteenth.

diciotto *agg.* eighteen.

dicitore *sm.* speaker.

dicitura *sf.* wording.

didascalìa *sf.* 1. explanation 2. (*cine*) subtitles (*pl.*).

didascàlico *agg.* didactic.

didàttica *sf.* didactics.

didàttico *agg.* didactic(al).

didentro *sm.* inside.

didietro *sm.* back.

dieci *agg.* ten.

diecina *sf.* ten, half a score.

diedro *sm.* dihedral.

dielèttrico *agg.* dielectric.

diesis *sm.* sharp.

dieta *sf.* diet.

dietètico *agg.* dietetic.

dietòlogo *sm.* dietician.

dietro *avv.* behind. ♦ dietro *prep.* behind, after. ♦ dietro *sm.* back, rear.

dietrofrònt *sm.* about turn!

difatti *avv.* as a matter of fact.

difèndere *vt.* to defend.

difendìbile *agg.* defensible.

difensiva *sf.* defensive.

difensivo *agg.* defensive.

difensore *agg.* defending 2. ♦ difensore *sm.* 1. defender 2. (*giur.*) defending counsel 3. (*di un'idea ecc.*) supporter.

difesa *sf.* defence.

difettare *vi.* to be wanting.

difettivo *agg.* defective.

difetto *sm.* defect.

difettoso *agg.* defective.

diffamare *vt.* to defame.

diffamatore *sm.* defamer.

diffamatorio *agg.* defamatory.

diffamazione *sf.* defamation.

differente *agg.* unlike, different.

differentemente *avv.* differently.

differenza *sf.* difference.

differenziale *agg.* e *sm.* differential.

differenziare *vt.* to differentiate.

differenziato *agg.* differentiated.

differenziazione *sf.* differentiation.

differìbile *agg.* that can be deferred.

differimento *sm.* deferment.

differire *vi.* (*essere diverso*) to differ (from). ♦ differire *vt.* to delay.

difficile *agg.* difficult.

difficilmente *avv.* with difficulty.

difficoltà *sf.* difficulty.

difficoltoso *agg.* difficult.

diffida *sf.* warning, intimation.

diffidare *vi.* to distrust. ♦ **diffidare** *vt.* to give (*v. irr.*) warning.

diffidente *agg.* suspicious.

diffidenza *sf.* **1.** distrust **2.** (*sospetto*) suspicion.

diffondere *vt.* to diffuse, to spread (*v. irr.*). ♦ **diffondersi** *vr.* to spread (*v. irr.*).

difforme *agg.* **1.** different **2.** shapeless.

difformità *sf.* difference, deformity.

diffrazione *sf.* diffraction.

diffusamente *avv.* diffusely.

diffusione *sf.* **1.** diffusion, spreading **2.** (*di giornale*) circulation.

diffuso *agg.* diffuse.

diffusore *sm.* diffusor.

difilato *avv.* straight.

diftèrico *agg.* diphtheric.

difterite *sf.* diphtheria.

diga *sf.* dam.

digerente *agg.* digestive.

digeribile *agg.* digestible.

digeribilità *sf.* digestibility.

digerire *vt.* to digest.

digestione *sf.* digestion.

digestivo *agg. e sm.* digestive.

digesto *sm.* digest.

digitale *agg.* digital ‖ *impronte digitali*, finger-prints. ♦ **digitale** *sf.* digitalis, (*fam.*) foxglove.

digiunare *vi.* to fast.

digiunatore *sm.* faster.

digiuno[1] *agg.* **1.** fasting **2.** (*fig.*) lacking (in).

digiuno[2] *sm.* fast.

dignità *sf.* dignity.

dignitario *sm.* dignitary.

dignitosamente *avv.* with dignity.

dignitoso *agg.* dignified.

digradante *agg.* **1.** sloping **2.** (*pitt.*) shading.

digradare *vi.* **1.** to slope down **2.** (*pitt.*) to shade off.

digressione *sf.* digression.

digressivo *agg.* digressive.

digrignare *vt.* to gnash.

digrossamento *sm.* **1.** reducing **2.** (*sbozzo*) rough-hewing.

digrossare *vt.* **1.** to reduce **2.** (*sbozzare*) to rough-hew.

dilacerare *vt.* to tear (*v. irr.*).

dilagare *vi.* to spread (*v. irr.*).

dilaniare *vt.* to tear (*v. irr.*) to pieces.

dilapidare *vt.* to squander.

dilapidatore *sm.* squanderer.

dilapidazione *sf.* squandering.

dilatàbile *agg.* dilatable.

dilatabilità *sf.* dilatability.

dilatare *vt.*, **dilatarsi** *vr.* **1.** to dilate **2.** (*fis.*) to expand.

dilatazione *sf.* dilatation.

dilatorio *agg.* dilatory.

dilavamento *sm.* washing away.

dilavare *vt.* to wash away.

dilazionare *vt.* to defer.

dilazione *sf.* delay, respite.

dileggiare *vt.* to mock.

dileggio *sm.* mockery.

dileguare *vt.* to disperse. ♦ **dileguarsi** *vr.* to disappear.

dilemma *sm.* dilemma.

dilettante *sm.* amateur.

dilettantismo *sm.* amateurism.

dilettare *vt.* to delight. ♦ **dilettarsi** *vr.* to take (*v. irr.*) delight (in).

dilettévole *agg.* delightful.

diletto *agg.* beloved. ♦ **diletto** *sm.* delight.

diligente *agg.* diligent.

diligenza *sf.* **1.** diligence **2.** (*carrozza*) stage-coach.

dilucidare *vt.* V. *delucidare*.

dilucidazione *sf.* V. *delucidazione*.

diluente *sm.* diluent.

diluire *vt.* **1.** to dilute **2.** (*fig.*) to water down.

diluizione *sf.* dilution.

dilungarsi *vr.* to speak (*v. irr.*) diffusely.

diluviale *agg.* **1.** torrential **2.** (*geol.*) diluvial.

diluviano *agg.* diluvial.

diluviare *vi.* **1.** to pour **2.** (*fig.*) to shower.

diluvio *sm.* deluge, flood.

dimagramento *sm.* thinning.

dimagrante *agg.* slimming.

dimagrare *vi.* to thin.

dimagrire *vi.* V. *dimagrare*.

dimenare *vt.* **1.** (*la coda*) to wag **2.** to wave. ♦ **dimenarsi** *vr.* to move about restlessly.

dimensione *sf.* dimension, size.

dimenticanza *sf.* **1.** (*svista*) oversight **2.** (*oblio*) oblivion.

dimenticare *vt.*, **dimenticarsi** *vr.* to forget (*v. irr.*).

diméntico *agg.* forgetful.

dimesso *agg.* **1.** modest **2.** (*trasandato*) shabby.

dimestichezza *sf.* familiarity.

dimetro *sm.* dimeter.

dimettere *vt.* to dismiss ‖ — *dall'ospedale*, to discharge. ◆ **dimettersi** *vr.* to resign.

dimezzamento *sm.* halving.

dimezzare *vt.* to halve.

diminuendo *sm.* **1.** (*mat.*) minuend **2.** (*mus.*) diminuendo.

diminuibile *agg.* diminishable.

diminuire *vt.* e *vi.* to lessen, to diminish.

diminutivo *agg.* e *sm.* diminutive.

diminuzione *sf.* lessening, reduction.

dimissionare *vt.* to oblige (so.) to resign.

dimissionario *agg.* resigning.

dimissione *sf.* resignation ‖ *dare le dimissioni*, to resign.

dimissoria *sf.* dimissory letter.

dimodoché *cong.* so that.

dimora *sf.* residence, lodgings (*pl.*).

dimorare *vi.* to stay, to live.

dimorfismo *sm.* dimorphism.

dimorfo *agg.* dimorphic.

dimostrabile *agg.* demonstrable.

dimostrabilità *sf.* demonstrability.

dimostrante *sm.* demonstrant.

dimostrare *vt.* **1.** to show (*v. irr.*) **2.** (*provare*) to demonstrate. ◆ **dimostrarsi** *vr.* to show oneself.

dimostrativo *agg.* e *sm.* demonstrative.

dimostratore *sm.* demonstrator.

dimostrazione *sf.* demonstration.

dina *sf.* dyne.

dinamica *sf.* dynamics.

dinamicamente *avv.* dynamically.

dinamicità *sf.* dynamism, energy.

dinamico *agg.* **1.** dynamic **2.** (*fig.*) energetic.

dinamismo *sm.* **1.** dynamism **2.** (*fig.*) energy.

dinamitardo *sm.* dynamiter.

dinamite *sf.* dynamite.

dinamo *sf.* dynamo.

dinamòmetro *sm.* dynamometer.

dinanzi *prep.* before, in front of. ◆ **dinanzi** *avv.* before, in front, forward.

dinaro *sm.* dinar.

dinasta *sm.* dynast.

dinastia *sf.* dynasty.

dinastico *agg.* dynastic(al).

dindo *sm.* turkey.

diniego *sm.* denial.

dinoccolato *agg.* slouching.

dinosauro *sm.* dinosaur.

dintorni *sm. pl.* surroundings.

dintorno *avv.* e *prep.* **1.** round, round about **2.** (*circa*) about.

dio *sm.* god: *Marte, il — della guerra*, Mars, the god of war. ◆ **Dio** *sm.* God: — *ci assista!*, — *non voglia!*, God help us, God forbid.

diocesano *agg.* diocesan.

diòcesi *sf.* diocese.

diodo *sm.* diode.

dionea *sf.* dionaea.

dionisiaco *agg.* Dionysiac.

diorama *sm.* diorama.

diorite *sf.* diorite.

diottria *sf.* diopter.

diòttrica *sf.* dioptrics.

diòttrico *agg.* dioptric.

dipanamento *sm.* winding into a ball.

dipanare *vt.* **1.** to wind (*v. irr.*) into a ball **2.** (*fig.*) to disentangle.

dipanatoio *sm.* skein-winder.

dipartimentale *agg.* departmental.

dipartimento *sm.* department.

dipartire *vi.* to depart. ◆ **dipartirsi** *vr.* **1.** to go (*v. irr.*) away **2.** (*morire*) to pass away.

dipartita *sf.* **1.** departure **2.** (*morte*) death.

dipendente *agg.* dependent (on). ◆ **dipendente** *sm.* employee.

dipendenza *sf.* dependence (on).

dipèndere *vi.* **1.** (*derivare*) to be due **2.** (*essere subordinato, vivere a carico*) to depend (on).

dipingere *vt.* to paint.

dipinto *agg.* painted. ◆ **dipinto** *sm.* painting.

diplegìa *sf.* diplegia.

diplococco *sm.* diplococcus (*pl.* -ci).

diploma *sm.* diploma.

diplomare *vt.* to confer a diploma (upon so.). ◆ **diplomarsi** *vr.* to get (*v. irr.*) a diploma.

diplomatica *sf.* diplomatics.

diplomaticamente *avv.* diplomatically.

diplomatico *agg.* diplomatic. ◆ **diplomàtico** *sm.* diplomat.

diplomato *agg.* holding a diploma. ◆ **diplomato** *sm.* graduate.

diplomazia *sf.* diplomacy.

diplopia *sf.* diplopia.

dipnoi *sm. pl.* Dipnoi.

dipodìa *sf.* dipody.

dipoi *avv.* then.

diporto *sm.* recreation, diversion ‖

viaggiare per —, to travel on pleasure.

dipresso *(nella loc. avv.) a un —,* approximately.

diptero *agg.* dipteral.

diradamento *sm.* **1.** thinning **2.** *(di nebbia, gas)* rarefaction.

diradare *vt.* **1.** to thin out **2.** *(rendere meno frequente)* to do *(v. irr.)* less frequent. ♦ **diradarsi** *vr.* **1.** to clear away **2.** *(divenire meno frequente)* to become *(v. irr.)* less frequent.

diramare *vt.* to issue, to spread *(v. irr.).*

diramazione *sf.* **1.** branching **2.** *(diffusione)* diffusion **3.** *(per radio)* broadcasting.

dire *vt.* **1.** *(nel senso di enunciare e quando introduce il discorso diretto)* to say *(v. irr.): dice che ha sonno,* he says he is sleepy; *« venite », ci disse, « come »,* he said to us **2.** *(nel senso di raccontare e quando è enunciata la persona cui si parla)* to tell *(v. irr.): gli dissi di venire,* I told him to come ‖ *si dice,* they say; *mi si dice,* I am told; *inutile — che,* it goes without saying that; *vale a —,* that is to say; *sentir —,* to hear *(v. irr.); voler —,* to mean *(v. irr.).*

dire *sm.* words *(pl.),* speech.

direttamente *avv.* directly.

direttissima *sf. per —,* summarily.

direttissimo *sm.* *(ferr.)* fast train.

direttiva *sf.* directions *(pl.).*

direttivo *agg.* **1.** leading **2.** *(comm.)* managing.

diretto *agg.* direct, straight.

direttore *sm.* **1.** *(comm.; amm.)* manager **2.** *(di scuola)* headmaster.

direttoriale *agg.* directorial.

direttorio *sm.* executive board.

direttrice *sf.* **1.** *(comm.; amm.)* manageress **2.** *(di scuola)* headmistress.

direzionale *agg.* directional ‖ *centro —,* office district.

direzione *sf.* **1.** direction, course **2.** *(di società)* management **3.** *(di giornale)* editorship **4.** *(di scuola)* headmastership **5.** *(sede)* administrative office.

dirigente *agg.* directing, leading. ♦ **dirigente** *sm.* director, manager, leader.

dirigere *vt.* **1.** *(indirizzare)* to direct **2.** *(guidare)* to lead *(v. irr.)* **3.** *(sovraintendere)* to supervise. ♦ **dirigersi** *vr.* to turn one's steps towards.

dirigibile *sm.* airship.

dirigismo *sm.* state planning.

dirigista *sm.* supporter of state planning.

dirimente *agg.* diriment.

dirimere *vt.* to settle.

dirimpettaio *sm.* person living just opposite.

dirimpetto *avv.* face to face, opposite.

diritta *sf.* right, right-hand: *a —,* on the right.

direttamente *avv.* straight.

diritto *agg.* straight, upright ‖ *rigare —,* to behave properly. ♦ **diritto** *sm.* **1.** right **2.** *(tassa, tributo)* due **3.** *(legge)* law.

dirittura *sf.* **1.** straight line **2.** *(rettitudine)* uprightness **3.** *(sport) — d'arrivo,* home stretch.

dirizzare *vt.* **1.** to direct **2.** *(erigere)* to raise **3.** *(raddrizzare; fig.)* to put *(v. irr.)* right, to straighten.

dirizzone *sm.* inconsiderate action.

diroccamento *sm.* demolition.

diroccare *vt.* to demolish.

diroccato *agg.* **1.** *(demolito)* dismantled **2.** *(in rovina)* crumbled.

dirompente *agg.* disruptive.

dirompere *vt.* **1.** *(di lino, canapa ecc.)* to scutch **2.** *(rompere)* to break *(v. irr.).*

dirottare *vt.* to divert. ♦ **dirottare** *vi.* to change course.

dirotto *agg.* excessive: *pianto —,* desperate crying; *piove a —,* it is pouring.

dirozzamento *sm.* **1.** *(lo sbozzare)* rough-hewing **2.** *(fig.)* refinement.

dirozzare *vt.* **1.** *(sbozzare)* to rough-hew **2.** *(fig.)* to refine.

dirugginire *vt.* to remove the rust from.

dirupamento *sm.* **1.** falling down **2.** *(di luogo)* abruptness.

dirupato *agg.* **1.** abrupt **2.** *(roccioso)* rocky.

dirupo *sm.* precipice.

disabbellire *vt.* to spoil the beauty of. ♦ **disabbellirsi** *vr.* to lose *(v. irr.)* one's beauty.

disabitato *agg.* **1.** uninhabited **2.** *(abbandonato)* deserted.

disabituare *vt.* to disaccustom. ♦ **disabituarsi** *vr.* to give *(v. irr.)*

up the habit of.

disaccordo *sm.* disagreement.

disacerbare *vt.* to appease.

disadatto *agg.* 1. unfit 2. (*che non si addice*) unbecoming.

disadornare *vt.* to disadorn.

disadorno *agg.* 1. unadorned 2. (*spoglio*) bare.

disaffezionarsi *vr.* to lose (*v. irr.*) one's affection (for).

disaffezionato *agg.* estranged.

disaffezione *sf.* estrangement.

disagévole *agg.* uncomfortable.

disagiatamente *avv.* uncomfortably.

disagiato *agg.* 1. uncomfortable 2. (*povero*) needy.

disagio *sm.* 1. uneasiness || essere a —, to be uneasy 2. (*disturbo*) inconvenience 3. (*pl.*; *privazioni*) privations.

disamare *vt.* to cease to love.

disàmina *sf.* examination.

disaminare *vt.* to examine carefully.

disancorarsi *vr.* 1. to weigh anchor 2. (*fig.*) to break (*v. irr.*) all connections (with).

disanimarsi *vr.* to lose (*v. irr.*) heart.

disappetenza *sf.* lack of appetite.

disapprèndere *vt.* to forget (*v. irr.*).

disapprovare *vt.* to disapprove (of).

disapprovazione *sf.* disapproval.

disappunto *sm.* disappointment.

disarcionare *vt.* to unsaddle.

disarmare *vt.* to disarm.

disarmato *agg.* disarmed.

disarmo *sm.* disarmament.

disarmonia *sf.* discord.

disarmonicamente *avv.* discordantly.

disarmònico *agg.* discordant.

disarmonizzare *vt.* to disharmonize.

disarticolare *vt.* to disjoint.

disarticolazione *sf.* disjointing.

disastro *sm.* disaster.

disastroso *agg.* disastrous.

disattento *agg.* inattentive.

disattenzione *sf.* inattention: errore di —, a slip of the pen.

disavanzo *sm.* deficit.

disavveduto *agg.* heedless.

disavventura *sf.* 1. mishap 2. (*sfortuna*) misfortune.

disavvertenza *sf.* inadvertence.

disavvezzo *agg.* unaccustomed.

disazotare *vt.* to remove nitrogen from.

disborso *sm.* disbursement.

disbrigo *sm.* dispatch.

disbrogliare *vt.* to disentangle.

discacciare *vt.* to turn out.

discapitare *vi.* to suffer damage.

discàpito *sm.* disadvantage.

discàrico *sm.* 1. discharge 2. (*scusa*) defence.

discendente *agg.* descending. ◆

discendente *sm.* descendant.

discendenza *sf.* 1. descent 2. (*discendenti*) offspring.

discéndere *vi.* 1. to descend, to go (*v. irr.*) down 2. (*di astri*) to sink (*v. irr.*) 3. (*di prezzi*) to fall (*v. irr.*).

discépolo *sm.* disciple.

discèrnere *vt.* 1. to discern 2. (*distinguere*) to distinguish.

discernìbile *agg.* discernible.

discernimento *sm.* discernment.

discesa *sf.* 1. descent 2. (*declivio*) slope 3. (*caduta*) fall 4. (*invasione*) invasion.

dischiùdere *vt.* to disclose.

dischiuso *agg.* disclosed.

discinto *agg.* ungirt.

disciplina *sf.* 1. (*materia di studio*) doctrine 2. (*regola*) discipline.

disciplinàbile *agg.* disciplinable.

disciplinare[1] *vt.* to discipline.

disciplinare[2] *agg.* disciplinary.

disciplinarmente *avv.* with discipline.

disciplinatamente *avv.* with discipline.

disciplinato *agg.* disciplined.

disco *sm.* 1. disk 2. (*mus.*) record 3. (*sport*) discus 4. (*ferr.*) disk signal.

discòbolo *sm.* discus-thrower.

discòide *agg.* discoid.

discolo *sm.* wild boy, little scamp.

discolpa *sf.* excuse.

discolpare *vt.* to clear.

disconoscente *aff.* ungrateful.

disconoscenza *sf.* ungratitude.

disconóscere *vt.* to refuse to recognize.

disconoscimento *sm.* 1. refusal to recognize 2. (*ingratitudine*) ingratitude.

discontinuità *sf.* discontinuity.

discontinuo *agg.* discontinuous.

discordante *agg.* 1. discordant 2. (*diverso*) different 3. (*di colori*) clashing.

discordanza *sf.* discordance.

discordare *vi.* **1.** to disagree **2.** (*di colori*) to clash **3.** (*di suoni*) to jar.

discorde *agg.* discordant (with).

discordemente *avv.* discordantly.

discordia *sf.* discord.

discòrrere *vi.* to talk.

discorsivo *agg.* talkative.

discorso *sm.* speech.

discostare *vt.* to shift.

discosto *agg.* far, distant. ◆ **discosto** *avv.* at some distance.

discoteca *sf.* record library.

discreditare *vt.* to discredit.

discrédito *sm.* discredit.

discrepante *agg.* differing.

discrepanza *sf.* discrepancy.

discretamente *avv.* **1.** (*con discrezione*) discreetly **2.** (*sufficientemente*) fairly **3.** (*piuttosto*) rather.

discreto *agg.* **1.** (*che ha discrezione*) discreet **2.** (*moderato*) moderate **3.** (*abbastanza buono*) fairly good.

discrezionale *agg.* discretionary.

discrezione *sf.* discretion.

discriminante *agg.* discriminating.

discriminare *vt.* to discriminate.

discriminazione *sf.* discrimination.

discussione *sf.* discussion.

discusso *agg.* discussed.

discùtere *vt.* to discuss.

discutìbile *agg.* questionable.

disdegnare *vt.* to disdain.

disdegno *sm.* disdain.

disdegnosamente *avv.* disdainfully.

disdegnoso *agg.* disdainful.

disdetta *sf.* **1.** (*giur.*) notice of leave **2.** (*sfortuna*) bad luck.

disdettare *vt.* to give (*v. irr.*) notice.

disdicévole *agg.* unbecoming.

disdire *vt.* **1.** (*ritrattare*) to take (*v. irr.*) back, to retract **2.** (*annullare*) to cancel.

disegnare *vt.* **1.** to draw (*v. irr.*) **2.** (*progettare*) to plan.

disegnatore *sm.* designer.

disegno *sm.* **1.** drawing **2.** (*di tessuto*) pattern **3.** (*di edificio*) plan **4.** (*schizzo*) sketch **5.** (*fig.*) design, plan.

diseredare *vt.* to disinherit.

diseredato *agg.* **1.** poor, destitute **2.** (*privato di eredità*) disinherited.

disertare *vt.* **1.** to desert **2.** (*abbandonare*) to leave (*v. irr.*).

disertore *sm.* deserter.

diserzione *sf.* desertion.

disfacimento *sm.* **1.** (*il disfare*) undoing **2.** (*decadimento*) decay.

disfare *vt.* **1.** to undo (*v. irr.*) **2.** (*slegare*) to untie.

lisfasia *sf.* dysphasia.

disfatta *sf.* defeat.

disfattismo *sm.* defeatism.

disfattista *agg.* e *s.* defeatist.

disfatto *agg.* **1.** (*distrutto*) ruined **2.** (*slegato*) undone **3.** (*molto stanco*) worn out.

disfavore *sm.* disfavour.

disfida *sf.* challenge.

disfunzione *sf.* disorder.

disgelare *vt.* e *vi.* to thaw.

disgelo *sm.* thaw.

disgiùngere *vt.* to disjoin.

disgiungimento *sm.* disjoining.

disgiuntamente *avv.* separately.

disgiuntivamente *avv.* disjunctively.

disgiuntivo *agg.* disjunctive.

disgiunto *agg.* disjoined.

disgiunzione *sf.* disjunction.

disgrazia *sf.* **1.** misfortune **2.** (*sfavore*) disfavour ‖ *cadere in —,* to lose (*v. irr.*) so.'s favour **3.** (*fatto involontario*) accident.

disgraziatamente *avv.* unfortunately.

disgraziato *agg.* **1.** unlucky, wretched **2.** (*deforme*) misshapen.

disgregamento *sm.* disintegration.

disgregare *vt.* to disgregate, to break (*v. irr.*) up.

disgregazione *sf.* disgregation.

disguido *sm.* miscarriage.

disgustare *vt.* to disgust, to sicken. ◆ **disgustarsi** *vr.* to become (*v. irr.*) disgusted (with).

disgusto *sm.* **1.** disgust **2.** (*avversione*) dislike.

disgustoso *agg.* disgusting.

disidratare *vt.* to dehydrate.

disidratazione *sf.* dehydration.

disillùdere *vt.* to undeceive.

disillusione *sf.* disillusion.

disilluso *agg.* undeceived, disappointed.

disimballaggio *sm.* unpacking.

disimballare *vt.* to unpack.

disimpacciare *vt.* to disembarrass.

disimparare *vt.* to forget (*v. irr.*).

disimpegnare *vt.* **1.** to redeem **2.** (*liberare da un impegno*) to release. ◆ **disimpegnarsi** *vr.* **1.** to disengage oneself **2.** (*cavarsela*) to manage.

disimpegno *sm.* **1.** redemption **2.** (*il liberarsi da un impegno*) disengagement.

disincagliare *vt.* to get (*v. irr.*) afloat.

disincantare *vt.* to disenchant.

disincantato *agg.* disenchanted.

disincanto *sm.* disenchantment.

disinfestare *vt.* to disinfest.

disinfettante *sm.* disinfectant.

disinfettare *vt.* to disinfect.

disinfezione *sf.* disinfection.

disingannare *vt.* to undeceive.

disinganno *sm.* **1.** undeceiving **2.** (*delusione*) disappointment.

disinnescare *vt.* to defuse.

disinnestare *vt.* to disengage.

disinnesto *sm.* disengagement, release.

disinserire *vt.* to disconnect.

disintegrare *vt.* to disintegrate.

disintegratore *sm.* disintegrator.

disintegrazione *sf.* disintegration.

disinteressare *vt.* **1.** to disinterest **2.** (*comm.*) to buy (*v. irr.*) out. ◆ **disinteressarsi** *vr.* to take (*v. irr.*) no interest (in).

disinteressato *agg.* **1.** disinterested **2.** (*altruistico*) unselfish.

disinteresse *sm.* **1.** indifference **2.** (*altruismo*) unselfishness.

disintossicare *vt.* to unpoison.

disintossicazione *sf.* unpoisoning.

disinvolto *agg.* unconstrained, free-and-easy.

disinvoltura *sf.* unconstraint, free-and-easy way.

disistima *sf.* disesteem.

disistimare *vt.* to disesteem.

dislivello *sm.* **1.** difference of level **2.** (*di acque*) rise **3.** (*di strade*) gradient **4.** (*ineguaglianza*) inequality.

dislocamento *sm.* **1.** displacement **2.** (*mil.*) dislocation.

dislocare *vt.* to displace **2.** (*mil.*) to dislocate.

dislocazione *sf.* removal, dislocation.

dismisura *sf.* excess ‖ *a —*, excessively.

disobbedire *vi.* V. *disubbidire*.

disobbligare *vt.* to release from duty. ◆ **disobbligarsi** *vr.* to free oneself from duty.

disoccupato *agg.* unemployed. ◆

disoccupato *sm.* unemployed person.

disoccupazione *sf.* unemployment.

disonestà *sf.* **1.** dishonesty **2.** (*atto disonesto*) fraud.

disonesto *agg.* dishonest, fraudulent.

disonorante *agg.* shameful.

disonorare *vt.* to dishonour.

disonore *sm.* dishonour, shame.

disonorévole *agg.* dishonourable.

disopra *avv.* **1.** above, over **2.** (*in cima*) on top **3.** (*ai piani superiori*) upstairs. ◆ **disopra** *sm.* top, upper part. ◆ **al disopra di**, **disopra a** *prep.* above.

disordinare *vt.* to disorder.

disordinatamente *avv.* untidily.

disordinato *agg.* untidy, disorderly.

disòrdine *sm.* **1.** disorder, untidiness **2.** (*sregolatezza*) disorderliness **3.** (*tumulto*) disorder, tumult.

disorgànico *agg.* inorganic.

disorganizzare *vt.* to disorganize.

disorganizzato *agg.* disorganized.

disorganizzazione *sf.* disorganization.

disorientamento *sm.* disorientation, confusion.

disorientare *vt.* **1.** to disorientate **2.** (*sconcertare*) to bewilder.

disorientato *agg.* bewildered, puzzled.

disormeggiare *vt.* to unmoor.

disossare *vt.* to bone.

disossidante *sm.* deoxidizer.

disossidare *vt.* to deoxidize.

disossidazione *sf.* deoxidation.

disotto *avv.* **1.** below, underneath **2.** (*al piano inferiore*) downstairs. ◆ **disotto** *sm.* underside, lower part. ◆ **al disotto di**, **disotto a** *prep.* under, beneath, below.

dispaccio *sm.* dispatch.

disparato *agg.* disparate.

disparere *sm.* difference of opinion.

dispari *agg.* odd.

disparità *sf.* disparity.

disparte *avv.* aside, apart: *starsene in —*, to stand (*v. irr.*) aside; (*fig.*) to stand aloof; *mettere in —*, to put (*v. irr.*) aside; (*per uno scopo*) to put by.

dispendio *sm.* **1.** heavy expense **2.** (*di forza, tempo*) waste.

dispendioso *agg.* expensive.

dispensa *sf.* **1.** pantry **2.** (*mobile*) sideboard **3.** (*pubblicazione perio-*

dica) number **4.** (*esenzione; eccl.*) dispensation.

dispensare *vt.* **1.** (*distribuire*) to deal (*v. irr.*) out **2.** (*esentare*) to exempt, to dispense.

dispensario *sm.* dispensary.

dispensato *agg.* exempted.

dispensatore *sm.* distributor, dispenser.

dispepsìa *sf.* dyspepsia.

dispèptico *agg.* dyspeptic.

disperare *vi.* to despair, to lose (*v. irr.*) all hope. ♦ **disperarsi** *vr.* to give (*v. irr.*) oneself up to despair.

disperatamente *avv.* desperately.

disperato *agg.* **1.** despairing **2.** (*senza speranza*) hopeless || essere — (*di malato*), to be far gone. ♦ **disperato** *sm.* **1.** (*miserabile*) destitute **2.** (*forsennato*) madman (*pl. -men*).

disperazione *sf.* despair.

dispèrdere *vt.* to disperse **2.** (*consumare*) to waste.

dispersione *sf.* **1.** dispersion **2.** (*elettr.*) leak.

dispersivo *agg.* dispersive.

disperso *agg.* missing, lost.

dispetto *sm.* **1.** spite: *a — di,* in spite of **2.** (*stizza*) vexation.

dispettoso *agg.* spiteful.

dispiacere [1] *vi.* **1.** to dislike || *mi dispiace,* I am sorry; (*in espressioni di cortesia*) *se non vi dispiace,* if you please **2.** (*essere sgradevole*) to be disagreeable.

dispiacere [2] *sm.* **1.** regret **2.** (*disapprovazione*) displeasure **3.** (*fastidio*) trouble.

dispiegare *vt.* **1.** (*allargare*) to spread (*v. irr.*) out **2.** (*le vele*) to unfurl.

displuvio *sm.* **1.** watershed || linea di —, ridge **2.** (*arch.*) hip.

disponìbile *agg.* available.

disponibilità *sf.* availability.

disporre *vt.* **1.** to arrange **2.** (*preparare*) to dispose **3.** (*deliberare*) to order.

dispositivo *sm.* (*mecc.*) device.

disposizione *sf.* **1.** disposition, arrangement **2.** (*ordine*) order, direction || *a —,* at one's disposal **3.** (*inclinazione*) bent.

disposto *agg.* **1.** ready, willing **2.** (*ben disposto fisicamente*) strong.

dispòtico *agg.* despotic.

dispotismo *sm.* despotism.

dispregiativamente *avv.* disparagingly.

dispregiativo *agg.* depreciative. ♦ **dispregiativo** *sm.* (*gramm.*) pejorative.

dispregiatore *sm.* contemner.

dispregio *sm.* contempt.

disprezzàbile *agg.* despicable.

disprezzare *vt.* **1.** to despise **2.** (*considerare di poco conto*) to look down on.

disprezzo *sm.* contempt.

disputa *sf.* discussion.

disputàbile *agg.* disputable.

disputare *vi* e *vt.* to discuss.

disquisizione *sf.* disquisition.

dissaldare *vt.* to unsolder.

dissanguamento *sm.* **1.** bleeding **2.** (*fig.*) impoverishment.

dissanguare *vt.* **1.** to bleed **2.** (*fig.*) to impoverish. ♦ **dissanguarsi** *vr.* (*fig.*) to become (*v. irr.*) impoverished.

dissanguato *agg.* **1.** bloodless **2.** (*fig.*) impoverished.

dissanguatore *sm.* (*fig.*) bloodsucker.

dissapore *sm.* disagreement.

dissecare *vt.* to dissect.

disseccamento *sm.* drying up.

disseccante *agg.* drying up. ♦ **disseccante** *sm.* desiccative.

disseccare *vt.* **1.** to dry up **2.** (*cibo*) to desiccate.

disselciare *vt.* to unpave.

disseminare *vt.* to disseminate.

disseminato *agg.* strewn.

disseminatore *agg.* disseminating. ♦ **disseminatore** *sm.* disseminator.

disseminazione *sf.* dissemination.

dissennatamente *avv.* madly.

dissennatezza *sf.* **1.** madness **2.** (*avventatezza*) rashness.

dissennato *agg.* **1.** mad **2.** (*avventato*) rash.

dissensione *sf.* dissension.

dissenso *sm.* dissent.

dissenterìa *sf.* dysentery.

dissentèrico *agg.* dysenteric.

dissentire *vi.* to dissent.

dissenziente *agg.* dissenting. ♦ **dissenziente** *sm.* dissenter.

disseppellimento *sm.* disinterment.

disseppellire *vt.* **1.** to disinter **2.** (*fig.*) to revive.

disserrare *vt.* to unfasten.

dissertare *vi.* to dissertate (on).

dissertatore *sm.* dissertator.

dissertazione sf. dissertation.

dissestare vt. 1. (finanziariamente) to ruin 2. (mettere fuori posto) to derange.

dissestato agg. (di persona) ruined.

dissesto sm. 1. trouble 2. (fallimento) bankruptcy.

dissetante agg. refreshing: bibita —, refreshing drink.

dissetare vt. to quench the thirst of. ♦ **dissetarsi** vr. 1. to quench one's thirst 2. (bere) to drink (v. irr.); (di animali) to water.

dissezione sf. dissection.

dissidente agg. e sm. dissident.

dissidenza sf. dissidence.

dissidio sm. 1. dissension, disagreement 2. (litigio) quarrel.

dissigillare vt. to unseal.

dissimile agg. unlike.

dissimmetria sf. dissymetry.

dissimulare vt. to dissemble.

dissimulatamente avv. dissemblingly.

dissimulatore sm. dissimulator.

dissimulazione sf. dissimulation.

dissipare vt. to dissipate. ♦ **dissiparsi** vr. to dissipate, to vanish.

dissipatezza sf. dissipation.

dissipatore sm. waster.

dissipazione sf. dissipation.

dissociàbile agg. dissociable.

dissociare vt. to dissociate.

dissociazione sf. dissociation.

dissodamento sm. tillage.

dissodare vt. to till.

dissolùbile agg. dissoluble.

dissolubilità sf. dissolubility.

dissolutezza sf. dissoluteness.

dissoluto agg. dissolute.

dissoluzione sf. dissolution.

dissolvente agg. e sm. dissolvent.

dissòlvere vt. 1. to dissolve 2. (disperdere) to dispel. ♦ **dissòlversi** vr. to dissolve.

dissolvimento sm. dissolution.

dissomigliante agg. dissimilar (to).

dissomiglianza sf. dissimilarity.

dissomigliare vi. to be unlike. ♦ **dissomigliarsi** vr. to differ from.

dissonante agg. dissonant.

dissonanza sf. 1. dissonance 2. (fig.) discordance.

dissonare vi. 1. to be out of tune 2. (fig.) to discord (with).

dissotterramento sm. disinterment.

dissotterrare vt. to disinter.

dissuadere vt. to dissuade.

dissuasione sf. dissuasion.

distaccamento sm. 1. detaching 2. (mil.) detachment.

distaccare vt. to detach. ♦ **distaccarsi** vr. to come (v. irr.) off.

distacco sm. 1. detaching 2. (partenza) leaving 3. (indifferenza) unconcern.

distante agg. distant. ♦ **distante** avv. far, far off, far away.

distanza sf. distance.

distanziare vt. 1. to space 2. (lasciare indietro) to distance.

distanziato agg. 1. spaced 2. (sport) outdistanced.

distare vi. to be far: quanto dista?, how far is it?

distèndere vt. 1. (allungare) to stretch 2. (spalmare) to spread (v. irr.) 3. (porre, stendere) to lay (v. irr.). ♦ **distèndersi** vr. 1. to spread (v. irr.) 2. (sdraiarsi) to lie (v. irr.) down 3. (rilassarsi) to relax.

distensione sf. 1. (di nervi, tensione) relaxation 2. (pol.) distension.

distensivo agg. relaxing.

distesa sf. expanse ‖ a —, continuously.

distesamente avv. diffusely.

disteso agg. 1. (teso) extended 2. (giacente) lying 3. (esteso) extensive ‖ per —, diffusely.

dìstico sm. couplet.

distillare vt. to distil.

distillato agg. distilled. ♦ **distillato** sm. distillate.

distillatoio sm. still.

distillatore sm. distiller.

distillazione sf. distillation.

distilleria sf. distillery.

distinguere vt. 1. to distinguish 2. (contrassegnare) to mark.

distinta sf. list.

distintivo agg. distinctive. ♦ **distintivo** sm. badge.

distinto agg. 1. distinct 2. (garbato) distinguished.

distinzione sf. 1. distinction 2. (riguardo) regard 3. (raffinatezza) refinement.

distògliere vt. 1. (dissuadere) to dissuade 2. (distrarre) to divert. ♦ **distògliersi** vr. to be distracted.

distorsione sf. distortion.

distrarre vt. 1. (distogliere) to divert 2. (divertire) to entertain.

distrattamente *avv.* **1.** absent-mindedly **2.** (*inavvertitamente*) inadvertently.

distratto *agg.* **1.** absent-minded **2.** (*disattento*) inattentive.

distrazione *sf.* **1.** absent-mindedness **2.** (*disattenzione*) inattention **3.** (*divertimento*) recreation.

distretta *sf.* urgent need.

distretto *sm.* district || — *militare*, recruiting centre.

distrettuale *agg.* district.

distribuibile *agg.* distributable.

distribuire *vt.* to distribute.

distributivo *agg.* e *sm.* distributive.

distributore *agg.* distributing. ♦ **distributore** *sm.* distributor || — *di benzina*, petrol pump.

distribuzione *sf.* distribution.

districare *vt.* to disentangle.

distrüggere *vt.* **1.** to destroy **2.** (*struggere*) to consume. ♦ **distrüggersi** *vr.* (*consumarsi*) to pine (away).

distruggibile *agg.* destroyable.

distruttivo *agg.* destroying.

distrutto *agg.* destroyed.

distruttore *agg.* destroying. ♦ **distruttore** *sm.* destroyer.

distruzione *sf.* destruction.

disturbare *vt.* to disturb.

disturbato *agg.* **1.** disturbed **2.** (*indisposto*) unwell.

disturbatore *sm.* disturber.

disturbo *sm.* **1.** trouble, inconvenience **2.** (*malattia*) trouble, illness **3.** (*radio*) disturbance.

disubbidiente *agg.* disobedient.

disubbidienza *sf.* disobedience.

disubbidire *vi.* to disobey.

disuguaglianza *sf.* **1.** inequality **2.** (*di terreno*) unevenness.

disuguale *agg.* **1.** unequal **2.** (*irregolare*) irregular **3.** (*differente*) different.

disumanamente *avv.* inhumanly.

disumanare *vt.* to divest of humanity.

disumanità *sf.* inhumanity.

disumano *agg.* inhuman.

disumidire *vt.* to dry.

disunione *sf.* disunion.

disunire *vt.* to disunite. ♦ **disunirsi** *vr.* to become (*v. irr.*) disunited.

disunito *agg.* disunited.

disusare *vt.* to disuse.

disusato *agg.* disused.

disuso *sm.* disuse.

ditale *sm.* thimble.

ditata *sf.* finger-mark.

ditirámbico *agg.* dithyrambic.

ditirambo *sm.* dithyramb.

dito *sm.* **1.** finger **2.** (*del piede*) toe.

ditta *sf.* firm.

dittàfono *sm.* dictaphone.

dittatore *sm.* dictator.

dittatoriale *agg.* dictatorial.

dittatorio *agg.* dictatorial.

dittatura *sf.* dictatorship.

dittico *sm.* diptych.

dittongo *sm.* diphthong.

diuresi *sf.* diuresis.

diurètico *agg.* diuretic.

diurno *agg.* diurnal, daytime.

diuturnamente *avv.* for a long time.

diuturno *agg.* diuturnal.

diva *sf.* **1.** goddess **2.** (*cine*) star.

divagare *vi.* to wander **2.** (*divertire*) to amuse. ♦ **divagarsi** *vr.* **1.** to be distracted **2.** (*divertirsi*) to amuse oneself.

divagazione *sf.* digression.

divampare *vi.* to blaze.

divano *sm.* divan, sofa.

divaricamento *sm.* straddle.

divaricare *vt.* to open wide || — *le gambe*, to part one's legs wide.

divario *sm.* difference.

divedere *vt.* (*nella loc. avv.*) *dare a* —, to show (*v. irr.*) clearly **2.** (*dar a credere*) to make (*v. irr.*) believe.

divèllere *vt.* to uproot.

divenire[1] *vi.* **1.** to become (*v. irr.*) **2.** (*mutarsi lentamente*) to grow (*v. irr.*).

divenire[2] *sm.* becoming: *l'essere e il* —, being and becoming.

diverbio *sm.* quarrel.

divergente *agg.* divergent.

divergenza *sf.* divergence.

divergere *vi.* **1.** to diverge **2.** (*scostarsi*) to wander.

diversamente *avv.* **1.** differently **2.** (*altrimenti*) otherwise.

diversificare *vt.* to diversify. ♦ **diversificarsi** *vr.* to differ.

diversione *sf.* diversion.

diversità *sf.* diversity.

diversivo *agg.* **1.** deviating **2.** (*che distrae*) diverting. ♦ **diversivo** *sm.* diversion, distraction.

diverso *agg.* different.

divertente *agg.* amusing.

divertimento *sm.* amusement.
divertire *vt.* to amuse, to entertain
♦ **divertirsi** *vr.* to enjoy oneself,
to have a good time.
divezzamento *sm.* weaning.
divezzare *vt.* to wean.
dividendo *sm.* dividend.
dividere *vt.* 1. to divide 2. (*condividere*) to share.
divieto *sm.* prohibition.
divinamente *avv.* divinely.
divinare *vt.* to divine.
divinatore *sm.* diviner.
divinatorio *agg.* divinatory.
divinazione *sf.* divination.
divincolarsi *vr.* to wriggle.
divinità *sf.* divinity.
divinizzare *vt.* to deify.
divino *agg.* divine.
divisa *sf.* 1. uniform 2. (*valuta*)
currency.
divisare *vt.* to plan.
divisibile *agg.* divisible.
divisibilità *sf.* divisibility.
divisionale *agg.* divisional.
divisione *sf.* 1. division 2. (*amm.*)
department.
divisionismo *sm.* pointillism.
divisionista *s.* pointillist.
divismo *sm.* stardom, star worship.
diviso *agg.* 1. divided 2. (*separato*)
separated 3. (*condiviso*) shared.
divisore *sm.* divisor.
divisorio *agg.* dividing.
divo *sm.* 1. deity 2. (*cine*) star.
divorare *vt.* to devour.
divoratore *agg.* devouring.
divorziare *vi.* to divorce, to be divorced.
divorziato *agg.* divorced. ♦ **divorziato** *sm.* divorcee.
divorzio *sm.* divorce (*anche fig.*).
divulgàbile *agg.* that may be divulged.
divulgare *vt.* to spread (*v. irr.*).
divulgativo *agg.* divulging.
divulgatore *sm.* divulger.
divulgazione *sf.* divulgation, spreading.
dizionario *sm.* dictionary.
dizionarista *s.* lexicographer.
dizione *sf.* 1. diction 2. (*pronuncia*)
pronunciation.
do *sm.* (*mus.*) C.
doccia *sf.* shower.
docente *agg.* teaching. ♦ **docente**
sm. teacher ‖ *libero —*, fully
established university lecturer.
docenza *sf.* teaching.

dòcile *agg.* docile.
docilità *sf.* docility.
documentare *vt.* to document.
documentario *sm.* documentary.
documentarista *s.* documentary
film-maker.
documentato *agg.* documented.
documentazione *sf.* 1. documentation 2. *pl.* (*documenti*) papers.
documento *sm.* document.
dodecaedro *sm.* dodecahedron.
dodecafonìa *sf.* dodecaphony.
dodecafònico *agg.* dodecaphonic.
dodecàgono *sm.* dodecagon.
dodecasìllabo *sm.* dodecasyllable.
dodicèsimo *agg.* twelfth.
dòdici *agg.* twelve.
doga *sf.* stave.
dogana *sf.* customs (*pl.*).
doganale *agg.* customs (*attr.*): *dichiarazione —*, customs entry.
doganiere *sm.* customs officer.
doge *sm.* doge.
doglia *sf.* 1. sharp pains 2. (*pl.
med.*) throes.
dogma *sm.* dogma.
dogmàtico *agg.* dogmatic(al).
dogmatismo *sm.* dogmatism.
dolce *agg.* 1. sweet 2. (*mite*) mild
3. (*tec.*) soft. ♦ **dolce** *sm.* 1.
sweet 2. (*torta*) cake.
dolcezza *sf.* 1. sweetness 2. (*di
clima*) mildness.
dolciario *agg.* confectionary.
dolciastro *agg.* sweetish.
dolcificare *vt.* 1. to sweeten 2.
(*fig.*) to mitigate.
dolcificazione *sf.* sweetening.
dolciumi *sm. pl.* sweets.
dolente *agg.* 1. afflicted, grieved 2.
(*spiacente*) sorry.
dolere *vi.* 1. to ache 2. (*rincrescere*)
to regret. ♦ **dolersi** *vr.* to regret.
dolicocèfalo *agg.* dolichocephalic.
dòllaro *sm.* dollar.
dolmen *sm.* dolmen.
dolo *sm.* fraud.
dolomite *sm.* dolomite.
dolomìtico *agg.* dolomitic.
dolorante *agg.* aching.
dolore *sm.* 1. pain, ache 2. (*fig.*)
sorrow, grief.
dolorosamente *avv.* 1. painfully
2. (*morale*) sadly.
doloroso *agg.* 1. painful 2. (*che
causa dolore*) grievous.
doloso *agg.* fraudulent.
domàbile *agg.* tamable.
domanda *sf.* 1. question, request

2. (*richiesta scritta*) application.

domandare *vt.* to ask (so. for sthg.). ♦ **domandarsi** *vr.* to wonder.

domani *avv.* tomorrow.

domare *vt.* 1. to tame 2. (*sottomettere*) to subdue.

domatore *sm.* tamer.

domattina *avv.* tomorrow morning.

doménica *sf.* Sunday.

domenicale *agg.* Sunday (*attr.*).

domenicano *agg.* dominican.

doméstica *sf.* maid.

doméstico *agg.* e *sm.* domestic || *lavori domestici*, household duties.

domiciliare *agg.* domiciliary.

domiciliarsi *vr.* to settle (in).

domiciliato *agg.* resident, living.

domicilio *sm.* 1. house, dwelling 2. (*giur.*) domicile.

dominante *agg.* dominant.

dominare *vt.* to dominate.

dominatore *sm.* ruler.

dominazione *sf.* domination.

dominio *sm.* 1. domination 2. (*territorio*) dominion 3. (*giur.*) domain || *di —* *pubblico*, known to everybody.

dòmino *sm.* domino.

donare *vt.* to give (*v. irr.*) ♦ **donare** *vi.* †(*addirsi*) to suit.

donatore *sm.* donor.

donazione *sf.* 1. donation 2. (*somma elargita per uno scopo*) grant.

donchisciottesco *agg.* quixotic.

donde *avv.* whence, from where || *ne ha ben —*, he has good reason for it.

dondolamento *sm.* swinging.

dondolare *vt.* e *vi.* to swing (*v. irr.*). ♦ **dondolarsi** *vr.* to swing, to rock.

dondolìo *sm.* swinging.

dòndolo *sm.* 1. (*altalena*) swing || *a —*, rocking.

donna *sf.* woman (*pl.* women).

donnaiolo *sm.* ladies' man (*pl.* men).

donnesco *agg.* womanlike.

dònnola *sf.* weasel.

dono *sm.* gift.

donzella *sf.* damsel.

dopo *avv.* 1. (*di luogo*) after, next 2. (*dietro*) behind 3. (*di tempo*) after, then 4. (*più tardi*) later. ♦ **dopo** *prep.* (*di luogo e tempo*) after.

dopodomani *avv.* the day after to-morrow.

dopoguerra *sm.* post-war period.

dopopranzo *sm.* afternoon.

dopotutto *avv.* after all.

doppiaggio *sm.* (*cine*) dubbing.

doppiamente *avv.* 1. doubly 2. (*con inganno*) deceitfully.

doppiare *vt.* 1. to double 2. (*cine*) to dub.

doppiato *agg.* 1. doubled 2. (*cine*) dubbed.

doppiatura *sf.* doubling.

doppietta *sf.* double-barrelled gun.

doppiezza *sf.* 1. doubleness 2. (*ambiguità*) double-dealing.

doppio *agg.* 1. double 2. (*ambiguo*) double-faced. ♦ **doppio** *sm.* twice as much, twice as many.

doppiofondo *sm.* double bottom.

doppione *sm.* 1. double 2. (*di parola*) doublet.

doppiopetto *sm.* double-breasted.

dorare *vt.* to gild.

dorato *agg.* 1. gilded 2. (*color oro*) golden.

doratore *sm.* gilder.

doratura *sf.* gilding.

dòrico *agg.* doric.

dorifora *sf.* potato-beetle.

dormicchiare *vi.* to doze.

dormiente *agg.* sleeping. ♦ **dormiente** *sm.* sleeper.

dormiglione *sm.* sleepy-head.

dormire *vi.* 1. to sleep (*v. irr.*) || *— tra due guanciali*, to set (*v. irr.*) one's mind at rest 2. (*fig.*) to remain inactive.

dormita *sf.* sleep.

dormitorio *sm.* dormitory.

dormiveglia *sm.* drowsiness.

dorsale *agg.* dorsal: *spina —*, backbone.

dorso *sm.* 1. back 2. (*di monte*) ridge.

dosàbile *agg.* measurable.

dosaggio *sm.* dosage.

dosare *vt.* to proportion: *— le parole*, to weigh one's words.

dosatura *sf.* dosage.

dose *sf.* dose: *una buona — di*, a good deal of.

dossale *sm.* dossal.

dosso *sm.* back: *togliersi di —*, to take (*v. irr.*) off.

dotare *vt.* 1. to give (*v. irr.*) a dowry 2. (*fornire di una rendita*) to endow 3. (*fornire*) to provide (with).

dotato *agg.* 1. gifted (with) 2. (*e-*

quipaggiato) provided (with).

dotazione *sf.* endowment.

dote *sf.* 1. dowry 2. (*qualità*) endowment.

dotto[1] *agg.* learned. ♦ **dotto** *sm.* scholar.

dotto[2] *sm.* (*anat.*) duct.

dottorale *agg.* doctoral.

dottorato *sm.* doctorate.

dottore *sm.* 1. doctor 2. (*laureato*) graduate.

dottoressa *sf.* 1. (*laureata*) graduate 2. (*in medicina*) lady doctor.

dottrina *sf.* doctrine.

dottrinale *agg.* doctrinal.

dottrinario *sm.* doctrinaire.

dottrinarismo *sm.* doctrinairism.

dove *avv.* where.

dovere[1] *vi.* 1. (*obbligo*) must (*v. dif.*): *devi lavorare,* you must work 2. to have to 3. (*possibilità, predestinazione*) to be to: *doveva diventare un grande scrittore,* he was to become a great writer 4. (*devo?, dobbiamo?, nel senso di: vuoi che?*) shall (*v. dif.*): *devo aprire la finestra?,* shall I open the window? 5. (*al condizionale*) ought to, should (*v. dif.*): *dovresti essere gentile,* you ought to be kind; *dovremmo partire,* we should leave 6. (*al congiuntivo*) should, were to: *se dovesse venire,* if he should come, if he were to come 7. (*essere obbligati*) to be obliged, to be forced 8. (*essere da attribuire, dover arrivare*) to be due: *lo si deve al mio ritardo,* this is due to my being late; *il treno deve arrivare alle 4,* the train is due at 4 a.m. ♦ **dovere** *vt.* (*essere debitore in tutti i sensi*) to owe: *ti devo 1000 lire,* I owe you one thousand lire; *ti devo la vita,* I owe you my life.

dovere[2] *sm.* duty: *fare il proprio —,* to do (*v. irr.*) one's duty.

doverosamente *avv.* dutifully.

doveroso *agg.* dutiful.

dovizia *sf.* plenty.

dovizioso *agg.* abundant.

dovunque *avv.* 1. everywhere 2. (*seguito da verbo*) wherever.

dovuto *agg.* 1. due 2. (*equo*) fair. ♦ **dovuto** *sm.* due.

dozzina *sf.* dozen.

dozzinale *agg.* cheap, common.

draconiano *agg.* draconian.

draga *sf.* dredger.

dragaggio *sm.* dredging.

dragamine *sm.* mine-sweeper.

dragare *vt.* to dredge.

draglia *sf.* stay.

drago *sm.* dragon.

dragona *sf.* sword-knot.

dragone *sm.* dragon.

dramma *sm.* drama.

drammàtica *sf.* dramatics.

drammaticamente *avv.* dramatically.

drammaticità *sf.* tragicalness.

drammàtico *agg.* dramatic.

drammatizzare *vt.* to dramatise.

drammaturgìa *sf.* dramaturgy.

drammaturgo *sm.* dramatist.

drappeggiare *vt.* to drape.

drappeggio *sm.* draping.

drappello *sm.* squad.

drapperìa *sf.* drapery.

drappo *sm.* cloth.

dràstico *agg.* drastic.

drenaggio *sm.* drainage.

drenare *vt.* to drain.

driade *sf.* 1. (*mit.*) dryad 2. (*bot.*) dryas (*pl.* -ades).

dribblare *vt.* to dribble.

dritta *sf.* 1. right hand, right 2. (*mar.*) starboard.

dritto *agg.* 1. (*non storto*) straight 2. (*eretto, onesto*) upright. ♦ **dritto** *sm.* right side.

drizza *sf.* halyard.

drizzare *vt.* to straighten.

droga *sf.* 1. drug 2. (*spezia*) spices (*pl.*).

drogare *vt.* 1. to drug 2. (*condire*) to spice.

drogherìa *sf.* grocery.

droghiere *sm.* grocer.

dromedario *sm.* dromedary.

drùido *sm.* druid.

drupa *sf.* drupe.

dualismo *sm.* dualism.

dualità *sf.* duality.

dubbiezza *sf.* dubiousness.

dubbio *sm.* doubt: *mettere in —,* to question. ♦ **dubbio** *agg.* dubious.

dubbioso *agg.* doubtful.

dubitare *vi.* to doubt.

dubitativo *agg.* dubitative.

duca *sm.* duke.

ducale *agg.* ducal.

ducato *sm.* 1. dukedom 2. (*moneta*) ducat.

duchessa *sf.* duchess.

due *agg.* two.

duecentèsimo *agg.* two hundredth.

duecentesco agg. thirteenth century (attr.).

duecento sm. two hundred ‖ il —, the thirteenth century.

duellare vi. to duel.

duello sm. duel: — all'ultimo sangue, duel to the death.

duetto sm. duet.

duna sf. dune.

dunque cong. 1. (perciò) therefore 2. (rafforzativo) well, then. ♦ **dunque** sm. venire al —, to come (v. irr.) to the point.

duodenale agg. duodenal.

duodeno sm. duodenum.

duomo sm. cathedral.

duplicare vt. to duplicate.

duplicato sm. duplicate.

dùplice agg. twofold.

duplicità sf. double-dealing.

durabilità sf. durability.

duralluminio sm. duralumin.

durante prep. during.

durare vi. 1. to last 2. (perseverare) to persist 3. (resistere) to hold (v. irr.) out. ♦ **durare** vt. to endure ‖ chi la dura la vince, slow and steady wins the race.

durata sf. 1. duration, length 2. (periodo) term 3. (di un oggetto) endurance.

duraturo agg. lasting.

durévole agg. durable.

durezza sf. 1. hardness 2. (rigidità) stiffness.

duro agg. 1. hard 2. (di voce) harsh ‖ avere il sonno —, to sleep (v. irr.) like a log; avere la testa dura, to be a block-head, to be stubborn.

durone sm. hard skin.

dùttile agg. ductile.

duttilità sf. ductility.

E

e cong. and: e... e, both... and.

ebanista sm. cabinet-maker.

ebanisterìa sf. 1. (bottega) cabinet-maker's shop 2. (arte) cabinet-making.

ebanite sf. ebonite.

èbano sm. ebony.

ebbene cong. well: —?, what about it?

ebbrezza sf. 1. drunkenness 2. (fig.) elation.

ebbro agg. 1. drunken 2. (fig.) mad.

ebdomadario agg. weekly. ♦ **ebdomadario** sm. weekly paper.

èbete agg. idiotic. ♦ **èbete** sm. idiot.

ebollizione sf. boiling.

ebràico agg. Hebrew.

ebreo agg. Hebrew, Jewish. ♦ **ebreo** sm. Hebrew, Jew.

ecatombe sf. massacre.

eccedente agg. excessive, in excess (pred.). ♦ **eccedente** sm. (comm.) exceeding.

eccedenza sf. excess, surplus: — di peso, overweight.

eccèdere vt. to exceed. ♦ **eccèdere** vi. to go (v. irr.) too far.

eccellente agg. excellent.

eccellenza sf. 1. excellence 2. (titolo) excellency.

eccèllere vi. to excel.

eccelso agg. sublime.

eccentricità sf. eccentricity.

eccèntrico agg. eccentric.

eccepire vi. to object.

eccessivo agg. excessive.

eccesso sm. excess.

eccètera sm. et cetera (abbr. etc.), and so on.

eccetto prep. except, but, save. ♦ **eccetto che** cong. 1. except that 2. (purché) provided that.

eccettuare vt. to except.

eccettuato agg. excluded.

eccezionale agg. exceptional.

eccezione sf. exception.

ecchìmosi sf. bruise.

eccidio sm. bloodshed.

eccitàbile agg. excitable.

eccitabilità sf. excitability.

eccitamento sm. excitement.

eccitante agg. e sm. excitant.

eccitare vt. to excite. ♦ **eccitarsi** vr. to get (v. irr.) excited.

eccitatore agg. excitative. ♦ **eccitatore** sm. exciter.

eccitazione sf. excitement.

ecclesiàstico agg. ecclesiastical.

ecco avv. here, there (in unione con le voci del verbo to be al pres. ind.): — il mio cappello!, here is my hat! ‖ — tutto, that's all; quand' —, when suddenly.

eccome inter. and how!

echeggiare vi. to echo (with sthg.).

echinoderma sm. echinoderm.

eclèttico agg. e sm. eclectic.

eclettismo *sm.* eclecticism.
eclissare *vt.* 1. to eclipse 2. (*fig.*) to overshadow.
eclisse, eclissi *sf.* eclipse.
eclittica *sf.* ecliptic.
eclittico *agg.* ecliptic.
eco *sf.* echo.
economato *sm.* 1. steward's office 2. (*in università*) bursar's office.
economìa *sf.* 1. economy 2. (*scienza*) economics.
econòmico *agg.* 1. economic 2. (*a buon prezzo*) cheap.
economista *s.* economist.
economizzare *vt.* to economize.
econòmo *agg.* economical. ♦ **econòmo** *sm.* 1. steward 2. (*di università*) bursar.
ecumènico *agg.* ecumenical.
eczema *sm.* eczema.
edema *sm.* oedema.
eden *sm.* Eden.
èdera *sf.* ivy.
edìcola *sf.* newspaper kiosk.
edicolista *sm.* news-agent.
edificante *agg.* edifying.
edificare *vt.* 1. to build (*v. irr.*) (up) 2. (*fig.*) to edify.
edificatore *sm.* 1. builder 2. (*fig.*) edifier.
edificazione *sf.* 1. building 2. (*fig.*) edification.
edificio *sm.* building.
edile *agg.* building: *perito* —, master-builder. ♦ **edile** *sm.* (*stor. romana*) aedile.
edilizia *sf.* building industry.
edilizio *agg.* building (*attr.*).
èdito *agg.* published.
editore *sm.* publisher.
editorìa *sf.* book industry.
editoriale *agg.* e *sm.* editorial.
editrice *agg.:* *casa* —, publishing house.
editto *sm.* edict.
edizione *sf.* edition, issue.
edonismo *sm.* hedonism.
edonista *s.* hedonist.
edotto *agg.* aware: *rendere* —, to inform.
educanda *sf.* boarding-school girl.
educandato *sm.* girls' boarding-school.
educare *vt.* 1. to educate 2. (*allevare*) to bring (*v. irr.*) up.
educativo *agg.* educational.
educato *agg.* well-bred, polite.
educatore *sm.* educator.
educazione *sf.* 1. education 2.

(*buone maniere*) good manners (*pl.*).
edulcorare *vt.* to edulcorate.
efebo *sm.* ephebe.
efèlide *sf.* freckle.
effemèride *sf.* ephemeris (*pl. -ides*).
effeminare *vt.* to effeminate. ♦ **effeminarsi** *vr.* to become (*v. irr.*) effeminate.
effeminatezza *sf.* effeminacy.
efferatezza *sf.* brutality.
efferato *agg.* brutal.
effervescente *agg.* sparkling.
effervescenza *sf.* effervescence.
effettivamente *avv.* actually, indeed.
effettivo *agg.* actual.
effetto *sm.* 1. effect, result ‖ *in effetti*, as a matter of fact 2. (*comm.*) bill.
effettuàbile *agg.* feasible.
effettuare *vt.* to carry out: — *un piano*, to carry out a plan. ♦ **effettuarsi** *vr.* (*aver luogo*) to take (*v. irr.*) place.
effettuazione *sf.* accomplishment.
efficace *agg.* effective, efficacious.
efficacia *sf.* efficacy.
efficiente *agg.* efficient.
efficienza *sf.* efficiency.
effigiare *vt.* to portray.
effigie *sf.* image.
effìmera *sf.* (*fam.*) mayfly.
effìmero *agg.* ephemeral.
effluvio *sm.* exhalation.
effóndere *vt.* to pour forth. ♦ **effóndersi** *vr.* to spread (*v. irr.*) (about).
effrazione *sf.* (*giur.*) house-breaking, burglary.
effusione *sf.* 1. shedding 2. (*cordialità*) cordiality 3. (*pl., manifestazioni*) effusions.
effusivo *agg.* effusive.
egemonìa *sf.* hegemony.
egemònico *agg.* hegemonic.
ègida *sf.* 1. aegis 2. (*fig.*) protection.
egiziano *agg.* e *sm.* Egyptian.
egli *pron. he:* — *stesso*, he himself.
ègloga *sf.* eclogue.
egocèntrico *agg.* egocentric. ♦ **egocèntrico** *sm.* egocentric man.
egocentrismo *sm.* egocentrism.
egoismo *sm.* selfishness.
egoista *agg.* e *sm.* egoist.
egotismo *sm.* self-conceit.
egregiamente *avv.* eminently.
egregio *agg.* eminent ‖ (*nelle lettere*) — *Signore*, Dear Sir.

eguaglianza, eguagliare, eguale ecc. V. *uguaglianza, uguagliare, uguale* ecc.

egualità *sf.* equality.

eiaculare *vi.* to ejaculate.

eiaculazione *sf.* ejaculation.

eiezione *sf.* ejection.

elaborare *vt.* to elaborate.

elaborato *agg.* elaborate.

elaborazione *sf.* **1.** elaboration **2.** (*di piano*) formulation.

elargire *vt.* to lavish.

elargizione *sf.* donation.

elasticità *sf.* **1.** elasticity **2.** (*agilità*) nimbleness.

elasticizzare *vt.* to make (*v. irr.*) elastic.

elàstico *agg.* **1.** elastic **2.** (*agile*) nimble. ♦ **elàstico** *sm.* rubber band.

elce *sm.* ilex.

elefante *sm.* elephant.

elefantesco *agg.* elephantine.

elefantìasi *sf.* elephantiasis.

elegante *agg.* elegant, smart.

eleganza *sf.* smartness.

elèggere *vt.* **1.** to elect **2.** (*nominare*) to appoint.

eleggìbile *agg.* eligible.

eleggibilità *sf.* eligibility.

elegìa *sf.* elegy.

elegìaco *agg.* elegiac.

elementare *agg.* elementary: *scuola —*, primary school.

elemento *sm.* **1.** element **2.** (*componente*) component **3.** (*pl., rudimenti*) rudiments **4.** (*persona*) person.

elemòsina *sf.* alms: *chiedere l'—*, to beg.

elemosinare *vt. e vi.* to beg (for).

elencare *vt.* to list.

elenco *sm.* list: *— telefonico*, telephone directory.

elettivo *agg.* elective.

eletto *agg.* elect, chosen.

elettorale *agg.* electoral.

elettorato *sm.* electorate.

elettore *sm.* voter.

elettràuto *sm.* **1.** (*officina*) car electrical repairs (*pl.*) **2.** (*meccanico*) car electrician.

elettricista *sm.* electrician.

elettricità *sf.* electricity.

elèttrico *agg.* electric.

elettrificare *vt.* to electrify.

elettrificazione *sf.* electrification.

elettrizzare *vt.* to electrify.

elettrocalamita *sf.* electro-magnet.

elettrocardiogramma *sm.* electro-cardiogram.

elettrodinàmica *sf.* electrody-namics.

elèttrodo *sm.* electrode.

elettrodomèstici *sm. pl.* electrical household appliances.

elettrògeno *agg.* generating electricity.

elettròlisi *sf.* elecrolysis.

elettromagnètico *agg.* electro-magnetic.

elettromotore *sm.* dynamo.

elettromotrice *sf.* electric rail car.

elettrone *sm.* electron.

elettrònica *sf.* electronics.

elettrònico *agg.* electronic.

elettrotècnica *sf.* electrical technology.

elettrotreno *sm.* electric train.

elevamento *sm.* elevation.

elevare *vt.* **1.** to elevate **2.** (*erigere*) to erect **3.** (*mat.*) to raise. ♦ **elevarsi** *vr.* to rise (*v. irr.*).

elevatezza *sf.* loftiness.

elevato *agg.* elevated, high.

elevatore *sm.* elevator.

elevazione *sf.* **1.** elevation **2.** (*l'elevare*) rising **3.** (*mat.*) raising.

elezione *sf.* election.

èlica *sf.* **1.** (*aer.*) propeller **2.** (*mar.*) screw.

elicoidale *agg.* helicoidal.

elicòttero *sm.* helicopter.

elìdere *vt.* to annul. ♦ **elìdersi** *vr. rec.* to annul each other.

eliminare *vt.* to eliminate. ♦ **eliminarsi** *vr.* to be eliminated.

eliminatòria *sf.* preliminary heat.

eliminazione *sf.* elimination, expulsion.

elio *sm.* helium.

eliocèntrico *agg.* heliocentric.

eliografia *sf.* heliography.

elioterapìa *sf.* heliotherapy.

eliotipìa *sf.* heliotypy.

elipòrto *sm.* heliport.

elisione *sf.* elision.

elisir *sm.* elixir.

èlitra *sf.* elytrum (*pl.* -ra).

ella *pron.* she: *— stessa*, she herself.

ellènico *agg.* Hellenic.

ellenismo *sm.* Hellenism.

ellenista *s.* Hellenist.

ellisse *sf.* ellipse.

ellissi *sf.* ellipsis (*pl.* -ses).

ellìttico *agg.* elliptic(al).

elmetto *sm.* helmet.

elmo *sm.* helmet.

elocuzione *sf.* elocution.

elogiàbile *agg.* praiseworthy.

elogiare *vt.* to eulogize, to praise.

elogiatore *sm.* eulogist.

elogio *sm.* eulogy, praise.

eloquente *agg.* eloquent.

eloquenza *sf.* eloquence.

elucubrare *vt.* to lucubrate: — *su, intorno a qc.*, to lucubrate on, about sthg.

elucubrazione *sf.* lucubration.

elùdere *vt.* to elude.

elusivo *agg.* elusive.

elvètico *agg.* Helvetic.

elzeviro *sm.* 1. elzevir 2. (*giorn.*) leading literary article.

emaciare *vt.* to emaciate. ♦ emaciarsi *vr.* to become (*v. irr.*) emaciated.

emaciato *agg.* emaciated.

emanare *vt.* 1. to issue 2. (*vapori, profumi*) to exhale.

emanazione *sf.* emanation.

emancipare *vt.* to emancipate.

emancipato *agg.* emancipated.

emancipazione *sf.* emancipation.

emàtico *agg.* haematic.

ematoma *sm.* haematoma (*pl.* -ata).

ematosi *sf.* haematosis.

embargo *sm.* embargo.

emblema *sm.* 1. emblem 2. (*simbolo*) symbol.

emblemàtico *agg.* emblematic.

embolìa *sf.* embolism.

èmbolo *sm.* embolus (*pl.* -li).

embrionale *agg.* embryonic.

embrione *sm.* embryo.

emendamento *sm.* 1. amendment 2. (*correzione*) emendation.

emendare *vt.* 1. to amend 2. (*correggere*) to emend.

emergenza *sf.* emergency.

emèrgere *vi.* 1. to emerge 2. (*fig.*) to emerge, to appear.

emèrito *agg.* emeritus.

emeroteca *sf.* newspaper library.

emersione *sf.* emersion.

eméttere *vt.* 1. to emit 2. (*di suono*) to utter 3. (*emanare*) to deliver 4. (*banconote*) to issue.

emiciclo *sm.* hemicycle.

emicrania *sf.* headache.

emigrante *agg. e sm.* emigrant.

emigrare *vi.* to emigrate.

emigrato *sm.* emigrant.

emigrazione *sf.* emigration.

eminente *agg.* outstanding, eminent.

eminenza *sf.* eminence.

emiro *sm.* emir.

emisfèrico *agg.* hemispheric(al).

emisfero *sm.* hemisphere.

emissario *sm.* emissary.

emissione *sf.* 1. emission 2. (*econ.*) issue.

emistichio *sm.* hemistich.

emittente *agg.* issuing || *stazione* — (*radio*), broadcasting station.

emofilìa *sf.* haemophilia.

emoglobina *sf.* haemoglobin.

emolliente *agg.* emollient.

emolumento *sm.* emolument.

emorragìa *sf.* haemorrhage.

emorròidi *sf. pl.* haemorrhoids.

emòstasi *sf.* haemostasis.

emostàtico *agg.* haemostatic.

emoteca *sf.* blood bank.

emotività *sf.* emotionality.

emotivo *agg.* emotional.

emottisi *sf.* haemoptysis.

emozionante *agg.* touching, exciting, thrilling.

emozionare *vt.* to move. ♦ emozionarsi *vr.* to get (*v. irr.*) excited.

emozione *sf.* emotion, thrill.

empiastro *sm.* plaster.

empietà *sf.* impiety.

empio *agg.* impious.

empire *vt.* to fill.

empìrico *agg. e sm.* empiric.

empirismo *sm.* empiricism.

emporio *sm.* department store.

emulare *vt.* to emulate.

emulazione *sf.* emulation.

èmulo *sm.* rival.

emulsionare *vt.* to emulsify.

emulsione *sf.* emulsion.

encefalite *sf.* encephalitis.

encèfalo *sm.* encephalon (*pl.* -ala).

encìclica *sf.* encyclic.

enciclopedìa *sf.* encyclopaedia.

enciclopèdico *agg.* encyclopaedic.

enclìtico *agg.* enclitic.

encomiàbile *agg.* praiseworthy.

encomiare *vt.* to commend.

encomio *sm.* panegyric.

endecasìllabo *agg.* hendecasyllabic. ♦ endecasìllabo *sm.* hendecasyllable.

endèmico *agg.* endemic.

endocardio *sm.* endocardium.

endocardite *sf.* endocarditis.

endòcrino *agg.* endocrine.

endocrinologìa *sf.* endocrinology.

endovenoso *agg.* intravenous. ♦ endovenosa *sf.* intravenous injection.

energètico *agg. e sm.* tonic.

energìa *sf.* energy.

energicamente *avv.* energetically.

enèrgico *agg.* energetic(al).

energùmeno *sm.* energumen.

ènfasi *sf.* emphasis.

enfàtico *agg.* emphatic.

enfiagione *sf.* swelling.

enfisema *sm.* emphysema.

enfitèusi *sf.* emphyteusis.

enigma *sm.* enigma, puzzle.

enigmàtico *agg.* puzzling.

enigmista *sm.* enigmatographer.

enigmìstica *sf.* enigmatography.

enigmìstico *agg.* puzzle (*attr.*).

ennèsimo *agg.* nth: *ennesima potenza,* nth power.

enologìa *sf.* oenology.

enòlogo *sm.* oenologist.

enorme *agg.* huge.

enormità *sf.* **1.** hugeness **2.** (*fig.*) absurdity.

ente *sm.* **1.** being **2.** (*comm.*) body, corporation.

enterite *sf.* enteritis.

enteroclisma *sm.* enema.

enterocolite *sf.* enterocolitis.

entità *sf.* entity.

entomologìa *sf.* entomology.

entomòlogo *sm.* entomologist.

entrambi *pron. e agg.* both.

entrante *agg.* (*con espressioni di tempo*) next, coming.

entrare *vi.* to enter, to come (*v. irr.*) in, to go (*v. irr.*) in ‖ *non c'entra,* this has got nothing to do with it; — *correndo,* to run (*v. irr.*) in; — *in carica,* to come (*v. irr.*) into office; — *in società,* to go into partnership (with); — *precipitosamente,* to rush in; — *in giuoco,* to come into play; — *in vigore,* to come into force.

entrata *sf.* **1.** entrance, entry **2.** (*rendita*) income.

entratura *sf.* entrance.

entro *prep.* **1.** (*luogo*) inside **2.** (*tempo*) in, within, by: — *due giorni,* within two days; — *lunedì,* by Monday.

entrobordo *sm.* inboard.

entroterra *sm.* inland.

entusiasmante *agg.* exciting.

entusiasmare *vt.* to raise enthusiasm in. ♦ **entusiasmarsi** *vr.* to become (*v. irr.*) enthusiastic.

entusiasmo *sm.* enthusiasm.

entusiasta *agg.* enthusiast: *essere — di qc.,* to be crazy about sthg.

entusiàstico *agg.* enthusiastic(al).

enucleare *vt.* to enucleate.

enucleazione *sf.* enucleation.

enumerare *vt.* to enumerate.

enumerazione *sf.* enumeration.

enunciare *vt.* to state: — *un teorema,* to enunciate a theorem.

enunciato *sm.* proposition, terms (*pl.*).

enunciazione *sf.* enunciation.

enuresi *sf.* enuresis.

enzima *sm.* enzyme.

eòlico *agg.* Aeolian.

epàtico *agg.* hepatic.

epatite *sf.* hepatitis.

èpica *sf.* epic.

èpico *agg.* epic.

epicentro *sm.* epicentre.

epicureìsmo *sm.* **1.** epicurism **2.** (*fil.*) epicureanism.

epicùreo *agg. e sm.* Epicurean.

epidemìa *sf.* epidemic.

epidèmico *agg.* epidemical.

epidèrmico *agg.* epidermic.

epidèrmide *sf.* epidermis, skin.

Epifanìa *sf.* Epiphany, Twelfth Night.

epìgono *sm.* imitator, follower.

epìgrafe *sf.* epigraph.

epigrafìa *sf.* epigraphy.

epigramma *sm.* epigram.

epigrammista *s.* epigrammatist.

epilessìa *sf.* epilepsy.

epilèttico *agg. e sm.* epileptic.

epìlogo *sm.* epilogue.

episcopale *agg.* episcopal.

episcopato *sm.* episcopacy.

episòdico *agg.* episodic(al).

episòdio *sm.* episode.

epìstola *sf.* epistle.

epistolare *agg.* epistolary.

epistolàrio *sm.* letters (*pl.*).

epitàffio *sm.* epitaph.

epitalàmio *sm.* epithalamium (*pl.* -ia).

epitèlio *sm.* epithelium.

epìteto *sm.* epithet.

epìtome *sf.* epitome.

època *sf.* **1.** epoch **2.** (*età*) age **3.** (*data*) date ‖ *far —,* to mark an epoch.

epopèa *sf.* **1.** epopee **2.** (*serie di fatti eroici*) epos.

eppure *cong.* yet.

epulone *sm.* glutton.

epurare *vt.* to purge.

epurazione *sf.* purge.

equamente *avv.* fairly.

equànime *agg.* equanimous.

equanimità *sf.* equanimity, impartiality.

equatore *sm.* equator.

equatoriale *agg.* equatorial.

equazione *sf.* equation.

equestre *agg.* equestrian.

equidistante *agg.* equidistant.

equidistanza *sf.* equidistance.

equilàtero *agg.* equilateral.

equilibrare *vt.* to balance.

equilibrato *agg.* **1.** balanced **2.** (*fig.*) well-balanced.

equilibrio *sm.* balance, equilibrium.

equilibrismo *sm.* acrobatics (*pl.*).

equilibrista *s.* acrobat.

equino *agg.* equine.

equinozio *sm.* equinox.

equipaggiamento *sm.* equipment, outfit.

equipaggiare *vt.* to equip, to fit out.

equipaggio *sm.* (*mar.; aer.*) crew.

equiparàbile *agg.* comparable.

equiparare *vt.* to equalize.

equiparazione *sf.* equalization.

equipollente *agg.* equipollent.

equipollenza *sf.* equipollence.

equità *sf.* equity, fairness.

equitazione *sf.* riding.

equivalente *agg.* equivalent.

equivalenza *sf.* equivalence.

equivalere *vi.* to be equivalent. ♦ **equivalersi** *vr.* to be equivalent.

equivocàbile *agg.* mistakable.

equivocare *vi.* to misunderstand (*v. irr.*).

equìvoco *agg.* equivocal, ambiguous. ♦ **equìvoco** *sm.* equivocation.

equo *agg.* fair.

era *sf.* era, epoch.

erariale *agg.* fiscal.

erario *sm.* Treasury.

erba *sf.* grass ‖ *in —,* green; (*fig.*) budding: *un poeta in —,* a budding poet.

erbaccia *sf.* weed.

erbàceo *agg.* herbaceous.

erbaggio *sm.* vegetable.

erbario *sm.* herbarium.

erbetta *sf.* new grass.

erbivéndolo *sm.* greengrocer.

erbìvoro *agg.* herbivorous.

erborista *s.* herborist.

erboso *agg.* grassy.

èrcole *sm.* Hercules.

ercùleo *agg.* Herculean.

erede *sm.* heir. ♦ **erede** *sf.* heiress.

eredità *sf.* inheritance.

ereditare *vt.* to inherit.

ereditarietà *sf.* hereditariness.

ereditario *agg.* hereditary.

ereditiera *sf.* heiress.

eremita *sm.* hermit.

eremitaggio *sm.* hermitage.

èremo *sm.* hermitage.

eresia *sf.* heresy.

erètico *agg.* heretical.

erèttile *agg.* erectile.

eretto *agg.* **1.** upright **2.** (*costruito*) built.

erezione *sf.* **1.** erection **2.** (*costruzione*) building.

ergastolano *sm.* convict (serving a life sentence).

ergàstolo *sm.* life imprisonment

èrgere *vt.* to raise. ♦ **èrgersi** *vr.* to rise (*v. irr.*).

èrica *sf.* heather.

erigere *vt.* to erect, to build (*v. irr.*). ♦ **erìgersi** *vr.* to set up (for).

erma *sf.* herma (*pl. -ae*).

ermafrodito *agg.* hermaphrodite.

ermellino *sm.* ermine.

ermenèuta *sm.* hermeneut.

ermenèutica *sf.* hermeneutics.

ermètico *agg.* **1.** (*tec.*) airtight **2.** (*oscuro*) obscure.

ermetismo *sm.* obscurity.

ernia *sf.* hernia.

erniario *agg.* hernial.

erodere *vt.* to wear (*v. irr.*) away.

eroe *sm.* hero.

erogare *vt.* **1.** to distribute **2.** (*elett.; idraulica*) to deliver.

erogazione *sf.* **1.** distribution **2.** (*elettr.; idraulica*) delivery.

eròico *agg.* heroic.

eroina *sf.* **1.** heroine **2.** (*farm.*) heroin.

eroismo *sm.* heroism.

eròmpere *vi.* to burst (*v. irr.*) forth.

erosione *sf.* erosion.

erosivo *agg.* erosive.

eròtico *agg.* erotic.

erotismo *sm.* eroticism.

erotòmane *s.* erotomaniac.

èrpete *sm.* herpes.

érpice *sm.* harrow.

errabondo *agg.* wandering.

errante *agg.* errant.

errare *vi.* **1.** (*vagare*) to wander **2.** (*sbagliare*) to err.

erràtico *agg.* erratic.

errato *agg.* wrong.

erròneo *agg.* erroneous.

errore *sm.* error, mistake.

erta *sf.* steep || *stare all'—*, to be on the look-out.

erto *agg.* steep.

erudire *vt.* to teach (*v. irr.*). ◆ **erudirsi** *vr.* to get (*v. irr.*) educated.

erudito *agg.* learned. ◆ **erudito** *sm.* scholar.

erudizione *sf.* erudition, learning.

eruttare *vt.* to erupt.

eruttivo *agg.* eruptive.

eruzione *sf.* eruption.

esacerbare *vt.* to embitter.

esacerbazione *sf.* embitterment.

esaedro *sm.* hexahedron.

esagerare *vt.* to exaggerate. ◆ **esagerare** *vi.* to go (*v. irr.*) too far, to exceed.

esagerato *agg.* 1. exaggerated 2. (*di prezzo*) exorbitant.

esagerazione *sf.* exaggeration.

esagitare *vt.* to stir violently.

esagonale *agg.* hexagonal.

esàgono *sm.* hexagon.

esalare *vt.* to exhale. ◆ **esalare** *vi.* to exhale, to rise (*v. irr.*).

esalazione *sf.* exhalation.

esaltare *vt.* to exalt. ◆ **esaltarsi** *vr.* 1. (*vantarsi*) to boast 2. (*infervorarsi*) to become (*v. irr.*) excited.

esaltato *agg.* excited. ◆ **esaltato** *sm.* hot-head.

esaltazione *sf.* 1. exaltation 2. (*eccitazione*) excitement.

esame *sm.* examination: *dare un —*, to take (*v. irr.*) an examination; *essere respinto ad un —*, to fail in an examination.

esàmetro *sm.* hexameter.

esaminando *sm.* candidate.

esaminare *vt.* to examine.

esaminatore *sm.* examiner.

esangue *agg.* bloodless.

esànime *agg.* lifeless.

esasperare *vt.* to exasperate. ◆ **esasperarsi** *vr.* to become (*v. irr.*) irritated.

esasperato *agg.* exasperated.

esasperazione *sf.* exasperation.

esattamente *avv.* exactly, just.

esattezza *sf.* exactitude.

esatto *agg.* exact, right.

esattore *sm.* collector.

esattoria *sf.* collector's office.

esaudimento *sm.* satisfaction.

esaudire *vt.* to grant.

esauriente *agg.* exhaustive.

esaurimento *sm.* exhaustion.

esaurire *vt.* to exhaust. ◆ **esaurirsi** *vr.* to get (*v. irr.*) exhausted.

esaurito *agg.* 1. exhausted 2. (*di persona*) worn out 3. (*che ha l'esaurimento nervoso*) suffering from a nervous breakdown 4. (*di libro*) out of print.

esàusto *agg.* exhausted.

esautorare *vt.* to deprive of authority.

esazione *sf.* collection.

esborso *sm.* outlay.

esca *sf.* 1. bait 2. (*materiale infiammabile*) tinder 3. (*di esplosivo*) fuse.

escandescenza *sf.* outburst of rage || *dare in escandescenze*, to lose (*v. irr.*) one's temper.

escatologia *sf.* eschatology.

escavatore *sm.* digger.

escavatrice *sf.* digger.

escavazione *sf.* digging out.

eschimese *agg.* e *sm.* Eskimo.

esclamare *vi.* to exclaim.

esclamativo *agg.* exclamatory: *punto —*, exclamation mark.

esclamazione *sf.* exclamation.

esclùdere *vt.* to exclude, to leave (*v. irr.*) out.

esclusione *sf.* exclusion || *ad — di*, except.

esclusiva *sf.* 1. patent 2. (*diritto esclusivo*) sole right.

esclusività *sf.* exclusiveness.

esclusivo *agg.* exclusive, sole.

escluso *agg.* 1. excluded 2. (*eccettuato*) excepted.

escogitare *vt.* to contrive.

escoriare *vt.* to graze.

escoriazione *sf.* abrasion.

escremento *sm.* excrement.

escrescenza *sf.* excrescence.

escursione *sf.* excursion, trip.

escursionista *s.* excursionist.

escussione *sf.* examination.

esecràbile *agg.* execrable.

esecrare *vt.* to execrate.

esecrazione *sf.* execration.

esecutivo *agg.* executive.

esecutore *sm.* 1. executor 2. (*di musica*) performer 3. (*carnefice*) executioner.

esecuzione *sf.* 1. execution 2. (*mus.*) performance.

esedra *sf.* exedra (*pl.* -ae).

esegesi *sf.* exegesis (*pl.* -ses).

esegeta *s.* exegete.

eseguìbile *agg.* feasible.

eseguire vt. **1.** to execute, to carry out **2.** (mus.) to perform.

esempio sm. **1.** example, instance **2.** (modello perfetto) pattern.

esemplare agg. exemplary. ◆ **esemplare** sm. **1.** pattern, specimen **2.** (di libro) copy.

esemplificare vt. to exemplify.

esemplificazione sf. exemplification.

esentare vt. to exempt.

esente agg. exempt, free.

esenzione sf. exemption.

esequie sf. pl. exequies.

esercente sm. shop-keeper.

esercire vt. to manage (a business) || — un negozio, to keep (v. irr.) a shop.

esercitare vt. **1.** to exercise **2.** (una professione) to practice **3.** (addestrare) to train. ◆ **esercitarsi** vr. to practice.

esercitazione sf. **1.** exercise **2.** (allenamento) training **3.** (mil.) drill.

esèrcito sm. army.

esercizio sm. **1.** exercise **2.** (negozio) shop **3.** (comm.) — finanziario, financial year.

esibire vt. to exhibit, to show (v. irr.).

esibizione sf. exhibition, show.

esibizionismo sm. exhibitionism, showing-off.

esibizionista s. exhibitionist.

esigente agg. exacting.

esigenza sf. **1.** demand, exigence **2.** (pretesa) pretension.

esigere vt. **1.** (comm.) to collect **2.** (richiedere con autorità) to insist on **3.** (pretendere) to exact.

esigibile agg. **1.** exigible **2.** (riscuotibile) collectable.

esiguità sf. exiguity.

esiguo agg. exiguous, scanty.

esilarante agg. exhilarating.

esilarare vt. to exhilarate.

èsile agg. slender.

esiliare vt. to exile. ◆ **esiliarsi** vr. to go (v. irr.) into exile.

esiliato agg. banished. ◆ **esiliato** sm. exile.

esilio sm. exile.

esìmere vt. to free, to excuse. ◆ **esìmersi** vr. to evade (sthg.).

esimio agg. excellent.

esistente agg. **1.** existing **2.** (di cose) extant.

esistenza sf. existence.

esistenziale agg. existential.

esistenzialismo sm. existentialism.

esistenzialista agg. e s. existentialist.

esìstere vi. to exist.

esitante agg. hesitating: voce —, faltering voice.

esitare vi. **1.** to hesitate **2.** (di voce) to falter.

esitazione sf. hesitation: senza —, unhesitatingly.

èsito sm. result, outcome.

esiziale agg. ruinous.

èsodo sm. exodus.

esòfago sm. oesophagus.

esògeno agg. exogenous.

esonerare vt. to exonerate.

esònero sm. exoneration.

esorbitante agg. exorbitant.

esorbitanza sf. exorbitance.

esorbitare vi. to exceed.

esorcismo sm. exorcism.

esorcista sm. exorcist.

esorcizzare vt. to exorcize.

esorcizzatore sm. exorcizer.

esordiente agg. beginning. ◆ **esordiente** sm. beginner.

esordio sm. preamble, beginning.

esordire vi. **1.** to begin (v. irr.) **2.** (in arte) to make (v. irr.) one's debut.

esortare vt. to exhort.

esortativo agg. exhortative.

esortazione sf. exhortation.

esosità sf. greediness.

esoso agg. greedy.

esotèrico agg. esoteric.

esotèrmico agg. exothermic.

esòtico agg. exotic.

esotismo sm. exoticism.

espàndere vt. to spread (v. irr.) (out). ◆ **espàndersi** vr. to spread.

espansione sf. expansion.

espansionismo sm. expansionism.

espansività sf. effusiveness.

espansivo agg. effusive.

espatriare vi. to emigrate.

espatrio sm. expatriation.

espediente sm. expedient.

espèllere vt. to expel.

esperanto sm. Esperanto.

esperienza sf. experience.

esperimento sm. **1.** experiment **2.** (esame) test **3.** (tentativo) trial.

esperire vt. to try.

esperto agg. e sm. expert.

espettorante agg. e sm. expectorant.

espettorare vt. to expectorate.

espettorazione *sf.* expectoration.

espiare *vt.* to expiate.

espiatorio *agg.* expiatory: *capro* —, scapegoat.

espiazione *sf.* expiation.

espirare *vt. e vi.* to expire.

espirazione *sf.* expiration.

espletare *vt.* to dispatch.

espletazione *sf.* dispatching.

esplicare *vt.* to explicate: — *un'attività*, to have an activity.

esplicativo *agg.* explanatory.

esplicazione *sf.* explication.

esplicito *agg.* explicit.

esplòdere *vi.* to explode, to burst (*v. irr.*).

esplorare *vt.* 1. to explore 2. (*mil.*) to scout.

esploratore *sm.* 1. explorer 2. (*mil.*) scout.

esplorazione *sf.* 1. exploration 2. (*mil.*) scouting expedition.

esplosione *sf.* 1. explosion, blast 2. (*fig.*) outbreak.

esplosivo *agg. e sm.* explosive.

esponente *sm.* exponent.

esporre *vt.* 1. to show (*v. irr.*) 2. (*a rischio*) to venture 3. (*spiegare*) to expound 4. (*mettere in vista*) to display. ♦ **esporsi** *vr.* to expose oneself.

esportare *vt.* to export.

esportatore *agg.* exporting. ♦ **esportatore** *sm.* exporter.

esportazione *sf.* export, exportation.

esposimetro *sm.* exposure-meter.

espositore *sm.* exhibitor.

esposizione *sf.* 1. exposure 2. (*mostra*) exhibition 3. (*eloquio*) exposition.

esposto *sm.* petition.

espressamente *avv.* 1. expressly 2. (*appositamente*) on purpose.

espressione *sf.* expression.

espressionismo *sm.* expressionism.

espressionista *s.* expressionist.

espressivo *agg.* expressive.

espresso *agg.* express.

esprìmere *vt.* to express.

esprimibile *agg.* expressible.

espropriare *vt.* to dispossess.

espropriazione *sf.* expropriation.

espugnare *vt.* to conquer.

espugnatore *sm.* conqueror.

espugnazione *sf.* conquest.

espulsione *sf.* expulsion.

espulsivo *agg. e sm.* expulsive.

espulsore *sm.* ejector.

espùngere *vt.* to expunge.

espurgare *vt.* 1. to expurgate 2. (*un libro*) to bowdlerize.

espurgazione *sf.* 1. expurgation 2. (*un libro*) to bowdlerize.

essa *pron.* 1. (*sogg.*) she, (*compl.*) her 2. (*riferito a cose o animali*) it.

esse *sf.* letter S.: *a* —, S-shaped.

essenza *sf.* essence.

essenziale *agg.* essential.

essenzialità *sf.* essentiality.

èssere *vi.* to be || *c'è, ci sono,* there is, there are.

èssere *sm.* 1. being 2. (*esistenza*) existence.

essi *pron.* 1. (*sogg.*) they, (*compl.*) them.

essiccare *vt.* to dry.

essiccatoio *sm.* drier.

essiccazione *sf.* drying process.

esso *pron.* 1. (*sogg.*) he, (*compl.*) him 2. (*per cose o animali*) it.

essudato *sm.* exudate.

essudazione *sf.* exudation.

est *sm.* east.

èstasi *sf.* ecstasy: *andare in* —, to go (*v. irr.*) into ecstasies; *mandare in* —, to throw (*v. irr.*) into ecstasies.

estasiare *vt.* to enrapture. ♦ **estasiarsi** *vr.* to be enraptured.

estate *sf.* summer.

estàtico *agg.* ecstatic.

estemporàneo *agg.* extempore.

estèndere *vt.* to extend.

estendìbile *agg.* extensible.

estensione *sf.* 1. extension 2. (*distesa*) expanse, extent 3. (*mus.*) range.

estensivo *agg.* extensive.

estensore *sm.* 1. compiler 2. (*giur.*) drafts-man (*pl.* -men) 3. (*sport*) chest-expander.

estenuante *agg.* exhausting.

estenuare *vt.* to tire out.

estenuazione *sf.* exhaustion.

esteriore *agg.* outward. ♦ **esteriore** *sm.* exterior, outside.

esteriorità *sf.* outward appearance.

esternamente *avv.* externally, outside.

esternare *vt.* to express, to utter.

esterno *agg.* outer, external.

èstero *agg.* foreign. ♦ **èstero** *sm.* foreign countries (*pl.*) || *all'*—, abroad.

esterofilia *sf.* xenomania.

esterrefatto *agg.* aghast, amazed.

esteso *agg.* large, wide || *per —,* in detail.

esteta *s.* aesthete.

estètica *sf.* aesthetics.

estètico *agg.* aesthetic.

estetismo *sm.* aestheticism.

èstimo *sm.* estimate.

estinguere *vt.* 1. to put (*v. irr.*) out 2. (*saldare*) to extinguish || *la propria sete,* to slake one's thirst. ♦ **estinguersi** *vr.* (*finire*) to die.

estinguìbile *agg.* extinguishable.

estinto *agg.* 1. extinct 2. (*morto*) dead. ♦ **estìnto** *sm.* deceased man.

estintore *sm.* extinguisher.

estinzione *sf.* 1. extinction 2. (*di sete*) quenching 3. (*di debito*) paying off.

estirpare *vt.* 1. to extirpate 2. (*di denti*) to pull out.

estirpazione *sf.* 1. extirpation 2. (*di denti*) extraction.

estivo *agg.* summer (*attr.*).

estòrcere *vt.* to extort.

estorsione *sf.* extortion.

estradare *vt.* to extradite.

estradizione *sf.* extradition.

estràneo *agg.* extraneous, alien. ♦ **estràneo** *sm.* stranger.

estraniare *vt.* to estrange. ♦ **estraniarsi** *vr.* to get (*v. irr.*) estranged.

estrarre *vt.* to draw (*v. irr.*) out: *— a sorte,* to draw by lot.

estrattivo *agg.* extractive.

estratto *sm.* 1. extract 2. (*riassunto*) excerpt 3. (*comm.*) *— conto,* statement of account.

estrattore *sm.* extractor.

estrazione *sf.* 1. extraction 2. (*di lotteria*) drawing.

estremamente *avv.* extremely.

estremismo *sm.* extremism.

estremista *s.* extremist: *— di destra,* extreme rightist; *— di sinistra,* extreme leftist.

estremità *sf.* extremity, end.

estremo *agg.* 1. utmost 2. (*eccessivo*) intense 3. (*drastico*) drastic. ♦ **estremo** *sm.* extreme.

estrinsecare *vt.* to express. ♦ **estrinsecarsi** *vr.* to be expressed.

estrinsecazione *sf.* expression.

estrìnseco *agg.* extrinsic(al).

estro *sm.* 1. inspiration 2. (*capriccio*) whim.

estrométtere *vt.* to turn out.

estromissione *sf.* expulsion.

estroso *agg.* 1. (*ispirato*) inspired 2. freakish.

estroverso *agg.* extroverted.

estuario *sm.* estuary.

esuberante *agg.* exuberant.

esuberanza *sf.* exuberance.

esulare *vi.* 1. to go (*v. irr.*) into exile 2. (*fig.*) to be beyond.

esulcerare *vt.* to exulcerate.

esulcerazione *sf.* exulceration.

èsule *sm.* 1. exile 2. (*profugo*) refugee.

esultante *agg.* rejoicing.

esultanza *sf.* exultation.

esultare *vi.* to rejoice.

esumare *vt.* to exhume.

esumazione *sf.* exhumation.

età *sf.* age || *che — hai?,* how old are you?; *avere la stessa —,* to be the same age; *una persona di mezza —,* a middle-aged person.

ètere *sm.* ether.

etèreo *agg.* ethereal.

eternare *vt.* to make (*v. irr.*) eternal.

eternità *sf.* eternity.

eterno *agg.* eternal, everlasting.

eteròclito *agg.* 1. heteroclite 2. (*fig.*) irregular.

eterodossìa *sf.* heterodoxy.

eterodosso *agg.* heterodox.

eterogeneità *sf.* heterogeneity.

eterogèneo *agg.* heterogeneous.

ètica *sf.* ethics.

etichetta *sf.* 1. label 2. (*galateo*) etiquette.

etichettare *vt.* to stick (*v. irr.*) a label (on).

ètico *agg.* ethical.

etilene *sm.* ethylene.

etìlico *agg.* ethylic.

etilismo *sm.* alcoholism.

etimologìa *sf.* etymology.

etimològico *agg.* etymologic(al).

ètnico *agg.* ethnic(al).

etnografìa *sf.* ethnography.

etnologìa *sf.* ethnology.

etnòlogo *sm.* ethnologist.

etrusco *agg.* e *sm.* Etruscan.

ettàgono *sm.* heptagon.

èttaro *sm.* hectare.

etto *sm.* hectogram.

ettòlitro *sm.* hectolitre.

ettòmetro *sm.* hectometre.

eucalipto *sm.* eucalyptus.

eucaristìa *sf.* Eucharist, Holy Communion.

eucarìstico agg. Eucharistic.
eufemismo sm. euphemism.
eufonìa sf. euphony.
eufònico agg. euphonic(al).
euforbia sf. Euphorbia.
euforìa sf. euphoria.
eufòrico agg. euphoric.
eunuco sm. eunuch.
euritmìa sf. eurhythmy.
europeismo sm. Europeanism.
europeo agg. e sm. European.
eurovisione sf. Eurovision.
eutanasia sf. euthanasia.
evacuare vt. to evacuate.
evacuazione sf. evacuation. ♦
evàdere vi. to escape. ♦ **evàdere**
vt. (burocratico) **1.** to dispatch **2.**
(eludere) to evade.
evanescente agg. vanishing.
evangèlico agg. evangelic(al).
evangelista sm. evangelist.
evangelizzare vt. to evangelize.
evaporare vi. to evaporate.
evaporazione sf. evaporation.
evasione sf. **1.** escape **2.** (comm.)
dare — a una pratica, to dispatch
a business.
evasivo agg. evasive.
evaso sm. runaway.
evasore sm. evader: — fiscale, tax
evader.
evenienza sf. event, occurrence:
per ogni —, for any occasion.
evento sm. event.
eventuale agg. possible.
eventualità sf. eventuality.
eventualmente avv. in case.
evidente agg. evident, obvious,
clear.
evidenza sf. evidence.
evincere vt. (giur.) to evict.
evirare vt. to evirate.
evitàbile agg. avoidable.
evitare vt. **1.** to avoid **2.** (sfuggire)
to escape.
evo sm. age: il Medio Evo, the
Middle Ages.
evocare vt. to evoke, to recall.
evocativo agg. evocative.
evocazione sf. evocation.
evolutivo agg. evolutive.
evoluto agg. well-developed, modern.
evoluzione sf. evolution.
evoluzionismo sm. evolutionism.
evòlvere vt. to evolve.
evviva inter. hurray.
ex libris sm. ex libris.
extra agg. extra.

extraterritoriale agg. extraterritorial.
eziologìa sf. aetiology.

F

fa¹ sm. (mus.) F.
fa² avv. ago: un anno —, a year ago.
fabbisogno sm. needs (pl.).
fàbbrica sf. **1.** factory; — di au-
tomobili, motor works; — di
mattoni, brickyard; — di carta,
paper-mill; capo —, fore-man (pl.
-men); marchio di —, trade-mark
2. (fabbricazione) manufacture.
fabbricàbile agg. manufacturable ||
area —, housing area.
fabbricante sm. manufacturer.
fabbricare vt. **1.** (produrre) to
manufacture **2.** (costruire) to build
(v. irr.) **3.** (fare) to make (v. irr.).
fabbricato sm. building || imposta
sui fabbricati, house tax.
fabbricazione sf. **1.** manufacture,
make **2.** (costruzione) building.
fabbro sm. blacksmith.
fabbroferraio sm. blacksmith.
faccenda sf. matter; business (solo
sing.) || — di stato, state affair
2. (lavori domestici) housework
(solo sing.).
faccendiere sm. busybody.
faccetta sf. little face **2.** (geom.)
facet.
facchinàggio sm. porterage.
facchino sm. porter.
faccia sf. **1.** face: che — tosta!,
what a face!; a — a —, face to face
2. (aspetto) look, expression **3.** (lato, superficie) face, side.
facciale agg. facial.
facciata sf. **1.** front, façade **2.** (pagina) page.
face sf. torch.
faceto agg. facetious, witty.
facezia sf. witty remark, joke: dire delle facezie, to crack jokes.
fachiro sm. fakir.
fàcile agg. **1.** easy **2.** (trattabile)
docile **3.** (pronto) ready **4.** (incline) inclined **3.** (probabile) likely.
facilità sf. **1.** facility **2.** (attitudine) aptitude.
facilitare vt. to make (v. irr.)
easier

facilitazione sf. 1. facilitation 2. (agevolazione) facility.

facilone sm. slipshod fellow.

facinoroso agg. lawless. ♦ **facinoroso** sm. lawless man.

facoltà sf. faculty.

facoltativo agg. facultative: *fermata facoltativa*, request stop.

facoltoso agg. wealthy.

facondia sf. eloquence.

facondo agg. eloquent.

facsìmile sm. facsimile.

factotum sm. factotum.

faggeto sm. beech-wood.

faggio sm. beech.

fagiano sm. pheasant.

fagiolino sm. French bean.

fagiolo sm. bean.

fagocita, fagocito sm. phagocyte.

fagocitare vt. 1. to phagocyte 2. (fig.) to absorb.

fagocitosi sf. phagocytosis.

fagotto[1] sm. bundle.

fagotto[2] sm. (mus.) bassoon.

faina sf. beech-marten.

falange sf. phalanx (pl. -nges).

falcata sf. 1. curvet 2. (di persona) stride.

falce sf. 1. sickle 2. (da fieno) scythe 3. (di luna) crescent.

falciare vt. 1. to mow (v. irr.) 2. (fig.) to mow down.

falciatore sm. mower.

falciatrice sf. mowing-machine.

falciatura sf. mowing.

falcidiare vt. to reduce.

falco sm. hawk: *avere occhi di —*, to be hawk-eyed.

falconeria sf. falconry.

falconiere sm. hawker.

falda sf. 1. (strato) stratum (pl. -ta) 2. (di neve) flake 3. (di cappello) brim 4. (di monte) slope.

falegname sm. joiner.

falegnameria sf. 1. joinery 2. (bottega) joiner's shop.

falena sf. moth.

falla sf. leak.

fallace agg. false, disappointing.

fallacia sf. fallacy.

fallibile agg. liable to make mistakes.

fàllico agg. phallic.

fallimentare agg. bankruptcy.

fallimento sm. 1. bankruptcy 2. (fig.) failure.

fallire vi. 1. to fail 2. (comm.) to go (v. irr.) bankrupt 3. (fam.) to go under.

fallito agg. 1. (comm.) bankrupt 2. (fig.) unsuccessful. ♦ **fallito** sm. 1. (comm.) bankrupt 2. (fig.) failure.

fallo sm. 1. fault: *senza —*, without fail 2. (anat.) phallus (pl. -li).

falò sm. bonfire.

falpalà sm. furbelow.

falsare vt. 1. to misrepresent 2. (falsificare) to falsify.

falsariga sf. 1. ruling paper 2. (fig.) pattern, model.

falsario sm. 1. forger 2. (di monete) coiner.

falsetto sm. falsetto.

falsificàbile agg. falsifiable.

falsificare vt. to falsify, to counterfeit.

falsificatore sm. 1. falsifier 2. (di monete) coiner.

falsificazione sf. falsification, forgery.

falsità sf. 1. falseness 2. (menzogna) falsehood 3. (ipocrisia) insincerity.

falso agg. 1. false 2. (falsificato) forged.

fama sf. fame, renown, reputation: *acquistarsi —*, to win (v. irr.) fame; *avere cattiva —*, to have a bad reputation.

fame sf. 1. hunger: *avere —*, to be hungry: *far morire di —*, to starve 2. (carestia) famine.

famèlico agg. ravenous.

famigerato agg. ill-famed.

famiglia sf. family.

familiare agg. 1. domestic, homely 2. (intimo, anche fig.) familiar 3. (senza cerimonie) informal. ♦ **familiare** sm. relative.

familiarità sf. familiarity: *avere — con qu.*, to be familiar with so.

famoso agg. famous, celebrated.

fanale sm. 1. lamp 2. (auto) light: *— anteriore*, head-light; *— di coda*, (aer.) tail light, (auto) rear lamp; *— di posizione*, parking lights (pl.).

fanàtico agg. fanatical. ♦ **fanàtico** sm. 1. fanatic 2. (fam.) fan.

fanatismo sm. fanaticism.

fanatizzare vt. to fanaticize.

fanciulla sf. young girl.

fanciullàggine sf. 1. childishness 2. (azione infantile) childish action.

fanciullesco agg. childish.

fanciullezza sf. childhood.

fanciullo *sm.* young boy, child (*pl.* children).

fandonia *sf.* lie.

fanello *sm.* linnet.

fanfara *sf.* 1. brass band 2. (*suono di trombe*) fanfare.

fanfaronata *sf.* boasting.

fanfarone *sm.* boaster.

fangaia *sf.* muddy road.

fanghiglia *sf.* slush.

fango *sm.* 1. mud: *gettare del — addosso a qu.*, to throw (*v. irr.*) mud at so.; *cadere nel —*, to fall (*v. irr.*) very low 2. (*med.*) mud-baths (*pl.*).

fangoso *agg.* muddy.

fannullone *sm.* idler.

fanone *sm.* whalebone.

fantaccino *sm.* foot-soldier.

fantascienza *sf.* science fiction.

fantasia *sf.* 1. imagination, fancy 2. (*inventiva*) inventiveness 3. (*articoli fantasia*) fancy goods.

fantasioso *agg.* fanciful.

fantasma *sm.* ghost.

fantasmagorìa *sf.* phantasmagoria.

fantasmagòrico *agg.* phantasmagoric.

fantasticare *vt.* to daydream.

fantasticherìa *sf.* daydream.

fantàstico *agg.* 1. fanciful 2. (*bizzarro*) queer 3. (*fam.*) extraordinary.

fante *sm.* 1. infantryman (*pl.* -men) 2. (*delle carte*) knave, jack.

fanterìa *sf.* infantry.

fantesca *sf.* maid-servant.

fantino *sm.* jockey.

fantoccio *sm.* puppet (*anche fig.*).

fantomàtico *agg.* mysterious.

farabutto *sm.* blackguard.

faraona *sf.* guinea-hen.

faraone *sm.* Pharaoh.

farcire *vt.* to stuff.

farcito *agg.* stuffed.

fardello *sm.* 1. bundle 2. (*fig.*) burden.

fare *vt.* 1. (*in senso generale*) to do (*v. irr.*): *cosa fai?*, what are you doing?; *ecco fatto!*, that's done!; *— del proprio meglio*, to do one's best; 2. (*fabbricare, produrre*) to make (*v. irr.*): *— amicizia*, to make friends; *— un errore*, to make a mistake; *— in fretta*, to make haste 3. (*essere, esercitare una professione*) to be: *faccio l'insegnante*, I am a teacher 4. (*reputare*) to think (*v. irr.*): *la facevo*

più intelligente, I thought she was more intelligent 5. (*segnare le ore*): *che ora fa il tuo orologio?*, what time is it by your watch? 6. (*praticare*) to go (*v. irr.*) in for || *— le carte*, to shuffle; *— fagotto*, to pack up; *— una passeggiata*, to go for a walk; *— colazione*, to have breakfast; *— bella, brutta figura*, to cut (*v. irr.*) a fine, a poor figure; *— compassione*, to rouse compassion; *— aspettare qu.*, to keep (*v. irr.*) so. waiting; *— avere, sapere, vedere a qu.*, to let (*v. irr.*) so. have, know, see. ♦ **fare** *vi.* 1. (*di condizioni atmosferiche*): *che tempo fa?*, what is the weather like? 2. (*far caldo, freddo*) to be hot, cold 3. (*essere adatto*) to suit. ♦ **farsi** *vr.* 1. to become (*v. irr.*), to grow (*v. irr.*) || *— animo*, to take (*v. irr.*) courage.

fare *sm.* manners (*pl*)

faretra *sf.* quiver.

farfalla *sf.* butterfly.

farfugliare *vt.* to mumble.

farina *sf.* meal, flour.

farinàceo *agg.* farinaceous.

faringe *sf.* pharynx (*pl.* -nges).

faringite *sf.* pharyngitis.

farinoso *agg.* mealy, floury.

fariseo *agg. e sm.* Pharisee.

farmacèutico *agg.* pharmaceutic.

farmacìa *sf.* 1. pharmacy 2. (*negozio*) chemist's shop.

farmacista *sm.* chemist.

fàrmaco *sm.* medicine, remedy (*anche fig.*).

farmacologìa *sf.* pharmacology.

farmacopea *sf.* pharmacopoeia.

farneticare *vi.* to rave.

faro *sm.* 1. lighthouse 2. (*auto*) headlight.

farràgine *sf.* medley, mixture.

farraginoso *agg.* confused.

farsa *sf.* farce.

farsesco *agg.* farcical.

fascetta *sf.* 1. small band 2. (*med.*) bandage 3. (*edit.*) wrapper.

fascia *sf.* 1. band 2. (*med.*) bandage 3. (*dei bambini*) swaddling-band.

fasciame *sm.* planking.

fasciare *vt.* 1. to bind (*v. irr.*) (up) 2. (*dei neonati*) to swaddle.

fasciatura *sf.* 1. dressing 2. (*di neonato*) swaddling.

fascìcolo *sm.* booklet.

fascina *sf.* faggot.

fàscino sm. charm, fascination.

fascio sm. 1. bundle 2. (geom.) sheaf 3. (di luce) beam.

fascismo sm. Fascism.

fascista agg. e s. Fascist.

fase sf. 1. stage 2. (elettr.) phase 3. (auto) stroke.

fastello sm. faggot.

fastidio sm. 1. trouble: dare — a qu., to give (v. irr.) so. trouble 2. (contrarietà) annoyance.

fastidioso agg. tiresome.

fastìgio sm. 1. pediment 2. (fig.) height.

fasto sm. pomp.

fastosità sf. pomp, splendour.

fastoso agg. magnificent.

fasullo agg. false.

fata sf. fairy.

fatale agg. fatal, inevitable.

fatalismo sm. fatalism.

fatalista agg. e s. fatalist.

fatalità sf. fatality.

fatìca sf. weariness, fatigue.

faticare vi. to toil, to work hard.

faticata sf. drudgery.

faticoso agg. hard, tiring.

fatìdico agg. fatidical.

fato sm. 1. fate, destiny 2. (sorte) lot.

fatta sf. kind, sort.

fattìbile agg. practicable.

fattispècie sf. case in point: nella —, in this case.

fattìvo agg. 1. effective 2. (attivo) busy.

fatto sm. 1. fact 2. (azione) deed 3. (avvenimento) event || sapere il — proprio, to know (v. irr.) one's business; venire al —, to go (v. irr.) to the point; in — di, as regards.

fattore sm. 1. factor 2. (agr.) farmer.

fattorìa sf. farm.

fattorino sm. errand-boy.

fattucchiere sm. wizard.

fattura sf. 1. making 2. (lavorazione) work 3. (comm.) invoice 4. (stregoneria) sorcery.

fatturare vt. 1. to adulterate 2. (comm.) to invoice.

fatturazione sf. (comm.) invoicing.

fatuità sf. fatuity.

fàtuo agg. 1. fatuous 2. (vanitoso) vain || fuoco —, will-o'-the-wisp.

fàuci sf. pl. 1. jaws 2. (di persona) throat (sing.).

fàuna sf. fauna.

fàuno sm. faun.

fàusto agg. propitious.

fautore sm. supporter.

fava sf. broad bean || pigliare due piccioni con una —, to kill two birds with one stone.

favella sf. speech.

favellare vi. to speak (v. irr.).

favilla sf. spark (anche fig.).

favo sm. 1. honeycomb 2. (med.) favus.

fàvola sf. 1. fable 2. (frottola) idle story 3. (oggetto di pettegolezzo) byword.

favoloso agg. fabulous.

favore sm. favour.

favoreggiamento sm. favouring.

favoreggiare vt. to favour.

favoreggiatore sm. abettor.

favorévole agg. favourable.

favorire vt. 1. to favour 2. (aiutare) to help 3. (promuovere) to foster.

favoritismo sm. favouritism.

favorito agg. e sm. favourite.

fazione sf. faction.

fazioso agg. factious.

fazzoletto sm. 1. handkerchief 2. (da collo) neckerchief.

febbraio sm. February.

febbre sf. fever.

febbricitante agg. feverish.

febbrìfugo agg. febrifugal. ♦ **febbrìfugo** sm. febrifuge.

febbrìle agg. feverish.

fecale agg. fecal.

feccia sf. dregs (pl.) (anche fig.).

feci sf. pl. excrement (sing.).

fècola sf. starch.

fecondare vt. to fecundate.

fecondazione sf. fecundation.

fecondità sf. fecundity.

fecondo agg. fecund.

fede sf. 1. faith, belief 2. (fiducia) trust.

fedele agg. faithful.

fedeltà sf. fidelity.

fèdera sf. pillow-case.

federale agg. federal.

federalismo sm. federalism.

federativo agg. federative.

federato agg. federate.

federazione sf. federation.

fedìfrago sm. traitor.

fedina sf. criminal record.

fégato sm. 1. liver 2. (fig.) courage.

fegatoso agg. 1. bilious 2. (fig.) irritable.

felce sf. fern.

feldspato sm. felspar.

felice *agg.* 1. happy 2. (*fortunato*) lucky 3. (*piacevole*) pleasant.

felicità *sf.* happiness.

felicitarsi *vr.* to congratulate (so. on sthg.).

felicitazioni *sf. pl.* congratulation (*sing.*).

felino *agg. e sm.* feline.

fellone *sm.* villain, traitor.

fellonìa *sf.* felony, treason.

felpato *agg.* 1. plushy 2. (*fig.*) soft || *a passi felpati*, stealthily.

feltro *sm.* felt.

feluca *sf.* 1. (*mar.*) felucca 2. (*cappello*) cocked hat.

fémmina *sf.* female || *mala —*, bad woman.

femminile *agg.* 1. female 2. (*da donna*) feminine.

femminilità *sf.* womanliness.

femminismo *sm.* feminism.

femminuccia *sf.* 1. simple woman 2. (*uomo senza coraggio*) coward.

femore *sm.* thigh-bone.

fendente *sm.* cutting blow.

fendere *vt.* to rend (*v. irr.*).

fenditura *sf.* cleft, fissure.

fenice *sf.* phoenix.

fenico *agg.* phenic.

fenolo *sm.* phenol.

fenomenale *agg.* phenomenal.

fenomenismo *sm.* phenomenalism.

fenòmeno *sm.* phenomenon (*pl. -na*).

fenomenologìa *sf.* phenomenology.

ferace *agg.* fruitful, rich (*anche fig.*).

ferale *agg.* feral, deadly.

fèretro *sm.* coffin.

ferie *sf. pl.* holidays.

feriale *agg.* working: *giorno —*, working-day.

ferimento *sm.* wounding.

ferino *agg.* ferine, wild.

ferire *vt.* to wound, to hurt (*v. irr.*).

ferita *sf.* wound (*anche fig.*).

ferito *agg.* wounded, injured.

feritoia *sf.* loophole.

ferma *sf.* 1. (*mil.*) service 2. (*caccia*) pointing.

fermacarte *sm.* paper-weight.

fermaglio *sm.* 1. clasp 2. (*per gioielli*) brooch 3. (*per carte*) clip.

fermare *vt.* 1. to stop, to arrest 2. (*fissare*) to fix (*anche fig.*). 3. (*giur.*) to hold (*v. irr.*). ♦ **fermarsi** *vr.* 1. to stop 2. (*soggiornare*) to stay 3. (*fare una pausa*) to pause.

fermata *sf.* 1. stop 2. (*pausa*) pause.

fermentare *vi.* to ferment (*anche fig.*).

fermentazione *sf.* fermentation.

fermento *sm.* 1. ferment 2. (*fig.*) turmoil, ferment.

fermezza *sf.* firmness, strength.

fermo *agg.* 1. still 2. (*irremovibile*) steady, firm || *mano ferma*, firm hand; *volontà ferma*, unfaltering will. ♦ **fermo** *sm.* 1. (*mecc.*) lock, catch, stop 2. (*giur.*) provisional arrest.

fermoposta *sm.* poste-restante.

feroce *agg.* fierce, cruel.

ferocia *sf.* fierceness.

ferraglia *sf.* scrap-iron.

ferragosto *sm.* 1. August holiday 2. (*in Inghilterra*) August Bank holiday.

ferraio *sm.* blacksmith.

ferramenta *sf. pl.* hardware (*sing.*).

ferramento *sm.* iron tool.

ferrare *vt.* 1. to fit with iron 2. (*di cavalli*) to shoe.

ferrato *agg.* 1. ironshod 2. (*di scarpe*) hobnailed 3. (*strada ferrata*) railway 4. (*fig.*) well read.

ferratura *sf.* shoeing.

fèrreo *agg.* iron (*attr.*).

ferriera *sf.* iron-foundry.

ferro *sm.* iron: *— battuto*, wrought iron; *— da stiro*, flat-iron; *— da calza*, knitting needle || *i ferri del mestiere*, the tools of the trade; *tocca —!*, touch wood!

ferroso *agg.* ferrous.

ferrovìa *sf.* railway.

ferroviario *agg.* railway (*attr.*).

ferroviere *sm.* railwayman (*pl. -men*).

ferruginoso *agg.* ferruginous.

fèrtile *agg.* fertile (*anche fig.*).

fertilità *sf.* fertility.

fertilizzante *agg.* fertilizing. ♦ **fertilizzante** *sm.* fertilizer.

fertilizzare *vt.* to fertilize.

fèrula *sf.* rod.

fervente *agg.* burning, ardent (*anche fig.*).

fèrvido *agg.* fervid, ardent || *fervidi auguri*, best wishes.

fervore *sm.* fervour, heat.

fessura *sf.* 1. crack 2. (*per liquidi*) leak.

festa *sf.* 1. (*giorno di riposo*) holiday 2. (*religiosa*) feast 3. (*anniversario*) birthday 4. (*onomasti-*

co) Saint's day **5.** (*banchetto, ballo*) feast, ball || *giorno di* —, festal day.

festaiolo *sm.* reveller.

festante *agg.* rejoicing.

festeggiamento *sm.* celebration.

festeggiare *vt.* **1.** to celebrate **2.** (*accogliere festosamente*) to give (*v. irr.*) a hearty welcome.

festévole *agg.* festive.

festino *sm.* feast.

festival *sm.* festival.

festività *sf.* festivity.

festivo *agg.* **1.** festive **2.** (*domenicale*) Sunday (*attr.*).

festone *sm.* festoon.

festoso *agg.* joyous.

festuca *sf.* straw.

feticcio *sm.* fetish.

feticismo *sm.* fetishism.

feticista *s.* fetishist.

fètido *agg.* foetid, foul.

feto *sm.* foetus.

fetore *sm.* stink.

fetta *sf.* **1.** slice **2.** (*piccolo pezzo*) piece.

fettuccia *sf.* tape.

feudale *agg.* feudal.

feudalésimo *sm.* feudalism.

feudatario *sm.* feudatory.

fèudo *sm.* feud.

fiaba *sf.* **1.** fable **2.** (*falsità*) falsehood.

fiabesco *agg.* fairy-like.

fiacca *sf.* weariness || *battere la* — (*fam.*), to be sluggish.

fiaccare *vt.* to exhaust. ♦ **fiaccarsi** *vr.* to break (*v. irr.*) down.

fiacchezza *sf.* weakness, weariness.

fiacco *agg.* weak, exhausted.

fiàccola *sf.* torch.

fiaccolata *sf.* torchlight procession.

fiala *sf.* phial.

fiamma *sf.* **1.** flame **2.** (*molto viva*) blaze.

fiammante *agg.* **1.** flaming **2.** (*fig.*) bright || *nuovo* —, brand-new.

fiammata *sf.* blaze.

fiammeggiante *agg.* blazing, burning.

fiammeggiare *vi.* to blaze, to flame, to burn.

fiammifero *sm.* match: *accendere un* —, to strike (*v. irr.*) a match.

fiammingo *agg.* Flemish. ♦ **fiammingo** *sm.* Fleming.

fiancata *sf.* **1.** side **2.** (*mar.*) broadside.

fiancheggiare *vt.* **1.** to flank **2.** (*fig.*) to support.

fiancheggiatore *sm.* flanker, supporter.

fianco *sm.* **1.** hip, side (*anche fig.*) **2.** (*di animali; mil.*) flank.

fiasca *sf.* flask.

fiasco *sm.* flask || *fare* —, to fail utterly.

fiatare *vi.* to breathe: *senza* —, without speaking.

fiato *sm.* breath.

fibbia *sf.* buckle.

fibra *sf.* **1.** fibre **2.** (*costituzione*) constitution.

fibroma *sm.* fibroma (*pl.* -ata).

fibroso *agg.* fibrous.

fibula *sf.* **1.** fibula **2.** (*med.*) splint-bone.

ficcanaso *sm.* meddler.

ficcare *vt.* to thrust (*v. irr.*): to drive (*v. irr.*) (in). ♦ **ficcarsi** *vr.* to interfere || — *in testa qc*, to get (*v. irr.*) sthg. into one's head.

fico *sm.* fig.

fidanzamento *sm.* engagement.

fidanzare *vt.* to engage. ♦ **fidanzarsi** *vr.* to become (*v. irr.*) engaged (to so.).

fidanzata *sf.* fiancée.

fidanzato *sm.* fiancé.

fidare *vi.* to trust. ♦ **fidarsi** *vr.* to trust (upon so., sthg.).

fidato *agg.* reliable.

fideiussione *sf.* suretyship.

fidente *agg.* confiding.

fido *agg.* faithful. ♦ **fido** *sm.* **1.** devoted follower **2.** (*comm.*) credit.

fiducia *sf.* trust, confidence: — *in se stessi*, self-confidence.

fiduciario *agg.* fiduciary. ♦ **fiduciario** *sm.* fiduciary, trustee.

fiducioso *agg.* trusting, hopeful.

fiele *sm.* **1.** gall **2.** (*fig.*) hatred.

fienagione *sf.* haymaking.

fienile *sm.* hay-loft.

fieno *sm.* hay: *asma da* —, hay-asthma.

fiera *sf.* **1.** fair **2.** (*esposizione*) exhibition || — *campionaria*, samples fair.

fierezza *sf.* fierceness.

fiero *agg.* proud.

fièvole *agg.* **1.** feeble **2.** (*di luce, suono*) dim.

figgere *vt.* to fix.

figlia *sf.* daughter.

figliare *vt.* to bring (*v. irr.*) forth.

figliastra *sf.* step-daughter.

figliastro *sm.* step-son.

figlio *sm.* son.

figlioccia *sf.* goddaughter.

figlioccio *sm.* godson.

figliolanza *sf.* children (*pl.*), family.

figliolo *sm.* son.

figura *sf.* **1.** figure **2.** (*illustrazione*) illustration, picture **3.** (*personaggio di romanzi, opere teatrali ecc.*) character ‖ *fare una bella, brutta* —, to cut (*v. irr.*) a fine, poor figure.

figurare *vt.* **1.** to represent **2.** (*far figura*) to look smart **3.** (*apparire*) to appear.

figurativo *agg.* figurative.

figurato *agg.* **1.** (*illustrato*) illustrated **2.** (*di linguaggio, senso*) figurative.

figurazione *sf.* figuration.

figurinista *s.* dress-designer.

figurino *sm.* fashion-plate.

figuro *sm.* scoundrel.

fila *sf.* **1.** row, file **2.** (*coda*) queue: *fare la* —, to queue (up).

filaccia *sf.* lint.

filamento *sm.* filament.

filamentoso *agg.* filamentous.

filanda *sf.* spinning-mill.

filandaia *sf.* spinner.

filante *agg.:* *stella* — **1.** (*astr.*) falling-star **2.** (*di carta*) (paper) streamer.

filantropia *sf.* philanthropy.

filàntropo *sm.* philanthrope.

filare[1] *vt.* **1.** to spin (*v. irr.*) **2.** (*correre*) to run (*v. irr.*) **3.** (*amoreggiare*) to flirt.

filare[2] *sm.* row, line.

filarmònico *agg.* e *sm.* philharmonic.

filastrocca *sf.* nursery rhyme.

filatelìa *sf.* stamp-collecting.

filatèlico *agg.* philatelic. ♦ **filatèlico** *sm.* philatelist.

filato *agg.* **1.** spun **2.** (*di seguito*) running.

filatura *sf.* spinning.

filettare *vt.* (*mecc.*) to thread.

filettatura *sf.* (*mecc.*) threading.

filetto *sm.* **1.** (*filo sottile*) thin thread **2.** (*mecc.*) thread ‖ — *della lingua*, fraenum.

filiale *agg.* filial. ♦ **filiale** *sf.* branch house.

filiazione *sf.* filiation.

filibustiere *sm.* **1.** filibuster **2.** (*fig.*) adventurer, rascal.

fillera *sf.* **1.** (*mecc.*) screw cutting die **2.** (*ind. tess.*) spinneret.

filiforme *agg.* threadlike.

filigrana *sf.* **1.** filigree **2.** (*di carta*) watermark.

filippica *sf.* philippic.

fillòssera *sf.* phylloxera.

film *sm.* picture ‖ *girare un* —, to shoot (*v. irr.*) a picture.

filmare *vt.* to film.

filo *sm.* **1.** thread **2.** (*ind. tessile*) yarn **3.** (*tec.*) wire ‖ *un* — *d'acqua*, a fine stream of water; *un* — *d'aria*, a breath of air.

filobus *sm.* trolley-bus.

filologìa *sf.* philology.

filòlogo *sm.* philologist.

filone *sm.* **1.** (*di pane*) long loaf **2.** (*min.*) vein.

filosofare *vi.* to philosophize.

filosofìa *sf.* philosophy.

filòsofo *sm.* philosopher.

filovìa *sf.* trolley-bus line.

filtrare *vt.* to filter, to strain.

filtro *sm.* **1.** filter **2.** (*colino*) strainer.

filza *sf.* **1.** string **2.** (*fig.*) series (*pl.*) **3.** (*cucito*) running stitch.

finale *agg.* last, final.

finalità *sf.* aim, end.

finalmente *avv.* **1.** at last **2.** (*in conclusione*) finally.

finanche *avv.* even.

finanza *sf.* finance.

finanziamento *sm.* financing.

finanziare *vt.* to finance.

finanziario *agg.* financial.

finanziatore *sm.* financing capitalist.

finanziere *sm.* financier.

finché *cong.* **1.** till, until **2.** (*per tutto il tempo che*) as long as.

fine[1] *sf.* end ‖ *alla fin* —, after all. ♦ *fine* (*scopo*) purpose.

fine[2] *agg.* fine, thin.

finestra *sf.* window.

finestrino *sm.* window.

finezza *sf.* **1.** thinness **2.** (*acume*) subtlety **3.** (*raffinatezza*) refinement **4.** (*gentilezza*) kindness.

fingere *vi.* to pretend. ♦ **fingersi** *vr.* to feign oneself.

finimenti *sm. pl.* harness (*sing.*).

finimondo *sm.* **1.** end of the world **2.** (*fig.*) catastrophe.

finire *vi.* **1.** to finish, to end **2.** (*interrompersi*) to stop ‖ — *con*, to end by: *finii con l'andare*, I ended by going.

finitezza *sf.* perfection.

finìtimo agg. bordering.

finito agg. 1. finished, ended 2. (rovinato) done for.

finitura sf. finishing.

fino prep. 1. (di tempo) till, until, up to: — a dicembre, till December 2. (di spazio) as far as: andammo fino a Roma, we went as far as Rome 3. (fino da) from 4. (a partire da) since.

finocchio sm. fennel.

finora avv. till now, so far.

finta sf. 1. sham 2. (scherma) feint.

fintantoché avv. V. finché.

finto agg. false.

finzione sf. pretence, duplicity.

fio sm. penalty: pagare il —, to pay (v. irr.) the penalty (of).

fioccare vi. 1. to snow 2. (fig.) to shower.

fiocco sm. 1. ribbon 2. (di lana) staple 3. (falda) flake 4. (di neve) snowflake.

fiòcina sf. harpoon.

fioco agg. 1. (rauco) hoarse 2. (debole) weak 3. (di luce) dim 4. (di voce) faint.

fionda sf. sling.

fioraio sm. florist.

fiorame sm. floral design.

fiordaliso sm. bluebottle.

fiordo sm. fjord.

fiore sm. 1. flower 2. (fioritura) bloom: essere in — (anche fig.), to be in bloom 3. (parte scelta) the best part 4. (nelle carte) clubs (pl.).

fiorente agg. 1. blooming 2. (fig.) flourishing.

fioretto sm. 1. little flower 2. (relig.) act of mortification 3. (scherma) foil.

fioricultore sm. floriculturist.

fiorino sm. florin.

fiorire vi. 1. to flower, to bloom, to blossom 2. (fig.) to flourish.

fiorista s. florist.

fiorito agg. 1. flowery 2. (in fiore) in bloom.

fioritura sf. 1. flowering 2. (fig.) flourishing.

fiotto sm. wave, stream: a fiotti, in streams.

firma sf. signature.

firmamento sm. firmament.

firmare vt. to sign.

firmatario sm. 1. signatory 2. (comm.) signer.

fisarmònica sf. accordion.

fisarmonicista s. accordionist.

fiscale agg. 1. fiscal 2. (inquisitorio) strict.

fiscalismo sm. rigorism.

fischiare vi. 1. to whistle 2. (di segnale acustico) to hoot 3. (di serpente; per disapprovare) to hiss 4. (nelle orecchie) to buzz 5. (di proiettili) to whiz.

fischiata sf. 1. whistling 2. (di disapprovazione) hissing.

fischiettare vt. to whistle softly.

fischietto sm. whistle.

fischio sm. 1. whistle 2. (di serpente; di disapprovazione) hiss 3. (segnali acustici) hoot 4. (nelle orecchie) buzzing.

fisco sm. public treasury.

fisica sf. physics.

fisico agg. physical, bodily. ♦ **físico** sm. 1. (scienziato) physicist 2. (costituzione) physique.

fisima sf. caprice, whim.

fisiologìa sf. physiology.

fisiològico agg. physiologic(al).

fisiòlogo sm. physiologist.

fisionomìa sf. 1. features (pl.) 2. (carattere) character.

fisionomista sm. physiognomist.

fisioterapìa sf. physiotherapy.

fissaggio sm. fixing.

fissare vt. 1. to fix 2. (guardare fisso) to gaze 3. (prenotare) to book. ♦ **fissarsi** vr. 1. to be fixed 2. (stabilirsi) to settle down.

fissato agg. 1. fixed 2. (fam.) obsessed.

fissatore sm. 1. fixer 2. (foto) fixing bath.

fissazione sf. fixed idea.

fissione sf. fission.

fissità sf. fixity.

fisso agg. fixed.

fistola sf. 1. Pan-pipe 2. (patol.) fistula.

fitologìa sf. phytology.

fitta sf. stitch.

fittàvolo sm. tenant farmer.

fittizio agg. fictitious.

fitto[1] agg. 1. (conficcato) driven in 2. (denso) thick.

fitto[2] sm. rent.

fiumana sf. 1. broad stream 2. (fig.) crowd, stream.

fiume sm. 1. river 2. (fig.) flood.

fiutare vt. 1. to smell (v. irr.) 2. (fig.) to guess.

fiuto sm. 1. scent, smell 2. (fig.) intuition.

flàccido *agg.* flabby.

flacone *sm.* vial.

flagellare *vt.* 1. to flagellate 2. *(fig.)* to scourge.

flagellazione *sf.* flagellation.

flagello *sm.* 1. scourge, whip 2. *(fig.)* scourge, plague.

flagrante *agg.* flagrant || *cogliere qu. in —*, to catch *(v. irr.)* so. in the open act.

flagranza *sf.* flagrancy.

flanella *sf.* flannel.

flato *sm.* flatus.

flatulenza *sf.* flatulence.

flautato *agg.* fluted.

flautista *sm.* flute-player.

flàuto *sm.* flute.

flèbile *agg.* plaintive, feeble.

flebite *sf.* phlebitis.

fleboclisi *sf.* phleboclysis.

flebòtomo *sm.* phlebotomist.

flemma *sf.* coolness, phlegm.

flemmàtico *agg.* phlegmatic.

flèmmone *sm.* phlegmon.

flessìbile *agg.* flexible, pliant *(anche fig.)*.

flessibilità *sf.* flexibility.

flessione *sf.* flexion, bending.

flessuosità *sf.* 1. flexuosity 2. *(di corpo)* suppleness.

flessuoso *agg.* 1. flexuous 2. *(di corpo)* supple.

flèttere *vt.* to bend *(v. irr.)*.

flirtare *vi.* to flirt.

flogìstico *agg. (med.)* phlogistic.

flora *sf.* flora.

floreale *agg.* floral.

floricoltore *sm.* floriculturist.

floricoltura *sf.* floriculture.

floridezza *sf.* prosperity.

flòrido *agg.* 1. prosperous 2. *(fig.)* buxom 3. *(di colorito)* ruddy.

florilegio *sm.* florilegium *(pl. -ia)*.

floscio *agg.* flabby.

flotta *sf.* fleet: — *metropolitana (in Gran Bretagna)*, the Home Fleet.

flottante *agg.* floating.

flottiglia *sf.* flotilla.

fluente *agg.* fluent *(anche fig.)*.

fluidità *sf.* fluency.

flùido *agg.* e *sm.* fluid.

fluire *vi.* to flow.

fluorescente *agg.* fluorescent.

fluorescenza *sf.* 1. *(fig.)* fluorescence 2. *(elettr.)* glow.

fluorìdrico *agg.* hydrofluoric.

fluorite *sf.* fluorite.

fluoro *sm.* fluorine.

fluoruro *sm.* fluoride.

flussione *sf.* fluxion.

flusso *sm.* 1. *(di marea)* flood(-tide) 2. *(fig.)* flux.

flutto *sm.* wave.

fluttuante *agg.* 1. fluctuating, floating 2. *(incerto)* irresolute.

fluttuare *vi.* to fluctuate, to waver.

fluttuazione *sf.* fluctuation.

fluviale *agg.* river *(attr.)*.

fobìa *sf.* phobia, aversion.

foca *sf.* seal.

focaccia *sf.* cake || *rendere pan per —*, to give *(v. irr.)* tit for tat.

focaia *agg. pietra —*, flint.

focale *agg.* focal.

foce *sf.* mouth.

focolaio *sm.* centre of infection.

focolare *sm.* 1. hearth 2. *(caminetto)* fireplace 3. *(fig.)* home.

focoso *agg.* hot, fiery.

fòdera *sf.* lining.

foderare *vt.* to line.

fòdero *sm.* scabbard, sheath.

foga *sf.* impetuosity.

foggia *sf.* 1. *(moda)* fashion 2. *(maniera)* way 3. *(forma)* shape.

foggiare *vt.* to shape.

foglia *sf.* leaf *(pl. leaves)* || *mangiare la —*, to take *(v. irr.)* the hint.

fogliame *sm.* foliage, leafage.

foglio *sm.* sheet.

fogna *sf.* sewer.

fognatura *sf.* sewage.

foia *sf.* lust.

fola *sf.* 1. fable 2. *(fandonia)* fib.

folata *sf. (di vento)* gust.

folclore *sm.* folklore.

folclorìstico *agg.* folkloristic.

folgorante *agg.* flashing, dazzling.

folgorare *vt.* to strike *(v. irr.)* with lightning.

folgorazione *sf.* 1. *(elettr.)* electrocution 2. *(fig.)* fulmination.

fòlgore *sf.* thunderbolt.

folla *sf.* crowd.

folle *agg.* 1. mad 2. *(mecc.)* idle 3. *(auto)* neutral.

folleggiare *vi.* 1. to behave foolishly 2. *(divertirsi)* to make *(v. irr.)* merry.

folletto *sm.* 1. imp 2. *(ragazzo)* restless child.

follìa *sf.* madness || *amare qu. alla —*, to be madly in love with so.

folto *agg.* thick. ♦ folto *sm.* thick.

fomentare *vt.* to foster.

fomentatore *sm.* fomenter.

fomento *sm.* fomentation

fonda sf. anchorage || nave alla —, ship at anchor.

fòndaco sm. draper's shop.

fondale sm. 1. (teat.) background 2. (mar.) depth.

fondamentale agg. fundamental.

fondamento sm. 1. foundation: gettare le fondamenta, to lay (v. irr.) the foundation 2. (fig.) basis, ground.

fondare vt. to found. ♦ **fondarsi** vr. to base oneself on.

fondatezza sf. foundation, ground.

fondato agg. well-grounded.

fondatore sm. founder.

fondazione sf. 1. foundation 2. (istituzione) institution.

fóndere vt. 1. to melt 2. (fondere in forma) to cast (v. irr.) 3. (unire) to blend.

fonderia sf. foundry.

fondiario agg. land (attr.).

fondista sm. long-distance runner.

fonditore sm. melter, caster.

fonditura sf. 1. melting 2. (colata) casting.

fondo agg. deep. ♦ **fondo** sm. 1. (parte inferiore) bottom 2. (estremità) end 3. (indole) nature 4. (possedimento) estate 5. (capitale) fund || articolo di —, leading article.

fonema sm. phoneme.

fonètica sf. phonetics.

fonogramma sm. phonogram.

fonologia sf. phonology.

fontana sf. fountain.

fontanella sf. (anat.) fontanel.

fonte sf. spring, source (anche fig.).

foraggio sm. forage.

foràneo agg. 1. rural 2. (mar.) outer.

forare vt. 1. to pierce 2. (di pneumatico) to puncture 3. (di biglietti) to punch.

foratura sf. 1. piercing 2. (di pneumatico) puncture.

fòrbici sf. pl. scissors.

forbire vt. 1. to clean 2. (di stile) to polish.

forbito agg. 1. elegant 2. (di stile) polished.

forca sf. 1. fork 2. (patibolo) gallows.

forcella sf. 1. forked stick 2. (mecc.) fork 3. (per capelli) hairpin.

forchetta sf. fork.

forcina sf. hairpin.

fòrcipe sm. forceps (pl.).

forcuto agg. forked.

forense agg. forensic.

foresta sf. forest (anche fig.), wood.

forestale agg. forestal: guardia —, forester.

foresterìa sf. guest-rooms (pl.).

forestiero agg. foreign. ♦ **forestiero** sm. foreigner.

fòrfora sf. dandruff, scurf.

forgiare vt. 1. to forge 2. (modellare) to shape.

forma sf. 1. form, shape 2. (tec.) mould.

formaggio sm. cheese.

formale agg. 1. formal 2. (solenne) solemn.

formalismo sm. formalism.

formalista agg. e s. formalist.

formalità sf. formality.

formalizzarsi vr. to be shocked (at, by).

formare vt. 1. to form 2. (fare) to make (v. irr.), to create 3. (modellare) to shape 4. (addestrare) to train. ♦ **formarsi** vr. 1. to form 2. (crescere, affinarsi) to grow (v. irr.), to develop.

formativo agg. formative.

formato sm. 1. form 2. (misura) size 3. (di libro) format.

formazione sf. formation.

formica sf. ant.

formichiere sm. ant-eater.

formicolare vi. 1. to swarm 2. (sentire un formicolio) to tingle.

formicolio sm. 1. swarming 2. (intorpidimento) tingling.

formidàbile agg. formidable.

fòrmula sf. formula (pl. -ae).

formulare vt. to formulate.

fornace sf. furnace.

fornaio sm. 1. baker 2. (negozio) baker's shop.

fornello sm. stove.

fornire vt. 1. to supply (with), to provide (with) 2. (equipaggiare) to equip (with).

fornito agg. 1. furnished (with), supplied (with) 2. (equipaggiato) equipped (with).

fornitore sm. furnisher, supplier.

fornitura sf. 1. (il fornire) supplying 2. (attrezzatura) furniture, fitting.

forno sm. 1. (da cucina) oven 2. (metal.) furnace.

foro[1] sm. hole.

foro[2] sm. 1. court of justice 2. (gli avvocati) the Bar 3. (stor.) forum.

forse *avv.* **1.** perhaps, maybe **2.** (*circa*) about.

forsennato *agg.* mad, frantic.

forte *agg.* **1.** strong (*anche fig.*) **2.** (*di mali*) severe **3.** (*violento*) heavy **4.** (*di suono*) loud. ♦ **forte** *sm.* **1.** strong man **2.** (*punto di forza*) strong point **3.** (*fortezza*) fortress. ♦ **forte** *avv.* strongly.

fortezza *sf.* stronghold, fortress.

fortificare *vt.* to strengthen, to fortify (*anche fig.*).

fortificazione *sf.* fortification.

fortino *sm.* block-house.

fortùito *agg.* fortuitous, accidental.

fortuna *sf.* **1.** luck **2.** (*ricchezza*) fortune, wealth **3.** (*riuscita*) success **4.** (*emergenza*) emergency.

fortunale *sm.* storm.

fortunato *agg.* lucky.

fortunoso *agg.* **1.** stormy **2.** (*fig.*) eventful.

forùncolo *sm.* boil.

foruncolosi *sf.* furunculosis.

forviare *vt.* to lead (*v. irr.*) astray.

forza *sf.* **1.** strength **2.** (*fig.*) power ‖ — *di volontà*, will-power; *a* — *di*, by dint of **3.** (*mil.*) force.

forzare *vt.* **1.** to force, to compel **2.** (*scassinare*) to pick the lock of.

forzato *agg.* forced. ♦ **forzato** *sm.* convict.

forziere *sm.* coffer.

forzoso *agg.* forced.

foschia *sf.* haze, mist.

fosco *agg.* **1.** dark, hazy **2.** (*di aspetto*) gloomy.

fosfato *sm.* phosphate.

fosforescente *agg.* phosphorescent.

fosforescenza *sf.* phosphorescence.

fòsforo *sm.* **1.** phosphorus **2.** (*fig.*) intelligence.

fossa *sf.* **1.** ditch **2.** (*cavità*) hollow **3.** (*tomba*) grave.

fossato *sm.* ditch.

fòssile *agg. e sm.* fossil ‖ *carbon* —, pit-coal.

fosso *sm.* ditch.

foto *sf.* photo.

fotocèllula *sf.* photoelectric cell.

fotocopia *sf.* photocopy.

fotogènico *agg.* photogenic.

fotografare *vt.* to photograph.

fotografia *sf.* **1.** (*arte fotografica*) photography **2.** (*immagine fotografica*) photograph ‖ — *istantanea*, snapshot; *fare una* —, to take (*v. irr.*) a photograph.

fotògrafo *sm.* photographer.

fotomontaggio *sm.* photomontage.

fra *prep.* V. *tra.*

fra' *sm.* (*relig.*) Brother.

frac *sm.* tail-coat.

fracassare *vt.* to smash, to shatter.

fracasso *sm.* **1.** noise, hubbub **2.** (*di cose rotte*) crash.

fracco *sm.* **1.** a great deal **2.** (*di botte*) a good thrashing.

fràdicio *agg.* **1.** rotten **2.** (*bagnato*) wet through.

fràgile *agg.* **1.** fragile **2.** (*fig.*) frail.

fragilità *sf.* fragility (*anche fig.*).

fràgola *sf.* strawberry.

fragore *sm.* loud noise.

fragoroso *agg.* noisy.

fragrante *agg.* fragrant.

fragranza *sf.* fragrance.

fraintèndere *vt.* to misunderstand (*v. irr.*).

frammassone *sm.* freemason.

frammassonerìa *sf.* freemasonry.

frammentario *agg.* fragmentary.

frammento *sm.* fragment.

frammèttere *vt.* to interpose. ♦ **frammèttersi** *vr.* to interpose, to intrude.

frammezzare *vt.* to intersperse.

frammezzo *prep.* V. *tra.*

frammischiare *vt.* to intermingle. ♦ **frammischiarsi** *vr.* to intermingle.

frana *sf.* landslide.

franare *vi.* **1.** (*di terreno*) to slide (*v. irr.*) down **2.** (*di casa*) to fall (*v. irr.*) in.

francescano *agg. e sm.* Franciscan.

francese *agg.* French. ♦ **francese** *sm.* Frenchman (*pl.* -men).

francesismo *sm.* Gallicism.

franchezza *sf.* frankness, outspokenness.

franchigia *sf.* **1.** immunity **2.** (*postale*) post-free **3.** (*mar.*) furlough.

franco¹ *agg.* **1.** frank, outspoken **2.** (*libero*; *comm.*) free: *un porto* —, a free port; — *a bordo*, free on board; — *di spese*, free of charge.

franco² *sm.* franc.

francobollo *sm.* stamp.

francotiratore *sm.* sharp-shooter.

frangente *sm.* **1.** (*mar.*) breaker **2.** (*situazione difficile*) emergency.

fràngere *vt.* **1.** to break (*v. irr.*) **2.** (*schiacciare*) to crush.

frangetta *sf.* fringe.

frangia *sf.* **1.** fringe **2.** (*fig.*) embellishment.

frangiare vt. to fringe.
frangibile agg. frangible.
frangibilità sf. frangibility.
frangiflutti agg. e sm. breakwater.
frangizolle sm. (agr.) clod-smasher.
franoso agg. crumbling.
frantoio sm. oil-mill.
frantumare vt. to shatter.
frantume sm. fragment || andare in frantumi, to break (v. irr.) into fragments.
frappé sm. shake.
frapporre vt. to interpose. ◆ **frapporsi** vr. to interpose.
frasario sm. jargon.
frasca sf. 1. leafy branch 2. (donna leggera) coquette.
frascheggiare vi. 1. to rustle 2. (civettare) to flirt.
fraschetta sf. 1. twig 2. (fig.) frivolous girl.
frase sf. sentence.
fraseggiare vi. to phrase.
fraseologia sf. phraseology.
fràssino sm. ash-tree.
frastagliare vt. to indent.
frastagliato agg. indented.
frastaglio sm. indentation.
frastornare vt. to disturb.
frastuono sm. noise, uproar, hub-bub.
frate sm. 1. friar 2. (come appellativo) Brother.
fratellanza sf. brotherhood, fraternity.
fratellastro sm. half-brother.
fratello sm. brother || fratelli siamesi, Siamese twins.
fraternità sf. brotherhood, fraternity.
fraternizzare vi. to fraternize.
fraternizzazione sf. fraternization.
fraterno agg. brotherly.
fratricida agg. fratricidal. ◆ **fratricida** s. fratricide.
fratricidio sm. fratricide.
fratta sf. thicket.
frattaglie sf. pl. chitterlings.
frattanto avv. meantime, meanwhile.
frattempo (nella loc. avv.) nel —, in the meanwhile.
fratto agg. broken, crushed.
frattura sf. fracture.
fratturare vt. to fracture, to break (v. irr.). ◆ **fratturarsi** vr. to fracture, to break.
fraudolento agg. fraudulent.
fraudolenza sf. fraudulence.

frazionamento sm. division.
frazionare vt. to divide.
frazionario agg. fractional.
frazione sf. fraction.
freccia sf. arrow.
frecciata sf. (fig.) gibe.
freddare vt. 1. to cool 2. (ammazzare) to kill.
freddezza sf. coldness, coldheartedness.
freddo agg. cold. ◆ **freddo** sm. cold: avere —, to be cold; tremare di —, to shiver with cold.
freddoloso agg. sensitive to cold.
freddura sf. pun.
fregagione sf. massage.
fregare vt. 1. to rub 2. (imbrogliare; volg.) to swindle.
fregata¹ sf. rubbing.
fregata² sf. (nave) frigate.
fregatura sf. swindle.
fregiare vt. to decorate, to adorn.
fregio sm. 1. ornament 2. (arch.) frieze.
frego sm. stroke: tirare un — su qc., to cross sthg. out.
frègola sf. heat.
fremente agg. quivering: — d'ira, fuming.
frèmere vi. to quiver, to tremble.
frèmito sm. quiver, thrill.
frenare vt. 1. to brake 2. (trattenere) to restrain.
frenata sf. braking.
frenesia sf. 1. frenzy 2. (desiderio sfrenato) immoderate desire.
frenètico agg. 1. frantic 2. (entusiastico) enthusiastic.
freno sm. 1. brake || bloccare i freni, to jam the brakes; togliere il —, to release the brake 2. (ritegno) check restraint || mordere il —, to fret under restraint; stringere i freni, to shorten the reins 3. (di cavallo) bit.
frenologia sf. phrenology.
frequentare vt. 1. to frequent 2. (di scuola) to attend 3. (di luogo pubblico) to patronize.
frequentato agg. 1. frequented 2. (di scuola) attended 3. (di luogo pubblico) patronized.
frequentatore sm. 1. frequenter 2. (cliente assiduo) regular customer.
frequente agg. frequent.
frequenza sf. 1. frequency 2. (affluenza) concourse 3. (assiduità) attendance.

fresa sf. milling machine.

fresatrice sf. milling machine.

freschezza sf. freshness (anche fig.), coolness.

fresco agg. 1. fresh 2. (di temperatura) cool.

frescura sf. coolness.

fretta sf. haste, hurry: avere —. to be in a hurry.

frettoloso agg. hurried.

freudiano agg. Freudian.

friàbile agg. crumbly.

friabilità sf. friability.

fricassea sf. fricassee.

friggere vt. to fry || andare a farsi —, to go (v. irr.) to the devil.

friggitoria sf. fried food shop.

frigidezza, frigidità sf. frigidity.

frigido agg. frigid (anche fig.).

frignare vi. to whimper.

frigorifero agg. refrigerant. ♦ **frigorifero** sm. 1. refrigerator 2. (fam.) fridge.

fringuello sm. finch.

frittata sf. omelette.

frittella sf. pancake.

fritto agg. fried.

frittura sf. fry.

frivolezza sf. 1. frivolity 2. (cosa frivola) trifle.

frivolo agg. frivolous.

frizionare vt. to rub, to massage.

frizione sf. 1. rub, rubbing, massage 2. (auto) clutch.

frizzante agg. 1. biting 2. (di bevanda) sparkling.

frizzare vi. 1. to tingle 2. (di bevanda) to sparkle.

frizzo sm. 1. witticism 2. (scherno) gibe.

frodare vt. to defraud.

frodatore sm. defrauder.

frode sf. fraud, swindle.

frodo sm. smuggling || cacciare di —, to poach; cacciatore di —, poacher.

frollare vt. to hang. ♦ **frollare** vi. to become (v. irr.) tender.

frollatura sf. hanging.

frollo agg. tender, high || pasta frolla, pastry.

fronda[1] sf. leafy branch.

fronda[2] sf. (rivolta) rebellion: vento di —, trouble brewing.

frondoso agg. leafy.

frontale agg. frontal.

fronte sf. 1. forehead: — ampia, sfuggente, broad, receding forehead 2. (arch.) front || di — a, in front

of; far — a, to face. ♦ **fronte** sm. 1. (mil.) front 2. (pol.) union.

fronteggiare vt. to face.

frontespizio sm. 1. (arch.) frontispiece 2. (di libro) title page.

frontiera sf. frontier, border.

frontone sm. 1. pediment 2. (di porta, finestra) gable.

fronzolo sm. frill || senza fronzoli, plain.

frotta sf. 1. crowd 2. (di animali) flock.

fròttola sf. fib.

frugacchiare vi. to rummage.

frugale agg. frugal.

frugalità sf. frugality.

frugare vi. to search, to rummage.

frùgolo sm. lively child.

fruire vi. to enjoy, to avail oneself of.

fruizione sf. fruition.

frullare vt. 1. to whip, to beat (v. irr.) up 2. (di ali) to whir.

frullato sm. — di frutta, fruit-shake.

frullatore sm. mill.

frullino sm. whisk.

frullio sm. whirring.

frullo sm. whir.

frumento sm. wheat.

frusciare vi. to rustle.

fruscio sm. rustle.

frusta sf. 1. whip 2. (cuc.) whisk.

frustare vt. to whip, to lash.

frustata sf. lash.

frustino sm. riding-whip.

frusto agg. worn-out, thread-bare.

frustrare vt. to frustrate.

frutta sf. fruit: — candita, candied fruit; — sciroppata, fruit in syrup; — cotta, compote.

fruttare vi. 1. to bear (v. irr.) fruit, to pay (v. irr.) 2. (comm.) to yield.

frutteto sm. orchard.

frutticultura sf. fruit-growing.

fruttiera sf. fruit-dish.

fruttifero agg. 1. fruitful 2. (econ.) interest-bearing: buono —, interest-bearing security.

fruttificare vi. to bear (v. irr.) fruit.

fruttivéndolo sm. greengrocer.

frutto sm. fruit || frutti di mare, edible mussels.

fruttuoso agg. fruitful, profitable.

fu agg. late.

fucilare vt. to shoot (v. irr.).

fucilata sf. shot.

fucilazione sf. shooting.

fucile *sm.* rifle, gun: — *ad aria compressa*, air-gun; — *da caccia*, shotgun; *calcio del* —, butt; *canna del* —, gun-barrel; *caricare un* —, to load a gun.

fucileria *sf.* 1. rifle fire 2. (*insieme di fucili*) musketry.

fuciliere *sm.* rifleman (*pl.* -men).

fucina *sf.* forge.

fucinare *vt.* to forge.

fuco *sm.* 1. drone 2. (*bot.*) fucus.

fucsia *sf.* fuchsia.

fuga *sf.* 1. flight, escape 2. (*di innamorati*) elopement 3. (*falla, apertura*) escape, leak 4. (*mus.*) fugue.

fugace *agg.* short-lived, transient.

fugacità *sf.* fugacity.

fugare *vt.* 1. to put (*v. irr.*) to flight, to disperse 2. (*scacciare*) to dispel.

fuggévole *agg.* flying, ephemeral.

fuggiasco *agg.* e *sm.* runaway.

fuggire *vi.* 1. to run (*v. irr.*) away, to flee (*v. irr.*) 2. (*di innamorati*) to elope. ♦ **fuggire** *vt.* to shun.

fuggitivo *agg.* e *sm.* fugitive.

fulcro *sm.* fulcrum (*pl.* -ra).

fulgido *agg.* shining.

fulgore *sm.* brightness.

fuliggine *sf.* soot.

fuligginoso *agg.* sooty.

fulminante *agg.* fulminant. ♦ **fulminante** *sm.* 1. (*chim.*) fulminate 2. (*di arma*) primer.

fulminare *vt.* 1. to strike (*v. irr.*) by lightning 2. (*colpire*) to strike.

fulminato *agg.* 1. struck by lightning 2. (*fig.*) thunder-struck.

fùlmine *sm.* lightning.

fulmineo *agg.* flashing.

fulvo *agg.* tawny.

fumaiolo *sm.* smoke-stack.

fumante *agg.* smoking, steaming.

fumare *vt.* e *vi.* to smoke.

fumarola *sf.* fumarole.

fumata *sf.* 1. smoke 2. (*segnale*) smoke signal.

fumatore *sm.* smoker.

fumetto *sm.* strip cartoon || *giornali a fumetti*, comics.

fumista *s.* stove-repairer.

fumo *sm.* 1. smoke || *venditore di* —, windbag; *andare in* —, to end in smoke 2. (*vapore*) fume (*anche fig.*) 3. (*di pentole*) steam.

fumògeno *agg.* smoke-producing.

fumoso *agg.* smoky.

funàmbolo *sm.* rope-dancer.

fune *sf.* 1. rope 2. (*cavo*) cable.

fùnebre *agg.* 1. funeral: *canto* —, dirge; *carro* —, hearse 2. (*cupo*) gloomy.

funerale *sm.* funeral || *i funerali*, the obsequies.

funerario *agg.* funerary.

funèreo *agg.* funereal.

funestare *vt.* to afflict.

funesto *agg.* baneful, woeful.

fungaia *sf.* mushroom-bed.

fùngere *vi.* to act (as).

fungo *sm.* mushroom.

funicolare *sf.* funicular.

funivìa *sf.* telpherage.

funzionale *agg.* functional.

funzionamento *sm.* working.

funzionare *vi.* 1. to act (as) 2. (*andar bene*) to work.

funzionario *sm.* official.

funzione *sf.* 1. function 2. (*carica*) office 3. (*relig.*) service.

fuochista *sm.* stoker.

fuoco *sm.* 1. fire 2. (*cine; foto; mat.*) focus: *mettere a* —, to focus.

fuorché *cong.* except, but.

fuori *avv.* 1. out, outdoors 2. (*all'estero*) abroad. ♦ **fuori (di)** *prep.* out of, outside.

fuoribordo *sm.* outboard motor.

fuoriclasse *sm.* first-rater.

fuorigioco *sm.*, *agg.* e *avv.* off-side.

fuorilegge *sm.* outlaw.

fuoriserie *agg.* e *sm.* special body car.

fuoruscito *sm.* exile, refugee.

fuorviare *vt.* to lead (*v. irr.*) astray.

furberìa *sf.* cunning.

furbo *agg.* cunning, shrewd.

furente *agg.* furious, mad.

furerìa *sf.* orderly room.

furetto *sm.* ferret.

furfante *sm.* rascal, scamp.

furgoncino *sm.* small van.

furgone *sm.* van.

furia *sf.* fury: *montare su tutte le furie*, to fly (*v. irr.*) into a fury.

furibondo *agg.* furious.

furioso *agg.* 1. furious 2. (*violento*) violent.

furore *sm.* fury: *far* —, to be a hit.

furoreggiare *vi.* to be all the rage.

furtivo *agg.* stealthy.

furto *sm.* theft.

fuscello *sm.* 1. twig, straw 2. (*fig.*) thin person.

fusibile *sm.* fuse.

fusione *sf.* 1. fusion 2. (*di società comm.*) merging.

fuso *sm.* spindle || — *orario*, time zone.

fusoliera *sf.* fuselage.

fustigare *vt.* to flog.

fusto *sm.* 1. (*bot.*) stalk 2. (*tronco umano*) trunk 3. (*per benzina*) drum 4. (*di legno per liquori*) barrel 5. (*giovane prestante*) muscle--man (*pl.* -men) 6. (*di colonna*) shaft.

fùtile *agg.* trifling.

futilità *sf.* trifle.

futurismo *sm.* futurism.

futurista *agg. e sm.* futurist.

futuro *agg. e sm.* future.

G

gabbamondo *sm.* swindler.

gabbare *vt.* to swindle.

gabbia *sf.* 1. cage 2. (*per imballaggio*) crate.

gabbiano *sm.* sea-gull.

gabellare *vt.* (*far credere*) to pass off as.

gabinetto *sm.* 1. (*studio*) study 2. (*pol.*) cabinet 3. (*latrina*) water-closet, toilet.

gagà *sm.* dandy.

gagliardamente *avv.* vigorously.

gagliardetto *sm.* pennon.

gagliardo *agg.* vigorous.

gaglioffo *sm.* rascal.

gaiezza *sf.* 1. cheerfulness 2. (*di colore*) brightness.

gaio *agg.* 1. cheerful 2. (*di colore*) bright.

gala *sf.* 1. (*trina*) frill 2. (*festa*) gala: *abito di* —, gala dress.

galante *agg. e sm.* gallant || *lettera* —, love letter; *fare il* —, to flirt.

galanteria *sf.* 1. gallantry 2. (*complimento*) compliment.

galantina *sf.* galantine.

galantuomo *sm.* honest man.

galassia *sf.* galaxy.

galateo *sm.* 1. good manners (*pl.*) 2. (*libro*) book of manners.

galena *sf.* galena.

galeone *sm.* galleon.

galeotto *sm.* 1. convict 2. (*mezzano*) pander 3. (*mar.*) galley-slave.

galera *sf.* 1. jail 2. (*mar.*) galley.

galileo *agg. e sm.* Galilean.

galla¹ (*nella loc. avv.*) *a* —, afloat || *stare a* —, to float; *venire a* —, to come (*v. irr.*) to the surface; (*fig.*) to come to light.

galla² *sf.* (*bot.*) gall.

galleggiamento *sm.* floating: *linea di* —, water-line.

galleggiante *agg.* floating, afloat (*pred.*). ♦ **galleggiante** *sm.* 1. float 2. (*boa*) buoy.

galleggiare *vi.* to float.

galleria *sf.* 1. tunnel 2. (*d'arte, in teatro*) gallery.

gallese *agg.* Welsh. ♦ **gallese** *sm.* Welshman (*pl.* -men).

galletta *sf.* biscuit.

gallina *sf.* 1. hen 2. (*cibo*) chicken.

gallináceo *agg. e sm.* gallinacean.

gallio *sm.* gallium.

gallismo *sm.* cocksure behaviour (towards women).

gallo *sm.* 1. cock 2. (*stor.*) Gaul.

gallonato *agg.* gallooned.

gallone *sm.* 1. braid, galloon 2. (*mil.*) chevron stripes (*pl.*) 3. (*misura*) gallon.

galoppante *agg.* galloping.

galoppare *vi.* to gallop.

galoppata *sf.* gallop.

galoppatoio *sm.* riding-track.

galoppino *sm.* 1. errand-boy 2. (*tirapiedi*) drudge.

galoppo *sm.* gallop: *al* —, at a gallop, (*fig.*) at full speed; *andare al gran* —, to ride (*v. irr.*) full gallop.

galoscia *sf.* galosh.

galvánico *agg.* galvanic.

galvanizzare *vt.* 1. to galvanize 2. (*rivestire di metallo*) to electroplate.

galvanizzazione *sf.* 1. galvanization 2. (*rivestitura di metallo*) electroplating.

galvanoplàstica *sf.* galvanoplastics.

gamba *sf.* leg || *avere le gambe lunghe*, to be long-legged; *male in* —, down at heel; *in* — (*fig.*), smart.

gambale *sm.* 1. legging 2. (*di armatura*) jamb.

gamberetto *sm.* shrimp.

gàmbero *sm.* 1. (*di mare*) lobster 2. (*d'acqua dolce*) crayfish || *andare come un* —, to go (*v. irr.*) backwards.

gambo *sm.* stem.

gamma *sf.* range: — *di lunghezza d'onda*, waveband.

ganascia *sf.* jaw || *mangiare a quattro ganasce*, to eat (*v. irr.*) voraciously.

gancio *sm.* hook.

ganga *sf.* gang.

gànghero *sm.* hinge || *andare fuori dai gangheri*, to lose (*v. irr.*) one's temper.

ganglio *sm.* ganglion (*pl.* -ia).

gangsterismo *sm.* gangsterism.

ganimede *sm.* dandy.

gara *sf.* competition.

garagista *sm.* garage keeper.

garante *sm.* 1. warranter 2. (*per un imputato*) bail || *essere —*, to answer for.

garantire *vt.* 1. to warrant 2. (*farsi garante per*) to answer for 3. (*un imputato*) to go (*v. irr.*) bail for.

garanzìa *sf.* 1. warranty, guarantee 2. (*somma di —*) security 3. (*cauzione*) bail || *dare, non dare —*, to be reliable, unreliable; *a — di*, as a guarantee for.

garbare *vi.* to like.

garbatamente *avv.* politely.

garbatezza *sf.* politeness.

garbato *agg.* polite.

garbo *sm.* politeness || *con bel —*, with a good grace.

garbuglio *sm.* entanglement.

gardenia *sf.* gardenia.

gareggiare *vi.* to compete.

garganella (*nella loc. avv.*) *bere a —*, to gulp down.

gargarismo *sm.* gargle.

gargarizzare *vi.* to gargle.

garibaldino *agg. e sm.* Garibaldian.

garitta *sf.* 1. sentry-box 2. (*torretta*) look-out turret 3. (*di guardiano*) cabin.

garòfano *sm.* carnation || *chiodo di —*, clove.

garrese *sm.* withers (*pl.*).

garretto *sm.* 1. back of heel 2. (*di animale*) hock.

garrire *vi.* 1. (*di bandiere*) to flutter, to flap 2. (*di uccelli*) to chirp.

gàrrulo *agg.* talkative.

garza *sf.* gauze.

garzone *sm.* shop-boy, apprentice.

gas *sm.* gas.

gasolio *sm.* gas oil.

gasometro *sm.* gasholder.

gassare *vt.* to gas.

gassato *agg.* aerated || *acqua gassata*, soda-water.

gassista *sm.* gas-fitter.

gassògeno *sm.* gas producer.

gassoso *agg.* 1. gaseous 2. (*gassato*) aerated.

gàstrico *agg.* gastric.

gastrite *sf.* gastritis.

gastroenterite *sf.* gastroenteritis.

gastronomìa *sf.* gastronomy.

gastronòmico *agg.* gastronomic(al).

gatta *sf.* she-cat.

gattabuia *sf.* jail.

gatto *sm.* cat.

gattopardo *sm.* leopard.

gaudente *agg.* 1. jolly 2. (*dissipato*) fast. ♦ **gaudente** *sm.* fast person.

gàudio *sm.* joy.

gavetta *sf.* mess-tin.

gavitello *sm.* buoy.

gazza *sf.* magpie.

gazzarra *sf.* din.

gazzella *sf.* gazelle.

gazzetta *sf.* gazette.

gelare *vt. e vi.* to freeze (*v. irr.*).

gelata *sf.* frost.

gelataio *sm.* ice-cream vendor.

gelaterìa *sf.* ice-cream shop.

gelatina *sf.* 1. (*cuc.*) jelly 2. (*chim.*) gelatine.

gelatinoso *agg.* gelatinous.

gelato *agg.* frozen, icy. ♦ **gelato** *sm.* ice-cream.

gèlido *agg.* icy (*anche fig.*).

gelo *sm.* 1. intense cold 2. (*fig.*) chill 3. (*ghiaccio*) ice 4. (*brina*) frost.

gelone *sm.* chilblain.

gelosìa *sf.* 1. jealousy 2. (*cura*) care 3. (*persiana*) shutter.

geloso *agg.* jealous.

gelso *sm.* mulberry(-tree).

gelsomino *sm.* jasmine.

gemebondo *agg.* groaning.

gemelli *sm. pl.* (*di polsino*) cuff-links.

gemello *agg. e sm.* twin.

gèmere *vi.* to groan.

gèmito *sm.* groan.

gemma *sf.* 1. gem 2. (*bot.*) bud.

gemmare *vi.* (*bot.*) to bud.

gendarme *sm.* policeman (*pl.* -men).

gendarmerìa *sf.* 1. police-force 2. (*caserma*) police-station.

genealogìa *sf.* genealogy.

genealògico *agg.* genealogical.

generàbile *agg.* generable.

generale[1] *agg.* general || *quartier —*, headquarters (*pl.*).

generale² *sm.* general.

generalità *sf.* generality ‖ dare le proprie —, to give (*v. irr.*) one's particulars.

generalizzare *vt.* to generalize.

generalizzazione *sf.* generalization.

generare *vt.* 1. to beget (*v. irr.*) 2. (*produrre, anche tec.*) to produce. ♦ generarsi *vr.* to be born.

generatore *agg.* generative. ♦ generatore *sm.* generator.

generazione *sf.* generation.

gènere *sm.* 1. kind 2. (*gramm.*) gender 3. (*letterario*) genre 4. (*prodotto*) product ‖ generi alimentari, foodstuffs; generi di prima necessità, commodities.

genèrico *agg.* generic, vague.

gènero *sm.* son-in-law.

generosità *sf.* generosity.

generoso *agg.* generous.

gènesi *sf.* genesis (*pl.* -es).

genètica *sf.* genetics.

genètico *agg.* genetic.

genetliaco *agg.* birthday.

gengiva *sf.* gum.

genìa *sf.* 1. race 2. (*spreg.*) tribe.

geniale *agg.* clever.

genialità *sf.* 1. cleverness 2. (*genio*) genius.

genio *sm.* genius ‖ andare a —, to please.

genitale *agg. e sm.* genital.

genitivo *sm.* genitive.

genitore *sm.* 1. parent 2. (*padre*) father.

genitrice *sf.* mother.

gennaio *sm.* January.

genocidio *sm.* genocide.

gentaglia *sf.* rabble.

gente *sf.* people: c'è molta —, there are a lot of people; le genti dell'Asia, the peoples of Asia.

gentildonna *sf.* lady.

gentile *agg.* 1. kind 2. (*cortese*) polite ‖ è — da parte sua, it is kind of him.

gentilezza *sf.* 1. kindness 2. (*cortesia*) politeness 3. (*favore*) favour.

gentilizio *agg.* noble: stemma —, coat of arms.

gentiluomo *sm.* gentleman (*pl.* -men).

genuflessione *sf.* genuflection.

genuflèttersi *vr.* to kneel down.

genuinità *sf.* genuineness.

genuino *agg.* genuine.

genziana *sf.* gentian.

geodesìa *sf.* geodesy.

geofisica *sf.* geophysics.

geografia *sf.* geography.

geogràfico *agg.* geographic(al) ‖ carta geografica, map.

geògrafo *sm.* geographer.

geologìa *sf.* geology.

geològico *agg.* geologic(al).

geòlogo *sm.* geologist.

geòmetra *sm.* 1. geometer 2. (*agrimensore*) land-surveyor.

geometrìa *sf.* geometry.

geomètrico *agg.* geometric(al).

geopolitica *sf.* geopolitics.

geòrgico *agg.* georgic.

geranio *sm.* geranium.

gerarca *sm.* leader.

gerarchìa *sf.* hierarchy.

gerente *sm.* manager.

gerenza *sf.* management.

gergo *sm.* 1. slang 2. (*di una classe professionale*) jargon.

germànico *agg.* Germanic.

germanio *sm.* germanium.

germanismo *sm.* Germanism.

germanista *s.* Germanist.

germanìstica *sf.* Germanic studies.

germano¹ *agg. e sm.* German.

germano² *agg.* german: fratello —, brother-german.

germe *sm.* germ.

germicida *agg.* germicidal. ♦ germicida *sm.* germicide.

germinare *vi.* V. germogliare.

germinazione *sf.* germination.

germogliare *vi.* 1. to sprout 2. (*fig.*) to spring (*v. irr.*) (up).

germoglio *sm.* germ.

geroglifico *sm.* hieroglyphic.

gerontologìa *sf.* gerontology.

gerundio *sm.* gerund.

gessetto *sm.* chalk.

gesso *sm.* 1. chalk 2. (*med.; scult.; edil.*) plaster.

gesta *sf. pl.* deeds.

gestante *sf.* pregnant woman.

gestazione *sf.* gestation.

gesticolare *vi.* to gesticulate.

gestione *sf.* management.

gestire¹ *vt.* to manage.

gestire² *vi.* to gesture.

gesto *sm.* gesture ‖ un bel —, a noble deed.

gestore *sm.* manager.

gesuita *sm.* Jesuit.

gesuìtico *agg.* Jesuitic(al).

gettare *vt.* 1. to throw (*v. irr.*), (*anche metal.; edil.*) to cast (*v. irr.*) 2. (*bot.*) to sprout 3. (*fruttare*) to yield ‖ — le fondamenta, to lay (v. irr.) the foundations; — un grido, to utter a cry. ♦ **gettarsi** vr. (di fiume) to flow.

gettata sf. 1. throw 2. (edil.; metal.) cast 3. (di arma) range 4. (molo) jetty.

gèttito sm. (delle imposte) yield.

getto sm. 1. throw 2. (mecc.; di liquidi) jet 3. (bot.) sprout 4. (metal.; edil.) casting || di —, effortlessly; a — continuo, continuously.

gettone sm. 1. counter: — telefonico, telephone counter 2. (contromarca) check || macchina a —, slot-machine.

geyser sm. geyser.

gheriglio sm. kernel.

gherminella sf. trick: fare una —, to play a trick (on).

ghermire vt. to clutch.

ghette sf. pl. spats.

ghetto sm. 1. ghetto 2. (insieme degli ebrei) Jewry.

ghiacciaia sf. 1. ice-box 2. (stanza) ice-house.

ghiacciaio sm. glacier.

ghiacciare vi e vt. to freeze (v. irr.).

ghiacciato agg. 1. frozen 2. (molto freddo) icy.

ghiaccio sm. ice.

ghiacciolo sm. icicle.

ghiaia sf. gravel.

ghiaioso agg. gravelly.

ghianda sf. acorn.

ghiàndola sf. gland.

ghibellino agg. e sm. Ghibelline.

ghigliottina sf. guillotine.

ghigliottinare vt. to guillotine.

ghignare vi. to grin.

ghigno sm. grin.

ghingheri (nella loc. avv.) mettersi in —, to dress up.

ghiotto agg. 1. greedy 2. (appetitoso) dainty.

ghiottone sm. glutton.

ghiottoneria sf. 1. gluttony 2. (cibo prelibato) dainty.

ghiribizzo sm. whim.

ghirigoro sm. doodle.

ghirlanda sf. wreath.

ghiro sm. dormouse (pl. dormice) || dormire come un —, to sleep (v. irr.) like a log.

ghisa sf. cast iron.

già avv. 1. already 2. (un tempo) once 3. (certamente) of course.

giacca sf. coat, jacket.

giacché cong. as, since.

giacente agg. 1. lying 2. (di capitale) uninvested 3. (di posta) unclaimed.

giacenza sf. lying || capitale in —, uninvested capital; lettera in —, unclaimed letter; merci in —, goods in stock.

giacere vi. to lie (v. irr.).

giaciglio sm. couch.

giacimento sm. (min.) deposit: — di petrolio, oil-field.

giacinto sm. hyacinth.

giacobino sm. e agg. Jacobin.

giada sf. jade.

giaggiolo sm. iris.

giaguaro sm. jaguar.

giallastro agg. yellowish.

giallo agg. yellow || romanzo, film, dramma —, thriller.

giammai avv. never.

giansenismo sm. Jansenism.

giansenista s. Jansenist.

giapponese agg. e sm. Japanese (invariato al pl.).

giara sf. jar.

giardinaggio sm. gardening.

giardinetta sf. station wagon.

giardiniere sm. gardener.

giardino sm. garden || — d'infanzia, nursery-school.

giarrettiera sf. garter.

giavellotto sm. javelin: lancio del —, javelin throwing.

gibbosità sf. hump.

giberna sf. cartridge-pouch.

gigante sm. giant || fare passi da —, to make (v. irr.) rapid progress.

gigantesco agg. gigantic.

gigantismo sm. giantism.

gigione sm. ham.

giglio sm. lily.

gilè sm. waistcoat.

gincana sf. gymkhana.

gineceo sm. gynaeceum (pl. -ea).

ginecologia sf. gynaecology.

ginecològico agg. gynaecological.

ginecòlogo sm. gynaecologist.

ginepraio sm. 1. juniper thicket 2. (fig.) fix: ficcarsi in un —, to get (v. irr.) into a scrape.

ginepro sm. juniper.

ginestra sf. broom.

gingillarsi vr. to dawdle.

gingillo sm. 1. knick-knack 2. (balocco) plaything.

ginnasio sm. 1. grammar school 2.

(in Italia e stor.) gymnasium *(pl. -ia).*

ginnasta *sm.* athlete.

ginnàstica *sf.* gymnastics.

ginnico *agg.* gymnastic, athletic.

ginocchiata *sf.* blow with the knee.

ginocchiera *sf.* 1. knee-guard 2. *(mecc.)* toggle.

ginocchio *sm.* 1. knee: *in —,* on one's knees 2. *(mecc.)* bend.

ginocchioni *avv.* on one's knees.

giocare *vi.* 1. to play 2. *(d'azzardo)* to gamble 3. *(scommettere)* to bet *(v. irr.)* 4. *(in borsa)* to speculate. ♦ **giocare** *vt.* 1. to play 2. *(ingannare)* to deceive. ♦ **giocarsi** *vr. (beffarsi)* to trifle (with).

giocata *sf.* 1. game 2. *(puntata)* stake.

giocatore *sm.* 1. player 2. *(d'azzardo)* gambler 3. *(in borsa)* stock-jobber.

giocàttolo *sm.* toy.

giocherellare *vi.* to toy.

gioco *sm.* 1. play 2. *(regolato da norme)* game 3. *(d'azzardo)* gambling 4. *(scherzo)* joke || *per —,* for fun; *— di pazienza,* puzzle; *— di parole,* pun; *essere in —,* to be involved.

giocoforza *sm.* necessary: *è —,* it is absolutely necessary.

giocoliere *sm.* juggler.

giocondità *sf.* gaiety.

giocondo *agg.* gay.

giocosità *sf.* playfulness.

giocoso *agg.* playful.

giogaia *sf.* mountain range.

giogo *sm.* 1. yoke 2. *(di monte)* summit.

gioia *sf.* 1. joy 2. *(gioiello)* jewel.

gioielleria *sf.* 1. jewelry 2. *(negozio)* jeweller's shop.

gioielliere *sm.* jeweller

gioiello *sm.* jewel

gioioso *agg.* joyful.

gioire *vi.* to rejoice (at).

giornalaio *sm.* newsman *(pl. -men).*

giornale *sm.* 1. newspaper 2. *(comm.)* journal || *— radio,* news bulletin; *cine —,* news-reel.

giornaliero *agg.* daily.

giornalismo *sm.* 1. journalism 2. *(la stampa)* press.

giornalista *s.* journalist, reporter.

giornalistico *agg.* journalistic || *ambiente —,* press.

giornalmente *avv.* daily.

giornata *sf.* day: *lavorare a —,* to work by the day || *donna a —,* charwoman *(pl. -women).*

giorno *sm.* day: *di —,* by day; *a giorni,* in a few days' time; *due volte al —,* twice a day; *un — (avv.),* one day || *— festivo,* holiday.

giovamento *sm.* benefit || *trarre — da,* to benefit by.

giòvane *agg.* young. ♦ **giòvane** *sm.* young man *(pl. -men).* ♦ **giòvane** *sf.* young woman *(pl. women).*

giovanetta *sf.* girl.

giovanetto *sm.* boy.

giovanile *agg.* 1. juvenile 2. *(da giovane)* youthful.

giovanotto *sm.* young man *(pl. men).*

giovare *vi.* to be of use. ♦ **giovare** *vt.* to be good (for). ♦ **giovarsi** *vr.* to benefit (by).

giovedì *sm.* Thursday.

giovenca *sf.* heifer.

gioventù *sf.* youth.

gioviale *agg.* jolly.

giovialità *sf.* jollity.

giovinastro *sm.* hooligan.

giovincello *sm.* lad.

giovinezza *sf.* youth.

giràbile *agg.* endorsable.

giradischi *sm.* record player.

giradito *sm.* whitlow.

giraffa *sf.* giraffe.

giramento *sm.* turning: *— di capo,* giddiness; *avere un —,* to feel *(v. irr.)* giddy.

giramondo *sm.* 1. wanderer 2. *(turista)* globe-trotter.

giràndola *sf.* 1. *(fuoco d'artificio)* Catherine-wheel 2. *(fig.)* fickle person.

girandolare *vi.* to saunter.

girandolone *sm.* saunterer.

girante *sm.* 1. *(comm.)* endorser 2. *(mecc.)* impeller *(di pompa),* wheel *(di turbina).*

girare *vi. e vt.* 1. to turn 2. *(evitare)* to avoid 3. *(viaggiare)* to tour 4. *(vagare)* to stroll 5. *(comm.)* to endorse 6. *(riprendere un film)* to shoot *(v. irr.).* ♦ **girarsi** *vr.* to turn.

girarrosto *sm.* spit.

girasole *sm.* sunflower.

girata *sf.* 1. turn 2. *(comm.)* endorsement.

giratario *sm. (comm.)* endorsee.

giravolta *sf.* 1. turning 2. (*fig.*) shift || *fare una —*, to turn round.

girello *sm.* 1. (*per bambini*) go-cart 2. (*parte di bue*) rump.

giretto *sm.* stroll: *fare un —*, to take (*v. irr.*) a short walk.

girévole *agg.* revolving.

girino *sm.* tadpole.

giro *sm.* 1. turn 2. (*viaggio*) tour 3. (*passeggiata*) stroll 4. (*percorso*) round || *a — di posta*, by return of post; *d'affari*, turnover; *nel — di pochi giorni*, in a few days' time; *fare un — in auto*, to go (*v. irr.*) for a drive in a car; *fare un — in bicicletta*, to take (*v. irr.*) a ride on a bicycle.

girondino *agg.* e *sm.* Girondist.

gironzolare *vi.* to stroll.

giroscopio *sm.* gyroscope.

girotondo *sm.* round dance.

girovagare *vi.* to wander.

giròvago *agg.* wandering. ♦ **giròvago** *sm.* tramp || *venditore —*, pedlar.

gita *sf.* trip: *fare una —*, to take (*v. irr.*) a trip.

gitano *sm.* Spanish gipsy.

gitante *s.* tripper.

giù *avv.* 1. down 2. (*dabbasso*) downstairs || *— per*, down; *su per —*, approximately.

giubba *sf.* coat.

giubbetto *sm.* 1. jacket 2. (*da donna*) bodice.

giubbotto *sm.* (heavy) coat.

giubileo *vi.* to exult.

giubileo *sm.* jubilee.

giùbilo *sm.* rejoicing.

giudàico *agg.* Judaic.

giudaismo *sm.* Judaism.

giudeo *agg.* Jewish. ♦ **giudeo** *sm.* Jew. ♦ **giudea** *sf.* Jewess.

giudicare *vt.* 1. to judge 2. (*pensare*) to think (*v. irr.*).

giùdice *sm.* judge || *i giudici*, the Bench.

giudiziario *agg.* judicial.

giudizio *sm.* 1. judgement 2. (*causa*) trial 3. (*sentenza*) sentence 4. (*buon*) *senso*) common sense || *far —*, to behave oneself; *rinviare a —*, to commit for trial.

giudizioso *agg.* sensible.

giùggiola *sf.* jujube || *andare in brodo di giuggiole*, to be extremely pleased.

giuggiolone *sm.* simpleton.

giugno *sm.* June.

giugulare *agg.* jugular.

giuliano *agg.* Julian.

giulivo *agg.* cheerful.

giullare *sm.* jester.

giumenta *sf.* (*cavalla*) mare.

giunca *sf.* junk.

giunco *sm.* reed.

giùngere *vi.* 1. to arrive (at), to reach (sthg.) 2. (*riuscire*) to succeed (in). ♦ **giùngere** *vt.* (*congiungere*) to join.

giungla *sf.* jungle.

giunta¹ *sf.* 1. addition: *per —*, in addition 2. (*di peso*) make-weight.

giunta² *sf.* *— comunale*, town council.

giunto *sm.* (*mecc.*) joint.

giuntura *sf.* juncture.

giunzione *sf.* 1. connection 2. (*giunto*) joint || *fare una —*, to joint.

giuramento *sm.* oath: *sotto —*, on oath.

giurare *vt.* to swear (*v. irr.*).

giurato *sm.* juryman (*pl.* -men) || *i giurati*, the jury (*sing.*).

giurìa *sf.* jury.

giurìdico *agg.* juridical: *stato —*, legal status.

giurisdizione *sf.* jurisdiction.

giurisprudenza *sf.* law.

giurista *sm.* jurist.

giustezza *sf.* 1. exactness 2. (*tip.*) measure.

giustificàbile *agg.* justifiable.

giustificare *vt.* to justify.

giustificazione *sf.* justification.

giustizia *sf.* justice.

giustiziare *vt.* to execute.

giustiziato *sm.* executed man.

giustiziere *sm.* 1. executioner 2. (*vendicatore*) avenger.

giusto *agg.* 1. just 2. (*esatto*) right 3. (*legittimo*) legitimate.

glabro *agg.* hairless.

glaciale *agg.* icy: *regione —*, ice region.

glaciazione *sf.* glaciation.

gladiatore *sm.* gladiator.

gladìolo *sm.* gladiolus.

glande *sm.* glans (*pl.* -ndes).

glàndola *sf.* V. *ghiandola.*

glandolare *agg.* glandular.

glassare *vt.* 1. (*con zucchero*) to ice 2. (*con gelatina*) to glaze.

glàuco *agg.* glaucous.

glaucoma *sm.* glaucoma.

gleba *sf.* clod || *servo della —*, serf.

gli¹ *art.* **1.** the **2.** (*in senso generico non si traduce*): — *stranieri amano l'Italia*, foreigners love Italy **3.** (*si traduce col possessivo coi capi di vestiario ecc.*): *si tolse — occhiali*, he took off his glasses.

gli² *pron.* **1.** (*per persona*) him, to him **2.** (*per cosa*) it, to it || — *mandai un libro*, I sent him a book, I sent a book to him.

glicerina *sf.* glycerine.

glicine *sm.* wistaria.

glicògeno *sm.* glycogen.

glielo *pron.* it (to) him; it (to) her; him to him; him to her; it to it.

globale *agg.* total.

globo *sm.* globe.

globulare *agg.* globular.

glòbulo *sm.* (*biol.*) corpuscle.

gloria *sf.* glory.

gloriarsi *vr.* to glory (in).

glorificare *vt.* to glorify.

glorificazione *sf.* glorification.

glorioso *agg.* glorious.

glossa *sf.* gloss.

glossario *sm.* glossary.

glòttide *sf.* glottis.

glottologia *sf.* glottology.

glottològico *agg.* glottological.

glottòlogo *sm.* glottologist.

glucosio *sm.* glucose.

glùteo *sm.* gluteus (*pl.* -ei).

glutinato *agg.* gluten (*attr.*).

glùtine *sm.* gluten.

gnomo *sm.* gnome.

gnosticismo *sm.* gnosticism.

gnòstico *agg. e sm.* gnostic.

gobba *sf.* **1.** hump (*anche fig.*) **2.** (*donna —*) humpbacked woman.

gobbo *agg.* **1.** humpbacked **2.** (*curvo*) bent. ♦ **gobbo** *sm.* humpback.

goccia *sf.* goccia *sm.* drop.

gocciolare *vi. e vt.* to drip.

gocciolìo *sm.* dripping.

godere *vi. e vt.* to enjoy || *godersela*, to have a good time.

godereccio *agg.* **1.** (*amante dei godimenti*) pleasure-loving **2.** (*che dà godimento*) pleasant.

godimento *sm.* enjoyment.

goffàggine *sf.* **1.** clumsiness **2.** (*atto goffo*) clumsy action.

goffo *agg.* clumsy.

gogna *sf.* pillory: *mettere alla —*, to pillory.

gola *sf.* **1.** throat: *aver mal di —*, to have a sorethroat **2.** (*golosità*) gluttony: *far —*, to tempt **3.** (*geogr.*) gorge.

goletta *sf.* (*mar.*) schooner.

golf *sm.* **1.** jersey **2.** (*gioco*) golf.

golfo *sm.* gulf.

goliàrdico *agg.* of students.

goliardo *sm.* university student.

golosità *sf.* **1.** greediness **2.** (*cibo prelibato*) dainty.

goloso *agg.* greedy. ♦ **goloso** *sm.* glutton.

gòmena *sf.* rope.

gomitata *sf.* nudge || *farsi avanti a gomitate*, to elbow one's way.

gòmito *sm.* **1.** elbow **2.** (*di strada*) sharp bend || — *a —*, side by side.

gomitolo *sm.* clew.

gomma *sf.* **1.** rubber **2.** (*sostanza resinosa*) gum **3.** (*pneumatico*) tyre.

gommapiuma *sf.* foam rubber.

gòndola *sf.* gondola.

gonfalone *sm.* standard.

gonfiare *vt.* **1.** to swell (*v. irr.*) **2.** (*esagerare*) to exaggerate. ♦ **gonfiarsi** *vr.* to swell (*anche fig.*).

gonfiatura *sf.* **1.** swelling **2.** (*esagerazione*) exaggeration.

gonfio *agg.* **1.** swollen **2.** (*di stile*) bombastic.

gonfiore *sm.* swelling.

gong *sm.* gong.

gongolante *agg.* rejoicing (at).

gongolare *vi.* to rejoice (at).

goniòmetro *sm.* goniometer.

gonna *sf.* **1.** skirt **2.** (*di costume storico anche maschile*) gown.

gonnellino *sm.* — *scozzese*, kilt.

gonzo *sm.* blockhead.

gorgheggiare *vi.* to trill.

gorgheggio *sm.* trill.

gorgo *sm.* whirlpool.

gorgogliare *vi.* to gurgle.

gorgoglìo *sm.* gurgling.

gorilla *sm.* gorilla.

gota *sf.* cheek.

gòtico *agg.* Gothic.

gotta *sf.* gout.

governàbile *agg.* governable.

governante *sm.* **1.** ruler **2.** (*statista*) statesman (*pl.* -men). ♦ **governante** *sf.* **1.** housekeeper **2.** (*bambinaia*) nurse.

governare *vt.* **1.** to govern, to rule **2.** (*badare a*) to look after **3.** (*mar.*) to steer.

governativo *agg.* government (*attributivo*).

governatore *sm.* governor.

governo *sm.* **1.** government **2.** (*dominio*) rule **3.** (*comm.*) management **4.** (*mar.*) steerage || — *della* *casa*, housekeeping.

gozzo *sm.* 1. goitre 2. (*di uccello*) crop.

gozzoviglia *sf.* revelry.

gozzovigliare *vi.* to revel.

gozzuto *agg.* goitrous.

gracchiare *vi.* to croak.

gracidare *vi.* to croak.

gracidìo *sm.* croaking.

gràcile *agg.* frail.

gracilità *sf.* frailty.

gradassata *sf.* boastfulness, brag.

gradasso *sm.* boaster, braggart.

gradatamente *avv.* gradually.

gradazione *sf.* 1. gradation 2. (*sfumatura*) shade.

gradévole *agg.* agreeable.

gradimento *sm.* 1. pleasure 2. satisfaction 3. (*approvazione*) approval.

gradinata *sf.* 1. flight of steps 2. (*negli stadi*) tiers of seats.

gradino *sm.* 1. step 2. (*di stadio*) stage.

gradire *vt.* 1. to like 2. (*accettare*) to accept.

gradito *agg.* 1. (*piacevole*) pleasant 2. (*ben accetto*) welcome.

grado *sm.* 1. degree 2. (*mil.*) rank || *essere in* —, to be able; *di buon* —, willingly.

graduale *agg.* gradual.

gradualità *sf.* graduality.

graduare *vt.* to graduate.

graduato *agg.* 1. graded 2. (*di strumento*) graduated. ♦ **graduato** *sm.* non-commissioned officer.

graduatoria *sf.* 1. classification 2. (*sport*) position.

graduazione *sf.* graduation.

graffa *sf.* clip.

graffiare *vt.* to scratch.

graffiatura *sf.* scratch.

graffio *sm.* scratch.

graffito *sm.* graffito (*pl.* -ti).

grafia *sf.* 1. writing 2. (*ortografia*) spelling.

gràfico *agg.* graphic. ♦ **gràfico** *sm.* graph.

grafite *sf.* graphite.

grafologia *sf.* graphology.

grafòlogo *sm.* graphologist.

grafòmane *s.* graphomaniac.

grafomania *sf.* graphomania.

gragnuola *sf.* 1. hail 2. (*fig.*) shower.

gramaglie *sf. pl.* mourning (*sing.*): *mettersi in* —, to go (*v. irr.*) into mourning.

gramigna *sf.* couch-grass.

graminàcee *sf. pl.* Gramineae.

grammàtica *sf.* grammar.

grammaticale *agg.* grammatical.

grammàtico *sm.* grammarian.

grammo *sm.* gram.

grammòfono *sm.* gramophone.

gramo *agg.* 1. miserable 2. (*scarso*) scanty.

grana *sf.* 1. grain 2. (*noia*) trouble 3. (*denaro*) dough.

granaglie *sf. pl.* corn (*sing.*).

granaio *sm.* barn.

granata[1] *sf.* (*scopa*) broom.

granata[2] *sf.* (*mil.*) grenade.

granatiere *sm.* grenadier.

granatina *sf.* grenadine.

granato *agg.* 1. garnet red 2. (*fatto a grani*) grainy.

grancassa *sf.* big drum.

granchio *sm.* crab || *prendere un* —, to make (*v. irr.*) a blunder.

grande *agg.* 1. great 2. (*esteso*) large 3. (*grosso*) big 4. (*alto*) high; (*di statura*) tall 5. (*adulto*) grownup.

grandeggiare *vi.* 1. to tower 2. (*ostentare*) to show (*v. irr.*) off.

grandezza *sf.* 1. greatness 2. (*dimensione*) size 3. (*estensione*) largeness 4. (*grandiosità*) grandeur 5. (*liberalità*) liberality 6. (*mat.*) quantity.

grandiloquenza *sf.* magniloquence.

grandinare *vi.* to hail (*anche fig.*).

grandinata *sf.* hail-storm.

gràndine *sf.* hail.

grandiosità *sf.* grandeur.

grandioso *agg.* grand.

granduca *sm.* Grand Duke.

granducato *sm.* Grand Duchy.

granduchessa *sf.* Grand Duchess.

granello *sm.* grain.

granita *sf.* grated-ice drink.

granìtico *agg.* granitic.

granito *sm.* granite.

granìvoro *agg.* granivorous.

grano *sm.* 1. grain 2. (*frumento*) wheat 3. (*ogni cereale*) corn.

granturco *sm.* maize.

granulare *agg.* granular.

granuloma *sm.* granuloma.

granuloso *agg.* granulose.

grappa[1] *sf.* (*per unire blocchi di legno ecc.*) cramp.

grappa[2] *sf.* (*liquore*) "grappa".

gràppolo *sm.* cluster.

grassaggio *sm.* greasing.

grassatore *sm.* robber.

grassazione sf. robbery.

grassetto sm. (tip.) heavytype.

grassezza sf. fatness.

grasso agg. fat. ◆ **grasso** sm. **1.** fat **2.** (lubrificante) grease.

grassoccio agg. plump.

grata sf. grating.

graticciata sf. trellis-work.

graticola sf. **1.** grill **2.** (di forno) grate.

graticolato sm. **1.** trellis **2.** (inferriata) grating.

gratifica sf. bonus.

gratificare vt. to gratify.

gratificazione sf. gratuity.

gratis avv. free.

gratitùdine sf. gratitude.

grato agg. **1.** grateful **2.** (gradito) welcome **3.** (piacevole) pleasant.

grattacapo sm. trouble.

grattacielo sm. skyscraper.

grattare vt. **1.** to scratch **2.** (grattugiare) to grate.

grattugia sf. grater.

grattugiare vt. to grate.

gratùito agg. **1.** free **2.** (ingiustificato) gratuitous.

gravame sm. **1.** burden **2.** (ipoteca) mortgage.

gravare vi. to weigh. ◆ **gravare** vt. to burden.

grave agg. **1.** grave **2.** (pesante) heavy **3.** (importante, pericoloso) serious.

gravezza sf. **1.** (pesantezza) heaviness **2.** (serietà) gravity **3.** (stanchezza) weariness.

gravidanza sf. pregnancy.

gràvido agg. **1.** (di femmina) pregnant **2.** (fig.) fraught (with).

gravità sf. **1.** gravity **2.** (severità) severity.

gravitare vi. to gravitate.

gravitazionale agg. gravitational.

gravitazione sf. gravitation.

gravosità sf. heaviness.

gravoso agg. heavy.

grazia sf. **1.** grace **2.** (favore) favour **3.** (clemenza) mercy **4.** (teol.) grace **5.** Sua, Vostra Grazia, His, Her, Your Grace || in — di, owing to.

graziare vt. to pardon.

grazie inter. thank you!, thanks! — tante, many thanks!

grazioso agg. pretty, graceful.

greca sf. **1.** (disegno) Greek fret **2.** (mil.) zig-zag braid.

grecale sm. north-east wind.

grecismo sm. Hellenism.

grecista s. Hellenist.

greco agg. e sm. Greek.

greco-romano agg. Graeco-Roman.

gregario sm. **1.** follower **2.** (aiutante) helper.

gregge sm. flock.

greggio agg. **1.** raw **2.** (di tessuto) unbleached **3.** (di metallo e fig.) unrefined.

gregoriano agg. Gregorian.

grembiale, grembiule sm. apron.

grembo sm. **1.** lap **2.** (ventre materno) womb **3.** (fig.) bosom.

gremire vt. to fill.

gremito agg. filled (with).

greppia sf. crib.

gres sm. stoneware.

greto sm. **1.** (di fiume) gravel bank **2.** (di mare) shingly shore.

grettezza sf. meanness.

gretto agg. mean, narrow-minded.

greve agg. heavy.

grezzo agg. V. greggio.

gridare vt. e vi. **1.** to cry **2.** (gridare forte, protestare) to cry out: gridò per il dolore, he cried out with pain.

grido sm. cry || di —, famous.

grifagno agg. **1.** rapacious **2.** (fig.) fierce.

grifo sm. snout.

grifone sm. griffin.

grigiastro agg. greyish.

grigio agg. grey: — perla, pearl grey.

grigiore sm. greyness.

griglia sf. **1.** (di finestra) shutter **2.** (di forno) grate **3.** (grata, graticola) grill || cuocere alla —, to grill.

grilletto sm. trigger.

grillo sm. **1.** cricket **2.** (fig.) fancy.

grillotalpa sm. mole-cricket.

grimaldello sm. picklock.

grinfia sf. clutch.

grinta sf. grim face.

grinza sf. **1.** (di pelle) wrinkle **2.** (di stoffa) crease || (fig.) non fa una —, it is quite correct.

grinzoso agg. **1.** (di pelle) wrinkly **2.** (di stoffa) creasy.

grisù sm. fire-damp.

gronda sf. eaves (pl.).

grondaia sf. **1.** gutter **2.** (tubo di discesa) gutter pipe.

grondante agg. dripping.

grondare vi. to drip || — sangue, to bleed (v. irr.).

groppa sf. back.

groppo sm. knot: avere un — in gola, to have a lump in one's throat.

groppone sm. back: piegare il —, to submit.

grossa sf. dormire della —, to sleep (v. irr.) soundly.

grossezza sf. 1. bigness 2. (dimensione) size 3. (spessore) thickness.

grossista s. wholesaler.

grosso agg. 1. (anche fig.) big 2. (denso) thick.

grossolanità sf. coarseness.

grossolano agg. coarse: errore —, blunder.

grotta sf. cave.

grottesco agg. grotesque.

groviera sf. gruyère.

groviglio sm. tangle.

gru sf. (zool.; mecc.) crane.

gruccia sf. 1. crutch 2. (per abiti) dress-hanger 3. (per uccelli) perch.

grufolare vi. to root.

grugnire vi. to grunt.

grugnito sm. grunt.

grugno sm. snout.

grumo sm. clot.

grumoso agg. clotted.

gruppo sm. group.

grùzzolo sm. hoard; (risparmi) savings (pl.).

guadàbile agg. fordable.

guadagnare vt. 1. to gain 2. (col lavoro) to earn.

guadagno sm. 1. earnings (pl.) 2. (comm.) profits (pl.) 3. (fig.) gain.

guadare vt. to ford.

guado sm. ford.

guai inter. woe!

guaìna sf. 1. (bot.; fodero per armi) sheath 2. (custodia, astuccio) case 3. (anat.) theca (pl. -ae).

guaio sm. trouble.

guaire vi. to yelp.

guaito sm. yelp.

gualcire vt. to rumple.

gualdrappa sf. saddle-cloth.

guancia sf. cheek.

guanciale sm. pillow || dormire fra due guanciali, to have no worries.

guantaio sm. glover.

guantiera sf. 1. (scatola per guanti) glove-box 2. (vassoio) tray.

guantificio sm. glove-factory.

guanto sm. glove.

guantone sm. boxing-glove.

guardabarriere sm. gate-keeper.

guardaboschi sm. forester.

guardacaccia sm. gamekeeper.

guardacoste sm. coastguard.

guardalinee sm. (sport) linesman (pl. -men).

guardamano sm. (di scala) hand-rail.

guardapesca sm. fishing warden.

guardaportone sm. doorkeeper.

guardare vt. 1. to look (at) 2. (proteggere) to protect. ♦ **guardare** vi. 1. (tentare) to try 2. (essere orientato) to face. ♦ **guardarsi** vr. (da), to beware (of).

guardaroba sm. 1. wardrobe 2. (in teatro ecc.) cloak-room.

guardarobiera sf. 1. (nei locali pubblici) cloak-room attendant 2. (in alberghi e case private) linen maid.

guardarobiere sm. (nei locali pubblici) cloak-room attendant.

guardasala sm. ticket-collector.

guardasigilli sm. keeper of the seals.

guardavìa sm. guard-rail.

guardia sf. guard || — medica, first-aid station; fare la — a, to guard; mettere in —, to warn.

guardiamarina sm. midshipman (pl. -men).

guardiano sm. 1. keeper 2. (di armenti) herdsman (pl. -men) || — notturno, night watchman (pl. -men).

guardina sf. guard-room.

guardingo agg. wary.

guardiola sf. guard-room.

guarìbile agg. 1. curable 2. (di ferita) healable.

guarigione sf. recovery.

guarire vt. 1. to cure 2. (una ferita) to heal. ♦ **guarire** vi. 1. to recover 2. (di ferita) to heal.

guaritore sm. healer.

guarnigione sf. garrison.

guarnire vt. 1. to trim 2. (cuc.) to garnish 3. (fornire) to furnish 4. (mecc.) to pack.

guarnitura, guarnizione sf. 1. trimming 2. (cuc.) garniture 3. (mecc.) packing.

guasconata sf. gasconade.

guascone agg. e sm. (anche fig.) Gascon.

guastafeste s. kill-joy.

guastamestieri sm. bungler.

guastare vt. 1. to spoil (v. irr.) 2. (danneggiare) to damage.

guastatore sm. 1. destroyer 2. (mil.) sapper.

guasto *agg.* **1.** damaged **2.** (*marcio*) rotten **3.** (*corrotto*) tainted **4.** (*mecc.*) out of order.

guasto *sm.* **1.** damage **2.** (*mecc.*) breakdown || ci deve essere un —, there must be something wrong.

guatare *vt.* to gaze (at).

guazzabuglio *sm.* mess.

guazzare *vi.* **1.** to paddle **2.** (*rotolarsi*) to wallow **3.** (*di liquidi in recipienti*) to splash about.

guazzo *sm.* (*pitt.*) gouache.

guelfo *agg. e sm.* Guelph.

guercio *agg.* squinting. ♦ **guercio** *sm.* squinter.

guerra *sf.* war.

guerrafondaio *sm.* warmonger.

guerreggiante *agg. e sm.* belligerent.

guerreggiare *vi.* to fight (v. irr.), to war.

guerresco *agg.* **1.** war (*attr.*) **2.** (*bellicoso*) warlike.

guerriero *agg.* warlike. ♦ **guerriero** *sm.* warrior.

guerriglia *sf.* guerrilla.

guerrigliero *sm.* **1.** guerrilla **2.** partisan.

gufo *sm.* owl.

guglia *sf.* spire.

gugliata *sf.* needleful.

guida *sf.* **1.** guide **2.** (*auto*) drive || patente di —, driving licence; — telefonica, telephone book.

guidare *vt.* **1.** to guide **2.** (*auto*) to drive (v. irr.).

guidatore *sm.* driver.

guidoslitta *sf.* bobsleigh.

guinzaglio *sm.* leash: mettere al —, to leash.

guisa *sf.* manner || a — di, like.

guitto *sm.* strolling player.

guizzante *agg.* **1.** darting **2.** (*di luce*) flashing **3.** (*di pesci*) wriggling.

guizzare *vi.* **1.** to dart **2.** (*di luce*) to flash **3.** (*di pesci*) to wriggle.

guizzo *sm.* **1.** dart **2.** (*di luce*) flash **3.** (*di pesci*) wriggle.

guscio *sm.* shell.

gustare *vt.* **1.** to enjoy **2.** (*assaggiare*) to taste.

gustativo *agg.* gustative.

gustatore *sm.* taster.

gusto *sm.* **1.** taste **2.** (*gradimento*) liking || di, con —, with relish.

gustoso *agg.* **1.** (*saporito*) tasty **2.** (*piacevole*) pleasant.

guttaperca *sf.* gutta-percha.

gutturale *agg.* guttural.

H

harem *sm.* harem.

hascisc *sm.* hashish.

hawaiano *agg. e sm.* Hawaiian.

hurrà *inter.* hurrah.

i *art.* the.

iarda *sf.* yard.

iato *sm.* hiatus.

iattanza *sf.* boastfulness.

iattura *sf.* misfortune.

iberico *agg. e sm.* Iberian.

ibernazione *sf.* hibernation.

ibisco *sm.* hibiscus.

ibridazione *sf.* hybridization.

ibridismo *sm.* hybridism.

ibrido *agg. e sm.* hybrid.

icona *sf.* icon.

iconoclasta *sm.* iconoclast.

idea *sf.* idea.

ideabile *agg.* imaginable.

ideale *agg. e sm.* ideal.

idealismo *sm.* idealism.

idealista *s.* idealist.

idealistico *agg.* idealistic.

idealizzare *vt.* to idealize.

idealizzazione *sf.* idealization.

ideare *vt.* to conceive, to devise.

ideatore *sm.* inventor, deviser.

ideazione *sf.* ideation.

identico *agg.* identic.

identificabile *agg.* identifiable.

identificare *vt.* to identify.

identificazione *sf.* identification.

identità *sf.* identity.

ideografia *sf.* ideography.

ideogramma *sm.* ideogram.

ideologia *sf.* ideology.

ideologico *agg.* ideologic(al).

ideologismo *sm.* ideology.

ideologo *sm.* ideologist.

idilliaco *agg.* idyllic.

idillio *sm.* idyl.

idioma *sm.* language.

idiomatico *agg.* idiomatic.

idiosincrasia *sf.* idiosyncrasy.

idiota *sm.* idiot. ♦ **idiota** *agg.* idiotic.

idiotismo *sm.* idiom.

idiozia *sf.* idiocy.

idolatra *sm.* idolater.

idolatrare vt. to worship.
idolatria sf. idolatry.
idolo sm. idol.
idoneità sf. fitness.
idòneo agg. fit.
idrante sm. hydrant.
idratare vt. to hydrate.
idrato sm. hydrate.
idràulica sf. hydraulics.
idràulico agg. hydraulic. ♦ **idràulico** sm. plumber.
idrico agg. water.
idrocarburo sm. hydrocarbon.
idrocefalìa sf. hydrocephalus.
idrocèfalo sm. hydrocephalus.
idroelèttrico agg. hydroelectric.
idròfilo agg. absorbent: *cotone* -, cotton wool.
idrofobìa sf. rabies.
idròfobo agg. **1.** rabid **2.** (fig.) furious.
idrògeno sm. hydrogen.
idrografìa sf. hydrography.
idròlisi sf. hydrolysis (pl. -ses).
idrologìa sf. hydrology.
idròpico agg. dropsical.
idropisìa sf. dropsy.
idroscalo sm. seaplane station.
idrostàtica sf. hydrostatics.
idrovolante sm. seaplane.
idròvora sf. water-scooping machine.
iella sf. bad luck.
iena sf. **1.** hyaena **2.** (fig.) vixen.
ieràtico agg. hieratic(al).
ieri avv. yesterday.
iettatore sm. evil-eyed man.
iettatura sf. evil-eye.
igiene sf. **1.** hygiene **2.** (sistema sanitario) sanitation.
igiènico agg. sanitary.
igienista s. hygienist.
ignaro agg. ignorant.
ignavia sf. laziness.
ignavo agg. lazy.
ìgneo agg. igneous.
ignòbile agg. mean.
ignominia sf. ignominy.
ignominioso agg. ignominious.
ignorante agg. e sm. ignorant.
ignoranza sf. ignorance.
ignorare vt. to ignore.
ignoto agg. unknown.
ignudo agg. naked.
igrometrìa sf. hygrometry.
iguana sf. iguana.
il art. the.
ilare agg. cheerful.
ilarità sf. hilarity.

ilìaco agg. iliac.
illanguidire vt. to weaken.
illazione sf. illation.
illécito agg. illicit.
illegale agg. illegal.
illegalità sf. illegality.
illeggìbile agg. illegible.
illegittimità sf. illegitimacy.
illegìttimo agg. illegitimate.
illeso agg. unhurt.
illibatezza sf. purity.
illibato agg. pure.
illiberale agg. illiberal.
illimitato agg. unlimited.
illividire vt. to make (v. irr.) livid. ♦ **illividire** vi. to turn livid.
illogicità sf. illogicality.
illògico agg. illogical.
illùdere vt. to delude. ♦ **illùdersi** vr. to delude oneself.
illuminante agg. illuminating.
illuminare vt. to light up.
illuminazione sf. lighting.
illuminismo sm. Illuminism.
illusione sf. illusion.
illusionismo sm. illusionism.
illusionista s. conjurer.
illuso agg. deluded. ♦ **illuso** sm. day-dreamer.
illusorio agg. illusory.
illustrare vt. to illustrate.
illustrativo agg. illustrative.
illustrato agg. illustrated || *cartolina illustrata*, picture post-card.
illustrazione sf. illustration.
illustre agg. renowned.
imbaccuccare vt. to muffle up.
imbaldanzire vt. to embolden. ♦ **imbaldanzirsi** vr. to grow (v. irr.) bold.
'mballaggio sm. packing.
imballare vt. to pack (up). ♦ **imballarsi** vr. (di motori) to race.
imbalsamare vt. **1.** to embalm **2.** (di animali) to stuff.
imbalsamatore sm. **1.** embalmer **2.** (di animali) stuffer.
imbalsamazione sf. **1.** embalming **2.** (di animali) stuffing.
imbambolato agg. dull.
imbandierare vt. to deck with flags.
imbandire vt. **1.** (la tavola) to lay (v. irr.) **2.** to prepare.
imbarazzante agg. embarrassing.
imbarazzare vt. to embarrass. ♦ **imbarazzarsi** vr. to meddle.
imbarazzato agg. embarrassed.
imbarazzo sm. embarrassment.

imbarcadero sm. landing-stage.
imbarcare vt. to take (v. irr.) on board. ♦ **imbarcarsi** vr. to embark.
imbarcazione sf. boat.
imbarco sm. embarkation.
imbastardire vt. to debase.
imbastardito agg. debased.
imbastire vt. 1. to tack 2. (fig.) to put (v. irr.) together.
imbastitura sf. tacking.
imbàttersi vr. to meet (v. irr.) (with).
imbattìbile agg. invincible.
imbattibilità sf. invincibility.
imbavagliare v. to gag.
imbeccare vt. 1. to feed (v. irr.) 2. (fig.) to prompt.
imbeccata sf. 1. beakful 2. (fig.) prompting.
imbecille agg. e sm. imbecile.
imbecillità sf. imbecility.
imbelle agg. weak.
imbellettare v. to make (v. irr.) up.
imbellire vt. to embellish.
imberbe agg. beardless.
imbestialire vi. to get (v. irr.) furious. ♦ **imbestialirsi** vr. to get furious.
imbévere vt. to imbue with.
imbiancamento sm. whitening.
imbiancare vt. 1. to whiten 2. (i muri) to whitewash.
imbiancatura sf. 1. (di muri) whitewashing 2. (di tessuti) bleaching.
imbianchino sm. house painter.
imbianchire vt. to make (v. irr.) fair. ♦ **imbiondire** vi. to become (v. irr.) fair.
imbizzarrirsi vr. 1. to become (v. irr.) restive (adirarsi) to fire up.
imboccare vt. 1. to feed (v. irr.) 2. (di strada) to enter.
imboccatura sf. 1. mouth 2. (di strumento) mouthpiece.
imbonimento sm. sales talk.
imbonire vt. to allure.
imbonitore sm. charlatan.
imborghesimento sm. getting into middle-class habits.
imborghesire vt. to give (v. irr.) middle-class habits. ♦ **imborghesirsi** vr. to acquire middle-class habits.
imboscare vt. 1. to put (v. irr.) into safe keeping 2. (mil.) to help to evade military service. ♦ **im-**

boscarsi vr. 1. to lie (v. irr.) in ambush 2. (mil.) to evade military service.
imboscata sf. ambush.
imboscato sm. shirker.
imboschimento sm. afforestation.
imboschire vt. to afforest.
imbottigliamento sm. bottling || — stradale, traffic jam.
imbottigliare vt. 1. to bottle 2. (fig.) to block.
imbottire vt. 1. to stuff 2. (di vestiti) to wad 3. (fig.) — la testa, to cram. ♦ **imbottirsi** vr. 1. to fill oneself (with), to stuff oneself (with) 2. (coprirsi) to wrap oneself (into).
imbottita sf. quilt.
imbottito agg. stuffed, filled || panino —, sandwich.
imbottitura sf. 1. stuffing 2. (di vestiti) wadding.
imbracciare vt. 1. to put (v. irr.) sthg. on one's hands 2. (di fucile) to bring (v. irr.) to firing position.
imbrancare vt. to herd.
imbrattacarte sm. scribbler.
imbrattamento sm. soiling.
imbrattare vt. to soil.
imbrattatele sm. dauber.
imbrigliamento sm. bridling.
imbrigliare vt. to bridle.
imbrigliatura sf. bridling.
imbroccare vt. 1. to hit (v. irr.) 2. (fig.) to guess.
imbrogliare vt. 1. to cheat 2. (confondere) to confuse.
imbroglio sm. cheat, swindle.
imbroglione sm. cheat, swindler.
imbronciarsi vr. to pout.
imbronciato agg. sulky.
imbrunire vi. 1. to brown 2. (farsi sera) to get (v. irr.) dark.
imbrunire sm. nightfall.
imbruttire vt. to make (v. irr.) ugly. ♦ **imbruttirsi** vr. to become (v. irr.) ugly.
imbucare vt. to post.
imburrare vt. to butter.
imbuto sm. funnel.
imene sm. hymen.
imeneo sm. wedding.
imenòttero sm. hymenopteron (pl. -ra).
imitare vt. to imitate.
imitativo agg. imitative.
imitatore sm. imitator.
imitazione sf. imitation.

immacolato *agg.* spotless.

immagazzinare *vt.* to store (up).

immaginàbile *agg.* imaginable.

immaginare *vt.* to imagine.

immaginario *agg.* imaginary.

immaginativa *sf.* imagination.

immaginativo *agg.* imaginative.

immaginazione *sf.* imagination.

immàgine *sf.* image.

immalinconire *vt.* to make (*v. irr.*) melancholy. ◆ **immalinconire** *vi.* to grow (*v. irr.*) sad.

immancàbile *agg.* unfailing.

immane *agg.* 1. huge 2. (*fig.*) frightful.

immanente *agg.* immanent.

immanenza *sf.* immanence.

immangiàbile *agg.* uneatable.

immarcescìbile *agg.* incorruptible.

immateriale *agg.* immaterial.

immaterialità *sf.* immateriality.

immatricolare *vt.* to matriculate. ◆ **immatricolarsi** *vr.* to matriculate.

immatricolazione *sf.* matriculation.

immaturità *sf.* immaturity.

immaturo *agg.* 1. (*di frutto*) unripe 2. (*di persona*) immature.

immedesimare *vt.* 1. to unify. ◆ **immedesimarsi** *vr.* to identify oneself (with).

immedesimazione *sf.* unifying.

immediatamente *avv.* at once.

immediatezza *sf.* immediateness.

immediato *agg.* immediate.

immemoràbile *agg.* immemorial.

immèmore *agg.* forgetful.

immensità *sf.* immensity.

immenso *agg.* immense.

immèrgere *vt.* to immerse. ◆ **immèrgersi** *vr.* to immerse oneself.

immeritato *agg.* undeserved.

immeritévole *agg.* undeserving.

immersione *sf.* immersion.

immèttere *vt.* to let (*v. irr.*) in. ◆ **immèttersi** *vr.* to penetrate.

immigrante *agg. e sm.* immigrant.

immigrare *vi.* to immigrate.

immigrato *agg.* immigrated. ◆ **immigrato** *sm.* immigrant.

immigrazione *sf.* immigration.

imminente *agg.* impending.

imminenza *sf.* imminence.

immischiare *vt.* to involve. ◆ **immischiarsi** *vr.* to meddle (with).

immiserimento *sm.* impoverishing.

immiserire *vt.* to impoverish. ◆

immiserirsi *vr.* 1. to become (*v. irr.*) poor 2. (*fig.*) to weaken.

immissario *sm.* affluent.

immissione *sf.* letting in.

immòbile *agg.* immobile || *beni immòbili*, immovables.

immobiliare *agg.* immovable.

immobilismo *sm.* ultra-conservatism.

immobilità *sf.* immobility.

immobilizzare *vt.* 1. to immobilize 2. (*comm.*) to lock up.

immobilizzazione *sf.* 1. immobilization 2. (*comm.*) locking up.

immoderato *agg.* immoderate.

immodestia *sf.* immodesty.

immodesto *agg.* immodest.

immolare *vt.* to immolate.

immondezza *sf.* dirtiness.

immondezzaio *sm.* garbage heap.

immondizia *sf.* 1. filth 2. (*spazzatura*) garbage.

immondo *agg.* dirty.

immorale *agg.* immoral.

immoralità *sf.* immorality.

immortalare *vt.* to immortalize.

immortale *agg.* immortal.

immortalità *sf.* immortality.

immoto *agg.* motionless.

immune *agg.* immune.

immunità *sf.* immunity.

immunizzare *vt.* to immunize.

immunizzazione *sf.* immunization.

immusonirsi *vr.* to sulk.

immusonito *agg.* sulky.

immutàbile *agg.* immutable.

immutabilità *sf.* immutability.

impacchettare *vt.* to package.

impacciare *vt.* to hamper.

impacciato *agg.* 1. embarrassed 2. (*goffo*) awkward.

impaccio *sm.* hindrance.

impacco *sm.* compress.

impadronirsi *vr.* to take (*v. irr.*) possession (of).

impagàbile *agg.* priceless.

impaginare *vt.* to make-up.

impaginatore *sm.* maker-up.

impaginazione *sf.* making-up.

impagliare *vt.* 1. to cover with straw 2. (*di animali*) to stuff with straw.

impagliatore *sm.* 1. chair-mender 2. (*di animali*) stuffer.

impagliatura *sf.* 1. chair-mending 2. (*di animali*) stuffing.

impalare *vt.* to impale.

impalato *agg.* stiff.

impalcatura *sf.* 1. scaffolding 2.

(di corna di cervo) antlers *(pl.)*.

impallidire *vi.* to turn pale.

impallinare *vt.* to shot.

impalmare *vt.* to marry.

impalpàbile *agg.* impalpable.

impalpabilità *sf.* impalpability.

impanare *vt.* 1. *(cuc.)* to bread 2. *(mecc.)* to thread.

impantanare *vt.* to swamp. ◆ **impantanarsi** *vr.* to swamp *(anche fig.)*.

impaperarsi *vr.* to slip up.

impappinarsi *vr.* to stammer.

imparagonàbile *agg.* incomparable.

imparare *vt.* to learn *(v. irr.)*.

impareggiàbile *agg.* unparalleled.

imparentare *vt.* to relate. ◆ **imparentarsi** *vr.* to become *(v. irr.)* related (to).

ìmpari *agg.* unequal.

imparisìllabo *agg. e sm.* imparisyllabic.

imparruccato *agg.* bewigged.

impartire *vt.* to impart.

imparziale *agg.* impartial.

imparzialità *sf.* impartiality.

impassìbile *agg.* impassive, unmoved.

impassibilità *sf.* impassibility.

impastare *vt.* to knead || — *i colori,* to impaste.

impastàto *agg.* 1. kneaded 2. *(fig.)* full.

impastatore *sm.* kneader.

impastatrice *sf.* kneading-machine.

impasto *sm.* 1. dough 2. *(miscuglio)* mixture.

impastoiare *vt.* *(fig.)* to impede.

impatto *sm.* impact.

impaurire *vt.* to frighten. ◆ **impaurirsi** *vr.* to get *(v. irr.)* scared.

impaurito *agg.* afraid: *sguardo* —, fearful look.

impàvido *agg.* fearless.

impaziente *agg.* impatient.

impazientirsi *vr.* to lose *(v. irr.)* one's patience.

impazienza *sf.* impatience.

impazzare *vi.* to be at one's height.

impazzata *(nella loc. avv.)* all'—, madly.

impazzire *vi.* to go *(v. irr.)* mad.

impeccàbile *agg.* faultless.

impeciare *vt.* to pitch.

impedimento *sm.* obstacle.

impedire *vt.* to prevent (from).

impegnare *vt.* 1. *(dare in pegno)* to pawn 2. *(prenotare)* to reserve,

to book. ◆ **impegnarsi** *vr.* to engage (oneself).

impegnativo *agg.* binding || *lavoro* —, exacting job.

impegno *sm.* engagement.

impegolarsi *vr.* *(fig.)* to get *(v. irr.)* involved.

impelagarsi *vr.* to get *(v. irr.)* in trouble.

impellente *agg.* urgent.

impellicciare *vt.* to fur.

impellicciatura *sf.* veneering.

impenetràbile *agg.* impenetrable.

impenetrabilità *sf.* impenetrableness.

impenitente *agg.* impenitent.

impennacchiare *vt.* to plume.

impennarsi *vr.* 1. *(di cavallo)* to rear 2. *(fig.)* to rear up.

impennata *sf.* *(di cavallo)* rearing 2. *(fig.)* bristling.

impensàbile *agg.* unthinkable.

impensato *agg.* unexpected.

impensierire *vt.* to worry.

imperante *agg.* ruling.

imperare *vi.* to rule (over).

imperativo *agg.* imperative.

imperatore *sm.* emperor.

imperatrice *sf.* empress.

impercettìbile *agg.* imperceptible.

impercettibilità *sf.* imperceptibility.

imperdonàbile *agg.* unpardonable.

imperfetto *agg.* 1. *(gramm.)* imperfect 2. *(fig.)* faulty.

imperfezione *sf.* imperfection.

imperiale[1] *agg.* imperial.

imperiale[2] *sm.* imperial.

imperialismo *sm.* imperialism.

imperialista *s.* imperialist.

imperialìstico *agg.* imperialistic.

imperio *sm.* command, authority.

imperioso *agg.* imperious.

imperito *agg.* unskilful.

imperituro *agg.* everlasting.

imperizia *sf.* unskilfulness.

imperlare *vt.* to bead. ◆ **imperlarsi** *vr.* to bead.

impermalirsi *vr.* to resent (sthg.).

impermeàbile *agg.* impermeable. ◆ **impermeàbile** *sm.* raincoat.

impermeabilità *sf.* impermeability.

impermeabilizzare *vt.* to waterproof.

impermeabilizzazione *sf.* waterproofing.

imperniare *vt.* to pivot (upon).

impero *sm.* empire.

imperscrutàbile *agg.* inscrutable.

imperscrutabilità sf. inscrutableness.

impersonale agg. impersonal.

impersonalità sf. impersonality.

impersonare vt. to impersonate. ♦ **impersonarsi** vr. to materialize.

imperterrito agg. undaunted.

impertinente agg. impertinent.

impertinenza sf. impertinence.

imperturbàbile agg. impassive.

imperturbabilità sf. imperturbability.

imperturbato agg. imperturbed.

imperversare vi. to rage.

impervio agg. inaccessible.

ímpeto sm. 1. rush, impetus 2. (impulso) impulse.

impetrare vt. to impetrate.

impettito agg. stiff.

impetuosità sf. impetuosity.

impetuoso agg. impetuous.

impiantare vt. to found.

impiantito sm. 1. (di legno) parquet floor 2. (di piastrelle) tiled floor.

impianto sm. plant, installation.

impiastricciare vt. to daub.

impiastro sm. 1. plaster 2. (fig.) bore.

impiccagione sf. hanging.

impiccare vt. to hang.

impiccato agg. hanged. ♦ **impiccato** sm. hanged man.

impicciare vt. to hinder. ♦ **impicciarsi** vr. to meddle (in).

impiccio sm. hindrance.

impiccolire vt. to make (v. irr.) smaller.

impiegare vt. 1. to employ 2. (spendere) to spend (v. irr.) 3. (comm.) to invest.

impiegatizio agg. white-collar (attributivo).

impiegato agg. employed. ♦ **impiegato** sm. employee, clerk.

impiego sm. 1. employment 2. (uso) use.

impietosire vt. to move to pity. ♦ **impietosirsi** vr. to feel (v. irr.) sorry (for).

impietrire vt. to petrify.

impigliare vt. to entangle.

impigrire vt. to make (v. irr.) lazy.

impinguare vt. to fatten 2. (fig.) to enrich.

impiombare vt. 1. to plumb 2. (otturare) to fill 3. (coprire di piombo) to lead.

impiombatura sf. 1. plumbing 2.

(otturazione) filling 3. (copertura di piombo) leading.

implacàbile agg. implacable.

implacabilità sf. implacability.

implicare vt. to involve.

implìcito agg. implicit.

implorare vt. to implore.

implorazione sf. entreaty.

implume agg. featherless.

impolìtico agg. impolitic.

impollinare vt. to pollinate.

impollinazione sf. pollination.

impoltronire vt. to make (v. irr.) lazy. ♦ **impoltronirsi** vr. to grow (v. irr.) lazy.

impolverare vt. to cover with dust.

impolverato agg. dusty.

impomatare vt. to pomade. ♦ **impomatarsi** vr. to pomade oneself.

imponderàbile agg. imponderable.

imponderabilità sf. imponderability.

imponente agg. imposing.

imponenza sf. grandeur, majesty.

imponìbile agg. taxable.

imponibilità sf. taxability.

impopolare agg. unpopular.

impopolarità sf. unpopularity.

imporporarsi vr. to purple.

imporre vt. to impose: — un nome, to give (v. irr.) a name. ♦ **imporsi** vr. 1. to impose oneself 2. (avere successo) to become (v. irr.) popular.

importante agg. important.

importanza sf. importance.

importare vi. imp. to matter, to care. ♦ **importare** vt. (comm.) to import.

importatore sm. importer.

importazione sf. import.

importo sm. amount.

importunare vt. to importune, to bother.

importunità sf. importunity.

importuno agg. boring. ♦ **importuno** sm. bore.

imposizione sf. imposition.

impossessarsi vr. to take (v. irr.) possession (of).

impossìbile agg. impossible.

impossibilità sf. impossibility.

impossibilitato agg. unable.

imposta sf. 1. tax 2. (edil.) shutter.

impostare vt. 1. to start 2. (di lettera) to post.

impostazione sf. general lines (pl.).

impostore sm. impostor.

impostura *sf.* 1. imposture 2. *(frode)* fraud.
impotente *agg.* powerless. ◆ impotente *agg. e sm. (med.)* impotent.
impotenza *sf.* impotence.
impoverimento *sm.* impoverishment.
impoverire *vt.* to impoverish. ◆ impoverirsi *vr.* to become *(v. irr.)* poor.
impraticàbile *agg.* impracticable: strada —, impassable road.
impraticabilità *sf.* impracticability.
impratichire *vt.* to train. ◆ impratichirsi *vr.* to get *(v. irr.)* trained.
imprecare *vi.* to curse.
imprecazione *sf.* curse.
imprecisàbile *agg.* indeterminable.
imprecisato *agg.* undetermined.
imprecisione *sf.* 1. vagueness 2. *(inesattezza)* inaccuracy.
impreciso *agg.* inaccurate.
impregnare *vt.* to impregnate (with). ◆ impregnarsi *vr.* to become *(v. irr.)* imbued (with).
imprèndere *vt.* to undertake *(v. irr.)*.
imprendìbile *agg.* elusive, invincible.
imprenditore *sm.* 1. entrepreneur 2. *(edil.)* contractor.
impreparato *agg.* unprepared.
impreparazione *sf.* unpreparedness.
impresa *sf.* 1. *(iniziativa)* undertaking 2. *(gesta)* deed 3. *(azienda)* firm, company.
impresario *sm.* 1. contractor 2. *(teat.)* manager.
imprescindìbile *agg.* unavoidable.
imprescrittìbile *agg.* indefeasible.
impressionàbile *agg.* impressionable.
impressionabilità *sf.* impressionability.
impressionante *agg.* frightening.
impressionare *vt.* 1. to impress 2. *(foto)* to expose.
impressione *sf.* impression.
impressionismo *sm.* impressionism.
impressionista *s.* impressionist.
impresso *agg.* imprest.
imprestare *vt.* to lend *(v. irr.)*.
imprevedìbile *agg.* unforeseeable.
impreveduto *agg.* unforeseen.
imprevidente *agg.* improvident.

imprevidenza *sf.* improvidence.
imprevisto *agg.* unexpected. ◆ imprevisto *sm.* unforeseen event.
impreziosire *vt.* to make *(v. irr.)* precious. ◆ impreziosirsi *vr.* to become *(v. irr.)* precious.
imprigionamento *sm.* imprisonment.
imprigionare *vt.* to imprison.
imprimere *vt.* to impress.
improbàbile *agg.* improbable.
improbabilità *sf.* improbability.
improbo *agg.* 1. dishonest 2. *(faticoso)* hard.
improduttività *sf.* unproductiveness.
improduttivo *agg.* unproductive.
impronta *sf.* 1. impression: — del piede, digitale, footprint, fingerprint 2. *(fig.)* mark.
improntare *vt.* 1. to prepare 2. *(fig.)* to mark.
improntitùdine *sf.* impudence.
impronunciàbile *agg.* unpronounceable.
improperio *sm.* insult.
improprietà *sf.* impropriety.
improprio *agg.* improper.
improrogàbile *agg.* undelayable.
improvvisamente *avv.* suddenly.
improvvisare *vt. e vi.* to improvise. ◆ improvvisarsi *vr.* to act.
improvvisata *sf.* surprise.
improvvisatore *sm.* improviser.
improvvisazione *sf.* improvisation.
improvviso *agg.* sudden.
imprudente *agg.* imprudent.
imprudenza *sf.* imprudence.
impudente *agg.* impudent.
impudenza *sf.* impudence.
impudicizia *sf.* immodesty.
impudico *agg.* shameless, immodest.
impugnàbile *agg. (giur.)* impugnable.
impugnabilità *sf. (giur.)* impugnment.
impugnare *vt.* 1. to grasp, to hold 2. *(giur.)* to impugn.
impugnatura *sf.* hilt.
impulsività *sf.* impulsiveness.
impulsivo *agg.* impulsive.
impulso *sm.* impulse.
impunemente *avv.* safely.
impunità *sf.* impunity.
impunito *agg.* unpunished.
impuntare *vi.* to stumbl: (over).

♦ **impuntarsi** *vr.* **1.** to jib **2.** (*ostinarsi*) to stick (*v. irr.*) (to).
impuntura *sf.* stitching.
impurità *sf.* impurity.
impuro *agg.* impure.
imputàbile *agg.* **1.** imputable **2.** (*giur.*) chargeable (with).
imputare *vt.* **1.** to impute **2.** (*giur.*) to charge (with).
imputato *sm.* defendant.
imputazione *sf.* imputation.
imputridimento *sm.* putrefaction.
imputridire *vi.* to rot.
in *prep.* (*stato in luogo*) in, at: *essere — campagna, — città*, to be in the country, in town; *essere — casa, — chiesa*, to be at home, at church **2.** (*moto a luogo*) to: *andò — America*, he went to America **3.** (*moto dentro luogo*) into: *va' nello studio*, go into the study **4.** (*coi mezzi di trasporto*) by: *sono venuto — treno*, I came by train.
inàbile *agg.* **1.** unable **2.** (*non idoneo*) unfit.
inabilità *sf.* **1.** inability **2.** (*inidoneità*) unfitness.
inabilitare *vt.* to disable.
inabilitazione *sf.* disability.
inabissamento *sm.* sinking.
inabissarsi *vr.* to sink (*v. irr.*).
inabitàbile *agg.* uninhabitable.
inabitabilità *sf.* uninhabitableness.
inabitato *agg.* **1.** uninhabited **2.** (*deserto*) deserted.
inaccessìbile *agg.* inaccessible.
inaccessibilità *sf.* inaccessibility.
inaccettàbile *agg.* unacceptable.
inaccettabilità *sf.* unacceptableness.
inacerbire *vt.* to exacerbate. ♦ **inacerbirsi** *vr.* to grow (*v. irr.*) bitter.
inacidire *vt.* to sour. ♦ **inacidirsi** *vr.* to turn sour.
inacidito *agg.* sour.
inadattàbile *agg.* unadaptable.
inadattabilità *sf.* inadaptability.
inadatto *agg.* **1.** unfit (for) **2.** (*sconveniente*) unbecoming.
inadeguato *agg.* inadequate.
inadempìbile *agg.* unfulfillable.
inadempiente *agg.* defaulting.
inadempienza *sf.* non-execution.
inafferràbile *agg.* unseizable.
inalare *vt.* to inhale.
inalatore *sm.* inhaler.
inalazione *sf.* inhalation.

inalberare *vt.* to hoist. ♦ **inalberarsi** *vr.* **1.** to rear up **2.** (*fig.*) to lose (*v. irr.*) one's temper.
inalienàbile *agg.* inalienable.
inalienabilità *sf.* inalienability.
inalteràbile *agg.* inalterable.
inalterabilità *sf.* inalterability.
inalterato *agg.* unaltered.
inalveare *vt.* to canalize.
inamidare *vt.* to starch.
inammissìbile *agg.* inadmissible.
inammissibilità *sf.* inadmissibility.
inamovìbile *agg.* irremovable.
inamovibilità *sf.* irremovability.
inane *agg.* inane.
inanellare *vt.* to curl.
inanimato *agg.* lifeless.
inanità *sf.* inanity.
inappagàbile *agg.* unsatisfiable.
inappagato *agg.* unsatisfied.
inappellàbile *agg.* unappellable.
inappetenza *sf.* inappetence.
inapplicàbile *agg.* inapplicable.
inapprezzàbile *agg.* priceless.
inappuntàbile *agg.* **1.** irreproachable **2.** (*nel vestire*) faultlessly dressed.
inarcamento *sm.* bending, arching.
inarcare *vt.* to bend (*v. irr.*) || — *le sopracciglia*, to raise one's brows. ♦ **inarcarsi** *vr.* to arch.
inargentare *vt.* to silver.
inaridire *vt.* to dry. ♦ **inaridirsi** *vr.* to dry up.
inarticolato *agg.* inarticulate.
inascoltato *agg.* unheard.
inaspettato *agg.* unexpected.
inasprimento *sm.* embitterment.
inasprire *vt.* to embitter. ♦ **inasprirsi** *vr.* to become (*v. irr.*) embittered.
inattaccàbile *agg.* unassailable.
inattendìbile *agg.* unreliable.
inatteso *agg.* unexpected.
inattività *sf.* inactivity.
inattivo *agg.* inactive.
inattuàbile *agg.* impracticable.
inattuale *agg.* outdated.
inaudito *agg.* unheard of.
inaugurale *agg.* inaugural.
inaugurare *vt.* to inaugurate.
inaugurazione *sf.* inauguration.
inavvedutezza *sf.* carelessness.
inavveduto *agg.* careless.
inavvertenza *sf.* inadvertence.
inavvertito *agg.* unperceived.
inazione *sf.* inaction.
incagliare *vt.* to hinder. ♦ **incagliarsi** *vr.* to strand.

incaglio *sm* **1.** stranding **2.** (*fig.*) obstacle.

incalcolàbile *agg.* incalculable.

incallire *vi.* to harden. ◆ **incallirsi** *vr.* to harden.

incallito *agg.* hardened.

incalzante *agg.* **1.** pursuing **2.** (*fig.*) pressing.

incalzare *vt.* **1.** to pursue **2.** (*fig.*) to urge.

incameramento *sm.* confiscation.

incamerare *vt.* to confiscate.

incamminare *vt.* to set (*v. irr.*) going. ◆ **incamminarsi** *vr.* to set out (for).

incanalamento *sm.* canalization.

incanalare *vt.* to canalize.

incancellàbile *agg.* indelible.

incancrenire *vi.* to become (*v. irr.*) gangrenous.

incandescente *agg.* white-hot.

incandescenza *sf.* incandescence.

incantamento *sm.* charm.

incantare *vt.* to charm. ◆ **incantarsi** *vr.* to be charmed.

incantato *agg.* enchanted.

incantatore *agg.* enchanting. ◆ **incantatore** *sm.* enchanter.

incantésimo *sm.* spell.

incantévole *agg.* charming.

incanto[1] *sm.* enchantment.

incanto[2] *sm.* (*comm.*) auction: *vendere all'—*, to sell (*v. irr.*) by auction.

incanutire *vi.* to grow (*v. irr.*) hoary.

incapace *agg.* unable.

incapacità *sf.* incapacity.

incaparbirsi *vr.* to become (*v. irr.*) obstinate.

incappare *vi.* to get (*v. irr.*) into, to stumble.

incappucciare *vt.* to hood. ◆ **incappucciarsi** *vr.* to put (*v. irr.*) on one's hood.

incapricciarsi *vr.* to take (*v. irr.*) a fancy (to).

incapsulare *vt.* to capsule.

incarcerare *vt.* to imprison.

incarcerazione *sf.* imprisonment.

incaricare *vt.* to charge (so. with). ◆ **incaricarsi** *vr.* to charge oneself (with).

incaricato *agg.* charged (with). ◆ **incaricato** *sm.* appointee.

incàrico *sm.* task, duty.

incarnare *vt.* to embody. ◆ **incarnarsi** *vr.* to take (*v. irr.*) body.

incarnato *sm.* complexion.

incarnazione *sf.* incarnation.

incarnire *vi.* to grow (*v. irr.*) into flesh.

incartamento *sm.* dossier.

incartapecorire *vi.* to wrinkle.

incartapecorito *agg.* 'wrinkled with age.

incartare *vt.* to wrap in paper.

incarto *sm.* set of papers.

incartocciare *vt.* to wrap up in a cornet.

incasellare *vt.* to put (*v. irr.*) in squares.

incassamento *sm.* **1.** boxing **2.** (*mecc.; arch.*) embedding.

incassare *vt.* **1.** to box **2.** (*riscuotere*) to cash.

incassatura *sf.* hollow.

incasso *sm.* **1.** collection **2.** (*di spettacoli*) receipts (*pl.*).

incastellamento *sm.* **1.** fortifications (*pl.*) **2.** (*arch.*) scaffolding.

incastellare *vt.* to fortify with battlements.

incastellatura *sf.* **1.** frame **2.** (*arch.*) scaffolding.

incastonare *vt.* to set (*v. irr.*).

incastonatura *sf.* setting.

incastrare *vt.* **1.** to embed **2.** (*adattare*) to fit in. ◆ **incastrarsi** *vr.* **1.** to fit **2.** (*impigliarsi*) to get (*v. irr.*) stuck.

incastro *sm.* joint.

incatenamento *sm.* chaining.

incatenare *vt.* to chain. ◆ **incatenarsi** *vr.* to be linked (with).

incatramare *vt.* to tar.

incattivire *vt.* to exasperate. ◆ **incattivirsi** *vr.* to get (*v. irr.*) crossed.

incàuto *agg.* rash.

incavare *vt.* to hollow out.

incavatura *sf.* hollowness.

incavo *sm.* hollow.

incèdere *vi.* to advance.

incendiare *vt.* to set (*v. irr.*) on fire.

incendiario *agg. e sm.* incendiary.

incendio *sm.* fire.

incenerire *vt.* to reduce to ashes.

incensamento *sm.* **1.** incensation **2.** (*fig.*) flattery.

incensare *vt.* **1.** to incense **2.** (*fig.*) to flatter.

incenso *sm.* incense.

incensuràbile *agg.* irreproachable.

incensurato *agg.* blameless: *essere —*, to be a first-offender.

incentivo *sm.* incentive.

inceppamento sm. 1. obstacle 2. (mecc.) jam.

inceppare vt. 1. to clog 2. (ostacolare) to encumber. ♦ **incepparsi** vr. to jam.

incerare vt. to wax.

incertezza sf. uncertainty, doubt.

incerto agg. uncertain. ♦ **incerto** sm. uncertainty.

incespicare vi. to stumble.

incessante agg. unceasing.

incesto sm. incest.

incestuoso agg. incestuous.

incetta sf. cornering: fare — di, to make (v. irr.) a corner in.

incettare vt. to corner.

incettatore sm. cornerer.

inchiesta sf. inquiry, investigation.

inchinare vt. to bow. ♦ **inchinarsi** vr. to bow (down).

inchino sm. bow.

inchiodare vt. to nail.

inchiodatura sf. nailing.

inchiostro sm. ink.

inciampare vi. to stumble.

inciampo sm. obstacle.

incidentale agg. 1. incidental 2. (gramm.) parenthetic.

incidente sm. incident. ♦ **incidente** sm. accident.

incidenza sf. incidence.

incidere[1] vt. 1. to cut (v. irr.) 2. (intagliare) to engrave 3. (su disco, nastro ecc.) to record.

incidere[2] vi. to weigh heavily: — sul bilancio, to weigh heavily on one's budget.

incinta agg. f. pregnant.

incipiente agg. incipient.

incipriare vt. to powder. ♦ **incipriarsi** vr. to powder (oneself).

incirca (nella loc. avv.) all'—, about.

incisione sf. 1. cut 2. (arte) engraving 3. (su disco, nastro ecc.) recording.

incisività sf. sharpness.

incisivo agg. incisive. ♦ **incisivo** sm. (anat.) incisor.

inciso sm. parenthetic clause: per —, incidentally.

incisore sm. engraver.

incitamento sm. urge.

incitare vt. to urge, to stimulate.

incitrullire vi. to become (v. irr.) silly.

incivile agg. 1. uncivilized 2. (scortese) rude.

incivilimento sm. civilization.

incivilire vt. to civilize. ♦ **incivilirsi** vr. to become (v. irr.) civilized.

inciviltà sf. 1. barbarism 2. (fig.) rudeness.

inclassificabile agg. unclassifiable.

inclemente agg. 1. inclement: tempo —, inclement weather 2. (spietato) merciless.

inclemenza sf. 1. (di tempo) inclemency 2. (crudeltà) mercilessness.

inclinare vt. to incline, to bend (v. irr.).

inclinato agg. inclined (anche fig.).

inclinazione sf. 1. inclination 2. (attitudine) bent.

incline agg. disposed.

inclito agg. famous.

includere vt. to include.

inclusione sf. inclusion.

inclusivo agg. inclusive.

incluso agg. 1. included 2. (accluso) enclosed.

incoccare vt. to nock.

incoercibile agg. irrepressible.

incoercibilità sf. irrepressibleness.

incoerente agg. incoherent.

incoerenza sf. incoherence.

incognita sf. 1. (mat.) unknown quantity 2. (fig.) uncertainty.

incognito agg. unknown. ♦ **incognito** sm. incognito (pl. -tos).

incollamento sm. pasting.

incollare vt. to stick (v. irr.). ♦ **incollarsi** vr. to stick.

incollatrice sf. sizing-machine.

incollatura[1] sf. sticking.

incollatura[2] sf. (ippica) neck.

incollerire vi. to get (v. irr.) angry. ♦ **incollerirsi** vr. to get angry.

incollerito agg. angry.

incolonnamento sm. column formation.

incolonnare vt. to form into columns. ♦ **incolonnarsi** vr. to rank.

incolore agg. colourless.

incolpabile agg. accusable.

incolpare vt. to charge (with), to accuse (of). ♦ **incolparsi** vr. to accuse oneself.

incolpévole agg. blameless.

incolto agg. uncultivated.

incolume agg. unhurt.

incolumità sf. safety.

incombente agg. impending.

incombenza sf. errand, task.

incombere vi. 1. (spettare) to be

one's job **2.** (*sovrastare*) to impend (over).

incombustìbile *agg.* incombustible.

incominciare *vt. e vi.* V. *cominciare.*

incommensuràbile *agg.* incommensurable.

incommensurabilità *sf.* incommensurability.

incommerciàbile *agg.* not negotiable.

incommutàbile *agg.* incommutable.

incomodare *vt.* to annoy. ◆ **incomodarsi** *vr.* to trouble.

incomodità *sf.* uncomfortableness.

incòmodo *agg.* uncomfortable ‖ *essere d' —*, to be in the way.

incomparàbile *agg.* incomparable.

incompatìbile *agg.* incompatible.

incompatibilità *sf.* incompatibility.

incompetente *agg.* incompetent.

incompetenza *sf.* incompetence.

incompiuto *agg.* unfinished.

incompletezza *sf.* incompleteness.

incompleto *agg.* incomplete.

incompostezza *sf.* disorder.

incomposto *agg.* disorderly.

incomprensìbile *agg.* incomprehensible.

incomprensibilità *sf.* incomprehensibility.

incomprensione *sf.* incomprehension.

incompreso *agg.* **1.** not understood **2.** (*non apprezzato*) unappreciated.

incomputàbile *agg.* incalculable.

incomunicàbile *agg.* incommunicable.

incomunicabilità *sf.* incommunicability.

inconcepìbile *agg.* inconceivable.

inconciliàbile *agg.* irreconcilable.

inconciliabilità *sf.* irreconcilability.

inconcludente *agg.* **1.** inconclusive **2.** (*di persona*) good-for-nothing.

inconcusso *agg.* unshaken.

incondizionato *agg.* unconditional.

inconfessàbile *agg.* unavowable.

inconfessato *agg.* unconfessed.

inconfondìbile *agg.* unmistakable.

inconfutàbile *agg.* irrefutable.

incongruente *agg.* incongruous.

incongruenza *sf.* incongruity.

incòngruo *agg.* incongruous.

inconsapévole *agg.* unconscious, unaware.

inconsapevolezza *sf.* unconsciousness, unawareness.

inconscio *agg. e sm.* unconscious.

inconseguente *agg.* inconsequent.

inconseguenza *sf.* inconsequence.

inconsideratezza *sf.* rashness.

inconsiderato *agg.* rash.

inconsistente *agg.* insubstantial.

inconsistenza *sf.* insubstantiality.

inconsolàbile *agg.* inconsolable.

inconsueto *agg.* unusual.

inconsulto *agg.* unadvised, rash.

incontaminato *agg.* unpolluted.

incontentàbile *agg.* insatiable.

incontentabilità *sf.* insatiability.

incontestàbile *agg.* incontestable.

incontinente *agg.* incontinent.

incontinenza *sf.* incontinence.

incontrare *vt.* to meet (*v. irr.*). ◆ **incontrarsi** *vr.* to meet ‖ *i nostri gusti non si incontrano*, our tastes do not agree.

incontrastàbile *agg.* incontestable.

incontrastato *agg.* uncontested.

incontro[1] *sm.* **1.** meeting **2.** (*sport*) match.

incontro[2] *prep. — a*, towards, to.

incontrollàbile *agg.* uncontrollable.

incontrollato *agg.* uncontrolled.

incontrovertìbile *agg.* indisputable.

inconveniente *sm.* inconvenience, drawback.

inconvertìbile *agg.* inconvertible.

inconvertibilità *sf.* inconvertibility.

incoraggiamento *sm.* encouragement.

incoraggiante *agg.* encouraging.

incoraggiare *vt.* to encourage.

incorniciare *vt.* to frame.

incorniciatura *sf.* framing.

incoronamento *sm.* V. *coronamento.*

incoronare *vt.* V. *coronare.*

incoronazione *sf.* coronation.

incorporare *vt.* to incorporate.

incorporazione *sf.* incorporation.

incorpòreo *agg.* incorporeal.

incorreggìbile *agg.* incorrigible.

incòrrere *vi.* to incur, to suffer (sthg.).

incorretto *agg.* incorrect.

incorrotto *agg.* incorrupt.

incorruttìbile *agg.* incorruptible.

incorruttibilità *sf.* incorruptibility.

incosciente *agg.* **1.** unconscious **2.** (*irresponsabile*) reckless. ◆ **incosciente** *sm.* irresponsible.

incoscienza *sf.* **1.** unconsciousness **2.** (*spericolatezza*) rashness.

incostante agg. inconstant: *tempo —*, changeable weather.

incostituzionale agg. unconstitutional.

incostituzionalità sf. unconstitutionality.

incredibile agg. incredible.

incredibilità sf. incredibility.

incredulità sf. incredulity.

incrèdulo agg. incredulous.

incrementare vt. to increase.

incremento sm. increase.

increscioso agg. unpleasant.

increspamento sm. **1.** (*di acque*) rippling **2.** (*di capelli*) ruffling.

increspare v., **incresparsi** vr. **1.** (*di acque*) to ripple **2.** (*di capelli*) to ruffle.

incretinire vt. to make (*v. irr.*) stupid. ♦ **incretinirsi** vr. to dull.

incriminàbile agg. impeachable.

incriminare vt. to impeach.

incriminazione sf. **1.** (*l'accusare*) crimination **2.** (*atto d'accusa*) indictment.

incrinare vt. to crack. ♦ **incrinarsi** vr. to crack.

incrinatura sf. crack.

incriticàbile agg. uncensurable.

incrociare vt. to cross. ♦ **incrociarsi** vr. to cross.

incrociatore sm. cruiser.

incrocio sm. **1.** crossing || *— stradale*, cross-road **2.** (*di razze*) crossbreed.

incrollàbile agg. unshakable.

incrostare vt. to incrust. ♦ **incrostarsi** vr. to become (*v. irr.*) incrusted.

incrostazione sf. incrustation.

incrudelimento sm. toughening.

incrudelire vi. to become (*v. irr.*) cruel || *— contro* qu., to be pitiless towards so.

incrudire vi. to grow (*v. irr.*) worse.

incruento agg. bloodless.

incubatrice sf. incubator.

incubazione sf. incubation.

incubo sm. nightmare.

incùdine sf. anvil.

inculcare vt. to inculcate.

incunàbolo sm. incunabulum.

incuneare vt. to wedge. ♦ **incunearsi** vr. to wedge oneself.

incupire vt. e vi. to darken. ♦ **incupirsi** vr. to become (*v. irr.*) gloomy.

incuràbile agg. e sm. incurable.

incurabilità sf. incurability.

incurante agg. careless, heedless.

incuria sf. heedlessness.

incuriosire vt. to make (*v. irr.*) curious. ♦ **incuriosirsi** vr. to become (*v. irr.*) curious.

incuriosito agg. made curious.

incursione sf. raid.

incurvare vt. e **incurvarsi** vr. to bend (*v. irr.*), to curve.

incurvatura sf. bend.

incustodito agg. unguarded.

incùtere vt. to rouse.

indaco sm. indigo.

indaffarato agg. busy.

indagare vt. to investigate.

indagatore agg. investigating.

indàgine sf. **1.** research, investigation **2.** (*giur.*) inquiry.

indebitare vt. to involve in debt. ♦ **indebitarsi** vr. to run (*v. irr.*) into debt.

indébito agg. undue.

indebolimento sm. weakening.

indebolire vt. to weaken. ♦ **indebolirsi** vr. to weaken.

indecente agg. indecent.

indecenza sf. indecency.

indecifràbile agg. **1.** indecipherable **2.** (*di calligrafia*) illegible.

indecisione sf. indecision.

indeciso agg. **1.** irresolute **2.** (*di cose*) undecided.

indeclinàbile agg. **1.** indeclinable **2.** (*che non si può eludere*) unavoidable.

indecoroso agg. unseemly.

indefesso agg. indefatigable.

indefinìbile agg. indefinable.

indefinito agg. indefinite.

indeformàbile agg. indeformable.

indegno agg. **1.** unworthy **2.** (*spregevole*) disgraceful.

indelèbile agg. indelible.

indelicatezza sf. indelicacy.

indelicato agg. tactless.

indemoniato agg. **1.** possessed **2.** (*fig.*) frantic. ♦ **indemoniato** sm. demoniac.

indenne agg. undamaged.

indennità sf. allowance.

indennizzare vt. to indemnify.

indennizzo sm. indemnity.

inderogàbile agg. intransgressible.

indescrivìbile agg. indescribable.

indesideràbile agg. undesirable.

indeterminàbile agg. indeterminable.

indeterminatezza sf. vagueness.

indeterminativo agg. (gramm.) indefinite.

indeterminato agg. indeterminate.

indeterminazione sf. indetermination.

indi avv. 1. (di tempo) then 2. (di luogo) (from) thence.

indiano agg. Indian: — d'America, Red Indian; in fila indiana, in Indian file.

indiavolato agg. frenzied, furious.

indicare vt. 1. to show (v. irr.) 2. (col dito) to point at.

indicativo agg. indicative.

indicato agg. 1. (adatto) suitable 2. (consigliabile) advisable.

indicatore agg. indicatory. ♦ **indicatore** sm. indicator.

indicazione sf. indication.

indice sm. 1. (dito della mano) forefinger 2. (di libro, statistica ecc.) index.

indicibile agg. inexpressible.

indietreggiare vi. to withdraw (v. irr.).

indietro avv. (di spazio, tempo) back, behind.

indifendibile agg. indefensible.

indifeso agg. undefended.

indifferente agg. indifferent.

indifferenza sf. indifference.

indifferibile agg. undelayable.

indigeno agg. e sm. native.

indigente agg. indigent, poor.

indigenza sf. indigence.

indigestione sf. indigestion.

indigesto agg. 1. indigestible 2. (fig.) heavy.

indignare vt. to make (v. irr.) indignant. ♦ **indignarsi** vr. to get (v. irr.) angry.

indignazione sf. indignation.

indimenticabile agg. unforgettable.

indimostrabile agg. indemonstrable.

indipendente agg. independent (of). ♦ **indipendente** sm. (pol.) independent.

indipendenza sf. independence.

indire vt. to call, to announce.

indiretto agg. indirect.

indirizzare vt. to address. ♦ **indirizzarsi** vr. 1. (dirigersi) to set (v. irr.) out (for) 2. (rivolgersi) to address oneself (to).

indirizzo sm. 1. address 2. (linea di condotta) trend.

indisciplina sf. indiscipline.

indisciplinato agg. undisciplined.

indiscretezza sf. indiscretion.

indiscreto agg. indiscreet.

indiscrezione sf. indiscretion.

indiscriminato agg. indiscriminate.

indiscusso agg. undiscussed.

indiscutibile agg. unquestionable.

indispensabile agg. indispensable.

indispettire vt. to vex. ♦ **indispettirsi** vr. to become (v. irr.) vexed.

indispettito agg. vexed.

indisponente agg. irritating.

indisporre vt. to irritate.

indisposizione sf. indisposition.

indisposto agg. unwell (pred.).

indissolubile agg. indissoluble.

indissolubilità sf. indissolubility.

indistinto agg. indistinct.

indistruttibile agg. indestructible.

indisturbato agg. undisturbed.

individuale agg. individual.

individualismo sm. individualism

individualista s. individualist.

individualistico agg. individualistic.

individuare vt. to single out.

individuo sm. individual.

indivisibile agg. indivisible.

indivisibilità sf. indivisibility.

indiviso agg. undivided.

indiziare vt. to make (v. irr.) suspect.

indiziario agg. presumptive.

indiziato agg. e sm. suspect.

indizio sm. 1. indication 2. (giur.) circumstantial proof.

indocile agg. indocile.

indocilità sf. indocility.

indoeuropeo agg. e sm. Indo-European.

indole sf. nature, disposition ‖ un ragazzo di buona —, a good-natured boy.

indolente agg. indolent.

indolenza sf. indolence.

idolenzimento sm. numbness.

indolenzire vt. to numb. ♦ **indolenzirsi** vr. to become (v. irr.) numb.

indolenzito agg. numb.

indolore agg. painless.

indomabile agg. untamable.

indomani sm. next day ‖ all' —, on the day after.

indòmito agg. indomitable.

indorare vt. V. dorare.

indossare vt. 1. (avere indosso) to wear (v. irr.) 2. (mettere indosso) to put (v. irr.) on.

indossatrice *sf.* mannequin.
indosso *avv.* on.
indotto *agg.* (*spinto*) driven.
indovinare *vt.* to guess.
indovinello *sm.* riddle.
indovino *sm.* soothsayer.
indubbio *agg.* undoubted.
indubitàbile *agg.* indubitable.
indugiare *vi.* to delay, to hesitate.
indugio *sm.* delay.
indulgente *agg.* indulgent.
indulgenza *sf.* indulgence.
indùlgere *vi.* to indulge (in).
indulto *sm.* 1. (*eccl.*) indult 2. (*giur.*) free pardon.
indumento *sm.* garment.
indurimento *sm.* hardening.
indurire *vt.* e *vi.* to harden. ♦ **indurirsi** *vr.* to harden.
indurre *vt.* to induce, to get (*v. irr.*) || — *in errore*, to mislead (*v. irr.*) ♦ **indursi** *vr.* to bring (*v. irr.*) oneself (to).
industria *sf.* industry.
industriale *agg.* industrial. ♦ **industriale** *sm.* industrialist, manufacturer.
industrialismo *sm.* industrialism.
industrializzare *vt.* to industrialize.
industrializzazione *sf.* industrialization.
industriarsi *vr.* to do (*v. irr.*) one's best.
industrioso *agg.* industrious.
induttivo *agg.* inductive.
induttore *agg.* inductor.
induzione *sf.* induction.
inebetire *vt.* e *vi.* to dull.
inebetito *agg.* dull.
inebriante *agg.* inebriating.
inebriare *vt.* 1. to make (*v. irr.*) drunk 2. (*fig.*) to inebriate. ♦ **inebriarsi** *vr.* 1. to get (*v. irr.*) drunk 2. (*fig.*) to go (*v. irr.*) into raptures.
ineccepìbile *agg.* unexceptionable.
inedia *sf.* starvation.
inèdito *agg.* unpublished.
ineducato *agg.* ill-bred.
ineffàbile *agg.* ineffable.
inefficace *agg.* ineffective.
inefficacia *sf.* inefficacy.
inefficiente *agg.* inefficient.
inefficienza *sf.* ineffectiveness.
ineguaglianza *sf.* inequality.
ineguale *agg.* 1. unlike 2. (*irregolare*) irregular 3. (*di superficie*) uneven.

ineleggìbile *agg.* ineligible.
ineleggibilità *sf.* ineligibility.
ineluttàbile *agg.* ineluctable.
ineluttabilità *sf.* inevitableness.
inenarràbile *agg.* unutterable.
inequivocàbile *agg.* unmistakable
'nerente *agg.* concerning.
inerme *agg.* unarmed.
inerpicarsi *vr.* to climb (up).
inerte *agg.* inert.
inerzia *sf.* inertness.
inesattezza *sf.* inaccuracy.
inesatto *agg.* incorrect.
inesaudito *agg.* ungranted.
inesauribile *agg.* inexhaustible.
inesàusto *agg.* unexhausted.
inseguìbile *agg.* unexecutable.
inesigibile *agg.* 1. uncollectable 2. (*di assegno*) worthless.
inesistente *agg.* inexistent.
inesistenza *sf.* inexistence.
inesoràbile *agg.* inexorable.
inesorabilità *sf.* inexorability.
inesperienza *sf.* inexperience.
inesperto *agg.* unskilled.
inespiàbile *agg.* inexpiable.
inesplicàbile *agg.* inexplicable.
inesploràbile *agg.* inexplorable.
inesplorato *agg.* unexplored.
inespressivo *agg.* inexpressive.
inespresso *agg.* implied.
inesprimìbile *agg.* inexpressible.
inespugnàbile *agg.* inexpugnable.
inespugnabilità *sf.* inexpugnability.
inestimàbile *agg.* inestimable.
inestinguìbile *agg.* unquenchable.
inestirpàbile *agg.* ineradicable.
inestricàbile *agg.* inextricable.
inettitùdine *sf.* unfitness.
inetto *agg.* 1. unapt 2. (*dappoco*) good-for-nothing.
inevaso *agg.* outstanding, unanswered.
inevitàbile *agg.* inevitable.
inezia *sf.* trifle.
infagottare *vt.* to muffle up. ♦ **infagottarsi** *vr.* to muffle oneself up.
infallìbile *agg.* infallible.
infallibilità *sf.* infallibility.
infamante *agg.* shameful.
infamare *vt.* to defame, to disgrace.
infame *agg.* wicked.
infamia *sf.* infamy.
infangare *vt.* to muddy. ♦ **infangarsi** *vr.* to become (*v. irr.*) muddy.
infanticida *s.* child-murderer.

infanticidio *sm.* child-murder.

infantile *agg.* childlike, childish.

infantilismo *sm.* infantilism.

infanzia *sf.* 1. infancy 2. *(coll.)* children *(pl.)*.

infarcire *vt.* V. *farcire*.

infarinare *vt.* to flour. ♦ **infarinarsi** *vr.* to get *(v. irr.)* covered with flour.

infarinatura *sf.* 1. flouring 2. *(fig.)* smattering.

infarto *sm.* infarct.

infastidire *vt.* to annoy. ♦ **infastidirsi** *vr.* to get *(v. irr.)* bored.

infaticàbile *agg.* tireless.

infatti *cong.* in fact.

infatuare *vt.* to infatuate. ♦ **infatuarsi** *vr.* to get *(v. irr.)* crazy (about).

infatuato *agg.* crazy (about).

infatuazione *sf.* infatuation.

infausto *agg.* unlucky.

infecondità *sf.* sterility.

infecondo *agg.* steril.

infedele *agg.* unfaithful. ♦ **infedele** *sm.* infidel.

infedeltà *sf.* unfaithfulness.

infelice *agg.* 1. unhappy 2. *(non appropriato)* ill-timed. ♦ **infelice** *s.* wretch.

infelicità *sf.* unhappiness.

inferiore *agg.* 1. inferior 2. *(più basso)* lower 3. *(al di sotto)* below. ♦ **inferiore** *sm.* inferior.

inferiorità *sf.* inferiority.

inferire *vt.* 1. *(dedurre)* to infer 2. *(dare)* to inflict.

infermería *sf.* infirmary.

infermiera *sf.* nurse.

infermiere *sm.* hospital attendant.

infermità *sf.* infirmity.

infermo *agg.* e *sm.* invalid.

infernale *agg.* 1. infernal 2. *(fig.)* awful.

inferno *sm.* hell.

inferocire *vt.* to enrage. ♦ **inferocire** *vi.* to get *(v. irr.)* fierce.

inferriata *sf.* grating.

infervorare *vt.* to excite. ♦ **infervorarsi** *vr.* to get *(v. irr.)* excited.

infervorato *agg.* fervent.

infestare *vt.* to infest.

infestazione *sf.* infestation.

infettare *vt.* to infect. ♦ **infettarsi** *vr.* to become *(v. irr.)* infected.

infettivo *agg.* contagious.

infetto *agg.* infected.

infezione *sf.* infection.

infiacchimento *sm.* weakening.

infiacchire *vt.* e *vi.* to weaken. ♦ **infiacchirsi** *vr.* to become *(v. irr.)* weak.

infiammàbile *agg.* inflammable.

infiammabilità *sf.* inflammability.

infiammare *vt.* 1. to set *(v. irr.)* on fire 2. *(fig.)* to inflame. ♦ **infiammarsi** *vr.* 1. to take *(v. irr.)* fire 2. *(fig.)* to get *(v. irr.)* excited.

infiammato *agg.* inflamed (with).

infiammatorio *agg.* inflammatory.

infiammazione *sf.* inflammation.

infiascare *vt.* to put *(v. irr.)* into flasks.

inficiare *vt.* 1. to invalidate 2. *(giur.)* to impugn.

infido *agg.* false.

infierire *vi.* to be pitiless.

infìggere *vt.* 1. to infix 2. *(conficcare)* to drive *(v. irr.)* (into).

infilare *vt.* 1. to thread 2. *(introdurre)* to insert 3. *(passare per)* to enter. ♦ **infilarsi** *vr.* to slip into.

infilata *sf.* row.

infiltrarsi *vr.* to penetrate.

infiltrazione *sf.* infiltration.

infilzare *vt.* 1. to transfix 2. *(conficcare)* to stick *(v. irr.)*. ♦ **infilzarsi** *vr.* 1. to run *(v. irr.)* oneself through 2. *(conficcarsi)* to get *(v. irr.)* stuck.

infilzata *sf.* string.

ìnfimo *agg.* lowest.

infine *avv.* at last.

infingardàggine *sf.* laziness.

infingardo *agg.* lazy.

infinità *sf.* infinity.

infinitamente *avv.* infinitely.

infinitesimale *agg.* infinitesimal.

infinito *agg.* boundless. ♦ **infinito** *sm.* 1. infinite 2. *(gramm.)* infinitive.

infioccare *vt.* to tassel.

infiorare *vt.* to flower.

infirmare *vt.* to invalidate.

infischiarsi *vr.* not to care (about).

infittire *vi.* to thicken. ♦ **infittirsi** *vr.* to thicken.

inflazione *sf.* inflation.

inflazionìstico *agg.* inflationary.

inflessìbile *agg.* inflexible.

inflessibilità *sf.* inflexibility.

inflessione *sf.* inflexion.

inflìggere *vt.* to inflict.

influente *agg.* influential.

influenza *sf.* 1. influence 2. *(med.)* *(fam.)* 'flu.

influenzare *vt.* to influence.

influire vi. to exert influence (on, upon, over).

influsso sm. influence.

infocare vt. 1. to heat up 2. to inflame.

infocato agg. 1. red hot 2. (fig.) inflamed.

infoltire vi. to thicken.

infondatezza sf. groundlessness.

infondato agg. groundless.

infòndere vt. to infuse.

inforcare vt. 1. to pitchfork 2. (montare a cavalcioni) to get (v. irr.) on || — gli occhiali, to put (v. irr.) on one's glasses.

informale agg. informal.

informare vt. 1. to inform 2. (dare forma) to shape. ♦ **informarsi** vr. to inquire (about).

informativo agg. informative.

informato agg. informed.

informatore sm. informer.

informazione sf. information (solo sing.), news (pl.).

informe agg. shapeless.

infornare vt. to put (v. irr.) into an oven.

infornata sf. batch.

infortunarsi vr. to get (v. irr.) injured.

infortunato agg. injured.

infortunio sm. accident.

infortunìstica sf. industrial accident research.

infossamento sm. hollow.

infossare vt. to hollow. ♦ **infossarsi** vr. to become (v. irr.) hollow.

infradiciare vt. 1. to drench 2. (marcire) to rot (v. irr.).

inframmettenza sf. interference.

inframméttere vt. to interpose. ♦ **inframméttersi** vr. to meddle (with).

infràngere vt. 1. to shatter 2. (trasgredire) to infringe. ♦ **infràngersi** vr. to break (v. irr.) (up).

infrangibile agg. unbreakable: vetro —, shatter-proof glass.

infranto agg. 1. shattered, broken 2. (di legge) infringed.

infrarosso agg. infrared.

infrasettimanale agg. midweek.

infrastruttura sf. infrastructure.

infrazione sf. infraction.

infreddolirsi vr. to feel (v. irr.) cold.

infreddolito agg. chilly.

infrequente agg. infrequent.

infrollirsi vr. 1. to become (v. irr.) tender 2. (di selvaggina) to become (v. irr.) high.

infruttifero agg. unfruitful.

infruttuoso agg. 1. unfruitful 2. (fig.) useless.

infuori (loc. prep.) all'—, except.

infuriare vi. to enrage. ♦ **infuriarsi** vr. to flare up.

infusione sf. infusion.

infuso agg. infused. ♦ **infuso** sm. infusion.

infusorio sm. infusorial.

ingabbiare vt. 1. to cage 2. (fig.) to lock up.

ingaggiare vt. to engage.

ingaggio sm. engagement.

ingagliardire vt. to strengthen. ♦ **ingagliardirsi** vr. to strengthen.

ingannare vt. to deceive || — il tempo, to while away the time. ♦ **ingannarsi** vr. to be mistaken.

ingannatore agg. deceiving. ♦ **ingannatore** sm. deceiver.

ingannévole agg. deceitful.

inganno sm. deception, fraud.

ingarbugliare vt. to entangle. ♦ **ingarbugliarsi** vr. to get (v. irr.) mixed up.

ingegnarsi vr. to contrive (to).

ingegnere sm. engineer.

ingegnerìa sf. engineering.

ingegno sm. talent.

ingegnosità sf. ingeniousness.

ingegnoso agg. ingenious.

ingelosire vt. to make (v. irr.) jealous. ♦ **ingelosirsi** vr. to become (v. irr.) jealous.

ingenerare vt. to engender.

ingeneroso agg. selfish.

ingente agg. huge.

ingentilire vt. to refine.

ingenuità sf. naïveness.

ingenuo agg. naïve.

ingerenza sf. interference.

ingerimento sm. swallowing.

ingerire vt. to swallow.

ingessare vt. to plaster.

ingessatura sf. 1. plastering 2. (med.) plaster cast.

inghiaiare vt. to gravel.

inghiottire vt. 1. to swallow 2. (di acque ecc.) to engulf 3. (sopportare) to lump.

inghirlandare vt. to wreathe.

ingiallire vt. e vi. to yellow.

ingigantire vt. to magnify. ♦ **ingigantire** vi. to become (v. irr.) gigantic.

inginocchiarsi *vr.* to kneel (*v. irr.*) (down).

inginocchiatoio *sm.* kneeler.

ingioiellare *vt.* to bejewel.

ingiù *avv.* down, downwards.

ingiùngere *vt.* to order.

ingiuntivo *agg.* injunctive.

ingiunzione *sf.* injunction.

ingiuria *sf.* insult.

ingiuriare *vt.* to insult.

ingiurioso *agg.* insulting.

ingiustamente *avv.* unjustly.

ingiustificàbile *agg.* unjustifiable.

ingiustificato *agg.* unjustified.

ingiustizia *sf.* unjustice.

ingiusto *agg.* unjust.

inglese *agg.* English. ♦ **inglese** *sm.* Englishman (*pl.* -men) ‖ *gli Inglesi,* the English (people).

inglobare *vt.* to inglobe.

inglorioso *agg.* inglorious.

ingobbire *vi.* to become (*v. irr.*) humpbacked. ♦ **ingobbirsi** *vr.* to become humpbacked.

ingoiare *vt.* to swallow.

ingolfarsi *vr.* (*fig.*) to throw (*v. irr.*) oneself (into).

ingollare *vt.* to gulp down.

ingolosire *vt.* to make (*v. irr.*) greedy.

ingombrante *agg.* cumbersome.

ingombrare *vt.* to encumber.

ingombro *agg.* encumbered (with). ♦ **ingombro** *sm.* encumbrance.

ingommare *vt.* 1. to gum 2. (*incollare*) to stick (*v. irr.*).

ingordigia *sf.* greed.

ingordo *agg.* greedy.

ingorgare *vt.* to choke. ♦ **ingorgarsi** *vr.* to become (*v. irr.*) choked.

ingorgo *sm.* 1. obstruction 2. (*del traffico*) traffic jam.

ingozzare *vt.* to gulp.

ingranaggio *sm.* 1. gear 2. (*fig.*) mechanism.

ingranare *vt.* 1. to put (*v. irr.*) into gear 2. (*auto*) — *una marcia,* to engage a gear. ♦ **ingranare** *vi.* (*fam.*) to get (*v. irr.*) along (with).

ingrandimento *sm.* 1. enlargement 2. (*ott.*) magnification.

ingrandire *vt.* 1. to enlarge 2. (*ott.*) to magnify. ♦ **ingrandirsi** *vr.* to become (*v. irr.*) larger.

ingrassare *vt.* 1. to fatten 2. (*lubrificare*) to grease. ♦ **ingrassare** *vi.* to grow (*v. irr.*) fat.

ingrasso *sm.* fattening.

ingratitùdine *sf.* ingratitude.

ingrato *agg.* ungrateful. ♦ **ingrato** *sm.* ingrate.

ingravidare *vt.* to make (*v. irr.*) pregnant. ♦ **ingravidare** *vi.* to become (*v. irr.*) pregnant.

ingraziarsi *vr.* to get (*v. irr.*) into so.'s good graces.

ingrediente *sm.* ingredient.

ingresso *sm.* 1. entry 2. (*entrata*) entrance 3. (*accesso*) admittance.

ingrossamento *sm.* enlargement.

ingrossare *vt.* e *vi.* to enlarge. ♦ **ingrossarsi** *vr.* to become (*v. irr.*) bigger.

ingrosso (*nella loc. avv.*) all'—, wholesale.

ingualcìbile *agg.* crease-resistant.

inguaribile *agg.* incurable.

inguinale *agg.* inguinal.

inguine *sm.* inguen.

ingurgitare *vt.* to swallow.

inibire *vt.* to inhibit.

inibito *agg.* inhibited.

inibizione *sf.* inhibition.

iniettare *vt.* to inject.

iniezione *sf.* injection.

inimicare *vt.* to alienate. ♦ **inimicarsi** *vr.* to estrange from oneself.

inimicizia *sf.* enmity.

inimitàbile *agg.* incomparable, inimitable.

inimmaginàbile *agg.* unimaginable.

inintelligibile *agg.* unintelligible.

ininterrotto *agg.* continuous, unceasing.

iniquità *sf.* iniquity.

iniquo *agg.* 1. unfair 2. (*malvagio*) wicked.

iniziale *agg.* initial, starting. ♦ **iniziale** *sf.* initial.

iniziare *vt.* 1. to begin (*v. irr.*), to start 2. (*introdurre*) to initiate.

iniziativa *sf.* initiative.

iniziato *agg.* e *sm.* initiate.

iniziazione *sf.* initiation.

inizio *sm.* beginning.

innaffiare *vt.* to water.

innaffiatoio *sm.* watering-pot.

innalzamento *sm.* elevation.

innalzare *vt.* 1. to raise 2. (*rendere più alto*) to heighten. ♦ **innalzarsi** *vr.* to rise (*v. irr.*).

innamoramento *sm.* falling in love.

innamorare *vt.* to charm. ♦ **innamorarsi** *vr.* to fall (*v. irr.*) in love (with).

innamorato *agg.* in love (with). ♦ **innamorato** *sm.* lover.

innanzi *avv.* 1. forward, on 2. *(di fronte)* in front of 3. *(più avanti)* further || **d'ora —**, from now on. ♦ **innanzi** *prep.* before.

innato *agg.* inborn.

innaturale *agg.* unnatural.

innegàbile *agg.* undeniable.

inneggiare *vi.* 1. to exalt 2. *(acclamare)* to cheer.

innervare *vt.* to innervate.

innervosire *vt.* to get *(v. irr.)* on so.'s nerves. ♦ **innervosirsi** *vr.* to get nervous.

innescamento *sm.* priming.

innescare *vt.* to prime.

innesco *sm.* primer.

innestare *vt.* 1. *(agr.; med.)* to graft 2. *(mecc.)* to engage.

innesto *sm.* 1. *(agr.; med.)* graft 2. *(mecc.)* clutch.

inno *sm.* hymn || **— nazionale**, national anthem.

innocente *agg.* e *sm.* innocent.

innocenza *sf.* innocence.

innocuità *sf.* innocuousness.

innocuo *agg.* harmless.

innominàbile *agg.* unmentionable.

innovare *vt.* to innovate.

innovatore *agg.* innovating. ♦ **innovatore** *sm.* innovator.

innovazione *sf.* innovation.

innumerévole *agg.* numberless.

inoculare *vt.* to inoculate.

inoculazione *sf.* inoculation.

inodoro *agg.* odourless.

inoffensivo *agg.* harmless.

inoltrare *vt.* to forward. ♦ **inoltrarsi** *vr.* to advance.

inoltrato *agg.* advanced, late.

inoltre *avv.* moreover, besides.

inoltro *sm.* 1. *(di merci)* forwarding 2. *(di documenti)* sending on.

inondare *vt.* to flood.

inondazione *sf.* flood.

inoperosità *sf.* inactivity.

inoperoso *agg.* inactive.

inopinàbile *agg.* inconceivable.

inopinato *agg.* unexpected.

inopportunità *sf.* inopportunity.

inopportuno *agg.* inopportune.

inoppugnàbile *agg.* incontestable.

inoppugnabilità *sf.* incontestability.

inorgànico *agg.* inorganic.

inorgoglire *vt.* to make *(v. irr.)* proud. ♦ **inorgoglirsi** *vr.* to become *(v. irr.)* proud.

inorridire *vt.* to horrify. ♦ **inorridire** *vi.* to be horrified.

inospitale *agg.* inhospitable.

inosservanza *sf.* inobservance.

inosservato *agg.* unobserved.

inossidàbile *agg.* rust-proof || **— acciaio —**, stainless steel.

inquadramento *sm.* framing.

inquadrare *vt.* 1. to frame 2. *(fig.)* to set *(v. irr.)* 3. *(mil.)* to rank 4. *(foto, cine)* to frame.

inquadratura *sf.* *(cine)* shot.

inqualificàbile *agg.* despicable.

inquietante *agg.* worrying.

inquietare *vt.* to worry. ♦ **inquietarsi** *vr.* to get *(v. irr.)* angry.

inquieto *agg.* 1. restless 2. *(preoccupato)* worried 3. *(arrabbiato)* angry.

inquietùdine *sf.* 1. restlessness 2. *(preoccupazione)* anxiety.

inquilino *sm.* tenant.

inquinamento *sm.* defilement.

inquinare *vt.* to defile.

inquirente *agg.* investigating.

inquisire *vt.* to investigate. ♦ **inquisire** *vi.* to inquire.

inquisitore *agg.* inquiring. ♦ **inquisitore** *sm.* inquisitor.

inquisizione *sf.* inquisition.

insabbiamento *sm.* *(fig.)* hindering.

insabbiare *vt.* 1. to sand 2. *(fig.)* to hinder.

insaccare *vt.* to sack.

insalata *sf.* salad.

insalatiera *sf.* salad-bowl.

insalubre *agg.* unhealthy.

insalubrità *sf.* insalubrity.

insanàbile *agg.* incurable.

insanguinare *vt.* to cover (with blood). ♦ **insanguinarsi** *vr.* to become *(v. irr.)* bloodstained.

insano *agg.* insane.

insaponare *vt.* to soap.

insaponatura *sf.* soaping.

insaporire *vt.* to flavour.

insaporo *agg.* flavourless.

insaputa *sf.* *(nella loc. avv.)* **all'— di**, unknown (to).

insaziàbile *agg.* insatiable.

insaziabilità *sf.* insatiability.

insaziato *agg.* unappeased.

inscatolare *vt.* to tin.

inscenare *vt.* to stage.

inscindìbile *agg.* inseparable.

inscrivere *vt.* 1. *(a una scuola, esame ecc.)* to enrol 2. *(scrivere, scolpire; geom.)* to inscribe.

insediamento *sm.* installation.
insediare *vt.* to install. ♦ **insediarsi** *vr.* to install oneself.
insegna *sf.* 1. insignia (*pl.*) 2. (*bandiera*) flag 3. (*di negozio*) signboard.
insegnamento *sm.* 1. teaching 2. (*precetto, lezione*) precept, lesson.
insegnante *agg.* teaching. ♦ **insegnante** *s.* teacher.
insegnare *vt.* to teach (*v. irr.*).
inseguimento *sm.* pursuit.
inseguire *vt.* to pursue.
inseguitore *sm.* pursuer.
insellare *vt.* to saddle.
inselvatichire *vi.* to grow (*v. irr.*) wild.
insenatura *sf.* inlet, creek.
insensatezza *sf.* 1. craziness 2. (*atto insensato*) foolish action.
insensato *agg.* foolish, crazy.
insensìbile *agg.* 1. insensible 2. (*indifferente*) indifferent 3. (*frigido*) unfeeling.
insensibilità *sf.* 1. insensibility 2. (*indifferenza*) indifference.
insensibilmente *avv.* 1. (*impercettibilmente*) imperceptibly, slightly 2. (*senza sentimento*) insensibly.
inseparàbile *agg.* inseparable.
insepolto *agg.* unburied.
inserimento *sm.* insertion.
inserire *vt.* 1. to insert 2. (*elettr.*) to connect.
inserto *sm.* 1. file, dossier 2. (*cine, stampa*) insert.
inservìbile *agg.* useless.
inserviente *sm.* attendant.
inserzione *sf.* 1. insertion 2. (*pubblicitaria*) advertisement.
inserzionista *sm.* advertiser.
insetticida *agg.* e *sm.* insecticide.
insettìvoro *agg.* insectivorous. ♦ **insettìvoro** *sm.* insectivore.
insetto *sm.* insect.
insicurezza *sf.* insecurity.
insìdia *sf.* 1. snare 2. (*pericolo*) danger.
insidiare *vt.* to endanger || — la vita di una persona, to attempt a person's life.
insidioso *agg.* insidious.
insieme *avv.* 1. together 2. (*allo stesso tempo*) at the same time. ♦ **insieme** *prep.* together (with). ♦ **insieme** *sm.* whole: nell'—, as a whole || sguardo d'—, comprehensive view.
insigne *agg.* famous.

insignificante *agg.* insignificant.
insignire *vt.* to confer (sthg. upon).
insincerità *sf.* insincerity.
insincero *agg.* insincere.
insindacàbile *agg.* undisputable.
insinuante *agg.* insinuating.
insinuare *vt.* to hint. ♦ **insinuarsi** *vr.* to insinuate oneself.
insinuazione *sf.* hint, insinuation.
insipidezza *sf.* insipidness.
insìpido *agg.* 1. tasteless 2. (*fig.*) insipid.
insistente *agg.* 1. insistent, steady 2. (*molesto*) irritating.
insistenza ·*sf.* insistence.
insìstere *vi.* to insist (on).
ìnsito *agg.* inborn, inherent.
insoddisfatto *agg.* dissatisfied (with).
insoddisfazione *sf.* dissatisfaction (with).
insofferente *agg.* intolerant.
insofferenza *sf.* intolerance.
insoffrìbile *agg.* unbearable.
insolazione *sf.* sunstroke.
insolente *agg.* e *sm.* insolent.
insolentire *vt.* to insult.
insolenza *sf.* insolence.
insòlito *agg.* unusual.
insolùbile *agg.* insoluble.
insolubilità *sf.* insolubility.
insoluto *agg.* 1. unsolved 2. (*non pagato*) unpaid.
insolvente *agg.* insolvent.
insolvenza *sf.* insolvency.
insolvìbile *agg.* 1. (*di debito*) unpayable 2. (*di persona*) insolvent.
insolvibilità *sf.* insolvency.
insomma *avv.* finally, in short.
insondàbile *agg.* unfathomable.
insonne *agg.* sleepless.
insonnia *sf.* insomnia.
insonnolito *agg.* drowsy, sleepy.
insopportàbile *agg.* unbearable.
insopprimìbile *agg.* insuppressible.
insòrgere *vi.* 1. to rise (*v. irr.*) 2. (*protestare*) to protest, to rebel 3. (*manifestarsi*) to arise (*v. irr.*).
insormontàbile *agg.* insurmountable.
insorto *sm.* rebel.
insospettàbile *agg.* beyond suspicion.
insospettato *agg.* unsuspected.
insospettire *vt.* to make (*v. irr.*) suspicious. ♦ **insospettirsi** *vr.* to grow (*v. irr.*) suspicious.
insostenìbile *agg.* unsustainable.
insostituìbile *agg.* irreplaceable.

insozzare vt. **1.** to soil **2.** (fig.) to disgrace.

insperàbile agg. beyond hope.

insperato agg. unhoped for.

inspiegàbile agg. inexplicable.

inspirare vt. to breathe in.

inspirazione sf. breathing in, inhalation.

instàbile agg. unstable ‖ tempo —, unsettled weather.

instabilità sf. **1.** instability **2.** (fig.) fickleness.

installare vt. to install. ♦ **installarsi** vr. to settle.

installazione sf. installation.

instancàbile agg. untiring.

instaurare vt. to set (v. irr.) up.

instaurazione sf. establishment.

instradare vt. to direct, to coach.

insù avv. up, upwards.

insubordinatezza sf. insubordination.

insubordinato agg. insubordinate.

insubordinazione sf. insubordination.

insuccesso sm. failure.

insudiciare vt. to soil.

insufficiente agg. insufficient.

insufficienza sf. **1.** insufficiency **2.** (scol.) low mark.

insulare agg. insular.

insulina sf. insulin.

insulsàggine sf. **1.** silliness **2.** (cosa insulsa) nonsense.

insulso agg. silly.

insultare vt. to insult.

insulto sm. insult.

insuperàbile agg. insuperable.

insuperato agg. unsurpassed.

insuperbire vt. to elate. ♦ **insuperbirsi** vr. to pride oneself (on).

insurrezionale agg. insurrectional.

insurrezione sf. insurrection.

insussistente agg. unfounded.

intaccare vt. **1.** to notch **2.** (chim.) to etch **3.** (fig.) to injure.

intacco sm. notch.

intagliare vt. **1.** to carve **2.** (incidere) to engrave.

intaglio sm. **1.** carving **2.** (incisione) engraving.

intangìbile agg. intangible.

intanto avv. meanwhile.

intarsiare vt. to inlay.

intarsio sm. inlay.

intasamento sm. obstruction.

intasare vt. to obstruct.

intascare vt. to pocket.

intatto agg. intact.

intavolare vt. **1.** to plank **2.** (iniziare) to begin (v. irr.), to start.

integèrrimo agg. strictly honest.

integràbile agg. integrable.

integrale agg. integral: (mat.) calcolo —, integral calculus.

integrante agg. integrant.

integrare vt. to integrate.

integrazione sf. integration.

integrità sf. integrity.

integro agg. **1.** integral **2.** (onesto) honest.

intelaiatura sf. **1.** framework **2.** (di finestre) sash.

intellettivo agg. intellective.

intelletto sm. intellect.

intellettuale agg. e sm. intellectual.

intellettualismo sm. intellectualism.

intelligente agg. intelligent.

intelligenza sf. intelligence.

intelligìbile agg. intelligible.

intelligibilità sf. intelligibility.

intemerata sf. reprimand.

intemerato agg. faultless.

intemperante agg. intemperate.

intemperanza sf. intemperance.

intemperie sf. pl. inclemency of the weather (sing.).

intempestività sf. untimeliness.

intempestivo agg. untimely.

intendente agg. expert. ♦ **intendente** sm. superintendent.

intendenza sf. superintendence.

intèndere vt. **1.** (capire) to understand (v. irr.) **2.** (significare) to mean (v. irr.) **3.** (avere intenzione di) to intend to. ♦ **intèndersi** vr. **1.** (avere cognizione) to be a good judge **2.** (mettersi d'accordo) to come (v. irr.) to an agreement.

intendimento sm. **1.** understanding **2.** (intenzione) intention.

intenditore sm. **1.** good judge **2.** (d'arte) connoisseur.

intenerimento sm. **1.** softening **2.** (fig.) tenderness.

intenerire vt. **1.** to soften **2.** (fig.) to move to pity. ♦ **intenerirsi** vr. to be moved to pity.

intensificare vt. to intensify.

intensificazione sf. intensification.

intensità sf. intensity.

intensivo agg. intensive.

intenso agg. intense.

intentàbile agg. **1.** unattemptable **2.** (giur.) suable.

intentare *vt.* to bring (*v. irr.*).
intento *agg.* intent. ♦ **intento** *sm.* aim, purpose.
intenzionale *agg.* deliberate.
intenzionato *agg.* disposed.
intenzione *sf.* intention.
intepidire *vt.* to warm, to make (*v. irr.*) tepid. ♦ **intepidirsi** *vr.* to get (*v. irr.*) tepid.
interamente *avv.* wholly, entirely.
intercalare *agg.* intercalary. ♦ **intercalare** *sm.* pet phrase.
intercalare *vt.* to intercalate.
intercambiàbile *agg.* interchangeable.
intercèdere *vi.* to intercede, to plead.
intercessione *sf.* intercession.
intercessore *sm.* intercessor.
intercettare *vt.* to intercept.
intercettatore *sm.* interceptor.
intercettazione *sf.* interception.
intercomunale *sf.* (*tel.*) long-distance call.
intercontinentale *agg.* intercontinental.
intercòrrere *vi.* **1.** to pass **2.** (*accadere*) to happen.
intercostale *agg.* intercostal.
interdetto. *agg.* **1.** prohibited **2.** (*giur.*) interdicted. ♦ **interdetto** *sm.* interdict.
interdipendente *agg.* interdependent.
interdipendenza *sf.* interdependence.
interdire *vt.* to interdict.
interdizione *sf.* interdiction.
interessamento *sm.* concern.
interessante *agg.* interesting.
interessare *vt.* **1.** to interest **2.** (*riguardare*) to concern. ♦ **interessarsi** *vr.* **1.** to be interested (in) **2.** (*provvedere*) to take (*v. irr.*) care (of).
interessato *agg.* interested.
interesse *sm.* interest.
interessenza *sf.* share, profit.
interezza *sf.* wholeness.
interferenza *sf.* interference.
interferire *vi.* to interfere.
interiezione *sf.* interjection.
interinale *agg.* temporary.
interiora *sf. pl.* entrails.
interiore *agg.* inner. ♦ **interiore** *sm.* interior, inside.
interiorità *sf.* inwardness.
interiormente *avv.* **1.** (*intimamente*) innerly **2.** (*nell'interno*) inside.

interlìnea *sf.* **1.** interline **2.** (*tip.*) lead.
interlineare *vt.* **1.** to interline **2.** (*tip.*) to lead (*v. irr.*).
interlineare *vt.* to interline.
interlocutore *sm.* interlocutor.
interlocutorio *agg.* interlocutory.
interloquire *vi.* to join in the conversation.
interludio *sm.* interlude.
intermediario *agg.* intermediary. ♦ **intermediario** *sm.* **1.** go-between **2.** (*comm.*) middleman (*pl.* -men).
intermedio *agg.* intermediate, middle.
intermezzo *sm.* **1.** intermission **2.** (*mus.*) intermezzo.
interminābile *agg.* endless.
intermittente *agg.* intermittent.
intermittenza *sf.* intermittence.
internamento *sm.* internment.
internare *vt.* to intern.
internato *agg.* interned. ♦ **internato** *sm.* (*scol.*) boarding-school.
internazionale *agg.* international.
internazionalismo *sm.* internationalism.
internazionalizzare *vt.* to internationalize.
interno *agg.* **1.** internal, interior **2.** (*interiore*) inner. ♦ **interno** *sm.* interior.
intero *agg.* **1.** whole **2.** (*intatto*) intact.
interpellanza *sf.* interrogation.
interpellare *vt.* **1.** (*pol.*) to interpellate **2.** (*giur.*) to summon **3.** (*chiedere*) to ask.
interplanetario *agg.* interplanetary.
interpolare *vt.* to interpolate.
interpolazione *sf* interpolation.
interporre *vt.* to interpose.
interpretare *vt.* **1.** to interpret, to render **2.** (*teat.*) to play.
interpretativo *agg.* interpretative.
interpretazione *sf* **1.** interpretation **2.** (*cine*) starring **3.** (*mus.*) performance **4.** (*teat.*) acting.
intèrprete *s.* **1.** interpreter **2.** (*teat.; cine*) actor, player.
interpunzione *sf.* punctuation.
interramento *sm.* burial.
interrare *vt.* **1.** to bury **2.** (*riempire di terra*) to fill up with earth.
interrogare *vt.* to question.
interrogativo *agg.* interrogative ‖ *punto —*, question mark. ♦ **interrogativo** *sm.* interrogative.

interrogatore agg. interrogating. ♦ **interrogatore** sm. examiner.

interrogatorio sm. examination.

interrogazione sf. 1. interrogation 2. (scol.) oral test.

interrompere vt. to interrupt. ♦ **interrompersi** vr. to stop.

interrotto agg. interrupted || strada interrotta, blocked road.

interruttore sm. (elettr.) switch.

interruzione sf. interruption.

intersecare vt. to intersect.

intersezione sf. intersection.

interstizio sm. interstice.

intervallare vt. to space.

intervallo sm. 1. interval 2. (spazio) space.

intervenire vi. 1. to intervene 2. (essere presenti) to be present.

interventismo sm. interventionism.

interventista s. interventionist.

intervento sm. 1. intervention 2. (presenza) presence 3. (chir.) operation.

intervenuto agg. present. ♦ **intervenuto** sm. person present.

intervista sf. interview.

intervistare vt. to interview.

intesa sf. agreement.

inteso agg. 1. agreed (upon) 2. (mirante) aiming (at).

intessere vt. to interweave (v. irr.).

intestare vt. to head, to register. ♦ **intestarsi** vr. to be determinated.

intestatario sm. holder.

intestato agg. 1. headed 2. (giur.) registered 3. (senza testamento) intestate 4. (ostinato) stubborn.

intestazione sf. 1. title 2. (di lettera ecc.) heading.

intestinale agg. intestinal.

intestino sm. intestine.

intimare vt. 1. (ordinare) to order 2. (ingiungere) to summon.

intimazione sf. 1. order 2. (ingiunzione) summons.

intimidatorio agg. intimidatory.

intimidazione sf. intimidation.

intimidire vt. 1. to make (v. irr.) shy 2. (impaurire) to intimidate.

intimità sf. 1. privacy 2. (familiarità) familiarity.

intimo agg. 1. intimate 2. (profondo) deep. ♦ **intimo** sm. 1. (amico) intimate 2. (animo) soul || nell'—, at heart.

intimorire vt. to frighten. ♦ **intimorirsi** vr. to get (v. irr.)

frightened.

intingere vt. to dip.

intingolo sm. 1. gravy 2. (salsa) sauce.

intirizzire vt. to benumb.

intitolare vt. 1. to entitle 2. (dedicare) to dedicate.

intoccabile agg. e sm. untouchable.

intollerabile agg. intolerable.

intollerante agg. intolerant.

intolleranza sf. intolerance.

intonacare vt. to plaster.

intonacatura sf. plastering.

intonaco sm. plaster.

intonare vt. 1. to tune 2. (cantilenare) to intone. ♦ **intonarsi** vr. 1. to harmonize (with) 2. (di colori) to match.

intonato agg. 1. in tune 2. (di colori) matching.

intonazione sf. 1. intonation 2. (di strumenti) tuning 3. (di colori, voce) tone.

intonso agg. (di libri) uncut.

intontimento sm. stunning.

intontire vt. to stun.

intoppare vt. to stumble (on).

intoppo sm. 1. obstacle 2. (fig.) hitch.

intorbidare vt. to make (v. irr.) muddy. ♦ **intorbidarsi** vr. to become (v. irr.) muddy.

intorno avv. round, around. ♦ **intorno a** prep. 1. round, around 2. (circa, su di) about.

intorpidimento sm. numbness.

intorpidire vt. to benumb. ♦ **intorpidirsi** vr. to grow (v. irr.) numb.

intossicare vt. to poison.

intossicazione sf. poisoning.

intraducibile agg. untranslatable.

intralciare vt. to hinder, to interfere.

intralcio sm. hindrance.

intrallazzo sm. 1. plotting 2. (imbroglio) swindle.

intramezzare vt. to interpose, to alternate.

intramontabile agg. everlasting.

intramuscolare agg. intermuscular.

intransigente agg. strict, intransigent.

intransigenza sf. intransigence.

intransitivo agg. e sm. intransitive.

intrappolare vt. to entrap.

intraprendente agg. enterprising.

intraprendenza sf. enterprise.

intraprèndere vt. 1. to undertake (v. irr.), to start 2. (una professione) to go (v. irr.) in for.

intrattàbile agg. intractable.

intrattenere vt. to entertain. ♦ **intrattenersi** vr. 1. to linger 2. (dilungarsi) to dwell (v. irr.).

intravedere vt. 1. (vedere di sfuggita) to catch (v. irr.) a glimpse of 2. (vedere indistintamente) to see (v. irr.) indistinctly.

intrecciare vt. 1. to interlace || — danze, to dance 2. (capelli, nastri) to plait.

intreccio sm. 1. interlacement 2. (di romanzi) plot.

intrèpido agg. brave, fearless.

intricare vt. to tangle. ♦ **intricarsi** vr. to get (v. irr.) entangled.

intrico sm. tangle.

intrìdere vt. to soak.

intrigante agg. crafty. ♦ **intrigante** sm. intriguer.

intrigare vi. to intrigue. ♦ **intrigarsi** vr. to meddle (with).

intrigo sm. intrigue, plot.

intrìnseco agg. intrinsic.

intristire vi. 1. to pine away 2. (incattivire) to grow (v. irr.) wicked.

introdotto agg. 1. (importato) imported 2. (conosciuto) well-known.

intriso agg. soaked (with), imbrued.

introdurre vt. 1. to introduce 2. (far entrare) to show (v. irr.) in. ♦ **introdursi** vr. to get (v. irr.) into, to slip into.

introduttivo agg. introductory.

introduzione sf. introduction.

introitare vt. to cash.

intròito sm. profit.

intromèttere vt. to introduce. ♦ **intromèttersi** vr. to interfere.

intromissione sf. intrusion.

intronare vt. to stun.

introspettivo agg. introspective.

introspezione sf. introspection.

introvàbile agg. not to be found.

introversione sf. introversion.

introverso agg. introverted. ♦ **introverso** sm. introvert.

intrufolarsi vr. to intrude (in).

intruglio sm. bad mixture.

intruppamento sm. trooping.

intrupparsi vr. to troop.

intrusione sf. intrusion.

intruso sm. intruder.

intuìbile agg. guessable.

intuire vt. to guess, to perceive.

intuitivo agg. intuitive.

intùito sm. intuition, insight.

intuizione sf. intuition.

inturgidimento sm. swelling.

inturgidire vi. to swell (up). **inturgidirsi** vr. to swell (up).

inuguale agg. unlike.

inumanità sf. inhumanity.

inumano agg. inhuman.

inumare vt. to inter.

inumazione sf. interment.

inumidire vt. to moisten. ♦ **inumidirsi** vr. to moisten.

inurbanità sf. incivility.

inurbano agg. uncivil.

inurbarsi vr. to inurbate.

inusitato agg. unusual.

inùtile agg. useless.

inutilità sf. uselessness.

inutilizzàbile agg. unusable.

invadente agg. intrusive.

invadenza sf. intrusiveness.

invàdere vt. to invade.

invaghimento sm. fancy (for).

invaghirsi vr. to take (v. irr.) a fancy (for), to fall (v. irr.) in love (with).

invaghito agg. fond (of), infatuated.

invalere vi. to prevail.

invalicàbile agg. impassable.

invalidare vt. to invalidate.

invalidazione sf. invalidation.

invalidità sf. invalidity.

invàlido agg. e sm. invalid.

invalso agg. prevailed.

invano avv. in vain.

invariàbile agg. 1. invariable 2. (di tempo) unchangeable.

invariabilità sf. invariability.

invariato agg. unchanged.

invasamento sm. obsession.

invasare vt. to possess.

invasato agg. possessed. ♦ **invasato** sm. possessed person.

invasione sf. invasion.

invasore sm. invader.

invecchiamento sm. ageing.

invecchiare vt. to make (v. irr.) old. ♦ **invecchiare** vi. to grow (v. irr.) old.

invece avv. on the contrary || — di, instead of.

inveire vi. to rail (at).

invelenire vt. to embitter.

invendibile agg. unsaleable.

invendicato agg. unavenged.

invenduto agg. unsold.

inventare *vt.* to invent.

inventariare *vt.* to inventory.

inventario *sm.* inventory || *con beneficio d'—*, with reservation.

inventiva *sf.* inventiveness.

inventivo *agg.* inventive.

inventore *sm.* inventor.

invenzione *sf.* invention.

inverdire *vi.* to turn green.

inverecondia *sf.* immodesty.

inverecondo *agg.* immodest.

inverificàbile *agg.* unverifiable.

invernale *agg.* **1.** winter (*attr.*) **2.** (*da inverno*) wintry.

invernata *sf.* wintertime.

inverno *sm.* winter.

invero *avv.* indeed.

inverosimiglianza *sf* unlikelihood.

inverosìmile *agg.* unlikely.

inversione *sf.* inversion.

inverso *agg.* **1.** (*mat.*) inverse **2.** opposite, contrary. ♦ **inverso** *sm.* opposite, contrary.

invertebrato *agg. e sm.* invertebrate.

invertìbile *agg.* invertible.

invertire *vt.* to invert || *— la marcia*, to reverse.

invertito *sm.* invert.

invertitore *sm.* reverse gear.

investigare *vt.* to inquire.

investigativo *agg.* investigative.

investigatore *sm.* detective.

investigazione *sf.* investigation.

investimento *sm.* **1.** investment **2.** collision **3.** (*stradale*) running down.

investire *vt.* **1.** to invest (with) **2.** (*comm.*) to invest **3.** (*assalire*) to assail **4.** (*auto*) to run (*v. irr.*) down.

investitore *sm.* (*comm.*) investor.

investitura *sf.* investiture.

inveterato *agg.* inveterate.

invetriata *sf.* glass window.

invettiva *sf.* invective.

inviare *vt.* to send (*v. irr.*).

inviato *sm.* **1.** messenger **2.** (*in diplomazia*) envoy **3.** (*in giornalismo*) correspondent.

invidia *sf.* envy; *per —*, out of envy.

invidiàbile *agg.* enviable.

invidiare *vt.* to envy.

invidioso *agg.* envious.

invigorire *vt.* to strengthen. ♦ **invigorirsi** *vr.* to strengthen.

inviluppare *vt.* to envelop, to wrap up.

invincìbile *agg.* invincible.

invincibilità *sf.* invincibility.

invio *sm.* **1.** (*per posta*) mailing **2.** (*di merci*) forwarding **3.** (*per nave*) shipment **4.** (*di danaro*) remittance.

inviolàbile *agg.* inviolable.

inviolabilità *sf.* inviolability.

inviperirsi *vr.* to become (*v. irr.*) furious.

inviperito *agg.* furious.

invischiare *vt.* **1.** to lime **2.** (*fig.*) to entangle. ♦ **invischiarsi** *vr.* to get (*v. irr.*) entangled.

invisìbile *agg.* invisible.

invisibilità *sf.* invisibility.

inviso *agg.* disliked.

invitante *agg.* inviting.

invitare *vt.* **1.** to invite **2.** (*domandare*) to request.

invitato *agg.* invited. ♦ **invitato** *sm.* guest.

invito *sm.* invitation.

invitto *agg.* unconquered.

invocare *vt.* to invoke.

invocazione *sf.* invocation.

invogliare *vt.* to tempt.

involare *vt.* to abduct. ♦ **involarsi** *vr.* to flee, to run (*v. irr.*) away.

involontario *agg.* unintentional.

involto *sm.* bundle, parcel.

invòlucro *sm.* **1.** envelope **2.** (*bot.*) involucre.

involutivo *agg.* involutionary.

involuto *agg.* involved.

involuzione *sf.* **1.** involution **2.** (*decadenza*) decline.

invulneràbile *agg.* invulnerable.

invulnerabilità *sf.* invulnerability.

inzaccherare *vt.* to muddy. ♦ **inzaccherarsi** *vr.* to get (*v. irr.*) muddy.

inzuppare *vt.* **1.** to soak **2.** (*intingere*) to dip.

io *pron.* I: *— stesso*, I myself.

iodato *agg.* iodized. ♦ **iodato** *sm.* iodate.

iodio *sm.* iodine.

iole *sf.* gig.

ione *sm.* ion.

iònico *agg.* Ionic.

ionizzazione *sf.* ionization.

ionosfera *sf.* ionosphere.

iosa (*nella loc. avv.*) *a —*, in plenty.

iperalimentazione *sf.* hypernutrition.

ipèrbole *sf.* hyperbole.

iperbòlico *agg.* hyperbolic(al).

iperbòreo *agg.* hyperborean.

ipercrìtico agg. hypercritical.
ipermetropìa sf. hypermetropia.
ipermètrope agg. hypermetropic.
ipernutrizione sf. hypernutrition.
ipersensìbile agg. hypersensitive.
ipersensibilità sf. hypersensitivity.
ipertensione sf. hypertension.
iperteso agg. e sm. hypertensive.
ipertrofìa sf. hypertrophy.
ipnòsi sf. hypnosis.
ipnòtico agg. hypnotic.
ipnotismo sm. hypnotism.
ipnotizzare vt. to hypnotize.
ipnotizzatore sm. hypnotizer.
ipocondrìa sf. hypochondria.
ipocondrìaco agg. e sm. hypochondriac.
ipocrisìa sf. hypocrisy.
ipòcrita agg. hypocritical. ♦ ipòcrita sm. hypocrite.
ipodèrmico agg. hypodermic.
ipodermoclisi sf. hypodermoclysis.
ipòfisi sf. hypophysis.
ipoteca sf. mortgage.
ipotecare vt. to mortgage.
ipotenusa sf. hypotenuse.
ipòtesi sf. 1. hypothesis (pl. -ses) 2.
(supposizione) supposition.
ipotètico agg. hypothetical.
ìppica sf. horse-racing.
ìppico agg. horse (attr.).
ippocampo" sm. hippocampus (pl.
-pi).
ippocastano sm. horse-chestnut.
ippòdromo sm. race-course.
ippopòtamo sm. hippopotamus.
ira sf. anger, rage.
iracondo agg. irascible.
irascìbile agg. irritable.
irascibilità sf. irritability.
irato agg. angry.
iridato agg. iridescent.
ìride sf. iris.
iridescente agg. iridescent.
iridescenza sf. iridescence.
irlandese agg. Irish.
ironìa sf. irony.
irònico agg. ironic(al).
ironizzare vi. to make (v. irr.)
ironical remarks.
iroso agg. wrathful.
irradiamento sm. irradiation.
irradiare vt. to irradiate.
irradiazione sf. V. irradiamento.
irraggiare vt. V. irradiare.
irraggiungìbile agg. unreachable.
irragionévole agg. unreasonable.
irrancidire vi. to grow (v. irr.)
rank.

irrazionale agg. irrational.
irrazionalità sf. irrationality.
irreale agg. unreal.
irrealizzàbile agg. unrealizable.
irrealtà sf. unreality.
irreconciliàbile agg. irreconcilable.
irrecuperàbile agg. irrecoverable.
irrefrenàbile agg. unrestrainable.
irrefutàbile agg. irrefutable.
irregolare agg. irregular.
irregolarità sf. irregularity.
irremovìbile agg. 1. immovable 2.
(inflessibile) inflexible.
irreparàbile agg. irreparable.
irreperìbile agg. elusive: rendersi —, to hide (v. irr.) oneself.
irreprensìbile agg. irreproachable.
irrequietezza sf. restlessness.
irrequieto agg. restless.
irresistìbile agg. irresistible.
irresolutezza sf. irresolution.
irresoluto agg. hesitating.
irrespiràbile agg. unbreathable.
irresponsàbile agg. irresponsible.
irresponsabilità sf. irresponsibility.
irrestringìbile agg. unshrinkable.
irretire vt. to snare.
irreversìbile agg. irreversible.
irreversibilità sf. irreversibility.
irrevocàbile agg. irrevocable.
irriconoscìbile agg. unrecognizable.
irridere vt. to laugh at.
irriducìbile agg. irreducible.
irriflessione sf. thoughtlessness.
irriflessivo agg. thoughtless.
irrigàbile agg. irrigable.
irrigare vt. to irrigate.
irrigazione sf. irrigation.
irrigidimento sm. stiffening.
irrigidire vt. to stiffen. ♦ irrigidirsi vr. to stiffen.
irriguo agg. well-watered.
irrilevante agg. insignificant.
irrimediàbile agg. irremediable.
irrisione sf. mockery.
irrisorio agg. derisory, paltry.
irrispettoso agg. disrespectful.
irritàbile agg. 1. (di persona) irritable 2. (di pelle) sensitive.
irritabilità sf. 1. (di persona) irritability 2. (di pelle) sensitiveness.
irritante agg. irritating.
irritare vt. to irritate. ♦ irritarsi
vr. 1. to grow (v. irr.) angry 2.
(di pelle) to become (v. irr.) irritated.
irritazione sf. 1. irritation 2. (di
pelle) inflammation.

irriverente *agg.* disrespectful.
irriverenza *sf.* irreverence.
irrobustire *vt.* to strengthen. ♦ **irrobustirsi** *vr.* to strengthen.
irrómpere *vi.* 1. to break (*v. irr.*) into 2. (*di acque*) to overflow.
irrorare *vt.* to sprinkle.
irroratrice *sf.* sprayer.
irruente *agg.* impetuous.
irruenza *sf.* impetuosity.
irruvidire *vt.* to roughen.
irruzione *sf.* irruption: *fare —*, to rush into.
irsuto *agg.* shaggy.
irto *agg.* bristling (with).
iscritto *sm.* member.
iscrìvere *vt.* 1. (*a scuola, esami ecc.*) to enrol 2. (*registrare*) to record 3. (*scolpire*) to engrave. ♦ **iscrìversi** *vr.* to enter, to join.
iscrizione *sf.* 1. inscription 2. (*a scuola, esami ecc.*) entry || *domanda d'—*, application.
islàmico *agg.* Islamic.
islamismo *sm.* Islamism.
isocronismo *sm.* isochronism.
isola *sf.* island.
isolamento *sm.* 1. isolation 2. (*elettr.*) insulation || *— acustico*, sound-proofing.
isolano *agg.* insular. ♦ **isolano** *sm.* islander.
isolante *agg.* insulating. ♦ **isolante** *sm.* insulator.
isolare *vt.* 1. to isolate 2. (*elettr.*) to insulate || *— acusticamente*, to soundproof. ♦ **isolarsi** *vr.* to seclude oneself.
isolato *agg.* 1. isolated 2. (*elettr.*) insulated. ♦ **isolato** *sm.* (*edil.*) block.
isolatore *sm.* insulator.
isolazionismo *sm.* isolationism.
isolazionista *s.* isolationist.
isolotto *sm.* islet.
isomorfismo *sm.* isomorphism.
isomorfo *agg.* isomorphous.
isòscele *agg.* isosceles.
isotèrmico *agg.* isothermal.
isòtopo *sm.* isotope.
isòtropo *sm.* isotrope.
ispànico *agg.* Hispanic.
ispanismo *sm.* Hispanicism.
ispanista *s.* Hispanist.
ispettorato *sm.* inspectorate.
ispettore *sm.* inspector.
ispezionare *vt.* to inspect.
ispezione *sf.* inspection.
ispido *agg.* hispid.

ispirare *vt.* to inspire (with). ♦ **ispirarsi** *vr* to draw (*v. irr.*) one's inspiration (from).
ispirato *agg.* 1. inspired 2. (*basato*) imbued (with).
ispiratore *agg.* inspiring. ♦ **ispiratore** *sm.* inspirer.
ispirazione *sf.* inspiration.
israeliano *agg.* e *sm.* Israeli.
israelita *agg.* e *s.* Israelite.
issare *vt.* to hoist.
istantànea *sf.* snapshot: *fare un'—*, to snapshot.
istantaneità *sf.* instantaneousness.
istantàneo *agg.* instantaneous.
istante *sm.* instant || *all'—*, *sull'—*, instantly.
istanza *sf.* 1. request, instance 2. (*supplica*) entreaty 3. (*domanda scritta*) application.
istèrico *agg.* hysteric(al). ♦ **istèrico** *sm.* hysterical man (*pl.* -men).
isterilire *vt.* to sterilize. ♦ **isterilirsi** *vr.* to become (*v. irr.*) barren.
isterismo *sm.* hysteria.
istigare *vt.* to instigate.
istigatore *sm.* instigator.
istigazione *sf.* instigation.
istintivo *agg.* instinctive.
istinto *sm.* instinct.
istituire *vt.* 1. to institute 2. (*fondare*) to found 3. (*giur.*) to appoint.
istituto *sm.* 1. institute 2. (*istituzione*) institution 3. (*scuola*) school.
istitutore *sm.* tutor.
istitutrice *sf.* governess.
istituzionale *agg.* institutional.
istituzione *sf.* institution.
istmo *sm.* isthmus (*pl.* -mi).
istologìa *sf.* histology.
istrice *sm.* hedgehog.
istrione *sm.* 1. (*teat.*) histrion 2. (*ciarlatano*) quack.
istriònico *agg.* histrionic.
istruire *vt.* 1. to teach (*v. irr.*) 2. (*dare istruzioni*) to instruct, to direct 3. (*giur.*) to institute. ♦ **istruirsi** *vr.* to educate oneself.
istruito *agg.* learned.
istruttivo *agg.* instructive.
istruttore *sm.* instructor: *giudice —*, examining magistrate.
istruttoria *sf.* examination || *aprire l'—*, to open proceedings.
istruzione *sf.* 1. education 2. (*cultura*) learning 3. (*insegnamento*) teaching 4. (*ordine*) instruction.

istupidire vt. to make (v. irr.) stupid. ✦ **istupidirsi** v.r. to become (v. irr.) stupid.

italiano agg. e sm. Italian.

itinerario sm. itinerary.

itterizia sf. jaundice.

ittiologia sf. ichthyology.

ittiòlogo sm. ichthyologist.

iugoslavo agg. e sm. Yugoslav.

iugulare agg. jugular.

iuta sf. jute.

ivi avv. there.

L

la[1] art. the. ✦ **la** pron. **1.** (per donna) her **2.** (per animale e cosa) it **3.** (forma di cortesia) you.

la[2] sm. (mus.) A.

là avv. there || l'al di —, the hereafter; — per —, on the spot; al di — di, beyond; più in —, (spazio) further on, (tempo) later on.

labbro sm. lip.

labiale agg. labial.

làbile agg. fleeting: memoria —, weak memory.

labirinto sm. labyrinth.

laboratorio sm. **1.** laboratory **2.** (artigianale) workshop.

laboriosità sf. laboriousness.

laborioso agg. laborious.

laburismo sm. labourism.

laburista agg. labour || partito —, Labour Party. ✦ **laburista** s. Labourite.

lacca sf. lacquer.

laccare vt. to lacquer.

laccatura sf. lacquering.

laccio sm. **1.** string || lacci da scarpe, shoe-laces **2.** (trappola) snare || prendere al — (fig.), to ensnare.

laceramento sm. tearing.

lacerante agg. rending.

lacerare vt. to tear (v. irr.) (up), to rend (v. irr.) (anche fig.). ✦ **lacerarsi** v.r. to tear.

lacerazione sf. laceration.

làcero agg. **1.** torn **2.** (med.) lacerated.

laconicità sf. laconicism.

lacònico agg. laconic(al).

làcrima sf. tear.

lacrimale agg. lachrymal.

lacrimare vi. to weep (v. irr.).

lacrimazione sf. lachrymation.

lacrimévole agg. tearful.

lacrimògeno agg. lachrymatory: gas —, tear-gas.

lacrimoso agg. tearful.

lacuna sf. gap.

lacunoso agg. lacunous.

lacustre agg. lacustrine.

laddove cong. whereas. ✦ **laddove** avv. (there) where.

ladra sf. woman thief.

ladro agg. thieving. ✦ **ladro** sm. thief: al —!, stop thief!

ladrocinio sm. theft.

ladrone sm. robber.

ladroneria sf. robbery.

laggiù avv. down there.

lagna sf. lament.

lagnanza sf. complaint.

lagnarsi vr. to complain (of).

lago sm. lake.

laguna sf. lagoon.

lagunare agg. lagoon (attr.).

laicato sm. laity.

laicismo sm. laicism.

laicizzare vt. to laicize.

làico agg. laic. ✦ **làico** sm. layman (pl. -men).

laidezza sf. ugliness, foulness.

làido agg. **1.** dirty **2.** (brutto) ugly.

lama[1] sf. blade.

lama[2] sm. (zool.) llama.

lama[3] sm. (monaco buddista) lama.

lambiccare vt. to distil || lambiccarsi il cervello, to rack one's brains.

lambiccato agg. **1.** distilled **2.** (ricercato) over-elaborate.

lambicco sm. alembic.

lambire vt. to lick.

lamella sf. lamella (pl. -lae).

lamentare vt. to lament. ✦ **lamentarsi** vr. to moan.

lamentazione sf. lamentation.

lamentela sf. complaint.

lamentévole agg. mournful.

lamento sm. moan.

lamentoso agg. mournful.

lametta sf. razor-blade.

lamiera sf. sheet.

làmina sf. lamina (pl. -nae).

laminare vt. to laminate.

laminato sm. **1.** (tessuto) lamé **2.** (metallo) rolled section.

laminatoio sm. rolling-mill.

làmpada sf. lamp.

lampadario sm. chandelier, lamp holder.

lampadina *sf.* bulb.

lampante *agg.* glaring, evident.

lampeggiamento *sm.* 1. flashing, lightning 2. (*di fari, semafori ecc.*) winking 3. (*di auto*) to blink.

lampeggiare *vi.* 1. to flash, to lighten 2. (*di fari, semafori ecc.*) to wink.

lampeggiatore *sm.* 1. winking light 2. (*di auto*) blinker.

lampione *sm.* street-lamp.

lampo *sm.* 1. lightning 2. (*luce istantanea, anche fig.*) flash || *chiusura* —, zip-fastener.

lampone *sm.* raspberry.

lampreda *sf.* lamprey.

lana *sf.* wool.

lancetta *sf.* 1. (*di quadrante*) hand 2. (*di chirurgo*) lancet.

lancia¹ *sf.* lance.

lancia² *sf.* (*mar.*) launch || — *di salvataggio*, lifeboat.

lanciafiamme *sm.* flame-thrower.

lanciare *vt.* 1. to throw (*v. irr.*) 2. (*fig.*) to launch || — *un'occhiata*, to cast (*v. irr.*) a glance. ♦ **lanciarsi** *vr.* to dash.

lanciatore *sm.* thrower.

lanciere *sm.* lancer.

lancinante *agg.* piercing.

lancio *sm.* 1. throwing 2. (*pubblicitario*) launching.

landa *sf.* moor.

languido *agg.* languid.

languire *vi.* to languish.

languore *sm.* languor.

laniero' *agg.* woollen.

lanificio *sm.* wool factory.

lanolina *sf.* lanolin.

lanoso *agg.* woolly.

lanterna *sf.* lantern.

lanùgine *sf.* down.

laparotomìa *sf.* laparotomy.

lapidare *vt.* to stone.

lapidario *agg.* lapidary.

lapidazione *sf.* lapidation.

làpide *sf.* 1. tablet 2. (*sepolcrale*) tombstone.

lapis *sm.* pencil.

lardellare *vt.* to .lard.

lardo *sm.* lard, bacon.

larga (*nella loc. avv.*) *alla* —, sway (from).

largheggiare *vi.* to abound (with).

larghezza *sf.* 1. breadth 2. (*liberalità*) liberality 3. (*abbondanza*) plenty.

largire *vt.* to bestow (upon).

largitore *sm.* bestower.

largizione *sf.* bestowal.

largo *agg.* broad, wide. ♦ **largo** *sm.* 1. (*mar.*) open sea 2. (*piazza*) square || *prendere il* —, to set (*v. irr.*) sail; (*fig.*) to run (*v. irr.*) away; *andare al* —, to take (*v. irr.*) to the open sea; *fare* —, to make (*v. irr.*) room.

làrice *sm.* larch.

laringe *sf.* larynx.

laringite *sf.* laryngitis.

larva *sf.* larva (*pl.* -ae).

lasciapassare *sm.* pass.

lasciare *vt.* 1. to leave (*v. irr.*) 2. (*permettere*) to let (*v. irr.*), to allow. ♦ **lasciarsi** *vr. rec.* (*separarsi*) to part.

làscito *sm.* legacy.

lascivia *sf.* lust.

lascivo *agg.* lustful.

lassativo *agg. e sm.* laxative.

lasso *sm.* lapse: *dopo un certo* — *di tempo*, after a lapse of time.

lassù *avv.* up there.

lastra *sf.* 1. (*vetro*) glass' sheet 2. (*di pietra*) slab 3. (*di metallo, foto*) plate.

lastricare *vt.* to pave.

lastricatura *sf.* paving.

làstrico *sm.* pavement || *essere sul* — (*fig.*), to be destitute.

latente *agg.* latent.

laterale *agg.* side: *via* —, by-street.

lateralmente *avv.* sideways.

laterizi *sm. pl.* bricks.

làtice *sm.* latex.

latifondista *sm.* landowner.

latifondo *sm.* large landed estate.

latinismo *sm.* Latinism.

latinista *s.* Latinist.

latinità *sf.* Latinity.

latino *agg. e sm.* Latin.

latitante *agg.* absconding: *essere* —, to be in hiding. ♦ **latitante** *s.* absconder.

latitanza *sf.* hiding: *darsi alla* —, to evade arrest.

latitùdine *sf.* latitude.

lato¹ *sm.* 1. side 2. (*fig.*) point of view || *d'altro* —, on the other hand; *da un* —, on the one hand.

lato² *agg.* wide || *in senso* —, in a broad sense.

latore *sm.* bearer.

latrare *vi.* to bark.

latrato *sm.* barking.

latrina *sf.* lavatory.

latta *sf.* tin.

lattaio *sm.* milkman (*pl.* -men).

lattante *agg.* unweaned. ♦ **lattante** *s.* suckling (baby).

latte *sm.* milk.

làtteo *agg.* milky.

latteria *sf.* dairy.

latticini *sm. pl.* dairy products.

lattiera *sf.* milk-jug.

lattiginoso *agg.* 1. milky 2. (*bot.*) lactescent.

lattoniere *sm.* tinker.

lattosio *sm.* lactose.

lattuga *sf.* lettuce.

laudativo *agg.* laudatory.

làurea *sf.* degree.

laureare *vt.* to confer a degree (on). ♦ **laurearsi** *vr.* to graduate.

laureato *agg.* graduated. ♦ **laureato** *sm.* graduate || — *in lettere*, Doctor of Literature Degree.

làuro *sm.* laurel.

làuto *agg.* sumptuous || *lauti guadagni*, large profits.

lava *sf.* lava.

lavàbile *agg.* washable.

lavabo *sm.* washbowl.

lavaggio *sm.* washing: — *a secco*, dry cleaning.

lavagna *sf.* 1. blackboard 2. (*ardesia*) slate.

lavanda[1] *sf.* 1. washing 2. (*med.*) lavage.

lavanda[2] *sf.* (*bot.*) lavender.

lavandaia *sf.* laundress.

lavanderìa *sf.* laundry.

lavandino *sm.* sink.

lavapiatti *s.* dish-washer.

lavare *vt.* to wash: — *a secco*, to dry-clean. ♦ **lavarsi** *vr.* to wash (oneself).

lavata *sf.* wash || *dare una — di capo* (fig.), to scold.

lavativo *sm.* 1. (*med.*) enema 2. (fig.) lazy-bones.

lavatoio *sm.* 1. wash-house 2. (*asse per lavare*) wash-board.

lavatrice *sf.* 1. washer 2. (*lavabiancheria*) washing machine.

lavatura *sf.* washing.

lavina *sf.* landslip.

lavorante *sm.* worker.

lavorare *vi.* e *vt.* to work.

lavorativo *agg.* working || *ora lavorativa*, man-hour.

lavoratore *agg.* working. ♦ **lavoratore** *sm.* worker || — *a giornata*, day-labourer.

lavorazione *sf.* 1. processing 2. (*fattura*) work 3. (*agr.*) tilling || —

a mano, handwork.

lavorìo *sm.* intense activity.

lavoro *sm.* 1. work 2. (*occupazione*) job || — *a ore*, work by the hour; *lavori di casa*, housework; — *su ordinazione*, work to order; *eccesso di* —, overwork; — *in proprio*, self-employment.

lazzaretto *sm.* lazaretto.

lazzarone *sm.* slacker.

lazzo *sm.* joke.

le *art.* the. ♦ **le** *pron.* 1. (*sing.*) her, to her 2. (*pl.*) them 3. (*forma di cortesia*) you, to you.

leale *agg.* 1. loyal 2. (*corretto*) fair.

lealtà *sf.* 1. loyalty 2. (*correttezza*) fairness.

lebbra *sf.* leprosy.

lebbrosario *sm.* leper hospital.

lebbroso *agg.* leprous. ♦ **lebbroso** *sm.* leper.

leccapiedi *sm.* bootlicker.

leccare *vt.* to lick. ♦ **leccarsi** *vr.* to lick (oneself).

leccata *sf.* licking.

leccornìa *sf.* dainty.

lécito *agg.* 1. lawful 2. (*giusto*) right 3. (*permesso*) allowed. ♦ **lécito** *sm.* right.

lèdere *vt.* 1. to injure 2. (*danneggiare*) to damage.

lega *sf.* 1. league 2. (*di metalli*) alloy || *di buona* —, genuine; *di cattiva* —, low.

legaccio *sm.* string.

legale *agg.* legal, lawful || *procedere per vie legali*, to have recourse to the law. ♦ **legale** *sm.* lawyer.

legalità *sf.* legality.

legalizzare *vt.* 1. to legalize 2. (*autenticare*) to authenticate.

legalizzazione *sf.* 1. legalization 2. (*autenticazione*) authentication.

legame *sm.* 1. string 2. (*vincolo*) tie 3. (*connessione*) link.

legamento *sm.* 1. string 2. (*anat.*) ligament.

legare[1] *vt.* 1. to tie 2. (*di metalli*) to alloy (with) 3. (*aver connessione*) to be connected. ♦ **legarsi** *vr.* to bind (*v. irr.*) oneself.

legare[2] *vt.* (*giur.*) to bequeath.

legatario *sm.* legatee.

legato[1] *sm.* 1. ambassador 2. (*eccl.*) legate.

legato[2] *sm.* (*giur.*) legacy.

legatore *sm.* binder.

legatorìa *sf.* bookbinder's establishment.

legatura *sf.* 1. binding 2. (*mus.*; *med.*) ligature.

legazione *sf.* legation.

legge *sf.* 1. law 2. (*singola*) act 3. (*regola*) rule || *progetto di* —, bill; *a norma di* —, according to the law; *a termini di* —, as by law enacted.

leggenda *sf.* legend.

leggendario *agg.* legendary.

leggere *vt.* to read (*v. irr.*).

leggerezza *sf.* lightness.

leggero *agg.* light.

leggiadria *sf.* loveliness.

leggiadro *agg.* lovely.

leggibile *agg.* readable.

leggio *sm.* 1. reading-desk 2. (*mus.*) music-stand.

legiferare *vi.* to legislate.

legionario *agg. e sm.* legionary.

legione *sf.* legion.

legislativo *agg.* legislative.

legislatore *sm.* legislator.

legislatura *sf.* legislature.

legislazione *sf.* legislation.

legittimare *vt.* to legitimate.

legittimazione *sf.* legitimation.

legittimità *sf.* legitimacy.

legittimo *agg.* legitimate.

legna *sf.* wood || — *da ardere*, fire-wood.

legnaia *sf.* wood-store.

legname *sm.* 1. wood 2. (*da costruzione*) timber.

legnata *sf.* blow with a cudgel.

legno *sm.* wood || *di* —, wooden.

legnosità *sf.* woodiness.

legnoso *agg.* 1. woody 2. (*duro*) tough.

legume *sm.* legume.

leguminoso *agg.* leguminous.

lei *pron.* 1. (*sogg.*) she, (*compl.*) her 2. (*forma di cortesia*) you.

lembo *sm.* 1. edge 2. (*pezzo*) strip.

lemma *sm.* lemma.

lemure *sm.* lemur. ♦ **lèmuri** *sm. pl.* (*mit.*) lemures.

lena *sf.* 1. energy 2. (*respiro*) breath.

lenire *vt.* to soothe.

lenone *sm.* pander.

lente *sf.* lens: — *d'ingrandimento*, magnifying lens || *lenti*, glasses.

lentezza *sf.* slowness.

lenticchia *sf.* lentil.

lentiggine *sf.* freckle.

lentigginoso *agg.* freckly.

lento *agg.* 1. slow 2. (*non teso*) loose.

lenza *sf.* fishing-line.

lenzuolo *sm.* sheet.

leone *sm.* lion.

leonessa *sf.* lioness.

leonino *agg.* leonine.

leopardo *sm.* leopard.

lepido *agg.* witty.

lepidòttero *sm.* lepidopteron (*pl.* -era).

leporino *agg.* leporine || *labbro* —, hare-lip.

lepre *sf.* hare.

lercio *agg.* filthy.

lèsbica *agg. e sf.* Lesbian.

lésina *sf.* awl.

lesinare *vi.* to be stingy. ♦ **lesinare** *vt.* to grudge.

lesionare *vt.* to damage, to injure.

lesione *sf.* 1. lesion, injury 2. (*danno*) damage.

lesivo *agg.* harmful.

leso *agg.* 1. injured 2. (*danneggiato*) damaged.

lessare *vt.* to boil.

lessicale *agg.* lexical.

lèssico *sm.* lexicon.

lessicografia *sf.* lexicography.

lessicologìa *sf.* lexicology.

lesso *agg.* boiled. ♦ **lesso** *sm.* boiled meat.

lestezza *sf.* quickness.

lesto *agg.* quick.

lestofante *sm.* swindler.

letale *agg.* lethal.

letamaio *sm.* dunghill.

letame *sm.* dung.

letàrgico *agg.* 1. lethargic 2. (*di animali, in inverno*) hibernating; (*id., in estate*) estivating.

letargo *sm.* 1. lethargy 2. (*di animali, in inverno*) hibernation; (*id., in estate*) estivation.

letizia *sf.* joy.

lèttera *sf.* letter || *alla* —, literally.

letterale *agg.* literal.

letterario *agg.* literary.

letterato *agg.* lettered. ♦ **letterato** *sm.* literary man.

letteratura *sf.* literature.

lettiga *sf.* stretcher.

letto *sm.* bed || *camera da* —, bedroom; *vagone* —, sleeping-car.

lettore *sm.* reader.

lettura *sf.* reading.

leucemia *sf.* leukaemia.

leucociti *sm. pl.* leucocytes.

leucoma *sm.* leucoma.

leva[1] *sf.* 1. lever 2. (*fig.*) stimulus || *far* — *sui sentimenti di qu.*, to play on so.'s feelings.

leva[2] *sf.* (*mil.*) draft: *essere di* —, to be due for draft.

levante *sm.* 1. east 2. (*vento*) levanter.

levare *vt.* 1. (*sollevare*) to raise 2. (*togliere*) to take (*v. irr.*) off. ◆ **levarsi** *vr.* 1. to rise (*v. irr.*) 2. (*togliersi*) to take off.

levata *sf.* 1. (*di sole*) rising 2. (*di posta*) collection || — *di scudi* rebellion.

levataccia *sf.* early rising.

levatoio *agg.* ponte —, drawbridge.

levatrice *sf.* midwife (*pl.* -wives).

levatura *sf.* intelligence.

levigare *vt.* to smooth.

levigatezza *sf.* smoothness.

levigato *agg.* smooth.

levitazione *sf.* levitation.

levriere *sm.* greyhound.

lezione *sf.* 1. lesson 2. (*universitaria*) lecture 3. (*lett.*) reading.

leziosàggine *sf.* affectation.

lezioso *agg.* affected.

lezzo *sm.* stench.

li *pron.* them.

lì *avv.* there: — *vicino*, near there; — *dentro*, in there || — *per* —, at first; *di* — *a poco*, soon after; *giù di* — (*press'a poco*), thereabouts; *essere* — *per*, to be on the point of.

liana *sf.* liana.

libagione *sf.* libation.

libbra *sf.* pound.

libeccio *sm.* Southwest wind.

libello *sm.* libel.

libèllula *sf.* dragonfly.

liberale *agg.* e *sm.* liberal.

liberalismo *sm.* liberalism.

liberalità *sf.* generosity.

liberalizzare *vt.* to liberalize.

liberare *vt.* 1. to free 2. (*da pericoli*) to rescue 3. (*sbarazzare*) to rid (*v. irr.*) (of). ◆ **liberarsi** *vr.* (*sbarazzarsi*) to get (*v. irr.*) rid (of).

liberatore *agg.* liberating. ◆ **liberatore** *sm.* deliverer.

liberazione *sf.* liberation.

libero *agg.* free.

liberoscambista *agg.* e *sm.* free-trader.

libertà *sf.* liberty, freedom.

libertario *agg.* e *sm.* libertarian.

liberticida *agg.* e *s.* liberticide.

libertinaggio *sm.* libertinage.

libertino *agg.* e *sm.* libertine.

libìdine *sf.* lust.

libidinoso *agg.* lustful.

libido *sf.* lustfulness.

libraio *sm.* bookseller.

librarsi *vr.* to hover.

librerìa *sf.* 1. bookshop 2. (*mobile*) bookcase.

libresco *agg.* bookish.

libretto *sm.* 1. booklet 2. (*d'opera*) libretto || — *di assegni*, cheque-book; — *di risparmio*, savings-book; — *personale*, record-book.

libro *sm.* book.

licenza *sf.* 1. (*abuso*) licence 2. (*permesso*) permission, leave 3. (*documento*) licence.

licenziamento *sm.* dismissal.

licenziare *vt.* to dismiss. ◆ **licenziarsi** *vr.* to give (*v. irr.*) up one's job.

licenziosità *sf.* licentiousness.

licenzioso *agg.* licentious.

lichene *sm.* lichen.

licitazione *sf.* sale by auction.

lido *sm.* shore.

lieto *agg.* glad.

lieve *agg.* slight.

lievitare *vi.* to rise (*v. irr.*). ◆ **lievitare** *vt.* to leaven.

lievitazione *sf.* leavening.

lièvito *sm.* 1. yeast 2. (*fermento*) ferment.

ligio *agg.* faithful, observant (of).

lignaggio *sm.* lineage.

ligneo *agg.* wooden.

lignite *sf.* lignite.

lillà *sm.* lilac.

lillipuziano *agg.* e *sm.* Lilliputian.

lima *sf.* file.

limaccioso *agg.* slimy.

limare *vt.* 1. to file 2. (*fig.*) to polish.

limatrice *sf.* (*mecc.*) shaping-machine.

limatura *sf.* filing.

limbo *sm.* limbo.

limitare *vt.* to limit. ◆ **limitarsi** *vr.* (*controllarsi*) to check oneself.

limitatezza *sf.* limitation.

limitativo *agg.* limitative.

limitato *agg.* limited.

limitazione *sf.* limitation: — *delle nascite*, birth-control.

limite *sm.* limit: — *di velocità*, speed-limit || — *di rottura*, breaking-point.

limìtrofo *agg.* neighbouring.

limo *sm.* slime.

limonata *sf.* lemonade.

limone *sm.* lemon.

limpidezza *sf.* clearness.

limpido *agg.* limpid, clear.

lince *sf.* lynx.

linciaggio *sm.* lynching.

linciare *vt.* to lynch.

lindo *agg.* neat.

linea *sf.* line || *aereo di* —, air-liner; *mantenere la* —, to keep (*v. irr.*) one's figure.

lineamenti *sm. pl.* features **2.** (*linee essenziali*) outlines.

lineare *agg.* **1.** linear **2.** (*fig.*) unswerving.

lineetta *sf.* **1.** dash **2.** (*trattino d'unione*) hyphen.

linfa *sf.* (*biol.*) lymph.

linfatico *agg.* lymphatic.

linfatismo *sm.* lymphatism.

lingotto *sm.* ingot.

lingua *sf.* **1.** tongue **2.** (*linguaggio*) language.

linguacciuto *agg.* talkative.

linguaggio *sm.* language.

linguetta *sf.* **1.** flap **2.** (*mecc.; di scarpe*) tongue.

linguista *s.* linguist.

linguistica *sf.* linguistics.

linguistico *agg.* linguistic.

linimento *sm.* liniment.

lino *sm.* flax.

linoleum *sm.* linoleum.

linone *sm.* lawn.

linotipia *sf.* linotyping.

linotipista *s.* linotypist.

liquefare *vt.* to liquefy. ♦ **liquefarsi** *vr.* to liquefy.

liquefazione *sf.* liquefaction.

liquidare *vt.* **1.** to liquidate **2.** (*comm.*) to sell (*v. irr.*) off, to settle || — *una questione*, to settle a question.

liquidatore *sm.* liquidator.

liquidazione *sf.* liquidation, sale.

liquido *agg. e sm.* liquid || *denaro* —, cash.

liquirizia *sf.* liquorice.

liquore *sm.* liqueur || *i liquori*, spirits.

liquoroso *agg.* liqueur-like.

lira *sf.* **1.** (*moneta*) lira **2.** (*mus.*) lyre.

lirica *sf.* **1.** lyric poetry **2.** (*teatro lirico*) opera.

lirico *agg.* lyric(al). ♦ **lirico** *sm.* lyrist.

lirismo *sm.* lyrism.

lisciare *vt.* **1.** to smooth **2.** (*adulare*) to flatter. ♦ **lisciarsi** *vr.* to sleek oneself.

liscio *agg.* **1.** smooth **2.** (*di bevanda*) undiluted **3.** (*semplice*) plain **4.** (*di capelli*) sleek.

lisciva *sf.* lye.

liso *agg.* threadbare.

lista *sf.* **1.** (*elenco*) list, note **2.** (*striscia*) stripe.

listare *vt.* **1.** to stripe **2.** (*bordare*) to border.

listino *sm.* list.

litania *sf.* litany.

lite *sf.* **1.** quarrel, wrangle **2.** (*giur.*) lawsuit.

litigante *sm.* **1.** wrangler **2.** (*giur.*) litigant.

litigare *vi.* **1.** to quarrel **2.** (*giur.*) to litigate.

litigio *sm.* quarrel.

litigioso *agg.* quarrelsome.

litografia *sf.* **1.** lithography **2.** (*pezzo singolo*) lithograph.

litografico *agg.* lithographic.

litorale *agg.* littoral. ♦ **litorale** *sm.* coast.

litro *sm.* litre.

liturgia *sf.* liturgy.

liturgico *agg.* liturgic(al).

liuto *sm.* lute.

livellamento *sm.* levelling.

livellare *vt.* to level.

livellatrice *sf.* bulldozer.

livello *sm.* level: *a* — *del mare*, at sea-level; *passaggio a* —, level-crossing; *essere allo stesso* — *di*, to be on a level with.

livido *agg.* livid. ♦ **livido** *sm.* bruise.

livore *sm.* **1.** (*invidia*) envy **2.** (*odio*) hatred.

livrea *sf.* livery.

lizza *sf.* competition, lists (*pl.*) || *essere in* — (*fig.*), to be competing.

lo *art.* the. ♦ **lo** *pron.* **1.** (*per uomo*) him **2.** (*per animale, cosa*) it || — *credo*, I think so.

lobo *sm.* lobe.

locale *agg.* local. ♦ **locale** *sm.* **1.** room **2.** (*ritrovo*) place.

località *sf.* locality, spot.

localizzare *vt.* to localize.

localizzazione *sf.* localization.

locanda *sf.* inn.

locandiere *sm.* innkeeper.

locandina *sf.* play-bill.

locare *vt.* to rent.

locatario *sm.* tenant.

locativo *agg.* locative || *valore* —, rental value.

locatore *sm.* lessor.

locazione *sf.* lease.

locomotiva *sf.* locomotive.

locomotore *agg. e sm.* locomotive.

locomozione *sf.* locomotion.

locusta *sf.* locust.

locuzione *sf.* locution.

lodàbile *agg.* laudable.

lodare *vt.* to praise

lodatore *sm.* praiser.

lode *sf.* praise.

lodévole *agg.* praiseworthy.

logaritmo *sm.* logarithm.

loggia *sf.* 1. (*arch.*) loggia 2. (*massonica*) lodge.

loggione *sm.* gallery.

lògica *sf.* logic.

logicità *sf.* logicality.

lògico *agg.* logical. ♦ **lògico** *sm.* logician.

logìstica *sf.* logistics.

logìstico *agg.* logistic(al).

loglio *sm.* darnel.

logomachìa *sf.* logomachy.

logoramento *sm.* 1. wear 2. (*fig.*) wasting away.

logorante *agg.* wearing.

logorare *vt.* to wear (*v. irr.*) (out, down). ♦ **logorarsi** *vr.* to wear (out, down).

logorìo *sm.* wear and tear.

lògoro *agg.* worn (out, down).

lombàggine *sf.* lumbago.

lombardo *agg. e sm.* Lombard.

lombare *agg.* lumbar.

lombi *sm. pl.* loins.

lombrico *sm.* earth-worm.

longànime *agg.* forbearing.

longanimità *sf.* forbearance.

longevità *sf.* longevity.

longevo *agg.* longevous.

longitudinale *agg.* longitudinal.

longitùdine *sf.* longitude.

lontananza *sf.* distance: *in* —, in the distance.

lontano *agg.* 1. far 2. (*nel tempo*) far off, distant 3. (*vago*) vague. ♦ **lontano** *avv.* far || *da* —, from afar.

lontra *sf.* otter.

loquace *agg.* talkative.

loquacità *sf.* talkativeness.

loquela *sf.* glibness.

lordare *vt.* to soil. ♦ **lordarsi** *vr.* to get (*v. irr.*) dirty.

lordo *agg.* 1. (*sporco*) filthy 2. (*di peso*) gross.

loro *agg. poss.* their. ♦ **loro** *pron. poss.* theirs. ♦ **loro** *pron. pers.*

1. (*sogg.*) they, (*compl.*) them 2. (*forma di cortesia*) you.

losanga *sf.* lozenge.

losco *agg.* 1. (*bieco*) sinister 2. (*sospetto*) suspicious.

loto *sm.* 1. (*fango*) mud 2. (*bot.*) lotus.

lotta *sf.* 1. struggle 2. (*sport*) wrestling.

lottare *vi.* 1. to struggle 2. (*sport*) to wrestle.

lottatore *sm.* 1. struggler 2. (*sport*) wrestler.

lotterìa *sf.* lottery.

lottizzare *vt.* to lot.

lottizzazione *sf.* division into lots.

lotto *sm.* 1. lot 2. (*gioco*) state lottery.

lozione *sf.* lotion.

lubricità *sf.* lubricity.

lùbrico *agg.* 1. lubricous 2. (*fig.*) lascivious.

lubrificante *agg.* lubricating. ♦ **lubrificante** *sm.* lubricant.

lubrificare *vt.* to lubricate.

lubrificazione *sf.* lubrication.

lucchetto *sm.* padlock.

luccicante *agg.* glittering.

luccicare *vi.* to glitter.

luccichìo *sm.* glitter.

lùcciola *sf.* 1. firefly 2. (*senz'ali*) glow-worm.

luce *sf.* light || *alla* — *del sole* (*fig.*), openly; *dare alla* — *un bambino*, to give (*v. irr.*) birth to a child; *mettere in* —, to show (*v. irr.*); *venire alla* — (*nascere*), to be born.

lucente *agg.* bright.

lucentezza *sf.* brightness.

lucerna *sf.* oil-lamp.

lucernario *sm.* skylight.

lucèrtola *sf.* lizard.

lucidare *vt.* to polish.

lucidatrice *sf.* 1. floor-polisher 2. (*mecc.*) polishing machine.

lucidatura *sf.* polishing.

lucidezza *sf.* 1. brightness 2. (*di mente*) lucidness.

lucidità *sf.* lucidity.

lùcido *agg.* 1. lucid 2. (*lucidato*) glossy. ♦ **lùcido** *sm.* 1. (*per scarpe*) shoe-polish 2. (*lucidezza*) shine.

lucignolo *sm.* wick.

lucrare *vt.* to profit.

lucrativo *agg.* profitable.

lucro *sm.* profit: *a scopo di* —, for the sake of gain.

ludibrio *sm.* mockery

luglio *sm.* July.
lùgubre *agg.* lugubrious.
lui *pron.* **1.** (*sogg.*) he **2.** (*compl.*) him.
lumaca *sf.* snail.
lume *sm.* light || *al — di candela,* by candle-light; *perdere il — della ragione,* to be blinded by anger.
lumeggiare *vt.* (*fig.*) to put (*v. irr.*) in evidence.
luminare *sm.* luminary.
luminescenza *sf.* luminescence.
luminosità *sf.* brightness.
luminoso *agg.* bright.
luna *sf.* moon: *— calante,* waning moon; *— crescente,* waxing moon || *chiaro di —,* moonlight; *— di miele,* honeymoon; *avere la —* (*fig.*), to be in the sulks.
lunare *agg.* lunar.
lunario *sm.* almanac || *sbarcare il —,* to make (*v. irr.*) both ends meet.
lunàtico *agg.* moody.
lunazione *sf.* lunation.
lunedì *sm.* Monday.
lunetta *sf.* lunette.
lungàggine *sf.* slowness, delay.
lunghezza *sf.* length.
lungimirante *agg.* far-sighted.
lungo *agg.* **1.** long: *a —,* long; *a — andare,* in the long run **2.** (*lento*) slow || *in — e in largo,* far and wide; *di gran lunga,* by far. ♦ **lungo** *prep.* **1.** along **2.** (*durante*) during.
lungofiume *sm.* embankment.
lungolago *sm.* lake-front.
lungomare *sm.* sea-front.
lungometraggio *sm.* feature film.
luogo *sm.* place: *— di nascita,* birthplace; *sul —,* on the spot; *aver —,* to take (*v. irr.*) place; *dar —,* to cause.
luogotenente *sm.* lieutenant.
lupa *sf.* she-wolf.
lupanare *sm.* brothel.
lupara *sf.* shotgun.
lupino *sm.* (*bot.*) lupine.
lupo *sm.* wolf || *— di mare,* sea-dog; *in bocca al —!,* good luck!
lùppolo *sm.* hop.
lùrido *agg.* dirty.
luridume *sm.* dirt.
lusinga *sf.* allurement, flattery.
lusingare *vt.* to allure, to flatter.
lusinghiero *agg.* alluring, flattering.
lussare *vt.* to dislocate.
lussazione *sf.* dislocation.

lusso *sm.* luxury.
lussuoso *agg.* luxurious, rich.
lussureggiante *agg.* luxuriant.
lussureggiare *vi.* to thrive (*v. irr.*).
lussuria *sf.* lust.
lussurioso *agg.* lustful.
lustrale *agg.* lustral.
lustrare *vt.* to polish.
lustrascarpe *sm.* shoeblack.
lustratura *sf.* polish.
lustrino *sm.* spangle.
lustro *agg.* shining, shiny. ♦ **lustro** *sm.* lustre.
luteranésimo *sm.* Lutheranism.
luterano *agg.* e *sm.* Lutheran.
lutto *sm.* mourning: *mettere il —,* to go (*v. irr.*) into mourning.
luttuoso *agg.* mournful.

M

ma *cong.* **1.** but **2.** (*tuttavia*) however, still.
màcabro *agg.* macabre.
macaco *sm.* **1.** macaque **2.** (*fig.*) runt.
macché *inter.* you don't say it!
maccheroni *sm. pl.* macaroni (*sing.*).
macchia[1] *sf.* spot, stain.
macchia[2] *sf.* (*boscaglia*) bush: *darsi alla —,* to take (*v. irr.*) to the bush.
macchiare *vt.* to stain. ♦ **macchiarsi** *vr.* **1.** to get (*v. irr.*) stained **2.** (*fig.*) to soil oneself.
macchiato *agg.* spotted.
macchietta *sf.* **1.** caricature **2.** (*di persona*) character.
màcchina *sf.* **1.** engine, machine: *— calcolatrice,* calculating machine; *— per cucire,* sewing-machine; *— da presa,* cine-camera; *— per scrivere,* typewriter; *— fotografica,* camera; *fatto a —,* machine-made; *andare in —* (*di giornali*), to go (*v. irr.*) to press **2.** (*automobile*) car.
macchinale *agg.* mechanical.
macchinare *vt.* to plot.
macchinario *sm.* machinery.
macchinazione *sf.* machination.
macchinista *sm.* **1.** (*ferr.*) engine-driver **2.** (*teat.*) scene-shifter.
macchinoso *agg.* complicated.

macedonia sf. (cuc.) fruit-salad.

macellaio sm. butcher.

macellare vt. to slaughter.

macelleria sf. butcher's shop.

macello sm. **1.** (luogo dove si macella) slaughter-house **2.** (massacro) slaughter.

macerare vt. **1.** to soak **2.** (di lino, canapa) to ret. ♦ **macerarsi** vr. (fig.) to waste (away).

maceratoio sm. rettery.

macerazione sf. **1.** soaking **2.** (industria tessile) retting.

macerie sf. pl. rubble (sing.), ruins.

màcero sm. (per canapa e lino) retting-ground: carta da —, wastepaper.

machiavèllico agg. Machiavellian.

machiavellismo sm. Machiavellism.

macigno sm. boulder.

macilento agg. emaciated.

macilenza sf. emaciation.

màcina sf. grindstone.

macinacaffè sm. coffee-mill.

macinapepe sm. pepper-mill.

macinare vt. **1.** to grind (v. irr.), to mince.

macinino sm. grinder.

maciullare vt. to crush.

macrocèfalo agg. macrocephalous.

macrocosmo sm. macrocosm.

macromolècola sf. macromolecule.

macroscòpico agg. macroscopic.

maculato agg. spotted.

madia sf. **1.** kitchen cupboard **2.** (per pane) kneading trough.

màdido agg. wet: — di sudore, bathed in sweat.

madonna sf. **1.** (titolo) Lady, My Lady **2.** (relig.) The Virgin Mary, Our Lady **3.** (pitt.) Madonna.

madornale agg. huge.

madre sf. mother.

madrepatria sf. mother-country.

madreperla sf. mother-of-pearl.

madreperlàceo agg. pearly.

madrèpora sf. madrepore.

madreporico agg. madreporic.

madrevite sf. **1.** nut screw **2.** (utensile) die.

madrigale sm. madrigal.

madrina sf. godmother.

maestà sf. majesty.

maestosità sf. majesty.

maestoso agg. majestic.

maestra sf. (scol.) teacher.

maestrale sm. mistral.

maestranza sf. skilled workers (pl.).

maestrìa sf. skill, ability.

maestro sm. **1.** (scol.) teacher **2.** (uomo dotto) master **3.** (mus.) conductor, "maestro" || albero —, mainmast.

mafia sf. "Mafia".

maga sf. sorceress.

magagna sf. flaw, imperfection.

magari inter. if only! ♦ **magari** avv. (forse) perhaps, maybe. ♦ **magari** cong. even if.

magazzinaggio sm. storage.

magazziniere sm. store-keeper.

magazzino sm. warehouse || fondi di —, unsold stock.

maggese sm. fallow land.

maggio sm. May.

maggiolino sm. May-bug.

maggiorana sf. marjoram.

maggioranza sf. majority, most (of).

maggiorare vt. to increase.

maggiorazione sf. increase, charge.

maggiordomo sm. butler.

maggiore agg. **1.** (più grande, ampio) greater, larger **2.** (più vecchio) older: il —, the oldest **3.** (di fratelli) elder (fra due), eldest (fra molti). ♦ **maggiore** sm. **1.** (mil.) major **2.** (superiore) superior.

maggiorenne agg. of age: diventare —, to come (v. irr.) of age. ♦ **maggiorenne** sm. major.

maggiorente sm. notable.

maggioritario agg. majority (attr.).

maggiormente avv. more, much more.

magìa sf. magic.

màgiaro agg. e sm. Magyar.

magicamente avv. magically.

màgico agg. magical.

magistrale agg. **1.** magisterial || scuola —, teachers' institute **2.** (eccellente) masterly.

magistralmente avv. skilfully.

magistrato sm. Magistrate.

magistratura sf. magistracy.

maglia sf. **1.** (di lavoro a maglia) stitch || lavorare a —, to knit (v. irr.) **2.** (indumento) vest **3.** (di catena) link.

magliaia sf. knitter.

maglierìa sf. hosiery.

maglificio sm. hosiery.

maglio sm. **1.** mallet **2.** (mecc.) hammer.

maglione sm. sweater.

magma sm. magma.

magnanimità sf. magnanimity.

magnànimo *agg.* magnanimous.

magnate *sm.* magnate.

magnesia *sf.* magnesia.

magnesio *sm.* magnesium. *lampo al* —, flash.

magnete *sm.* magnet.

magnètico *agg.* magnetic.

magnetismo *sm.* magnetism.

magnetite *sf.* magnetite.

magnetizzare *vt.* to magnetize.

magnetizzatore *sm.* magnetizer.

magnetizzazione *sf.* magnetization.

magnetòfono *sm.* tape-recorder.

magnetòmetro *sm.* magnetometer.

magnificamente *avv.* magnificently.

magnificare *vt.* to extol, to glorify.

magnificenza *sf.* magnificence.

magnifico *agg.* magnificent.

magniloquente *agg.* magniloquent.

magniloquenza *sf.* magniloquence.

magnolia *sf.* magnolia.

mago *sm.* wizard.

magra *sf.* (*di fiumi*) low water.

magrezza *sf.* thinness.

magro *agg.* **1.** thin **2.** (*di carni*) lean.

mah *inter.* who knows!

mai *avv.* **1.** ever **2.** (*non mai*) never: — *e poi* —, never never; — *più*, never more; *caso* —, if; *non si sa* —, you never can tell; *meglio tardi che* —, better late than never.

maiale *sm.* **1.** pig **2.** (*carne*) pork.

maièutica *sf.* maieutics.

maiòlica *sf.* majolica.

maionese *sf.* mayonnaise.

mais *sm.* maize.

malùscola *sf.* capital letter.

maiuscoletto *sm.* small capitals.

malùscolo *agg.* capital.

malaccorto *agg.* ill-advised.

malachite *sf.* malachite.

malacreanza *sf.* rudeness.

malafede *sf.* bad faith.

malaffare *sm.* **1.** *donna di* —, whore **2.** *gente di* —, crooks (*pl.*).

malagévole *agg.* difficult, hard.

malagrazia *sf.* bad grace.

malalingua *sf.* backbiter.

malamente *avv.* badly.

malandato *agg.* in bad condition.

malandrino *sm.* **1.** brigand **2.** (*fam.*) rogue.

malànimo *sm* malevolence.

malanno *sm.* **1.** calamity **2.** (*malattia*) illness.

malapena (*nella loc. avv.*) *a* —, hardly.

malaria *sf.* malaria.

malaticcio *agg.* sickly.

malato *agg.* sick, ill. ♦ **malato** *sm.* patient.

malattia *sf.* sickness, disease.

malauguratamente *avv.* unluckily.

malaugurato *agg.* ill-fated.

malaugurio *sm.* ill-omen.

malavita *sf.* underworld.

malavoglia *sf.* unwillingness || *di* —, reluctantly.

malcapitato *agg.* unlucky. ♦ **malcapitato** *sm.* victim.

malconcio *agg.* **1.** battered **2.** (*contuso*) bruised.

malcontento *agg.* dissatisfied (with). ♦ **malcontento** *sm.* discontent.

malcostume *sm.* immorality, corruption.

maldestro *agg.* awkward.

maldicente *agg.* disparaging. ♦ **maldicente** *sm.* slanderer.

maldicenza *sf.* backbiting.

maldisposto *agg.* ill-disposed, hostile.

male *sm.* **1.** evil **2.** (*malattia*) illness, disease **3.** (*dolore fisico*) pain || — *di testa*, headache. ♦ **male** *avv.* badly, ill.

maledettamente *avv.* awfully.

maledetto *agg.* cursed.

malèdico *agg.* slanderous.

maledire *vt.* to curse.

maledizione *sf.* curse, malediction || —! (*inter.*), damn!

maleducato *agg.* rude, impolite.

maleducazione *sf.* rudeness.

malefatta *sf.* mischief.

maleficio *sm.* sorcery.

malèfico *agg.* harmful.

malerba *sf.* weed.

malese *agg.* e *sm.* Malay.

malèssere *sm.* **1.** malaise **2.** (*disagio*) uneasiness.

malestro *sm.* mischief.

malevolenza *sf.* malevolence.

malèvolo *agg.* malevolent.

malfamato *agg.* ill-famed.

malfatto *agg.* **1.** ill-shaped **2.** (*di abito*) ill-fitting.

malfattore *sm.* evil-doer.

malfermo *agg.* shaky || *salute malferma*, poor health.

malfido *agg.* unreliable.

malfondato *agg.* ill-grounded.

malformato *agg.* malformed.

malformazione *sf.* malformation.

malgarbo *sm.* bad grace.

malgoverno *sm.* misgovernment, misrule.

malgrado *prep. e avv.* in spite of. ♦ malgrado (che) *cong.* though, although.

malìa *sf.* (*fascino*) fascination.

maliarda *sf.* 1. (*donna affascinante*) fascinating woman 2. (*maga*) witch.

malignamente *avv.* maliciously.

malignare *vi.* to speak (*v. irr.*) ill (of).

malignità *sf.* malice.

maligno *agg.* malicious: *tumore* —, malignant tumor.

malinconìa *sf.* melancholy.

malinconicamente *avv.* sadly.

malincònico *agg.* melancholy.

malincuore (*nella loc. avv.*) *a* —, unwillingly.

malintenzionato *agg.* ill-disposed.

malinteso *agg.* misplaced. ♦ malinteso *sm.* misunderstanding.

malìzia *sf.* 1. malice 2. (*astuzia*) cunning.

maliziosamente *avv.* artfully.

malizioso *agg.* malicious, mischievous.

malleàbile *agg.* malleable.

malleabilità *sf.* malleability.

malleverìa *sf.* bail.

malloppo *sm.* swag.

malmenare *vt.* to manhandle.

malmesso *ag.* poorly dressed.

malnato *agg.* ill-bred.

malocchio *sm.* evil eye.

malora *sf.* ruin || *va alla* —!, go to the devil!

malore *sm.* illness.

malpensante *agg.* wrong-thinking.

malsano *agg.* unhealthy.

malsicuro *agg.* unsafe.

malta *sf.* mortar.

maltempo *sm.* bad weather.

maltenuto *agg.* untidy.

maltese *agg. e sm.* Maltese.

malto *sm.* malt.

maltolto *agg.* ill-gotten. ♦ maltolto *sm.* ill-gotten property.

maltosio *sm.* maltose.

maltrattamento *sm.* maltreatment.

maltrattare *vt.* to maltreat.

maltusianìsmo *sm.* Malthusianism.

maltusiano *agg. e sm.* Malthusian.

malumore *sm.* ill-humour.

malva *sf.* mallow.

malvagio *agg.* wicked.

malvagità *sf.* wickedness.

malversatore *sm.* embezzler.

malversazione *sf.* embezzlement.

malvisto *agg.* unpopular (with).

malvivente *sm.* gangster.

malvivenza *sf.* delinquency.

malvolere *sm.* ill-will.

malvolere *vi.* to dislike.

malvolentieri *avv.* unwillingly.

mamma *sf.* mama, mummy.

mammalucco *sm.* (*fam.*) simpleton.

mammella *sf.* 1. mamma (*pl.* -ae) 2. (*di animali da latte*) udder.

mammìfero *agg.* mammiferous. ♦ mammìfero *sm.* mammal.

màmmola *sf.* sweet-smelling violet.

mammùt *sm.* mammoth.

manata *sf.* slap.

manca *sf.* 1. left hand 2. (*parte sinistra*) left || *a dritta e a* —, on all sides.

mancante *agg.* incomplete.

mancanza *sf.* 1. lack, shortage 2. (*fallo*) fault || *sentire la* — *di qu.*, to miss so.

mancare *vi.* 1. to be lacking (in) 2. (*non esserci*) to be missing 3. (*venir meno*) to fail 4. (*agire scorrettamente*) to wrong (so.).

mancato *agg.* unsuccessful.

manchévole *agg.* defective.

manchevolezza *sf.* defect, fault.

mancia *sf.* tip || *dare la* — *a qu.*, to tip so.

manciata *sf.* handful.

mancina *sf.* left-hand.

mancino *agg.* left-handed. ♦ mancino *sm.* left-hander.

manco *avv.* not even.

mandamento *sm.* district.

mandante *sm.* 1. instigator 2. (*giur.*) principal.

mandare *vt.* 1. to send (*v. irr.*) 2. (*spedire*) to forward 3. (*emettere*) to give (*v. irr.*) out.

mandarino *sm.* mandarin.

mandata *sf.* batch || — *di chiave*, turn.

mandatario *sm.* mandatary.

mandato *sm.* 1. mandate 2. (*comm.*) agency 3. (*giur.*) warrant.

mandìbola *sf.* mandible.

mandola *sf.* mandola.

mandolinista *s.* mandolinist.

mandolino *sm.* mandolin.

màndorla *sf.* almond.

màndorlo *sm.* almond-tree.

mandràgora *sf.* mandrake.

mandria *sf.* herd.

mandriano *sm.* herdsman (*pl.* -men).

maneggévole *agg.* handy.

maneggiare *vt.* to handle.

maneggio *sm.* 1. (*equitazione*) riding-ground 2. (*uso*) use 3. (*intrigo*) plot.

manesco *agg.* rough, aggressive.

manette *sf. pl.* handcuff (*sing.*).

manforte *sf.* help.

manganellare *vt.* to cudgel.

manganello *sm.* cudgel.

manganese *sm.* manganese.

mangereccio *agg.* eatable.

mangiàbile *agg.* eatable.

mangiare *vt.* to eat (*v. irr.*).

mangiata *sf.* square meal.

mangiatoia *sf.* manger.

mangime *sm.* fodder.

mangiucchiare *vt.* to nibble (at).

manìa *sf.* mania.

maniaco *agg.* 1. maniac 2. (*fig.*) crazy. ♦ **maniaco** *sm.* maniac.

mànica *sf.* sleeve || *essere di larga, stretta,* to be indulgent, strict.

manicheìsmo *sm.* Manicheism.

manicheo *agg. e sm.* Manichean.

manichino *sm.* manikin.

mànico *sm.* handle.

manicomio *sm.* mental hospital.

manicotto *sm.* 1. muff 2. (*mecc.*) sleeve.

maniera *sf.* manner, way.

manierato *agg.* affected.

manierismo *sm.* mannerism.

maniero *sm.* castle.

manifattura *sf.* manufacture.

manifatturiero *agg.* manufacturing.

manifestante *s.* demonstrator.

manifestare *vt.* 1. to manifest, to show (*v. irr.*) 2. (*pol.*) to demonstrate.

manifestazione *sf.* 1. manifestation 2. (*pol.*) demonstration.

manifesto *agg.* manifest, clear, obvious. ♦ **manifesto** *sm.* 1. (*affisso*) poster 2. (*volantino*) leaflet 3. (*dichiarazione*) manifesto.

maniglia *sf.* handle.

manigoldo *sm.* scoundrel.

manioca *sf.* manioc.

manipolare *vt.* to manipulate.

manipolatore *sm.* manipulator.

manipolazione *sf.* manipulation.

manìpolo *sm.* (*eccl.; stor.*) maniple.

maniscalco *sm.* blacksmith.

manna *sf.* 1. manna 2. (*fig.*) blessing.

mannaia *sf.* 1. axe 2. (*della ghigliottina*) knife.

mannaro *agg. lupo* —, werewolf.

mano *sf.* hand: *fatto a* —, hand-made; *stringere la* —, to shake (*v. irr.*) hands with || *a — armata,* by force of arms; *sotto* —, underhand.

manodòpera *sf.* labour.

manòmetro *sm.* manometer.

manométtere *vt.* to tamper with.

manomissione *sf.* tampering.

manòpola *sf.* 1. knob 2. (*impugnatura*) handle.

manoscritto *agg.* handwritten. ♦ **manoscritto** *sm.* manuscript.

manovale *sm.* hodman (*pl.* -men).

manovella *sf.* crank.

manovra *sf.* manoeuvre, operation.

manovràbile *agg.* manoeuvrable.

manovrare *vt.* 1. to manoeuvre 2. (*mecc.*) to operate.

manovratore *sm.* operator, driver.

manrovescio *sm.* back-handed slap.

mansarda *sf.* mansard.

mansione *sf.* function.

mansuefare *vt.* to tame.

mansueto *agg.* meek, mild.

mansuetùdine *sf.* meekness.

mantella *sf.* cape.

mantello *sm.* cloak.

mantenere *vt.* to keep (*v. irr.*), to maintain: — *la parola,* to keep one's word.

mantenimento *sm.* maintenance.

màntice *sm.* bellows (*pl.*).

manto *sm.* cloak.

manuale *agg.* manual. ♦ **manuale** *sm.* handbook.

manubrio *sm.* 1. handle 2. (*di bicicletta ecc.*) handle-bar.

manufatto *agg.* hand-made. ♦ **manufatto** *sm.* hand-manufactured article.

manutèngolo *sm.* abettor.

manutenzione *sf.* maintenance, servicing.

manzo *sm.* 1. (*zool.*) steer 2. (*carne*) beef.

maomettano *agg. e sm.* Mohammedan.

mappa *sf.* map.

mappamondo *sm.* globe.

marachella *sf.* trick.

marasma *sm.* 1. (*med.*) marasmus 2. (*fig.*) decadence.

maratona *sf.* marathon race.

marca *sf.* brand: — *di fabbrica*, trade mark.

marcare *vt.* **1.** to mark **2.** (*sport*) to score.

marcato *agg.* marked, branded.

marcatore *sm.* **1.** marker **2.** (*sport*) scorer.

marcatura *sf.* **1.** marking **2.** (*sport*) scoring.

marchesa *sf.* **1.** marchioness **2.** (*se non è inglese*) marquise.

marchesato *sm.* marquisate.

marchese *sm.* marquis.

marchiano *agg.* enormous, glaring.

marchiare *vt.* to brand.

marchiatura *sf.* branding.

marchio *sm.* **1.** stamp **2.** (*a fuoco*) brand **3.** (*fig.; comm.*) mark.

marcia *sf.* **1.** (*auto*) gear **2.** (*mil.; mus.*) march.

marciapiede *sm.* **1.** pavement **2.** (*ferr.*) platform.

marciare *vi.* to march.

marciatore *sm.* (*sport*) road-walker.

marcio *agg.* **1.** rotten **2.** (*fig.*) corrupted. ♦ **marcio** *sm.* (*fig.*) corruption.

marcire *vi.* **1.** (*guastarsi*) to go (*v. irr.*) bad **2.** (*decomporsi*) to rot (*v. irr.*).

marciume *sm.* rottenness.

marco *sm.* mark.

marconigrafia *sf.* marconigraphy.

mare *sm.* sea.

marea *sf.* tide.

mareggiata *sf.* sea-storm.

maremma *sf.* maremma (*pl.* -me).

maremoto *sm.* seaquake.

mareògrafo *sm.* tide-gauge.

maresciallo *sm.* marshal.

margarina *sf.* margarine.

margherita *sf.* daisy.

marginale *agg.* marginal.

marginare *vt.* **1.** to border **2.** (*tip.*) to margin.

marginatura *sf.* **1.** edging **2.** (*tip.*) furniture.

màrgine *sm.* **1.** border, edge **2.** (*fig.*) margin.

marina *sf.* **1.** navy **2.** (*costa*) sea-shore **3.** (*pitt.*) sea-scape.

marinaio *sm.* sailor.

marinara *sf.* **1.** (*cappotto*) duffle coat **2.** (*cappello*) sailor hat.

marinare *vt.* (*cuc.*) to pickle || — *la scuola*, to play truant.

marinaresco *agg.* sailor-like.

marinaro *agg.* **1.** maritime **2.** sail-or-like. ♦ **marinaro** *sm.* sailor.

marinerìa *sf.* **1.** seamanship **2.** (*marina*) navy.

marino *agg.* sea (*attr.*).

mariolo *sm.* rogue.

marionetta *sf.* puppet.

maritale *agg.* marital.

maritare *vt.* to marry. ♦ **maritarsi** *vr.* to get (*v. irr.*) married.

marito *sm.* husband.

marittimo *agg.* maritime || *città marittima*, sea-town; *commercio* —, shipping business. ♦ **marittimo** *sm.* seafarer || *i marittimi*, seafolk (*sing.*).

marmaglia *sf.* rabble.

marmellata *sf.* **1.** jam **2.** (*d'arance*) marmalade.

marmista *sm.* marble-cutter.

marmitta *sf.* **1.** (*cuc.*) stock-pot **2.** (*auto*) silencer's muffler.

marmo *sm.* marble.

marmocchio *sm.* kid.

marmòreo *agg.* marble.

marmotta *sf.* **1.** marmot **2.** (*di persona*) lazy-bones.

marna *sf.* marl.

marocchino *agg.* Moroccan. ♦ **marocchino** *sm.* **1.** (*persona*) Moroccan **2.** (*cuoio*) Morocco leather.

maroso *sm.* billow.

marra *sf.* **1.** (*agr.*) hoe **2.** (*mar.*) fluke.

marrone *agg.* brown. ♦ **marrone** *sm.* chestnut.

martedì *sm.* Tuesday.

martellamento *sm.* hammering.

martellare *vt.* **1.** to hammer **2.** (*mil.*) to pound **3.** (*pulsare*) to throb.

martellata *sf.* hammer-blow.

martello *sm.* hammer.

martinetto *sm.* jack.

martingala *sf.* half-belt.

màrtire *sm.* martyr.

martirio *sm.* martyrdom.

martirizzare *vt.* to martyrize.

martirologio *sm.* martyrology.

màrtora *sf.* marten.

martoriare *vt.* to torture.

marxismo *sm.* Marxism.

marxista *agg. e s.* Marxist.

marzapane *sm.* marzipan.

marziale *agg.* martial.

marziano *sm.* Martian.

marzo *sm.* March.

mascalzonata *sf.* knavery.

mascalzone *sm.* rascal.

mascella *sf.* jaw.

mascellare agg. jaw (attr.).
màschera sf. 1. mask 2. (figura mascherata) masker 3. (cosmesi) face-pack 4. (inserviente di cinema, teatro) usher.
mascheramento sm. masking.
mascherare vt. to mask.
mascherata sf. masquerade.
maschietto sm. male.
maschile agg. male.
maschio[1] agg. 1. male 2. (virile) manly. ♦ **maschio** sm. 1. (di animale) (uccelli) cock, (mammiferi) bull (attributivi) 2. (di uomo) male 3. (bambino) boy.
maschio[2] sm. (torre) donjon.
mascolinità sf. masculinity.
masnada sf. gang.
masnadiere sm. highwayman (pl. -men).
masochismo sm. masochism.
masonite sf. masonite.
massa sf. mass, heap.
massacrante agg. exhausting.
massacrare vt. to massacre.
massacratore sm. slaughterer.
massacro sm. massacre.
massaggiare vt. to massage.
massaggiatore sm. masseur.
massaggiatrice sf. masseuse.
massaggio sm. massage.
massaia sf. housewife (pl. -wives).
massello sm. ingot.
masseria sf. farm.
masserizie sf. pl. household goods.
massicciata sf. road-bed.
massiccio agg. solid. ♦ **massiccio** sm. massif.
màssima sf. maxim, rule || in linea di —, on the whole; accordo di —, general agreement.
massimalismo sm. Maximalism.
massimalista s. Maximalist.
màssimo agg. 1. greatest, highest 2. (l'estremo) utmost 3. (il più lungo) longest. ♦ **màssimo** sm. 1. most 2. (il meglio) best 3. (mat.; fis.) maximum.
masso sm. boulder.
massone sm. freemason.
massoneria sf. freemasonry.
mastello sm. tub.
masticare vt. to chew.
masticazione sf. mastication.
màstice sm. rubber.
mastino sm. mastiff.
mastite sf. mastitis.
mastodonte sm. 1. (zool.) mastodon 2. (fig.) giant.

mastodòntico agg. colossal.
mastòide sf. mastoid.
mastoidite sf. mastoiditis.
mastro sm. 1. (libro) ledger 2. (ap pellativo) Master.
masturbazione sf. masturbation.
matassa sf. 1. hank 2. (fig.) tangle.
matemàtica sf. mathematics.
matemàtico agg. mathematical. ♦
matemàtico sm. mathematician.
materasso sm. mattress.
materia sf. matter, subject.
materiale agg. 1. material 2. (rozzo) rough. ♦ **materiale** sm. material.
materialismo sm. materialism.
materialista s. materialist.
materialistico agg. materialistic.
materializzare vt. to materialize.
maternità sf. maternity.
materno agg. motherly, maternal || scuola materna, nursery-school.
matita sf. pencil.
matriarcato sm. matriarchy.
matrice sf. 1. matrix (pl. matrices) 2. (comm.) counterfoil.
matricida s. matricide.
matricidio sm. matricide.
matricola sf. 1. matricula, register || numero di —, matriculation number 2. (scol.) freshman (pl. -men).
matricolato agg. matriculated || briccone —, arrant knave.
matrigna sf. stepmother.
matrimoniale agg. matrimonial.
matrimonio sm. 1. marriage 2. (cerimonia nuziale) wedding.
matrona sf. matron.
matta sf. 1. mad woman (pl. women) 2. (al gioco) jolly joker.
mattacchione sm. joker.
mattatoio sm. slaughter-house.
matterello sm. rolling-pin.
mattina sf. morning.
mattinata sf. 1. morning 2. (teat.) matinée.
mattiniero agg. early-rising.
mattino sm. morning.
matto[1] agg. mad, crazy. ♦ **matto** sm. madman (pl. -men).
matto[2] agg. 1. (non lucido) mat 2. (di gioielli) false.
mattone sm. 1. brick 2. (fig.) bore.
mattonella sf. tile.
mattutino agg. morning (attr.). ♦
mattutino sm. (eccl.) matins (pl.).
maturare vi. e vt. to ripen, to mature (anche fig.).

maturazione sf. maturation, ripening (anche fig.).

maturità sf. ripening, maturity (anche fig.).

maturo agg. ripe, mature (anche fig.).

mausoleo sm. mausoleum.

mazurca sf. mazurka.

mazza sf. 1. (clava) club 2. (martello di legno) mallet.

mazzata sf. heavy blow (anche fig.).

mazziere sm. 1. mace-bearer 2. (di carte) dealer.

mazzo sm. 1. bunch 2. (di carte) pack || fare il —, to shuffle 3. (di fiori) bouquet.

mazzolino sm. (di fiori) posy.

mazzuolo sm. mallet.

me pron. 1. me 2. (me stesso) myself.

meandro sm. 1. meander 2. (labirinto) maze.

meato sm. meatus.

meccanica sf. mechanics.

meccànico agg. mechanical. ♦ **meccànico** sm. mechanic.

meccanismo sm. 1. gear 2. (movimento) motion.

meccanizzare vt. to mechanize.

meccanizzazione sf. mechanization.

meccanografìa sf. mechanography.

meccanogràfico agg. mechanographic.

mecenate sm. Maecenas.

mecenatismo sm. patronage.

medaglia sf. medal.

medaglione sm. 1. locket 2. (arch.) medallion.

medaglista sm. 1. (incisore) medallist 2. (collezionista) collector of medals.

medésimo agg. e pron. V. stesso.

media sf. 1. average: alla — di, at an average of 2. (mat.) mean.

mediana sf. median line.

medìanico agg. mediumistic.

mediano agg. 1. medial, middle (attr.) 2. (geom.; anat; bot.) median. ♦ **mediano** sm. (sport) half-back.

mediante prep. by, by means of, through.

mediato agg. indirect.

mediatore sm. 1. mediator 2. (comm.) broker.

mediazione sf. 1. mediation 2. (comm.) brokerage.

medicamento sm. medicament.

medicare vt. to dress.

medicastro sm. quack (doctor).

medicazione sf. 1. medication 2. (di ferita) dressing.

medicina sf. medicine.

medicinale sm. medicinal.

mèdico agg. medical. ♦ **mèdico** sm. physician, doctor.

medievale agg. medieval.

medio agg. 1. (dito) middle finger 2. (mat.) mean. ♦ **medio** agg. 1. middle 2. (normale, che risulta da una media) average.

mediocre agg. second-rate.

mediocrità sf. mediocrity.

medioevo sm. Middle Ages (pl.).

meditabondo agg. thoughtful.

meditare vt. 1. to ponder 2. (avere in'intenzione) to meditate.

meditativo agg. meditative.

meditazione sf. meditation.

mediterràneo agg. 1. inland 2. Mediterranean.

medium sm. medium.

medusa sf. medusa (pl. -ae).

mefistofèlico agg. satanic.

mefìtico agg. poisonous.

megaciclo sm. megacycle.

megàfono sm. megaphone.

megalòmane sm. megalomaniac.

megalomanìa sf. megalomania.

megatone sm. megaton.

mèglio avv. 1. (comp.) better 2. (superl. rel.) best. ♦ **mèglio** agg. 1. (comp.) better: questo vestito è — di quello, this dress is better than that 2. (superl. rel.) best. ♦ **mèglio** sm. best, best thing || in mancanza di —, for lack of anything better. ♦ **mèglio** sf. avere la —, to have the better || alla —, as well as possible.

mela sf. apple.

melacotogna sf. quince.

melagrana sf. pomegranate.

melanismo sm. melanism.

melanzana sf. aubergine.

melassa sf. molasses (pl.).

melato agg. 1. sweetened with honey 2. (fig.) honeyed.

melenso agg. dull, silly.

mellifluo agg. honeyed.

melma sf. slime.

melmoso agg. slimy.

melo sm. apple-tree.

melodìa sf. melody.

melòdico agg. melodic.

melodìoso agg. melodious.

melodramma sm. 1. opera 2. (fig.) melodrama.

melodrammàtico agg. **1.** operatic **2.** (fig.) melodramatic.

melograno sm. pomegrancte-tree.

melòmane s. melomaniac.

melomanìa sf. melomania.

melone sm. melon.

membra sf. pl. limbs.

membrana sf. membrane.

membratura sf. structure.

membro sm. **1.** member **2.** (anat.) limb.

memoràbile agg. memorable.

memorandum sm. memorandum (pl. -da).

mèmore agg. mindful.

memoria sf. **1.** memory: — di ferro, cast-iron memory || a —, by heart **2.** (ricordo) memory, recollection.

memoriale sm. **1.** (petizione) memorial **2.** (libro di memorie) memoirs (pl.).

memorialista s. memorialist.

menabò sm. dummy.

menadito (nella loc. avv.) a —, perfectly || sapere qc. a —, to have sthg. at one's finger-tips.

menagramo sm. bearer of ill-luck.

menare vt. (condurre) to lead (v. irr.) || — vanto, to boast; — il can per l'aia, to beat (v. irr.) about the bush; — buono, gramo, to bring (v. irr.) good, bad luck.

mendace agg. mendacious, false.

mendacia sf. mendacity.

mendicante sm. beggar.

mendicare vi. to beg.

mendicità sf. mendicity.

mendico agg. e sm. mendicant.

menestrello sm. minstrel.

meninge sf. meninx (pl. meninges).

menisco sm. meniscus.

meno avv. **1.** (comp.) less **2.** (superl. rel.) least || fare a —, to do (v. irr.) without; non poter fare a —, cannot help; non posso fare a — di andare, I cannot help going **3.** (mat.) minus. ♦ **meno** prep. but for || a — che (non), unless. ♦ **meno** agg. **1.** (comp. sing.) less: è — bella di sua sorella, she is less beautiful than her sister **2.** (comp. con s. pl.) fewer: ho — libri di te, I have fewer books than you **3.** (superl. rel. sing.) the least: è il — intelligente dei miei amici, he is the least intelligent of my friends **4.** (superl. rel. con s. pl.) the fewest (raro).

♦ **meno** sm. **1.** (comp.) less **2.** (superl. rel.) the least.

menomare vt. to lessen.

menomato agg. **1.** lessened **2.** (di vista, udito) impaired.

menomazione sf. **1.** lessening **2.** (di arti, sensi) impairment **3.** (di persona) disablement.

menopàusa sf. menopause.

mensa sf. table.

mensile agg. monthly. ♦ **mensile** sm. **1.** (salario) month's salary **2.** (pubblicazione mensile) monthly.

mensilità sf. monthly instalment || tredicesima —, Christmas bonus.

mensilmente avv. monthly, once a month.

mènsola sf. **1.** bracket **2.** (scaffale) shelf (pl. -lves).

menta sf. mint.

mentale agg. mental.

mentalità sf. mentality.

mente sf. mind: persona dalla — ristretta, narrow-minded person; aguzzare la —, to sharpen one's wits.

mentecatto agg. insane. ♦ **mentecatto** sm. madman (pl. -men).

mentina sf. peppermint-drop.

mentire vi. to lie.

mentito agg. false: sotto mentite spoglie, under false pretences.

mentitore sm. liar.

mento sm. chin.

mentolo sm. menthol.

mèntore sm. mentor.

mentre cong. **1.** (temporale) while, as, when **2.** (avversativo) whereas, while **3.** (finché) as long as, while. ♦ **mentre** sm. moment: in quel —, at that moment.

menzionare vt. to mention.

menzione sf. mention.

menzogna sf. falsehood.

menzognero agg. **1.** (di persona) mendacious **2.** (di cosa) false.

meraviglia sf. wonder: sopraffatto dalla —, wonder-struck; non fa — che, nessuna — che, no wonder.

meravigliare vt. to astonish.

meravigliarsi vr. to be astonished (at).

meravigliato agg. astonished.

meraviglioso agg. wonderful.

mercante sm. merchant.

mercanteggiare vi. (tirare sul prezzo) to bargain, to haggle.

mercantile agg. mercantile. ♦ **mercantile** sm. cargo boat.

mercantilismo *sm.* mercantilism.

mercanzia *sf.* merchandise.

mercato *sm.* market || *a buon —,* cheap.

merce *sf.* goods (*pl.*).

mercé *sf.* mercy.

mercede *sf.* pay, reward.

mercenario *agg. e sm.* mercenary.

merceologìa *sf.* technology of marketable goods.

mercerìa *sf.* 1. haberdashery 2. (*negozio*) haberdasher's shop.

mercerizzato *agg.* mercerized.

merciaio *sm.* haberdasher.

mercoledì *sm.* Wednesday: *— delle Ceneri,* Ash Wednesday.

mercurio *sm.* mercury, quicksilver.

merenda *sf.* afternoon snack.

meretrice *sf.* prostitute.

meretricio *sm.* prostitution.

meridiana *sf.* sun-dial.

meridiano *agg. e sm.* meridian.

meridionale *agg.* Southern. ♦ **meridionale** *sm.* Southerner.

meridione *sm.* south.

meringa *sf.* meringue.

merino *sm.* merino.

meritare *vt.* to deserve.

meritévole *agg.* deserving.

mèrito *sm.* merit || *in — a,* as to.

meritorio *agg.* meritorious, deserving.

merletto *sm.* lace.

merlo *sm.* 1. blackbird 2. (*sciocco*) simpleton.

merluzzo *sm.* codfish.

mero *agg.* 1. pure 2. (*fig.*) mere.

mesata *sf.* 1. month 2. (*paga di un mese*) month's pay.

méscere *vt.* to pour (out).

meschinità *sf.* meanness.

meschino *agg.* mean. ♦ **meschino** *sm.* wretch.

méscita *sf.* pouring (out).

mescolanza *sf.* 1. mixing 2. (*miscuglio*) mixture.

mescolare *vt.* 1. to mix 2. (*tè, caffè, liquori, tabacco*) to blend. ♦ **mescolarsi** *vr.* to mingle.

mescolatrice *sf.* mixer.

mese *sm.* month.

messa *sf.* 1. (*eccl.*) Mass 2. (*azione del mettere*) putting, setting: *— a punto,* setting up || *— a fuoco,* focusing.

messaggero *sm.* messenger.

messaggio *sm.* 1. message 2. (*allocuzione*) address.

messale *sm.* missal.

messe *sf.* crop, harvest.

messìa *sm.* Messiah.

messiànico *agg.* Messianic.

messianismo *sm.* Messianism.

messicano *agg. e sm.* Mexican.

messinscena *sf.* staging.

mestare *vt.* to stir.

mestiere *sm.* 1. trade 2. (*perizia*) skill 3. (*lavoro*) work.

mestizia *sf.* sadness.

méstola *sf.* ladle.

méstolo *sm.* ladle.

mestruazione *sf.* menstruation.

meta *sf.* 1. destination 2. (*scopo*) aim, purpose: *senza —,* aimless.

metà *sf.* 1. half (*pl.* halves) 2. (*parte mediana*) middle 3. (*coniuge*) la *mia —,* my better half.

metabolismo *sm.* metabolism.

metafìsica *sf.* metaphysics.

metàfora *sf.* metaphor.

metafòrico *agg.* metaphoric(al).

metàllico *agg.* metallic.

metallo *sm.* metal.

metallurgìa *sf.* metallurgy.

metallùrgico *agg.* metallurgic(al). ♦ **metallùrgico** *sm.* metallurgist.

metalmeccànico *sm.* metallurgist and mechanic.

metamòrfico *agg.* metamorphic.

metamorfismo *sm.* metamorphism.

metamòrfosi *sf.* metamorphosis (*pl.* -ses).

metano *sm.* methane.

metapsìchica *sf.* metapsychics.

metapsìchico *agg.* metapsychic(al).

metàstasi *sf.* metastasis (*pl.* -ses).

metempsicosi *sf.* metempsychosis (*pl.* -ses).

metèora *sf.* meteor.

meteòrico *agg.* meteoric.

meteorite *sm.* meteorite.

meteorologìa *sf.* meteorology.

meteorològico *agg.* meteorological || *previsioni meteorologiche,* weather-forecast (*sing.*).

meteoròlogo *sm.* meteorologist.

meticcio *agg. e sm.* mestizo (*pl.* -za).

meticoloso *agg.* meticulous.

metodicità *sf.* methodicalness.

metòdico *agg.* methodical.

metodista *agg. e s.* Methodist.

mètodo *sm.* method.

metodologìa *sf.* methodology.

metodològico *agg.* methodological.

mètopa *sf.* metope.

metraggio *sm.* 1. length (in metres) 2. (*cine*) *corto, lungo —,* short, full-length film.

mètrica sf. prosody.

mètrico agg. metric.

metrite sf. metritis.

metro sm. 1. metre 2. (strumento per misurare) rule.

metrònomo sm. metronome.

metronotte sm. night-watch.

metròpoli sf. metropolis (pl. -ses).

metropolitana sf. underground.

metropolitano agg. metropolitan.

méttere vt. 1. to put (v. irr.) || — in chiaro qc., to make (v. irr.) sthg. clear; — in dubbio qc., to doubt sthg.; — in serbo, to lay (v. irr.) aside; — in moto, to start; — in luce, to emphasize; — in guardia qu., to put so. on his guard; — le mani su qc., to take (v. irr.) possession of; — le mani sul fuoco per qu., to speak (v. irr.) for so. 2. (impiegare, di tempo) to take 3. (indossare) to put on 4. (paragonare) to compare. ♦ **mettersi** vr. 1. to put oneself || — in contatto còn qu., to get (v. irr.) in touch with so.; — in testa di fare qc., to take into one's head to do sthg.; — sotto, to get down to it 2. (incominciare) to begin (v. irr.) 3. (indossare) to put (v. irr.) on.

mettifoglio sm. (tip.) feeder.

mezzadrìa sf. métayage.

mezzadro sm. métayer.

mezzaluna sf. 1. half-moon 2. (emblema islamico) crescent 3. (cuc.) mincing-knife.

mezzana¹ sf. (mar.) mizzen sail.

mezzana² sf. procuress.

mezzano agg. middle. ♦ **mezzano** sm. go-between.

mezzanotte sf. midnight.

mezzatinta sf. half-tone.

mezzo¹ agg. 1. half 2. (medio) middle. ♦ **mezzo** avv. half. ♦ **in mezzo a** prep. 1. in the middle of 2. (fra molti) among 3. (fra due) between.

mezzo² sm. 1. means 2. (fis.) medium.

mezzo³ agg. (marcio) rotten.

mezzobusto sm. bust.

mezzocerchio sm. semicircle.

mezzodì sm. midday, noon.

mezzofondo sm. middle-distance race.

mezzogiorno sm. 1. midday 2. (Sud) South.

mezzosoprano sm. mezzo-soprano.

mi¹ pron. 1. me 2. (me stesso) myself 3. (a me) to me.

mi² sm. (mus.) E, mi.

miagolare vi. to mew

miagolio sm. mewing

miasma sm. miasma.

mica sf. mica.

miccia sf. fuse.

michetta sf. roll.

micidiale agg. lethal,, deadly.

micino sm. kitten, pussy.

micosi sf. mycosis (pl. -ses).

microbio sm. microbe.

microbiologìa sf. microbiology.

microcosmo sm. microcosm.

microfilm sm. microfilm.

micròfono sm. microphone.

microfotografìa sf. microphotography.

micrometrìa sf. micrometry.

micròmetro sm. micrometer.

micron sm. micron.

microrganismo sm. microorganism.

microscopìa sf. microscopy.

microscòpico agg. microscopic(al).

microscopio sm. microscope.

microsolco sm. long-playing record.

microtelèfono sm. microtelephone.

midolla sf. crumb.

midollare agg. medullar.

midollo sm. marrow: — spinale, spinal cord.

miele sm. honey.

mietere vt. to reap.

mietitrice sf. reaper.

mietitura sf. reaping.

migliaio sm. thousand.

miglio¹ sm. (bot.) millet.

miglio² sm. (misura di lunghezza) mile.

miglioramento sm. improvement.

migliorare vt. to better, to improve.

migliore agg. 1. (comp.) better: questo libro è — di quello, this book is better than that 2. (superl.) the best: è il — alunno della classe, he is the best pupil in his class.

migliorìa sf. improvement.

mignatta sf. leech.

mìgnolo sm. little finger.

migrare vi. to migrate.

migratore agg. migratory. ♦ **migratore** sm. migrant.

migratorio agg. migratory.

migrazione sf. migration.

miliardario sm. multi-millionaire.

miliardo sm. a thousand millions.
miliare agg. pietra —, milestone.
milionario sm. millionaire.
milione sm. million.
milionèsimo agg. millionth.
militante agg. militant.
militare[1] agg. military. ♦ militare sm. soldier.
militare[2] vi. 1. to be a soldier 2. (lavorare a favore di) to support.
militaresco agg. soldierlike.
militarismo sm. militarism.
militarista sm. militarist.
militarizzare vt. to militarize.
militarizzazione sf. militarization.
militarmente avv. militarily.
milite sm. militiaman (pl. -men).
milizia sf. Army.
miliziano sm. militiaman (pl. -men).
millantare vt. to boast of. ♦ millantarsi vr. to boast.
millantatore sm. boaster.
millanteria sf. boasting.
mille agg. one thousand.
millenario agg. e sm. millenary.
millennio sm. millennium.
millepiedi sm. millepede.
millèsimo agg. thousandth.
milligrammo sm. milligram.
millìmetro sm. millimetre.
milza sf. spleen.
mimare vt. e vi. to mime.
mimètico agg. mimetic.
mimetismo sm. 1. (di animali) mimicry 2. (mil.) camouflage.
mimetizzare vt. to camouflage.
mimetizzazione sf. camouflage.
mìmica sf. 1. (teat.) mimic art 2. (di gesti) gesticulation.
mìmico agg. miming, mimic.
mimo sm. mime.
mimosa sf. mimosa.
mina sf. mine.
minaccia sf. threat.
minacciare vt. to threaten.
minaccioso agg. threatening.
minare vt. 1. to mine 2. (fig.) to undermine.
minareto sm. minaret.
minatore sm. miner.
minatorio agg. threatening.
minchione sm. simpleton.
minerale agg. mineral. ♦ minerale sm. mineral.
mineralizzare vt. to mineralize.
mineralogìa sf. mineralogy.
minerario agg. mining (attr.).
minestra sf. soup.
mingherlino agg. slim.

miniare vt. 1. to paint in miniature 2. (di manoscritti) to illuminate.
miniato agg. illuminated.
miniatura sf. miniature.
miniaturista sm. miniaturist.
miniera sf. mine.
minigonna sf. miniskirt.
minimamente avv. not in the least.
minimizzare vt. to minimize.
mìnimo agg. least, slightest, smallest. ♦ mìnimo sm. minimum.
minio sm. red lead.
ministeriale agg. ministerial.
ministero sm. ministry: — dell'Istruzione, ministry of Education || — degli Esteri, dell'Interno, Foreign, Home Office; — del Tesoro, Treasury.
ministro sm. minister.
minoranza sf. minority.
minorare vt. to diminish.
minorato agg. disabled.
minorazione sf. 1. (diminuzione) reduction 2. (invalidità) disablement.
minore agg. 1. (comp.) (più piccolo) smaller, less; (più basso) lower; (più corto) shorter; (più giovane) younger 2. (superl.) the smallest, least, lowest, shortest, youngest.
minorile agg. juvenile.
minorenne agg. under age. ♦ minorenne s. minor.
minorile agg. juvenile.
minorità sf. minority.
minoritario agg. minority (attr.).
minuetto sm. minuet.
minugia sf. gut.
minùscolo agg. small letter.
minuta sf. rough copy.
minutaglia sf. bits and pieces (pl.).
minuto[1] agg. 1. minute 2. (dettagliato) detailed.
minuto[2] sm. minute.
minuto[3] sm. (comm.) retail.
minuzia sf. trifle.
minuziosamente avv. minutely.
minuziosità sf. minuteness.
minuzioso agg. minute, detailed.
minùzzolo sm. crumb.
mio agg. my. ♦ mio pron. mine.
miocardìa sf. myocardia.
miocardio sm. myocardium.
miocardite sf. myocarditis.
miocene sm. miocene.
mìope agg. short-sighted.
miopìa sf. myopia.

mira *sf.* **1.** aim: *prendere la —,* to take (*v. irr.*) aim **2.** (*fig.*) aim, design.

miràbile *agg.* admirable.

mirabilia *sf. pl.* wonders.

mirabolante *agg.* astonishing.

miràcolo *sm.* miracle: *fare miracoli,* to do (*v. irr.*) miracles, (*fig.*) to work wonders.

miracoloso *agg.* miraculous.

miraggio *sm.* mirage.

mirare *vt.* to look at. ♦ **mirare** *vi.* to aim (at).

mìriade *sf.* myriad.

miriagrammo *sm.* myriagram.

miriàmetro *sm.* myriametre.

miriàpodi *sm. pl.* Myriapoda.

mirìfico *agg.* wondrous.

mirino *sm.* **1.** sight **2.** (*foto*) view-finder.

mirra *sf.* myrrh.

mirtillo *sm.* bilberry.

mirto *sm.* myrtle.

misantropìa *sf.* misanthropy.

misàntropo *sm.* misanthrope.

miscela *sf.* **1.** mixture **2.** (*di caffè, tè, liquori, tabacco*) blend.

miscelare *vt.* **1.** to mix **2.** (*di caffè, tabacco, liquori ecc.*) to blend.

miscellànea *sf.* miscellany.

mischia *sf.* fray.

mischiare *vt.* to mix, to mingle.

mischiatura *sf.* **1.** (*il mischiare*) mixing **2.** (*miscuglio*) mixture.

misconòscere *vt.* not to acknowledge.

miscredente *agg.* misbelieving. ♦ **miscredente** *sm.* misbeliever.

miscredenza *sf.* misbelief.

miscuglio *sm.* **1.** mixture **2.** (*amalgama*) blend.

miseràbile *agg.* **1.** miserable **2.** (*scarso*) poor **3.** (*vile*) despicable, mean. ♦ **miseràbile** *sm.* wretch.

miserando *agg.* miserable.

miserévole *agg.* miserable, pitiable.

miseria *sf.* **1.** misery, poverty **2.** (*scarsità*) lack **3.** (*inezia*) trifle.

misericòrdia *sf.* mercy.

misericordioso *agg.* merciful.

mìsero *agg.* **1.** poor, scanty **2.** (*meschino*) wretched.

misfatto *sm.* misdeed.

misogìnìa *sf.* misogyny.

misògino *agg.* misogynous. ♦ **misògino** *sm.* misogynist.

misoneismo *sm.* misoneism.

missaggio *sm.* mixing.

mìssile *sm.* missile.

missionario *sm.* missionary.

missione *sf.* mission.

missiva *sf.* letter.

misteriosamente *avv.* mysteriously.

misterioso *agg.* mysterious.

mistero *sm.* mystery.

mìstica *sf.* mysticism.

misticismo *sm.* mysticism.

mìstico *agg.* mystic.

mistificare *vt.* to mystify.

mistificatore *sm.* mystifier.

mistificazione *sf.* mystification.

misto *agg.* mixed.

mistura *sf.* mixture.

misura *sf.* **1.** (*misurazione, precauzione*) measure **2.** (*taglia*) size **3.** (*limite*) limit.

misuràbile *agg.* measurable.

misurare *vt.* **1.** to measure **2.** (*tec.*) to gauge **3.** (*limitare*) to limit. ♦ **misurarsi** *vr.* to compete.

misurato *agg.* measured.

misuratore *sm.* **1.** (*persona che misura*) measurer **2.** (*strumento*) gauge.

misurazione *sf.* measurement.

misurino *sm.* small measure.

mite *agg.* gentle, meek.

mitezza *sf.* gentleness, meekness.

mìtico *agg.* mythical.

mitigare *vt.* **1.** to mitigate **2.** (*passioni*) to appease **3.** (*dolori*) to relieve. ♦ **mitigarsi** *vr.* to be appeased.

mitigazione *sf.* **1.** mitigation **2.** (*di passioni*) appeasement **3.** (*di dolore*) relief.

mìtilo *sm.* mussel.

mito *sm.* myth.

mitologìa *sf.* mythology.

mitològico *agg.* mythological.

mitòmane *s.* mythomaniac.

mitomanìa *sf.* mythomania.

mitra[1] *sf.* (*eccl.*) mitre.

mitra[2] *sm.* (*mil.*) tommy-gun.

mitraglia *sf.* grape-shot.

mitragliare *vt.* to machine-gun.

mitragliatore *sm.* machine-gunner.

mitragliatrice *sf.* machine-gun.

mitragliere *sm.* machine-gunner.

mitrale *agg.* mitral.

mitrato *agg.* mitred.

mitridàtico *agg.* mithridatic.

mitridatismo *sm.* mithridatism.

mittente *sm.* sender.

mnemònica *sf.* mnemonics.

mnemònico *agg.* mnemonic.

mo' (*nella loc. prep.*) *a — di,* like.

mòbile *agg.* **1.** movable ‖ *scala* —, escalator; *beni mobili*, personal property **2.** (*mutevole*) inconstant. ♦ **mòbile** *sm.* piece of furniture.

mobilia *sf.* furniture.

mobiliare[1] *agg.* movable, personal.

mobiliare[2] *vt.* to furnish.

mobilità *sf.* **1.** mobility **2.** (*fig.*) inconstancy.

mobilitare *vt.* to mobilize.

mobilitazione *sf.* mobilization.

mocassino *sm.* moccasin.

moccioso *agg.* snivelling. ♦ **moccioso** *sm.* young scoundrel, brat.

mòccolo *sm.* **1.** candle-end **2.** (*bestemmia*) curse.

moda *sf.* **1.** fashion: *di* —, in fashion; *fuori* —, out of fashion ‖ *alla* —, fashionable **2.** (*abitudine, modo*) manner, way: *alla* — *di*, after the manner of.

modale *agg.* modal.

modalità *sf.* modality.

modanatura *sf.* moulding.

mòdano *sm.* model.

modella *sf.* model.

modellare *vt.* to model, to shape.

modellatore *sm.* modeller.

modellazione *sf.* modelling.

modello *sm.* **1.** model, pattern **2.** (*stampo*) mould.

moderare *vt.* to moderate, to check.

moderato *agg.* moderate.

moderatore *agg.* moderating. ♦ **moderatore** *sm.* moderator.

moderazione *sf.* moderation.

modernismo *sm.* modernism.

modernità *sf.* modernity.

modernizzare *vt.* to modernize.

moderno *agg.* modern, up-to-date (*attr.*).

modestia *sf.* modesty: — *a parte*, modesty apart.

modesto *agg.* modest.

modicità *sf.* **1.** moderateness **2.** (*di prezzi*) cheapness.

mòdico *agg.* moderate: *a prezzo* —, cheap.

modifica *sf.* alteration, change.

modificare *vt.* to modify.

modificazione *sf.* V. *modifica*.

modista *sf.* milliner.

modisterìa *sf.* milliner's shop.

modo *sm.* **1.** way, manner **2.** (*gramm.*) mood **3.** (*mezzo*) means: *in nessun* —, by no means ‖ *di* — *che*, so (that); *in* — *da*, so as to; *in che* —, how; *in qualche* —, anyhow; *oltre* —, beyond measure.

modulare *vt.* to modulate.

modulato *agg.* modulated.

modulazione *sf.* modulation

mòdulo *sm.* form.

moffetta *sf.* skunk.

mògano *sm.* mahogany.

moggio *sm.* bushel.

mogio *agg.* depressed.

moglie *sf.* wife (*pl.* wives).

moina *sf.* simpering.

mola[1] *sf.* **1.** (*di mulino*) millstone **2.** (*per arrotare*) grindstone.

mola[2] *sf.* (*itt.*) sun-fish.

molare[1] *vi.* to grind (*v. irr.*).

molare[2] *agg.* molar. ♦ **molare** *sm.* (*dente*) molar (tooth).

molatura *sf.* grinding.

molazza *sf.* muller.

mole *sf.* **1.** mass, bulk **2.** (*dimensione*) size.

molècola *sf.* molecule.

molecolare *agg.* molecular.

molestare *vt.* to molest, to tease.

molestatore *agg.* molesting. ♦ **molestatore** *sm.* molester.

molestia *sf.* nuisance, trouble.

molesto *agg.* troublesome.

molibdeno *sm.* molybdenum.

molitorio *agg.* molinary.

molla *sf.* **1.** spring **2.** (*incentivo*) spur.

mollare *vt.* **1.** (*allentare*) to slacken **2.** (*mar.*) to let (*v. irr.*) go. ♦ **mollare** *vi.* to give (*v. irr.*) in.

molle *agg.* **1.** soft **2.** (*floscio*) flabby **3.** (*debole*) weak **4.** (*inzuppato*) soaking wet. ♦ **molle** *sf. pl.* tongs.

molleggiamento *sm.* **1.** (*elasticità*) springiness **2.** (*di veicoli*) springing system.

molleggiare *vi.* to be springy.

molleggiato *agg.* sprung.

molleggio *sm.* (*di veicoli*) suspension.

molletta *sf.* **1.** (*per il bucato*) clothes-peg **2.** (*per i capelli*) hair-pin.

mollettiere *sf. pl.* puttees.

mollettone *sm.* thick flannel.

mollezza *sf.* **1.** (*morbidezza*) softness **2.** (*debolezza*) weakness.

mollica *sf.* crumb.

mollo *agg.* damp: *mettere a* —, to steep.

mollusco *sm.* mollusc.

molo *sm.* pier, wharf.

moltéplice *agg.* manifold.

molteplicità *sf.* multiplicity.

moltiplica sf. (mecc.) chain gearing.

moltiplicando sm. multiplicand.

moltiplicare vt. to multiply.

moltiplicatore sm. multiplier.

moltiplicazione sf. multiplication.

moltissimo agg. indef. **1.** very much (pl. very many) **2.** (di tempo) very long. ♦ **moltissimo** avv. a great deal, very much.

moltitudine sf. multitude.

molto agg. indef. **1.** (sing.) much, a great deal of, a lot of, plenty of **2.** (pl.) many, a good many, a lot of, plenty of **3.** (di tempo) long. ♦ **molto** avv. **1.** very **2.** (con comp.) much, far **3.** (di tempo) long, a long time.

momentaneamente avv. at the moment.

momentaneo agg. momentary.

momento sm. **1.** moment ‖ dal — che, since **2.** (tempo, circostanza) time **3.** (opportunità) chance.

mònaca sf. nun.

monacale agg. monastic.

mònaco sm. monk.

mònade sf. monad.

monarca sm. monarch.

monarchìa sf. monarchy.

monàrchico agg. monarchic.

monastero sm. monastery.

monàstico agg. monastic.

moncherino sm. stump.

monco agg. **1.** maimed **2.** (fig.) incomplete.

moncone sm. stump.

mondanità sf. **1.** society life **2.** worldliness.

mondano agg. worldly.

mondare vt. **1.** to clean ‖ — il grano, to winnow the corn **2.** (fig.) to cleanse.

mondiale agg. world-wide, world (attr.).

mondina sf. rice-weeder.

mondo[1] sm. world: fare il giro del —, to go (v. irr.) round the world; da che — è —, since the world began.

mondo[2] agg. clean.

monellerìa sf. prank.

monello sm. little rascal, urchin.

moneta sf. **1.** money (solo sing.) **2.** (ogni singolo pezzo) coin **3.** (spiccioli) change.

monetario agg. monetary.

monetizzare vt. to monetize.

mongolfiera sf. montgolfier.

mongolismo sm. mongolism.

mòngolo agg. Mongolian. ♦ **mòngolo** sm. Mongol.

mongolòide agg. e sm. mongoloid.

monile sm. jewel.

monismo sm. monism.

mònito sm. warning.

monoblocco sm. monobloc.

monòcolo sm. monocle.

monocromàtico agg. monochromatic.

monòcromo agg. monochrome.

monodìa sf. monody.

monogamìa sf. monogamy.

monògamo agg. monogamous. ♦ **monògamo** sm. monogamist.

monografìa sf. monograph.

monogràfico agg. monographic.

monogramma sm. monogram.

monolìtico agg. monolithic.

monòlogo sm. monologue, soliloquy.

monometallismo sm. monometallism.

monomio sm. monomial.

monopàttino sm. scooter.

monoplano sm. monoplane.

monopolio sm. monopoly.

monopolista sm. monopolist.

monopolizzare vt. to monopolize.

monoposto agg. e sm. single-seater.

monorotaia sf. monorail.

monosillàbico agg. monosyllabic.

monosìllabo sm. monosyllable.

monoteismo sm. monotheism.

monoteista s. monotheist.

monoteìstico agg. monotheistic.

monotìpo sm. monotype.

monotonìa sf. monotony.

monòtono agg. monotonous.

monovalente agg. monovalent.

monsignore sm. monsignor (pl. -ri).

monsone sm. monsoon.

montacàrichi sm. goods-lift.

montaggio sm. **1.** assembly: linea di —, assembly line **2.** (cine) editing **3.** (foto) montage.

montagna sf. mountain.

montagnoso agg. mountainous.

montanaro sm. mountain (attr.). ♦ **montanaro** sm. mountaineer.

montante sm. **1.** (boxe) uppercut **2.** (mecc.; edil.) vertical rod.

montare vt. **1.** (mettere insieme) to assemble **2.** (cavalcare) to ride (v. irr.) **3.** (di panna) to whip. ♦ **montare** vi. **1.** to climb **2.** (alzarsi, aumentare) to rise (v. irr.). ♦ **montarsi** vr. to get (v. irr.) excited.

montatore *sm.* assembler.
montatura *sf.* 1. fitting 2. (*fig.*) hot hair.
montavivande *sm.* dumb-waiter.
monte *sm.* 1. mount (*seguito dal nome*) 2. mountain || *andare a* —, to come (*v. irr.*) to nothing; *mandare a* —, to cause to fail.
montone *sm.* 1. ram 2. (*carne*) mutton.
montuosità *sf.* hilliness.
montuoso *agg.* hilly.
monumentale *agg.* monumental.
monumento *sm.* monument.
mora[1] *sf.* (*bot.*) mulberry.
mora[2] *sf.* (*giur.*) delay.
morale *agg.* moral. ♦ **morale** *sm.* morale. ♦ **morale** *sf.* 1. morals (*pl.*) 2. (*fil.*) ethics 3. (*conclusione*) moral.
moralismo *sm.* moralism.
moralista *s.* moralist.
moralistico *agg.* moralistic.
moralità *sf.* morality.
moralizzare *vt.* to moralize.
moralizzazione *sf.* moralization.
moratorio *sm.* moratory.
morbidezza *sf.* softness.
mòrbido *agg.* soft.
morbillo *sm.* measles (*pl.*).
morbo *sm.* disease, plague.
morbosità *sf.* morbidity.
morboso *agg.* morbid.
mordace *agg.* biting, pungent.
mordacità *sf.* mordacity.
mordente *sm.* 1. (*mus.*) mordent 2. (*spirito aggressivo*) bite.
mòrdere *vt.* 1. to bite (*v. irr.*) 2. (*tormentare*) to torment || — *il freno*, to strain at the leash; — *la polvere*, to bite the dust.
morena *sf.* moraine.
morènico *agg.* morainic.
morente *agg.* dying. ♦ **morente** *sm.* dying man.
moresco *agg.* Moorish.
morfina *sf.* morphine.
morfinòmane *s.* morphinomaniac.
morfologia *sf.* morphology.
morfològico *agg.* morphologic(al).
morganàtico *agg.* morganatic.
moribondo *agg.* dying. ♦ **moribondo** *sm.* dying man.
morigeratezza *sf.* moderation.
morigerato *agg.* moderate, sober.
morire *vi.* 1. to die 2. (*di luci e colori*) to fade 3. (*di suoni*) to die out 4. (*tramontare*) to set (*v. irr.*) ♦ **morire** *sm.* death.

mormone *agg. e sm.* Mormon.
mormorare *vt.* to murmur. ♦ **mormorare** *vi.* (*parlar male*) to gossip.
mormorio *sm.* 1. murmur 2. (*lamento*) complaining 3. (*malignità*) evil gossip.
moro *agg.* dark. ♦ **moro** *sm.* 1. moor 2. (*bot.*) mulberry-tree.
morra *sf.* "morra".
morsa *sf.* vice.
morsetto *sm.* (*mecc.*) clamp.
morsicare *vt.* to bite (*v. irr.*).
morsicatura *sf.* bite.
morsicchiare *vt.* to nibble.
morso *sm.* 1. bite 2. (*puntura, stimolo*) sting, pang 3. (*del cavallo*) bit 4. (*boccone*) morsel, bit.
mortaio *sm.* mortar.
mortale *agg.* mortal, deadly.
mortalità *sf.* mortality.
mortalmente *avv.* mortally.
mortaretto *sm.* cracker.
morte *sf.* death || *pena di* —, capital punishment; *dar la* — *a qu.*, to kill so.; *odiare a* — *qu.*, to hate so. like poison.
mortella *sf.* myrtle.
mortìfero *agg.* lethal.
mortificare *vt.* 1. to humiliate 2. (*reprimere*) to mortify.
mortificato *agg.* humiliated.
mortificazione *sf.* mortification.
morto *agg.* 1. dead || *natura morta* (*pitt.*), still life; *stanco* —, dead tired 2. (*senza vivacità*) dull. ♦ **morto** *sm.* dead man.
mortorio *sm.* funeral.
mortuario *agg.* mortuary.
mosaicista *s.* mosaicist.
mosàico *sm.* mosaic.
mosca *sf.* fly.
moscatello *sm.* muscatel.
moscato *sm.* (*vino*) muscatel. ♦ **moscato** *agg.* noce moscata, nutmeg.
moscerino *sm.* gnat.
moschea *sf.* mosque.
moschettiere *sm.* musketeer.
moschetto *sm.* musket.
moscio *agg.* flabby.
moscone *sm.* blue-bottle.
mossa *sf.* 1. movement 2. (*spostamento al gioco*; *fig.*) move 3. (*sport*) starting post.
mossiere *sm.* (*sport*) starter.
mosso *agg.* 1. (*di mare*) rough 2. (*di capelli*) wavy.
mosto *sm.* must.

mostra sf. 1. (esposizione) show, exhibition 2. (vetrina) shop-window 3. (ostentazione) display.

mostrare vt. 1. to show (v. irr.) 2. (ostentare) to show (v. irr.) off 3. (dimostrare) to prove 4. (fingere) to pretend.

mostrina sf. collar badge.

mostro sm. monster.

mostruosamente avv. monstrously.

mostruosità sf. monstrosity.

mostruoso agg. monstrous. for 2. (giur.) to allege.

mota sf. mud, mire.

motivare vt. to state the reason

motivazione sf. 1. motivation 2. (giur.) opinion.

motivo sm. 1. reason ‖ a — di, owing to; senza —, groundless 2. (mus.) theme.

moto sm. 1. motion, movement 2. (esercizio fisico) exercise 3. (impulso) impulse. ♦ **moto** sf. motor-cycle.

motobarca sf. motor-boat.

motocarrozzetta sf. side-car.

motocicletta sf. motor-cycle.

motociclismo sm. motor-cycling.

motociclista s. motor-cyclist.

motofurgone sm. van.

motore agg. motor, driving. ♦ **motore** sm. engine, motor.

motorista sm. engineer.

motorizzare vt. to motorize. ♦ **motorizzarsi** vr. to buy (v. irr.) a car, a motor-cycle.

motorizzazione sf. motorization.

motoscafo sm. motor-boat.

motoveicolo sm. motor vehicle.

motrice sf. 1. tractor 2. (ferr.) engine.

motteggiare vt. to make (v. irr.) fun of. ♦ **motteggiare** vi. to joke.

motteggiatore agg. joking. ♦ **motteggiatore** sm. joker.

motteggio sm. 1. (il motteggiare) raillery 2. (detto arguto) joke.

mottetto sm. motet.

motto sm. 1. word 2. (proverbio) saying 3. (facezia) witticism.

movente sm. motive, cause.

movenza sf. movements (pl.).

movibile agg. movable.

movimentare vt. to enliven.

movimentato agg. 1. lively 2. (pieno di movimento) eventful.

movimento sm. 1. movement 2.

(traffico, trambusto) traffic, bustle.

moviola sf. film-editing machine.

mozione sf. motion.

mozzare vt. to cut (v. irr.) off.

mozzicone sm. 1. stump 2. (di sigaretta) butt.

mozzo¹ agg. cut (off).

mozzo² sm. 1. (di ruota) hub 2. (mar.) ship-boy.

mucca sf. cow.

mucchio sm. heap, mass.

mùcido agg. mouldy. ♦ **mùcido** sm. mould.

muco sm. mucus.

mucosa sf. mucous membrane.

mucoso agg. mucous.

muffa sf. mould.

muffire vi. to mildew.

muflone sm. moufflon.

mugghiare vi. 1. to bellow 2. (fig.) to roar 3. (del vento) to howl.

mugghio sm. 1. bellow 2. (fig.) roar 3. (del vento) howl.

muggire vi. V. mugghiare.

muggito sm. V. mugghio.

mughetto sm. lily of the valley.

mugnaio sm. miller.

mugolare vi. 1. to howl 2. (piagnucolare) to whimper.

mugolìo sm. 1. howling 2. (piagnucolìo) whimpering.

mugugnare vi. to mumble.

mulattiera sf. mule-track.

mulattiere sm. mule-driver.

mulatto sm. mulatto.

muliebre agg. feminine, womanly.

mulinare vt. 1. to whirl 2. (fig.) to brood (over).

mulinello sm. 1. (d'acqua) whirlpool 2. (d'aria) whirlwind 3. (rapido movimento) twirl.

mulino sm. mill.

mulo sm. mule.

multa sf. fine.

multare vt. to fine.

multicolore agg. many-coloured.

multiforme agg. multiform.

mùltiplo agg. e sm. multiple.

mummia sf. mummy.

mummificare vt. to mummify.

mummificazione sf. mummification.

mùngere vt. to milk.

mungitore sm. milker.

mungitura sf. milking.

municipale agg. municipal.

municipalità sf. municipality.

municipalizzare vt. to municipalize.

municipalizzazione *sf.* municipalization.

municipio *sm.* **1.** municipality **2.** (*palazzo*) townhall **3.** (*stor.*) municipium (*pl.* -ia).

munificenza *sf.* munificence.

munifico *agg.* munificent.

munire *vt.* **1.** (*fortificare*) to fortify **2.** (*provvedere*) to supply (with).

munizione *sf.* munition.

muòvere *vt.* to move. ◆ **muòversi** *vr.* to move, to stir || *muoviti!* hurry up!

mura¹ *sf.* (*mar.*) tack.

mura² *sf. pl.* walls.

muraglia *sf.* wall.

muraglione *sm.* massive wall.

murale *agg.* mural.

murare *vt.* **1.** to wall up **2.** (*cingere di mura*) to wall.

murario *agg.* building (*attr.*).

murata *sf.* ship's side.

muratore *sm.* bricklayer.

muratura *sf.* masonry || *lavoro in* —, brickwork.

murena *sf.* moray.

muriàtico *agg.* muriatic.

muricciolo *sm.* low wall.

murice *sm.* murex.

muro *sm.* wall || *armadio a* —, built-in cupboard; — *del suono*, sound barrier.

musa *sf.* muse.

muschiato *agg.* musky.

muschio¹ *sm.* (*sostanza odorosa*) musk.

muschio² *sm.* (*bot.*) moss.

muscolare *agg.* muscular.

muscolatura *sf.* musculature.

muscolo *sm.* muscle.

muscoloso *agg.* muscular.

muscoso *agg.* mossy.

museo *sm.* museum.

museruola *sf.* muzzle.

musica *sf.* music.

musicale *agg.* musical.

musicalità *sf.* musicality.

musicante *sm.* musician.

musicare *vt.* to set (*v. irr.*) to music.

musicista *sm.* musician.

musico *sm.* musician.

musicologia *sf.* musicology.

musicòlogo *sm.* musicologist.

musivo *agg.* mosaic (*attr.*).

muso *sm.* **1.** muzzle **2.** (*broncio*) long face: *fare il* —, to pull a long face.

musone *sm.* **1.** large muzzle **2.** (*per-*

sona che tiene il broncio) sulky person.

musoneria *sf.* sulkiness.

mussare *vi.* to froth.

mussolina *sf.* muslin.

mustèlidi *sm. pl.* mustelidae.

musulmano *agg.* e *sm.* Muslim.

muta *sf.* **1.** (*di cani*) pack of hounds **2.** (*della guardia*) change **3.** (*biol.*) moult.

mutàbile *agg.* changeable.

mutabilità *sf.* **1.** (*di cosa*) changeability **2.** (*di persona*) fickleness.

mutamento *sm.* change.

mutande *sf. pl.* drawers.

mutandine *sf. pl.* trunks.

mutare *vt.* **1.** to change **2.** (*di animali*) to shed (*v. irr.*), to moult. ◆ **mutarsi** *vr.* to change.

mutazione *sf.* change.

mutévole *agg.* changeable.

mutilare *vt.* **1.** to maim **2.** (*fig.*) to mutilate.

mutilato *agg.* **1.** maimed **2.** (*fig.*) mutilated. ◆ **mutilato** *sm.* cripple.

mutilazione *sf.* **1.** maiming **2.** (*fig.*) mutilation.

mùtilo *agg.* mutilated.

mutismo *sm.* dumbness.

muto *agg.* **1.** dumb || *carta geografica muta*, blank map **2.** (*fonetica*) mute.

mutria *sf.* stand-offishness.

mutua *sf.* national insurance || *medico della* —, panel doctor.

mutualistico *agg.* insurance (*attr.*).

mutualità *sf.* mutual help.

mutuare *vt.* **1.** (*dare in mutuo*) to lend (*v. irr.*) **2.** (*prendere a mutuo*) to borrow.

mutuatario *sm.* borrower.

mutuato *agg.* insured.

mutuo *agg.* mutual. ◆ **mutuo** *sm.* loan.

N

nababbo *sm.* nabob.

nàcchera *sf.* castanet.

nafta *sf.* **1.** oil **2.** (*chim.*) naphtha.

naftalina *sf.* moth-balls (*pl.*).

naia¹ *sf.* (*zool.*) cobra.

naia² *sf.* (*mil.*) *fare la* —, to do (*v. irr.*) one's bit.

nàiade *sf.* naiad.

nàilon *sm.* nylon.

nandù *sm.* nandu.

nanismo *sm.* nanism.

nano *sm.* dwarf.

nappa *sf.* tassel.

narcisismo *sm.* narcissism.

narcisista *sm.* narcissist.

narciso *sm.* narcissus.

narcosi *sf.* narcosis (*pl.* -ses).

narcòtico *agg. e sm.* narcotic.

narcotizzare *vt.* to narcotize.

narice *sf.* nostril.

narrare *vt.* to tell (*v. irr.*).

narrativa *sf.* fiction.

narrativo *agg.* narrative.

narratore *sm.* **1.** story-teller **2.** (*scrittore*) writer.

narrazione *sf.* narration.

narvalo *sm.* narwhal.

nasale *agg.* nasal.

nascente *agg.* rising.

nàscere *vi.* **1.** to be born **2.** (*di piante*) to spring (*v. irr.*) up **3.** (*di fiume; sorgere*) to rise (*v. irr.*) **4.** (*avere origine*) to originate ‖ *far —,* to give (*v. irr.*) rise to.

nàscita *sf.* **1.** birth **2.** (*origine*) origin.

nascituro *sm.* unborn child.

nascòndere *vt.* to hide (*v. irr.*). ♦ **nascòndersi** *vr.* to hide (oneself).

nascondiglio *sm.* hiding-place.

nascosto *agg.* hidden ‖ *di —,* secretly.

nasello *sm.* (*itt.*) whiting.

naso *sm.* nose ‖ *a lume di —,* by guesswork; *ficcare il — in qc.,* to poke one's nose into sthg.; *avere buon —,* to be shrewd.

nassa *sf.* bow-net.

nastro *sm.* **1.** ribbon **2.** (*tec.*) tape.

natale *agg.* native. ♦ **Natale** *sm.* Christmas.

natalità *sf.* birth-rate.

natalizio *agg.* Christmas (*attr.*).

natante *agg.* floating. ♦ **natante** *sm.* watercraft.

natatoia *sf.* fin.

natatorio *agg.* swimming (*attr.*).

nàtica *sf.* buttock.

natività *sf.* nativity.

nativo *agg.* **1.** native **2.** (*innato*) inborn.

nato *agg.* born.

natura *sf.* nature.

naturale *agg.* natural.

naturalezza *sf.* naturalness, simplicity.

naturalismo *sm.* naturalism.

naturalista *s.* naturalist.

naturalizzare *vt.* to naturalize.

naturalizzazione *sf.* naturalization.

naturalmente *avv.* naturally, of course.

naturismo *sm.* naturism.

naturista *s.* naturist.

naufragare *vi.* **1.** to be shipwrecked **2.** (*fig.*) to be wrecked.

naufragio *sm.* **1.** shipwreck **2.** (*fig.*) wreck.

nàufrago *sm.* shipwrecked person.

nàusea *sf.* disgust, nausea ‖ *avere la —,* to feel (*v. irr.*) sick.

nauseabondo *agg.* nauseating.

nauseare *vt.* to make (*v. irr.*) sick.

nàutica *sf.* navigation.

nàutico *agg.* nautical.

navale *agg.* naval.

navata *sf.* **1.** (*centrale*) nave **2.** (*laterale*) aisle.

nave *sf.* ship.

navetta *sf.* shuttle.

navicella *sf.* (*aer.*) nacelle.

navigàbile *agg.* navigable.

navigabilità *sf.* navigability.

navigare *vi.* to sail.

navigato *agg.* (*fig.*) cunning.

navigatore *sm.* navigator.

navigazione *sf.* navigation.

naviglio *sm.* **1.** fleet **2.** (*nave*) craft.

nazionale *agg.* national.

nazionalismo *sm.* nationalism.

nazionalista *s.* nationalist.

nazionalità *sf.* nationality.

nazionalizzare *vt.* to nationalize.

nazionalizzazione *sf.* nationalization.

nazionalsocialismo *sm.* National Socialism.

nazione *sf.* nation.

nazismo *sm.* Nazism.

nazista *agg. e sm.* Nazi.

nazzareno *agg. e sm.* Nazarene.

ne *pron.* **1.** of him, about him; of her, about her; of it, about it; of them, about them; of this, about this; of that, about that **2.** (*partitivo*) some: *— ho,* I have some; any: *non — ho,* I haven't any. ♦ **ne** (*particella avv. di moto da luogo*) from there.

né *cong.* **1.** neither, nor **2.** (*né... né...*) neither... nor; (*in presenza di altra negazione*) either... or.

neanche *avv.* not even. ♦ **neanche** *cong.* neither; nor: *essi non anda-*

rono e — io, they did not go and neither did I.

nebbia *sf.* fog.

nebbioso *agg.* foggy.

nebulizzare *vt.* to nebulize.

nebulizzatore *sm.* nebulizer.

nebulosa *sf.* nebula (*pl.* -ae).

nebulosità *sf.* 1. nebulosity 2. (*fig.*) haziness.

nebuloso *agg.* 1. nebulous 2. (*fig.*) vague.

necessario *agg.* necessary. ♦ **necessario** *sm.* 1. necessary 2. (*l'indispensabile*) necessities (*pl.*).

necessità *sf.* 1. necessity 2. (*bisogno*) need.

necessitare *vi.* to need.

necrologia *sf.* obituary-notice.

necrologio *sm.* 1. necrology 2. (*annuncio*) obituary.

necropoli *sf.* necropolis.

necrosi *sf.* necrosis (*pl.* -ses).

necrotizzare *vt.* to necrotize.

nefandezza *sf.* wickedness.

nefando *agg.* wicked.

nefasto *agg.* ill-omened.

nefrite *sf.* nephritis.

nefritico *agg.* nephritic. ♦ **nefritico** *sm.* nephritic subject.

negare *vt.* 1. to deny 2. (*rifiutare*) to refuse.

negativa *sf.* (*anche foto*) negative.

negativo *agg.* negative.

negato *agg.* 1. refused, denied 2. (*inadatto*) unfit (for).

negatore *agg.* negatory. ♦ **negatore** *sm.* denier.

negazione *sf.* 1. denial 2. (*gramm.*) negative 3. (*cosa diametralmente opposta all'altra*) negation.

neghittoso *agg.* slothful.

negletto *agg.* 1. neglected 2. (*di aspetto*) slovenly.

negligente *agg.* negligent, careless.

negligenza *sf.* negligence, carelessness.

negoziabile *agg.* negotiable.

negoziante *sm.* 1. merchant, trader 2. (*chi ha negozio*) shopkeeper.

negoziare *vt.* to negotiate.

negoziato *agg.* negotiated. ♦ **negoziato** *sm.* negotiation.

negozio *sm.* 1. shop 2. (*commercio*) trade 3. (*faccenda*) affair.

negriero *agg.* slave (*attr.*). ♦ **negriero** *sm.* slave-trader.

negro *agg. e sm.* 1. negro 2. (*spreg.*) nigger.

negroide *agg. e s.* negroid.

negromante *sm.* necromancer.

negromanzia *sf.* necromancy.

nembo *sm.* 1. raincloud 2. (*fig.*) multitude.

nemesi *sf.* nemesis (*pl.* -ses).

nemico *agg.* 1. adverse 2. (*del nemico*) enemy (*attr.*). ♦ **nemico** *sm.* enemy.

neo¹ *sm.* 1. mole 2. (*fig.*) flaw.

neo² *agg.* neo.

neocapitalismo *sm.* neo-capitalism.

neocapitalista *agg. e sm.* neo-capitalist.

neocapitalistico *agg.* neo-capitalistic.

neoclassicismo *sm.* neo-classicism.

neoclassico *agg.* neo-classic.

neofascismo *sm.* neofascism.

neofascista *agg. e s.* neofascist.

neòfita *sm.* 1. neophyte 2. (*fig.*) beginner.

neolitico *agg.* .Neolithic.

neologismo *sm.* neologism.

neon *sm.* neon: *insegna al —,* neon sign.

neonato *agg.* new-born. ♦ **neonato** *sm.* (new-born) baby.

neorealismo *sm.* Neorealism.

neorealista *agg. e sm.* neorealist.

neozelandese *agg.* New Zealand (*attr.*). ♦ **neozelandese** *s.* New Zealander.

nepotismo *sm.* 'nepotism.

nerastro *agg.* blackish.

nerbo *sm.* 1. sinew 2. (*fig.*) strength, vigour.

nerboruto *agg.* brawny.

neretto *sm.* (*tip.*) boldface.

nerezza *sf.* blackness.

nero *agg.* black.

nerofumo *sm.* lamp-black.

nerògnolo *agg.* blackish.

nerume *sm.* mass of black.

nervatura *sf.* ribbing.

nervo *sm.* nerve.

nervosamente *agg.* nervously.

nervosismo *sm.* nervousness.

nervoso *agg.* nervous, irritable.

nèspola *sf.* medlar.

nèspolo *sm.* medlar(-tree).

nesso *sm.* connection.

nessuno *agg.* 1. no 2. (*in presenza di altra neg.*) any. ♦ **nessuno** *pron.* 1. (*per persone*) nobody, no one; (*per cose*) none 2. (*in presenza di altra neg.*) anybody (*solo per persone*), anyone, any ‖ — *di,* none of, (*in presenza di altra neg.*) any of.

nèttare *sm.* nectar.

nettare *vt.* to clean.

nettezza *sf.* cleanness: — *urbana*, municipal street cleansing.

netto *agg.* 1. clean, spotless (*anche fig.*) 2. (*comm.*) net.

nettùnio *sm.* neptunium.

neurite *sf.* neuritis.

neurochirurgìa *sf.* neurosurgery.

neurologìa *sf.* neurology.

neuròlogo *sm.* neurologist.

neuropàtico *agg.* neuropathic. ♦ **neuropàtico** *sm.* neuropath.

neuropatologìa *sf.* neuropathology.

neuròsi *sf.* neurosis (*pl.* -ses).

neurovegetativo *agg.* vegetative nervous.

neutrale *agg.* neutral.

neutralìsmo *sm.* neutralism.

neutralista *s.* neutralist.

neutralità *sf.* neutrality.

neutralizzare *vt.* to neutralize.

neutralizzazione *sf.* neutralization.

nèutro *agg.* 1. neutral 2. (*gramm.*; *bot.*; *zool.*) neuter.

neutróne *sm.* neutron.

neve *sf.* snow.

nevicare *vi.* to snow: *nevica*, it is snowing.

nevicata *sf.* snowfall.

nevìschio *sm.* sleet.

nevóso *agg.* snowy.

nevralgìa *sf.* neuralgia.

nevràlgico *agg.* neuralgic.

nevrastenìa *sf.* neurasthenia.

nevrastènico *agg.* neurasthenic.

nevròtico *agg.* e *sm.* neurotic.

nìbbio *sm.* kite.

nìcchia *sf.* niche.

nicchiare *vi.* to shilly-shally.

nìchel *sm.* nickel.

nichelare *vt.* to nickel.

nichelatura *sf.* nickel-plating.

nichelìno *sm.* nickel coin.

nichilìsmo *sm.* nihilism.

nichilista *sm.* nihilist.

nicotìna *sf.* nicotine.

nidiata *sf.* 1. nest 2. (*covata*) brood || *una* — *di bambini*, a swarm of children.

nidificare *vi.* to nest.

nìdo *sm.* nest.

niente *pron.* 1. nothing 2. (*in presenza di altre negazioni*) anything.

nimbo *sm.* halo.

ninfa *sf.* nymph.

ninfèa *sf.* water-lily.

ninfòmane *sf.* nymphomaniac.

ninnananna *sf.* lullaby.

nìnnolo *sm.* 1. knick-knack 2. (*balocco*) plaything.

nipóte *sm.* 1. (*di nonno*) grand-son 2. (*di zio*) nephew. ♦ **nipóte** *sf.* 1. (*di nonno*) grand-daughter 2. (*di zio*) niece.

nippònico *agg.* e *sm.* Japanese.

nirvana *sm.* nirvana.

nitidézza *sf.* neatness.

nìtido *agg.* neat, clear.

nitrato *sm.* nitrate.

nìtrico *agg.* nitric.

nitrìre *vi.* to whinny.

nitrìto¹ *sm.* (*di cavallo*) whinny.

nitrìto² *sm.* (*chim.*) nitrite.

nitroglicerìna *sf.* nitroglycerin.

nìveo *agg.* snowy.

no *avv.* no.

nòbile *agg.* e *sm.* noble.

nobiliare *agg.* nobiliary.

nobilitare *vt.* to ennoble.

nobilitazione *sf.* ennobling.

nobilménte *avv.* nobly.

nobiltà *sf.* nobility.

nòcca *sf.* knuckle.

nocchiére *sm.* helmsman (*pl.* -men).

nocciòla *sf.* hazel-nut.

nòcciolo *sm.* 1. stone 2. (*ciò che è essenziale*) heart.

nocciòlo *sm.* (*bot.*) hazel-tree.

nóce *sm.* walnut-tree. ♦ **nóce** *sf.* walnut || *guscio di* — (*barchetta*), cockle-shell; — *moscata*, nutmeg.

nocìvo *agg.* noxious, harmful.

nòdo *sm.* knot.

nodóso *agg.* knotty.

nói *pron.* 1. (*sogg.*) we 2. (*compl.*) us.

nòia *sf.* 1. boredom 2. (*fastidio*) worry, nuisance.

noióso *agg.* 1. boring 2. (*molesto*) annoying.

noleggiante *sm.* (*mar.*) charterer.

noleggiare *vt.* 1. to hire 2. (*di navi*) to charter.

noleggiatore *sm.* hirer.

noléggio *sm.* 1. hire 2. (*mar.*) freight.

nolènte *agg.* unwilling || *volente o* —, willy-nilly.

nòlo *sm.* 1. hire 2. (*mar.*) freight.

nòmade *agg.* e *s.* nomad.

nomadìsmo *sm.* nomadism.

nóme *sm.* 1. name 2. (*di battesimo*) Christian name || *senza* —, nameless; *a* — *di*, on behalf of; *per* —, by name 3. (*gramm.*) noun.

nomèa *sf.* notoriety.

nomenclatura *sf.* nomenclature.

nomìgnolo *sm.* nickname.

nòmina *sf.* appointment.

nominale *agg.* nominal.

nominalismo *sm.* nominalism.

nominalista *s.* nominalist.

nominalmente *avv.* nominally.

nominare *vt.* 1. to name 2. (*eleggere*) to appoint.

nominativo *agg.* 1. nominative 2. (*comm.*) registered. ♦ **nominativo** *sm.* name.

non *avv.* not.

nona *sf.* 1. (*eccl.*) Nones (*pl.*) 2. (*mus.*) ninth.

nonagenario *agg.* ninety years old (*pred.*); ninety-year-old (*attr.*). ♦ **nonagenario** *sm.* nonagenarian.

nonconformista *s.* non-conformist.

noncurante *agg.* careless.

noncuranza *sf.* carelessness.

nondimeno *avv.* nevertheless.

nonna *sf.* grandmother.

nonno *sm.* grandfather: *i miei nonni*, my grandparents.

nonnulla *sm.* trifle.

nono *agg.* ninth.

nonostante *prep.* notwithstanding || — *che*, though, although.

nonsenso *sm.* nonsense.

non-ti-scordar-di-me *sm.* forget-me-not.

nord *sm.* north.

nordamericano *agg. e sm.* North American.

nòrdico *agg.* 1. northern 2. (*dell'Europa settentrionale*) Nordic. ♦ **nòrdico** *sm.* 1. Northerner 2. (*dell'Europa settentrionale*) Nordic.

nordista *sm.* (*stor. amer.*) Federal.

norma *sf.* 1. rule, norm 2. (*istruzioni*) instruction, direction || — *di legge*, according to law.

normale *agg. e sm.* 1. normal 2. (*che dà una norma*) standard.

normalità *sf.* normality.

normalizzare *vt.* to normalize.

normalizzazione *sf.* normalization.

normalmente *avv.* usually.

normanno *agg. e sm.* Norman: *anglo—*, (*stor.*) Anglo-Norman.

normativo *agg.* normative.

normògrafo *sm.* stencil.

norvegese *agg. e sm.* Norwegian.

nosocòmio *sm.* hospital.

nostalgìa *sf.* home-sickness.

nostàlgico *agg.* homesick.

nostrano *agg.* home (*attr.*), national.

nostro *agg.* our: *i nostri amici*, our friends. ♦ **nostro** *pron.* ours: *questa casa è nostra*, this house is ours. ♦ **nostro** *sm.* 1. *viviamo del —*, we live on our own income 2. *il Nostro (di autore)*, the Author 3. *i nostri*, our family.

nostromo *sm.* boatswain.

nota *sf.* 1. note 2. (*lista*) list.

notàbile *agg.* notable.

notaio *sm.* notary.

notare *vt.* to note.

notariato *sm.* profession of notary.

notarile *agg.* notarial.

notazione *sf.* notation.

notévole *agg.* remarkable, notable.

notevolmente *avv.* remarkably.

notìfica *sf.* 1. notification 2. (*giur.*) service.

notificare *vt.* 1. to notify 2. (*informare*) to inform 3. (*giur.*) to serve.

notizia *sf.* 1. news (*pl. con costruzione sing.*), piece of news (*solo sing.*) 2. (*informazione*) information (*solo sing.*) 3. (*dato*) note: *notizie biografiche*, biographical notes.

notiziario *sm.* news (*pl.*, con costruzione sing.).

noto *agg.* well-known. ♦ **noto** *sm.* the known.

notoriamente *avv.* notoriously.

notorietà *sf.* notoriety.

notorio *agg.* 1. (*in senso sfavorevole*) notorious 2. well-known.

nottàmbulo *agg.* noctambulous. ♦ **nottàmbulo** *sm.* night-bird.

nottata *sf.* night.

notte *sf.* night.

nottetempo *avv.* by night.

notturno *agg.* night (*attr.*). ♦ **notturno** *sm.* (*mus.*) nocturne.

novanta *agg.* ninety.

novantenne *agg.* 1. ninety years old (*pred.*) 2. ninety-year-old (*attr.*).

novantèsimo *agg.* ninetieth.

novatore *sm.* innovator.

nove *agg.* nine.

novecento *agg.* nine hundred.

novella *sf.* short story, tale.

novellino *agg.* inexperienced. ♦ **novellino** *sm.* beginner.

novellista *s.* short-story writer.

novellìstica *sf.* story-telling.

novello *agg.* 1. new, spring (*attr.*) 2. (*nuovo*) second: *un — Raffaello*, a second Raffaello.

novembre sm. November.
novena sf. novena (pl. -ae).
nòvero sm. number 2. (categoria) class.
novilunio sm. new moon.
novità sf. 1. novelty 2. (notizia) news (pl. con costruzione sing.), piece of news (solo sing.).
noviziato sm. novitiate.
novizio sm. novice.
nozione sf. notion.
nozze sf. pl. wedding (sing.).
nube sf. cloud.
nubifragio sm. downpour.
nùbile agg. unmarried, single. ♦ **nùbile** sf. single woman.
nuca sf. nape.
nucleare agg. nuclear.
nucleina sf. nuclein.
nùcleo sm. nucleus (pl. -ei).
nudismo sm. nudism.
nudista s. nudist.
nudità sf. nakedness.
nudo agg. naked, bare.
nùgolo sm. cloud.
nulla pron. V. niente.
nullaosta sm. permit.
nullatenente agg. without property. ♦ **nullatenente** s. person without property.
nullità sf. 1. (di cose) nullity 2. (di persone) nonentity.
nullo agg. (giur.) null, void.
nume sm. numen, deity.
numeràbile agg. numerable.
numerabilità sf. numerability.
numerale agg. numeral.
numerare vt. 1. to count 2. (segnare con numero) to number.
numerato agg. 1. counted 2. (segnato con un numero) numbered.
numerario agg. numerary. ♦ **numerario** sm. (comm.) ready cash.
numeratore sm. (mat.) numerator.
numerazione sf. 1. numbering 2. (mat.) numeration.
numericamente avv. numerically.
numèrico agg. numerical.
nùmero sm. number.
numeroso agg. numerous.
numismàtica sf. numismatics.
numismàtico agg. numismatic. ♦ **numismàtico** sm. numismatist.
nunziatura sf. (eccl.) nunciature.
nunzio sm. nuncio.
nuòcere vi. to damage, to harm.
nuora sf. daughter-in-law.
nuotare vi. to swim (v. irr.).
nuotata sf. swim.

nuotatore sm. swimmer.
nuoto sm. swimming: gara di —, swimming-race.
nuova sf. news (pl. con costruzione sing.), piece of news (solo sing.).
nuovamente avv. again.
nuovo agg. new: — di zecca, fiammante, brand-new.
nutazione sf. nutation.
nutrice sf. wet-nurse.
nutriente agg. nourishing.
nutrimento sm. 1. feeding 2. (fig.) nourishment.
nutrire vt. 1. to feed (v. irr.) 2. (mantenere) to maintain 3. (di sentimenti, passioni) to foster. ♦ **nutrirsi** vr. to feed (on).
nutritivo agg. nourishing.
nutrito agg. fed, nourished.
nutrizione sf. 1. feeding 2. (fig.) nourishment.
nùvola sf. cloud.
nuvoloso agg. overcast, cloudy.
nuziale agg. wedding (attr.).

O

o cong. or || o ... o, either ... or: — tu — tua madre dovete venire, either you or your mother must come; — l'uno — l'altro, either: prendi — l'uno — l'altro, take either.
òasi sf. oasis (pl. -ses).
obbligare vt. to compel. ♦ **obbligarsi** vr. to bind (v. irr.) oneself.
obbligatorietà sf. compulsoriness.
obbligatorio agg. compulsory.
obbligazione sf. 1. obligation 2. (comm.) bond.
obbligazionista sm. bond-holder.
òbbligo sm. obligation: assumersi l'—, to undertake (v. irr.).
obbrobrio sm. disgrace.
obbrobrioso agg. disgraceful.
obelisco sm. obelisk.
oberare vt. to burden.
obesità sf. obesity.
obeso agg. obese.
òbice sm. howitzer.
obiettare vt. to object.
obiettivamente avv. objectively.
obiettivismo sm. objectivism.
obiettività sf. objectivity.

obiettivo *agg.* objective. ◆ **obiettivo** *sm.* **1.** (*mil.*) objective **2.** (*scopo*) aim **3.** (*foto*) lens.

obiettore *sm.* objector: — *di coscienza,* conscientious objector.

obiezione *sf.* objection.

obitorio *sm.* morgue.

oblatore *sm.* donor.

oblazione *sf.* donation.

obliare *vt.* to forget (*v. irr.*).

oblio *sm.* oblivion.

obliquamente *avv.* obliquely.

obliquità *sf.* obliquity.

obliquo *agg.* oblique.

obliterare *vt.* to obliterate.

obliterazione *sf.* obliteration.

oblò *sm.* porthole.

oblungo *agg.* oblong.

òboe *sm.* oboe.

òbolo *sm.* offering.

obsoleto *agg.* obsolete.

oca *sf.* goose (*pl.* geese): *pelle d'—,* goose flesh; *penna d'—,* goose-quill.

occasionale *agg.* occasional.

occasionalismo *sm.* occasionalism.

occasionalmente *avv.* occasionally.

occasione *sf.* occasion.

occhiaia *sf.* eye-socket || *avere le occhiaie,* to have rings under one's eyes.

occhiali *sm. pl.* spectacles, glasses.

occhialuto *agg.* spectacled, wearing spectacles (*pred.*).

occhiata *sf.* look, glance.

occhiataccia *sf.* glare.

occhieggiare *vt.* to cast (*v. irr.*) glances (at). ◆ **occhieggiare** *vi.* to peep (at).

occhiello *sm.* **1.** button-hole **2.** (*mecc.*) eye.

occhietto *sm.* fare l'— *a qu.,* to wink at so.

occhio *sm.* eye || *costare un — || avere le occhiaie,* to be terribly expensive; *chiudere un — su,* to turn a blind eye to; *dare nell'—,* to strike (*v. irr.*) the eye; *tenere d'—,* to keep (*v. irr.*) an eye on; *in un batter d'—,* in the twinkling of an eye.

occidentale *agg.* west, western. ◆ **occidentale** *s.* westerner.

occidentalizzare *vt.* to occidentalize.

occidente *sm.* west.

occipitale *agg.* occipital.

occìpite *sm.* occiput (*pl.* occipita).

occlusione *sf.* occlusion.

occlusivo *agg.* occlusive.

occorrente *agg.* necessary. ◆ **occorrente** *sm.* the necessary.

occorrenza *sf.* all'—, in case of need.

occòrrere *vi.* **1.** (*imp.*) to be necessary **2.** (*abbisognare*) to need.

occultamento *sm.* concealment.

occultare *vt.* to hide (*v. irr.*), to conceal. ◆ **occultarsi** *vr.* to hide.

occultatore *sm.* hider.

occultismo *sm.* occultism.

occulto *agg.* **1.** occult **2.** (*nascosto*) hidden.

occupante *agg.* occupying. ◆ **occupante** *s.* occupant.

occupare *vt.* **1.** to occupy **2.** (*ingaggiare*) to employ. ◆ **occuparsi** *vr.* **1.** (*impiegarsi*) to find (*v. irr.*) a job **2.** (*badare*) to attend (to).

occupato *agg.* engaged || *essere — (fare un lavoro),* to work.

occupazione *sf.* **1.** occupation **2.** (*lavoro*) job.

oceànico *agg.* oceanic.

oceàno *sm.* ocean.

oceanografia *sf.* oceanography.

ocello *sm.* ocellus (*pl.* -li).

ocra *sf.* ochre.

oculare *agg.* ocular, eye (*attr.*). ◆ **oculare** *sm.* (*fis.*) eyepiece.

oculatezza *sf.* shrewdness.

oculato *agg.* prudent.

oculista *sm.* oculist.

oculìstica *sf.* ophthalmology.

odalisca *sf.* odalisque.

ode *sf.* ode.

odiare *vt.* to hate.

odierno *agg.* of today, today's.

odio *sm.* hatred.

odioso *agg.* hateful.

odontàlgico *agg.* odontalgic.

odontoiatra *s.* odontologist, dentist.

odontoiatrìa *sf.* odontology.

odontoiàtrico *agg.* odontological.

odorare *vt. e vi.* to smell (*v. irr.*).

odorato *sm.* smell.

odore *sm.* smell.

odorìfero *agg.* odoriferous.

odoroso *agg.* fragrant.

offèndere *vt.* to offend. ◆ **offendersi** *vr.* to be offended (at, by); to feel (*v. irr.*) hurt (by).

offensiva *sf.* offensive.

offensivo *agg.* offensive.

offensore *sm.* offender.

offerente *s.* **1.** offerer **2.** (*a un'asta*) bidder.

offerta *sf.* offer, donation.

offesa *sf.* offence.

offeso *agg.* offended, injured.

officiare *vi.* to officiate.

officina *sf.* workshop.

officinale *agg.* officinal.

offrire *vt.* to offer. ♦ **offrirsi** *vr.* to offer (oneself).

offuscamento *sm.* **1.** dimming **2.** (*oscurità*) dimness.

offuscare *vt.* to dim. ♦ **offuscarsi** *vr.* to grow (*v. irr.*) dim.

oftalmìa *sf.* ophthalmia.

oftàlmico *agg.* ophthalmic.

oftalmologìa *sf.* ophthalmology.

oftalmoscopìa *sf.* ophthalmoscopy.

oftalmoscopio *sm.* ophthalmoscope.

oggettivamente *avv.* objectively.

oggettivare *vt.* to objectify.

oggettivazione *sf.* objectification.

oggettivismo *sm.* objectivism.

oggettività *sf.* objectivity.

oggettivo *agg.* objective.

oggetto *sm.* object.

oggi *avv.* today.

ogiva *sf.* ogive.

ogivale *agg.* ogival.

ogni *agg.* every, each || *in — modo*, anyhow; *in — luogo*, everywhere.

ogniqualvolta *cong.* whenever.

ognuno *pron.* everybody, everyone || *— di*, each of.

oleandro *sm.* oleander.

oleario *agg.* oil (*attr.*).

oleato *agg.* oiled || *carta oleata*, grease-proof paper.

oleificio *sm.* oil mill.

oleodotto *sm.* oil pipeline.

oleografìa *sf.* **1.** oleography **2.** (*pezzo singolo*) oleograph.

oleoso *agg.* oily.

olezzare *vi.* to smell (*v. irr.*) sweetly.

olezzo *sm.* fragrance.

olfattivo *agg.* olfactory.

olfatto *sm.* smell.

ollare *vt.* to oil.

oliatore *sm.* oil-can.

oliera *sf.* cruet.

oligarca *sm.* oligarch.

oligarchìa *sf.* oligarchy.

oligàrchico *agg.* oligarchic(al).

oligocene *sm.* Oligocene.

olimpìaco *agg.* V. *olimpico*.

olimpìade *sf.* Olympiad || *le Olimpiadi*, Olympic games.

olìmpico *agg.* Olympic.

olimpiònico *agg.* Olympic games (*attr.*). ♦ **olimpiònico** *sm.*

Olympic champion.

olio *sm.* oil.

oliva *sf.* olive.

olivastro *agg.* olive.

oliveto *sm.* olive-grove.

olivo *sm.* olive.

olmo *sm.* elm.

olocàusto *sm.* holocaust.

ològrafo *agg.* holograph.

oltraggiare *vt.* to outrage.

oltraggio *sm.* outrage.

oltraggioso *agg.* outrageous.

oltramontano *agg. e sm.* ultramontane.

oltranza *sf.* (*nella loc. avv.*) *a —*, to the bitter end.

oltranzista *sm.* extremist.

oltre *avv.* **1.** (*di luogo*) further, farther **2.** (*di tempo*) longer. ♦ **oltre** *prep.* **1.** (*di luogo*) beyond **2.** (*più di*) over **3.** (*in aggiunta*) in addition to. ♦ **oltre a, che** *cong.* besides.

oltrecortina *avv.* beyond the Iron Curtain.

oltremare *avv.* overseas: *d'—*. overseas (*attr.*).

oltremodo *avv.* extremely.

oltrepassare *vt.* to go (*v. irr.*) beyond || *— i limiti* (*fig.*), to go (*v. irr.*) too far.

oltretomba *sm.* hereafter.

omaccione *sm.* burly man (*pl.* men).

omaggio *sm.* **1.** homage **2.** (*offerta*) gift.

ombelicale *agg.* umbilical.

ombelico *sm.* navel.

ombra *sf.* **1.** shade (*anche spettro*) **2.** (*immagine proiettata, parvenza*) shadow || *dar — a qu.*, to overshadow so.

ombreggiare *vt.* to shade.

ombreggiatura *sf.* shading.

ombrella *sf.* (*bot.*) umbel.

ombrellìfero *agg.* umbelliferous.

ombrellino *sm.* parasol.

ombrello *sm.* umbrella.

ombrellone *sm.* sunshade.

ombretto *sm.* eye shadow.

ombrina *sf.* umbrina.

ombrosità *sf.* **1.** shadiness **2.** (*di persona*) touchiness **3.** (*di cavallo*) skittishness.

ombroso *agg.* **1.** shady **2.** (*di persona*) touchy **3.** (*di cavallo*) skittish.

omega *sm.* omega.

omelìa *sf.* homily.

omeopatìa *sf.* homeopathy.

omeopàtico *agg.* homeopathic. ♦
omeopàtico *sm.* homeopath

omèrico *agg.* Homeric.

òmero *sm.* humerus (*pl.* -ri).

omertà *sf.* silence.

omesso *agg.* omitted.

ométtere *vt.* to omit, to leave out.

omicida *agg.* homicidal. ♦ omicida *s.* homicide.

omicidio *sm.* homicide.

omissione *sf.* omission.

òmnibus *sm.* bus.

omogeneità *sf.* homogeneity.

omogeneizzare *vt.* to homogenize.

omogèneo *agg.* homogeneous.

omologare *vt.* 1. to homologate 2. (*sport*) to ratify.

omologazione *sf.* 1. homologation 2. (*sport*) ratification.

omòlogo *agg.* homologous.

omonimia *sf.* homonymy.

omònimo *agg.* homonymous. ♦ omònimo *sm.* homonym.

omosessuale *agg.* e *s.* homosexual.

omosessualità *sf.* homosexuality.

oncia *sf.* ounce.

onda *sf.* wave || mettere in — (*radio*), to broadcast (*v. irr.*).

ondata *sf.* wave: *a ondate*, in waves.

onde *avv.* 1. whence 2. (*affinché*) so that 3. (*cosicché*) therefore 4. (*da, con cui*) from, by, with which.

ondeggiamento *sm.* 1. waving 2. (*di barca*) rolling 3. (*esitazione*) wavering.

ondeggiante *agg.* 1. waving 2. (*di barca*) rolling 3. (*esitante*) wavering.

ondeggiare *vi.* 1. to wave 2. (*di barca*) to roll 3. (*esitare*) to waver.

ondina *sf.* undine.

ondoso *agg.* undulatory.

ondulare *vt.* to wave.

ondulato *agg.* 1. wavy 2. (*tec.*) corrugated.

ondulatorio *agg.* undulatory.

ondulazione *sf.* 1. undulation 2. (*di capelli*) wave.

onerare *vt.* to burden.

ònere *sm.* burden || — *fiscale*, tax.

oneroso *agg.* burdensome.

onestà *sf.* 1. honesty 2. (*castità*) chastity.

onesto *agg.* 1. honest 2. (*casto*) chaste.

onice *sf.* onyx.

onirico *agg.* oneiric.

onnipotente *agg.* omnipotent. ♦
Onnipotente (l') *sm.* the Almighty.

onnipotenza *sf.* omnipotence.

onnipresente *agg.* omnipresent.

onnisciente *agg.* omniscient.

onniscienza *sf.* omniscience.

onniveggente *agg.* omnipercipient.

onnivoro *agg.* omnivorous. ♦ onnivoro *sm.* omnivore.

onomàstico *agg.* onomastic. ♦
onomàstico *sm.* name-day.

onomatopea *sf.* onomatopoeia.

onomatopèico *agg.* onomatopoeic.

onoràbile *agg.* honourable.

onorabilità *sf.* honourableness.

onoranza *sf.* honour.

onorare *vt.* to honour. ♦ onorarsi *vr.* to be proud (of).

onorario *agg.* honorary. ♦ onorario *sm.* fee.

onorato *agg.* 1. honoured 2. (*onesto*) honourable.

onore *sm.* honour || *farsi* —, to excel; *a onor del vero*, to tell (*v. irr.*) the truth; *serata d'*—, gala night.

onorévole *agg.* honourable.

onorificenza *sf.* 1. honour 2. (*decorazione*) decoration.

onorifico *agg.* honorific(al).

onta *sf.* 1. shame 2. (*offesa*) insult || *ad* — *di*, in spite of.

ontano *sm.* alder.

ontologia *sf.* ontology.

ontològico *agg.* ontological.

opacità *sf.* opacity.

opaco *agg.* 1. opaque 2. (*di suoni, colori*) dull.

opale *sm.* opal.

opalescente *agg.* opalescent.

opalino *agg.* opaline.

òpera *sf.* 1. work 2. (*melodramma*) opera 3. (*istituto*) institution.

operàbile *agg.* 1. workable. 2. (*chir.*) operable.

operaio *agg.* working. ♦ operaio *sm.* worker: — *specializzato*, skilled worker.

operante *agg.* operating.

operare *vi.* to work, to operate (*anche med.*).

operativo *agg.* operative.

operato *agg.* (*di tessuto*) diapered. ♦ operato *sm.* 1. (*condotta*) behaviour 2. (*chi ha subito un'operazione*) operated patient.

operatore *sm.* 1. operator 2. (*cine*) cameraman (*pl.* -men).

operatorio *agg.* operating.
operazione *sf.* operation: *fare un'* — *a qu.*, to perform an operation on so.; *subire un'* —, to undergo (*v. irr.*) an operation.
operetta *sf.* operetta.
operistico *agg.* opera (*attr.*).
operosità *sf.* industry.
operoso *agg.* industrious.
opificio *sm.* factory.
opimo *agg.* fertile.
opinàbile *agg.* thinkable.
opinare *vi.* to think (*v. irr.*).
opinione *sf.* opinion: *secondo l'— di qu.*, in so.'s opinion.
opòssum *sm.* opossum.
oppiare *vt.* to opiate.
oppiato *agg. e sm.* opiate.
oppio *sm.* opium.
oppiòmane *s.* opium-addict.
opponente *agg. e sm.* opponent.
oppinibile *agg.* opposable.
opporre *vt.* **1.** to oppose **2.** (*obiettare*) to object. ♦ **opporsi** *vr.* to object (to), to be opposed.
opportunismo *sm.* opportunism.
opportunista *s.* opportunist.
opportunistico *agg.* opportunistic.
opportunità *sf.* **1.** (*occasione*) opportunity **2.** (*l'essere opportuno*) timeliness.
opportuno *agg.* **1.** opportune **2.** (*giusto*) right.
oppositore *sm.* opponent.
opposizione *sf.* opposition || *fare* — (*a qu., qc.*), to oppose (so., sthg.).
opposto *agg. e sm.* opposite.
oppressione *sf.* oppression.
oppressivo *agg.* oppressive.
oppresso *agg.* oppressed.
oppressore *sm.* oppressor.
opprimente *agg.* oppressive.
opprìmere *vt.* to oppress.
oppugnare *vt.* to assail.
oppure *cong.* **1.** or **2.** (*altrimenti*) or else.
optare *vi.* to opt.
opulento *agg.* opulent.
opulenza *sf.* opulence.
opùscolo *sm.* pamphlet.
opzione *sf.* option.
ora¹ *sf.* **1.** hour **2.** (*tempo*) time: *che — è?*, what time is it?; — *di punta*, rush hour; *all'*—, by the hour; *di* — *in* —, hourly; *di buon'*—, early; — *legale*, summer time; *non veder l'* — *di*, to look forward to.

ora² *avv.* now || — *come* —, at the moment; *d'* — *in poi*, from now on; *fino ad* —, so far; *sin d'*—, now; *prima d'* —, before; *or* —, just. ♦ **ora che** *cong.* now (that).
oràcolo *sm.* oracle.
òrafo *sm.* goldsmith.
orale *agg. e sm.* oral.
oralmente *avv.* orally.
oramai *avv.* V. *ormai*.
orango *sm.* orang-outang.
orario *agg.* **1.** time (*attr.*) **2.** (*all'ora*) per hour. ♦ **orario** *sm.* **1.** hours (*pl.*) **2.** (*tabella*) time-table || *in* —, on time.
orata *sf.* dory.
oratore *sm.* orator.
oratoria *sf.* oratory.
oratorio *sm.* oratory.
orazione *sf.* **1.** oration **2.** (*preghiera*) prayer.
orbare *vt.* to bereave (*v. irr.*).
orbene *avv.* well.
òrbita *sf.* orbit.
orbitale *agg.* orbital.
orbo *agg.* (*di un occhio*) one-eyed.
orchestra *sf.* orchestra.
orchestrale *agg.* orchestral. ♦ **orchestrale** *s.* member of an orchestra.
orchestrare *vt.* to orchestrate.
orchestrazione *sf.* orchestration.
orchestrina *sf.* band.
orchidea *sf.* orchid.
orcio *sm.* pitcher.
orco *sm.* ogre.
orda *sf.* horde.
ordigno *sm.* device.
ordinale *agg. e sm.* ordinal.
ordinamento *sm.* **1.** arrangement **2.** (*regolamento*) code, system.
ordinanza *sf.* **1.** order **2.** (*attendente mil.*) batman (*pl.* -men).
ordinare *vt.* **1.** to order **2.** (*mettere in ordine*) to put (*v. irr.*) in order **3.** (*eccl.*) to ordain **4.** (*med.*) to prescribe. ♦ **ordinarsi** *vr.* **1.** to straighten up **2.** (*mil.*) to draw (*v. irr.*) up.
ordinario *agg. e sm.* ordinary.
ordinata *sf.* **1.** (*mat.*) ordinate **2.** (*aer.; mar.*) frame.
ordinatamente *avv.* tidily.
ordinato *agg.* tidy, orderly.
ordinazione *sf.* **1.** order **2.** (*med.*) prescription **3.** (*eccl.*) ordination.
òrdine *sm.* order || — *d'idee*, scheme of things; *all'* — *del giorno*,

on the agenda; *per — di*, by order of; *parola d'—*, password; *di primʾ—*, firstclass (*attr.*).

ordire *vt.* **1.** to warp **2.** (*fig.*) to plot.

ordito *sm.* warp.

orecchiàbile *agg.* catchy.

orecchino *sm.* earring.

orecchio *sm.* ear.

orecchioni *sm. pl.* mumps.

oréfice *sm.* jeweller.

oreficeria *sf.* **1.** jeweller's art **2.** (*negozio*) jeweller's shop.

òrfano *agg.* e *sm.* orphan.

orfanotrofio *sm.* orphanage.

organetto *sm.* barrel-organ || *suonatore di —*, organ-grinder.

organicità *sf.* organic unity.

organico[1] *agg.* organic.

organico[2] *sm.* staff.

organismo *sm.* **1.** organism **2.** (*ente*) body.

organista *s.* organist.

organizzàbile *agg.* organizable.

organizzare *vt.* to organize.

organizzatore *sm.* organizer.

organizzazione *sf.* organization.

òrgano *sm.* organ.

organza *sf.* organza.

organzino *sm.* organzine.

orgasmo *sm.* orgasm.

orgia *sf.* orgy.

orgiàstico *agg.* orgiastic.

orgoglio *sm.* pride.

orgoglioso *agg.* proud.

orientale *agg.* eastern.

orientalista *s.* orientalist.

orientamento *sm.* orientation || *perdere l'—*, to lose (*v. irr.*) one's bearings.

orientare *vt.* to orient. ♦ **orientarsi** *vr.* **1.** to find (*v. irr.*) one's bearings **2.** (*tendere*) to tend.

oriente *sm.* east.

orifiamma *sf.* oriflamme.

orifizio *sm.* orifice.

origano *sm.* origan.

originale *agg.* **1.** original **2.** (*strano*) odd. ♦ **originale** *sm.* **1.** original **2.** (*persona eccentrica*) eccentric.

originalità *sf.* **1.** originality **2.** (*stranezza*) oddity.

originare *vt.* e *vi.* to originate.

originariamente *avv.* originally.

originario *agg.* original.

origine *sf.* origin || *avere —*, to originate; *dare —*, to cause.

origliare *vi.* to eavesdrop.

orina *sf.* urine.

orinale *sm.* chamber pot.

orinare *vi.* to urinate.

orinatolo *sm.* public lavatory.

orizzontale *agg.* horizontal.

orizzontalmente *avv.* horizontally.

orizzontare *vt.*, **orizzontarsi** *vr.* V. *orientare, orientarsi*.

orizzonte *sm.* horizon.

orlare *vt.* **1.** (*bordare*) to edge **2.** (*fare l'orlo*) to hem.

orlatura *sf.* hemming.

orlo *sm.* **1.** (*di abito ecc.*) hem **2.** (*bordatura*) border **3.** (*estremità*) edge **4.** (*di oggetto rotondo*) rim || *— a giorno*, hem-stitch; *sull'—della rovina*, on the verge of ruin.

orma *sf.* **1.** mark **2.** (*traccia*) trace **3.** (*di piede*) footprint || *seguire le orme di qu.*, to follow in so.'s footsteps; *tornare sulle proprie orme*, to go (*v. irr.*) back on one's tracks.

ormai *avv.* **1.** (by) now **2.** (*al passato*) (by) then.

ormeggiare *vt.* to moor. ♦ **ormeggiarsi** *vr.* to moor.

ormeggio *sm.* mooring.

ormone *sm.* hormone.

ormònico *agg.* hormonic.

ornamentale *agg.* ornamental.

ornamentazione *sf.* ornamentation.

ornamento *sm.* ornament.

ornare *vt.* to adorn.

ornato *agg.* **1.** adorned (with) **2.** (*di stile*) ornate.

ornitologia *sf.* ornithology.

ornitològico *agg.* ornithological.

ornitòlogo *sm.* ornithologist.

oro *sm.* gold || *d'—*, golden.

orografia *sf.* orography.

orogràfico *agg.* orographic(al).

orologeria *sf.* **1.** (*arte*) horology **2.** (*negozio*) watchmaker's shop || *movimento d'—*, clock movement.

orologiaio *sm.* watchmaker.

orologio *sm.* **1.** watch **2.** (*a muro, da tavolo*) clock.

oròscopo *sm.* horoscope.

orpello *sm.* tinsel.

orrendamente *avv.* dreadfully.

orrendo *agg.* dreadful.

orrìbile *agg.* horrible.

orribilmente *avv.* horribly.

òrrido *agg.* frightful.

orripilante *agg.* terrifying.

orrore *sm.* horror.

orsa *sf.* she-bear: *— Maggiore*,

Great Bear; — *Minore*, Little Bear.

orsacchiotto *sm.* **1.** young bear **2.** (*giocattolo*) Teddy bear.

orso *sm.* bear.

ortaggio *sm.* vegetable.

ortensia *sf.* hydrangea.

ortica *sf.* nettle.

orticaria *sf.* nettle-rash.

orticoltore *sm.* horticulturist.

orticultura *sf.* horticulture.

orto *sm.* **1.** kitchen garden **2.** (*di orticoltore*) market garden.

ortodossia *sf.* orthodoxy.

ortodosso *agg.* orthodox.

ortofrutticolo *agg.* horticultural.

ortogonale *agg.* orthogonal.

ortografia *sf.* orthography, spelling.

ortografico *agg.* orthographic(al).

ortolano *sm.* **1.** market-gardener **2.** (*negoziante*) greengrocer.

ortopedia *sf.* orthopedics.

ortopèdico *agg.* orthopedic. ♦ **ortopèdico** *sm.* orthopedist.

orzaiolo *sm.* sty.

orzata *sf.* (*bibita*) orgeat.

orzo *sm.* barley.

osanna *sf.* hosanna.

osare *vi.* to dare (*v. semidif.*). ♦ **osare** *vt.* (*tentare*) to attempt.

oscenità *sf.* obscenity.

osceno *agg.* obscene.

oscillare *vi.* **1.** to swing (*v. irr.*) **2.** (*di fiamma; opinioni*) to waver **3.** (*elettr.*) to oscillate **4.** (*di prezzi*) to fluctuate.

oscillatore *sm.* oscillator.

oscillatorio *agg.* oscillatory.

oscillazione *sf.* **1.** swing **2.** (*di fiamma; opinioni*) wavering **3.** (*elettr.*) oscillation **4.** (*di prezzi*) fluctuation.

oscillògrafo *sm.* oscillograph.

oscurantismo *sm.* obscurantism.

oscurantista *agg. e s.* obscurantist.

oscurare *vt.* **1.** to darken **2.** (*fig.*) to overshadow. ♦ **oscurarsi** *vr.* to darken.

oscurità *sf.* **1.** darkness **2.** (*fig.*) obscurity.

oscuro *agg.* **1.** dark **2.** (*sconosciuto, umile*) obscure **3.** (*difficile*) hard, difficult **4.** (*sconosciuto*) unknown.

osmosi *sf.* osmosis (*pl.* -ses).

ospedale *sm.* hospital.

ospedaliero *agg.* hospital (*attr.*).

ospitale *agg.* hospitable.

ospitalità *sf.* hospitality.

ospitare *vt.* to entertain.

òspite *s.* **1.** (*chi ospita, uomo*) host; (*id., donna*) hostess **2.** (*chi è ospitato*) guest.

ospizio *sm.* **1.** (*per poveri*) alms-house **2.** (*per trovatelli*) foundling hospital **3.** (*per vecchi ecc.*) home (for the old etc.).

ossario *sm.* charnel-house, ossuary.

ossatura *sf.* **1.** skeleton **2.** (*di edificio, discorso*) framework.

òsseo *agg.* bony.

ossequente *agg.* respectful.

ossequio *sm.* **1.** homage **2.** (*obbedienza*) obedience **3.** (*saluti*) regards (*pl.*).

ossequiosità *sf.* deference.

ossequioso *agg.* deferential.

osservàbile *agg.* observable.

osservante *agg.* observant.

osservanza *sf.* **1.** observance **2.** (*ossequio*) regards (*pl.*).

osservare *vt.* **1.** to observe **2.** (*esaminare*) to examine.

osservatore *agg.* observing. ♦ **osservatore** *sm.* observer.

osservatorio *sm.* observatory.

osservazione *sf.* **1.** observation: *in —*, under observation **2.** (*rimprovero*) reproach.

ossessionante *agg.* haunting.

ossessionare *vt.* to haunt.

ossessione *sf.* obsession.

ossessivo *agg.* haunting.

ossesso *sm.* person possessed.

ossia *cong.* (*cioè*) that is.

ossidàbile *agg.* oxidizable.

ossidare *vt.* to oxidize. ♦ **ossidarsi** *vr.* to oxidize.

ossidazione *sf.* oxidation.

òssido *sm.* oxide.

ossidrico *agg.* oxyhydrogen.

ossificare *vt.* to ossify. ♦ **ossificarsi** *vr.* to ossify.

ossificazione *sf.* ossification.

ossigenare *vt.* **1.** to oxygenate **2.** (*di capelli*) to peroxide.

ossigenato *agg.* **1.** oxygenated **2.** (*di capelli*) peroxided ‖ *acqua ossigenata*, hydrogen peroxide.

ossigeno *sm.* oxygen.

osso *sm.* bone ‖ *in carne e ossa*, in flesh and blood; *avere le ossa rotte*, to be aching all over.

ossuto *agg.* bony.

ostacolare *vt.* to hamper.

ostàcolo *sm.* **1.** obstacle **2.** (*sport*) hurdle ‖ *corsa ippica ad ostacoli*, steeple-chase.

ostaggio *sm.* hostage.

oste *sm.* innkeeper.

osteggiare *vt.* to oppose.

ostello *sm.* — *della gioventù,* (youth) hostel.

ostensorio *sm.* monstrance.

ostentare *vt.* 1. to show (*v. irr.*) off 2. (*fingere*) to feign.

ostentatamente *avv.* ostentatiously.

ostentazione *sf.* ostentation.

osteologia *sf.* osteology.

osteria *sf.* pub.

ostètrica *sf.* midwife (*pl.* -wives).

ostetricia *sf.* obstetrics.

ostètrico *sm.* obstetrician.

ostia *sf.* 1. wafer 2. (*eccl.*) host.

òstico *agg.* 1. irksome 2. (*di sapore*) unpalatable 3. (*fig.*) difficult.

ostile *agg.* hostile.

ostilità *sf.* hostility.

ostinarsi *vr.* to persist (in).

ostinato *agg.* stubborn.

ostinazione *sf.* obstinacy.

ostracismo *sm.* ostracism.

òstrica *sf.* oyster.

ostricaio *sm.* oyster-seller.

ostricultura *sf.* oyster-breeding.

ostruire *vt.* to obstruct.

ostruzione *sf.* obstruction.

ostruzionismo *sm.* obstructionism.

ostruzionista *s.* obstructionist.

otaria *sf.* otary.

otite *sf.* otitis.

otorinolaringoiatra *s.* otorhino-laryngologist.

otorinolaringoiatrìa *sf.* otorhino-laryngology.

ottaedro *sm.* octahedron.

ottagonale *agg.* octagonal.

ottàgono *sm.* octagon.

ottanta *agg.* eighty.

ottantenne *agg.* eighty years old, eighty-year-old (*attr.*).

ottantèsimo *agg.* eightieth.

ottava *sf.* octave.

ottavo *agg. e sm.* eighth.

ottemperanza *sf.* compliance.

ottemperare *vi.* to comply (with).

ottenebrare *vt.* to cloud.

ottenere *vt.* to obtain, to get (*v. irr.*).

ottetto *sm.* octet.

òttica *sf.* optics.

òttico *agg.* optic(al). ♦ **òttico** *sm.* optician.

ottimismo *sm.* optimism.

ottimista *s.* optimist.

ottimìstico *agg.* optimistic.

òttimo *agg.* best, very good. ♦ **òttimo** *sm.* optimum (*pl.* -ma).

otto *agg.* eight.

ottobre *sm.* October.

ottocento *agg.* eight hundred. ♦ **ottocento** *sm. l'—,* the nineteenth century.

ottomana *sf.* ottoman.

ottomano *agg. e sm.* Ottoman.

ottone *sm.* brass.

ottuagenario *agg. e sm.* octogenarian.

otturare *vt.* to stop. ♦ **otturarsi** *vr.* to stop.

otturatore *sm.* (*foto*) shutter.

otturazione *sf.* stopping.

ottusità *sf.* obtuseness.

ottuso *agg.* obtuse.

ovaia *sf.* ovary.

ovale *agg. e sm.* oval.

ovatta *sf.* 1. wadding 2. (*cotone idròfilo*) cotton-wool.

ovattare *vt.* to stuff with wadding.

ovazione *sf.* ovation.

ove *avv.* where.

ovest *sm.* west.

ovile *sm.* fold.

ovino *agg.* ovine. ♦ **ovino** *sm.* sheep (*invariato al pl.*).

ovìparo *agg.* oviparous.

ovòide *agg.* egg-shaped.

òvolo *sm.* (*fungo*) agaric.

ovulazione *sf.* ovulation.

òvulo *sm.* ovule.

ovunque *avv.* 1. everywhere 2. (*in qualsiasi posto*) anywhere. ♦ **o-vunque** *cong.* wherever.

ovvero *cong.* or.

ovviare *vi.* to obviate (sthg.).

ovvio *agg.* obvious.

oziare *vi.* to loaf, to idle.

ozio *sm.* idleness.

oziosamente *avv.* idly.

ozono *sm.* ozone.

P

pacare *vt.* to calm.

pacatezza *sf.* calmness.

pacato *agg.* calm.

pacca *sf.* slap.

pacchetto *sm.* packet.

pacchia *sf.* godsend.

pacchianata *sf.* coarse action.

pacchiano *agg.* coarse.

pacco *sm.* 1. (*postale*) parcel 2. (*collo*) package.

paccottiglia sf. cheap stuff.
pace sf. peace || darsi —, to set (v. irr.) one's mind at rest.
pachiderma sm. pachyderm.
pachistano agg. e sm. Pakistani.
pacificare vt. 1. to pacify 2. (riconciliare) to reconcile. ♦ **pacificarsi** vr. to become (v. irr.) reconciled.
pacificazione sf. 1. pacification 2. (riconciliazione) reconciliation.
pacìfico agg. 1. pacific 2. (evidente) self-evident.
pacifismo sm. pacifism.
pacifista s. pacifist.
pacioccone sm. easy-going person.
padella sf. frying-pan.
padiglione sm. pavilion.
padre sm. father.
padrino sm. godfather.
padronale agg. (privato) private || casa —, manor-house.
padronanza sf. mastery: — di sé, self-control.
padrone sm. 1. master 2. (proprietario) owner 3. (di casa, albergo) landlord || essere — di sé, to have self-control; padronissimo!, do as you like!
paesaggio sm. landscape.
paesano agg. rural. ♦ **paesano** sm. peasant.
paese sm. 1. (nazione, territorio) country 2. (villaggio) village.
paesista s. landscape painter.
paffuto agg. chubby.
paga sf. pay, wages (pl.): libro —, wages book; giorno di —, pay day.
pagàbile agg. payable.
pagaia sf. paddle.
pagamento sm. payment.
paganésimo sm. paganism.
pagano agg. e sm. pagan.
pagare vt. to pay (v. irr.).
pagella sf. schoolreport.
paggio sm. page.
pagherò sm. promissory note.
pàgina sf. page.
paglia sf. straw.
pagliacciata sf. buffoonery.
pagliaccio sm. clown.
paglialo sm. strawstack.
pagliericcio sm. paillasse.
paglierino agg. straw-coloured.
vaglietta sf. 1. (cappello) straw-hat 2. (paglia di ferro) steel-wool 3. (trucioli per imballaggio) wood-shavings (pl.) 4. (trucioli, di carta) paper-wool.

pagnotta sf. round loaf (pl. -aves).
pagoda sf. pagoda.
paio sm. 1. (di cose necessariamente unite) pair 2. (due) couple.
pala sf. 1. shovel 2. (di remo, elica) blade 3. (di ruota) paddle || — d'altare, altar-piece.
paladino sm. 1. paladin 2. (fig.) champion.
palafitta sf. 1. pile 2. (abitazione) pile-dwelling.
palafreniere sm. groom.
palafreno sm. palfrey.
palanchino sm. palanquin.
palata sf. 1. shovelful 2. (colpo) blow with a shovel || a palate (fig.), in plenty.
palatale agg. palatal.
palatino agg. palatine.
palato sm. palate.
palazzo sm. palace.
palco sm. 1. (di teatro) box 2. (pedana) stand.
palcoscènico sm. stage.
paleocristiano agg. paleo-christian.
paleografia sf. paleography.
paleògrafo sm. paleographer.
paleontologìa sf. paleontology.
paleontològico agg. paleontologic(al).
paleontòlogo sm. paleontologist.
palesare vt. to reveal.
palese agg. evident.
palestra sf. gymnasium.
paletta sf. (di capostazione) signal stick.
palinodìa sf. palinode.
palissandro sm. rosewood.
palizzata sf. palisade.
palla sf. 1. ball 2. (pallottola) bullet.
pallacanestro sf. basket-ball.
pallanuoto sf. water-polo.
pallavolo sf. volley-ball.
palleggiare vi. (calcio) to dribble. ♦ **palleggiare** vt. to toss. ♦ **palleggiarsi** vr. rec. to shift on one another.
palleggio sm. 1. (calcio) dribbling 2. (tennis) tossing.
palliativo agg. e sm. palliative.
pallidezza sf. paleness.
pàllido agg. pale.
pallino sm. 1. (di -fucile) shot 2. (mania) craze.
palloncino sm. 1. balloon 2. (lampioncino) Chinese lantern.
pallone sm. ball || gioco del —, football.

pallore *sm.* pallor.
pallòttola *sf.* **1.** pellet **2.** *(mil.)* bullet.
pallottoliere *sm.* abacus *(pl. -ci).*
palma[1] *sf. (della mano)* palm.
palma[2] *sf. (albero)* palm(-tree).
palmare *agg.* **1.** *(anat.)* palmar **2.** *(evidente)* clear.
palmato *agg.* **1.** *(bot.)* palmate **2.** *(zool.)* webbed.
palmeto *sm.* palm-grove.
palmìpede *agg.* e *sm.* palmiped.
palmo *sm.* palm.
palo *sm.* **1.** pole **2.** *(per fondamenta, ormeggio)* pile || — *indicatore*, signpost; *fare il* —, to be on the lookout.
palombaro *sm.* diver.
palpàbile *agg.* tangible.
palpare *vt.* **1.** to finger **2.** *(med.)* to palpate.
pàlpebra *sf.* eyelid || *battere le palpebre*, to blink.
palpitante *agg.* **1.** throbbing **2.** *(fig.)* fascinating.
palpitare *vi.* to throb (with sthg.).
palpitazione *sf.* **1.** throbbing **2.** *(med.)* palpitation.
pàlpito *sm.* throb.
paltò *sm.* overcoat.
palude *sf.*-marsh.
paludoso *agg.* marshy.
pàmpino *sm.* vine-leaf *(pl. -leaves).*
panacea *sf.* panacea.
panare *vt.* to bread.
panca *sf.* bench.
pancetta *sf.* **1.** *(cu persona)* pot-belly.
panchina *sf.* bench.
pancia *sf.* belly.
panciera *sf.* body-belt.
panciotto *sm.* waistcoat.
panciuto *agg.* pot-bellied.
pancotto *sm.* panada.
pàncreas *sm.* pancreas.
pancreàtico *agg.* pancreatic.
pandemonio *sm.* pandemonium.
pane *sm.* bread.
panegìrico *sm.* panegyric.
panetteria *sf.* bakery.
panettiere *sm.* baker.
pànfilo *sm.* yacht.
pangermanismo *sm.* Pan-Germanism.
pànico *agg.* e *sm.* panic.
panico *sm.* *(bot.)* millet.
paniere *sm.* basket.
panificare *vi.* to make *(v. irr.)* bread.

panificazione *sf.* bread-making.
panificio *sm.* bakery.
panino *sm.* roll: — *imbottito*, sandwich.
panna[1] *sf.* cream: — *montata*, whipped cream.
panna[2] *sf. restare in* —, to have a breakdown.
pannello *sm.* **1.** *(edil.)* panel **2.** *(di stoffa)* light cloth.
panno *sm.* **1.** cloth *(pl. cloths)* **2.** *pl. (vestiti)* clothes.
pannocchia *sf.* cob.
pannolino *sm.* **1.** *(per bambini)* napkin **2.** *(assorbente igienico)* sanitary towel.
panorama *sm.* view.
panslavismo *sm.* Pan-slavism.
pantagruèlico *agg.* Pantagruelian.
pantaloni *sm. pl.* trousers || — *corti*, shorts.
pantano *sm.* **1.** mire **2.** *(luogo pantanoso; fig.)* quagmire.
panteismo *sm.* pantheism.
panteista *s.* pantheist.
panteìstico *agg.* pantheistic(al).
pantera *sf.* panther.
pantòfola *sf.* slipper.
pantògrafo *sm.* pantograph.
pantomima *sf.* pantomime.
panzana *sf.* fib.
paonazzo *agg.* purple.
papa *sm.* pope.
papà *sm.* daddy.
papale *agg.* papal.
papalina *sf.* skull-cap.
papato *sm.* papacy.
papàvero *sm.* poppy || *alto* —, *(fig.)* bigwig.
pàpera *sf.* **1.** *(zool.)* duckling **2.** *(errore)* slip **3.** *(teat.)* fluff.
papilla *sf.* papilla *(pl. -ae).*
papillare *agg.* papillary.
papiro *sm.* papyrus *(pl. -ri).*
papirologìa *sf.* papyrology.
papismo *sm.* popery.
papista *s.* papist.
pappa *sf.* pap.
pappagallo *sm.* parrot || *ripetere a* —, to parrot.
pappagorgia *sf.* double chin.
pappare *vt.* to gorge, ♦ **papparsi** *vr.* to eat up.
pàprica *sf.* paprika.
paràbola *sf.* **1.** parable **2.** *(geom.; mil.)* parabola.
parabòlico *agg.* parabolic.
parabrezza *sm.* windscreen.
paracadutare *vt.* to parachute. ♦

paracadutarsi *vr.* to bail out.
paracadute *sm.* parachute.
paracadutismo *sm.* parachutism.
paracadutista *sm.* **1.** parachutist **2.** *(mil.)* paratrooper.
paracarro *sm.* wayside post.
paradigma *sm.* paradigm.
paradisiaco *agg.* paradisiac(al).
paradiso *sm.* paradise.
paradossale *agg.* paradoxical.
paradosso *sm.* paradox.
parafango *sm.* mudguard.
paraffina *sf.* paraffin.
parafrasare *vt.* to paraphrase.
paràfrasi *sf.* paraphrase.
parafùlmine *sm.* lightning-rod.
paragonàbile *agg.* comparable.
paragonare *vt.* to compare.
paragone *sm.* comparison: *a — di,* in comparison with.
paràgrafo *sm.* paragraph.
paràlisi *sf.* palsy.
paralìtico *agg.* e *sm.* paralytic.
paralizzare *vt.* to paralyze.
parallela *sf.* parallel: *le parallele* (*sport*), parallel bars.
parallelepìpedo *sm.* parallelepiped (*pl.* -da).
parallelismo *sm.* parallelism.
parallelo *agg.* e *sm.* parallel.
parallelogrammo *sm.* parallelogram.
paralume *sm.* lamp-shade.
paramento *sm.* **1.** hanging **2.** *(eccl.)* vestment.
paràmetro *sm.* parameter.
paraninfo *sm.* paranymph.
paranoia *sf.* paranoia.
paranòico *agg.* e *sm.* paranoiac.
paraocchi *sm. pl.* blinkers.
parapetto *sm.* **1.** parapet **2.** *(davanzale)* sill.
parapiglia *sm.* turmoil.
parapioggia *sm.* umbrella.
parare *vt.* **1.** *(riparare)* to shield **2.** *(evitare)* to parry **3.** *(ornare)* to decorate || *andare a —,* to drive (*v. irr.*) at. ♦ **pararsi** *vr.* **1.** *(comparire)* to appear **2.** *(adornarsi)* to deck oneself.
parasole *sm.* parasol.
parassita *agg.* parasitic. ♦ **parassita** *s.* parasite.
parassitismo *sm.* parasitism.
parastatale *agg.* State controlled || *ente —,* semi-governmental body.
parata *sf.* **1.** parade **2.** *(sport)* parry || *fare una — (sport)*, to parry.
paratìa *sf.* bulkhead.

paratifo *sm.* paratyphoid.
parato *sm.* hanging || *carta da parati,* wallpaper.
paratoia *sf.* cataract.
paraurti *sm.* bumper.
paravento *sm.* screen.
parcella *sf.* fee.
parcheggiare *vt.* to park.
parcheggio *sm.* **1.** parking **2.** *(luogo)* car park.
parco[1] *sm.* park: *— di divertimenti,* fun-fair.
parco[2] *agg.* sparing.
parecchio *agg.* quite a lot of. ♦ **parecchio** *avv.* quite a lot, quite (+ *agg.*). ♦ **parecchio** *pron.* a good deal of it, several (*pl.*).
pareggiare *vt.* **1.** *(livellare)* to level **2.** *(comm.)* to balance **3.** *(parificare una scuola)* to recognize officially. ♦ **pareggiare** *vi.* (*sport*) to draw (*v. irr.*).
pareggio *sm.* **1.** *(comm.)* balance **2.** *(sport)* draw, tie.
parentado *sm.* V. *parentela.*
parente *sm.* relative.
parentela *sf.* **1.** relationship **2.** *(i parenti)* relatives.
parèntesi *sf.* **1.** parenthesis (*pl.* -ses) **2.** *(segno gràfico)* bracket.
parere[1] *vi.* **1.** to seem **2.** *(essere simile a)* to look like **3.** *(pensare)* to think (*v. irr.*) (of).
parere[2] *sm.* opinion.
paresi *sf.* paresis.
parete *sf.* wall: *— divisoria,* partition.
pàrgolo *sm.* little child (*pl.* children).
pari *agg.* **1.** equal, same **2.** *(simile)* like **3.** *(divisibile per due)* even. ♦ **pari** *sm.* equal, peer.
paria *sm.* pariah.
parietale *agg.* parietal.
parificazione *sf.* **1.** *(comm.)* balance **2.** *(scuola)* official recognition **3.** *(livellamento)* levelling.
parigino *agg.* e *sm.* Parisian.
pariglia *sf.* pair.
parimenti *avv.* likewise.
parità *sf.* equality.
paritario *agg.* equalitarian.
parlamentare[1] *agg.* parliamentary. ♦ **parlamentare** *sm.* Member of Parliament.
parlamentare[2] *vi.* to parley.
parlamentarismo *sm.* parliamentarianism.

parlamento *sm.* parliament.
parlantina *sf.* talkativeness || *aver buona —*, to be a glib talker.
parlare *vi.* to speak (*v. irr.*), to talk.
parlare *sm.* 1. (*discorso*) speech 2. (*chiacchiere*) talk 3. (*idioma*) language.
parlato *agg. cinema —*, talkies (*pl.*).
parlatore *sm.* speaker.
parlatorio *sm.* parlour.
parlottare *vi.* to mutter.
parodìa *sf.* parody.
parodiare *vt.* to parody.
parodista *s.* parodist.
parola *sf.* 1. word 2. (*facoltà di parlare, discorso*) speech || *parole incrociate*, crosswords; *gioco di parole*, pun; *far —*, to mention; *restare senza —*, to be left speechless; *venire a parole con*, to have words with; *rivolgere la — a qu.*, to address so.; *avere la — facile*, to be a glib talker.
parolaccia *sf.* nasty word: *dire parolacce*, to swear (*v. irr.*).
parolaio *sm.* 1. chatterbox 2. (*di scrittore*) word-monger.
paroliere *sm.* « lyrics » writer.
parossismo *sm.* paroxysm.
paròtide *sf.* parotid.
parricida *s.* parricide.
parricidio *sm.* parricide.
parrocchia *sf.* parish.
parrocchiale *agg.* parish (*attr.*).
parrocchiano *sm.* parishioner.
pàrroco *sm.* 1. (*cattolico*) parish priest 2. (*protestante*) parson.
parrucca *sf.* wig.
parrucchiere *sm.* hairdresser.
parsimonia *sf.* thriftiness.
parsimonioso *agg.* thrifty.
parte *sf.* 1. part 2. (*lato*) side 3. (*porzione*) share 4. (*pol.; comm.; giur.*) party || *da —*, aside: *da di*, from; *da — a —*, right through; *da una — ... dall'altra*, on one hand ... on the other; *la maggior di*, most (of); *a — ciò*, apart from that; *farsi da —*, to get (*v. irr.*) out of the way; *fare la — di*, to play.
partecipante *s.* 1. sharer 2. (*chi annuncia*) spokesman (*pl. -men*) 3. (*chi presenzia*) the bystander.
partecipare *vi.* 1. to share (in) 2. (*esser presente*) to be present. ◆ **partecipare** *vt.* to announce.
partecipazione *sf.* 1. sharing 2.

(*esser presente*) presence 3. (*annuncio*) announcement 4. (*biglietto*) card.
partécipe *agg.* 1. sharing 2. (*informato*) acquainted || *rendere — qu. di qc.*, to acquaint so. with sthg.
parteggiare *vi.* to take (*v. irr.*) sides (with).
partenogènesi *sf.* parthenogenesis.
partenza *sf.* 1. departure, leaving 2. (*sport*) start || *punto di —*, starting-point; *essere in —*, to be leaving.
particella *sf.* particle.
participiale *agg.* participial.
participio *sm.* participle.
particolare *agg.* particular. ◆ **particolare** *sm.* detail.
particolareggiato *agg.* detailed.
particolarismo *sm.* particularism.
particolarità *sf.* 1. particularity 2. (*dettaglio*) detail.
partigiano *agg. e sm.* partisan.
partire¹ *vi.* 1. to leave (*v. irr.*) 2. (*muoversi, iniziare, anche fig.*) to start || *a — da*, (*beginning*) from.
partire² *vt.* to separate.
partita *sf.* 1. (*giocata*) game, match 2. (*di merci*) lot 3. (*in contabilità*) entry || *dar — vinta* (*fig.*), to give (*v. irr.*) in.
partitivo *agg. e sm.* partitive.
partito *sm.* party.
partitura *sf.* (*mus.*) score.
partizione *sf.* division.
parto *sm.* 1. delivery 2. (*fig.*) product.
partoriente *agg.* parturient. ◆ **partoriente** *sf.* lying-in woman.
partorire *vt.* to bring (*v. irr.*) forth, to beget (*v. irr.*) (*anche fig.*).
parvenza *sf.* 1. appearance 2. (*ombra*) shadow.
parziale *agg.* partial.
parzialità *sf.* partiality.
parzialmente *avv.* partially.
pàscere *vt. e vi.* 1. to feed (*v. irr.*) 2. (*al pascolo*) to graze. ◆ **pàscersi** *vr.* to feed (on).
pascià *sm.* pasha.
pasciuto *agg.* fed.
pascolare *vt. e vi.* to pasture.
pàscolo *sm.* pasture || *essere al —*, to be grazing.
Pasqua *sf.* Easter.
pasquale *agg.* Easter (*attr.*).
passabile *agg.* passabl▸

passabilmente *avv.* passably.
passaggio *sm.* 1. passage 2. (*traversata*) crossing || *dare un — in macchina*, to give (*v. irr.*) a lift; *vietato il —*, no thoroughfare; *di —*, of transition; (*incidentalmente*) incidentally.
passamaneria *sf.* passementerie.
passamano *sm.* (*fettuccia*) braid.
passamontagna *sm.* snow-cap.
passante *sm.* 1. (*di cinghia ecc.*) loop 2. (*persona*) passer-by.
passaporto *sm.* passport.
passare *vi.* 1. to pass 2. (*andare*) to call (on so., at sthg.). ♦ **passare** *vt.* 1. to pass 2. (*di tempo*) to spend (*v. irr.*) 3. (*sopportare, trafiggere*) to pass through.
passatempo *sm.* pastime.
passatista *s.* traditionalist.
passato *agg.* 1. past 2. (*scorso*) last. ♦ **passato** *sm.* 1. past 2. (*cuc.*) mash.
passaverdura *sm.* vegetable masher.
passeggero *agg.* passing. ♦ **passeggero** *sm.* passenger.
passeggiare *vi.* to walk, to take (*v. irr.*) a walk.
passeggiata *sf.* 1. walk 2. (*in auto*) drive 3. (*in bicicletta, a cavallo*) ride 4. (*lungomare*) promenade.
passeggino *sm.* perambulator.
passeggio *sm.* 1. walk 2. (*gente che passeggia*) promenaders (*pl.*) || *andare a —*, to go (*v. irr.*) for a walk.
passeràceo *sm. e agg.* passerine.
passerella *sf.* 1. (*ponte pedonale*) footbridge 2. (*provvisoria*) trestle-bridge 3. (*mar.; edil.*) gangway 4. (*teat.*) parade.
pàssero *sm.* sparrow.
passibile *agg.* liable (to).
passiflora *sf.* passion-flower.
passino *sm.* strainer.
passionale *agg.* 1. passional 2. (*appassionato*) passionate.
passione *sf.* passion.
passivamente *avv.* passively.
passività *sf.* 1. passivity 2. (*comm.*) liabilities (*pl.*).
passivo *agg.* passive. ♦ **passivo** *sm.* 1. passive 2. (*comm.*) liabilities (*pl.*).
passo *sm.* 1. step 2. (*andatura*) pace 3. (*di montagna*) pass 4. (*brano, passaggio*) passage 5. (*cine*)

gauge 6. (*tec.*) pitch || *passo passo*, very slowly; *segnare il —*, to mark time; *camminare a grandi passi*, to stride (*v. irr.*).
pasta *sf.* 1. paste 2. (*pasticcino*) cake 3. (*per minestre*) "pasta".
pasteggiare *vi.* to feed (*v. irr.*) (on).
pastella *sf.* (*cuc.*) batter.
pastello *sm.* pastel: *matita, disegno a —*, pastel.
pastica *sf.* tablet.
pasticceria *sf.* confectionery.
pasticciare *vt. e vi.* to make (*v. irr.*) a mess (of).
pasticciere *sm.* confectioner.
pasticcino *sm.* cake.
pasticcio *sm.* 1. (*cuc.*) pie 2. (*fig*) mess || *essere nei pasticci*, to be in trouble.
pasticcione *sm.* bungler.
pastificio *sm.* « pasta » factory.
pastiglia *sf.* tablet.
pasto *sm.* meal.
pastoia *sf.* hobble.
pastone *sm.* mash.
pastorale *agg.* pastoral.
pastore *sm.* 1. shepherd 2. (*relig.*) parson.
pastorizia *sf.* stock-raising.
pastorizzare *vt.* to pasteurize.
pastorizzazione *sf.* pasteurization.
pastosità *sf.* 1. mellowness 2. (*morbidezza*) doughiness.
pastoso *agg.* 1. mellow 2. (*morbido*) doughy.
pastrano *sm.* overcoat.
pastura *sf.* pasture.
patacca *sf.* 1. (*macchia*) spot 2. (*cosa senza valore*) worthless object.
patata *sf.* potato: — *americana*, sweet potato || — *fritta*, chip; (*id., croccante*) crisp.
patema *sm.* worry.
patentato *agg.* licenced.
patente *agg.* patent. ♦ **patente** *sf.* licence.
patereccio *sm.* whitlow.
paternale *sf.* scolding || *fare una — a qu.*, to lecture so.
paternalismo *sm.* paternalism.
paternalìstico *agg.* paternalistic.
paternità *sf.* paternity.
paterno *agg.* paternal.
pateticamente *avv.* pathetically.
patètico *agg. e sm.* pathetic.
patibolare *agg.* sinister.
patìbolo *sm.* scaffold.
patimento *sm.* pain.
pàtina *sf.* 1. patina 2. (*di vernice*)

coat of varnish 3. (*sulla lingua*) coat 4. (*su carta, terracotta*) glaze.

patinare *vt.* 1. to varnish 2. (*caria, terracotta*) to glaze.

patire *vt. e vi.* to suffer: — *il freddo*, to suffer from the cold || — *la fame*, to starve.

patito *agg.* sickly. ♦ **patito** *sm.* (*fig.*) fan.

patògeno *agg.* pathogenic.

patologia *sf.* pathology.

patològico *agg.* pathologic(al).

patòlogo *sm.* pathologist.

patria *sf.* 1. country, fatherland 2. (*luogo natale*) birthplace.

patriarca *sm.* patriarch.

patriarcale *agg.* patriarchal.

patriarcato *sm.* patriarchate.

patricida *s.* V. **parricida**.

patrigno *sm.* stepfather.

patrimoniale *agg.* patrimonial.

patrimonio *sm.* patrimony.

patrio *agg.* 1. native 2. (*paterno*) paternal.

patriota *s.* patriot.

patriottardo *sm. e agg.* jingoist.

patriòttico *agg.* patriotic.

patriottismo *sm.* patriotism.

patriziato *sm.* patriciate.

patrizio *sm. e agg.* patrician.

patrocinante *sm.* pleader.

patrocinare *vt.* 1. (*sostenere*) to support 2. (*giur.*) to plead.

patrocinio *sm.* 1. support 2. (*giur.*) pleading.

patronato *sm.* 1. patronage 2. (*istituto benefico*) charitable institution.

patronessa *sf.* patroness.

patrono *sm.* 1. patron 2. (*giur.*) counsel for the defence.

patteggiare *vi.* to come (*v. irr.*) to terms.

pattinaggio *sm.* skating.

pattinare *vi.* to skate.

pattinatore *sm.* skater.

pàttino *sm.* 1. (*a rotelle*) roller-skate 2. (*da ghiaccio*) ice-skate 3. (*di slitta*) shoe 4. (*aer.*) skid 5. (*mecc.*) sliding-block.

patto *sm.* 1. agreement, pact 2. (*condizione*) term || *a — che*, provided that; *a nessun —*, by no means.

pattuglia *sf.* patrol.

pattugliare *vi.* to patrol.

pattuire *vi.* to reach an agreement (upon). ♦ **pattuire** *vt.* to agree (on).

pattume *sm.* rubbish.

pattumiera *sf.* dust-bin.

pauperismo *sm.* pauperism.

paura *sf.* 1. fear, dread 2. (*spavento*) fright, scare.

pauroso *agg.* fearful.

pàusa *sf.* pause.

pavesare *vt.* to dress (with flags).

pavese *sm.* (*mar.*) hoist.

pavimentare *vt.* 1. to pave 2. (*una stanza*) to floor.

pavimento *sm.* floor.

pavone *sm.* peacock.

pavoneggiarsi *vr.* to show (*v. irr.*) off.

pazientare *vi.* to have patience.

paziente *agg. e sm.* patient.

pazienza *sf.* patience || —!, never mind!

pazzesco *agg.* foolish.

pazzìa *sf.* madness 2. (*azione, idea pazza*) folly || *fare pazzie*, to act like a fool.

pazzo *agg.* mad. ♦ **pazzo** *sm.* madman (*pl.* -men).

pecca *sf.* fault || *senza —*, faultless.

pe càminoso *agg.* sinful.

peccare *vi.* 1. to sin 2. (*errare*) to err 3. (*esser mancheuole*) to lack (sthg.).

peccato *sm.* sin || *che —!*, what a pity!; *è un — che*, it is a pity that.

peccatore *sm.* sinner.

pece *sf.* pitch.

pècora *sf.* 1. sheep (*pl. invariato*) 2. (*femmina*) ewe.

pecoraio *sm.* shepherd.

peculato *sm.* peculation.

peculiare *agg.* peculiar.

peculiarità *sf.* peculiarity.

peculio *sm.* money.

pecuniario *agg.* pecuniary.

pedaggio *sm.* toll.

pedagogìa *sf.* pedagogy.

pedagògico *agg.* pedagogic(al).

pedagogista *s.* pedagogist.

pedagogo *sm.* pedagogue.

pedalare *vi.* to pedal.

pedale *sm.* pedal.

pedaliera *sf.* 1. (*aer.*) rudder-bar 2. (*mus.*) pedal keyboard.

pedana *sf.* 1. (*sport*) spring-board 2. (*piedistallo*) stand.

pedante *agg.* pedantic. ♦ **pedante** *s.* pedant.

pedanteria *sf.* pedantry.

pedantesco *agg.* pedantic.

pedata *sf.* 1. kick 2. (*impronta*) footprint.

pedemontano agg. piedmont.

pederasta sm. homosexual.

pederastia sf. homosexuality.

pedestre agg. pedestrian.

pediatra s. pediatrist.

pediatria sf. pediatrics.

pedicure s. chiropodist.

pediluvio sm. foot-bath.

pedina sf. **1.** (alla dama) piece **2.** (agli scacchi) pawn || muovere una — (anche fig.), to make (v. irr.) a move.

pedinare vt. to shadow.

pedonale agg. pedestrian (attr.): passaggio —, pedestrian crossing.

pedone sm. pedestrian || strada riservata ai pedoni, footpath.

peduncolo sm. stalk.

peggio agg. (comp.) worse. ♦ **peggio** sm. the worst. ♦ **peggio** avv. **1.** (comp.) worse **2.** (superl. rel.) the worst || — per lui, so much the worse for him; alla —, at worst; avere la —, to get (v. irr.) the worst of it.

peggioramento sm. aggravation.

peggiorare vt. to make (v. irr.) worse. ♦ **peggiorare** vi. to get (v. irr.) worse.

peggiorativo agg. e sm. pejorative.

peggiore agg. **1.** (comp.) worse: questo libro è — di quello, this book is worse than that **2.** (superl. rel.) the worst: era il suo — nemico, he was his worst enemy.

pegno sm. pledge || dare qc. in —, to pledge sthg.; polizza di —, pawn-ticket; agenzia di pegni, pawnshop.

pelagico agg. pelagic.

pelame sm. hair.

pelapatate sm. potato peeler.

pelare vt. **1.** to unhair **2.** (sbucciare) to peel **3.** (spellare) to skin **4.** (far pagare caro) to fleece. ♦ **pelarsi** vr. to lose (v. irr.) one's hair.

pelato agg. bald.

pelatura sf. **1.** unhairing **2.** (sbucciatura) peeling.

pellaio sm. furrier.

pellame sm. hides (pl.).

pelle sf. skin; (di animale grosso) hide || articoli in —, leather articles; amici per la —, bosom friends.

pellegrina sf. (mantella) tippet.

pellegrinaggio sm. pilgrimage: in —, on a pilgrimage.

pellegrinare vi. to wander, to roam.

pellegrino sm. pilgrim.

pellerossa agg. e sm. redskin.

pelletteria sf. **1.** leather goods **2.** (negozio) leather goods shop.

pellicano sm. pelican.

pelliccerìa sf. furriery **2.** (negozio) furrier's shop

pelliccia sf. fur.

pellicciaio sm. furrier.

pellicola sf. film: — a passo ridotto, substandard film.

pelo sm. hair: per un —, by a hair's breadth; cercare il — nell'uovo, to split (v. irr.) hairs || non avere peli sulla lingua, to be outspoken.

peloso agg. hairy.

pelota sf. pelota.

peltro sm. pewter.

peluria sf. down || coperto di —, downy.

pelvi sf. pelvis.

pelvico agg. pelvic.

pena sf. **1.** (punizione) punishment **2.** (dolore) pain **3.** (disturbo) trouble || essere in —, to worry; aver — di, to pity; a mala —, hardly; non ne vale la —, it is not worth while.

penale agg. **1.** criminal **2.** (relativo alla pena) penal.

penalista sm. criminal lawyer.

penalità sf. penalty.

penalizzare vt. to penalize.

penare vi. **1.** to suffer **2.** (far fatica) to be hardly able.

pendaglio sm. pendant.

pendente agg. **1.** pendent **2.** (inclinato) leaning. ♦ **pendente** sm. pendant.

pendenza sf. **1.** slope **2.** (grado d'inclinazione) gradient **3.** (giur.) pending suit **4.** (comm.) outstanding account.

pendere vi. **1.** to hang (v. irr.) **2.** (inclinare) to lean (v. irr.) **3.** (essere in declivio) to slope **4.** (incombere) to overhang (v. irr.) **5.** (essere incerto) to waver.

pendio sm. slope.

pendola sf. pendulum-clock.

pendolare agg. pendular.

pendolo sm. pendulum.

pendulo agg. pendulous.

pene sm. penis.

penetrabile agg. penetrable.

penetrabilità sf. penetrability.

penetrante *agg.* piercing.

penetrare *vi. e vt.* 1. to penetrate 2. *(con fatica; di freddo, suono)* to pierce 3. *(furtivamente)* to steal *(v. irr.)* (into).

penetrazione *sf.* penetration.

penicillina *sf.* penicillin.

peninsulare *agg.* peninsular.

penisola *sf.* peninsula.

penitente *agg. e s.* penitent.

penitenza *sf.* 1. *(teol.)* penance 2. *(pentimento)* repentance 3. *(nei giochi)* forfeit.

penitenziale *agg.* penitential.

penitenziario *agg.* penitentiary. ♦ penitenziario *sm.* jail.

penna *sf.* 1. pen 2. *(di uccello)* feather.

pennacchio *sm.* 1. plume 2. *(mil.)* panache.

pennecchio *sm.* wool on the distaff.

pennellare *vi.* 1. to brush 2. *(med.)* to paint.

pennellata *sf.* touch (of the brush).

pennellessa *sf.* flat brush.

pennello *sm.* brush.

pennino *sm.* nib.

pennone *sm.* *(mar.)* yard.

pennuto *agg.* feathered. ♦ pennuto *sm.* bird.

penombra *sf.* half-light.

penoso *agg.* painful.

pensare *vi. e vt.* 1. to think *(v. irr.)* (of) 2. *(badare)* to look after || *pensa ai fatti tuoi*, mind your own business.

pensata *sf.* thought, idea.

pensatore *sm.* thinker.

pensiero *sm.* 1. thought 2. *(opinione)* mind, opinion 3. *(ansia)* worry.

pensieroso *agg.* thoughtful.

pensile *agg.* hanging || *giardino —*, roof garden.

pensilina *sf.* 1. penthouse 2. *(di attesa)* shelter.

pensionabile *agg.* pensionable.

pensionante *s.* boarder.

pensionato[1] *agg.* retired. ♦ pensionato *sm.* pensioner, retired person.

pensionato[2] *sm.* *(istituto)* hostel.

pensione *sf.* 1. *(assegno vitalizio)* pension || *essere in —*, to be retired; *mettere in —*, to pension off 2. *(albergo)* boarding-house || *essere a —*, to be boarding (at); *— completa*, full board.

pensoso *agg.* pensive.

pentaedro *sm.* pentahedron.

pentagono *sm.* pentagon.

pentagramma *sm.* *(mus.)* pentagram.

pentametro *sm.* pentameter.

pentano *sm.* pentane.

Pentecoste *sf.* Pentecost, Whit-sunday.

pentimento *sm.* repentance.

pentirsi *vr.* 1. to repent 2. *(rimpiangere)* to regret.

pentodo *sm.* pentode,

pentola *sf.* pot.

penultimo *agg. e sm.* last but one.

penuria *sf.* shortage, penury.

penzolare *vi.* to dangle.

penzoloni *agg.* 1. *(dondolante)* dangling 2. *(pendente)* hanging.

peocio *sm.* mussel.

peonia *sf.* peony.

pepaiola *sf.* pepper-box.

pepare *vt.* to pepper.

pepato *agg.* peppery *(anche fig.).*

pepe *sm.* pepper.

peperone *sm.* pepper: *peperoni sott'aceto*, pickled peppers.

pepita *sf.* nugget.

peplo *sm.* peplum.

pepsina *sf.* pepsin.

peptone *sm.* peptone.

per *prep.* 1. for: *fallo — me*, do it for me 2. *(moto per luogo)* through: *passai per Roma*, I passed through Rome 3. *(entro, per mezzo di)* by: *devo farlo — la fine dell'anno*, I have to do it by the end of the year; *— telegramma*, by telegram 4. *(causa)* owing to, because of: *non potemmo andare — la nebbia*, we couldn't go owing to (because of) fog || *— l'addietro*, in the past; *— caso*, by chance; *— nulla*, not at all; *— sempre*, for ever; *— tempo*, early. ♦ per *cong.* 1. *(finale)* to, in order to 2. *(causale)* for.

pera *sf.* pear.

peracido *sm.* peracid.

perbacco *inter.* by Jove.

perbene *agg.* respectable.

percalle *sm.* percale.

percentuale *agg.* per cent. ♦ percentuale *sf.* percentage.

percepibile *agg.* 1. perceptible 2. *(di somme)* receivable.

percepire *vt.* 1. to perceive 2. *(di stipendio)* to receive.

percettìbile agg. perceptible.

percettivo agg. perceptive.

percezione sf. perception.

perché cong. 1. (int.) why 2. (nelle risposte) because 3. (affinché) so that. ♦ **perché** sm. reason, why: chiedersi il —, to wonder why.

perciò cong. therefore, so.

perclorato sm. perchlorate.

percòrrere vt. 1. to cover 2. (attraversare) to run (v. irr.) through.

percorso sm. 1. (distanza) distance 2. (tragitto) way 3. (tracciato) course.

percossa sf. blow.

percuòtere vt. to strike (v. irr.).

percussione sf. percussion.

percussore sm. percussion-pin.

perdente agg. losing. ♦ **perdente** s. loser.

pèrdere vt. 1. to lose (v. irr.) 2. (di treno, occasione) to miss 3. (far acqua) to leak. ♦ **pèrdersi** vr. 1. to get (v. irr.) lost 2. (svanire) to fade 3. (rovinarsi) to be ruined || — d'animo, to lose heart.

perdifiato (nella loc. avv.) a —, with all one's strength.

perdigiorno sm. idler.

pèrdita sf. 1. loss 2. (falla, fuga) leak.

perditempo sm. waste of time.

perdizione sf. perdition.

perdonàbile agg. pardonable.

perdonare vt. 1. to forgive (v. irr.) 2. (risparmiare) to spare. ♦ **perdonarsi** vr. to forgive oneself. ♦ **perdonarsi** v. rec. to forgive each other (one another).

perdono sm. forgiveness || chiedere —, to beg one's pardon.

perdurare vi. to continue.

perdutamente avv. desperately.

perduto agg. lost.

peregrinare vi. to wander, to roam.

peregrinazione sf. wandering, roaming.

peregrino agg. rare.

perenne agg. 1. perennial 2. (eterno) everlasting.

perennemente avv. 1. perennially 2. (per sempre) for ever.

perentorio agg. peremptory.

perequazione sf. equalization.

perfettamente avv. perfectly.

perfettìbile agg. perfectible.

perfettibilità sf. perfectibility.

perfetto agg. perfect. ◄ **perfetto** sm. (gramm.) perfect.

perfezionamento sm. perfecting.

perfezionare vt. 1. to perfect 2. (migliorare) to improve. ♦ **perfezionarsi** vr. to improve.

perfezione sf. perfection: alla —, to perfection.

perfidamente avv. wickedly.

perfidia sf. wickedness.

pèrfido agg. wicked.

perfino avv. even.

perforare vt. 1. to pierce 2. (d biglietti, schede) to punch 3. (mecc.) to drill, to bore.

perforante agg. perforating. ♦ **perforatore** sm. perforator.

perforatrice sf. (macchina) drill, punch.

perforazione sf. 1. perforation 2. (mecc.) drilling 3. (di biglietti, schede) punching.

pergamena sf. parchment.

pèrgola sf. bower.

pergolato sm. arbour.

pericardio sm. pericardium (pl. -ia).

pericolante agg. tottering.

perìcolo sm. danger || mettere in —, to endanger; correre un —, to be in danger.

pericolosamente avv. dangerously.

pericoloso agg. dangerous.

periferìa sf. 1. periphery 2. (di città) suburbs (pl.).

perifèrico agg. 1. peripheral 2. (suburbano) suburban.

perìfrasi sf. periphrasis (pl. -ses).

perifràstico agg. periphrastic.

perigeo sm. perigee.

perìmetro sm. perimeter.

periodicità sf. periodicity.

periòdico agg. e sm. periodical.

perìodo sm. period.

peripezìa sf. vicissitude.

perìplo sm. circumnavigation.

perire vi. to perish.

periscopio sm. periscope.

peristilio sm. peristyle.

perito sm. 1. expert 2. (comm.) estimator.

peritonite sf. peritonitis.

perituro agg. perishable.

perizia sf. 1. (abilità) skill 2. (valutazione) survey.

perla sf. pearl.

perlàceo agg. pearly.

perlìfero agg. pearl (attr.).

perlomeno avv. at least.

perlustrare vt. 1. to reconnoitre 2. (di polizia) to patrol.

perlustratore *sm.* scout.
perlustrazione *sf.* 1. reconnaissance 2. *(di polizia)* patrol || *essere in* —, to be on a reconnaissance.
permalosità *sf.* touchiness.
permaloso *agg.* touchy.
permanente *agg.* permanent. ♦ **permanente** *sf.* permanent wave.
permanentemente *avv.* permanently.
permanenza *sf.* 1. permanence 2. *(soggiorno)* stay.
permanere *vi.* 1. to remain 2. *(durare)* to last.
permanganato *sm.* permanganate.
permeàbile *agg.* permeable.
permeabilità *sf.* permeability.
permeare *vt.* to permeate.
permesso *agg.* allowed. ♦ **permesso** *sm.* 1. leave: *in* —, on leave 2. *(autorizzazione)* licence || *documento di* —, permit.
perméttere *vt.* to allow || *permetteté?*, may I? ♦ **perméttersi** *vr.* *(prendersi la libertà)* to take *(v. irr.)* the liberty (of) || *il lusso*, to afford.
pèrmuta *sf.* exchange.
permutàbile *agg.* exchangeable.
permutare *vt.* to exchange.
permutazione *sf.* permutation.
pernice *sf.* partridge.
pernicioso *agg.* pernicious.
perno *sm.* pivot.
pernottamento *sm.* overnight stay.
pernottare *vi.* to stay overnight.
pero *sm.* pear-tree.
però *cong.* but.
peronòspora *sf.* mildew.
perorare *vt.* to plead.
perorazione *sf.* pleading.
peròssido *sm.* peroxide.
perpendicolare *agg. e sf.* perpendicular.
perpetrare *vt.* to perpetrate.
perpetuamente *avv.* perpetually.
perpetuare *vt.* to perpetuate. ♦ **perpetuarsi** *vr.* to last.
perpetuità *sf.* perpetuity.
perpetuo *agg.* perpetual: *in* —, perpetually.
perplessità *sf.* perplexity.
perplesso *agg.* perplexed: *rendere* —, to perplex.
perquisire *vt.* to search.
perquisizione *sf.* search.
persecutore *sm.* persecutor.
persecuzione *sf.* persecution.
perseguìbile *agg.* (*giur.*) prosecu-

table.
perseguìre *vt.* 1. to pursue 2. *(giur.)* to prosecute.
perseguitare *vt.* to persecute.
perseguitato *sm.* persecuted person.
perseverante *agg.* persevering.
perseveranza *sf.* perseverance.
perseverare *vi.* to persevere.
persiana *sf.* shutter.
persiano *agg. e sm.* Persian.
persistente *agg.* persistent.
persistenza *sf.* persistence.
persìstere *vi.* to persist.
persona *sf.* person: *di* —, personally; — *giuridica*, artificial person.
personaggio *sm.* 1. personage 2. *(di romanzo ecc.)* character.
personale *agg.* personal. ♦ **personale** *sm.* 1. staff 2. *(corporatura)* figure.
personalità *sf.* personality: — *giuridica*, legal status.
personalmente *avv.* personally.
personificare *vt.* 1. to personify 2. *(teat.)* to play.
personificazione *sf.* personification.
perspicace *agg.* shrewd.
perspicacia *sf.* shrewdness.
perspicuo *agg.* perspicuous.
persuadere *vt.* to persuade. ♦ **persuadersi** *vr.* to convince oneself.
persuasione *sf.* persuasion.
persuasivo *agg.* persuasive.
pertanto *cong.* therefore.
pèrtica *sf.* perch.
pertinace *agg.* pertinacious.
pertinacia *sf.* pertinacity.
pertinente *agg.* pertinent.
pertinenza *sf.* pertinence.
pertosse *sf.* whooping cough.
pertugio *sm.* hole.
perturbare *vt.* to disturb.
perturbatore *agg.* disturbing. ♦ **perturbatore** *sm.* disturber.
perturbazione *sf.* disturbance.
pervàdere *vt.* to pervade.
pervenire *vi.* to arrive (at).
perversione *sf.* perversion.
perversità *sf.* perversity.
perverso *agg.* perverse.
pervertire *vt.* to pervert. ♦ **pervertirsi** *vr.* to go (*v. irr.*) astray.
pervicace *agg.* obstinate.
pervicacia *sf.* obstinacy.
pervinca *sf.* periwinkle.
pesa *sf.* 1. *(luogo)* weigh-house 2. *(apparecchio)* weighing-machine.
pesante *agg.* heavy.

pesantezza *sf.* heaviness.

pesare *vt.* to weigh. ♦ **pesare** *vi.* 1. to weigh 2. (*fig.*) to lie (*v. irr.*) heavy.

pesata *sf.* weighing.

pesca¹ *sf.* (*bot.*) peach.

pesca² *sf.* 1. (*il pescare*) fishing 2. (*industria*) fishery 3. (*il pescato*) catch.

pescaggio *sm.* (*mar.*) draught.

pescare *vt.* 1. to fish 2. (*fig.*) to fish out 3. (*cogliere sul fatto*) to catch (*v. irr.*) red-handed 4. (*carte*) to draw (*v. irr.*). ♦ **pescare** *vi.* to draw.

pescatore *sm.* 1. fisher 2. (*con lenza*) angler.

pesce *sm.* fish: — *rosso*, goldfish; — *persico*, perch.

pescecane *sm.* shark.

peschereccio *agg.* fishing. ♦ **peschereccio** *sm.* fishing-boat.

pescheria *sf.* 1. fish-shop 2. (*mercato*) fish-market.

peschiera *sf.* fish-pond.

pesciaiola *sf.* (*cuc.*) fish-kettle.

pesco *sm.* peach-tree.

pescoso *agg.* fishy.

pesista *sm.* weight thrower.

peso *sm.* weight: *a* —, by weight.

pessimismo *sm.* pessimism.

pessimista *agg.* pessimistic. ♦ **pessimista** *s.* pessimist.

pessimistico *agg.* pessimistic.

pessimo *agg.* worst, very bad.

pesta *sf.* 1. track 2. (*difficoltà*) difficulty.

pestaggio *sm.* scuffle.

pestare *vt.* 1. to pound 2. (*picchiare*) to beat (*v. irr.*) 3. (*calpestare*) to tread (*v. irr.*) on.

pestata *sf.* 1. (*lo schiacciare*) pounding 2. (*il calpestare*) treading.

peste *sf.* plague.

pestello *sm.* pestle.

pestifero *agg.* pestiferous.

pestilenza *sf.* plague.

pestilenziale *agg.* pestilential.

pesto *agg.* pounded: *buio* —, pitch dark; *avere gli occhi pesti*, to have rings under one's eyes.

petalo *sm.* petal.

petardo *sm.* petard.

petizione *sf.* petition.

petraia *sf.* 1. (*cava*) quarry 2. (*mucchio di pietre*) heap of stones.

petrografia *sf.* petrography.

petroliera *sf.* tanker.

petrolifero *agg.* oil (*attr.*).

petrolio *sm.* oil.

pettegola *sf.* gossiper.

pettegolare *vi.* to gossip.

pettegolezzo *sm.* gossip.

pettegolo *agg.* gossipy. ♦ **pettegolo** *sm.* gossiper.

pettinare *vt.* to comb. ♦ **pettinarsi** *vr.* to comb one's hair.

pettinato *sm.* worsted.

pettinatrice *sf.* 1. hairdresser 2. (*industria tessile*) comber.

pettinatura *sf.* 1. hairdo 2. (*industria tessile*) combing.

pettine *sm.* comb.

pettirosso *sm.* robin.

petto *sm.* 1. breast 2. (*torace*) chest || — *a* —, face to face; *prendere di* —, to face.

pettorale *agg.* e *sm.* pectoral.

pettorina *sf.* stomacher.

pettoruto *agg.* 1. full-breasted 2. (*fig.*) haughty.

petulante *agg.* pert.

petulanza *sf.* pertness.

petunia *sf.* petunia.

pezza *sf.* 1. patch 2. (*macchia*) spot || — *di stoffa*, roll.

pezzato *agg.* spotted.

pezzente *agg.* beggarly. ♦ **pezzente** *s.* ragamuffin.

pezzo *sm.* piece: *fare a pezzi*, to tear (*v. irr.*) to pieces; *a pezzi e bocconi*, piecemeal; — *grosso* (*fig.*), bigwig; — *di ricambio*, spare part.

pezzuola *sf.* handkerchief.

piacente *agg.* pleasant.

piacere¹ *sm.* 1. pleasure 2. (*favore*) favour || *per* —, please; — ! (*nelle presentazioni*), how do you do!

piacere² *vi.* to like: *gli piace leggere*, he likes reading, he likes to read; *come pare e piace*, as one pleases.

piacevole *agg.* pleasant.

piacimento *sm.* pleasure, liking: *a* —, as much as one likes.

piaga *sf.* 1. sore 2. (*calamità*) plague 3. (*fig.*) nuisance.

piagnisteo *sm.* moaning.

piagnucolare *vi.* to whimper.

piagnucollo *sm.* whimper.

piagnucoloso *agg.* whimpering.

pialla *sf.* plane.

piallare *vt.* to plane.

piallatrice *sf.* planer.

piallatura *sf.* 1. planing 2. (*trucioli*) shavings (*pl.*).

piana *sf.* plane.

pianeggiante *agg.* level.

pianella *sf.* **1.** (*pantofola*) slipper **2.** (*mattonella*) flat tile.

pianeròttolo *sm.* landing.

pianeta *sm.* planet.

piangente *agg.* weeping, crying.

piàngere *vi.* to cry, to weep (*v. irr.*). ◆ **piàngere** *vt.* to weep **2.** (*un lutto*) to mourn || — *a calde lacrime*, to weep one's heart out.

pianificare *vt.* to plan.

pianificazione *sf.* planning.

pianista *s.* pianist.

piano¹ *agg.* **1.** flat **2.** (*chiaro*) clear **3.** (*semplice*) simple.

piano² *sm.* **1.** (*di casa*) floor, storey **2.** (*strato*) layer **3.** (*superficie piana, livello*) plane **5.** (*progetto*) plan **6.** (*cine*) primo —, close up || — *stradale*, roadway; *in primo* —, in the foreground.

piano³ *avv.* **1.** (*lentamente*) slowly **2.** (*sommessamente*) softly **3.** (*con cautela*) gently.

pianoforte *sm.* piano.

pianola *sf.* barrel-organ.

pianta *sf.* **1.** plant **2.** (*carta topografica*) map **3.** (*del piede*) sole || *di sana* — (*completamente*), completely; (*di nuovo*) anew.

piantagione *sf.* plantation.

piantare *vt.* **1.** to plant **2.** (*conficcare*) to drive (*v. irr.*) **3.** (*lasciare*) to leave (*v. irr.*) || *piantarla*, to stop.

piantatore *sm.* planter.

pianterreno *sm.* ground-floor.

pianto *sm.* **1.** tears (*pl.*): *scoppiare in* —, to burst (*v. irr.*) into tears **2.** (*dolore*) grief.

piantonamento *sm.* guarding.

piantonare *vt.* to guard.

piantone¹ *sm.* soldier on guard.

piantone² *sm.* (*agr.*) shoot.

pianura *sf.* plain.

piastra *sf.* **1.** plate **2.** (*di marmo*) slab **3.** (*moneta*) piastre.

piastrella *sf.* tile.

piastrellare *vt.* to tile.

piastrellatura *sf.* tiling.

piastrina *sf.* plaque.

piattaforma *sf.* platform.

piattello *sm.* pan || *tiro al* —, trap-shooting.

piattino *sm.* saucer.

piatto¹ *agg.* flat.

piatto² *sm.* **1.** dish **2.** (*portata*) course **3.** (*di lama*) flat **4.** (*di grammofono*) turn-table.

piazza *sf.* **1.** square **2.** (*comm.*) market || *mettere qc. in* —, to make (*v. irr.*) sthg. public.

piazzaforte *sf.* stronghold.

piazzale *sm.* large square.

piazzamento *sm.* place.

piazzare *vt.* to place. ◆ **piazzarsi** *vr.* (*sport*) to be placed.

piazzista *sm.* salesman (*pl.* -men).

picaresco *agg.* picaresque.

picca *sf.* pike || *picche* (*alle carte*), spades (*pl.*).

piccante *agg.* **1.** piquant **2.** (*salace*) spicy.

piccarsi *vr.* to plume oneself (on).

piccato *agg.* resentful.

picchettare *vt.* **1.** to peg out **2.** (*mil.*) to picket.

picchetto *sm.* peg **2.** (*mil.*) picket: *essere di* —, to be on picket.

picchiare *vt. e vi.* **1.** (*percuotere*) to beat (*v. irr.*) **2.** (*battere*) to strike (*v. irr.*) **3.** (*bussare*) to knock **4.** (*aer.*) to pitch || — *in testa* (*di motore*), to ping. ◆ **picchiarsi** *vr. rec.* to fight (*v. irr.*).

picchiata *sf.* **1.** beating **2.** (*aer.*) dive || *scendere in* —, to dive.

picchiatello *agg.* slightly crazy.

picchiettare *vt.* **1.** (*battere*) to tap **2.** (*chiazzare*) to spot.

picchiettato *agg.* spotted.

picchiettio *sm.* tapping.

picchio¹ *sm.* **1.** (*colpo*) blow **2.** (*alla porta*) knock.

picchio² *sm.* (*zool.*) woodpecker.

picchiotto *sm.* door-knocker.

piccineria *sf.* meanness.

piccino *agg.* **1.** little **2.** (*fig.*) mean.

piccionaia *sf.* **1.** pigeon-house **2.** (*teat.*) gallery.

piccione *sm.* pigeon.

picco *sm.* peak || *a* —, vertically; *colare a* —, *mandare a* —, to sink (*v. irr.*).

piccolezza *sf.* **1.** smallness **2.** (*meschinità*) meanness **3.** (*inezia*) trifle.

piccolo *agg.* **1.** small, little **2.** (*di statura, breve*) short **3.** (*giovane*) young **4.** (*meschino*) mean **5.** (*leggero*) light.

piccone *sm.* pick(axe).

piccozza *sf.* axe.

pidochieria *sf.* meanness.

pidocchio *sm.* **1.** louse (*pl.* lice) **2.** (*fig.*) miser.

pidocchioso *agg.* **1.** lousy **2.** (*fig.*) stingy.

piede *sm.* foot (*pl.* feet): *a piedi*, on foot ‖ *a — libero*, on bail; *prender —*, to get (*v. irr.*) a footing.

piedistallo *sm.* pedestal.

piega *sf.* 1. fold 2. (*fatta ad arte*) pleat 3. (*segno*) crease ‖ *messa in — (di capelli)*, set.

piegabile *agg.* folding.

piegamento *sm.* 1. folding 2. (*flessione*) flexing.

piegare *vt.* 1. to fold 2. (*flettere, anche fig.*) to bend (*v. irr.*). ♦ **piegare** *vi.* 1. (*voltare*) to turn 2. (*curvarsi*) to bend. ♦ **piegarsi** *vr.* to bend.

piegatrice *sf.* (*mecc.*) bending-machine.

pieghettare *vt.* to pleat.

pieghévole *agg.* 1. pliable 2. (*atto a essere piegato*) folding. ♦ **pieghévole** *sm.* folder.

pieghevolezza *sf.* pliability.

piena *sf.* 1. flood, spate 2. (*folla*) crowd.

pienamente *avv.* fully.

pienezza *sf.* 1. fullness 2. (*massimo grado*) height.

pieno *agg.* full: — *zeppo*, full up; *in — (completamente)*, fully, (*esattamente*) exactly, (*nel mezzo*) in the middle; *in — giorno*, in broad daylight. ♦ **pieno** *sm.* (*il colmo*) middle ‖ *fare il — (auto)*, to fill up.

pietà *sf.* 1. piety 2. (*relig.*) piety ‖ *aver — di*, to have mercy on; *far —*, to arouse pity; *per —!*, for pity's sake!

pietanza *sf.* 1. main course 2. (*piatto*) dish.

pietismo *sm.* pietism.

pietosamente *avv.* pitifully.

pietoso *agg.* pitiful.

pietra *sf.* stone: *posare la prima —*, to lay the foundation stone.

pietraia *sf.* V. *petraia*.

pietrificare *vt.* to petrify. ♦ **pietrificarsi** *vr.* to petrify.

pietrina *sf.* flint.

pietrisco *sm.* rubble.

pietroso *agg.* stony.

piffero *sm.* pipe.

pigiama *sm.* pyjamas (*pl.*).

pigia pigia *sm.* awful crush.

pigiare *vt.* to press. ♦ **pigiarsi** *vr.* to crowd.

pigione *sf.* rent: *stare a — presso*, to lodge with.

pigmentato *agg.* pigmented.

pigmentazione *sf.* pigmentation.

pigmento *sm.* pigment.

pigmeo *sm.* pigmy.

pigna *sf.* pinecone.

pignatta *sf.* pot.

pignoleria *sf.* faultfinding.

pignolo *sm.* 1. (*bot.*) pine-seed 2. (*fig.*) faultfinder.

pignoramento *sm.* attachment.

pignorare *vt.* to distrain.

pigolare *vi.* to peep.

pigolìo *sm.* peep.

pigramente *avv.* 1. lazily 2. (*lentamente*) sluggishly.

pigrizia *sf.* 1. laziness 2. (*lentezza*) sluggishness.

pigro *agg.* 1. lazy 2. (*lento*) sluggish.

pila *sf.* pile: — *a secco*, dry battery.

pilastro *sm.* pillar.

pillola *sf.* pill: — *anticoncezionale*, contraceptive (pill), the "pill".

pilone *sm.* 1. pylon 2. (*di ponte*) pier ‖ — *d'ormeggio*, mooringmast.

piloro *sm.* pylorus (*pl.* -ri).

pilota *sm.* 1. pilot 2. (*di auto*) driver.

pilotaggio *sm.* pilotage: *scuola di —*, flying-school.

pilotare *vt.* 1. to pilot 2. (*un'auto*) to drive (*v. irr.*).

piluccare *vt.* to nibble.

piluccone *sm.* nibbler.

pinacoteca *sf.* picture-gallery.

pinastro *sm.* pinaster.

pindàrico *agg.* Pindaric.

pineta *sf.* pinewood.

pingue *agg.* 1. fat 2. (*ricco*) rich.

pinguèdine *sf.* fatness.

pinguino *sm.* penguin.

pinna *sf.* 1. fin 2. (*sport*) flipper.

pinnàcolo[1] *sm.* pinnacle.

pinnàcolo[2] *sm.* (*gioco*) pinochle.

pino *sm.* pine (-tree).

pinolo *sm.* pine-seed.

pinta *sf.* pint.

pinza *sf.* pliers (*pl.*), pincers (*pl.*).

pinzetta *sf.* tweezers (*pl.*).

pio *agg.* pious ‖ *opera pia*, charitable organization.

pioggia *sf.* rain: *sotto la —*, in the rain.

piolo *sm.* V. *piuolo*.

piombare *vt.* 1. to plumb 2. (*tip*) to lead ‖ — *un dente*, to stop a tooth ♦ **piombare** *vi.* 1. (*cade-*

re) to fall (*v. irr.*) heavily **2.** (*assalire*) to assail **3.** (*precipitarsi*) to rush.

piombatura *sf.* sealing, leading.

piombino *sm.* **1.** plummet **2.** (*sigillo*) leaden seal.

piombo *sm.* **1** lead **2.** (*sigillo*) leaden seal **3.** (*pallottola*) bullet || *filo a* —, plumb line; *a* —, perpendicularly; *di* —, leaden; *andare coi piedi di* —, to proceed very cautiously.

pioniere *sm.* pioneer.

pioppeto *sm.* poplargrove.

pioppo *sm.* poplar.

piorrea *sf.* pyorrhoea.

piovano *agg.* rain (*attr.*).

piovasco *sm.* shower.

piòvere *vi.* to rain, to pour (*anche fig.*).

piovigginare *vi.* to drizzle.

piovigginoso *agg.* drizzly, rainy.

piovoso *agg.* rainy.

piovra *sf.* octopus.

pipa *sf.* pipe.

pipetta *sf.* (*chim.*) pipette.

pipistrello *sm.* bat.

pipita *sf.* agnail.

pira *sf.* pyre.

piramidale *ag.* pyramidal.

piràmide *sf.* pyramid.

pirata *sm.* pirate || — *della strada*, hit-and-run driver.

pirateria *sf.* piracy.

pìrico *agg. polvere pirica*, gunpowder.

pirite *sf.* pyrite(s).

piroetta *sf.* pirouette.

piroettare *vi.* to pirouette.

piroga *sf.* pirogue.

pirografia *sf.* pyrography.

piròscafo *sm.* steamer.

pirotècnica *sf.* pyrotechnics.

pirotècnico *agg.* pyrotechnic(al): *spettacolo* —, fireworks. ◆ **pirotècnico** *sm.* pyrotechnist.

piscia *sf.* piss.

pisciare *vi.* to piss.

pisciata *sf.* piss.

pisciatoio *sm.* urinal.

piscicoltura *sf.* pisciculture.

piscina *sf.* swimming-pool.

pisello *sm.* pea.

pisolino *sm.* nap.

pista *sf.* **1.** (*traccia*) track **2.** (*di animale*) trail **3.** (*aer.*) strip.

pistacchio *sm.* pistachio.

pistillo *sm.* pistil.

pistola *sf.* pistol

pistone *sm.* piston.

pitagòrico *agg. e sm.* Pythagorean: *tavola pitagorica*, multiplication table.

pitale *sm.* chamber pot.

pitocco *agg.* **1.** mean **2.** (*fig.*) stingy. ◆ **pitocco** *sm.* **1.** beggar **2.** (*fig.*) mean person.

pitone *sm.* python.

pitonessa *sf.* pythoness.

pittore *sm.* painter.

pittoresco *agg.* picturesque.

pittòrico *agg.* pictorial.

pittrice *sf.* paintress.

pittura *sf.* **1.** painting **2.** (*dipinto, descrizione*) picture **3.** (*vernice*) paint.

pitturare *vt.* to paint.

più *avv.* **1.** (*comp. di maggioranza con agg. polisillabi, con s., v. e avv.*) more: *questo libro è* — *costoso di quello*, this book is more expensive than that; *ho* — *libri di te*, I have more books than you; *lavoro* — *di te*, I work more than you **2.** (*comp. di maggioranza con agg. e avv. monosillabi e bisillabi terminanti in* y, er, ow) ...*er*: *è* — *gentile di lui*, he is kinder than he is **3.** (*superl. rel., corrispondente a "more"*) the most, the more (*fra due*): *è il libro* — *costoso di tutti*, it is the most expensive book of all; *la* — *bella delle due sorelle*, the more beautiful of the two sisters **4.** (*superl. rel., corrispondente a "...er"*) the ...est, the ...er (*fra due*): *è la persona* — *felice che conosca*, she is the happiest person I know; *è la* — *graziosa delle due sorelle*, she is the prettier of the sisters **4.** (*di tempo*) no longer, no more, not again || *mai* —, never again. ◆ **più** *agg.* **1.** more **2.** (*diversi*) several. ◆ **più** *sm.* most: *il* — *è fatto*, most of it is done || *i* —, most people (*al sing.*).

piuma *sf.* **1.** feather, down **2.** (*ornamento*) plume.

piumaggio *sm.* plumage.

piumino *sm.* **1.** down **2.** (*copriletto*) eiderdown **3.** (*per la cipria*) powder-puff **4.** (*per spolverare*) duster.

piuttosto *avv.* rather. ◆ **piuttosto che** *di cong.* rather than.

piuolo *sm.* **1.** peg: *scala a piuoli*, ladder **2.** (*paletto*) post.

piva *sf.* bagpipe.
pivello *sm.* greenhorn.
piviere *sm.* plover.
pizzicàgnolo *sm.* delicatessen seller.
pizzicare *vt.* **1.** to pinch, to nip **2.** (*di insetti*) to bite (*v. irr.*) **3.** (*di sostanza acre*) to burn (*v. irr.*) **4.** (*con parole*) to tease **5.** (*sorprendere*) to catch (*v. irr.*). ♦ **pizzicare** *vi.* (*prudere*) to itch, to tingle.
pizzicherìa *sf.* **1.** delicatessen shop **2.** (*merci*) delicatessen.
pizzico *sm.* **1.** pinch **2.** (*pizzicore*) itch **3.** (*fig.*) bit.
pizzicore *sm.* itch.
pizzicotto *sm.* pinch.
pizzo *sm.* **1.** lace (*solo sing.*) **2.** (*di montagna*) peak **3.** (*barba*) pointed beard.
placare *vt.* to appease: — *la fame di qu.*, to satisfy so.'s hunger; — *la sete di qu.*, to quench so.'s thirst. ♦ **placarsi** *vr.* to calm down.
placca *sf.* plaque.
placcare *vt.* to plate (sthg. with).
placcatura *sf.* plating.
placenta *sf.* placenta.
placidità *sf.* placidity.
plàcido *agg.* placid.
plaga *sf.* region.
plagiare *vt. e vi.* to plagiarize.
plagiario *agg.* plagiaristic. ♦ **plagiario** *sm.* plagiarist.
plagio *sm.* plagiarism.
planare *vi.* to glide down.
planata *sf.* glide.
plancia *sf.* (*mar.*) deck.
plancton *sm.* plankton.
planetario *agg.* planetary. ♦ **planetario** *sm.* planetarium (*pl.* -ia).
planimetrìa *sf.* planimetry, plan.
planimètrico *agg.* planimetric(al).
planisfero *sm.* planisphere.
plantìgrado *agg. e sm.* plantigrade.
plasma *sm.* plasma.
plasmare *vt.* to mould.
plàstica *sf.* **1.** (*operazione*) plastic operation **2.** (*materiale*) plastic.
plasticare *vt.* to plasticize.
plasticità *sf.* plasticity.
plàstico *agg.* plastic. ♦ **plàstico** *sm.* **1.** plastic model **2.** (*carta topografica*) relief map.
plastilina *sf.* plasticine.
plàtano *sm.* plane (-tree).
platea *sf.* pit: *poltrona di —*, stall.
plateale *agg.* coarse.

platinare *vt.* **1.** to platinize **2.** (*di capelli*) to bleach.
plàtino *sm.* platinum.
platònico *agg.* Platonic.
plaudente *agg.* applauding.
plausibile *agg.* plausible.
plàuso *sm.* **1.** applause **2.** (*lode*) praise.
plebàglia *sf.* mob.
plebe *sf.* populace.
plebeo *agg. e sm.* plebeian.
plebiscitario *agg.* plebiscitary.
plebiscito *sm.* plebiscite.
plenario *agg.* plenary.
plenilunio *sm.* plenilune.
plenipotenziario *agg. e sm.* plenipotentiary.
pleonasmo *sm.* pleonasm.
pleonàstico *agg.* pleonastic.
plesso *sm.* plexus.
plètora *sf.* plethora.
plètorico *agg.* plethoric.
plettro *sm.* plectrum (*pl.* -ra).
pièura *sf.* pleura (*pl.* -rae).
pleurite *sf.* pleurisy.
plico *sm.* **1.** packet **2.** (*busta*) cover: *in — separato*, under separate cover.
plotone *sm.* platoon.
plùmbeo *agg.* leaden.
plurale *agg. e sm.* plural.
pluralismo *sm.* pluralism.
pluralità *sf.* plurality.
pluricellulare *agg.* multicellular.
plusvalore *sm.* plus value.
plutòcrate *sm.* plutocrat.
plutocrazìa *sf.* plutocracy.
pneumàtico *agg.* pneumatic, inflatable. ♦ **pneumàtico** *sm.* (*di auto*) tyre.
pneumatorace *sm.* pneumothorax.
pochezza *sf.* (*scarsità, ristrettezza*) scantiness, insufficiency.
pochìssimo *agg. e avv.* **1.** very little **2.** (*rarissimamente*) very seldom. ♦ **pochìssimi** *sm. pl.* very few.
poco *avv.* **1.** not very (*con agg. e avv.*), little (*con comp., p. passati, verbi*): *a — a —*, little by little; — *per volta*, a little at a time **2.** (*di tempo*) a short time || *fra —*, soon. ♦ **poco** *agg.* **1.** little (*pl.* few) **2.** (*di tempo*) short. ♦ **poco** *pron. e sm.* little (*pl.* few): *un —*, di, a little.
podere *sm.* farm.
poderoso *agg.* powerful.
podio *sm.* platform.

podismo *sm.* **1.** walking **2.** (*sport*) foot-racing.

podista *sm.* (*sport*) foot-racer.

podìstico *agg.* foot (*attr.*).

poema *sm.* poem.

poesìa *sf.* **1.** poetry **2.** (*composizione poetica*) poem.

poeta *sm.* poet.

poetare *vi.* to write (*v. irr.*) poetry.

poètico *agg.* poetic(al).

poggiapiedi *sm.* footstool.

poggiare *vi.* e *vt.* to rest. ♦ **poggiarsi** *vr.* to lean (*v. irr.*) against.

poggio *sm.* hillock.

poi *avv.* **1.** then **2.** (*più tardi*) later || *d'ora in* —, from now on.

poiché *cong.* since, as.

polacca *sf.* (*mus.*) polonaise.

polacco *agg.* Polish. ♦ **polacco** *sm.* Pole.

polare *agg.* polar || *stella* —, pole-star.

polarità *sf.* polarity.

polarizzare *vt.* to polarize.

polarizzatore *agg.* polarizing. ♦ **polarizzatore** *sm.* polarizer.

polarizzazione *sf.* polarization.

polca *sf.* polka.

polèmica *sf.* polemic.

polèmico *agg.* e *sm.* polemic.

polemista *s.* polemist.

polemizzare *vi.* to polemize.

poliandrìa *sf.* polyandry.

policlìnico *sm.* polyclinic.

policromìa *sf.* polychromy.

policromo *agg.* polychrome.

polièdrico *agg.* **1.** polyhedral **2.** (*fig.*) versatile.

poliedro *sm.* polyhedron.

polifonìa *sf.* polyphony.

polifònico *agg.* polyphonic.

poligamia *sf.* polygamy.

polìgamo *agg.* polygamous. ♦ **polìgamo** *sm.* polygamist.

poliglotta *s.* polyglot.

polìgono *sm.* polygon || — *di tiro*, shooting-range.

polimerizzazione *sf.* polymerization.

polìmero *agg.* polymeric. ♦ **polìmero** *sm.* polymer.

polimorfismo *sm.* polymorphism.

poliomielite *sf.* poliomyelitis.

poliomielìtico *agg.* polio (*attr.*). ♦ **poliomielìtico** *sm.* person who has had polio.

polìpo *sm.* polyp.

polisillabo *agg.* polysyllabic(al). ♦ **polisìllabo** *sm.* polysyllable.

politècnico *agg.* e *sm.* polytechnic.

politeismo *sm.* polytheism.

politeista *agg.* polytheistic. ♦ **politeista** *s.* polytheist.

politica *sf.* **1.** politics **2.** (*linea di condotta*) policy.

politicante *sm.* petty politician.

politico *agg.* **1.** political **2.** (*sagace*) politic || *uomo* —, politician.

polivalente *agg.* polyvalent.

polizia *sf.* police (*us. al pl.*).

poliziesco *agg.* **1.** police (*attr.*) **2.** (*di film ecc.*) detective (*attr.*).

poliziotto *sm.* policeman (*pl.* -men).

pòlizza *sf.* **1.** policy **2.** (*ricevuta*) bill.

polla *sf.* spring.

pollaio *sm.* hen-house.

pollame *sm.* poultry.

pollastra *sf.* pullet.

pollastro *sm.* cockerel.

pòllice *sm.* **1.** thumb **2.** (*del piede*) big toe **3.** (*misura*) inch.

pollicoltore *sm.* poultryman (*pl.* -men).

pollicoltura *sf.* poultry-farming.

pòlline *sm.* pollen.

pollivéndolo *sm.* poulterer.

pollo *sm.* **1.** chicken **2.** (*fig.*) dupe.

polmonare *agg.* pulmonary.

polmone *sm.* lung: — *d'acciaio*, iron lung.

polmonite *sf.* pneumonia.

polo[1] *sm.* pole.

polo[2] *sm.* (*sport*) polo.

polpa *sf.* **1.** (*di frutta*) pulp **2.** (*carne*) lean meat.

polpaccio *sm.* calf (*pl.* calves).

polpastrello *sm.* finger-tip.

polpetta *sf.* meat-ball, croquette.

polposo *agg.* pulpy.

polsino *sm.* cuff.

polso *sm.* **1.** wrist **2.** (*fig.*) energy **3.** (*pulsazione*) pulse **4.** (*polsino*) cuff || *tastare il* — *a qu.*, to feel (*v. irr.*) so.'s pulse; *uomo di* —, energetic man.

poltiglia *sf.* **1.** pulp **2.** (*fanghiglia*) mud.

poltrire *vi.* to idle.

poltrona *sf.* **1.** armchair **2.** (*teat.*) stall.

poltrone *agg.* idle. ♦ **poltrone** *sm.* idler.

poltronerìa *sf.* idleness.

pòlvere *sf.* **1.** dust **2.** (*sostanza polverizzata*) powder || *togliere la* —, to dust.

polveriera *sf.* powder-magazine.

polverizzare *vt.* to pulverize. ♦
    polverizzarsi *vr.* to pulverize.
polverone *sm.* cloud of dust.
polveroso *agg.* dusty.
pomata *sf.* salve.
pomello *sm.* 1. (*di porta ecc.*) knob
    2. (*di guancia*) cheek-bone.
pomeridiano *agg.* 1. afternoon
    (*attr.*) 2. (*con le ore*) p. m. (post
    meridiem): *alle 5 pomeridiane*,
    at five o'clock.
pomeriggio *sm.* afternoon.
pòmice *sf.* pumice.
pomo *sm.* 1. (*mela*) apple 2. (*di
    porta ecc.*) knob.
pomodoro *sm.* tomato.
pompa *sf.* 1. pump 2. (*fasto*) pomp
    3. (*ostentazione*) display || *impresa
    di pompe funebri*, undertaker's
    business; *far — di sé*, to show (*v.
    irr.*) off.
pompare *vt.* 1. to pump 2. (*fig.*)
    to puff up.
pompelmo *sm.* grapefruit.
pompiere *sm.* fireman (*pl.* -men).
pompòsità *sf.* pomposity.
pomposo *agg.* pompous.
ponderàbile *agg.* ponderable.
ponderabilità *sf.* ponderability.
ponderare *vt.* to ponder.
ponderatamente *avv.* after reflec-
    tion.
ponderatezza *sf.* circumspection.
ponderato *agg.* pondered.
ponderazione *sf.* consideration.
ponderoso *agg.* ponderous.
ponente *sm.* west.
ponte *sm.* 1. bridge: *— girevole*,
    swing bridge 2. (*mar.*) deck 3.
    (*impalcatura*) scaffold || *rompere i
    ponti con* (*fig.*), to break (*v. irr.*)
    with.
pontéfice *sm.* pope.
pontificale *agg.* pontifical.
pontificare *vi.* to pontificate.
pontificato *sm.* pontificate.
pontificio *agg.* papal.
pontile *sm.* landing-stage.
pontone *sm.* pontoon.
ponzare *vi.* to rack one's brains.
popolamento *sm.* peopling.
popolano *agg.* common. ♦ **popola-
    no** *sm.* man of the people || *i
    popolani*, the common people.
popolare[1] *vt.* to people. ♦ **popo-
    larsi** *vr.* to become (*v. irr.*) pop-
    ulated.
popolare[2] *agg.* 1. popular 2. (*tradi-
    zionale*) folk (*attr.*).

popolaresco *agg.* popular-like.
popolarità *sf.* popularity.
popolarizzare *vt.* to popularize.
popolazione *sf.* population.
pòpolo *sm.* 1. (*gente*) people (*pl.*)
    2. (*nazione*) people.
popoloso *agg.* populous.
popone *sm.* melon.
poppa[1] *sf.* 1. (*mar.*) stern || *avere il
    vento in —*, to sail before the
    wind; *a —*, astern.
poppa[2] *sf.* breast.
poppante *s.* suckling.
poppare *vt.* to suck.
poppata *sf.* suck: *ora della —*,
    feeding-time.
poppatoio *sm.* feeding-bottle.
populismo *sm.* populism.
populista *agg.* populistic. ♦ **popu-
    lista** *s.* populist.
porcaro *sm.* swineherd.
porcellana *sf.* china (*solo sing.*).
porcheria *sf.* 1. dirt 2. (*azione di-
    sonesta*) dirty trick 3. (*detto in-
    decente*) obscene word 4. (*atto in-
    decente*) obscene act 5. (*cibo cat-
    tivo*) revolting stuff 6. (*cose senza
    valore*) rubbish.
porcile *sm.* pigsty.
porcino *agg.* pig (*attr.*). ♦ **por-
    cino** *sm.* (*fungo*) boletus.
porco *sm.* 1. pig 2. (*cuc.*) pork.
porcospino *sm.* porcupine.
pòrfido *sm.* porphyry.
pòrgere *vt.* 1. to hand 2. (*offrire*)
    to offer.
pornografia *sf.* pornography.
pornogràfico *agg.* pornographic
poro *sm.* pore.
porosità *sf.* porosity.
poroso *agg.* porous.
pòrpora *sf.* purple.
porporato *sm.* Cardinal.
porre *vt.* 1. to put (*v. irr.*) 2. (*sup-
    porre*) to suppose || *— le fonda-
    menta*, to lay (*v. irr.*) the founda-
    tions; *— mano*, to begin (*v. irr.*).
porro *sm.* 1. leek 2. (*med.*) wart.
porta *sf.* 1. door 2. (*di mura ecc.*)
    gate 3. (*sport*) goal.
portabagagli *sm.* 1. luggage-rack
    2. (*facchino*) porter.
portabandiera *sm.* ensign.
portacarte *sm.* portfolio.
portacénere *sm.* ash-tray.
portachiavi *sm.* key-holder.
portacipria *sm.* compact.
portaèrei *sf.* aircraft carrier.
portaferiti *sm.* stretcher-bearer.

portafiori *sm.* flower-holder.

portafoglio *sm.* **1.** wallet **2.** (*pol.*) portfolio.

portafortuna *sm.* mascot.

portagioielli *sm.* jewel-case.

portalèttere *sm.* postman (*pl.* -men).

portamento *sm.* **1.** gait **2.** (*condotta*) behaviour.

portamonete *sm.* purse.

portantina *sf.* sedan-chair.

portaombrelli *sm.* umbrella-stand.

portaòrdini *sm.* messenger.

portapacchi *sm.* carrier.

portapenne *sm.* penholder.

portare *vt.* **1.** (*verso chi parla o ascolta*) to bring (*v. irr.*) **2.** (*lontano da chi parla, accompagnare*) to take (*v. irr.*) **3.** (*trasportare*) to carry **4.** (*condurre*) to lead (*v. irr.*) **5.** (*indossare*) to wear (*v. irr.*) **6.** (*avere*) to have.

portasapone *sm.* soap-dish.

portasigarette *sm.* cigarette-case.

portaspilli *sm.* pincushion.

portata *sf.* **1.** (*di pranzo*) course **2.** (*di arma, strumento ottico*) range **3.** (*di fiume*) flow **4.** (*di ponte, auto ecc.*) capacity **5.** (*stazza*) tonnage **6.** (*fig.*) importance.

portàtile *agg.* portable.

portatore *sm.* bearer.

portauovo *sm.* egg-cup.

portavoce *sm.* spokesman (*pl.* -men).

portello *sm.* hatch.

portento *sm.* prodigy.

portentosamente *avv.* prodigiously.

portentoso *agg.* prodigious.

porticato *sm.* arcade.

pòrtico *sm.* **1.** (*loggia*) porch **2.** (*porticato*) arcade.

portiera[1] *sf.* (*porta*) door.

portiera[2] *sf.* doorkeeper.

portiere *sm.* **1.** (*sport*) goal-keeper **2.** porter.

portinaio *sm.* door keeper.

portineria *sf.* porter's lodge.

porto[1] *sm.* **1.** port (*anche fig.*) **2.** (*bacino*) harbour (*anche fig.*).

porto[2] *sm.* (*trasporto*) carriage: *franco di* —, carriage paid || — *d'armi*, shooting licence; *condurre in* — (*fig.*), to carry out.

portoghese *agg. e sm.* Portuguese.

portone *sm.* main door.

portuale *agg.* harbour (*attr.*): *città* —, port. ♦ **portuale** *sm.* docker.

porzione *sf.* portion.

posa *sf.* **1.** (*il porre*) laying **2.** (*posizione*) posture **3.** (*affettazione*) pose **4.** (*pausa*) pause **5.** (*foto*) exposure || *mettersi in* —, to pose; *senza* —, incessantly.

posare *vt.* to lay (*v. irr.*). ♦ **posare** *vi.* **1.** (*aver fondamento*) to rest **2.** (*assumere un atteggiamento non spontaneo*) to pose **3.** (*di liquido*) to stand (*v. irr.*). ♦ **posarsi** *vr.* **1.** to settle **2.** (*aer.; di uccello*) to alight.

posata *sf.* **1.** (*coltello*) knife (*pl.* knives) **2.** (*forchetta*) fork **3.** (*cucchiaio*) spoon.

posato *agg.* staid.

poscritto *sm.* postscript.

positiva *sf.* (*foto*) positive.

positivamente *avv.* positively.

positivismo *sm.* positivism.

positivista *s.* positivist.

positivo *agg.* positive.

posizione *sf.* position.

posologìa *sf.* posology.

posporre *vt.* **1.** to place after **2.** (*posticipare*) to postpone.

possedere *vt.* to possess.

possedimento *sm.* V. *possesso*.

possente *agg.* powerful.

possessivo *agg.* possessive.

possesso *sm.* **1.** possession **2.** (*proprietà*) property.

possessore *sm.* possessor, owner.

possìbile *agg.* possible: *il più presto* —, as soon as possible; *fare il* —, to do (*v. irr.*) one's best.

possibilità *sf.* **1.** possibility **2.** (*potere*) power || — *finanziarie*, means.

possidente *sm.* man (*pl.* -men) of property **2.** (*terriero*) landowner.

posta *sf.* **1.** post, mail **2.** (*ufficio postale*) post-office || *fermo* —, poste restante; *a giro di* —, by return of post; *per* —, by mail **3.** (*al gioco*) stake.

postale *agg.* postal, post (*attr.*), mail (*attr.*): *per pacco* —, by parcel post; *spese postali*, postage.

postazione *sf.* stationing.

postbèllico *agg.* post-war (*attr.*).

postdatare *vt.* to postdate.

posteggiare *vt.* to park.

posteggiatore *sm.* **1.** car-park attendant **2.** (*venditore*) stall-keeper.

posteggio *sm.* car-park || — *di taxi*, taxi rank.

postelegrafònico *agg.* postal telegraph and telephone (*attr.*).

postelegrafònico *sm.* post-office clerk.

postema *sf.* aposteme.

pòsteri *sm. pl.* descendants.

posteriore *agg.* 1. (*nel tempo*) following 2. (*nello spazio*) back, rear.

posterità *sf.* posterity.

posticcio *agg.* false. ♦ **posticcio** *sm.* toupee.

posticipare *vt.* to postpone.

posticipazione *sf.* deferment.

postiglione *sm.* postilion.

postilla *sf.* (*marginal*) note.

postillare *vt.* to annotate.

postino *sm.* postman (*pl.* -men).

posto *sm.* 1. place 2. (*spazio*) room 3. (*lavoro*) job 4. (*posto a sedere*) seat 5. (*stazione*) station || *al — di*, instead of.

postoperatorio *agg.* postoperative.

postribolo *sm.* brothel.

postulante *sm.* 1. petitioner 2. (*eccl.*) postulant.

postulare *vt.* to petition (for sthg.).

postulato *sm.* postulate.

pòstumo *agg.* posthumous.

potàbile *agg.* drinkable.

potare *vt.* to prune.

potassa *sf.* potash.

potàssico *agg.* potassic.

potassio *sm.* potassium.

potatore *sm.* pruner.

potatura *sf.* pruning.

potente *agg.* powerful.

potenza *sf.* power || *in —* (*avv.*), potentially, (*agg.*) potential.

potenziale *agg.* e *sm.* potential.

potenzialità *sf.* potentiality.

potenziamento *sm.* 1. (*rafforzamento*) strengthening 2. (*sviluppo*) development.

potenziare *vt.* 1. (*rafforzare*) to strengthen 2. (*sviluppare*) to develop.

potere[1] *vi.* 1. can (*pres.*), could (*pass., condiz.*), to be able: *non può venire*, he cannot come 2. (*eventualità, augurio, permesso*) may (*pres.*), might (*pass., condiz.*), to be allowed to: *può darsi*, maybe; *può darsi che venga*, he may come.

potere[2] *sm.* power.

potestà *sf.* power, authority.

poveraccio *sm.* poor devil.

pòvero *agg.* poor.

povertà *sf.* poverty.

pozione *sf.* potion.

pozza *sf.* pool.

pozzànghera *sf.* puddle.

pozzetto *sm.* 1. (*di motore*) sump 2. (*di fognatura*) drain well.

pozzo *sm.* well: *— nero*, cesspool; *— carbonifero*, coal-pit.

pragmatismo *sm.* pragmatism.

pragmatista *s.* pragmatist.

pragmatìstico *agg.* pragmatist.

prammàtica *sf.* custom: *di —*, customary.

prammàtico *agg.* pragmatic.

pranzare *vi.* to dine.

pranzo *sm.* 1. dinner 2. (*di mezzogiorno*) lunch.

prassi *sf.* praxis.

prataiolo *agg.* field (*attr.*).

praterìa *sf.* prairie.

pratica *sf.* 1. practice 2. (*affare*) matter 3. (*esperienza*) experience 4. (*incartamento*) file 5. (*trattativa*) dealing 6. (*passo presso un'autorità*) step || *far —*, to practise; *aver — di*, to be familiar with.

praticàbile *agg.* practicable.

praticabilità *sf.* practicability.

praticaccia *sf.* practical knowledge.

praticante *agg.* practising.

praticare *vt.* 1. to practise 2. (*frequentare*) to frequent 3. (*fare*) to make (*v. irr.*).

praticità *sf.* practicality.

pràtico *agg.* 1. practical 2. (*esperto*) skilled || *esser — di*, to be familiar with.

prativo *agg.* grass (*attr.*).

prato *sm.* 1. meadow 2. (*artificiale*) lawn.

pratolina *sf.* daisy.

pravo *agg.* perverse.

preallarme *sm.* prewarning.

preàmbolo *sm.* preface.

preannunziare *vt.* to portend.

preavvertire *vt.* to forewarn.

preavvisare *vt.* to forewarn.

preavviso *sm.* 1. forewarning 2. (*disdetta*) notice.

prebèllico *agg.* pre-war (*attr.*).

prebenda *sf.* 1. (*eccl.*) prebend 2. (*salario*) salary.

precarietà *sf.* precariousness.

precario *agg.* precarious.

precauzionale *agg.* precautionary.

precauzione *sf.* 1. precaution 2. (*cautela*) caution.

precedente *agg.* previous. ♦ **precedente** *sm.* precedent || *i precedenti* (*condotta*), record.

precedenza *sf.* precedence || *in —*, previously.

precèdere *vt.* to precede. ♦ **precèdere** *vi.* to come (*v. irr.*) first.

precessione *sf.* precession.

precettare *vt.* 1. (*giur.*) to summon 2. (*mil.*) to call to arms.

precetto *sm.* 1. precept 2. (*mil.*) call-up notice.

precettore *sm.* tutor.

precipitare *vt.* to precipitate. ♦ **precipitare** *vi.* 1. to fall (*v. irr.*) 2. (*chim.*) to precipitate. ♦ **precipitarsi** *vr.* to rush.

precipitato *agg. e sm.* precipitate.

precipitazione *sf.* 1. (*atmosferica*) precipitation 2. (*furia*) haste.

precipitoso *agg.* 1. (*impetuoso*) headlong 2. (*frettoloso*) hasty 3. (*scosceso*) precipitous.

precipizio *sm.* precipice: *a —* (*precipitosamente*), headlong; (*a picco*) perpendicularly.

precipuo *agg.* principal.

precisare *vt.* to specify.

precisazione *sf.* specification.

precisione *sf.* 1. precision 2. (*chiarezza*) clarity.

preciso *agg.* 1. precise 2. (*accurato*) careful 3. (*definito*) definite 4. (*identico*) identical 5. (*di ore*) sharp.

preclaro *agg.* prominent.

preclùdere *vt.* to preclude.

precoce *agg.* 1. precocious 2. (*di frutto, stagione*) early 3. (*prematuro*) premature.

precocità *sf.* precociousness.

preconcetto *agg.* preconceived. ♦ **preconcetto** *sm.* prejudice.

preconizzare *vt.* to foretell (*v. irr.*).

precordi *sm. pl.* praecordia.

precòrrere *vt.* to anticipate.

precursore *agg.* precursory. ♦ **precursore** *sm.* forerunner.

preda *sf.* 1. prey 2. (*bottino*) booty ‖ *cadere in — a*, to fall (*v. irr.*) a prey to; *far — di*, to plunder.

predace *agg.* predacious.

predare *vt.* to plunder.

predatore *agg.* predatory. ♦ **predatore** *sm.* plunderer.

predatorio *agg.* predatory.

predecessore *sm.* forerunner.

predella *sf.* 1. platform 2. (*sgabello*) stool.

predellino *sm.* 1. (*di vettura*) footboard 2. (*poggiapiedi*) footstool.

predestinare *vt.* to predestine.

predestinazione *sf.* 1. predestina-

tion 2. (*destino*) destiny.

predeterminare *vt.* to predetermine.

predeterminazione *sf.* predetermination.

predetto *agg.* 1. (*suddetto*) above mentioned 2. (*presagito*) foretold (*pred.*).

prediale *agg.* praedial.

prèdica *sf.* sermon: *fare la — a qu.*, to lecture so.

predicàbile *agg.* predicable.

predicare *vt. e vi.* to preach.

predicativo *agg.* predicative.

predicato *sm.* predicate: *essere in — per*, to be considered for.

predicatore *sm.* preacher.

predicatorio *agg.* preachifying.

predicazione *sf.* preaching.

predicozzo *sm.* lecture.

predigestione *sf.* preliminary digestion.

prediletto *agg.* favourite. ♦ **prediletto** *sm.* pet.

predilezione *sf.* predilection.

predilìgere *vt.* to prefer.

predire *vt.* to foretell (*v. irr.*).

predisporre *vt.* 1. to predispose 2. (*provvedere*) to arrange. ♦ **predisporsi** *vr.* to prepare oneself.

predisposizione *sf.* 1. (*med.*) predisposition 2. (*inclinazione*) bent.

predizione *sf.* prediction.

predominante *agg.* prevailing.

predominanza *sf.* prevalence.

predominare *vi.* to prevail.

predominio *sm.* predominance.

predone *sm.* plunderer.

preesistente *agg.* pre-existing.

preesistenza *sf.* pre-existence.

preesistere *vi.* to pre-exist.

prefabbricare *vt.* to prefabricate.

prefazio *sm.* preface.

prefazione *sf.* preface.

preferenza *sf.* preference: *di —*, generally.

preferenziale *agg.* preferential.

preferibile *agg.* preferable.

preferire *vt.* to prefer.

preferito *agg. e sm.* V. prediletto.

prefettizio *agg.* prefectorial.

prefetto *sm.* prefect.

prefettura *sf.* prefecture.

prefìggere *vt.* to (pre-)establish. ♦ **prefìggersi** *vr.* to be resolved: *— uno scopo*, to propose an aim to oneself.

prefigurare *vt.* to prefigure.

prefigurazione *sf.* prefiguration.

prefisso *sm.* prefix.

preformare *vt.* to preform.

pregare *vt.* **1.** to pray **2.** (*chiedere*) to beg.

pregévole *agg.* valuable.

preghiera *sf.* **1.** prayer **2.** (*domanda*) request.

pregiare *vt.* to esteem. ♦ **pregiarsi** *vr.* to beg (to).

pregiato *agg.* valuable: *vino* —, vintage wine.

pregio *sm.* **1.** (*valore*) value **2.** (*merito*) merit || *di* —, valuable.

pregiudicare *vt.* to prejudice.

pregiudicato *sm.* previous offender.

pregiudiziale *agg.* prejudicial.

pregiudizio *sm.* prejudice.

pregnante *agg.* pregnant.

pregno *agg.* **1.** pregnant (with) **2.** (*pieno*) full (of).

pregustare *vt.* to foretaste.

preistoria *sf.* prehistory.

preistòrico *agg.* prehistoric.

prelatizio *agg.* prelatic.

prelato *sm.* prelate.

prelazione *sf.* pre-emption.

prelevamento *sm.* drawing: *fare un* — (*comm.*), to draw (*v. irr.*).

prelevare *vt.* to draw (*v. irr.*).

prelibare *vt.* to foretaste.

prelibato *agg.* excellent.

prelievo *sm.* V. *prelevamento*.

preliminare *agg.* preliminary.

prelùdere *vi.* to prelude (sthg.), to foreshadow (sthg.).

preludiare *vi.* to prelude.

preludio *sm.* prelude.

prematuro *agg.* premature.

premeditare *vt.* to premeditate.

premeditato *agg.* premeditated.

premeditazione *sf.* premeditation.

prèmere *vi.* **1.** to press **2.** (*importare*) to interest **3.** (*essere urgente*) to be urgent. ♦ **prèmere** *vt.* to press.

premessa *sf.* introduction.

premesso *agg.* previous.

premèttere *vt.* **1.** to premise **2.** (*mettere prima*) to put (*v. irr.*) before.

premiare *vt.* **1.** to give (*v. irr.*) a prize **2.** (*ricompensare*) to reward.

premiazione *sf.* awarding of prizes.

preminente *agg.* pre-eminent.

preminenza *sf.* pre-eminence.

premio *sm.* **1.** prize **2.** (*ricompensa*) reward **3.** (*comm.*) premium.

prèmito *sm.* tenesmus.

premolare *agg.* e *sm.* premolar.

premonitore *agg.* premonitory.

premorire *vi.* to predecease.

premunire *vt.* to forearm. ♦ **premunirsi** *vr.* to secure.

premura *sf.* **1.** (*cura*) care **2.** (*fretta*) hurry **3.** (*gentilezza*) kindness || *aver* —, to be in a hurry.

premuroso *agg.* (*servizievole*) helpful **2.** (*gentile*) obliging.

prèndere *vt.* **1.** to take (*v. irr.*) **2.** (*sorprendere, afferrare*) to catch (*v. irr.*) **3.** (*comprare, ottenere*) to get (*v. irr.*). ♦ **prèndersi** *vr.* to take || *che ti prende?*, what's the matter with you?

prendisole *sm.* sun-suit.

prenome *sm.* praenomen (*pl.* -mina).

prenotare *vt.* to book. ♦ **prenotarsi** *vr.* to engage oneself.

prenotazione *sf.* booking.

prènsile *agg.* prehensile.

prensione *sf.* prehension.

preoccupante *agg.* worrying.

preoccupare *vt.* to worry. ♦ **preoccuparsi** *vr.* to be worried (about).

preoccupazione *sf.* worry.

preordinare *vt.* to prearrange.

preparare *vt.* to prepare. ♦ **prepararsi** *vr.* to get (*v. irr.*) ready.

preparativo *sm.* preparation.

preparato *agg.* ready. ♦ **preparato** *sm.* (*med.*) preparation.

preparatore *sm.* preparer.

preparatorio *agg.* preparatory.

preparazione *sf.* preparation.

preponderante *agg.* preponderant.

preponderanza *sf.* preponderance.

preporre *vt.* **1.** to put (*v. irr.*) before **2.** (*preferire*) to prefer **3.** (*mettere a capo*) to put at the head.

prepositivo *agg.* prepositional.

preposizione *sf.* preposition.

preposto *sm.* **1.** provost **2.** (*relig., prevosto*) parish priest.

prepotente *agg.* overbearing.

prepotentemente *avv.* overbearingly.

prepotenza *sf.* **1.** arrogance **2.** (*azione*) overbearing action.

preraffaellismo *sm.* Pre-Raphaelitism.

preraffaellita *agg.* e *s.* Pre-Raphaelite.

prerogativa *sf.* **1.** prerogative **2.** (*di persona*) faculty **3.** (*di cosa*) property

presa *sf.* **1.** taking **2.** (*stretta*) grip

3. (*cattura*) capture **4.** (*elettr.*) plug **5.** (*pizzico*) pinch ‖ *macchina da* —, camera; *far* — (*di cemento*), to set (*v. irr.*).

presagio *sm.* presage, omen.

presagire *vt.* **1.** to foresee (*v. irr.*) **2.** (*essere presagio di*) to forebode.

presago *agg.* essere — *di* (*prevedere*), to have a presentiment of.

presbiopia *sf.* long-sightedness.

presbite *agg.* long-sighted.

presbiterianismo *sm.* Presbyterianism.

presbiteriano *agg. e sm:* Presbyterian.

presbiterio *sm.* presbytery.

prescégliere *vt.* to choose (*v. irr.*).

prescelto *agg.* chosen.

prescienza *sf.* prescience.

prescindere *vi.* to leave (*v. irr.*) out of consideration: *a* — *da*, apart from.

prescritto *sm.* prescript.

prescrivere *vt.* to prescribe.

prescrizione *sf.* **1.** regulation **2.** (*med.; giur.*) prescription: *caduto in* —, invalidated by prescription.

presentàbile *agg.* presentable.

presentare *vt.* **1.** to present **2.** (*mostrare*) to show (*v. irr.*) **3.** (*far conoscere*) to introduce. ♦ **presentarsi** *vr.* **1.** to present oneself **2.** (*capitare*) to occur.

presentatore *sm.* **1.** announcer **2.** (*teat.*) showman (*pl. -men*).

presentazione *sf.* **1.** presentation **2.** (*di una persona*) introduction.

presente *agg. e s.* present ‖ *i presenti*, the people present; *la* — (*lettera*), this letter.

presentemente *avv.* now.

presentimento *sm.* presentiment.

presentire *vt.* to foresee (*v. irr.*).

presenza *sf.* **1.** presence **2.** (*frequenza*) attendance.

presenziare *vt. e vi.* to be present (at).

presepio *sm.* crib.

preservare *vt.* to preserve.

preservativo *agg. e sm.* preservative.

preservazione *sf.* preservation.

prèside *sm.* headmaster. ♦ **prèside** *sf.* headmistress.

presidente *sm.* **1.** president **2.** (*di assemblea*) chairman (*pl. -men*).

presidenza *sf.* **1.** presidency **2.** (*di assemblea*) chairmanship **3.** (*di società*) management **4.** (*insieme di*

direttori) board of directors **5.** (*di scuola*) headmastership.

presidenziale *agg.* presidential.

presidiare *vt.* to garrison.

presidio *sm.* garrison.

presièdere *vt. e vi.* to preside (over, at).

pressa *sf.* press.

pressacarte *sm.* paper-weight.

pressante *agg.* pressing.

pressantemente *avv.* pressingly.

pressappoco *avv.* approximately.

pressare *vt.* to press.

pressi *sm. pl.* **1.** neighbourhood (*sing.*) **2.** (*sobborghi*) outskirts.

pressione *sf.* pressure: *fare* — *su qu.* (*fig.*), to put (*v. irr.*) pressure on so.

presso *avv.* nearly: *a un di* —, *press'a poco*, approximately; *da* —, closely. ♦ **presso** *prep.* **1.** near **2.** (*a casa di*) at **3.** (*nell'ufficio di*) with **4.** (*fra*) among **5.** (*negli indirizzi*) c/o (care of).

pressoché *avv.* almost.

pressurizzare *vt.* to pressurize.

pressurizzazione *sf.* pressurization.

prestabilire *vt.* to pre-arrange.

prestamente *avv.* quickly.

prestanome *sm.* man of straw.

prestante *agg.* good-looking.

prestanza *sf.* fine appearance.

prestare *vt.* V. imprestare. ♦ **prestarsi** *vr.* to volunteer.

prestatore *sm.* lender: — *d'opera*, workman (*pl. -men*).

prestazione *sf.* **1.** (*prestito*) loan **2.** (*servizio*) service **3.** (*sport*) performance.

prestezza *sf.* quickness.

prestidigitatore *sm.* conjurer.

prestigio *sm.* prestige ‖ *gioco di* —, conjuring trick.

prestigioso *agg.* **1.** (*affascinante*) glamorous **2.** (*favoloso*) fabulous.

prèstito *sm.* loan: *prendere in* —, to borrow; *dare in* —, to lend (*v. irr.*).

presto[1] *agg.* — *di mano*, dexterous.

presto[2] *avv.* **1.** soon **2.** (*di buon'ora*) early **3.** (*in fretta*) quickly ‖ — *o tardi*, sooner or later; *al più* —, as soon as possible. ♦ **presto!** *inter.* quick!

presùmere *vt.* to presume.

presumìbile *agg.* presumable.

presumibilmente *avv.* presumably.

presuntivo *agg.* presumptive.

presunto *agg.* supposed.

presuntuosamente *avv.* presumptuously.

presuntuosità *sf.* conceit.

presuntuoso *agg.* presumptuous.

presunzione *sf.* presumption.

presupporre *vt.* **1.** to presuppose **2.** (*supporre*) to suppose.

presupposizione *sf.* **1.** presupposition **2.** (*supposizione*) supposition.

presupposto *sm.* V. *presupposizione*.

prete *sm.* priest.

pretendente *sm.* **1.** pretender **2.** (*corteggiatore*) suitor.

pretèndere *vt.* **1.** to pretend **2.** (*esigere*) to want. ♦ **pretèndere** *vi.* to claim.

pretensione *sf.* pretension.

pretenzioso *agg.* **1.** pretentious **2.** (*presuntuoso*) conceited.

preterintenzionale *agg.* unintentional.

pretèrito *agg. e sm.* past.

pretesa *sf.* **1.** pretence **2.** (*richiesta*) claim || *avere molte pretese*, to be hard to please; *avanzare pretese su*, to claim rights over.

pretesto *sm.* **1.** pretext **2.** (*occasione*) occasion.

pretore *sm.* magistrate.

prettamente *avv.* purely.

pretto *agg.* pure.

pretura *sf.* magistrate's court.

prevalente *agg.* prevailing.

prevalenza *sf.* prevalence.

prevalere *vi.* to prevail.

prevaricare *vi.* **1.** to prevaricate **2.** (*abusare del potere*) to abuse one's office.

prevaricatore *sm.* prevaricator.

prevaricazione *sf.* **1.** prevarication **2.** (*abuso di potere*) abuse of office.

prevedere *vt.* **1.** to foresee (*v. irr.*) **2.** (*di legge, contratto*) to provide (for).

prevedibile *agg.* foreseeable.

preveggente *agg.* foreseeing.

preveggenza *sf.* foresight.

prevenire *vt.* **1.** (*precedere*) to forestall **2.** (*evitare*) to prevent **3.** (*avvertire*) to warn.

preventivamente *avv.* **1.** beforehand **2.** (*in modo preventivo*) preventively.

preventivare *vt.* to estimate.

preventivo *agg.* **1.** preventive **2.** (*comm.*) estimated || *bilancio* —, budget. ♦ **preventivo** *sm.* estimate

preventorio *sm.* preventive sanatorium.

prevenuto *agg.* essere — *contro*, to have a prejudice against.

prevenzione *sf.* **1.** prejudice **2.** (*il prevenire*) prevention.

previdente *agg.* provident.

previdenza *sf.* providence: — *sociale*, social security.

previdenziale *agg.* social security (*attr.*).

previo *agg.* **1.** previous **2.** (*soggetto a*) subject to.

previsione *sf.* **1.** forecast **2.** (*comm.*) estimate.

previsto *agg.* **1.** foreseen **2.** (*comm.*) estimated **3.** (*giur.*) provided.

prevosto *sm.* V. *preposto*.

preziosismo *sm.* preciosity.

preziosità *sf.* preciousness.

prezioso *agg.* precious. ♦ **prezioso** *sm.* jewel.

prezzèmolo *sm.* parsley.

prezzo *sm.* **1.** price, cost **2.** (*valore*) value || *a* — *di*, at the cost of.

prezzolare *vt.* to hire.

prezzolato *agg.* (*mercenario*) mercenary.

prigione *sf.* **1.** prison **2.** (*pena*) imprisonment.

prigionia *sf.* imprisonment.

prigioniero *agg.* imprisoned. ♦ **prigioniero** *sm.* prisoner.

prillare *vi.* to twirl.

prima[1] *avv.* **1.** before **2.** (*in anticipo*) in advance **3.** (*un tempo*) once **4.** (*più presto*) earlier, sooner **5.** (*per prima cosa*) first || — *o poi*, sooner or later; *quanto* —, soon. ♦ **prima** *prep.* before. ♦ **prima che, di** *cong.* before.

prima[2] *sf.* **1.** (*ferr.; scuola*) first class **2.** (*teat.*) première.

primario *agg.* primary. ♦ **primario** *sm.* head physician.

primate *sm.* (*eccl.*) primate.

primati *sm. pl.* (*zool.*) Primates.

primaticcio *agg.* early.

primatista *s.* record-holder.

primato *sm.* **1.** supremacy **2.** (*sport*) record.

primavera *sf.* spring.

primaverile *agg.* spring (*attributivo*), springlike.

primeggiare *vi.* to excel.

primigenio *agg.* primigenial.

primipara *sf.* primipara (*pl.* -ae).

primitivo *agg. e sm.* primitive.

primizia *sf.* **1.** (*frutta*) early fruit

2. (*verdura*) early vegetable **3.** (*novità*) novelty.

primo agg. **1.** first **2.** (*principale*) chief **3.** (*iniziale*) early **4.** (*prossimo*) next || in un — tempo, at first.

primogènito agg. e sm. first-born.

primogenitura sf. primogeniture.

primordiale agg. primeval.

primordi sm. pl. beginnings.

primula sf. primrose.

principale agg. principal. ♦ **principale** sm. master, boss.

principato sm. principality.

principe sm. prince.

principesco agg. princely.

principessa sf. princess.

principiante sm. beginner.

principiare vt. e vi. to begin (v. irr.).

principio sm. **1.** (*inizio*) beginning **2.** (*norma*) principle: per —, on principle.

priora sf. prioress.

priorato sm. priorate.

priore sm. prior.

priorità sf. priority.

prisma sm. prism.

prismàtico agg. prismatic(al).

pristino agg. former.

privare vt. to deprive.

privatista s. external student.

privativa sf. **1.** (*esclusiva*) sole right **2.** (*monopolio*) monopoly **3.** (*tabaccheria*) tobacconist's shop.

privativo agg. privative.

privato agg. **1.** private **2.** (*privo*) deprived. ♦ **privato** sm. private citizen.

privazione sf. **1.** (*disagio*) privation **2.** (*perdita*) loss.

privilegiare vt. to privilege.

privilegiato agg. **1.** privileged **2.** (*comm.*) preferred.

privilegio sm. privilege.

privo agg. devoid of: — di padre, fatherless; — di madre, motherless.

pro¹ prep. for.

pro² sm. a che —?, what is the use of?

proavo sm. great grandfather.

probàbile agg. probable.

probabilismo sm. probabilism.

probabilità sf. probability.

probante agg. probatory.

probativo agg. probative.

probità sf. uprightness.

probiviri sm. pl. arbiters.

problema sm. problem.

problematicità sf. problematic nature.

problemàtico agg. problematic(al).

probo agg. upright.

proboscidati sm. pl. Proboscidea.

probòscide sf. trunk.

procaccia sm. postman (pl. -men).

procacciare vt. to get (v. irr.). ♦ **procacciarsi** vr. to get.

procacciatore sm. procurer.

procace agg. **1.** (*provocante*) provoking **2.** (*inverecondo*) immodest.

procacità sf. **1.** provocativeness **2.** (*inverecondia*) immodesty.

pro capite loc. avv. each.

procèdere vi. **1.** to proceed, to go (v. irr.) on **2.** (*agire*) to act.

procedimento sm. **1.** (*progressione*) course **2.** (*condotta*) behaviour **3.** (*giur.*) proceedings (pl.) **4.** (*tec.*) process.

procedura sf. **1.** procedure **2.** (*giur.*) practice.

procedurale agg. procedural.

procella sf. storm.

procellaria sf. stormy-petrel.

procelloso agg. stormy.

processare vt. to try: far —, to prosecute.

processionaria sf. processioner.

processione sf. procession.

processo sm. **1.** (*giur.*) trial **2.** (*med.; chim.; tec.*) process || andare sotto —, to be tried; intentare un —, to bring (v. irr.) an action.

processuale agg. trial (attr.).

procinto (*nella loc. avv.*) in — di, on the point of.

proclama sm. proclamation.

proclamare vt. to proclaim.

proclamatore sm. proclaimer.

proclamazione sf. proclamation.

proclive agg. inclined.

proclività sf. inclination.

procònsole sm. proconsul.

procrastinare vt. to postpone. ♦ **procrastinare** vi. to procrastinate.

procrastinazione sf. procrastination.

procreare vt. to procreate.

procreatore sm. procreator.

procreazione sf. procreation.

procura sf. **1.** proxy: per —, by proxy **2.** (*documento*) letter of attorney.

procurare vt. **1.** to get (v. irr.) **2.** (*causare*) to cause **3.** (*cercare*) to try. ♦ **procurarsi** *vr.* to get (*v. irr.*).

procuratore *sm.* attorney.

prode *agg.* brave.

prodezza *sf.* 1. bravery 2. (*azione*) brave deed.

prodiere *sm.* bowman (*pl.* -men).

prodiero *agg.* forward.

prodigalità *sf.* lavishness.

prodigare *vt.* to lavish. ♦ **prodigarsi** *vr.* to do (*v. irr.*) all one can.

prodigio *sm.* prodigy.

prodigiosità *sf.* prodigiousness.

prodigioso *agg.* prodigious.

prodigo *agg.* lavish.

proditoriamente *avv.* treacherously.

proditorio *agg.* treacherous.

prodotto *sm.* 1. product 2. (*risultato*) result 3. (*agr.*) produce.

pròdromo *sm.* 1. warning sign 2. (*med.*) symptom.

produrre *vt.* to produce. ♦ **prodursi** *vr.* 1. (*causarsi*) to cause oneself 2. (*accadere*) to happen 3. (*esibirsi*) to perform (before).

produttività *sf.* productivity.

produttivo *agg.* productive.

produttore *agg.* productive. ♦ **produttore** *sm.* producer.

produzione *sf.* production.

proemio *sm.* proem.

profanamente *avv.* profanely.

profanare *vt.* to profane.

profanatore *agg.* profaning. ♦ **profanatore** *sm.* profaner.

profanazione *sf.* profanation.

profanità *sf.* profanity.

profano *agg.* profane. ♦ **profano** *sm.* (*persona inesperta*) layman (*pl.* -men) ‖ *i profani*, the laity.

proferire *vt.* 1. to pronounce 2. (*dire*) to utter.

professare *vt.* to profess.

professionale *agg.* professional: *scuola* —, vocational school.

professione *sf.* profession.

professionismo *sm.* professionalism.

professionista *sm.* 1. professional man 2. (*sport*) professional.

professorale *agg.* professorial.

professore *sm.* 1. teacher 2. (*ordinario di università*) professor.

profeta *sm.* prophet.

profetare *vt.* to prophesy.

profetico *agg.* prophetic(al).

profetizzare *vt.* V. *profetare*.

profezìa *sf.* prophecy.

profferire *vt.* 1. (*offrire*) to offer 2. (*pronunciare*) to utter.

profferta *sf.* offer.

proficuo *agg.* profitable.

profilare *vt.* 1. to profile 2. (*orlare*) to edge. ♦ **profilarsi** *vr.* 1. to be outlined 2. (*apparire*) to loom.

profilassi *sf.* prophylaxis.

profilato *agg.* 1. (*delineato*) outlined 2. (*affilato*) sharp 3. (*orlato*) edged. ♦ **profilato** *sm.* section.

profilàttico *agg. e sm.* prophylactic.

profilo *sm.* 1. (*contorno*) outline 2. (*di viso*) profile 3. (*studio letterario*) monograph.

profittare *vi.* 1. (*trar profitto*) to avail oneself (of) 2. (*progredire*) to make (*v. irr.*) progress 3. (*guadagnare*) to make profits.

profittatore *sm.* profiteer.

profittévole *agg.* profitable.

profitto *sm.* profit: *trar* —, to profit (by); *mettere qc. a* —, to make (*v. irr.*) good use of sthg.

profluvio *sm.* flood.

profondamente *avv.* deeply: *dormire* —, to sleep (*v. irr.*) soundly.

profóndere *vt.* to lavish. ♦ **profóndersi** *vr.* to be profuse (in, of).

profondità *sf.* depth.

profondo *agg.* deep. ♦ **profondo** *sm.* depth.

pròfugo *sm.* refugee.

profumare *vt.* to scent. ♦ **profumarsi** *vr.* to spray oneself with scent.

profumatamente *avv.* (*fig.*) dearly.

profumerìa *sf.* perfumery.

profumiere *sm.* perfumer.

profumo *sm.* perfume, scent.

profusamente *avv.* 1. profusely 2. (*lungamente*) at length.

profusione *sf.* profusion.

progenerare *vt.* to procreate.

progenie *sf.* progeny.

progenitore *sm.* ancestor.

progettare *vt.* to plan.

progettazione *sf.* planning.

progettista *s.* planner.

progetto *sm.* plan.

prognatismo *sm.* prognathism.

prognato *agg.* prognathous.

prògnosi *sf.* prognosis (*pl.* -ses).

programma *sm.* program(me).

programmare *vt.* to program(me).

programmatore *sm.* programmist.

programmazione *sf.* programming.

programmista *sm.* programmer.
progredire *vi.* **1.** to advance **2.** (*fig.*) to get (*v. irr.*) on **3.** (*far progressi*) to make (*v. irr.*) progress.
progressione *sf.* progression.
progressista *agg.* e *s.* progressive.
progressivamente *avv.* progressively.
progressivo *agg.* progressive.
progresso *sm.* progress.
proibire *vt.* **1.** to forbid (*v. irr.*) **2.** (*impedire*) to prevent.
proibitivo *agg.* prohibitive.
proibizione *sf.* prohibition.
proibizionismo *sm.* prohibitionism.
proibizionista *agg.* e *s.* prohibitionist.
proiettare *vt.* **1.** to project **2.** (*cine*) to show (*v. irr.*) ◆ **proiettare** *vi.* to project. ◆ **proiettarsi** *vr.* to be projected.
proiettile *sm.* shell.
proiettore *sm.* **1.** (*riflettore*) searchlight **2.** (*cine*) projector.
proiezione *sf.* **1.** projection **2.** (*cine*) movie show || *macchina da —*, projector; *sala di —*, projection room.
prole *sf.* issue.
proletariato *sm.* proletariat.
proletario *agg.* e *sm.* proletarian.
proliferare *vi.* to proliferate.
proliferazione *sf.* proliferation.
prolifico *agg.* prolific.
prolissità *sf.* prolixity.
prolisso *agg.* prolix.
prologo *sm.* prologue.
prolungabile *agg.* extendable.
prolungamento *sm.* extension.
prolungare *vt.* **1.** to extend **2.** (*differire*) to postpone. ◆ **prolungarsi** *vr.* **1.** to extend **2.** (*dilungarsi*) to dwell (*v. irr.*) (on).
prolusione *sf.* opening lecture.
promemoria *sm.* memorandum (*pl.* -da).
promessa *sf.* promise.
promettente *agg.* promising.
promettere *vt.* to promise: *— bene*, to be full of promise.
prominente *agg.* prominent.
prominenza *sf.* prominence.
promiscuità *sf.* promiscuity.
promiscuo *agg.* mixed, promiscuous.
promontorio *sm.* promontory.
promosso *agg.* **1.** (*a scuola*) successful **2.** (*sostenuto*) promoted.

promotore *sm.* promoter.
promozione *sf.* promotion.
promulgare *vt.* to promulgate.
promulgatore *sm.* promulgator.
promulgazione *sf.* promulgation.
promuovere *vt.* **1.** to promote **2.** (*a scuola*) to pass.
pronao *sm.* pronaos (*pl.* -aoi).
pronipote *sm.* **1.** (*di bisnonno*) great-grandson, great-grandchild (*pl.* -children) **2.** (*di prozio*) grand-nephew || *i pronipoti* (*discendenti*), descendants. ◆ **pronipote** *sf.* **1.** (*di bisnonno*) great-granddaughter, great-grandchild **2.** (*di prozio*) grandniece.
prono *agg.* prone.
pronome *sm.* pronoun.
pronominale *agg.* pronominal.
pronosticare *vt.* **1.** to forecast (*v. irr.*) **2.** (*predire*) to foretell (*v. irr.*) **3.** (*far prevedere*) to portend.
pronostico *sm.* forecast.
prontezza *sf.* readiness.
pronto *agg.* **1.** (*preparato*) ready **2.** (*veloce*) prompt **3.** (*al telefono*) hallo || *— soccorso*, first aid.
prontuario *sm.* handbook.
pronuncia *sf.* pronunciation.
pronunciamento *sm.* pronouncement.
pronunciare *vt.* **1.** to pronounce **2.** (*proferire*) to utter || *— un discorso*, to deliver a speech. ◆ **pronunciarsi** *vr.* to give (*v. irr.*) one's opinion.
pronunciato *agg.* pronounced.
propaganda *sf.* **1.** propaganda **2.** (*comm.*) advertising: *far —* (*comm.*), to advertise **3.** (*pol.*) canvass.
propagandare *vt.* **1.** to propagandize **2.** (*comm.*) to advertise.
propagandista *s.* **1.** propagandist **2.** (*comm.*) advertiser.
propagandistico *agg.* **1.** propagandist **2.** (*comm.*) advertising.
propagare *vt.* to propagate. ◆ **propagarsi** *vr.* to propagate.
propagatore *sm.* propagator.
propagazione *sf.* propagation.
propagginare *vt.* (*agr.*) to layer.
propaggine *sf.* **1.** (*agr.*) layer **2.** (*geogr.*) ramification **3.** (*discendenza*) offspring.
propalare *vt.* to spread (*v. irr.*).
propano *sm.* propane.
propedeutica *sf.* propaedeutics.
propedeutico *agg.* propaedeutic(al).

propellente *agg.* propellent. ◆ **propellente** *sm.* propellant.

propèndere *vi.* to be inclined. ,

propensione *sf.* propensity.

propenso *agg.* inclined.

propilene *sm.* propylene.

propileo *sm.* propylaeum (*pl.* -laea).

propina *sf.* examiner's fee.

propinare *vt.* to give (*v. irr.*).

propiziare *vt.* to propitiate. ◆ **propiziarsi** *vr.* to gain so.'s favour.

propiziatore *sm.* propitiator.

propiziatorio *agg.* propitiatory.

propiziazione *sf.* propitiation.

propizio *agg.* favourable.

proponimento *sm.* resolution: *far —,* to resolve.

proporre *vt.* 1. to propose 2. (*suggerire*) to suggest. ◆ **proporsi** *vr.* to intend, to mean (*v. irr.*).

proporzionale *agg.* proportional.

proporzionalità *sf.* proportionality.

proporzionare *vt.* to proportion.

proporzionato *agg.* (*adeguato*) proportionate: *ben —,* well-proportioned.

proporzione *sf.* 1. proportion 2. (*rapporto*) ratio.

propòsito *sm.* 1. purpose 2. (*intenzione*) intention || *di —,* on purpose; *a — di,* with regard to; *a — (inter.)* by the way; *a — (al momento giusto),* at the right moment.

proposizione *sf.* sentence.

proposta *sf.* proposal.

proprietà *sf.* 1. property 2. (*l'essere proprietario*) ownership 3. (*correttezza*) propriety || *— letteraria,* copyright.

proprietario *agg.* proprietary. ◆ **proprietario** *sm.* 1. owner 2. (*di locanda*) landlord 3. (*possidente*) man of property || *— terriero,* landowner.

proprio *agg.* 1. (*rafforzativo del poss.*) own 2. (*adatto*) suitable 3. (*mat.; gramm.*) proper || *vero e —,* real. ◆ **proprio** *avv.* 1. (*esattamente*) exactly 2. (*veramente*) really || *— ora,* just now; *— così,* just like that.

propugnare *vt.* to support.

propugnatore *sm.* supporter.

propulsione *sf.* propulsion.

propulsivo *agg.* propulsive.

propulsore *sm.* propeller.

prora *sf.* bow.

proravìa (*nella loc. avv.*) *a —,* at the bow.

pròroga *sf.* 1. (*giur.*) adjournment 2. (*dilazione*) extension.

prorogàbile *agg.* 1. (*giur.*) adjournable 2. extensible.

prorogare *vt.* 1. to delay, to extend 2. (*giur.*) to postpone.

prorompente *agg.* bursting (out). ◆

prorómpere *vi.* 1. to burst (*v. irr.*) (out) 2. (*di liquidi*) to gush out.

prosa *sf.* prose || *teatro di —,* drama; *compagnia di —,* dramatic company.

prosaicità *sf.* prosaism.

prosàico *agg.* prosaic.

prosàpia *sf.* race.

prosàstico *agg.* prose (*attr.*).

prosatore *sm.* prose-writer.

proscenio *sm.* proscenium.

proscimmie *sf. pl.* lemurs.

prosciògliere *vt.* 1. (*da un obbligo*) to release 2. (*giur.*) to acquit.

proscioglimento *sm.* 1. release 2. (*giur.*) acquittal.

prosciugamento *sm.* 1. drying up 2. (*artificiale*) draining.

prosciugare *vt.* 1. to dry up 2. (*artificialmente*) to drain. ◆ **prosciugarsi** *vr.* to dry up.

prosciutto *sm.* ham.

proscritto *sm.* exile.

proscrivere *vt.* to banish.

proscrizione *sf.* banishment.

prosecuzione *sf.* prosecution.

proseguimento *sm.* continuation.

proseguire *vt.* to continue. ◆ **proseguire** *vi.* to go (*v. irr.*) on.

proselitismo *sm.* proselytism.

prosèlito *sm.* proselyte.

prosieguo *sm.* course.

prosodia *sf.* prosody.

prosopopea *sf.* (*fig.*) haughtiness.

prosperare *vi.* to prosper.

prosperità *sf.* prosperity.

pròspero *agg.* prosperous.

prosperoso *agg.* 1. prosperous 2. (*in salute*) healthy.

prospettare *vt.* 1. (*indicare*) to point out 2. (*guardare*) to look on to.

prospèttico *agg.* perspective (*attr.*).

prospettiva *sf.* 1. perspective 2. (*possibilità*) prospect.

prospetto *sm.* 1. view 2. (*fronte*) front 3. (*specchietto, programma*) prospectus.

prospezione *sf.* prospecting.

prospiciente *agg.* facing.

prossimità *sf.* closeness: *in — di*, near.

pròssimo *agg.* 1. (*vicino*) near 2. (*seguente*) next. ♦ **pròssimo** *sm.* fellow creatures (*pl.*), neighbour.

pròstata *sf.* prostate.

prosternare *vt.* to prostrate.

prostituire *vt.* to prostitute.

prostituta *sf.* prostitute.

prostituzione *sf.* prostitution.

prostrare *vt.* to prostrate. ♦ **prostrarsi** *vr.* to bow down.

prostrazione *sf.* prostration.

protagonista *s.* protagonist.

protèggere *vt.* to protect.

protèico *agg.* protein (*attr.*).

proteina *sf.* protein.

protèndere *vt.* to stretch (out): *— lo sguardo*, to gaze. ♦ **protèndersi** *vr.* to stretch oneself.

protervia *sf.* insolence.

protervo *agg.* insolent.

pròtesi *sf.* prosthesis.

protesi *sf.* protest.

protestante *agg.* e *s.* protestant.

protestantésimo *sm.* Protestantism.

protestare *vt.* e *vi.* to protest.

protesto *sm.* protest: *in —*, under protest; *lasciar andare una cambiale in —*, to dishonour a bill.

protettivo *agg.* protective.

protetto *agg.* protected. ♦ **protetto** *sm.* favourite.

protettorato *sm.* protectorate.

protettore *sm.* 1. protector 2. (*patrono*) patron.

protezione *sf.* 1. protection 2. (*patronato*) patronage.

protezionismo *sm.* protectionism.

protezionista *s.* protectionist.

proto *sm.* overseer.

protocollare *agg.* protocol (*attr.*).

protocollo *sm.* 1. protocol 2. (*registro*) record || *mettere a —*, to record; *carta —*, foolscap.

protone *sm.* proton.

protoplasma *sm.* protoplasm.

protòtipo *sm.* prototype.

protozoi *sm. pl.* Protozoa.

protrarre *vt.* 1. to protract 2. (*differire*) to defer. ♦ **protrarsi** *vr.* to go (*v. irr.*) on.

protrazione *sf.* 1. protraction 2. (*differimento*) deferment.

protuberanza *sf.* bulge.

prova *sf.* 1. proof 2. (*giur.*) evidence (*solo sing.*) 3. (*esperimento*, *esame*) test 4. (*tentativo*) try 5.

(*sventura*) trial 6. (*teat.*) rehearsal 7. (*di abito*) fitting || *in —*, on trial; *dar — di essere*, to prove to be; *superare una —*, to pass a test.

provare *vt.* 1. to prove 2. (*tentare*, *mettere alla prova*) to try 3. (*sentire*) to feel (*v. irr.*) 4. (*di abiti*) to try on 5. (*teat.*) to rehearse 6. (*collaudare*) to test. ♦ **provarsi** *vr.* 1. (*tentare*) to try 2. (*cimentarsi*) to engage (in).

provenienza *sf.* origin.

provenire *vi.* to come (*v. irr.*).

provento *sm.* 1. proceeds (*pl.*) 2. (*reddito*) income.

proverbiale *agg.* proverbial.

proverbio *sm.* proverb.

provetta *sf.* test-tube.

provetto *agg.* skilled.

provincia *sf.* province.

provinciale *agg.* e *s.* provincial: *strada —*, main road.

provincialismo *sm.* provincialism.

provino *sm.* 1. (*teat.*) tryout 2. (*cine*) test film.

provocante *agg.* 1. provocative 2. (*procace*) immodest.

provocare *vt.* 1. to provoke 2. (*causare*) to cause.

provocatore *sm.* provoker.

provocazione *sf.* provocation.

provvedere *vi.* 1. to provide (for) 2. (*badare a*) to see (*v. irr.*) to) 3. (*aver cura di*) to take (*v. irr.*) care of. ♦ **provvedere** *vt.* 1. to provide 2. (*preparare*) to prepare.

provvedimento *sm.* measure.

provveduto *agg.* 1. provided (with) 2. (*accorto*) wary.

provvidenza *sf.* providence: *essere una —*, to be providential.

provvidenziale *agg.* providential.

pròvvido *agg.* provident.

provvigione *sf.* 1. (*comm.*) commission 2. (*provvista*) supply.

provvisorietà *sf.* temporariness.

provvisorio *agg.* temporary: *in via provvisoria*, temporarily.

provvista *sf.* supply, provision (*specialmente di cibo*).

provvisto *agg.* 1. supplied (with) 2. (*fig.*) well-off.

prua *sf.* bow.

prudente *agg.* 1. prudent 2. (*cauto*) careful.

prudenza *sf.* 1. prudence 2. (*cautela*) care 3. (*precauzione*) precaution.

prùdere *vi.* to itch.

prugna *sf.* plum.

prugno *sm.* plum-tree.

pruno *sm.* 1. thorn-bush 2. (*spina*) thorn.

pruriginoso *agg.* itching

prurito *sm.* itch.

prùssico *agg.* prussic.

pseudònimo *sm.* pseudonym.

psicanàlisi *sf.* psychoanalysis.

psicanalista *s.* psychoanalyst.

psicanalìtico *agg.* psychoanalytic(al).

psicanalizzare *vt.* to psychoanalyze.

psiche *sf.* psyche.

psichiatra *s.* psychiatrist.

psichiatrìa *sf.* psychiatry.

psichiàtrico *agg.* psychiatric(al).

psichico *agg.* psychic(al).

psicologìa *sf.* psychology.

psicològico *agg.* psychologic(al).

psicòlogo *sm.* psychologist.

psicometrìa *sf.* psychometry.

psicopatìa *sf.* psychopathy.

psicopàtico *agg.* e *sm.* psychopathic.

psicopatologìa *sf.* psychopathology.

psicosi *sf.* psychosis (*pl.* -ses).

psicoterapìa *sf.* psychotherapy.

psittacosi *sf.* psittacosis.

pubblicàbile *agg.* publishable.

pubblicano *sm.* publican.

pubblicare *vt.* 1. to publish 2. (*di leggi ecc.*) to issue.

pubblicazione *sf.* publication: *fare le pubblicazioni di matrimonio*, to put up the banns.

pubblicista *s.* journalist.

pubblicità *sf.* 1. publicity 2. (*propaganda*) advertising ‖ *fare —*, to advertise.

pubblicitario *agg.* advertising.

pùbblico *agg.* public. ♦ **pùbblico** *sm.* 1. public 2. (*in teatro ecc.*) audience 3. (*cine*) moviegoers (*pl.*).

pube *sm.* pubis (*pl.* -bes).

pubertà *sf.* puberty.

pudibondo *agg.* demure.

pudicizia *sf.* demureness.

pudìco *agg.* demure.

pudore *sm.* decency.

puericoltura *sf.* puericulture.

puerile *agg.* childish.

puerilità *sf.* childishness.

puèrpera *sf.* childwife (*pl.* -wives)

pugilato *sm.* boxing: *fare del —*, to box

pùgile *sm.* boxer.

pugnalare *vt.* to stab.

pugnalata *sf.* 1. stab 2. (*fig.*) blow.

pugnale *sm.* dagger.

pugno *sm.* 1. fist 2. (*colpo*) punch 3. (*manciata*) handful ‖ *colpire col —*, to punch; *in —*, in one's hand; *di proprio —*, in one's own handwriting; *fare a pugni*, to fight (*v. irr.*), (*fig.*) to clash.

pula *sf.* chaff.

pulce *sf.* flea: *— in un orecchio*, suspicion.

pulcino *sm.* chick.

puledro *sm.* colt.

puleggia *sf.* pulley.

pulire *vt.* to clean: *pulirsi la bocca*, to wipe one's mouth.

pulito *agg.* clean.

pulitore *sm.* cleaner.

pulizia *sf.* 1. (*il pulire*) cleaning 2. (*l'essere pulito*) cleanliness.

pullulare *vi.* to swarm (with).

pùlpito *sm.* pulpit.

pulsante *sm.* push button.

pulsare *vi.* to beat (*v. irr.*)

pulsazione *sf.* beat.

pulverulento *agg.* dusty.

pulvìscolo *sm.* dust: *— atmosferico*, motes (*pl.*).

puma *sm.* puma.

pungente *agg.* 1. prickly 2. (*fig.*) biting.

pùngere *vt.* 1. to sting (*v. irr.*) 2. (*di ago*) to prick 3. (*fig.*) to tease. ♦ **pùngersi** *vr.* to prick oneself.

pungiglione *sm.* sting.

pungitopo *sm.* (*bot.*) butcher's broom.

pungolare *vt.* to goad.

pùngolo *sm.* goad.

punìbile *agg.* punishable.

punire *vt.* to punish: *— una offesa*, to revenge an insult.

punitivo *agg.* punitive.

punitore *agg.* punitory. ♦ **punitore** *sm.* punisher.

punizione *sf.* punishment.

punta *sf.* 1. point 2. (*estremità*) tip 3. (*cima*) top 4. (*un po'*) bit 5. (*dolore, fitta*) twinge ‖ *sulla — dei piedi*, on tiptoe; *avere qc. sulla — delle dita*, to have sthg. at one's finger-tips.

puntale *sm.* (*di bastone ecc.*) ferrule.

puntamento *sm.* aim.

puntare *vt.* 1. to point (at) 2. (*mirare*) to aim (at) 3. (*spingere*) to push 4. (*scommettere*) to bet (*v. irr.*) ‖ — i piedi (*fig.*), to put (*v. irr.*) one's foot down. ♦ **puntare** *vi.* to head.

puntata *sf.* 1. (*al gioco*) stake 2. (*di romanzo*) instalment.

puntatore *sm.* 1. (*mil.*) marksman (*pl. -men*) 2. (*al gioco*) better.

punteggiare *vt.* 1. to punctuate 2. (*nel disegno*) to dot.

punteggiatura *sf.* 1. punctuation 2. (*nel disegno*) dotting.

punteggio *sm.* (*sport*) score.

puntellare *vt.* to prop.

puntellatura *sf.* propping.

puntello *sm.* prop.

punteruolo *sm.* punch.

puntiglio *sm.* 1. punctilio 2. (*ostinazione*) obstinacy ‖ per —, out of pique.

puntigliosamente *avv.* 1. punctiliously 2. (*ostinatamente*) obstinately.

puntiglioso *agg.* 1. punctilious 2. (*ostinato*) obstinate.

puntina *sf.* 1. (*da fonografo*) needle 2. (*da disegno*) drawing-pin.

puntino *sm.* dot: *puntini di sospensione*, dots ‖ a —, properly.

punto[1] *sm.* 1. point 2. (*di cucito*) stitch 3. (*voto*) mark 4. (*gramm.*) full stop 5. (*macchiolina*) dot ‖ due punti, colon; — e virgola, semicolon; mettere a —, to set (*v. irr.*) up.

punto[2] *avv.* not at all.

punto[3] *agg.* e *pron.* not ... any.

puntone *sm.* (*edil.*) strut.

puntuale *agg.* punctual.

puntualità *sf.* punctuality.

puntualizzare *vt.* to stress.

puntualmente *avv.* punctually.

puntura *sf.* 1. (*di insetto*) sting 2. (*di ago*) prick 3. (*iniezione*) injection 4. (*dolore, fitta*) pain.

puntuto *agg.* pointed.

punzecchiamento *sm.* 1. (*d'insetto*) stinging 2. (*d'ago*) pricking 3. (*fig.*) teasing.

punzecchiare *vt.* 1. (*di insetti*) to sting (*v. irr.*) 2. (*fig.*) to tease.

punzonare *vt.* to punch.

punzonatrice *sf.* (*mecc.*) punch.

punzonatura *sf.* punching.

punzone *sm.* punch.

pupàttola *sf.* doll.

pupazzetto *sm.* (*disegno*) sketch.

pupazzo *sm.* puppet.

pupilla *sf.* pupil.

pupillo *sm.* pupil.

pupo *sm.* baby.

purché *cong.* provided (that).

pure *avv.* 1. (*anche*) also, too 2. (*eppure*) yet 3. (*di concessione*) as you like, of course. ♦ **pure** *cong.* 1. (*con frasi concessive*) even though 2. (*tuttavia*) but, yet. ♦ **pure** di *cong.* if only.

purè *sm.* purée: — di patate, mashed potatoes; fare un — di verdura, to mash vegetables.

purezza *sf.* purity.

purga *sf.* purgative, purge.

purgante *sm.* purgative, purge.

purgare *vt.* 1. to purge 2. (*di scritti*) to expurgate.

purgativo *agg.* purgative.

purgatorio *sm.* purgatory.

purificare *vt.* to purify.

purificatore *agg.* purificatory.

purificazione *sf.* purification.

purismo *sm.* purism.

purista *s.* purist.

puritanésimo *sm.* Puritanism.

puritano *agg.* e *sm.* Puritan.

puro *agg.* 1. pure 2. (*mero*) mere.

purosangue *sm.* thoroughbred.

purpùreo *agg.* purple.

purpurina *sf.* purpurin.

purtroppo *avv.* unfortunately.

purulento *agg.* purulent.

pus *sm.* pus.

pusillànime *agg.* pusillanimous. ♦ **pusillànime** *s.* coward.

pusillanimità *sf.* pusillanimity.

pùstola *sf.* pustule.

putacaso *loc. avv.* supposing.

putativo *agg.* putative.

putiferio *sm.* uproar: sollevare un —, to make (*v. irr.*) an uproar.

putrèdine *sf.* 1. putridness 2. (*cosa putrefatta*) rot.

putrefare *vi.* to rot. ♦ **putrefarsi** *vr.* to rot.

putrefatto *agg.* rotten.

putrefazione *sf.* putrefaction.

putrella *sf.* iron beam.

putrescenza *sf.* putrescence.

putrescìbile *agg.* putrescible.

putridità *sf.* rottenness.

pùtrido *agg.* rotten.

putridume *sm.* rot.

putto *sm.* putto (*pl. -ti*).

puzza *sf.* V. puzzo.

puzzare *vi.* to stink (*v. irr.*).

puzzo *sm.* stench.

pùzzola *sf.* polecat.

puzzolente *agg.* stinking.

Q

qua *avv.* here: *di — di*, on this side of; *per di —*, this way; *da quando in —?*, since when?

quàcchero *agg. e sm.* Quaker.

quaderno *sm.* exercise-book.

quadrangolare *agg.* quadrangular.

quadràngolo *sm.* quadrangle.

quadrante *sm.* 1. quadrant 2. *(di orologio)* dial.

quadrare *vt.* 1. *(geom.)* to square 2. *(formare)* to shape. ♦ **quadrare** *vi. (corrispondere)* to suit.

quadrato *agg.* 1. square 2. *(fig.)* strong. ♦ **quadrato** *sm.* 1. square 2. *(sport)* ring.

quadratura *sf.* 1. squaring 2. *(mat.)* quadrature.

quadrettato *agg.* 1. squared 2. *(di tessuto)* chequered.

quadriennale *agg.* quadrennial.

quadriennio *sm.* quadrennium *(pl. -ia)*.

quadrifoglio *sm.* four-leaved clover.

quadriglia *sf.* quadrille.

quadrilàtero *sm.* quadrilateral.

quadrimotore *sm.* four-engined aircraft.

quadrivio *sm.* cross-roads.

quadro *agg.* V. *quadrato*. ♦ **quadro** *sm.* 1. picture 2. *(tabella)* table 3. *(teat.)* scene 4. *(elettr.)* board 5. *(mil.)* cadre || *galleria di quadri*, picture-gallery; — *riassuntivo*, summary; — *degli interruttori*, switch board.

quadrùmane *agg.* quadrumanous. ♦ **quadrùmane** *sm.* quadrumane.

quadrùpede *agg. e sm.* quadruped.

quadruplicare *vt.* to quadruple. ♦ **quadruplicarsi** *vr.* to quadruple.

quàdruplo *agg. e sm.* 1. quadruple 2. *(quattro volte tanto)* four times as much.

quaggiù *avv.* down here.

quaglia *sf.* quail.

qualche *agg.* *(in frasi affermative e interrogative che aspettano risposta affermativa)* some; *(in frasi interrogative, dubitative, condizionali)* any || — *volta*, sometimes; *in — luogo*, somewhere; *in — modo*, somehow.

qualcosa *pron.* something, anything *(per l'uso V. qualche)*.

qualcuno *pron.* 1. somebody, someone 2. *(alcuni)* some, any: — *di*,

some, any of *(per l'uso V. qualche)*.

quale *pron. rel.* 1. *(per persone)* who *(sogg.)*, whom *(altri casi)* 2. *(per animali, cose)* which 3. *(per tutti, solo sogg. e ogg.)* that || *del* — *(poss.)*, whose: *l'uomo la casa del* —, the man whose house. ♦ **quale** *agg. e pron. int.* 1. *(di che tipo)* what 2. *(scelta tra numero limitato)* which. ♦ **quale** *agg. escl.* what. ♦ **quale** *pron.* *(correlativo di "tale")* as || *è tale e* — *suo fratello*, he is just like his brother.

qualifica *sf.* 1. qualification 2. *(titolo)* title.

qualificare *vt.* to qualify.

qualificativo *agg.* qualifying.

qualificato *agg.* qualified: *operaio* —, skilled worker.

qualificazione *sf.* qualification.

qualità *sf.* 1. quality 2. *(specie)* kind 3. *(ufficio)* capacity.

qualitativo *agg.* qualitative.

qualora *cong.* in case.

qualsìasi *agg.* V. *qualunque*.

qualunque *agg.* 1. any 2. *(quale che sia)* whatever; *(riferito a numero limitato)* whichever 3. *(comune)* ordinary || *uno* —, anybody; — *cosa*, anything; *in — posto*, anywhere; *in — modo*, anyhow.

quando *avv. e cong.* when || *da* —, since; *da* —?, since when?; *quand'anche*, even though; *di — in* —, now and then.

quantità *sf.* quantity: *una gran — di*, a great deal of.

quantitativo *agg.* quantitative. ♦ **quantitativo** *sm.* V. *quantità*.

quanto *agg.* how much *(pl.* how many*)* || *tanto...* —, as much... as; *tanti... quanti*, as many... as; — *tempo?* how long? ♦ **quanto** *avv.* how, how much || *tanto...* —, as much as; *tanto...* —, as... as; *tanto...* — *(sia... sia)*, both ...and; — *più... tanto più*, the more... the more; — *più...* — *tanto meno*, the more... the less; — *a*, as for; — *prima*, soon; *per* —, however; — *fa?*, how much is it?

quantunque *cong.* though, although.

quaranta *agg.* forty.

quarantena *sf.* quarantine.

quarantenne *agg.* forty years old, forty-year-old *(attr.)*.

quarantèsimo *agg.* fortieth.

quarantina *sf.* about forty: *aver*

passato la —, to be over forty.

quaresima *sf.* Lent.

quartetto *sm.* quartet.

quartiere *sm.* 1. (*di una città*) quarter 2. (*rione amministrativo*) district || — *generale*, headquarters (*pl.*).

quartina *sf.* quatrain.

quarto *agg.* fourth. ♦ **quarto** *sm.* quarter.

quarzo *sm.* quartz.

quasi *avv.* almost: — *mai*, hardly ever.

quassù *avv.* up here.

quaterna *sf.* set of four numbers.

quaternario *agg.* quaternary. ♦ **quaternario** *sm.* (*verso di una poesia*) line of four syllables.

quatto *agg.* 1. squatting 2. (*silenzioso*) silent || —, very quietly.

quattordicesimo *agg.* fourteenth.

quattòrdici *agg.* fourteen.

quattrini *sm. pl.* money (*us. al sing.*): *star male a* —, to be hard up.

quattro *agg.* four || *in* — *e* — *otto*, in no time; *fare il diavolo a* —, to make (*v. irr.*) a hullabaloo; *farsi in* —, to do (*v. irr.*) one's utmost.

quattrocchi (*nella loc. avv.*) *a* —, privately.

quattrocento *agg.* four hundred. ♦ **quattrocento** *sm. il* — *the*, fifteenth century.

quattromila *agg.* four thousand.

quegli *agg.* V. *quelli*. ♦ **quegli** *pron.* V. *egli*.

quei *agg. e pron.* V. *quelli*.

quella *agg. e pron.* V. *quello*.

quelle *agg. e pron.* V. *quelli*.

quelli *agg.* those. ♦ **quelli** *pron.* those, the ones.

quello *agg.* that. ♦ **quello** *pron.* that, the one || — *che* (*ciò che*), what; *tutto* — *che*, all that.

quercia *sf.* oak.

querela *sf.* 1. complaint 2. (*giur.*) action; *sporger* —, to bring (*v. irr.*) an action.

querelante *s.* plaintiff.

querelare *vt.* to proceed (against).

querelato *sm.* defendant.

quèrulo *agg.* querulous.

quesito *sm.* question.

questa *agg. e pron.* V. *questo*.

queste *agg. e pron.* V. *questi*.

questi *agg.* these. ♦ **questi** *pron.* 1. these 2. (*sing.*) this (man).

questionare *vi.* to quarrel.

questionario *sm.* questionnaire.

questione *sf.* 1. question 2. (*lite*) quarrel.

questo *agg.* this. ♦ **questo** *pron.* this, that || —*...quello* (*il primo... il secondo*) the former... the latter.

questore *sm.* questor.

questua *sf.* 1. begging 2. (*in chiesa*) collection.

questuante *agg.* begging. ♦ **questuante** *s.* beggar.

questuare *vi.* to beg.

questura *sf.* police-headquarters (*pl.*).

questurino *sm.* cop.

qui *avv.* here: *per di* —, this way; — *vicino*, close by; *da* — *innanzi*, from now on; *di* — *a un anno*, a year from now; *di* — *a otto giorni*, a week today; *fin* — (*di tempo*), so far.

quiescenza *sf.* quiescence.

quietanza *sf.* receipt.

quietare *vt.* to quiet. ♦ **quietarsi** *vr.* to quiet down.

quiete *sf.* quiet.

quietismo *sm.* quietism.

quieto *agg.* quiet || *star* — (*zitto*), to keep (*v. irr.*) quiet; *star* — (*fermo*), to keep (*v. irr.*) still; — —, very quietly.

quindi *avv.* 1. therefore 2. (*poi*) then.

quindicenne *agg.* fifteen years old, fifteen-year-old (*attr.*).

quindicèsimo *agg.* fifteenth.

quìndici *agg.* fifteen.

quindicina *sf.* 1. about fifteen 2. (*salario*) a fortnight's wages || *una* — *di giorni*, about a fortnight.

quindicinale *agg.* fortnightly.

quinquennale *agg.* quinquennial.

quinta *sf.* (*teat.*) wing || *dietro le quinte*, behind the scenes.

quintale *sm.* quintal.

quinterno *sm.* five sheets (*pl.*).

quintessenza *sf.* quintessence.

quintetto *sm.* quintet(te).

quinto *agg.* fifth.

quintuplicare *vt.* to quintuple.

quintuplo *agg. e sm.* quintuple.

quisquilia *sf.* trifle.

quivi *avv.* here.

quota *sf.* 1. share 2. (*aer.*) altitude 3. (*mar.*) depth || *perdere* —, to lose (*v. irr.*) height; *prender* —, to climb.

quotare vt. to quote. ♦ **quotarsi** vr. to subscribe.

quotato agg. 1. quoted 2. (fig.) esteemed.

quotazione sf. quotation.

quotidianamente avv. daily.

quotidiano agg. e sm. daily: vita quotidiana, everyday life.

quoziente sm. quotient.

R

rabàrbaro sm. rhubarb.

rabberciamento sm. patching (up).

rabberciare vt. to patch (up).

rabbia sf. 1. rage 2. (idrofobia) rabies || far — a qu., to make (v. irr.) so. angry.

rabbino sm. rabbi.

rabbioso agg. 1. (med.) rabid 2. (fig.) angry.

rabbonire vt. to calm down.

rabbrividire vi. 1. (di freddo) to shiver 2. (di paura ecc.) to shudder.

rabbuffare vt. 1. to ruffle 2. (rimproverare) to reprimand.

rabbuffo sm. rebuke.

rabbuiarsi vr. to darken.

rabdomante s. dowser.

rabdomanzia sf. dowsing.

rabesco sm. V. arabesco.

raccapezzare vt. 1. (raccogliere) to gather 2. (capire) to understand (v. irr.). ♦ **raccapezzarsi** vr. to see (v. irr.) one's way.

raccapricciante agg. horrifying.

raccapricciare vt. to horrify. ♦ **raccapricciarsi** vr. to be horrified.

raccapriccio sm. horror.

raccattare vt. to pick up.

racchètta sf. racket.

racchio agg. ugly.

racchiùdere vt. to contain.

raccògliere vt. 1. to pick (up) 2. (radunare) to gather 3. (far collezione) to collect 4. (accogliere) to shelter 5. (agr.) to reap. ♦ **raccògliersi** vr. 1. to gather 2. (concentrarsi) to collect one's thoughts.

raccoglimento sm. 1. concentration 2. (meditazione) meditation.

raccoglitìccio agg. picked up at random.

raccoglitore sm. 1. picker 2. (collezionista) collector 3. (cartella) folder.

raccolta sf. 1. (agr.) harvest; (di frutta, cotone) picking 2. (collezione) collection 3. (adunanza) gathering || fare la —, to harvest; chiamare a —, to collect.

raccoltamente avv. intently

raccolto sm. harvest.

raccomandàbile agg. recommendable.

raccomandare vt. 1. to recommend 2. (esortare) to urge 3. (di lettere, pacchi) to register. ♦ **raccomandarsi** vr. to beg (so.).

raccomandata sf. registered letter: fare una —, to register a letter.

raccomandazione sf. 1. recommendation 2. (consiglio) advice 3. (di lettere, pacchi) registration.

raccomodare vt. to mend.

raccontare vt. to tell (v. irr.) || si racconta, it is said.

racconto sm. 1. tale 2. (resoconto) relation.

raccorciare vt. to shorten. ♦ **raccorciarsi** vr. to grow (v. irr.) shorter.

raccordare vt. to connect.

raccordo sm. 1. connection 2. (mecc.) union 3. (ferr.) siding.

ràchide sf. rachis (pl. -ides).

rachitico agg. rickety.

rachitismo sm. rickets.

racimolare vt. to glean.

rada sf. roadstead.

radar sm. radar.

raddobbare vt. 1. (mar.) to repair 2. (riparare) to refit.

raddobbo sm. (mar.) repair.

raddolcimento sm. 1. sweetening 2. (fig.) softening.

raddolcire vt. 1. to sweeten 2. (fig.) to soften 3. (alleviare) to soothe. ♦ **raddolcirsi** vr. 1. to soften 2. (alleviarsi) to grow milder 3. (mitigarsi) to grow (v. irr.) milder.

raddoppiamento sm. doubling.

raddoppiare vt. to double. ♦ **raddoppiarsi** vr. to double.

raddoppio sm. doubling.

raddrizzamento sm. 1. straightening 2. (correzione) redressing.

raddrizzare vt. 1. to straighten 2. (correggere) to redress.

radente agg. 1. shaving 2. (rasente) grazing.

ràdere *vt.* **1.** to shave **2.** (*sfiorare*) to graze **3.** (*distruggere*) to raze.

radezza *sf.* **1.** thinness **2.** (*rarità*) infrequency.

radiale *agg.* radial.

radiante *agg.* radiant.

radiare *vt.* **1.** to radiate **2.** (*espellere*) to expel **3.** (*un nome*) to strike (*v. irr.*) off.

radiatore *sm.* radiator.

radiazione *sf.* **1.** radiation **2.** (*espulsione*) expulsion.

radicale *agg.* radical.

radicalismo *sm.* radicalism.

radicare *vi.* to root. ♦ **radicarsi** *vr.* to root.

radicato *agg.* deep-rooted.

radice *sf.* root.

radio[1] *sm.* (*anat.*) radius (*pl.* -dii).

radio[2] *sm.* (*chim.*) radium.

radio[3] *sf.* radio, wireless: *ponte —,* radiolink; *alla —,* on the radio; *— portatile ricevente e trasmittente,* walkie-talkie.

radioattività *sf.* radioactivity.

radioattivo *agg.* radioactive.

radioaudizione *sf.* **1.** broadcasting **2.** (*ascolto*) listening.

radiocomunicazione *sf.* wireless communication.

radiocrònaca *sf.* running commentary, radio account.

radiocronista *s.* radio commentator, wireless commentator.

radiodiffusione *sf.* broadcast.

radioestesìa *sf.* sensitivity to radiation.

radiofaro *sm.* radio beacon.

radiogoniòmetro *sm.* radio compass.

radiografare *vt.* to radiograph.

radiografìa *sf.* **1.** radiograph **2.** (*scienza*) radiography.

radiogramma *sm.* radiogram.

radiogrammòfono *sm.* radio--gramophone.

radiologìa *sf.* radiology.

radiòlogo *sm.* radiologist.

radioscopìa *sf.* radioscopy.

radioscòpico *agg.* radioscopic.

radiosità *sf.* radiance.

radioso *agg.* bright.

radiotècnica *sf.* radioengineering.

radiotècnico *sm.* radioengineer.

radiotelefonìa *sf.* radiotelephony.

radiotelèfono *sm.* radiotelephone.

radiotelegrafìa *sf.* radiotelegraphy.

radiotelegràfico *agg.* radiotelegraphic, wireless (*attr.*).

radiotelegrafista *s.* telegraphist.

radiotelevisione *sf.* radio and television.

radioterapìa *sf.* radiotherapy.

radiotrasméttere *vt.* to broadcast (*v. irr.*).

rado *agg.* **1.** thin **2.** (*non frequente*) infrequent || *di —,* seldom.

radunare *vt.* to gather. ♦ **radunarsi** *vr.* to gather.

raduno *sm.* gathering.

radura *sf.* glade.

raffazzonare *vt.* to patch up.

raffermo *agg.* stale.

ràffica *sf.* **1.** gust **2.** (*di arma*) burst **3.** (*fig.*) hail.

raffigurare *vt.* to represent. ♦ **raffigurarsi** *vr.* (*immaginare*) to imagine.

raffinamento *sm.* **1.** refining **2.** (*fig.*) refinement.

raffinare *vt.* to refine. ♦ **raffinarsi** *vr.* to become (*v. irr.*) refined, to refine.

raffinatamente *avv.* refinedly.

raffinatezza *sf.* refinement.

raffinato *agg.* refined (*anche fig.*).

raffinazione *sf.* refining.

raffinerìa *sf.* refinery.

raffio *sm.* grapnel.

rafforzamento *sm.* strengthening.

rafforzare *vt.* to strengthen. ♦ **rafforzarsi** *vr.* to grow (*v. irr.*) stronger.

raffreddamento *sm.* **1.** cooling **2.** (*fig.*) coolness.

raffreddare *vt.* **1.** to cool **2.** (*fig.*) to lessen. ♦ **raffreddarsi** *vr.* **1.** to cool **2.** (*fig.*) to wane **3.** (*prendere un raffredore*) to catch (*v. irr.*) a cold.

raffreddato *agg. essere —,* to have a cold.

raffreddatore *sm.* cooler.

raffreddore *sm.* cold.

raffrenare *vt.* to restrain.

raffrontare *vt.* to compare.

raffronto *sm.* comparison.

rafia *sf.* raffia.

ràgadi *sf. pl.* rhagades.

raganella *sf.* **1.** tree-frog **2.** (*strumento*) rattle.

ragazza *sf.* girl.

ragazzaglia *sf.* crowd of youngsters.

ragazzata *sf.* escapade.

ragazzo *sm.* boy: *da —,* as a boy.

raggelare *vt.* to freeze (*v. irr.*). ♦ **raggelarsi** *vr.* to freeze.

raggiante *agg.* radiant (with).

raggiare *vi.* 1. to shine (*v. irr.*) (with sthg.) 2. (*fig.*) to beam (with sthg.). ♦ **raggiare** *vt.* to radiate.

raggiera *sf.* halo of rays: *a —*, radially.

raggio *sm.* 1. ray 2. (*geom.*) radius 3. (*d'azione*) range 4. (*di ruota*) spoke || *— di sole*, sunbeam.

raggirare *vt.* to cheat.

raggiro *sm.* cheat.

raggiùngere *vt.* to reach.

raggiungimento *sm.* reaching.

raggiustare *vt.* 1. to repair 2. (*riordinare*) to rearrange.

raggomitolare *vt.* to roll up. ♦ **raggomitolarsi** *vr.* to roll oneself up.

raggranellare *vt.* to scrape together.

raggrinzire *vt.* to wrinkle. ♦ **raggrinzirsi** *vr.* to wrinkle, to become (*v. irr.*) wrinkled.

raggrumare *vt.* to clot. ♦ **raggrumarsi** *vr.* to clot.

raggruppamento *sm.* 1. grouping 2. (*gruppo*) group.

raggruppare *vt.* to group. ♦ **raggrupparsi** *vr.* to gather.

ragguagliare *vt.* 1. (*livellare*) to level 2. (*informare*) to inform 3. (*paragonare*) to compare 4. (*comm.*) to balance.

ragguaglio *sm.* 1. (*informazione*) information (*solo sing.*) 2. (*paragone*) comparison 3. (*comm.*) balance.

ragguardévole *agg.* considerable.

ragìa *sf.* resin: *acqua —*, turpentine.

ragionamento *sm.* reasoning.

ragionare *vi.* 1. to reason (about) 2. (*discutere*) to discuss (sthg.).

ragionatore *sm.* reasoner.

ragione *sf.* 1. reason 2. (*diritto*) right 2. (*rapporto*) rate || *la — per cui*, the reason why; *a — veduta*, after due consideration; *aver —*, to be right; *a maggior —*, all the more reason; *aver — di qu.*, to get (*v. irr.*) the better of so.; *— sociale* (*comm.*), style.

ragioneria *sf.* bookkeeping.

ragionévole *agg.* 1. reasonable 2. (*di buon senso*) sensible.

ragionevolezza *sf.* reasonableness.

ragioniere *sm.* bookkeeper.

ragliare *vi.* to bray.

raglio *sm.* bray.

ragnatela *sf.* cobweb.

ragno *sm.* spider.

ragù *sm.* ragout.

raion *sm.* rayon.

rallegramenti *sm. pl.* congratulations.

rallegrare *vt.* to cheer (up). ♦ **rallegrarsi** *vr.* 1. to rejoice (at) 2. (*congratularsi*) to congratulate (so. on sthg.).

rallentamento *sm.* slowing down.

rallentare *vt.* to slacken. ♦ **rallentare** *vi.* 1. to slacken 2. (*di velocità*) to slow down. ♦ **rallentarsi** *vr.* to get (*v. irr.*) slack.

rallentatore *sm.* (*cine*) slow motion.

ramaiolo *sm.* ladle.

ramanzina *sf.* scolding.

ramare *vt.* to copper.

ramarro *sm.* green lizard.

ramazza *sf.* broom.

rame *sm.* copper.

ramìfero *agg.* copper-bearing (*attr.*).

ramificare *vi.* to ramify. ♦ **ramificarsi** *vr.* to ramify.

ramificazione *sf.* ramification.

ramingo *agg.* roving.

rammagliare *vt.* to mend a run.

rammaricare *vt.* to afflict. ♦ **rammaricarsi** *vr.* 1. to be sorry 2. (*lamentarsi*) to complain (of).

rammàrico *sm.* sorrow.

rammendare *vt.* to darn.

rammendatrice *sf.* darner.

rammendo *sm.* 1. darning 2. (*parte rammendata*) darn.

rammentare *vt.* to remember: *— qc. a qu.*, to remind so. of sthg. ♦ **rammentarsi** *vr.* to remember.

rammollimento *sm.* softening.

rammollire *vt.* to soften. ♦ **rammollirsi** *vr.* to soften, to go (*v. irr.*) soft.

rammollito *agg.* soft: *un vecchio —*, a dotard. ♦ **rammollito** *sm.* imbecile.

ramo *sm.* branch.

ramoscello *sm.* twig.

ramoso *agg.* branched.

rampa *sf.* 1. ramp 2. (*di scale*) flight.

rampante *agg.* rampant.

rampicante *agg.* climbing: *pianta —*, creeper.

rampino *sm.* hook.

rampogna *sf.* reproach.

rampollare *vi.* to spring (*v. irr.*).

rampollo *sm.* 1. (*d'acqua*) spring 2. (*di albero*) shoot 3. (*discendente*) offspring.

rampone sm. 1. (*mar.*) harpoon 2. (*da montagna*) crampon.

rana sf. frog: *uomo* —, frogman (*pl.* -men); *nuotare a* —, to swim (*v. irr.*) the breast stroke.

ràncido agg. 1. rancid 2. (*fig.*) trite || *sapere di* —, to have a rancid taste.

rancio sm. (*mil.*) mess.

rancore sm. grudge.

randagio agg. stray.

randellare vt. to cudgel.

randellata sf. blow with a cudgel.

randello sm. cudgel.

ranetta sf. rennet.

rango sm. rank.

rannicchiarsi vr. to crouch.

rannuvolamento sm. clouding over.

rannuvolare vi. to become (*v. irr.*) cloudy, to cloud over. ♦ **rannuvolarsi** vr. to get (*v. irr.*) cloudy.

ranocchio sm. frog.

rantolare vi. 1. to wheeze 2. (*in punto di morte*) to have the death-rattle.

ràntolo sm. 1. wheeze 2. (*di morte*) death-rattle.

ranùncolo sm. buttercup.

rapa sf. turnip.

rapace agg. greedy. ♦ **rapace** sm. bird of prey.

rapacità sf. greed.

rapare vt. to crop (so.'s hair).

rapato agg. shorn.

ràpida sf. rapid.

rapidità sf. swiftness.

ràpido agg. swift. ♦ **ràpido** sm. express (train).

rapimento sm. 1. kidnapping 2. (*di donna*) abduction 3. (*fig.*) rapture.

rapina sf. robbery.

rapinare vt. to rob.

rapinatore sm. robber.

rapire vt. 1. to kidnap 2. (*una donna*) to abduct 3. (*fig.*) to ravish.

rapitore sm. 1. kidnapper 2. (*di donna*) abductor.

rappacificare vt. to reconcile. ♦ **rappacificarsi** vr. to become (*v. irr.*) reconciled.

rappacificazione sf. reconciliation.

rappezzare vt. to patch.

rappezzatura sf. 1. patching 2. (*parte rappezzata*) patch.

rapporto sm. 1. relation 2. (*relazione*) report 3. (*mat.*) ratio || *chiamare a* —, to summon; *andare a* — *da*, to report; *essere in buoni rapporti*, to be on good terms; *sotto tutti i rapporti*, in every respect.

rapprèndere vi. to coagulate. ♦ **rapprèndersi** vr. to coagulate.

rappresaglia sf. retaliation: *far* —, to retaliate.

rappresentàbile agg. performable.

rappresentante s. 1. representative 2. (*comm.*) agent.

rappresentanza sf. 1. representation 2. (*comm.*) agency || *in* — *di*, on behalf of.

rappresentare vt. 1. to represent 2. (*comm.*) to be agent (for) 3. (*una parte*) to play 4. (*un'opera teatrale*) to stage. ♦ **rappresentarsi** vr. to imagine.

rappresentativo agg. representative.

rappresentazione sf. 1. representation 2. (*teat.*) performance 3. (*cine*) exhibition.

rapsodìa sf. rhapsody.

rarefare vt. to rarefy. ♦ **rarefarsi** vr. to rarefy.

rarefatto agg. rarefied.

rarefazione sf. rarefaction.

rarità sf. rarity.

raro agg. rare: *rare volte*, seldom; *una bestia rara* (*fig.*), a queer fish.

rasare vt. 1. to shave 2. (*un prato*) to mow (*v. irr.*) 3. (*lisciare*) to smooth. ♦ **rasarsi** vr. to shave.

rasato agg. 1. shaven 2. (*liscio*) smooth 3. (*simile a raso*) satin (*attributivo*).

rasatura sf. 1. shave 2. (*di prato*) mowing.

raschiamento sm. 1. scraping 2. (*med.*) curettage.

raschiare vt. 1. to scrape 2. (*med.*) to curette || *raschiarsi la gola*, to clear one's throat.

raschiata sf. scraping.

raschiatoio sm. 1. scraper 2. (*med.*) curette.

raschiatura sf. scraping.

raschietto sm. 1. scraper 2. (*per cancellare*) eraser.

rasciugare vt. to dry.

rasentare vt. 1. to graze 2. (*confinare*) to border (on).

rasente prep. close to: *passare* —, to skim.

raso agg. V. rasato. ♦ **raso** sm. satin.

rasoio sm. razor.

raspa sf. rasp.

raspamento sm. rasping.

raspare vt. 1. to rasp 2. (con le unghie) to scratch 3. (frugare) to rummage.

rassegna sf. 1. (rivista, recensione) review 2. (esame) survey ‖ passare in —, to inspect.

rassegnare vt. to hand in: — le dimissioni, to resign. ♦ **rassegnarsi** vr. to resign oneself.

rassegnato agg. resigned.

rassegnazione sf. resignation.

rasserenare vt. 1. to clear 2. (fig.) to cheer up. ♦ **rasserenarsi** vr. to clear up.

rassettare vt. 1. to tidy 2. (riparare) to mend.

rassicurante agg. reassuring.

rassicurare vt. to reassure. ♦ **rassicurarsi** vr. to be reassured.

rassicurazione sf. reassurance.

rassodamento sm. consolidation.

rassodare vt. 1. to consolidate 2. (indurire) to harden. ♦ **rassodarsi** vr. to harden.

rassomigliante agg. like, alike (pred.).

rassomiglianza sf. likeness.

rassomigliare vi. to be like. ♦ **rassomigliarsi** vr. rec. to be alike.

rassottigliare vt. V. assottigliare.

rastrellamento sm. 1. raking 2. (mil.) mopping up 3. (di polizia) combing 4. (draggaggio) dragging.

rastrellare vt. 1. to rake 2. (mil.) to mop up 3. (di polizia) to comb 4. (dragare) to drag.

rastrelliera sf. rack.

rastrello sm. rake.

rastremare vt. to taper. ♦ **rastremarsi** vr. to taper.

rata sf. instalment: a rate, by instalments.

rateale agg. by instalments.

rateare vt. to divide into instalments.

ratifica sf. ratification.

ratificare vt. to ratify.

ratificatore sm. ratifier.

ratificazione sf. V. ratifica.

ratto[1] sm. 1. kidnapping 2. (di donna) rape.

ratto[2] sm. (topo) rat.

rattoppare vt. to patch (up).

rattoppo sm. 1. patching up 2. (toppa) patch.

rattrappimento sm. 1. (intorpidi-mento) benumbing 2. (contrazione) contraction.

rattrappire vt. 1. (contrarre) to contract 2. (intorpidire) to benumb.

rattristare vt. to grieve. ♦ **rattristarsi** vr. 1. (divenir triste) to become (v. irr.) sad 2. (essere triste) to be sad.

raucèdine sf. hoarseness: avere la —, to have a hoarse voice.

ràuco agg. hoarse.

ravanello sm. radish.

ravvedersi vr. to mend one's way.

ravvedimento sm. reformation.

ravviamento sm. tidying (up).

ravviare vt. to tidy (up).

ravvicinamento sm. 1. approach 2. (conciliazione) reconciliation.

ravvicinare vt. 1. to bring (v. irr.) closer 2. (riconciliare) to reconcile 3. (confrontare) to compare. ♦ **ravvicinarsi** vr. 1. to draw (v. irr.) closer 2. (riconciliarsi) to become (v. irr.) reconciled.

ravvisàbile agg. recognizable.

ravvisare vt. to recognize.

ravvivamento sm. revival.

ravvivare vt. 1. to revive 2. (rallegrare) to brighten up ‖ — il fuoco, to poke the fire. ♦ **ravvivarsi** vr. 1. to revive 2. (rallegrarsi) to brighten up.

raziocinante agg. reasoning.

raziocìnio sm. 1. reason 2. (buon senso) common sense.

razionale agg. rational.

razionalismo sm. rationalism.

razionalista s. rationalist.

razionalità sf. rationality.

razionamento sm. rationing.

razionare vt. to ration.

razione sf. ration.

razza[1] sf. 1. race 2. (di animali) breed 3. (genere) kind.

razza[2] sf. (itt.) ray.

razzìa sf. 1. raid 2. (insetticida) insecticide ‖ far —, to plunder.

razziale agg. racial.

razziare vt. to plunder.

razziatore sm. plunderer.

razzismo sm. racialism.

razzista s. racialist.

razzo sm. rocket.

razzolare vi. to scratch about.

re[1] sm. king.

re[2] sm. (mus.) D, re.

reagente sm. reagent.

reagire vi. to react.

reale[1] agg. real.

reale[2] agg. (del re) royal.

realismo sm. realism.

realista[1] agg. e s. realist.

realista[2] agg. e s. (del re) royalist.

realistico agg. realistic.

realizzàbile agg. realizable.

realizzare vt. to realize. ♦ realizzarsi vr. 1. to be realized 2. (avverarsi) to come (v. irr.) true.

realizzatore sm. realizer.

realizzazione sf. 1. realization 2. (teat.) staging 3. (cine) production.

realtà sf. reality.

reame sm. kingdom.

reato sm. 1. offence 2. (crimine) crime.

reattivo agg. reactive. ♦ reattivo sm. reagent.

reattore sm. 1. reactor 2. (aereo) jet.

reazionario agg. e sm. reactionary.

reazione sf. reaction: motore a —, jet engine; aereo a —, jet.

reboante agg. 1. thundering 2. (fig.) bombastic.

rebus sm. rebus.

recalcitrare vi. V. ricalcitrare.

recapitare vt. to deliver.

recàpito sm. 1. (consegna) delivery 2. (indirizzo) address.

recare vt. 1. to bring (v. irr.) 2. (fig.) to bear (v. irr.) 3. (causare) to cause. ♦ recarsi vr. to go (v. irr.).

recèdere vi. to withdraw (v. irr.).

recensione sf. review.

recensire vt. to review.

recensore sm. reviewer.

recente agg. recent.

recentemente avv. recently.

recentissime sf. pl. latest news.

recessione sf. recession.

recessivo agg. receding.

recesso sm. 1. recess 2. (recessione) recession 3. (giur.) withdrawal.

recettivo agg. V. ricettivo.

recezione sf. reception.

recìdere vt. to cut (v. irr.) off.

recidiva sf. relapse.

recidività sf. 1. (giur.) recidivism 2. (med.) relapse.

recidivo agg. 1. (giur.) recidivous 2. (med.) relapsing. ♦ recidivo sm. 1. (giur.) recidivist 2. (med.) relapser.

recintare vt. to fence.

recinto sm. enclosure.

recipiente sm. vessel.

reciprocamente avv. reciprocally.

reciprocità sf. reciprocity.

recìproco agg. reciprocal.

recisamente avv. resolutely.

recisione sf. excision.

reciso agg. 1. cut 2. (fig.) resolute.

rècita sf. performance.

recitare vt. 1. to recite 2. (teat.) to act || — una parte, to play a part.

recitativo sm. recitative.

recitazione sf. 1. recitation 2. (teat.) acting.

reclamante sm. claimant.

reclamare vt. to claim. ♦ reclamare vi. to complain.

reclamìstico agg. advertising.

reclamizzare vt. to advertise.

reclamo sm. complaint.

reclinare vt. to bow.

reclusione sf. 1. seclusion 2. (prigionia) imprisonment.

recluso agg. 1. secluded 2. (imprigionato) imprisoned. ♦ recluso sm. prisoner.

rècluta sf. 1. recruit 2. (fig.) novice.

reclutamento sm. enlistment.

reclutare vt. to enlist, to recruit.

recòndito agg. hidden.

recriminare vi. 1. to recriminate 2. (lamentarsi) to complain.

recriminazione sf. 1. recrimination 2. (lamentela) complaint.

recrudescente agg. recrudescent.

recrudescenza sf. recrudescence.

redarguire vt. to reproach.

redattore sm. 1. drawer 2. (di giornale) member of the editorial staff || — capo, editor.

redazionale agg. editorial.

redazione sf. 1. drawing up 2. (di giornale) editing 2. (i redattori) editorial staff 3. (ufficio) editorial office.

redditività sf. profitableness.

redditizio agg. profitable.

rèddito sm. 1. income 2. (dello Stato) revenue.

redento agg. redeemed.

redentore sm. redeemer.

redenzione sf. redemption.

redìgere vt. to draw (v. irr.) up.

redìmere vt. to redeem.

redimìbile agg. redeemable.

rèdini sf. pl. reins.

redivivo agg. 1. restored to life 2. (nuovo) new.

rèduce agg. back from. ♦ rèduce sm. veteran.

referendum *sm.* referendum.

referenza *sf.* reference.

referenziare *vt.* to give (*v. irr.*) references.

referto *sm.* report.

refettorio *sm.* refectory.

refezione *sf.* meal.

refrattario *agg.* refractory: *terra refrattaria,* fireclay.

refrigerante *agg.* e *sm.* refrigerant.

refrigerare *vt.* to refrigerate.

refrigeratore *sm.* refrigerator.

refrigerazione *sf.* refrigeration.

refrigerio *sm.* **1.** cool **2.** (*sollievo*) relief.

refurtiva *sf.* stolen goods (*pl.*).

refuso *sm.* misprint, wrong fount.

regalare *vt.* **1.** to present (so. with sthg.) **2.** (*vendere a poco prezzo*) to sell (*v. irr.*) cheap.

regalato *agg.* (*venduto a buon prezzo*) cheap.

regale *agg.* regal.

regalia *sf.* (*mancia*) gratuity.

regalo *sm.* present: *in —,* as a present.

regata *sf.* regatta.

reggente *agg.* e *sm.* regent.

reggenza *sf.* regency.

règgere *vt.* **1.** (*sorreggere*) to hold (*v. irr.*) **2.** (*dirigere*) to run (*v. irr.*) **3.** (*gramm.*) to govern ‖ — *una prova,* to stand (*v. irr.*) a test. ♦ **règgere** *vi.* **1.** (*resistere*) to hold (out) **2.** (*stare in piedi, anche fig.*) to stand. ♦ **règgersi** *vr.* **1.** (*sostenersi*) to stand **2.** (*appoggiarsi a*) to hold (on, to).

reggia *sf.* royal palace.

reggicalze *sm.* girdle.

reggimento *sm.* (*mil.*) regiment.

reggipetto *sm.* bra.

reggiseno *sm.* V. *reggipetto.*

reggitore *sm.* ruler.

regia *sf.* **1.** (*teat.*) production **2.** (*cine*) direction ‖ — *di,* produced, directed by.

regicida *sm.* regicide.

regicidio *sm.* regicide.

regime *sm.* **1.** regime **2.** (*mecc.*) speed **3.** (*dieta*) diet ‖ *essere a —,* to be on a diet.

regina *sf.* queen.

regio *agg.* royal.

regionale *agg.* regional.

regionalismo *sm.* regionalism.

regionalista *s.* regionalist.

regione *sf.* **1.** region **2.** (*divisione amministrativa; fig.*) province.

regista *sm.* **1.** (*teat.*) producer **2.** (*cine*) director.

registràbile *agg.* registrable, recordable.

registrare *vt.* **1.** to register **2.** (*comm.*) to book **3.** (*segnare; cine*) to record **4.** (*su nastro*) to tape-record **5.** (*mecc.*) to adjust.

registratore *sm.* **1.** (*persona*) registrar **2.** (*strumento*) register: — *di cassa,* cash-register **3.** (*magnetofono*) taperecorder.

registrazione *sf.* **1.** registration **2.** (*comm.*) entry **3.** (*di suoni*) recording.

registro *sm.* **1.** register **2.** (*comm.*) book **3.** (*ufficio governativo*) registry.

regnante *agg.* reigning. ♦ **regnante** *s.* sovereign.

regnare *vi.* to reign.

regno *sm.* **1.** reign **2.** (*territorio; fig.*) kingdom.

règola *sf.* **1.** rule **2.** (*esempio*) example **3.** (*misura*) moderation ‖ *in —,* in order; *è di —,* it is the custom.

regolamentare *agg.* prescribed: *non essere —,* to be against the rules.

regolamentarmente *avv.* according to the rules.

regolamentazione *sf.* regulations (*pl.*).

regolamento *sm.* regulation: — *dei conti,* settlement.

regolare[1] *vt.* **1.** to regulate **2.** (*sistemare*) to settle **3.** (*sintonizzare*) to tune (in). ♦ **regolarsi** *vr.* **1.** to act **2.** (*controllarsi*) to control oneself.

regolare[2] *agg.* regular.

regolarità *sf.* regularity.

regolarizzare *vt.* to regularize.

regolarizzazione *sf.* regularization.

regolatamente *avv.* **1.** regularly **2.** (*con moderazione*) moderately.

regolatezza *sf.* sobriety.

regolato *agg.* regular.

regolatore *agg.* regulating: *piano —,* townplan. ♦ **regolatore** *sm.* regulator.

regolazione *sf.* regulation.

règolo *sm.* rule: — *calcolatore,* slide rule.

regredire *vi.* to regress.

regressione *sf.* regression.

regressivo *agg.* regressive.

regresso *sm.* regress.

reietto agg. rejected. ♦ **reietto** sm. outcast.

reiezione sf. rejection.

reincarnare vt. to reincarnate. ♦ **reincarnarsi** vr. to be reincarnated.

reincarnazione sf. reincarnation.

reintegrare vt. 1. to restore 2. (risarcire) to indemnify.

reintegrazione sf. 1. restoration 2. (risarcimento) indemnification.

reità sf. 1. (colpevolezza) guiltiness 2. (malvagità) wickedness.

reiterare vt. to reiterate.

reiterazione sf. reiteration.

relativamente avv. comparatively: — a, as regards.

relativismo sm. relativism.

relativistico agg. relativistic.

relatività sf. relativity.

relativo agg. 1. relative 2. (rispettivo) respective 3. (attinente) pertinent.

relatore sm. 1. relator 2. (di leggi) proposer.

relazionare vt. to relate.

relazione sf. 1. report 2. (legame) relation 3. (contatto) touch 4. (conoscenza) acquaintance || aver — con, to be connected with; essere in buone relazioni, to be on good terms; mettersi in — con, to get (v. irr.) into touch with; — amorosa, love affair.

relegare vt. to relegate.

relegazione sf. relegation.

religione sf. 1. religion 2. (culto) worship.

religiosità sf. piety.

religioso agg. e sm. religious.

reliquia sf. relic.

reliquario sm. reliquary.

relitto sm. 1. wreckage 2. (di persona) outcast.

remare vi. 1. to row 2. (con pagaia) to paddle.

remata sf. 1. row 2. (colpo di remo) stroke.

rematore sm. oarsman (pl. -men).

remiganti sf. pl. remiges.

remigare vi. 1. to row 2. (di ali) to flap.

reminiscenza sf. reminiscence.

remissione sf. (giur.) remission.

remissività sf. submissiveness.

remissivo agg. submissive.

remo sm. oar.

rèmora sf. 1. (ostacolo) obstacle 2. (indugio) delay 3. (zool.) remora.

remoto agg. remote: passato — (gramm.) past simple tense.

remunerare vt. to remunerate.

remunerativo agg. remunerative.

remunerazione sf. remuneration.

rena sf. sand.

renale agg. renal.

rèndere vt. 1. to render 2. (fruttare) to yield || — conto di, to account for; — giustizia a qu., to do (v. irr.) so. justice. ♦ **rèndersi** vr. to become (v. irr.) || — conto di, to realize.

rendiconto sm. 1. statement 2. (resoconto) report.

rendimento sm. 1. rendering 2. (resa) output 3. (efficienza) efficiency.

rèndita sf. 1. revenue 2. (privata) income.

rene sm. kidney.

renella sf. gravel.

reni sf. pl. back (sing.).

renitente agg. reluctant || essere — alla leva, to fail to appear at the draft.

renitenza sf. reluctance || — alla leva, failure to register for national service.

renna sf. reindeer (pl. invariato).

renoso agg. sandy.

reo agg. guilty. ♦ **reo** sm. culprit.

reòmetro sm. rheometer.

reòstato sm. rheostat.

reparto sm. 1. department 2. (mil.) detachment.

repellente agg. repulsive.

repentaglio sm. danger: a —, in danger.

repentino agg. sudden.

reperibile agg. to be found (pred.).

reperire vt. to find (v. irr.).

reperto sm. 1. (giur.) evidence 2. (med.) report.

repertorio sm. (teat.) repertoire.

rèplica sf. 1. reply 2. (obiezione) objection 3. (copia) copy 4. (teat.) performance || avere molte repliche (teat.), to have a long run.

replicare vt. 1. to reply 2. (obiettare) to object 3. (ripetere) to repeat.

reprensìbile agg. reprehensible.

reprensione sf. reprehension.

repressione sf. repression.

repressivo agg. repressive.

represso agg. repressed.

reprimenda sf. reprimand.

reprimere vt. to repress.

rèprobo *agg. e sm.* reprobate.

repùbblica *sf.* republic.

repubblicano *agg. e sm.* republican.

reputare *vt.* **1.** to consider **2.** (*pensare*) to think (*v. irr.*).

reputazione *sf.* reputation.

requie *sf.* rest.

requisire *vt.* to requisition.

requisito *sm.* qualification.

requisitoria *sf.* **1.** indictment **2.** (*giur.*) summing up.

requisizione *sf.* requisition.

resa *sf.* (*rendimento*) yield **2.** (*capitolazione*) surrender ‖ — *dei conti*, rendering of accounts.

rescìndere *vt.* to rescind.

rescindìbile *agg.* rescindable.

rescissione *sf.* rescission.

reseda *sf.* reseda.

resezione *sf.* resection.

residente *agg. e sm.* resident.

residenza *sf.* residence.

residenziale *agg.* residential.

residuare *vi.* to be left.

residuato *agg.* residual. ♦ **residuato** *sm.* — *di guerra*, war surplus.

residuo *agg.* remaining. ♦ **residuo** *sm.* residue: *residui radioattivi*, radioactive waste.

rèsina *sf.* resin.

resinoso *agg.* resinous.

resipiscenza *sf.* resipiscence.

resistente *agg.* **1.** resistant **2.** (*forte*) strong.

resistenza *sf.* resistance.

resìstere *vi.* **1.** to resist **2.** (*sopportare*) to endure.

resoconto *sm.* report.

respingente *sm.* buffer.

respìngere *vt.* **1.** to repel **2.** (*rimandare*) to return **3.** (*rifiutare*) to reject **4.** (*scol.*) to pluck.

respinta *sf.* V. *parata*.

respiràbile *agg.* breathable.

respirare *vt. e vi.* to breathe.

respiratore *sm.* respirator.

respiratorio *agg.* respiratory.

respirazione *sf.* respiration, breathing.

respiro *sm.* **1.** breath **2.** (*riposo*) respite.

responsàbile *agg.* responsible (for).

responsabilità *sf.* responsibility.

responso *sm.* **1.** response **2.** (*opinione*) opinion.

responsorio *sm.* responsory.

ressa *sf.* crowd: *far — intorno a*

qu., to crowd round so.

resta *sf.* **1.** (*di cipolla, aglio ecc.*) string **2.** (*di lancia*) rest.

restante *agg. e sm.* V. *rimanente*.

restare *vi.* V. *rimanere*.

restaurare *vt.* to restore.

restauratore *sm.* restorer.

restaurazione *sf.* restoration.

restàuro *sm.* restoration: *in* —, under repair.

restìo *agg.* loath, reluctant.

restituire *vt.* **1.** to return **2.** (*reintegrare*) to restore.

restituzione *sf.* **1.** return **2.** (*reintegrazione*) restoration.

resto *sm.* **1.** rest **2.** (*mat.*) remainder **3.** (*di denaro*) change ‖ *resti*, remains; *del* —, on the other hand.

restringente *agg.* astringent.

restrìngere *vt.* **1.** (*contrarre*) to contract **2.** (*limitare*) to limit **3.** (*un vestito*) to tighten. ♦ **restrìngersi** *vr.* **1.** to get (*v. irr.*) narrower **2.** (*contrarsi*) to contract **3.** (*affollarsi*) to close up **4.** (*di tessuti*) to shrink (*v. irr.*).

restringimento *sm.* **1.** narrowing **2.** (*contrazione*) contraction **3.** (*limitazione*) limitation **4.** (*di tessuto*) shrinking **5.** (*di vestito*) tightening.

restrittivo *agg.* restrictive.

restrizione *sf.* restriction.

retaggio *sm.* heritage.

retata *sf.* **1.** haul **2.** (*di polizia*) roundup.

rete *sf.* **1.** net **2.** (*di letto*) wire netting **3.** (*intreccio*) network.

reticella *sf.* **1.** (*per capelli*) hair-net **2.** (*per bagagli*) luggage-rack.

reticente *agg.* reticent.

reticenza *sf.* reticence.

reticolato *sm.* **1.** (*mil.*) barbed-wire entanglement **2.** (*tracciato di linee*) network.

retìcolo *sm.* **1.** (*anat.*) reticulum (*pl.* -la) **2.** (*ott.*) reticle.

rètina *sf.* retina.

retina *sf.* V. *reticella*.

rètore *sm.* rhetorician.

retòrica *sf.* rhetoric.

retòrico *agg.* rhetorical.

retrarre *vt.* to retract.

retràttile *agg.* retractile.

retrattilità *sf.* retractility.

retribuire *vt.* to pay (*v. irr.*).

retribuzione *sf.* payment.

retrivo *agg.* reactionary.

retro *sm.* back.

retroattività *sf.* retroactivity.

retroattivo *agg.* retroactive.

retrobottega *sm.* back of the shop.

retrocèdere *vi.* to withdraw (*v. irr.*). ◆ retrocèdere *vt.* 1. (*mil.*) to degrade 2. to retrocede.

retrocessione *sf.* 1. retrocession 2. (*mil.*) degradation.

retrodatare *vt.* to date back.

retrògrado *agg.* 1. out-of-date 2. (*reazionario*) reactionary.

retroguardia *sf.* rear-guard.

retromarcia *sf.* reverse-gear.

retroscena *sm.* 1. back of the stage 2. (*fig.*) intrigue.

retrospettivo *agg.* retrospective.

retrostante *agg.* at the back.

retroterra *sm.* hinterland.

retroversione *sf.* 1. retroversion 2. (*di traduzione*) back version.

retrovie *sf. pl.* zone behind the front (*sing*).

retrovisore *sm.* specchietto —, driving mirror.

retta[1] *sf.* (*geom.*) straight line.

retta[2] *sf.* (*di pensione*) terms (*pl.*).

retta[3] *sf.* dar — a qu., to listen to so.

rettale *agg.* rectal.

rettamente *avv.* 1. (*giustamente*) rightly 2. (*onestamente*) honestly.

rettangolare *agg.* rectangular.

rettàngolo *sm.* rectangle.

rettìfica *sf.* 1. rectification 2. (*mecc.*) grinding.

rettificare *vt.* 1. to rectify 2. (*mecc.*) to grind (*v. irr.*).

rettificatrice *sf.* grinder.

rettificazione *sf.* V. rettìfica.

rettifilo *sm.* straight, stretch.

rèttile *sm.* reptile.

rettilineo *agg.* rectilinear. ◆ rettilineo *sm.* straight, stretch.

rettitùdine *sf.* righteousness, honesty.

retto *agg.* 1. straight 2. (*geom.; giusto*) right. ◆ retto *sm.* (*anat.*) rectum (*pl.* -ta).

rettorato *sm.* rectorship.

rettore *sm.* 1. rector 2. (*di università*) chancellor.

rèuma *sm.* rheumatism.

reumàtico *agg. e sm.* rheumatic.

reumatismo *sm.* V. rèuma.

reverendo *agg.* reverend. ◆ reverendo *sm.* clergyman (*pl.* -men).

reversìbile *agg.* reversible.

reversibilità *sf.* reversibility.

reversione *sf.* reversion.

revisionare *vt.* 1. (*mecc.*) to overhaul 2. (*comm.*) to audit.

revisione *sf.* 1. revision 2. (*mecc.*) overhaul 3. (*comm.*) audit.

revisionismo *sm.* revisionism.

revisore *sm.* 1. reviser 2. (*comm.*) auditor.

reviviscenza *sf.* reviviscence.

rèvoca *sf.* revocation.

revocàbile *agg.* revocable.

revocare *vt.* 1. (*richiamare*) to recall 2. (*giur.*) to revoke.

revocazione *sf.* revocation.

revolverata *sf.* revolver shot.

revulsione *sf.* revulsion.

revulsivo *agg.* revulsive.

riabbottonare *vt.* to button again.

riabilitare *vt.* to rehabilitate.

riabilitazione *sf.* rehabilitation.

riaccèndere *vt.* 1. to relight 2. (*radio, luce ecc.*) to turn on again. ◆ riaccèndersi *vr.* 1. to brighten again 2. (*riprender fuoco*) to catch (*v. irr.*) fire again.

riaccompagnare *vt.* to take (*v. irr.*) home.

riacquistare *vt.* 1. to buy (*v. irr.*) again 2. (*riprendere*) to recover.

riadattare *vt.* to adapt again. ◆ riadattarsi *vr.* (*rassegnarsi*) to resign oneself again.

riaddormentare *vt.* to send (*v. irr.*) to sleep again. ◆ riaddormentarsi *vr.* to fall (*v. irr.*) asleep again.

riaffacciare *vt.* to present again. ◆ riaffacciarsi *vr.* to reappear, to appear again.

riaffermare *vt.* to affirm again. ◆ riaffermarsi *vr.* to reaffirm oneself.

riafferrare *vt.* to grasp again. ◆ riafferrarsi *vr.* to catch (*v. irr.*) hold of (so., sth.) again.

riallacciare *vt.* 1. to fasten again 2. (*riprendere*) to resume.

riallargare *vt.* to widen again. ◆ riallargarsi *vr.* to widen again.

rialto *sm.* rise, height.

rialzamento *sm.* 1. raising 2. (*rialzo*) rise, height.

rialzare *vt.* 1. to raise 2. (*rendere più alto*) to make (*v. irr.*) higher. ◆ rialzarsi *vr.* to rise (*v. irr.*) again.

rialzato *agg.* piano —, ground floor.

rialzo *sm.* 1. rise 2. (*di sostegno*) support.

riamare *vt.* to love again.

riamméttere vt. to readmit.

rianimare vt. to revive. ♦ **rianimarsi** vr. 1. (riprendere allegria) to cheer up 2. (riprendere coraggio) to take (v. irr.) courage again.

riapertura sf. reopening.

riapparire vi. to reappear.

riaprire vt. to open again. ♦ **riaprirsi** vr. to open again.

riarmare vt. to rearm. ♦ **riarmarsi** vr. to rearm.

riarmo sm. rearmament.

riarso agg. parched.

riassestare vt. to readjust. ♦ **riassestarsi** vr. to readjust.

riassettare vt. to put (v. irr.) in order again.

riassetto sm. rearrangement.

riassorbire vt. to reabsorb.

riassùmere vt. 1. (assumere di nuovo) to take (v. irr.) on again 2. (riepilogare) to sum up 3. (riprendere) to resume.

riassuntivo agg. summarizing.

riassunto sm. summary.

riattaccare vt. 1. (con colla) to stick (v. irr.) again 2. (ricucire) to sew (v. irr.) 3. (riprendere) to begin (v. irr.) again 4. (mil.) to attack again 5. (tel.) to hang (v. irr.) up. ♦ **riattaccarsi** vr. to stick again.

riattamento sm. repair.

riattare vt. to repair.

riattivare vt. to restore.

riavere vt. 1. to have again 2. (ricuperare) to get (v. irr.) back. ♦ **riaversi** vr. to recover.

riavvicinare vt. 1. to approach again 2. (riconciliare) to reconcile. ♦ **riavvicinarsi** vr. to approach again 2. (riconciliarsi) to be reconciled.

ribadire vt. to rivet.

ribalderìa sf. rascality.

ribaldo sm. rascal.

ribalta sf. 1. (teat.) footlights (pl.) 2. (fig.) limelight.

ribaltàbile agg. overturnable.

ribaltare vt. to overturn. ♦ **ribaltarsi** vr. to capsize.

ribassare vt. to reduce. ♦ **ribassare** vi. to fall (v. irr.).

ribasso sm. 1. fall 2. (sconto) discount.

ribàttere vt. 1. to beat (v. irr.) again 2. (ribadire) to rivet 3. (confutare) to confute. ♦ **ribàttere** vi. to insist.

ribattezzare vt. to rename.

ribellarsi vr. to rebel.

ribelle agg. rebellious. ♦ **ribelle** s. rebel.

ribellione sf. rebellion.

ribes sm. gooseberry.

riboccante agg. overflowing (with).

riboccare vi. to overflow (with).

ribollimento sm. ebullition.

ribollire vi. to boil.

ribollitura sf. reboiling.

ribrezzo sm. disgust: fare —, to disgust.

ributtante agg. disgusting.

ributtare vt. 1. to throw (v. irr.) again 2. (respingere) to repel 3. (disgustare) to disgust.

ricacciare vt. 1. (respingere) to push (out, back) 2. (ficcare di nuovo) to thrust (v. irr.) again. ♦ **ricacciarsi** vr. to plunge again.

ricadere vi. 1. to fall (v. irr.) again 2. (avere una ricaduta) to relapse 3. (pendere) to hang (v. irr.).

ricaduta sf. relapse.

ricalcare vt. 1. to pull down 2. (un disegno) to transfer || — le orme di qu., to tread (v. irr.) in so.'s steps.

ricalcitrante agg. recalcitrant.

ricalcitrare vi. to recalcitrate.

ricamare vt. e vi. to embroider.

ricamatore sm. embroiderer.

ricamatrice sf. embroideress.

ricambiare vt. 1. to change again 2. (contraccambiare) to return.

ricambio sm. 1. replacement 2. (med.) metabolism || di —, spare (agg. attr.).

ricamo sm. embroidery: un —, a piece of embroidery.

ricapitolare vt. to summarize || ricapitolando, in short.

ricapitolazione sf. summary.

ricaricare vt. 1. to reload 2. (di batteria) to recharge 3. (di orologio) to wind (v. irr.) up again.

ricascare vi. V. ricadere.

ricattare vt. to blackmail.

ricattatore sm. blackmailer.

ricattatorio agg. blackmailing.

ricatto sm. blackmail.

ricavare vt. 1. to draw (v. irr.) 2. (ottenere) to get (v. irr.).

ricavato sm. proceeds (pl.).

ricavo sm. V. ricavato.

riccamente avv. richly.

ricchezza sf. wealth (solo sing.).

riccio[1] agg. curly.

riccio[2] *sm.* **1.** curl **2.** (*bot.*) chestnut husk **3.** (*zool.*) hedgehog **4.** (*di mare*) sea-urchin.

ricciuto *agg.* curly.

ricco *agg.* rich: — *di*, rich in.

ricerca *sf.* **1.** search **2.** (*scientifica*) research **3.** (*indagine*) investigation.

ricercare *vt.* **1.** (*cercare*) to seek (*v. irr.*) for **2.** (*investigare*) to investigate **3.** (*cercare di nuovo*) to look for (so., sthg.) again.

ricercatezza *sf.* refinement.

ricercato *agg.* **1.** (*richiesto*) sought-after **2.** (*raffinato*) refined **3.** (*insolito*) far-fetched **4.** (*dalla polizia*) wanted.

ricercatore *sm.* **1.** searcher **2.** (*scientifico*) researcher.

ricetta *sf.* **1.** (*med.*) prescription **2.** (*cuc.*) recipe.

ricettàcolo *sm.* receptacle.

ricettare *vt.* (*custodire cose rubate*) to receive.

ricettario *sm.* **1.** (*med.*) book of prescriptions **2.** (*cuc.*) book of recipes.

ricettatore *sm.* receiver.

ricettazione *sf.* receiving of stolen goods.

ricettività *sf.* receptivity.

ricettivo *agg.* receptive.

ricevente *agg.* receiving. ♦ **ricevente** *s.* receiver.

ricévere *vt.* to receive.

ricevimento *sm.* **1.** receipt **2.** (*festa*) party.

ricevitore *sm.* receiver.

ricevitoria *sf.* receiving-office.

ricevuta *sf.* receipt: *accusare* —, to acknowledge receipt.

ricezione *vt.* reception.

richiamare *vt.* **1.** to call again **2.** (*far tornare*) to recall **3.** (*attirare*) to attract **4.** (*rimproverare*) to rebuke ‖ — *all'ordine*, to call to order. ♦ **richiamarsi** *vr.* (*riferirsi*) to refer.

richiamata *sf.* recall.

richiamato *sm.* (*mil.*) re-drafted soldier.

richiamo *sm.* **1.** recall **2.** (*allettamento*) call.

richiedente *s.* applicant.

richièdere *vt.* **1.** to ask (for sthg., so.) again **2.** (*chiedere*) to ask for **3.** (*in restituzione*) to ask (for sthg.) back **4.** (*necessitare di*) to require.

richiesta *sf.* **1.** request: *dietro* —, at request **2.** (*comm.*) demand.

richiùdere *vt.* to close again. ♦ **richiùdersi** *vr.* to close again.

ricino *sm.* castor-oil plant: *olio di* —, castor-oil.

ricognitore *sm.* (*mil.*) scout.

ricognizione *sf.* reconnaissance.

ricollegare *vt.* to connect. ♦ **ricollegarsi** *vr.* to be connected.

ricollocamento *sm.* replacement.

ricolmare *vt.* **1.** to fill up **2.** (*fig.*) to load.

ricolmo *agg.* **1.** full **2.** (*fig.*) loaded (with).

ricominciare *vt.* to begin (*v. irr.*) again.

ricomparire *vi.* to reappear.

ricompensa *sf.* reward: *in* —, as a reward.

ricompensare *vt.* to reward.

ricomprare *vt.* to buy (*v. irr.*) again.

ricomporre *vt.* to recompose.

ricomposizione *sf.* recomposition.

riconciliare *vt.* to reconcile. ♦ **riconciliarsi** *vr.* to be reconciled.

riconciliatore *sm.* reconciler.

riconciliazione *sf.* reconciliation.

ricondurre *vt.* to take (*v. irr.*) back, to bring (*v. irr.*) back.

riconferma *sf.* reconfirmation.

riconfermare *vt.* to reconfirm.

riconfortare *vt.* to cheer up. ♦ **riconfortarsi** *vr.* to cheer up.

ricongiùngere *vt.* to join again. ♦ **ricongiùngersi** *vr.* to join again.

ricongiungimento *sm.* reunion.

riconnèttere *vt.* to connect again.

riconoscente *agg.* grateful.

riconoscenza *sf.* gratitude.

riconóscere *vt.* to recognize.

riconoscìbile *agg.* recognizable.

riconoscimento *sm.* **1.** recognition **2.** (*ammissione*) admission.

riconquista *sf.* recapture.

riconquistare *vt.* to conquer again.

riconsegna *sf.* return.

riconsegnare *vt.* to redeliver.

riconsiderare *vt.* to reconsider.

riconversione *sf.* reconversion.

riconvocare *vt.* to resummon.

riconvocazione *sf.* resummons.

ricopiare *vt.* to copy.

ricopiatura *sf.* (re)copying.

ricoprire *vt.* **1.** to cover **2.** (*coprire di nuovo*) to cover again **3.** (*fig.*) to load.

ricordare vt. 1. to remember 2. (chiamare alla memoria altrui) to remind (so. of sthg.) 3. (nominare) to mention. ♦ **ricordarsi** vr. to remember.

ricordo sm. 1. memory 2. (oggetto ricordo) souvenir 3. (memorie) (lett.) memoirs (pl.).

ricorrente agg. recurrent.

ricorrenza sf. 1. recurrence 2. (anniversario) anniversary 3. (occasione) occasion.

ricòrrere vi. 1. (ripetersi) to recur 2. (rivòlgersi) to apply 3. (fare appello) to appeal 4. (valersi) to resort.

ricorso sm. 1. (ritorno) return 2. (appello) appeal || su — di, on a petition by.

ricostituente agg. e sm. tonic.

ricostituire vt. to form again. ♦ **ricostituirsi** vr. to form again.

ricostituzione sf. reconstitution.

ricostruire vt. to reconstruct.

ricostruttore agg. reconstructive. ♦ **ricostruttore** sm. reconstructor.

ricostruzione sf. reconstruction.

ricoverare vt. to shelter: — in ospedale, to hospitalize. ♦ **ricoverarsi** vr. to take (v. irr.) shelter.

ricòvero sm. 1. sheltering 2. (in ospedale) hospitalization 3. (ospizio) home.

ricreare¹ vt. to re-create.

ricreare² vt. (divertire) to recreate. ♦ **ricrearsi** vr. to recreate.

ricreativo agg. recreative.

ricreazione sf. recreation: ora della —, playtime.

ricrédersi vr. to change one's mind.

ricréscere vi. to grow (v. irr.) again.

ricréscita sf. fresh growth.

ricucire vt. 1. to sew (v. irr.) up 2. (cucire di nuovo) to sew (v. irr.) again.

ricucitura sf. sewing up.

ricuòcere vt. e vi. 1. to cook again 2. (al forno) to bake again.

ricuperàbile agg. recoverable.

ricuperare vt. 1. to recover 2. (di tempo) to make (v. irr.) up for.

ricùpero sm. recovery.

ricurvare vt. 1. to bend (v. irr.) 2. (curvare di nuovo) to bend again.

ricurvo agg. bent.

ricusàbile agg. refusable.

ricusare vt. to refuse.

ridacchiare vi. to giggle.

ridanciano agg. jolly.

ridare vt. 1. to give (v. irr.) again 2. (restituire) to return.

ridda sf. turmoil.

ridente agg. 1. smiling 2. (di luogo) charming.

rìdere vi. to laugh (at): per —, for fun. ♦ **rìdersi** vr. to make (v. irr.) fun (of).

ridestare vt. 1. to wake (v. irr.) (up) again 2. (destare) to awaken. ♦ **ridestarsi** vr. 1. to wake (up) again 2. (destarsi) to awake.

ridicolàggine sf. nonsense (solo sing.).

ridìcolo agg. ridiculous. ♦ **ridìcolo** sm. ridicule.

ridimensionare vt. to reorganize.

ridire vt. 1. to say (v. irr.) again, to tell (v. irr.) again 2. (riferire) to repeat 3. (obiettare) to object.

ridiscéndere vi. to come (v. irr.) down again, to go (v. irr.) down again.

ridiscòrrere vi. to talk again.

ridiventare vi. to become (v. irr.) again.

ridomandare vt. to ask again.

ridonare vt. 1. to give (v. irr.) again 2. (restituire) to give back.

ridondante agg. redundant.

ridondanza sf. redundancy.

ridondare vi. 1. to be redundant 2. (risultare) to redound.

ridosso (nella loc. avv.) a — di, close to.

ridotta sf. redoubt.

ridotto agg. 1. reduced 2. (di libro) abridged || mal —, in a sorry plight. ♦ **ridotto** sm. (teat.) foyer.

riducente agg. reducing. ♦ **riducente** sm. reducer.

riducìbile agg. reducible.

ridurre vt. 1. to reduce 2. (adattare) to adapt 3. (un libro) to abridge. ♦ **ridursi** vr. 1. to be reduced 2. (restringersi) to shrink (v. irr.).

riduttore agg. e sm. V. riducente.

riduzione sf. 1. reduction 2. (sconto) discount 3. (cine; tv) adaptation 4. (di libro) abridgement.

riecheggiare vt. e vi. to re-echo.

riedificare vt. to rebuild (v. irr.).

riedificazione sf. rebuilding.

rieducare vt. to re-educate.

rieducazione sf. re-education.

rielaborare vt. to re-elaborate.

rieleggere vt. to re-elect.

rieleggibile agg. re-eligible.

rielezione sf. re-election.

riemergere vi. to re-emerge.

riemersione sf. re-emergence.

riempire vt. to fill. ♦ **riempirsi** vr. to fill.

riempitivo sm. filling.

rientrante agg. receding.

rientranza sf. recess.

rientrare vi. 1. to re-enter 2. (tornare) to return 3. (far parte) to be part (of) 4. (piegare in dentro) to recede.

rientro sm. 1. recess 2. (astronautica) retro-firing 3. (ritorno) return.

riepilogare vt. to recapitulate.

riepilogo sm. recapitulation.

riesame sm. re-examination.

riesaminare vt. to re-examine.

riessere vi. to be again.

riesumare vt. 1. to exhume 2. (fig.) to bring (v. irr.) to light.

rievocare vt. to recall.

rievocazione sf. recalling.

rifacimento sm. 1. reconstruction 2. (adattamento) adaptation.

rifare vt. 1. to do (v. irr.) again, to make (v. irr.) again 2. (ripercorrere) to retrace 3. (riparare) to repair 4. (imitare) to imitate 5. (indennizzare) to indemnify. ♦ **rifarsi** vr. 1. to make up 2. (vendicarsi) to revenge oneself 3. (risalire) to go (v. irr.) back.

rifasciare vt. 1. to bandage again 2. (un bambino) to swaddle again.

riferibile agg. 1. referable 2. (raccontabile) fit to be told.

riferimento sm. reference: linea, punto di —, datum-line, datum-point.

riferire vt. 1. to report 2. (attribuire) to ascribe. ♦ **riferirsi** vr. to refer.

rificcare vt. to thrust (v. irr.) again.

rifilare vt. 1. to spin again 2. (tagliare a filo) to trim 3. (appioppare) to palm off.

rifilatura sf. 1. trimming 2. (bordo) border.

rifinimento sm. finishing touch.

rifinire vt. to finish.

rifinitura sf. V. rifinimento.

rifiorire vi. 1. to blossom again 2. (fig.) to flourish again.

rifioritura sf. reflorescence.

rifiutàbile agg. refusable.

rifiutare vt. to refuse.

rifiuto sm. refusal || rifiuti, waste (solo sing.); i rifiuti della società, the dregs of society.

riflessione sf. reflection.

riflessivo agg. 1. reflective 2. (gramm.) reflexive.

riflesso agg. reflected, reflex (anche fig.). ♦ **riflesso** sm. 1. reflection 2. (di colore) tint 3. (med.) reflex || di —, as a consequence; per —, indirectly.

riflèttere vt. e vi. to reflect. ♦ **riflèttersi** vr. to be reflected.

riflettore sm. 1. reflector 2. (lampada) searchlight.

rifluire vi. 1. to flow again 2. (fluire indietro) to flow back.

riflusso sm. ebb.

rifocillare vt. to give (v. irr.) refreshment. ♦ **rifocillarsi** vr. to take (v. irr.) refreshment.

rifòndere vt. 1. to melt again 2. (rimborsare) to refund.

riforma sf. reformation.

riformare vt. 1. to reform 2. (mil.) to declare unfit for military service.

riformatore sm. reformer.

riformatorio sm. reformatory.

riformismo sm. reformism.

riformista s. reformist.

rifornimento sm. 1. supplying 2. (aer.; auto) refuelling 3. (scorta) supply || stazione di —, filling-station; far — di benzina, to fill up the tank.

rifornire vt. to supply (so. with).

rifornitore sm. supplier.

rifràngere vt. to refract. ♦ **rifràngersi** vr. to be refracted.

rifrangibilità sf. refrangibility.

rifrattore sm. refractor.

rifrazione sf. refraction.

rifritto agg. 1. fried again 2. (fig.) stale.

rifuggire vi. 1. to escape again 2. (essere alieno) to shrink (v. irr.).

rifugiarsi vr. to take (v. irr.) shelter.

rifugiato agg. e sm. refugee.

rifugio sm. 1. shelter 2. (di montagna) mountain hut.

rifulgere vi. to shine (v. irr.) brightly (with sthg.).

rifusione sf. 1. re-melting 2. (rimborso) repayment.

riga sf. 1. line 2. (fila) row 3. (regolo) rule 4. (striscia) stripe 5. (scriminatura) parting 6. (mus.

stave || *mettersi in* —, to line up.

rigaglie *sf. pl.* giblets.

rigàgnolo *sm.* 1. rivulet 2. (*scolo*) gutter.

rigare *vt.* 1. to rule 2. (*solcare*) to furrow || — *diritto*, to behave well.

rigato *agg.* 1. ruled 2. (*a strisce*) striped 3. (*solcato*) furrowed.

rigattiere *sm.* second-hand dealer.

rigatura *sf.* 1. ruling 2. (*di arma*) rifling.

rigenerare *vt.* 1. to regenerate 2. (*mecc.*) to repair.

rigeneratore *agg.* regenerative. ◆ **rigeneratore** *sm.* regenerator.

rigenerazione *sf.* regeneration.

rigettare *vt.* 1. to throw (*v. irr.*) again 2. (*gettare indietro*) to throw back 3. (*vomitare*) to vomit 4. (*respingere*) to reject..

rigetto *sm.* rejection.

righello *sm.* ruler.

rigidezza *sf.* 1. stiffness 2. (*di clima*) rigour.

rigidità *sf.* V. *rigidezza*.

rìgido *agg.* 1. stiff 2. (*di clima*) rigorous.

rigirare *vt.* 1. to turn again 2. (*cambiare*) to change. ◆ **rigirare** *vi.* to walk about. ◆ **rigirarsi** *vr.* to turn about.

rigiro *sm.* 1. turning round 2. (*di parole*) involved expression.

rigo *sm.* V. *riga*.

rigòglio *sm.* bloom.

rigogliosità *sf.* luxuriancy.

rigoglioso *agg.* flourishing.

rigonfiamento *sm.* swelling.

rigonfiare *vt.* to swell (*v. irr.*). ◆ **rigonfiarsi** *vr.* to swell.

rigonfio *agg.* swollen (with). ◆ **rigonfio** *sm.* swelling.

rigore *sm.* 1. rigour 2. (*esattezza*) exactness || *di* —, compulsory; *a* —, according to the rules; *a* — *di termini*, in the strict sense, *area di* — (*sport*), penalty-area.

rigorismo *sm.* rigorism.

rigorista *s.* rigorist.

rigorosità *sf.* 1. rigour 2. (*esattezza*) preciseness.

rigoroso *agg.* 1. rigorous 2. (*esatto*) exact.

rigovernare *vt.* 1. to govern again 2. (*di piatti*) to wash up.

rigovernatura *sf.* washing-up.

riguadagnare *vt.* 1. to earn again

2. (*ricuperare, raggiungere*) to regain.

riguardare *vt.* 1. to look at (so., sthg.) again 2. (*esaminare*) to examine 3. (*considerare*) to regard. ◆ **riguardarsi** *vr.* to take (*v. irr.*) care of oneself.

riguardata *sf.* look.

riguardévole *agg.* 1. considerable 2. (*importante*) important.

riguardo *sm.* 1. regard 2. (*cura*) care || *persona di* —, person of consequence; — *a*, as regards; *a questo* —, in this connection.

riguardoso *agg.* respectful.

rigurgitare *vi.* 1. to overflow 2. (*di stomaco*) to regurgitate 3. (*brulicare*) to swarm (with).

rigùrgito *sm.* 1. overflow 2. (*di stomaco*) regurgitation 3. (*travaso*) extravasation 4. (*gorgo*) eddy.

rilanciare *vt.* 1. to throw (*v. irr.*) again 2. (*lanciare indietro*) to throw back 3. (*un'offerta*) to raise.

rilancio *sm.* 1. new throw 2. (*di offerta*) raising.

rilasciare *vt.* 1. to release 2. (*concedere*) to grant 3. (*emettere*) to issue. ◆ **rilasciarsi** *vr.* 1. to slacken 2. (*med.*) to prolapse 3. (*rilassarsi*) to relax.

rilascio *sm.* 1. release 2. (*concessione*) granting 3. (*emissione*) issue.

rilassamento *sm.* 1. slackening 2. (*med.*) prolapse 3. (*riposo*) relaxation.

rilassare *vt.,* 1. to slacken 2. (*distendere*) to relax. ◆ **rilassarsi** *vr.* 1. to slacken 2. (*distendersi*) to relax.

rilassatezza *sf.* laxity.

rilegare *vt.* 1. to tie again 2. (*libri*) to bind (*v. irr.*).

rilegatura *sf.* binding.

rilèggere *vt.* to reread (*v. irr.*), to read (*v. irr.*) again.

rilento (*nella loc. avv.*) *a* —, slowly.

rilevamento *sm.* 1. (*topografico*) survey 2. (*mar.*) bearing 3. (*cambio*) relieving.

rilevante *agg.* prominent.

rilevare *vt.* 1. to take (*v. irr.*) off again 2. (*notare*) to notice 3. (*far notare*) to point out 4. (*prendere*) to take 5. (*topografia*) to survey 6. (*sostituire*) to relieve 7. (*comm.*) to take over.

rilevazione sf. V. rilievo.

rilievo sm. 1. relief 2. (importanza) importance 3. (osservazione) remark 4. (topografico) survey 5. (comm.) taking over ‖ mettere in —, to stress.

rilucente agg. glittering.

rilùcere vi. to glitter.

riluttante agg. reluctant.

riluttanza sf. reluctance.

riluttare vi. to reluct (at).

rima sf. rhyme ‖ rispondere per le rime, to give (v. irr.) tit for tat.

rimandare vt. 1. to send (v. irr.) again 2. (restituire) to send back 3. (posporre) to postpone 4. (far riferimento) to refer 5. (agli esami) to make (v. irr.) (so.) repeat (an exam).

rimando sm. 1. returning 2. (differimento) postponement 3. (segno di richiamo) reference-mark.

rimaneggiamento sm. 1. rearrangement 2. (di opera letteraria) adaptation 3. (pol.) shuffle.

rimaneggiare vt. 1. to rearrange 2. (modificare) to change 3. (pol.) to shuffle.

rimanente agg. remaining. ♦ **rimanente** sm. rest.

rimanenza sf. remainder.

rimanere vi. 1. to remain 2. (avanzare) to be left 3. (essere sorpreso) to be astonished.

rimangiare vt. to eat (v. irr.) again. ♦ **rimangiarsi** vr. to take (v. irr.) back.

rimarchévole agg. remarkable.

rimare vt. e vi. to rhyme.

rimarginare vt. to heal. ♦ **rimarginarsi** vr. to heal.

rimaritare vt. to marry again. ♦ **rimaritarsi** vr. to marry again.

rimasticare vt. 1. to chew again 2. (fig.) to muse.

rimasuglio sm. remains (pl.).

rimatore sm. rhymer.

rimbalzare vi. to rebound.

rimbalzello sm. ducks and drakes.

rimbalzo sm. rebound: di —, on the rebound.

rimbambimento sm. dotage.

rimbambire vi. to reach one's dotage.

rimbambito agg. in one's dotage (pred.): un vecchio —, a dotard.

rimbeccare vt. to retort.

rimbecco sm. retort.

rimbecillire vi. 1. to grow (v. irr.) stupid 2. (per età) to reach one's dotage.

rimbecillito agg. doting.

rimboccare vt. to tuck up. ♦ rimboccarsi vr. to tuck up.

rimbombante agg. thundering.

rimbombare vi. 1. to thunder 2. (risuonare) to resound.

rimbombo sm. roar.

rimborsàbile agg. repayable.

rimborsare vt. to reimburse.

rimborso sm. reimbursement.

rimboscare vt. V. rimboschire.

rimboschimento sm. reafforestation.

rimboschire vt. to reafforest. ♦ rimboschirsi vr. to become (v. irr.) wooded again.

rimbrottare vt. to reproach.

rimbrotto sm. reproach.

rimediàbile agg. remediable.

rimediare vi. to find (v. irr.) a remedy (for).

rimedio sm. remedy.

rimembranza sf. memory.

rimembrare vt. to remember.

rimeritare vt. to reward.

rimescolamento sm. 1. stir 2. (turbamento) shock.

rimescolare vt. 1. to stir again 2. (mescolare) to stir. ♦ **rimescolarsi** vr. to be upset ‖ gli si rimescolò il sangue (per rabbia), his blood boiled, (per paura), his blood ran cold.

rimescolìo sm. confusion.

rimessa sf. 1. replacing 2. (per auto) garage 3. (di denaro) remittance 4. (di merci) consignment ‖ — in gioco, throw-in.

rimesso agg. 1. (falso) false 2. (ristabilito) well again 3. (perdonato) forgiven.

rimestare vt. V. rimescolare.

riméttere vt. 1. to put (v. irr.) again, to put back 2. (consegnare) to hand 3. (mandare, perdonare) to remit 4. (affidare) to leave (v. irr.) 5. (vomitare) to vomit ‖ — in gioco, to throw (v. irr.) in; rimetterci, to lose (v. irr.). ♦ **riméttersi** vr. 1. (affidarsi) to rely on 2. (ristabilirsi) to recover 3. (rasserenarsi) to clear up.

rimirare vt. to gaze (at). ♦ **rimirarsi** vr. to admire oneself.

rimisurare vt. to measure again.

rimodellare vt. to remodel.

rimodernamento *sm.* modernization.

rimodernare *vt.* to modernize. ◆ **rimodernarsi** *vr.* to become up-to-date.

rimondare *vt.* to clean again.

rimonta *sf.* 1. (*mil.*) remount 2. (*sport*) catching up.

rimontare *vt.* 1. to go (*v. irr.*) up 2. (*ricomporre*) to reassemble. ◆ **rimontare** *vi.* 1. to remount 2. (*fig.*) to go back 3. (*sport*) to catch (*v. irr.*) up ‖ — *in auto*, to get (*v. irr.*) into a car again.

rimorchiare *vt.* to tow.

rimorchiatore *sm.* tug.

rimorchio *sm.* 1. tow 2. (*veicolo*) trailer.

rimòrdere *vt.* 1. to bite (*v. irr.*) again 2. (*fig.*) to prick.

rimorso *sm.* remorse.

rimosso *agg.* removed.

rimostranza *sf.* remonstrance: *fare le proprie rimostranze*, to remonstrate.

rimostrare *vi.* to remonstrate.

rimovìbile *agg.* removable.

rimozione *sf.* removal.

rimpacchettare *vt.* to package again.

rimpadronirsi *vr.* to seize again.

rimpagliare *vt.* 1. to re-cover with straw 2. (*imbottire*) to re-stuff with straw.

rimpallo *sm.* counterblow.

rimpannucciarsi *vr.* (*fig.*) to improve one's financial position.

rimpastare *vt.* 1. to knead again 2. (*fig.*) to rearrange.

rimpasto *sm.* 1. kneading again 2. (*fig.*) rearrangement 3. (*pol.*) reshuffle.

rimpatriare *vt.* to repatriate. ◆ **rimpatriare** *vi.* to return to one's country.

rimpatrio *sm.* repatriation.

rimpetto *avv.* opposite.

rimpiàngere *vt.* 1. to regret 2. (*una perdita*) to mourn.

rimpianto *sm.* regret.

rimpiattarsi *vr.* to hide (*v. irr.*) oneself.

rimpiattino *sm.* hide-and-seek.

rimpiazzare *vt.* to replace.

rimpiazzo *sm.* replacement.

rimpicciolire *vt.* to lessen. ◆ **rimpicciolirsi** *vr.* to lessen.

rimpiegare *vt.* to re-employ.

rimpiego *sm.* re-employment.

rimpinguare *vt.* 1. to fatten 2. (*arricchire*) to enrich. ◆ **rimpinguarsi** *vr.* 1. to fatten 2. (*arricchirsi*) to grow (*v. irr.*) rich.

rimpinzare *vt.* to stuff (with).

rimpolpare *vt.* V. *rimpinguare*.

rimproverare *vt.* to reproach.

rimpròvero *sm.* reproach: *muovere un —*, to reproach.

rimuginare *vt.* to brood over.

rimunerare *vt.* to remunerate.

rimuòvere *vt.* 1. to remove 2. (*dissuadere*) to dissuade 3. (*da una carica*) to dismiss.

rimutare *vt.* to change again.

rinascenza *sf.* Renaissance.

rinàscere *vi.* to revive.

rinascimentale *agg.* Renaissance (*attr.*).

rinascimento *sm.* Renaissance.

rinàscita *sf.* 1. rebirth 2. (*fig.*) revival.

rincagnarsi *vr.* to frown.

rincagnato *agg.* pug (*attr.*).

rincalzare *vt.* 1. (*rimboccare*) to tuck in 2. (*sostenere*) to prop up.

rincalzo *sm.* support: *a — di*, in support of.

rincantucciare *vt.* to put (*v. irr.*) in a corner. ◆ **rincantucciarsi** *vr.* to hide (*v. irr.*) in a corner.

rincarare *vt.* 1. to raise the price of 2. (*esagerare*) to exaggerate. ◆ **rincarare** *vi.* to become (*v. irr.*) more expensive.

rincaro *sm.* rise in prices.

rincasare *vi.* to return home.

rinchiùdere *vt.* to shut (*v. irr.*) up.

rincitrullire *vt.* to make (*v. irr.*) silly. ◆ **rincitrullirsi** *vr.* to grow (*v. irr.*) silly.

rincivilire *vt.* to civilize. ◆ **rincivilirsi** *vr.* 1. to become (*v. irr.*) civilized 2. (*raffinarsi*) to become refined.

rincollare *vt.* to paste again.

rincominciare *vt.* to begin (*v. irr.*) again.

rincontrare *vt.* to meet (*v. irr.*) again. ◆ **rincontrarsi** *vr.* to meet again.

rincontro *sm.* meeting.

rincoramento *sm.* encouragement.

rincorare *vt.* to encourage. ◆ **rincorarsi** *vr.* to pluck up courage.

rincòrrere *vt.* to run (*v. irr.*) after.

rincorsa *sf.* run-up.

rincréscere *vi.* 1. to be sorry: *mi*

rincresce, I am sorry 2. (dar noia) to mind: ti rincresce aprire la finestra?, do you mind opening the window?

rincrescimento sm. regret: con mio —, to my regret.

rincrudimento sm. aggravation.

rincrudire vi. 1. to aggravate 2. (esacerbare) to embitter 3. (del tempo) to get (v. irr.) worse.

rinculare vi. to recoil.

rinculo sm. recoil.

rinfacciare vt. to throw (v. irr.) (sthg.) in so.'s face.

rinfiancare vt. to support.

rinfilare vt. 1. to thread again 2. (rinserire) to insert again. ♦ rinfilarsi vr. 1. (introdursi) to slip again 2. (rindossare) to slip on again.

rinfiorare vt. to adorn with flowers again.

rinfittire vt. 1. to thicken 2. (rendere più frequenti) to make (v. irr.) more frequent. ♦ rinfittirsi vr. (di lana) to shrink (v. irr.).

rinfocolare vt. 1. to poke 2. (fig.) to stir up (again).

rinfoderare vt. to sheathe (again).

rinforzamento sm. strengthening.

rinforzare vt. 1. to strengthen 2. (mecc.) to stiffen. ♦ rinforzarsi vr. to become (v. irr.) stronger.

rinforzo sm. 1. strengthening 2. (mil.) reinforcements (pl.) 3. (fig.) support 4. (mecc.) stiffener.

rinfrancare vt. to encourage. ♦ rinfrancarsi vr. 1. (migliorare) to improve 2. (riprendere coraggio) to pluck up courage.

rinfrescamento sm. cooling.

rinfrescante agg. refreshing.

rinfrescare vt. 1. to cool 2. (ristorare) to refresh 3. (rinnovare) to renovate. ♦ rinfrescare vi. to cool.

rinfresco sm. 1. refreshments (pl.) 2. (ricevimento) cocktail party.

rinfusa (nella loc. avv.) alla —, in confusion.

ringalluzzire vt. to make (v. irr.) cocky. ♦ ringalluzzirsi vr. to become (v. irr.) cocky.

ringentilire vt. to refine.

ringhiare vi. to snarl.

ringhiera sf. 1. railing 2. (di scale) banisters (pl.).

ringhio sm. snarl.

ringhioso agg. snarling

ringiovanimento sm. rejuvenation.

ringiovanire vt. 1. to make (v. irr.) young again 2. (far sembrare più giovane) to make (so.) look younger. ♦ ringiovanire vi. 1. to grow (v. irr.) young again 2. (sembrare più giovane) to look younger.

ringioire vt. to swallow up again.

ringranare vt. to re-engage.

ringraziamento sm. thanks (pl.).

ringraziare vt. to thank.

ringuainare vt. V. rinfoderare.

rinite sf. rhinitis.

rinnegàbile agg. deniable.

rinnegamento sm. disowning.

rinnegare vt. to disown.

rinnegato agg. e sm. renegade.

rinnegatore sm. disowner.

rinnestare vt. 1. (agr.) to graft again 2. (mecc.) to re-engage.

rinnesto sm. 1. (agr.) new grafting 2. (mecc.) re-engagement.

rinnovàbile agg. renewable.

rinnovamento sm. renewal.

rinnovare vt. to renew. ♦ rinnovarsi vr. (riaccadere) to happen again.

rinnovatore sm. renewer.

rinnovazione sf. renewal.

rinnovellare vt. to renew. ♦ rinnovellarsi vr. to be renewed.

rinnovo sm. renewal.

rinoceronte sm. rhinoceros.

rinolaringite sf. rhinolaryngitis.

rinologia sf. rhinology.

rinomanza sf. renown.

rinomato agg. renowned.

rinominare vt. 1. to name again 2. (designare di nuovo) to reappoint.

rinoplàstica sf. rhinoplasty.

rinoscopia sf. rhinoscopy.

rinoscopio sm. rhinoscope.

rinsaccare vt. to pack again. ♦ rinsaccarsi vr. to shrug one's shoulders.

rinsaldamento sm. consolidation.

rinsaldare vt. to consolidate.

rinsanguare vt. 1. to supply with new blood 2. (fig.) to reinvigorate. ♦ rinsanguarsi vr. 1. to recover 2. (finanziariamente) to re-establish one's financial condition.

rinsanire vi. 1. to recover 2. (rinsavire) to return to reason.

rinsavimento sm. return to reason.

rinsavire vi. to recover one's wits.

rinsecchire vi. 1. to dry up 2. (di persone) to get (v. irr.) thin 3.

(*avvizzire*) to wither.

rinserrare *vt.* to shut (*v. irr.*) up (again).

rintanarsi *vr.* to shut (*v. irr.*) oneself up.

rintascare *vt.* to pocket again.

rintavolare *vt.* to start again.

rintoccare *vi.* 1. (*di orologio*) to strike (*v. irr.*) 2. (*di campana*) to toll.

rintocco *sm.* 1. (*di orologio*) stroke 2. (*di campana*) toll.

rintontire *vt.* to stun. ♦ **rintontirsi** *vr.* to be stunned.

rintracciare *vt.* 1. to trace 2. (*trovare*) to find (*v. irr.*) out.

rintronamento *sm.* booming.

rintronare *vt.* 1. to deafen 2. (*stordire*) to stun. ♦ **rintronare** *vi.* to boom.

rintuzzare *vt.* 1. to blunt 2. (*ribattere*) to retort.

rinuncia *sf.* renouncement.

rinunciare *vi.* to renounce (sthg.).

rinunciatario *agg.* releasee.

rinvenimento *sm.* recovery.

rinvenire *vt.* to find (*v. irr.*). ♦ **rinvenire** *vi.* 1. to recover one's senses 2. (*riprendere freschezza*) to revive 3. (*riprendere morbidezza*) to soften.

rinverdire *vt.* (*ravvivare*) to reawaken. ♦ **rinverdire** *vi.* 1. to turn green again 2. (*ravvivarsi*) to revive.

rinvestimento *sm.* reinvestment.

rinvestire *vt.* 1. to restore to the possession of 2. (*comm.*) to reinvest.

rinviare *vt.* 1. to put (*v. irr.*) off 2. (*mandare indietro*) to return.

rinvigorimento *sm.* reinvigoration.

rinvigorire *vt.* to reinvigorate. ♦ **rinvigorirsi** *vr.* to regain strength.

rinvilire *vt.* to lower. ♦ **rinvilire** *vi.* to become (*v. irr.*) cheaper.

rinvio *sm.* 1. postponement 2. (*il rimandare indietro*) returning.

rinvoltare *vt.* to wrap up again.

rinzaffare *vt.* 1. to bung again 2. (*arch.*) to rough in.

rinzaffatura *sf.* (*arch.*) roughing-in coat.

rio¹ *sm.* rivulet.

rio² *agg.* evil.

rioccupare *vt.* to reoccupy.

rioccupazione *sf.* reoccupation.

rionale *agg.* local, ward (*attr.*).

rione *sm.* ward, district.

riordinare *vt.* 1. to tidy up 2. (*riorganizzare*) to reorganize 3. (*comandare di nuovo*) to order again.

riordinatore *sm.* 1. rearranger 2. (*riorganizzatore*) reorganizer.

riordinazione *sf.* 1. rearrangement 2. (*riorganizzazione*) reorganization 3. (*nuova ordinazione*) new order.

riòrdino *sm.* V. *riordinazione*.

riorganizzare *vt.* to reorganize.

riorganizzatore *sm.* reorganizer.

riorganizzazione *sf.* reorganization.

riottosità *sf.* 1. turbulence 2. (*indocilità*) indocility.

riottoso *agg.* 1. turbulent 2. (*indocile*) indocile.

ripa *sf.* 1. bank 2. (*scarpata*) scarp.

ripagare *vt.* 1. to repay (*v. irr.*) 2. (*pagare di nuovo*) to pay (*v. irr.*) again.

riparare *vt.* 1. (*proteggere*) to shelter 2. (*aggiustare*) to repair 3. (*risarcire*) to redress || — *un esame*, to repeat an exam. ♦ **riparare** *vi.* 1. (*porre rimedio*) to remedy 2. (*rifugiarsi*) to take (*v. irr.*) shelter. ♦ **ripararsi** *vr.* to take shelter.

riparatore *agg.* repairing. ♦ **riparatore** *sm.* repairer.

riparazione *sf.* 1. repair: *in* —, under repair 2. (*fig.*) reparation.

riparlare *vi.* to speak (*v. irr.*) again.

riparo *sm.* 1. shelter 2. (*rimedio*) remedy 3. (*mecc.*) guard.

ripartire¹ *vi.* to start again.

ripartire² *vt.* to divide.

ripartizione *sf.* division.

ripassare *vi.* to pass again 2. (*far vista*) to call again. ♦ **ripassare** *vt.* 1. (*riattraversare*) to cross again 2. (*dare di nuovo*) to pass again 3. (*rileggere, rivedere*) to go (*v. irr.*) through 4. (*mecc.*) to overhaul.

ripassata *sf.* 1. (*revisione*) revision 2. (*mecc.*) overhauling 3. (*pulita*) cleaning 4. (*mano di vernice*) new coat.

ripasso *sf.* 1. (*ritorno*) return 2. (*revisione*) revision 3. (*di lezioni*) review.

ripensamento *sm.* reflection: *avere un* —, to change one's mind.

ripensare *vi.* 1. to think (*v. irr.*) (of sthg., so.) again 2. (*riconside-*

rare) to think over **3.** (*cambiar parere*) to change one's mind: *ci ho ripensato*, I have changed my mind.

ripercorrere *vt.* to travel over (sthg.) again.

ripercuòtere *vt.* to strike (*v. irr.*) again. ♦ **ripercuòtersi** *vr.* **1.** to reverberate **2.** (*fig.*) to influence (so., sthg.).

ripercussione *sf.* repercussion.

ripescare *vt.* **1.** to catch (*v. irr.*) again **2.** (*ritrovare*) to find (*v. irr.*) again.

ripetente *s.* repeater.

ripètere *vt.* to repeat.

ripetitore *sm.* **1.** repeater **2.** (*scol.*) private tutor.

ripetizione *sf.* **1.** (*rifacimento*) repetition **2.** (*ripasso*) revision **3.** (*lezione privata*) private lesson ‖ *arma a* —, repeater.

ripetuto *agg.* repeated.

ripiano *sm.* **1.** (*terreno*) terrace **2.** (*pianerottolo*) landing **3.** (*scaffale*) shelf (*pl.* -lves).

ripicco *sm.* spite: *per* —, out of spite.

ripidezza *sf.* steepness.

rìpido *agg.* steep.

ripiegamento *sm.* **1.** folding **2.** (*il curvare*) bending **3.** (*mil.*) withdrawal.

ripiegare *vt.* **1.** to bend (*v. irr.*) again **2.** (*piegare*) to fold. ♦ **ripiegare** *vi.* **1.** to bend **2.** (*ritirarsi*) to withdraw (*v. irr.*). ♦ **ripiegarsi** *vr.* to bend.

ripiegatura *sf.* **1.** folding **2.** (*piega*) fold **2.** (*curva*) bend.

ripiego *sm.* expedient **2.** (*rimedio*) remedy.

ripienezza *sf.* fullness.

ripieno *agg.* **1.** full **2.** (*cuc.*) stuffed (with). ♦ **ripieno** *sm.* **1.** filling **2.** (*cuc.*) stuffing.

ripigliare *vt.* V. *riprendere.*

ripiombare *vt.* to plunge back. ♦ **ripiombare** *vi.* to fall (*v. irr.*) again.

ripopolamento *sm.* **1.** repeopling **2.** (*di animali*) restocking.

ripopolare *vt.* **1.** to repeople **2.** (*di animali*) to restock.

riporre *vt.* **1.** to replace **2.** (*metter via*) to put (*v. irr.*) away **3.** (*porre*) to place. ♦ **riporsi** *vr.* (*riprendere*) to resume.

riportare *vt.* **1.** to bring (*v. irr.*)

again, to take (*v. irr.*) again **2.** (*portare indietro*) to bring back, to take back **3.** (*riferire*) to report **4.** (*citare*) to quote **5.** (*ricevere*) to get (*v. irr.*) **6.** (*mat.*) to carry. ♦ **riportarsi** *vr.* (*tornare*) to go (*v. irr.*) back.

riporto *sm.* **1.** (*mat.*) carry over **2.** (*in borsa*) contango **3.** (*ornamento*) appliqué.

riposante *agg.* restful.

riposare *vt.* to rest **2.** (*posare di nuovo*) to place back. ♦ **riposare** *vi.* to rest. ♦ **riposarsi** *vr.* to rest.

riposato *agg.* **1.** (*fresco*) fresh **2.** (*tranquillo*) quiet.

riposo *sm.* rest: *andare a* —, to retire.

ripostiglio *sm.* cupboard.

riprèndere *vt.* **1.** to take (*v. irr.*) again **2.** (*riavere*) to take back **3.** (*riassumere, ricominciare*) to resume **4.** (*ricuperare*) to recover **5.** (*rimproverare*) to reprove **6.** (*teat.*) to revive **7.** (*cine*) to shoot (*v. irr.*). ♦ **riprèndersi** *vr.* **1.** to recover **2.** (*da turbamento*) to collect oneself **3.** (*correggersi*) to correct oneself.

riprensione *sf.* reprehension.

riprensivo *agg.* reprehensible.

ripresa *sf.* **1.** renewal **2.** (*teat.; rinascita*) revival **3.** (*riconquista*) recapture **4.** (*da malattia*) recovery **5.** (*cine*) shot **6.** (*auto*) acceleration **7.** (*registrazione*) recording **8.** (*di pugilato*) round **9.** (*sport*) second half.

ripresentare *vt.* to present again.

ripristinare *vt.* **1.** to restore **2.** (*rimettere in vigore*) to re-establish.

ripristino *sm.* **1.** restoration **2.** (*il rimettere in vigore*) re-establishment.

riproducìbile *agg.* reproducible.

riprodurre *vt.* to reproduce. ♦ **riprodursi** *vr.* to reproduce.

riproduttivo *agg.* reproductive.

riproduttore *agg.* reproducing. ♦ **riproduttore** *sm.* reproducer.

riproduzione *sf.* reproduction.

ripromèttere *vt.* to promise again. ♦ **ripromèttersi** *vr.* **1.** to intend **2.** (*aspettarsi*) to expect.

riproporre *vt.* to re-propose. ♦ **riproporsi** *vr.* to re-propose.

riprova *sf.* (new) proof.

riprovare *vt.* **1.** to try again **2.** (*sentire di nuovo*) to feel (*v. irr.*)

again **3.** *(disapprovare)* to criticize **4.** *(scol)* to fail.

riprovazione *sf.* reprobation.

riprovévole *agg.* **1.** blamable **2.** *(spregevole)* despicable.

ripubblicare *vt.* to republish.

ripudiare *vt.* to repudiate.

ripudio *sm.* repudiation.

ripugnante *agg.* repugnant.

ripugnanza *sf.* repugnance.

ripugnare *vi.* **1.** *(disgustare)* to disgust **2.** *(essere contrario)* to be repugnant.

ripulire *vt.* **1.** to clean again **2.** *(pulire)* to clean **3.** *(fig.)* to polish **4.** *(saccheggiare)* to ransack.

ripulita *sf.* clean: *darsi una —,* to tidy one;self up.

ripulsa *sf.* repulse.

ripulsione *sf.* repulsion.

ripulsivo *agg.* repulsive.

riquadrare *vt.* **1.** to square **2.** *(una stanza)* to decorate.

riquadratura *sf.* **1.** square **2.** *(decorazione)* decoration.

riquaḍro *sm.* **1.** square **2.** *(su parete)* panel.

risacca *sf.* surf.

risaia *sf.* rice-field.

risalire *vt.* **1.** to go *(v. irr.)* up again **2.** *(contro corrente)* to go up: *— la corrente,* to go upstream. ♦ **risalire** *vi.* **1.** to go up again **2.** *(nel tempo)* to go back.

risaltare[1] *vi.* **1.** to show *(v. irr.)* up **2.** *(di persona)* to stand *(v. irr.)* out.

risaltare[2] *vt.* to jump again.

risalto *sm.* **1.** prominence **2.** *(rilievo)* relief.

risanàbile *agg.* **1.** curable **2.** *(bonificabile)* reclaimable.

risanamento *sm.* **1.** curing **2.** *(guarigione)* recovery **3.** *(bonifica)* reclamation **4.** *(fig.)* reformation ‖ *— di quartiere,* slum-clearance.

risanare *vt.* **1.** to cure **2.** *(bonificare)* to reclaim **3.** *(un quartiere)* to clear (a slum). ♦ **risanare** *vi.* to recover.

risanatore *agg.* healing. ♦ **risanatore** *sm.* healer.

risapere *vt.* to come *(v. irr.)* to know.

risaputo *agg.* well-known.

risarcìbile *agg.* that can be indemnified.

risarcimento *sm.* indemnity.

risarcire *vt.* to indemnify.

risata *sf.* laugh: *scoppiare in una —,* to burst *(v. irr.)* out laughing.

riscaldamento *sm.* heating.

riscaldare *vt.* **1.** to warm (up) **2.** *(di casa)* to heat **3.** *(fig.)* to excite. ♦ **riscaldarsi** *vr.* to warm up.

riscaldo *sm.* inflammation.

riscattàbile *agg.* redeemable.

riscattare *vt.* to redeem.

riscatto *sm.* **1.** ransom **2.** *(redenzione)* redemption.

rischiaramento *sm.* brightening.

rischiarare *vt.* to light *(v. irr)* (up). ♦ **rischiararsi** *vr.* **1.** to light up **2.** *(diventare più chiaro)* to get *(v. irr.)* clearer **3.** *(di cielo)* to clear up.

rischiare *vt.* to risk. ♦ **rischiare** *vi.* to run *(v. irr.)* the risk (of).

rischio *sm.* risk.

rischioso *agg.* risky.

risciacquare *vt.* to rinse. ♦ **risciacquarsi** *vr.* to rinse.

risciacquata *sf.* rinse.

risciacquatura *sf.* **1.** rinsing **2.** *(acqua)* dish-water.

riscontare *vt.* to rediscount.

risconto *sm.* rediscount.

riscontrare *vt.* **1.** *(controllare)* to check **2.** *(trovare)* to find *(v. irr)* **3.** *(confrontare)* to compare.

riscontro *sm.* **1.** *(controllo)* checking **2.** *(confronto)* comparison **3.** *(risposta)* reply **4.** *(corrispondenza simmetrica)* pendant.

riscoprire *vt.* to discover again.

riscossa *sf.* **1.** *(rivolta)* revolt **2.** *(riscatto)* redemption ‖ *andare alla —,* to counterattack.

riscossione *sf.* collection.

riscotìbile *agg.* collectable.

riscotimento *sm.* collection.

riscrivere *vt.* **1.** to rewrite *(v. irr.)* **2.** *(in risposta)* to write *(v. irr)* back.

riscuòtere *vt.* **1.** *(denaro)* to collect **2.** *(conseguire)* to win *(v. irr.)* **3.** *(scuotere)* to shake *(v. irr.)* ♦ **riscuòtersi** *vr.* *(trasalire)* to start.

riseccare *vt.* to dry up. ♦ **riseccarsi** *vr.* to dry up.

risedersi *vr.* to sit *(v. irr.)* down again.

risega *sf.* **1.** *(arch.)* offset **2.** *(della pelle)* fold.

riseminare *vt.* to sow *(v. irr)* again.

risentimento *sm.* resentment: *con —,* resentfully.

risentire vt. 1. (sentire di nuovo) to feel (v. irr.) again 2. (riudire) to hear (v. irr.) again 3. (sentire) to feel || — di qc., to show (v. irr.) traces of sthg.; (di persona) to feel the effect of sthg. ♦ **risentirsi** vr. to take (v. irr.) offence (at).

risentito agg. (sdegnato) resentful.

riserbare vt. V. riservare.

riserbo sm. 1. reserve 2. (discrezione) discretion.

riserva sf. 1. reserve 2. (di caccia, pesca) preserve.

riservare vt. to reserve. ♦ **riservarsi** vr. (ripromettersi) to intend: — la diagnosi, to refuse to formulate a definite diagnosis.

riservatezza sf. reservedness.

riservato agg. 1. reserved 2. (segreto) private.

risibile agg. laughable.

risicoltore sm. rice-grower.

risicoltura sf. rice-growing.

risièdere vi. to reside.

risma sf. 1. ream 2. (fig.) kind.

riso¹ sm. (bot.) rice.

riso² sm. laugh.

risolare vt. to resole.

risolatura sf. resoling.

risollevare vt. 1. to raise again 2. (confortare) to cheer up. ♦ **risollevarsi** vr. 1. to rise again 2. (confortarsi) to cheer up.

risolutezza sf. resolution.

risolutivo agg. resolutive.

risoluto agg. resolute.

risoluzione sf. 1. resolution 2. (giur.) cancellation.

risòlvere vt. 1. to resolve 2. (rescindere) to rescind. ♦ **risòlversi** vr. 1. (decidersi) to make (v. irr.) up one's mind 2. (mutarsi) to turn (into) 3. (di malattia) to clear up.

risolvìbile agg. 1. resolvable 2. (rescindibile) rescindable.

risonante agg. resonant.

risonanza sf. resonance.

risonare vt. 1. to play again 2. (un campanello) to ring (v. irr.) again. ♦ **risonare** vi. to resound.

risòrgere vi. 1. to rise (v. irr.) again 2. (rifiorire) to revive || far —, to revive.

risorgimento sm. revival.

risorsa sf. resource.

risparmiare vt. 1. to save 2. (evitare, salvare) to spare.

risparmiatore agg. thrifty. ♦ **risparmiatore** sm. saver.

risparmio sm. saving: senza —, lavishly.

rispecchiare vt. to reflect. ♦ **rispecchiarsi** vr. to be reflected.

rispedire vt. 1. to send (v. irr.) again 2. (spedire indietro) to send back.

rispettàbile agg. respectable.

rispettabilità sf. respectability.

rispettare vt. 1. to respect 2. (onorare) to honour.

rispettivo agg. respective.

rispetto sm. respect: — a, as regards; a — di, in comparison to; mancare di — a, to be disrespectful to.

rispettoso agg. respectful.

risplendente agg. shining.

risplèndere vi. to shine (v. irr.).

rispolverare vt. 1. to dust again 2. (fig.) to brush up.

rispondente agg. answering (to).

rispondenza sf. correspondence.

rispòndere vt. e vi. 1. to answer (so., sthg.) 2. (obbedire) to respond || — di qu., qc., to answer for so., sthg.

risposare vt. V. rimaritare.

risposta sf. answer, reply.

rispuntare vi. 1. to reappear 2. (risorgere) to rise (v. irr.) again 3. (di germogli) to sprout again.

rissa sf. brawl.

rissare vi. to brawl.

rissoso agg. quarrelsome.

ristabilimento sm. 1. restoration 2. (di salute) recovery.

ristabilire vt. to restore. ♦ **ristabilirsi** vr. 1. to settle again 2. (rimettersi) to recover.

ristagnamento sm. 1. stagnation 2. (di sangue) staunching.

ristagnare vi. to stagnate. ♦ **ristagnare** vt. to staunch.

ristagno sm. (econ.) slackness.

ristampa sf. reprint: essere in —, to be reprinting.

ristampare vt. to reprint.

ristare vi. 1. (cessare) to stop 2. (rimanere) to remain.

ristoràbile agg. restorable.

ristorante sm. restaurant.

ristorare vt. to refresh, to restore (anche fig.).

ristoratore agg. refreshing. ♦ **ristoratore** sm. restorer.

ristoro sm. 1. relief 2. (cibo, be-

vanda) refreshment || *luogo di —*, refreshment-room.

ristrettezza *sf.* **1.** narrowness **2.** (*insufficienza*) lack || *— di idee*, narrow-mindedness.

ristretto *agg.* **1.** narrow **2.** (*condensato*) condensed.

ristringere *vt.* **1.** to tighten again **2.** (*premere di nuovo*) to press again || *— la mano a qu.*, to shake (*v. irr.*) hands with so. again.

ristuccare *vt.* **1.** (*edil.*) to replaster **2.** (*nauseare*) to surfeit.

ristuccatura *sf.* (*edil.*) replastering.

ristudiare *vt.* to study again.

risucchiare *vt.* to suck (again).

risucchio *sm.* whirlpool.

risultante *agg.* e *sf.* resultant.

risultanza *sf.* result.

risultare *vi.* **1.** to result **2.** (*venire a sapere*) to turn out || *mi risulta*, I know.

risultato *sm.* result.

risurrezione *sf.* resurrection.

risuscitamento *sm.* resuscitation.

risuscitare *vt.* e *vi.* to resuscitate.

risvegliare *vt.* to wake (*v. irr.*) (up). ♦ **risvegliarsi** *vr.* to wake up.

risveglio *sm.* **1.** awakening **2.** (*fig.*) revival.

risvoltare *vt.* to turn up.

risvolto *sm.* **1.** (*di giacca*) lapel **2.** (*di calzoni*) turn-up.

ritagliare *vt.* **1.** to cut (*v. irr.*) out **2.** (*tagliare di nuovo*) to cut again.

ritaglio *sm.* **1.** (*di stoffa*) remnant **2.** (*di giornale*) clipping || *ritagli di tempo*, odd moments.

ritardare *vt.* to delay. ♦ **ritardare** *vi.* **1.** to be late **2.** (*di orologio*) to be slow.

ritardatario *sm.* late-comer.

ritardo *sm.* delay: *in —*, late.

ritegno *sm.* **1.** reserve **2.** (*freno*) restraint **3.** (*riluttanza*) reluctance.

ritemprare *vt.* **1.** to strengthen **2.** (*metalli*) to harden again. ♦ **ritemprarsi** *vr.* to get (*v. irr.*) stronger.

ritenere *vt.* **1.** to hold (*v. irr.*) **2.** (*giudicare*) to consider **3.** (*pensare*) to think (*v. irr.*).

ritentare *vt.* **1.** to tempt again **2.** (*riprovare*) to try again.

ritenuta *sf.* deduction.

ritenzione *sf.* retention.

ritingere *vt.* to dye again.

ritirare *vt.* **1.** to withdraw (*v. irr.*)

2. (*farsi consegnare*) to collect. ♦ **ritirarsi** *vr.* **1.** to retire **2.** (*di stoffa*) to shrink (*v. irr.*).

ritirata *sf.* **1.** retreat **2.** (*latrina*) lavatory.

ritiro *sm.* **1.** withdrawal **2.** (*il ritirarsi*) retirement **3.** (*luogo appartato*) retreat **4.** (*il farsi consegnare*) collection.

ritmare *vt.* to mark.

ritmica *sf.* rhythmic(s).

ritmico *agg.* rhythmic(al).

ritmo *sm.* rhythm.

rito *sm.* rite: *essere di —*, to be customary.

ritoccare *vt.* to retouch.

ritoccatore *sm.* retoucher.

ritocco *sm.* retouch.

ritògliere *vt.* **1.** to take (*v. irr.*) off again **2.** (*riappropriarsi*) to take back. ♦ **ritògliersi** *vr.* to take off again.

ritòrcere *vt.* **1.** to twist again **2.** (*torcere*) to twist **3.** (*rivolgere*) to retort. ♦ **ritòrcersi** *vr.* **1.** to get (*v. irr.*) twisted **2.** (*fig.*) to recoil (on, upon).

ritorcitura *sf.* twisting.

ritornare *vi.* to return.

ritornello *sm.* refrain.

ritorno *sm.* return: *— di fiamma*, backfire; *essere di —*, to be back.

ritorsione *sf.* retortion.

ritorto *agg.* twisted.

ritrarre *vt.* **1.** to withdraw (*v. irr.*) **2.** (*distogliere*) to turn away **3.** (*rappresentare*) to represent **4.** (*dedurre*) to understand (*v. irr.*). ♦ **ritrarsi** *vr.* to withdraw.

ritrattare *vt.* **1.** to retract **2.** (*trattare di nuovo*) to treat again.

ritrattazione *sf.* **1.** retraction **2.** (*nuova trattazione*) new treatment.

ritrattista *s.* portraitist.

ritrattìstica *sf.* portraiture.

ritratto *sm.* portrait.

ritrazione *sf.* retraction.

ritrito *agg.* stale.

ritrosìa *sf.* **1.** (*riluttanza*) reluctance **2.** (*timidezza*) shyness.

ritroso *agg.* **1.** (*riluttante*) reluctant **2.** (*timido*) shy || *a —*, backwards.

ritrovamento *sm.* finding.

ritrovare *vt.* **1.** to find (*v. irr.*) again **2.** (*ricuperare*) to recover **3.** (*scoprire*) to discover. ♦ **ritrovarsi** *vr.* **1.** to find oneself **2.** (*rincontrarsi*) to meet (*v. irr.*) again.

ritrovato sm. **1.** invention **2.** (scoperta) discovery.

ritrovo sm. meeting-place, haunt.

ritto agg. upright.

rituale agg. e sm. ritual.

rituffare vt. to plunge again. ◆ **rituffarsi** vr. to plunge again.

riudire vt. to hear (v. irr.) again.

riunione sf. meeting.

riunire vt. **1.** to re-unite (2. (raccogliere) to gather **3.** (unire) to join. ◆ **riunirsi** vr. **1.** to come (v. irr.) together again **2.** (unirsi) to unite **3.** (incontrarsi) to meet (v. irr.).

riuscire vi. **1.** to succeed (in), to be good (at) **2.** (risultare) to be **3.** (uscire di nuovo) to go (v. irr.) out again.

riuscita sf. **1.** issue **2.** (successo) success.

riutilizzare vt. to utilize again.

riva sf. **1.** (di mare, lago) shore **2.** (di fiume) bank.

rivale agg. e sm. rival.

rivaleggiare vi. to rival (so., sthg.).

rivalersi vr. **1.** to make (v. irr.) up for one's losses **2.** (valersi di nuovo) to make use again.

rivalicare vt. to recross.

rivalità sf. rivalry.

rivalsa sf. **1.** (rivincita) revenge **2.** (risarcimento) compensation **3.** (comm.) recourse.

rivalutare vt. to revalue **2.** (elevare) to raise.

rivalutazione sf. **1.** revaluation **2.** (aumento) rise.

rivangare vt. e vi. to dig (v. irr.) up again.

rivedere vt. **1.** to see (v. irr.) again **2.** (revisionare) to revise.

riveduta sf. look, revision.

rivelare vt. **1.** to reveal. ◆ **rivelarsi** vr. **1.** to reveal oneself **2.** (dimostrarsi) to prove.

rivelatore agg. revealing. ◆ **rivelatore** sm. **1.** revealer **2.** (radio) detector.

rivelazione sf. **1.** revelation **2.** (fis ; radio) detection.

rivéndere vt. **1.** to resell (v. irr.) **2.** (al dettaglio) to retail.

rivendicare vt. **1.** to claim **2.** (vendicare) to revenge.

rivendicatore agg. **1.** claiming **2.** (vendicatore) revenging. ◆ **rivendicatore** sm. **1.** claimant **2.** (vendicatore) revenger.

rivendicazione sf. claim.

rivéndita sf. **1.** resale **2.** (spaccio) shop.

rivenditore sm. retailer.

rivendùgliolo sm. V. rigattiere.

riverberare vt. to reverberate. ◆ **riverberarsi** vr. to reverberate.

rivèrbero sm. reverberation: di —, indirectly.

riverente agg. reverent.

riverenza sf. **1.** reverence **2.** (inchino) bow.

riverenziale agg. reverential.

riverire vt. **1.** to revere (v. irr.) **2.** (salutare) to pay (v. irr.) one's respects (to).

riversare vt. **1.** to pour again **2.** (versare) to pour **3.** (di fiume) to flow. ◆ **riversarsi** vr. to flow.

riverso avv. on one's back.

rivestimento sm. **1.** covering **2.** (interno) lining.

rivestire vt. **1.** to dress again **2.** (foderare) to line (with sthg.) **3.** (coprire) to cover (with sthg.) **4.** (fig.) to hold (v. irr.).

riviera sf. coast || la Riviera, the Riviera.

rivierasco agg. coast (attr.).

rivincere vt. **1.** to win (v. irr.) again **2.** (recuperare) to win back.

rivincita sf. **1.** (vendetta) revenge **2.** (sport) return match **3.** (al gioco) return game.

rivista sf. **1.** review **2.** (teat.) revue **3.** (mil.) parade || passare in —, to review.

rivivere vi. e vt. to live again.

rivo sm. stream.

rivolere vt. **1.** to want again **2.** (volere indietro) to want back.

rivòlgere vt. **1.** to turn **2.** (indirizzare) to address. ◆ **rivòlgersi** vr. **1.** to turn **2.** (parlando) to address (so.) **3.** (ricorrere, riferirsi) to apply (to).

rivolgimento sm. **1.** upheaval **2.** (cambio) change.

rivolo sm. streamlet.

rivolta sf. revolt.

rivoltante agg. revolting.

rivoltare vt. **1.** to turn (over) again **2.** (rovesciare) to turn **3.** (capovolgere) to turn upside-down **4.** (con l'interno all'esterno) to turn inside out **5.** (fig.) to upset (v. irr.). ◆ **rivoltarsi** vr. **1.** to turn round **2.** (rigirarsi) to turn over **3.** (ribellarsi) to revolt **4.** (fig.) to turn.

rivoltella sf. revolver.

rivoltoso *agg. e sm.* rebel.

rivoluzionare *vt.* to revolutionize.

rivoluzionario *agg. e sm.* revolutionary.

rivoluzione *sf.* revolution.

rizoma *sm.* rhizome.

rizzare *vt.* to raise: — *le orecchie,* to prick one's ears. ♦ **rizzarsi** *vr.* 1. to stand (*v. irr.*) up 2. (*di capelli*) to stand on end.

roba *sf.* stuff, things (*pl.*).

robaccia *sf.* rubbish.

robinia *sf.* locust-tree.

robustezza *sf.* robustness.

robusto *agg.* robust.

rocambolesco *agg.* daring.

rocca¹ *sf.* 1. stronghold 2. (*roccia*) rock.

rocca² *sf.* (*conocchia*) distaff.

roccaforte *sf.* stronghold.

rocchetto *sm.* 1. spool 2. (*elettr*) coil.

rocchio *sm.* 1. (*di tronco*) log 2. (*di colonna*) drum.

roccia *sf.* rock.

rocciatore *sm.* rock-climber.

roccioso *agg.* rocky.

roco *agg.* hoarse.

rodaggio *sm.* (*auto*) running in.

rodare *vt.* to run (*v. irr.*) in.

ròdere *vt.* 1. to gnaw 2. (*corrodere*) to corrode. ♦ **ròdersi** *vr.* 1. to worry 2. (*di rabbia ecc.*) to be consumed (with).

rodimento *sm.* 1. gnawing 2. (*fig.*) anxiety.

roditore *agg. e sm.* rodent.

rododendro *sm.* rhododendron.

rogare *vt.* to draw (*v. irr.*) up.

rogatoria *sf.* request.

rogazioni *sf. pl.* rogations.

roggia *sf.* irrigation ditch.

rògito *sm.* deed.

rogna *sf.* 1. scabies 2. (*fig.*) trouble.

rognone *sm.* kidney.

rognoso *agg.* scabby.

rogo *sm.* 1. fire 2. (*pira*) pyre 3. (*supplizio*) stake.

rollare *vi.* to roll.

rollìo *sm.* roll.

romancio *agg.* Romansh.

romànico *agg.* 1. (*arch.*) Romanesque 2. Romanic.

romano *agg. e sm.* Roman.

romanticherìa *sf.* 1. (*atteggiamento*) romantic attitude 2. (*azione*) romantic deed.

romanticismo *sm.* Romanticism.

romàntico *agg. e sm.* romantic.

romanza *sf.* romance.

romanzare *vt.* to romanticize.

romanzesco *agg.* romantic.

romanziere *sm.* novelist.

romanzo¹ *agg.* Romance.

romanzo² *sm.* 1. novel 2. (*storia incredibile*) romance ‖ — *a puntate,* serial; — *a fumetti,* comics.

romba *sf.* roar.

rombare *vi.* to rumble.

ròmbico *agg.* rhombic(al).

rombo¹ *sm.* (*rumore*) rumble.

rombo² *sm.* (*geom.*) rhomb.

rombo³ *sm.* (*itt.*) brill.

romboèdrico *agg.* rhombohedral.

romboedro *sm.* rhombohedron (*pl.* -ra).

romboidale *agg.* rhomboid(al).

rombòide *agg. e sm.* rhomboid.

romeno *agg. e sm.* Rumanian.

romeo *sm.* pilgrim.

romitaggio *sm.* hermitage.

romito *agg.* solitary. ♦ **romito** *sm.* hermit.

romitorio *sm.* hermitage.

ròmpere *vt.* to break (*v. irr.*): — *i ponti con qu.,* to break with so. ♦ **rompersi** *vr.* to break (up).

rompicapo *sm.* puzzle.

rompicollo *sm.* madcap: *a —,* headlong.

rompighiaccio *sm.* ice-breaker.

rompiscàtole *s.* nuisance.

rompitore *sm.* breaker.

ronca *sf.* pruning-knife (*pl.* -ives).

ronciglio *sm.* hook.

ròncola *sf.* pruning-hook.

ronda *sf.* 1. rounds (*pl.*) 2. (*pattuglia*) patrol.

rondella *sf.* washer.

ròndine *sf.* swallow: *a coda di —,* swallow-tailed.

rondinotto *sm.* young swallow.

rondò *sm.* 1. (*mus.*) rondo 2. (*poet*) rondel 3. (*piazza circolare*) circus.

rondone *sm.* swift.

ronfare *vi.* to snore.

ronzare *vi.* 1. to buzz 2. (*fig.*) to hang (*v. irr.*) around.

ronzino *sm.* jade.

ronzìo *sm.* buzz.

ròrido *agg.* 1. (*bagnato*) wet 2. (*rugiadoso*) dewy.

rosa *sf.* rose ‖ *all'acqua di rose* (*fig.*), moderate. ♦ **rosa** *agg. e sm.* pink.

rosàceo *agg.* rosy.

rosaio *sm.* rose-bush.

rosario *sm.* rosary.

rosato *agg.* rosy.

ròseo *agg.* rosy.

roseòla *sf.* roseola.

roseto *sm.* rose-garden.

rosetta *sf.* **1.** rosette **2.** (*diamante*) rose **3.** (*mecc.*) washer.

rosicchiare *vt.* to gnaw.

rosmarino *sm.* rosemary.

rosolare *vt.* to brown. ♦ **rosolarsi** *vr.* **1.** to get (*v. irr.*) brown **2.** (*prendere il sole*) to bask.

rosolìa *sf.* German measles (*pl.*).

rosolio *sm.* rosolio.

rosone *sm.* rose-window.

rospo *sm.* toad.

rossastro *agg.* reddish.

rosseggiare *vi.* to be reddish.

rossetto *sm.* **1.** (*per labbra*) lipstick **2.** (*per guance*) rouge.

rossiccio *agg.* ruddy.

rosso *agg. e sm.* red: — *d'uovo,* yolk; *diventar —,* to flush.

rossore *sm.* flush.

rosticcerìa *sf.* rotisserie.

rosticciere *sm.* owner of a rotisserie.

rostro *sm.* **1.** rostrum (*pl.* -ra) **2.** (*becco*) beak.

rotàbile *agg.* carriage (*attr.*).

rotàia *sf.* **1.** rail **2.** (*solco*) rut.

rotare *vi. e vt.* to rotate, to revolve.

rotativa *sf.* rotary press.

rotativo *agg.* rotary.

rotatòrio *agg.* rotating.

rotazione *sf.* rotation.

roteare *vt.* **1.** to swing (*v. irr.*) **2.** (*gli occhi*) to roll. ♦ **roteare** *vi.* to wheel.

rotella *sf.* small wheel.

rotocalco *sm.* **1.** rotogravure **2.** (*rivista*) illustrated magazine.

rotolamento *sm.* rolling.

rotolare *vt. e vi.* to roll. ♦ **rotolarsi** *vr.* to roll.

ròtolo *sm.* roll || *andare a rotoli,* to go (*v. irr.*) to rack and ruin; *mandare a rotoli,* to ruin.

rotolone *sm.* V. *ruzzolone.*

rotonda *sf.* rotunda.

rotondità *sf.* roundness.

rotondo *agg.* **1.** round **2.** (*grassoccio*) plump.

rotore *sm.* rotor.

rotta *sf.* **1.** course **2.** (*rottura*) breach **3.** (*sconfitta*) rout || *a — di collo,* headlong; *essere in — con,* to be on bad terms with; *mettere in —,* to rout.

rottame *sm.* **1.** wreck **2.** (*di scarto*) scraps (*pl.*).

rotto *agg.* **1.** broken **2.** (*stracciato*) torn **3.** (*avvezzo*) accustomed.

rottura *sf.* break(ing).

rovente *agg.* red-hot.

ròvere *sm.* oak.

rovesciamento *sm.* **1.** overthrowing **2.** (*cambiamento*) reversal.

rovesciare *vt.* **1.** to overturn **2.** (*capovolgere*) to turn upside down **3.** (*gettare*) to throw (*v. irr.*) **4.** (*rivoltare*) to turn inside out **5.** (*versare intenzionalmente*) to pour **6.** (*versare accidentalmente*) to spill **7.** (*abbattere*) to overthrow (*v. irr.*). ♦ **rovesciarsi** *vr.* **1.** to overturn **2.** (*riversarsi*) to pour.

rovescio *sm.* **1.** reverse **2.** (*opposto*) opposite **3.** (*di pioggia*) heavy shower **4.** (*di critiche ecc.*) hail || *a — (capovolto),* upside down.

roveto *sm.* bramble-bush.

rovina *sf.* ruin.

rovinare *vt.* **1.** to ruin **2.** (*sciupare*) to spoil (*v. irr.*). ♦ **rovinare** *vi.* to crash.

rovinìo *sm.* **1.** downfall **2.** (*rumore*) crash.

rovinoso *agg.* ruinous.

rovistare *vt. e vi.* to rummage.

rovo *sm.* blackberry bush.

rozza *sf.* jade.

rozzezza *sf.* roughness.

rozzo *agg.* rough.

ruba *sf.* *andare a —,* to sell (*v. irr.*) like wildfire.

rubacchiare *vt.* to pilfer.

rubacuori *agg.* bewitching. ♦ **rubacuori** *sm.* lady-killer.

rubare *vt.* to steal (*v. irr.*).

ruberìa *sf.* theft.

rubicondo *agg.* ruddy.

rubinetterìa *sf.* plumbing fixtures (*pl.*).

rubinetto *sm.* tap.

rubino *sm.* ruby.

rubizzo *agg.* hale.

rublo *sm.* rouble.

rubrica *sf.* **1.** (*di giornale*) column **2.** (*per indirizzi*) addressbook.

rude *agg.* rough.

rùdere *sm.* ruin.

rudezza *sf.* roughness.

rudimentale *agg.* rudimentary.

rudimento *sm.* rudiment.

ruffiano *sm.* pander.

ruga *sf.* wrinkle.

ruggente *agg.* roaring.

ruggine *sf.* **1.** rust **2.** (*fig.*) grudge.

rugginoso *agg.* rusty.

ruggire *vi.* to roar.

ruggito *sm.* roar.

rugiada *sf.* dew: *goccia di —*, dew-drop.

rugiadoso *agg.* dewy.

rugosità *sf.* **1.** wrinkledness **2.** (*scabrosità*) ruggedness.

rugoso *agg.* **1.** wrinkled **2.** (*scabro*) rugged.

rullaggio *sm. pista di —*, taxi-track.

rullare *vi.* **1.** to roll **2.** (*di aereo*) to taxi.

rullino *sm.* roll.

rullio *sm.* roll.

rullo *sm.* **1.** roll **2.** (*mecc.*) roller.

rum *sm.* rum.

ruminante *agg. e sm.* ruminant.

ruminare *vt.* to ruminate.

ruminazione *sf.* rumination.

rùmine *sm.* rumen.

rumore *sm.* **1.** noise **2.** (*diceria*) rumour || *far —* (*fig.*), to arouse great interest.

rumoreggiare *vi.* **1.** to rumble **2.** (*fig.*) to rumour.

rumorìo *sm.* noise.

rumorista *sm.* noise-maker.

rumoroso *agg.* noisy.

ruolino *sm.* (*di marcia*) time schedule.

ruolo *sm.* **1.** roll, list **2.** (*teat.*) role **3.** (*amm.*) roster.

ruota *sf.* wheel.

rupe *sf.* cliff.

rupestre *agg.* rocky.

rurale *agg.* rural || *i rurali*, country people.

ruscello *sm.* brook.

ruspa *sf.* scraper.

ruspare *vi.* (*razzolare*) to scratch about.

russare *vi.* to snore.

russo *agg. e sm.* Russian.

rusticità *sf.* rusticity.

rùstico *agg.* **1.** rustic **2.** (*ritroso*) unsociable.

ruta *sf.* rue.

rutilante *agg.* glowing.

ruttare *vi.* to belch.

rutto *sm.* belch.

rùvido *agg.* rough.

ruzzare *vi.* to romp.

ruzzolare *vt.* to roll. ♦ **ruzzolare** *vi.* **1.** to roll **2.** (*cadere*) to tumble down.

ruzzolone *sm.* tumble: *fare un —*, to tumble down.

S

sàbato *sm.* Saturday.

sabba *sm.* witches' Sabbath.

sabbia *sf.* sand.

sabbiare *vt.* to sand.

sabbiatura *sf.* sand-bath.

sabbioso *agg.* sandy.

sabotaggio *sm.* sabotage.

sabotare *vt.* to sabotage.

sabotatore *sm.* saboteur.

sacca *sf.* bag.

saccarina *sf.* saccharine.

saccarosio *sm.* saccharose.

saccente *agg.* pedantic. ♦ **saccente** *s.* pedant.

saccheggiare *vt.* to sack.

saccheggio *sm.* sack.

sacchetto *sm.* small bag.

sacco *sm.* **1.** sack, bag || *colazione al —*, picnic; *mettere qu. nel —*, to take (*v. irr.*) so. in **2.** (*grande quantità*) a lot of.

saccoccia *sf.* pocket.

saccone *sm.* palliasse.

sacerdotale *agg.* sacerdotal.

sacerdote *sm.* priest.

sacerdozio *sm.* priesthood.

sacrale *agg.* sacral.

sacramentale *agg.* sacramental.

sacramentare *vi.* (*fig.*) to swear (*v. irr.*).

sacramento *sm.* sacrament.

sacrario *sm.* shrine.

sacrificare *vt.* to sacrifice.

sacrificio *sm.* sacrifice.

sacrilegio *sm.* sacrilege.

sacrìlego *agg.* sacrilegious.

sacrista *sm.* sacristan.

sacro *agg.* sacred, holy.

sacrosanto *agg.* **1.** sacrosanct **2.** (*indiscutibile*) absolute.

sàdico *agg.* sadistic. ♦ **sàdico** *sm.* sadist.

sadismo *sm.* sadism.

saetta *sf.* **1.** arrow **2.** (*fulmine*) thunderbolt.

saettare *vt.* **1.** to shoot (*v. irr.*) arrows at **2.** (*fig.*) to dart. ♦ **saettare** *vi.* to dart.

sàffico *agg.* Sapphic.

sagace *agg.* sagacious.

sagacia *sf.* sagacity.

saggezza *sf.* wisdom.

saggiare *vt.* to assay, to test.

saggiatore *sm.* **1.** assayer **2.** (*bilancia*) assay balance.

saggina *sf.* sorghum.

saggio¹ *agg.* wise. ♦ **saggio** *sm.* wise man (*pl.* men).

saggio² *sm.* **1.** essay **2.** (*campione*) sample **3.** (*saggio ginnico*) display.

saggista *s.* essayist.

sagittario *sm.* **1.** archer **2.** (*astr.*) Sagittarius.

sàgoma *sf.* shape ‖ *è una —!* (*fam.*), he is a character!

sagomare *vt.* to shape.

sagra *sf.* festival.

sagrato *sm.* church-square.

sagrestano *sm.* sacristan.

sagrestìa *sf.* sacristy.

saia *sf.* serge.

saio *sm.* habit.

sala *sf.* hall, room: *— da pranzo*, dining-room.

salace *agg.* salacious.

salacità *sf.* salacity.

salamandra *sf.* salamander.

salame *sm.* salami (*pl.*).

salamelecco *sm.* salaam.

salamoia *sf.* pickle.

salare *vt.* to salt.

salariale *agg.* salary (*attr.*).

salariato *agg.* wage-earning. ♦ **salariato** *sm.* wage-earner.

salario *sm.* wages (*pl.*).

salassare *vt.* to bleed (*v. irr.*).

salasso *sm.* **1.** bleeding **2.** (*fig.*) extortion.

salato *agg.* **1.** salty **2.** (*costoso*) dear **3.** (*salace*) keen.

salatura *sf.* salting.

salda *sf.* starch-water.

saldamente *avv.* firmly.

saldare *vt.* **1.** to solder, to weld **2.** (*un conto*) to settle.

saldatore *sm.* solderer, welder.

saldatrice *sf.* welding machine.

saldatura *sf.* soldering, welding.

saldezza *sf.* firmness.

saldo¹ *agg.* firm.

saldo² *sm.* balance: *— attivo, passivo*, credit, debit balance.

sale *sm.* salt.

salesiano *agg.* e *sm.* Salesian.

salgemma *sm.* rock-salt.

sàlice *sm.* willow.

salicilato *sm.* salicylate.

saliente *agg.* important.

saliera *sf.* salt-cellar.

salina *sf.* salt-pit.

salino *agg.* saline, salt (*attr.*).

salire *vi.* **1.** to rise (*v. irr.*), to go (*v. irr.*) up **2.** (*di prezzi*) to increase.

saliscendi *sm.* **1.** latch **2.** (*alter-*

narsi di salite e discese) ups and downs (*pl.*).

salita *sf.* **1.** slope, ascent **2.** (*aumento*) rise.

saliva *sf.* saliva, spittle.

salivare *agg.* salivary.

salivare *vi.* to salivate.

salivazione *sf.* salivation.

salma *sf.* corpse.

salmastro *agg.* saltish.

salmo *sm.* psalm.

salmodìa *sf.* psalmody.

salmodiare *vi.* to sing (*v. irr.*) psalms.

salmone *sm.* salmon.

salnitro *sm.* saltpetre.

salone *sm.* large hall, reception-room.

salottiero *agg.* drawing-room (*attr.*).

salotto *sm.* sitting-room.

salpare *vi.* to set (*v. irr.*) sails.

salsa *sf.* sauce.

salsèdine *sf.* saltness.

salsiccia *sf.* sausage.

salsiera *sf.* sauce-boat.

salso *agg.* salt (*attr.*).

saltare *vt.* e *vi.* to jump, to leap (*v. irr.*): *— di palo in frasca*, to jump from one subject to another; *far — una serratura*, to break (*v. irr.*) a lock.

saltatore *agg.* jumping. ♦ **saltatore** *sm.* jumper.

saltellare *vi.* to hop.

saltimbanco *sm.* tumbler.

salto *sm.* jump, leap.

saltuario *agg.* desultory.

salubre *agg.* healthy.

salubrità *sf.* healthiness.

salume *sm.* salted meat.

salumiere *sm.* delicatessen seller.

salumeria *sf.* delicatessen.

salutare¹ *agg.* healthy.

salutare² *vt.* to greet, to hail.

salute *sf.* health.

saluto *sm.* greeting, salute.

salva *sf.* volley (*anche fig.*): *colpo a —*, blank shot.

salvacondotto *sm.* safe-conduct.

salvadanaio *sm.* money-box.

salvagente *sm.* **1.** life-belt **2.** (*marciapiede*) traffic island.

salvaguardare *vt.* to safeguard.

salvaguardia *sf.* safeguard.

salvare *vt.* **1.** to save (*anche fig.*) **2.** (*trarre in salvo*) to rescue. ♦ **salvarsi** *vr.* to save oneself.

salvataggio *sm.* rescue.

salvatore *sm.* saviour, saver.

salve *inter.* hail.

salvezza *sf.* salvation.

salvia *sf.* sage.

salvietta *sf.* towel.

salvo *agg.* safe. ♦ **salvo** *prep.* except, save. ♦ **salvo che** *cong.* except that, unless.

sanàbile *agg.* curable, remediable.

sanare *vt.* to heal.

sanatorio *sm.* sanatorium (*pl.* -ia).

sancire *vt.* to sanction.

sanculotto *sm.* sansculotte.

sàndalo[1] *sm.* (*calzatura*) sandal.

sàndalo[2] *sm.* (*mar.*) punt.

sandolino *sm.* small canoe.

sangue *sm.* blood: *spargimento di* —, bloodshed; *perdita di* —, bleeding; — *freddo,* coolness; *a* — *freddo,* in cold blood; *farsi cattivo* —, to worry over; *buon* — *non mente,* blood will tell.

sanguigno *agg.* sanguineous, blood (*attr.*).

sanguinaccio *sm.* blood-sausage.

sanguinante *agg.* bleeding.

sanguinare *vi.* to bleed (*v. irr.*).

sanguinario *agg. e sm.* sanguinary; *uomo* —, bloodthirsty man.

sanguinoso *agg.* bloody.

sanguisuga *sf.* leech.

sanità *sf.* soundness, sanity.

sanitario *agg.* sanitary.

sano *agg.* 1. healthy 2. (*fig.*) sound 3. (*intero, intatto*) intact.

sansa *sf.* husk.

sànscrito *sm.* Sanskrit.

santarellina *sf.* goody-goody.

santificante *agg.* sanctifying.

santificare *vt.* to canonize: — *le feste,* to observe holy days.

santificazione *sf.* sanctification.

santino *sm.* small holy picture.

santissimo *agg.* most holy: *il* — *Sacramento,* the Blessed Sacrament.

santità *sf.* holiness.

santo *agg.* 1. holy 2. (*seguito da nome proprio*) saint. ♦ **santo** *sm.* saint.

santone *sm.* santon.

santuario *sm.* sanctuary.

sanzionare *vt.* to ratify.

sanzione *sf.* sanction.

sapere[1] *vt.* 1. to know (*v. irr.*): *non* — *che fare,* to be at a loss what to do; *chi sa!,* who knows!; *non si sa mai,* you never know; *venire a* —, to hear (*v. irr.*); *(essere capace)* can, to be able: *sai parlare inglese?,* can you speak

English?; *non so farlo,* I am not able to do it. ♦ **sapere** *vi.* (*aver sapore*) to taste.

sapere[2] *sm.* 1. knowledge 2. (*cultura*) learning.

sàpido *agg.* sapid.

sapiente *agg.* wise. ♦ **sapiente** *sm.* sage.

sapienza *sf.* wisdom.

saponaria *sf.* soapwort.

saponata *sf.* lather (*solo sing.*).

sapone *sm.* soap: — *da barba,* shaving-soap; — *da bagno,* bath soap.

saponetta *sf.* cake of soap.

saponificare *vt.* to saponify.

saponificazione *sf.* saponification.

saponificio *sm.* soap-works (*pl. con costruzione sing.*).

sapore *sm.* taste, flavour (*anche fig.*).

saporire *vt.* to flavour

saporitamente *avv.* savourily || *dormire* —, to sleep (*v. irr.*) soundly.

saporito *agg.* savoury, tasty.

saputello *sm.* wiseacre.

saputo *agg.* 1. learned 2. (*noto*) well-known.

sarabanda *sf.* saraband.

saraceno *sm.* saracen.

saracinesca *sf.* rolling-shutter.

sarcasmo *sm.* sarcasm.

sarcàstico *agg.* sarcastic.

sarchiare *vt.* to weed.

sarchiatore *sm.* weeding. ♦ **sarchiatore** *sm.* weeder.

sarchiatura *sf.* weeding.

sarchio *sm.* hoe.

sarcòfago *sm.* sarcophagus (*pl.* -gi).

sardina *sf.* sardine.

sardònico *agg.* sardonic.

sarmento *sm.* runner.

sarta *sf.* dressmaker.

sartie *sf. pl.* shrouds.

sartina *sf.* grisette.

sarto *sm.* tailor.

sartorìa *sf.* 1. (*da uomo*) tailor's 2. (*da donna*) dressmaker's.

sassaia *sf.* stony place.

sassaiuola *sf.* 1. shower of stones 2. (*battaglia di sassi*) stone-fight.

sassata *sf.* blow with a stone.

sasso *sm.* stone: *a un tiro di* — *da,* within a stone's throw of.

sassofonista *sm.* saxophonist

sassòfono *sm.* saxophone.

sassolino *sm.* pebble.

sàssone *agg. e sm.* Saxon.

sassoso *agg.* stony.

satànico *agg.* Satanic.

satèllite *sm.* satellite.

sàtira *sf.* satire.

satìrico *agg.* satirical.

sàtiro *sm.* satyr.

satollare *vt.* to satiate.

satollo *agg.* satiated.

sàtrapo *sm.* satrap.

saturare *vt.* to saturate.

saturazione *sf.* saturation.

saturnali *sm. pl.* saturnalia.

sàturo *agg.* saturated.

sàuro *agg.* sorrel.

savana *sf.* savannah.

savio *agg.* wise. ♦ savio *sm.* sage.

saziàbile *agg.* satiable.

saziare *vt.* to satisfy, to glut. ♦ saziarsi *vr.* to get (*v. irr.*) full.

sazietà *sf.* satiety: *mangiare, bere a —*, to eat (*v. irr.*), to drink (*v. irr.*) one's fill.

sazio *agg.* replete, full.

sbaciucchiare *vt.* to smother with kisses.

sbadatàggine *sf.* carelessness.

sbadato *agg.* careless.

sbadigliare *vi.* to yawn.

sbadiglio *sm.* yawn.

sbafare *vi.* to scrounge.

sbafatore *sm.* scrounger.

sbafo (*nella loc. avv.*) *prendere qc. a —,* to scrounge sthg.

sbagliare *vi.* to mistake (*v. irr.*). ♦ sbagliarsi *vr.* to make (*v. irr.*) a mistake.

sbagliato *agg.* wrong.

sbaglio *sm.* mistake.

sbalestrare *vt.* 1. to send (*v. irr.*) 2. (*fig.*) to flounder.

sballare *vt.* to unpack.

sballato *agg.* (*fig.*) foolhardy.

sballottamento *sm.* jolting.

sballottare *vt.* to jolt (about), to toss (about).

sbalordimento *sm.* amazement.

sbalordire *vt.* to amaze.

sbalorditivo *agg.* amazing.

sbalordito *agg.* amazed.

sbalzamento *sm.* 1. overthrow 2. (*fig.*) dismissal.

sbalzare[1] *vt.* to throw (*v. irr.*), to toss.

sbalzare[2] *vt.* (*arte*) to emboss.

sbalzato *agg.* (*arte*) embossed.

sbalzo *sm.* 1. bound, jump 2. (*cambio*) change.

sbancare *vt.* to leave (*v. irr.*) broke.

sbandamento *sm.* 1. dispersal 2. (*auto*) skid 3. (*mar.*) list.

sbandare *vt.* 1. to disperse 2. (*auto*) to cause a skid.

sbandata *sf.* V. *sbandamento.*

sbandato *sm.* straggler.

sbandierare *vt.* (*fig.*) to display.

sbaragliare *vt.* to rout.

sbaraglio *sm.* jeopardy; *mettere allo —,* to jeopardize.

sbarazzare *vt.* to clear up. ♦ sbarazzarsi *vr.* to get (*v. irr.*) rid (of).

sbarazzino *agg.* free and easy. ♦ sbarazzino *sm.* little scamp.

sbarbare *vt.* to shave.

sbarbatello *sm.* young colt.

sbarcare *vt. e vi.* to land, to disembark.

sbarco *sm.* 1. (*di passeggeri*) landing 2. (*di merci*) unloading.

sbarra *sf.* 1. bar 2. (*del timone*) tiller.

sbarramento *sm.* 1. barricade 2. (*di acque*) dam 3. (*mil.*) barrage.

sbarrare *vt.* 1. to bar: *— un assegno,* to cross a cheque 2. (*spalancare*) to open wide.

sbarrato *agg.* blocked || *occhi sbarrati,* wide open eyes.

sbatacchiamento *sm.* banging, slamming.

sbatacchiare *vt.* to bang, to slam.

sbàttere *vt.* 1. (*urtare contro*) to knock 2. (*scaraventare*) to throw (*v. irr.*) 3. (*chiudere violentemente*) to slam 4. (*di panna, uova*) to whip, to beat (*v. irr.*).

sbattezzare *vt.* to force to abjure Christianity.

sbattimento *sm.* banging.

sbattiuova *sm.* egg-whisk.

sbattuto *agg.* 1. depressed: *viso —,* tired face 2. (*di uova*) beaten.

sbavare *vi.* 1. to dribble 2. (*tip.*) to smudge.

sbavatura *sf.* 1. dribble 2. (*tip.*) smudge.

sbellicarsi *vr. — dalle risa,* to split (*v. irr.*) one's sides with laughter.

sbendare *vt.* to unbandage.

sberla *sf.* slap.

sberleffo *sm.* grimace.

sbertucciare *vt.* 1. to mock 2. (*sgualcire*) to crumple.

sbiadire *vi.* to fade.

sbiancare *vt.* to bleach. ♦ sbiancare *vi* to turn white. ♦ sbiancarsi *vr.* to turn white.

sbieco agg. slanting: *guardare qu. di —*, to look askance at so.; *tagliare una stoffa di —*, to cut (v. irr.) a cloth on the bias.

sbigottimento sm. dismay.

sbigottire vt. to dismay. ♦ **sbigottirsi** vr. to be dismayed.

sbigottito agg. dismayed.

sbilanciare vt. to unbalance. ♦ **sbilanciarsi** vr. 1. to lose (v. irr.) one's balance 2. (fig.) to commit oneself.

sbilancio sm. lack of balance; disproportion.

sbilenco agg. crooked.

sbirciare vt. to cast (v. irr.) a sidelong glance.

sbirraglia sf. police (us. al pl.).

sbirro sm. policeman (pl. -men).

sbizzarrirsi vr. to satisfy one's whims.

sbloccare vt. to raise the blockade: *— gli affitti*, to decontrol rents.

sblocco sm. 1. raising the blockade 2. (mecc.) releasing the brake 3. (econ.) decontrol.

sboccare vi. 1. (di corso d'acqua) to flow 2. (di strada) to lead (v. irr.).

sboccato agg. (fig.) coarse.

sbocciare vi. to open, to blossom.

sboccio sm. blooming.

sbocco sm. outlet, exit.

sbocconcellare vt. to nibble.

sbollire vi. (fig.) to cool down.

sbolognare vt. to palm off.

sbornia sf. drunkenness: *prendere la —*, to get (v. irr.) drunk.

sborsamento sm. paying out.

sborsare vt. to pay (v. irr.) out.

sborso sm. 1. payment 2. (denaro sborsato) outlay.

sbottare vi. to burst (v. irr.) out.

sbotto sm. outburst.

sbottonare vt. to unbutton. ♦ **sbottonarsi** vr. 1. to undo (v. irr.) one's buttons 2. (fig.) to disclose one's feelings.

sbozzare vt. to sketch out.

sbracare vt. to unbreech.

sbracato agg. (fig.) unseemly.

sbracciare vi. to gesticulate. ♦ **sbracciarsi** vr. 1. to roll up one's sleeves 2. (agitarsi) to strive (v. irr.).

sbracciato agg. (di persona) with bare arms.

sbraitare vi. to shout.

sbranamento sm. tearing to pieces.

sbranare vt. to tear (v. irr.) to pieces.

sbrancare vt. to separate. ♦ **sbrancarsi** vr. to scatter.

sbrattare vt. to clean.

sbriciolamento sm. crumbling.

sbriciolare vt. to crumble.

sbrigare vt. to finish off, to get (v. irr.) through. ♦ **sbrigarsi** vr. to hurry up.

sbrigativo agg. quick, hasty.

sbrigliare vt. to unbridle.

sbrinamento sm. defrosting.

sbrinare vt. to defrost.

sbrindellare vt. to tear (v. irr.) to ribbons.

sbrodolare vt. to spill (v. irr.).

sbrodolone sm. 1. slovenly eater 2. (chi parla a lungo) babbler.

sbrogliare vt. to disentangle. ♦ **sbrogliarsi** vr. to extricate oneself.

sbronza sf. V. sbornia.

sbronzarsi vr. to get (v. irr.) drunk.

sbronzo agg. drunk.

sbruffare vt. to besprinkle. ♦ **sbruffare** vi. (fig.) to brag.

sbruffo sm. sprinkle.

sbruffone sm. braggart.

sbucare vi. 1. to come (v. irr.) out 2. (fig.) to spring (v. irr.).

sbucciare vt. 1. to peel 2. (sgranare) to shell.

sbucciatura sf. 1. peeling 2. (scalfittura) scratch.

sbudellamento sm. stabbing.

sbudellare vt. to stab.

sbuffare vi. 1. to pant, to puff 2. (per noia, ira) to snort.

sbuffo sm. 1. puff 2. (per noia, ira) snort.

sbugiardare vt. to give (v. irr.) the lie to.

sbullonare vt. to unbolt.

scabbia sf. scabies.

scabbioso agg. scabby.

scabro agg. rough.

scabrosità sf. 1. roughness 2. (fig.) difficulty.

scabroso agg. 1. rough 2. (fig.) scabrous.

scacchiera sf. chess-board.

scacchiere sm. (stor.) Exchequer.

scacchista sm. chess-player.

scacciacani sf. dummy pistol.

scacciare vt. 1. to drive (v. irr.) away 2. (da scuola) to expel.

scacciata sf. expulsion.

scaccino sm. church cleaner.

scacco sm. 1. (quadratino) square 2. (disegno su tessuti) check 3. (giuoco) chess || — matto, checkmate.

scadente agg. 1. poor 2. (comm.) falling due.

scadenza sf. (comm.) maturity: a breve, lunga scadenza (comm.), at short, long maturity || a breve —, in a short time.

scadenzario sm. discount bill-book.

scadere vi. 1. to expire 2. (di pagamenti ecc.) to become (v. irr.) due 3. (peggiorare) to fall (v. irr.) off.

scadimento sm. decay.

scafandro sm. diving-suit.

scaffalare vt. to shelve.

scaffalatura sf. shelving.

scaffale sm. shelf (pl. shelves).

scafo sm. hull, body.

scagionare vt. to acquit. ♦ scagionarsi vr. to exculpate oneself.

scaglia sf. 1. scale 2. (di legno, pietra) chip.

scagliare vt. to fling (v. irr.), to throw (v. irr.).

scaglionare vt. to divide into groups.

scaglione sm. 1. group 2. (mil.) echelon.

scaglioso agg. scaly.

scala sf. 1. stairs (pl.) 2. (trasportabile) ladder 3. (scala graduata) scale || salire, scendere le scale, to go (v. irr.) upstairs, downstairs.

scalare[1] agg. gradual.

scalare[2] vt. 1. to climb (up) 2. (diminuire) to scale down.

scalata sf. climbing.

scalatore sm. climber.

scalcagnato agg. down-at-heel, shabby.

scalciare vi. to kick.

scalcinato agg. 1. unplastered 2. (sciatto) shabby.

scaldabagno sm. water-heater.

scaldaletto sm. bed-warmer.

scaldapiedi sm. foot-warmer.

scaldare vt. to heat, to warm. ♦ scaldarsi vr. to warm oneself, to get (v. irr.) warm.

scaldavivande sm. dish-warmer.

scaldino sm. hand-warmer.

scalea sf. flight of stairs.

scaleno agg. scalene.

scalfire vt. to scratch.

scalfittura sf. scratch.

scalinata sf. flight of steps.

scalino sm. step.

scalmanarsi vr. (fig.) to get (v. irr.) excited.

scalmanato agg. out of breath, excited.

scalmo sm. rowlock.

scalo sm. 1. (mar.; aer.) port of call: volo senza —, non-stop flight 2. (ferr.) goods station || fare — a, to touch at.

scalogna sf. bad luck.

scalognato agg. unlucky.

scalone sm. great staircase.

scaloppina sf. veal cutlet.

scalpellare vt. to chisel.

scalpellino sm. stone-cutter.

scalpello sm. chisel.

scalpicciare vi. to shuffle.

scalpiccio sm. shuffling.

scalpitare vi. 1. to paw 2. (di persona) to stamp.

scalpitio sm. 1. pawing 2. (di persona) stamping.

scalpore sm. fuss, noise.

scaltrezza sf. shrewdness.

scaltrire vt. to sharpen so.'s wits. ♦ scaltrirsi vr. to become (v. irr.) sharp.

scaltro agg. shrewd.

scalzacane sm. 1. (incompetente) botcher 2. (malridotto) down-and-out.

scalzare vt. 1. to take (v. irr.) so.'s shoes and socks off 2. (fig.) to undermine.

scalzo agg. barefoot.

scambiare vt. 1. to exchange 2. (sbagliarsi) to mistake (v. irr.).

scambiévole agg. reciprocal.

scambio sm. 1. exchange 2. (ferr.) points (pl.).

scambista sm. (ferr.) pointsman (pl. -men).

scamiciato agg. shirt-sleeved (attr.).

scamosciare vt. to chamois.

scamosciato agg. shammy.

scampagnata sf. trip into the country.

scampanare vt. to chime.

scampanellare vi. to ring (v. irr.) long and loudly.

scampanellata sf. loud long ring.

scampare vi. to escape || l'hai scampata bella!, you have had a narrow escape.

scampato sm. survivor.

scampo[1] sm. escape: via di —, escape.

scampo² *sm.* (*itt.*) shrimp.

scàmpolo *sm.* remnant.

scanalare *vt.* to channel.

scanalatura *sf.* groove.

scandagliare *vt.* to sound.

scandaglio *sm.* sounding-lead.

scandalizzare *vt.* to shock.

scandalizzato *agg.* shocked.

scàndalo *sm.* scandal: *fare uno —*, to stir up a scandal.

scandaloso *agg.* scandalous, shocking.

scandire *vt.* **1.** to scan **2.** (*parole*) to syllabize **3.** (*mus.*) to stress.

scannare *vt.* **1.** to cut (*v. irr.*) so.'s throat **2.** (*uccidere crudelmente*) to slaughter.

scannatoio *sm.* slaughter-house.

scanno *sm.* seat.

scansafatiche *sm.* lazy-bones.

scansare *vt.* to avoid, to shun. ♦ **scansarsi** *vr.* to step aside.

scansìa *sf.* shelves (*pl.*).

scantinato *sm.* basement.

scantonamento *sm.* (*l'evitare*) avoiding.

scantonare *vt.* (*evitare*) to avoid. ♦ **scantonare** *vi.* to turn the corner.

scanzonato *agg.* unconventional.

scapaccione *sm.* slap.

scapataggine *sf.* recklessness.

scapestrato *agg. e sm.* madcap.

scapigliare *vt.* to dishevel.

scapigliato *agg.* **1.** dishevelled **2.** (*fig.*) unruly.

scàpito *sm.* damage, detriment: *a — di*, to the detriment of.

scàpola *sf.* shoulder-blade.

scapolare *agg. e sm.* scapular.

scàpolo *agg.* single. ♦ **scàpolo** *sm.* bachelor.

scappamento *sm.* **1.** escape **2.** (*di motori*) exhaust.

scappare *vi.* to escape, to run (*v. irr.*) away || *lasciarsi —*, to miss.

scappata *sf.* **1.** escape **2.** (*breve visita*) call.

scappatella *sf.* prank.

scappatola *sf.* loop-hole.

scappellarsi *vr.* to take (*v. irr.*) off one's hat.

scappellata *sf.* raising one's hat.

scappellotto *sm.* slap.

scarabeo *sm.* scarab.

scarabocchiare *vt. e vi.* to scribble.

scarabocchio *sm.* scribble.

scarafaggio *sm.* black-beetle.

scaramanzia *sf. per —*, for luck.

scaramuccia *sf.* skirmish.

scaraventare *vt.* to hurl.

scarcerare *vt.* to release (from prison).

scarcerazione *sf.* release (from prison).

scardinare *vt.* to unhinge.

scàrica *sf.* **1.** (*di armi da fuoco; elettr.*) discharge **2.** (*di proiettili, frecce; fig.*) shower.

scaricabarili *sm. fare a —*, to lay (*v. irr.*) the blame on so. else.

scaricamento *sm.* unloading.

scaricare *vt.* to discharge.

scaricatoio *sm.* **1.** wharf **2.** (*tubo*) waste-pipe.

scaricatore *sm.* unloader: *— di porto*, docker.

scàrico *sm.* **1.** (*scolo*) drain **2.** (*di merci*) discharge. ♦ **scàrico** *agg.* **1.** (*di arma*) unloaded **2.** discharged.

scarlattina *sf.* scarlet fever.

scarlatto *agg.* scarlet.

scarmigliare *vt.* to dishevel.

scarnire *vt.* to take (*v. irr.*) flesh off.

scarno *agg.* thin, lean.

scarpa *sf.* shoe: *— col tacco alto*, high-heeled shoe; *lucido per scarpe*, shoe polish.

scarpata *sf.* scarp.

scarpone *sm.* boot.

scarroccio *sm.* (*mar.*) leeway.

scarrozzare *vt. e vi.* to drive (*v. irr.*) about.

scarsamente *avv.* scarcely.

scarseggiare *vi.* to be lacking (in).

scarsità *sf.* shortage, lack.

scarso *agg.* scanty, lacking in.

scartabellare *vt.* to look through.

scartafaccio *sm.* note-book.

scartamento *sm.* (*ferr.*) gauge: *— ridotto*, narrow gauge.

scartare¹ *vt.* (*mettere da parte*) to reject.

scartare² *vi.* to unwrap.

scartare³ *vt.* (*sport*) to swerve.

scarto¹ *sm.* **1.** (*cosa scartata*) discard **2.** (*lo scartare*) discarding.

scarto² *sm.* (*deviazione*) swerve.

scartocciare *vt.* to unwrap.

scartoffie *sf. pl.* heap of papers.

scassare *vt.* (*rompere*) to force open.

scassinare *vt.* to break (*v. irr.*) open.

scassinatore *sm.* **1.** house-breaker **2.** (*di notte*) burglar.

scasso *sm.* lock-picking, house-breaking: *furto con —* (*di giorno*), house-breaking; (*di notte*) burglary.

scatenamento *sm.* (*fig.*) outburst.

scatenare *vt.* 1. (*aizzare*) to stir up 2. (*suscitare*) to rouse. ♦ **scatenarsi** *vr.* 1. to break (*v. irr.*) loose 2. (*fig.*) to break out.

scàtola *sf.* 1. box 2. (*di latta*) tin.

scatolame *sm.* 1. tins (*pl.*) 2. (*cibo in scatola*) tinned food.

scattare *vi.* 1. (*adirarsi*) to lose (*v. irr.*) one's temper 2. to go (*v. irr.*) off; to spring (*v. irr.*). ♦ **scattare** *vt.* (*foto*) to shoot (*v. irr.*).

scatto *sm.* 1. (*d'ira*) outburst || *di —*, suddenly; *a scatti*, in jerks 2. (*rumore*) click 3. (*di stipendio*) increase.

scaturire *vi.* 1. to spring (*v. irr.*) 2. (*derivare*) to originate.

scavalcare *vt.* 1. (*gettare da cavallo*) to unhorse 2. (*fig.*) to supplant 3. (*passare sopra*) to step, to jump over.

scavare *vt.* 1. to dig (*v. irr.*) 2. (*archeologia*) to excavate.

scavatrice *sf.* excavator.

scavezzacollo *sm.* reckless fellow.

scavo *sm.* 1. digging 2. (*archeologia*) excavation.

scégliere *vt.* to choose (*v. irr.*), to pick out.

sceicco *sm.* sheik.

scelleratezza *sf.* 1. wickedness 2. (*atto scellerato*) misdeed. ♦ **scellerato** *sm.* wicked person.

scellerato *agg.* wicked.

scellino *sm.* shilling: *mezzo —*, sixpence.

scelta *sf.* choice.

scelto *agg.* choice, selected.

scemare *vi.* to diminish.

scemenza *sf.* stupidity.

scemo *agg. e sm.* stupid.

scempiare *vt.* to halve.

scempio¹ *agg.* stupid, foolish.

scempio² *sm.* havoc.

scena *sf.* 1. scene 2. (*palcoscenico*) stage: *colpo di —*, stage effect.

scenario *sm.* scenery.

scenata *sf.* row.

scéndere *vi.* 1. to go (*v. irr.*) down, to come (*v. irr.*) down 2. (*da un veicolo*) to get (*v. irr.*) off; (*da cavallo*), to dismount (from a horse) 3. (*declinare*) to slope down 4. (*di astri*) to sink (*v. irr.*) 5. (*avere origini*) to descend.

scendiletto *sm.* bedside-carpet.

sceneggiare *vt.* to arrange into scenes.

sceneggiatore *sm.* scenarist.

sceneggiatura *sf.* screenplay.

scenicamente *avv.* scenically.

scenografia *sf.* scenography.

scèrnere *vt.* to choose (*v. irr.*).

scervellarsi *vr.* to rack one's brains.

scervellato *agg.* brainless. ♦ **scervellato** *sm.* brainless person.

scetticismo *sm.* scepticism.

scèttico *agg.* sceptical. ♦ **scèttico** *sm.* sceptic.

scettro *sm.* sceptre.

sceverare *vt.* to discern.

scevro *agg.* exempt.

scheda *sf.* card: *— elettorale*, voting-paper.

schedario *sm.* card-index.

scheggia *sf.* splinter, chip.

scheggiare *vt.* to chip, to splinter.

schelètrico *agg.* skeletal.

schèletro *sm.* skeleton.

schema *sm.* 1. scheme 2. (*tec.*) diagram.

schemàtico *agg.* schematic.

schematismo *sm.* schematism.

scherma *sf.* fencing.

schermaglia *sf.* skirmish.

schermare *vt.* 1. to screen 2. (*elettr.*) to shield.

schermirsi *vr.* to act coy.

schermitore *sm.* fencer.

schermo *sm.* 1. protection 2. (*cine*) screen 3. (*fis.*) shield 4. (*foto*) filter.

schernire *vt.* to laugh at.

scherno *sm.* mockery, derision.

scherzare *vi.* 1. to joke 2. (*considerare con leggerezza*) to trifle with.

scherzo *sm.* 1. joke: *per —*, for fun 2. (*effetto*) effects (*pl.*).

scherzosamente *avv.* playfully.

scherzoso *agg.* playful.

schettinare *vi.* to roller-skate.

schettini *sm. pl.* roller-skates.

schiaccianoci *sm.* nut-cracker.

schiacciante *agg.* (*decisivo*) overwhelming.

schiacciare *vt.* to crush, to squash.

schiacciasassi *sm.* steam-roller.

schiaffare *vt.* to hurl.

schiaffeggiare *vt.* to slap.

schiaffo *sm.* 1. slap 2. (*affronto*) slap in the face.

schiamazzare *vi.* to make (*v. irr.*) a din.

schiamazzo *sm.* din, uproar.

schiantare *vt.* to break (*v. irr.*). ♦ **schiantarsi** *vr.* to break, to crash.

schiarimento *sm.* (*spiegazione*) explanation.

schiarire *vt.* to clear, to make (*v. irr.*) clear: — *i capelli*, to bleach one's hair. ♦ **schiarirsi** *vr.* (*di tempo*) to brighten.

schiarita *sf.* 1. clearing 2. (*miglioramento*) improvement.

schiattare *vi.* to burst: — *di rabbia*, to burst with rage.

schiavista *sm.* 1. anti-abolitionist 2. (*mercante di schiavi*) slave-trader.

schiavitù *sf.* slavery.

schiavo *agg. e sm.* slave.

schidionata *sf.* spitful.

schidione *sm.* spit.

schiena *sf.* 1. back 2. (*di monte*) ridge.

schienale *sm.* back.

schiera *sf.* 1. formation 2. (*gruppo di persone*) group.

schieramento *sm.* array.

schierare *vt.* to array. ♦ **schierarsi** *vr.* 1. to draw (*v. irr.*) up 2. (*parteggiare*) to side with.

schiettezza *sf.* openness, purity.

schietto *agg.* pure, open.

schifare *vt.* to loathe. ♦ **schifarsi** *vr.* to feel (*v. irr.*) disgusted (at).

schifezza *sf.* disgusting thing.

schifiltoso *agg.* squeamish.

schifo[1] *sm.* disgust.

schifo[2] *sm.* (*mar.*) skiff.

schifoso *agg.* disgusting.

schioccare *vi.* 1. to crack 2. (*le dita*) to snap 3. (*le labbra*) to smack.

schiocco *sm.* 1. crack 2. (*di labbra*) smack.

schiodare *vt.* to unnail.

schiodatura *sf.* unnailing.

schioppettata *sf.* shot.

schioppo *sm.* gun.

schiùdere *vt.* to open. ♦ **schiùdersi** *vr.* to open.

schiuma *sf.* 1. foam 2. (*di vino, birra*) froth 3. (*di sapone*) lather.

schiumare *vt.* to skim. ♦ **schiumare** *vi.* 1. to foam 2. (*di bevande*) to froth.

schiumarola *sf.* skimmer.

schiumoso *agg.* 1. (*di mare*) foamy 2. (*di bevande*) frothy 3. (*di sapone*) lathery.

schiuso *agg.* open.

schivare *vt.* to avoid.

schivata *sf.* dodge.

schivo *agg.* shy, bashful.

schizofrenìa *sf.* schizophrenia.

schizofrènico *agg.* schizophrenic. ♦ **schizofrènico** *sm.* schizophrene.

schizzare *vt.* 1. to splash, to spatter 2. (*abbozzare*) to sketch. ♦ **schizzare** *vi.* to spurt.

schizzata *sf.* splashing.

schizzatoio *sm.* spray.

schizzetto *sm.* spray.

schizzinoso *agg.* squeamish, fussy.

schizzo *sm.* 1. splash, squirt 2. (*pitt.*) sketch.

sci *sm.* ski.

scia *sf.* 1. (*mar.*) wake 2. (*traccia*) trail.

scià *sm.* shah.

sciàbica *sf.* trawl.

sciàbola *sf.* sabre.

sciabolata *sf.* sabre-cut.

sciabolatore *sm.* sabreur.

sciabordare *vi.* to wash.

sciabordìo *sm.* washing, lapping.

sciacallo *sm.* 1. jackal 2. (*fig.*) profiteer.

sciacquare *vt.* to rinse (out).

sciacquatura *sf.* 1. rinsing 2. (*acqua*) rinsing-water.

sciacquìo *sm.* rinsing.

sciacquone *sm.* flush.

sciagura *sf.* misfortune.

sciagurato *agg.* 1. unlucky 2. (*malvagio*) wicked. ♦ **sciagurato** *sm.* wretch.

scialacquare *vt.* to squander.

scialacquatore *sm.* squanderer.

scialacquìo *sm.* squandering.

scialare *vt.* to squander money.

scialbare *vt.* to plaster.

scialbo *agg.* pale, wan.

scialle *sm.* shawl.

scialo *sm.* waste.

scialuppa *sf.* boat.

sciamannato *agg.* slovenly.

sciamano *sm.* shaman.

sciamare *vi.* to swarm.

sciame *sm.* swarm.

sciancarsi *vr.* to become (*v. irr.*) lame.

sciancato *agg.* lame.

sciarada *sf.* charade.

sciare[1] *vi.* to ski.

sciare[2] *vi.* (*mar.*) to back water.

sciarpa *sf.* scarf.

sciàtica *sf.* sciatica.

sciàtico *agg.* sciatic.

sciatore *sm.* skier.

sciatterìa *sf.* slovenliness.

sciatto *agg.* **1.** slovenly, untidy **2.** (*di stile ecc.*) careless.

scìbile *sm.* knowledge.

sciccherìa *sf.* smartness.

scientìfico *agg.* scientific.

scienza *sf.* science.

scienziato *sm.* scientist.

scilinguàgnolo *sm.* glib tongue.

scimitarra *sf.* scimitar.

scimmia *sf.* monkey, ape (*anche fig.*).

scimmiesco *agg.* monkeyish.

scimmiottare *vt.* to ape.

scimmiotto *sm.* young monkey.

scimpanzé *sm.* chimpanzee.

scimunito *agg.* silly. ◆ **scimunito** *sm.* blockhead.

scìndere *vt.* to divide: — *le questioni*, to deal (*v. irr.*) with each matter separately.

scintilla *sf.* spark.

scintillamento *sm.* sparkling.

scintillante *agg.* sparkling.

scintillare *vi.* to sparkle.

scintillìo *sm.* sparkling.

scintoismo *sm.* Shintoism.

scintoista *sm.* Shintoist.

scioccamente *avv.* foolishly.

scioccchezza *sf.* **1.** foolishness **2.** foolish thing **3.** trifle.

sciocco *agg.* silly.

sciògliere *vt.* **1.** to melt **2.** (*slegare, disfare*) to untie **3.** (*liberare*) to release **4.** (*risolvere*) to solve. ◆ **sciògliersi** *vr.* to dissolve, to get (*v. irr.*) loose.

scioglilingua *sm.* tongue-twister.

scioglimento *sm.* **1.** dissolution, breaking up **2.** (*epilogo*) unravelling.

sciolina *sf.* ski wax.

scioltezza *sf.* **1.** agility **2.** (*spigliatezza*) ease **3.** (*nel parlare*) fluency.

sciolto *agg.* **1.** melted **2.** (*slegato*) untied **3.** (*agile*) agile **4.** (*disinvolto*) easy || *capelli sciolti*, loose hair; *avere la lingua sciolta*, to have a ready tongue; — *da obblighi*, free from obligations.

scioperante *sm.* striker.

scioperare *vi.* to strike (*v. irr.*).

scioperatàggine *sf.* laziness.

scioperato *agg.* lazy. ◆ **scioperato** *sm.* lazy fellow.

sciòpero *sm.* strike.

sciorinare *vt.* to air, to display (*anche fig.*).

sciovìa *sf.* ski-lift.

sciovinismo *sm.* chauvinism.

sciovinista *sm.* chauvinist.

scipitàggine *sf.* insipidity (*anche fig.*).

scipito *agg.* insipid.

scirocco *sm.* sirocco.

sciroppare *vt.* to syrup.

sciroppato *agg.* in syrup.

sciropposo *agg.* syrupy.

scisma *sm.* schism.

scismàtico *agg.* e *sm.* schismatic.

scissione *sf.* **1.** scission, split (*anche fig.*) **2.** (*fis.; biol.*) fission.

scisso *agg.* divided.

scissura *sf.* **1.** cleft, split **2.** (*fig.*) dissension.

sciupare *vt.* **1.** to spoil (*v. irr.*), to damage **2.** (*sprecare*) to waste.

sciupato *agg.* **1.** spoilt **2.** (*sprecato*) wasted.

sciupìo *sm.* waste.

sciupone *agg.* wasteful. ◆ **sciupone** *sm.* waster.

scivolamento *sm.* sliding.

scivolare *vi.* **1.** to slide (*v. irr.*) **2.** (*involontariamente*) to slip.

scivolata *sf.* **1.** slide **2.** (*involontaria*) slip.

scìvolo *sm.* **1.** (*aer.; mar.*) slipway **2.** skid.

scivolone *sm.* slip.

scivoloso *agg.* slippery.

sclerosi *sf.* sclerosis.

scleròtica *sf.* sclerotic.

scleròtico *agg.* sclerotic.

scoccare *vt.* e *vi.* **1.** to shoot (*v. irr.*) **2.** (*l'ora*) to strike (*v. irr.*).

scocciare *vt.* to bother.

scocciatore *sm.* bore.

scocciatura *sf.* bother.

scodella *sf.* bowl.

scodellare *vt.* to dish up.

scodinzolare *vi.* to wag the tail.

scodinzolìo *sm.* tail-wagging.

scogliera *sf.* cliff.

scòglio *sm.* **1.** rock **2.** (*fig.*) difficulty.

scoiare *vt.* V. *scuoiare*.

scoiàttolo *sm.* squirrel.

scolapasta *sm.* colander.

scolara *sf.* pupil, schoolgirl.

scolare *vt.* **1.** to drain **2.** (*in un colabrodo*) to strain.

scolaresca *sf.* student-body.

scolaro *sm.* pupil, schoolboy.

scolàstica *sf.* scholasticism.

scolàstico *agg.* **1.** school (*attr.*) **2.** (*dispregiativo*) bookish.

scolatoio *sm.* drain.

scolatura *sf.* draining.

scoliosi *sf.* scoliosis.

scollacciato *agg.* 1. (*di abito*) low--necked 2. (*fig.*) coarse.

scollare¹ *vt.* to cut (*v. irr.*) away the neck of.

scollare² *vt.* (*staccare*) to unglue.

scollato¹ *agg.* (*di abito*) low-necked.

scollato² *agg.* unglued.

scollatura *sf.* neckline.

scollo *sm.* neck-opening.

scolo *sm.* draining.

scolorare *vt.* to discolour. ◆ **scolorarsi** *vr.* to grow (*v. irr.*) pale.

scolorimento *sm.* discolouration.

scolorire *vt.* to bleach.

scolorito *agg.* faded, pale.

scolpare *vt.* to exculpate.

scolpire *vt.* to sculpture.

scombinare *vt.* to upset (*v. irr.*).

scombinato *agg.* screwy.

scombussolamento *sm.* upsetting.

scombussolare *vt.* to upset (*v. irr.*).

scommessa *sf.* bet.

scommettere *vt.* to bet (*v. irr.*).

scommettitore *sm.* bettor.

scomodamente *avv.* uncomfortably.

scomodare *vt.* to trouble, to bother.

scomodità *sf.* lack of comfort.

scòmodo *agg.* uncomfortable.

scompaginamento *sm.* upsetting, upset.

scompaginare *vt.* to upset (*v. irr.*).

scompagnare *vt.* to break (*v. irr.*) up (a pair).

scompagnato *agg.* odd.

scomparire *vi.* 1. to disappear 2. (*non spiccare*) not to stand (*v. irr.*) out.

scomparsa *sf.* 1. disappearance 2. (*morte*) death.

scomparso *agg.* 1. disappeared 2. (*morto*) dead.

scompartimento *sm.* 1. partition 2. (*ferr.*) compartment.

scompartire *vt.* to divide, to share out.

scomparto *sm.* V. *scompartimento*.

scompenso *sm.* lack of balance: — *cardiaco*, cardiac decompensation.

scompiacenza *sf.* unkindness.

scompigliare *vt.* 1. to upset (*v. irr.*) 2. (*arruffare*) to ruffle.

scompigliatamente *avv.* confusedly.

scompiglio *sm.* confusion, disorder.

scomponìbile *agg.* decomposable.

scomponimento *sm.* decomposition.

scomporre *vt.* 1. to decompose 2. (*i lineamenti*) to distort.

scompostamente *avv.* in an unseemly manner.

scompostezza *sf.* unseemliness.

scomposto *agg.* 1. (*sguaiato*) unseemly 2. decomposed.

scomùnica *sf.* excommunication.

scomunicare *vt.* to excommunicate.

scomunicato *agg.* e *sm.* excommunicate.

sconcertante *agg.* disconcerting.

sconcertare *vt.* to disconcert, to baffle.

sconcertato *agg.* disconcerted.

sconcerto *sm.* perturbation.

sconcezza *sf.* indecency.

sconciamente *avv.* indecently.

sconcio *agg.* indecent.

sconclusionatamente *avv.* inconclusively.

sconclusionato *agg.* inconclusive.

scondito *agg.* 1. unseasoned 2. (*di insalata*) undressed.

sconfessare *vt.* to disown.

sconfessione *sf.* disowning.

sconfìggere *vt.* to defeat.

sconfinamento *sm.* 1. (*in paese straniero*) crossing the frontier 2. (*in proprietà privata*) trespass.

sconfinare *vi.* 1. (*in paese straniero*) to cross the frontier 2. (*in proprietà privata*) to trespass.

sconfinato *agg.* boundless.

sconfitta *sf.* defeat.

sconfitto *agg.* defeated.

sconfortante *agg.* discouraging.

sconfortare *vt.* to discourage.

sconfortato *agg.* discouraged.

sconforto *sm.* 1. discouragement 2. (*dolore*) sorrow.

scongiurare *vt.* 1. to beseech (*v. irr.*) 2. (*evitare*) to avoid.

scongiuro *sm.* exorcism.

sconnessione *sf.* disconnectedness.

sconnesso *agg.* 1. disconnected 2. (*fig.*) rambling.

sconnèttere *vt.* to disconnect. ◆ **sconnèttere** *vi.* to wander.

sconoscente *agg.* ungrateful.

sconoscenza *sf.* ingratitude.

sconòscere *vt.* to disown.

sconosciuto *agg.* unknown. ◆ **sconosciuto** *sm.* stranger.

sconquassare *vt.* to shatter.

sconquassato *agg.* ramshackle.

sconquasso *sm.* mess, disorder.

sconsacrare *vt.* to deconsecrate.

sconsideratezza *sf.* rashness.

sconsiderato *agg.* thoughtless.

sconsigliare *vt.* to advise against.

sconsigliato *agg.* rash.

sconsolante *agg.* discouraging.

sconsolare *vt.* to dishearten.

sconsolato *agg.* disconsolate.

scontàbile *agg.* discountable.

scontare *vt.* **1.** (*comm.*) to discount **2.** (*detrarre*) to deduct **3.** (*espiare*) to expiate.

scontato *agg.* (*previsto*) expected.

scontentare *vt.* to displease.

scontentezza *sf.* discontent.

scontento *agg.* displeased.

sconto *sm.* discount.

scontrarsi *vr.* to clash.

scontrino *sm.* ticket, check.

scontro *sm.* **1.** encounter **2.** (*di veicoli*) crash **3.** (*fig.*) clash.

scontrosamente *avv.* peevishly.

scontrosità *sf.* bad temper.

scontroso *agg.* bad-tempered.

sconveniente *agg.* **1.** unprofitable **2.** (*indecente*) unseemly.

sconvenientemente *avv.* unbecomingly.

sconvenienza *sf.* **1.** unprofitableness **2.** (*mancanza di correttezza*) unseemliness.

sconvolgente *agg.* upsetting.

sconvòlgere *vt.* to upset (*v. irr.*).

sconvolgimento *sm.* upsetting, confusion.

sconvolto *agg.* upset.

scopa *sf.* broom.

scopare *vt.* to sweep (*v. irr.*).

scoperchiare *vt.* to take (*v. irr.*) off the lid.

scoperta *sf.* discovery.

scopertamente *avv.* openly.

scoperto *agg.* uncovered ‖ *automobile scoperta*, open car; *a capo —*, bare-headed; *giocare a carte scoperte*, to act openly.

scopino *sm.* street-sweeper.

scopo *sm.* aim, purpose: *senza —*, aimless.

scopolamina *sf.* scopolamine.

scoppiare *vi.* **1.** to burst (*v. irr.*) **2.** (*di guerre, epidemie ecc.*) to break (*v. irr.*) out.

scoppiettante *agg.* crackling.

scoppiettare *vi.* to crackle.

scoppiettìo *sm.* crackling.

scoppio *sm.* **1.** burst, explosion: *motore a —*, piston-engine **2.** (*di guerre, rivoluzioni ecc.*) outbreak.

scoprimento *sm.* **1.** discovering **2.** (*di monumento*) unveiling.

scoprire *vt.* **1.** to discover **2.** (*avvistare*) to sight **3.** (*togliere ciò che copre*) to uncover **4.** (*palesare*) to show (*v. irr.*). ◆ **scoprirsi** *vr.* (*rivelarsi*) to reveal oneself.

scopritore *sm.* discoverer.

scoraggiamento *sm.* discouragement.

scoraggiante *agg.* discouraging.

scoraggiare *vt.* to discourage. ◆ **scoraggiarsi** *vr.* to get (*v. irr.*) discouraged.

scoraggiato *agg.* discouraged.

scoramento *sm.* discouragement.

scorato *agg.* disheartened.

scorbùtico *agg.* **1.** (*med.*) scorbutic **2.** (*fig.*) ill-tempered.

scorbuto *sm.* scurvy.

scorciare *vt.* to shorten.

scorciatola *sf.* short cut.

scorcio *sm.* **1.** foreshortening **2.** (*spazio di tempo*) end, close.

scordare[1] *vt.* to forget (*v. irr.*).

scordare[2] *vt.* (*mus.*) to untune.

scordato[1] *agg.* forgotten.

scordato[2] *agg.* (*mus.*) untuned.

scòrfano *sm.* **1.** sea-scorpion **2.** (*di persona*) fright: *che —!*, what a fright!

scòrgere *vt.* to perceive, to discern.

scoria *sf.* **1.** (*metal.*) dross **2.** (*fig.*) scum.

scornare *vt.* **1.** to horn **2.** (*fig.*) to humiliate.

scornato *agg.* humiliated.

scorno *sm.* shame.

scorpacciata *sf.* blow out: *fare una — di*, to stuff oneself with.

scorpione *sm.* scorpion.

scorporare *vt.* to disembody.

scòrporo *sm.* breaking up.

scorrazzare *vi.* to run (*v. irr.*) about.

scòrrere *vi.* **1.** to run (*v. irr.*) **2.** (*scivolare*) to glide **3.** (*fluire*) to flow **4.** (*di tempo*) to fly (*v. irr.*).

scorreria *sf.* raid.

scorrettezza *sf.* incorrectness.

scorretto *agg.* **1.** incorrect **2.** (*di costumi*) dissolute **3.** (*maleducato*) rude.

scorrévole *agg.* **1.** sliding **2.** (*fig.*) fluent.

scorrevolezza *sf.* fluency.

scorribanda *sf.* incursion, raid.

scorrimento *sm.* sliding.

scorsa *sf.* glance.

scorso *agg.* last, past.

scorsolo *agg.* running.

scorta *sf.* **1.** escort **2.** (*provvista*) supply ‖ *ruota di —*, spare wheel.

scortare *vt.* to escort.

scortecciare *vt.* **1.** to peel **2.** (*un albero*) to bark.

scortese *agg.* rude, impolite.

scortesia *sf.* rudeness.

scorticare *vt.* to skin.

scorticatura *sf.* scratch.

scortichino *sm.* flaying-knife.

scorza *sf.* **1.** (*corteccia*) bark **2.** (*buccia*) skin, rind.

scoscéndere *vt.* to split (*v. irr.*).

scoscendimento *sm.* **1.** collapse **2.** (*di terreno*) break.

scosceso *agg.* steep, sloping.

scossa *sf.* shock, shake.

scosso *agg.* **1.** shaken **2.** (*fig.*) upset.

scossone *sm.* **1.** shake **2.** (*strattone*) jerk.

scostare *vt.* to shift, to move away. ♦ **scostarsi** *vr.* **1.** to move away **2.** (*staccarsi*) to turn off.

scostumatezza *sf.* dissoluteness.

scostumato *agg.* dissolute. ♦ **scostumato** *sm.* dissolute person.

scotennare *vt.* to scalp.

scottante *agg.* burning.

scottare *vt.* **1.** to burn (*v. irr.*) **2.** (*cuc.*) to half-cook **3.** (*fig.*) to hurt (*v. irr.*).

scottatura *sf.* burn.

scotto[1] *sm.* score: *pagare lo —,* to pay (*v. irr.*) one's piper.

scotto[2] *agg.* overdone.

scovare *vt.* **1.** to put (*v. irr.*) up **2.** (*scoprire*) to discover.

scozzare *vt.* to shuffle.

scozzese *agg.* Scotch, Scottish. ♦ **scozzese** *sm.* Scotchman (*pl.* -men).

scozzonare *vt.* **1.** to break (*v. irr.*) in **2.** (*fig.*) to teach (*v. irr.*) the first elements.

screanzatamente *avv.* rudely.

screanzato *agg.* rude, impolite. ♦ **screanzato** *sm.* rude person.

screditare *vt.* to discredit.

screditato *agg.* discredited.

scrédito *sm.* discredit.

scremare *vt.* to skim.

scremato *agg.* skimmed: *latte —,* skim-milk.

scrematura *sf.* skimming.

screpolare *vi.* **1.** to crack **2.** (*della pelle*) to get (*v. irr.*) chapped.

screpolatura *sf.* **1.** crack **2.** (*della pelle*) chap.

screziare *vt.* to variegate.

screziato *agg.* variegated.

screziatura *sf.* variegation.

screzio *sm.* disagreement.

scribacchiare *vt. e vi.* to scribble.

scribacchino *sm.* scribbler.

scricchiolare *vi.* **1.** to creak **2.** (*di denti*) to grind (*v. irr.*).

scricchiolìo *sm.* **1.** creaking **2.** (*di denti*) grinding.

scrigno *sm.* casket: *— di gioielli,* jewel-case.

scriminatura *sf.* (hair-)parting.

scriteriato *agg.* senseless.

scritta *sf.* **1.** inscription **2.** (*cartello*) notice **3.** (*dicitura*) caption.

scritto *sm.* writing.

scrittoio *sm.* writing-desk.

scrittore *sm.* writer.

scrittrice *sf.* woman writer.

scrittura *sf.* **1.** writing: *— a macchina,* typewriting; *— a mano,* handwriting **2.** (*teat.*) engagement **3.** (*giur.*) deed.

scritturare *vt.* to engage.

scrivanìa *sf.* writing-desk.

scrivano *sm.* clerk, copyist.

scrivere *vt.* to write (*v. irr.*): *— a mano,* to write by hand; *— a penna, a matita,* to write in pen, in pencil; *— sotto dettatura,* to write from dictation; *— a macchina,* to typewrite (*v. irr.*) **2.** (*registrare*) to enter, to record.

scroccare *vt.* to scrounge.

scrocco *sm.* *vivere a —,* to sponge one's living.

scroccone *sm.* sponger.

scrofa *sf.* sow.

scrofoloso *agg.* scrofulous.

scrollamento *sm.* **1.** shaking **2.** (*di spalle*) shrugging.

scrollare *vt.* **1.** to shake (*v. irr.*) **2.** (*le spalle*) to shrug.

scrollata *sf.* **1.** (*di testa*) shake **2.** (*di spalle*) shrug.

scrosciante *agg.* (*di risa ecc.*) roaring: *pioggia —,* pelting rain.

scrosciare *vi.* **1.** (*di pioggia*) to pelt down **2.** (*fig.*) to roar.

scroscio *sm.* **1.** (*di cascata, torrente ecc.*) roar **2.** (*fig.*) roar, burst ‖ *— di pioggia,* shower.

scrostamento *sm.* peeling.

scrostare *vt.* 1. to take (*v. irr.*) the crust off, to peel off 2. (*dei muri*) to remove the plaster from a wall. ♦ **scrostarsi** *vr.* to fall (*v. irr.*) off, to peel off.

scrùpolo *sm.* scruple.

scrupolosamente *avv.* scrupulously.

scrupolosità *sf.* scrupulosity.

scrupoloso *agg.* scrupulous.

scrutare *vt.* to search, to scan.

scrutatore *agg.* searching, inquisitive. ♦ **scrutatore** *sm.* 1. searcher 2. (*di elezioni*) scrutineer.

scrutinare *vt.* to scrutinize.

scrutinio *sm.* 1. (*di elezioni*) poll 2. (*scolastico*) assignment of a term's marks 3. (*attento esame*) scrutiny.

scucire *vt.* to unsew (*v. irr.*), to unstitch. ♦ **scucirsi** *vr.* to rip.

scucito *agg.* 1. unsewn 2. (*fig.*) incoherent.

scucitura *sf.* unsewing.

scuderìa *sf.* stable.

scudetto *sm.* 1. small shield 2. (*sport*) (championship) shield.

scudiero *sm.* squire.

scudisciare *vt.* to lash.

scudisciata *sf.* lash.

scudiscio *sm.* switch, lash.

scudo *sm.* shield.

scuffia *sf.* (*sbornia*) drunkenness.

sculacciare *vt.* to spank.

sculacciata *sf.* spank.

scullettare *vi.* to waddle.

scultore *sm.* sculptor.

scultòreo *agg.* sculptural.

scultura *sf.* sculpture.

scuolare *vt.* to skin.

scuola *sf.* school: — *diurna*, day-classes; — *elementare*, primary school; — *media inferiore, superiore*, secondary school; — *pubblica*, State school; *maestro di* —, schoolmaster.

scuòtere *vt.* 1. to shake (*v. irr.*) (*anche fig.*) 2. (*agitare*) to stir.

scuotimento *sm.* shaking.

scure *sf.* axe.

scurire *vt.* 1. to darken 2. (*pitt.*) to tone down. ♦ **scurirsi** *vr.* to grow (*v. irr.*) dark.

scuro *agg.* dark || *faccia scura*, grim face.

scurrile *agg.* scurrilous.

scurrilità *sf.* scurrility.

scusa *sf.* 1. excuse, apology 2. (*pretesto*) pretext.

scusàbile *agg.* excusable.

scusare *vt.* to excuse, to forgive (*v. irr.*) || *scusi!, scusate!*, sorry!, excuse me! ♦ **scusarsi** *vr.* to apologize.

sdebitarsi *vr.* 1. to pay (*v. irr.*) off one's debts 2. (*disobbligarsi*) to return a kindness.

sdegnare *vt.* 1. to disdain 2. (*provocare lo sdegno*) to enrage.

sdegnato *agg.* indignant.

sdegno *sm.* disdain, indignation.

sdegnosamente *avv.* disdainfully.

sdegnoso *agg.* 1. (*di atti e parole*) disdainful 2. (*di persona*) haughty.

sdentare *vt.* to break (*v. irr.*) the teeth.

sdentato *agg.* toothless.

sdilinquimento *sm.* mawkishness.

sdilinquirsi *vr.* to melt away.

sdoganamento *sm.* clearing (through the customs).

sdolcinato *agg.* sugary, affected.

sdolcinatura *sf.* mawkishness.

sdoppiamento *sm.* splitting.

sdoppiare *vt.* to split.

sdraia *sf.* deck-chair.

sdraiarsi *vr.* to lie (*v. irr.*) down.

sdrucciolare *vi.* to slip, to slide.

sdrucciolévole *agg.* slippery.

sdrucciolone *sm.* slip.

sdrucire *vt.* to tear (*v. irr.*).

sdrucito *agg.* torn.

se *cong.* 1. if 2. (*dubitativo*) whether || — *mai*, in case; — *non altro*, at least; — *non che*, except that; *anche* —, even if.

sé *pron. pers.* 1. one, him, her, it, them 2. (*riflessivi*) oneself, himself, herself, itself, themselves || *una donna piena di* —, a conceited woman; *essere fuori di* —, to be beside oneself; *tornare in* —, to recover consciousness; *amore di* —, selfishness; *padronanza di* —, self-control; *un uomo sicuro di* —, a self-confident man; *un uomo che si è fatto da* —, a self-made man; *rispetto di* —, self-respect.

sebàceo *agg.* sebaceous.

sebbene *cong.* though, although.

sebo *sm.* sebum.

secante *sf.* secant.

secca *sf.* 1. shoal 2. (*siccità*) drought.

seccamente *avv.* coldly.

seccante *agg.* (*fig.*) annoying, irritating || *una cosa, persona* —, a nuisance.

seccare *vt.* 1. to dry up 2. (*annoiare*) to annoy, to irritate. ◆ **seccarsi** *vr.* (*infastidirsi*) to be annoyed (with).

seccatore *sm.* bother.

seccatura *sf.* 1. (*essicamento*) drying 2. (*noia*) bother, nuisance.

secchia *sf.* pail, bucket.

secchiello *sm.* bucket.

secchio *sm.* V. *secchia*.

secco *agg.* 1. dry 2. (*appassito*) withered 3. (*magro*) thin 4. (*brusco*) sharp 5. (*freddo*) cold.

secentesco *agg.* of the seventeenth century.

secèrnere *vt.* to secrete.

secessione *sf.* secession.

secessionista *agg. e sm.* secessionist.

seco *pron.* with him, with her, with them.

secolare *agg.* 1. secular 2. (*in opposizione a ecclesiastico*) lay.

secolarizzare *vt.* to secularize.

secolarizzazione *sf.* secularization.

sècolo *sm.* 1. century 2. (*epoca*) epoch, age || *Padre Carlo, al — John Smith*, Father Charles, in the world John Smith.

seconda *sf.* (*auto*) second gear || *a — di* (*loc. prep.*), according to.

secondare *vt.* to favour.

secondario *agg.* secondary.

secondino *sm.* warder.

secondo[1] *agg.* 1. second 2. (*favorevole*) favourable. ◆ **secondo** *sm.* 1. (*minuto*) second 2. (*ufficiale in seconda*) executive officer.

secondo[2] *prep.* according to. ◆ **secondo** *avv.* second.

secrezione *sf.* secretion.

sèdano *sm.* celery.

sedare *vt.* to soothe.

sedativo *agg. e sm.* sedative.

sede *sf.* 1. seat, centre 2. (*residenza*) residence 3. (*eccl.*) see 4. (*edificio per pubblici uffici*) office.

sedentario *agg.* sedentary.

sedere[1] *vi.* 1. (*stare seduto*) to sit (*v. irr.*), to be sitting 2. (*mettersi a sedere*) to sit (down).

sedere[2] *sm.* bottom.

sedia *sf.* chair: — *a dondolo*, rocking-chair.

sedicenne *agg.* 1. (*attr.*) sixteen--year-old 2. (*pred.*) sixteen years old.

sedicente *agg.* would-be.

sedicèsimo *agg.* sixteenth.

sédici *agg.* sixteen.

sedile *sm.* seat, chair.

sedimentario *agg.* sedimentary.

sedimentazione *sf.* sedimentation.

sedimento *sm.* sediment.

sedizione *sf.* sedition.

sedizioso *agg.* seditious.

seducente *agg.* 1. alluring 2. (*affascinante*) charming.

sedurre *vt.* to seduce, to tempt.

seduta *sf.* sitting, session.

seduttore *agg.* seducing. ◆ **seduttore** *sm.* seducer.

seduzione *sf.* 1. seduction 2. (*attrazione*) attraction.

sega *sf.* saw.

ségala *sf.* rye.

segaligno *agg.* 1. rye (*attr.*) 2. (*di persona*) wiry.

segare *vt.* to saw (*v. irr.*).

segatura *sf.* sawdust.

seggio *sm.* chair, seat: — *elettorale*, poll.

sèggiola *sf.* chair.

seggiovia *sf.* chair-lift.

segherìa *sf.* saw-mill.

seghettare *vt.* to jag.

segmentazione *sf.* segmentation.

segmento *sm.* segment.

segnalare *vt.* 1. to signal 2. (*far notare*) to point out. ◆ **segnalarsi** *vr.* to distinguish oneself.

segnalatore *sm.* 1. signaller 2. (*segnalatore di direzione*) direction indicator.

segnalazione *sf.* signal: — *stradale*, traffic signal.

segnale *sm.* signal: — *di pericolo, allarme*, danger, alarm signal; — *di linea libera, occupata* (*tel.*), ringing, engaged tone; — *di passaggio a livello*, level-crossing signal.

segnalètica *sf.* signals (*pl.*).

segnalètico *agg.* descriptive.

segnalibro *sm.* book-mark.

segnare *vt.* 1. to mark 2. (*indicare*) to show (*v. irr.*) 3. (*sport*) to score. ◆ **segnarsi** *vr.* to cross oneself.

segnatura *sf.* 1. marking 2. (*sport*) scoring.

segno *sm.* 1. sign, mark: *passare il —*, to overstep the mark 2. (*limite*) limit 3. (*simbolo*) symbol.

sego *sm.* tallow.

segregare *vt.* to segregate.

segregazione *sf.* segregation.

segreta *sf.* dungeon.

segretamente *avv.* in secret.

segretariato *sm.* secretariate.

segretario *sm.* secretary.

segreteria *sf.* 1. secretariat 2. (*di ministero*) secretariat of State.

segretezza *sf.* secrecy.

segreto *agg.* secret. ♦ **segreto** *sm.* 1. secret: *nel — del cuore*, in the depths of one's heart 2. (*parte interna, intimità*) secrecy.

seguace *sm.* follower, supporter.

seguente *agg.* following, next.

segugio *sm.* bloodhound.

seguire *vt. e vi.* 1. to follow 2. (*sorvegliare*) to supervise 3. (*frequentare regolarmente*) to attend.

séguito *sm.* 1. (*corteo*) retinue 2. (*successione, sequela*) series 3. (*continuazione*) continuation || *il — alla prossima puntata*, to be continued 4. (*comm.*): *a — di*, following up.

sei *agg.* six.

seicento *agg.* six hundred. ♦ **seicento** *sm.* the seventeenth century.

selce *sf.* flint.

selciare *vt.* to pave.

selciato *sm.* pavement.

selenio *sm.* selenium.

selenite *agg.* lunar. ♦ **selenite** *sf.* selenite.

selettività *sf.* selectivity.

selettivo *agg.* selective.

selettore *sm.* selector.

selezionare *vt.* to select.

selezione *sf.* selection.

sella *sf.* saddle.

sellaio *sm.* saddler.

sellare *vt.* to saddle.

sellino *sm.* saddle.

selva *sf.* 1. wood 2. (*fig.*) mass.

selvaggina *sf.* game.

selvaggio *agg.* wild, primitive. ♦ **selvaggio** *sm.* savage.

selvàtico *agg.* 1. wild 2. (*non socievole*) unsociable.

selvoso *agg.* woody.

semàforo *sm.* traffic-lights (*pl.*).

semàntica *sf.* semantics.

semàntico *agg.* semantic.

semblanza *sf.* features (*pl.*).

sembrare *vi.* 1. to seem 2. (*somigliare*) to look like.

seme *sm.* 1. seed 2. (*carte da giuoco*) suit.

sementa *sf.* 1. seeds (*pl.*) 2. (*epoca della semina*) seed-time.

semente *sf.* seeds (*pl.*).

semenza *sf.* seeds (*pl.*).

semenzaio *sm.* seed-bed.

semestrale *agg.* six-monthly (*attr.*).

semestralmente *avv.* twice a year.

semestre *sm.* half-year.

semiaperto *agg.* half-open.

semicerchio *sm.* semicircle.

semichiuso *agg.* half-closed.

semicircolare *agg.* semicircular.

semiconduttore *sm.* semiconductor.

semidiàmetro *sm.* semi-diameter.

semidio *sm.* demigod.

semifinale *sf.* semifinal.

semilavorato *agg. e sm.* semi-manufactured.

sémina *sf.* sowing.

seminàbile *agg.* fit to be sown.

seminagione *sf.* sowing.

seminare *vt.* to sow (*v. irr.*).

seminario *sm.* seminary.

seminarista *sm.* seminarist.

seminato *agg.* 1. sown 2. (*fig.*) strewn.

seminatore *sm.* sower.

seminfermità *sf.* partial infirmity: — *mentale*, partial insanity.

seminudo *agg.* half-naked.

semiserio *agg.* half-serious.

semisfera *sf.* hemisphere.

semita *s.* Semite.

semitico *agg.* Semitic.

semitono *sm.* semitone.

semivivo *agg.* half-alive.

sémola *sf.* bran.

semolino *sm.* semolina.

semovente *agg.* self-moving.

sempiterno *agg.* everlasting.

sémplice *agg.* simple.

semplicione *sm.* simpleton.

semplicismo *sm.* superficiality.

semplicìstico *agg.* superficial.

semplicità *sf.* simplicity.

semplificare *vt.* to simplify.

semplificazione *sf.* simplification

sempre *avv.* 1. always: — *avanti!* always onward!; — *meglio, peggio*, better and better, worse and worse; *per —*, for ever; *una volta per —*, once for all 2. (*tuttora*) still: *vivi — qui?*, do you still live here?

sempreverde *sm.* evergreen.

sènape *sf.* mustard.

senato *sm.* senate.

senatore *sm.* senator.

senatoriale *agg.* senatorial.

senescenza *sf.* senescence.

senile *agg.* senile.

senilità *sf.* senility.

senno *sm.* sense, wisdom.

seno *sm.* 1. breast, bosom 2. (*grembo*) womb.

sensale *sm.* broker.

sensatezza *sf.* good sense.

sensato *agg.* sensible.

sensazionale *agg.* sensational.

sensazione *sf.* sensation, feeling.

sensibile *agg.* sensitive.

sensibilità *sf.* sensitiveness.

sensibilizzare *vt.* to sensitize.

sensibilmente *avv.* 1. sensitively 2. (*notevolmente*) sensibly.

sensitività *sf.* sensitivity.

sensitivo *agg.* 1. sensory 2. (*sensibile*) sensitive.

senso *sm.* 1. sense 2. (*sensazione*) sensation 3. (*direzione*) direction, way 4. (*modo*) way, manner.

sensorio *agg.* sensorial.

sensuale *agg.* sensual.

sensualità *sf.* sensuality.

sensualmente *avv.* sensually.

sentenza *sf.* 1. sentence 2. (*massima*) saying.

sentenziare *vi.* to judge, to hold (*v. irr.*).

sentenziosamente *avv.* sententiously.

sentenzioso *agg.* sententious.

sentiero *sm.* path.

sentimentale *agg.* sentimental.

sentimentalismo *sm.* sentimentalism.

sentimentalità *sf.* sentimentality.

sentimento *sm.* 1. sentiment 2. (*disposizione spirituale*) feeling.

sentinella *sf.* sentry.

sentire *vt.* 1. to feel (*v. irr.*) 2. (*udire*) to hear (*v. irr.*) 3. (*gustare*) to taste 4. (*odorare*) to smell (*v. irr.*) 5. (*ascoltare*) to listen to. ◆ **sentirsi** *vr.* to feel.

sentitamente *avv.* heartily.

sentito *agg.* 1. heart-felt 2. (*udito*) heard || *per — dire*, by hearsay.

sentore *sm.* inkling: *aver — di*, to suspect.

senza *prep.* without: — *scarpe*, barefoot; — *fine*, endless; — *confronto*, unrivalled; — *numero*, countless; — *testa*, thoughtless.

senzatetto *s.* homeless person.

separare *vt.* to separate. ◆ **separarsi** *vr.* to separate.

separatamente *avv.* separately.

separatismo *sm.* separatism.

separatista *s.* separatist.

separativo *agg.* separative.

separato *agg.* separated.

separazione *sf.* separation.

sepolcrale *agg.* sepulchral.

sepolcro *sm.* sepulchre, tomb.

sepolto *agg.* buried.

sepoltura *sf.* burial.

seppellimento *sm.* burial.

seppellire *vt.* to bury.

seppia *sf.* cuttle-fish.

seppure *cong.* even if.

sequela *sf.* series (*invariato al pl*).

sequenza *sf.* 1. series 2. (*cine*) sequence.

sequestrabile *agg.* seizable.

sequestrare *vt.* to seize.

sequestro *sm.* 1. seizure 2. (*per debiti*) distress.

sequoia *sf.* sequoia.

sera *sf.* evening.

seràfico *agg.* seraphic.

serafino *sm.* seraph.

serale *agg.* evening (*attr.*).

serata *sf.* 1. evening 2. (*ricevimento serale*) party.

serbare *vt.* 1. (*mettere in serbo*) to put (*v. irr.*) aside 2. (*conservare*) to keep (*v. irr.*) || — *odio*, *rancore*, to nourish hatred, rancour. ◆ **serbarsi** *vr.* to keep, to remain.

serbatoio *sm.* reservoir, tank.

serbo (*nella loc.*) *tenere in —*, to keep (*v. irr.*) aside.

serenamente *avv.* serenely.

serenata *sf.* serenade.

serenissimo *agg.* Serene Highness.

serenità *sf.* serenity.

sereno *agg.* serene, clear || *giudizio —*, objective judgement.

sergente *sm.* sergeant.

sèrico *agg.* silk (*attr.*), silky.

sericoltore *sm.* silkgrower.

sericoltura *sf.* sericulture.

serie *sf.* 1. series (*invariato al pl.*): *in —*, mass-produced 2. (*assieme*) set 3. (*fila*) row.

serietà *sf.* seriousness.

serio *agg.* serious, earnest.

sermone *sm.* 1. sermon 2. (*rimprovero*) lecture.

seròtino *agg.* evening (*attr.*).

serpe *sf.* snake.

serpeggiante *agg.* winding.

serpeggiare *vi.* to wind (*v. irr.*).

serpente *sm.* snake, serpent.

serpentina *sf.* 1. coil 2. (*di strada*) winding road.

serpentino *agg.* snakelike. ◆ **serpentino** *sm.* serpentine.

serra *sf.* greenhouse.

serraglio sm. **1.** menagerie **2.** (del sultano) seraglio.

serramànico (nella loc. avv.) coltello a —, flick-knife.

serramento sm. lock.

serrare vt. **1.** to shut (v. irr.), to close **2.** (a chiave) to lock **3.** (stringere) to tighten **4.** (concludere) to conclude.

serrata sf. (econ.) lockout.

serratura sf. lock: buco della —, keyhole.

serva sf. maid-servant.

servìbile agg. usable.

servigio sm. service, favour.

servile agg. servile.

servilismo sm. servility.

servire vt. **1.** to serve **2.** (di persona di servizio) to wait on **3.** (le carte) to deal (v. irr.). ♦ **servire** vi. (occorrere) to need: vi serve qualcosa?, can I help you? ♦ **servirsi** vr. **1.** to use **2.** (a tavola) to help oneself (to).

servitore sm. servant.

servitù sf. **1.** servitude, slavery **2.** (personale di servizio) servants (pl.).

serviziévole agg. obliging.

servizio sm. **1.** service **2.** (lavoro) work: fuori —, off duty **3.** (favore) favour.

servo sm. **1.** servant **2.** (schiavo) slave.

servofreno sm. brake booster.

sèsamo sm. sesame.

sessanta agg. sixty.

sessantenne agg. **1.** (attr.) sixty-year-old **2.** (pred.) sixty years old. ♦ **sessantenne** s. sixty-year-old person.

sessantèsimo agg. sixtieth.

sessantina sf. about sixty: un uomo sulla —, a man in his sixties.

sessione sf. session.

sesso sm. sex.

sessuale agg. sexual.

sessualità sf. sexuality.

sestante sm. sextant.

sesterzio sm. sesterce.

sestetto sm. sextet.

sesto¹ agg. sixth.

sesto² sm. **1.** order **2.** (arch.) curve.

sèstuplo agg. e sm. sextuple.

seta sf. silk.

setacciare vt. to sieve.

setaccio sm. sieve.

sete sf. thirst: avere —, to be thirsty.

seterìa sf. **1.** silk factory **2.** (negozio di seta) silk shop.

setificio sm. silk factory.

sétola sf. **1.** bristle **2.** (crine) hair.

setta sf. sect.

settanta agg. seventy.

settantenne agg. **1.** (attr.) seventy-year-old **2.** (pred.) seventy years old. ♦ **settantenne** s. seventy-year-old person.

settantèsimo agg. seventieth.

settario agg. sectarian.

settarismo sm. sectarianism.

sette agg. seven.

settecentesco agg. of eighteenth century.

settecento agg. seven hundred. ♦ **settecento** sm. the eighteenth century.

settembre sm. September.

settentrionale agg. northern.

settentrione sm. north.

setticemia sf. septicaemia.

sèttico agg. septic.

settimana sf. week.

settimanale agg. weekly. ♦ **settimanale** sm. weekly magazine.

settimino sm. seven months' child.

setto sm. septum (pl. -ta).

settore sm. **1.** (geom.) sector **2.** (campo) field.

settoriale agg. sectorial.

severità sf. severity.

severo agg. severe, strict.

sevizia sf. torture.

seviziare vt. to torture.

sezionamento sm. dissection.

sezionare vt. (anat.) to dissect.

sezione sf. **1.** section **2.** (reparto) department **3.** (di scuola) side.

sfaccendato agg. idle. ♦ **sfaccendato** sm. idler.

sfaccettare vt. to facet.

sfacchinare vi. to drudge.

sfacciatàggine sf. impudence.

sfacciato agg. **1.** impudent, cheeky **2.** (di colori) gaudy.

sfacelo sm. break-up.

sfaldamento sm. flaking.

sfaldarsi vr. to flake away.

sfamare vt. to appease so.'s hunger.

sfarfallare vi. to flutter about.

sfarzo sm. pomp.

sfarzoso agg. sumptuous.

sfasamento sm. **1.** (mecc.; elettr.) phase-displacement, phase-difference **2.** (fig.) inconsequence.

sfasato agg. **1.** out of phase **2.** (fig.) inconsequent.

sfasciare[1] *vt.* (*togliere le fasce*) to unbandage.

sfasciare[2] *vt.* to smash. ♦ **sfasciarsi** *vr.* to collapse.

sfasciato *agg.* (*rotto*) in pieces.

sfatare *vt.* to discredit.

sfaticato *agg.* lazy. ♦ **sfaticato** *sm.* lazy-bones.

sfatto *agg.* undone.

sfavillante *agg.* shining.

sfavillare *vi.* to shine (*v. irr.*), to sparkle.

sfavore *sm.* disfavour, discredit.

sfavorévole *agg.* unfavourable.

sfebbrato *agg.* without a temperature.

sfegatarsi *vr.* to wear (*v. irr.*) oneself out.

sfegatato *agg.* fanatic.

sfenòide *sm.* sphenoid.

sfera *sf.* 1. sphere 2. (*lancetta*) hand 3. (*mecc.*) ball.

sfericità *sf.* sphericity.

sfèrico *agg.* spherical.

sferragliare *vi.* to clang.

sferrare *vt.* 1. (*un attacco*) to launch 2. (*un colpo*) to land a blow. ♦ **sferrarsi** *vr.* to hurl oneself (at).

sferruzzare *vi.* to knit (*v. irr.*).

sferza *sf.* whip, lash (*anche fig.*).

sferzare *vt.* 1. to whip, to lash 2. (*fig.*) to reprimand.

sferzata *sf.* 1. lash 2. (*fig.*) sharp rebuke.

sfiancare *vt.* to wear (*v. irr.*) out.

sfiatare *vi.* to leak. ♦ **sfiatarsi** *vr.* to talk oneself hoarse.

sfiatato *agg.* out of breath.

sfiatatoio *sm.* vent.

sfibbiare *vt.* to unbuckle.

sfibramento *sm.* enfeeblement.

sfibrante *agg.* exhausting.

sfibrare *vt.* to weaken, to wear (*v. irr.*) out.

sfibratura *sf.* breaking.

sfida *sf.* challenge: *in tono di —,* defiantly.

sfidante *sm.* challenger.

sfidare *vt.* 1. to challenge 2. (*affrontare*) to face, to dare: *— la morte,* to face death.

sfiducia *sf.* mistrust: *avere —,* to mistrust.

sfiduciare *vt.* to discourage. ♦ **sfiduciarsi** *vr.* to become (*v. irr.*) discouraged.

sfiduciato *agg.* discouraged.

sfigurare *vt.* to spoil (*v. irr.*). ♦

sfigurare *vi.* to cut (*v. irr.*) a poor figure.

sfigurato *agg.* disfigured.

sfilacciare *vt.* to fray.

sfilacciato *agg.* frayed.

sfilare[1] *vt.* to unthread, to unstring (*v. irr.*).

sfilare[2] *vi.* to parade.

sfilata *sf.* 1. march, parade 2. (*fila*) line, string.

sfinge *sf.* sphinx.

sfinimento *sm.* exhaustion.

sfinire *vt.* to exhaust.

sfinitezza *sf.* extreme weakness.

sfinito *agg.* worn out.

sfintere *sm.* sphincter.

sfiorare *vt.* to graze, to touch on.

sfiorire *vi.* to wither, to fade.

sfiorito *agg.* faded, withered (*anche fig.*).

sfittare *vt.* to vacate.

sfitto *agg.* vacant.

sfocato *agg.* out of focus.

sfociare *vi.* to flow.

sfoderare *vt.* 1. to unline 2. (*sguainare*) to unsheathe 3. (*ostentare*) to display.

sfoderato *agg.* 1. unlined 2. (*sguainato*) unsheathed.

sfogare *vt.* to give (*v. irr.*) vent to. ♦ **sfogarsi** *vr.* to relieve one's feelings.

sfoggiare *vi.* to show (*v. irr.*) off.

sfoggio *sm.* show, ostentation.

sfoglia *sf.* 1. (*lamina*) foil 2. (*cuc.*) pastry.

sfogliare[1] *vt.* to pluck the petals off.

sfogliare[2] *vt.* 1. (*voltare le pagine*) to turn over the pages 2. (*dare un'occhiata*) to glance through.

sfogliata *sf.* 1. (*cuc.*) puff-pastry 2. (*di libro*) thumbing.

sfogo *sm.* vent, outlet.

sfolgoramento *sm.* blazing.

sfolgorante *agg.* flaming.

sfolgorare *vi.* to blaze.

sfolgorìo *sm.* blaze.

sfollagente *sm.* truncheon.

sfollamento *sm.* 1. dispersal 2. (*mil.*) evacuation.

sfollare *vt.* e *vi.* to disperse 2. (*mil.*) to evacuate.

sfollato *agg.* 1. evacuated. ♦ **sfollato** *sm.* evacuee.

sfoltire *vt.* to thin.

sfondamento *sm.* breaking.

sfondare *vt.* 1. (*rompere il fondo*) to break (*v. irr.*) the bottom 2.

(*mil.*) to break through. ♦ **sfondare** *vi.* to have success.

sfondato *agg.* **1.** without a bottom || *scarpe sfondate*, worn-out shoes **2.** (*insaziabile*) voracious.

sfondo *sm.* background.

sforbiciare *vt.* to cut (*v. irr.*) with scissors.

sformare *vt.* **1.** to pull out of shape **2.** (*togliere dalla forma*) to remove from the mould. ♦ **sformarsi** *vr.* to get (*v. irr.*) out of shape.

sformato *agg.* shapeless.

sfornare *vt.* **1.** to take (*v. irr.*) out of the oven **2.** (*produrre*) to bring (*v. irr.*) out.

sfornito *agg.* destitute, lacking (in).

sfortuna *sf.* bad luck.

sfortunato *agg.* unlucky.

sforzare *vt.* to strain, to force. ♦ **sforzarsi** *vr.* to try hard.

sforzatamente *avv.* **1.** with much effort **2.** (*in modo forzato*) forcedly.

sforzato *agg.* **1.** forced **2.** (*fig.*) false.

sforzatura *sf.* (*cosa sforzata*) far-fetched thing.

sforzo *sm.* **1.** effort **2.** (*mecc.*) stress.

sfòttere *vt.* to pull so.'s legs.

sfracellare *vt.* to smash. ♦ **sfracellarsi** *vr.* to smash.

sfrangiare *vt.* to undo (*v. irr.*), to form a fringe. ♦ **sfrangiarsi** *vr.* to fray.

sfrangiatura *sf.* fraying.

sfrattare *vt.* to evict.

sfratto *sm.* eviction.

sfrecciare *vi.* to dart.

sfregamento *sm.* rubbing.

sfregare *vt.* to rub.

sfregiare *vt.* to disfigure.

sfregiato *agg.* disfigured.

sfregio *sm.* slash, scar.

sfrenare *vt.* to unbridle.

sfrenatezza *sf.* unrestraint.

sfrenato *agg.* wild, unbridled.

sfrigolare *vi.* to sizzle.

sfrigolìo *sm.* sizzle.

sfringuellare *vi.* to twitter.

sfrondare *vt.* **1.** to strip off leaves **2.** (*fig.*) to curtail.

sfrontatezza *sf.* effrontery.

sfrontato *agg.* brazen, impudent. ♦ **sfrontato** *sm.* impudent fellow.

sfrusciare *vi.* to rustle.

sfruscìo *sm.* rustling.

sfruttamento *sm.* exploitation.

sfruttare *vt.* to exploit.

sfruttatore *sm.* profiteer.

sfuggente *agg.* receding: *sguardo* —, elusive look.

sfuggévole *agg.* transitory.

sfuggire *vi.* to escape, to slip. ♦ **sfuggire** *vt.* to avoid.

sfuggita *sf. di* —, quickly: *vedere qu. di* —, to have a glimpse of so.

sfumare *vt.* to shade. ♦ **sfumare** *vi.* **1.** to evaporate **2.** (*fig.*) to come (*v. irr.*) to nothing.

sfumatamente *avv.* softly.

sfumato *agg.* **1.** vanished **2.** (*di colori*) soft.

sfumatura *sf.* **1.** (*lo sfumare*) shading **2.** (*gradazione*) shade.

sfuriata *sf.* outburst.

sgabello *sm.* stool.

sgabuzzino *sm.* closet.

sgambettare *vi.* to kick (one's legs) about.

sgambetto *sm.* trip: *fare lo* —, to trip (so.); (*fig.*) to supplant.

sganasciamento *sm.* dislocation (of so.'s jaw).

sganasciarsi *vr.* — *dalle risa*, to laugh oneself silly.

sganascione *sm.* slap.

sganciare *vt.* **1.** to unhook **2.** (*ferr.*) to uncouple **3.** (*di bombe*) to release. ♦ **sganciarsi** *vr.* (*liberarsi di qu.*) to get (*v. irr.*) away (so.).

sgangherare *vt.* to unhinge.

sgangherato *agg.* **1.** unhinged **2.** (*sguaiato*) wild.

sgarbatamente *avv.* impolitely.

sgarbato *agg.* rude, impolite.

sgarberìa *sf.* rudeness.

sgarbo *sm.* offence.

sgargiante *agg.* gaudy.

sgarrare *vi.* **1.** to be wrong **2.** (*di orologio*) (*se è avanti*) to gain; (*se è indietro*) to lose (*v. irr.*).

sgattaiolare *vi.* to slip away.

sgelare *vi.* to thaw. ♦ **sgelarsi** *vr.* to thaw.

sgelo *sm.* thawing.

sghembo *agg.* oblique: *di* —, obliquely.

sgherro *sm.* hired assassin.

sghignazzare *vi.* to guffaw.

sghignazzata *sf.* guffaw.

sghimbescio (*nella loc. avv.*) *di* —, awry.

sghiribìzzo *sm.* whim.

sgobbare *vi.* to work hard.

sgobbone *sm.* **1.** hard worker **2.** (*studentesco*) swot.

sgocciolare vi. to drip.

sgocciolìo sm. dripping.

sgolarsi vr. to shout oneself hoarse.

sgombrare vt. to clear.

sgombro agg. 1. clear (of) 2. (fig.) free (from).

sgomentare vt. to dismay.

sgomento agg. dismayed. ♦ **sgomento** sm. dismay.

sgominare vt. to rout.

sgonfiamento sm. deflation.

sgonfiare vt. to deflate.

sgonfio agg. deflated.

sgorbia sf. gouge.

sgorbiare vt. to scrawl.

sgorbio sm. 1. scrawl 2. (pittura mal fatta) daub 3. (fig.) deformed man (pl. men).

sgorgare vi. to gush, to flow.

sgozzare vt. to cut (v. irr.) so.'s throat.

sgradévole agg. unpleasant.

sgradito agg. 1. disagreeable 2. (mal accetto) unwelcome.

sgrammaticato agg. ungrammatical.

sgranare vt. 1. to shell: — gli occhi, to open one's eyes wide 2. (mangiare) to devour.

sgranatrice sf. husker.

sgranchire vt. to stretch.

sgranocchiare vt. to munch.

sgrassare vt. to take (v. irr.) the grease off: — il brodo, to skim the grease from the broth.

sgravare vt. 1. to lighten 2. (fig.) to relieve.

sgravio sm. 1. lightening 2. (fig.) relief.

sgraziato agg. awkward.

sgretolamento sm. pounding.

sgretolare vt. to pound. ♦ **sgretolarsi** vr. to crumble.

sgridare vt. to scold.

sgroppare¹ vt. (sciogliere) to untie.

sgroppare² vi. (di cavallo) to buck.

sgroppata sf. bucking.

sgrossamento sm. rough-shaping.

sgrossare vt. 1. to rough 2. (dirozzare) to refine.

sgrovigliare vt. to unravel.

sguaiato agg. 1. unbecoming 2. (volgare) coarse.

sguainare vt. to unsheathe.

sgualcire vt. to crease.

sgualdrina sf. harlot, whore.

sguardo sm. look, glance: dare uno —, to have a look.

sguarnire vt. 1. to untrim 2. (mil.) to dismantle.

sguattero sm. scullery-boy.

sguazzare vi. to wallow.

sguinzagliare vt. to unleash.

sgusciare vt. to shell. ♦ **sgusciare** vi. to slip away.

sì¹ pron. 1. (riflessivo) oneself, himself, herself, itself, themselves 2. (rec.) (fra due) each other; (fra molti) one another 3. (pron. indef.) one, people, we, they: — dice, people say.

sì² sm. (mus.) si, B.

sì avv. yes: penso di —, I think so; — certo, certainly; e — che, yet; uno —, uno no, every other one; forse che —, forse che no, maybe yes, maybe no.

sia cong. 1. (o l'uno o l'altro) whether... or, either... or 2. (entrambi) both... and.

siamese agg. e s. Siamese.

sibarita s. sybarite.

siberiano agg. Siberian.

sibilante agg. 1. hissing 2. (fonetica) sibilant.

sibilare vi. to whistle, to hiss.

sibilla sf. sibyl.

sibillino agg. sibylline.

sibilo sm. hiss, whistle.

sicario sm. cut-throat.

sicché cong. 1. so... that 2. (dunque) therefore.

siccità sf. drought.

siccome cong. as, since.

siciliano agg. e sm. Sicilian.

sicomoro sm. sycamore.

sicumera sf. presumption.

sicura sf. safety belt.

sicurezza sf. 1. (certezza) certainty 2. (immunità da pericoli) safety || dispositivo di —, safety device; misura di —, precautionary measure; uscita di —, emergency door; rasoio, spilla di —, safety-razor, pin.

sicuro agg. 1. (certo) sure: — di sé, self-confident 2. (immune da pericoli) safe 3. (che non sbaglia) unfailing 4. (calmo, saldo) calm, steady 5. (esperto) skilful.

siderale agg. sidereal.

siderurgìa sf. metallurgy of iron.

siderùrgico agg. iron (attr.): stabilimento di —, iron-works (pl.). ♦ **siderùrgico** sm. iron worker.

sidro sm. cider.

siepe sf. hedge.

siero *sm.* serum.

sieroso *agg.* serous.

sieroterapia *sf.* serotherapy.

siesta *sf.* nap.

siffatto *agg.* such.

sifilide *sf.* syphilis.

sifone *sm.* siphon.

sigaraia *sf.* cigar-seller.

sigaretta *sf.* cigarette.

sigaro *sm.* cigar.

sigillare *vt.* to seal.

sigillatura *sf.* scaling.

sigillo *sm.* seal.

sigla *sf.* monogram.

siglare *vt.* to initial.

significare *vt.* **1.** to mean (*v. irr.*) **2.** (*comunicare*) to signify **3.** (*simboleggiare*) to represent.

significativo *agg.* meaningful.

significato *sm.* **1.** meaning **2.** (*valore*) import.

signora *sf.* **1.** lady, woman (*pl.* women) **2.** (*seguito da cognome*) Mrs: *la — Smith*, Mrs. Smith **3.** (*vocativo*) Madam: *buon giorno —*, good morning Madam **4.** (*padrona*) mistress **5.** (*donna ricca*) rich lady **6.** (*moglie*) wife (*pl.* wives).

signore *sm.* **1.** gentleman, man (*pl.* -men) **2.** (*seguito da cognome*) Mr.: *il — Smith*, Mr. Smith **3.** (*padrone*) master **4.** (*vocativo*) Sir: *sì —*! yes, Sir! **5.** (*uomo ricco*) lord **6.** (*Dio*) God, Lord.

signoreggiare *vt.* to rule.

signoria *sf.* **1.** (*di uomo*) Lordship; (*di donna*) Ladyship **2.** (*dominio*) dominion.

signorile *agg.* **1.** (*riferito a uomo*) gentlemanlike; (*riferito a donna*) ladylike **2.** (*elegante*) luxury.

signorilità *sf.* distinction, high class.

signorina *sf.* **1.** young lady **2.** (*seguito da cognome*) Miss: *la — Smith*, Miss Smith **3.** (*vocativo*) Madam: *Buon giorno —*, good morning Madam **4.** (*padroncina*) young mistress **5.** (*donna non sposata*) unmarried woman.

signorotto *sm.* squire.

silenziatore *sm.* silencer.

silenzio *sm.* silence.

silenzioso *agg.* silent || *una strada silenziosa*, a noiseless street.

silfide *sf.* sylph.

silfo *sm.* sylph.

silice *sf.* silica.

silicio *sm.* silicon.

silicone *sm.* silicone.

silicosi *sf.* silicosis.

sillaba *sf.* syllable.

sillabare *vt.* to syllabize.

sillabo *sm.* summary.

sillogismo *sm.* syllogism.

sillogistico *agg.* syllogistic.

silo *sm.* silo (*pl.* silos).

siluramento *sm.* **1.** torpedoing **2.** (*fig.*) firing.

silurante *sf.* torpedo-boat.

silurare *vt.* **1.** to torpedo **2.** (*fig.*) to dismiss.

siluriano *agg. e sm.* Silurian.

siluro *sm.* (*mil.; zool.*) torpedo.

silvestre *agg.* sylvan.

silvicoltore *sm.* forester.

silvicoltura *sf.* forestry.

simbiosi *sf.* symbiosis.

simboleggiare *vt.* to symbolize.

simbolico *agg.* **1.** symbolic **2.** (*nominale*) nominal.

simbolismo *sm.* symbolism.

simbolista *agg. e sm.* symbolist.

simbolo *sm.* symbol.

similare *agg.* similar.

simile *agg.* **1.** like, similar **2.** (*pred.*) alike **3.** (*tale*) such. ♦ **simile** *sm.* fellow-creature.

similitudine *sf.* **1.** likeness **2.** (*lett.*) simile.

simmetria *sf.* symmetry.

simmetrico *agg.* symmetric(al).

simonia *sf.* simony.

simoniaco *agg. e sm.* simoniac.

simpatia *sf.* liking.

simpatico *agg.* nice, pleasant.

simpatizzante *agg.* sympathizing. ♦ **simpatizzante** *s.* sympathizer.

simpatizzare *vi.* **1.** to sympathize **2.** (*rec.*) to take (*v. irr.*) a liking to each other.

simposio *sm.* symposium (*pl.* -ia).

simulacro *sm.* **1.** simulacre **2.** (*finzione*) sham.

simulare *vt.* to feign.

simulato *agg.* simulated.

simulatore *sm.* simulator.

simulazione *sf.* simulation.

simultaneità *sf.* simultaneity.

simultaneo *agg.* simultaneous (with).

sinagoga *sf.* synagogue.

sincerarsi *vr.* to make (*v. irr.*) sure.

sincerità *sf.* sincerity.

sincero *agg.* sincere, true.

sincopare *vt.* to syncopate.

sincopato agg. syncopated.

sincope sf. 1. (med.) syncope 2. (mus.; gramm.) syncopation.

sincronismo sm. synchronism.

sincronizzare vt. to synchronize.

sincronizzazione sf. synchronization.

sindacale agg. trade-union (attr.).

sindacalismo sm. trade-unionism.

sindacalista s. trade-unionist.

sindacare vt. 1. to control 2. (criticare) to criticize.

sindacato sm. trade-union.

sindaco sm. 1. mayor 2. (di società) auditor.

sindrome sf. syndrome.

sinecura sf. sinecure.

sinfonia sf. symphony.

sinfonico agg. symphonic.

singhiozzare vi. to sob.

singhiozzo sm. 1. hiccup 2. (di pianto) sob.

singolare agg. 1. singular 2. (singolo) single.

singolarità sf. singularity.

singolarmente avv. 1. (ad uno ad uno) singly 2. (segnatamente) particularly.

singolo agg. single, individual.

singulto sm. 1. hiccup 2. (di pianto) sob.

sinistra sf. 1. left: alla mia —, on my left 2. (mano) left hand 3. (parte) left-hand side || uomo di — (pol.), left-winger.

sinistramente avv. sinisterly.

sinistrato agg. 1. (di edificio) bomb-damaged 2. (di persona) injured. ♦ **sinistrato** sm. (damage) sufferer.

sinistro agg. 1. left 2. (truce) sinister, grim. ♦ **sinistro** sm. 1. accident, mishap 2. (boxe) left.

sinologo sm. Sinologist.

sinonimia sf. synonymy.

sinonimo agg. synonymous. ♦ **sinonimo** sm. synonym.

sinora avv. till now, so far.

sinovite sf. synovitis.

sintassi sf. syntax.

sintattico agg. syntactic(al).

sintesi sf. synthesis (pl. -ses).

sintetico agg. synthetic.

sintetizzare vt. to synthetize.

sintomatico agg. symptomatic.

sintomo sm. symptom.

sintonia sf. syntony.

sintonizzare vt. to tune in.

sinuosità sf. winding.

sinuoso agg. winding.

sinusite sf. sinusitis.

sionismo sm. Zionism.

sionista s. Zionist.

sipario sm. curtain.

sirena sf. 1. (mit.) siren, mermaid 2. (acustica) hooter.

siringa sf. syringe.

siringare vt. to syringe.

sismico agg. seismic.

sismografo sm. seismograph.

sismologia sf. seismology.

sismologo sm. seismologist.

sistema sm. system: — di vita, way of life.

sistemare vt. 1. (mettere in ordine) to arrange 2. (definire) to settle.

sistematico agg. systematic(al).

sistemazione sf. 1. (ordine) arrangement 2. (collocazione di macchinari) layout 3. (il sistemarsi) settling 4. (lavoro) job.

sito sm. place.

situare vt. to place.

situazione sf. situation.

slabbrare vt. to chip the rim of.

slabbratura sf. chipping.

slacciare vt. 1. to untie 2. (sbottonare) to unbutton.

slanciarsi vr. to rush.

slanciato agg. slim.

slancio sm. 1. rush 2. (energia) energy.

slargare vt. to widen.

slattamento sm. weaning.

slattare vt. to wean.

slavato agg. pale.

slavina sf. landslide; (di neve) snowslide.

slavo agg. e sm. Slav.

sleale agg. unfair.

slealtà sf. disloyalty.

slegare vt. to untie.

slegato agg. 1. untied 2. (di discorso ecc.) disconnected.

slitta sf. sleigh.

slittamento sm. skidding.

slittare vi. 1. to slide (v. irr.) 2. (di ruote) to skid.

slogamento sm. dislocation.

slogare vt. to dislocate.

slogatura sf. dislocation.

sloggiare vi. to clear out. ♦ **sloggiare** vt. to drive (v. irr.) out.

smaccato agg. sickly-sweet.

smacchiare vt. to clean.

smacchiatore sm. stain-remover.

smacchiatura sf. cleaning.

smacco sm. mortification.

smagliante *agg.* dazzling.

smagliare *vt.* to unravel. ♦ **smagliarsi** *vr.* (*di calze*) to ladder.

smagliato *agg.* unravelled.

smagliatura *sf.* 1. (*di calze*) ladder.

smagnetizzare *vt.* to demagnetize.

smagnetizzazione *sf.* demagnetization.

smagrire *vt.* e *vi.* to thin.

smagrito *agg.* thin, grown thin.

smaliziare *vt.* to smarten up. ♦ **smaliziarsi** *vr.* to wisen.

smaliziato *agg.* cunning.

smaltare *vt.* to enamel: — *le unghie*, to paint one's nails.

smaltato *agg.* 1. enamelled 2. (*di unghie*) painted.

smaltire *vt.* to digest: — *la sbornia*, to get (*v. irr.*) over one's drunkenness.

smalto *sm.* enamel: — *per unghie*, nail-polish.

smanceria *sf.* mawkishness.

smangiare *vt.* to corrode.

smania *sf.* 1. great desire 2. (*agitazione*) frenzy.

smaniare *vi.* 1. to yearn (for) 2. (*essere agitati*) to be restless.

smanioso *agg.* 1. eager 2. (*agitato*) restless.

smantellamento *sm.* dismantling.

smantellare *vt.* to dismantle.

smarcare *vt.* to unmark.

smargiassata *sf.* swagger.

smargiasseria *sf.* bragging.

smargiasso *sm.* braggart.

smarginare *vt.* to trim the edge.

smarrimento *sm.* 1. loss 2. (*turbamento*) bewilderment.

smarrire *vt.* to lose (*v. irr.*). ♦ **smarrirsi** *vr.* 1. to lose one's way 2. (*di lettera, pacco*) to miscarry 3. (*turbarsi*) to be bewildered.

smascellarsi *vr.* to dislocate one's jaws.

smascherare *vt.* to unmask.

smembramento *sm.* dismemberment.

smembrare *vt.* to dismember.

smemorataggine *sf.* 1. lack of memory 2. (*dimenticanza*) lapse of memory.

smemorato *agg.* absent-minded.

smentire *vt.* to deny. ♦ **smentirsi** *vr.* 1. to contradict oneself 2. (*venir meno*) to be untrue to oneself.

smentita *sf.* denial.

smeraldo *sm.* emerald.

smerciare *vt.* to sell (*v. irr.*) off.

smercio *sm.* sale.

smerigliare *vt.* 1. to polish with emery 2. (*di vetri*) to frost glass.

smerigliato *agg.* emery: *carta smerigliata*, emery paper; *vetro —*, frosted glass.

smeriglio *sm.* emery.

smerlo *sm.* scallop.

smesso *agg.* cast off.

smettere *vt.* to stop, to leave (*v. irr.*) off: — *un vestito*, to cast (*v. irr.*) off a dress.

mezzare *vt.* to halve.

smidollato *agg.* (*di persona*) spineless.

smilitarizzare *vt.* to demilitarize.

smilitarizzazione *sf.* demilitarization.

smilzo *agg.* thin.

sminuire *vt.* to diminish. ♦ **sminuirsi** *vr.* to belittle oneself.

sminuzzare *vt.* 1. (*tritare*) to mince 2. (*tagliuzzare*) to chop up 3. (*sbriciolare*) to crumble.

smistamento *sm.* 1. clearing 2. (*ferr.*) shunting 3. (*di corrispondenza*) sorting.

smistare *vt.* 1. (*di corrispondenza*) to sort out 2. (*ferr.*) to shunt.

smisuratamente *avv.* beyond measure.

smisurato *agg.* enormous, huge.

smobilitare *vt.* to demobilize.

smobilitazione *sf.* demobilization.

smoccolare *vt.* to snuff.

smoccolatoio *sm.* snuffers (*pl.*).

smoccolatura *sf.* snuffing.

smodato *agg.* immoderate.

smoderatezza *sf.* immoderateness.

smoderato *agg.* immoderate.

smontabile *agg.* demountable.

smontaggio *sm.* disassembling.

smontare *vt.* 1. (*far scendere*) (*da cavallo*) to unhorse; (*da un'automobile*) to drop 2. (*scomporre in parti*) to take (*v. irr.*) to pieces 3. (*mecc.*) to disassemble 4. (*fig.*) to dishearten, to cool. ♦ **smontare** *vi.* 1. (*da un treno, tram ecc.*) to get (*v. irr.*) off 2. (*da un'automobile*) to get (*v. irr.*) out 3. (*da cavallo*) to dismount 4. (*dal lavoro*) to go (*v. irr.*) off duty 5. (*sbiadire*) to fade.

smorfia *sf.* grimace.

smorfioso *agg.* affected.

smorto *agg.* pale.

smorzamento *sm.* 1. (*di luci*) shading 2. (*di colori*) toning down 3. (*di suoni*) lowering 4. (*di sete; fig.*) quenching.

smorzare *vt.* 1. (*di luci*) to shade 2. (*di colori*) to tone down 3. (*di suoni*) to lower 4. (*di sete; fig.*) to quench 5. (*spegnere*) to put (*v. irr.*) down.

smottamento *sm.* landslip.

smottare *vi.* to slip.

smozzicare *vt.* 1. to hack to pieces 2. (*di parole*) to clip.

smunto *agg.* pale.

smuovere *vt.* 1. to shift 2. (*fig.*) to move.

smussare *vt.* 1. to round off 2. (*fig.*) to soften.

smussato *agg.* 1. blunted 2. (*fig.*) softened.

snaturare *vt.* to pervert.

snaturato *agg.* unnatural.

snazionalizzare *vt.* to denationalize.

snebbiare *vt.* 1. to dispel the fog 2. (*fig.*) to clear.

snellezza *sf.* slenderness.

snellire *vt.* 1. to make (*v. irr.*) slender 2. (*fig.*) to simplify. ♦ **snellirsi** *vr.* to grow (*v. irr.*) slender.

snello *agg.* slender.

snervante *agg.* enervating.

snervare *vt.* to enervate.

snidare *vt.* 1. to flush 2. (*fig.*) to dislodge.

snobbare *vt.* to snob.

snobismo *sm.* snobbery.

snocciolare *vt.* 1. to stone 2. (*fig.*) to tell (*v. irr.*).

snodare *vt.* 1. to untie 2. (*rendere agile*) to make (*v. irr.*) supple. ♦ **snodarsi** *vr.* (*di strade*) to wind (*v. irr.*).

snodato *agg.* 1. supple 2. (*di cosa*) jointed.

snodo *sm.* joint.

soave *agg.* sweet.

soavità *sf.* sweetness.

sobbalzare *vi.* 1. to jerk 2. (*trasalire*) to start.

sobbalzo *sm.* 1. jerk 2. (*sussulto*) start.

sobbarcarsi *vr.* to take (*v. irr.*) upon oneself.

sobborgo *sm.* suburb.

sobillare *vt.* to stir up.

sobillatore *sm.* instigator.

sobrietà *sf.* sobriety.

sobrio *agg.* sober.

socchiùdere *vt.* 1. to half-close 2. (*aprire un po'*) to half-open.

socchiuso *agg.* half-closed, half-open.

sòccida *sf.* agistment.

soccómbere *vi.* to succumb.

soccòrrere *vt.* to help, to assist.

soccorritore *agg.* helpful. ♦ **soccorritore** *sm.* helper.

soccorso *sm.* help || **pronto —**, first aid.

socialdemocràtico *agg.* socialdemocratic.

socialdemocrazìa *sf.* socialdemocracy.

sociale *agg.* social.

socialismo *sm.* Socialism.

socialista *agg. e sm.* Socialist.

socialità *sf.* sociality.

socializzare *vt.* to socialize.

socializzazione *sf.* socialization.

società *sf.* 1. society 2. (*comm.*) company: **— anonima**, joint-stock company; **— a responsabilità limitata**, limited company || **entrare in —**, to enter into partnership.

sociévole *agg.* sociable.

socievolezza *sf.* sociability.

socio *sm.* 1. member 2. (*comm.*) partner.

sociologìa *sf.* sociology.

sociològico *agg.* sociological.

sociòlogo *sm.* sociologist.

socràtico *agg.* Socratic.

soda *sf.* soda.

sodalizio *sm.* 1. society 2. (*confraternita*) brotherhood.

sodare *vt.* to consolidate.

sodatura *sf.* (*tessile*) fulling.

soddisfacente *agg.* satisfactory.

soddisfare *vt.* 1. to satisfy 2. (*adempiere*) to fulfil 3. (*far fronte a*) to discharge 4. (*riparare*) to make (*v. irr.*) amends.

soddisfazione *sf.* satisfaction.

sodio *sm.* sodium.

sodo *agg.* solid, firm: **uovo —**, hard-boiled egg; **darle sode a qu.**, to strike (*v. irr.*) so. hard.

sofferente *agg.* 1. suffering 2. (*malaticcio*) poorly.

sofferenza *sf.* pain.

soffermare *vt.* to stop. ♦ **soffermarsi** *vr.* to stop.

soffiare *vt. e vi.* to blow (*v. irr.*): **soffiarsi il naso**, to blow one's nose.

soffiata *sf.* puff.

soffiato *agg.* puffed.

soffiatore *sm.* blower.

soffiatura *sf.* blowing.

sòffice *agg.* soft.

soffietto *sm.* **1.** bellows (*pl.*) **2.** (*edit.*) blurb.

soffio *sm.* puff, whiff.

soffione *sm.* **1.** blow-pipe **2.** (*geol.*) fumarole.

soffitta *sf.* garret.

soffitto *sm.* ceiling.

soffocamento *sm.* choking.

soffocante *agg.* choking: *caldo —,* sultry heat.

soffocare *vt.* **1.** to choke **2.** (*re-primere*) to repress.

soffocato *agg.* choked.

sòffoco *sm.* sultriness.

soffóndere *vt.* to suffuse.

soffriggere *vt.* to fry slightly.

soffrire *vt.* **1.** to suffer **2.** (*soppor-tare*) to stand (*v. irr.*).

soffuso *agg.* suffused.

sofisma *sm.* sophism.

sofista *sm.* sophist.

sofistica *sf.* sophistry.

sofisticare *vi.* to quibble. ♦ **so-fisticare** *vt.* to adulterate.

sofisticato *agg.* **1.** sophisticated **2.** (*adulterato*) adulterated.

sofisticazione *sf.* adulteration.

sofisticheria *sf.* quibbling.

sofistico *agg.* sophistical.

soggettista *sm.* scenario writer.

soggettivismo *sm.* subjectivism.

soggettività *sf.* subjectivity.

soggettivo *agg.* subjective.

soggetto *agg. e sm.* subject.

soggezione *sf.* **1.** subjection **2.** (*ti-midezza*) shyness.

sogghignare *vi.* to sneer.

sogghigno *sm.* sneer.

soggiacere *vi.* to be subjected.

soggiogare *vt.* to subdue.

soggiornare *vi.* to stay.

soggiorno *sm.* stay: *stanza di —,* living-room.

soggiùngere *vt.* to add.

soglia *sf.* threshold.

sògliola *sf.* sole.

sognante *agg.* dreaming: *occhi so-gnanti,* dreamy eyes.

sognare *vt.* to dream (*v. irr.*): — *ad occhi aperti,* to have day-dreams.

sognatore *agg.* dreaming. ♦ **so-gnatore** *sm.* dreamer.

sogno *sm.* dream.

soia *sf.* soya.

solaio *sm.* attic.

solamente *avv.* only.

solare *agg.* **1.** solar **2.** (*radioso*) ra-diant.

solatìo *agg.* sunny.

solcare *vt.* **1.** to plough **2.** (*fig.*) to furrow.

solcato *agg.* **1.** ploughed **2.** (*fig.*) furrowed.

solcatura *sf.* ploughing, furrowing.

solco *sm.* **1.** (*agr.*) furrow **2.** (*ruga*) wrinkle **3.** (*mar.*) wake **4.** (*di ruo-ta sul terreno*) track.

solcòmetro *sm.* log.

soldataglia *sf.* soldiery.

soldatesco *agg.* soldierly.

soldato *sm.* soldier.

soldo *sm.* **1.** penny **2.** (*denaro*) money **3.** (*salario*) pay: *essere al — di qu.,* to be in so.'s pay.

sole *sm.* sun: *bagno di —,* sun-bathing; *colpo di —,* sunstroke; *un giorno di —, senza —,* a sunny day, a sunless day; *tramonto del —,* sunset.

soleggiare *vt.* to sun-dry.

soleggiato *agg.* sunny.

solenne *agg.* solemn.

solennità *sf.* **1.** solemnity **2.** (*cer-imonia*) ceremony.

solennizzare *vt.* to solemnize.

solenòide *sm.* solenoid.

solere *vi.* to use (*usato solo al pas-sato*).

solerte *agg.* diligent.

solerzia *sf.* diligence.

soletta *sf.* sole.

solfa *sf.* **1.** scale **2.** (*fig.*) old story.

solfara *sf.* sulphur mine.

solfare *vt.* to sulphur.

solfatara *sf.* solfatara.

solfato *sm.* sulphate.

solfeggiare *vt.* to sol-fa.

solfeggio *sm.* solfeggio.

solfito *sm.* sulphite.

solfuro *sm.* sulphide.

solidale *agg.* solid (for).

solidamente *avv.* solidly.

solidarietà *sf.* solidarity.

solidarizzare *vi.* to be solid (for).

solidificare *vt.* to solidify.

solidificazione *sf.* solidification.

solidità *sf.* **1.** solidity **2.** (*di colori*) fastness.

sòlido *agg.* **1.** solid **2.** (*di colori*) fast **3.** (*fig.*) sound. ♦ **sòlido** *sm.* solid.

soliloquio *sm.* soliloquy.

solipsismo *sm.* solipsism.

solista *s.* soloist.

solitamente *avv.* usually.

solitario¹ *agg.* solitary. ♦ **solitario** *sm.* 1. hermit 2. (*brillante*) solitaire.

solitario² *sm.* (*a carte*) solitaire.

sòlito *agg.* usual, customary: essere —, to be used to (doing); di —, usually.

solitùdine *sf.* loneliness.

sollazzare *vt.* to amuse.

sollazzo *sm.* amusement.

sollecitante *agg.* urging.

sollecitare *vt.* 1. (*far premura*) to urge 2. (*brigare*) to solicit 3. (*affrettare*) to hurry up.

sollecitazione *sf.* 1. solicitation 2. (*preghiera*) entreaty.

sollécito *agg.* 1. (*rapido*) prompt 2. (*preoccupato*) solicitous 3. (*premuroso*) obliging.

sollecitùdine *sf.* 1. (*rapidità*) promptness 2. (*interessamento*) concern 3. (*gentilezza*) kindness.

solleone *sm.* dog-days (*pl.*).

solleticante *agg.* alluring.

solleticare *vt.* to tickle.

sollético *sm.* 1. tickle: soffrire il —, to be ticklish 2. (*fig.*) itch.

sollevamento *sm.* lifting.

sollevare *vt.* 1. to lift 2. (*issare*) to hoist 3. (*fig.*) to raise 4. (*dar sollievo*) to relieve. ♦ **sollevarsi** *vr.* 1. to rise (*v. irr.*) 2. (*riaversi*) to recover 3. (*insorgere*) to rebel.

sollevato *agg.* (*rasserenato*) cheered up.

sollevazione *sf.* (*rivolta*) rising.

sollievo *sm.* relief.

sollùchero *sm.* andare in —, to go (*v. irr.*) into raptures.

solo *agg.* 1. alone (*pred.*): da —, by oneself 2. (*unico*) only. ♦ **solo** *avv.* only.

solstizio *sm.* solstice.

soltanto *avv.* only.

solùbile *agg.* soluble.

solubilità *sf.* solubility.

soluzione *sf.* solution.

solvente *agg.* e *sm.* solvent.

solvenza *sf.* (*comm.*) solvency.

solvìbile *agg.* solvent.

solvibilità *sf.* solvency.

soma *sf.* load, burden.

somaràggine *sf.* stupidity.

somaro *sm.* ass.

somàtico *agg.* somatic.

somigliante *agg.* alike, similar.

somiglianza *sf.* likeness.

somigliare *vi.* to look like.

somma *sf.* 1. (*mat.*) addition 2. (*di denaro*) sum.

sommamente *avv.* extremely.

sommare *vt.* to add.

sommariamente *avv.* summarily.

sommario *agg.* e *sm.* summary.

sommèrgere *vt.* to submerge.

sommergìbile *agg.* submersible. ♦ **sommergìbile** *sm.* submarine.

sommergibilista *sm.* submariner.

sommersione *sf.* submersion.

sommerso *agg.* submerged.

sommessamente *avv.* 1. submissively 2. (*a bassa voce*) in a low voice.

sommesso *agg.* 1. submissive 2. (*di voce*) low.

somministrare *vt.* to administer.

somministratore *sm.* giver.

somministrazione *sf.* giving.

sommissione *sf.* V. sottomissione.

sommità *sf.* summit, top.

sommo¹ *agg.* 1. highest 2. (*fig.*) supreme.

sommo² *sm.* summit, top.

sommossa *sf.* rising.

sommovimento *sm.* movement, agitation.

sommozzatore *sm.* frogman (*pl.* -men).

sommuòvere *vt.* to stir up.

sonagliera *sf.* collar with bells.

sonaglio *sm.* 1. harness-bell 2. (*giocattolo*) rattle || serpente a sonagli, rattlesnake.

sonante *agg.* resounding || denaro —, ready money.

sonare *vt.* 1. to sound 2. (*musica*) to play 3. (*di orologio*) to strike (*v. irr.*). ♦ **sonare** *vi.* (*di campanello*) to ring (*v. irr.*).

sonata *sf.* (*mus.*) sonata.

sonatore *sm.* player.

sonda *sf.* 1. (*mar.*) sounding line 2. (*med.*) probe 3. (*min.*) drill.

sondaggio *sm.* 1. sounding 2. (*med.*) probing 3. (*min.*) drilling.

sondare *vt.* 1. to sound 2. (*fig.*) to throw (*v. irr.*) out.

sonerìa *sf.* 1. (*di orologio*) striking-mechanism 2. alarm.

sonetto *sm.* sonnet.

sonnacchiosamente *avv.* drowsily.

sonnacchioso *agg.* 1. sleepy 2. (*fig.*) torpid.

sonnambulismo *sm.* sleep-walking.

sonnàmbulo *sm.* sleep-walker.

sonnecchiare *vi.* to doze.

sonnellino *sm.* nap.

sonnìfero *sm.* sleeping pills (*pl.*).
sonno *sm.* sleep; — *profondo*, sound sleep.
sonnolento *agg.* drowsy.
sonnolenza *sf.* drowsiness.
sonoramente *avv.* sonorously.
sonorità *sf.* sonority.
sonorizzare *vt.* to post-score.
sonorizzazione *sf.* post-scoring.
sonoro *agg.* 1. sonorous 2. (*rumoroso*) loud 3. (*cine*) sound.
sontuosamente *avv.* sumptuously.
sontuosità *sf.* sumptuousness.
sontuoso *agg.* sumptuous.
soperchierìa *sf.* V. *soverchierìa*.
sopire *vt.* 1. to make (*v. irr.*) drowsy 2. (*calmare*) to soothe.
sopore *sm.* doze.
soporìfero *agg.* soporific.
sopperire *vi.* 1. to provide (for) 2. (*supplire*) to make (*v. irr.*) up (for).
soppesare *vt.* 1. to weigh in one's hand 2. (*considerare*) to weigh.
soppiantare *vt.* to supplant.
soppiatto (*nella loc. avv.*) *di* —, stealthily.
sopportàbile *agg.* bearable.
sopportabilità *sf.* bearableness.
sopportabilmente *avv.* bearably.
sopportare *vt.* to bear (*v. irr.*).
sopportazione *sf.* endurance.
soppressare *vt.* to press.
soppressione *sf.* 1. suppression 2. (*abolizione*) abolition.
soppresso *agg.* 1. suppressed 2. (*abolito*) abolished.
sopprìmere *vt.* 1. to suppress 2. (*abolire*) to abolish.
sopra *prep.* 1. (*con contatto*) on, upon 2. (*senza contatto*) over 3. (*al di sopra*) above. ♦ **sopra** *avv.* 1. above 2. (*al piano superiore*) upstairs.
soprabbondanza *sf.* V. *sovrabbondanza*.
soprabbondare *vi.* V. *sovrabbondare*.
sopràbito *sm.* overcoat.
sopraccaricare *vt.* V. *sovraccaricare*.
sopraccàrico *sm.* V. *sovraccàrico*.
sopraccennato *agg.* above-mentioned.
sopracciglio *sm.* eyebrow.
sopraccitato *agg.* V. *sopraddetto*.
sopraccoperta *sf.* 1. (*di libro*) jacket 2. (*di letto*) counterpane. ♦ **sopraccoperta** *avv.* (*mar.*) on

deck.
sopraddetto *agg.* above-mentioned.
sopraelevare *vt.* 1. (*edil.*) to increase the height of 2. (*di strade, rotaie ecc.*) to bank.
sopraelevazione *sf.* 1. (*edil.*) heightening 2. (*di strade, rotaie ecc.*) superelevation.
sopraffare *vt.* to overwhelm.
sopraffazione *sf.* 1. overwhelming 2. (*abuso*) abuse.
sopraffino *agg.* first-rate.
sopraggiùngere *vi.* 1. to arrive 2. (*accadere*) to happen.
sopraggiunta *sf.* addition.
sopraindicato *agg.* V. *sopraddetto*.
sopralluogo *sm.* investigation on the spot.
soprammercato (*nella loc. avv.*) *per* —, moreover.
sopramméttere *vt.* to place on.
soprammòbile *sm.* knick-knack.
soprannaturale *agg.* supernatural.
soprannome *sm.* nickname.
soprannominare *vt.* to nickname.
soprannùmero *sm.* excess.
soprano *sm.* soprano.
soprappassaggio *sm.* overbridge.
soprappensiero *avv.* lost in thought.
soprappiù *sm.* extra, addition.
soprapprezzo *sm.* extra charge.
soprascarpa *sf.* galosh.
soprascritta *sf.* inscription.
soprascritto *agg.* above-written.
soprasensìbile *agg.* supersensible.
soprassalto *sm.* jerk; *di* —, all of a sudden.
soprassedere *vi.* 1. to wait 2. (*rimandare*) to postpone.
soprassoldo *sm.* extra pay.
soprastruttura *sf.* superstructure.
soprattassa *sf.* extra tax.
soprattutto *avv.* above all.
sopravanzare *vt.* 1. (*superare*) to surpass 2. (*avanzare*) to be left over.
sopravanzo *sm.* surplus.
sopravvalutare *vt.* to overrate.
sopravvenire *vi.* 1. (*di persone*) to turn up 2. (*di cose*) to come (*v. irr.*) about.
sopravvento *sm.* 1. (*mar.*) windward 2. (*fig.*) upper hand; *prendere il* —, to get (*v. irr.*) the upper hand.
sopravvissuto *agg.* e *sm.* surviving. ♦ **sopravvissuto** *sm.* survivor.
sopravvivenza *sf.* survival.

sopravvìvere *vi.* to survive.

sopruso *sm.* abuse of power.

soqquadro *sm.* confusion: *a —*, topsy-turvy.

sorbettare *vt.* to freeze (*v. irr.*).

sorbetto *sm.* sherbet.

sorbire *vt.* to sip. ◆ **sorbirsi** *vr.* to put (*v. irr.*) up with.

sorcio *sm.* mouse (*pl.* mice).

sordamente *avv.* dully.

sordidamente *avv.* filthily.

sordidezza *sf.* filthiness.

sòrdido *agg.* filthy.

sordina *sf.* (*mus.*) mute: *in —* (*fig.*), on the sly.

sordità *sf.* deafness.

sordo *agg.* deaf.

sordomuto *sm.* deaf-mute.

sorella *sf.* sister.

sorellastra *sf.* half-sister.

sorgente *sf.* spring, source.

sòrgere *vi.* to rise (*v. irr.*).

sorgiva *sf.* spring-water.

sorgivo *agg.* spring (*attr.*).

soriano *agg.* syrian: *gatto —*, tabby cat.

sormontare *vt.* **1.** to surmount **2.** (*superare*) to overcome (*v. irr.*).

sornione *agg.* sly. ◆ **sornione** *sm.* sly person.

sorpassare *vt.* **1.** to overtake (*v. irr.*) **2.** (*sport*) to outrun (*v. irr.*).

sorpassato *agg.* old-fashioned.

sorpasso *sm.* overtaking.

sorprendente *agg.* surprising.

sorprèndere *vt.* **1.** (*cogliere inaspettatamente*) to catch (*v. irr.*) **2.** (*meravigliare*) to surprise.

sorpresa *sf.* surprise: *di —*, by surprise.

sorrèggere *vt.* to support.

sorridente *agg.* smiling.

sorrìdere *vi.* **1.** to smile **2.** (*attrarre*) to appeal.

sorriso *sm.* smile.

sorsata *sf.* sip.

sorseggiare *vt.* to sip.

sorso *sm.* gulp, sip.

sorta *sf.* kind, sort.

sorte *sf.* **1.** destiny, lot **2.** (*avvenire*) future.

sorteggiare *vt.* to draw (*v. irr.*) lots (for).

sorteggio *sm.* draw.

sortilegio *sm.* witchcraft.

sortire[1] *vt.* to get (*v. irr.*).

sortire[2] *vi.* to come (*v. irr.*) out.

sortita *sf.* sally.

sorvegliante *sm.* overseer.

sorveglianza *sf.* overseeing.

sorvegliare *vt.* to oversee (*v. irr.*).

sorvolare *vt.* **1.** to fly (*v. irr.*) over **2.** (*passar sopra*) to pass over.

sorvolo *sm.* flying over.

sosia *sm.* double.

sospèndere *vt.* **1.** (*attaccare*) to suspend **2.** (*interrompere*) to defer.

sospensione *sf.* **1.** (*incertezza; chim*) suspension **2.** (*interruzione*) interruption.

sospensiva *sf.* suspension.

sospensivo *agg.* suspensive.

sospeso *agg.* **1.** hanging **2.** (*interrotto*) suspended.

sospettàbile *agg.* liable to suspicion.

sospettare *vt.* to suspect.

sospetto *sm.* suspicion.

sospettosamente *avv.* suspiciously.

sospettoso *agg.* suspicious.

sospìngere *vt.* to drive (*v. irr.*) || *ad ogni piè sospinto*, at every moment.

sospirare *vi.* **1.** to sigh **2.** (*fig.*) to pine. ◆ **sospirare** *vt.* to long (for).

sospirato *agg.* (*desiderato*) longed for.

sospiro *sm.* sigh.

sosta *sf.* **1.** (*fermata*) stop **2.** (*pausa*) pause.

sostantivamente *avv.* substantively.

sostantivare *vt.* to substantivize.

sostantivo *sm.* substantive, noun.

sostanza *sf.* substance || *in —* (*in breve*), in short.

sostanziale *agg.* substantial.

sostanzialmente *avv.* substantially.

sostanzioso *agg.* substantial.

sostare *vi.* to stop.

sostegno *sm.* support.

sostenere *vt.* **1.** to support **2.** (*affermare*) to maintain **3.** (*tener alto*) to keep (*v. irr.*) up.

sostenìbile *agg.* **1.** supportable **2.** (*di opinioni*) maintainable.

sostenimento *sm.* **1.** support **2.** (*sostentamento*) sustenance.

sostenitore *sm.* supporter.

sostentamento *sm.* sustenance.

sostenuto *agg.* **1.** stiff, distant **2.** (*comm.*) steady.

sostituìbile *agg.* replaceable.

sostituire *vt.* to replace.

sostituto *sm.* substitute.

sostituzione *sf.* replacement.

sostrato *sm.* substratum (*pl.* -ta).

sottacere vt. to keep (v. irr.) (sthg.) from.

sottaceti sm. pl. pickles.

sottana sf. 1. skirt 2. (di prete) cassock.

sottecchi (nella loc. avv.) di —, stealthily.

sotterfugio sm. subterfuge.

sotterramento sm. burial.

sotterrànea sf. underground.

sotterràneo agg. underground. ◆ **sotterràneo** sm. 1. (di basilica) vault 2. (di castello) dungeon.

sotterrare vt. to bury.

sottigliezza sf. 1. thinness 2. (acutezza) subtlety.

sottile agg. 1. thin 2. (fig.) subtle.

sottilizzare vi. to split (v. irr.) hairs.

sottilmente avv. 1. finely 2. (con acutezza) subtly.

sottintèndere vt. to imply.

sottinteso agg. implied. ◆ **sottinteso** sm. allusion.

sotto prep. 1. under 2. (al di sotto, più in basso) below, beneath 3. (in espressioni di tempo) — Natale, at Christmas; essere — gli esami, to be close to the exams. ◆ **sotto** avv. 1. underneath, below 2. (al piano di sotto) downstairs.

sottobanco loc. avv. underthecounter.

sottobosco sm. underbrush.

sottocchio avv. in front of: tenere qc. —, to keep (v. irr.) an eye on sthg.

sottochiave avv. under lock and key.

sottocoperta sf. (mar.) below deck.

sottocoppa sf. saucer.

sottocutàneo agg. subcutaneous.

sottofondo sm. 1. (edil.) foundation 2. (sfondo) background.

sottogamba (nella loc. avv.) prendere qc. —, to make (v. irr.) light of sthg.

sottolineare vt. 1. to underline 2. (fig.) to lay (v. irr.) stress (on).

sottolineatura sf. underlining.

sottomano avv. 1. (di nascosto) underhand 2. (a portata di mano) at hand.

sottomarino agg. e sm. submarine.

sottomesso agg. 1. subdued 2. (obbediente) submissive.

sottométtere vt. to subject. ◆ **sottométtersi** vr. to submit (oneself).

sottomissione sf. 1. subdual 2. (obbedienza) submission.

sottopassaggio sm. subway.

sottoporre vt. 1. (al giudizio di qu.) to submit 2. (subire, far subire) to subject 3. (esporre) to expose.

sottoposto sm. subordinate.

sottoprodotto sm. by-product.

sottoscritto agg. subscribed. ◆ **sottoscritto** sm. undersigned.

sottoscrivere vt. 1. to sign 2. (comm.) to underwrite. ◆ **sottoscrivere** vi. to subscribe.

sottoscrizione sf. subscription.

sottosegretario sm. under-secretary.

sottosopra avv. 1. upside down 2. (in disordine) topsy-turvy.

sottospecie sf. subspecies (invariato al pl.).

sottostante agg. below.

sottostare vi. 1. (essere sotto) to be below 2. (essere soggetto) to be subjected 3. (sottomettersi) to submit.

sottosuolo sm. subsoil.

sottotenente sm. second lieutenant.

sottotìtolo sm. subtitle.

sottovalutare vt. to undervalue.

sottovento avv. (mar.) leeward.

sottoveste sf. petticoat.

sottovoce avv. in a low voice.

sottrarre vt. 1. (mat.) to subtract 2. (portar via) to take (v. irr.) away 3. (rubare) to steal (v. irr.) 4. (salvare da) to deliver. ◆ **sottrarsi** vr. to avoid (sthg.).

sottrazione sf. subtraction.

sottufficiale sm. non-commissioned officer.

sovente avv. often, frequently.

soverchiare vi. to overcome (v. irr.).

soverchierìa sf. oppression.

soviètico agg. e sm. Soviet.

sovrabbondante agg. superabundant.

sovrabbondanza sf. superabundance.

sovrabbondare vi. to superabound.

sovraccaricare vt. to overload.

sovraccàrico sm. overload.

sovraccoperta sf. e avv. V. sopraccoperta.

sovranità sf. 1. sovereignty 2. (supremazia) supremacy.

sovrannaturale agg. V. soprannaturale.

sovrano *agg.* sovereign.

sovrappopolare *vt.* to overpopulate.

sovrappopolato *agg.* overpopulated.

sovrappopolazione *sf.* overpopulation.

sovrapporre *vt.* to superimpose.

sovrapposizione *sf.* superimposition.

sovrastampa *sf.* overprint.

sovrastante *agg.* impending, overhanging.

sovrastare *vi.* **1.** to overhang (*v. irr.*) over **2.** (*fig.*) to impend **3.** (*essere superiore*) to be superior.

sovreccedente *agg.* superabundant.

sovreccedenza *sf.* surplus.

sovreccitàbile *agg.* overexcitable.

sovreccitabilità *sf.* overexcitability.

sovreccitare *vt.* to overexcite.

sovreccitazione *sf.* overexcitement.

sovrimposta *sf.* additional tax.

sovrimpressione *sf.* (*foto; cine*) superimposure.

sovrintendente *sm.* superintendent.

sovrintendenza *sf.* superintendence.

sovrumano *agg.* superhuman.

sovvenzionare *vt.* to subsidize.

sovvenzione *sf.* subsidy.

sovversione *sf.* overthrow.

sovversivo *agg.* subversive. ♦ **sovversivo** *sm.* subverter.

sovvertimento *sm.* subversion.

sovvertire *vt.* to overthrow (*v. irr.*).

sozzo *agg.* filthy.

sozzume *sm.* filth.

spaccalegna *sm.* wood-cutter.

spaccamontagne *sm.* braggart.

spaccapietre *sm.* stone-breaker.

spaccare *vt.* **1.** to split (*v. irr.*) **2.** (*rompere*) to break (*v. irr.*) || *il mio orologio spacca il minuto*, my watch is dead right; *il sole spacca le pietre*, the sun is blazing down.

spaccatura *sf.* split, cleft.

spacchettare *vt.* to unpack.

spacciare *vt.* **1.** (*vendere*) to sell (*v. irr.*) **2.** (*mettere in circolazione*) to circulate **3.** (*far credere*) to make (*v. irr.*) (so.) believe **4.** (*uccidere*) to kill. ♦ **spacciarsi** *vr.* to pretend to be || *lo danno per spacciato* (*di malato*), they give him up.

spacciato *agg.* done for.

spacciatore *sm.* **1.** seller **2.** (*di monete false*) forger.

spaccio *sm.* **1.** shop **2.** (*vendita*) sale.

spacco *sm.* **1.** split **2.** (*di abiti*) vent.

spacconata *sf.* bluff.

spaccone *sm.* boaster.

spada *sf.* sword.

spadaccino *sm.* fencer.

spadino *sm.* court-sword.

spadroneggiare *vi.* to lord it.

spaesato *agg.* (*fig.*) lost.

spaghetto *sm.* **1.** (*piccolo spago*) string **2.** (*fam.*) (*paura*) fright.

spagliare *vt.* to take (*v. irr.*) the straw off.

spagnoletta *sf.* **1.** (*di filo*) spool **2.** (*arachide*) peanut.

spagnolismo *sm.* Hispanicism.

spagnolo *agg.* Spanish. ♦ **spagnolo** *sm.* Spaniard.

spago *sm.* string.

spaiare *vt.* to uncouple.

spaiato *agg.* odd.

spalancare *vt.* to open wide.

spalancato *agg.* wide open.

spalare *vt.* to shovel away.

spalatore *sm.* shoveller.

spalatura *sf.* shovelling.

spalla *sf.* **1.** shoulder **2.** (*pl.*) back (*sing.*) **3.** (*teat.*) stooge man || *alle spalle*, behind; *vivere alle spalle di qu.*, to live on so.

spallata *sf.* **1.** push with the shoulders **2.** (*alzata di spalle*) shrug.

spalleggiare *vt.* to back.

spalletta *sf.* parapet.

spalliera *sf.* **1.** back **2.** (*di piante*) espalier.

spallina *sf.* **1.** shoulder-strap **2.** (*mil.*) epaulette.

spalluccia *sf.* *far spallucce*, to shrug one's shoulders.

spalmare *vt.* to smear.

spalto *sm.* glacis.

spampanare *vt.* to strip a vine of its leaves.

spàndere *vt.* **1.** to spread (*v. irr.*) **2.** (*versare*) to shed (*v. irr.*) **3.** (*scialacquare*) to squander.

spanna *sf.* span.

spannare *vt.* to skim.

spannocchiare *vt.* to husk.

spappolare *vt.* to pulp. ♦ **spappolarsi** *vr.* to become (*v. irr.*) mushy.

sparare[1] *vt.* to shoot (*v. irr.*), to fire.

sparare[2] *vt.* (*squartare*) to split (*v. irr.*).

sparata *sf.* 1. discharge 2. (*spacconata*) brag.

sparato *sm.* (*di camicia*) shirt-front.

sparatore *sm.* shooter.

sparatoria *sf.* shooting.

sparecchiare *vt.* to clear.

spareggio *sm.* 1. disparity 2. (*sport*) deciding game.

spàrgere *vt.* 1. to scatter 2. (*divulgare*) to spread (*v. irr.*) 3. (*versare; di luce*) to shed (*v. irr.*).

spargimento *sm.* 1. spreading 2. (*versamento*) shedding || — *di sangue*, bloodshed.

sparigliare *vt.* to unmatch.

sparire *vi.* to disappear.

sparizione *sf.* disappearance.

sparlare *vi.* to speak (*v. irr.*) badly.

sparo *sm.* shot.

sparpagliare *vt.* to scatter. ♦ **sparpagliarsi** *vr.* to scatter.

sparso *agg.* 1. (*versato*) shed 2. (*sciolto*) loose.

spartano *agg.* Spartan.

spartiacque *sm.* watershed.

spartineve *sm.* snow-plough.

spartire *vt.* to share out.

spartito *sm.* score.

spartizióne *sf.* sharing.

sparuto *agg.* lean, spare.

sparviero *sm.* sparrow-hawk.

spasimante *sm.* wooer.

spasimare *vi.* 1. to suffer agonies 2. (*fig.*) to yearn.

spàsimo *sm.* pang.

spasmo *sm.* spasm.

spasmodicamente *avv.* spasmodically.

spasmòdico *agg.* spasmodic.

spassare *vt.* to amuse || *spassarsela*, to have a very good time.

spassionato *agg.* impartial.

spasso *sm.* 1. amusement: *che —!*, what fun! 2. (*passeggiata*) *andare a —*, to go (*v. irr.*) for a walk; *essere a —*, to be out of work.

spassoso *agg.* funny, amusing.

spàstico *agg.* spastic.

spato *sm.* spar.

spàtola *sf.* broad knife.

spatriare *vt.* V. *espatriare*.

spauracchio *sm.* 1. scarecrow 2. (*fig.*) bugbear.

spaurire *vt.* to frighten. ♦ **spaurirsi** *vr.* to get (*v. irr.*) frightened.

spaurito *agg.* frightened.

spavalderìa *sf.* boldness.

spavaldo *agg.* bold, arrogant.

spaventapàsseri *sm.* scarecrow.

spaventare *vt.* to frighten, to scare. ♦ **spaventarsi** *vr.* to be frightened.

spaventato *agg.* frightened, scared.

spavento *sm.* fright.

spaventoso *agg.* dreadful, frightful.

spaziale *agg.* space (*attr.*).

spaziare *vt.* to space. ♦ **spaziare** *vt.* to range.

spaziatura *sf.* spacing.

spazieggiare *vt.* to space.

spazientirsi *vr.* to lose (*v. irr.*) one's patience.

spazio *sm.* 1. space 2. (*posto*) room.

spazioso *agg.* wide.

spazzacamino *sm.* chimney-sweep.

spazzamine *sm.* mine-sweeper.

spazzaneve *sm.* snow-plough.

spazzare *vt.* to sweep (*v. irr.*).

spazzata *sf.* sweep.

spazzatura *sf.* (*rifiuti*) sweepings (*pl.*): *bidone della —*, dust-bin; *carro della —*, dust-cart.

spazzino *sm.* 1. road-sweeper 2. (*spazzaturaio*) dustman (*pl.* -men).

spàzzola *sf.* brush || *capelli a —*, crew-cut.

spazzolare *vt.* to brush.

spazzolata *sf.* brush.

spazzolino *sm.* (small) brush: *da denti*, tooth-brush.

spazzolone *sm.* scrubbing-brush.

specchiarsi *vr.* 1. to look at oneself in a mirror 2. (*riflettersi*) to be mirrored.

specchiera *sf.* looking-glass.

specchietto *sm.* 1. hand-mirror 2. (*tabella*) table || — *retrovisore*, driving-mirror.

specchio *sm.* 1. mirror 2. (*prospetto*) register 3. (*modello*) model || — *d'acqua*, sheet of water.

speciale *agg.* special.

specialista *s.* specialist.

specialità *sf.* speciality.

specializzare *vt.* to specialize. ♦ **specializzarsi** *vr.* to specialize.

specializzazione *sf.* specialization.

specie *sf.* 1. kind 2. (*scientifico; teol.*) species (*pl. invariato*) || *far —*, to surprise.

specificamente *avv.* specifically.

specificare *vt.* to specify.

specificazione *sf.* specification.

specìfico *agg. e sm.* specific.

specioso *agg.* specious.

speculare¹ *vi.* to speculate (on): — *al rialzo*, *al ribasso*, to speculate for the advance, for the fall.

speculare² *agg.* mirror-like.

speculativo *agg.* speculative.

speculatore *agg.* speculative. ◆ **speculatore** *sm.* speculator.

speculazione *sf.* speculation.

spedire *vt.* **1.** to send (*v. irr.*) **2.** (*via mare*) to ship **3.** (*via terra*) to forward.

speditamente *avv.* **1.** quickly **2.** (*correntemente*) fluently.

speditezza *sf.* **1.** quickness **2.** (*nel parlare*) fluency.

spedito *agg.* **1.** (*svelto*) quick **2.** (*nel parlare*) fluent.

speditore *sm.* sender.

spedizione *sf.* **1.** forwarding **2.** (*per mare*) shipment **3.** (*di lettere, pacchi*) dispatch **4.** (*scientifico; mil.*) expedition || — *per via aerea*, air-freight.

spedizioniere *sm.* forwarding agent.

spègnere *vt.* **1.** (*un fuoco*) to put (*v. irr.*) out **2.** (*gas, luce ecc.*) to turn off **3.** (*fig.*) to stifle || — *la sete*, to quench one's thirst. ◆ **spègnersi** *vr.* **1.** to go (*v. irr.*) out **2.** (*fig.*) to fade **3.** (*morire*) to pass away.

spegnimento *sm.* extinction.

spegnitoio *sm.* snuffer.

spelacchiare *vt.* to tear (*v. irr.*) out the hair of. ◆ **spelacchiarsi** *vr.* to lose (*v. irr.*) one's hair.

spelacchiato *agg.* **1.** scanty-haired **2.** (*di stoffe, pellicce*) worn-out.

spelare *vt.* to balden. ◆ **spelarsi** *vr.* V. spelacchiarsi.

spelato *agg.* **1.** hairless **2.** (*di indumento*) worn.

spelatura *sf.* **1.** hairless patch **2.** (*di indumento*) worn patch.

speleologia *sf.* speleology.

speleològico *agg.* speleological.

speleòlogo *sm.* speleologist.

spellare *vt.* to skin. ◆ **spellarsi** *vr.* to peel.

spellatura *sf.* **1.** skinning **2.** (*parte spellata*) graze.

spelonca *sf.* den.

spendaccione *sm.* spendthrift.

spèndere *vt.* to spend (*v. irr.*) (*anche fig.*).

spennacchiare *vt.* to pluck. ◆ **spennacchiarsi** *vr.* to lose (*v. irr.*) one's feathers.

spennare *vt.* to pluck.

spennellare *vt.* **1.** to brush **2.** (*med.*) to paint.

spennellata *sf.* touch of the brush.

spennellatura *sf.* (*med.*) painting.

spensieratamente *avv.* thoughtlessly.

spensieratezza *sf.* thoughtlessness.

spensierato *agg.* thoughtless.

spento *agg.* **1.** extinguished, out (*pred.*) **2.** (*estinto*) extinct **3.** (*smorto*) dull.

speràbile *agg.* to be hoped (for).

speranza *sf.* hope.

speranzoso *agg.* hopeful.

sperare *v.* e *vi.* to hope (for sthg., in so.).

spèrdersi *vr.* **1.** to get (*v. irr.*) lost **2.** (*dileguare*) to vanish.

sperduto *agg.* **1.** scattered **2.** (*isolato*) secluded **3.** (*smarrito*) lost.

sperequazione *sf.* inequality.

spergiurare *vi.* to swear (*v. irr.*) falsely: *giurare e —*, to swear again and again.

spergiuro *sm.* **1.** perjury **2.** (*di persona*) perjurer.

spericolato *agg.* reckless. ◆ **spericolato** *sm.* daredevil.

sperimentale *agg.* experimental.

sperimentalismo *sm.* experimentalism.

sperimentalmente *avv.* experimentally.

sperimentare *vt.* **1.** to experiment (with) **2.** (*mettere alla prova*) to test.

sperimentato *agg.* **1.** (*provato*) tried **2.** (*esperto*) experienced.

sperimentatore *sm.* experimenter.

sperimentazione *sf.* experimentation.

sperma *sm.* sperm.

spermatozoo *sm.* spermatozoon (*pl.* -zoa).

speronare *vt.* **1.** (*mar.*) to ram **2.** (*un cavallo*) to spur.

speronata *sf.* **1.** (*mar.*) ramming **2.** (*colpo di sperone*) spur.

sperone *sm.* V. sprone.

sperperamento *sm.* squandering.

sperperare *vt.* to squander.

sperperatore *sm.* squanderer.

spèrpero *sm.* dissipation.

sperticato *agg.* excessive.

spesa *sf.* **1.** expense: *far fronte a una —*, to meet (*v. irr.*) an expense **2.** (*compera*) shopping: *andare a far spese*, to go (*v. irr.*) shopping.

spesare vt. to maintain.

spesato agg. essere —, to have all expenses paid.

spessire vt. to thicken. ♦ **spessirsi** vr. to thicken.

spesso¹ agg. 1. thick 2. (frequente) frequent.

spesso² avv. often.

spessore sm. thickness.

spettàbile agg. respectable.

spettàcolo sm. 1. spectacle 2. (teat.) performance.

spettacoloso agg. spectacular.

spettante agg. due.

spettanze sf. pl. dues.

spettare vi. 1. to be (for so.) 2. (essere dovuto) to be due.

spettatore sm. 1. spectator 2. (testimone) witness || gli spettatori, the audience.

spettegolare vi. to gossip.

spettinare vt. to ruffle so.'s hair. ♦ **spettinarsi** vr. to ruffle one's hair.

spettinato agg. uncombed.

spettrale agg. spectral.

spettro sm. 1. ghost 2. (fis.) spectrum (pl. -ra).

spettroscopìa sf. spectroscopy.

spettroscòpico agg. spectroscopic(al).

spettroscòpio sm. spectroscope.

speziale sm. (farmacista) chemist.

spezie sf. pl. spices.

spezzàbile agg. breakable.

spezzare vt. to break (v. irr.). ♦ **spezzarsi** vr. to break.

spezzatino sm. stew.

spezzato agg. broken.

spezzettamento sm. chopping.

spezzettare vt. to chop.

spezzone sm. 1. (mil.) incendiary bomb 2. (metal.) cut-down size.

spia sf. 1. spy 2. (indizio) evidence 3. (di porta) peep-hole || — luminosa, warning light; fare la —, to play the spy.

splaccicare vt. to squash. ♦ **splaccicarsi** vr. to get (v. irr.) squashed.

splacente agg. sorry.

splacere vi. V. dispiacere.

splacévole agg. unpleasant.

splacevolmente avv. unpleasantly.

splaggia sf. 1. beach 2. (riva) (sea)shore.

splanamento sm. 1. levelling 2. (il radere al suolo) razing.

splanare vt. 1. to level 2. (radere al suolo) to raze 3. (appianare, lisciare) to smooth. ♦ **spianarsi** vr. to become (v. irr.) smooth.

splanata sf. 1. levelling 2. (luogo spianato) open space 3. (arch.) esplanade 4. (in un bosco) clearing.

splanato agg. 1. levelled 2. (liscio) smooth.

splano (nella loc. avv.) a tutto —, profusely; (sodo) hard.

splantare vt. 1. to pull out 2. (rovinare) to ruin. ♦ **spiantarsi** vr. (rovinarsi) to go (v. irr.) to ruin.

splantato agg. (fig.) penniless.

splantato sm. (fig.) pauper.

splare vt. 1. to spy (upon) 2. (aspettare) to watch (for).

splattellare vt. to blab (out).

splazzo sm. 1. open space 2. (nel bosco) clearing.

splccare vt. 1. to pick 2. (tagliare) to cut (v. irr.) off 3. (pronunciare) to enunciate distinctly 4. (emettere) to issue || — un salto, to take (v. irr.) a leap; — il volo, to fly (v. irr.) up; — una tratta, to draw (v. irr.) a bill. ♦ **spiccare** vi. to stand (v. irr.) out.

splccatamente avv. distinctly.

splccato agg. 1. (marcato) marked 2. (nitido) clear.

splcchio sm. 1. slice 2. (di agrumi) segment 3. (di aglio) clove 4. (geom.) sector || a spicchi, sliced.

splcclare vt. to dispatch. ♦ **spicciarsi** vr. to hurry up.

splcclativo agg. V. spiccio.

splcclcare vt. 1. to detach 2. (pronunciare) to utter.

splccio agg. 1. quick 2. (franco) straightforward || andar per le spicce, to go (v. irr.) straight to the point; moneta spiccia, small change.

splcciolata (nella loc. avv.) alla —, few at a time.

splccioli sm. pl. change (solo sing.).

splcco sm. far —, to stand (v. irr.) out.

splpocchiare vt. to delouse.

spledo sm. spit.

splegàbile agg. explainable.

splegamento sm. 1. spreading out 2. (mil.) deployment.

splegare vt. 1. to explain 2. (stendere) to spread (v. irr.) out 3. (di vele) to unfurl 4. (mil.) to deploy. ♦ **spiegarsi** vr. 1. (farsi *capire*) to make (*v. irr.*) oneself understood 2. (*stendersi*) to spread out.

spiegazione *sf.* explanation.

spiegazzare *vt.* to crumple.

spietatamente *avv.* ruthlessly.

spietatezza *sf.* ruthlessness.

spietato *agg.* ruthless.

spifferare *vt.* to blurt out.

spiffero *sm.* draught.

spiga *sf.* 1. spike 2. (*di cereali*) ear.

spigare *vi.* to ear.

spighetta *sf.* braid.

spigliatamente *avv.* easily.

spigliatezza *sf.* ease.

spigliato *agg.* easy.

spigo *sm.* lavender.

spigolare *vt.* to glean (*anche fig.*).

spigolatore *sm.* gleaner.

spigolatrice *sf.* gleaner.

spigolatura *sf.* gleaning.

spigolo *sm.* edge.

spigoloso *agg.* edgy.

spilla *sf.* 1. pin 2. (*gioiello*) brooch.

spillare *vt.* 1. to draw (*v. irr.*) 2. (*fig.*) to worm.

spillo *sm.* pin: — *da balia*, safety-pin.

spillone *sm.* (*per cappello*) hat-pin.

spilorceria *sf.* stinginess.

spilorcio *agg.* stingy. ♦ **spilorcio** *sm.* miser.

spilungona *sf.* lanky woman.

spilungone *sm.* lanky man.

spina *sf.* 1. thorn 2. (*lisca*) fishbone 3. (*elettr.*) plug 4. (*mecc.*) pin 5. (*di botte*) bung 6. (*fig.*) sorrow, grief || — *dorsale*, backbone; *a — di pesce*, herring-bone.

spinacio *sm.* spinach (*solo sing.*).

spinale *agg.* spinal.

spinare *vt.* (*pesce*) to bone.

spinato *agg.* (*a spina di pesce*) herring-bone || *filo —*, barbed wire.

spinetta *sf.* spinet.

spingere *vt.* 1. to push 2. (*condurre*) to drive (*v. irr.*) 3. (*stimolare*) to urge 4. (*portare*) to carry. ♦ **spingersi** *vr.* to push.

spino *sm.* thorn.

spinone *sm.* (*cane*) griffon.

spinosità *sf.* thorniness.

spinoso *agg.* thorny.

spinta *sf.* 1. push 2. (*stimolo*) incentive 3. (*mecc.; edil.*) thrust.

spinterogeno *sm.* (battery) coil ignition.

spinto *agg.* 1. (*eccessivo*) excessive 2. (*audace*) risky.

spintone *sm.* shove || *farsi avanti a spintoni*, to elbow one's way forward.

spiombare *vt.* to unseal.

spionaggio *sm.* espionage.

spioncino *sm.* peep-hole.

spione *sm.* spy.

spiovente *agg.* 1. drooping 2. (*inclinato*) sloping. ♦ **spiovente** *sm.* 1. slope 2. (*sport*) high kick.

spiòvere *vi.* 1. to stop raining 2. (*ricadere*) to come (*v. irr.*) down.

spira *sf.* coil.

spiraglio *sm.* 1. small hole 2. (*barlume*) gleam.

spirale *sf.* 1. spiral 2. (*molla*) spring.

spirante *agg.* 1. (*soffiante*) blowing 2. (*morente*) passing away 3. (*esalante*) exhaling.

spirare *vi.* 1. (*soffiare*) to blow (*v. irr.*) 2. (*morire*) to pass away 3. (*scadere*) to expire 4. (*emanare*) to emanate. ♦ **spirare** *vt.* to exhale.

spiritato *agg.* 1. possessed 2. (*spaventato*) frightened.

spiritico *agg.* spiritualistic.

spiritismo *sm.* spiritualism.

spiritista *s.* spiritualist.

spiritìstico *agg.* V. *spiritico*.

spìrito *sm.* 1. spirit 2. (*fantasma*) ghost 3. (*arguzia*) wit 4. (*alcool*) alcohol || *far dello —*, to be witty.

spiritosàggine *sf.* witticism.

spiritosamente *avv.* wittily.

spiritoso *agg.* 1. witty 2. (*alcoolico*) alcoholic.

spirituale *agg.* spiritual.

spiritualismo *sm.* spiritualism.

spiritualista *agg.* spiritualistic. ♦ **spiritualista** *s.* spiritualist.

spiritualità *sf.* spirituality.

spiritualizzare *vt.* to spiritualize.

spiritualmente *avv.* spiritually.

spizzicare *vt.* to nibble.

spizzico (*nella loc. avv.*) *a —*, little by little.

splendente *agg.* bright.

splèndere *vi.* to shine (*v. irr.*).

splèndido *agg.* splendid.

splendore *sm.* splendour.

spocchia *sf.* haughtiness.

spocchioso *agg.* haughty.

spodestamento *sm.* 1. dispossession 2. (*da posizione autorevole*) dethronement.

spodestare *vt.* 1. to dispossess 2. (*detronizzare*) to dethrone.

spoetizzare *vt.* to disenchant.

spoglia *sf.* **1.** (*di animale*) skin **2.** (*veste*) dress **3.** (*bottino*) spoils (*pl.*) ‖ *spoglie mortali*, mortal remains.

spogliare *vt.* **1.** to strip **2.** (*derubare*) to rob **3.** (*saccheggiare*) to plunder. ◆ **spogliarsi** *vr.* **1.** to strip **2.** (*di alberi*) to shed (*v. irr.*) **3.** (*privarsi*) to strip oneself (of).

spogliarello *sm.* strip-tease.

spogliatoio *sm.* **1.** dressing-room **2.** (*teat. ecc.*) cloak-room.

spoglio *agg.* bare. ◆ **spoglio** *sm.* **1.** (*computo*) counting **2.** (*esame*) examination **3.** (*vestito smesso*) cast-off ‖ *fare lo —*, to go (*v. irr.*) through.

spola *sf.* shuttle.

spoletta *sf.* **1.** spool **2.** (*di arma*) fuse.

spoliazione *sf.* spoliation.

spolmonarsi *vr.* to talk oneself hoarse.

spolpare *vt.* **1.** to take (*v. irr.*) the flesh off **2.** (*fig.*) to skin.

spolpato *agg.* **1.** stripped of the flesh **2.** (*fig.*) skinned.

spolverare *vt.* to dust.

spolveratura *sf.* **1.** dusting **2.** (*fig.*) smattering.

spolverino *sm.* dust-coat.

spolverizzare *vt.* to dust.

spòlvero *sm.* **1.** dusting **2.** (*disegno*) perforated pattern.

sponda *sf.* **1.** edge **2.** (*di fiume*) bank **3.** (*di mare*) shore **4.** (*parapetto*) parapet.

sponsali *sm. pl.* nuptials.

spontaneamente *avv.* spontaneously.

spontaneità *sf.* spontaneity.

spontàneo *agg.* spontaneous.

spopolamento *sm.* depopulation.

spopolare *vt.* to depopulate. ◆ **spopolarsi** *vr.* to become (*v. irr.*) depopulated.

spopolato *agg.* (*deserto*) deserted.

spora *sf.* spore.

sporàdico *agg.* sporadic.

sporcaccione *sm.* dirty man

sporcare *vt.* to dirty.

sporcizia *sf.* dirt.

sporco *agg.* dirty.

sporgente *agg.* protruding.

sporgenza *sf.* protrusion.

spòrgere *vi.* to put (*v. irr.*) out. ◆ **spòrgere** *vt.* to put (*v. irr.*) out. ◆ **spòrgersi** *vr.* to lean (*v. irr.*) out.

sport *sm.* sport.

sporta *sf.* basket.

sportello *sm.* **1.** door **2.** (*di biglietteria*) ticket-window **3.** (*di ufficio postale ecc.*) counter.

sportivamente *avv.* sportingly.

sportivo *agg.* sporting. ◆ **sportivo** *sm.* sportsman (*pl.* -men).

sporto *agg.* **1.** leaning out **2.** (*proteso*) outstretched.

sposa *sf.* bride.

sposalizio *sm.* wedding.

sposare *vt.* to marry. ◆ **sposarsi** *vr.* to get (*v. irr.*) married.

sposo *sm.* bridegroom.

spossamento *sm.* exhaustion.

spossante *agg.* exhausting.

spossare *vt.* to exhaust.

spossatezza *sf.* V. *spossamento*.

spossato *agg.* weary.

spossessare *vt.* to dispossess.

spostàbile *agg.* shiftable.

spostamento *sm.* **1.** shifting **2.** (*cambiamento*) change.

spostare *vt.* **1.** to shift, to move **2.** (*cambiare*) to change. ◆ **spostarsi** *vr.* to shift.

spostato *agg.* out of one's place (*pred.*). ◆ **spostato** *sm.* misfit.

spranga *sf.* bar.

sprangare *vt.* to bar.

sprazzo *sm.* flash: *— d'ingegno*, brain-wave.

sprecare *vt.* to waste.

spreco *sm.* waste.

sprecone *sm.* waster.

spregévole *agg.* despicable.

spregiare *vt.* to scorn.

spregiativo *agg.* **1.** scornful **2.** (*gramm.*) pejorative. ◆ **spregiativo** *sm.* (*gramm.*) pejorative.

spregio *sm.* contempt.

spregiudicatamente *avv.* open-mindedly.

spregiudicatezza *sf.* open-mindedness.

spregiudicato *agg.* open-minded.

sprèmere *vt.* **1.** to squeeze **2.** (*torcere*) to wring (*v. irr.*) out. ◆ **spremersi** *vr.* to rack oneself.

spremilimoni *sm.* lemon-squeezer.

spremitura *sf.* **1.** squeezing **2.** (*di panni bagnati*) wringing.

spremuta *sf.* squash.

spremuto *agg.* **1.** squeezed **2.** (*di panni*) wrung.

spretare *vt.* to unfrock. ◆ **spretarsi** *vr.* to renounce one's priesthood.

spretato *agg.* unfrocked. ♦ **spretato** *sm.* unfrocked priest.
sprezzante *agg.* scornful.
sprezzare *vt.* V. *disprezzare*.
sprezzo *sm.* scorn.
sprigionamento *sm.* **1.** exhalation **2.** (*violento*) bursting out.
sprigionare *vt.* to emit. ♦ **sprigionarsi** *vr.* **1.** to be emitted **2.** (*con violenza*) to burst (*v. irr.*) out.
sprimacciare *vt.* to shake (*v. irr.*) up.
sprizzare *vt. e vi.* to spurt: — *scintille*, to spit (*v. irr.*) sparks; — *gioia*, to burst (*v. irr.*) with joy.
sprizzo *sm.* spurt.
sprofondamento *sm.* **1.** sinking **2.** (*crollo*) collapse.
sprofondare *vt.* (*far cadere*) to cause to collapse. ♦ **sprofondare** *vi.* **1.** to sink (*v. irr.*) **2.** (*crollare*) to collapse **3.** (*fig.*) to be absorbed. ♦ **sprofondarsi** *vr.* **1.** to sink **2.** (*crollare*) to collapse **3.** (*fig.*) to be absorbed.
sproloquio *sm.* long rigmarole.
spronare *vt.* to spur.
spronata *sf.* spurring.
sprone *sm.* **1.** spur **2.** (*mar.*) ram ‖ *a spron battuto*, at full speed.
sproporzionato *agg.* disproportionate, out of proportion (*pred.*).
sproporzione *sf.* disproportion.
spropositato *agg.* **1.** full of blunders **2.** (*fig.*) enormous.
spropòsito *sm.* **1.** blunder **2.** (*eccesso*) excess ‖ *a* —, off the point.
sprovveduto *agg.* **1.** (*incauto*) unwary **2.** (*sprovvisto*) devoid **3.** (*impreparato*) unprepared.
sprovvisto *agg.* devoid ‖ *alla sprovvista*, unawares.
spruzzare *vt.* **1.** to spray **2.** (*inzaccherare*) to splash.
spruzzata *sf.* spray.
spruzzatore *sm.* sprayer.
spruzzatura *sf.* spraying.
spruzzo *sm.* **1.** spray **2.** (*di liquido sporco*) splash.
spudoratezza *sf.* shamelessness.
spudorato *agg.* shameless.
spugna *sf.* **1.** sponge **2.** (*tessuto*) sponge-cloth ‖ *cancellare con la* —, to sponge; *bere come una* —, to drink (*v. irr.*) like a fish.
spugnatura *sf.* sponge down.
spugnosità *sf.* sponginess.

spugnoso *agg.* spongy.
spulciare *vt.* **1.** to look for fleas (on) **2.** (*esaminare; fig.*) to peruse **3.** (*raccogliere; fig.*) to gather here and there.
spuma *sf.* foam.
spumante *agg.* foaming. ♦ **spumante** *sm.* sparkling wine.
spumare *vi.* to foam.
spumeggiante *agg.* foaming.
spumeggiare *vi.* to foam.
spumoso *agg.* foamy.
spuntare¹ *vt.* **1.** (*smussare*) to blunt **2.** (*tagliare*) to trim **3.** (*staccare*) to unpin ‖ *spuntarla*, to succeed. ♦ **spuntarsi** *vr.* **1.** (*smussarsi*) to get (*v. irr.*) blunt **2.** (*staccarsi*) to become (*v. irr.*) unpinned.
spuntare² *vi.* **1.** (*sorgere*) to rise (*v. irr.*) **2.** (*germogliare*) to sprout **3.** (*di capelli*) to begin (*v. irr.*) to grow **4.** (*apparire*) to appear.
spuntato *agg.* pointless.
spuntatura *sf.* **1.** (*lo smussare*) blunting **2.** (*il tagliare*) trimming.
spuntino *sm.* snack.
spunto *sm.* **1.** cue **2.** (*punto di partenza*) starting point.
spuntone *sm.* spike.
spurgare *vt.* **1.** to clean **2.** (*med.*) to discharge. ♦ **spurgarsi** *vr.* (*espettorare*) to expectorate.
spurgo *sm.* **1.** (*lo spurgare*) discharging **2.** (*l'espettorare*) expectorating **3.** (*ciò che viene espulso*) discharge.
spurio *agg.* spurious.
sputacchiare *vi.* V. *sputare*.
sputacchiera *sf.* spittoon.
sputacchio *sm.* spittle.
sputare *vt.* to spit (*v. irr.*).
sputasentenze *sm.* wiseacre.
sputo *sm.* spit.
squadra *sf.* **1.** (*da disegno*) square **2.** (*gruppo; sport*) team **3.** (*di operai*) gang **4.** (*mil.*) squad **5.** (*mar.*) squadron ‖ — *mobile*, flying squad.
squadrare *vt.* **1.** to square **2.** (*guardare*) to look (*so.*) up and down.
squadratura *sf.* squaring.
squadriglia *sf.* squadron.
squadro *sm.* squaring.
squadrone *sm.* squadron.
squagliamento *sm.* melting.
squagliare *vt.* to melt. ♦ **squagliarsi** *vr.* **1.** to melt **2.** (*andar via*) to steal (*v. irr.*) away.
squalìfica *sf.* disqualification.

squalificare vt. to disqualify.

squàllido agg. dreary.

squallore sm. dreariness.

squalo sm. shark.

squama sf. scale.

squamare vt. to scale. ♦ **squamarsi** vr. to scale.

squamoso agg. scaly.

squarciagola (nella loc. avv.) a —, at the top of one's voice.

squarciamento sm. tearing.

squarciare vt. 1. to tear (v. irr.) 2. (fig.) to dispel. ♦ **squarciarsi** vr. to be torn.

squarcio sm. gash.

squartare vt. to mangle.

squartatore sm. mangler.

squassare vt. to jolt.

squasso sm. jolt.

squattrinato agg. penniless.

squilibrare vt. to unbalance. ♦ **squilibrarsi** vr. to lose (v. irr.) one's balance.

squilibrio agg. unbalanced. ♦ **squilibrato** sm. lunatic.

squilibrio sm. 1. lack of balance 2. (mentale) derangement.

squillante agg. 1. shrill 2. (di trombe) blaring 3. (di campane) pealing.

squillare vi. 1. to ring (v. irr.) 2. (di trombe) to blare.

squillo sm. 1. ring 2. (di tromba) blare.

squinternare vt. 1. to ruin 2. (fig.) to upset (v. irr.).

squisitezza sf. exquisiteness.

squisito agg. exquisite.

squittìo sm. squeak.

squittire vi. to squeak.

sradicare vt. to uproot.

sragionare vi. to talk nonsense.

sregolatezza sf. disorderliness.

sregolato agg. disorderly.

stabbio sm. 1. sty 2. (letame) manure.

stàbile . sm. building. ♦ **stàbile** agg. 1. stable 2. (permanente) permanent: in pianta —, on the permanent staff.

stabilimento sm. 1. (fabbrica) factory 2. (edificio, lo stabilire) establishment.

stabilire vt. 1. to establish 2. (decidere) to decide. ♦ **stabilirsi** vr. to settle.

stabilità sf. stability.

stabilizzare vt. to stabilize.

stabilizzatore sm. stabilizer.

stabilizzazione sf. stabilization.

stabilmente avv. firmly.

stacanovismo sm. Stakhanovism.

staccàbile agg. detachable.

staccare vt. 1. to take (v. irr.) off 2. (tagliare) to cut (v. irr.) off 3. (separare) to separate 4. (slegare) to unfasten || — un assegno, to issue a cheque. ♦ **staccarsi** vr. 1. to come (v. irr.) off 2. (sciogliersi) to break (v. irr.) loose 3. (scostarsi) to move away 4. (separarsi) to part 5. (distaccarsi) to pull ahead (of) 6. (esser diverso) to differ.

stacciare vt. to sieve.

staccio sm. sieve.

staccionata sf. fence.

stacco sm. detachment.

stadera sf. steelyard.

stadio sm. 1. stadium (pl. -ia), sports ground 2. (fase) stage.

staffa sf. stirrup || perder le staffe (fig.), to lose (v. irr.) one's self--control.

staffetta sf. 1. courier 2. (sport) relay race.

staffilare vt. to lash.

staffilata sf. lash.

staffile sm. whip.

stafilococco sm. staphylococcus (pl. -ci).

staggio sm. 1. (di scala) shaft 2. (di sedia) back leg.

stagionale agg. seasonal.

stagionare vt. to season.

stagionato agg. 1. seasoned 2. (fig.) oldish.

stagionatura sf. seasoning.

stagione sf. season.

stagnaio sm. tinsmith.

stagnante agg. stagnant.

stagnare[1] vi. to stagnate.

stagnare[2] vt. 1. to tin 2. (saldare) to solder 3. (impermeabilizzare) to waterproof 4. (fermare) to staunch.

stagnatura sf. tinning.

stagnino sm. tinker.

stagno[1] sm. tin.

stagno[2] sm. (bacino d'acqua) pond.

stagno[3] agg. water-tight.

stagnola sf. tin-foil.

staio sm. bushel.

stalagmite sf. stalagmite.

stalattite sf. stalactite.

stalla sf. stable.

stalliere sm. stable-boy.

stallo sm. stall.

stallone sm. stallion.

stamattina *avv.* this morning.

stambecco *sm.* ibex.

stamberga *sf.* hovel.

stambugio *sm.* hole.

stame *sm.* (*bot.*) stamen.

stamigna *sf.* bunting.

stampa *sf.* 1. print 2. (*atto di stampare*) printing 3. (*periodici, giornali*) press 4. (*genere*) stamp || *agenzia di —*, news-agency; *errore di —*, misprint.

stampare *vt.* 1. to print 2. (*mecc.*) to press 3. (*coniare*) to coin. ◆ **stamparsi** *vr.* — *in mente*, to impress (sthg.) firmly on one's mind.

stampatello *sm.* block letters (*pl.*).

stampato *sm.* 1. printed matter 2. (*modulo*) form.

stampatore *sm.* printer.

stampatrice *sf.* printing-press.

stampella *sf.* crutch.

stamperìa *sf.* printing-office.

stampigliare *vt.* to stamp.

stampo *sm.* 1. die, mould 2. (*genere*) stamp.

stanare *vt.* to drive (*v. irr.*) out.

stancare *vt.* 1. to tire 2. (*infastidire*) to annoy. ◆ **stancarsi** *vr.* 1. to get (*v. irr.*) tired 2. (*annoiarsi*) to get bored.

stanchezza *sf.* tiredness.

stanco *agg.* tired.

standardizzare *vt.* to standardize.

stanga *sf.* 1. bar 2. (*di carro*) shaft 3. (*di passaggio a livello*) barrier.

stangare *vt.* 1. to bar 2. (*percuotere*) to thrash.

stanghetta *sf.* 1. (*degli occhiali*) bar 2. (*di serratura*) bolt.

stanotte *avv.* tonight.

stantio *agg.* stale.

stantuffo *sm.* 1. piston 2. (*di pompa ecc.*) plunger.

stanza *sf.* 1. room 2. (*strofa*) stanza || *prendere, avere —*, to settle.

stanziamento *sm.* appropriation.

stanziare *vt.* to appropriate. ◆ **stanziarsi** *vr.* to settle.

stappare *vt.* to uncork.

stare *vi.* 1. to stay 2. (*abitare*) to live 3. (*di salute, essere*) to be 4. (*in piedi*) to stand (*v. irr.*) 5. (*dipendere*) to depend (on) 6. (*spettare*) to be up 7. (*andare*) to go (*v. irr.*) 8. (*di abito*) to suit || *— per,* to be going (to); *lasciar —,* to leave (*v. irr.*) alone; *sta' a sentire!,* listen!; *ben ti sta!,* it

serves you right!

starnazzare *vi.* to flutter.

starnutire *vi.* to sneeze.

starnuto *sm.* sneeze.

stasare *vt.* to unclog.

stasera *avv.* this evening.

stasi *sf.* 1. standstill 2. (*med.*) stasis (*pl.* -ses).

statale *agg.* State (*attr.*), of the State. ◆ **statale** *s.* State employee.

stàtica *sf.* statics.

stàtico *agg.* static.

statista *sm.* statesman (*pl.* -men).

statìstica *sf.* statistics.

statizzare *vt.* to nationalize.

statizzazione *sf.* nationalization.

stato *sm.* 1. state, condition (*anche posizione sociale*) 2. (*giur.*) status 3. (*pol.*) State || *ufficio di — civile,* registry office; *ufficiale di — civile,* registrar.

statua *sf.* statue.

statuaria *sf.* statuary.

statuario *agg.* statuesque.

statuire *vt.* to decree.

statunitense *agg.* United States (*attr.*). ◆ **statunitense** *sm.* United States citizen.

statura *sf.* stature.

statuto *sm.* statute.

stazionamento *sm.* standing.

stazionare *vi.* 1. to stay 2. (*di vetture*) to be parked.

stazionario *agg.* stationary.

stazione *sf.* station.

stazza *sf.* tonnage.

stazzare *vt.* to have the tonnage of.

stecca *sf.* 1. (*di ombrello, ventaglio*) rib 2. (*da biliardo*) cue 3. (*di persiana*) slat 4. (*di busto*) whalebone 5. (*stonatura*) false note.

steccare *vt.* 1. (*chiudere con steccato*) to fence in 2. (*mus.*) to fluff. ◆ **steccare** *vi.* 1. (*cantando*) to sing (*v. irr.*) a false note 2. (*suonando*) to play a false note.

steccato *sm.* fence.

stecchito *agg.* 1. (*secco*) dried up 2. (*magro*) skinny 3. (*morto*) stone dead.

stecco *sm.* 1. stick 2. (*persona magra*) bag of bones.

stecconata *sf.* paling.

stele *sf.* stele (*pl.* -lae).

stella *sf.* star: *— marina,* starfish; *a forma di —,* starlike.

stellare *agg.* 1. stellar 2. (*a forma di stella*) star-shaped.

stellato *agg.* starry.

stelletta sf. 1. (tip.) asterisk 2. (mil.) star.

stelloncino sm. short paragraph.

stelo sm. stem.

stemma sm. coat-of-arms.

stemperare vt. 1. to mix 2. (diluire) to spin out. ♦ **stemperarsi** vr. to dissolve.

stempiarsi vr. to go (v. irr.) bald.

stendardo sm. standard.

stèndere vt. 1. to spread (v. irr.) 2. (allungare) to stretch 3. (scrivere) to draw (v. irr.) up 4. (rilassare) to relax || — il bucato, to hang (v. irr.) out the washing. ♦ **stèndersi** vr. 1. to stretch 2. (adagiarsi) to lie (v. irr.) down.

stenodattilografia sf. shorthand and typewriting.

stenografare vt. to write (v. irr.) down in shorthand.

stenografia sf. shorthand.

stenògrafo sm. shorthand-writer.

stentare vi. 1. to have difficulty (in) 2. (mancare del necessario) to be in need.

stentato agg. 1. hard 2. (cresciuto a stento) stunted.

stento sm. privation: a —, hardly, with difficulty.

stentòreo agg. stentorian.

steppa sf. steppe.

sterco sm. dung.

stereofonia sf. stereophony.

stereofònico agg. stereophonic.

stereografia sf. stereography.

stereogràfico agg. stereographic(al).

stereoscopìa sf. stereoscopy.

stereoscòpio sm. stereoscope.

stereotipato agg. stereotyped.

stereotipìa sf. stereotyping.

stèrile agg. barren.

sterilità sf. barrenness.

sterilizzare vt. to sterilize.

sterilizzatore agg. sterilizing. ♦ **sterilizzatore** sm. sterilizer.

sterilizzazione sf. sterilization.

sterlina sf. pound.

sterminare vt. to exterminate.

sterminatezza sf. immensity.

sterminato agg. (smisurato) immense.

sterminatore sm. exterminator.

sterminio sm. extermination.

sterno sm. breast-bone.

sterpaglia sf. brushwood.

sterpo sm. dry twig.

sterrare vt. to dig (v. irr.) up.

sterratore sm. navvy.

sterzare vt. to steer.

sterzata sf. sudden turn.

sterzo sm. (auto) steering-gear.

stesso agg. 1. (medesimo) same 2. (intensivo) se —, oneself; io, me —, myself; tu, te — yourself; egli, lui —, himself; elia, lei stessa, herself; esso —, itself; noi stessi, ourselves; voi stessi, yourselves; loro stessi, themselves 3. (proprio) very. ♦ **stesso** sm. same. ♦ **stesso** avv. all the same.

stesura sf. 1. (redazione) draft 2. (di contratto) drawing up.

stetoscòpio sm. stethoscope.

stigmate sf. pl. 1. stigmata (pl.) 2. (marchio) brand (sing.).

stigmatizzare vt. to stigmatize.

stilare vt. to draw (v. irr.) up.

stile sm. style: aver —, to be stylish; con —, stylishly.

stilettata sf. stab.

stilista s. stylist.

stilistica sf. stylistics.

stilizzare vt. to stylize.

stilizzazione sf. stylization.

stilla sf. drop.

stillare vi. e vt. to ooze. ♦ **stillarsi** vr. — il cervello, to rack one's brain.

stillicìdio sm. dripping.

stilo sm. stylus.

stilogràfica sf. fountainpen.

stilogràfico agg. stylographic(al).

stima sf. 1. (valutazione) estimate 2. (buona opinione) esteem.

stimàbile agg. estimable.

stimare vt. 1. (valutare) to estimate 2. (tenere in considerazione) to esteem 3. (ritenere) to consider.

stimatore sm. estimator.

stimolante agg. stimulating. ♦ **stimolante** sm. stimulant.

stimolare vt. to stimulate.

stìmolo sm. 1. stimulus (pl. -li) 2. (pungolo) goad.

stinco sm. shin.

stìngere vt. to fade. ♦ **stìngersi** vr. to fade.

stinto agg. faded.

stipare vt. to cram.

stipato agg. crammed (with).

stipendiare vt. to pay (v. irr.) a salary (to so.).

stipendio sm. salary.

stìpite sm. jamb.

stipulante agg. stipulating. ♦ **stipulante** s. stipulator.

stipulare vt. to stipulate.

stipulazione *sf.* stipulation.

stiracchiare *vt.* **1.** to stretch **2.** (*distorcere*) to twist.

stiracchiato *agg.* (*fig.*) forced.

stiramento *sm.* **1.** stretching **2.** (*muscolare*) strain.

stirare *vt.* **1.** to stretch **2.** (*col ferro da stiro*) to iron.

stiratura *sf.* ironing.

stireria *sf.* (*e tintoria*) laundry shop.

stirpe *sf.* **1.** stock **2.** (*progenie*) issue.

stitichezza *sf.* constipation.

stitico *agg.* constipated.

stiva *sf.* hold.

stivale *sm.* boot.

stivaletto *sm.* ankle-boot.

stizza *sf.* anger.

stizzire *vt.* to vex. ♦ **stizzirsi** *vr.* to get (*v. irr.*) cross.

stizzito *agg.* cross.

stizzoso *agg.* peevish.

stoccata *sf.* thrust: *lanciare una —* (*fig.*), to gibe (at).

stoffa *sf.* **1.** cloth **2.** (*fig.*) stuff.

stoicismo *sm.* stoicism.

stòico *agg. e sm.* stoic.

stoino *sm.* door-mat.

stola *sf.* stole.

stolidità *sf.* stolidity.

stòlido *agg.* stolid.

stoltezza *sf.* foolishness.

stolto *agg.* foolish. ♦ **stolto** *sm.* fool.

stomacare *vt.* to sicken. ♦ **stomacarsi** *vr.* to sicken.

stomachévole *agg.* sickening.

stòmaco *sm.* stomach: *dare di —*, to vomit; *restare sullo —*, to lie (*v. irr.*) on one's stomach.

stomatite *sf.* stomatitis.

stomatologia *sf.* stomatology.

stonare *vi.* **1.** to be out of tune **2.** (*fig.*) to be out of place **3.** (*di colori*) to clash. ♦ **stonare** *vt.* to upset (*v. irr.*).

stonato *agg.* **1.** out of tune **2.** (*fig.*) out of place **3.** (*turbato*) upset **4.** (*di nota*) false.

stonatura *sf.* false note.

stoppa *sf.* tow.

stoppaccio *sm.* wad.

stoppare *vt.* **1.** to plug **2.** (*sport*) to stop.

stoppia *sf.* stubble.

stoppino *sm.* wick.

stopposo *agg.* **1.** towy **2.** (*di carne*) stringy.

stòrcere *vt.* **1.** to twist **2.** (*un'articolazione*) to sprain || *— gli occhi*, to roll one's eyes. ♦ **stòrcersi** *vr.* **1.** to twist **2.** (*lussarsi, slogarsi*) to wrench.

stordimento *sm.* **1.** dizziness **2.** (*meraviglia*) bewilderment.

stordire *vt.* **1.** to stun **2.** (*di alcoolici*) to dull **3.** (*assordare*) to deafen **4.** (*innervosire*) to drive (*v. irr.*) crazy. ♦ **stordirsi** *vr.* to dull one's senses.

stordito *agg.* **1.** (*sbalordito*) bewildered **2.** (*sbadato*) heedless **3.** (*sciocco*) foolish.

storia *sf.* **1.** history **2.** (*racconto*) story.

storicismo *sm.* historical method.

storicità *sf.* historicity. ♦ **stòrico** *agg.* historical. ♦ **stòrico** *sm.* historian.

storiografia *sf.* historiography.

storiògrafo *sm.* historiographer.

stormire *vi.* to rustle.

stormo *sm.* **1.** flight **2.** (*folla*) crowd || *suonare a —*, to ring (*v. irr.*) the tocsin.

stornare *vt.* to divert.

stornello[1] *sm.* ditty.

stornello[2] *sm.* (*zool.*) starling.

storno[1] *agg.* dapple-grey.

storno[2] *sm.* (*zool.*) starling.

storno[3] *sm.* (*comm.*) transfer.

storpiare *vt.* **1.** to cripple **2.** (*rovinare*) to mangle.

storpiatura *sf.* **1.** crippling **2.** (*fig.*) mangling **3.** (*cosa malfatta*) botch.

stòrpio *sm.* cripple.

storta *sf.* **1.** twist **2.** (*in una articolazione*) sprain **3.** (*chim.*) retort.

storto *agg.* **1.** twisted **2.** (*piegato*) crooked **3.** (*di occhi*) squinting **4.** (*sbagliato*) wrong.

stortura *sf.* **1.** deformity **2.** (*errore*) mistake.

stoviglie *sf. pl.* kitchenware (*sing.*).

stràbico *agg.* squinting. ♦ **stràbico** *sm.* squinter.

strabiliante *agg.* amazing.

strabiliare *vt.* to amaze (*anche far strabiliare*). ♦ **strabiliare** *vi.* to be amazed. ♦ **strabiliarsi** *vr.* to be amazed.

strabismo *sm.* squint.

straboccare *vi.* **1.** to overflow **2.** (*fig.*) to abound (in).

strabocchévole *agg.* overflowing.

strabuzzare *vt. — gli occhi*, to roll one's eyes.

stracàrico agg. overloaded (with).

stracciare vt. to tear (v. irr.). ◆ **stracciarsi** vr. to tear.

stracciato agg. **1.** torn **2.** (di persona) in rags.

straccio agg. torn, in rags || carta straccia, waste paper. ◆ **straccio** sm. rag: — per la polvere, duster.

straccione sm. ragamuffin.

straccivéndolo sm. rag-and-bone-man (pl. -men).

stracotto agg. overdone. ◆ **stracotto** sm. stew.

strada sf. **1.** road **2.** (di città) street **3.** (percorso; fig.) way || — a senso unico, one-way street; — ferrata, railway; — maestra, main road.

stradale agg. road (attr.), of the road: fondo —, road-bed.

stradino sm. roadman (pl. -men).

strafalcione sm. blunder.

strafare vi. to overdo (v. irr.).

strafottente agg. **1.** (noncurante) unconcerned **2.** (arrogante) arrogant.

strage sf. **1.** slaughter **2.** (distruzione) destruction || fare una —, to slaughter.

stragrande agg. enormous.

stralciare vt. **1.** (comm.) to remove **2.** (fig.) to take (v. irr.) off.

stralcio sm. **1.** removal **2.** (estratto) extract.

strale sm. dart.

stralunare vt. — gli occhi, to roll one's eyes, to open one's eyes wide.

stralunato agg. **1.** (di occhi) rolling, wild-eyed **2.** (di persona) upset.

stramazzare vi. to fall (v. irr.) heavily.

stramberìa sf. oddity.

strambo agg. odd.

strame sm. litter.

strampalato agg. queer.

stranezza sf. oddity.

strangolamento sm. strangling.

strangolare vt. to strangle.

strangolatore sm. strangler.

straniero agg. foreign. ◆ **straniero** sm. foreigner.

strano agg. strange.

straordinario agg. extraordinary.

strapazzare vt. **1.** to ill-u°e **2.** (sgridare) to scold **3.** (far lavorare troppo) to overwork **4.** (di uova) to scramble. ◆ **strapazzarsi** vr. to overwork oneself.

strapazzata sf. **1.** scolding **2.** (fatica) overwork.

strapazzo sm. overwork: abiti da —, working-clothes; scrittore da —, hack.

strapieno agg. full up.

strapiombare vi. **1.** to lean (v. irr.) **2.** (scendere a precipizio) to fall (v. irr.) perpendicularly.

strapiombo sm. precipice: a —, sheer.

strapotente agg. very powerful.

strappare vt. **1.** (lacerare) to tear (v. irr.) **2.** (togliere) to snatch **3.** (estirpare) to pull up **4.** (un dente) to pull out **5.** (estorcere) to wring (v. irr.). ◆ **strapparsi** vr. (lacerarsi) to tear.

strappo sm. **1.** tear **2.** (strappata) pull **3.** (infrazione) breach || — muscolare, sprain.

strapuntino sm. folding seat.

straricco agg. immensely rich.

straripamento sm. overflowing.

straripare vi. to overflow.

strascicare vt. **1.** to drag **2.** (i piedi) to shuffle **3.** (le parole) to drawl.

strascico sm. **1.** train **2.** (residuo) after-effect **3.** (rete) trawl.

strascinare vt. V. trascinare.

stratagemma sm. stratagem.

stratega sm. strategist.

strategìa sf. strategy.

stratègico agg. strategic(al).

stratificare vt. to stratify.

stratificazione sf. stratification.

strato sm. **1.** layer **2.** (di rivestimento) coat **3.** (della società) class.

stratosfera sf. stratosphere.

stratosfèrico agg. stratospheric(al).

strattone sm. **1.** pull **2.** (sobbalzo) jerk || a strattoni, jerkily; (a intervalli) by fits and starts.

stravagante agg. odd, queer.

stravaganza sf. oddity.

stravecchio agg. very old.

stravedere vt. to see (v. irr.) badly: — per qu., to be crazy about so.

stravincere vt. to crush. ◆ **stravincere** vi. to win (v. irr.) all along the line.

stravizio sm. excess.

stravòlgere vt. **1.** to twist **2.** (gli occhi) to roll.

stravolto agg. **1.** (turbato) upset **2.** (di occhi) rolling.

straziante agg. tormenting, heart-rending (solo fig.).

straziare vt. to tear (v. irr.).

strazio sm. torment: far — di, to play havoc with.

strega sf. witch.

stregare vt. to bewitch.

stregone sm. wizard.

stregoneria sf. witchcraft.

stremare vt. to exhaust.

stremo sm. extreme.

strenna sf. gift.

strenuo agg. brave.

strepitare vi. to shout.

strepito sm. din, uproar.

strepitoso agg. uproarious: successo —, striking success.

streptococco sm. streptococcus (pl. -ci).

streptomicina sf. streptomycin.

stretta sf. 1. grasp 2. (calca) press 3. (gola) gorge || — di mano, handshake; essere alle strette, to be in dire straits; mettere alle strette qu., to put (v. irr.) so. with his back against the wall.

strettezza sf. 1. narrowness 2. (povertà) financial difficulty.

stretto agg. 1. narrow 2. (serrato, piccolo) tight 3. (rigoroso) strict 4. (pigiato) packed. ♦ **stretto** sm. strait.

strettoia sf. narrow passage.

stria sf. streak.

striare vt. to streak.

stricnina sf. strychnine.

stridente agg. 1. shrill 2. (discordante) jarring.

stridere vi. 1. to creak 2. (di insetti) to chirp 3. (contrastare) to jar.

stridio sm. 1. creaking 2. (di insetti) chirping.

strido sm. 1. scream 2. (di animale) screech.

stridulo agg. shrill.

striglia sf. curry-comb.

strigliare vt. 1. to curry 2. (fig.) to rebuke.

strillare vi. to scream.

strillo sm. scream.

strillone sm. newsboy.

striminzito agg. 1. stunted 2. (di persona) thin.

strimpellare vt. 1. (di violino) to scrape 2. (di pianoforte) to strum.

strinare vt. to singe.

stringa sf. lace.

stringare vt. 1. to lace tightly 2. (fig.) to condense.

stringato agg. 1. laced 2. (fig.) concise.

stringente agg. 1. (urgente) urgent 2. (convincente) persuasive.

stringere vt. 1. to press 2. (restringere, avvitare) to tighten 3. (abbracciare) to clasp 4. (impugnare) to grasp 5. (fare) to make (v. irr.) || — la mano a, to shake (v. irr.) hands with; — i pugni, to clench one's fists; stringi stringi, in conclusion. ♦ **stringere** vi. to be tight. ♦ **stringersi** vr. 1. to press (against) 2. (far spazio) to squeeze up || — nelle spalle, to shrug one's shoulders.

stringimento sm. 1. pressing 2. (restringimento, legamento, avvitamento) tightening 3. (l'impugnare) clasp 4. (fitta) pang.

striscia sf. 1. strip 2. (riga) stripe 3. (scia) trail || a strisce, striped.

strisciante agg. 1. creeping 2. (servile) fawning.

strisciare vi. 1. to creep (v. irr.) 2. (fig.) to grovel. ♦ **strisciare** vt. 1. to drag 2. (i piedi) to shuffle 3. (radere) to graze 4. (fig.) to fawn (on).

stritolamento sm. crushing.

stritolare vt. to crush.

strizzare vt. 1. to squeeze 2. (torcere) to wring (v. irr.) || — l'occhio, to wink (at so.).

strizzata sf. 1. squeeze 2. (il torcere) wring.

strofa sf. stanza.

strofinaccio sm. 1. duster 2. (per asciugare) towel.

strofinamento sm. rubbing.

strofinare vt. to rub.

strombatura sf. splay.

strombazzare vt. e vi. to trumpet.

strombettare vi. 1. to blow (v. irr.) a trumpet 2. (auto) to honk.

stroncare vt. 1. to break (v. irr.) off 2. (fig.) to demolish.

stroncatura sf. harsh criticism.

stronzio sm. strontium.

stropicciare vt. 1. to rub 2. (i piedi) to shuffle 3. (sgualcire) to crease. ♦ **stropicciarsi** vr. 1. (gli occhi) to rub oneself 2. (sgualcirsi) to crease.

stropiccio sm. — di piedi, shuffling.

strozzare vt. 1. to strangle 2. (ostruire) to obstruct 3. (fig.) to choke.

strozzato agg. 1. strangled 2. (soffocato) choked 3. (con strozzature) with narrow passages 4. (med.)

strangulated **5.** (*ostruito*) obstructed.

strozzatura *sf.* **1.** strangling **2.** (*il soffocare*) choking **3.** (*ostruzione*) obstruction **4.** (*restringimento*) narrow passage **5.** (*med.*) strangulation.

strozzinaggio *sm.* usury.

strozzino *sm.* usurer.

struggente *agg.* pining.

struggere *vt.* **1.** to melt **2.** (*fig.*) to wear (*v. irr.*) out. ♦ **struggersi** *vr.* **1.** to melt **2.** (*affliggersi*) to be distressed **3.** (*languire*) to be consumed (with), to pine (for).

struggimento *sm.* longing.

strumentale *agg.* instrumental.

strumentalismo *sm.* instrumentalism.

strumentare *vt.* to instrument.

strumentazione *sf.* instrumentation.

strumento *sm.* instrument.

strusciare *vt.* **1.** to rub **2.** (*adulare*) to fawn (on). ♦ **strusciarsi** *vr.* to rub (oneself).

strutto *sm.* lard.

struttura *sf.* structure.

strutturale *agg.* structural.

strutturare *vt.* to structure.

strutturazione *sf.* structure.

struzzo *sm.* ostrich.

stuccare[1] *vt.* **1.** to stucco **2.** (*turare*) to fill.

stuccare[2] *vt.* **1.** (*nauseare*) to sicken **2.** (*annoiare*) to bore. ♦ **stuccarsi** *vr.* **1.** to get (*v. irr.*) sick **2.** (*annoiarsi*) to get bored.

stuccatura *sf.* **1.** plastering **2.** (*di dente*) filling.

stucchévole *agg.* **1.** filling **2.** (*nauseante*) sickening **3.** (*noioso*) boring.

stucco *sm.* **1.** stucco **2.** (*per vetri*) putty ‖ *restare di* —, to be nonplussed.

studente *sm.* student.

studentesco *agg.* student (*attr.*).

studiacchiare *vt.* to study fitfully.

studiare *vt.* to study. ♦ **studiarsi** *vr.* to try.

studiato *agg.* (*affettato*) affected.

studio *sm.* **1.** study **2.** (*progetto*) plan **3.** (*cine*) studio ‖ *programma di studi*, curriculum; *essere allo* —, to be under consideration.

studioso *agg.* studious. ♦ **studioso** *sm.* scholar.

stufa *sf.* stove.

stufare *vt.* **1.** to stew **2.** (*fig.*) to bore. ♦ **stufarsi** *vr.* to get (*v. irr.*) bored.

stufato *sm.* stew.

stufo *agg.* fed up (with).

stuoia *sf.* mat.

stuolo *sm.* crowd.

stupefacente *agg.* stupefying. ♦ **stupefacente** *sm.* drug.

stupefare *vt.* to stupefy. ♦ **stupefarsi** *vr.* to be stupefied.

stupefazione *sf.* stupefaction.

stupendamente *avv.* wonderfully.

stupendo *agg.* wonderful.

stupidàggine *sf.* stupidity.

stupidità *sf.* stupidity.

stùpido *agg.* e *sm.* stupid.

stupire *vt.* to astonish. ♦ **stupirsi** *vr.* to be astonished.

stupìto *agg.* astonished.

stupore *sm.* astonishment.

stupro *sm.* rape.

sturare *vt.* **1.** to uncork **2.** (*botti*) to unbung.

stuzzicadenti *sm.* tooth-pick.

stuzzicare *vt.* **1.** to prod **2.** (*frugare*) to pick **3.** (*molestare*) to tease **4.** (*stimolare*) to whet.

su *prep.* **1.** on **2.** (*senza contatto; rivestimento*) over **3.** (*al di sopra di*) above **4.** (*circa*) about ‖ *nove volte* — *dieci*, nine times out of ten. ♦ **su** *avv.* **1.** up **2.** (*al piano superiore*) upstairs **3.** (*indosso*) on ‖ — *per giù*, more or less; *in* — (*in avanti*), onwards; *più* —, further up; —, *andiamo!*, come on!

sua *agg.* e *pron.* V. *suo.*

suadente *agg.* persuasive.

subàcqueo *agg.* underwater (*attr.*). ♦ **subàcqueo** *sm.* frogman (*pl.* -men).

subaffittare *vt.* to sublease.

subaffitto *sm.* sublease.

subalpino *agg.* subalpine.

subalterno *agg.* e *sm.* subaltern.

subbuglio *sm.* **1.** turmoil **2.** (*disordine*) mess.

subconscio *sm.* subconscious.

subcosciente *agg.* e *sm.* subconscious.

subdolamente *avv.* underhand.

sùbdolo *agg.* sly.

subentrare *vi.* to take (*v. irr.*) the place (of).

subire *vt.* to undergo (*v. irr.*).

subissare *vt.* **1.** (*sprofondare*) to sink (*v. irr.*) **2.** (*fig.*) to overwhelm.

subisso *sm.* (*gran quantità*) shower.

subitaneità *sf.* suddenness.

subitàneo *agg.* sudden.

sùbito *avv.* 1. at once 2. (*presto*) soon || — *prima*, just before; — *dopo*, just after.

sublimare *vt.* to sublimate.

sublimato *sm.* sublimate.

sublimazione *sf.* sublimation.

sublime *agg. e sm.* sublime.

sublimità *sf.* sublimity.

sublocazione *sf.* subletting.

sublunare *agg.* sublunar.

subodorare *vt.* to suspect.

subordinare *vt.* to subordinate.

subordinata *sf.* subordinate clause.

subordinato *agg. e sm.* subordinate.

subordinazione *sf.* subordination.

subornare *vt.* to suborn.

subornazione *sf.* subornation.

substrato *sm.* substratum (*pl.* -ta).

suburbano *agg.* suburban.

suburbio *sm.* suburb.

succèdere *vi.* 1. to succeed 2. (*capitare*) to happen. ◆ **succèdersi** *vr.* to follow one another.

successione *sf.* succession.

successivamente *avv.* afterwards.

successo *sm.* 1. success 2. (*esito*) outcome || *aver* —, to be successful.

successore *sm.* successor.

succhiare *vt.* to suck.

succhiata *sf.* suck.

succhiello *sm.* gimlet.

succinto *agg.* 1. (*di abiti*) scanty 2. (*conciso*) concise.

succo *sm.* 1. juice 2. (*fig.*) pith.

succosità *sf.* 1. juiciness 2. (*fig.*) pithiness.

succoso *agg.* 1. juicy 2. (*fig.*) pithy.

sùccubo *agg.* entirely dominated (by).

succulento *agg.* 1. juicy 2. (*gustoso*) rich.

succursale *sf.* branch.

sud *sm.* south: *del* —, southern, south (*attr.*); *verso* —, southwards.

sudare *vi.* to sweat: — *sette camicie*, to toil hard; — *freddo*, to be in a cold sweat.

sudario *sm.* shroud.

sudata *sf.* sweat.

sudaticcio *agg.* clammy.

sudato *agg.* 1. sweaty 2. (*fig.*) hard-earned.

suddetto *agg.* above-mentioned.

suddiàcono *sm.* subdeacon.

sudditanza *sf.* subjection.

sùddito *sm.* subject.

suddivìdere *vt.* to subdivide.

suddivisione *sf.* subdivision.

sùdicio *agg.* dirty.

sudicione *sm.* dirty fellow.

sudiciume *sm.* dirt.

sudore *sm.* 1. sweat 2. (*fig.*) toil.

sudorìfero *agg.* 1. (*che secerne sudore*) sudoriferous 2. (*che produce sudore*) sudorific.

sue *agg. e pron.* V. *suo.*

sufficiente *agg.* 1. sufficient 2. (*altezzoso*) conceited 2. (*voto sufficiente*) pass mark.

sufficienza *sf.* 1. sufficiency 2. (*alterigia*) conceit 3. (*voto sufficiente*) pass mark || *aria di* —, superior air; *a* —, enough.

suffisso *sm.* suffix.

suffragare *vt.* 1. to support 2. (*eccl.*) to pray for.

suffragio *sm.* 1. suffrage 2. (*approvazione*) approval.

suggellare *vt.* to seal.

suggello *sm.* seal.

suggerimento *sm.* 1. suggestion 2. (*teat.*) prompting.

suggerire *vt.* 1. to suggest 2. (*dar l'imbeccata; teat.*) to prompt.

suggeritore *sm.* prompter.

suggestionàbile *agg.* impressionable.

suggestionabilità *sf.* impressionability.

suggestionare *vt.* to influence. ◆ **suggestionarsi** *vr.* to will oneself (to do sthg.), to be influenced.

suggestione *sf.* suggestion.

suggestività *sf.* suggestiveness.

suggestivamente *avv.* evocatively.

suggestivo *agg.* evocative.

sùghero *sm.* 1. cork 2. (*albero*) cork-tree.

sugna *sf.* pork fat.

sugo *sm.* 1. juice 2. (*di carne*) gravy 3. (*di pomodoro*) sauce 4. (*fig.*) gist.

sugosità *sf.* V. *succosità.*

sugoso *agg.* V. *succoso.*

suicida *agg.* suicidal. ◆ **suicida** *s.* suicide.

suicidarsi *vr.* to commit suicide.

suicìdio *sm.* suicide.

suino *agg.* swine (*attr.*) || *carne suina*, pork. ◆ **suino** *sm.* swine (*pl. invariato*).

sulfamìdico *sm.* sulphonamide.

sulfùreo agg. sulphureous.

sultanato sm. sultanate.

sultanina sf. sultana.

sultano sm. sultan.

summenzionato agg. aforesaid.

sunto sm. summary.

suo agg. 1. (di lui) his 2. (di lei) her 3. (di esso) its 4. (formula di cortesia) your. ♦ **suo** pron. 1. (di lui) his 2. (di lei) hers 3. (di esso) its 4. (formula di cortesia) yours || i suoi (famigliari), his, her family.

suòcera sf. mother-in-law.

suòcero sm. father-in-law.

suoi agg. e pron. V. suo.

suola sf. sole.

suolo sm. soil, ground.

suonare vt. V. sonare.

suono sm. sound.

suora sf. nun, sister.

superàbile agg. surmountable.

superaffollato agg. overcrowded.

superalimentare vt. 1. to overrish 2. (mecc.) to overcharge.

superalimentazione sf. 1. overfeeding 2. (mecc.) overcharging.

superamento sm. 1. overcoming 2. (auto) overtaking.

superare vt. 1. (oltrepassare) to exceed 2. (auto) to overtake (v. irr.) 3. (attraversare) to cross 4. (vincere) to overcome (v. irr.) 5. (una persona) to surpass 6. (un esame, una prova) to pass.

superbia sf. pride.

superbo agg. 1. proud 2. (magnifico) superb.

superdotato agg. highly gifted.

superficiale agg. superficial.

superficialità sf. superficiality.

superficie sf. 1. surface 2. (area) area.

superfluo agg. superfluous. ♦ **superfluo** sm. surplus.

superiora sf. Mother Superior.

superiore agg. 1. superior 2. (sovrastante) upper 3. (più avanzato) advanced. ♦ **superiore** sm. superior.

superiorità sf. superiority.

superlativo agg. e sm. superlative.

supermercato sm. supermarket.

supernutrizione sf. overfeeding.

supersònico agg. supersonic.

supèrstite agg. surviving. ♦ **supèrstite** s. survivor.

superstizione sf. superstition.

superstizioso agg. superstitious.

superuomo sm. superman (pl. -men).

supervisione sf. supervision.

supervisore sm. supervisor.

supinamente avv. supinely.

supino agg. supine.

suppellèttile sf. furnishings (pl.).

supplementare agg. supplementary.

supplemento sm. 1. supplement 2. (spesa supplementare) additional charge 3. (di biglietto ferroviario) excess fare.

supplente agg. temporary. ♦ **supplente** s. temporary teacher.

supplenza sf. temporary post.

suppletivo agg. supplementary.

sùpplica sf. 1. entreaty 2. (petizione) petition.

supplicante agg. e s. suppliant.

supplicare vt. to entreat.

supplichévole agg. entreating.

supplire vi. 1. (compensare) to make (v. irr.) up (for) 2. (sostituire) to substitute (for). ♦ **supplire** vt. to take (v. irr.) the place of.

supplizio sm. torment: andare al —, to go (v. irr.) to the scaffold.

supporre vt. to suppose.

supporto sm. support.

supposizione sf. supposition.

supposta sf. suppository.

supposto che cong. suppose (that).

suppurare vi. to suppurate.

suppurazione sf. suppuration.

supremazìa sf. supremacy.

supremo agg. supreme: Comando — (mil.), headquarters (pl.).

surclassare vt. to outclass.

surgelare vt. to deep-freeze (v. irr.).

surrealismo sm. surrealism.

surrealista agg. e s. surrealist.

surrealistico agg. surrealistic.

surrenale agg. suprarenal.

surrettizio agg. surreptitious.

surriscaldamento sm. overheating.

surriscaldare vt. to overheat. ♦ **surriscaldarsi** vr. to get (v. irr.) overheated.

surrogàbile agg. replaceable.

surrogare vt. to replace.

surrogato sm. substitute.

surrogazione sf. (giur.) surrogation.

suscettibile agg. 1. susceptible 2. (permaloso) touchy.

suscettibilità sf. 1. susceptibility 2. (permalosità) touchiness || urtare la — di qu., to hurt (v. irr.) so.'s feelings.

suscitare vt. 1. to provoke 2. (eccitare) to stir up.

suscitatore sm. provoker.

susina sf. plum.

susino sm. plum-tree.

susseguente agg. following.

susseguire vi. to follow.

sussidiare vt. 1. to support 2. (di governo) to subsidize.

sussidiario agg. subsidiary.

sussidio sm. subsidy.

sussiego sm. haughtiness.

sussistenza sf. 1. existence 2. (sostentamento) subsistence 3. (mil.) Catering Corps.

sussistere vi. 1. to subsist 2. (reggere) to hold (v. irr.) water.

sussultare vi. 1. to start 2. (di cose) to shake (v. irr.).

sussulto sm. start.

sussurrare vt. e vi. 1. to whisper 2. (criticare) to murmur.

sussurro sm. whisper.

sutura sf. suture.

suturare vt. to suture.

svagare vt. 1. to divert 2. (divertire) to amuse. ♦ svagarsi vr. 1. to divert one's mind 2. (divertirsi) to amuse oneself.

svagatezza sf. absent-mindedness.

svagato agg. absent-minded.

svago sm. amusement.

svaligiamento sm. 1. robbery 2. (di una casa) burglary.

svaligiare vt. 1. to rob 2. (una casa) to burgle.

svaligiatore sm. 1. robber 2. (di case) burglar.

svalutare vt. 1. to devaluate 2. (sottovalutare) to undervalue.

svalutazione sf. devaluation.

svanire vi. 1. to disappear 2. (dileguarsi, di luce ecc.) to fade.

svanito agg. 1. (dileguato) vanished 2. (di mente) feeble-minded.

svantaggio sm. disadvantage.

svantaggioso agg. disadvantageous.

svaporamento sm. evaporation.

svaporare vi. to evaporate.

svariare vt. to vary.

svariato agg. various.

svarione sm. blunder.

svasare vt. (mecc.) to flare.

svasato agg. (di abito) bell-shaped.

svasatura sf. 1. (di abito) bell-shaping 2. (mecc.; lo svasare) flaring 3. (apertura) countersink.

svàstica sf. swastika.

svecchiamento sm. renewal.

svecchiare vt. to renew.

svedese agg. Swedish. ♦ svedese sm. Swede.

sveglia sf. 1. early call 2. (orologio) alarm clock 3. (mil.) reveille.

svegliare vt. to wake (v. irr.) (up). ♦ svegliarsi vr. to wake (up).

sveglio agg. 1. awake (pred.) 2. (fig.) quick-witted.

svelare vt. 1. to reveal, to disclose 2. (togliere il velo) to unveil.

svelenire vt. (fig.) to remove the sting from.

svèllere vt. to extirpate.

sveltezza sf. quickness.

sveltire vt. 1. to quicken 2. (scaltrire) to wake (v. irr.) up || — la figura, to slim. ♦ sveltirsi vr. 1. to become (v. irr.) quick(er) 2. (scaltrirsi) to wake up.

svelto agg. 1. quick 2. (slanciato) slender 3. (intelligente) smart. ♦ svelto avv. fast || —!, hurry up!

svenare vt. to open so.'s veins. ♦ svenarsi vr. to cut (v. irr.) one's veins.

svéndere vt. to undersell (v. irr.).

svéndita sf. (clearance) sale.

svenévole agg. maudlin.

svenimento sm. faint.

svenire vi. to faint.

sventagliare vt. to fan.

sventare vt. to baffle.

sventatezza sf. 1. thoughtlessness 2. (atto sventato) thoughtless action.

sventato agg. (sbadato) thoughtless. ♦ sventato sm. scatter-brain.

svèntola sf. (schiaffo) slap.

sventolare vt. e vi. to wave. ♦ sventolarsi vr. to fan oneself.

sventolio sm. waving.

sventramento sm. 1. disembowelment 2. (demolizione) demolition.

sventrare vt. 1. to disembowel 2. (demolire) to demolish.

sventura sf. misfortune: per —, unluckily; per colmo di —, to crown it all.

sventuratamente avv. unfortunately.

sventurato agg. unfortunate.

svenuto agg. unconscious.

svergognare vt. to shame.

svergognatamente avv. shamelessly.

svergognato agg. shameless.

svernamento sm. wintering.

svernare vi. to winter.

svestire *vt.* to undress. ♦ **svestirsi** *vr.* to undress.

svettare *vt.* to lop. ♦ **svettare** *vi.* to stand (*v. irr.*) out.

svezzamento *sm.* weaning.

svezzare *vt.* to wean.

sviamento *sm.* 1. diversion 2. (*il traviare*) leading astray 3. (*il traviarsi*) going astray.

sviare *vt.* 1. to divert 2. (*traviare*) to lead (*v. irr.*) astray. ♦ **sviarsi** *vr.* 1. to be diverted 2. (*traviarsi*) to go (*v. irr.*) astray.

sviato *agg.* led astray (*pred.*).

svignàrsela *vr.* to slink (*v. irr.*) away.

svigorire *vt.* to weaken. ♦ **svigorirsi** *vr.* to grow (*v. irr.*) weak.

svilimento *sm.* depreciation.

svilire *vt.* to depreciate.

sviluppare *vt.* 1. to develop 2. (*sciogliere*) to loosen 3. (*sprigionare*) to generate. ♦ **svilupparsi** *vr.* to develop.

sviluppatore *sm.* (*foto*) developer.

sviluppo *sm.* 1. development 2. (*sprigionamento*) generation.

svincolamento *sm.* 1. release 2. (*doganale*) clearance 3. (*riscatto*) redemption.

svincolare *vt.* 1. to release 2. (*sdoganare*) to clear 3. (*riscattare*) to redeem. ♦ **svincolarsi** *vr.* to get (*v. irr.*) free.

svisare *vt.* (*travisare*) to twist.

sviscerare *vt.* 1. to disembowel 2. (*fig.*) to dissect.

sviscerato *agg.* passionate.

svista *sf.* oversight.

svitare *vt.* to unscrew.

svizzero *agg.* e *sm.* Swiss.

svogliatezza *sf.* 1. unwillingness 2. (*pigrizia*) laziness.

svogliato *agg.* 1. unwilling 2. (*pigro*) lazy. ♦ **svogliato** *sm.* lazy-bones.

svolazzare *vi.* to flutter.

svolazzo *sm* 1. fluttering 2. (*tratto di penna*) flourish.

svòlgere *vt.* 1. to unwind (*v. irr.*) 2. (*trattare*) to develop 3. (*mettere in opera*) to carry out. ♦ **svòlgersi** *vr.* 1. to unwind 2. (*svilupparsi*) to develop 3. (*accadere*) to take (*v. irr.*) place.

svolgimento *sm.* 1. unwinding 2. (*trattazione*) treatment 3. (*corso*) course 4. (*sviluppo*) development.

svolta *sf.* 1. turn 2. (*fig.*) turning point || *fare una* —, to turn.

svoltare *vi.* to turn.

svuotamento *sm.* emptying.

svuotare *vt.* 1. to empty 2. (*fig.*) to deprive.

T

tabaccaio *sm.* tobacconist.

tabaccare *vt.* to snuff.

tabaccheria *sf.* tobacconist's.

tabacchiera *sf.* snuff-box.

tabacco *sm.* tobacco.

tabella *sf.* 1. (*lista*) list 2. (*quadro*) board.

tabellone *sm.* notice board.

tabernàcolo *sm.* tabernacle.

tabù *sm.* taboo.

tabulatore *sm.* tabulator.

tacca *sf.* 1. notch 2. (*fig.*) condition.

taccagneria *sf.* stinginess.

taccagno *agg.* stingy. ♦ **taccagno** *sm.* miser.

tacchino *sm.* turkey.

taccia *sf.* 1. reputation 2. (*accusa*) charge.

tacciare *vt.* to charge (with).

tacco *sm.* heel.

taccuino *sm.* note-book.

tacere *vi.* to be silent: *far* —, to silence.

tachicardìa *sf.* tachycardia.

tachìmetro *sm.* tachometer.

tacitare *vt.* 1. to hush up 2. (*un creditore*) to pay (*v. irr.*) off.

tàcito *agg.* 1. silent 2. (*non espresso*) tacit.

taciturno *agg.* silent.

tafano *sm.* gad-fly.

tafferuglio *sm.* brawl.

taglìa *sf.* 1. (*riscatto*) ransom 2. (*ricompensa*) reward 3. (*misura*) size.

tagliacarte *sm.* paper-knife (*pl.* -knives).

taglialegna *sm.* wood-cutter.

tagliando *sm.* coupon.

tagliapietre *sm.* stone-cutter.

tagliare *vt.* 1. to cut (*v. irr.*) 2. (*attraversare*) to cut across: — *via*, to cut off || — *a pezzi*, to cut into pieces; — *la corda* (*fig.*), to run (*v. irr.*) away; — *la strada a qu*, to bar so.'s way. ♦ **tagliarsi** *vr.* to cut.

tagliatelle *sf. pl.* noodles.

tagliato *agg.* 1. cut 2. (*inclinato, disposto*) cut out, fit: *essere — fuori*, to be cut off.

tagliatore *sm.* cutter.

taglieggiare *vt.* to ransom.

tagliente *agg.* sharp.

tagliere *sm.* trencher.

taglio *sm.* 1. cut 2. (*il tagliare*) cutting 3. (*parte tagliente, orlo*) edge 4. (*dimensione*) size 5. (*raccolto*) harvest.

tagliola *sf.* snare.

taglione *sm.* retaliation.

tagliuzzare *vt.* to mince.

talare *agg.* talaric: *veste —*, cassock.

talco *sm.* talc: *— borato*, talcum powder.

tale *agg.* 1. such 2. (*per tralasciare i dati determinati*) such and such: *il — giorno*, on such and such day 3. (*suddetto*) above-mentioned 1. *— e quale*, exactly like, exactly as. ♦ **tale** *pron. indef.* someone.

talea *sf.* scion.

talento *sm.* talent.

talismano *sm.* talisman.

tallonare *vi.* to follow.

talloncino *sm.* slip.

tallone *sm.* heel.

talora *avv.* sometimes.

talpa *sf.* mole.

taluno *agg.* some. ♦ **taluno** *pron.* someone (*pl.* some people).

talvolta *avv.* V. *talora*.

tamarindo *sm.* tamarind.

tamburegglare *vi.* to drum.

tamburellare *vi.* to drum one's fingers on.

tamburino *sm.* drummer.

tamburo *sm.* 1. drum 2. (*mecc.*) cylinder.

tamponamento *sm.* 1. plugging 2. (*med.*) tamponage 3. (*auto*) bumping.

tamponare *vt.* 1. to plug 2. (*med.*) to tampon 3. (*auto*) to bump (against).

tampone *sm.* 1. plug 2. (*med.*) tampon 3. (*di carta asciugante*) blotter.

tana *sf.* den.

tanfo *sm.* stench.

tangente *agg.* e *sf.* tangent.

tangenza *sf.* tangency: *punto di —*, tangential point.

tangenziale *agg.* tangential.

tànghero *sm.* boor.

tangibile *agg.* tangible.

tangibilità *sf.* tangibility.

tànnico *agg.* (*chim.*) tannic.

tannino *sm.* tannin.

tanto *avv.* 1. so 2. (*coi verbi*) so much 3. (*di tempo*) so long 4. (*ad ogni modo*) anyhow || *— quanto*, as much as; *— ... quanto*, as... as (*sia... sia*) both ... and; *— meglio*, so much the better; *— per cambiare*, just for a change. ♦ **tanto** *agg.* so much (*pl.* so many): *— ... quanto*, as much... as (*pl.* as many... as). ♦ **tanto che** *cong.* so (that).

tapiro *sm.* tapir.

tappa *sf.* 1. (*luogo*) halting-place 2. (*parte di viaggio*) stage 3. (*sport*) lap.

tappare *vt.* 1. to stop 2. (*con tappo*) to cork.

tapparella *sf.* rolling shutter.

tappeto *sm.* carpet.

tappezzare *vt.* 1. (*con carta*) to paper 2. (*coprire*) to cover 3. (*foderare*) to upholster.

tappezzerìa *sf.* 1. (*di carta*) paper 2. (*di stoffa*) tapestry.

tappezziere *sm.* 1. (*per pareti*) paper hanger 2. (*per divani ecc.*) upholsterer.

tappo *sm.* 1. plug 2. (*per bottiglia*) cap.

tara *sf.* 1. tare 2. (*med.; difetto*) taint.

taràntola *sf.* tarantula.

tarare *vt.* 1. (*mecc.*) to set (*v. irr.*) 2. (*calibrare*) to calibrate 3. (*comm.*) to tare.

tarato *agg.* 1. (*comm.*) tared 2. (*mecc.*) set 3. (*med.*) with a taint 4. (*fig.*) corrupted.

tarchiato *agg.* sturdy.

tardare *vi.* to be late. ♦ **tardare** *vt.* to delay.

tardi *avv.* late: *far —*, to be late.

tardivo *agg.* 1. (*arretrato*) backward 2. (*che viene tardi*) tardy.

tardo *agg.* 1. tardy 2. (*ottuso*) dull 3. (*di tempo*) late || *a tarda notte*, late in the night; *tarda età*, old age.

targa *sf.* 1. (*di metallo*) plate 2. (*di marmo*) slab 3. (*auto*) number-plate.

targare *vt.* (*auto*) to give (*v. irr.*) a number-plate (to a car).

tariffa *sf.* tariff.

tarlarsi *vr.* to get (*v. irr.*) worm-caten.

tarlatura *sf.* worm-hole.

tarlo *sm.* **1.** woodworm **2.** (*fig.*) gnawings (*pl.*).

tarma *sf.* moth.

tarmarsi *vr.* to get (*v. irr.*) moth-eaten.

tarpare *vt.* to clip.

tartagliare *vi.* to stammer.

tartàrico *agg.* tartaric.

tàrtaro *sm.* tartar.

tartaruga *sf.* tortoise.

tartassare *vt.* to harass.

tartina *sf.* canapé.

tartufo *sm.* truffle.

tasca *sf.* pocket.

tascàbile *agg.* pocket (*attributivo*).

tassa *sf.* **1.** tax **2.** (*d'iscrizione*) fee.

tassàbile *agg.* taxable.

tassàmetro *sm.* taximeter: — *di parcheggio*, parking meter.

tassare *vt.* to tax.

tassativo *agg.* peremptory.

tassazione *sf.* taxation.

tassello *sm.* dowel.

tassì *sm.* taxi.

tassista *sm.* taxi-driver.

tasso[1] *sm.* (*comm.*) rate.

tasso[2] *sm.* (*bot.*) yew.

tasso[3] *sm.* (*zool.*) badger.

tastare *vt.* to feel (*v. irr.*): — *il terreno* (*fig.*), to feel one's way.

tastiera *sf.* keyboard.

tasto *sm.* **1.** key **2.** (*tatto*) feel **3.** (*argomento*) subject.

tastoni *avv.* *a* —, gropingly; *andare a* —, to grope.

tàttica *sf.* tactics.

tàttico *agg.* tactical. ♦ **tàttico** *sm.* tactician.

tàttile *agg.* tactile.

tatto *sm.* **1.** touch **2.** (*fig.*) tact || *con* —, tactfully.

tatuaggio *sm.* tattoo.

tatuare *vt.* to tattoo.

taumatùrgico *agg.* thaumaturgic(al).

taumaturgo *sm.* thaumaturge.

taurino *agg.* bull-like (*attr.*): *dal collo* —, bull-necked.

tauromachìa *sf.* bullfight.

tautologìa *sf.* tautology.

taverna *sf.* tavern.

taverniere *sm.* tavern-keeper.

tàvola *sf.* **1.** table **2.** (*asse*) board **3.** (*di marmo*) slab **4.** (*illustrazione*) plate.

tavolaccio *sm.* plank-bed.

tavolata *sf.* table.

tavolato *sm.* **1.** (*di pavimento*) plank floor **2.** (*mar.*) planking **3.** (*geogr.*) plateau.

tavolozza *sf.* palette.

tazza *sf.* cup: — *da tè*, tea-cup.

te *pron.* you.

tè *sm.* tea.

teatrale *agg.* theatrical.

teatro *sm.* theatre: — *di posa*, studio.

tècnica *sf.* technique.

tecnicìsmo *sm.* technicality.

tècnico *agg.* technical. ♦ **tècnico** *sm.* technician.

tecnologìa *sf.* technology.

tecnològico *agg.* technological.

tedesco *agg.* e *sm.* German.

tediare *vt.* to bore.

tedio *sm.* boredom.

tedioso *agg.* boring.

tegame *sm.* saucepan.

teglia *sf.* bakepan.

tégola *sf.* tile: *coprire di tegole*, to tile.

teiera *sf.* tea-pot.

teismo *sm.* theism.

tela *sf.* **1.** cloth **2.** (*teat.*) curtain **3.** (*dipinto*) painting **4.** (*per dipingere*) canvas || — *cerata*, oilcloth; — *di sacco*, sackcloth; — *di lino*, linen; — *di ragno*, cobweb.

telaio *sm.* **1.** loom **2.** (*ossatura, cornice*) frame.

telecàmera *sf.* camera.

telecomandare *vt.* to radiocontrol.

telecomunicazione *sf.* telecommunication.

teleférica *sf.* cableway.

telefonare *vt.* to (tele)phone.

telefonata *sf.* (telephone) call.

telefonìa *sf.* telephony.

telefònico *agg.* telephone (*attr.*): *cabina telefonica*, telephone booth.

telefonista *sf.* (telephone) operator. ♦ **telefonista** *sf.* switchboard girl.

telèfono *sm.* (tele)phone: *dare un colpo di* —, to ring (*v. irr.*) up.

telefoto *sf.* telephotograph.

telegiornale *sm.* (television) news (-reel).

telegrafare *vt.* to telegraph.

telegrafìa *sf.* telegraphy.

telegràfico *agg.* telegraphic(al).

telegrafista *sm.* telegraphist.

telègrafo *sm.* **1.** telegraph **2.** (*uffici*) telegraph-office.

telegramma *sm.* telegram, wire: *fare un* — *a qu.*, to wire so.

telèmetro *sm.* **1.** telemeter **2.** (*in arma da fuoco; foto*) rangefinder.

teleobbiettivo *sm.* telephoto lens.
teleologia *sf.* teleology.
telepatia *sf.* telepathy.
telerie *sf. pl.* linen (*sing.*): *commerciante in* —, linen-draper.
teleschermo *sm.* television screen.
telescopio *sm.* telescope.
telescrivente *sf.* teletypewriter.
teleselezione *sf.* long distance dialing.
telespettatore *sm.* televiewer.
teletipia *sf.* teletype.
teletrasméttere *vt.* to telecast (*v. irr.*).
televisione *sf.* television: *guardare la* —, to watch television; *alla* —, on television; *trasmettere per* —, to telecast.
televisivo *agg.* televisional, television (*attr.*): *trasmissione televisiva*, telecast.
televisore *sm.* television set.
tellùrico *agg.* telluric.
telo *sm.* sheet.
telone *sm.* **1.** (*teat.*) curtain **2.** (*cine*) screen.
tema¹ *sf.* (*paura*) fear: *per — che*, lest.
tema² *sm.* **1.** theme **2.** (*scolastico*) composition.
temàtica *sf.* themes (*pl.*).
temàtico *agg.* thematic(al).
temerarietà *sf.* rashness.
temerario *agg.* rash.
temere *vt.* e *vi.* **1.** to fear **2.** (*patire*) not to stand (*v. irr.*) || *·temo di sì*, I fear so; *temo di no*, I fear not.
temìbile *agg.* dreadful.
tèmpera *sf.* **1.** (*metal.*) hardening **2.** (*pitt.*) distemper || *dipingere a* —, to distemper.
temperamatite *sm.·* pencil-sharpener.
temperamento *sm.* **1.** temperament **2.** (*alleviamento*) mitigation.
temperante *agg.* temperate.
temperanza *sf.* temperance.
temperare *vt.* **1.** to temper **2.** (*matite*) to sharpen.
temperato *agg.* **1.** temperate **2.** (*di matita*) sharpened.
temperatura *sf.* temperature.
temperino *sm.* penknife (*pl.* -knives).
tempesta *sf.* tempest, storm.
tempestare *vt.* **1.** (*assalire*) to assail **2.** (*importunare*) to harass **3.** (*cospargere*) to strew (*v. irr.*) (sthg.

with). ◆ **tempestare** *vi.* **1.** to storm **2.** (*grandinare*) to hail.
tempestività *sf.* timeliness.
tempestivo *agg.* timely.
tempestoso *agg.* stormy.
tempia *sf.* temple.
tempio *sm.* temple.
tempo *sm.* **1.** time **2.** (*atmosferico*) weather **3.** (*gramm.*) tense **4.** (*fase*) stage **5.** (*cine*) part || *un* —, once; *col passare del* —, in the long run; *molto — prima, dopo*, long before, after; *a — perso*, in one's spare time; *per* —, early.
temporale¹ *agg.* temporal.
temporale² *agg.* (*anat.*) temporal.
temporale³ *sm.* storm.
temporalesco *agg.* stormy.
temporaneità *sf.* temporariness.
temporàneo *agg.* temporary.
temporeggiare *vi.* to temporize.
tempra *sf.* **1.** temper **2.** (*metal.*) hardening **3.** (*fig.*) character.
temprare *vt.* **1.** to temper **2.** (*fig.*) to strengthen **3.** (*plasmare*) to form.
temprato *agg.* (*abituato*) inured.
tenace *agg.* tenacious.
tenacia *sf.* tenacity.
tenaglia *sf.* pincers (*pl.*).
tenda *sf.* **1.** curtain **2.** (*da campo*) tent.
tendaggio *sm.* curtain.
tendente *agg.* tending.
tendenza *sf.* **1.** tendency **2.** inclination.
tendenziale *agg.* tendential.
tendenziosità *sf.* tendentiousness.
tendenzioso *agg.* tendentious.
tèndere *vt.* **1.** (*protendere*) to stretch (out) **2.** (*mettere in tensione*) to tighten. ◆ **tèndere** *vi.* **1.** to tend **2.** (*mirare*) to aim (at).
tendina *sf.* curtain.
tèndine *sm.* tendon.
tenditore *sm.* turnbuckle.
tènebra *sf.* darkness.
tenebroso *agg.* **1.** dark **2.** (*sinistro*) sinister.
tenente *sm.* lieutenant.
tenere *vt.* **1.** to keep (*v. irr.*) **2.** (*sostenere, considerare, contenere*) to hold (*v. irr.*) || *— una lezione*, to give (*v. irr.*) a lesson. ◆ **tenersi** *vr.* (*seguire*) to follow: *— al corrente*, to keep tabs on.
tenerezza *sf.* tenderness.
tènero *agg.* tender. ◆ **tènero** *sm.* **1.** (*parte tenera*) tender part **2.** (*affetto*) sympathy.

tenia *sf.* tapeworm.
tennis *sm.* tennis.
tennista *s.* tennis-player.
tenore *sm.* tenor.
tenorile *agg.* tenor (*attr.*).
tensione *sf.* tension.
tentacolare *agg.* tentacular.
tentàcolo *sm.* tentacle.
tentare *vt.* 1. to tempt 2. (*provare*) to try.
tentativo *sm.* attempt.
tentatore *agg.* tempting. ♦ **tentatore** *sm.* tempter.
tentazione *sf.* temptation.
tentennamento *sm.* 1. shaking 2. (*traballamento*) tottering 3. (*esitazione*) hesitation.
tentennare *vt.* to shake (*v. irr.*). ♦ **tentennare** *vi.* 1. to totter 2. (*esitare*) to waver.
tentoni *agg.* gropingly.
tenue *agg.* 1. small 2. (*leggero*) soft.
tenuità *sf.* 1. smallness 2. (*levità*) slightness.
tenuta *sf.* 1. (*proprietà*) estate 2. (*capacità*) capacity 3. (*abiti*) clothes (*pl.*) 4. (*tec.*) seal || — *di strada*, roadability; *a* — *d'acqua*, watertight.
teocràtico *agg.* theocratic(al).
teocrazìa *sf.* theocracy.
teologale *agg.* theological.
teologìa *sf.* theology.
teològico *agg.* theologic(al).
teòlogo *sm.* theologian.
teorema *sm.* theorem.
teorìa *sf.* 1. theory 2. (*fila*) string.
teòrico *agg.* theoretic(al).
teorizzare *vi.* to theorize.
tepore *sm.* lukewarmness.
teppa *sf.* rabble.
teppista *sm.* teddy-boy.
terapèutico *agg.* therapeutic(al).
terapìa *sf.* therapy.
terebinto *sm.* terebinth.
tèrgere *vt.* to wipe (off).
tergicristallo *sm.* windscreen wiper.
tergiversare *vi.* to hesitate.
tergiversazione *sf.* hesitation.
tergo *sm.* back: *segue a* —, please turn over.
termale *agg.* thermal: *stazione* —, spa.
terme *sf. pl.* thermal springs.
tèrmico *agg.* thermic.
terminale *agg.* terminal.
terminare *vt. e vi.* to end.

tèrmine *sm.* 1. term 2. (*limite*) limit 3. (*fine*) end || *contratto a* —, time-contract; *portare a* —, to carry out.
terminologìa *sf.* terminology.
tèrmite *sf.* termite.
termocoperta *sf.* thermal blanket.
termodinàmica *sf.* thermodynamics.
termoelèttrico *agg.* thermoelectric(al).
termòforo *sm.* warming pad.
termògeno *agg.* thermogenetic.
termoiònico *agg.* thermionic.
termòmetro *sm.* thermometer: *il* — *segna...*, the thermometer stands at...
termonucleare *agg.* thermonuclear.
termos *sm.* vacuum bottle.
termosifone *sm.* (*radiatore*) radiator.
termòstato *sm.* thermostat.
ternario *agg.* ternary.
terno *sm.* tern. ♦ **terno** *agg.* triple.
terra *sf.* 1. (*globo terracqueo*) earth 2. (*paese; l'opposto del mare*) land 3. (*terreno*) ground || — —, earth bound; *raso* —, to the ground.
terracotta *sf.* terracotta: *vasellame di* —, earthenware.
terraferma *sf.* dry land.
terraglia *sf.* pottery.
terranova *sm.* (*cane*) Newfoundland dog.
terrapieno *sm.* 1. bank 2. (*di fiume*) embankment.
terràqueo *agg.* terraqueous.
terrazza *sf.* 1. terrace 2. (*balcone*) balcony.
terrazziere *sm.* digger.
terrazzo *sm.* V. *terrazza*.
terremoto *sm.* earthquake.
terreno[1] *agg.* earthly.
terreno[2] *sm.* ground.
tèrreo *agg.* 1. earthy 2. (*di colorito*) wan, sallow.
terrestre *agg.* terrestrial, earthly.
terrìbile *agg.* terrible.
terriccio *sm.* mould.
terriero *agg.* land (*attr.*).
terrificante *agg.* terrifying.
terrificare *vt.* to terrify.
terrina *sf.* tureen.
territoriale *agg.* territorial.
territorio *sm.* territory.
terrore *sm.* terror: *incutere* — *a qu.*, to strike (*v. irr.*) so. with terror.
terrorismo *sm.* terrorism.

terrorista *s.* terrorist.
terrorìstico *agg.* terroristic.
terrorizzare *vt.* to terrorize.
terroso *agg.* earthy.
terso *agg.* clear.
terza *sf.* 1. (*di scuola, treno*) third class 2. (*di auto*) third gear.
terzetto *sm.* trio.
terziario *agg.* e *sm.* tertiary.
terzina *sf.* tercet.
terzino *sm.* (*sport*) full back.
terzo *agg.* third. ♦ **terzo** *sm.* 1. third 2. (*terza persona*) third person || *terzi*, third party.
terzùltimo *agg.* e *sm.* last but two.
tesa *sf.* brim.
tesaurizzare *vt.* to treasure.
teschio *sm.* skull.
tesi *sf.* thesis (*pl.* -ses).
teso *agg.* taut.
tesoreria *sf.* treasury.
tesoriere *sm.* treasurer.
tesoro *sm.* 1. treasure 2. (*pol.*) treasury.
tèssera *sf.* 1. card 2. (*di mosaico*) tessera (*pl.* -rae).
tesseramento *sm.* 1. rationing 2. (*reclutamento*) enrolment.
tesserare *vt.* 1. to ration 2. (*arruolare*) to enrol.
tèssere *vt.* to weave (*v. irr.*).
tèssile *agg.* textile. ♦ **tèssile** *sm.* weaver.
tessitore *sm.* weaver.
tessitura *sf.* 1. weaving 2. (*disposizione dei fili*) texture.
tessuto *sm.* 1. fabric 2. (*med.; fig.*) tissue || *negozio di tessuti*, draper's shop.
testa *sf.* head: *colpo di* —, rash act; *essere in* — *a tutti*, to be ahead of everybody.
testamentario *agg.* testamentary.
testamento *sm.* will.
testardàggine *sf.* stubbornness.
testardo *agg.* stubborn.
testata *sf.* 1. head 2. (*colpo*) butt 3. (*di giornale*) heading.
teste *s.* witness: — *d'accusa, di difesa*, witness for the prosecution, the defence.
testìcolo *sm.* testicle.
testimonianza *sf.* 1. witness 2. (*prova*) evidence || *far* —, to bear (*v. irr.*) witness.
testimoniare *vt.* e *vi.* 1. to witness 2. (*attestare*) to testify.
testimonio *sm.* witness.
testo *sm.* text.

testuale *agg.* 1. textual 2. (*esatto*) exact.
tetànico *agg.* tetanic.
tètano *sm.* tetanus.
tetraedro *sm.* tetrahedron.
tetràggine *sf.* gloom.
tetràgono *agg.* (*fig.*) steadfast.
tetralogìa *sf.* tetralogy.
tetro *agg.* gloomy.
tettarella *sf.* dummy.
tetto *sm.* roof: — *a capanna*, saddle roof.
tettoia *sf.* shed.
tettònica *sf.* tectonics.
teutònico *agg.* Teutonic. ♦ **teutònico** *sm.* Teuton.
ti *pron.* 1. you, to you 2. (*r.*) yourself.
tiara *sf.* tiara.
tibia *sf.* tibia.
tic *sm.* tic.
ticchettare *vi.* to tick.
ticchettìo *sm.* ticking.
tìcchio *sm.* fancy.
tièpido *agg.* tepid.
tifo *sm.* 1. typhus 2. (*fig.*) fanaticism.
tifone *sm.* typhoon.
tifoso *sm.* 1. typhus patient 2. (*fig.*) fan.
tìglio *sm.* lime.
tigna *sf.* ringworm.
tignola *sf.* moth.
tigrato *agg.* striped.
tigre *sf.* tiger.
timbrare *vt.* 1. to stamp 2. (*lettere*) to postmark || — *a secco*, to emboss.
timbratura *sf.* 1. stamping 2. (*postale*) postmarking.
timbro *sm.* 1. stamp 2. (*di suono*) timbre 3. (*postale*) postmark || — *a secco*, embossed stamp.
timidezza *sf.* shyness.
tìmido *agg.* shy.
†timo *sm.* thyme.
timone *sm.* helm.
timoniere *sm.* helmsman (*pl.* -men).
timorato *agg.* 1. respectful 2. (*scrupoloso*) scrupulous.
timore *sm.* fear: *aver* —, to fear, to be afraid.
timoroso *agg.* fearful.
tìmpano *sm.* 1. eardrum 2. (*mus.*) kettle-drum 3. (*arch.*) gable.
tinca *sf.* tench.
tinello *sm.* living-room.
tìngere *vt.* to dye (*v. irr.*). ♦ **tìngersi** *vr.* to dye oneself.

tino *sm.* vat.

tinozza *sf.* tub.

tinta *sf.* 1. (*colore*) hue 2. (*materia colorante*) dye 3. (*tintura*) dyeing.

tinteggiare *vt.* to paint.

tintinnare *vi.* to tinkle.

tintinnio *sm.* tinkling.

tintore *sm.* 1. dyer 2. (*anche per lavature a secco*) cleaner.

tintoria *sf.* 1. dyeworks (*pl.*) 2. (*negozio anche per lavature a secco*) dry cleaners' shop.

tintura *sf.* V. tinta.

tipico *agg.* typical.

tipo *sm.* 1. type 2. (*modello*) pattern 3. (*individuo*) fellow.

tipografia *sf.* 1. typography 2. (*mecc.*) letterpress printing.

tipografico *agg.* typographic(al).

tipografo *sm.* typographer.

tiraggio *sm.* draught.

tiralinee *sm.* drawing-pen.

tiranneggiare *vt.* to tyrannize.

tirannia *sf.* tyranny.

tirannico *agg.* tyrannical.

tirannide *sf.* tyranny.

tiranno *sm.* tyrant.

tirante *sm.* 1. (*mecc.*) connecting rod 2. (*arch.*) tie-beam.

tirapiedi *sm.* drudge.

tirare *vt.* 1. to draw (*v. irr.*), to pull 2. (*scagliare*) to throw (*v. irr.*). ♦ **tirare** *vi.* 1. (*sparare*) to shoot (*v. irr.*) 2. (*di tiraggio*) to draw 3. (*di vestito*) to be tight. ♦ **tirarsi** *vr.* to draw.

tirata *sf.* 1. pull 2. (*invettiva*) tirade.

tiratore *sm.* shooter.

tiratura *sf.* 1. (*tip.*) printing 2. (*numero di copie stampate*) circulation.

tirchieria *sf.* niggardliness.

tirchio *agg.* niggardly.

tiritera *sf.* rigmarole.

tiro *sm.* 1. (*trazione*) draught 2. (*lancio*) throw 3. (*sparo*) shot 4. (*scherzo*) trick.

tirocinio *sm.* apprenticeship.

tiroide *sf.* thyroid.

tisana *sf.* ptisan.

tisi *sf.* consumption.

tisico *agg. e sm.* consumptive.

tisiologia *sf.* phthisiology.

tisiologo *sm.* phthisiologist.

titanico *agg.* titanic.

titillare *vt.* to tickle.

titolare *agg.* 1. regular 2. (*nominale*) titular. ♦ **titolare** *s.* 1. regular holder 2. (*proprietario*) owner 3. (*capo*) principal.

titolato *agg.* titled.

titolo *sm.* 1. title 2. (*qualifica*) qualification 3. (*documento*) document 4. (*comm.*) security.

titubante *agg.* hesitating.

titubanza *sf.* hesitation.

titubare *vi.* to hesitate.

tizianesco *agg.* 1. Titianesque 2. (*di capelli*) titian.

tizio *sm.* fellow.

tizzone *sm.* brand.

toccare *vt.* to touch || — un porto, to call at. ♦ **toccare** *vi.* 1. (*capitare*) to happen 2. (*spettare*) to fall (*v. irr.*).

toccasana *sm.* cure-all.

tocco[1] *agg.* (*pazzoide*) touched.

tocco[2] *sm.* 1. touch 2. (*battito*) knock 3. (*rintocco*) toll || al —, at one o'clock.

tocco[3] *sm.* (*berretto*) toque.

toga *sf.* gown.

togato *agg.* gowned.

togliere *vt.* 1. to take (*v. irr.*) 2. (*liberare*) to relieve. ♦ **togliersi** *vr.* 1. to get (*v. irr.*) off 2. (*un indumento*) to take off || — la vita, to commit suicide.

toletta *sf.* toilet.

tollerabile *agg.* tolerable.

tollerante *agg.* tolerant.

tolleranza *sf.* tolerance.

tollerare *vt.* 1. to tolerate 2. (*sopportare*) to bear (*v. irr.*).

tomaia *sf.* vamp.

tomba *sf.* grave.

tombale *agg.* grave (*attr.*).

tombino *sm.* manhole.

tombola *sf.* 1. (*gioco*) "tombola" 2. (*caduta*) tumble.

tombolare *vi.* to tumble down.

tomismo *sm.* Thomism.

tomista *agg. e sm.* Thomist.

tomo *sm.* 1. tome 2. (*persona*) chap.

tonaca *sf.* frock: gettare la —, to give (*v. irr.*) up the frock.

tonalità *sf.* tonality.

tonante *agg.* thundering.

tondeggiante *agg.* roundish.

tondeggiare *vi.* to be roundish.

tondello *sm.* round.

tondo *agg. e sm.* round || chiaro e —, clearly.

tonfo *sm.* splash.

tonico *agg. e sm.* tonic.

tonificare *vt.* to brace.

tonnellaggio *sm.* tonnage.

tonnellata *sf.* ton.

tonno *sm.* tunny.

tono *sm.* **1.** tone **2.** (*accordo*) tune **3.** (*mus.*) strain.

tonsilla *sf.* tonsil.

tonsillectomìa *sf.* tonsillectomy.

tonsillite *sf.* tonsillitis.

tonsura *sf.* tonsure.

tonsurare *vt.* to tonsure.

tonto *agg.* dull. ♦ **tonto** *sm.* dunce.

topaia *sf.* (*fig.*) hovel.

topazio *sm.* topaz.

tòpica *sf.* **1.** topic **2.** (*errore*) blunder.

tòpico *agg.* topical.

topo *sm.* mouse (*pl.* mice), rat || — *di biblioteca* (*fig.*), bookworm; — *di albergo* (*fig.*), hotel thief.

topografia *sf.* topography.

topogràfico *agg.* topographic(al).

topologìa *sf.* topology.

toponomàstica *sf.* toponymy.

toppa *sf.* **1.** (*pezza*) patch **2.** (*di serratura*) keyhole || *mettere una* —, to patch up.

torace *sm.* thorax, chest.

torba *sf.* peat.

torbidezza *sf.* **1.** turbidity **2.** (*esser fosco*) gloominess.

tòrbido *agg.* **1.** turbid **2.** (*fosco*) gloomy **3.** (*inquieto*) troubled. ♦ **tòrbido** *sm.* (*disordine*) disorder: *pescare nel* —, to fish in troubled water.

torbiera *sf.* peat-bog.

tòrcere *vt.* **1.** to wring (*v. irr.*) **2.** (*attorcigliare*) to twist || *dare del filo da* —, to give (*v. irr.*) a lot of trouble; — *il naso* (*fig.*), to turn up one's nose (at). ♦ **tòrcersi** *vr.* to twist.

torchiare *vt.* to press.

torchiatura *sf.* pressing.

torchio *sm.* press.

torcia *sf.* torch.

torcicollo *sm.* stiff- neck.

torcitore *sm.* twister.

torcitura *sf.* twist.

tordo *sm.* thrush.

torero *sm.* bullfighter.

torma *sf.* swarm.

tormalina *sf.* tourmaline.

tormenta *sf.* blizzard.

tormentare *vt.* to torment. ♦ **tormentarsi** *vr.* to worry.

tormentato *agg.* (*inquieto*) restless.

tormento *sm.* torment.

tormentoso *agg.* tormenting.

tornaconto *sm.* profit.

tornado *sm.* tornado.

tornante *sm.* bend.

tornare *vi.* **1.** to return **2.** (*di conti*) to be correct.

tornasole *sm.* litmus.

torneo *sm.* tournament.

tornio *sm.* lathe.

tornire *vt.* **1.** (*mecc.*) to turn **2.** (*fig.*) to polish.

tornito *agg.* **1.** (*rotondo*) round **2.** (*ben fatto*) well-shaped.

tornitore *sm.* turner.

toro *sm.* bull.

torpediniera *sf.* torpedo-boat.

torpedo *sf.* torpedo.

torpedone *sm.* (motor-)coach.

tòrpido *agg.* torpid.

torpore *sm.* torpor.

torre *sf.* tower.

torrefare *vt.* **1.** to torrefy **2.** (*caffè*) to roast.

torrefazione *sf.* **1.** torrefaction **2.** (*di caffè*) roasting **3.** (*negozio*) coffee store.

torreggiare *vi.* to tower.

torrente *sm.* torrent.

torrentizio *agg.* torrent-like.

torrenziale *agg.* torrential.

torretta *sf.* (*mil.; mar.*) turret.

tòrrido *agg.* torrid.

torrione *sm.* donjon.

torrone *sm.* nougat.

torsione *sf.* torsion.

torso *sm.* **1.** trunk **2.** (*di statua*) torso.

tòrsolo *sm.* **1.** (*di verdura*) stump **2.** (*di frutta*) core.

torta *sf.* cake.

tortiera *sf.* bakepan.

torto *agg.* **1.** (*piegato*) bent **2.** (*contorto*) twisted.

torto *sm.* **1.** wrong **2.** (*colpa*) fault || *aver* —, to be wrong; *far* — *a qu.*, to wrong so.; *a* —, wrongly.

tòrtora *sf.* turtle-dove.

tortuosità *sf.* tortuosity.

tortuoso *agg.* tortuous.

tortura *sf.* torture.

torturare *vt.* to torture. ♦ **torturarsi** *vr.* to worry.

torvo *agg.* grim.

tosare *vt.* to shear (*v. irr.*).

tosatrice *sf.* clippers (*pl.*).

tosatura *sf.* shearing.

toscano *agg.* e *sm.* Tuscan.

tosse *sf.* cough.

tossicchiare *vi.* to keep (*v. irr.*) on coughing.

tossicità *sf.* toxicity.

tòssico *agg.* toxic. ♦ **tòssico** *sm.* toxicant.

tossicologìa *sf.* toxicology.

tossicòlogo *sm.* toxicologist.

tossicomanìa *sf.* toxicomania.

tossina *sf.* toxin.

tossire *vi.* to cough.

tostapane *sm.* toaster.

tostare *vt.* 1. to toast 2. (*caffè*) to roast.

tosto[1] *avv.* at once.

tosto[2] *agg.* hard || *faccia tosta*, cheek.

tosto[3] *sm.* toast.

totale *agg.* e *sm.* total: *in —*, in all.

totalità *sf.* 1. totality 2. (*numero complessivo*) mass.

totalitario *agg.* totalitarian.

totalitarismo *sm.* totalitarianism.

totalizzare *vt.* 1. to totalize 2. (*sport*) to score.

totalizzatore *sm.* totalizer.

tovaglia *sf.* (table-)cloth.

tovagliolo *sm.* napkin.

tozzo[1] *agg.* squat, stocky.

tozzo[2] *sm.* piece: *un — di pane*, a crust of bread.

tra *prep.* 1. (*fra due persone, cose, gruppi*) between 2. (*fra più di due*) among 3. (*nel mezzo di*) amid 4. (*di tempo*) (with)in.

traballare *vi.* 1. to stagger 2. (*di vettura*) to jolt || *entrare, uscire traballando*, to stagger in, out.

trabeazione *sf.* trabeation.

trabìccolo *sm.* ramshackle vehicle.

traboccare *vi.* to overflow.

trabocchetto *sm.* trap.

tracagnotto *agg.* squat.

tracannare *vt.* to gulp down.

traccia *sf.* 1. trace 2. (*segno*) mark 3. (*orme*) footsteps (*pl.*) 4. (*schema*) outline.

tracciare *vt.* to trace (out): *— a grandi linee*, to outline.

tracciato *sm.* layout.

tracciatore *sm.* tracer.

trachea *sf.* windpipe.

tracheale *agg.* tracheal.

tracheite *sf.* tracheitis.

tracolla *sf.* baldric: *portare qc. a —*, to carry sthg. across one's back.

tracollare *vi.* 1. to lose (*v. irr.*) one's balance 2. (*cadere*) to collapse.

tracollo *sm.* collapse: *portare al —*, to bring (*v. irr.*) to ruin.

tracoma *sm.* trachoma.

tracotante *agg* haughty.

tracotanza *sf.* haughtiness.

tradimento *sm.* 1. treason 2. (*infedeltà*) betrayal || *a —* (*agg.*), treacherous, (*avv.*) treacherously.

tradire *vt.* 1. to betray 2. (*di coniuge*) to be unfaithful (to).

traditore *agg.* treacherous. ♦ **traditore** *sm.* traitor.

tradizionale *agg.* traditional.

tradizionalismo *sm.* traditionalism.

tradizionalista *s.* traditionalist.

tradizione *sf.* tradition: *per —*, traditionally.

tradotta *sf.* troop-train.

traducìbile *agg.* translatable.

tradurre *vt.* to translate: *— in atto*, to carry out; *— in carcere*, to take (*v. irr.*) to prison.

traduttore *sm.* translator.

traduzione *sf.* translation.

traente *s.* (*comm.*) drawer.

trafelato *agg.* breathless.

trafficante *sm.* dealer.

trafficare *vi.* 1. to deal (*v. irr.*) 2. (*affaccendarsi*) to bustle about.

tràffico *sm.* 1. traffic 2. (*comm.*) trade.

trafiggere *vt.* to pierce (through).

trafila *sf.* 1. procedure 2. (*mecc.*) draw-plate.

trafilare *vt.* to draw (*v. irr.*).

trafiletto *sm.* paragraph.

traforare *vt.* 1. to perforate 2. (*ricamare*) to embroider with open-work.

traforato *agg.* 1. perforated 2. (*ricamato a traforo*) open-work (*attr.*).

traforatrice *sf.* fret-sawing machine.

traforo *sm.* 1. perforation 2. (*galleria*) tunnel 3. (*falegnameria*) fretwork 4. (*ricamo*) open-work.

trafugamento *sm.* stealing.

trafugare *vt.* to steal (*v. irr.*).

tragedia *sf.* tragedy.

tragediògrafo *sm.* tragedian.

traghettare *vt.* to ferry.

traghetto *sm.* ferry-boat.

tragicità *sf.* tragicalness.

tràgico *agg.* tragical. ♦ **tràgico** *sm.* tragedian.

tragicòmico *agg.* tragicomic(al).

tragicommedia *sf.* tragicomedy.

tragitto *sm.* 1. way 2. (*viaggio*) journey.

traguardo *sm.* goal.

traiettòria *sf.* trajectory.

trainare *vt.* to haul.

tràino *sm.* 1. haulage 2. (*carro*) truck.

tralasciare *vt.* to leave (*v. irr.*) out, to omit.

tralcio *sm.* shoot.

traliccio *sm.* 1. (*tela*) ticking 2. (*per costruzioni*) trellis || — *di ferro*, iron framework.

tralice (*nella loc. avv.*) in —, askance.

tralignamento *sm.* degeneration.

tralignare *vi.* to degenerate.

tralùcere *vi.* to shine (*v. irr.*) (through).

tram *sm.* tramcar.

trama *sf.* 1. weft 2. (*fig.*) plot.

tramaglio *sm.* trammel.

tramandare *vt.* to hand down.

tramare *vt.* 1. to weave (*v. irr.*) 2. (*fig.*) to plot.

trambusto *sm.* bustle.

tramenare *vt.* e *vi.* to move about.

tramenìo *sm.* bustle.

tramestare *vt.* to rummage.

tramestìo *sm.* 1. rummaging 2. (*trepestio*) stamping.

tramezzare *vt.* to partition.

tramezzino *sm.* sandwich.

tramezzo *sm.* partition.

tràmite *sm.* path: — *qu.*, through so.

tramoggia *sf.* hopper.

tramontana *sf.* 1. north 2. (*vento*) north wind || *perder la* —, to lose (*v. irr.*) one's head.

tramontare *vi.* 1. to set (*v. irr.*) 2. (*svanire*) to fade.

tramonto *sm.* 1. setting 2. (*del sole*) sunset 3. (*declino*) decline.

tramortimento *sm.* swoon.

tramortire *vt.* to stun.

trampoliere *sm.* wader.

trampolino *sm.* spring-board.

tràmpolo *sm.* stilt.

tramutare *vt.* to change. ♦ **tramutarsi** *vr.* to change.

trancia *sf.* 1. shears (*pl.*) 2. (*fetta*) slice.

tranciare *vt.* to shear.

tranello *sm.* snare.

trangugiare *vt.* to swallow.

tranne *prep.* but.

tranquillante *agg.* tranquillizing. ♦ **tranquillante** *sm.* tranquillizer.

tranquillità *sf.* calmness.

tranquillizzare *vt.* 1. to calm 2. (*rassicurare*) to reassure.

tranquillo *agg.* calm: *star* —, to keep (*v. irr.*) quiet; *sta' —!*, do not worry!

transalpino *agg.* transalpine.

transatlàntico *agg.* transatlantic. ♦ **transatlàntico** *sm.* liner.

transazione *sf.* 1. transaction 2. (*accomodamento*) arrangement 3. (*compromesso*) compromise.

transcontinentale *agg.* transcontinental.

transetto *sm.* transept.

trànsfuga *s.* runaway.

transìgere *vt.* e *vi.* to compromise.

transistore *sm.* transistor.

transitàbile *agg.* practicable.

transitabilità *sf.* practicability.

transitare *vi.* to pass through.

transitivo *agg.* e *sm.* transitive.

trànsito *sm.* transit.

transitorio *agg.* transitory.

transizione *sf.* transition.

transoceànico *agg.* transoceanic.

transustanziazione *sf.* transubstantiation.

tranvìa *sf.* tramway.

tranviario *agg.* tramcar (*attr.*).

tranviere *sm.* 1. tram-driver 2. (*bigliettario*) tram-conductor.

trapanare *vt.* 1. to drill 2. (*med*) to trepan.

trapanazione *sf.* 1. drilling 2. (*med.*) trepanation.

tràpano *sm.* 1. drill 2. (*med.*) trepan.

trapassare *vt.* to pierce through. ♦ **trapassare** *vi.* (*morire*) to die.

trapasso *sm.* 1. (*morte*) death 2. (*giur.; comm.*) transfer.

trapelare *vi.* to leak out.

trapezio *sm.* 1. trapezium 2. (*da ginnastica*) trapeze.

trapiantare *vt.* to transplant. ♦ **trapiantarsi** *vr.* (*stabilirsi*) to settle.

trapianto *sm.* 1. transplantation 2. (*tessuto trapiantato*) graft.

trappista *sm.* Trappist.

tràppola *sf.* trap: *prendere in* —, to trap.

trapunta *sf.* quilt.

trapuntare *vt.* 1. to quilt 2. (*ricamare*) to embroider.

trapunto *agg.* 1. quilted 2. (*ricamato*) embroidered || — *di stelle*, starry.

trarre *vt.* 1. to draw (*v. irr*) 2. (*ottenere*) to get (*v. irr.*). ♦ **trarsi** *vr.* to draw.

trasalire *vi.* to startle: *far* —, to startle.

trasandato *agg.* shabby.

trasbordare *vt.* **1.** to transfer **2.** (*traghettare*) to ferry.

trasbordo *sm.* **1.** transfer **2.** (*traghetto*) ferrying across.

trascendentale *agg.* transcendental.

trascendentalismo *sm.* transcendentalism.

trascendente *agg.* transcendent.

trascendenza *sf.* transcendence.

trascéndere *vt.* to transcend. ♦ **trascéndere** *vi.* to let (*v. irr.*) oneself go.

trascinare *vt.* **1.** to drag **2.** (*affascinare*) to fascinate.

trascórrere *vt.* (*il tempo*) to spend (*v. irr.*). ♦ **trascórrere** *vi.* (*di tempo*) to pass **2.** (*lasciar correre*) to pass over.

trascorso *agg.* past. ♦ **trascorso** *sm.* (*errore*) slip.

trascrittore *sm.* transcriber.

trascrivere *vt.* **1.** to transcribe **2.** (*giur.*) to register.

trascrizione *sf.* **1.** transcription **2.** (*giur.*) registration **3.** (*trapasso*) transfer.

trascuràbile *agg.* negligible.

trascurare *vt.* to neglect. ♦ **trascurarsi** *vr.* not to care of oneself.

trascuratezza *sf.* **1.** negligence **2.** (*sciatteria*) slovenliness.

trascurato *agg.* **1.** (*negligente*) careless **2.** (*sciatto*) sloven.

trasecolare *vi.* to be amazed.

trasecolato *agg.* amazed.

trasferìbile *agg.* transferable.

trasferimento *sm.* transfer.

trasferire *vt.* to transfer. ♦ **trasferirsi** *vr.* to (re)move.

trasferta *sf.* **1.** transfer **2.** (*indennità*) travelling allowance || in —, on transfer; *partita in* — (*sport*), out match.

trasfigurare *vt.* to transfigure. ♦ **trasfigurarsi** *vr.* to become (*v. irr.*) transfigured.

trasfigurazione *sf.* transfiguration.

trasfóndere *vt.* **1.** to transfuse **2.** (*fig.*) to instil.

trasformàbile *agg.* convertible.

trasformare *vt.* to change, to turn. ♦ **trasformarsi** *vr.* to change.

trasformatore *sm.* transformer.

trasformazione *sf.* transformation.

trasformismo *sm.* transformism.

trasfusione *sf.* transfusion.

trasgredire *vt. e vi.* to infringe.

trasgressione *sf.* infringement.

trasgressore *sm.* infringer.

traslazione *sf.* **1.** transfer **2.** (*fis.; eccl.*) translation.

traslocare *vt. e vi.* to move.

trasloco *sm.* removal.

traslùcido *agg.* translucent.

trasméttere *vt.* to transmit.

trasmettitore *sm.* transmitter.

trasmigrare *vi.* to transmigrate.

trasmigrazione *sf.* transmigration.

trasmissìbile *agg.* transmissible.

trasmissione *sf.* **1.** transmission **2.** (*giur.*) transfer **3.** (*mecc.*) drive || — *radio*, broadcast; — *televisiva*, telecast.

trasmittente *agg.* transmitting.

trasognato *agg.* dreamy.

trasparente *agg.* transparent.

trasparenza *sf.* transparence.

trasparire *vi.* **1.** to shine (*v. irr.*) through **2.** (*esser trasparente*) to be transparent || *lasciar* —, to betray.

traspirare *vi.* to transpire.

traspirazione *sf.* transpiration.

trasporre *vt.* to transpose.

trasportàbile *agg.* transportable.

trasportare *vt.* **1.** to carry **2.** (*fig.*) to carry away. ♦ **trasportarsi** *vr.* to go (*v. irr.*).

trasportatore *sm.* conveyer: — *a nastro*, belt-conveyer.

trasporto *sm.* transport: *nave da* —, cargo; *spese di* —, carriage.

trasposizione *sf.* transposition.

trastullare *vt.* to amuse. ♦ **trastullarsi** *vr.* **1.** (*giocare*) to play **2.** (*scherzare*) to trifle.

trastullo *sm.* **1.** plaything **2.** (*divertimento*) amusement.

trasudamento *sm.* sweating.

trasudare *vt. e vi.* to sweat.

trasversale *agg.* transversal, cross (*attr.*). ♦ **trasversale** *sf.* **1.** transversal **2.** (*strada*) cross-road.

trasvolare *vt.* to fly (*v. irr.*) across.

trasvolata *sf.* flight (across).

tratta *sf.* **1.** (*traffico*) trade **2.** (*comm.*) draft || — *a vista*, sight draft; *spiccare una* — *su qu.*, to draw (*v. irr.*) upon so.

trattàbile *agg.* **1.** tractable **2.** (*di argomento*) that can be dealt with.

trattabilità *sf.* tractability.

trattamento *sm.* **1.** treatment **2.** (*paga*) salary.

trattare *vt.* **1.** to treat **2.** (*maneggiare*) to handle **3.** (*commerciare*) to deal (*v. irr.*) (in) **4.** (*negoziare*) to negotiate **5.** (*un argomento*) to deal (with). ♦ **trattarsi** *v. imp.* to be a question of, to be involved.

trattativa sf. negotiation.

trattato sm. **1.** (patto) treaty **2.** (libro) treatise.

trattazione sf. treatment.

tratteggiare vt. **1.** to outline **2.** (ombreggiare) to hatch.

tratteggio sm. **1.** (abbozzo) outline **2.** (ombreggiatura) hatching.

trattenere vt. **1.** to keep (v. irr.) **2.** (dedurre) to deduct **3.** (frenare) to refrain || — il respiro, to hold (v. irr.) one's breath. ♦ **trattenersi** vr. (fermarsi) to stay || non posso trattenermi dal fare, I cannot help doing.

trattenimento sm. (festa) party.

trattenuta sf. deduction.

trattino sm. **1.** dash **2.** (di unione) hyphen.

tratto sm. **1.** (tirata) pull **2.** (colpo) stroke **3.** (linea) line **4.** (brano) passage **5.** (estensione di spazio) way **6.** (lineamento) feature **7.** (comportamento) manners (pl.) || d'un —, suddenly; di — in —, now and then.

trattore[1] sm. (mecc.) tractor.

trattore[2] sm. (oste) inn-keeper.

trattoria sf. inn.

tratturo sm. cattle-track.

tràuma sm. trauma.

traumàtico agg. traumatic.

traumatologia sf. traumatology.

travagliare vt. V. tormentare.

travaglio sm. **1.** (fatica) labour **2.** (cruccio) trouble.

travasare vt. to pour off.

travaso sm. **1.** pouring off **2.** (med.) effusion.

travatura sf. truss.

trave sf. beam.

travéggole sf. pl. avere le —, to mistake (v. irr.) one thing for another.

traversa sf. **1.** (sbarra) cross-bar **2.** (via) side-road.

traversata sf. crossing.

traversia sf. misfortune.

traversina sf. sleeper.

traverso agg. **1.** transverse, cross (attr.) **2.** (obliquo) slanting || di —, askance; andare per — (fig.), to go (v. irr.) wrong with.

travestimento sm. disguise.

travestire vt. to disguise (as).

traviamento sm. corruption.

traviare vt. to mislead (v. irr.). ♦ **traviarsi** vr. to go (v. irr.) astray.

travisamento sm. alteration.

travisare vt. to alter.

travolgente agg. sweeping.

travòlgere vt. **1.** to sweep (v. irr.) away **2.** (investire) to run (v. irr.) over.

trazione sf. traction.

tre agg. three.

trebbiare vt. to thrash.

trebbiatrice sf. thrasher.

trebbiatura sf. thrashing.

treccia sf. plait: farsi le trecce, to plait one's hair.

trecento agg. three hundred || il — (secolo), the fourteenth century.

tredicenne agg. thirteen years old, thirteen-year-old (attr.).

tredicèsimo agg. thirteenth.

trédici agg. thirteen.

tregua sf. **1.** truce **2.** (riposo) rest.

tremante agg. **1.** trembling **2.** (di freddo) shivering.

tremare vi. **1.** to tremble **2.** (di freddo) to shiver.

tremendo agg. awful.

trementina sf. turpentine.

tremila agg. three thousand.

trèmito sm. **1.** tremble **2.** (di freddo) shiver.

tremolante agg. **1.** trembling **2.** (di luce) flickering **3.** (di stelle) twinkling.

tremolare vi. **1.** to tremble **2.** (di luce) to flicker **3.** (di stelle) to twinkle.

tremolio sm. **1.** tremble **2.** (di luce) flickering **3.** (di stelle) twinkle.

♦**tremore** sm. V. trèmito.

treno sm. **1.** train: — accelerato, slow train; — direttissimo, fast train; — rapido, express train **2.** (tenore) way of living, routine.

trenta agg. thirty.

trentenne agg. thirty years old, thirty-year-old (attr.).

trentennio sm. period of thirty years.

trentèsimo agg. thirtieth.

trentina sf about thirty.

trepestio sm. stamping.

trepidante agg. anxious.

trepidare vi. to be anxious.

trepidazione sf. anxiety.

treppiede sm tripod.

tresca sf. intrigue.

tréspolo sm. trestle.

triade sf. triad.

triangolare agg. triangular.

triangolazione sf. triangulation.

triàngolo sm. triangle.

tribale agg. tribal.

tribolare vi. 1. to toil 2. (soffrire) to suffer. ♦ **tribolare** vt. to vex.

tribolazione sf. suffering.

tribordo sm. starboard.

tribù sf. tribe.

tribuna sf. 1. (per oratori) platform 2. (sport) stand.

tribunale sm. court.

tribuno sm. tribune.

tributare vt. to bestow.

tributario agg. 1. tributary 2. (fiscale) fiscal. ♦ **tributario** sm. tributary.

tributo sm. tribute.

tricheco sm. walrus.

triciclo sm. tricycle.

triclinio sm. triclinium (pl. -nia).

tricolore agg. e sm. tricolour.

tricorno sm. tricorn.

tricromìa sf. 1. trichromatism 2. (pezzo singolo) trichromatic print.

tridente sm. 1. trident 2. (per fieno) hayfork.

tridimensionale agg. tridimensional.

triedro sm. trihedron.

triennale agg. e sm. triennial.

triennio sm. period of three years.

trifase agg. three-phase (attr.).

trifoglio sm. clover.

trigèmino agg. e sm. trigeminal: parto —, birth of triplets.

trigèsimo agg. thirtieth: nel — della sua morte, on the thirtieth day after his death.

trigonometrìa sf. trigonometry.

trilione sm. 1. (in sistema italiano, francese e americano = 1000⁴) billion; (amer.) trillion 2. (in sistema inglese e tedesco = 1000⁶) trillion; (amer.) quintillion.

trillare vi. 1. to trill 2. (squillare) to ring (v. irr.).

trillo sm. 1. trill 2. (di sveglia, telefono) ring.

trilogìa sf. trilogy.

trimestrale agg. quarterly.

trimestre sm. 1. quarter 2. (scol.) term 3. (paga trimestrale) quarterage.

trimotore agg. three-engined aeroplane.

trina sf. lace.

trincare vt. to gulp. ♦ **trincare** vi. to drink (v. irr.).

trincea sf. trench.

trincerare vt. to entrench.

trincetto sm. shoemaker's knife (pl. knives).

trinchetto sm. albero di —, foremast; vela di —, foresail.

trinciante agg. sharp. ♦ **trinciante** sm. carver.

trinciare vt. 1. to cut (v. irr.) (up) 2. (carne) to carve || — giudizi, to judge rashly.

trinciato sm. cut-tobacco.

trinità sf. trinity.

trinomio sm. trinomial.

trionfante agg. triumphant.

trionfare vt. to triumph.

trionfatore sm. triumpher.

trionfo sm. triumph.

tripartito agg. tripartite.

tripartizione sf. tripartition.

triplicare vt. to treble.

triplo agg. triple. ♦ **triplo** sm. 1. triple 2. (tre volte tanto) three times as much.

trippa sf. (cuc.) tripe.

tripudiare vi. to exult.

tripudio sm. exultation.

trisàvolo sm. great-great-grand-father.

trisìllabo agg. trisyllabic. ♦ **trisìllabo** sm. trisyllable.

triste agg. sad.

tristezza sf. 1. sadness 2. (dolore) grief.

tristo agg. wicked.

tritacarne sm. mincer.

tritare vt. to mince.

tritatutto sm. mincer.

trito agg. (fig.) trite.

tritolo sm. trinitrotoluene.

trìttico sm. triptych.

trittongo sm. triphthong.

tritume sm. crumbs (pl.).

triturare vt. to triturate.

triumvirato sm. triumvirate.

triùmviro sm. triumvir.

trivalente agg. trivalent.

trivella sf. 1. (min.) drill 2. (falegnameria) auger.

trivellare vt. to drill.

trivellazione sf. drilling: torre di —, derrick.

triviale agg. coarse.

trivialità sf. 1. coarseness 2. (detto triviale) coarse expression.

trofeo sm. trophy.

troglodita sm. troglodyte.

troglodìtico agg. troglodytic(al).

trògolo sm. trough.

troia sf. (zool.) sow.

tromba sf. 1. trumpet 2. (di scale)

well ǁ — *d'aria*, tornado; — *d'acqua*, water-spout.

trombettiere *sm.* trumpeter.

trombone *sm.* 1. (*mus.*) trombone 2. (*schioppo*) blunderbuss ǁ *suonatore di* —, trombonist.

trombosi *sf.* thrombosis.

troncare *vt.* 1. to cut (*v. irr.*) off 2. (*fig.*) to break (*v. irr.*) off.

tronco¹ *agg.* 1. cut off 2. (*fig.*) broken.

tronco² *sm.* 1. trunk 2. (*d'albero abbattuto*) log 3. (*geom.*) frustum ǁ — *ferroviario*, railway section; *licenziare in* —, to sack on the spot.

troncone *sm.* stump.

troneggiare *vi.* to dominate (sthg.).

tronfio *agg.* 1. conceited 2. (*di stile*) bombastic.

trono *sm.* throne.

tropicale *agg.* tropical.

tròpico *sm.* tropic.

tropismo *sm.* tropism.

troposfera *sf.* troposphere.

troppo *avv.* 1. (*con agg. e avv*) too 2. (*con v.*) too much 3. (*di tempo*) too long. ◆ **troppo** *agg. e pron.* too much (*pl.* too many): *anche* —, only too; *essere di* —, to be unwelcome.

trota *sf.* trout (*pl. invariato*).

trottare *vi.* to trot: *far* — *qu.* (*fig.*) to make (*v. irr.*) so. run.

trottata *sf.* trot.

trottatore *sm.* trotter.

trotterellare *vi.* 1. to trot along 2. (*di bambini*) to toddle.

trotto *sm.* trot: *mettere un cavallo al* —, to trot a horse.

tròttola *sf.* top.

trovare *vt.* 1. to find (*v. irr.*) 2. (*far visita*) to see (*v. irr.*) 3. (*pensare*) to think (*v. irr.*). ◆ **trovarsi** *vr.* 1. (*essere*) to be 2. (*sentirsi*) to feel (*v. irr.*).

trovata *sf.* trick.

trovatello *sm.* foundling.

trovatore *sm.* troubadour.

truccare *vi.* 1. to make (*v. irr.*) up 2. (*sport*) to fix.

truccatore *sm.* maker-up.

truccatura *sf.* make-up.

trucco *sm.* 1. trick 2. (*cosmetici*) make-up 3. (*inganno*) deceit.

truce *agg.* grim.

trucidare *vt.* to slay (*v. irr.*).

trùciolo *sm.* shaving.

truculento *agg.* truculent.

truffa *sf.* cheat.

truffaldino *agg.* cheating.

truffare *vt.* to cheat.

truffatore *sm.* cheat.

truismo *sm.* truism.

truppa *sf.* troop.

tu *pron.* you.

tua *agg. e pron.* V. *tuo*.

tuba *sf.* 1. tuba 2. (*cappello*) top-hat.

tubare *vi.* to coo.

tubatura *sf.* piping.

tubercolare *agg.* tubercular.

tubercolina *sf.* tuberculin.

tubercolosario *sm.* sanatorium.

tubercolosi *sf.* tuberculosis: — *polmonare*, consumption.

tubercoloso *agg.* tuberculous. ◆ **tubercoloso** *sm.* consumptive.

tùbero *sm.* tuber.

tuberosa *sf.* tuberose.

tubino *sm.* bowler-hat.

tubo *sm.* 1. tube 2. (*di conduttura*) pipe 3. (*anat.*) canal.

tubolare *agg.* tubular.

tue *agg. e pron.* V. *tuo*.

tuffare *vt.* to plunge, to dip. ◆ **tuffarsi** *vr.* to plunge, to dive.

tuffatore *sm.* diver.

tuffo *sm.* plunge, dive.

tufo *sm.* tuff.

tugurio *sm.* hovel.

tulipano *sm.* tulip.

tumefare *vt.* to swell (*v. irr.*). ◆ **tumefarsi** *vr.* to swell.

tumefatto *agg.* swollen.

tumefazione *sf.* swelling.

tùmido *agg.* tumid: *labbra tumide*, thick lips.

tumore *sm.* tumour.

tumulare *vt.* to bury.

tumulazione *sf.* burial.

tùmulo *sm.* 1. tumulus (*pl.* -li) 2. (*tomba*) grave.

tumulto *sm.* tumult.

tumultuante *agg.* riotous.

tumultuare *vi.* to riot.

tumultuoso *agg.* tumultuous.

tundra *sf.* tundra.

tungsteno *sm.* tungsten.

tùnica *sf.* tunic.

tunnel *sm.* tunnel.

tuo *agg. your.* ◆ **tuo** *pron* yours.

tuoi *agg. e pron.* V. *tuo* ǁ *i* —, your family.

tuonare *vi.* to thunder.

tuono *sm.* thunder.

tuorlo *sm.* yolk.

turàcciolo *sm.* 1. stopper 2. (*di su-*

ghero) cork || *mettere il — a una bottiglia,* to cork a bottle.

turare *vt.* to stop, to fill up. ♦ **turarsi** *vr.* **1.** to stop **2.** *(chiudersi)* to shut oneself up.

turba[1] *sf.* crowd.

turba[2] *sf. (med.)* trouble.

turbamento *sm.* **1.** perturbation **2.** *(eccitazione)* excitement **3.** *(sconvolgimento)* upsetting.

turbante *sm.* turban.

turbare *vt.* **1.** to upset *(v. irr.)* **2.** *(agitare intorbidando)* to muddy. ♦ **turbarsi** *vr.* to get *(v. irr.)* upset.

turbina *sf.* turbine.

turbinare *vi.* to whirl.

turbine *sm.* **1.** whirl **2.** *(uragano)* hurricane.

turbinìo *sm.* whirling.

turbinoso *agg.* **1.** whirling **2.** *(tumultuoso)* tumultuous.

turbolento *agg.* boisterous.

turbolenza *sf.* boisterousness.

turbomotore *sm.* turbojet engine.

turbonave *sf.* turboship.

turboreattore *sm. (aer.)* turbojet.

turcasso *sm.* quiver.

turchese *sm.* turquoise.

turchino *agg.* deep blue.

turco *agg.* Turkish. ♦ **turco** *sm.* Turk.

turgidezza *sf.* turgidity.

tùrgido *agg.* turgid.

turìbolo *sm.* censer.

turismo *sm.* tourism.

turista *s.* tourist.

turìstico *agg.* tourist *(attr.).*

turlupinare *vt.* to swindle.

turlupinatura *sf.* swindle.

turno *sm.* **1.** turn **2.** *(servizio)* duty || *di —,* on duty; *a —,* on turn.

turpe *agg.* filthy.

turpilòquio *sm.* coarse language.

turpitùdine *sf.* baseness.

turrito *agg.* turreted.

tuta *sf.* overalls *(pl.):* — *spaziale,* spacesuit.

tutela *sf.* **1.** guardianship **2.** *(protezione)* protection.

tutelare *vt.* to guard.

tutelare *agg.* tutelary.

tutore *sm.* guardian.

tuttavìa *cong.* yet.

tutto *agg.* all, whole *(pl.* all); *(ogni)* every || *tutt'e due,* both; *tutt'al più,* at the most; *tutt'altro che,* anything but; *tutt'altro!,* on the contrary! ♦ **tutto** *pron.* all,

everything *(pl.* alì); *(ognuno)* everybody. ♦ **tutto** *s.n.* whole: *del —,* quite.

tuttofare *agg. cameriera —,* maid-of-all-work.

tuttora *avv.* still.

U

ubbìa *sf.* whim.

ubbidiente *agg.* obedient.

ubbidienza *sf.* obedience.

ubbidire *vi.* to obey (so., sthg.).

ubicare *vt.* to locate.

ubicato *agg.* situated.

ubicazione *sf.* location.

ubiquità *sf.* ubiquity.

ubriacare *vt.* to make *(v. irr.)* drunk. ♦ **ubriacarsi** *vr.* to get *(v. irr.)* drunk.

ubriacatura *sf.* intoxication.

ubriachezza *sf.* drunkenness.

ubriaco *agg.* drunk. ♦ **ubriaco** *sm.* drunken man *(pl.* men).

ubriacone *sm.* drunkard.

uccellagione *sf.* feathered game.

uccellare *vi.* to fowl.

uccelliera *sf.* aviary.

uccello *sm.* bird.

uccìdere *vt.* **1.** to kill **2.** *(assassinare)* to murder **3.** *(con pugnale)* to stab to death **4.** *(con arma da fuoco)* to shoot *(v. irr.).* ♦ **uccìdersi** *vr.* **1.** to get *(v. irr.)* killed **2.** *(suicidarsi)* to commit suicide, to kill oneself.

uccisione *sf.* killing.

uccisore *sm.* killer.

udìbile *agg.* audible.

udienza *sf.* hearing.

udire *vt.* to hear *(v. irr.).*

uditivo *agg.* auditory.

udito *sm.* hearing.

uditore *sm.* **1.** listener **2.** *(nella scuola)* auditor.

uditorio *sm.* audience.

ufficiale *agg.* official. ♦ **ufficiale** *sm.* **1.** officer **2.** *(governativo, postale)* official.

ufficialità *sf.* official character.

ufficialmente *avv.* officially.

ufficiare *vi.* to officiate.

ufficio *sm.* office: *capo —,* head clerk; *d'—,* officially; — *informazioni,* information bureau.

ufficiosamente *avv.* unofficially.

ufficioso *agg.* unofficial.

ufo (*nella loc. avv.*) *a* —, without paying.

ugello *sm.* nozzle.

uggia *sf.* boredom: *questo libro mi è venuto in* —, I have grown tired of this book.

uggiolare *vi.* to whine.

uggioso *agg.* dull.

ùgola *sf.* 1. uvula 2. (*voce*) voice.

uguaglianza *sf.* equality.

uguagliare *vt.* 1. to be equal (to) 2. (*rendere uguale*) to make (*v. irr.*) equal.

uguale *agg.* 1. equal 2. (*simile*) like, alike (*pred.*) 3. (*stesso*) same.

ugualitario *agg.* equalitarian.

ugualmente *avv.* 1. equally 2. (*lo stesso*) all the same.

ùlcera *sf.* ulcer.

ulcerare *vt.* to ulcerate. ♦ **ulcerarsi** *vr.* to ulcerate.

ulcerato *agg.* ulcerated.

ulcerazione *sf.* ulceration.

ulceroso *agg.* ulcerous.

ulteriore *agg.* further.

ulteriormente *avv.* further on.

ultimamente *avv.* 1. recently 2. (*da ultimo*) finally.

ultimare *vt.* to finish.

ultimazione *sf.* conclusion.

ultimo *agg.* 1. last 2. (*il più recente*) latest 3. (*estremo*) utmost.

ultramicroscòpico *agg.* ultramicroscopic(al).

ultramoderno *agg.* ultramodern.

ultrasensìbile *agg.* ultrasensitive.

ultrasònico *agg.* ultrasonic.

ultrasuono *sm.* ultrasound.

ultraterreno *agg.* supernatural.

ultravioletto *agg.* ultraviolet.

ululare *vi.* 1. to howl 2. (*di sirena*) to hoot.

ululato *sm.* 1. howl 2. (*di sirena*) hoot.

umanésimo *sm.* Humanism.

umanista *s.* humanist.

umanistico *agg.* humanistic.

umanità *sf.* humanity.

umanitario *agg.* humanitarian.

umanitarismo *sm.* humanitarianism.

umanizzare *vt.* to humanize.

umano *agg.* 1. human 2. (*comprensivo*) humane.

umerale *agg.* humeral.

umettare *vt.* to moisten.

umidità *sf.* humidity, dampness.

ùmido *agg.* damp.

ùmile *agg.* humble.

umiliante *agg.* humiliating.

umiliare *vt.* to humble.

umiliazione *sf.* humiliation.

umiltà *sf.* 1. humbleness 2. (*virtù dell'umile*) humility.

umore *sm.* humour: *essere di buon* —, to be in a good humour.

umorismo *sm.* humour.

umorista *s.* humorist.

umoristico *agg.* humorous.

una *art. e agg.* V. **uno**.

unànime *agg.* unanimous.

unanimità *sf.* unanimity: *all'*—, unanimously.

uncinare *vt.* to hook.

uncinato *agg.* hooked ‖ *croce uncinata*, swastika.

uncinetto *sm.* crochet-hook: *lavorare all'*—, to crochet.

uncino *sm.* hook.

undicèsimo *agg.* eleventh.

ùndici *agg.* eleven.

ùngere *vt.* to grease.

unghia *sf.* 1. nail 2. (*di equino*) hoof 3. (*fig.*) clutch.

unghiata *sf.* scratch: *dare un'*—, to scratch.

unguento *sm.* ointment.

ungulato *agg.* hoofed.

unicamente *avv.* only.

unicellulare *agg.* unicellular.

unicità *sf.* uniqueness.

ùnico *agg.* 1. only 2. (*senza uguale*) unique.

unificare *vt.* 1. to unify 2. (*uniformare*) to standardize.

unificatore *agg.* unifying. ♦ **unificatore** *sm.* uniher.

unificazione *sf.* 1. unification 2. (*uniformazione*) standardization.

uniformare *vt.* 1. to conform 2. (*rendere conforme*) to standardize. ♦ **uniformarsi** *vr.* to conform (to).

uniforme[1] *agg.* uniform.

uniforme[2] *sf.* uniform.

uniformemente *avv.* uniformly.

uniformità *sf.* uniformity.

unigènito *agg.* only child.

unilaterale *agg.* unilateral.

unilateralmente *avv.* unilaterally.

uninominale *agg.* uninominal.

unione *sf.* union.

unionista *sm.* unionist.

unipolare *agg.* unipolar.

unire *vt.* to unite, to join. ♦ **unirsi** *vr.* to unite, to join.

unìsono *sm.* unison.

unità *sf.* 1. unity 2. (*fis.; mat.; mil.*) unit.

unitamente *avv.* unitedly: — *a*, together with.

unitario *agg.* unitary.

unito *agg.* 1. united 2. (*accluso*) enclosed.

universale *agg.* universal.

universalità *sf.* universality.

universalizzare *vt.* to universalize.

università *sf.* university.

universitario *agg.* university (*attr.*). ♦ **universitario** *sm.* university student.

universo *agg.* whole. ♦ **universo** *sm.* universe.

univoco *agg.* univocal.

uno, un, una *art.* a, an (*davanti a vocale e h muta*). ♦ **uno, un, una** *agg.* one. ♦ **uno, una** *pron.* 1. one 2. (*un tale*) a man; (*una tale*) a woman || — *a* —, one by one; *l' — e l'altro*, both; *l' — o l'altro*, either; *né l' — né l'altro*, neither; *l' — l'altro*, each other; *un po' per* —, a part each; *costano 5 sterline l'—*, they cost 5 pounds each.

unto *agg.* greasy.

untume *sm.* grease.

untuosamente *avv.* (*fig.*) unctuously.

untuosità *sf.* 1. greasiness 2. (*fig.*) unctuousness.

untuoso *agg.* 1. greasy 2. (*fig.*) unctuous.

unzione *sf.* unction.

uomo *sm.* man (*pl.* men): *un — da nulla*, a nobody.

uopo *sm.* esser *d'*—, to be necessary; *all'*—, if necessary.

uovo *sm.* egg: *rosso d'*—, yolk; *cercare il pelo nell'*—, to split (*v. irr.*) hairs.

uragano *sm.* hurricane.

uranifero *agg.* uranic.

uranio *sm.* uranium.

uranite *sf.* uranite.

uranografìa *sf.* uranography.

urbanésimo *sm.* urbanization.

urbanista *s.* town planner.

urbanìstica *sf.* town-planning.

urbanìstico *agg.* town-planning.

urbanità *sf.* urbanity.

urbanizzare *vt.* to urbanize.

urbanizzazione *sf.* urbanization.

urbano *agg.* 1. urban 2. (*cortese*) urbane.

ùrea *sf.* urea.

uremìa *sf.* uraemia.

urèmico *agg.* uraemic.

uretra *sf.* urethra.

urgente *agg.* urgent.

urgentemente *avv.* urgently.

urgenza *sf.* urgency.

ùrgere *vt.* to urge. ♦ **ùrgere** *vi.* to be urgent.

uricemìa *sf.* uricaemia.

ùrico *agg.* uric.

urina *sf.* V. *orina*.

urinare *vi.* V. *orinare*.

urlare *vt. e vi.* 1. to shout, to scream 2. (*di vento, animale; per il dolore*) to howl.

urlatore *agg.* shouting. ♦ **urlatore** *sm.* shouter.

urlo *sm.* 1. shout 2. (*di vento, animale; per il dolore*) howl.

urna *sf.* 1. urn 2. (*per i voti*) ballot-box || *andare alle urne*, to go (*v. irr.*) to the polls.

urogallo *sm.* grouse.

urologìa *sf.* urology.

uròlogo *sm.* urologist.

urtante *agg.* irritating.

urtare *vt.* 1. to knock 2. (*infastidire*) to irritate 3. (*offendere*) to hurt (*v. irr.*). ♦ **urtarsi** *vr.* to get (*v. irr.*) cross. ♦ **urtarsi** *vr. rec.* to collide.

urticante *agg.* urticating.

urticaria *sf.* nettle rash.

urto *sm.* 1. push 2. (*scontro, contrasto*) collision || *essere in* —, to be at variance.

urtone *sm.* shove.

usanza *sf.* 1. custom 2. (*abitudine personale*) habit.

usare *vt.* to use: — *una cortesia*, to do (*v. irr.*) a favour. ♦ **usare** *vi.* 1. to be accustomed; (*solo al passato*) to use 2. (*essere di moda*) to be fashionable.

usato *agg.* 1. used 2. (*in uso*) in use 3. (*abituale*) usual 4. (*non nuovo*) second-hand.

uscente *agg.* 1. retiring 2. (*con espressioni di tempo*) closing.

usciere *sm.* 1. usher 2. (*ufficiale giudiziario*) bailiff.

uscio *sm.* door: *abitare — a — (con)*, to live next door (to).

uscire *vi.* 1. to go (*v. irr.*) out, to come (*v. irr.*) out 2. (*sboccare*) to lead (*v. irr.*) out 3. (*uscire di strada*) to go off || *uscirne bene, male*, to come off well, badly.

uscita *sf.* **1.** way out **2.** (*atto di uscire*) going out, coming out **3.** (*spese*) expense || *strada senza —*, blind-alley.

usignolo *sm.* nightingale.

uso¹ *agg.* accustomed.

uso² *sm.* use: *d'—*, usual; *all'— di*, after the fashion of.

ùssaro *sm.* hussar.

ustionare *vt.* to scald.

ustionato *agg.* scalded.

ustione *sf.* scald.

usuale *agg.* usual.

usufruire *vi.* to benefit (by).

usufrutto *sm.* usufruct.

usufruttuario *agg. e sm.* usufructuary.

usura *sf.* **1.** usury **2.** (*logorio*) wear and tear.

usuraio *sm.* usurer.

usurpare *vt.* to usurp.

usurpatore *agg.* usurping. ♦ **usurpatore** *sm.* usurper.

usurpazione *sf.* usurpation.

utènsile *sm.* utensil.

utente *s.* user.

uterino *agg.* uterine.

ùtero *sm.* uterus (*pl.* -ri).

ùtile *agg.* useful. ♦ **ùtile** *sm.* profit.

utilità *sf.* **1.** usefulness **2.** (*vantaggio*) profit || *non ne vedo l'—*, I do not see the use of it.

utilitaria *sf.* (*auto*) utility car.

utilitario *agg. e sm.* utilitarian.

utilitarismo *sm.* utilitarianism.

utilitarìstico *agg.* V. *utilitario*.

utilizzàbile *agg.* utilizable.

utilizzare *vt.* to utilize.

utilizzatore *agg.* utilizing. ♦ **utilizzatore** *sm.* utilizer.

utilizzazione *sf.* utilization.

utopìa *sf.* utopia.

utopista *s.* utopian.

utopìstico *agg.* utopian.

uva *sf.* grapes (*pl.*): — *passa*, raisin.

uxoricida *sm.* uxoricide.

uxoricidio *sm.* uxoricide.

V

vacante *agg.* vacant.

vacanza *sf.* **1.** holiday **2.** (*posto vacante*) vacancy.

vacca *sf.* cow.

vaccaro *sm.* cowherd.

vaccherìa *sf.* cowhouse.

vacchetta *sf.* cowhide.

vaccinàbile *agg.* that can be vaccinated.

vaccinare *vt.* to vaccinate.

vaccinazione *sf.* vaccination.

vaccino *sm.* vaccine.

vaccinògeno *agg.* vaccinogenous.

vaccinoterapìa *sf.* vaccinotherapy.

vacillamento *sm.* **1.** unsteadiness **2.** (*di luce*) flickering **3.** (*fig.*) wavering.

vacillante *agg.* **1.** unsteady **2.** (*di luce*) flickering **3.** (*fig.*) uncertain.

vacillare *vi.* **1.** to be unsteady **2.** (*di luce*) to flicker **3.** (*fig.*) to waver.

vacuità *sf.* vacuity.

vacuo *agg.* vacuous.

vademecum *sm.* vade-mecum.

vagabondaggio *sm.* vagrancy.

vagabondare *vi.* to wander.

vagabondo *agg.* vagabond. ♦ **vagabondo** *sm.* vagrant.

vagamente *avv.* vaguely.

vagante *agg.* wandering.

vagare *vi.* to wander.

vagheggiamento *sm.* longing (for).

vagheggiare *vt.* to long (for).

vagheggino *sm.* gallant.

vaghezza *sf.* **1.** charm **2.** (*indeterminatezza*) vagueness.

vagina *sf.* vagina (*pl.* -nae).

vagire *vi.* to wail.

vagito *sm.* wail.

vaglia¹ *sf.* (*valore*) worth.

vaglia² *sm.* money order: — *postale*, postal order.

vagliare *vt.* to sieve **2.** (*fig.*) to weigh.

vagliatura *sf.* screening.

vaglio *sm.* **1.** sieve **2.** (*fig.*) sifting.

vago *agg.* **1.** vague **2.** (*leggiadro*) pretty.

vagoncino *sm.* wag(g)on.

vagolare *vi.* to rove.

vagone *sm.* carriage, coach.

vaio¹ *agg.* dark grey.

vaio² *sm.* vair.

vaiolo *sm.* smallpox.

valanga *sf.* avalanche.

valchiria *sf.* Walkyrie.

valente *agg.* **1.** skilful **2.** (*valoroso*) brave.

valentemente *avv.* **1.** skilfully **2.** (*valorosamente*) bravely.

valentìa *sf.* **1.** skill **2.** (*valore*) worth.

valentuomo *sm.* worthy man.

valenza *sf.* valence.

valere *vi.* 1. to be worth: — *la pena*, to be worth while; *far — i propri diritti*, to assert one's rights; *farsi —*, to make (*v. irr.*) oneself appreciated 2. (*contare*) to count 3. (*servire*) to be of use 4. (*essere valido*) to be valid. ♦ valersi *vr.* to avail oneself (of).

valeriana *sf.* valerian.

valévole *agg.* valid.

valicàbile *agg.* that can be crossed.

valicare *vt.* to cross.

valico *sm.* pass.

validamente *avv.* validly.

validità *sf.* validity.

vàlido *agg.* 1. valid 2. (*fondato*) well-grounded 3. (*forte*) strong.

valigeria *sf.* leatherware shop.

valigia *sf.* suit-case; *fare le valigie*, to pack up.

vallata *sf.* valley.

valle *sf.* valley.

valletto *sm.* valet.

vallo *sm.* rampart.

vallone *agg. e sm.* Walloon.

valore *sm.* 1. value 2. (*coraggio*) bravery.

valorizzare *vt.* 1. to turn to account 2. (*accentuare*) to emphasize.

valorizzazione *sf.* 1. turning to account 2. (*comm.*) valorization.

valorosamente *avv.* bravely.

valoroso *agg.* brave.

valsente *sm.* commercial value.

valuta *sf.* 1. value 2. (*moneta*) currency: — *estera*, foreign currency.

valutàbile *agg.* valuable.

valutare *vt.* 1. to value 2. (*considerare*) to consider.

valutazione *sf.* 1. evaluation 2. (*considerazione*) careful consideration.

valva *sf.* valve.

vàlvola *sf.* 1. valve 2. (*elettr.*) fuse 3. (*radio*) valve, tube.

valvolare *agg.* valvular.

valzer *sm.* waltz: *ballare il —*, to waltz.

vampa *sf.* 1. blaze 2. (*al viso*) flush.

vampata *sf.* 1. blaze 2. (*folata*) blast 3. (*al viso*) flush.

vampeggiante *agg.* blazing.

vampeggiare *vi.* to blaze.

vampiro *sm.* vampire.

vanagloria *sf.* vainglory.

vanagloriarsi *vr.* to boast.

vanaglorioso *agg.* boastful.

vanamente *avv.* vainly.

vandàlico *agg.* vandalic.

vandalismo *sm.* vandalism.

vàndalo *agg. e sm.* vandal.

vaneggiamento *sm.* raving.

vaneggiare *vi.* to rave.

vanesio *agg.* foppish. ♦ vanesio *sm.* fop.

vanga *sf.* spade.

vangare *vt.* to spade.

vangata *sf.* blow with a spade.

vangatore *sm.* spademan.

vangatura *sf.* spading.

vangelo *sm.* Gospel.

vaniglia *sf.* vanilla.

vanigliato *agg.* vanilla-flavoured.

vaniloquio *sm.* empty talk.

vanità *sf.* vanity.

vanitoso *agg.* conceited.

vano[1] *agg.* vain.

vano[2] *sm.* space, room.

vantaggio *sm.* 1. advantage 2. (*sport*) lead.

vantaggiosamente *avv.* advantageously.

vantaggioso *agg.* advantageous.

vantare *vt.* 1. to boast (of) 2. (*lodare*) to praise 3. (*millantare*) to brag. ♦ vantarsi *vr.* to boast (of).

vanteria *sf.* boast.

vanto *sm.* boast.

vànvera (*nella loc. avv.*) *a —*, at random.

vapore *sm.* 1. steam 2. (*mar.*) steamer.

vaporetto *sm.* steamboat.

vaporiera *sf.* steam-engine.

vaporizzare *vt.* to vaporize.

vaporizzatore *sm.* vaporizer.

vaporizzazione *sf.* vaporization.

vaporosità *sf.* 1. haziness 2. (*di abito*) gauziness.

vaporoso *agg.* 1. hazy 2. (*di abito*) gauzy.

varare *vt.* to launch (*anche fig.*).

varcare *vt.* to cross, to pass.

varco *sm.* passage, opening: *aprirsi un — fra la folla*, to force one's way through the crowd.

variàbile *agg.* variable, unsteady.

variabilità *sf.* variability, unsteadiness.

variante *sf.* variant.

variare *vt.* 1. to vary 2. (*di mercato*) to fluctuate.

variato *agg.* V. *vario*.

variazione *sf.* variation, change.

varice sf. varix (pl. varices).
varicella sf. chicken-pox.
varicoso agg. varicose.
variegato agg. variegated.
varietà sf. variety.
vario agg. 1. varied 2. (differente) various 3. (parecchi) several.
variopinto agg. many-coloured.
varo sm. launch.
vasaio sm. potter.
vasca sf. basin: — da bagno, bath (tub).
vascello sm. vessel.
vascolare agg. vascular.
vaselina sf. vaseline.
vasellame sm. 1. (di terracotta) earthenware 2. (di porcellana) china 3. (d'argento, d'oro) silver, gold plate.
vaso sm. 1. vase 2. (rotondo) pot 3. (recipiente; anat.) vessel.
vasocostrittore agg. e sm. vasoconstrictor.
vasodilatatore agg. e sm. vasodilator.
vasomotore agg. vasomotor.
vasomotorio agg. vasomotor.
vassallaggio sm. 1. (stor.) vassalage 2. subjection.
vassallo agg. e sm. 1. (stor.) vassal 2. subject.
vassoio sm. tray.
vastità sf. 1. vastness 2. (estensione) expanse.
vasto agg. wide, large.
vate sm. 1. prophet 2. (poeta) poet.
Vaticano agg. Vatican.
vaticinare vt. to prophesy.
vaticinio sm. prophecy.
vattelappesca inter. who knows!
ve pron: you: — lo scrissi, I wrote it to you. ♦ ve avv. there: — ne sono due, there are two.
ve' inter. look, see.
vecchiaia sf. old age.
vecchiezza sf. great age.
vecchio agg. 1. old 2. (antico) ancient 3. (stantio) stale. ♦ vecchio sm. old man.
veccia sf. vetch.
vece sf. stead, place.
vedere vt. to see (v. irr.): — la luce (nascere), to be born; far —, to show (v. irr.); farsi —, to show oneself; non — l'ora di, to look forward to (con gerundio). ♦ vedersi vr. 1. to see oneself 2. (vedersela) to deal (v. irr. with).
vedetta sf. 1. (sentinella) watchman

(pl. -men) 2. (posto di osservazione) look-out.
védova sf. widow.
vedovanza sf. widowhood.
vedovile agg. 1. (di vedova) of a widow 2. (di vedovo) of a widower.
védovo sm. widower.
vedretta sf. small steep glacier.
veduta sf. 1. sight, view 2. (opinione) view, idea.
veemente agg. vehement.
veemenza sf. vehemence.
vegetale agg. e sm. vegetable.
vegetare vi. to vegetate.
vegetariano agg. e sm. vegetarian.
vegetativo agg. vegetative.
vegetazione sf. vegetation.
vègeto agg. 1. (di pianta) thriving 2. (di persona) vigorous, strong || vivo e —, hale and hearty
veggente sm. seer.
veglia sf. 1. waking 2. (il vegliare) watch.
vegliardo sm. old man.
vegliare vi. 1. to be awake 2. (far la veglia) to watch.
veglione sm. masked ball.
veicolo sm. vehicle.
vela sf. sail.
velame sm. 1. veil 2. (mar.) sails (pl.).
velare vt. to veil.
velario sm. curtain.
velatura sf. sails (pl.).
veleggiare vi. to sail.
veleno sm. poison.
velenoso agg. poisonous, venomous.
veletta sf. 1. (mar.) topsail 2. (di cappello) veil.
veliero sm. sailing-ship.
velina sf. tissue-paper.
velismo sm. sailing.
velivolo sm. aeroplane.
velleità sf. foolish ambition, fancy.
vellicare vt. to tickle.
vello sm. fleece.
vellutato agg. velvety: pelle vellutata, downy skin.
velluto sm. velvet.
velo sm. veil.
veloce agg. fast, quick, swift.
velocipede sm. velocipede.
velocità sf. speed, velocity: a tutta —, at full speed; limite di —, speed limit; cambio di — (auto), gearbox; indicatore di —, speedometer.
velòdromo sm. cycle-racing track.

veltro *sm.* greyhound.
vena *sf.* vein.
venale *agg.* venal.
venalità *sf.* venality.
venare *vt.* 1. to vein 2. (*di legno*) to grain.
venato *agg.* 1. veined 2. (*di legno*) grained.
venatorio *agg.* venatorial.
venatura *sf.* 1. vein 2. (*di legno*) grain.
vendemmia *sf.* vintage.
vendemmiare *vi.* to gather grapes.
vendemmiatore *sm.* vintager.
véndere *vt.* to sell (*v. irr.*): — *a buon mercato*, to sell cheaply; — *a credito*, to sell on credit; — *all'ingrosso, al minuto*, to sell wholesale, by retail; — *a rate*, to sell by instalments.
vendetta *sf.* revenge.
vendibile *agg.* salable.
vendicare *vt.* to revenge.
vendicativo *agg.* revengeful.
vendicatore *sm.* revenger.
véndita *sf.* sale: — *all'asta*, auction.
venditore *sm.* seller.
venduto *agg.* 1. sold 2. (*fig.*) corrupted.
veneficio *sm.* poisoning.
venèfico *agg.* poisonous.
veneràbile *agg.* venerable.
venerando *agg.* venerable.
venerare *vt.* to worship.
venerazione *sf.* worship.
venerdì *sm.* Friday: — *Santo*, Good Friday.
vènere *sf.* 1. Venus 2. (*fig.*) beauty.
venèreo *agg.* venereal.
veneziana *sf.* Venetian-blind.
veniale *agg.* venial.
venire *vi.* 1. to come (*v. irr.*): — *al sodo*, to come to the point; — *in mente*, to come into one's head; — *meno*, to faint; — *alla luce*, to come to light 2. (*riuscire*) to turn out 3. (*derivare*) to derive.
venoso *agg.* venous.
ventaglio *sm.* fan.
ventata *sf.* gust of wind.
ventèsimo *agg.* twentieth.
venti *agg.* twenty.
ventilare *vt.* to ventilate.
ventilato *agg.* airy, windy.
ventilatore *sm.* fan.
ventilazione *sf.* ventilation.
ventina *sf.* score: *essere sulla* — (*di anni*), to be about twenty.

vento *sm.* wind.
ventosa *sf.* sucker.
ventosità *sf.* flatulence.
ventoso *agg.* windy.
ventrale *agg.* ventral.
ventre *sm.* 1. abdomen 2. (*fam.*) tummy.
ventricolo *sm.* ventricle.
ventriera *sf.* body-belt.
ventriglio *sm.* gizzard.
ventriloquio *sm.* ventriloquism.
ventriloquo *sm.* ventriloquist.
ventura *sf.* chance, fortune.
venturo *agg.* next, coming.
venustà *sf.* beauty.
venusto *agg.* beautiful.
venuta *sf.* coming, arrival.
vera *sf.* wedding-ring.
verace *agg.* true.
veracità *sf.* veracity, truth.
veramente *avv.* really, truly, indeed.
veranda *sf.* verandah.
verbale *agg.* verbal. ♦ **verbale** *sm.* minutes (*pl.*).
verbalizzare *vt.* to record.
verbo *sm.* 1. verb 2. (*parola*) word.
verbosità *sf.* verbosity.
verboso *agg.* verbose.
verdastro *agg.* greenish.
verde *agg.* green.
verdeggiante *agg.* verdant.
verdeggiare *vi.* to be verdant.
verdemare *sm.* sea-green.
verderame *sm.* verdigris.
verdetto *sm.* verdict.
verdògnolo *agg.* greenish.
verdura *sf.* vegetables (*pl.*).
verecondia *sf.* modesty.
verecondo *agg.* modest.
verga *sf.* 1. twig 2. (*bacchetta*) rod.
vergare *vt.* (*scrivere*) to write (*v. irr.*).
vergata *sf.* blow with a rod.
vergato *agg.* 1. striped 2. (*scritto*) written || *carta vergata*, laid paper.
verginale *agg.* virginal.
vérgine *agg. e sf.* virgin.
vergineo *agg.* virginal.
verginità *sf.* virginity.
vergogna *sf.* shame: *aver* —, to be ashamed.
vergognarsi *vr.* to be, to feel (*v. irr.*) shamed.
vergognosamente *avv.* shamefully.
vergognoso *agg.* 1. shameful 2. (*timido*) shy.
veridicamente *avv.* veraciously.
veridicità *sf.* veracity.

verìdico *agg.* veracious.

verìfica *sf.* verification.

verificàbile *agg.* verifiable.

verificare *vt.* to verify, to check.

verificatore *sm.* verifier.

verificazione *sf.* V. *verìfica*.

verismo *sm.* realism.

verista *sm.* realist.

verìstico *agg.* realistic.

verità *sf.* truth: *dire la —*, to tell (*v. irr.*) the truth.

veritiero *agg.* truthful.

verme *sm.* worm.

vermìfugo *agg. e sm.* vermifuge.

vermiglio *agg.* bright red.

verminoso *agg.* verminous.

vernàcolo *agg.* vernacular.

vernice *sf.* 1. paint 2. (*apparenza*) varnish.

verniciare *vt.* to paint, to varnish.

verniciatura *sf.* painting, varnishing.

vero *agg.* true, real.

verosimigliante *agg.* likely.

verosimiglianza *sf.* likelihood.

verosìmile *agg.* likely, probable.

verricello *sm.* windlass.

verro *sm.* boar.

verruca *sf.* wart.

versamento *sm.* 1. pouring 2. (*comm.*) payment, deposit.

versante *sm.* side, slope.

versare *vt.* 1. to pour 2. (*rovesciare*) to spill (*v. irr.*) 3. (*comm.*) to pay (*v. irr.*).

versàtile *agg.* versatile.

versatilità *sf.* versatility.

versato *agg.* 1. poured out 2. (*esperto*) versed.

verseggiare *vt.* to versify.

verseggiatore *sm.* versifier.

versetto *sm.* 1. short line 2. (*della Bibbia*) verse.

versificare *vt.* to versify.

versificatore *sm.* versifier.

versificazione *sf.* versification.

versione *sf.* version, translation.

verso[1] *sm.* 1. verse, line 2. (*suono*) sound 3. (*direzione*) way.

verso[2] *prep.* 1. towards, to 2. (*contro*) against 3. (*circa*) about.

vèrtebra *sf.* vertebra (*pl.* -rae).

vertebrale *agg.* vertebral.

vertebrato *agg. e sm.* vertebrate.

vertenza *sf.* 1. dispute 2. (*giur.*) litigation.

vèrtere *vi.* to be about, to concern.

verticale *agg.* vertical.

verticalità *sf.* verticality.

vèrtice *sm.* 1. vertex (*pl.* vertices) 2. (*fig.*) height, top.

vertìgine *sf.* dizziness (*solo sing.*).

vertiginoso *agg.* dizzy.

verza *sf.* cabbage.

vescìca *sf.* bladder.

vescovado *sm.* bishop's residence.

vescovile *agg.* episcopal.

véscovo *sm.* bishop.

vespa *sf.* wasp.

vespaio *sm.* 1. wasps' nest 2. (*fig.*) hornets' nest.

vespro *sm.* 1. evening 2. (*relig.*) evensong.

vessare *vt.* to vex.

vessatorio *agg.* vexatious.

vessazione *sf.* vexation.

vessillo *sm.* flag.

vestaglia *sf.* dressing-gown.

vestale *sf.* vestal.

veste *sf.* 1. dress 2. (*eccl.*) vestment 3. (*qualità*) capacity.

vestiario *sm.* clothes (*pl.*).

vestìbolo *sm.* hall.

vestigio *sm.* vestige.

vestimento *sm.* V. *veste*.

vestire *vt.* 1. to dress 2. (*fig.*) to clothe 3. (*indossare*) to wear (*v. irr.*). ◆ vestirsi *vr.* to dress oneself.

vestito *sm.* 1. (*da uomo*) suit 2. (*da donna*) frock, dress.

vestizione *sf.* 1. (*eccl.*) ceremony of taking the habit 2. (*di monaca*) ceremony of taking the veil.

veterano *sm.* veteran.

veterinaria *sf.* veterinary science.

veterinario *sm.* veterinary.

veto *sm.* veto.

vetraio *sm.* glazier.

vetrame *sm.* glassware.

vetrata *sf.* glass partition: *— a colori*, stained glass window.

vetrato *agg.* glazed: *carta vetrata*, glass-paper.

vetreria *sf.* glass-work.

vetrificàbile *agg.* vitrifiable.

vetrificare *vt.* to vitrify.

vetrificazione *sf.* vitrification.

vetrina *sf.* shop-window.

vetrioleggiare *vt.* to vitriolize.

vetriolo *sm.* vitriol.

vetro *sm.* 1. glass 2. (*di finestra*) window-pane.

vetrocromìa *sf.* glass-painting.

vetroso *agg.* glassy.

vetta *sf.* top, summit.

vettore *sm.* vector.

vettoriale *agg.* vectorial.

vettovagliamento *sm.* provisining.

vettovagliare *vt.* to provision.

vettura *sf.* 1. coach 2. (*automobile*) car || — *di piazza,* taxi-cab.

vetturino *sm.* cabman (*pl.* -men).

vetustà *sf.* antiquity.

vetusto *agg.* ancient.

vezzeggiare *vt.* to fondle.

vezzeggiativo *sm.* petname.

vezzo *sm.* 1. habit 2. (*collana*) necklace.

vezzosamente *avv.* charmingly.

vezzoso *agg.* charming.

vi' *pron.* you, to you.

vi² *avv.* 1. (*qui*) here 2. (*là*) there.

via¹ *sf.* 1. street 2. (*strada di comunicazione*) road 3. (*cammino*) way (*anche fig.*) 4. (*linea di condotta*) course. ♦ **via** *sm.* dare il —, to give (*v. irr.*) the starting.

via² *avv.* away: *andar —,* to go (*v. irr.*) away.

viabilità *sf.* state of a road.

viadotto *sm.* viaduct.

viaggiante *agg.* travelling.

viaggiare *vi.* to travel: — *in treno, automobile, aereo,* to travel by train, by car, by air.

viaggiatore *sm.* traveller: — *di commercio,* commercial traveller.

viaggio *sm.* 1. journey, trip 2. (*per mare*) voyage 3. (*in aereo*) flight.

viale *sm.* avenue; (*di giardino*) alley.

viandante *sm.* wayfarer.

viatico *sm.* viaticum (*pl.* -ca).

viavai *sm.* coming-and-going.

vibrante *agg.* vibrating (with).

vibrare *vi.* 1. to vibrate 2. (*colpi*) to strike (*v. irr.*).

vibratile *agg.* vibratile.

vibrato *agg.* energetic.

vibratore *sm.* vibrator.

vibrazione *sf.* vibration.

vicariato *sm.* vicariate.

vicario *sm.* vicar.

viceconsole *sm.* vice-consul.

vicedirettore *sm.* assistant-director.

vicegovernatore *sm.* vice-governor.

vicenda *sf.* 1. vicissitude 2. (*evento*) event 3. (*successione*) succession.

vicendévole *agg.* mutual.

vicendevolmente *avv.* mutually.

vicepresidente *sm.* vice-president.

viceré *sm.* viceroy.

vicesegretario *sm.* vice-secretary.

viceversa *avv.* vice versa. ♦ **viceversa** *cong.* whereas.

vicinale *agg.* local road

vicinanza *sf.* 1. vicinity: *in — di,* close to 2. (*adiacenze*) neighbourhood: *nelle vicinanze,* in the neighbourhood.

vicinato *sm.* 1. neighbourhood 2. (*i vicini*) neighbours (*pl.*).

vicino¹ *agg.* near, close. ♦ **vicino** *sm.* neighbour.

vicino² *avv.* near, near by. ♦ **vicino** *prep.* near, close to.

vicissitudine *sf.* vicissitude.

vicolo *sm.* lane, alley.

video *sm.* video.

vidimare *vt.* 1. (*firmare*) to sign 2. (*autenticare*) to authenticate.

vidimazione *sf.* 1. (*firma*) signature 2. (*autenticazione*) authentication.

vietare *vt.* to forbid (*v. irr.*).

vietato *agg.* forbidden: — *fumare,* no smoking; — *entrare,* no admittance.

vieto *agg.* antiquated.

vigente *agg.* in force.

vigere *vi.* to be in force.

vigilante *agg.* watchful.

vigilanza *sf.* watch.

vigilare *vt.* to watch over.

vigilato *agg.* watched.

vigile *agg.* watchful. ♦ **vigile** *sm.* policeman (*pl.* -men).

vigilia *sf.* 1. eve 2. (*relig.*) fast.

vigliaccamente *avv.* in a cowardly way.

vigliaccheria *sf.* 1. cowardice 2. (*azione vigliacca*) cowardly action.

vigliacco *agg.* cowardly.

vigna *sf.* vineyard.

vigneto *sm.* vineyard.

vignetta *sf.* cartoon.

vigore *sm.* vigour: *in —,* in force.

vigoroso *agg.* vigorous.

vile *agg.* 1. cowardly 2. (*meschino*) mean 3. (*basso*) low.

vilipèndere *vt.* to despise.

vilipendio *sm.* contempt.

villa *sf.* villa.

villaggio *sm.* village.

villania *sf.* 1. rudeness 2. (*azione villana*) rude action.

villano *agg.* rude. ♦ **villano** *sm.* peasant, countryman (*pl.* -men).

villeggiante *s.* holiday-maker.

villeggiatura *sf.* holiday: *luogo di —,* (holiday) resort.

villino *sm.* cottage.

villoso *agg.* hairy.

viltà *sf.* 1. cowardice 2. (*azione vile*) cowardly action.

vilucchio *sm.* bearbind.

viluppo *sm.* tangle.

vimine *sm.* withe: *paniere di vimini*, wicker basket.

vinaccia *sf.* dregs of pressed grapes (*pl.*).

vinaio *sm.* wine-merchant.

vinario *agg.* wine (*attr.*).

vincente *agg.* winning. ◆ **vincente** *sm.* winner.

vincere *vt.* **1.** to win (*v. irr.*) **2.** (*battere*) to beat (*v. irr.*) **3.** (*sopraffare*) to overcome (*v. irr.*) **4.** (*superare*) to outdo (*v. irr.*).

vincibile *agg.* conquerable.

vincita *sf.* **1.** win **2.** (*denaro vinto*) winnings (*pl.*).

vincitore *agg.* winning. ◆ **vincitore** *sm.* winner.

vinco *sm.* withe.

vincolare *vt.* **1.** to bind (*v. irr.*) **2.** (*comm.*) to lock up.

vincolato *agg.* **1.** bound **2.** (*comm.*) locked up.

vincolo *sm.* tie, bond.

vinello *sm.* light wine.

vinicolo *agg.* wine (*attr.*).

vinificazione *sf.* wine-making.

vino *sm.* wine.

vinto *agg.* **1.** that has been won **2.** (*sconfitto*) beaten **3.** (*sopraffatto*) overcome ‖ *darsi* —, to give (*v. irr.*) in. ◆ **vinto** *sm.* **1.** (*al giuoco o in qualsiasi contesa*) loser **2.** (*in battaglia*) vanquished man.

viola[1] *sf.* **1.** violet: — *del pensiero*, pansy. ◆ **viola** *agg. e sm.* violet.

viola[2] *sf.* (*mus.*) viola.

violacee *sf. pl.* violaceae.

violaceo *agg.* violet.

violare *vt.* to violate.

violatore *sm.* violator.

violazione *sf.* violation: — *di domicilio*, house-breaking.

violentare *vt.* **1.** to violate, to rape **2.** (*fig.*) to do (*v. irr.*) violence to.

violento *agg.* violent.

violenza *sf.* violence, rape.

violetto *agg.* violet.

violinista *s.* violin-player.

violino *sm.* violin.

violoncellista *s.* violoncellist.

violoncello *sm.* violoncello.

viòttola *sf.* path, lane.

viòttolo *sm.* path, lane.

vipera *sf.* **1.** adder **2.** (*fig.*) viper.

viperino *agg.* viperous.

viraggio *sm.* (*foto*) toning.

virago *sf.* virago.

virare *vt. e vi.* **1.** to veer: — *di bordo*, to veer round **2.** (*fig.*) to turn about.

virata *sf.* veer.

virginale *agg.* virginal.

virginia *sm.* Virginia.

virgola *sf.* **1.** (*gramm.*) comma **2.** (*mat.*) point.

virgolette *sf. pl.* inverted commas: *tra* —, in inverted commas.

virgulto *sm.* shoot.

virile *agg.* manly.

virilità *sf.* **1.** manliness **2.** (*età virile*) manhood.

virilmente *avv.* manfully.

virologìa *sf.* virology.

virosi *sf.* virosis (*pl.* -ses).

virtù *sf.* virtue.

virtuale *agg.* virtual.

virtualità *sf.* virtuality.

virtuosismo *sm.* virtuosity.

virtuoso *agg.* virtuous.

virulento *agg.* virulent.

virulenza *sf.* virulence.

virus *sm.* virus.

viscerale *agg.* visceral.

viscere *sm.* **1.** vital organ **2.** (*f. pl.*) *le viscere*, viscera.

vischio *sm.* **1.** mistletoe **2.** (*pania*) bird-lime.

vischiosità *sf.* stickiness.

vischioso *agg.* sticky.

viscidità *sf.* viscidity.

viscido *agg.* **1.** sticky **2.** (*scivoloso*) slippery.

visciola *sf.* wild cherry.

visconte *sm.* viscount.

viscontessa *sf.* viscountess.

viscosità *sf.* viscosity.

viscoso *agg.* viscous.

visibile *agg.* visible, clear.

visibilio *sm.* great number: *andare in* —, to go (*v. irr.*) into raptures.

visibilità *sf.* visibility.

visiera *sf.* **1.** (*di elmo*) visor **2.** (*di berretto*) peak.

visionario *agg. e sm.* visionary.

visione *sf.* vision: *prendere* — *di*, to look over; *prima* — (*cine*) first screening.

visita *sf.* **1.** visit, call: *fare una* —, to pay (*v. irr.*) a visit **2.** (*persona che visita*) visitor **3.** (*med.*) examination.

visitare *vt.* to visit.

visitatore *sm.* visitor.

visivo *agg.* visual.

viso *sm.* face: — *a* —, face to face.

visone *sm.* mink.

vispo *agg.* lively, brisk.

vista *sf.* 1. sight 2. (*occhi*) eyes (*pl.*).

vistare *vt.* to visa.

visto[1] *sm.* visa.

visto[2] *agg.* seen || — *che,* since as.

vistoso *agg.* 1. showy 2. (*fig.*) considerable.

visuale *agg.* visual. ♦ **visuale** *sf.* sight.

vita[1] *sf.* 1. life (*pl.* lives): *a* —, for life; *in* —, during one's life 2. (*necessario per vivere*) living: *costo della* —, cost of living.

vita[2] *sf.* (*anat.*) waist.

vitalolo *sm.* bon viveur.

vitalba *sf.* clematis.

vitale *agg.* vital.

vitalità *sf.* vitality.

vitalizio *agg.* for life. ♦ **vitalizio** *sm.* annuity.

vitamina *sf.* vitamin.

vitaminico *agg.* vitaminic.

vite[1] *sf.* vine.

vite[2] *sf.* (*mecc.*) screw.

vitello *sm.* calf (*pl.* calves).

viticcio *sm.* vine-tendril.

viticolo *agg.* viticultural.

viticoltore *sm.* viticulturist.

viticoltura *sf.* grape-growing.

vitreo *agg.* vitreous.

vittima *sf.* victim.

vittimismo *sm.* victimization.

vitto *sm.* 1. food 2. (*pasti in pensione o albergo*) board: — *e alloggio,* board and lodging.

vittoria *sf.* victory.

vittorioso *agg.* victorious.

vituperare *vt.* to vituperate.

vituperio *sm.* insult.

viuzza *sf.* lane.

viva *inter.* hurrah!

vivacchiare *vi.* to live poorly.

vivace *agg.* 1. lively, sprightly 2. (*pronto, sveglio*) quick 3. (*di colori*) bright.

vivacemente *avv.* 1. lively 2. (*prontamente*) quickly 3. (*vivamente*) brightly.

vivacità *sf.* 1. liveliness 2. (*di colori*) brightness.

vivaio *sm.* 1. (*di pesci*) fish-pond 2. (*di piante*) nursery.

vivamente *avv.* deeply, keenly.

vivanda *sf.* food.

vivandiere *sm.* sutler.

vivente *agg.* alive (*pred.*), living. ♦ **vivente** *sm.* living being.

vivere *vt.* e *vi.* to live: *cessare di*

—, to die; *insegnare a* — *a qu.,* to teach (*v. irr.*) so. good manners; — *alle spalle di qu.,* to sponge on so.

viveri *sm pl.* victuals.

vivido *agg.* vivid.

vivificare *vt.* to enliven.

vivificatore *agg.* vivifying. ♦ **vivificatore** *sm.* vivifier.

viviparo *agg.* e *sm.* viviparous.

vivisezione *sf.* vivisection.

vivo *agg.* 1. living, alive (*pred.*) || *a viva forza,* by main force; *argento* —, quicksilver; *calce viva,* quicklime; *farsi* —, to turn up 2. (*vivace*) lively 3. (*profondo, acuto*) deep, sharp 4. (*vivido*) vivid 5. (*di colori*) bright.

viziare *vt.* 1. to spoil (*v. irr.*) 2. (*guastare*) to vitiate.

viziato *agg.* 1. spoilt 2. (*guasto*) vitiated.

vizio *sm.* 1. vice 2. (*cattiva abitudine*) bad habit.

vizioso *agg.* vicious. ♦ **vizioso** *sm.* vicious man.

vocabolario *sm.* 1. vocabulary 2. (*dizionario*) dictionary.

vocabolo *sm.* word.

vocale[1] *agg.* vocal.

vocale[2] *sf.* vowel.

vocalizzare *vt.* e *vi.* to vocalize.

vocalizzo *sm.* vocalization.

vocativo *agg.* e *sm.* vocative.

vocazione *sf.* vocation, bent.

voce *sf.* 1. voice: *a* — *alta, bassa,* in a loud, low voice; *parlare sotto* —, to whisper 2. (*diceria*) rumour 3. (*articolo di elenco*) item.

vociare *vi.* to shout.

vociferare *vi.* 1. to shout 2. (*spargere una voce*) to rumour.

vocio *sm.* shouting.

voga[1] *sf.* (*mar.*) rowing.

voga[2] *sf.* 1. (*moda*) fashion 2. (*energia*) energy.

vogare *vi.* (*mar.*) to row.

vogata *sf.* row.

vogatore *sm.* rower.

voglia *sf.* 1. wish: *aver* —, to feel (*v. irr.*) like 2. (*volontà*) will.

voglioso *agg.* desirous, willing.

voi *pron.* you: — *stessi,* you yourselves.

volano *sm.* battledore and shuttlecock.

volante[1] *agg.* flying: *cervo* —, kite; *foglio* —, loose sheet. ♦ **volante** *sf.* (*di polizia*) flying squad.

volante² *sm.* steering-wheel.

volantino *sm.* leaflet.

volare *vi.* to fly (*v. irr.*): *far —,* to blow (*v. irr.*).

volata *sf.* **1.** flight **2.** (*corsa*) rush **3.** (*sport*) final sprint.

volàtile¹ *agg.* (*chim.*) volatile.

volàtile² *sm.* bird.

volatilizzare *vt.* to volatilize. ♦ **volatilizzarsi** *vr.* to volatilize.

volente *agg.* — *o nolente,* willy-nilly.

volenterosamente *avv.* willingly.

volenteroso *agg.* V. *volonteroso.*

volentieri *avv.* willingly.

volere¹ *vt.* **1.** (*forte volontà*) (*pres. indicativo e congiuntivo*) will; (*passato indicativo e congiuntivo, condizionale*) would **2.** (*desiderio*) to want, to wish: *voglio che egli venga,* I want him to come **3.** (*gradire*) to like (*costr. pers.*): *vorrei, avrei voluto,* I should like, I should have liked **4.** (*desiderio intenso*) to wish: *vorrei essere ricco!,* I wish I were rich! **5.** (*aver bisogno di*) to need, to require **6.** (*con espressioni di tempo*) to take (*v. irr.*): *ci vogliono due ore per andare alla stazione,* it takes two hours to go to the station **7.** (*cercare*) to ask for: *c'è qualcuno che ti cerca,* there is somebody asking for you **8.** (*essere disposti*) to be willing || *che tu voglia o no,* whether you like it or not; *vuoi ... vuoi* (*sia ... sia*), both ... and; *Dio lo voglia, Dio non voglia!,* God grant it, God forbid!

volere² *sm.* will, wish.

volgare *agg.* vulgar, common.

volgarità *sf.* vulgarity.

volgarizzare *vt.* to divulge.

volgarizzatore *sm.* popularizer.

volgarizzazione *sf.* popularization.

volgarmente *avv.* vulgarly, commonly.

vòlgere *vt.* to turn.

vòlgere *sm.* course.

volgo *sm.* common people.

voliera *sf.* aviary.

volitivo *agg.* **1.** strong-willed **2.** (*gramm.*) volitive.

volo *sm.* flight: *prendere il —,* to run (*v. irr.*) away; *capire qc. al —,* to grasp sthg. immediately.

volontà *sf.* will: *di sua spontanea —,* of his own free-will.

volontariamente *avv.* voluntarily.

volontario *agg.* voluntary. ♦ **volontario** *sm.* volunteer.

volontarismo *sm.* voluntarism.

volonteroso *agg.* willing.

volontieri *avv.* V. *volentieri.*

volpe *sf.* fox.

volpino *agg.* foxy: *cane —,* Pomeranian.

volpone *sm.* old fox.

volta¹ *sf.* **1.** time: *una —,* once; *due, tre volte,* twice, three times; *ancora una —,* once again; *una — e mezzo,* half as much; *una — o l'altra,* sooner or later; *rare volte,* seldom; *una — tanto,* once in a while; *c'era una —,* once upon a time there was **2.** (*turno*) turn: *a mia —,* in my turn.

volta² *sf.* **1.** (*curva*) bend **2.** (*arch.*) vault.

voltafaccia *sm.* volte-face.

voltaggio *sm.* voltage.

voltàmetro *sm.* voltameter.

voltare *vt.* to turn.

voltastòmaco *sm.* sickness.

voltata *sf.* bend, turning, curve.

volteggiare *vi.* **1.** to whirl **2.** (*svolazzare*) to fly (*v. irr.*) about.

volteggio *sm.* vaulting.

volto¹ *sm.* **1.** face **2.** (*aspetto*) aspect.

volto² *agg.* **1.** turned **2.** (*rivolto*) directed.

volùbile *agg.* changeable.

volubilità *sf.* inconstancy.

volume *sm.* volume.

volumètrico *agg.* volumetric.

voluminoso *agg.* voluminous, bulky.

voluta *sf.* volute.

volutamente *avv.* intentionally.

voluttà *sf.* **1.** delight **2.** (*dei sensi*) voluptuousness.

voluttuario *agg.* voluptuary.

voluttuosamente *avv.* voluptuously.

voluttuoso *agg.* voluptuous.

vòmere *sm.* **1.** ploughshare **2.** (*anat.*) vomer.

vomitare *vt.* to vomit, to be sick.

vòmito *sm.* vomiting: *conato di —,* retch.

vòngola *sf.* mussel.

vorace *agg.* voracious, greedy.

voracità *sf.* voracity, greed.

voràgine *sf.* chasm.

vorticare *vi.* to whirl.

vòrtice *sm.* whirl: — *di vento,* whirlwind.

vorticosamente *avv.* in whirls.

vorticoso *agg.* whirling.

vostro *agg. poss.* your || *in vece vostra*, instead of you. ♦ vostro *pron. poss.* yours || *rispondiamo alla vostra del 3 giugno (comm.)*, in reply to your letter of June 3rd; *sono dalla vostra*, I am on your side.

votante *agg.* voting. ♦ votante *sm.* voter.

votare *vt.* to vote. ♦ votarsi *vr.* to devote oneself.

votato *agg.* 1. passed 2. (*dedicato*) devoted.

votazione *sf.* voting.

votivo *agg.* votive.

voto *sm.* 1. (*promessa solenne*) vow 2. (*augurio*) wish 3. (*per elezioni*) vote 4. (*scolastico*) mark: *prendere un bel, brutto —*, to get (*v. irr.*) a good, bad mark.

vulcànico *agg.* volcanic.

vulcanismo *sm.* vulcanism.

vulcanizzare *vt.* to vulcanize.

vulcanizzato *agg.* vulcanized.

vulcanizzazione *sf.* vulcanization.

vulcano *sm.* volcano.

vulneràbile *agg.* vulnerable.

vulnerabilità *sf.* vulnerability.

vuotare *vt.* to empty: *— il sacco*, to speak (*v. irr.*) out one's mind.

vuoto *agg.* 1. empty 2. (*sprovvisto*) devoid. ♦ vuoto *sm.* 1. empty space 2. (*recipiente vuoto*) empty 3. (*vacuità*) emptiness.

X

xenofobìa *sf.* xenophobia.

xenòfobo *sm.* xenophobe.

xilòfono *sm.* xylophone.

xilografìa *sf.* 1. (*incisione*) xylograph 2. (*arte*) xylography.

Z

zaffata *sf.* whiff.

zafferano *sm.* saffron.

zaffiro *sm.* sapphire.

zàino *sm.* knapsack.

zampa *sf.* 1. paw 2. (*con zoccolo*)

hoof 3. (*di uccello*) claw 4. (*di insetto*) leg || *zampe di gallina (scrittura)*, scrawl; (*rughe*) crow's feet.

zampata *sf.* blow with a paw.

zampettare *vt.* to toddle.

zampillante *agg.* gushing.

zampillare *vi.* to gush.

zampillo *sm.* gush.

zampino *sm.* little paw || *mettere lo — in una faccenda*, to have a hand in the matter.

zampogna *sf.* 1. reed-pipe 2. (*cornamusa*) bag-pipe.

zampognaro *sm.* piper.

zanna *sf.* 1. fang 2. (*di elefante*) tusk.

zanzara *sf.* mosquito.

zanzariera *sf.* mosquito-net.

zappa *sf.* hoe.

zappare *vt.* to hoe.

zappata *sf.* blow with a hoe.

zappatore *sm.* 1. hoer 2. (*mil.*) pioneer.

zappatura *sf.* hoeing.

zar *sm.* czar.

zarina *sf.* czarina.

zarista *s.* czarist.

zàttera *sf.* raft.

zavorra *sf.* 1. ballast 2. (*fig.*) rubbish.

zavorrare *vt.* to ballast.

zàzzera *sf.* mane.

zazzeruto *agg.* shockheaded.

zebra *sf.* zebra.

zebrato *agg.* striped.

zebratura *sf.* stripes (*pl.*).

zebù *sm.* zebu.

zecca[1] *sf.* mint: *nuovo di —*, brand-new.

zecca[2] *sf.* (*zool.*) tick.

zecchino *sm.* sequin: *oro —*, first-quality-gold.

zèfiro *sm.* zephyr.

zelante *agg.* zealous.

zelantemente *avv.* zealously.

zelo *sm.* zeal.

zenit *sm.* zenith.

zénzero *sm.* ginger.

zeppo *agg.* crammed (with).

zerbino *sm.* door-mat.

zerbinotto *sm.* dandy.

zero *sm.* 1. nought 2. (*in graduazioni*) zero 3. (*tel.*) O || *ridursi a —*, to come (*v. irr.*) to nought.

zia *sf.* aunt.

zibaldone *sm.* miscellany.

zibellino *sm.* sable.

zigano *agg. e sm.* tzigane.

zigomo *sm.* cheek-bone.

zigrinare *vt.* to knurl.

zigrinato *agg.* knurled.

zig-zag (*nella loc. avv.*) *a* —, zigzag.

zigzagare *vi.* to zigzag.

zimbello *sm.* **1.** decoy **2.** (*fig.*) laughing-stock.

zincare *vt.* to zinc.

zincatura *sf.* zinc-plating.

zinco *sm.* zinc.

zincografia *sf.* zincography.

zingaresco *agg.* gipsy (*attr.*).

zingaro *sm.* gipsy.

zio *sm.* uncle.

zircone *sm.* zircon.

zirconio *sm.* zirconium.

zitella *sf.* spinster.

zittire *vt.* to hiss.

zitto *agg.* silent: *star* —, to be silent.

zizzania *sf.* **1.** darnel **2.** (*fig.*) discord.

zoccolaio *sm.* clog-maker.

zoccolare *vi.* to clatter about with one's clogs.

zoccolo *sm.* **1.** clog **2.** (*di animale*) hoof **3.** (*piedistallo*) base.

zodiacale *agg.* zodiacal.

zodiaco *sm.* zodiac.

zolfanello *sm.* match.

zolfatara *sf.* V. *solfatara*.

zolfatura *sf.* sulfurization.

zolfo *sm.* sulphur

zolla *sf.* clod.

zolletta *sf.* lump.

zona *sf.* zone, area.

zonzo (*nella loc. avv.*) *andare a* —, to loaf.

zoo *sm.* zoo.

zoofilia *sf.* zoophilia.

zoòfilo *agg.* zoophilous. ♦ **zoòfilo** *sm.* animal-lover.

zoofobia *sf.* zoophobia.

zoologia *sf.* zoology.

zoològico *agg.* zoological.

zoòlogo *sm.* zoologist.

zootecnia *sf.* zootechny.

zootècnico *agg.* zootechnic: *patrimonio* —, live-stock. ♦ **zootècnico** *sm.* animal expert.

zoppicamento *sm.* limping.

zoppicante *agg.* lame.

zoppicare *vi.* **1.** to limp **2.** (*di mobile*) to be shaky.

zoppo *agg.* **1.** lame **2.** (*di mobile*) shaky. ♦ **zoppo** *sm.* lame person.

zoticàggine *sf.* boorishness.

zòtico *agg.* boorish. ♦ **zòtico** *sm.* boor.

zuavo *sm.* zouave ‖ *calzoni alla zuava*, knickerbockers.

zucca *sf.* **1.** pumpkin **2.** (*testa*) pate.

zuccherare *vt.* to sugar.

zuccherato *agg.* sugared.

zuccheriera *sf.* sugar-basin.

zuccherificio *sm.* sugar-refinery.

zuccherino *sm.* **1.** sweet **2.** (*fig.*) sugar-plum.

zùcchero *sm.* sugar.

zucchina *sf.* vegetable marrow.

zucconàggine *sf.* **1.** (*ottusità*) dullness **2.** (*ostinatezza*) stubbornness.

zuccone *sm.* **1.** (*ottuso*) blockhead **2.** (*testardo*) donkey.

zuffa *sf.* brawl.

zufolare *vt.* e *vi.* to whistle.

zufolo *sm.* whistle.

zùfolo *sm.* **1.** whistle **2.** (*mus.*) pipe.

zuppa *sf.* soup.

zuppiera *sf.* tureen.

zuppo *agg.* soaked.

zuzzurellone *sm.* skittish boy.

NOMI PROPRI, STORICI E GEOGRAFICI

Abele Abel.
Abissinia Abyssinia.
Abramo Abraham.
Achille Achilles.
Ada Ada.
Adamo Adam.
Adolfo Adolph.
Adone Adonis.
Adriano Hadrian.
Adriatico (Mar) Adriatic Sea.
Afganistan Afghanistan.
Africa Africa.
Afrodite Aphrodite.
Agamennone Agamemnon
Agata Agatha.
Agnese Agnes.
Agostino Augustin.
Aia (L') The Hague.
Alace Ajax.
Albania Albania.
Alberto Albert.
Aldo Aldous.
Alessandra Alexandra.
Alessandro Alexander.
Alessio Alexis.
Alfredo Alfred.
Algeri Algiers.
Algeria Algeria.
Alice Alice.
Alpi Alps pl.
Alsazia Alsace.
Amazzoni (Rio delle) Amazon.
Ambrogio Ambrose.
Amburgo Hamburg.
Amelia Amelia.
America America.
Amleto Hamlet.
Andalusia Andalusia.
Ande Andes pl.
Andrea Andrew.
Angelo Angel.
Anna Ann(e).
Annibale Hannibal.
Antartide Antarctica.
Antonino Antoninus.
Antonio Ant(h)ony.
Apollo Apollo.
Appennini Apennines pl.
Arabia Arabia.
Aragona Aragon.
Arcadia Arcadia.
Archimede Archimedes.

Argentina Argentina.
Arianna Ariadne.
Aristofane Aristophanes.
Aristotele Aristotle.
Armando Armand.
Arnaldo Arnold.
Aroldo Harold.
Arrigo Henry.
Arturo Arthur.
Asia Asia.
Atene Athens.
Atlantico Atlantic.
Augusta Augusta.
Augusto Augustus.
Australia Australia.
Austria Austria.
Azzorre Azores pl.

Babele Babel.
Babilonia Babylon.
Bacco Bacchus.
Balcani Balkans pl.
Baldassarre Balthazar.
Baleari Balearic Islands pl.
Baltico (Mar) Baltic Sea.
Baltimora Baltimore.
Barbara Barbara.
Barcellona Barcelona.
Barnaba Barnaby, Barnabas.
Bartolomeo Bartholomew.
Basilea Basel.
Basilio Basil.
Battista Baptist.
Beatrice Beatrix.
Belgio Belgium.
Belgrado Belgrade.
Benedetto Benedict.
Bengala Bengal.
Beniamino Benjamin.
Berenice Berenice.
Berlino Berlin.
Bermude Bermudas pl.
Bernardo Bernard.
Berta Bertha.
Betlemme Bethlehem.
Bianca Blanche.
Birmania Burma.
Boemia Bohemia.
Bolivia Bolivia.
Bonifacio Boniface.
Bosforo Bosporus.

Brandeburgo Brandenburg.
Brasile Brazil.
Bretagna Brittany.
Bruto Brutus.
Bulgaria Bulgaria.

Cadice Cadiz.
Caino Cain.
Caio Caius.
Cairo Cairo.
California California.
Calvino Calvin.
Cambogia Cambodia.
Campidoglio Capitol.
Canadà Canada.
Caraibi (Mar dei) Caribbean Sea.
Carlo Charles.
Carlomagno Charlemagne.
Carlotta Charlotte.
Carolina Caroline.
Carpazi Carpathian Mountains *pl.*
Cartagine Carthage.
Cascemir Cashmere, Kashmir.
Caspio (Mar) Caspian Sea.
Cassio Cassius.
Cassiopea Cassiopeia.
Castiglia Castile.
Caterina Catherine.
Catone Cato.
Caucaso Caucasus.
Cecilia Cecily.
Cecilio Cecil.
Cecoslovacchia Czechoslovakia.
Cenerentola Cinderella.
Cesare Caesar.
Chiara Clara.
Cicerone Cicero.
Cile Chile.
Cina China.
Cinzia Cynthia.
Cipro Cyprus.
Cirillo Cyril.
Ciro Cyrus.
Clara Clara.
Claudio Claudius, Claude.
Clemente Clement.
Clementina Clementine.
Cleopatra Cleopatra.
Clitennestra Clytemnestra.
Colombia Colombia.
Colonia Cologne.
Congo Congo.
Corea Korea.
Corfù Corfu.
Corinto Corinth.
Cornelio Cornelius.
Cornovaglia Cornwall.
Corrado Conrad.

Corsica Corsica.
Costantino Constantine.
Costantinopoli Constantinople.
Costanza Constance.
Creta Crete.
Crimea Crimea.
Cristina Christine.
Cristo Christ.
Cristoforo Christopher.
Cuba Cuba.

Dafne Daphne.
Damasco Damascus.
Damocle Damocles.
Daniele Daniel.
Danimarca Denmark.
Danubio Danube.
Danzica Danzig.
Dardanelli Dardanelles *pl.*
Dario Darius.
Davide David.
Debora Debórah.
Delfo Delphi.
Democrito Democritus.
Demostene Demosthenes.
Desdemona Desdemona.
Diana Diana.
Didone Dido.
Diocleziano Diocletian.
Diogene Diogenes.
Dionigi, Dionisio Dionysius.
Domenico Dominic.
Domiziano Domitian.
Dorotea Dorothy.
Dublino Dublin.

Ebridi Hebrides *pl.*
Edgardo Edgar.
Edimburgo Edinburgh.
Edipo Oedipus.
Edmondo Edmund.
Edoardo Edward.
Egeo (Mar) Aegean Sea.
Egitto Egypt.
Elena Helen.
Eleonora Eleanor.
Elettra Electra.
Elia Elias, Elijah.
Elisa Eliza.
Elisabetta Elizabeth.
Ellade Hellas.
Emanuele Emanuel.
Emilia Emily.
Enea Aeneas.
Enrichetta Henrietta, Harriet.
Enrico Henry, Harry.
Epaminonda Epaminondas.

Epicuro Epicurus.
Eraclito Heraclitus.
Erasmo Erasmus.
Erberto Herbert.
Ercole Hercules.
Eritrea Eritrea.
Ermete Hermes.
Ernesto Ernest.
Erode Herod.
Erodoto Herodotus.
Esaù Esau.
Eschilo Aeschylus.
Esiodo Hesiod.
Esopo Aesop.
Ester Esther.
Etiopia Ethiopia.
Ettore Hector.
Euclide Euclid.
Eufrate Euphrates.
Eugenio Eugene.
Euripide Euripides.
Europa Europe.
Eva Eve.
Evelina Evelyn.
Ezechiele Ezekiel.

Farsalo Pharsalus.
Fausto Faust(us).
Federico Frederic.
Fedra Phaedra.
Felice Felix.
Ferdinando Ferdinand.
Filadelfia Philadelphia.
Filippi Philippi.
Filippine Philippines pl.
Filippo Philip.
Finlandia Finland.
Firenze Florence.
Formosa Formosa.
Francesca Frances.
Francesco Francis.
Francia France.
Franco Frank.
Francoforte Frankfurt.

Gabriele Gabriel.
Galilea Galilee.
Galles Wales.
Gallia Gaule.
Genova Genoa.
Geova Jehovah.
Gerardo Gerard.
Geremia Jeremiah.
Gerico Jericho.
Germania Germany.
Gerolamo Jerome.
Gerusalemme Jerusalem.

Gesù Jesus.
Giacobbe Jacob.
Giacomo James.
Giamaica Jamaica.
Giappone Japan.
Giasone Jason.
Giava Java.
Gibilterra Gibraltar.
Gilberto Gilbert.
Ginevra Geneva.
Giobbe Job.
Giona Jonah, Jonas.
Gionata Jonathan.
Giordano Jordan.
Giorgio George.
Giosuè Joshua.
Giovanna Jane, Jean, Joan.
Giovanni John.
Giove Jove, Jupiter.
Giovenale Juvenal.
Giuda Judas, Jude.
Giudea Judea.
Giuditta Judith.
Giulia Julia, Julie.
Giuliana Juliana.
Giuliano Julian.
Giulietta Juliet.
Giulio Julius.
Giunone Juno.
Giuseppe Joseph.
Giuseppina Josephine.
Goffredo Geoffrey, Jeffrey.
Golgota Golgotha.
Golia Goliath.
Gran Bretagna Great Britain.
Grazia Grace.
Grecia Greece.
Gregorio Gregory.
Groenlandia Greenland.
Guaiana Guiana.
Gualtiero Walter.
Guascogna Gascony.
Guglielmo William.
Guido Guy.
Guinea Guinea.
Gustavo Gustavus.

Iacopo James.
Iberia Iberia.
Icaro Icarus.
Ignazio Ignatius.
Ilario Hilary.
Imalaia Himalaya.
India India.
Indostan Hindustan.
Inghilterra England.
Innocenzo Innocent.
Ionio (Mar) Ionian Sea.

Ippolito Hippolytus.
Irene Irene.
Iride Iris.
Irlanda Ireland.
Irlanda (Stato Libero di) Eire.
Isabella Isabel.
Isacco Isaac.
Isaia Isaiah.
Iside Isis.
Islanda Iceland.
Ismaele Ishmael.
Israele Israel.
Italia Italy.
Iugoslavia Yugoslavia.

Lamberto Lambert.
Lancillotto Launcelot.
Laocoonte Laocoon.
Lapponia Lapland.
Laura Laura.
Lazio Latium.
Lazzaro Lazarus.
Leandro Leander.
Leonardo Leonard.
Leone Leo(n).
Leonida Leonidas.
Leopoldo Leopold.
Lete Lethe.
Letizia Letitia.
Libano Lebanon.
Libia Libya.
Licurgo Lycurgus.
Lidia Lydia.
Liegi Liege.
Lione Lyons.
Lisbona Lisbon.
Livio Livy.
Livorno Leghorn.
Lodovico Ludwig.
Lombardia Lombardy.
Londra London.
Lorena Lorraine.
Lorenzo Lawrence.
Losanna Lausanne.
Lotario Lothar.
Lovanio Louvain.
Luca Luke.
Lucerna Lucerne.
Lucia Lucy.
Luciano Lucian.
Lucifero Lucifer.
Lucio Lucius.
Lucrezio Lucretius.
Luigi Louis, Lewis.
Luigia, Luisa Louise.
Lussemburgo Luxemburg.
Lutero Luther.

Maddalena Magdalene.
Maiorca Majorca.
Malesia Malaya.
Malta Malta.
Manciuria Manchuria.
Manfredi Manfred.
Manica (La) The Channel.
Mantova Mantua.
Maometto Mohammed.
Maratona Marathon.
Marcello Marcellus.
Marco Mark.
Margherita Margaret.
Maria Mary.
Marianna Marianne.
Mario Marius.
Marocco Morocco.
Marta Martha.
Marte Mars.
Martino Martin.
Marziale Martial.
Massimiliano Maximilian.
Matilde Matilda.
Matteo Matthew.
Matusalemme Methuselah.
Maurizio Maurice.
Mecca, La Mecca.
Mecenate Maecenas.
Mediterraneo Mediterranean.
Medusa Medusa.
Mefistofele Mephistopheles.
Melanesia Melanesia.
Menelao Menelaus.
Mercurio Mercury.
Merlino Merlin.
Mesopotamia Mesopotamia.
Messalina Messalina.
Messico Mexico.
Micene Mycenae.
Michele Michael.
Mida Midas.
Milano Milan.
Minerva Minerva.
Minosse Minos.
Minotauro Minotaur.
Mitridate Mithridates.
Molucche Moluccas *pl.*
Monaco (Principato di) Monaco.
Monaco di Baviera Munich.
Mongolia Mongolia.
Mosa Meuse.
Mosca Moscow.
Mosè Moses.
Mozambico Mozambique.

Napoleone Napoleon.
Napoli Naples.
Narciso Narcissus.

Nerone Nero.
Nettuno Neptune.
Nicola, Niccolò Nicholas.
Nilo Nile.
Nizza Nice.
Noè Noah.
Normandia Normandy.
Norvegia Norway.
Nuova Zelanda New Zealand.

Oceania Oceania.
Ofelia Ophelia.
Olanda Holland.
Olimpo Olympus.
Oliviero Oliver.
Omero Homer.
Orazio Horace, Horatio.
Orcadi Orkneys pl.
Oreste Orestes.
Orfeo Orpheus.
Orione Orion.
Orlando Roland.
Orsola Ursula.
Osiride Osiris.
Osvaldo Oswald.
Otello Othello.
Ovidio Ovid.

Pacifico Pacific.
Padova Padua.
Paesi Bassi Netherlands p..
Palestina Palestine.
Pancrazio Pancras.
Paola Paula.
Paolina Pauline.
Paolo Paul.
Papuasia Papua.
Paride Paris.
Parigi Paris.
Parnaso Parnassus.
Partenone Parthenon.
Patagonia Patagonia.
Patrizia Patricia.
Patrizio Patrick.
Pechino Peking.
Peloponneso Peloponnesus.
Penelope Penelope.
Pensilvania Pennsylvania.
Pericle Pericles.
Perseo Perseus.
Persia Persia.
Perù Peru.
Piemonte Piedmont.
Pietro, Piero Peter.
Pigmalione Pigmalion.
Pindaro Pindar.
Pio Pius.

Pirenei Pyrenees pl.
Pireo Piraeus.
Pitagora Pythagoras.
Platone Plato.
Plinio Pliny.
Plutarco Plutarch.
Polinesia Polynesia.
Polonia Poland.
Pompeo Pompey.
Portogallo Portugal.
Praga Prague.
Prometeo Prometheus.
Prussia Prussia.
Puglia Apulia.

Quintino Quentin.

Rachele Rachel.
Raffaele, Raffaello Raphael.
Raimondo Raymond.
Ramsete Ramses.
Rebecca Rebecca.
Remo Remus.
Reno Rhine.
Riccardo Richard.
Roberto Robert.
Rodano Rhone.
Rodi Rhodes.
Rodolfo Rudolph.
Rodrigo Roderick.
Rolando Roland.
Roma Rome.
Romania Ro(u)mania.
Romeo Romeo.
Romolo Romulus.
Rosa Rose.
Rosalia Rosalie.
Rosalinda Rosalind.
Rossana Roxana.
Rubicone Rubicon.
Ruggero Roger.
Russia Russia.

Saffo Sappho.
Salomone Solomon.
Samuele Samuel.
Sansone Samson.
Sara Sarah.
Sardegna Sardinia.
Sassonia Saxony.
Satana Satan.
Saturno Saturn.
Saul Saul.
Savoia Savoy.
Scandinavia Scandinavia.
Scipione Scipion.

Scozia Scotland.
Sebastiano Sebastian.
Sempione Simplon.
Serse Xerxes.
Siam Siam.
Siberia Siberia.
Sibilla Sibyl.
Sicilia Sicily.
Silla Sulla.
Silvestro Silvester.
Silvia Sylvia.
Simeone Simeon.
Simone Simon.
Siracusa Syracuse.
Siria Syria.
Smirne Smyrna.
Socrate Socrates.
Sodoma Sodom.
Sofia Sophia.
Sofocle Sophocles.
Somalia Somaliland.
Spagna Spain.
Sparta Sparta.
Stati Uniti United States (of America - U.S.A.).
Stefano Stephen.
Stoccolma Stockholm.
Strasburgo Strasbourg.
Sudan S(o)udan.
Susanna Susan(nah).
Svezia Sweden.
Svizzera Switzerland.

Tacito Tacitus.
Tailandia Thailand.
Tamigi Thames.
Tangeri Tangier(s).
Tasmania Tasmania.
Tebe Thebes.
Telemaco Telemachus.
Temistocle Themistocles.
Teodorico Theodoric.
Terenzio Terence.
Teresa Theresa.
Termopili Thermopylae pl.
Terranova Newfoundland.
Teseo Theseus.
Tevere Tiber.
Tiberio Tiberius.
Tirolo Tirol, Tyrol.

Tirreno (Mar) Tyrrhenian Sea.
Tito Titus.
Tiziano Titian.
Tobia Tobias.
Tolomeo Ptolemy.
Tommaso Thomas.
Tonchino Tonkin, Tongking.
Torino Turin.
Toscana Tuscany.
Traiano Trajan.
Tristano Tristan, Tristram.
Troia Troy.
Tullio Tully.
Tunisi Tunis.
Tunisia Tunisia.
Turchia Turkey.

Uberto Hubert.
Ucraina Ukraine.
Ugo Hugh.
Ulisse Ulysses.
Umberto Humbert.
Ungheria Hungary.
Urbano Urban.
URSS USSR (Union of Socialist Soviet Republics).

Valentino Valentine.
Valeria Valeria.
Valerio Valerius.
Varsavia Warsaw.
Vaticano Vatican.
Venere Venus.
Veneto Venetia.
Venezia Venice.
Vesuvio Vesuvius.
Vienna Vienna.
Vincenzo Vincent.
Virgilio Virgil.
Virginia Virginia.
Vittoria Victoria.
Vittorio Victor.
Viviana, Viviano Vivian.
Vulcano Vulcan.

Zaccaria Zachary.
Zurigo Zurich.

SIGLE E ABBREVIAZIONI USATE IN ITALIA

A., *alto:* H., high.

A.C., *Automobile Club:* A.A., Automobile Association.

a.C., *avanti Cristo:* B.C. Before Christ.

A.D., *Anno Domini, nell'anno del Signore:* A.D., Anno Domini, (After Christ).

ago., *Agosto:* Aug., August.

A.M., *Aeronautica Militare:* A.F., Air Force.

am., amer., *americano:* Am., American.

anon., *anonimo:* anon., anonymous.

app., *appendice:* app., appendix.

approx., *approssimativo:* approx., approximate.

apr., *aprile:* Apr., April.

A.R., *altezza reale:* R.H., Royal Highness.

ar., *arrivo:* arr., arrival.

ass., *associazione:* ass., association.

b.f., *bassa frequenza:* L.F., low frequency.

boll., *bollettino:* bull., bulletin.

brev., *brevetto:* pat., patent.

C., *centigradi:* cent., centigrade.

c., 1. *conto:* acc., account 2. *cubico:* cu., cubic.

ca., 1. *circa:* a., about 2. *corrente alternata:* a.c., alternating current.

cad., *cadauno:* ea., each.

Cap., *capitano:* Capt., captain.

cap., *capitolo:* c., chapter.

capit., *capitolo:* c., chapter.

Capp., *capitoli:* cc., chapters.

Card., *Cardinale:* Card., cardinal.

C/c, *conto corrente:* c/a, current account.

cc., *corrente continua:* dc., direct current.

C.D., *Corpo Diplomatico:* C.D., Corps Diplomatique.

C.E.E.A., *Comunità europea per l'energia atomica:* A.E.C., Atomic Energy Commission.

cent., centg., *centigrado:* cent., centigrade.

Cf., *confronta:* cp., compare.

cm., *centimetro:* cent., centimetre.

c.m., *corrente mese:* inst., instant.

cm.c., *centimetro cubo:* c.c., cubic centimetre.

Col., *colonnello:* col., colonel.

coll., *collegio:* coll., college.

coop., *cooperativa:* coop., co-operative.

C.P., *Casella Postale:* P.O.B., Post Office Box.

C.S., *Corte Suprema:* Sup. Ct., Supreme Court.

D., *dottore:* dr., doctor.

d.C., *dopo Cristo:* A.D., Anno Domini.

dic., *dicembre:* Dec., December.

Dirett., *direttore:* dir., director.

dom., *domenica:* Sun., Sunday.

dott., *dottore:* dr., doctor.

dozz., *dozzina:* doz., dozen.

E., *est:* E, East.

ecc., *eccetera:* etc., and so on.

ed., 1. *edito:* ed., edited 2. *edizione:* ed., edition.

Egr., *egregio:* Esq., Esquire.

es., *esempio:* ex., example.

feb., *febbraio:* Feb., February.

fed., *federazione:* fed., federation.

F.lli, *fratelli:* br., brothers.

g., *grammo:* g., gram.

Gen., *generale:* Gen., General.

gen., 1. *generale:* gen., general 2. *gennaio:* Jan., January.

giov., *giovedì:* Thur., Thursday.

h., *ora:* h., hour.

H.P., *cavallo vapore:* H.P., horse power.

ibid., *ibidem, nello stesso luogo:* ibid., in the same place.

id., *idem, come sopra:* id., the same.

iun., *iunior, giovane:* jr., junior.

kg., *chilogrammo:* kg., kilogram.
km., *chilometro:* km., kilometre.
kw., *chilowatt:* kw., kilowatt.

l., 1. *latino:* Lat., Latin 2. *litro:* l., litre.
lat., *latitudine:* lat., latitude.
lib., *libro:* b., book.
long., *longitudine:* long., longitude.
L.st., *Lira sterlina:* L., pound.
lun., *lunedì:* Mon., Monday.

M., *monte:* Mt., mount.
m., 1. *morto:* d., dead 2. *mese:* m., month 3. *metro:* m., metre 4. *minuto:* m., minute.
M.AA.EE., *Ministero degli Affari Esteri:* F.O., Foreign Office.
Magg., *Maggiore:* Maj., Major.
mar., *marzo:* Mar., March.
mart., *martedì:* Tues., Tuesday.
mass., *massimo:* max., maximum.
m.c.d., *minimo comun denominatore:* L.C.D., Lowest Common Denominator.
m.c.m., *minimo comune multiplo:* L.C.M., Least Common Multiple.
M.E.C., *Mercato Comune Europeo:* E.C.M., European Common Market.
mer(c)., *mercoledì:* Wed., Wednesday.
mg., *milligrammo:* mg., milligram.
mm., *millimetro:* mm., millimetre.
M/n., *motonave:* Ms., motorship.
ms., *manoscritto:* ms., manuscript.
mss., *manoscritti:* mss., manuscripts.
Mus., *museo:* mus., museum.

N., 1. *nato:* b., born 2. *Nord:* N., North 3. *numero:* N., Number.
nov., *novembre:* Nov., November.
N.U., *Nazioni Unite:* U.N., United Nations.

O., *ovest:* W., West.
on., *onorevole:* hon., honourable.
O.N.U., *Organizzazione Nazioni Unite:* U.N.O., United Nations Organization.
ott., *ottobre:* Oct., October.

P., *padre:* fr., father.
p., *pagina:* p., page.
P.A., *Patto Atlantico:* N.A.T.O., North Atlantic Treaty Organization.
paragr., *paragrafo:* par., paragraph.
p.at., *peso atomico:* a.w., atomic weight.
P.C., *Partito Comunista:* C.P., Communist Party.
p.e., *per esempio:* e.g., for example (exempli gratia).
pres., *presidente:* pres., president.
proc., *procuratore:* att., attorney.
prof., *professore:* prof., professor.
P.S., *poscritto:* P.S., postscript.
p.za, *piazza:* sq., square.

Q.G., *Quartier Generale:* G.H., General Headquarters.

ref., *referenze:* ref., reference.
reg., *registro:* reg., register.
Rev., *Reverendo:* rev., Reverend.
R.M., *ricchezza mobile:* PAYE, Pay As You Earn.
R.U., *Regno Unito:* U.K., United Kingdom.

S., 1. *Santo:* St., Saint 2. *secolo:* cen., century 3. *società:* co., Company 4. *Sud:* S., South.
sab., *sabato:* Sat., Saturday.
S.A.R., *Sua Altezza Reale:* H.R.H., His (Her) Royal Highness.
Sc., *scuola:* sch., school.
S.E., *Sua Eccellenza:* H.E., His Excellency.
segg., *seguenti:* fol., following.
segr., *segretario:* sec., secretary.
serg., *sergente:* sergt., sergeant.
sett., *settembre:* Sept., September.
sig., *signore:* Mr., Mister.
sig.na, *signorina:* Miss.
sig.ra, *signora:* Mrs., Mistress.
S.M.B., *Sua Maestà Britannica:* H.B.M., His (Her) Britannic Majesty.
S.O., *Sud Ovest:* S.W., South West.
s.p.a., *società per azioni:* inc., incorporated.
spec., 1. *speciale:* spec., special 2. *specialmente:* spec., specially.
s.r.l., *società a responsabilità limitata:* ltd., limited (in inglese); corp., corporation (in americano).
S.S., *Sua Santità:* H.H., His Holiness.
S.U., *Stati Uniti:* U.S., United States.

S.U.A., *Stati Uniti d'America:* U.S.A., United States of America.

T., *tonnellata:* t., ton.
T.B.C., *tubercolosi:* T.B., Tuberculosis.
tel., *telefono:* tel. telephone.

U., *unione:* U., Union.
U.P., *Unione postale:* P.U., Postal Union.
U.R.S.S., *Unione Repubbliche So-*

cialiste Sovietiche: U.S.S.R., Union of Socialist Soviet Republics.

V., 1. *vaglia:* P.O., Postal Order **2.** *volume:* vol., volume.
v., *verso:* v., verse.
Ven., *Venerabile:* Ven., Venerable.
ven., *venerdì:* Fr., Friday.
vesc., *vescovo:* Bp., Bishop.
v.le, *viale:* Ave., Avenue.
vol., *volume:* vol., volume.
voll., *volumi:* voll., volumes.
vv., *versi:* vv., verses.